W0007810

長江之帆船与舢板

長江之帆船与舢板

THE JUNKS & SAMPANS OF THE YANGTZE

G. R. G. WORCESTER

River Inspector (retired), Chinese Maritime Customs

Seaforth
PUBLISHING

First published in Great Britain in 2020 by
Seaforth Publishing,
A division of Pen & Sword Books Ltd,
47 Church Street,
Barnsley S70 2AS

www.seaforthpublishing.com

First published in the USA 1971

British Library Cataloguing in Publication Data
A catalogue record for this book is available from the British Library

ISBN 978 1 5267 8490 2 (hardback)
ISBN 978 1 5267 8491 9 (epub)
ISBN 978 1 5267 8492 6 (kindle)

Pen & Sword Books Limited incorporates the imprints of Atlas, Archaeology, Aviation, Discovery, Family History, Fiction, History, Maritime, Military, Military Classics, Politics, Select, Transport, True Crime, Air World, Frontline Publishing, Leo Cooper, Remember When, Seaforth Publishing, The Praetorian Press, Wharncliffe Local History, Wharncliffe Transport, Wharncliffe True Crime and White Owl

Printed and bound in India by Replika Press Pvt. Ltd.

PREFATORY NOTE

My friend and colleague, the late G. R. G. Worcester, Esquire, the author of this beautiful book, had a long and notable career in the Chinese Customs Service. He was for many years an officer in the Customs River Inspectorate, which was responsible for the control and improvement of navigation on the Yangtze River. It was during his years on this great river—which he came to know like the back of his hand—that he devoted himself to the study of the junks described in his book.

Mr. Worcester died in England in 1969, happy in the knowledge that his work was to be published in its present form.

In a despatch to Lord Salisbury in 1885, Sir Robert Hart, Inspector General of the Chinese Customs Service, wrote: "*The Service which I direct is called the Customs Service, but its scope is wide and its aim is to do good work for China in every possible direction.*"

This simple creed has guided the unique Chinese Customs Service ever since it was founded in 1854. Its chief function was, of course, the collection of the revenue on an extensive foreign trade, but it also did "good work for China" in many fields far removed from conventional customs responsibilities.

This versatile civil service actively encouraged the writing and publication of books by its members on a broad range of subjects concerning the great country they served. The most recent of the noteworthy books by a Customs author was Mr. Worcester's definitive work on Chinese junks. Originally published by the Customs in Shanghai in a rather limited edition, the books are now out of print and collectors' items.

With the growing interest in, and concern with, China and the Far East, it is therefore timely and fitting that *The Junks and Sampans of the Yangtze*, revised and expanded, should be published by the United States Naval Institute and thus permit a wide reading public to enjoy the romantic story of these age-old craft.

In the prefatory note to Mr. Worcester's first book, *Junks and Sampans of the Upper Yangtze* (1940), Sir Frederick Maze, then Inspector General of Customs, pointed out that the Chinese have probably shown more originality than any other people in the art of shipbuilding, and commented on their ingenuity in designing vessels to suit special requirements and different conditions.

We of the West are inclined to think that the construction of ships for specialized purposes—tankers, bulk carriers, ore boats—is a relatively recent development. Mr. Worcester shows that centuries ago the Chinese built highly sophisticated vessels for a great variety of special purposes.

Local waters, of course, called for special vessels. The shallow waters of western Szechwan; the tumultuous rapids between Chungking and Ichang; the broad reaches of the lower river; and the open ocean demanded different kinds of craft.

Within these broad categories—from the humble and ubiquitous sampan to the great three-masted junks of Foochow—there are hundreds of different types, each designed for efficient and economical use.

This unique book is a comprehensive and authoritative record of the vessels which for centuries provided practically the sole means of communication and transportation in the vast area drained by one of the world's greatest waterways.

Mr. Worcester pays deserved respect and admiration to the generations of humble but skilled men who built the junks. These shipwrights, working with crude tools, designed and constructed boats which incorporated such advanced features as the watertight bulkhead and the balance rudder.

The men—and women—who sailed the junks were, as Mr. Worcester says, a simple, unlettered yet highly skilled people who for generations have cheerfully and unquestioningly accepted a life of unmitigated hardship. That he can add that, in his long experience, he has never met an unpleasant junkman, is high praise for these fine sailors.

As in other maritime countries, steam and internal combustion engines, with their superior speed and economy, have already supplanted the sail and the oar on certain routes and in certain types of vessels in China, and this development must inevitably continue. Yet even today an immense tonnage of cargo and uncounted thousands of passengers are carried by the junks described in this book.

Moreover, they may figure prominently in future naval and military operations, as, in fact, the craft indigenous to Southeast Asia are doing as this is being written.

These remarkable craft deserve an unusual biographer, and in Mr. Worcester they have found one—sailor, artist, and student of history.

He was first of all a sailor, whose lifetime career was concerned with ships—steam and sail.

He was also a talented artist and produced not only a profusion of scale drawings of many junks and their accessories but also the delicate sketches which illustrate the text.

Lastly, he went deeply into the history of his subject and gave us the results of his research, which happily include the folklore, legends, and romance which have followed in the wake of these fascinating craft.

L. K. Little

L. K. Little
Inspector General (Retired)
Chinese Customs Service

Cornish, New Hampshire, 12 August 1970

ACKNOWLEDGEMENT

My thanks are due to Dr. Vernon D. Tate, formerly Professor-Librarian of the U.S. Naval Academy Library, Annapolis, Maryland, for initiating the reproduction of these out-of-print volumes on the Chinese junk.

Thanks are also due to Mr. L. K. Little who, following Sir Frederick Maze as Inspector General of the Chinese Maritime Customs, made possible the writing of the original treatises.

While traveling in the byways of China to gather material for this book, I was often accompanied by my first wife, who shared many of the inevitable dangers and discomforts and made them tolerable by her cheerful acceptance of every situation.

The task of preparation of this revised edition has been in like manner lightened for me by the assistance afforded by my present wife.

Finally, I would like to record my indebtedness to Mr. T. C. Germain, formerly of the Chinese Maritime Customs, who has more than once read through the entire manuscript and proffered welcome criticism and advice.

CONTENTS

4 *Craft of the Upper Yangtze & Tributaries* 471

PROLOGUE

THE Yangtze River is China's most important inland highway. It is the country's great trade artery, carrying an enormous amount of traffic both up and down its 2,000 miles of navigable water.

The story of the craft of the Lower and Middle Yangtze and of the simple and every-day types of the littoral lacks the spice of peril and romance to be found in the rapids and races of the Upper Yangtze; yet there is much on the lower sections of the great river to arouse interest and admiration. Moreover there is an infinite variety, ranging from the ancient sea-going junks in the estuary, manned by crews whose skill is equal to their hardihood and daring, to the stately polished junks of the broad, quiet reaches of the Lower and Middle Yangtze. Interspersed with these are the humble little junks whose only claim to interest lies in their inherent usefulness and adaptability to local conditions.

Dragon boats and Snail boats, Duck-boats and Kettle-boats, each has an individual attractiveness, and each, in its way, plays a part, however lowly, in the magical and little-known story of the age-old craft of China.

The steamer, which first made its appearance in China in the mid-nineteenth century, had a great effect on the junk. Further, a large part of China's inland produce, which had been for centuries carried by small craft on the creeks and canals, was soon, owing to the recent large-scale programme of road construction throughout the country, to be conveyed by the trucks of Mr. Henry Ford and Mr. Dodge.

It must be remembered that many of the vessels herein described belong to the old China, the China that has now faded, and the immense and picturesque junk traffic so vividly remembered by those of us whose knowledge goes back 30 years or more has correspondingly dwindled.

Nevertheless, alas, with depleted numbers, some of the junks of China still more than hold their own and, without doubt, will do so untouched by the hand of modern scientific development. Should they continue to exist, it would be interesting indeed to know what the seamen of 100 years will think of them.

For generations the junkmen of China have cheerfully accepted a life of unmitigated hardship, and it is surely time some acknowledgment were made to their endurance and resourceful ingenuity. Chinese sailors served in the East India Company's ships, and even today they are to be found in the Merchant Navies of many different countries.

The junkmen are marvellously adaptable. It is just this adaptability of theirs that astonishes one beyond all else in China. An instance of this is the fact that the best ricksha men in Shanghai and the most careful lorry drivers on the Burma Road came from the junks of Langshan. There is, of course, nothing remarkable in the fact that the Chinese can do wonderful things along their own particular lines, but the extraordinary thing is that after a lesson or two even a coolie can be taught to drive a trolley-car or a taxi-cab. The only disadvantage to their adaptability is that they will persist in adhering to their own way of doing things. If they are shown the right way of doing a thing, they obey, go home, think out a new way, and follow their own method ever after.

Some Chinese mythical legends have found their way into these pages. Many, of course, sound trivial and cannot always be regarded with uniform gravity; but they cannot be excluded, for they are, taken as a whole, so important a part of the junkman's life and throw a valuable light on his mental attitude.

Modern young China is scornful of these stories and dismisses them contemptuously as superstitious nonsense; but, apart from the interest and pleasure entailed in collecting them and associating them with the locality where they originated, there is the satisfaction of conserving these interesting legends and superstitions of the old-time junkmen lest they too pass away unrecorded.

I am a sailor by profession. My early days at sea were served in sail, with the great-hearted sailors of a bygone age in a severe school of seamanship. Although I turned my back on salt water and joined the Chinese Maritime Customs at a fairly early age, I lived on the Yangtze River for a great number of years, and so it came about that all my active life (including even the three years I spent in Japanese prison camps) has been spent within sight and sound of water of some sort.

My 30 years' service in the Chinese Maritime Customs and my numerous wanderings up and down the coast and rivers of China throughout that time with theodolite and sketch book obliged me to live among Chinese sailors of all kinds and bred in me a deep interest and affection for the junkmen, their craft, and their story. So it came about that the Inspector General of Customs, Sir Frederick Maze, detached me to carry out Chinese nautical research, and I was thus able to visit many places in the interior not always accessible to foreigners.

Some seven years or more have gone into the making of these volumes on Yangtze junks, the material for which was collected over a very much longer period. It has been compiled from field research carried out during perhaps the most disturbed period of China's eventful history and in China's recognized trouble spots, amid almost continual fighting, bandit raids, enemy occupation, floods and droughts, culminating in a Japanese prison camp.

A review of the period during which I have been collecting this material makes me rather sad, for I fear it was begun too late. Some of the finest types, as a result of the last few difficult years, have gone forever. But an imperfect record is better than none at all, and in spite of its many shortcomings enough has, I hope, been written to show that the Chinese know how to build for their own particular needs, even if their methods are crude by the standard of a Lloyd's surveyor.

Mr. John Hay, former Secretary of State of the United States, once said: "*The storm centre of the world has gradually shifted to China . . . whoever fully understands that mighty Empire . . . has the key to world politics for the next five centuries.*" Although uttered more than half a century ago, the words of this famous advocate of the "Open Door" to China have recently taken on an additional meaning. The changing political conditions of the Far East, as they affect the other nations of the world, should bring the realization to everyone that an understanding of China, ancient as well as modern, is a vital necessity.

I do not wish it to be assumed that this book will help very much towards a greater knowledge of China; but, if the reader feels stirred to a deeper interest in the boats, places, and peoples I have written about, I shall be happy indeed.

Be all this as it may, it will perhaps be appropriate to conclude this section with the words of an earlier author: "Here then we will begin the narration; let this be enough by the way of a preface; for it is a foolish thing to make a long prologue and to be short in the story itself."

Windlesham, Surrey, 1967 G. R. G. Worcester.

MAP & NOTES

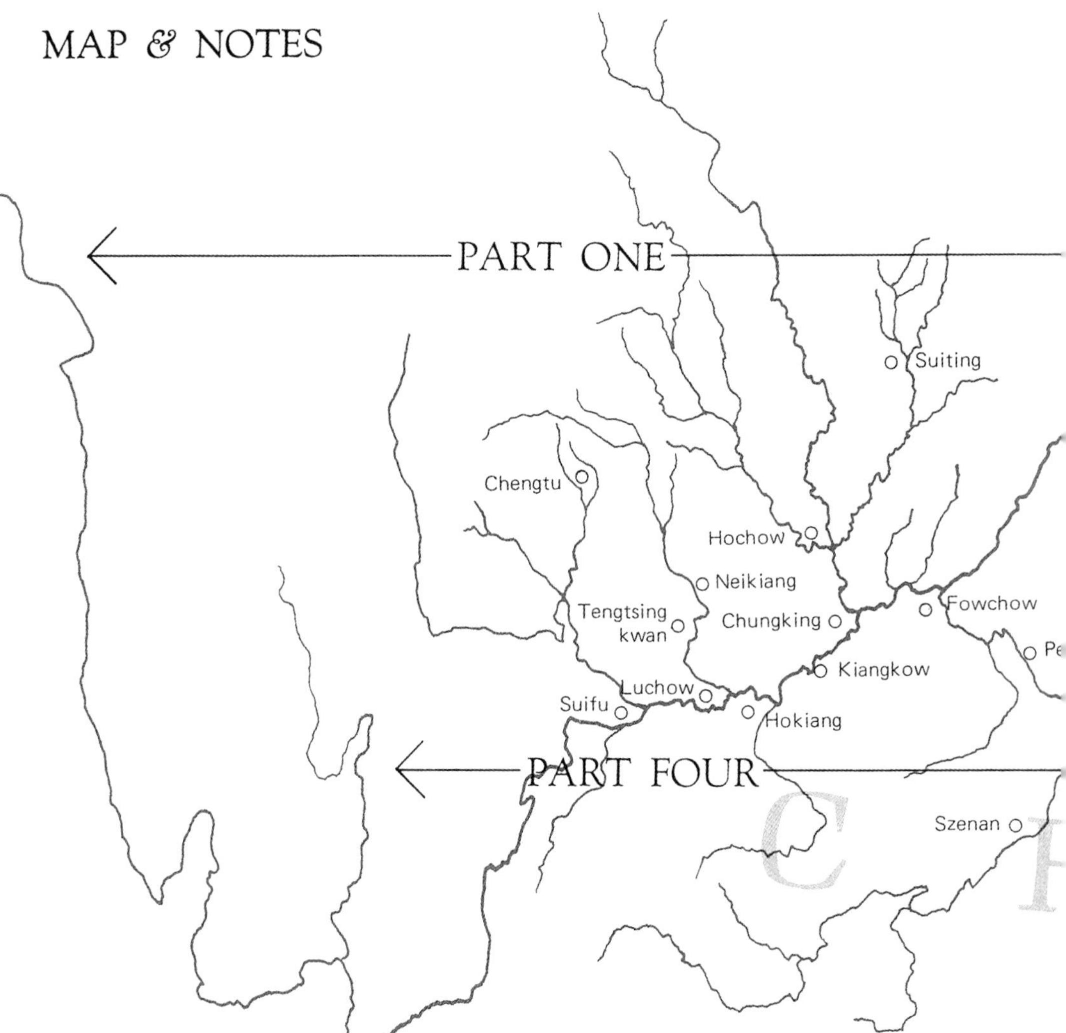

EDITOR'S NOTES:

Mr. Worcester's four volumes dealing with the craft of the Yangtze River were originally published in Shanghai between 1940 and 1948 by order of the Inspector General of Customs of the Chinese Maritime Customs Service. They were *Junks and Sampans of the Upper Yangtze; Notes on the Crooked-bow and Crooked-stern Junks of Szechwan;* and Volumes I and II of *The Junks and Sampans of the Yangtze,* which covered the craft of the estuary and Shanghai area and of the Lower and Middle Yangtze. The books have been long out of print, and the few existing copies are now collectors' items.

The aim of this presentation is to preserve Mr. Worcester's great work for a scholarly audience while at the same time presenting it in an attractive manner to the general reader.

In order to compatibly combine in one volume four books that were written as separate entities, editing was necessary to eliminate repetition and to ensure continuity. Part One of this volume consists of general material, gleaned from all four books, covering the River, its craft, and its people, and ending with a previously unpublished section on the coming of the steamer to the Yangtze. One of the few changes has been the division of this material into eleven chapters for which new titles have been supplied. A discussion of the *Keying,* a junk brought to England, has been transferred from the text to an appendix, as has material on Chinese junk models and a list of Chinese war vessels. Parts Two, Three, and Four are the plans and descriptions of the craft on the three sections of the Yangtze, reproduced as they appeared in the original texts. In Part Four, previously unpublished material has been added to the descriptions of the Upper River and its tributaries, just as the author wished.

Mr. Worcester's footnotes were reset and now appear as margin notes. Editor's notes are printed in brown.

The glossary of nautical terms appeared in two of the original books. None of the previous books contained an index; therefore, the index for this volume is entirely new.

THE English foot rather than the Chinese has been used throughout this book as a unit of measurement, the reason being that in actual practice a Chinese foot (*ch'ih*) varies from 8.6 to 27.8 inches. The Chinese Commercial Guide gives a hundred different values of the *ch'ih* as actually in use. The English mile, too, has been accepted rather than the Chinese *li*, for distances in China depend on the difficulty in getting over the ground. On level ground a mile is called 2 *li;* on ordinary hill roads, not very steep, one mile is 5 *li;* on mountainous roads one mile is called 15 *li*. It will be sufficient to assume 3 *li* as being the equivalent of one mile. Standards of weight also vary all over the country. The piculs and catties in this book are respectively equal to about 133¼ pounds or 60.48 kilogrammes and 1¼ pounds or 0.6048 kilogrammes.

So, too, with place names. Even the most unobservant traveller soon discovers that a level of uniformity cannot be safely assumed. The names vary in perhaps unaccountable ways: Pahsien is the alternative name for Tch'ongk'ing, Tchongkin, or Chungking. To make matters worse, there is an interesting variety of romanizing them. For instance, Anking, Nganking, or Nganking must not be confused with Nanking, Nankin, or Nankeen. Both are on the Yangtze, and both provincial capitals but different towns, 157 miles apart. Moreover, the junkmen, who seldom can read or write, often have their own private place names.

If therefore mistakes have crept in, it is probably due to these irritating circumstances.

G. R. G. W.

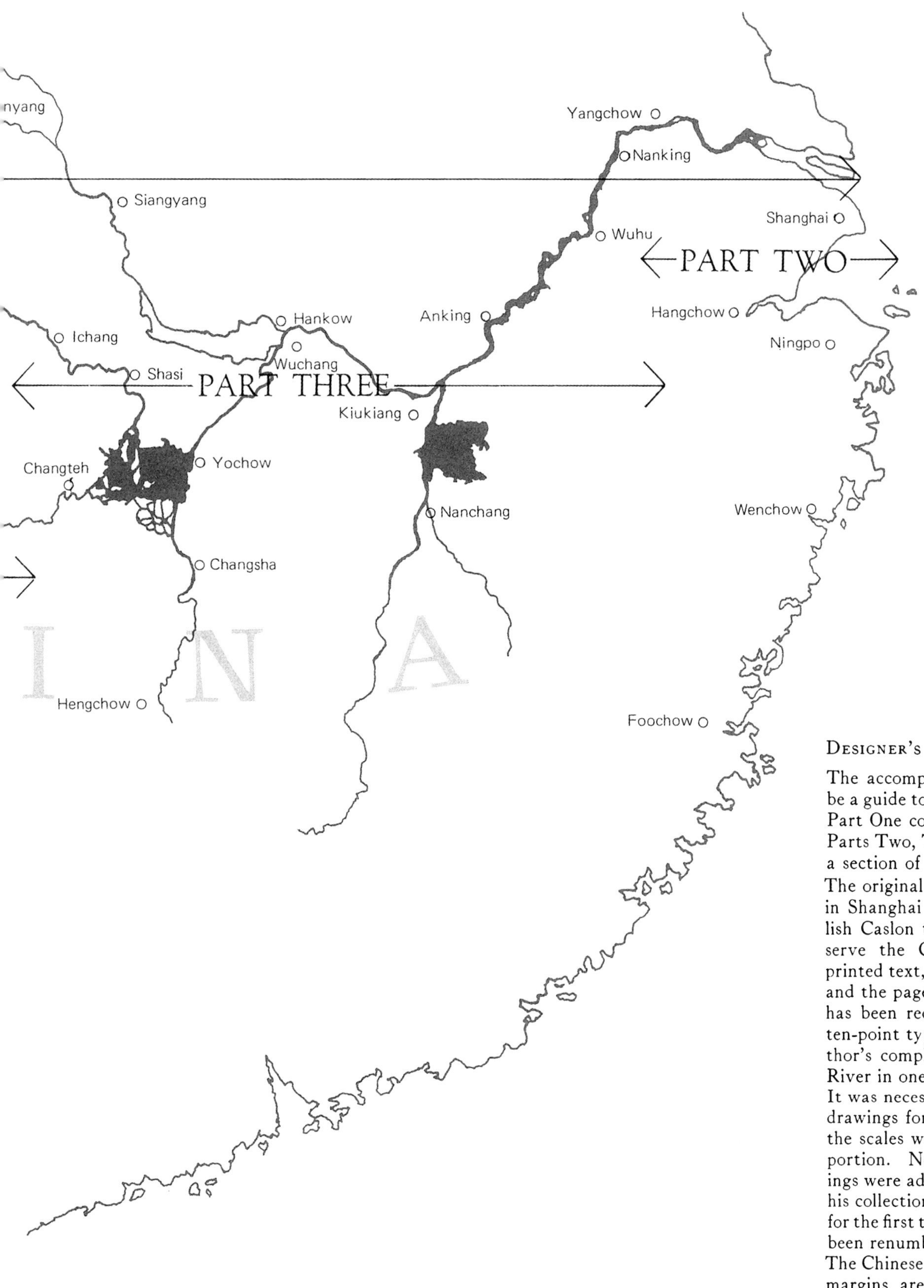

DESIGNER'S NOTES:

The accompanying map is designed to be a guide to the four parts of this book: Part One covers the River as a whole; Parts Two, Three, and Four each cover a section of the Yangtze.

The original four volumes were printed in Shanghai using a twelve-point English Caslon typeface. In order to preserve the Chinese characters in the printed text, the bindings were removed and the pages photographed. The text has been reduced to the equivalent of ten-point type to accommodate the author's complete works on the Yangtze River in one volume.

It was necessary to reduce many of the drawings for this new page design, but the scales were retained in correct proportion. New photographs and drawings were added by Mr. Worcester from his collection and appear in this volume for the first time. The illustrations have been renumbered in this new format.

The Chinese characters appearing in the margins are the work of calligrapher Peter W. T. Ho and replace the original typecast characters.

The redesigned format for this important work was submitted to the author and approved shortly before his death. It is hoped the finished volume would have pleased Mr. Worcester.

PART ONE

THE YANGTZE RIVER— ITS CRAFT & PEOPLE

There are thoſe who affirm there are more veſſels in China than in all the reſt of the known world. This will ſeem incredible to many Europeans; but I who have not ſeen the eighth part of the veſſels in China, and have travelled a great part of the world, do look upon it as moſt certain.

THE NEW HISTORY OF CHINA, 1688
by Gabriel Magaillans,
Miſſionary Apoſtolick.

THE RIVER

THE Yangtzekiang, the fourth largest river in the world, being over 3,000 miles in length but, together with its tributaries, navigable by junks for 5,500 miles, traverses six of the provinces of China and forms a vital artery for the trade of the country, which for thousands of years has passed up and down its length.

Rising beyond the western border of China Proper in the mountains of Tibet, it flows for its first 2,000 odd miles through narrow ravines carved through mountainous country. On emerging from these deep ravines it winds its way in rather more leisurely fashion through the alluvial plains of Central China, which were at one time an inland sea studded with occasional islands, now represented by mountain ranges or isolated hills.

The importance of these water communications was very soon recognized by the Chinese, who sought further to improve them by linking up the Yangtze with an elaborate system of canals and creeks. The great Emperor Yü (大 禹), 2205–2198 B.C., utilized the surplus waters of the rivers by draining them off into specially dug canals and thereby combining flood-control with a signal service to commerce and irrigation. He is said to have worked unceasingly for eight years, tracking the rivers to their sources, constructing bunds and dikes, deepening channels, and making cuts through hills. His inspiration for the network of waterways was said to have been derived from the markings on the back of a tortoise.

No other river in the world provides such an ideal natural network of waterways whereby the most distant parts are accessible. The basin thus drained is estimated at 750,000 square miles, or one-half of the area of the Eighteen Provinces of China Proper; the Yangtze, therefore, constitutes one of China's chief assets for the development of commercial prosperity and inland communications, and nearly 200,000,000 industrious people convey their merchandise down this main artery.

The Yangtze affords direct communication by small steamers and the largest junks up to Suifu, 1,750 miles from its mouth, and its limit of navigability for all craft is only reached 40 miles above Suifu at a point above Pingshan. Vessels of 24 feet draught can reach Wuhu, 264 miles from Shanghai, at all seasons of the year, and ships of 10 feet draught in winter and over 29 feet in summer can reach Hankow, a distance farther up of 334 miles; while vessels drawing 5 feet in winter and 14 feet in summer can reach Ichang, 1,000 miles from the sea.

The Yangtze, which divides China almost precisely in half, has figured very largely in the story of the Empire from its earliest days. Every succeeding dynasty was faced anew with the problem of reconquering provinces distant from the capital; and so, throughout the long Imperial history, there are ever-recurrent accounts of how the Yangtze was crossed and crossed again, punctuated with checks when the opposing armies were held up on one bank or the other of the vast river.

Like most large rivers in China, the Yangtze is known by several different names. Friar Odoric, in the account of his travels in the early fourteenth century, calls it the Talay, a Mongol version of the Chinese name. Both Père Huc and the Russian explorer, Prjevalsky, use the Mongol name of Murui-Usu. It has also been well named the Girdle of China. The best-known Chinese title and that which applies to the longest stretch is Kinho (Gold River), or Kinshakiang (Golden Sand River), extending from Batang down to Suifu. From Suifu down to the Tungting Lake it is called the Takiang, or Great River; thence the Ch'angkiang, or Long River; and in its lower reaches it becomes the Yangtze-kiang. A picturesque, but erroneous, rendering of this name is "Son of the Sea" and owes its origin to a misinterpretation in the translation of the character *yang*, which is actually derived from the ancient Kingdom of Yang, both of which have the same sound. Twenty miles north of Chinkiang the old capital of Yang still exists under its former name of Yangchow and is famous as being the town where Marco Polo once held office under the Great Khan. Strictly speaking, it is only from here to the sea that the name of Yangtzekiang is really applicable. For the most part the people who live on or near the Yangtze refer to it simply as "Kiang," or the River, for it looms too largely in their lives to be confused with any lesser stream. Under the generic title of Kiang, too, it has its influence on the names of two of the provinces through which it flows, Kiangsi and Kiangsu.

Unlike the Yellow River, China's Sorrow, which by reason of its floods and tremendous changes of direction has been a source of constant trouble and expense, the Yangtze, despite the losses and dangers of ordinary annual floods and occasional tremendous inundations, has been an immense blessing to China.

It has also in the main, except for minor vagaries, retained its course more or less unaltered. Evidence, however, exists of two changes which have affected its upper and lower portions. The first concerns the head waters and main course of the Kinsha and probably dates back to the early Pleistocene period. In the opinion of eminent scientific authorities the upper reaches of the Yangtze before that time ran into the Red River and thence through Indo-China into the Gulf of Tonkin. Some great geographical disturbance then occurred, such as the sinking of the Red basin or an upheaval of the Yunnan plateau, which so obstructed the course of the Kinsha that it was forced to carve out a passage for itself eastwards to the Yangtze. It is interesting that a belief still obtains among the aboriginal tribe of the Moso that the upper waters of the Yangtze once ran through a different channel, though, according to them, the Mekong and not the Red River was the receiving stream. This, if it was not the reason for, must have had a considerable bearing on, the commonly held Chinese opinion that the Min River and not the Kinsha is the parent stream; for, at that early stage in the world's story, when the upper reaches of the Yangtze flowed south instead of east, the beheaded waters of the Kinsha would have formed only a lesser tributary, and, as the "Yü Kung" (禹 貢) says in the Sixth Book of the Chinese Classics, the course of the Kiang, or the River, indeed began in the mountains of the Min Range.

Geological authorities, in discussing the interesting problems of their science connected with the many great parallel streams that rise in the Tibetan mountains, think that it is not unlikely that the Mekong River may so alter its course as to become a tributary of the Salween River, and consider there are grounds for the belief, if this happens, that the upper reaches of the Yangtze may in consequence be once again diverted, but this time to flow into the Indian Ocean.

The second great change in the direction of the course of the Yangtze concerns its outlet. Authorities are agreed that the river formerly flowed into the sea not, as now, through an estuary but through a number of multiple mouths then commonly known as the Northern, Middle, and Southern Rivers. Actually the reference to three ancient mouths is rather misleading, for there were in reality four.

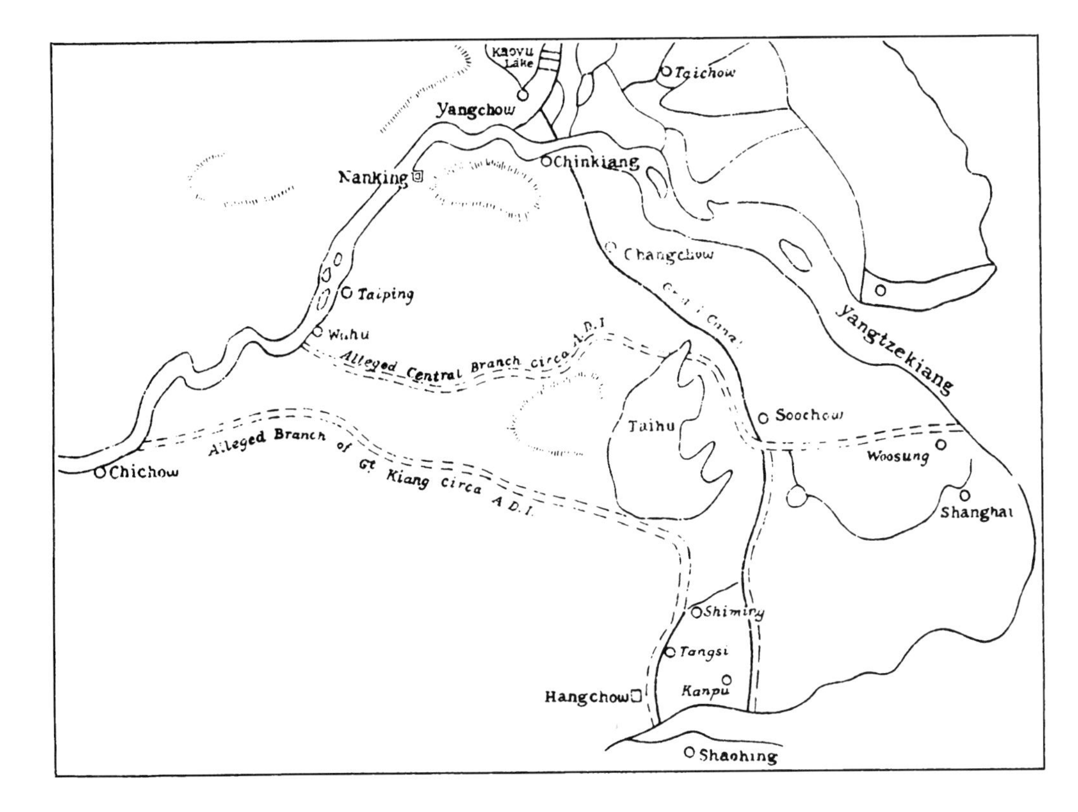

The ancient mouths of the Yangtze.

The northern branch seems to have more or less followed the course of the estuary as it is to-day. The middle portion branched off in the vicinity of Wuhu and ran in an easterly direction into Southern Kiangsu, past and through the northern tip of the Great T'aihu; farther south below Soochow it branched again into two widely diverging streams, one arm becoming the Woosung River, now known as the Soochow Creek, and the other flowing out into Hangchow Bay in Chekiang Province. The last, or southern, portion was then considered the principal stream. It separated from the Yangtze at Chihchow (池 州), nearly 400 miles from the sea, and, after skirting or passing through the southern end of the T'aihu, formed the present channel of the Grand Canal and finally, about 30 miles west of Ningpo, emptied itself into Hangchow Bay near Yüyao (餘 姚), south of and near to the southern arm of the middle branch. The site of this southern branch has been established by a reference in the "Ch'ien Han Shu" (前 漢 書), or "History of the Former Han Dynasty," 206 B.C. to A.D. 25, compiled by Pan Ku (班 固), who lived at the beginning of the Christian era. Still earlier mentions in Chinese history date back to the ancient geographical description of the country in the "Yü Kung," prepared by the Emperor Yü, 2205–2198 B.C., after he had completed his great task of subduing the waters caused by the great flood. In this account he alludes to the three separate embouchements of the river.

The silt brought down in such vast quantities gradually filled the southern and middle branches, while the force of the current at the same time gradually deepened and enlarged the northern branch, until finally in the third century the waters ceased to flow in the Chekiang Channel, and in the seventh century the embankment was made, which cut off all communication with the sea along the north bank of Hangchow Bay.

This alluvial deposit of the Yangtze is a formidable factor to be reckoned with. Its waters are so highly charged with sediment that the continual layers of loamy silt constitute an unending process of reclamation by means of which the land frontier is being gradually extended. Each year every yard of ground thus naturally reclaimed is embanked and cultivated by the Chinese. A great part of South-eastern Kiangsu owes its origin to this fertile mixture of silt and detritus, and at the same time the level of the ocean-bed is being raised over an area of hundreds of miles.

Each waterway has its different problems and its different conditions, and the Chinese shipwrights, in their own inimitable way, have designed their craft accordingly. And so we find an endless variety of different types, while throughout them all simplicity is the keynote. Nevertheless, for all their simplicity, some of the devices are both efficient and ingenious.

And so down the Yangtze River come junks laden with hemp, beans, straw braid, graphites, lead, and silk; others bring vegetable tallow, bamboos, paper, and silver. From far beyond Wuhu they bring copper, iron, coal, dates, fungus, varnish, and, of course, rice. Down the vast waterways from Anking come joss sticks, roots, and paper, and across the Poyang Lake the grasscloth of Ningtu (甯都), the tobacco leaves of Juikin (瑞 金), and the rice of Nanchang. Kingtehchen, the well-known porcelain-manufacturing centre in Kiangsi Province, is not accessible to steam-launches, and shipments of porcelain from that area are carried to Kiukiang in specially constructed junks. From the far interior, fed by the Han River, junks bring beans, bristles, flour, fans, hides, silk, tea, and wood oil to Hankow, the commercial, industrial, and financial heart of Central China. The junks of Hunan carry coal, lead, zinc, antimony, manganese, and other minerals across the Tungting Lake to the factories of Hankow, and the produce of Yochow, such as rice, timber, bamboos, and fish, for consumption in the great city. From Shasi junks bring cotton and silk, and hither come from Ichang, the large transhipment port, the produce of Szechwan, white wax, bristles, forest trees, wheat, fruit, herbs, and medicines.

THE CHINESE JUNK IN HISTORY, ART, AND LITERATURE

AMONG the meagre arts and crafts practised by primitive man, the knowledge of how to propel himself in or on some form of floating vessel was so certainly acquired from the very earliest time that this fact has been taken for granted by all ethnologists and antiquaries.

The floating trunk of a tree doubtless inspired early man's first nautical venture, and in this connection, in an old Chinese book the "Huai Nan Tzŭ" (淮 南 子), dating back to about 122 B.C., it is suggested that rafts owe their genesis to man's observation of leaves drifting by on the stream, and it is said that "he who looked on a hollow log floating on the water was the first shipbuilder."

In the earliest writings of any country there are always allusions, albeit lamentably vague, to ships and boats. Vague of course, for we cannot expect to find documents describing how early man came to build the first boats, and histories of various nations in the world contain no records of the initial stages of navigation, for the good and sufficient reason that boatbuilding came before writing.

According to Chinese legendary history, all useful inventions, together with the philosophy of the sages, were said to be mentioned in the earliest of the classics, the "I Ching" (易 經), or "Book of Changes," and its appendices. The art of boatbuilding is also claimed by some (although this is difficult to believe) to be represented in the system of symbols of which the "I Ching" consists. One of these appendices, written after the time of Confucius, describes how Fu Hsi (伏 羲), the first of the five great rulers, traditionally dated 2852 B.C., taught the people many useful arts, including that of fishing with nets and how to make the first boats. These were built by "hewing planks and shaping and planing wood."

Tradition makes a lot of Fu Hsi, who was credited with being the offspring of a nymph and a rainbow. One of the most outstanding of the legends describes how celestial aid was sent him in his efforts for the enlightenment of his people by the sudden appearance of a "dragon" horse bearing a scroll on which were inscribed the eight mystic trigrams known as the *pa-kua* (八 卦) which play so important a part in Chinese divination and philosophy. Little more is told us of this interesting personality except that he "dwelt in a hall, wore robes, introduced rafts and carts," and fittingly terminated his picturesque career by ascending to heaven on a dragon's back.

There is so large a substratum of truth upon which Chinese myths and legends have grown up through the efforts of the unlearned to explain some noticed fact or phenomenon that the staging of the important incidents of Fu Hsi's life by the banks of the Yellow River seems the Chinese way of designating that area as the cradle of their civilization. Certainly it is a tradition among the junkmen that the craft of the Yellow River antedate those of the Yangtze, which, in their turn, preceded the ocean-going junks.

This young industry of shipbuilding then, so it was said, was fostered and developed about 700 years later by the great Emperor Yü (禹 王), sometimes called the first shipbuilder.

The Emperor Yü has played such an important part in the history of the rivers of China that a few remarks on his spectacular achievements are apposite. According to tradition, his mother saw a star falling through one of the constellations and in a dream connected with it swallowed a magic pearl. And so, in due season, Yü entered the world. He started life with the handicap of having, according to the bamboo books, "a tiger's nose, a large mouth, and ears with three openings." The Emperor became ancient China's most famous and efficient conservancy engineer. His labours are too numerous to mention, but chief among them were the "bringing to order of the Nine Kiangs," including the T'o (沱) and the Ch'ien (潛) Rivers, and the draining of the marshes of Yün (雲) and Mêng (夢). He carried out repairs to the existing works of the T'aiyüan (太 原), moving from thence on to the "cross-flowing stream of Chang (漳)." It is said that he is buried near Ningpo.

Early Chinese writers attribute boatbuilding and other inventions to one or other of the mythical sages with a bewildering lack of discrimination, for according to another of the Chinese Histories, the "Ch'un Ch'iu" (春 秋), edited by Confucius (who put forward the claims of Fu Hsi above as the first naval authority), and also the writings of Mo Tzŭ (墨 子), it is claimed that the boat was introduced by Yü Jên (虞 訒), Hua Hu (化 狐), Kung Shui (工 倕), P'an Yü (番 愚), Pai I (伯 益), and Ku Huo Ti (鼓 貨 狄), all officers of the Emperor Huang Ti (黃 帝), and so the Emperor Huang Ti as well as Fu Hsi is very generally credited with building the first boat.

In the "Shih I Chi" (拾 遺 記) it is stated that the Emperor learned the importance of maritime power during his campaign in Hopeh against his great enemy Ch'ih Yu (蚩 尤). The Emperor, who lived over 4,000 years ago, must have been something of an inventor, for in addition to boats he is said to have introduced the oar as a propelling agent, the smoke screen, and finally the compass.

As has been indicated, it seems that the art of shipbuilding in a country with so old a civilization as that of China probably dates back very much further than these legendary periods, for a crude form of navigation was one of primitive man's earliest discoveries, wherein he was, no doubt, inspired by the desire for food and suitable surroundings.

The calm and sheltered waters of China's rivers and lakes were admirably adapted to the development of craft from the floating log, man's first nautical venture.

The ubiquity of the bamboo must probably have caused rafts of this material to have been used most generally where it was to be found. In the north it would appear to have been replaced by skin rafts, still in use in some places to-day. From these primitive beginnings gradually evolved the built-up craft which were the forbears of the junks and sampans we know to-day.

Indeed, we have it on the authority of the "Shih I Chi," written by Wang Chia (王 嘉) in the Ch'in dynasty, more than 2,000 years ago, that before the invention of the boat the ancients used a form of raft for ferrying purposes.

Between neolithic man and modern man in China there is, despite gaps, a fairly clear continuity, so that it is reasonable to suppose that the first attempts at boatbuilding were handed down and perfected generation by generation, until various kinds of simple craft evolved which were efficient enough to be eventually stabilized into types. These types must have been the progenitors of all those still in use to-day in China.

More or less authentic descriptions and paintings, dating back to 2600 B.C., exist of the ships of ancient Egypt, Greece, and Rome, and even of India and Persia. That is to say, the data available can be safely assumed to be so tolerably accurate in general that these ships can be reasonably reconstructed, and many old pictures of them are to be found which would not offend the historian or the sailor; but there is nothing of the kind relating to ancient Chinese junks.

No chapter in the history of China is so incomplete as that concerning ships and sailors. There is no general collection of pictures, nor can literary sources be regarded as satisfactory.

In the effort to trace back the earliest mention of floating craft, therefore, a brief survey of the origin of Chinese writing is necessary, particularly considering the pictographic character it showed in its initial stages.

The rise of the art of writing, even more than that of shipbuilding, will always be a mystery quite impossible to solve. It is claimed by many Chinese scholars that the kindred arts of writing and drawing came into existence together from one and the same source. Legend tells how, under the same Yellow Emperor, Huang Ti, from whose reign date the principal arts and crafts of the Chinese, there were two inspired sages.

The first was Ts'ang Chieh (倉 頡), who was a Minister of Huang Ti. He was born a sage and was, naturally enough, precocious as a child. He is said to have invented writing by imitating the footprints of birds and animals on the ground, and thus doing away with the old clumsy method of using knots.

The other sage was Shih Huang (史 皇), who was also a Minister of Huang Ti; indeed, some authorities state this is another name for Ts'ang Chieh. This official is credited with the introduction of drawing and of himself making the first picture. According to some, however, the first painter was a younger sister of the Emperor Shun (舜 帝) named Lai (萊), *circa* 2255 B.C.

The written characters in use in very early days were originally crude pictures of men, houses, and the like. It is possible to trace in the modified modern forms of those characters resemblances more or less to the objects intended. Thus, for sun the ancient Chinese drew a circle with a dot in it; for mouth, a round hole; and so on. These are called pictograms. Later, ideograms came into being, that is to say, ideas. Thus, a pig under a roof indicated home; one woman under a roof, peace; two women under a roof, strife; a woman with a broom, a wife; and so on.

By Shang (商) times, however, the art of writing had progressed beyond this primitive order, although early pictograms in some form or other still survived. Indeed, in some cases, though still further modified, they are in use to-day. This is the case with various pictograms relating to boats, as will be shown later.

The most ancient surviving Chinese writing as yet discovered is that found on the bone and shell fragments known as the oracle bones.* These, therefore, constitute the earliest references yet found to boats in China.

These bones formed a part of the royal archives of the Shang dynasty, which flourished from 1766 to 1122 B.C. The Shang people were the successors of the stone-bronze age men, the site of their capital being at Anyang (安 陽), in North China.

The bone fragments vary in size from pieces only large enough to carry

* Towards the end of the last century some inscribed turtle shells and animal bones were unearthed by farmers in Honan, who decided they must be "dragon" bones. The villagers, after scraping off the invaluable inscriptions, sold the bones to the local medicine shops, where they were ground into powder and were considered to be of the very highest efficacy in curing ailments, particularly nervous disorders. A curio dealer, being struck by the antique writing on some of the pieces, showed them to a Chinese scholar. The discovery caused a sensation, and so came to light by accident the earliest examples of Chinese writings and the most ancient records of the Chinese people. Some hundreds of thousands of fragments are in the hands of collectors, and now all have been catalogued. Needless to say, as soon as it was realized that these bones were worth money they were immediately forged in considerable numbers.

	A.—CHOU: A BOAT.	B.—PAN: TO PROPEL A BOAT BY MEANS OF AN OAR.
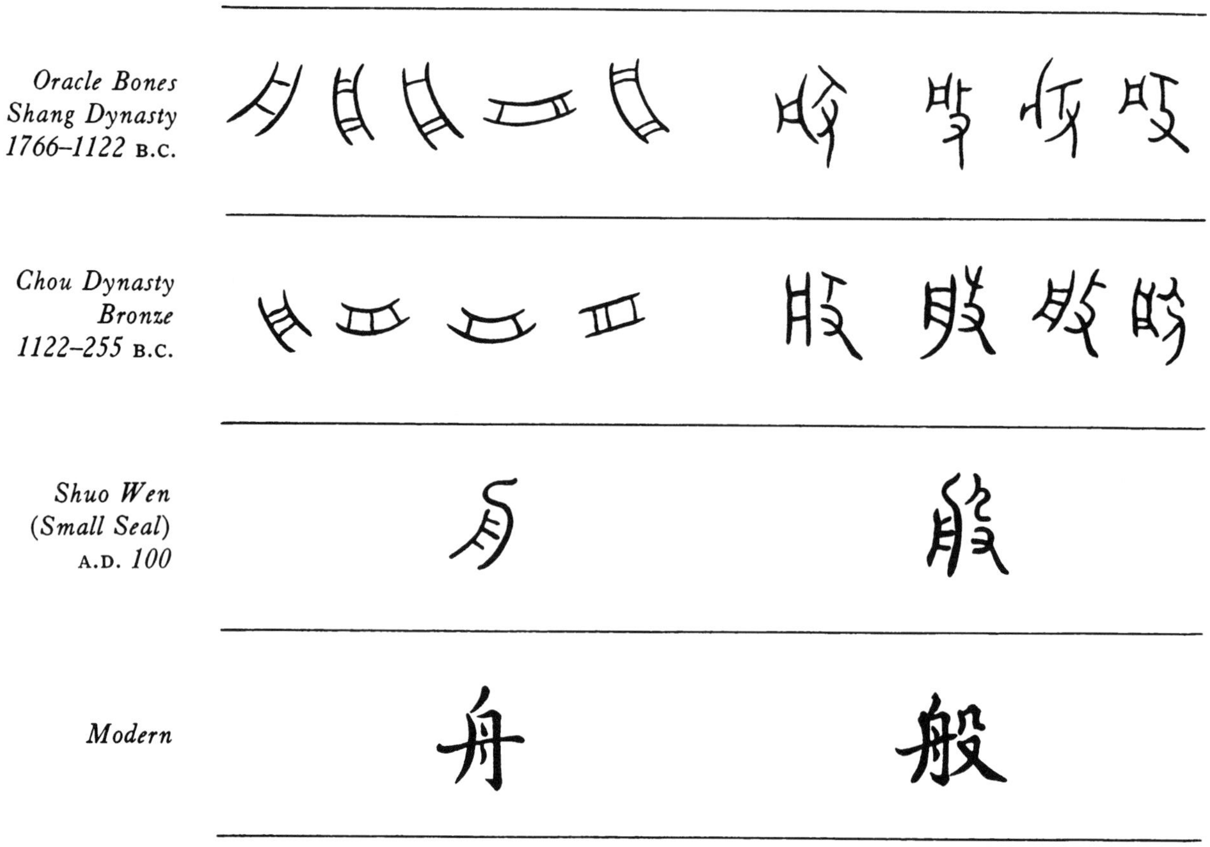 *Oracle Bones Shang Dynasty 1766–1122* B.C.		
Chou Dynasty Bronze 1122–255 B.C.		
Shuo Wen (Small Seal) A.D. *100*		
Modern	舟	般

one character to those of a couple of feet in length. They were used for divination purposes and are of two kinds. First, the shoulder-blades of oxen or large deer and, secondly, the under side of turtles, the latter being caught by fishermen in the autumn and offered to the Government. The surface was smoothed and polished, and then shallow, siim, oval indentations were hollowed out of the back of the bone surface. The number of these pits varied with the size of the bone. There were as many as 72 in a large tortoise-shell. Heat was then applied to any spot on the edge of the oval, probably by means of a heated bronze skewer. This resulted in the cracks intersecting somewhere on the centre line of the hollowed oval in a T-shaped figure which constituted the utterances of the oracle, the shapes and direction being interpreted according to fixed rules. Essentially, however, the answer was either affirmative or negative.

Apparently the Shang people did very little without first consulting the oracle. If ever they got into any sort of trouble they told the spirits about it and asked their advice; and the bone and shell fragments are the results of various questions put to their ancestors and the gods by these careful people.

They always kept the spirits fully informed, and asked advice and guidance on all possible subjects, not only on important matters such as making wars on hostile neighbours, political moves, and so on, but on comparatively unimportant details connected with their daily life—also, of course, boats (*see illustration above*, Fig. A).

So cautious were they about leaving nothing to chance that they would make full and detailed inquiries before proceeding on a voyage and all the routine matters connected with travel.

In the matter of hunting and fishing they were just as particular, and they

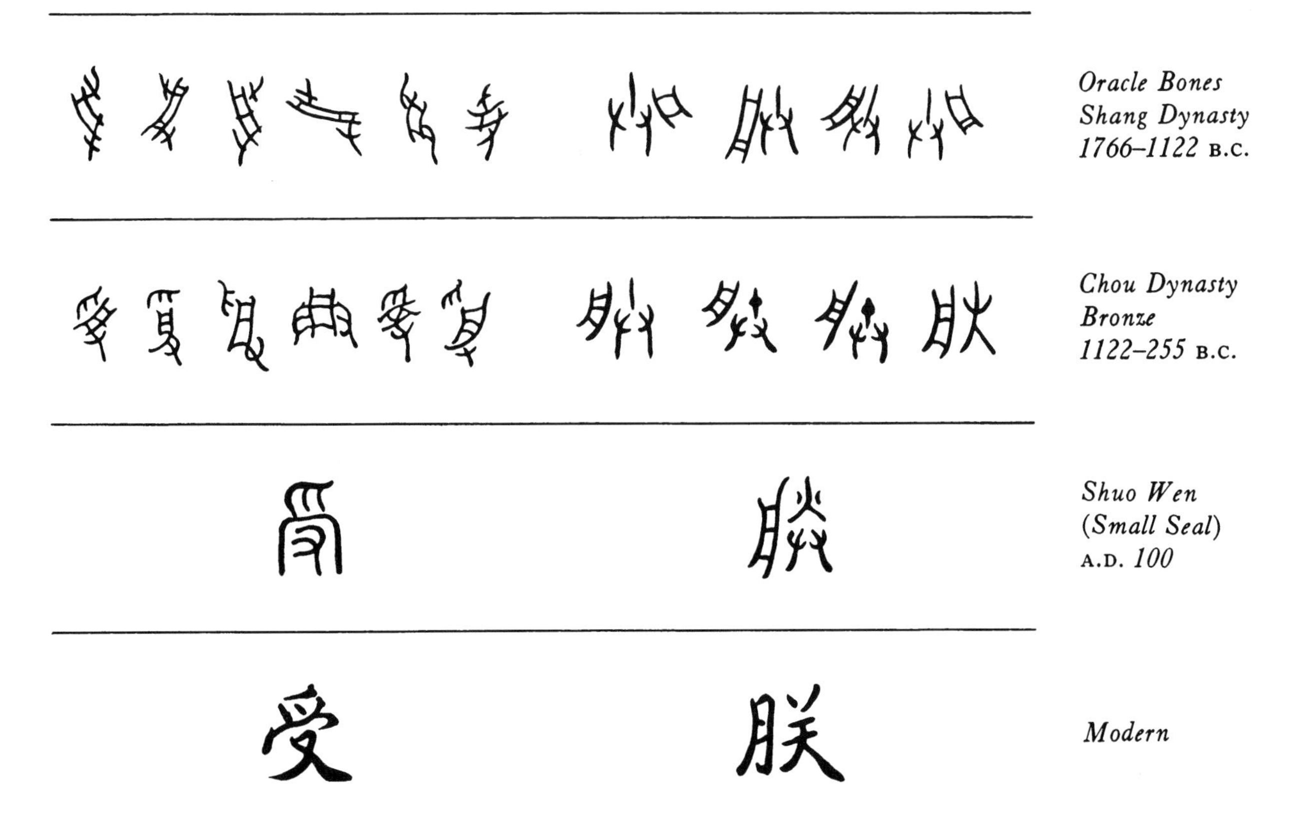

had, apparently, so little confidence in themselves that the oracle was called upon to supply answers to the most elementary questions.

The Shang people lived by agriculture, herding flocks and cattle, and by hunting. They were by no means a nautical people, but we do know that they traded by boats over considerable distances; indeed, by inference, it is supposed that they had trade relations with portions at least of the Yangtze Valley.* No doubt a considerable part of the journey was water borne, indeed, the pictogram for a boat is as commonly found on the oracle bones as that of a horse,† so that it is hard to determine which form of transport was most in use.

It is disappointing that so far no evidence of the use of sails has come to light on the oracle bones. The character *pan* (般) (*see illustration*, Fig. B), to propel a boat by means of an oar, oars, or by a sweep, appears in their pictograms. This, however, is no proof that sails did not also exist. The Shang writers were masters of the art of shorthand, and sails may have been omitted in the interests of simplicity just as the cart is always shown without a horse, horse-lovers though the Shang people were.†

The men of Shang had a considerable culture and showed outstanding freshness and artistry in their handicrafts, sculpture, and bronze. We may safely assume that their boatbuilding, although we know so little of this aspect of their life, was not inferior in efficiency to their other activities. From the word *chêng* (朕), meaning to caulk the seams of a boat, which appears on the oracle bones, we know, for instance, that the boats were caulked, and this indicates that they had progressed beyond the dug-out stage of naval architecture.‡

That water transport played a very important part in their daily life is abundantly evidenced by the fact that the pictograph *shou* (受), which has the archaic meaning of to "receive from hand to hand," is illustrated by the character

* "The Birth of China," Herrlee Glessner Creel. Strongly recommended to all readers anxious to follow up this fascinating subject.

† "Communications in China during the Shang Period." "China Journal," Vol. XXVI, May 1937. A most able article by Mr. H. E. Gibson.

‡ In Monsieur E. Sigaut's opinion, although adjacent countries such as Burma, Malaya, Netherlands East Indies, and Philippine Islands developed their craft through the dug-out, it by no means follows that China did the same. This contention is much strengthened by the fact that there are no dug-outs to be seen to-day in China, although many of these survivals still exist in the countries named. He argues, therefore, very convincingly for China's development of her built-up craft straight from the raft. Evidence against this opinion, however, is the statement attributed to the Emperor Huang Ti, *circa* 2697 B.C., that "boats were made by hollowing out logs." ("Monsieur Sigaut" is Etienne Sigaut, a Frenchman who lived in Shanghai and was a good friend of the Worcesters. After the Worcesters' internment in a Japanese concentration camp from March 1943 to August 1945, they stayed with the Sigauts in Shanghai.)

for a boat being, according to Mr. H. E. Gibson, loaded or unloaded. This pictograph will be seen on Page No. 11, Fig. C, the crosses at bow and stern being pictographs of hands, it is thought, at work on the cargo. The cargo cannot be seen* in the oracle bone characters but becomes apparent (with a little imagination) in those of the "Shuo Wên"† and Chou bronzes. This pictograph persisted, with comparatively small change, down to A.D. 100, and even to-day forms the basis of the modern character for boat.

Excavations carried out at Anyang show that the Shang people buried with their dead a great variety of objects, some of exquisite workmanship. Moreover, their royal tombs were most elaborately constructed and decorated. It is infinitely to be regretted that nothing nautical, apparently, has come down to us. The inclusion of but one model boat would have been of inestimable assistance to nautical research. So cultured were these people, unlike some of the dynasties which followed them, that great reliance could have been placed on any contribution they made. The Anyang sites, it is comforting to know, are still being excavated, and it is possible that some nautical artifacts may yet come to light.

The Shangs were conquered by the Chous, who founded the dynasty of that name. At first they were vastly inferior in their culture and quite unimportant from a nautical point of view except that they produced that great man the Duke Chou, who is credited by some with the invention of the compass, and this dynasty provided much literary material, notably the "I Ching" (易 經), or "Book of Changes"; the "Shang Shu" (尙 書), or "Book of History"; the "Shih Ching" (詩 經), or "Book of Poetry," and others which will be referred to later.

Interesting as all this may be, it casts no real light on the subject of nautical research in China. In default, therefore, of any reliable records of Chinese craft, the would-be historian, in trying to trace their evolution, is naturally led to make researches into the craft of contemporary or more ancient civilizations in that cradle of all civilizations, the Near East, and then to endeavour to link up with, or in some way explain, the Chinese types. The more this method is pursued, the more similarities come to light, so that it would seem that so many likenesses could not be due to mere coincidence. Yet, unhappily, the exact opposite is equally easy to prove.‡

The views of those seeking to solve the problem may be divided into two distinct schools of thought. The one insists that in very ancient times a Western people with great natural abilities and a high type of culture migrated to China and settled there, first in the Wei (渭) River Valley and then in that of the Yellow River. From these areas, it is believed, they gradually spread their civilization among their backward neighbours and thus evolved present China.

Another school of thought, equally insistent, affirms that the Chinese civilization has evolved without any outside aid whatsoever. The discovery and study of the oracle bones, already referred to, and the excavation of the Shang dynasty site at Anyang has given a solid foundation for the beginning of history in China about 1500 B.C., and the neolithic discoveries in recent years (revealing the cultures of the black pottery people) push the indigenous civilization still further back.

The prevailing opinion, therefore, to-day is that Chinese civilization is indigenous, though probably influenced from time to time by outside elements.

That there is some resemblance, however it arose, between Chinese craft and the early Nilotic types may be taken as an accepted fact. Various theories have been put forward as to the channels by which this influence flowed and the grounds for the likeness, real or fancied.

These influences, according to some authorities, had incontestably reached

* Perhaps it was down in the hold.

† "Shuo Wên" (說 文), the celebrated dictionary of the Lesser Seal character, by Hsü Shên (許 愼), who died in A.D. 120. It is a collection of all the Chinese characters then in existence, amounting to about 10,000, analysed by the author into their original picture elements with a view to showing the hieroglyphic origin of the Chinese language.

‡ Those interested in following up this subject are referred to the "China Review," Vol. II, of 1873, page 194, where 17 most convincing similarities in the cultures of Egypt and China are given.

India and were certainly apparent there by about the seventh century B.C., when Psammetichius I in Egypt and Nebuchadnezzar the Great in Babylon first organized trade in the Mediterranean and the Indian Ocean. If they journeyed to China by land, these contacts must have travelled by the old Central Asia routes which entered through the remote western provinces.

That there was before the Christian era communication by sea with the Far East we know, and these voyages of the ancients from the Eastern Mediterranean would account for the many traces in the Far East reminiscent of Egyptian and Arabian craft, and for the retention by the conservative junkmen of many devices such as were known to those early civilizations of the West.

Which of these interesting survivals, however, were communicated to, and which borrowed from, the Far East by the Near East is a matter for endless conjecture.

However they evolved, the early Chinese formed their settlements in the valley of the Yellow River, which must have been the stimulus to their efforts at boatbuilding.

Before reaching the sea the early inhabitants of China must have had experience of wide spaces of water. In neolithic days the great plain of North China, across which the Yellow River flowed, was more marshy than at present and included many lakes and lagoons.

The inhabitants soon separated themselves into tribes under local chieftains. Wars were of constant occurrence, and the use of boats for fighting or moving troops must have begun very early in a country so well provided with natural waterways—too well, perhaps, for there is frequent mention of a great flood in the twenty-third century B.C. which was said to have lasted for 13 years and which, it seems not improbable, was due to the Yellow River cutting a new passage for itself to the sea, causing the devastation described by geographical writers, until in time the waters drained away, assisted by the efforts of the great Emperor Yü, who built embankments and cut channels to control and carry off the great waters.

It has for long been conceded that the sea-going junks of North China are among the oldest known types of vessels, with a basic structure dating back perhaps some thousands of years. A factor contributing very largely to the unchanging continuity of design in these northern craft is that they were never subjected to any modifying outside influences, as in the southern China seas; for their inter-colony coastal operations crossed no trade routes, but served a sparsely populated area devoid of commercial opportunities for foreign shipping. Of these ancient coastal types, the Antung trader, so often to be seen in Shanghai, has, it is thought, probably changed the least during the last 2,500 years.

Without disputing the age of the northern sea-going junks, the contention that they represent the oldest existing basically unchanged types would appear open to serious question. For if, as is affirmed by all the eminent authorities, the Chinese race settled by the rivers first, it is only logical to assume that the flat-bottomed riverine craft, the descendants of the raft, are the earliest of all types in China. The argument in favour of the priority of the riverine craft would seem to be borne out by the fact that the farther inland and away from outside modifying influences these craft are to be found plying, the nearer they seem in basic design to the ancient simple conception of a boat. This premised, it may well be, though it has yet to be proved, that many of the craft of the Yangtze derive directly from the craft of the Yellow River, and must have altered little in their main structure from their early prototypes, if only because there is fundamentally so little to change. This, of course, applies to craft of the delta, particularly to those indigenous to waterways in direct communication with the Grand Canal.

The Han Bas Reliefs,
A.D. *25–221.*

In seeking to trace the origins of the various types of craft it is natural to study not only the sculpture, literature, drawing, and painting of a country, but also its ceramic art, together with coins and seals, which have all, in the West, proved such a fruitful field for nautical research.

Very little can be gleaned from the earliest known representations of Chinese craft. Probably the oldest are three sampans on a sculptured slab of stone from a rock tomb of the Later Han dynasty, A.D. 25–221, situated fairly close to the tomb of Confucius at Hsiao T'ang Shan (孝 堂 山). These are depicted as assisting in the operation entitled "the Urn of Chou being brought out of the river." The seated occupants of the boats use a paddle, while in one boat a man stands with a pole, which he may be using either as a quant or as a sounding-pole.

Probably the second oldest portrayal of sampans is similarly sculptured on the walls of a stone tomb of a family named Wu, at Tzŭ Yün Shan (紫 雲 山), also in Shantung, dated about A.D. 147. These craft are heavier in type and have a more characteristic shape. The method of propulsion seems to be more in the nature of an oar than a paddle and is still operated from the stern.

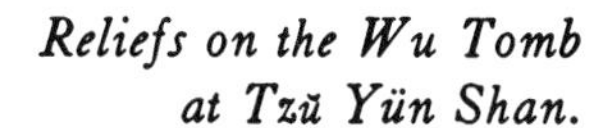

Reliefs on the Wu Tomb at Tzŭ Yün Shan.

As sculptors in stone the Chinese have produced very little else that is of interest to the nautically-minded. It is notable that in their stone or earthenware tomb figures and articles junks play no part at all. Except for those described above and the much-quoted fresco at Ajunta, in India, to be described later, which, even if it represents a Chinese junk, was probably not executed by a Chinese artist, there are no other murals of note showing junks, and the only examples of junks carved in stone are the fanciful jade or soapstone objets d'art from the curio shops or, last and worst of all, the Dowager Empress's marble boat in the Summer Palace in Peking. This stone atrocity of dreadful design was built from funds which had been ear-marked for the navy.

As regards drawing and painting, junks and sampans frequently appear as motifs in early Chinese paintings of all dynasties after the Han dynasty, of which no authentic drawing or painting has come down to us. Some of the early representations clearly incorporate many features and fittings still in use to-day; but these are accidents reflecting more credit on the artist's powers of observation than his knowledge of rigging and seamanship. It is noteworthy that the Chinese artists confine themselves to painting the craft of river and lake, never do they attempt the sea-going type of junk. They never drew a boat for the sake of the boat, but only as an accessory because a sage, philosopher, or high official happened to be meditating in the vicinity.

Landscapes, in particular those depicting mountains and streams, rank highest in Chinese paintings, after which come studies of birds and flowers, dragons, and mythical creatures and animals. Chinese art is so stylistic that everything is cast in a stereotype mould. The rules require that any large sheet of water portrayed should be studded with sails, and a recognized technique was developed for depicting boats in a strictly conventional manner. Thus most of the junks that appear in old pictures have little connection with reality and show exaggerated and bizarre features—from a nautical research point of view—from which little can be deduced. In the case of sampans, however, some degree of comparative accuracy is shown. For instance, in a "Winter Landscape" by Wang Wei (王 維), of the T'ang period, A.D. 618–907, there is a perfect representation of a sampan, banked-in, complete with stick-in-the-mud anchor, a contrivance which will be described later. Wang Wei was a high official during the T'ang dynasty, and a celebrated artist of whom it was said that in his drawings there was poetry, and in his poetry pictures, for in China these two arts are inseparably linked. There seems little reason to doubt that Wang Wei drew the sampan more or less correctly.

It is difficult to arrive at any conclusion from many of these drawings owing to the obviously inadequate knowledge some of the artists had of the craft they illustrated. The Chinese practice of repeating famous pictures, with variations sometimes, and their habit of copying earlier masters is a great help to the student of the periods and styles of ancient artists but it is unfortunately no help to nautical research. In the study of Chinese art due allowance must always be made for the conventionality of the drawing, and this applies with equal force in the matter of Chinese junks.

In Chinese literature there is much more material upon which to draw, although the allusions are not very specific or instructive. There are always references to junks and sampans in the classics and the old dictionaries. Vague mention is made to the tribute brought by various tribes to the Emperor Yü, which are described as "floating along down the rivers Huai (淮), Ssŭ (泗), and Huang (黃)." The semi-barbarous kingdom of Yüeh (越), comprising what is now Chekiang, about 472 B.C. had the largest navy of any of the feudal states and fought always on water, never using war chariots. There was a 21-years' war between this tribe and the state of Wu (吳). The state of Yüeh became a maritime power, and it is probable that, when it is said that the Chinese reached the Yangtze cape in 1200 B.C., this was the occasion of the foundation of this maritime tribe.

Although the date of 1200 B.C. has been asserted with some confidence as being the time that the sea coast in the vicinity of the Yangtze was first reached, it seems far more probable that the Chinese had started their maritime adventures at a very much earlier date, although their excursions would have doubtless been at first confined to fishing, fighting, and other purely local activities.

Sea fights are specifically mentioned as early as 473 B.C., and it is stated in the "Shih Chi" (史 記), the first general history of China, dating back to about 90 B.C., that:

> The King of the Wu kingdom made an attack upon the Ch'i kingdom from the sea, but was defeated and turned home. (吳王從海中(原作上據正義徐廣說改)攻齊齊人敗吳吳王乃引兵歸)

Two years later, in a contest between these two marine kingdoms, the ruler of the Yüeh ordered his general to proceed along the coast and carry out an attack up the Huai River (淮 水), which at that time entered the sea by its own estuary.

Among the many voluminous Chinese dictionaries there is the "Shuo Wên" (說 文) by Hsü Shên (許 愼), who died in A.D. 120. It comprises some 10,000 characters, but, despite numerous references to ships, there is nothing really descriptive of any craft that can be used as evidence of the existence of any definite type at any particular time.*

In respect of one of the earliest mentioned voyages to the East, researches

* References to junks and boats in Chinese literature are innumerable, if not very illuminating. Those interested in following up the subject are referred to the following: "Han Shu" (漢書), "Huai Nan Tzŭ" (淮南子), "Shan Hai Ching" (山海經), "Shuo Wên" (說文), "Han Shu Chu" (漢書注), "Shih I Chi" (拾遺記), "Shu I Chi" (述異記), "Fei Yen Wai Chuan" (飛燕外傳), "Hua Shan Chi" (華山記), "Hou Han Shu" (後漢書), "T'ai P'ing Ching Hua" (太平精華).

into the "Book of History" and the "Book of Odes" reveal how it is recorded that in 219 B.C. the Emperor Shih Huang (秦始皇), of the Ch'in dynasty, ordered Hsü Shih (徐市) to go on an expedition with "several tens of thousands of youths and maidens to search for the three fairy Isles of the Blest." Other authorities have described how they started off from Shantung, and it is confirmed by various sources that they actually reached Japan. Unhappily, history does not appear to relate what success attended their mission. Although no material result was brought to the avaricious Emperor, the story goes to show that sea navigation was widely opened—at least along the north part of the China coast—by that time.

As a result of the incursions and campaigns of the Chinese, the aboriginal tribes gradually withdrew south to the regions now known as Fukien and Kwangtung. In the "Han Shu" (漢書), or "History of the Former Han Dynasty," written by Pan Ku (班固), *circa* A.D. 90, mention is made of the "Crossing Sea General" Han Yüeh, who was ordered to

> "Float on the sea and proceed eastward *via* Kuchang (故鄞)," now Ningpo. (上遣橫海將軍韓說浮海從東方往)

The result of the fighting was that the tribes were subjected and forced to migrate by Imperial orders to the regions north of the Yangtze.

To leave the realms of war and return to those of peace, we find frequent references to floating craft in the works of China's various poets who flourished during the eighth century.

About a thousand years ago there lived a man who ranks among China's most famous poets. His name was Li T'ai-po (李太白). He wrote mainly of wine, sadness of lonely hearts, crows calling each other to rest, sages resting in pavilions, birds singing at dusk, and so forth; but he produced a poem which should make an instant appeal to every ship-lover. It is called the "Song of the River,"* and runs as follows:

> My boat is of ebony;
> The holes in my flute are golden.
>
> As a plant takes out stains from silk,
> So wine takes sadness from the heart.
>
> When one has good wine,
> A graceful boat,
> And a maiden's love,
> Why envy the immortal gods?

But writing odes to the moon and lolling in boats on quiet waters are habits which, desirable as they may be from a literary point of view, are quite sterile as regards nautical research.

Apart from the pottery rafts, which will be mentioned later, the ceramic greatness of China yields no help in tracing the evolution of the junk through the centuries. Such representations as are to be seen on porcelain are of the usual stereotyped nature and not very informative.

The potter, like the poet and landscape painter, views the junk and sampan through romantic and non-technical eyes. Nevertheless, their evidence cannot be altogether disregarded, as it must have been at least a reflection, accurate or not, of what they saw around them. In this connection it is interesting to speculate as to why, in the painting after Ku K'ai-chih (顧愷之) as well as in the paintings on various articles of chinaware, boats are shown with tiled roofs.† Before ruling them out as fantastic it must be remembered that on the Upper Yangtze there are many types of craft to be found with tall built-in brick kitchen chimneys, or galley funnels as the sailors would call them.

* "Chinese Lyrics." Translated from the French of Judith Gautier by James Whitall.

† Monsieur Sigaut suggests that maybe they were made of bamboo and designed to look like tiled roofs.

The lovely old blue willow pattern plate, with its complete disregard for the laws of perspective, is the classical example of the sampan in the ceramic art, and should remind the West of the extent of its obligation to China in this great industry.

The ever interesting story which is illustrated by this design has often been told. It is as follows. The palace on the right-hand side of the picture is where a high official and his only daughter lived after the death of her mother. He took with him his Secretary, Chang; and herein lies the whole trouble and the foundation of the immortal story. At sunset each day the daughter used to linger in the garden to see Chang. Unhappily their secret meetings were discovered, Chang was dismissed and the daughter shut up in a room facing the sea.

One day, feeling more desolate than usual, her attention was aroused by a half coconut-shell with a miniature sail floating gently past. The fact that she was incarcerated did not apparently prevent her from fishing it out with her parasol. In it she found a bead she had given her lover, which was sufficient proof that he had sent it. There was also a message which read "cast your thoughts upon the water as I have done and I shall hear your words." Meanwhile her father had selected for her a man whom he thought was a more suitable husband. Just as the feast of the betrothal had commenced Chang suddenly appeared in her chamber and rescued her, after which we see them crossing the bridge. First comes the daughter, followed by Chang, and then the irate father with a whip in his hand. The story has a sad ending.

They make good their escape in the small boat we see on the left-hand side of the plate, meaning to reach Chang's island home in the upper part of the picture. But the wrath of the official was quite uncontrollable. He raised the whole countryside against them and their lives were in great danger.

The gods, however, took pity on them in their distress and transformed them into the two doves seen on the top of the plate. These immortal birds, floating in the air, were the fit emblems of the loving constancy of their affections which had rendered them so remarkable in life that now they were to be undivided by death.

In Europe, coins and, later, seals form a useful source of our knowledge of the craft of the ancients. From seals especially the evolution of the sailing ship can be followed. By their aid the development of the rudder, the growth of the forecastle and poop, rigging, the bowsprit, and even fenders can be accurately traced and, which is so important, dated. Unhappily there is nothing of the kind in China.

The Ku Pu spade coins, so called on account of their shape, are said to originate from the middle of the Chou dynasty, 1122–255 B.C., but it was not until some 2,000 years later, in 1931 to be exact, that anything nautical made its appearance. This was on the Sun Yat Sen 1 yuan. The very fine representation of a junk thereon is said to typify the ship of state, with Sun Yat Sen's Three Principles depicted by the three birds overhead, the Kuo-min-tang (國 民 黨) being the sun's rays. This was issued at a time when Japan took the Three Eastern Provinces. The issue was recalled and the dies changed as it was thought that the three birds were the three provinces flying away from China under the influence of the sun rays of Japan. This coin is now very valuable and is extremely artistic.

And so we leave our researches with a final regret that Chinese painting, literature, and culture in all its many forms and with its amazing and continuous tradition of 2,000 years should contain so little about her ships and sailors.

A great deal has been written about the first Europeans to visit China but little or nothing in the case of the earliest Chinese to visit Europe or to come into

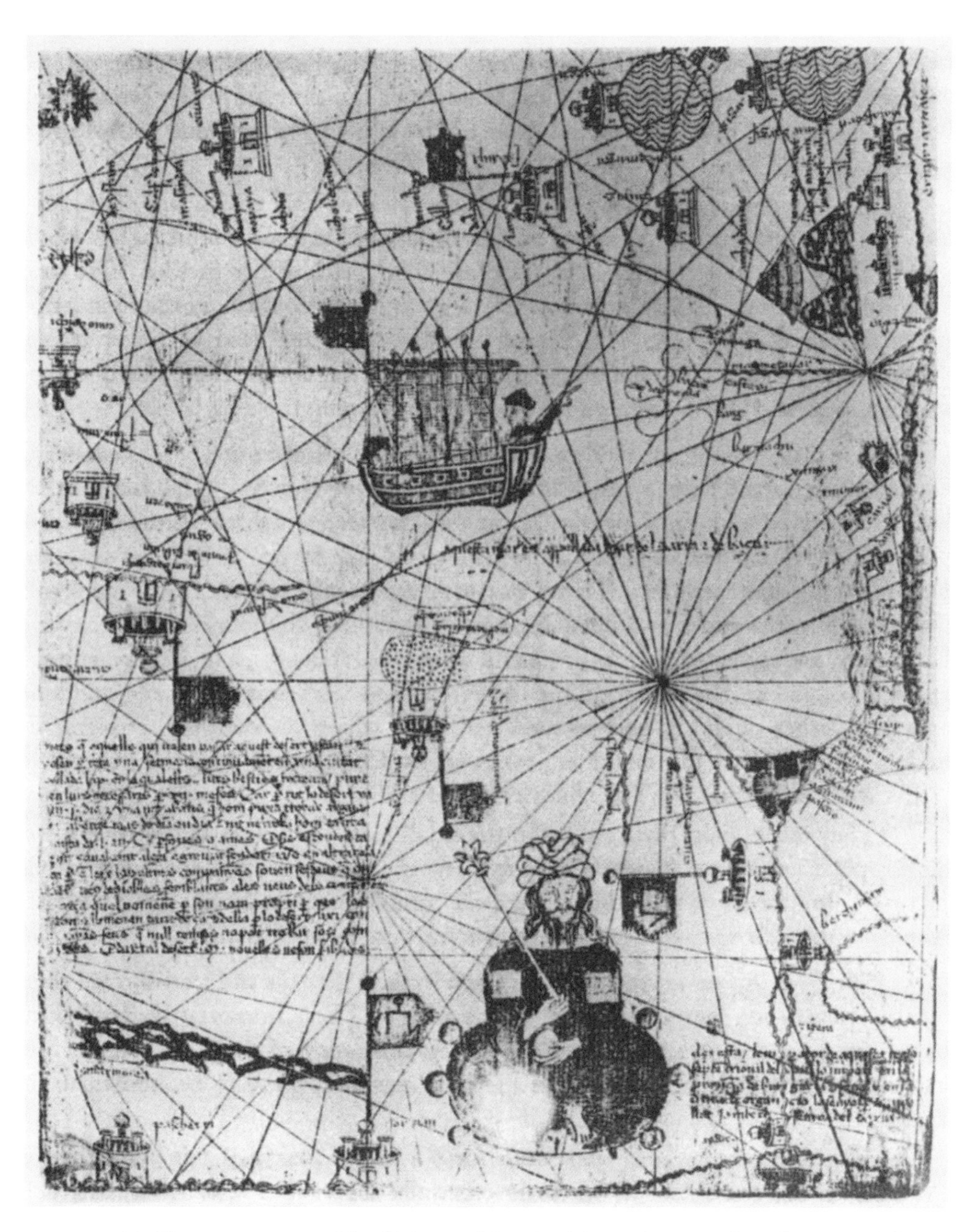

The Catalan Map, A.D. *1375.*

contact with Europeans outside China. Nor is this to be wondered at considering the prohibition placed by the early Ming Emperors on their subjects trading and residing abroad. Those Chinese who went abroad in defiance of this ban were, no doubt, confined to seamen, smugglers, pirates, vagabonds, and the like classes of people who do not as a rule leave written records of their adventures, that is, if they are wise. Scholars of the literary class or even well-educated merchants must needs have been singularly few and far between in those far-off days and, even so, it is doubtful if they would have interested themselves in nautical research or chronicled the adventures and habits of sailors or fisherfolk. This is probably the reason why we cannot expect to find anything of importance on our subject in Chinese annals.

Western historians and writers are unfortunately not much more helpful in clearing up the mystery surrounding the date of origin of types of Chinese craft, or indeed as regards anything concerning the craft in current use.

The Catalan Map, dated 1375, is said to have served to introduce the Chinese junk to European eyes, although it cannot claim to add very substantially to our knowledge. The map (*reproduced above*), however, is extremely interesting. It consists of six plates drawn on parchment, attached in the middle to wooden boards and bound in book form. It is considered to be the most comprehensive cartographic work of the fourteenth century and shows the known coasts of the world at that time. Cordier and Nordenskold agree that the unknown cartographer took almost all his facts about China from the accounts of Marco Polo's travels.

True, almost any nautical book of reference has something to say about Far Eastern craft, but it is astonishing how uninformed are most of the comments on the Chinese junk.

Western paintings and etchings of the nineteenth century depicting junks are quite valueless, as they are too unconvincing and inaccurately portrayed to facilitate any recognition of definite types. An exception to this must be made in favour of William Alexander of the Macartney Mission in 1792.

It is greatly to be regretted that so many erroneous and misleading statements about, and drawings* of junks have crept into the pages of modern books by well-known and respected writers on nautical subjects. Doubtless in the absence of first-hand knowledge they were obliged to tap such sources as were available to them, notably the Far Eastern models in various museums, which models, alas, are sometimes far from being correct.

The Chinese carpenter has a wide reputation for the excellence of his work, and so it might be expected that he would provide material for nautical research. Unhappily this is not so.

Model-making, *per se*, was scarcely ever practised in China. One of the few old specimens is on display in the Musée Heude of the Aurora University in Shanghai. It was presented in the thirteenth century to the Emperor by a well-known scholar, Chao Yu-jen. Later, in the nineteenth century, it was removed to Ningpo, where it was preserved in a temple. Artistically, or rather from a craftsman's point of view, it is a fine piece of delicate carving, but as an historical record it is quite useless. The same applies to the expensive objets d'art produced by the silversmiths, ivory-workers, and stone-carvers.

The next type of models to be reviewed are the votive offerings. The ancients were accustomed to suspend in their temples shields with appropriate inscriptions and other offerings in honour of their gods. Dædalus, after his safe return from his first flight, is said to have consecrated his wings to Apollo. The Romans, when saved from shipwreck, hung up their wet clothing in the temple of Neptune. The custom of making votive offerings is still observed in Catholic countries, as their various churches amply testify. In the West nowadays, however, the numerous ingenious inventions and improvements in navigational instruments have so greatly diminished the difficulties and perils of ocean travel that this pleasing custom has fallen into desuetude. In China, however, it still persists, and fairly reasonable models may sometimes be seen hanging in the temples frequented by junkmen. These models, though, are quite unreliable from a nautical research point of view, despite their sentimental and romantic interest.

Towards the latter part of the nineteenth century the Chinese model-maker made his appearance for the benefit of the tourists or the retiring foreigner anxious for souvenirs of his years of service in the Far East. These craftsmen are unsurpassed in the art of producing fancy junks of no known type. The trap for the innocent buyer is often baited with fluttering pennants and carving and paint in a riot of colour.

Unlike a drawing, which however inaccurate may yet present a faithful impression of a ship, a model, since it deals with three dimensions, increases the possibility of error, whereby not only is all true likeness destroyed, but the result is made infinitely more misleading than a bad drawing.

* Actually the correct drawing of ships of any sort under sail is, perhaps, the most difficult subject in art. For instance, apart from the actual craft itself, the force and direction of the wind and sea must be apparent and the sails must be shown as they would appear in nature, to say nothing of the delineation of the rigging in motion. All these must harmonize if they are not to offend the practised eye of the sailor.

Mr. Worcester had Chinese carpenters build scale models of the crooked-bow and crooked-stern junks. These are described in the Appendix.

Casual model-making of this sort is, of course, prevalent everywhere, but is nowhere more in evidence than in China, where not only is the idea of a scale model unknown to the Chinese carpenter, but almost invariably a due sense of proportion is lacking.* Add to this a lively imagination, and the effect is a mere conventional work of art with little if any relation to reality.

And so it came about that illustrious visitors to the Far East, on their return home, brought with them gorgeous-looking models of Chinese junks. These, in time, found their way into museums, where they have been accepted in all good faith as true replicas.

It is very distressing to see these spurious models convincingly labelled and displayed in museums of repute. It is to be hoped that all such institutions will take careful stock of their Chinese craft in order that wrong information may not be perpetuated.

The civilizations of Europe and China developed independently, each being for a long time ignorant of the other's existence. Overland trade routes, however, must have indirectly served to connect them by means of trade marts from very early times, for Herodotus, writing of the fifth century B.C., refers to the description of a caravan route by a traveller 200 years earlier, and the estimated date of the first arrival of foreign influence by sea is placed as far back as 650 B.C.

There are records innumerable of early contacts with the West. The Phœnicians, the Babylonians, the Arabs, the Romans, and others all established connections with China by one route or another, but prolonged research gives no authentic records of the Chinese having at this time ventured farther west in their own craft than Cochin-China, Annam, and the Straits of Malacca, and north as far as Japan.

The first mention of Thinæ by Western writers occurs, says the "Chinese Repository," in a book ascribed to Aristotle. Eratosthenes, who lived 250 B.C., placed Thinæ at the end of the earth, bordering upon the Eastern Ocean. Arrian, *circa* A.D. 150, after describing an island, says:

> Still farther towards the north, beyond the sea which bounds the country of the Sinæ, is the great city of Thinæ, in the interior from which raw and manufactured silks are brought. It is extremely difficult to reach Thinæ because it lies at a great distance, and few go there.

The Chinese did little in ancient as well as in modern times towards making themselves acquainted with other nations, so that it is not surprising that, while there are innumerable records of contacts from the West reaching China, first by land and then by sea, there is the greatest difficulty in establishing proof that the Chinese themselves travelled overseas in their own ships. Probably the main obstacle to long ocean voyages on the part of the Chinese, for which their ships were quite sufficiently seaworthy, was their inferiority in mathematical knowledge. This lack of mathematical science was accentuated by the fact that their language and writing were quite unsuited to the exact science of working out mathematical navigational problems. That they did penetrate as far as India and beyond by "guess and by God" methods is therefore vastly to their credit.

They seem to have obtained their first definite knowledge of Rome during the reign of the Han Emperor Wu Ti (漢 武 帝), 140–86 B.C., and the recorded attempt to establish communication was made in A.D. 97 by Pan Ch'ao (班 超), who sent an official named Kan Ying (甘 英) on a mission to the West to acquire information. This seems to have marked the beginning of extensive trade relations. Contacts with the West increased. It is known, in the second century B.C., jugglers (male and female), dancers, and musicians, famous in Alexandria, were transported

* An exception must, however, be made in the case of the model-makers of Ichang. Some of their models, which are often to be seen in the shops of Shanghai, are excellent in every way.

from there by sea, entering China through Burma, the earliest means of access. It is claimed in the "Han Shu," or "Han History," that Wu Ti established a sea route to India, and that in 140 B.C. a cargo of gold and silks was carried to a town near Madras. We may therefore, with great respect, assume that Mr. Rockhill was incorrect in affirming that at the beginning of our era there were no Chinese vessels at all in the Indian Ocean, although the Chinese "often crossed it in ships of the barbarians."*

It is probable that soon after this period other Chinese vessels must have reached Hindustan, but it is clear that, until the Alexandrine merchants had established a regular trade with the coasts of Malabar, and probably for some considerable time after, the chief Chinese commercial traffic with the West was conducted by means of caravans overland.

A century later sea-borne trade entered by what is now Indo-China, through the port of Tonkin, as the maritime peoples of Western Asia were finding out the easier sea route to China *via* the Straits of Malacca. Burma then ceased to be the high road between East and West. An important early terminus for the sea route was Hanoi, then known as Cattigara, and, of course, Canton. The Arab merchants were welcomed in China on their first arrival there in A.D. 787, and although the Chinese imposed upon them strange modes of selling goods, yet the founding of agencies was permitted, the traders were exempted from fiscal burdens, and justice was permitted to be administered by their own judges. Few ships, however, ventured on a voyage so full of risk as that to the distant seas of China. The Arab trade which later carried on such a thriving business was probably responsible for the Egyptian influence on Chinese junks as evidenced by the oculus, for the Arab ships themselves derived from the Egyptian or Nilotic types. There is another possible source for these alien influences in the earlier sea contacts with the Mediterranean peoples, for it is believed that the Phœnician merchants, in their voyages in search of the "land of fine silk," reached Indo-China about 650 B.C.

Lin Yu (林 幽), writing in the "T'ien Hsia Monthly" (天 下), gives it as his opinion that the end of the Liu Sung period (劉 宋), A.D. 420–479, was the probable time when China first began to build craft for her sea-going trade. These were known as the bull-head ships, and the largest were said to be capable of carrying 300,000 catties of cargo. The descriptive title is not an inapt one; for if, as seems probable, the Kiangsu trader evolved from the earlier bull-head type, it fits this latter-day descendant very well.

The Kiangsu Trader is described in Part Two, page 163.

All that is known of early China and the industry and enterprise of its merchants tends to show that they would not have confined their marine activities to the rivers and estuaries only for the many centuries of their highly advanced form of civilization and culture which obtained before the Liu Sung period. Without desiring to enter any controversial field as to the date and extent of their overseas trade with outside nations, it seems pretty definite that they must have made use of junks for coastal trade considerably more than 1,500 years ago.†

The earliest concrete evidence of the antiquity of the Chinese sea-going junk is in the shape of a representation said to be that of a three-masted North China junk in a fresco in the caves of Ajunta, in Hyderabad, India. These 29 caves were the centre of the Buddhist religion in those days. Although no date can be given for the portrayal of the junk, it must have been completed some time during the process of digging out the caves, which spread over a period of 800 years from the second century A.D. That Chinese travellers had visited the caves we know, too, by the records of that amazing pilgrim Hsüan Chuang (玄奘), who journeyed overland from Shensi to Ajunta in the early seventh century. This fresco has been quoted in Torr's "Ancient Ships" as a representation of a

* W. W. Rockhill. Chao Ju-kua (趙汝适): his work on the Chinese and the Arab trade in the twelfth and thirteenth centuries, entitled "Chu Fan Chih" (諸蕃志).

† "China's International Relations," Harley F. MacNair. "Journal of the R.A.S.," 1925.

Chinese junk. There are others who believe the drawing is meant to depict an Indian vessel.

In the year A.D. 417 Fa Hsien (法顯), the Buddhist monk, travelled from India to China, and was probably the first Chinese to leave any real record of a voyage. He describes the ships of that day as each carrying 200 souls, and says:

> "Behind the large vessel was a smaller one, to be used in case of disaster to the larger one."

The voyage from Java to Canton was estimated to take 50 days; actually the ship was driven far from her course by contrary winds and bad weather, and finally, after 90 days, reached Shantung instead. During the latter half of the seventh century 37 holy men made the trip to India by sea. Ardent Buddhists and keen observers they may have been, but they were astonishingly poor recorders on nautical matters.

It is generally believed, but in no way proved, that the ships they sailed in were foreign, that is to say, not Chinese ships, but Indian or Arab, or, as one of the pilgrims says, quoting his own case, Persian. The port of departure was usually Hsüwên (徐聞), slightly north of Hoihow.

In the early days of the T'ang dynasty, at the start of the seventh century, the greater part of China's sea-borne trade was in the hands of the Arabs, who were not slow in perceiving the advantages to be gained by adopting devices used in Chinese junks. The Western world, therefore, through the medium of Arab shipping, is indebted to China for the lee-board, the centre-board, the balance and slotted rudder, the windlass, and, above all, the watertight compartment, unknown in the Mediterranean at that time. Another feature common to both Chinese and Arabian craft is the practice in some cases of painting their boats with a mixture of lime and wood oil.*

Gradually the Chinese maritime traders were growing bolder, and they soon penetrated to the Persian Gulf and the Red Sea. During the early days of Hsiao Tsung (孝宗), 1162–89, the ocean liners of the period were known as the single-mast ships, with a capacity of 200 tons; next in size with one-third of the capacity were the bull-head ships, already mentioned; and thirdly, a class of junks known merely as wooden ships with the same capacity, and another type of equal size, *i.e.*, less than 80 tons capacity.

The main impetus for trade had been the Western desire for silk; and with the introduction of silk culture into Europe by two Nestorian monks who smuggled the secret out, silk imports decreased and trade languished. Under the Yüan dynasty of Mongolian Khans the old sea routes which had lapsed were re-established.

The large junks in the Yüan dynasty are said to have been of 36 feet beam with a length of more than 100 feet. No writer of nautical experience has described these vessels or provided us with information on which reliance can be placed. Writers on shipping were, or seemed to be, practically unknown in those days; the few that refer to it are so inaccurate and laconic, or both, that their works have little if any real value, and so everything relating to the ships of the period is in a great degree a matter for conjecture. The opinion of a contemporary Chinese traveller on the hazards of sea voyages in those days is worth quoting†:

> The great ocean spreads out over a boundless expanse. There is no knowing east or west; only by observing the sun, moon, and stars was it possible to go forward. In the darkness of the night only the great waves were to be seen, emitting a brightness like that of fire, with huge turtles and other monsters of the deep all about. The merchants were full of terror, not knowing where they were going.

Although the existence of junks and some conception of their appearance must have been known in the West long before his day, Marco Polo is the first traveller to provide any authentic description of Chinese craft, and with one or

* The following is taken from the Customs "Annual Reports on Trade," China, 1869:

> "A characteristic of the junks mentioned by Friar Odoric of Pordenone in the fourteenth century attracts the attention of every visitor of the present day. He remarks that 'all the vessels are as white as snow, being coated with whitewash,' and this whitewashing of the junks is as much in vogue now—especially with the junks of Chinchew (the Zaitun of the Middle Ages)—as it was apparently five centuries ago. This whitewash is a mixture of lime with wood oil (extracted from the poisonous seeds of the *Dryandra cordifolia*), which preserves the ship's bottom and keeps out the worm."

† Chao Ju-kua (趙汝适), author of the "Chu Fan Chih" (諸蕃志).

two notable exceptions few have since interested themselves in the subject, the tendency being to classify all Chinese craft merely as junks without recognizing any individual difference or characteristic. Polo, in his memoirs, gave a detailed description of a Chinese merchant trader of his day:

> They have a single deck, and below this the space is divided into about 60 small cabins, fewer or more according to the size of the vessel, each of them affording accommodation for one merchant. They are provided with a good helm. They have four masts and as many sails, and some have two masts which can be set up and lowered again.

His reference to the craft he saw navigating the Yangtze in 1295 is not very illuminating and savours of exaggeration, for he puts the number seen in Chinkiang as being 15,000. Elsewhere he speaks of Yangtze junks with a mast and one sail and "covered with a kind of deck." *

Marco finally left China in a fleet, provided and equipped by the Khan, of 14 ships, each of which he tells us had "four masts and was capable of being navigated with nine sails." He here admits that "the construction and rigging would admit of ample description, but is for the present omitted." He goes on to say "among these vessels there were at least four or five that had crews of 250 to 260 men and stores and provisions for two years." They took three months to reach Java.

Of his actual voyage Marco Polo has recorded little, but in another connection he describes the ocean-going ships of the Chinese merchantmen as being four-masters, made of fir, double planked, with a single deck. They had stout iron nails and huge wooden anchors, and wood oil took the place of pitch. Their compartments were watertight, a novelty at that time. It took four men to wield one of the massive oars held in reserve for calms. These sweeps were very long, heavy, and designed for emergency use. In the West until comparatively recent times even tolerably large sailing vessels used sweeps to set them round when they missed stays, but more especially, it would appear, in case of being chased by the enemy. Thus the combined oars and sails of the ancients may be said to have survived almost to our own time.

After Marco Polo many—albeit sketchy and unreliable—accounts of junks are to be found in the annals of mediæval travellers. One of the most adventurous of these was Ibn Batuta, a pious Mohammedan pilgrim, who left his native town of Tangier in 1324 and for a period of nearly 30 years travelled over a great portion of Asia. He describes how, on the Malabar Coast, he found 15 Chinese junks at anchor. One of the most interesting things about his story is the evidence it gives us of the great activity of shipping in the Persian Gulf and beyond. Much of this was Arab, but we also hear of large and luxurious Chinese junks. Literary giants, sinologues, and authorities of various sorts dispute every place name, phrase, nay, even every word of the travels of this great man as he approaches China. To avoid the many pitfalls, Yule's version of Ibn Batuta's description of the Chinese junks he saw is quoted verbatim:

> The greater ships had from three to 12 sails, made of strips of bamboo woven like mats. Each of them had a crew of 1,000 men, viz., 600 sailors and 400 soldiers, and had three tenders attached which were called respectively the half, the third, and the quarter, names apparently indicating their proportionate size. The vessels for the trade were built nowhere but at Zaitun, Sinkalan, and at the city also called Sinulsin, and were all made with triple sides, fastened with enormous spikes 3 cubits in length. Each vessel had four decks, and numerous private and public cabins for the merchant passengers, with closets and all kinds of conveniences. The sailors had frequently pit-herbs, ginger, etc., growing on board in wooden tubs. The commander of the ship was a great personage, and when he landed the soldiers belonging to his ship marched before him with sword and spear and martial music. The oars and sweeps used on these great junks were more like masts than oars, pulling by means of a strong cable fastened to the oar, and singing out to the stroke la! la! la!

* Actually this would seem to be a mistranslation on Yule's part, for in "Le Livre de Marco Polo," by A. S. H. Charignon, the French word used is "*paillasson*," which means a straw mat.

Whenever a Chinese junk is about to undertake a voyage, it is the custom for the Admiral of the port and his Secretaries to go on board, and to take note of the number of soldiers, servants, and sailors who are embarked. The ship is not allowed to sail till this form has been complied with. And when the junk returns to China the same officials again visit her, and compare the persons found on board with the numbers entered in the register. If anyone is missing the Captain is responsible, and must furnish evidence of the death or desertion of the missing individual, or otherwise account for him. If he cannot, he is arrested and punished. The Captain is then obliged to give a detailed report of all the items of the junk's cargo, be their value great or small. Everybody then goes ashore, and the Custom House Officers commence an inspection of what everybody has. If they find anything has been kept back from their knowledge, the junk and all its cargo is forfeited.*

The next series of voyages were made in A.D. 1407 by a famous eunuch Chêng Ho (鄭和), who was by no means too emasculated to make long sea voyages of conquest to the south. He, in company with another eunuch Wang Ching-hung (王景弘), was commissioned by the Emperor Yung Lo (永樂), and they visited many foreign "tribes" and brought back many valuable commodities as tributes to the Emperor and succeeded in impressing on them the grandeur and power of the Empire. Their voyages were recorded in the books "Ying Yai Shêng Lan" (瀛涯勝覽), by Ma Huan (馬歡), and "Hsing Ch'a Shêng Lan" (星槎勝覽), by Fei Hsin (費信), and made the subject of a romantic novel entitled "San Pao T'ai Chien Hsia Hsi Yang" (三保太監下西洋). The description of their journey, compiled by Huang Shêng-tsêng (黃省曾) in the fifteenth century, states:

With 100 mighty ships they began their journey from Fuhchow at the river mouth of the Five Tigers. With rudders hoisted and sails unfurled they took their course where sea and sky are blended. Hence forth, amid the thundering billows and surges rearing mountains high, helped by their flying masts and labouring oars, now with their cordage tightly strained and now under loosened sails, they journeyed many myriads of *li*, and in their voyaging to and fro spent nigh on 30 years. And yet the lands they saw were but a score or so in number . . . Beyond Sumatra . . . Cochin-China is the most remote, and on again of the six or seven countries more, Arabia is the farthest.

Huang Shêng-tsêng also quotes from a treatise on navigation by compass called "Chen Wei Pien," but no copy can be traced of this work, which it would be indeed interesting to read.

From this time onwards practically all the exploration and writings on China were made by men who made their journeys in the interests of religion, from the Franciscan Friar Odoric, 1286–1331, to John de Marignolli; and all the many early adventurous Jesuits from Ricci in the early seventeenth century to Du Halde in the eighteenth century. All these missionaries must have frequently travelled long distances by junk. Friar Odoric has recorded that he sailed from India in a Chinese junk *via* Sumatra, Java, Borneo, and Cochin-China to Canton, then known as Chin-Kalan, and described by the friar as being "as big as three Venices, and all Italy has not the amount of craft that this one city hath."

The Jesuit, Mattheo Ricci, also went long voyages in junks during his 27 years in China as one of the founders of the modern missions to that country. He travelled by junk from Canton up the Yangtze and lived for several months in that craft under the walls of Nanking. Completely alone among the Chinese, and with nothing but his faith, courage, and enthusiasm to protect and sustain him, he presented himself before the gates of that impenetrable city and peacefully forced them open.

These saintly adventurers were, of course, utterly unskilled in all nautical matters, and their spelling of place names caused Colonel Yule and other authorities to expend years of research in their efforts to straighten out the tangle they had made.

All alike bear witness to the great volume of shipping they saw in Chinese ports. A point much stressed by these early writers was the astonishingly large crews carried by Chinese junks. Ibn Batuta's ship, as we have already seen,

* "Ibn Batuta's Travels in Bengal and China." "Cathay and the Way Thither." Yule.

carried 1,000 men, 400 of whom were soldiers; Odoric speaks of 700 souls on board; while Marco's ships each carried 600, excluding the crew, but "nearly all died by the way, so that only eight survived," from which it would appear that the passengers were not very well looked after.

But most astonishing of all is the alleged practice of constructing the vessels of that day with three skins. Marco Polo (who usually gives a little more than anyone else) mentions six. He says:

> When the ship has been a year in work and they wish to repair her, they nail on a third plank over the first two and caulk and pay it well: and when another repair is wanted they nail on yet another plank, and so on year by year as it is required. Howbeit, they do this only for a certain number of years, and until there are six thicknesses of planking.

The Jesuit, Gabriel Magaillans, writing in 1688, contented himself, in alluding to junks, in estimating that the number of rice junks he saw on the Yangtze was 9,999. He could, one would have thought, have added one to the number without fear of being accused of undue exaggeration. The same number of tribute junks is quoted by E. Ysbrand Ides, the Russian Ambassador from Moscow. This could hardly be coincidence. It would be interesting to know if he echoed the number of junks as stated by Magaillans, or if by any chance that was a symbolic number as used by the Chinese to suggest magnitude. Ides, in his book "Three Years' Travels from Moscow Overland to China," published in 1706, graphically describes Yangtze junks thus:

> In China the quantity of the ships is innumerable as the sand of the sea. Those that carry corn only to Peking amounting to 9,999 large ships sufficient to carry above thirty to forty thousand weight, and their passage from Nanking to Peking, being seven or eight hundred Italian miles mostly through artificial channels, takes up fully six months' time. Besides this there is an equal number of ships made to carry silk, stuffs, and other goods thither; so that they are prodigiously numerous, besides the ships which belong to particular merchants; so that it is not only feasible to step from ship to ship as on a water key [*sic*] from Nanking to Peking, but as the Jesuits expressing their incredible number say, if it were but practicable here are ships enough to make a bridge from China to Europe.
>
> Besides these smaller ships there are at Nanking, and also at several other havens of the Empire, ships which are twice as large as these, being of seventy or eighty thousand weight burden: and these serve to carry salt throughout the whole land. There are also abundance of magnificent barks or ships which belong to the Mandarins, Governors, and others of the Nobles, which are provided with spacious halls and apartments, very richly furnished as also with galleries, rails, windows, and doors for convenience and pleasure. There are likewise several pleasure boats made use of by the Chinese for diversion and mutual merry making: these are also provided with chambers and apartments which are finely painted so that indeed they deserve rather to be termed floating houses than ships. Besides all which all parts are abundantly provided with all sorts of necessary barks or boats for travellers: for there is scarce a city whether large or small of which there is not a passage by water. And what is yet more, there are a sort of driving floats on which whole families live by keeping ducks or following some other trade. So that indeed when one sees such various sorts of craft in one row, they seem like nothing more than a floating city in which the vessels run together like ants.

There is, of course, and always must be, an uncommon interest attached to the recorded impressions of the early travellers, but it is a mistake to attach any very profound meaning to much of their descriptions, which, on careful analysis, often prove to be superficial, and their impressions and writings on the subject of ships and craft of all sorts are more often than not almost pathetically inept.

If their descriptions are to be unreservedly accepted, the theory that the basic types of present-day junks are little changed from those of hundreds of years ago breaks down. This period is in the dark ages of nautical history, but we may justly assume that the sea-going junks of Marco Polo's day were considerably larger than those of the present day, and moreover were probably larger than ships used in Europe up to, and even after, Drake's *Golden Hind.*

After the vigorous policy of the Mings was abandoned, Chinese shipping grew less venturesome, and Malacca was about the uttermost limit of their voyages. With the arrival of European ships in the China seas in the sixteenth century,

Chinese shipping became more and more tied to home waters, and thereafter it has hardly been possible to speak of a Chinese mercantile marine on the high seas, though, of course, the junk traffic on the inland waterways remained unchanged.

An ambassadorial mission productive of a sketchy description of the construction of riverine craft is provided by Sir George Leonard Staunton, Secretary to Lord Macartney's Mission to China in 1792, who wrote:

> The boats in common use among them consist of five planks only, united together with ribs and timbers. These planks are rendered flexible by being exposed, sometimes, to a flame of fire, and are then brought to the desired degree of inflexion, the ends being thus connected together in a line. The edges are joined and fixed by tree nails (wooden nails) and stitches with flexible threads of bamboo. The seams are afterwards payed with paste, made by mixing water and quicklime from sea shells. Other boats are made with wicker work, the interstices of which are payed, or filled up with the same composition as used by the former, and this luting, as it may be styled, renders them watertight. They are remarked for withstanding the violence of the waves, and being stiff upon the water, and for sailing with expedition.

It is disappointing that Sir George, who wrote so fully and so entertainingly of comparatively unimportant matters, should, when he touched on the subject of junks, have provided such a meagre account, and an account, moreover, which is open to serious question as regards most of the statements contained therein.

Engraving on copper by William Alexander, representing a Fukien junk in 1801.

The British mission travelled back from the capital to Canton in junks, escorted for part of the way by war junks. As their route led down the Grand Canal, and by devious rivers and waterways through several provinces, they had unrivalled facilities for studying junks, and must have seen a representative assortment of most of the types of North, South, and Central China. This cross-country journey would be a unique experience even in this century. It must have been stupendous a hundred and fifty or so years ago; but this golden opportunity for recording interesting facts about ancient types of craft was wasted. With the exception of Sir George Staunton, none of the learned gentlemen on Lord Macartney's staff showed any interest in this neglected subject, although voluminous reports, official and unofficial, were compiled describing the voyage, the country, and the people and their customs.

The only valuable record made on the journey in respect of Chinese craft is a set of eight engravings and a water-colour made by William Alexander, the official artist attached to the mission. These are probably the oldest Western drawings of any accuracy of Chinese junks now extant.*

Unfortunately there are few who bridge the gap between this period and the early fifties. That great and instructive publication the "Chinese Repository," and writers like Gutzlaff, John Henry Gray, and others give pleasing albeit superficial word pictures of the Chinese junk, mostly in Kwangtung. All these should be read by the serious student of the Chinese junk.

There is, however, one other source of voluminous and accurate information on all subjects connected even remotely with Chinese affairs, and in the Customs Trade and other Reports the enthusiast, if he can only get access to these out-of-print publications, will find a wealth of knowledge even on the subject of junks.

The Chinese Customs was, and still is, far from being merely a revenue-collecting machine, for from it there sprang into being that wonderful series of Trade Reports and Decennial Reports, and later the Marine Department Reports.†

These interesting documents are now relegated to the most inaccessible shelves of Reference Libraries because they look dull and because the gems they contain are hidden beneath a conglomeration of statistics. Actually no serious

* William Alexander was the first to hold the appointment of Keeper of Oriental Prints at the British Museum, where reproductions of his drawings of junks may be seen.

† The Shanghai Custom House seems to have published Trade Returns before 1854, although little can have been done before 1863. In 1874 regular Annual Trade Reports began to be issued. In 1892 there appeared the first issue of the Decennial Reports, of which by now five issues have been published. Monthly and Annual Returns are now issued by the Customs. The compilation of statistics have become a science. Junk statistics are based on the control of certain Native Customs Districts by the Maritime Customs, 19 such districts being at one time controlled by the Inspector General.

student of China, her history, people, or industries should neglect these publications. Written in faultless prose by men of a bygone generation who were scholars as well as administrators, their work is bound to be of the greatest historical value. Nothing was too unimportant, nothing too trivial for these earnest, lucid compilers of the Trade Reports. Statistics on the movement of umbrellas in Canton, vermicelli from Chinchew, animal tallow from Chinghai, and coal dust from Putien were all treated with the same care and attention to detail as was vast "Treasure, Imported and Exported." The statistical tables were prefaced with masterly summaries of the trade and history of the period. The old Commissioners of Customs wrote on every subject under the sun and drew conclusions from everything, and so, of course, they wrote about junks in a general sort of way from a revenue point of view. Nevertheless, in these pages a picture, or rather an impression, is given of what the Chinese junk meant to China before the coming of the steamer, the chicken-boat, and the dreadful Japanese "puff-puff." From a nautical research point of view it must have been a wonderful period in which to have lived.

It is interesting to make a comparative review of Chinese and Western European sea-going craft. England, the greatest maritime power of Europe, has, comparatively speaking, a very short sea history. The sailing ship period may be said to date from the long ships of Alfred the Great to the *Victory* at Trafalgar only, for a few years later the era of the steamship set in and ranged, in just over a hundred years, from the *Comet* to the *Queen Elizabeth*. The whole process of evolution from ships of 100 or more feet long, pulling some 30 oars, to square-rigged sailing ships and thence to the steamer of 1,032 feet in length and 85,000 tons displacement covers a period of just over a thousand years.

In the beginning then, as regards sailing ships, China must have for long been far ahead, with stout seaworthy craft fitted with watertight compartments, hoisting rudders, and various valuable devices. Up to a period about 400 years ago her craft must have equalled, if not surpassed, the ships which sailed under Magellan, Cabot, and even perhaps Drake. Even to-day, unaltered as they are from designs dating centuries back, the junks of China compare very favourably with the coasting craft of many Western countries.

Similarly, too, as is always the case where there is a deeply indented coast-line as in Britain, the Scandinavian countries, and Brittany, a breed of hardy Chinese seamen grew up to man their craft.

When the ships of the West began to make advances in design and ingenuity, the only way China could have maintained her former position as a maritime nation was by copying Western models and keeping pace with foreign ideas.

But, though the West recognized its need for Chinese co-operation in trade, China in their early days of contact felt no need for, or interest in, the West; and in China stagnation in maritime affairs may be traced to the fact that it was not until after the wars with Britain and France that she realized that she had anything to learn from the intruders despite her ancient apathy and dislike of change in any form.

The junk, therefore, like so many customs and articles in China, has survived down the ages as a sort of perpetual and useful anachronism, and is in most essentials very little altered from its ancient prototypes.

THE JUNKS AND SAMPANS OF THE YANGTZE

THE word "junk" in its present form is really a product of the age of the East India Company, but its origin dates back some hundreds of years to the thirteenth century.

The first reference to junks in European literature is in the year 1555. Richard Eden, in a translated work from the Italian entitled "The Decades of the Newe World," says:

> From the Ilandes (the Moluccas) they are brought to India in shyps or barkes made without any iron tooles . . . these they call *giunche*.

Nowadays the word junk has come to be applied to all types of Far Eastern native sailing vessels and even, more loosely, to Southern India craft.

According to various dictionaries the word has several meanings. In the first place it signifies a rush; a form of splint; an old or inferior cable or rope; pieces of old rope used in making a fender; any discarded or waste material that can be put to some use; a piece or lump of anything; the mass of thick tissue beneath the nostril of a sperm whale; waste film, such as old unwanted cut-outs; a name for a join in the bedding of slate or other rock; to discard or throw away film; and, lastly, it is a name for "the common type of sailing vessel in the China seas."

Other early references are disparaging, such as "all manner of odd-looking craft, but none so odd as the Chinese junk." One dictionary describes the word "junkman" not as the member of the crew of a junk, but as "a man who sells junk or waste material."

One world-famous encyclopædia dismisses the Chinese junk in 40 words, none of them being flattering or even accurate, and another encyclopædia devotes one slightly longer and no less uninformative paragraph to the same topic, equally unflattering. It is surprising that so little interest has been shown in this subject by standard works of reference.

The English word junk has its counterpart in many languages: the French *jonque* (or *joncque* in old French), Portuguese and Spanish *junco*, Dutch *jonk*, German *dschonke*, and Italian *giunco* sprang from the Javanese word *djong* which was applied by the first Portuguese and Dutch merchants to the vessels which they found established as traders with Java and the Malay Archipelago. This word *djong* in turn derived, so it is said, from the Chinese *ch'uan* for boat or ship. This derivation is more clearly demonstrated by the Amoy dialect pronunciation of the word as *ch'un*.

As we have already seen, the Chinese attained to a high degree of civilization long before most portions of the world, and since then have been jogging along for ages without any alteration in their institutions. They were satisfied that they had perfected the art of living with the minimum outlay of money and effort; their costume was cheap, comfortable, and practical, this latter markedly so in the case of small children, who wear trousers of a design which is the acme of labour-saving devices. From the most primitive looms they produce the best silks in the world; a mere handful of fuel will suffice to cook a meal for a dozen people; finally, to omit numerous other such instances of common-sense inexpensive methods and

The children are dressed with a gap in the seat of their trousers that is overhung by the tail of their coats when standing, but facilitates when a gap in clothing is required.

contraptions, their junks have been unchanged for centuries, precisely because they have been so excellently suited to their needs.

When a man decides to build a junk he is not confronted with any difficulty in choosing his design; that was decided for him centuries ago, for certain types are proper to certain districts. Some slight modifications are permitted to meet peculiar requirements, but these are in no way allowed to interfere with the essential design, which is scrupulously adhered to.

In parenthesis, it may be mentioned that this is not only true of China, it is true of every great nation of sailing ship seamen: England, France, the Netherlands, the Scandinavian countries, and others. Sailors the world over are a conservative people. They seem to have an inordinate horror of any change. Nationality, suitability, pride of locality, materials available, and local customs must, of course, account for the lack of any sort of uniformity in dealing with shipbuilding problems. These factors, however, only inadequately account for this. What is the basic reason?

Conversely, the dullest uniformity seems to govern the design of steam craft, the same type of tug or small launch being equally at home on the waters of the Thames or the Yangtze. The sad conclusion is forced upon us that when sailing craft eventually die out, by this is meant useful rather than pleasure craft, with them will vanish all individuality and local colour.

To return, however, to the Chinese junk, such differences as there are, however, do not materially alter the main structural principle of junk design, which depends for its strength upon a system of bulkheads interspersed with frames or timbers.

It is, of course, well known that the Chinese were the first to adopt the watertight bulkhead, not only as a strengthening device, but as a safety arrangement. Marco Polo describes this in the following words:

> Moreover, the larger of their vessels have some 13 compartments or severances in the interior, made with planking strongly framed, in case mayhap the ship should spring a leak, either by running on a rock or by the blow of a hungry whale (as shall betide oftentimes, for when the ship in her course by night sends a ripple back alongside of the whale, the creature seeing the foam fancies there is something to eat afloat, and makes a rush forward, whereby it often shall stave in some part of the ship). In such case the water that enters the leak flows to the bilge, which is always kept clear, and the mariners having ascertained where the damage is, empty the cargo from the compartment into those adjoining, for the planking is so well fitted that the water cannot pass from one compartment to another. They then stop the leak and replace the lading.*

It will be of interest to American readers to know that an unpublished letter from Benjamin Franklin, written about 1787, contains a paragraph referring to the mail packets between France and the United States, and says:

> As these packets are to be laden with goods, their holds may, without inconvenience, be divided into separate compartments after the Chinese manner, and each of their compartments caulked tight so as to keep out the water. In which case if a leak should happen in one compartment that only would be affected by it and the others would be free, so that the ship would not be so subject as others to founder and sink at sea. This being known would be a great encouragement to the passengers.

The famous *Nemesis*, well known in China as the first steamer ever to enter the Whangpoo, was also probably the first to be built with watertight compartments, of which she had seven.†

There is much about Chinese shipbuilding analogous to that carried out by the sturdy master shipwrights in the days when England was laying the foundations of her shipping industry. Usually the most experienced sailor was chosen to design and build a ship, and the naval constructor of those days was

* These accidents were not perhaps so extravagant as they sound. The American "Neptune," Vol. 1, page 393, quotes several classical examples of attacks made on ships by angry whales.

† It was in 1850 that the Marine Department of the Board of Trade in England came into being, and one of its first enactments was that all steamers should be divided by watertight compartments.

therefore always a man with practical experience in the art of seamanship. This is almost invariably the case in China to-day. The junkmen have a proverb, thus:

Yao t'sao tzŭ-sun-ch'uan (要造子孫船),
Sha pai tzŭ chang nan (杉柏梓樟楠).

Yao: (If you) want	*Sha: sha-mu*
Ts'ao: to build	*Pai:* cypress
Tzŭ: (for) son (and)	*Tzŭ: tzŭ-mu*
Sun: grandson	*Chang:* camphor-wood
Ch'uan: (a) junk,	*Nan: nan-mu.*

Chinese sentences of this sort are always rather cryptically telegraphic and need a specialized sort of interpretation. This one may be read as meaning:

"To build a junk strong enough to last for generations, it is necessary to use these kinds of wood together."

Once a design has been tested, the Chinese craftsman of whatever calling sees no point in changing from what is as well suited to himself as it was to his ancestors; and herein may be seen the reason for the conformity to ancient types. The tenacity with which they have held to their traditional design is nowhere more plainly demonstrated than in their junks.

Many different sizes of each type of junk are to be found, since the details of build are at the discretion of the owner, and they often vary according to the funds available. To enable the observer to tell the approximate capacity at a glance, the junkmen have a saying: "*San t'o, ssŭ chiao, wu mao ch'ih*" (三拖四絞五毛廁), a literal translation being "Three, towing; four, winding; five, portable latrine"; which means that a junk of a capacity of 300 piculs, about 1¼ tons, or over, usually has a sampan in tow; those junks of a capacity of 400 piculs or above hoist their sails by a form of windlass or capstan; and those of a capacity of 500 piculs and over are equipped with a portable latrine. Junks below 300 piculs have none of these refinements.

With the exception of the big salt-junks and those from Tsungming Island (崇明島) and Tungchow (通州), the maximum load rarely exceeds 600 piculs, the minimum being about 150 piculs. Kiangsu junks were naturally the most numerous, each important trade centre having its own special class of junk. Thus there were three kinds of Nanking junks employed in the carriage of grain and other foodstuffs, the best-known type being the *liang-p'êng* (涼篷), of 160 to 320 piculs capacity. Four varieties were peculiar to Luho (六合), while Yangchow (揚州), Tsingkiangpu, and Hwaian (淮安), on the Grand Canal, and Soochow, Kiangyin, Tsungming, and Tungchow each send vessels which have their own distinguishing characteristics and designations. The majority were grain-carriers, but the large vessels from Tungchow bring raw cotton and cotton cloth.

There used to be about eight main types of junks trading to Kiukiang, namely, the *man-kiang-hung* (滿江紅), *ch'ê-p'ai* (車牌), *tiao-kou* (釣鉤), *fu-ch'uan* (撫船), *hsiao-po-ch'uan* (小駁船), *ch'en-ch'uan* (辰船), *shan-ch'uan* (山船), and *ya-shao* (鴨梢).* All of these are divided into different sizes varying from 60 to 100 feet, with a maximum capacity of 3,500 piculs and a minimum of 1,200 piculs.

Practical always, the Chinese planned their vessels primarily for utility, each type being designed to meet some special contingency or local requirement, on the Yangtze not the least being the successful evasion or limitation of tax payments based on hull measurement, for the junkowner of China shares to the full that common human instinct—an aversion to paying taxes.

The *kiang-tung-tzŭ* (江東子), which are built below Chinkiang, are broad and deep, but short, so as to meet the over-all measurements on which taxes were payable at the Wuhu tax barriers.

The Kiangsi junks, such as the *fu-tiao-tzŭ* (府 凋 子), and those from Hupeh Province are always narrow in the vicinity of the mast and astonishingly broad elsewhere. This mode of construction, which is not at all unpleasing to the eye in the case of a loaded junk, was devised to meet the situation obtaining at Kiukiang, where duty was at one time assessed according to the beam measurement at the mast. This may be said to have sponsored the turret-built types of naval architecture in China, which antedated by many centuries a similar idea in the West in the turret-built steamers designed to lessen the dues payable in the Suez Canal.

Rice from Fuchow (撫 州) paid its *shih-fen*, or local tax, at Hwangkiangkow (黃 江 口); on reaching Hsiehpu (謝 埠) it was called on to pay an extra levy of 11 cash per *shih*, or 5 per cent on the original *shih-fen*; when passing Tuchang (都 昌) the extra levy was 22 cash per *shih*, or 10 per cent of the *shih-fen*; and at Kutang it was 29 cash, or 13 per cent of the *shih-fen*. At Hukow the export levy, with its inevitable *hao-yin* (耗 銀), came to more than three times the *shih-fen*, being 616 cash for export duty and 62 cash, or 10 per cent of this duty, for *hao-yin*; in addition there was the railway tax of 20 cents, and the *chiu-chiu* tax of 15 cents, each per *shih*.* In other words, a consignment of rice from Fuchow to Kiukiang had to make eight distinct payments in five places over a distance of only 175 miles.

In the Poyang Lake the port dues used to be levied according to the cubic capacity, the length being taken from the first movable plank in the bow to the rudder-post; and junks were designed to meet and, as far as possible, defeat this rule. Thus we have the remarkable craft called locally the *hung-hsiu-hsieh* (紅 繡 鞋).

At Hankow taxes were levied according to the draught, and it is not surprising, therefore, that Hupeh junks such as the *pien-tzŭ* (扁 子), the *ch'iu-tzŭ* (秋 子), and the *pai-tzŭ* (擺 子) should be broad in the beam but of relatively light draught.

The methods employed in building junks vary, of course, according to the locality and the type and size of the junk, but essentially the initial operation in the building of a small-sized junk is to lay the flat planks for the bottom boards side by side on the site selected as the shipbuilding yard and to secure them together. These planks number eight or more, according to the size of the junk, and have, where necessary, extra lengths scarfed on to make them of uniform measurement. Usually the planks are flat on the inside, but unhewn and left in their natural state on the outer side where exposed to the water.

At suitable intervals, according to the length of the junk and the strength of construction desired, transverse bulkheads and/or ribs are placed in position on the bottom planks to act as stiffening. Longitudinal strength is provided by heavy wales. The bulkheads consist of planks laid vertically one upon the other, edge to edge, and built up to deck level. If they are not too large to be easily handled, they are first assembled and secured together on the ground and then moved bodily into their positions, where they are retained in position by shores and ribbands. The heavy side planks of the hull and the wales are cut to shape by the sawmen, who work without a foot rule, using only the carpenter's string.

The side planks are then placed longitudinally in position and hove down by a Chinese windlass, after which they are firmly nailed to the edges of the bulkheads. The spacing of the transverse frames, or ribs, varies according to the work for which the junk is intended and the number and disposition of the bulkheads. The ideal, of course, would be to make the ribs in one piece, but very seldom is this possible, and they are therefore composed of two, three, or more

* "Kiangsi Native Trade and its Taxation." Stanley F. Wright.

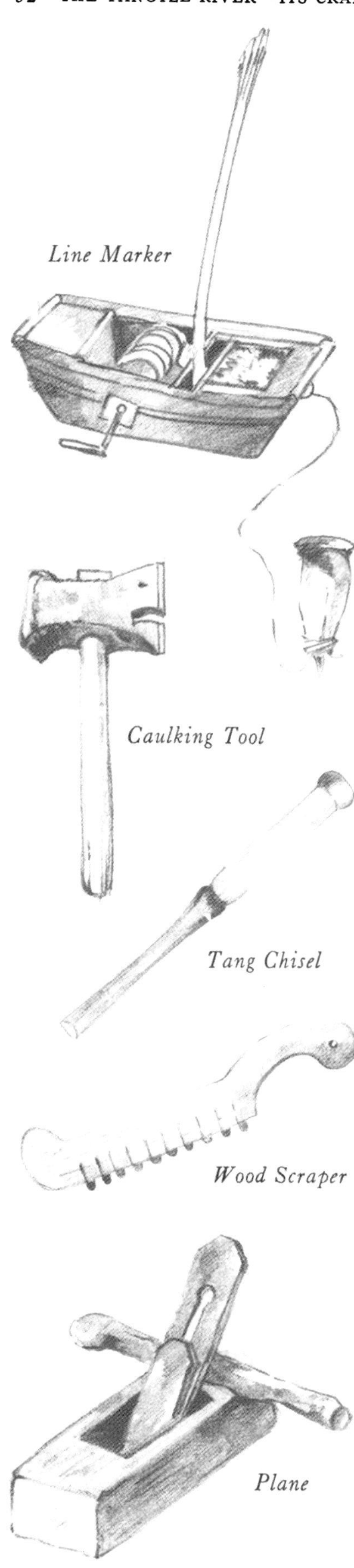

members or parts bolted and joined by heavy nails or scarfed according to the circumstances. In the smaller junks a remarkable fact is that the roots of trees are often utilized, and timber grown to shape is used in all junks whenever possible. The natural shapes of trees, branches, and spars are used also to the fullest advantage, not only for ribs and knees, but for rudder-posts, sweeps, thole-pins, stick-in-the-mud anchors, and countless lesser fittings.

The string line-marker referred to above is of outstanding interest and consists of a wooden cup filled with cotton waste soaked in ink and 2 or 3 yards of string wound round a movable bar running through the middle. When required, the string is pulled out. Attached to the outer end of the string is an awl which is stuck into the plank at the spot where the required line is to begin. With the fingers the thread is taken to where the line is to end and there held. The carpenter then grasps the inked line in the middle with his other hand, lifts it and allows it to rebound against the wood. A straight black line is thus obtained between the points.* An allusion in the Chinese classics in A.D. 560 shows the antiquity of this device. The line-marker of the shipwright differs in appearance from that used by other carpenters, for it is roughly boat-shaped and divided into three compartments by bulkheads. The foremost compartment carries the drum round which the string is wound, the midship compartment carries the bamboo brush for line ruling, while in the after one is stowed the inked cotton waste through which the string passes. Imitation wales, a handsome bow, and a transom stern complete the illusion. When the brush for ruling a short line is in position it gives the appearance of a mast.

The nails used are wrought iron. Those most generally used are the *yang-yen* (羊眼), or sheep's eye; the *tsao-huo-ting* (棗活釘), or date stone, a double-ended pinning nail; the *ch'an-ting* (鏠釘), or joining nail, an unheaded, all-purpose nail; the *pa-t'ou-ting* (耙頭釘), or scratch-head nail, a large sized, rectangular-headed, tapering nail; and the *t'ieh-ting-tzŭ* (鐵錠子), or iron bobbin, with a split tail so that the ends may be fared. This type is used for pinning large planks, such as hatches and the like. This method of pinning is preferred in Shanghai, where the use of iron dogs and clamps is not common.

The Chinese shipwright's tools are far inferior to those of his brother in the West. The axe, the chisel, the plane, the drill, and the saw are all different in design and they are all used in a different manner.

In the West there is a great variety of hammers, each used in a different type of work; the Chinese junk carpenter, however, only uses one type for all his work—the back of his axe. This axe is interesting, since its blade is usually of a rounded shape and sharpened on one side only.

The European carpenter uses the tang type of chisel, that is to say, the chisel fits into the handle, whereas the Chinese carpenter uses the socket type in which the handle fits into the chisel. With the former type the foreign carpenter uses a wooden mallet, but the Chinese uses the back of an axe, and, to avoid splitting the handle through this unnecessarily violent method, a buffalo-hide grummet or an iron ring is placed on the butt or extremity.

The Chinese plane differs very much from the foreign variety. In the first place it has no back-iron, and consequently it tends to tear up the wood on the cross grain. It would be simple and effective to fit one, but the Chinese carpenter has never used one in times past and sees no reason to change now. He manages to reduce the tendency of wood destruction by pushing the plane and working the wood away from him, for which purpose a cross handle is fitted. Secondly, the cutting irons of a Chinese plane are placed well in rear of the centre line and not well forward of it as in the West. Lastly, the irons are removed by the European carpenter by tapping a small metal button placed for the purpose on the fore part of the plane, whereas the Chinese method is to hit the rear side of the plane sharply with an axe.

* The carpenter of the West uses a white chalk line and dry, while the Chinese use a black line and wet. The Chinese mason uses a red line.

The Chinese hand-drill has doubtless changed little through the centuries. It consists of a hardwood stick into the lower end of which a drill is introduced. At least two men are required to operate the drill: one man to hold the handle, or stock, which revolves freely, and another to pull the buffalo-hide thong which causes the drill to revolve. The action is a "backwards-and-forwards" motion rather than "round-and-round" as in the West, and the tendency is to wear through rather than cut through the wood.

At least 10 different types of saw are used by the shipwright of the West. The Chinese junkbuilder, however, accomplishes all his work with one type—a frame saw.

In shipbuilding two sizes of saw are used. One is a small hand-saw for general use, measuring about 2 feet with a width, including the frame, of about 1 foot. All its teeth run in the same way as in a foreign-type saw; the teeth are set to cut on the push. The other type of saw much in use with Chinese shipwrights is the large log-cutting variety measuring about 5 feet in length and 3 feet over-all in width. Mainly similar in design to the small saw, it requires two men to operate it. The teeth on the blade run in opposite directions from a 4-inch long central area without any cutting edge. This arrangement of the teeth has been evolved so that each saw-man does the same amount of cutting work. To saw through a log longitudinally, one man stands on the tilted end of it and pulls the saw up towards him, after which his colleague sitting on the ground below pulls the saw down again. In the West, where the teeth of the saw run in the same direction, only the man below does the actual cutting while the man above merely pulls the saw back into place again for the next stroke. In China the saw blades are always set at an angle to the plane of the frame. Why this is done is not clear, and no Chinese carpenter so far has, when questioned, been able to give a completely satisfactory reason. The tautening of the blade is effected by putting a stick between the separate strands and twisting the rope joining the extremities of the side pieces, on the principle of a tourniquet.

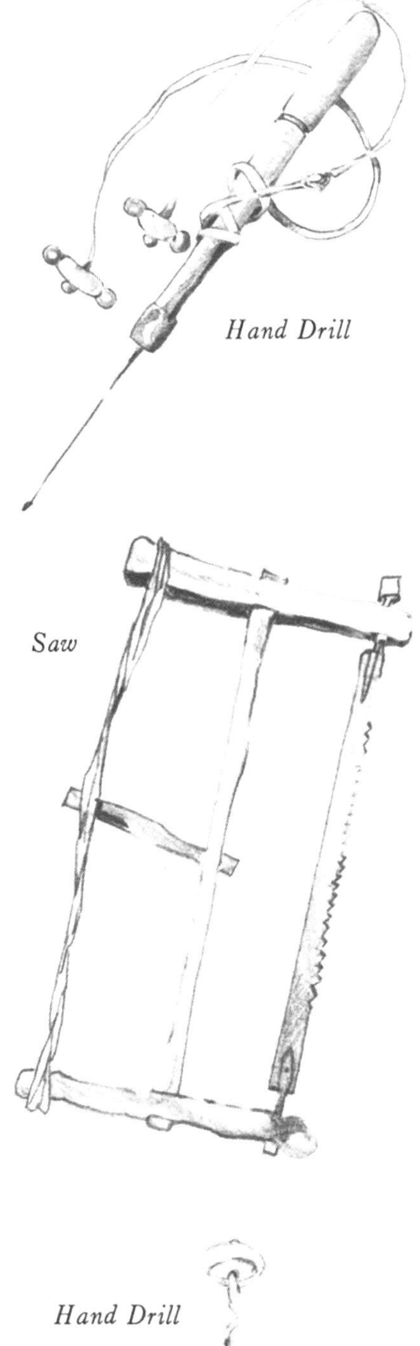

Hand Drill

Saw

There are many different methods of holding the log in place during the process of sawing, but essentially the wood to be sawn is supported in various ways upon two trestles, to which it is secured sometimes by long iron "dogs," often as long as 6 inches, and sometimes by an ingenious arrangement of interlocking.

Although the tools used on the Upper Yangtze are much the same as those employed in other parts of China, there are a few which may be considered peculiar to Szechwan. In the field of drills and saws there is some variety. The principle, in the case of drills, as in other parts of China, is always that of reciprocal motion and not the more advanced continuous rotary action used in the West. Two of the most common varieties are illustrated. A bow-drill, for instance, is fixed vertically in a spindle rotated by means of a hide thong which turns the spindle back and forth as an attached bow is pulled backwards and forwards. This bow can be any length according to the power required. When extra power is desired, two men, one at each extremity, can work the bow, a third holds and guides the revolving grip.

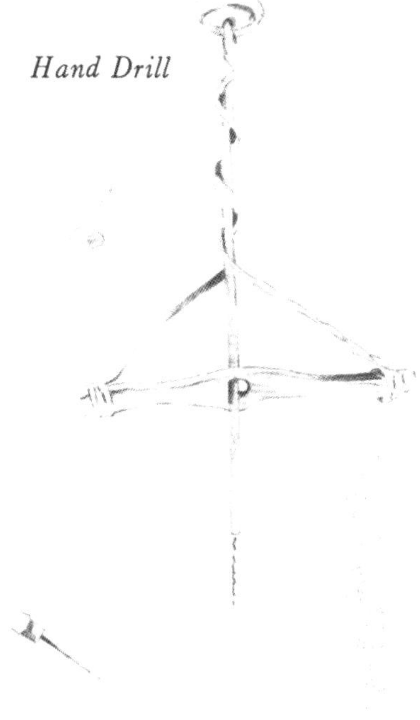

Hand Drill

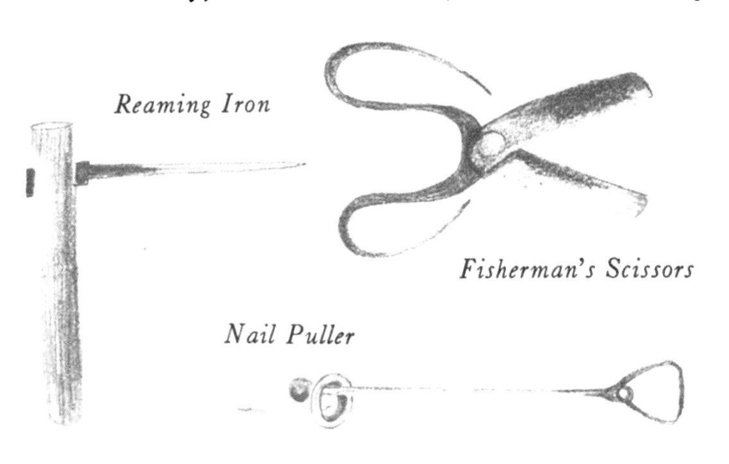

Reaming Iron

Fisherman's Scissors

Nail Puller

Bow Drill

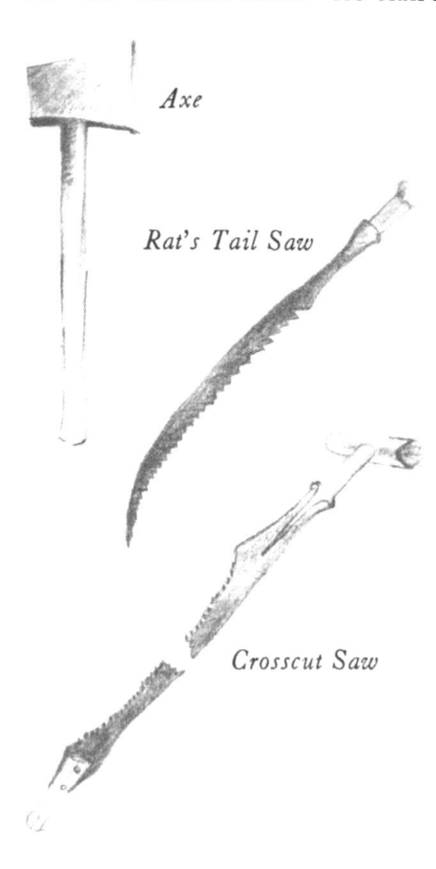

Another and simpler type is the hand drill, which is used for light work, and consists of a smooth shaft having a fixed disc fitted at the top. Immediately below this a hole is bored in the shaft through which passes two hide thongs. These are wound round the central rod and the two ends are secured to the opposite ends of a horizontal wooden bar, or governor, which, with a centre hole, rotates on the shaft. With downward pressure the wooden governor uncoils the thong at the same time rotating the rod in one direction. When the pressure is released the thong uncoils, while the rod continues to rotate and winds the thong around itself in the opposite direction. By this means an alternating motion is transmitted to the drill at the base.

The carpenter's reamer is simple in construction and is used by caulkers for opening the seams of the planks, so that the oakum and chunam may be more readily hammered in. The same tool is also used to make holes in the wood for the insertion of dowels or treenails. For this reason it is made square and tapering.

The scissors of China are characteristically original; there are two varieties, the open and the closed. The former is used by men and the latter by women. The obvious reason is that a man's hand is usually larger. The type illustrated is used by fishermen when net-making.

The band saw is a variety of the cross cut or pit saw. It consists of a thin blade, one edge of which is cut into angular teeth. It is worked by two men and can be as long as four feet. That illustrated has been shown as being divided into two parts, in the interests of space.

The rat's tail saw, in common use in the West, is only occasionally to be found in Szechwan. It is used in scarfing and for mortise-and tenon joins.

Nails used in junk-building in Szechwan are fearsome objects, usually large and always crude. Once hammered in, they are difficult to dislodge. During overhauls or for repairs it becomes necessary to remove them with the minimum amount of damage to the rest of the boat. For this purpose a very simple tool has been devised. It consists of a short iron rod having a solid knob at its extremity over which is a loose ring. The ring is placed over the head of the nail. Leverage on the nail to be extracted is obtained by pivoting the iron rod downwards and away from the nail on its knob extremity. A refinement consists of a ring at the other end, by means of which the instrument can be hung up when not in use.

The Chinese carpenter, moreover, does not require a tool bag. He manages to transport all his tools suspended from a saw which he slings over his shoulder on an axe.

All Chinese tools are hammered out by hand from mild "bamboo steel"* except the saws, which are often made from the iron hoops of cotton bales.

With these primitive tools no finish in the Western sense of the word is possible, but nevertheless it is amazing what excellent work the junk carpenter can produce, and, like all other good craftsmen, he does take a pride in his work.

The boatbuilders are an industrious class. After an early meal they start work at 8 a.m. With an interval of an hour at noon for another meal they work on until dark, and finish off their day with a third and last meal. It is usual for the master shipwright to supply the food.

Between the 5th day of the 5th moon, that is to say the Dragon Boat Festival, and the 15th day of the 8th moon, the Mid-Autumn Festival, they have an extra hour for the midday meal, which is usually devoted to sleep.

* The following story is taken from "The Principal Articles of Chinese Commerce," by Ernest Watson. Chinese Maritime Customs publication, Special Series, No. 38. "Many years ago a large consignment of steel was very urgently required from Europe by a Chinese merchant. The order was given to a British firm, who, on coming to roll the steel, found that their rollers were not exactly suited for the particular size required, and that there was no time to make or procure new rollers. Accordingly, small grooves or notches were made in the old rollers to enable them to get a better grip on the bars of metal, with the result that the finished bars all bore small transverse ridges on the surface. The consignment was sent out and proved to be a great suc-

The saw-men start their career as children. The planks are divided into two lengths, 7 and 14 feet long, and two skilled men can saw 40 planks a day, or 30 if less adept. It does not rank high as a trade, as is evidenced by the saying *yi tan mi hu-ch'in; yi wan fan chü-chiang* (一担米胡琴；一碗飯鋸匠), meaning 1 picul rice, fiddle; one bowl rice, sawing workman.

A free translation of this is that it needs more than the time taken to consume a picul of rice than to learn to play the fiddle, even passably; whereas the time taken to eat a bowl of rice will suffice to train a *k'ai-chiang*. Nothing, it may be said, could be more unjust to the saw-men.

Most of the timber used in junk-building is obtained from firs and pines. Fir is found in the Southern Provinces and is about the fastest growing coniferous tree in China. Generally the trees are cut for sale when they are 20 to 30 years old and about 50 feet high. The wood is light, soft, and fairly tough.

Pine (*Cunninghamia sinensis*) known as *sha-mu* (杉木) is the pine most commonly found in China. This particular tree yields a timber which, varying in colour from white to red, is much used for junk-building. Laurel is another wood much in favour for bulkheads. It is close grained and very durable. Camphor-wood comes from the Nan Ling and Nan Shan Ranges, from Fukien, and it is also found scattered in Szechwan.

In building an iron ship the angle bars are simply heated in a furnace and then bent to the required curve, but in a wooden junk it is a matter of careful and skilful workmanship to saw or hew from the rough logs curved timbers, many of which have to be scarfed to form a single rib. The sawing of planks, too, requires great skill.

The caulkers are a different class and are known as *nien-fêng-chiang* (黏縫匠). Caulking is, of course, of very antique origin. In the West the ancients appear to have used it in very early times by introducing pounded sea shells into the seams between the planks, a process which was found to be satisfactory only for a short time.

In later days other methods were adopted, one of which, according to Lindsay, is attributed by Pliny to the Belgæ, and consisted in beating pounded seeds into the fissures between the planks of vessels—a substitute, he says, found to be more tenacious than glue and more to be relied upon than pitch. This is evidently the same in principle as the modern practice of caulking.

The first mention of caulking in China would appear to be on the oracle bones, to which Chinese tradition assigns the dates 1766–1122 B.C. The character *chêng* is of surpassing interest, for it shows a boat (see Page No. 11, Fig. D) and two hands with caulking tool.

Methods of caulking in China were noticed and recorded by Marco Polo in the thirteenth century, who says:

> The fastenings are all of good iron nails and the sides are double, one plank laid over the other, and caulked outside and in. The planks are not pitched, for these people do not have any pitch, but they daub the sides with another matter, deemed by them far better than pitch; it is this. You see, they take some lime and chopped hemp, and these they knead together with a certain wood oil; and when the three are thoroughly amalgamated, they hold like any glue. And with this mixture they do pay their ships.

The mixture alluded to was, of course, what is known to-day in China as chunam (油石灰), which is a compound of lime and wood oil, a product of the *t'ung* nut. As a point of interest it should be added that despite Marco Polo's reference to the excellent qualities of *t'ung* oil, it did not become known to the outside world until 1516, through the Portuguese traders. Even then the first

cess. Later on the same Chinese firm ordered more of the same class of steel. In the meantime, the firm in Great Britain, who were rather ashamed of the rough state in which the former shipment had been turned out, had procured new rollers, and were able to deliver the next consignment in perfectly smooth well-finished bars. The Chinese merchant, however, refused to take delivery of the shipment, on the ground that as the bars were quite smooth they could not be of the same quality as those formerly sent, which were marked like a 'bamboo.' Since that time, this class of steel intended for shipment to China has always been prepared 'with the transverse ridges on the surface, and is still known as bamboo steel.' "

shipment did not reach America until 1875, and the wood-oil trade did not develop to any appreciable extent until the twentieth century.

Sir George Staunton, Secretary to the Embassy sent to China in 1792, wrote of quite a different form of caulking, for, as he describes it, the "seams are payed with paste, made by mixing water with quicklime from sea shells."

Caulking in China nowadays is carried out exactly in the manner described by Marco Polo 700 years ago; that is to say, oakum is laid along the outside of the seam for a distance of about a foot, and then bit by bit inserted and hammered home together with small portions of chunam, which are picked up with a caulking chisel from a kind of crude pallet carried by the caulker.

Caulking of large seams is carried out with a mixture of oakum and old discarded fish-nets. The net is beaten soft, cut into strips, smeared with chunam, and mixed with oakum. Considerable extra strength is thereby imparted to the area to be caulked. Old caulking is jerried out by means of a caulking knife.

In addition to its use as a vehicle for chunam, the junkmen on the Yangtze use nothing else but wood oil to varnish or finish the surface of their junks. A liberal coating is rubbed in with the hands, and this is repeated, as a rule, until three or more coats have been applied at intervals of a few days. At the annual overhaul, carried out in the dry winter season, fresh coats of wood oil are applied.

Small numbers are used in the text to correspond with the parts or parts referred to in the plate or diagram.

Riverine junks are not as a rule painted, as are the sea-going junks. Instead they are coated with wood oil. This oil is obtained from the seeds of the *t'ung* trees. They are handsome, very hardy, and fast growing trees, about 20 feet in height. In the middle of September each year the apple-like fruit is collected from fully matured trees. The seeds when dried contain 36 per cent oil. This oil is a thick, semi-solid substance varying from pale yellow to dark brown in colour, and it is said to be the best drying and waterproofing oil of vegetable origin known to technical science. Of China's total output of *t'ung* oil, Szechwan produces nearly one-third, Hunan nearly one-fourth, Hupeh and Kiangsi furnishing the remainder. Hankow is the chief exporting centre.

Junkbuilding or repair yards are usually situated up the smaller creeks. Sometimes craft have to travel a mile or more up a narrow waterway before being hauled up on the bank for overhaul, though a convenient foreshore is also very generally used.

The vessels are slipped by means of a primitive form of capstan (*illustrated in margin*) which consists of a wooden barrel [1] revolving on a heavy iron pivot [2] fitted in a wooden bed[3]. Posts are driven into the ground, and the portable capstan is secured thereto by ropes leading to the hook[4].

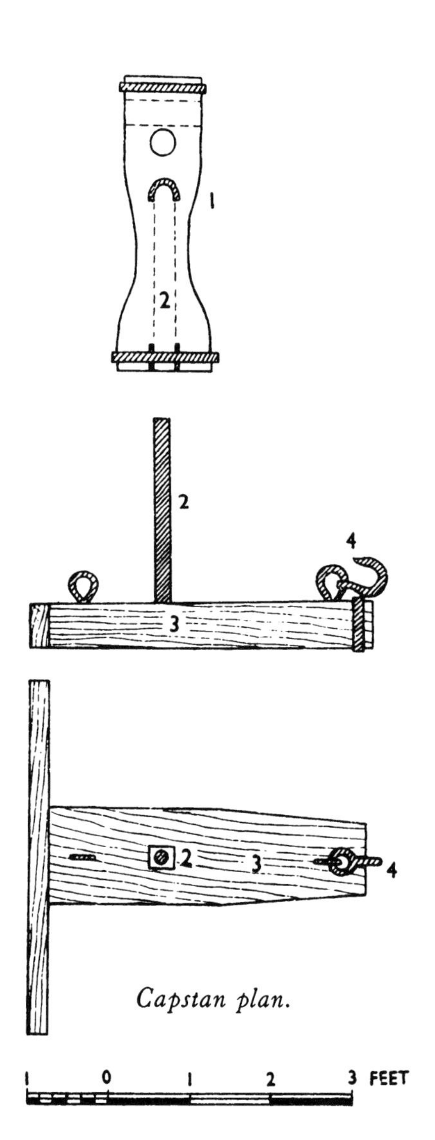

Capstan plan.

In many types of junks, both sea-going and riverine, the foremost compartment (and sometimes the after compartment as well) is made free flooding by boring holes in the bottom. The sailors of the Lower Yangtze claim for this practice that it has a tendency to stop junks flying up into the wind, while those on the Upper Yangtze affirm that resistance to the water is thus reduced to a minimum. It is difficult to understand these theories, although it may perhaps reduce pounding in a heavy sea or a rapid.

A more probable explanation is that these holes are made for the purpose of draining water shipped over the bow or getting in through slack seams. This compartment is very difficult to keep dry owing to the method of construction, and the practice of free flooding saves bailing and at the same time prevents the accumulated water from remaining dead.

It is quite possible that the idea of the fathom and the word "sounding-lead" were both derived from the Chinese. It is recorded that an envoy sent to Korea used a sounding-lead (鐵 鍋) in order to ascertain the depth of water and found 32 fathoms (三十二托). The word *t'o* is still used by the junkmen to mean "a two-arm reach," which is what fathom means.

According to Notes and Queries in the "China Review," the correct word for fathom is *t'o* (拓 or 托). In the chapter regarding navigation contained in the "Tung Hsi Yang K'ao" (東西洋考), Chapter 9, it is stated that, when heaving the lead to ascertain the depth of the sea, the depth is expressed in so many *t'o* (沉繩水底打量某處水深淺幾托), and an explanatory note is added saying that, according to the "Fang Yen" (方言), the length of the two arms extended makes one *t'o*. This quite corresponds with the original meaning of our word fathom.

Sailors of all ages from the time of the Phœnicians have taken pleasure in adorning their ships; indeed Platus, the historian, classes together ships and women as equally greedy of ornament.

In China the decoration of junks is largely bound up with religion, mythology, and symbolism. The worship of Shang Ti (上帝), the supreme spirit, is regarded as the most ancient belief of the Chinese. Later this worship was extended to spirits of the river, mountains, and so forth. They did not make images of these supernatural beings but they were suggested by symbols.

And so from the time when the *pa-kua* (八卦) was first revealed to Fu Hsi (伏羲) the Chinese have been the greatest exponents of the art of symbolism. It first made its appearance in the early bronzes, and so on down the ages until to-day, when symbolism still plays its part in every phase of life throughout the Middle Kingdom.

In a modified form the symbol figures on the masthead devices or wind vanes carried by nearly all junks. Although the original religious meaning, if any, has probably been forgotten, these picturesque pennants serve as distinguishing marks and are, in addition, regarded as securing good luck and prosperity, and are portents of happy omen.

Wind vanes are illustrated in the Appendix.

The wind vanes of sea-going and estuary craft are not, as on the Upper Yangtze, altogether and solely indicative of the actual port of origin of the craft but rather denote in a general way the district from which the junk hails.

There is not complete uniformity. For instance, two junks of different types from the same district will differ albeit in small details only as regards their wind vanes; two junks of the same type from the same district will carry wind vanes still more alike.

The single-masted junks of the Whangpoo seldom have a wind vane. Some Tsungming junks also are to be found without one, although generally speaking they follow the design of those of the Kiangsu craft. The wind vanes of the now defunct lorchas were dull indeed, consisting of no more than a wooden fish and a red streamer mounted on an iron rod.

The most favoured motif in the wind vanes is the fish, which is a symbol of wealth on account of the similarity in the pronunciation of the words *yü* (魚), fish, and *yü* (餘), superfluity. Moreover, it is happy in its own element or sphere and is regarded as a symbol of harmony. The fish, too, never closes its eyes and is therefore considered to be a fit model of vigilance.

The mirror is a charm or anti-spectral device for protection against demons or warding off evil influences. If a fish forms part of the masthead device, a mirror, usually diamond-shaped, is very often superimposed on the centre of its body. This serves to frighten away the evil spirits when they see their ugly faces reflected therein.

Red is the prevailing colour of the pennants, for it is a powerful devil-dispelling colour and constitutes a formidable agent against malicious spirits.

The wind vanes illustrated (*see endsheets*) are by no means complete but are sufficient to give a good indication of this interesting feature of junk decoration.

Particularly interesting are the many forms of distinguishing devices and symbols carried by some small craft, always at a small staff on the mizzen. A device in fibre at the masthead denotes the port of origin or the district. There would seem to be at least eight different kinds of these. Below this are three pennants. The highest is the "wind flag" or vane, the second denotes the association to which the owner belongs, and the third the firm or company in control of the junk. This short bamboo, therefore, can convey a good deal of information to the initiated. Junks belonging to, or chartered by, a Government organization such as the Salt Gabelle paint their mastheads white, including the truck. A sprig of bamboo, less the leaves, covered at its base with yellow cloth denotes that the junk has recently been on an ocean pilgrimage to Pootoo.

Signalling is carried out by the laodah by hoisting and lowering the mizzen at specified intervals, this forming a code to indicate various requirements.

Other signals used are the hoisting of a matting raincoat at the masthead to hail the Fishing Guild, or a basket at the foremast summons the tax collector, hard as it may be to believe that anyone would willingly invite his officious attentions.

All the larger types of junks working between Chungking and Ichang carry devices on a light staff at the masthead, which differ a great deal in shape, colour, and design, and denote the town to which the owner belongs.

This practice is not followed by junks regularly trading above Chungking. When, however, they operate in waters where these devices are general, all junks from the upper reaches fly a small red flag. If a parent of a junkowner dies, a plain, small, white flag is flown, inferior to the normal device, as a mark of respect and is kept flying for three years, which is the normal period of mourning. A number of the more common distinguishing emblems of various home ports are illustrated in the endpapers. It is possible they have a religious significance.

The most elaborate design comes from the town of Fowchow (涪 州) and consists of two small pennants, and below, suspended obliquely, a sword terminating in an open hand. From the middle of the palm hangs by a cord and decorative knot a multi-coloured swallow-tailed banner.

Another more common custom is the use of two twists of wire, not unlike loose wire springs, which droop like antennæ from either side of the staff at the masthead and end in small bells, or pom-poms. Many of the designs include a number of *tan* (蛋), or coloured wooden "eggs." These rest in tin receptacles, one above the other, vertically down the staff.

The principal part of the device is the flag, or flags, which are nearly always red, and may be large or small, square or oblong, pennants or burgees. Sometimes they are plain, but more often they carry the name of the junkowner, the *pa-kua* (八 卦), the *yin* and *yang* (陰 陽), or a motto such as *shun* (順), meaning "a fair wind."

The *lao-hua-ch'iu* (老 划 秋) type of junk, which plies on the Suiningho (遂 寧 河), a tributary of the Kialing River, is often to be seen with what might be described as an open umbrella lashed at the masthead just above the blocks for the halyards. This contrivance, which measures about 4 feet across, is like an umbrella of the official presentation type (萬 民 傘), that is to say, it is circular, with deep vertical sides after the fashion of a lampshade, and with cross-pieces to give it support. Constructed on a bamboo frame, it is made of oiled cloth, or of the outer husks of bamboo shoots (筍 殼).

Repeated questioning always results in the same reply that it is designed to "keep off the rain." The rainfall on the Suiningho is no heavier—indeed, rather less—than in the neighbouring districts, nevertheless the officials of the junk guilds and the junkmen all give this explanation.

Despite its resemblance in shape—and allegedly in function—to an umbrella, it is never known as such, but is referred to as a *fêng-pao* (風 包), a rather ambiguous title which may be translated variously as a "wind parcel," "wind wrapping," or "wind collector or container." It appears not unlikely that the *fêng-pao* may be a form of masthead talisman, particularly as its use is entirely confined to the Suiningho.

Although its explanation and origin remain obscure, its presence at the top of the lofty masts of the longest junks of the Upper Yangtze regions adds an unusual touch of local colour here and there to the closely clustered junks which lie inside the Kialing River below the east wall of the city of Chungking.

With at most two exceptions the oculus* as a form of decoration is never to be found on Yangtze craft and on only some of the estuary types mentioned in these pages. Broadly speaking, the oculus is present sporadically in the north, but its main habitat is from the mouth of the Yangtze to Amoy. It reappears in Tonkin and even in Singapore, though there and in Indo-China it is more akin to the Egyptian sacred boat oculus, that is to say, elongated more in the form of the human eye than the round eye of the Chinese junk.

Actually the use of the oculus in the Far East has given rise to a great deal of interesting but rather unproductive discussion in learned treatises and technical periodicals, since little can be deduced as to its origin. It is usually accepted as a truism that the eye on the bows of Chinese junks is not indigenous but was borrowed from the Arabian craft; but even that is by no means proved.

If that is so, why is the eye not universally used in Canton, for so long the greatest sphere of Arab influence, while it persists (indeed, it is its chief stronghold) in and around Ningpo? Why is it that on the Song Ca River, where Annam joins Tonkin, in Indo-China, on one bank the Chinese staring oculus is to be seen on craft while on the other is to be found the long oval eye suggestive of Arab influence?

Why again do the traders from Hangchow, one of the most important Arab trading stations, have no oculus but instead the *pa-kua* (八 卦), while those just across the estuary at Shaohing have neither? Further, the eye is not unknown in Shantung and Manchuria, places where no ancient Arab ever set foot.

The theory, which is so often quoted, that the oculus is only to be found in craft hailing from ports which in ancient days were Arab trading stations needs considerably more proof than is at present available to make it convincing.

A great number of fishing-junks off the estuary are lost through being caught in typhoons; but the Observatory at Siccawei, under Father E. Gherzi, Director of Meteorology, has done a great service to the junkmen in instituting wireless warnings. It has been said that Padre Gherzi is the father of typhoons, although unable to control these unruly children of his. Actually the term "sky pilot," as applied to a priest of any denomination, seems a more apt designation, for with the aid of wireless he has been the means of guiding countless junks to safety. On the approach of a typhoon, telegrams are sent out from Siccawei to the chief fishing ports telling the junks not to leave harbour. In the fishing fleet at sea one junk is equipped with a small wireless set, and on receipt of the wireless warning she hoists a black ball at the masthead and leads the fishing fleet to the safety of the nearest refuge.

* In fishing-junks the eyeball is often set low in the white so as to be on the alert to observe the fish, unlike the trading junk, wherein the eye looks straight ahead so as to perceive and avoid distant perils invisible to mortal sight.

The number of sea-going junks trading to Chinkiang in 1901 was estimated at 1,000 all told and the number of trips performed in the year at 3,000 or more. They usually spent from one to three months waiting for a cargo. The merchandise carried consisted principally of paper, sea blubber, and softwood poles as imports, and of grain, mainly rice, as export.

In the same year it was estimated that about double that number of inland-water junks visited the port. About one-fourth of these carried between 1,000 and 2,000 piculs each, while the rest ranged from 50 to 800 piculs in carrying capacity. Chinkiang is an important junction for interprovincial water-borne traffic, for the greater part of China's inland waterways can be reached from this point. A very large proportion of the surface of the Province of Kiangsu and, to a lesser degree, that of Anhwei is covered with water, forming a network, partly artificial and partly natural, of creeks and canals connected by numberless lakes. Access to these is available by the Grand Canal, which also provides communication to the North and South for large junks from Hangchow to Tsingkiangpu (淸 江 浦), where connection is then made *via* the Hwai River (淮 河) with Northern Anhwei. An extension of the canal supplies good navigation to Tsining (濟 甯) in Shantung, and rice-boats followed a direct route to Peiping. Owing to the heavy likin charges introduced in the middle of the nineteenth century, much of this traffic was diverted from the more obvious main routes. On the Grand Canal, for instance, the likin barriers followed each other at 29-mile intervals, and it was not surprising that much of the distribution of merchandise was effected *via* devious lesser-known routes.

A likin tax is a Chinese provincial tax levied at inland stations on imports or articles in transit.

In addition to the riverine craft, sea-going junks are to be found on the lower reaches of the Yangtze. There used to be a regular service of junks trading from Ningpo to Chinkiang and another from Foochow. They consisted of vessels varying in size from 300 to 6,000 piculs in carrying capacity. Junks of the larger type used to anchor at a place some 25 miles farther down river, while the smaller types anchored on the north shore opposite Chinkiang. Previous to the Tai-ping Rebellion in 1865 the sea-going junk anchorage was close to the city; but, owing to the riotous character of the junkmen and their readiness to assist the rebels, the authorities forbade them access to the harbour limits and assigned them to a distant anchorage.

Sea-going junks used to be met with as far up river as Nanking, but in no large numbers. The kind most usually seen, perhaps because they were most easily distinguished, were the ordinary Ningpo *tiao-tzŭ* (刁 子), but even these did not often come much beyond Chinkiang, where, as already stated, they had a special anchorage set apart for them.

Sea-going junks are never to be seen at Kiukiang. Many different classes of riverine craft have access to good water communications through the Poyang Lake to Nanchang, the capital of Kiangsi, and the Kan River in the south of the province, where connection is made with the overland Meiling Pass (梅 嶺) crossing the watershed to Namyung Cheo (南 雄) in Kwangtung, where riverine communication again becomes possible by means of the eastern branch of the North River.

From the Native Customs returns for 1901 it is apparent that altogether 109 craft, comprising six varieties of sea-going junks of different capacity, traded as far into the interior as Nanking. Sugar from Fukien and Formosa and kerosene oil from Hongkong appear to have been the principal goods carried.

Before the port was open to foreign shipping in the spring of 1899, practically the whole of Nanking's junk trade was done in river and inland-water junks. The Native Customs returns of 40 years ago give 35 distinct classes of junks engaged in this trade, excluding small fishing and passenger boats and cargo-sampans. Each of these classes was represented by junks of different carrying capacity, as many as six different sizes of the same variety being met with.

Of extra-provincial junks, Hunan and Anhwei send the greatest variety and were each represented by five different kinds of vessel. Of Hunan junks, the class known locally as the *ya-shao-tzŭ* (鴨 梢 子) comes in the greatest number and brings coal and other fuel. Kiangsi junks are represented by three different varieties.

Situated as it is at the mouth of the Han, where it enters the Yangtze, Hankow is not only in the middle of China, but forms, even more than does Chinkiang, a well-placed junction whereby much widespread connection can be made with waterways leading to the farthest corners of China. Creek routes for shallow-draught craft considerably shorten the passage to the Western Hupeh *entrepôt* of Shasi, and have, moreover, the advantage of little or no current to contend with on the upward journey. Other creek routes form a network of water communications with the hinterland. Contact may also be made *via* the Han River with the North.

From up and down the Yangtze and all its innumerable tributaries and creeks, from the Grand Canal, the Poyang and Tungting Lakes, and the Han and Siang Rivers, a vast collection of craft converges on Hankow, where the Great River, despite being distant 600 miles from the sea, is a mile wide.

Junks from as far afield as Chekiang and Kiangsu, Anhwei and Kiangsi, Hunan, Honan, Shensi, and Szechwan may be seen at Hankow. The number of Szechwan junks, however, is comparatively few, for the bulk of these junks find Shasi a more convenient terminal port.

The Native Customs at Wuhu gave a return of 15,000 craft of all kinds dealt with in a year early this century, but considered this to be a very conservative estimate. They embraced about 21 types varying in capacity from 50 to 2,000 piculs, with a length of 100 feet downwards and a crew of from two to 16 men. Tonnage dues were collected from upwards of 4,200 craft in 1901, but in the conditions under which tonnage dues were paid these figures give no adequate basis for reckoning the number of entries. These vessels trade with places as far up river as Ichang, as far down as Shanghai, and with inland places in both sections of the Anhwei Province, that is to say, north and south of the Yangtze. The largest vessels frequenting Wuhu were traders from Hankow, Chinkiang, and Shanghai, some having a capacity up to 2,700 piculs, but the smallest tubs paddled with the hands may also be met with at this port as well as a very small variety of bamboo raft.

The greatest number of junks entering at any one Yangtze port, however, is to be found at the Wu-Han cities (武 漢), where the Customs returns of 1891 computed that 23,500 junks entered the Han or the mouth of the Han, with a total tonnage of about 1 million and an estimated aggregate figure of 165,000 crew. This extremely conservative estimate gives some idea of the enormous trade involved. These craft range from vessels of 40 feet in length, 7 feet beam, with a carrying capacity of 150 piculs, to those of 70 feet, having a beam of 15½ feet, with a carrying capacity of 1,100 piculs and a crew of 12 men.

The Wu-Han Cities are Wuchang, Hanyang, and Hankow. See Part Three, page 353.

At Wuhu it is estimated that one-tenth of the merchandise is carried by barrow or pack-animal, two-tenths by porters, and the rest by water. Here sea-going junks are very rarely seen, but inland-water junks are to be found in great numbers frequenting the waterways which lead both north and south, for Wuhu is admirably situated for trade. It is connected with the important city of Ningkwofu (寧國府), in Southern Anhwei, by a large canal carrying a fair depth of water; another runs south-west for 8 miles towards the tea district of Taipinghsien (太平縣) and on to the silk areas of Nanling (南陵) and Kinghsien (涇縣). There are also additional canals joining a system of waterways which serve to convey thence coal and timber from the interior.

The Appendix to the "I Ching" (易經), called "Hsi Tz'ŭ" (繫辭), states laconically "during the reign of Huang Ti boats were made first by hollowing out logs, and oars by shaping and planing planks." This is probably the first reference to sampans in Chinese history. A junkmen's legend, however, attributes the conception of boats to Ho Hsien-ku (何仙姑), one of the eight Taoist fairies and the only female member of that roistering band of fantastic immortals.* It is said that her first effort was a raft, but that while washing clothes in the river she got the inspiration of adding oars and a rudder from watching a fish pass by. She is always represented as standing on a floating lotus petal—a most unsailor-like practice.

Between the log and the complete boat there must have come into existence all sorts of intermediate forms of craft, such as skin boats, skin rafts, coracles, basket boats, calabash floats, bundle-boats, and pottery-rafts. All these are still to be found in various parts of China to-day.

We do not know, of course, and it is quite useless to speculate on the order in which they came first into being. Tung Fang-shuo (東方朔), the great Chinese scholar who was born in 154 B.C., writing in the "Shen I Ching" (神異經), says:

> In the extreme southland there grew gigantic bamboos . . . the stems are used for making ships. (南方荒中有涕竹長數百丈可以爲船)

That basket boats existed in ancient China is borne out by the frequent references to them in the "Pao P'o Tzŭ" (抱朴子), one of which says:

> Paddling a basket boat, he crossed the great river. (棹藍舟而濟大川)

The basket boats of Indo-China are still in existence to-day. They are very simple in construction and caulked with a mixture of cattle-dung and coconut oil. It is not thought that the Chinese invented basket boats but that they derived from the Mesopotamian "goofa" *via* Persia and Northern India.

The skin boat of China is also a survival of ancient culture and must have co-existed with the early rafts. There is an illustration in the "San Ts'ai T'u Huei" (三才圖會), a Chinese encyclopædia of the mediæval period. The skin boat is still to be found on the upper courses of the Yangtze.

The skin raft is almost international, being found to this day in Japan, the Ganges and Sutlej, Baghdad, Babylon, Syria, Morocco, and Peru. In China it is to be found on the Yellow River.

Another illustration also to be found in the "San Ts'ai T'u Huei" represents a *mu-ying* (木罌), or pottery-raft. It is described therein as consisting of many earthen jars or pots tied together so as to form a raft.

In the illustration the jars are not visible, being beneath the raft. The pottery-rafts in use to-day usually consist of about 78 jars, 13 rows of six jars in each. This type of raft is also in use in India, on the Nile, and in Japan, as well as on the Upper Yangtze.

The pottery-raft was probably the first "assault craft" in the world, for in "Ssŭ-ma Ch'ien's History" (史記淮陰侯傳), written in 95 B.C., it is

* This is a typical example of the vague unrelated sense of time displayed by the early historians of China, for Ho Hsien-ku is said to have been born in Canton in A.D. 700, which, as fairies go, is comparatively modern and centuries after the art of boatbuilding was perfected by the Chinese.

recorded that *mu-ying* were used by the troops of General Han Hsin (韓 信), of the Han kingdom, who made a surprise crossing of the Yellow River and subsequently achieved a remarkable victory. A short footnote to the term *mu-ying* was added by Fu Ch'ien (服 虔), of the Later Han dynasty, to the effect that the rafts used were made of earthen pots with a wooden framework.

The calabash as a means of water transport is mentioned in the "Yen Fan Lou," written during the Sung dynasty, wherein it is described as a waist boat. It goes on to say:

> . . . a full-grown fruit, which is very large and strong, may be cut into two parts and made into pots for crossing the water. It is so strong that it can cross even deep water without mishap.

The book does not mention in what way the calabash was used in crossing the water, but presumably it was made airtight and fastened to the waist or under the arms of the user as a primitive form of water wings. In the "Shih Ching" (詩 經) there is a poem which suggests the use of the calabash for ferrying across the streams among the ancient people of China. One verse runs:

> Bitter are the leaves of the calabash.
> Deep is the ferry sometimes, though shallow at other times.

Again it is recorded in the "Chuang Tzŭ" (莊 子) how the King of Wei (魏 王) was presented with a calabash seed by one of his loyal subjects.

He sowed it and cultivated it with the greatest diligence, and was both pleased and surprised to find his care rewarded when the seed developed into a gigantic growth of strange design. The King tried various experiments with the produce of this novel plant. He found it was extremely unpalatable; it was too heavy to move when used for storing water; it made an indifferent ladle and an even worse receptacle. The King was at his wit's end to know what to do with this embarrassing present, indeed he was, it was reported, on the verge of having it destroyed when some nautically-minded official of his court recommended it should be made into a boat. And so it was.

This practical suggestion proved a complete success, and the King of Wei was frequently to be seen disporting himself in or on his calabash. It is pleasant to be able to record that the amateur yachtsman who was responsible for the idea was suitably rewarded.

The word sampan (三 板) is derived from the Chinese *san*, meaning three, and *pan*, meaning planks, the whole being a symbolic definition of a small boat. This form of spelling has arisen from the fact that early foreign intercourse with China was more or less limited to Canton, where the pronunciation of "*san*," for three, is "*sam*." The presence of the "m" is further explained by the Annamese name of *tam* (for *san*), again meaning three, and the Spanish *cempan* and Portuguese *champana*. The first recorded mention of this word in Europe dates as far back as 1620, from which time it has been recognized as the generic term for any small boat of Chinese design and as such has found its way into the "Oxford English Dictionary."

Curiously enough, despite the Chinese flavour of the word, the Chinese themselves, unless dealing with foreigners, never use it, but have other names which vary in different parts of the country. In the Shanghai district, for instance, they always refer to a *hua-tzŭ* (划 子), literally, a "small boat." The word sampan, nevertheless, however it attained its present popularity, has during the last 300 years become so firmly established as to need no apology for its use here.

From Mr. Worcester's notes: The types of sampan in use on the upper reaches of the Yangtze and its tributaries differ completely from those on the Lower River. All are admirably designed for their work, and the sampanmen are probably the best of their kind in the world. To them the rapid is not a dangerous navigable element but an intimate companion and lifelong friend—a friend they respect, a friend they take advantage of whenever possible, but not one they fear.

VARIOUS METHODS OF PROPULSION

NO matter in what part of the world primitive man's first attempt to propel his crude craft was made, doubtless it was by paddling with his hands and later with the branch of a tree. So, with dawning intelligence, the shaped paddle gradually developed.

From the paddle was evolved the oar, for it was not long before it was discovered that much more power could be exerted by rowing than by paddling. In the latter case the stroke depends on the strength of the arms alone, but in rowing the oarsman is able to make use of the long leverage of his oars and can in addition use the whole weight of his body.

In China, as elsewhere, nothing of course is known of the early history of propulsion, but one thing is pretty certain, and that is that the Chinese oar as in use to-day is probably very little changed from that which the mythical Emperor Fu Hsi is said to have taught the early people of China to use in 2852 B.C. It should be remembered that at this early date there seems nothing to indicate the use of wind as an aid to propulsion.

Probably the first delineation of an oar in Chinese history is to be found in the early Chinese character *pan* (般), to propel, as shown on the oracle bones, (see Page No. 10, Fig. B). In this character the oar can easily be seen, or rather imagined, in the hand.

Although reliable descriptive references to junks and sampans are quite lacking in Chinese history in the main, there are early allusions to rowing which would seem to prove that the methods in use to-day are identical with those of over 2,000 years ago, and are very likely vastly older. The first reference to oars is in the "Shang Shu" (尚 書), a history of the Shang dynasty, 1400 B.C. The latest of these documents is supposed to have been written in 600 B.C., but many are forgeries of later dates up to the third century A.D. In one place it makes the rather obvious statement:

> When you want to cross a big river, you require a boat and oars. (若 濟 巨 川 用 汝 作 舟 楫)

The "Han Shu" (漢 書), or "History of the Former Han Dynasty," written by Pan Ku (班 固), *circa* A.D. 90, describes how the Emperors of the Han dynasty, 206 B.C. to A.D. 25, were rowed on the Yangtze in boats with "oars resting on pivots far in front and a rudder at the stern."

The oars of China may be classified under three main headings:

(*a*) The paddle.
(*b*) The *chiang*, or oar proper.
(*c*) The yuloh, or sculling oar.

It is more than probable that oars in China developed in that order, the reason being that the paddle was obviously the most primitive, to be followed by the oar, which is merely a paddle with a fixed fulcrum. Finally, the yuloh, which is a much more scientific instrument of propulsion.

All the early Western travellers of note made references to the Chinese oar, and indeed, accustomed as they were to seeing galleys with their banks of oars, it is not surprising that the old writers should have expatiated on the Chinese sweeps.

The wonderment expressed is the measure of their novelty. Marco Polo, although he remarked on their size, did not describe them so fully as the Arab traveller, Ibn Batuta, who is quoted by Yule as saying:

> They are moved by large oars which might be compared with great masts in respect of size, over which 25 men are sometimes placed, who work standing.

The oar proper—that is to say, in the sense of an implement to propel by means of pushing or pulling—is hardly ever used in the Shanghai area except in one or two types of small sampan, although it has a very considerable vogue in many other parts of China, notably on the Yangtze.

In rowing, as in many other arts, the Chinese again show their great independence of thought. In the West the blade of the oar must be just nicely covered, it is important that it should not go deeply into the water.

With the junkman of China the exact contrary is the case. With him nothing matters beyond propelling his heavy boat at a moderate speed with a minimum of exertion. This is necessary because he may be required to row sometimes with hardly a stop for most of the daylight hours.

On large junks the loom of the heavy oar may extend above the oarsman's head.

He stands to row instead of sits, and pushes his oar rather than pulls it. The rowers stand on the opposite side of the junk to that on which the oar is operating, so as to give greater leverage. There are, however, further differences which require to be noted. The oar, instead of making a stroke just below the surface of the water and then returning in the reverse direction just above it, dips deeply, indeed very deep, and moves in more or less of a vertical plane. The whole curve of the blade in the water is therefore A B C D in China as against A E D in the West. The "catch," or instantaneous application of weight and muscles to the oar at the moment it enters the water, is made with the arms partially extended, in the case of heavy junks, the loom of the oar being actually above the head of the standing oarsman. Then comes the push, with force of arms and legs pressure being exerted against the thole pin. The blade is at an angle, and for the first part of the stroke goes down sharply in the water at an angle of perhaps 60°. The "recovery," or those movements at the end of the stroke that are necessary before another stroke can be commenced, is short and sharp, the arms being shot out full length.

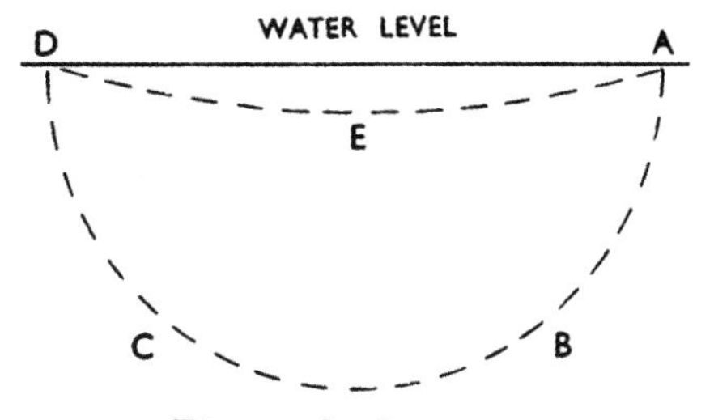

The track of an oar.

More work is therefore done by the Chinese per stroke. Pushing the oar tends to increase the lunge, and the legs and body certainly play an important part in propulsion. In sampans the crossing of the oars in front of the rower is essentially Chinese and is inspired by the idea of economy of effort.

The junkman of China stands to row.

Working the yuloh.

From this oar doubtless developed the more scientific yuloh. The word *lu* (櫓) is first mentioned in the "Shih Ming" (釋名), a dictionary written by Liu Hsi (劉熙) in the Later Han dynasty, A.D. 25–221, where it is defined as denoting:

> "The thing on the boat's sides which is to be managed by strong muscles before the boat moves." (在旁曰櫓櫓膂也用膂力然後舟行也)

The word is again used in the "History of the Three Kingdoms" (三國志), by Ch'ên Shou (陳壽), written during the third century A.D. The word *yao* (搖) is the verb to wave, shake, or sway, and from this derives the word yuloh, denoting the act of sculling.

The yuloh, as such, is mentioned in the "Tung Ming Chi" (洞冥記), a book which dates back to the Later Han dynasty, A.D. 25–221.

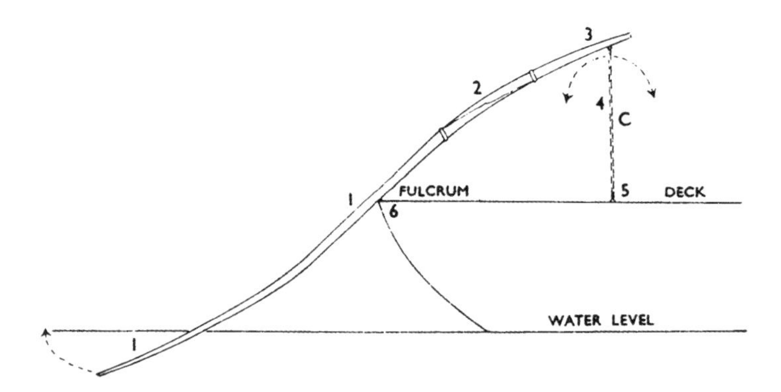

Diagram of a yuloh.

Generally speaking, it is a broad blade[1] of hardwood joined to a shaft[2] and a loom[3]. On the extremity of the loom is a cut-away portion to which a fibre rope[4] is made fast (or alternatively, to a ring in the loom), the other end being attached to a ring-bolt in the deck[5]. The yuloh rests at about its centre of balance upon a fulcrum in the shape of a sloping iron pivot[6].

This pivot is either set into a beam situated over the stern or, if used anywhere else, into a removable hardwood bumkin, to be described later.

Briefly, the yuloh operates on the principle of a screw. It is a bent sculling oar working on a fixed point[6], and having the extremity of the loom attached to another fixed point on the hull—by a rope[4]. The loom being thus attached by the rope, the yuloh is compelled to move in the arc of a circle. Equally, the blade of the oar must, on the other side of the fulcrum, or bearing pin, be likewise compelled to move in the arc of a circle but in the reverse direction.

If the blade of the oar remained tangential to the curve there would be no movement ahead, and if the boat were under weigh the yuloh would float up and off the pin. For propulsion the oar is more efficient if angled, and here is to be found the reason why the yuloh is usually bent. A pull or push of the hand at the point C puts the feather on the oar, that is to say, a pull or push on the rope primarily controls the feather.

The motion of the yuloh is now reduced to a reversible screw, and the problem naturally arises how propulsion is maintained when the angle of the blade is altered and it must pass through the tangential position. The answer is to be found in the jerk given to the centre of the rope just when the feather changes. This not only changes the feather but the temporary shortening of the rope decreases the radius of the circle in the arc in which the blade of the oar works. Thus propulsion is absolutely continuous, with the yuloh travelling in a zigzag path through the wake of the boat. Thus:

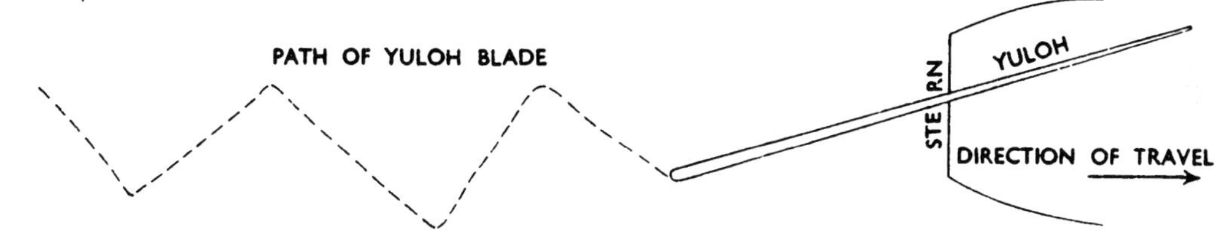

As previously stated, the yuloh rests at about its centre of balance upon a fulcrum in the shape of a sloping iron pivot. This pivot is set either into a beam situated over the stern or, if used anywhere else, into a removable hardwood bumkin (see Page No. 48). The angle of inclination of the yuloh over the stern is nicely calculated to obtain the best results.

The bumkin,* as used in China for this purpose, is of ancient origin, for it is mentioned in a footnote in the "Fang Yen" (方言), a dictionary compiled by Kuo P'o (郭璞) in the third century A.D., in the following words:

> A small wood to bear the yuloh (搖櫓) is called *hu-jên* (胡人) by the Kiangtung people. (籆搖櫓小橛也江東又名爲胡人)

An interesting feature is that the friction is reduced to the absolute minimum by the fact that the fulcrum is an iron tenon or bearing pin. Moreover, Chinese attention to economy provides a small wooden block fitted flush into the yuloh on the under side for the pin to take into, so that when it shows signs of wear the block can be replaced without damage to the yuloh itself.

In junks of light draught, such as the *pai-ch'uan*, the block extends for about 10 inches on the under side of the neck, whereas in deep-draught craft, such as the wharf-boat (碼頭船), the block is as long as 5 feet. The reason for this is not far to seek, and may be found in the fact that the yuloh requires to be adjusted to the trim of the junk.

In the Whangpoo and around Shanghai there are two distinct and easily recognized types of yuloh. The first, the *p'i-p'a* (琵琶), so named after the form of guitar to which fancy may compare its lines, is shaped in a gentle curve. This is achieved by making the loom, the neck, and the blade in three different overlapping sections, scarfed, pinned, and lashed together with rattan. The second type is known as the *shaohing* (紹興), so named after a town, or, more commonly, the *pan-lu* (板櫓), or plank oar. This yuloh is quite straight in shape with a substantial overlap, the ends being bound together with iron bands.

* This fulcrum was called *chiang* (籆) in the Former Han dynasty, 206 B.C. to A.D. 25. In the third century A.D. it was known as *hu-jên* (胡人), and to-day it is spoken of as *lu-ni-t'ou* (櫓泥頭).

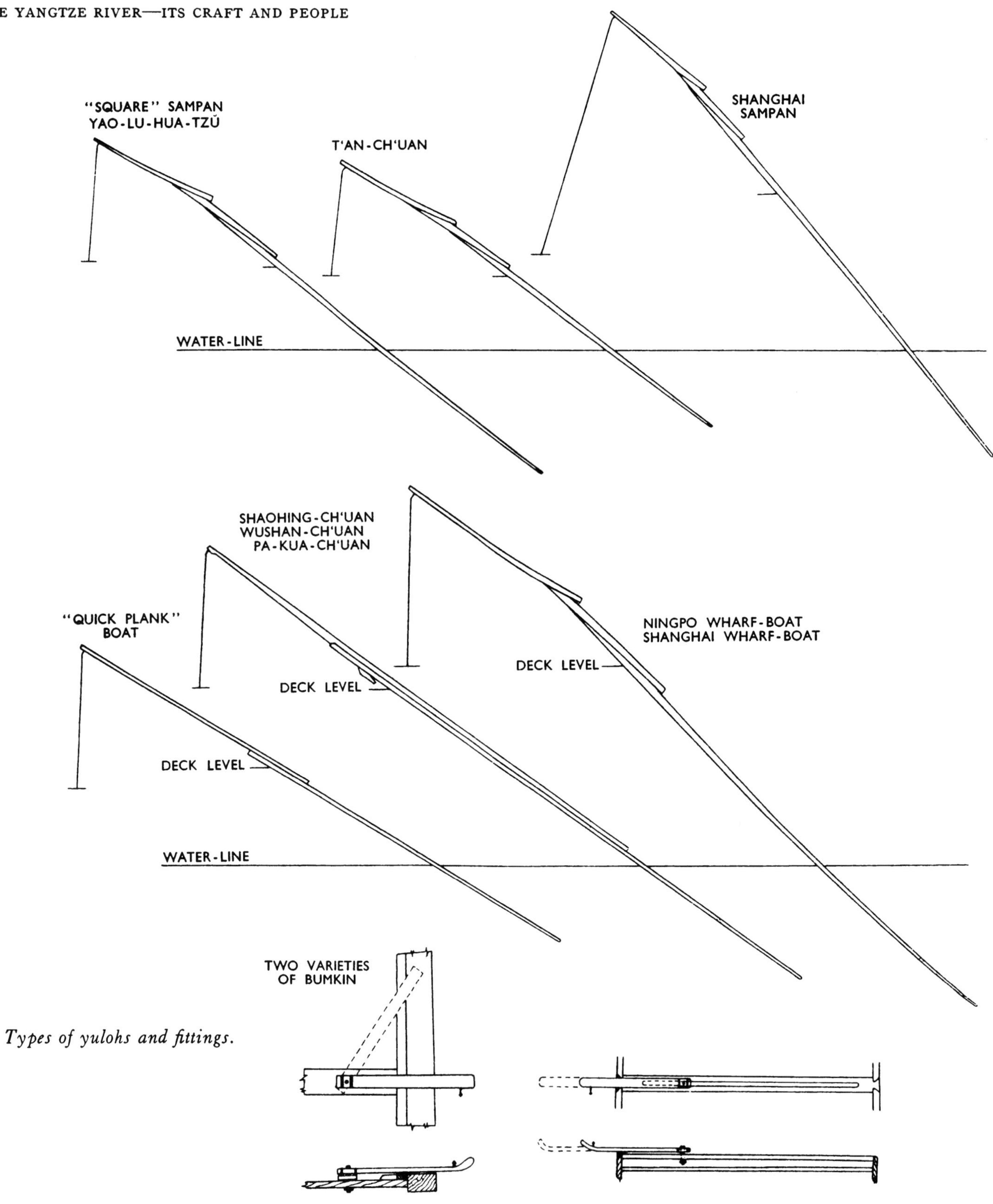

Types of yulohs and fittings.

These drawings show variations of the yuloh. Very slight differences in both types occur, according to the whim or custom of local boatbuilders.

It would seem that the junks from Chusan, South Chekiang, and Fukien, and indeed many sea-going junks, have generally straight yulohs, which is probably the most primitive variety. The curved yuloh is more generally found on the rivers.

It is difficult to ascertain why some junks use the straight and others the curved yuloh, and it is utterly impossible to lay down any hard-and-fast rules as to which districts use one kind or the other. It is, however, a fact that all the boats of a certain type keep to their own kind of yuloh.

Some yulohs are iron bound round the blade. There are two reasons for this. Firstly, it is to provide weight to the blade, and secondly it is to give a smooth cut when entering the water.

The oar as used in the West is a far more powerful lever than the yuloh, or indeed any form of scull, and even as used in China it still probably has the lead for power, although the junkmen claim that a given number of men at the yulohs will make better speed than the same crew under oars.

Leaving out the question of speed, the Chinese method of propelling by yuloh is probably unrivalled for its purpose. Not only can it be handled by a child or old woman with the minimum of physical fatigue and expenditure of effort over a long distance, but also, when worked over the stern or from short bumkins over the bow or quarter, the yuloh, as it takes up no room laterally, is ideal for working in crowded waterways which may be narrow also and are generally shallow.

In narrow waters the rudder, if present, or lowered for use, is seldom used, for the yuloh imitates the action of a fish, which with a flick of its tail can shift the balance of impulse as desired to either side. In 1740 the Jesuit Du Halde, with an observant eye which does credit to a landsman, was sufficiently impressed to write of the yuloh with considerable detail. He noticed the same likeness, for he says:

> . . . being continually moved to the right and the left in the water like a fish's tail, cuts obliquely in the same manner as your birds of prey in the air when they fly with their wings extended, making use of their tails as oars.

The obvious inference to be drawn is that nothing of the kind had been seen elsewhere.

The man or woman at the yuloh holds the rope in one hand and with the other works the yuloh to and fro in a circular manner. If more than one is at the yuloh, the second works the rope while the others work on the loom.

It is not uncommon to see children of all ages working in with the men and women and so learning the peculiar swinging motion of the yuloh.

In the West power is gained by increasing the number of oars, but in China more men are put to work on the yuloh. Eight men on a yuloh is no very uncommon sight, with two at least on the rope. This latter is a very highly specialized branch of the art; the rope-men throw themselves backwards with great abandon until they lie almost flat on their backs, their opposite numbers, doing the same thing, bringing them to their feet again. The speed of different junks varies considerably, but under favourable circumstances an average rate of 3½ miles, or 10 *li*, per hour is a fair average under yulohs.

It is interesting to compare the Shanghai type of yuloh with that of Szechwan. The Shanghai yuloh has a large blade which plunges into the water at an angle of 45° or more and rests on an iron nail-head, while the Szechwan yuloh is slightly straighter with a narrower blade and meets the water at a much more oblique angle. Each is designed for its own particular sphere and type of work and craft, yet it would be instructive to compare their leverage power and respective merits. The Shanghai yuloh might well prove to have more power, yet be unsuitable for use in swift waters.

In the yuloh, as in other inventions, the Chinese have never bothered to investigate the principles of mechanics, and indeed have never pursued their investigations beyond the point where they ceased to be of practical use. The yuloh is probably the most scientific of the Chinese inventions, but seemingly its mechanical aspect has never been investigated.* The many problems connected with the yuloh are here mentioned not to solve them, but to provide some data for the purpose.

To summarize. The difference between sculling in the West and in China is that in the West the feather, or twist, is put on by hand instead of, as in China, by means of a pull on the rope. The Western method is more wasteful of energy in that it lacks the continuous propulsion obtained by the little kick at the end of each stroke, and is therefore all the less efficient.

Next in importance, after the almost universal means of propulsion by yuloh, is tracking, which is resorted to when conditions of wind, tide, or current are adverse. Tracking is much easier work than yulohing, and although the speed of the junk may be somewhat less it is more certain. About 3 miles per hour should be made good unless against a head wind or current. This very obvious method of progress is carried on in much the same manner all over the world, except that horses, so much in demand in the West, are never used for junks.

By indirect allusion it would appear that horses were used in China for tracking, even perhaps very extensively, but unfortunately no definite references can be obtained as proof of the indirect hints of early travellers.

Marco Polo described how junks were tracked up-river by as many as 10 or 12 horses. No other foreign writers make any reference to tracking by horses, so there is no reliable indication as to when this custom was started or when it was discontinued, nor can exhaustive search produce any other written evidence to show that they were used on the Yangtze.

Du Halde, in his "Description of the Empire of China," 1736, writes with some detail on tracking. He mentions horses, but in a curious way, for according to him each mandarin was assessed at so much horse-power, and this was then multiplied by three and translated into man-power for tracking purposes, thus:

> The barks have their rowers and, in case of necessity, are also drawn with a rope along the bank by men who are furnished by the mandarins of each city and changed each day. The number of the horses appointed by the Kiang Ho, or Patent of the Emperor, namely, three men for every horse; hence, if eight horses are appointed for an envoy, they supply him with 24 men to draw the bark.

Although tracking is nowhere in the delta area developed to the science that it is on the Upper Yangtze, nevertheless it may often be necessary for six or eight men to track a heavily-laden junk for weeks at a time.

Along the creeks, canals, and waterways there are regular tow-paths with bridges over the mouths of any tributary creeks, and these are kept up by the nearest villagers. In many cases, however, there are no tow-paths, and only very slow progress is made, particularly when unbridged side creeks have to be negotiated. In such cases the trackers wade out with the tow-line and board the junk, slipping off again into the water to regain the shore when the obstacle is passed.

In order to overcome such difficulties, quite a different form of harness has evolved from that in use on the Upper Yangtze.

The Shanghai and district type of harness consists of a wooden breast batten, 25 inches long by 2 inches broad and ½ inch thick, forming the base of a 2-foot bridle into which an 11-foot hemp tail is made fast. The wooden batten ensures that the harness will float in the water and be easily retrieved when it

* Photographs taken with a slow-motion camera would be of the greatest interest.

becomes necessary to throw it through the arches of bridges or across a narrow creek. Unlike the gear of the Upper Yangtze trackers, there is no elaborate knot and bamboo button, for the delta tracker merely attaches himself to the thin hemp tow-line with a half hitch about 18 inches from the end of the tail of the harness, while the knotted end of the tail is made fast again farther down the line by the ordinary tracker's knot.

Tracking is never done by hired professional men as on the Upper Yangtze, but always by the junks' crews themselves. Unless there is a fair wind, they may have to track from dawn to dusk, with intervals for meals on board three times a day.

The routine of this arduous work, through constant rehearsal, has become a fixed drill requiring the minimum of orders from the laodah or of discussion among the men themselves, who carry out their duties almost automatically. Indeed, the absence of the usual argument and noise that accompanies so much of China's labour is a marked feature of the navigation of the waterways around Shanghai.

Tracking has been developed almost to a science on the Upper Yangtze. Junks on passage between Ichang and Chungking always carry a small gang of long-distance trackers to haul the junks along in the comparatively calm reaches between rapids when they cannot operate under sail alone. On arrival at one of the bad rapids the junks bank in and wait their turn to be hauled over the rapid. Sometimes as many as 200 or more additional men have to be engaged for this work. On the banks below each of the larger rapids there are a number of mat houses forming a temporary village—temporary, for the ground on which they stand is under

Hauling a junk over the Yeh T'an. The extra tracking hawser can be seen, as can the sampan which supports the bamboo rope.

A junk being hauled up the Yeh T'an.

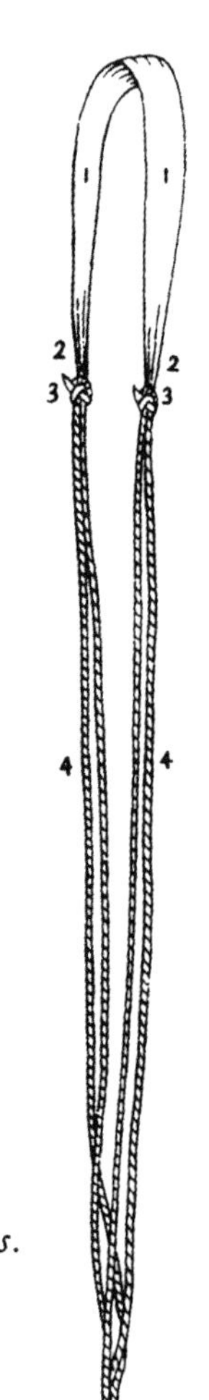

Tracker's harness.

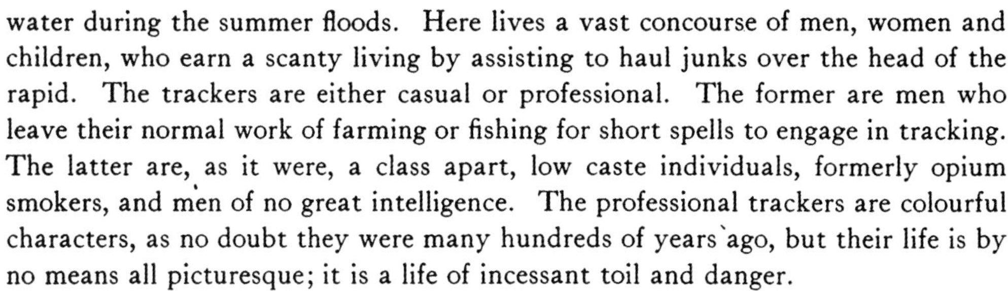

water during the summer floods. Here lives a vast concourse of men, women and children, who earn a scanty living by assisting to haul junks over the head of the rapid. The trackers are either casual or professional. The former are men who leave their normal work of farming or fishing for short spells to engage in tracking. The latter are, as it were, a class apart, low caste individuals, formerly opium smokers, and men of no great intelligence. The professional trackers are colourful characters, as no doubt they were many hundreds of years ago, but their life is by no means all picturesque; it is a life of incessant toil and danger.

When tracking, they attach themselves fanwise to the bamboo tracking-line by a simple, but practical, form of harness, consisting of a loop of rope,[1] or more often white cloth,[2] passed over one shoulder and round the body and joined to a short length of square sennit [6] which takes into a bone, or wooden button,[8] terminating through it in a wale knot.[7] A half-hitch is made with this round the bamboo rope, which bears against the button when the strain is on, but loosens directly the tension relaxes, forming a safety device whereby the tracker can easily release himself in an emergency.

The summer costume of the professional trackers often consists solely of a rag bound round their heads. They wear woven straw shoes in rainy weather or on stony ground; otherwise they go barefooted.

Once harnessed to the junk, the men display perfect discipline and teamwork and are controlled by the rhythmic beat of a drum from the junk, the note being varied from the signal "stop," denoted by a short sharp beat; "slow," indicated by a slow and even rhythm; and "full speed," denoted by a rapid, constant drumming. The throbbing sound of the drum is a marked characteristic of the Upper Yangtze.

Most up-bound junks are accompanied by a sampan, to land the trackers and the bamboo hawsers. Failing this, they have to bank in to do so. In the ordinary way, about a dozen men track a large junk, and two or more follow behind them to clear the line, which may extend for 800 yards in a difficult rapid. When such a rope is out, it has to be supported by a sampan ahead in the slack water above the rapid.

The tracking paths, where possible, follow a natural shelf in the precipitous sides of the Gorges, but in many cases this has to be widened, and in other places the whole path has to be cut out of the vertical face of the rock. Along these narrow winding paths which climb up and down the cliff at varying levels, the trackers scramble, sometimes level with the river, at others suspended far up the sides of a high cliff. Harnessed as they are to the long heavy line, and liable at any moment to be brought up with a sudden jerk, or to a full stop, it is one of the many wonders of the Upper Yangtze that they manage to keep a foothold at all, far less haul their clumsy craft for some hundreds of miles. At times the trackers have to make their way over a foreshore composed of gigantic boulders in vast mounds such as none but men trained to them from childhood would attempt to climb over.

Occasionally the leading men come to a steep sloping surface of rock down which they have to slide in a stilting position. When this has been negotiated, the end of the rope is flung down to them, and they are off again, shouting as they go, sometimes creeping almost on all fours, at others running round points or projecting rocks, pattering barefoot, or in straw sandals, over steep slippery paths, yet always keeping a strain on the rope. One or two special trackers always remain behind in order to clear the line from snags or jutting obstacles.

The wonder is that the fatalities are not heavier, for it frequently seems inevitable that one or more must be pulled over to be drowned in the wild waters below.

As may be seen in the illustration, the inboard end of the tracking-line,[1] which is always made of bamboo rope, is firmly secured on the after cross-beam,[2] whence it travels to the mast, where it passes through a primitive form of snatch-block [3] which is secured to the mast by a strong bamboo-rope grummet.[4] Halyards,[5] passing through the block at the masthead,[6] are fitted to the grummet so that the snatch-block can be maintained at any desired height on the mast to suit the conditions obtaining and the height of the trackers' path, as well as to "masthead" the tracking-lines when overhauling another junk. The snatch-block as illustrated is designed to take three tracking-lines and is made of cast iron crudely finished. One ring [7] takes the halyards, while those marked [8,9] and [10] carry the tracking-lines. A downhaul is attached to the ring.[11] A lizard is used from the bow of the junk to bowse down the tracking-line when rounding an obstacle such as an isolated rock or

A tracking path cut out of the vertical face of the rock.
R. V. DENT

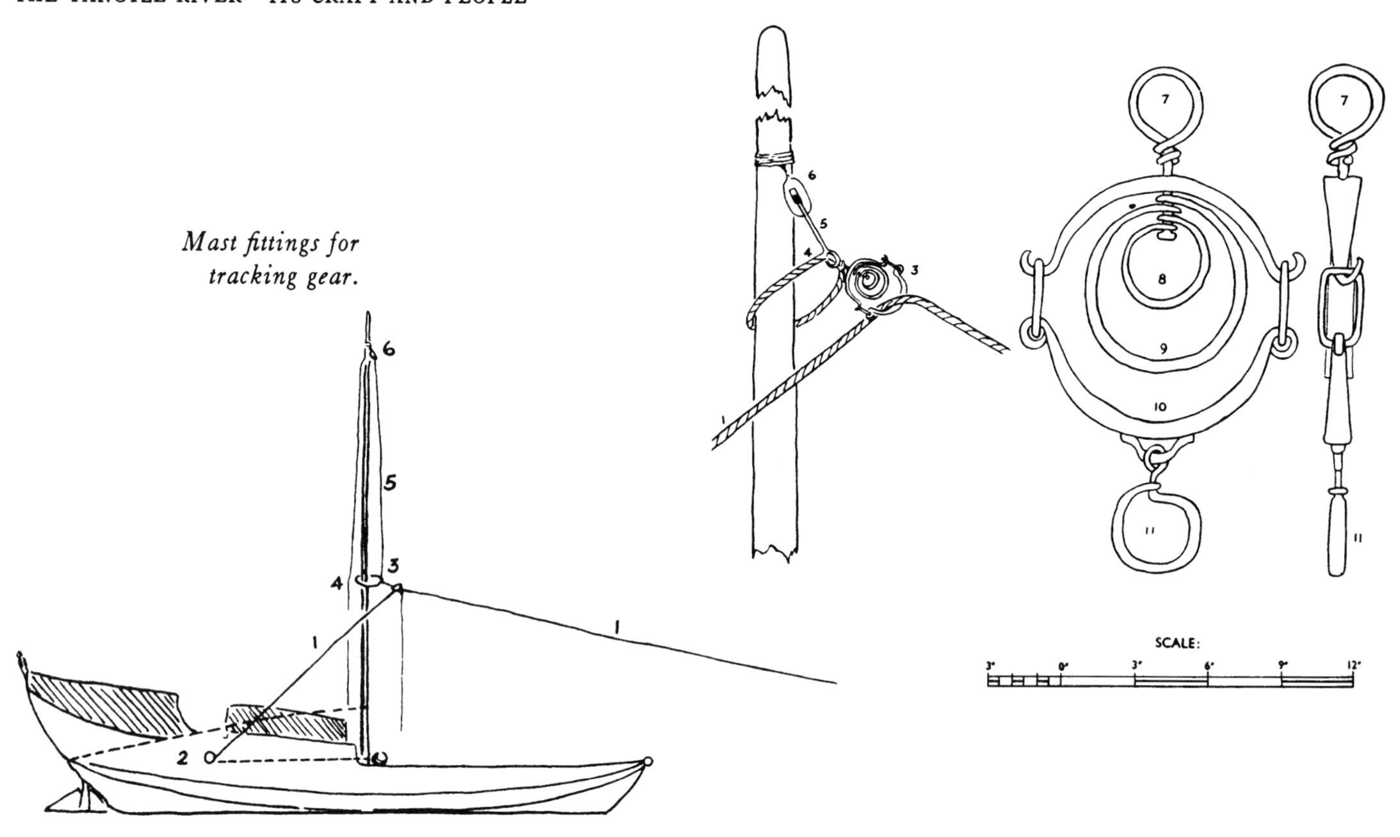

Mast fittings for tracking gear.

a projecting crag. By this means the point of towage is moved from the mast to whichever side of the bow it is desired, so that the junk may be caused to sheer out into the current.

Often to deaden the shock of being driven against a rock, a strong hardwood spar is wedged against the threatening rock. A few turns are taken round the spar with the tail of a rope of which the inboard end is made fast to a ring bolt or cross-beam in the bow. The spar is braced and steadied by the united efforts of three or four men and so the first impact is successfully withstood. The whole manoeuvre calls for exceptional skill and celerity.

Ascending a rapid in a large junk is an operation that requires the nicest skill and judgement and the most prompt and ready obedience to the slightest signal given by the laodah or pilot. The smallest error or delay in executing an order would often be fatal.

Before attempting a difficult rapid, the junk is usually lightened as much as possible by the removal of some of her heavy cargo, and sometimes hours are spent laying out warps. One leads straight up the rapid, and two others—preventers—are made fast ashore, so that, if the main rope parts, the junk would surge back to the place from which she started, provided, of course, she did not come into contact with one or more of the vicious-looking rocks in the process or collide with a down-bound junk.

When it becomes necessary to "hang-off" a bamboo hawser (which is always highly polished and slippery) a special kind of stopper is employed. The secret of its success is, of course, the number of strands forming the stopper. When the strain comes on, each strand buries itself between the strands below, and so not only obviates slipping but also distributes the strain.

At a rapid all hands go ashore except the half dozen or so at the bow sweep, which is used to shoot her out into the current so as to clear rocks which the helmsman unaided would be unable to avoid, and two men to attend to the paying out and hauling in of the tracking line or to pole off rocks.

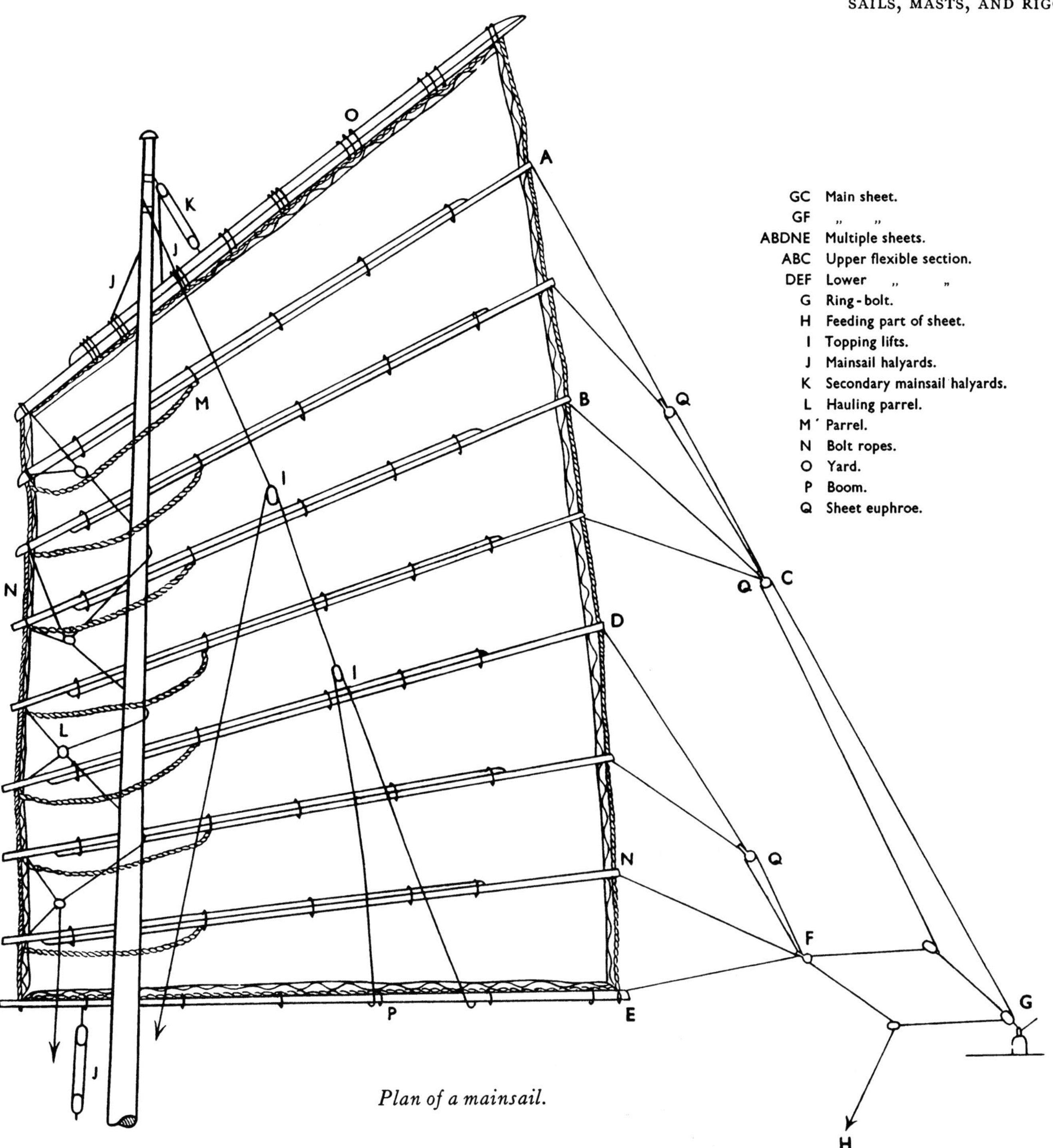

Plan of a mainsail.

In the case of the fore-sail a possible explanation is that the foremast is often raked forward and so the upper part of the sail would provide a better lead. In types where the foremast is vertical the primary pull is usually on the lower part of the sail. A plausible explanation for the lead of the main sheet is so as to avoid fouling.

It is interesting—but not at all illuminating—to find that in certain of the heavier types, such as the Kiangsu trader and the Tsungming junk, the primary pull is always on the lower sections of all three sails. In the case of the Foochow pole-junk, the primary pull is almost invariably found to be on the upper portion of the fore-sail and the lower portions of the main and mizzen. The same rule seems to apply to the lorcha.

A study of six types of Ningpo and Chusan junks shows that the primary pull, while practically always on the upper portion of the fore-sail and lower part of the mizzen, may be almost equally on either portion of the mainsail.

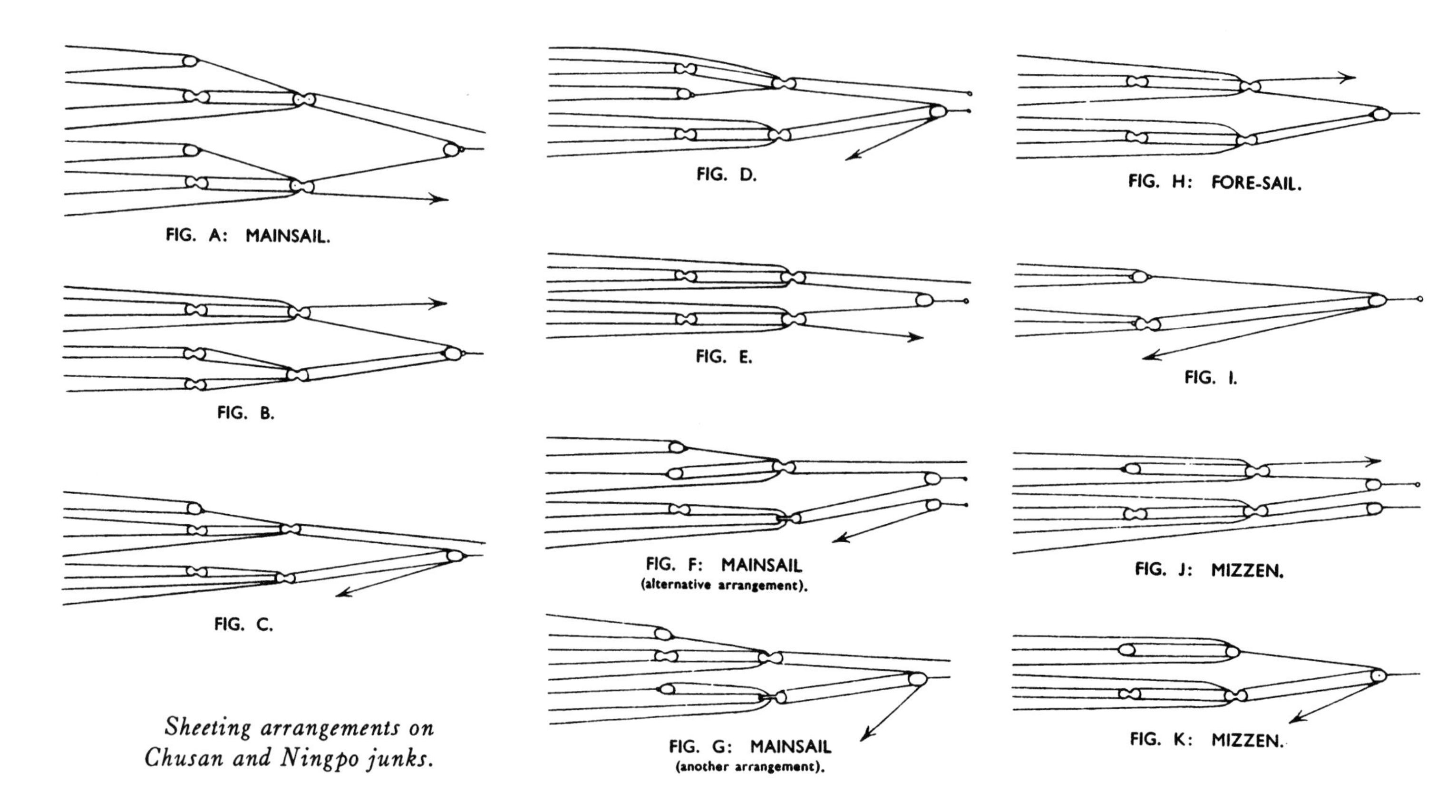

Sheeting arrangements on Chusan and Ningpo junks.

A careful mathematical analysis of the respective areas of the sails of the Foochow pole-junk, for example, yields some interesting results. To begin with, by the arrangement of the battens into groups, the total sail area is, in each case, split up into two distinct sections connected by flexible joints, as already described.

Taking the fore-sail first, this division falls between the third and fourth battens in the specimen illustrated on Page No. 80, Fig. C. This area, controlled by the upper part of the main sheet, comprises 43 per cent of the whole sail as against 57 per cent controlled by the lower part of the main sheet. As there are two ropes or bights to the upper section, each receives a pull equivalent to 21 per cent of the sail area. The lower section is controlled by three ropes, each of which covers an area of approximately 19 per cent. The total multiplication of force is therefore 5, that is to say, for every 5 feet of sheet hauled in the sail moves 1 foot. The strain on all five ropes, therefore, disregarding friction, approximates very closely, and it is interesting to see how the Chinese methods of rule-of-thumb and trial-and-error have been perfected through the centuries until they have achieved results which are mathematically so well balanced. When the fore-sheet is hauled in, the top portion of the fore-sail receives more of the initial pull and comes over, batten by batten.

In the case of the mainsail (Page No. 80, Fig. A) of the same craft, the upper portion contains about 51 per cent of the sail area as opposed to 49 per cent in the lower portion below the flexible joint, and the strain on all four ropes is about equal, the multiplication of force being only 4 to 1.

When a junk, instead of the ordinary Chinese lug-sails with battens, carries spritsails (see Page No. 79), the sheeting follows much the same lines. The multiple sheets, however, instead of being each connected to a batten, start at the leech from the end of each seam of the horizontal and nearly parallel sailcloths making up the sail. These multiple sheets, which usually number about 20 for the mainsail and about eight or less for the small fore-sail, may be arranged in one or two groups in the case of the mainsail but always one only for the fore-sail. Sometimes a bonnet[1] is fitted, that is to say, an extra portion comprising a few feet of sail is laced to the foot of the mainsail (illustrated below, Fig. B). When this is the case, whatever the grouping in the mainsail itself, the sheets of the bonnet are always arranged in a separate group[2] and the primary pull is almost always on the upper portion of the sail. An alternative method of grouping the sheets may be seen in the same sketch, Fig. C. Fig. A shows a fore-sail. Page No. 71 shows a sail with two bonnets, which is unusual, and the junkman's method of dealing with the difficult problem of the sheet.

It is impossible here to give an analysis of all the various sheeting arrangements of each type of junk. A selection only, therefore, is given of the methods adopted by the more striking junks.

The Foochow pole-junk is perhaps one of the better-known types, and an examination of the systems used for this craft will be of value, not only in itself, but because it has probably provided models for other types. In this craft, which always has three masts, the sheeting arrangements vary according to the number of battens on each sail, which are not always identical. The mainsail, for instance, may have eight or nine battens; all of them, however, are always to be found on the port side of the sail. When there are eight battens they are divided into two groups of four, both groups being identically arranged with the main sheet connecting and controlling them (Page No. 80, Fig. A). When there are nine battens they are still arranged in two groups, but the uppermost group contains five battens while the lower one has four. The presence of five battens

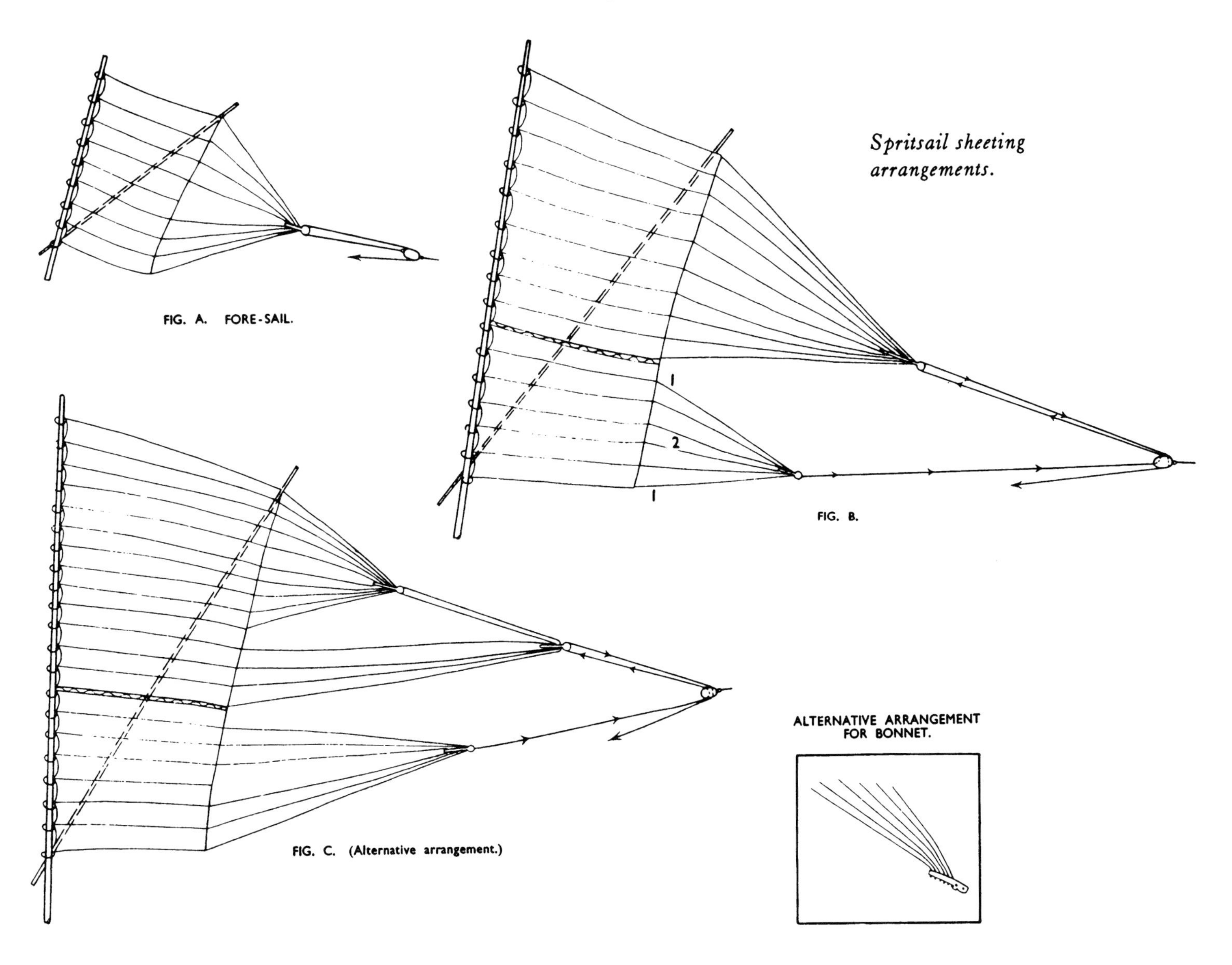

Spritsail sheeting arrangements.

FIG. A. FORE-SAIL.

FIG. B.

FIG. C. (Alternative arrangement.)

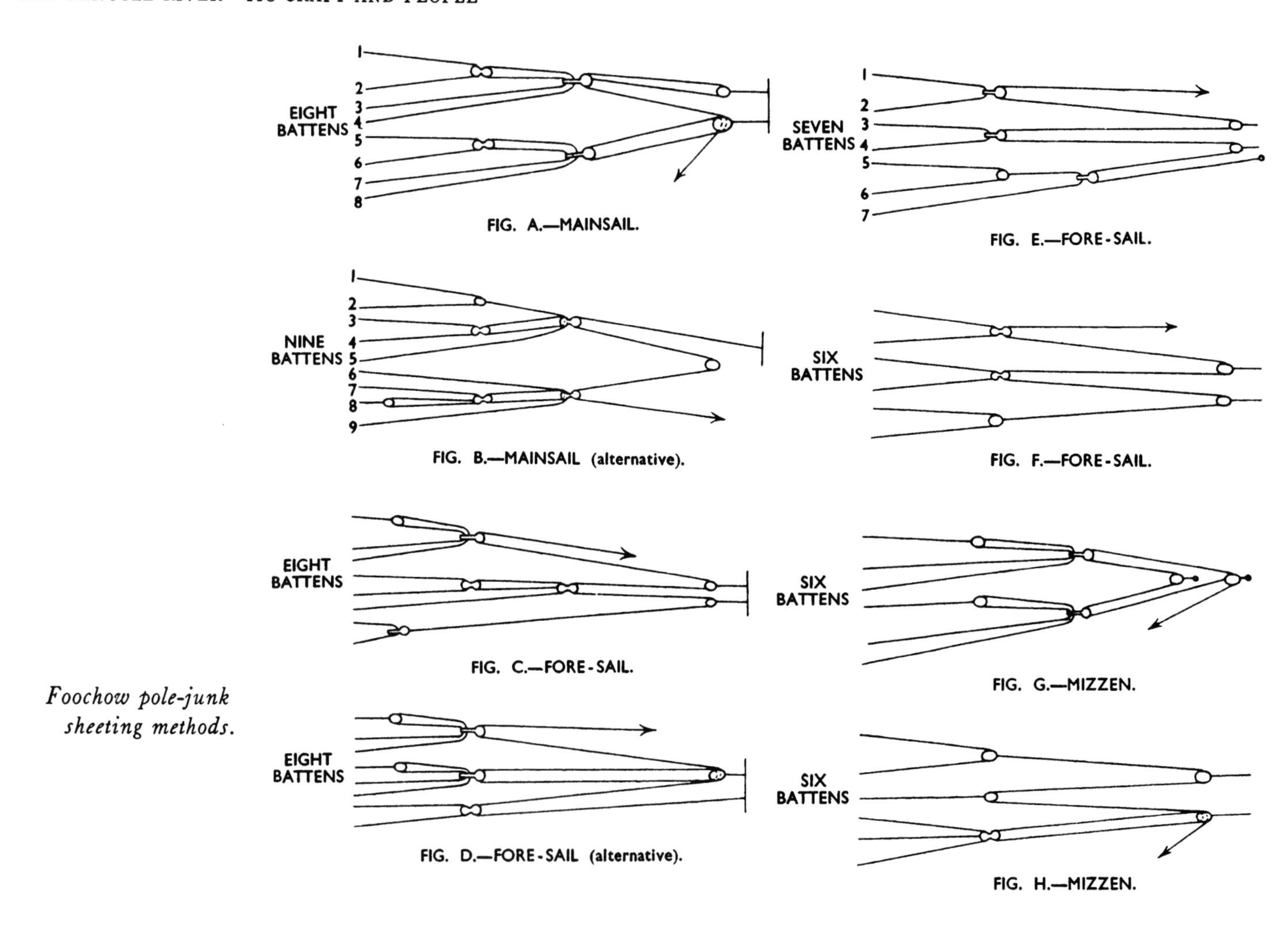

Foochow pole-junk sheeting methods.

naturally necessitates a different arrangement, but oddly enough when there are nine battens the lower group of four could be arranged according to Fig. B, although there seems to be no apparent reason why they should not follow the same system as the less complicated groups of four in Fig. A. In both cases the primary pull is on the lower section of the mainsail.

With regard to the fore-sail, the number of battens on this sail ranges from six to eight and appears to have no relation to the number of battens on the mainsail. All are always situated on the starboard side of the sail. Where there are eight battens they are arranged in three groups of three, three, and two battens respectively. There are, however, two alternative ways of reeving the middle group of three whereby the main sheet exerts a primary pull on the top section of the sail as in Figs. C and D. The latter arrangement is usually to be found accompanying a mainsail with nine battens. Usually the standing part which passes through a large double block in the case of D, or two smaller blocks in the case of C, is made fast to a ring-bolt attached to an iron band round the mainmast or to ring-bolts situated on either side of the junk. Sometimes the ring-bolt may be found situated farther forward than the mainmast and on one side of the ship.

Where the fore-sail has seven battens they are arranged in four groups of two, two, two, and one (see Fig. E), the primary pull being at the upper end. The main sheet may pass either through one big double block or two single blocks. In the case of six battens the system is greatly simplified. The groups resolve themselves into three pairs of battens, with the primary pull still at the upper end of the sail as in Fig. F.

In the case of the mizzen this usually carries six battens, which are always on the port side of the sail, that is to say, on the same side as the battens on the mainsail. These six battens may be arranged either into two groups of three (see Fig. G), or in descending order, in groups of two, one, and three (see Fig. H). Sometimes there may be seven or even eight battens, and when this occurs they are arranged in a similar manner to those of the mizzen-sail on the lorcha (see *illustration below*, Figs. D and E).

The sheeting arrangements of the lorcha (*illustrated below*) for the most part follow those of the Foochow pole-junk, from which they were very likely adopted. The battens are on the same side of the sail as the Foochow pole-junk, that is to say, on the port side of the mainsail, the starboard side of the fore-sail, and the port side again for the mizzen.

Sheeting system on the Lorcha.

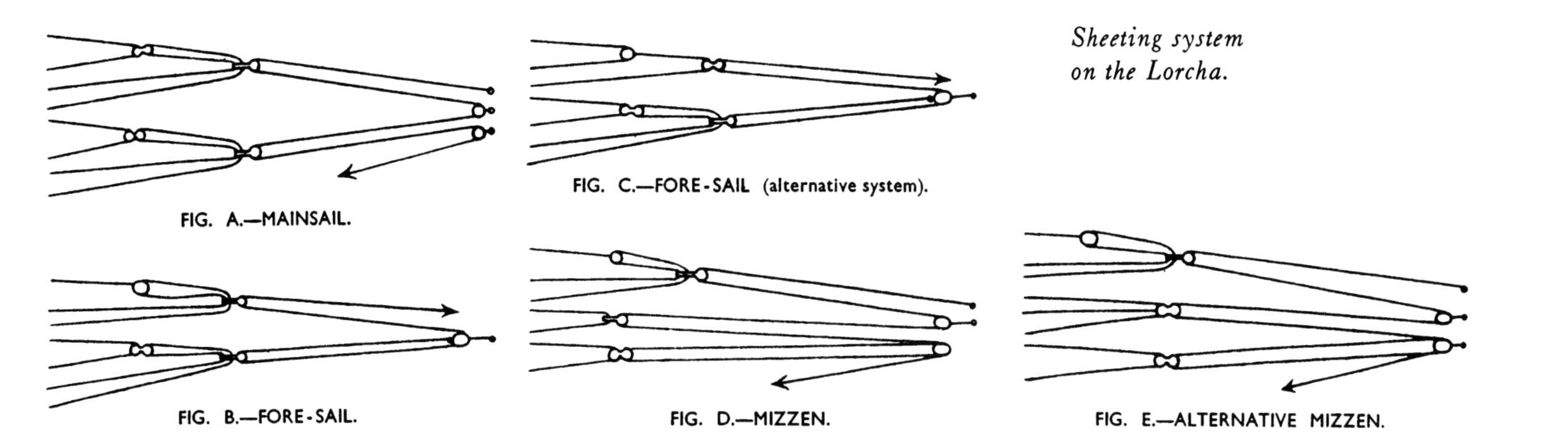

The mainsail always has eight battens arranged in four groups of two, the multiple sheet arrangements being in two groups of four, and the division of the main strain areas falling between the fourth and fifth battens (Fig. A). The primary pull is always on the lower section of the sail.

The fore-sail (Fig. B), too, has always a stereotyped number of battens, that is to say, seven, which are arranged in groups of three and four, the primary pull being always on the upper section and exerted between the third and fourth battens. The internal arrangement of the two groups, however, can be according to two alternative systems which will be seen in Figs. B* and C. The large double block of the main sheet is secured to a ring-bolt on the mainmast.

The mizzen may have either seven battens arranged in groups of three, two, and two (Fig. D), or eight battens arranged in groups of three, three, and two (Fig. E). In both cases the main division of the strain area of the sail is always exerted on the lower portion of the sail. Occasionally the mizzen has no multiple sheets and a Western style of sheeting is used. The lowest batten is then used as a boom, from either end of which two sheets lead to short bumkins projecting one on either side in the fore and aft line over the stern.

The Hangchow trader is another interesting type (see Page No. 82). A marked peculiarity of this junk is the fact that the foot of each of the three sails is on the same level; this line, being unusually high, allows ample head room for bulky deck cargo, such as firewood, charcoal, bamboos, and so forth.

In the largest type of these junks trading to Shanghai the battens are on the port side of all the sails, but on the smaller types which frequent the Ch'ient'ang River the battens are generally on the starboard side of the fore-sail,

* This is the system adopted on the lorcha in the Maze Collection in the South Kensington Museum.

the port side of the mainsail, and the port side of the mizzen, if any, similar to the usage of the Foochow pole-junk. Generally speaking, and certainly in all old junks, the mainsail has 12 battens, with 10 on the fore-sail and eight on the mizzen. In the case of more modern junks, the number of battens is reduced to nine on the mainsail, eight on the fore-sail, and five on the mizzen. The old type of junk with 12 battens on the mainsail has them arranged in two similar groups of six each, with the division between the sixth and seventh battens. The standing part of the main sheet is secured to a crude type of cleat fair-lead[1]—a word coined for want of a better—in the shape of a hole in the top of a cross-piece, the running part after passing through the topmost euphroe [2] (*drawing below*, Fig. **A**) returns to pass through a second hole in the cleat fair-lead, thence back through a third

Sheet leads on a Hangchow Bay Trader.

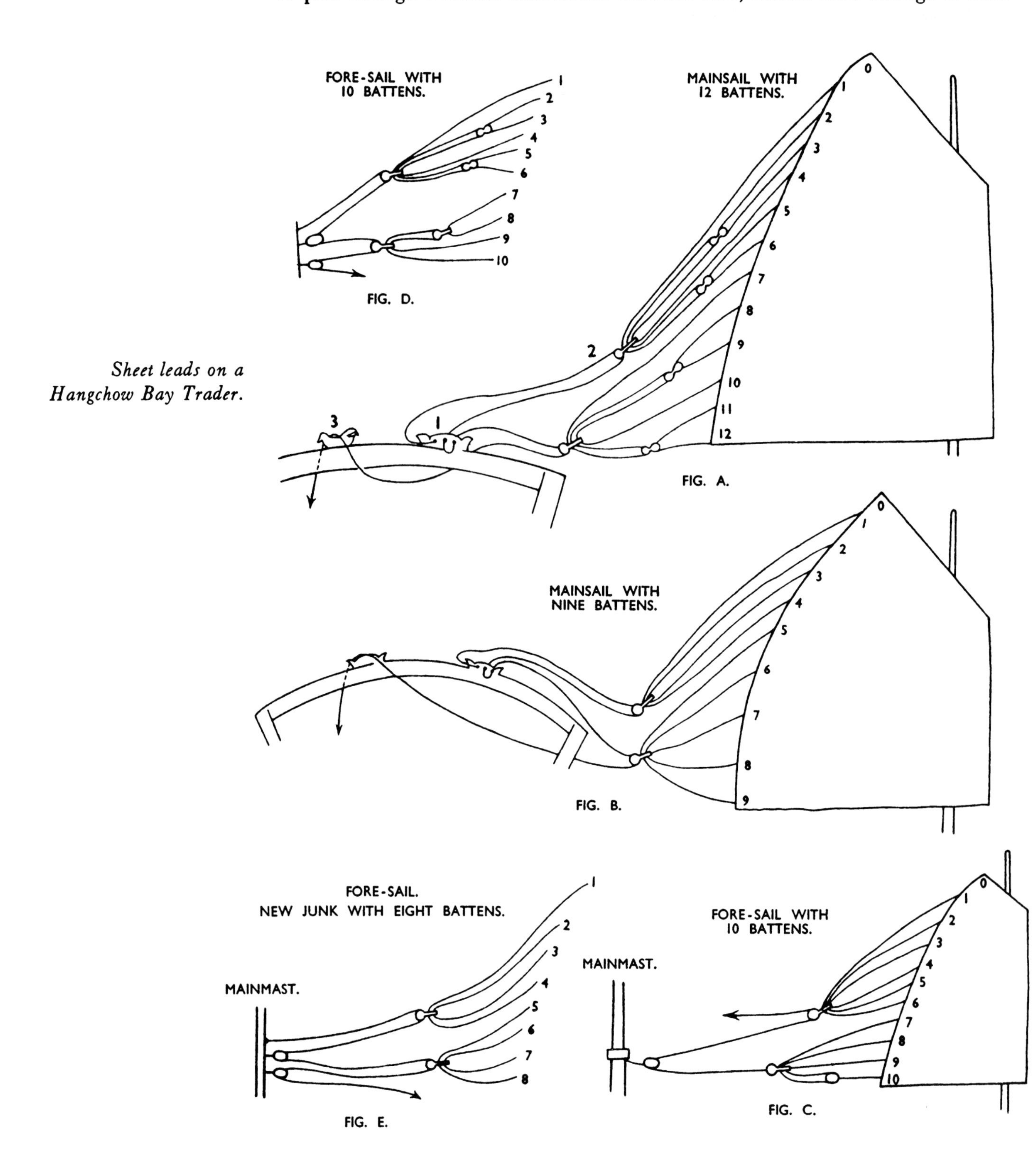

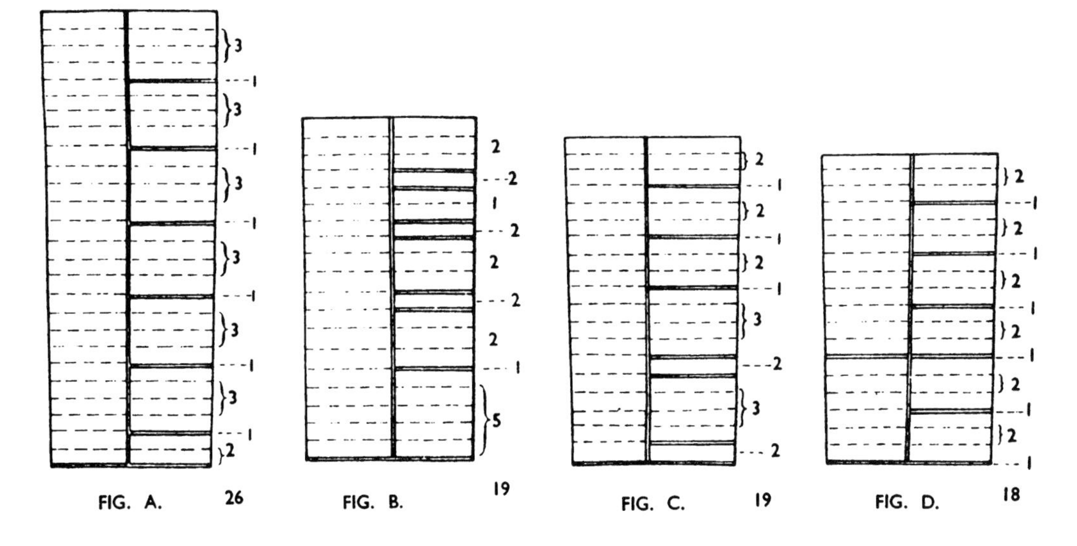

Arrangement of battens.

hole in the lower block, from where it returns to the starboard side of the transom[3]. When there are nine battens in the new-style Hangchow trader they are more simply arranged (Fig. B) in two groups of four and five with the flexible joint between them. The primary pull is in both cases on the lower part of the sail.

The fore-sail when it comprises 10 battens has them arranged in two groups of six and four, the division thus falling rather low down between the sixth and seventh battens (Fig. D), the primary pull being on the lower part of the sail. An alternative arrangement of the two groups of 10 battens with six and four may be seen in the same Plate, Fig. C, where it will be noticed that the primary pull is now exerted on the upper portion of the fore-sail. Fig. E shows the fore-sail of the new-type junk, wherein the eight battens are grouped into two lots of four, identically arranged. The primary pull is on the lower part of the sail.

In the matter of sheeting the Ningpo and Chusan junks, frequent visitors to Shanghai, show the influence of the Foochow pole-junk and the Shaohing types. The sizes of these craft vary, as does, of course, the height of the mast, and these factors necessarily govern the sail areas and especially the number of battens. The number of battens varies between eight and 10 for the mainsail, seven or eight for the fore-sail, and six or seven for the mizzen. Page No. 78 shows the arrangement of some of these types. In the case of the larger craft, such as the Ningpo trader, the battens are situated as on the Foochow pole-junk, that is to say, on the starboard side for the fore-sail and on the port side for the main and mizzen. The smaller types, however, such as those hailing from Chusan, the fishing-junks, and the fish-carriers, vary as to the side of the sail on which the battens are placed. The fishing craft, for instance, often carry all the battens of all their sails on the port side. None, however, has all their battens on the starboard side.

The sails of the Tsungming junks are particularly interesting as they may be said to be the connecting link between the sea-going visitors here described and the riverine sails proper (see Page No. 84).

As their masts are actually, as well as relatively, very tall, there are necessarily a great number of battens. The masts vary a good deal in height, however, and this, together with a by no means uniform spacing of the battens, makes for some variation in the number of the latter.

They are generally to be found on the starboard side of the sails, although there are exceptions to this rule, particularly in the case of the mizzen, the battens of which are sometimes to be seen on the port side. Although hailing from the broad waters of the estuary, this type chiefly operates in the narrower inland waters of the Whangpoo and the adjacent creeks; for this reason it carries the tall masts and flat-headed lug-sails characteristic of inland waterscraft.

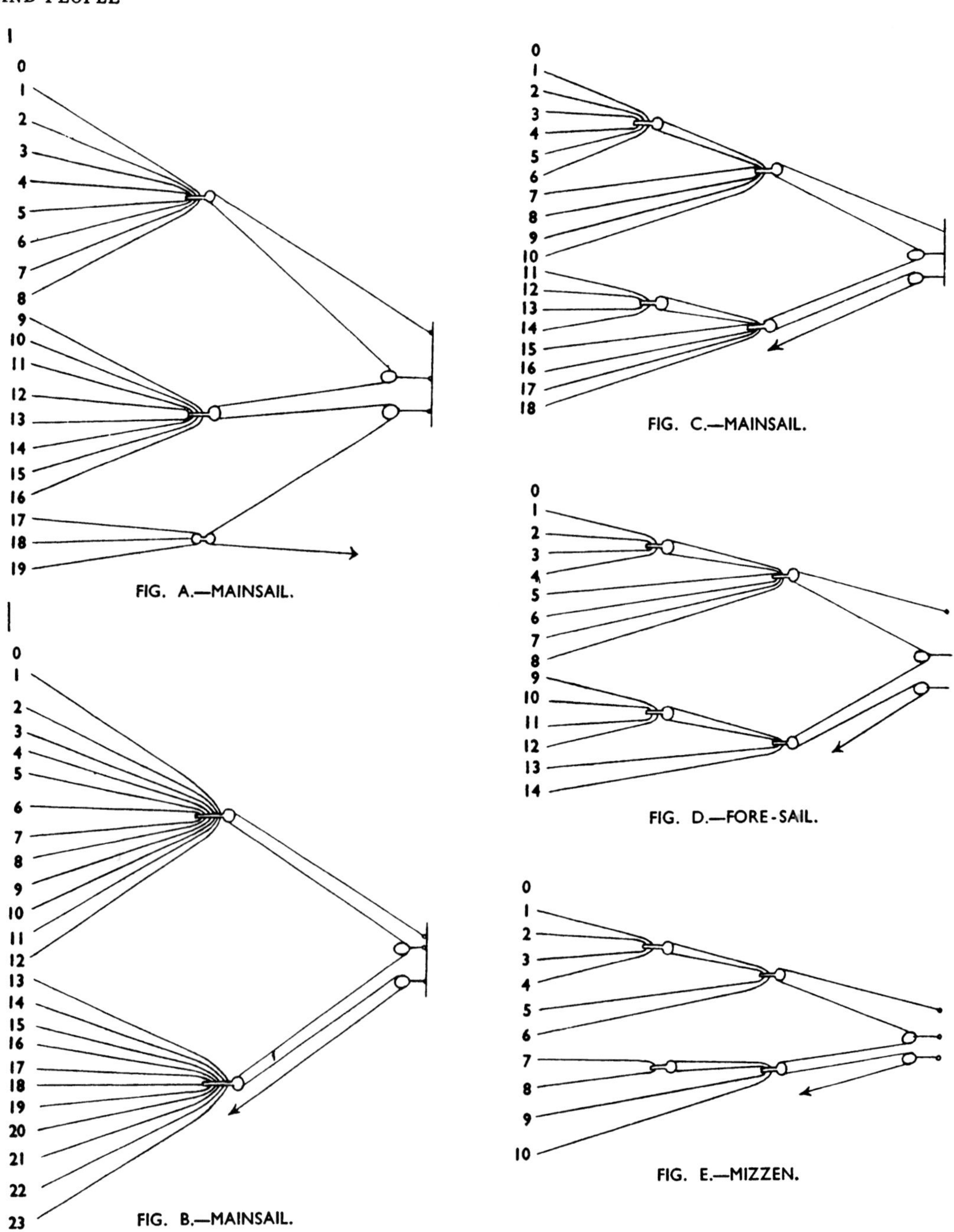

FIG. A.—MAINSAIL.

FIG. B.—MAINSAIL.

FIG. C.—MAINSAIL.

FIG. D.—FORE-SAIL.

FIG. E.—MIZZEN.

Sheeting arrangements on Tsungming junks.

The lofty mainsail of this type is always rigged with what has already been termed in the discussion on sails as a vertical bonnet, that is to say, it consists of two almost equal portions of sail joined vertically down the middle by lacings. As has been said, the average junk of this type has all the battens of its mainsail on the starboard side of the sail except for one batten, or sometimes a pair of battens, which, commencing on the starboard side of the sail, pass through the central lacing on to the port side of the sail. The number of battens on the mainsail ranges from 18 to 20 up to as many as 25 or 26. Where the maximum number is reached they are more closely grouped together, and the arrangement is as shown on Page No. 83, Fig. A, every fourth batten passing through from the starboard to the port side of the sail. In another junk with only 19 battens the arrangement is not only different but not uniform throughout the sail area (see Fig. B). The third and fourth battens pass through, one is missed and another pair of battens pass through, two are missed and another pair pass through, two are again missed and then only one batten passes through, and no more, though there are five more battens to follow.

Another arrangement of 19 battens appears in Fig. C, where the system is two, one, two, one until half way down the sail, and then becomes three, two, three, two. For a mainsail with 18 battens exactly the same grouping is used except that the last groups are three, two, three, one. Another arrangement of 18 battens consists of two, one alternately the length of the sail six times (see Fig. D).

The sheeting arrangements are, considering the number of battens, surprisingly simple and, in most junks of this type, resolve themselves into two large groups and sometimes a third quite small group. The large groups on the crowfoot principle consist of eight or 10 battens connected by four or five bights of rope which all pass through the same euphroe (see Page No. 84, Figs. A and B). In some cases, however, the system is less simple, as may be seen in Fig. C, when the grouping is six and four in the upper portion of the flexible joint and four and four in the lower portion.

The number of battens in the fore-sail varies from 12 to 16. A typical example is shown in Fig. D, with a similar but rather more complicated method of grouping to that shown in Fig. C, and the flexible joint rather below the centre line between the eighth and ninth battens. Euphroes are still, of course, used if necessary to carry the multiple sheets.

In the case of the mizzen (see Fig. E), there is slightly less variation in the number of battens, which may range from 12 to 14. The arrangement followed is very similar to those of Figs. C and D. On all three sails the primary pull is exerted on the lower portion of the sail.

The Kiangsu trader, frequently met in the estuary, carries a very great number of battens. There is comparatively little variation in the number of these battens, which range between 20 and 30 for the mainsail, 24 to 26 for the fore-sail,

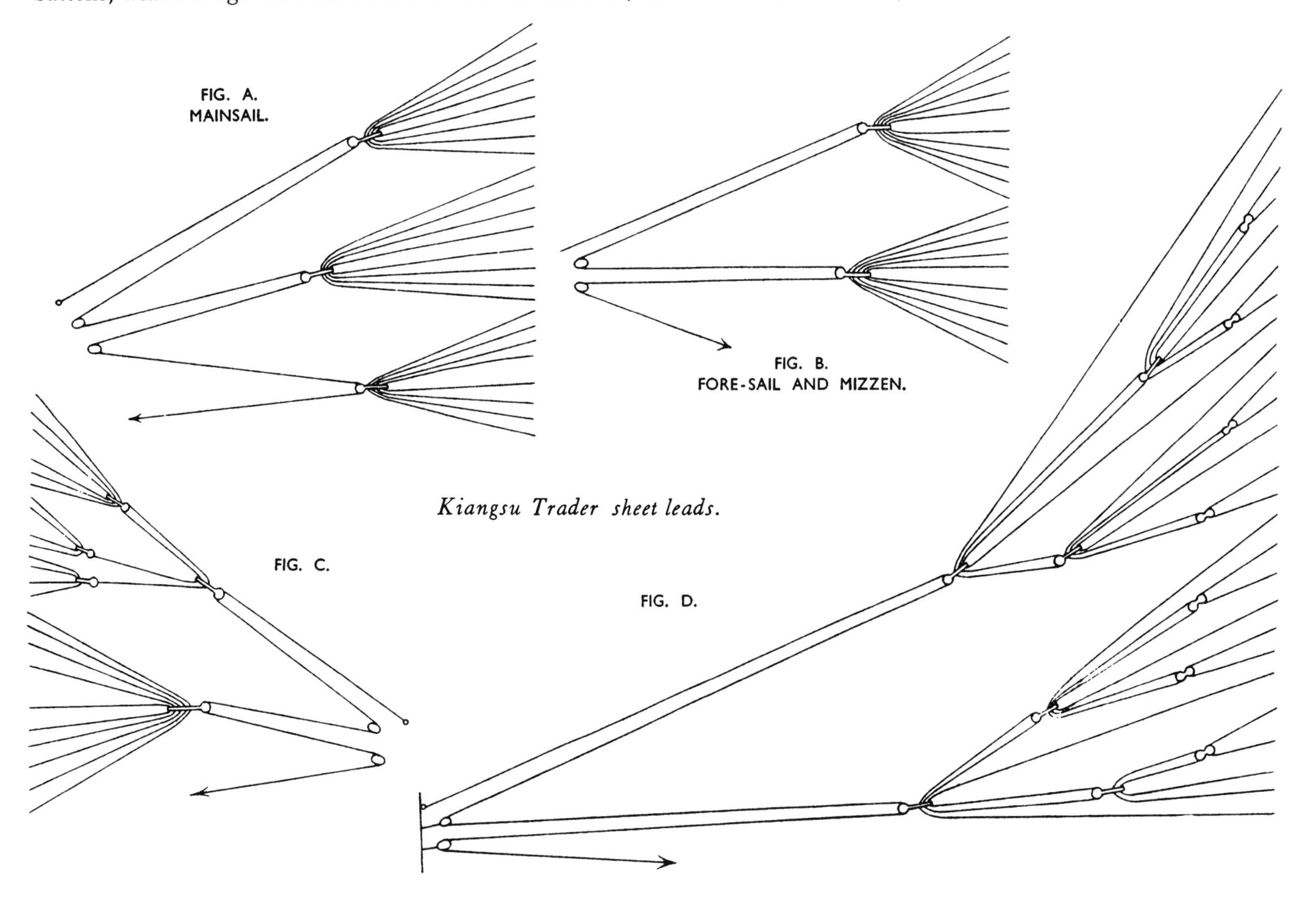

Kiangsu Trader sheet leads.

17 to 22 for the mizzen, 16 to 18 for the port or small fore-sail, and 12 or 13 for the port or small mizzen. All the battens are on the starboard side of the sails, which is usual for all northern and Kiangsu types and, generally speaking, for all tall rectangular sails.

Another common feature often to be found is the presence of supplementary strengthening battens on the port side of the sail. These supplementary battens may number three or four and are fitted on the mainsail and/or fore-sail only. They are always to be seen on the lower half of the sail and are usually placed against every third batten on the opposite side of the sail. This is to prevent chafing of the sail by the topping lifts and blocks, to facilitate the quick dousing of the sail, and to ensure its coming down cleanly between its topping lifts.

Sometimes the sheeting is greatly simplified as on Page No. 85, Fig. A, where a mainsail of 24 battens has the latter arranged in three large groups of eight each rove through a euphroe with four holes, the primary pull being on the lower part of the sail. The fore and mizzen are similarly arranged in two groups of 10 each (see Fig. B).

The sheeting system adopted in some of these junks, however, is the most complicated of all the types here studied; indeed, to the Western mind it often seems quite unnecessarily so. As centuries of their highly practical trial-and-error methods would tend, however, to eliminate any superfluous intricacy, it may be assumed there is good reason for every additional rope and block. It is possible that one reason is to be found in the impracticability of having more than a limited number of ropes pass through the euphroe.

The breadth of the sailcloths and the number of battens seem to influence the scheme of sheeting but, as with other features of the Chinese junk, it is difficult, if not quite impossible, to lay down any definite rules or draw any conclusions.

As a very general rule, however, it would appear that the greater the number of battens the greater the number of multiple sheets, and, consequently, a flatter sail and a greater degree of finer adjustment in the leech of the sail is possible.

For this reason probably, sea-going traders and especially fishing craft have fewer battens to their sails, for, in narrow waters such as rivers, lakes, and canals, where any progress under sail depends on short tacks, a greater windward work is required than at sea where, in the case of traders, quick passages are not matters of moment, and junks can rely on known winds, usually following ones. Even more does this apply to fishing-junks, much of whose time is spent lying by the wind with a trawl down or to drift nets. There are, unfortunately, at least three exceptions to this rule and all trade with the north. They are the Antung, Shantung, and Kiangsu traders. The reason for their large number of battens may, perhaps, be found in the fact that some of their work lies up estuaries.

What has been said in connection with propulsion applies with equal, if not more, force to sheeting, namely, that the many problems are here mentioned not to solve them, but to provide some data for the purpose of further study in this interesting albeit baffling field of seamanship.

ANCHORS, RUDDERS, AND COMPASSES

THE first use of anchors in the West, like that of masts and sails, is of very uncertain date and presumably considerably later origin. J. B. Bury in his "History of Greece" says, rather cryptically, that about the time of Hesiod, which he places *circa* 700 B.C., "an important advance in sea craft was made by the discovery of the anchor." Yet the ancients had most certainly been using anchors before then. Authorities differ as to the date of Homer, but he lived not later than 850 B.C. and probably some time nearer the tenth or eleventh centuries B.C. He makes definite reference in the "Odyssey" to anchors. These in his day consisted of large stones thrown over from the bow to act as anchors.*

Metal anchors were certainly known from about the seventh century B.C., and it is possible that the discovery mentioned by Bury refers to them, for the logical surmise would be that stones as anchors were in use countless years before then, and possibly the "stick-in-the-mud" anchor also, for a dug-out found near Rotterdam and dating back to the seventh century B.C. shows the vertical hole for the spar and even the remains of the pole itself standing in the clay soil beneath it.† A similar method was in use in ancient times in Ireland, for an oak dug-out canoe was discovered about 19½ feet long with a beam of 3 feet, and in the bows a hole 2 inches in diameter for the anchor pole.‡ Unfortunately no date is ascribed to the dug-out.

The invention of the metal anchor in Europe has been attributed by some to the Scythian traveller and philosopher, Anacharsis, 594 B.C., who acquired his knowledge of Greek culture from Solon and has been reckoned as one of the Seven Wise Men. Strabo, however, only claims for Anacharsis that he added the second fluke to the existing anchor, which had but one fluke. Pausanias gives the credit of the first fluke or tooth to Midas, King of Phrygia, and Pliny, on the other hand, to the Tuscans. Pliny ascribes the addition of the second fluke to Eupalamus of Sicyonia, and in support of his theory it is noteworthy that the Grecian city of Sicyon was not only famous for its bronze work, but for its shipping and harbour, which played a large part in the development of trade.

The theory that the Greeks probably originated the anchor rather than any of the older Near Eastern civilizations would seem to be borne out by the fact that the word anchor is derived from the Greek word *ancyra*, which is found in "Pindar," 522 B.C. The ancient Greeks and Romans used the symbol of an anchor on their coins, seals, rings, and even badges, and the portrayals were frequently executed with great fidelity. Those shown on the early Greek coins § and, later, on those of Rome therefore serve to fix on numismatic evidence the types of anchor in current use during those eras, which show for the most part all the features of the present-day anchors of the West. On some of the Greek coins and most of the Roman ones a ring is shown on the crown, so as to facilitate tripping the anchor, a method still carried out to-day in many countries. It is of interest to note that, while some are without a stock, in no single instance when the stock is present is it placed anywhere but close to the ring.

The "Encyclopædia Britannica" claims that anchors with curved arms were not introduced into the British Navy until 1813, this innovation being attributed to a clerk named Pering in the Plymouth Yard. If true, it is astonishing to think that

* Macao fishing craft (about 30 feet long) still use stones with a hole for the rope and have no other anchors.

† "The Mariner's Mirror," Vol. XII, page 350.

‡ Those interested in pursuing this subject are referred to the "Mariner's Mirror," Vol. XXVII, No. 1, January 1941. The writer also mentions having seen the same device in the Philippines.

§ There are at least 15 Greek anchor-bearing coins dating between 450–125 B.C. Some of these are attractively laid out in the Coin and Seal Room at the National Maritime Museum at Greenwich and should be consulted by the serious student of the anchor.

the British Navy should be more than 2,000 years behind the Greeks in adopting this method of design. Another feature in which the British Navy has been slow in following an example set by the ancients is in the matter of anchor cable. Until 1811 the Navy used rope, but we read instances of iron chain being used for this purpose as far back as the Siege of Tyre, 332 B.C., when Alexander used chain to defeat the efforts of the Tyrian divers, who repeatedly cut the rope cables so that his galleys drifted away. In 56 B.C. also, Cæsar, in recording his campaign against the Veneti in Brittany, remarks that the enemy made use of iron chain.

In Europe the anchor has, from ancient times, been a symbol of hope. At the start of our era it was frequently carved on the tombs of the early Christians, as hidden within its design was the cross which they could not openly display without risk of persecution, and which served as an emblem of hope through redemption.

In mediæval times the anchor has figured on coats of arms, on armorial bearings, and on Masons' marks. In England, pre-eminently a maritime nation, the anchor is to be found everywhere: in watermarks, in advertisements, on "peace and plenty" tokens, and on flags, badges, and buttons. It signifies truth, prudence, steadfastness, and hope in nearly all countries. There is, however, no evidence that it has ever meant anything at all symbolic to the Chinese.

Dr. Moll, the great authority on the anchor, quotes Giles as saying that Chinese anchors date back to 2000 B.C., which would agree with the legendary belief that they were invented by the great Emperor Yü. Nevertheless, it would appear that no evidence to support the theory of any great antiquity for the anchor is to be found in the early Chinese classics.

In the old Chinese dictionary the "Erh Ya,"* and again in another named the "Shih Ming," written in the Later Han dynasty, A.D. 25–221, no mention is made of anchors, although oars, rudders, masts and sails, and boats in general are often referred to. As far as can be ascertained, it was not until the third century A.D. that reference to anchors, or, more correctly, something to hold a vessel in mid-stream, was first made, wherein it is said:

> Two fighting ships were connected with large palm ropes to the stones used as anchors by General Huang Tsu. (黃祖橫兩蒙衝以栟閭大紲繫石爲矴)

The character used for anchor was composed of two parts, the left, called the radical, means a stone, while the right-hand part gives the pronunciation, that is to say, *ting* (矴). Fȧ Hsien (法 顯), the first Chinese who has left a record of a voyage from India to China, in A.D. 417, makes use of this word, meaning literally "let down a stone." He says:

> The sea was deep and bottomless, and there was no place they could anchor (下 石).

Later a variation of the word *ting*, but still with the stone radical and identical pronunciation, came into use: 碇.

The primitive method whereby a vessel was held merely by the weight and friction of a large stone dragging along the bottom was next superseded by something more elaborate. The Chinese, with their economical genius for utilizing what is to hand, doubtless improved their first "hook" anchor by weighting the fork of a tree with a cunningly adjusted stone. Another branch would suggest a stock, and so probably evolved the single-fluked wooden anchors they use to-day. These in comparatively recent times were alternated by iron anchors.

The time of this transition can be gauged with some measure of certainty by the fact that a new word for anchor came into use about the sixth century A.D. It makes its first appearance in a dictionary, the "Yü P'ien" (玉 篇), written in A.D. 543. The character used was likewise composed of two parts, the left-hand one meaning metal, while the other gave the pronunciation: 錨.

* The "Êrh Ya" was compiled by an unknown author. Its date is uncertain, but although often attributed to the Duke Chou in the twelfth century B.C., it seems improbable it could have been written before the second century B.C., when it only consisted of three chapters. Although traditionally believed to be the first of the ancient Chinese lexicographies, it would seem there are one or two others better qualified for this title.

By this it is clear that a type of anchor was now made with metal in some form as a component part. Nevertheless, despite her general progress in shipbuilding, China was still very far behind the Greeks and Romans in the matter of anchors.

Another type of anchor in use in former times was what may be termed unofficially the "stick-in-the-mud" anchor. This type of anchor is known, very aptly, as the *shui-yen* (水 眼), or water eye. Delineations of this type of anchor are extant dating back to the Sung dynasty, about A.D. 960, proving that it was in use at least at that time, if not before. The method employed is to drive a pole right through the junk by means of a round or more generally a square boxed-in form of navel pipe and out through an aperture in the bottom of the junk into the bed of the river. This form of anchoring is much in vogue on the Yangtze. It is usually situated in the foremost compartment of the vessel, although sometimes it is to be seen in the stern. More than one type of junk is known to have one in both bow and stern. Among many obvious advantages of this method is its adaptability to fluctuating levels of water, for the junk can travel up or down the stationary pole as the water rises and falls. As a general rule it may be said that the higher one penetrates up the river, the more universally is the custom to be found.

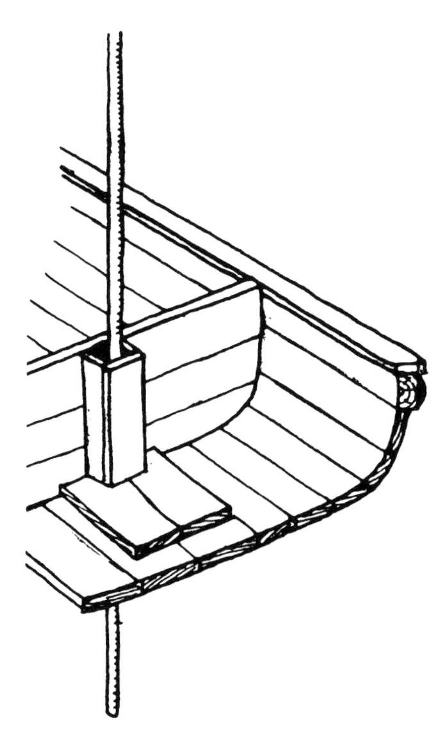

Typical "stick-in-the-mud" anchor.

The modern anchor in use to-day is known as *mao* (錨). The radical is "metal," and the phonetic identical with that of the word *mao* (貓) for "cat," which has the "dog" radical.

By the evidence of obviously unchanged types of anchor in use to-day it seems probable that the old Chinese anchors had straight arms and that the curves which were introduced later in some of their anchors were the result of foreign influence.

It is not known at what date flukes made their appearance in the Far East. The use of one fluke only is obviously a survival of an antique pattern. That illustrated in Fig. K is of the simplest construction. It consists of a 15-foot baulk of hardwood with a single arm set at an angle of about 45°.* Shaft and arm are bound together at the crown by iron wire and a 2-inch iron band below. The bill is iron tipped. The aperture in which the stock engages is situated about 2 feet above the crown. This type of anchor is usually to be found on sea-going junks hailing from southern ports. It is very useful for work in soft mud, for it does not sink into it as does a heavy iron anchor. If they are found to be too light they can readily be weighted with stones in the manner of the ancients.

Another type of Chinese anchor in use to-day, which probably differs little from that of the ancient Greeks, is that shown in the margin, Fig. A, except that the position of the stock in the Greek anchor was near the ring whereas in China the stock is always just above or below the crown. This is the more or less standard pattern anchor of the estuary. With one fluke (Fig. A) it is used as a stream anchor, with two it functions as a bower (Page No. 91, Fig. L).

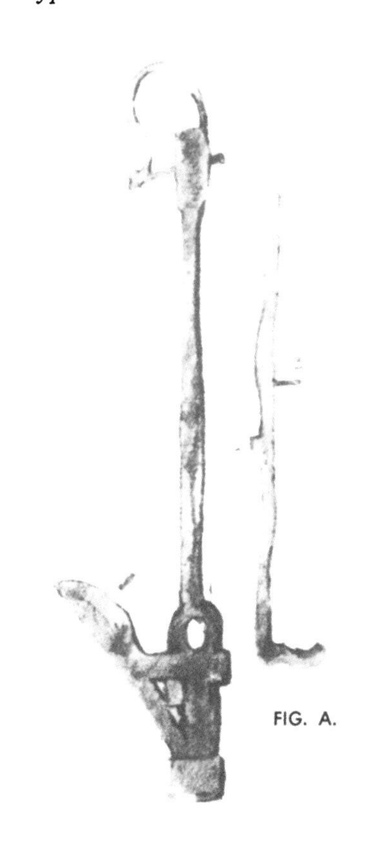

FIG. A.

The essential parts of an anchor proper consist of a vertical beam in the case of a wooden anchor and an iron shaft in a metal anchor, called in either case the shank, with a ring at its upper end. At the lower extremity is the crown from which branch out one or more arms. Each arm spreads out in a broad palm in a foreign anchor or a sharp fluke in most Chinese anchors. A transverse piece called the stock is placed below the ring in foreign anchors, but in the true Chinese anchor it is always just above the crown, indeed in some varieties it is actually below it. The stock is used to cant the anchor and is a most important part, for it is the agent by means of which the flukes are brought into a position to bite.

* An oak anchor recovered from Lake Nemi, in Italy, near one of Caligula's galleys, *circa* A.D. 35, shows a striking resemblance to the Chinese wooden anchor.

When the anchor is let go the crown first strikes the bottom and then falls over in such a manner that one end of the stock rests upon the ground, and the subsequent movement of the junk and the cable cause one or other of the flukes to enter the ground.

In the Chinese anchor when not in use the stock can always be unshipped for ease in stowing (see Fig. A). When required for use, the stock is inserted through the aperture[1]. A cotter[2] on the stock prevents it travelling too far and fits against the lower part of the shank. A pin[3], usually of bamboo, passing through another small aperture in the stock itself, retains the whole in place. Should the iron stock rust through, a wooden one is used in its place, or it is covered with a wooden sheathing (see Fig. B).

Sometimes the foreign type of anchor is to be found fitted with a removable wooden stock. This ingenious device is shown in Fig. J. It consists of an iron strop passing round the lower part of the arms through which the wooden stock is inserted, being set up with wedges. When the stock, which consists of a *sha-mu* pole, is withdrawn the iron strop can be passed up the shank and removed altogether when not required. The reason for having the stock below the crown of the anchor is to lessen the risks of fouling. A grapnel anchor with four flukes is commonly used on the Yangtze. The advantage of this is that at least two flukes take hold of the ground at once, no matter how the anchor falls, and consequently no stock is required, although one is often fitted. Its use is to prevent the anchor from sinking too deep into the mud. For work in very soft ground a variation of this pattern of anchor is sometimes found with an iron extension joining one of the flukes to the shank.

The cable when made of hemp is attached to the grapnel-type of anchor by passing it through the ring, down the shank, and securing it to the crown, the loose end being made fast to one of the flukes by a succession of stoppings.

All who have had experience of the various types of small landing craft used in the late war will surely be interested to learn that the latest development of the anchors used by those craft—the Danforth anchor—is in effect basically formed on the same plan as the Chinese anchor, that is to say, it has the stock at the crown of the anchor, a practice never hitherto employed in the West. The maker's claim that this anchor is non-fouling is justified, for this is true of the Chinese counterpart.

As mentioned above, the Greeks and Romans, like some countries to-day, used to trip their anchors by means of a ring below the crown or a strop round the crown. The junkman, always original, fits a ring and block to one of the four flukes of his anchor to achieve the same purpose. This is usually seen only in kedge, or stern, anchors and in shallow water, and in such a case the anchor is lowered slowly to the bottom and not "let go."

Shoeing, that is to say, covering, the flukes with additional pieces of wood or iron is a very common practice with Chinese seamen. The area of the additional fitting is, of course, much greater than the flukes, in order to give the anchor a stronger hold in soft ground.

In England rules for the buying or selling of an anchor for ships is controlled by Act of Parliament. No anchor may be bought or sold for use in a British ship until it has passed certain tests which are required by the Act. The junkman knows no such hampering influence. He is not restricted by any Lloyd's or Board of Trade regulations requiring him to have his anchors and cables tested. He evolves his own "safe working strains" by bitter experience. When he finds his anchor too small he enlarges it by the simple device of adding

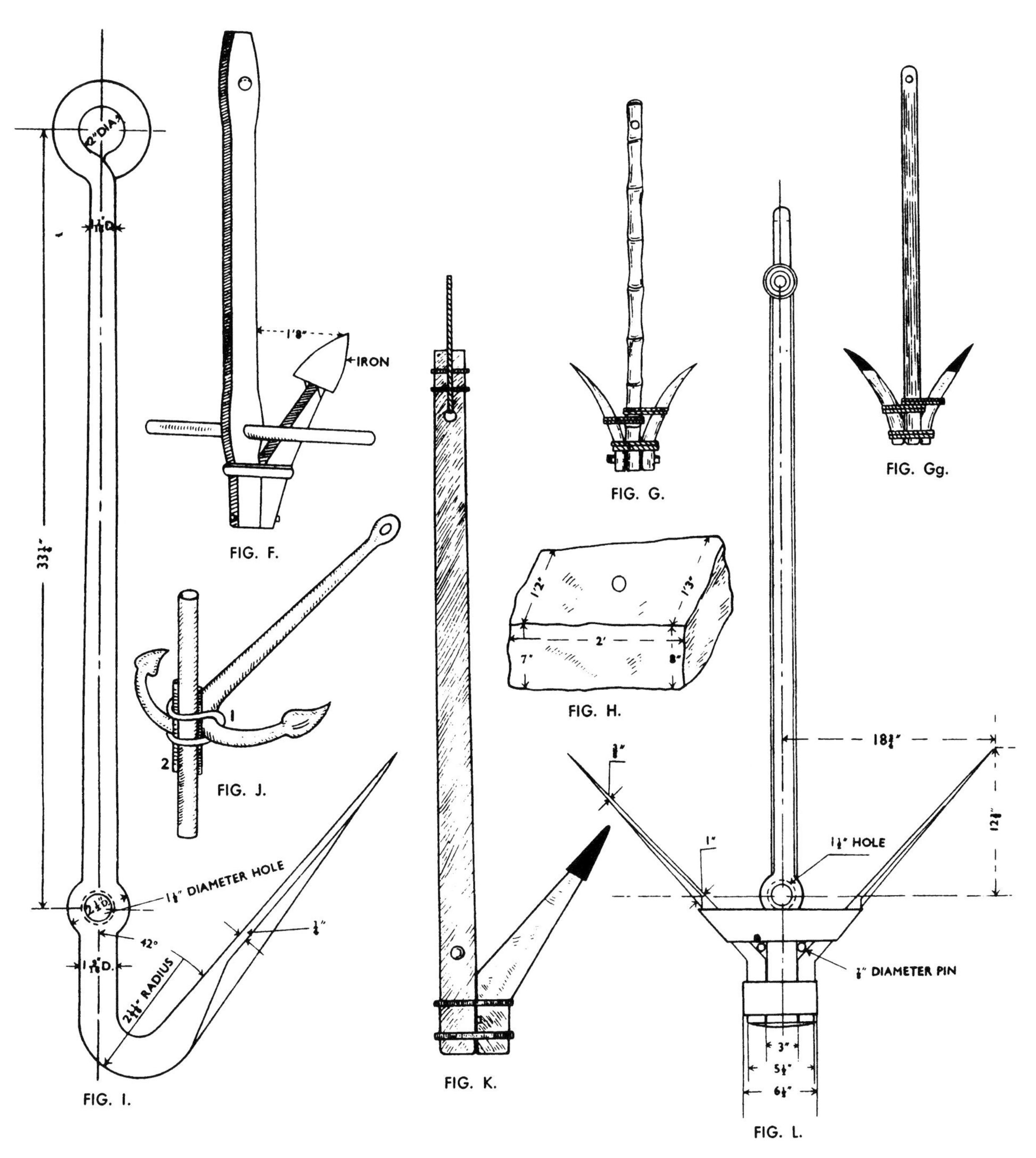

Fig. F. Wooden Anchor, Foochow.
Fig. G. Bamboo Anchor, filled with sand and plugged, Foochow.
Fig. Gg. Double-fluke Wooden Anchor (size varies from 6 to 20 feet).
Fig. H. Stone Anchor, T'an T'ou.
Fig. I. Single-fluke Iron Anchor.
Fig. J. Method of Securing Stock.
Fig. K. Wooden Anchor (obsolete type).
Fig. L. Double-fluke Iron Anchor.

a wooden frame carrying heavy iron peaks (see Page No. 90, Fig. B). If it is merely too light he weights it with stones.

When a fluke is broken a wooden one is sometimes lashed to the jagged edge where it broke off (see Page No. 90, Fig. C). Indeed, there is no limit to his ingenuity in improvising, adding to, or taking chances with his ground tackle. No seaman in the world tempts providence more and with less impunity.

It must be remembered that the Chinese anchor is only to be seen at its best in sea-going or large riverine junks. The small craft of the Yangtze and its tributaries and waterways either anchor with very light ground tackle in the shoalest water or dispense with its use altogether by banking in.

The handling of heavy ground tackle was one of the first problems which had to be solved by the early sailors when the size of their sea-going vessels increased. The use of the handspike and the capstan for this purpose was known to the ancients of both East and West. In China, as has been shown, the ground tackle was probably lighter than in the West; nevertheless the problem was much the same.

Method of putting a stopper on the cable.

The Chinese use a crude form of winch or windlass for hoisting their anchors, masts, and sails. This simple and eminently practical device must, for many centuries, have proved sufficiently satisfactory for the needs of the junkmen. There is no available evidence to show when the Chinese style of wooden capstan was first used, but it would appear that it must have been considerably later than the windlass. With the exception of the huge drum-like wooden capstan in the big Yangtze timber rafts, the true Chinese capstan in use on inland waters is usually an insignificant light framework, just strong enough to hoist the light masts. Since the arrival of the foreign sailing ship in China, the junkmen have adopted a wooden capstan designed on Western lines for use in craft with heavier anchors or sails.

There are many different ways of putting a stopper on the cable, that in most general use is illustrated.

Finally, mention must here be made of the sea anchor. No sailor in the world needs it more than the Chinese or is more skilled in its use. The sea anchor, of course, floats on the surface of the water and is used to keep the ship's head to the wind and to decrease her drift. The Chinese sailor for this purpose uses a huge bamboo basket, and well it serves its purpose.

The earliest method of steering a ship or boat in the West was by means of an oar over the stern. This was followed by the adoption of what might be termed rudder-oars, which operated from the quarter or the stern.

Contemporary Egyptian stone carvings show the boats of about 3000 B.C. propelled and steered by paddles. Fifteen hundred years later we find small bladed oars being used for rowing, and large paddles attached to the quarter or over the stern for steering. Virtually this was the dawn of the rudder.

Where, instead of an oar or oars on the quarter, a rudder-oar was used it operated on a short pillar, the forerunner of the rudder-post, which in turn stood on the stern between two projecting wings.

As the Egyptian boats were built with little or no keel so as to negotiate the sandbanks of the Nile, the advantages of bodily raising this oar under certain conditions, such as in shallow channels, would soon occur to the nautical mind. Representations of Queen Hatshepsut's Expedition to the unidentified land of Punt show two rudder-oars.

The Greek ships of later date usually had two "rudders." They were often joined by cross-bars or rudder-bands* attached to the pair of tillers, which were set at an angle to the rudder-oars.

The Viking ships which sailed the seas some thousands of years later were steered in exactly the same way save that they had only one rudder-oar on the starboard or "steor-borde" side.

The use of quarter rudders and rudder-oars persisted in Europe down to the Middle Ages with only comparatively small improvements and adaptations.

All authorities are agreed that in Europe it was not until the beginning or middle of the thirteenth century that the true stern-post rudder came to be slung by pintles and gudgeons. The slowness of progression in this respect is

* An allusion to rudder-bands occurs in Acts XXVII: "loosing withal the rudder-bands."

attributed to the difficulty experienced by the ancient shipwrights in adapting a rudder to the sloping stern of that day. This innovation marked a most important advance in shipbuilding, as it at last made it possible to have a large increase in tonnage. The shifting of the steering gear from the starboard quarter to hinges on the stern-post brought about the first big change in the form of the ship, resulting in a definite difference being made between the bow and stern of the hull. In order to hang a rudder firmly it was necessary for the stern-post to be more or less straight; at the same time the stern planking had to be squared off in its upper part and a small transom introduced in which the hole for the tiller was pierced. It is almost unbelievable that so many thousands of years should have passed before this simple and apparently obvious way of fitting a rudder occurred to anyone, but the explanation, as already stated, is almost certainly to be found in the curved shape of the sterns in all early ships, which would have made the fitting of a stern rudder rather difficult. Once the idea was thought of, the stern-post was made as straight and as square as possible.

The slow, indeed surprisingly slow, process by which the rudder-oar in the West was gradually superseded by its modern counterpart can be traced down through the ages with comparative certainty by means of illustrations on coins and seals; but in China, despite all her historians, her culture, and her scholars, the development of the rudder, like that of other parts of the ship, is very obscure and a matter for conjecture only.

Twelfth century Chinese painting, "The Nymph of the Lo River."
COURTESY OF THE FREER MUSEUM OF ART, WASHINGTON, D. C.

It was, however, mentioned in the "Han Shu" (漢書), written by Pan Ku (班固), *circa* A.D. 90, where it is recorded that the Han Emperors were rowed in boats with a rudder in the stern. Such a craft is illustrated.

A study of this picture, named "The Nymph of the Lo River,"* will show that there is a contraption over the stern. This would seem to be a fairly accurate representation of a rudder in the hoisted position to facilitate the use of the yuloh over the stern. The fact that quants are being used shows the craft is in shoal water. This picture is by an unknown artist of the twelfth century, after an

* According to the history of the Han dynasty, Fu Fei, the unusually beautiful and remarkably intelligent daughter of the legendary Emperor Fu Hsi, drowned herself, for reasons which are obscure, in the Lo River and became the goddess of that river. The painting illustrates the poem by Ts'ao Chih, *circa* A.D. 192–232, who wrote it as an expression of his grief over her untimely death.

original attributed to Ku K'ai-chih. The point at stake is that if this twelfth century painting was known to be an accurate copy in this respect of the lost original fourth century painting by Ku K'ai-chih, then it would be definite proof that the rudder in China was in common use in the fourth century A.D.

The date of the Chinese stern post rudder can be pushed back still further by the discovery of a pottery model boat found in a Han Dynasty tomb in the environs of Canton. This model, which dates from between 206 B.C. and A.D. 220 and is now in the Canton Museum, is of a flat-bottomed boat fitted with deck houses. An anchor and thole pins can also be seen, as well as the protruding deck beams, a characteristic of many of China's riverine craft.

Pottery Model of a Han Dynasty boat: From a tomb at Canton, 206 B.C.–A.D. 220.

Certain facts, however, are incontrovertible. The origin of the rudder was, as in the West, doubtless from an oar over the stern, that is to say, the prototype in China of the rudder was the stern-sweep. In Siam, India, and especially the Maldives and Malaya, the paddle, or steering-oar, does in some cases give an indication of the influence of the quarter rudders of the ancients in Europe. But in the Chinese junk there is no such indication, and it would seem fairly safe to assume that in China there was no transitional stage between the stern-sweep or steering-oar and the rudder; that is to say, they had no equivalent of the rudder-oar, but progressed direct from stern-sweep to rudder. The reason for this surmise is to be found in the fact that the ancient Chinese shipwrights were in no way embarrassed, as were their brothers in the West, by the shape of the stern of their junks, which in China from time immemorial had been square, and was therefore as eminently adapted to the rudder as it was unsuitable to the paddle or rudder-oar. By the thirteenth century the art of Chinese sea-going navigation had made considerable progress, due principally to the use made of the compass,* and Chinese ships began to be seen in Western harbours. As already stated, the rudder slung from the stern-post did not make its appearance in Europe until the middle of the thirteenth century; therefore, although we have no definite proof, it is not unreasonable to suppose it possible that the rudder, the forbear of that used to-day the world over, came directly or indirectly to Europe from China through the medium of the Arabs.

While it is, of course, impossible to be sure which form of rudder came first, it seems not illogical to presume that some form of the balance type was the earliest variety to evolve. When confronted with the same problem that defeated the Western shipwrights, that is to say, when the hull of the vessel was too rounded to receive a rudder in the obvious way, the Chinese evolved the rudder-trunk. Moreover, they improved upon it still further by installing mechanism to hoist the deep rudder up by means of winches when entering shallow water. From this it was but a step to extend this hoisting principle to the centre-board.

* "Chinese and Arab Trade in the Twelfth and Thirteenth Centuries." Translated by Hirth and Rockhill.

It is a truism that in China no records exist in respect of any form of shipbuilding; and we have, therefore, no means of knowing when the rudder was first adopted or whether its first appearance was substantially different from what it is to-day. A knowledge of the Chinese methods of solving their problems and their conservatism in retaining old and well-tried customs inclines one to the opinion that the rudders of to-day are little changed from their prototypes.

The word for rudder in use before our era was *t'o* (柭), a character which is now obsolete and had the archaic meaning of "a branch of a tree." Chinese scholars think that this suggests an oar over the stern. The word occurs in the philosophical writings of Liu An (劉安), 122 B.C., entitled the "Huai Nan Tzŭ" (淮南子).

An argument in favour of the unchanged character of the rudder since that date is to be found in its present name. The character *t'o* (柁) for rudder (but with a different radical) is to be found in the "Shih Ming" of the first century A.D.,

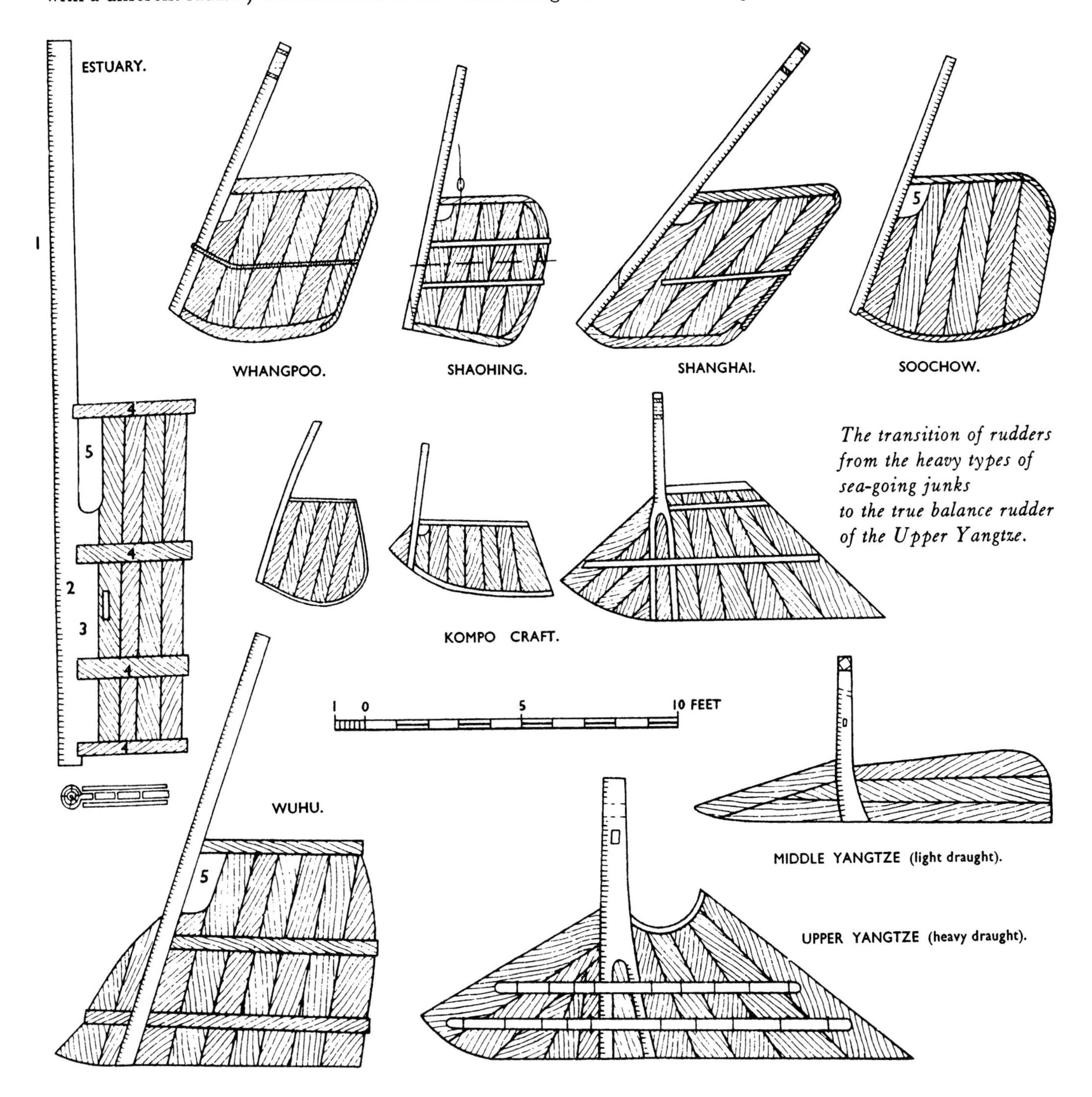

The transition of rudders from the heavy types of sea-going junks to the true balance rudder of the Upper Yangtze.

and the same word is in use to-day. In the above-mentioned book the meaning given is to draw, or tow from the stern. This would imply a rudder in the accepted meaning of the term, and not a quarter or side rudder.

It is not surprising that the people who were presumably the first to invent the rudder should still have the lead in the amazing number and variety of their rudders and steering arrangements, each designed for a special kind of work. Indeed, it is no exaggeration to say that practically every type of junk has its own particular rudder specially built for that craft and that craft alone. Nor are the differences small.

For instance, in vessels of deep draught, such as the Ningpo and Amoy fishing-junks, the rudder is narrow and extends only a short distance from the stern-post (see Page No. 95). The heavier types of rudder repay close study. They are usually made up of an ingenious collection of different sizes of wood and are extremely strong. The rudder-post[1] and what at first sight appears to be the next adjoining plank, marked[2] and[3], are actually one and the same piece of hard-wood. Plank succeeds plank until the required length is arrived at, when they are locked together by retaining pieces[4] kept in place by heavy iron spikes with iron bands at strategic points.

In those of light draught, such as those on the Middle Yangtze craft, it is proportionally wide or extends farther out, until in the large flat-bottomed junks

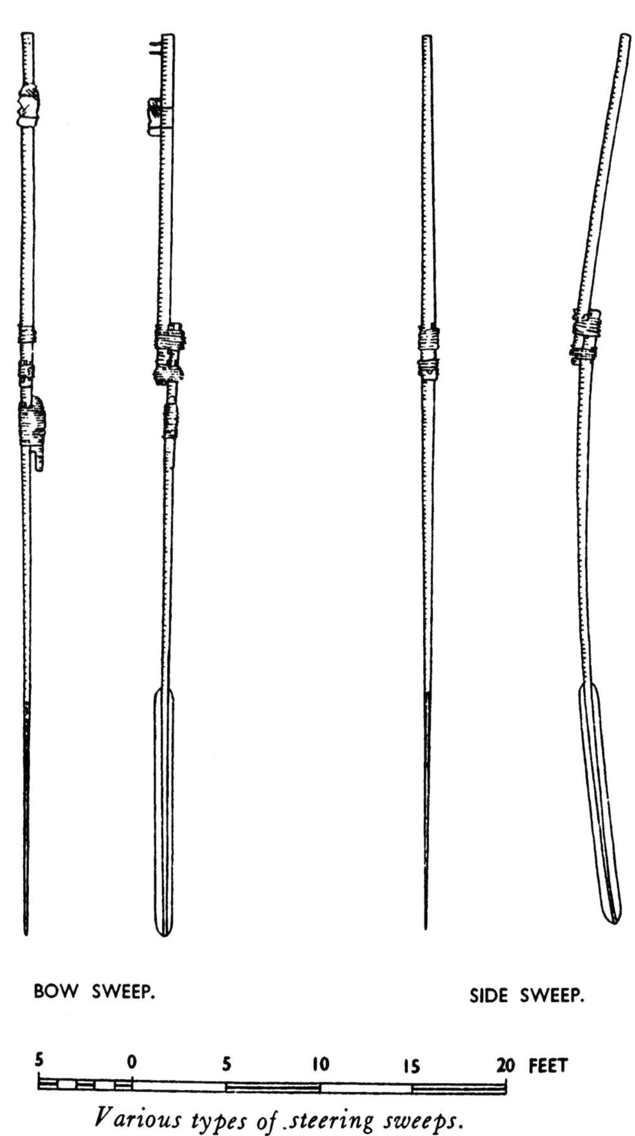

STERN SWEEP.

Various types of steering sweeps.

The crooked-stern junk of the Upper Yangtze is steered by a huge sweep. Note the stone lashed to the sweep for balance.

of the lighter variety, as on the Upper Yangtze, it is very wide and deep. In shallow-draught junks on the Ch'ient'ang River the rudder is little more than a plank 6 feet long. In small sailing craft of the delta we find the rudder larger and deeper than on the coast, for riverine craft carry a proportionally greater spread of sail. Finally, there are types of craft used exclusively in rapids which use no rudder at all but are instead steered by huge sweeps. In this case the sweep is about the same length as the junk itself. Some other sweeps are as much as 100 feet long, balanced with great dexterity by stones placed at convenient points.

In the main it may be said that rudders in China are large in proportion to the craft and are operated by suitably large tillers. The reason may be found in the fact that, when sailing, the rudder in a great measure takes the place of the keel in keeping the vessel to the wind.

It is noticeable that the balance rudder is seldom to be seen in the Shanghai area, where in the inter-communicating shallow creeks and waterways all rudders have necessarily to be hoisted in the case of the larger craft or unshipped in the case of small sampans. Moreover, a balance rudder requires a particular kind of stern.

Shanghai and the Whangpoo district show many styles, but the most typical rudders of that district are those of the Ningpo and Shanghai wharf-boats. They are specially designed to fit the characteristically square, yet sloping, sterns and have therefore a considerable rake. Most Shanghai craft, irrespective of size, have an aperture in the upper end of the rudder close to the rudder-post so as to enable the helm to be put hard over without touching any part of the socket[5]. The apparently unnecessary length of this aperture is so as to legislate for any height at which the rudder may be operating. In port a fid is often inserted in this aperture to relieve the strain on the tackles.

Although the Chinese may appear to have made little progress in investigating the principles and forces of mechanics, yet in all their shipwrights' work they have brought the construction of each part to an astonishing degree of efficiency. This particularly applies to all matters connected with balance. For instance, every rudder for every type of craft is accurately adjusted to the exact weight which can be handled comfortably by the number of men designed to man the rudder. Generally, of course, this is one man, but occasionally in some types and under certain conditions it may be necessary to have two or more men at the tiller, and in such cases the weight is always proportionate. Similarly, their ingenuity, and again their sense of balance, shows up strongly in their construction of windlasses and labour-saving devices, in which respect they would seem to have been always far ahead of the standard reached by European nations until about two centuries ago.

The hoisting type of rudder is slung from a windlass. When the rudder is so heavy as to require hoisting gear, this consists of a rope, or chain, passing from the windlass through a single block or a purchase shackled to a strengthening piece in the rudder and back to the windlass, or sometimes instead through a sheave inserted in the rudder.

When the rudder projects farther aft than usual, the stern is elongated by means of a gallery, or even merely a pair of spars, to which the rope from the rudder block or sheave travels and passes through another sheave on its way to the windlass.

There are three distinct methods of retaining the rudder, which for convenience may be classified as the open, half-open, and closed gudgeons or sockets, as illustrated at the left.

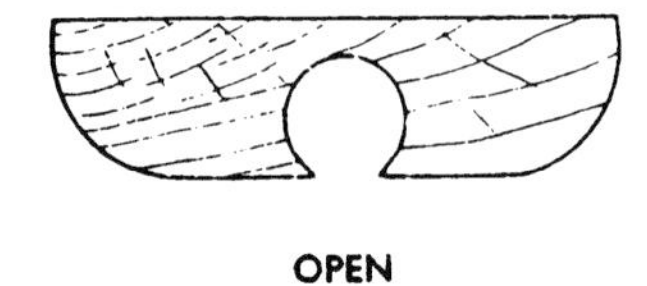

OPEN

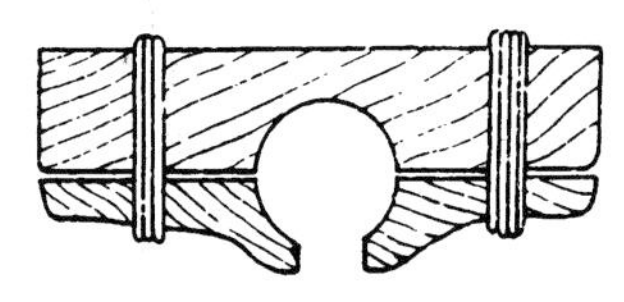

HALF-OPEN

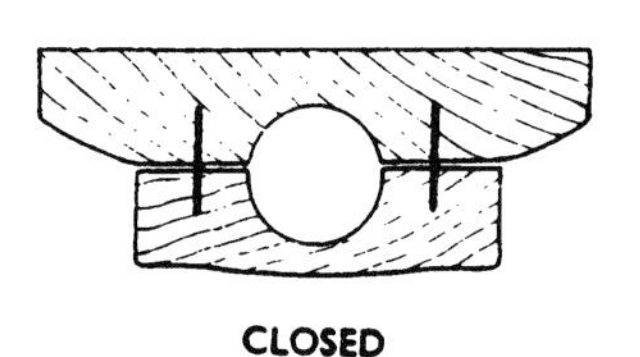

CLOSED

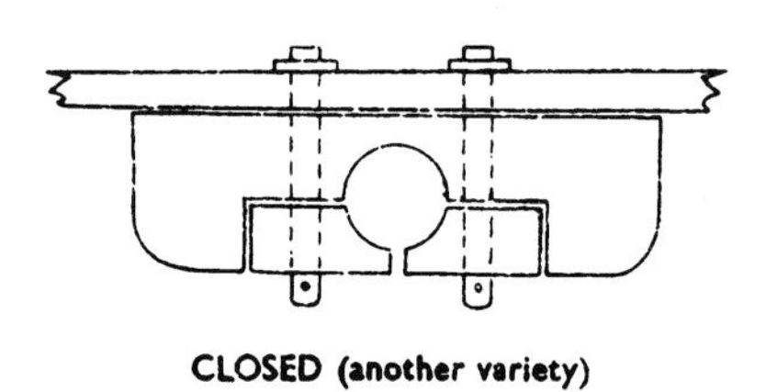

CLOSED (another variety)

Types of gudgeons or sockets.

In the case of the former or open variety the rudder is inserted from above through the wooden gudgeon, the open jaws of which permit its free passage. It is retained at the desired level by the windlass or any other device that may serve in lieu. The rudder-post, being too thick to slip through the open jaws of the gudgeon, is thereby kept from any lateral movement.

In the closed type of gudgeon, which consists of two parts, the rudder is set in place in the fixed part, the other half of which is then lashed into position.

The "Kompo" craft of the Shanghai area and the Hangchow Bay trader, that is to say, those that hail from the north bank of the Yangtze, show the first beginnings of the balance type of rudder. As the Yangtze is ascended, the more pronounced becomes the balance rudder, until it attains its true form, that is to say, with about one-third of its area before the axis, about which the rudder rotates.

Page No. 95 shows the transition from a typical example of the heavy type used by sea-going junks to the true balance rudder of the Upper Yangtze. The two latter examples selected show, Fig. A, a light-draught type of rudder with an area of 6.12 sq. feet forward of the rudder-post and 19.03 sq. feet abaft it. Fig. B shows a heavy-draught balance rudder with an area of 19 sq. feet before the rudder-post and 30 sq. feet abaft it. That is to say, those two rudders are within 5 and 10 per cent respectively of the recognized proportions for the modern balance rudder, and form an excellent example of how the junkbuilders by trial-and-error methods, and apparently without knowing it, have accurately arrived at a correct mathematical solution of their problem.

There is no component part of a junk which displays more variety than the rudder. Two or more classes of craft may have identical bows and very similar sterns, but seldom will the rudder be the same. This marked distinctiveness indicates much to the initiated, who at a glance will recognize the junk's port of origin, and know if she was designed for calm or rough weather, for sea or river, for shoal or deep water, for tortuous rapids or broad, quiet reaches.

The individuality and importance of this part of a boat's equipment may be summarized by the fact that the words a "rudderless boat" (無舵之舟) signify in Chinese a widowed woman.

It has for long been commonly accepted that the Arabians and the Chinese were acquainted with the mariner's compass from remote ages. The Chinese themselves claim the discovery was made by Huang Ti (黃 帝), the Yellow Emperor, in mythical days. He was, so runs the legend, engaged in battle at Cholu, in Hopeh, with his great enemy Ch'ih Yu (蚩 尤). The latter made use of a secret weapon, for, being possessed of supernatural powers, he was able to conjure up a fog. This early use of the smoke screen would seem to place yet another invention to China's credit, used, as is almost invariably the case, in exactly the opposite way to that employed by the West, for in modern warfare the smoke screen hides an intended movement or attack, whereas the Chinese design in this case was to cause their enemies to lose their way. With most commendable promptitude Huang Ti instantly invented "a certain kind of instrument" which always pointed south, and by this means he was able to lead his bewildered troops through the artificially-produced fog to victory.

This instrument, the *chih-nan-chên* (指 南 針), is mentioned in "The Imperial History," which describes how in 1130 B.C., during the time that the famous Duke Chou (周 公)* was acting as regent for his young nephew, ambassadors from Cochin-China to the Imperial Court had long outstayed their welcome on the plea that they had forgotten their way home. The resourceful Duke immediately gave them five chariots in each of which was placed one of the same instruments, which, no matter which direction the drivers took, always pointed to the south. This enabled them to reach the sea without difficulty, and they finally arrived home after a year's voyage.

Beyond this purely legendary evidence, which might, or might not, be interpreted to mean that the "south-pointing chariots" contained something in the nature of a magnet, there seems no indication, historical or otherwise, to support the long-established claim that the Chinese invented the compass. Indeed, the known facts might even be interpreted to show the reverse, for that observant traveller Marco Polo, who made voyages on the China seas in Chinese junks, never once mentions it; while Nicolo Conti, who navigated Indian waters in 1420, after the magnetic properties were known in Italy, expressly states that the mariners had no compass, but were "guided by the stars of the southern pole."

In "An Introductory Difcourse suppofed to be written by the celebrated Mifter Locke," entitled "An whole Hiftory of Navigation from its original to this present time," written in the year 1669, the discovery of the compass is attributed to Flavius of Amalfi. The date of the discovery is said to be about the year 1300, and the writer continues:

> The compafs opened ways in the unknown ocean, and made them as plain and eafy in the blackeft night as in the brighteft day . . . Upon diligent search all modern inquirers into antiquity unanimoufly agree that they cannot find the leaft ground to believe it was known before rather than give credit to some few writers, who rather suppofe such a thing to have been used by the Phœnicians, that pretend to prove it have nothing but their own fancies, raifed upon weak and groundlefs surmifes, to build upon.

Du Halde, writing in 1736, says:

> It is said that the Chinese were the first inventors of the mariner's compass, which if true, they have made little advantage of it.

Lindsay, in "The History of Merchant Shipping," also gave it as his opinion that there is no reason to believe the Chinese in the Middle Ages used a mariner's compass, despite allusions in Chinese books to the physical fact that by constant hammering iron becomes magnetized; in other words, has imparted to it the property of pointing to the north and the south.

In the "History of India, Notes and Observations," the same opinion is held, for it states that there is really abundant evidence to show that the compass had long been in use among the nations of the West before it was adopted by the Chinese.

* Duke Chou, it is recorded, was so energetic that he could hardly take a bath without rushing forth several times in the middle of it, holding his long wet hair in his hand, to consult with some official on matters of public importance. Several times during every meal he would put the food out of his mouth for the same purpose. He is said to have had a wrist like a swivel, on which his hand could turn completely round.

From all this conflicting evidence no very convincing case can be made for either side. Even if the early Chinese had had some form of compass, it would seem that it was far from being efficient, and such a discovery in any really practical form would have been so important an aid to navigation that its existence could not have been kept secret for so many centuries, or escaped the inquiring and recording observation of the early travellers from Marco Polo onwards.

H. G. Wells, in his "Outline of History," makes a most apt summing up of the case and draws from it what would appear the most logical and probable conclusions. He says:

> It is doubtful if the Chinese knew of the mariner's compass. Hirth, "Ancient History of China," page 126, comes to the conclusion, after a careful examination of all data, that, although it is probable something like a compass was known in high antiquity, the knowledge of it was lost for a long time afterwards until, in the Middle Ages, it reappears as an instrument in the hands of geomancers. The earliest unmistakable mention of its use as a guide to mariners occurs in a work of the twelfth century and refers to its use on foreign ships trading between China and Sumatra. Hirth is rather inclined to assume that Arab travellers may have seen it in the hands of Chinese geomancers and applied its use to navigation, so that it was afterwards brought back by them to China as the "mariner's compass."

The Chinese compass.

However the Chinese mariner's compass evolved, they certainly make good use of it to-day. The riverine junks and small craft which are never out of sight of land have, of course, no need for a compass, but the sea-going junks and craft of the estuary carry as many as three, which serve as a check on each other.

This is the only nautical instrument to be found on board a junk, and a more primitive one can hardly be conceived. It consists essentially of a round box $3\frac{1}{2}$ inches in diameter cut out of a solid block of wood. Inside a shallow circular shelf is left, measuring about $\frac{1}{2}$ an inch. The central portion of rather under 2 inches diameter is then hollowed out to a depth of about $\frac{3}{4}$ of an inch. In this cavity, which is painted white, a black arrow-shaped needle is balanced, none too accurately, on a central pin, its point of suspension slightly below its centre of gravity, and is very sensitive. The circular shelf surrounding the top of the cavity is painted black and serves as a compass card, for it is divided by white lines into 24 points of the compass. These are designated by characters selected from the "twelve earthly branches" and the "ten heavenly stems" of the eight trigrams. As there are 30 of these characters from which to choose, two stems and four diagrams are omitted.* *Tung* (東), meaning east, is derived from the conventional figure of the sun rising above the tops of the trees; while *hsi* (西), west, is a form derived from the image of a bird sitting on its nest at sunset.

In this connection it is interesting to note that in order to express the phrase "to explain something in detail" the four cardinal points are used. A Chinese thereby understands that when he is asked for the north, south, east, and west of the matter he is required to give the whole story. To talk east and west is to talk in an irrelevant manner. Completely happy east and south means host and guests thoroughly enjoying themselves.

The compass is usually kept on a shelf inside a junk "port," which is really a square glass window. In this way it is visible to those on deck, and at night it is illuminated by a small vegetable-oil lamp, or by a typical Chinese tallow candle mounted on a short bamboo wand and stuck into a shallow circle of wood, for which an iron bracket with the legs stuck into either side serves as a handle.

In the catalogue of the "Maze Collection of Chinese Junk Models," Sir Frederick Maze recounts how an interesting detail was brought to light in 1907 in connection with the Hainan junks which trade with the Malay States, when it was noted that each compass was set on a small tray of human bone ash which, so it was believed by the junkmen, had the property of annulling the attraction of any iron or steel that might happen to be in the vicinity of the compass.

There is no lubber's line to the Chinese compass. Instead, a string running parallel to the ship's head is sometimes fastened to the deck in front of the box when

* Giles defines the "earthly branches" as horary characters which, combined with the "heavenly stems," give names to the 60 years of the Chinese cycle, and the "eight diagrams" as arrangements or combinations of a divided line. There seems no reason in the selection of the branches and stems. The whole subject, however, is controversial and full of pitfalls even to the sinologue.

it is desired to place the compass in the true fore and aft line. A piece of brass wire is permanently fastened across the whole face of the compass, dividing it into two equal parts, the opposite ends being placed at the north and south points respectively.

The Chinese method of using the compass has been described by Du Halde as follows:

> They put the head of the ſhip upon the rhumb that they desire to ſteer in by the help of a ſilken ſtring, which cuts the outward ſurface of the compaſs in two equal parts, north and ſouth, which they do in two different manners: for inſtance, to ſail north-eaſt they put this rhumb parallel to the keel of the ſhip, and then turn it about until the needle is parallel to the ſtring; or elſe, which is the ſame thing, they put the ſtring parallel to the keel, and let the needle point to the north-weſt. The needle of the largest compaſs is not above 3 inches long.

In former days lighted joss sticks suspended from the deck head were the only timepieces whereby the time a ship had been on a certain course could be roughly judged. The advent of Western civilization in the form of the cheap alarm clock has greatly simplified navigation for the junkmaster. The junks carry no charts of any kind. The laodahs find their way by means of a skilful combination of sea instinct, keen eyesight, good memory, and an instinct for direction nearly as well developed as that of a homing pigeon. By long practise they are enabled to feel their way from headland to headland. If they get blown out to sea by bad weather and manage to survive, they stand in for the land, depending entirely upon their knowledge of its appearance and the depth and nature of the soundings to give them their position, for to them the bottom of the sea has its hills and valleys like the land, and they acquire an intimate acquaintance with its contours and the type of bottom to be expected in each locality.

To the sailor of the West, accustomed to radar, gyro-compasses, radio-beacons, and such modern refinements of navigational aid, it is almost incredible that a junk, with no nautical instruments save its primitive compass, a hand-lead and line, and a rusty alarm clock, should seldom overrun its port.

NOTES ON ROPEMAKING AND KNOTTING

THE making of rope is, of course, of very ancient origin. Ezekiel XXVII mentions the vessels of Tyre as having sails of Egyptian linen and palm rope for tackle; and Pliny records the use of hemp for ships, stating that it was in common use among the Romans in the first century.*

Rope is made very extensively in Shanghai. There are many varieties, not all of which are used in junks as cordage, although most of them are used for tying the bundles, bales, and other cargo.

In the Shanghai area at least eight kinds of rope are made from coir, hemp, and rice stalks, and it is perhaps surprising that with so many different varieties, not only in size but in fibre, they are all made on the same jenny.

The first operation in the making of rope is known as "softening," which makes the fibres more supple. This is done in Shanghai by beating the material with a heavy top-maul, a simple and inexpensive treatment.

A rope is composed of a certain number of strands, which are in turn made up of many yarns. The rope spinner walks backwards, feeding in even proportions of fibre as he goes, regulating his pace so that the amount of twist communicated to the yarn is uniform. He draws the fibre from the basket at his waist with his left hand and works it into the rope that is forming in his right hand. At the same time he draws the rope towards him with a jerking movement which serves to revolve the spool on its stand. When a length of 15 feet or so has been laid it is wound back on to the spool and the spinning is renewed.

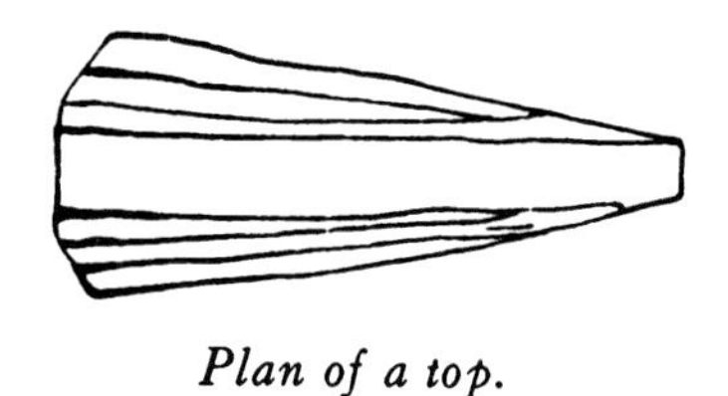

Plan of a top.

The next process is to carry these strands to some unfrequented street, where they are made up into rope. This is done in a "walk" of 300 feet between the spinning machines at both ends. At one end is a spinning jenny consisting of three hooks in a frame, on to which the strands are hung. The whole is set in motion by a wooden bar. At the other end of the rope walk is a frame with only a single hook, on to which the opposite ends of the rope are secured. A conical block of wood, technically known as a top (*see sketch*), is inserted between the strands, which fall into the equidistant grooves cut therein. The single hook is now rotated, and the three hooks holding the strands at the other end are correspondingly revolved in the opposite direction so as to maintain the requisite amount of twist. The framework carrying the single hook carries a large stone as ballast together with a boy standing on it and engaged in winding in the rope. Nevertheless, despite its weight, the whole structure is dragged down the walk by the process of shortening the strands as they are wound together in the finished rope.

A man and two boys working together will in a day produce 70 to 90 lengths of rope, each measuring 50 feet. Lack of space for the rope walks precludes the making of greater lengths in Shanghai, where the public roads may not be used. In the suburb of Nantao, where this objection does not exist, a small compensation is paid to the shopowners for the use of the road or shop frontage and longer ropes are spun. Only hemp and coir is made into rope in this way, as the rice stalks are now spun into cord by machinery. There are two kinds of hemp rope: one from hemp produced in Hangchow, which is known as *hung-ma* (紅 麻), red fibre; and the other from Hankow hemp, known as white hemp (白 麻).

* Hemp was introduced into China in the beginning of the seventeenth century B.C. when it was brought in by the Chou (周), who, according to Mr. E. T. C. Werner, may have learned its use from the Scythians of Central Asia.

Bamboo rope is used to the exclusion of all else for tracking on the Upper Yangtze, but is not, however, so easy to handle as hemp, and will not coil so quickly or in so small a space, nor will it stand a sudden cross-strain nearly so well. Nevertheless, it will endure a greater pulling strain and is lighter in weight than any hempen hawser of the same size, which could never hold out against the severe friction of the ragged rocks and would probably rot with the sudden changes of temperature and constant immersion.

Hemp ropes when wet lose about 25 per cent of their strength, whereas, as will be seen later from the results of a test carried out by the Whangpoo Conservancy Board, it would appear that the strength of the bamboo rope is actually increased by about 20 per cent when saturated with water.

Although bamboo-rope makers are to be found all up and down the Yangtze, the best bamboo rope is said to come from a village about 20 miles above Ichang, known as Hwanglingmiao (黃陵廟), which is famous for the excellence of its bamboos. An up-bound junk usually stops there to embark her new supplies of tracking-rope for the voyage up stream. An average junk requires the astonishing figure of about 1 mile of bamboo rope of varying lengths and sizes, and could, up to 1938, acquire this for $53. This is accounted a heavy item of expenditure, for, tough as they are, these ropes only last one trip despite the utmost care. Economy in tracking-lines is a dangerous policy and has been responsible for many an accident on the Upper Yangtze.

Not infrequently a bamboo rope carries away, or has to be cut to avoid an accident; when this is the case, the rope is very rarely joined by splicing, as this is a technical matter, but by laying the two ends side by side and securely seizing the rope at the overlaps at an interval of about 1 foot. A large rope may have three, or even as many as four, seizings at 1-foot intervals.

Discarded bamboo rope is used as fuel, and is also cut into lengths of a few feet and sold as torches, which last about 20 minutes.

The method of making the rope, which varies very little in the different localities, is surprisingly simple and quick. The most tedious process, and that demanding the most skill, is the preliminary splitting of the bamboo into narrow strips about ¼ to ½ inch in width, according to the diameter of the rope required, the canes being first soaked in water to make them soft and pliable. The splitting is done with a large sharp knife by a man who wears a finger-stall made of bamboo and who sits on a low bamboo stool. The plaiting of the rope is carried out by another man who stands facing a long, steep, downward slope or, where the country is too flat to permit of this, is perched on a flimsily-built bamboo tower.

He wears a protective apron and grips between his knees an 18-inch long half-cylinder of bamboo, slung on a string round his hips, into which he presses the coil as it leaves his fingers. The finished rope thus passes through a sort of crude "fair-lead" and slips easily away from where he stands, either falling down the height of the tower or else sliding down the beaten earth slope before him. The twist consists of a varying number of bamboo strips, always in multiples of four, the joints being irregularly placed for extra strength.

The method used on the Upper Yangtze is then to coil the rope, which is usually in lengths of 1,000 to 1,800 Chinese feet (about 400 to 700 yards), into a large, high, wooden tub permanently fixed over a cement stove. A solution of lime and water is poured through a funnel in the base of the cement framework above which rests the rope, supported by a small, circular, projecting shelf which keeps it clear of the water by some inches. The whole is covered with another tub turned down over that containing the rope, and the rope is steamed for four hours over a coal fire, the lime in the water serving to harden the bamboos. The water is replenished through the outer funnel as it becomes exhausted. Draught and outlet for smoke is provided by an immensely tall, four-sided chimney, reinforced at each corner with the ubiquitous bamboo.

A variation is the larger calibre of bamboo rope as made near Ichang, in which the strands are laid as in a hemp rope instead of being plaited. This rope is used for moorings and never for tracking.

The following report on a test carried out by the Whangpoo Conservancy Board has a special interest:

NOTES REGARDING TESTS ON BAMBOO ROPE FROM THE YANGTZE GORGES.

The plaited ropes from the Yangtze Gorges consist of a middle cord of straight bamboo material split off from thin and weak specimens of the bamboo, serving only as a support for the fibres plaited round them forming an outer layer which carries the load. This outer layer consists of the outer fibres, or ⅛ of an inch, of big and strong bamboo stems. In the joints of the fibres forming the rope, the outer ones are overlapping each other by about 1 foot while the inner ones are having no overlap at all.

The rope of 1½ inches diameter being tested in November 1923 by me had a square section area of about 0.7 square inch of solid bamboo material, the central cord being 0.3 and the effective outer fibres being 0.4 square inch.

Some difficulties arose in finding a reliable device for fixing the testing specimen in the machine. The best results were obtained when both ends were stuffed full of tar-filled rope and the ends then carefully wound with the same sort of rope in the way indicated on the sketch. The specimens for testing were 2 feet 6 inches long.

The rope was capable of carrying about 11,000 pounds or nearly *5 tons* when being absolutely dry. The middle cord already breaking at 8,000 pounds. The stress in the outer fibres being 26,500 pounds per square inch, this being in average of three tests, the result comparing favourably with my statement in "Tests of Mec. Prop. of Bamboo," page 16, where same is given as 25,000 pounds per square inch.

I did not succeed in obtaining any reliable results as to the strength of the rope when being saturated with water, as the specimen slipped out of the grips before the final break-down, but the tests indicated a 20 per cent increase of the strength, corresponding to a total carrying capacity of about *6 tons*.

(Signed) H. F. MEYER,
Engineering Assistant.

28th January 1924.

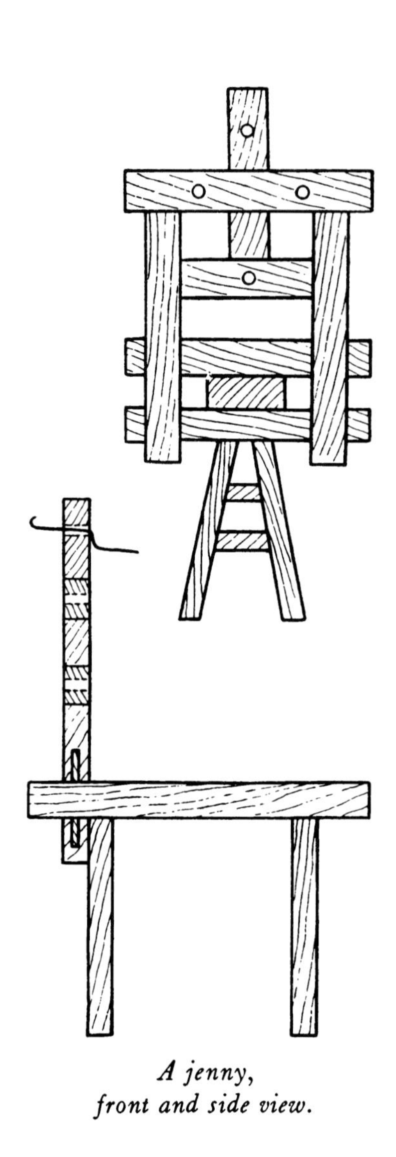
A jenny, front and side view.

Palm-fibre rope, called *tsung-shêng* (棕 繩), is extensively made in Chungking and at other ports on the Upper Yangtze. The laying, or spinning, of the rope is done on the foreshore, the rope-walk being about 50 yards in length.

The sequence of operations in this "rope-walk" method of spinning can be divided into three parts, namely, hacking the fibre, spinning the yarn, and laying these strands into rope.

The fibre comes in from the country in bundles. The hacking consists of taking a handful of fibre from the bundle and dashing it against the hacking-board, which is a wooden block about 1 foot long, studded with five or six strong, sharp-pointed, iron prongs, after the fashion of a broom-head, and secured to a trestle. The raw material is drawn through these prongs to separate the fibres and to lay them parallel. As the operator proceeds, a gradually increasing length is thrown onto and drawn through the prongs.

Spinning the rope is carried out on a jenny, a device consisting of a number of cross-pieces nailed together to form a convenient framework to carry four hooks, which have their long iron ends passed through the boards and bent at an angle to make handles. Only one of these hooks is used in the spinning process. The operator walks backwards down the rope-walk away from the revolving hook, to which is attached one end of the fibre; the other he draws out with his left hand as he walks, while constantly inserting and weaving in a few more strands with his right hand. An assistant turns the handle revolving the hook, whereby a twist is imparted to the strands. When a sufficient length has been spun, the process of laying it into rope with the three hooks, or occasionally the whole four when four-stranded rope is required, is commenced.

The method adopted is to make fast the end of a strand to each of the hooks, the other ends being collected together on to one similarly revolving hook on another jenny at the other end of the rope-walk.

As the multiple hooks twist in one direction against the twist of the single hook in the other, the operator again walks backwards from the separated hooks, laying or guiding the strands by means of a truncated hardwood cone, about 1 foot long, on which are cut three equidistant, longitudinal grooves which converge at the smaller end of the cone. The strands which enter separately into these grooves slip off the cone as they become the finished rope.

This crudely made rope, which can be as large as 5 inches in circumference, is exclusively used on the Upper Yangtze for the running rigging of junks, roping of sails, and, indeed, for all purposes save tracking.

The art of knotting in China probably dates back to the nomad period, during which men counted and even corresponded by means of knots made in cords, and it seems strange to the sailor that so much has been written on this form of knotting while its more recent and general use in China is neglected.

Crooked-stern and crooked-bow salt junks have no sails, carry no boats, use no rudder, and have no rope but the clumsy bamboo hawser and an occasional length of palm-fibre rope. Moreover, astonishing as it may seem, only one of the craft has even a block. The crews of these junks, therefore, have small need for knots and bends, and their knowledge of them is necessarily elementary. The science of seamanship as known in the West, which includes knotting and splicing, does not of course exist in Szechwan in any stereotyped form, for the junkmen learn in no school save that of experience.

Mr. Worcester is referring to the crooked-stern salt junks of Fowchow, described in Part Four, page 507, and the crooked bow salt junks of Tzeliut-sing, Part Four, page 564.

Nevertheless, their few hitches are eminently practical and perfectly suited to the craft and the work required, and their manner of application has sufficient novelty to warrant some description of the more outstanding varieties.

THE TRACKER'S KNOT

Quite the most simple and efficient Chinese knot is what may be termed the tracker's knot, which, in one form or another, is used all over China. In Szechwan it is, of course, more in evidence than anywhere else, for through this western province, the largest in China, flows the Yangtze, still tumultuous and rock bound after its headlong descent from the uplands of Tibet, and fed by innumerable tributaries, large and small, but all torrential, with gorges and rapids of their own. It may therefore be said to be the home of trackers and tracking, and the harness in use there is unlikely to have been much affected by outside influences.

The tracker's harness (see diagram, Page 52) consists of a band of blue or white folded cloth [1] about 3 feet in length, which passes over the shoulder and round the body. To each extremity [2] of this cloth band are secured by single-sheet bends [3] the two ends of a pair of small ropes [4] 9 feet long. Thus a loop is formed 12 feet in circumference, composed of the 3 feet of cloth [1] and 9 feet of the two parallel ropes.[4] At the middle of the rope section, that is to say, 4½ feet from each end of the cloth, the two ropes are secured by a double-sheet bend [5] to a 15-inch length of square sennit,[6] at the far, or outer, end of which is a bone or wooden button [7] about 1 inch in diameter. The sennit passes through a central hole in this button, and is secured from slipping by terminating in the ordinary wale, or wall, knot [8] as it is called in the West. This knot is made by unlaying and intertwining the strands.

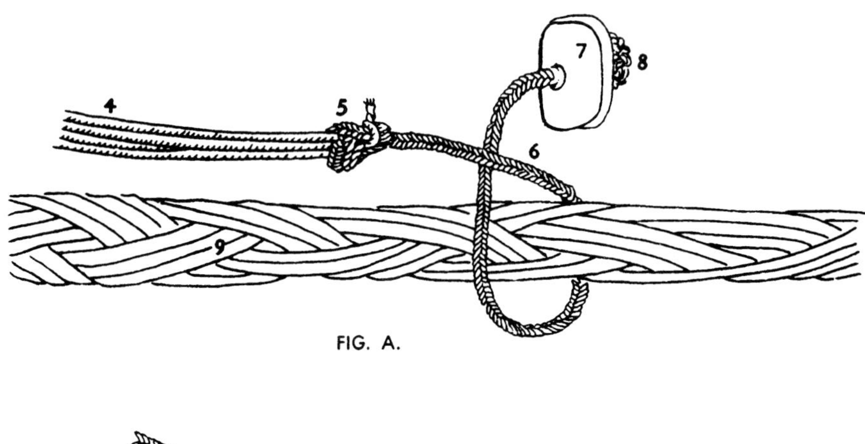

FIG. A.

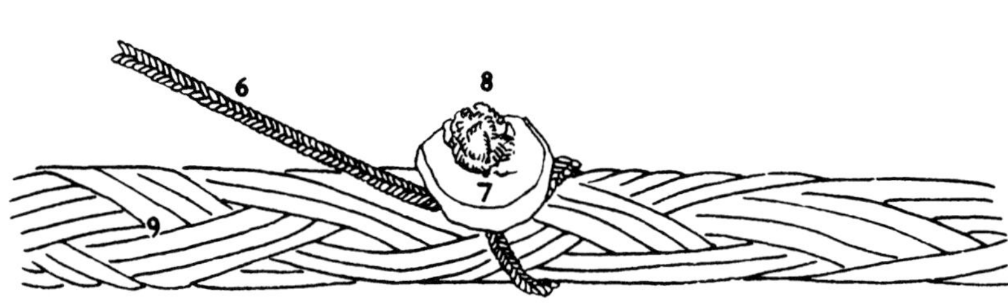

Tracker's knot.

FIG. B.

The complete tracker's harness, therefore, consists of a cloth band joined by double ropes into a loop to which is connected a short sennit stopper, or tail.[6]

Parenthetically it may be mentioned that in the days when cash were in current use, one of these coins—which have a square hole in the middle—was generally used in lieu of the button.[7]

The old sailor in the days of the China clippers would have used precisely these knots or bends, and the question naturally arises, how do they come to be found in daily use on the Yangtze and its tributaries, 1,500 miles and more from the sea? Is the coincidence due to foreign influence, to a common source of civilisation, or to the process of evolution unfolding along parallel lines in widely separated areas?

The trackers hitch themselves to the bamboo hawser[9] (*sketched above*, Fig. A) with the sennit tail of their harness,[6] which bears against the button[7] when the strain is on (Fig. B), but loosens directly the tension relaxes, forming a safety device whereby the tracker can easily release himself in an emergency, such as when the junk "takes charge" and sheers out into the current. *Ta-san* (打 散), meaning "break loose," is the technical term for this accident. Once a junk is cast off, her safety depends on the skill and cool head of the laodah, who must get some steerage way on to prevent her getting broadside on to the current and colliding with a rock.

Harness such as this, the knot and button being precisely the same, is used by the Italian fishermen to haul their boats up the beach. They throw the knot on, that is to say, they hold the tail of the harness, and with a deft swing the button is made to encircle the rope, and the harness is pulled tight, jamming the knot. The Chinese trackers use the same technique. Szechwan was visited by Marco Polo, and tracking was mentioned by him as long ago as the thirteenth century. Can it be that Marco Polo introduced the practice into Europe?

The trackers' harness used in the Shanghai area, and on some parts of the Yangtze River where tracking is only of comparatively short duration and low bridges have to be negotiated, is totally different.

THE KUNGT'ANHO CAPSTAN

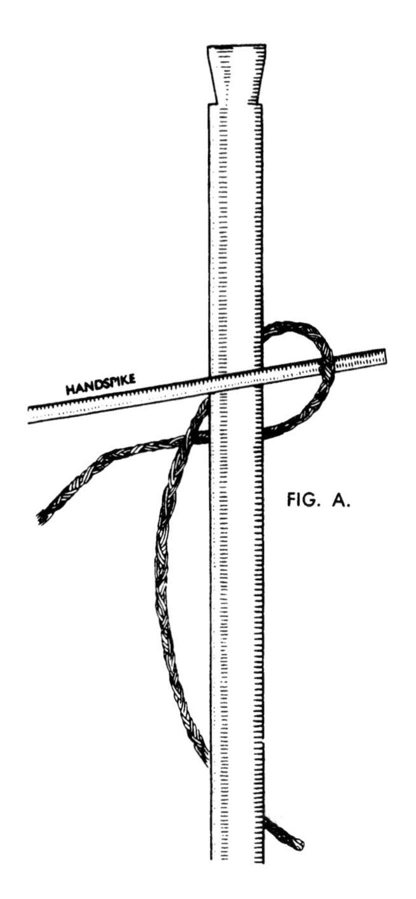

From the writings of Herodotus, who lived from 486 to 408 B.C., we know that the ancients were conversant with the handspike and capstan, and a painting in Herculaneum, which is said to represent the ship of Theseus, demonstrates that some form of capstan was then in use.

Unfortunately we have no such proof in respect to China, but it may not be wide of the mark to suggest that, generally speaking, what was known in the West was known also in the Far East, and the primitive type of capstan used on the Kungt'anho would seem to point to its antiquity.

Each particular rapid of the Yangtze and its affluents calls for a different method of approach, but the skill in each case lies in taking advantage of the eddies whenever possible. Hawsers, sometimes as many as six at a time, are sent ashore. These are all manned by trackers in the normal way, except for one which is made fast to a rock or a tree and hove in as necessary. Actually the capstan is used only to get the junk over the head of a rapid, where the belt of water having the maximum strength is sometimes only a few yards in width.

The distinct disadvantage normal to all Spanish windlasses, in that the rope cannot be readily slipped in an emergency, is obviated here, for the reason that the line, being made fast ashore, can be let go very easily at the shore end.

The capstan in general use on the Kungt'anho has already been described elsewhere in this book as being a tall, hardwood, removable timber standing on the fore part of the junk, some 8 feet above the deck. This contrivance has several uses. It can be employed as a bollard, or to assist the trackers when the tracking-lines are made fast ashore. Its chief function, however, is as a means of heaving in on these lines when so made fast. Actually this device corresponds almost precisely with the definition given in the Oxford Dictionary for a Spanish windlass, namely:

> "A wooden roller having a rope wound round about it through the bight of which rope an iron bolt is inserted as a lever for heaving it round."

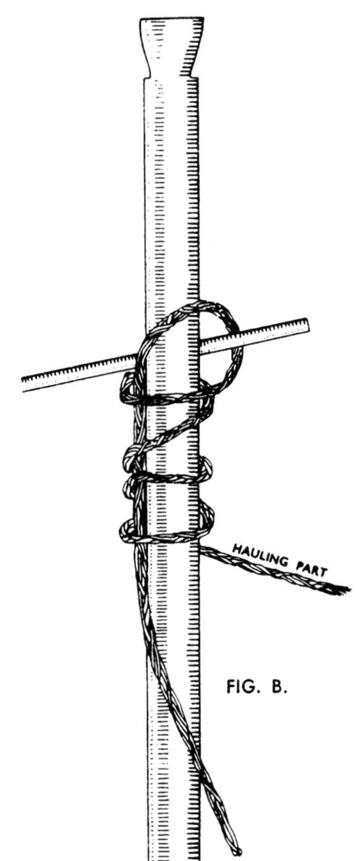

When used in this way, it is surprisingly efficient. Bamboo rope, it must be remembered, is very difficult to handle and will not coil so quickly, or easily, or in so small a space as other varieties of rope, neither will it stand a sudden cross-strain nearly so well. Nevertheless, it is admirably adapted for the service required of it, as, for instance, if used as a tracking-rope, when it has to withstand the friction of being hauled over stony foreshores and ragged rocks.

Besides being tough, it possesses the quality of buoyancy so valuable in a tow-rope. An average junk, astonishing as it may seem, requires about a mile of bamboo rope of varying sizes and lengths, and it is not uncommon to have a tracking-line a quarter of a mile long.

The Spanish windlass as known in the West is laid horizontally, with the barrel engaging with two uprights. Space is a matter of vital importance when working a rapid, and so the Kungt'anho Spanish windlass is vertical. The tracking-rope is put on in such a manner that the part through which the lever—in this case a handspike—is inserted is jammed by the standing part, thus retaining the lever in place and keeping the bamboo rope under control. As the rope is hove in, it accumulates on the capstan, and the resultant increase of girth is naturally an advantage.

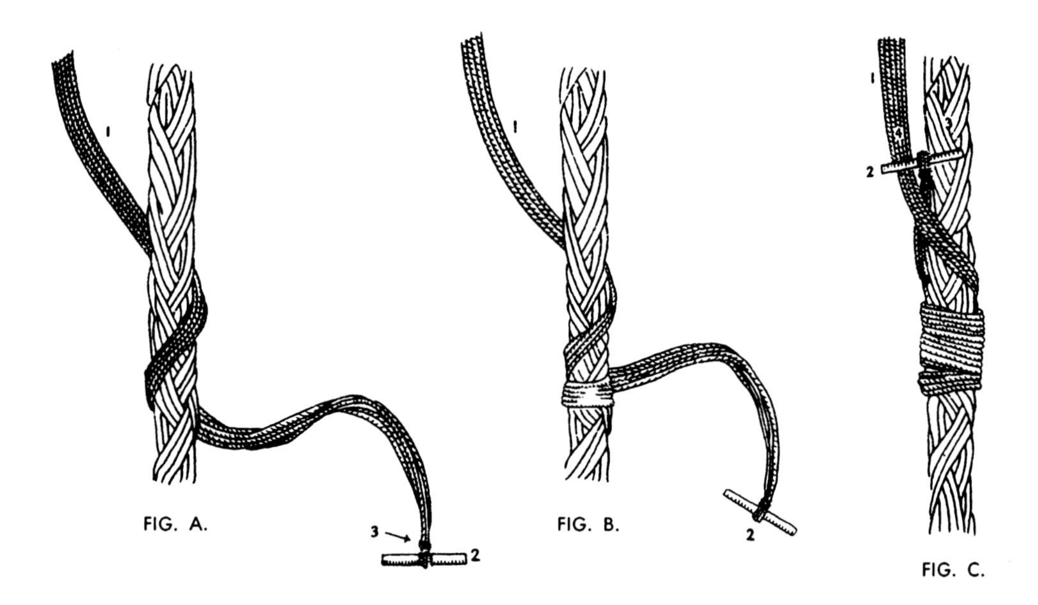

METHOD OF PUTTING ON A STOPPER, KUNGT'ANHO

The bamboo towing hawsers lead from a faked, or coiled, position inside the house to the fore-deck and thence to the trackers ashore, passing over the towing beams, to which they are secured by stoppers.

A pair of stoppers is put on to each hawser, and to avoid overlapping the stoppers are rendered unequal in length by securing one to a bamboo-rope grummet from the towing beam while the other is made fast to the same beam.

As the bamboo rope is subjected to constant friction over rocks, it becomes highly polished and slippery, and the ordinary single-rope strop as used in the West would be inadequate to hold it. The junkmen with innate ingenuity have devised a satisfactory remedy in a stopper (see Figs. **A**, **B**, and **C**). This consists of a small rope looped seven times to form a 6-foot becket.[1] Where the two ends coincide, a wooden toggle[2] is inserted through all the loops and seized with yarn[3] to make it secure.

The stopper is put on the bamboo hawser by taking five or six turns round the bamboo rope (Fig. **B**), some of the turns being on top of each other, and the toggle[2] is finally jammed in between the bamboo rope[3] and the standing part of the stopper, as will be seen in Fig. **C** (*drawing above*). The secret of the success of this is, of course, the number of strands forming the stopper. When the strain comes on, each strand buries itself between the strands below, and so not only obviates slipping by providing a better grip but also distributes the strain.

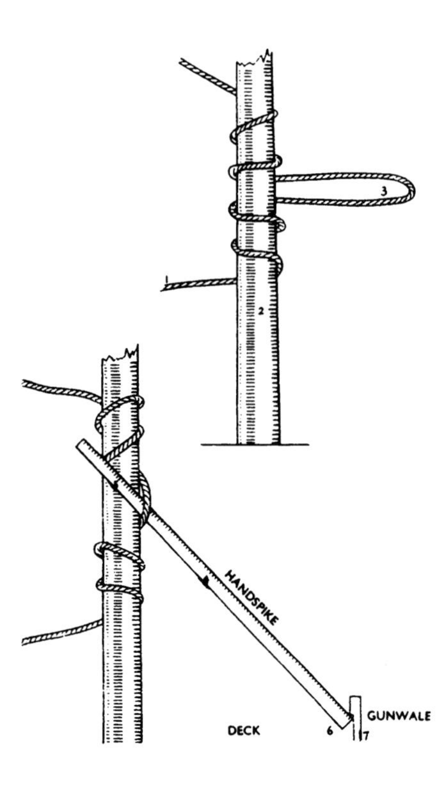

METHOD OF SECURING A TRACKING-LINE IN A RAPID

The method of securing the bamboo tracking-line used in the rapids of the Yentsingho is particularly worthy of mention, in that by a simple device it can be almost instantly slipped in an emergency.

The bamboo rope[1] leads from the trackers on the shore to the mast,[2] where, at a height of about 2 feet above the deck, several turns round the mast are taken with the bight,[3] through the end of which a handspike is finally inserted,[4] with the upper end[5] resting against the mast and the lower end[6] against the gunwale.[7] The strain on the tracking-line keeps the handspike in position, but it can in a moment be slipped by kicking the lower end[6] clear from the gunwale,[7] when the handspike[4] automatically falls out of the bight and the rope disappears over the side.

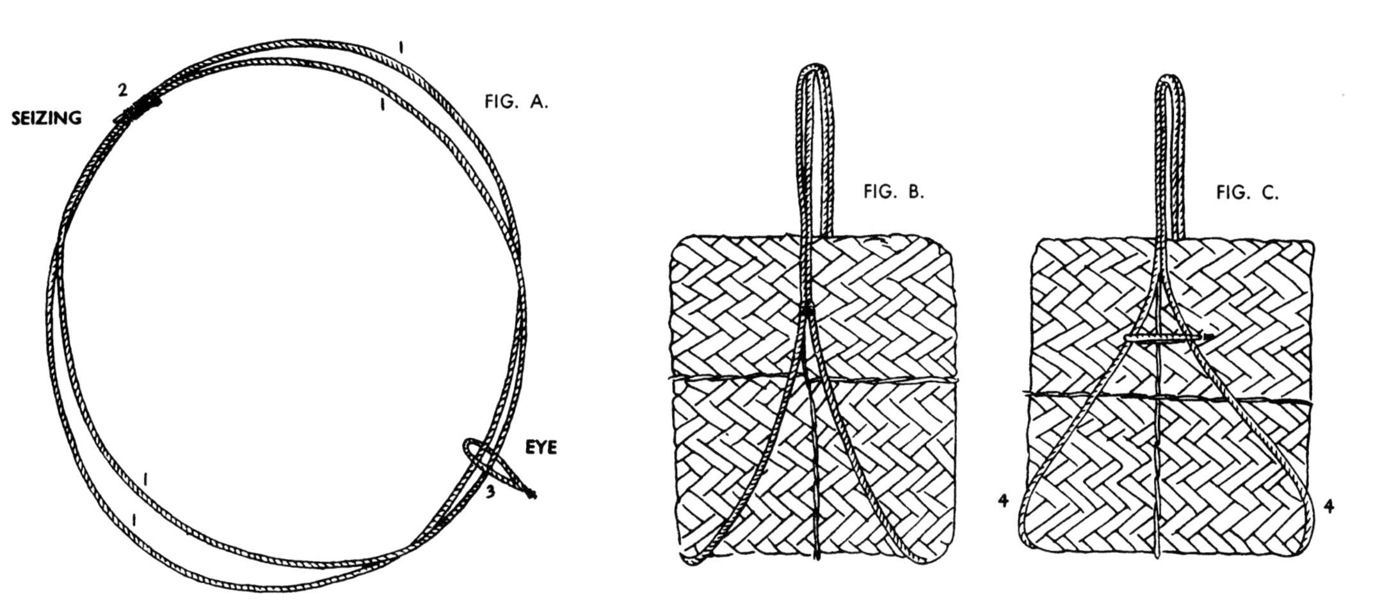

SALT-BASKET SLING, TZELIUTSING

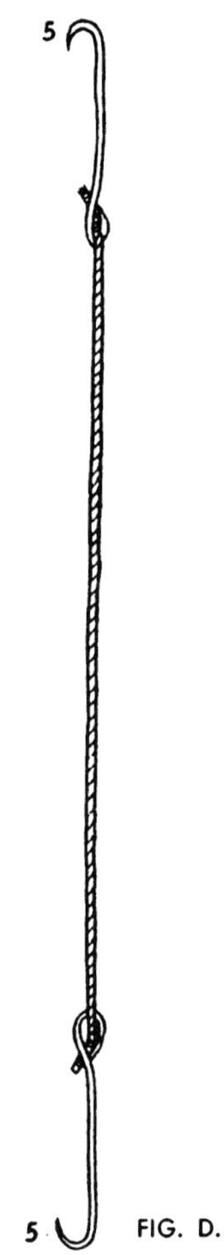

FIG. D.

From the time when the brine crystallises in the pans until it is eaten, the salt that comes from Tzeliutsing is lifted or carried by man-power in some form or other.

A very original form of sling is used to carry the salt baskets from factory to salt sampan or junk. As it is much used on board for stowing cargo or transporting it from one compartment to another, it seems reasonable to suppose that it owes its origin to the junkmen. The sling consists of a length of rope measuring about 16 feet, and laid up into two overlapping loops,[1] the whole being seized at the join of the two ends [2] (see Fig. **A**). The essential part of the device is a movable eye,[3] seized-in at its ends, which lies loosely round the two strands of the sling, being free to travel back and forth.

The sling is put on as shown (*see sketch above*, Fig. **B**), the eye [3] being pulled down to secure rigidity (Fig. **C**). It is of interest to remark that practically the same device is used in the West to tighten the bass and side drums used in naval and military brass bands.

It should be noted that the sling on the eye side does not pass under the bottom of the salt basket but round its sides.[4] This is, of course, a regular feature in Chinese methods of slinging, in the art of which they are past masters.

When the salt travels by road, it is made up into long bricks, two being the convenient load for a carrying-coolie. A special type of basket is used for this purpose, and a sling as illustrated in Fig. **D** is employed. The method of using this sling is destructive rather than ingenious, for the two hooks [5] at either end are jabbed into the sides of the salt basket, and the bight of the sling is raised and twisted so as to lock the bamboo carrying pole.

Bamboo, it may be mentioned, is so important to the life of Szechwan that it might well be called the national emblem. Nowhere is it more in evidence than in Szechwan, where it is put to many uses unknown to the rest of China. Its functions range from bridging rivers to making paper, or providing a succulent vegetable. The scholar, the farmer, the fisherman, the carpenter, the policeman, and the baby would be lost without it. But above all, it is utterly indispensable to the junkmen. A conservative estimate can readily provide 70 important uses for it in a junk, ranging from rafts to rope and from shoe soles to chopsticks, or a comb in the hair of the laodah's wife.

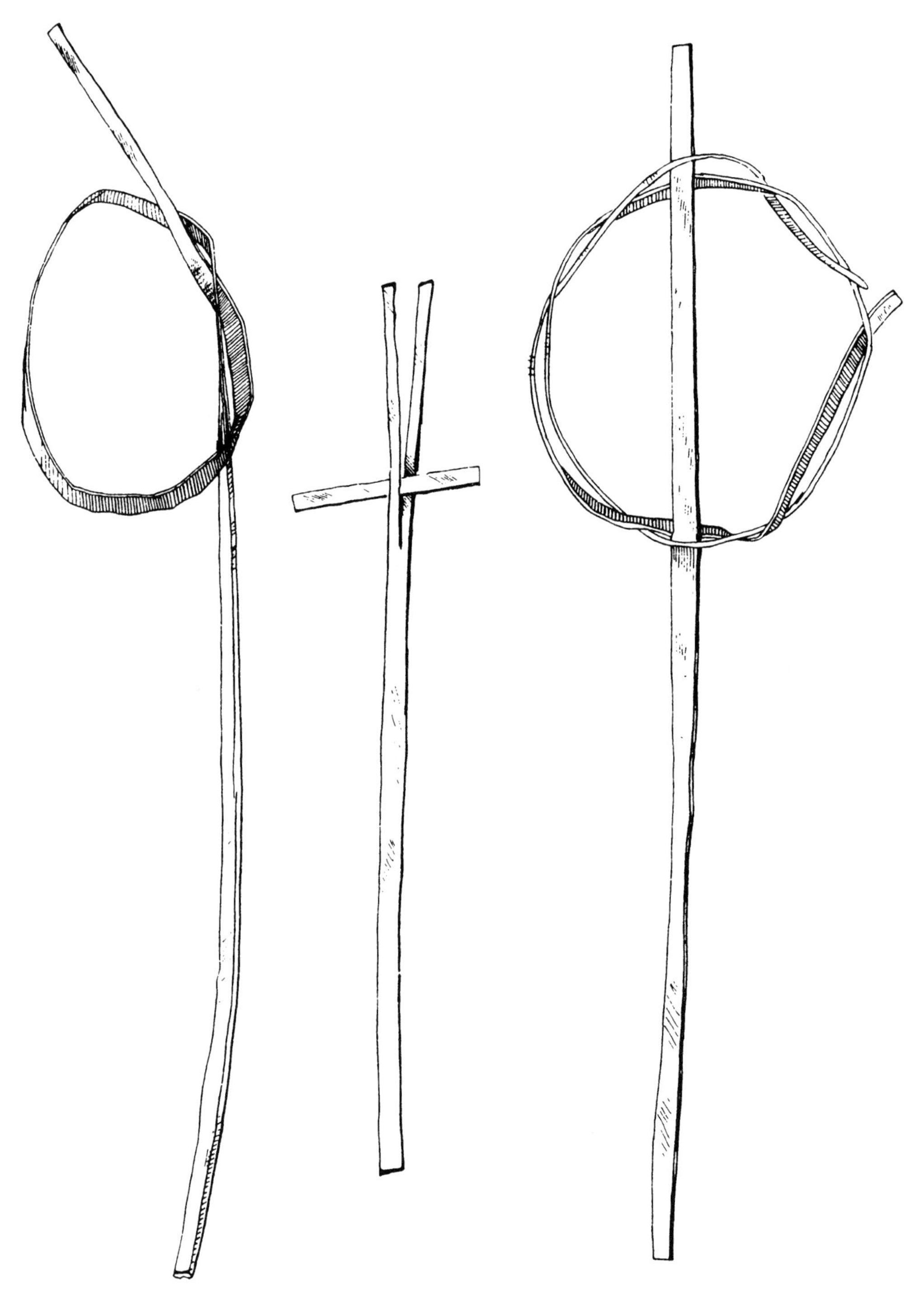

THE GRASS KNOT

Although not perhaps, strictly speaking, a knot in the accepted meaning of the word, the bamboo twist, known to foreigners in Szechwan as the pig's tail, may very well be included here. Called *ts'ao-chieh* (草 節) by the Chinese, it is of very ancient origin and is used only by people who are not professional hawkers.

In Chungking three varieties may commonly be seen, and are illustrated in the drawing. In each case the emblem is made of bamboo or rattan, although it can be made of straw, and is about 9 inches over-all measurement. It is carried in the hand to denote that the pedestrian exhibiting the sign has something for sale, the article in question being carried on the other arm.

When exhibited from a boat, it takes the form of a bamboo grummet, about a foot in diameter, made fast to a boat-hook standing erect in a thole-pin hole. It then represents one of the saddest sights to a sailor's eye, namely, a ship for sale.*

* An interesting analogy to this is to be found in certain parts of England, where a broom at the masthead signifies the boat is for disposal.

THE JUNKMEN

NO less than their junks do the people that man them form an unfailing subject of interest. Different from the sea-going junks, most of the Yangtze craft are owner-run. On the Yangtze the junkmasters for the most part carry their wives with them, and hundreds of thousands of such families with their children live, move, and have their being afloat in junks, where they continue to work their boats as long as life itself endures, and finally die, as they have lived, unknown to the rest of the community. The women may not be able to read, but they can help at the yulohs and oars, with babies strapped to their backs, and handle the ropes and take a turn at the tiller like the good sailors they are. No one would call them laconic in an argument and, like good seamen too, they are possessed of "topsail-halyard voices," which they use to the full in any altercation.

Despite the economy of running expenses, the junkmen maintain that there are no very large profits to be made in the business, but at least they can make a more comfortable living than most of their compatriots ashore and, provided their boat holds together, are always sure of a means of livelihood.

The junkmen's calling has descended for generations from father to son; sometimes a junk has been sailed by three or more generations of laodah. The inherited instincts, reinforced by their daily experience, have bred a race of hardy, resourceful sailors. They are rough and tough, with plenty of pluck and endurance, and will work from daylight to dusk without shirking or grumbling. No craft in the world are more skilfully handled than the so-called "lumbering junks"; and nowhere else do sailors work so desperately hard on such poor fare, or face so many risks for so little pay. Their amazing staying power, combined with the ability to stand hardships, has trained them in the best of schools. China, did she but know it, possesses in these industrious and fearless junkmen a treasure of immeasurable value to the country.

Comfort, in the Western sense of the word, is unknown to these frugal people. Their bedding consists of a quilt, about 3 by 6 feet, made of cotton wadding enclosed in coarse blue cloth. This is laid on a strip of rush matting in which, in the daytime, it is rolled up out of the way. If the luxury of a pillow is not available, their outer garments rolled into a bundle or a log of wood will serve.*

The raincoat of the junkman is made from the coir palm. It is a hardy plant, able to weather the frosty winters of the Yangtze Valley. The large brown bracts, which protect the stems from the cold, are natural pieces of fibre cloth resembling coconut fibre but superior in quality. The fibre is woven into a raincoat, which is the indispensable wear of the junkman.

Naturally parsimonious, they spend the minimum on their food. They seem content with a monotonous repetition of inferior rice served with cabbage or some other inexpensive vegetable fried in oil. Occasionally and on festivals this is supplemented by a bit of pork or fish. The main staple is, of course, rice. Each man fills his bowl from the great rice-pot boiling on the galley fire and with this as a basis, deftly, with his chopsticks or with a porcelain short-handled spoon, helps himself into the same bowl from the smaller dishes, which are placed in a circle on the deck in the small craft and on a table in the larger and more spacious junks.

In 1926 the junk hands used to be paid a regular wage of $4 or $5 per month in addition to free board and lodging from the owner, and this, together with their perquisites from the owners of the cargo, augmented their monthly earnings

* In the porcelain trade a pillow made of chinaware is used.

to $8 or $9 at most. With free food their daily personal expenses, however, amounted to much less than those of other classes of workers, and on this pay they could generally manage to support a family.

Following the capture of Nanking by the Kuo-min-tang Army in 1927, labour unions were immediately organized on the Russian model, and the picturesque customs and organizations of the guilds gave place to the more modern and rather dull "collective bargaining." As a matter of interest, the Seamen's Union was formed in 1927, the entrance fee being $1, the annual subscription $2.40, and its avowed purpose to "unite Chinese seamen all over the world and promote common interests."

There are three varieties of guilds in China. The *kung-so*, public halls, or trade union guilds with which alone we are concerned here are very old in origin and, it is claimed, date back in some instances to the Former Han dynasty or even before. All the craftsmen of every calling were more or less obliged by public opinion to join a trade guild, which derived its income from entrance fees and percentage on sales. The guilds were purely democratic in their administration, which was under a Manager and Committee elected annually, each member serving in rotation as Manager. Rules were made to govern the price of products and hours of work, and to regulate questions of storage, packing, insurance, and prices. An important function was to arbitrate in any dispute between members. The guilds would also subscribe handsomely to the funeral expenses of even the poorer members, sometimes donating a coffin, and generally care for the bereaved widows and orphans. A newly-joined member, for his part, was expected to make a donation in the form of a scroll or set of lanterns.

To-day, sad to relate, the ancient guilds representing the interests of the silk and tea merchants, the goldsmiths, butchers, bakers, tailors, barbers, and innumerable others, even including the thieves and beggars, are said to be passing away, and an association which claims to have similar objects has taken their place. There are, however, still four nautical guilds in Shanghai, namely, the Owners of Sea-going Junks, the Shipwrights, the Cargo-boat Owners, and the Coal and Stone Lighters Guild.

The junk guilds in Chungking are represented by three main associations dealing respectively with the Yangtze River above Chungking, the river below Chungking, and the Kialing River. These comprise in all 22 branch guilds, each usually named after a district, although there are exceptions, such as the Salt Guilds and the Red Flag Guild. Eight guilds cover the section of the river below Chungking, and four different guilds deal with various areas on the Kialing River. The rest function above Chungking in small sections, except for the Chungking–Chengtu Junk Guild (渝蓉綫民船商業同業公會), which functions in the area from Chungking to Chengtu *via* the Yangtze River and Minkiang, and the Chungking–Kintang Junk Guild (渝金綫民船商業同業公會), from Chungking to Chengtu *via* the T'o River. The latter guild, the oldest of them all, was established in the reign of the Emperor Ch'ien Lung (乾隆), about 150 years ago.

It would seem that, in their present form, though some of the guilds date from about the middle of the Ch'ing dynasty (清朝), most of them only came into being 20 or 30 years ago, for in the early days of the Republic the guilds were reorganised, and as recently as 1938 further changes were inaugurated, in that the Chinese Government approved of the establishment of all the branches under one Central Guild. Each branch is controlled by a committee of not less than three or more than eleven, and each has a representative on the Committee of the Central Guild, which body elects a chairman.

The origin of these guilds is lost in antiquity, but probably in a modified form they are as old as the junks themselves. Their history, even in comparatively modern times, is hard to trace, but before the evolution of the present organisation a guild was known as *pang* (幫), or group, and a *pang-t'ou* (幫 頭), or elder, was elected every year on the anniversary of the birthday of Chên Chiang Wang Yeh (鎮 江 王 爺), the River God, which falls on the 6th day of the 6th moon. This ancient practice is still carried out by most of the branch guilds.

The guilds usually maintain their offices and records on the first floor above a tea-house, in which members can conveniently meet and discuss matters of business and pick up contracts for cargo from the merchants. A registration book is kept, in which each junk is entered with relative particulars and containing the name and chop of each junkmaster, together with his age and birthplace, and the number of his craft as assigned by the guild.

After registration with the appropriate guild, the junkowner is given a copy of the guild's regulations, a certificate, and Ch'uanchao (船 照).

The Central Guild estimates the number of junks on the Upper Yangtze and its tributaries at 30,000, excluding small boats, ferries, and the like. The crews of the registered junks are said to be between 300,000 and 400,000. It is probable that these figures are very conservative.

Mention must here be made of another institution which is closely interwoven with the fabric of Chinese daily life, and that is the tea-house. In addition to being a centre for social intercourse, fulfilling the functions of a club, it is closely associated with the commercial side of life, and the average man from every class of the community patronizes his own particular tea-house, wherein he spends a leisure hour or so, transacts some bargain of buying or selling, or merely looks round for an opportunity to do so.

Others who frequent the tea-houses, though not to use them as a club or a business rendezvous, are the dealers, pedlars, beggars, and, more welcome than these, the professional story-tellers, who sit on stools or upturned boxes and recount their endless tales of a bygone age. Occasionally the proprietor will hire a vocalist as an additional attraction.

The tea-house, moreover, serves as a sort of Labour Exchange. Each has a regular clientele of customers who attend at different hours of the day.

The junkowners, the laodahs, and the junkmen in particular are ardent devotees of the tea-house system and meet there constantly to exchange gossip, render mutual aid, and find or give employment. If a junkowner obtains a cargo too big for him to handle, he divides it up among his friends, and the whole transaction will be carried through at his favourite tea-house. It may be said, and said with confidence, that more business is done over the tea-cups than is ever done on the waterfront or on board a junk. Here the junkowners arrange for their cargoes, discuss the details of their negotiations, settle their outstanding accounts, and arrange for credits, for most of the borrowing is done in tea-houses, where loan contracts are kept ready in case of demand. Here, too, cargoes are insured. Marine insurance in England may be said to have first seen the light in the equivalent of a tea-house, for Lloyd's in 1688 was a coffee-house which served as a meeting place for those interested in shipping.

It would be interesting and salutary for the present day great insurance companies of the West, ensconced in their vast temples of commerce, to reflect that in this, as in so many other respects, the Chinese were before them by numberless centuries. The origin of insurance as practised in China is lost in antiquity, but it is certain that from a very early period the merchants took steps to secure recompense for loss or damage to their goods through the perils of sea transit. Not only was the ship and cargo insured, but also the life of the laodah. One of the earliest forms of contract was in respect of capture by pirates.*

* The "Customs Trade Report" for 1869 described the system of life insurance forced upon the guilds because of the difficulty in obtaining sailors on a coast so badly infested by pirates. Every Shantung junk on entering port paid a fee of $100 to the guild, which in turn provided an escorting convoy and paid a refund for loss or damages to the junk and her cargo provided these were occasioned by pirates and not due to natural causes. If a junkman was captured the guild paid the ransom, and in the case of his death a fee in compensation was paid to his family. Junks from Chinkiang and Fukien were similarly insured by their respective guilds.

In every coastal town, all up and down the Yangtze, and along all the creek routes, wherever junks bank in for the night, are to be found tea-houses which, besides catering for all classes of the community, are specially frequented by the floating fraternity. In some towns the prosaic bath-houses perform the same functions as tea-houses and are used for business transactions, while barbers, ear-pickers, and others are always in attendance.

An instructive and amusing hour or two may be spent in Shanghai in the Foochow Road (福州路), which is the street of tea-houses. Those interested in the craft themselves, however, rather than in their crews and owners, can spend an enthralling hour on a seat in the Bund Public Gardens, where they can command a view not only of the harbour and the Whangpoo, but also of the Soochow Creek. Here within a short space of time may be seen passing in procession the brick-boats of Wusih, the Soochow *kang* boats, wine-boats from the Ningpo hinterland, firewood boats, fishing-boats, and junks and sampans of all sorts taking in and discharging cargo. Some are laden with rice, beans, cabbage, grain, and eggs; others with brooms, poles, or ricks of straw with scarcely a part of the boat discernible. Boats with flowers, lime-boats, and drag-boats. Boats carrying beancake resembling grindstones or with firewood neatly arranged. Bamboo rafts and rafts made of enormous tree trunks add a character of their own to the scene. Boats containing sugar from Swatow, others with millet and blocks of paper, wood oil from Szechwan, seaweed and salt fish from Bangkok, oranges from Swatow and Canton, pumeloes from Amoy, and bale after bale of cotton, the product of Chinese toil and industry.

Not only the craft but the workers too. Among the army of coolies who, day after day, carry heavy loads to and from the junks, the great majority come from Shantung. Almost all the men connected with the fishing trade, such as fish hawkers, dealers, and fishermen, come from Ningpo, the vegetable-boats' crews alone being Shanghai men, because they have a better connection with the local farmers.

To keep time by singing in chorus when at work on the oars or when hauling on ropes is a practice amongst sailors which has existed from the most ancient days. It has never been scientifically investigated in China, and there is ample scope on the Yangtze for research work in this respect.

John Barrow, Private Secretary, and a member of the suite of Lord Macartney's Mission to the Emperor of China, writing on this subject in 1805, makes an initial contribution.* He says:

"To lighten their labour, and assist in keeping time with the strokes, the following rude air was generally sung by the master, to which the whole crew used to join in chorus:

Song of the Yangtze boatmen.

"On many a calm still evening, when a dead silence reigned upon the waters, have we listened with pleasure to this artless and unpolished air, which was sung with little alteration through the whole fleet. Extraordinary exertions of bodily strength, depending, in a certain degree, on the willingness of the mind, are frequently accompanied with exhilarating exclamations among the most savage people; but the Chinese song could not be considered in this point of view. Like the exclamations of our seamen in hauling on ropes, or the oar song of the Hebrideans, which as Doctor Johnson has observed, resembled the proceleusmatic verse by which the rowers of Grecian galleys were animated, the chief objects of the Chinese chorus seemed to be that of combining cheerfulness with regularity."

* "Travels in China, containing Descriptions, Observations and Comparisons made and collected in the Course of a Journey through the Country from Peking to Canton," by John Barrow.

Life on the foreshore, Kiukiang.

Sailors the world over are commonly believed to be more superstitious than landsmen; and seamen of the West still cling to tales of Neptune, Mother Cary's Chickens, the Flying Dutchman, and St. Elmo's Fire. The junkmen too, like all good sailors, have many customs and superstitions, legends and myths. Several of these concern food; for instance, when afloat, chopsticks must not be placed across a rice-bowl, as is commonly done on shore, as such a position suggests a junk aground. Even more ominous would it be to turn a bowl upside down, as it would too pointedly signify what might happen to the junk. Grains of rice left adhering to the copper in which it has been boiled must not be called by the usual name *fan-chih* (飯 滯), because the character 滯 also signifies an obstruction or stoppage, and the sound is similar to that of 遲, meaning "slow." The characters 飯 快 are therefore used instead, meaning "quick."

Superstitions of the junkmen are discussed at length on pages 118–27.

There are many days when it is considered unlucky to start on a trip. Danger can often, the junkmen hope, be averted by buying a charm as a protection from the 100 unlucky days.

Many junks, when first built, have small wooden knobs under the overhanging square bows. From these are suspended strips of red, green, and yellow cloth, which are believed to prevent the approach of evil spirits. These strips, which represent the four seasons of the year, are never removed, but allowed to remain until they drop off. Any craft that is suspected not to have been constructed according to the principles of geomancy has these additions affixed, if they have been omitted in the building, or readjusted if they appear to have failed in their purpose. They are also installed after any large overhaul. Sometimes ingots of paper money, that is to say, silver-paper sycee, are also attached to the cloth strips in order to attract riches during the coming year or to propitiate the spirits and so allow the junk to pass unmolested. When on a journey in a junk it is highly undesirable to inquire the distance to the next port of call; for if this be mentioned, the junk, it is said, will immediately be slowed down by the jealous deities guarding its fortunes.

There are superstitions to fit most contingencies. It is thought to be unlucky to pass under a bridge when a woman is crossing it. Another interesting belief is the existence of bridges known as "dumb bridges," for no one should speak while passing under them. These, it would seem, are mainly confined to the Shanghai and Soochow areas.

Brass gongs, so much in demand in religious ceremonies in China, are always carried in junks, where they are much in use for the frightening of evil spirits as well as for various other purposes. Junks of the same fleet or hailing from the same port often salute each other when passing by banging on the gong. From this custom arises the idiom "不 擂 鑼" (not to beat gongs), that is to say, "not to salute," said of persons no longer on speaking terms. If a junk be wrecked, the survivors are most careful to save the gong and will not part with it for any consideration.

These superstitions vary a good deal according to the localities, some being indigenous to one place or province, whilst others are more or less widespread. Nor are they so easily to be discovered as in former days. The tendency nowadays is to diverge sharply from the former manners and ways of thought and shamefacedly to repudiate any connection with the old folklore. Nevertheless, when the last of the old Chinese sailors' superstitions have withered away under the scorn of an enlightened and sceptical generation, with them will vanish much of the romance of the river.

No race is so amphibious as the Chinese, and their genius for adapting themselves to the most uncomfortable living conditions is here amply illustrated. The sampan men and women and their families know exactly how to stow themselves away in the smallest possible space, and it is surprising that they can so cheerfully accustom themselves to the conditions under which they have to live. It is fortunate that they have this gift, for it is often necessary for them to remain for hours in the same position, which they do without apparent weariness or need of a change.

When the day's work is over the sampanmen fall asleep huddled together in their limited quarters in a perfectly stifling atmosphere which would be sufficient to suffocate the ordinary person. In the cramped space at his disposal a sampanman sleeps restfully, regardless of the fact that throughout the night he can probably neither stretch himself nor even change his position, and that his pillow, if he has one, is a log of wood. Such a night's rest would be a misnomer to the ordinary person, but the tough dwellers in sampans awake as refreshed as though they had retired to a comfortable bunk—or rather bed—in a luxury liner.

The generations of children born in sampans very soon acquire their sea legs and display an aptitude for the life. Their inherited and/or acquired sense of equilibrium is extraordinary, and they rarely fall overboard. It is a lesson in the effect of environment to watch the bearing of a small junk baby, still too young to be promoted to real trousers instead of the utility sternless type devised by economical Chinese mothers for their children of both sexes. The child of an age to be unsteady on its feet, even on land, will instinctively straddle its legs and sway to the motion of the sampan in a choppy sea.

The junior members of the family soon become important members of the crew and at a very early age learn to "hand, reef, and steer" and to "catch a turn" round a bollard in a manner which would do credit to an old sailing ship sailor. Occasionally a more cautious mother will tether her offspring to the mast or provide against a fatal accident by tying on an improvised lifebelt in the shape of a large dried gourd or small baulk of wood. The hard but healthy outdoor life inures these children to climatic changes. In warm weather they are often to be seen wearing little more than two such "lifebelts." In cold weather, in voluminous padded coats they cheerfully face all extremes of the China coast winter. At the age of about four or five a child learns to handle an oar, an art which with its attendant rhythm must be subconsciously inculcated almost from birth, for the sampanwoman will row for hours with a young baby strapped to her back. Small wonder if, in this practical school of experience, the sampan folk, whatever their sex, develop into expert sailors. The women and their daughters usually act as crew for the ferry and cargo sampans, while the fathers and husbands act as sailors in the larger junks. From a Chinese point of view these families enjoy comparative prosperity. They very seldom have need to go ashore, for smaller boats, laden with various commodities, ply the harbour and satisfy the needs of their floating customers.

Even the livestock carried in a sampan—or junk too for that matter—readily become adjusted to an unstable and restricted mode of life. Fowls, when free, congregate on the transom or roost together in groups wherever opportunity offers, but as a general rule they are herded together in a miserable improvised coop which consists of a box with a sloping roof and a small hole to enable the incarcerated fowl to put out its head and long for freedom. The coop is hung over the stern. The ducks are freer in that they are usually tethered by a long string to one leg and so permitted a good deal of cruising about in home waters. Cats and dogs and even pigs all make themselves completely at home and show marked sagacity in avoiding disaster.

Altogether, community life in a sampan is very sociable and demonstrates a form of communism as practical as the seamanship. All the family, including the furred and feathered members, live amicably together, satisfied with the very barest necessities. The women in particular are an object lesson in contentment with their lot.

More complex and variable conditions obtain at Kiukiang, although here, too, the longshoremen may be divided into two classes and are careful never to stray into each other's business preserves. One type carries the cargo on a bamboo carrying-pole in the normal way; the other is known as the *ch'ien-fu* (縴 夫), or "junk worker," and carries his load on his shoulders. Here this class of coolie is always used for carrying rice and for unloading the delicate porcelain cargoes from the potteries of Kingtehchen. Both types are engaged by contractors, usually on a piece-work basis, and these sharks pocket about half of the coolies' daily earnings by way of commission. Sometimes the contractor farms his job out to a sub-contractor, who also requires his share of commission and moreover acts as the private detective of the organization, keeping watch lest one class should trespass on the other's beat.

The stowage of cargo in foreign ships has been the subject for much skilled attention and many books, and has developed into an exact science. The junkmen, however, have no publications, such as "Stevens: on Stowage," to guide them and use no art in the arrangement of cargo, which very often is merely dumped into the open holds of the junks regardless of all considerations. Nevertheless, their skill and ingenuity in the stowing of difficult cargoes, such as bamboo arm-chairs, porcelain, straw, pigs, wood, and so forth, is amazing.

At one time it was usual for the junks to advertise the cargoes they had on board by hoisting a small portion of the commodity at the masthead, such as a bundle of firewood, a rice measure, a fish basket, or a bundle of reeds. This picturesque custom is now seldom seen on the river, although it is still common on the coast.

The sailing-ship sailor of the West is apt to idealize his ship, be she Clipper or Bawley. To him she has nobility, grace, and strength, and not even the most unimaginative would deny her the possession of a special personality or soul. The junkman, however, prosaic and practical, is proud of his craft to a certain extent, but from first to last she is pre-eminently a conveyance to afford him shelter of a sort and the means whereby he can buy food to sustain life in his tough and leathery body.

BELIEFS AND SUPERSTITIONS OF THE JUNKMEN

THE old pilots and junkmen, although they may well rely on their own consummate skill and judgement in negotiating the rapids and other dangers which play so large a part in their daily life, yet feel the need for some supernatural assistance to give them moral support.

They are more ethically than religiously inclined and are practically devoid of what, in the west, would be considered the quality of reverence towards their gods and their temples. Nevertheless a very lively superstition remains, and few would be superior to the commonly accepted methods of placating the supernatural being who may or may not be responsible for or able to relieve disaster—"it can do no harm, and it may do some good."

The junkmen believe themselves to be surrounded by a multitude of spirits, powerful for evil but subject to bribes, flattery, and cajolery and capable of being cheated. On days set apart for the purpose they will worship the fox, snake, rat, and countless others, all of which are addressed as Excellencies.

Although Kuan Yin, the Best Beloved, is the supreme and favourite patroness of those who go down to the sea in ships and has to a certain extent supplanted all other maritime goddesses in popular favour, there are certain local deities, notably Chen Chiang Wang Yeh, the River Guardian King. Actually, his profession was that of a pirate in the twelfth century, with a stronghold in the Tungting Lake. So secure did he feel in his fortress that he arrogantly announced that the Government forces could not "capture the place unless they could fly and come from the air." However, without recourse to this modern form of warfare, he was finally defeated by General Yo Fei and in his despair cast himself into the lake, there to join many others of China's mythical personages. Nearly every junk has a model of him. The figure is often handed down from father to son and may serve in several junks.

Any description of tools, carpentry, or boatbuilding would be incomplete without a reference to Lu Pan (魯班), the carpenter god. Opinions vary as to when he lived, some placing it as far back as 506 B.C. and others some hundreds of years later. There is a similar disagreement as to whether he lived in Shantung, Kansu, or Kiangsu. It seems probable there were two or more master carpenters. Now, regardless of his origin or whether he be one or two personalities, he, or a composite deity of his name, is revered by all the guilds of the carpenters. He had a wife and a concubine, and images of these two, the one red and the other black, are objects of veneration to the varnishers.

Twice a year, on the 13th of the 5th moon and the 21st of the 7th moon, the guild members meet at a temple dedicated to Lu Pan.* On the latter date they celebrate Lu Pan's birthday and make food offerings on a plate with nine compartments.

Besides being the cleverest man of his generation, he was credited with founding the art of carpentry and inventing oars, paddles, and many improved types of boats. In this connection there is an interesting association in his name Lu (魯) with the word *lu* (櫓), to scull.

* The temple dedicated to Lu Pan in Shanghai is situated in the Hsiao P'i Lung (硝皮弄).

He is also said to have designed various mechanical tools, including the wooden irrigation pumps still used by the Chinese farmers. He also made a "self-moving chariot" or automatic wheelbarrow for his aged mother-in-law.

It was said that his skill was so great that he never wasted any wood, and could cut or saw a plank without the help of a guiding line. Many are the stories of his exploits. It is believed by the junkmen that when the pillars upholding the sky were in danger of collapse, Lu Pan successfully repaired them.

Under the reign of the Ming Emperor, Yung Lo, he was given the title of Grand Supporter of the Empire and became the patron saint of all artisans.

One of his most notable inventions was a ladder which reached the sky and raised and lowered itself as required when he attacked his enemies from the air. He also carved magpies out of wood with such skill that they flew into the air and remained away, some say for several days and others for three years. Unfortunately, as this flight was not authenticated by the Aero Club of that day it must be regarded as strictly unofficial.

Nor was this his only venture in aeronautics, for the carpenter god invented a wooden machine into which his father climbed, and on his knocking three times on the door, it rose into the air and transported him to a place near Soochow, whereupon the men of Wu (吳), taking the visitant to be a devil, killed him.

The indignant Lu Pan avenged his father's death by carving a wooden effigy of one of the immortals and placing it to the south of the town of Soochow. The image was represented as shaking an angry fist towards the south-east, and this produced a three-years' drought which only ceased when the proper apologies were sent to Lu Pan. Placated, the great artisan cut off the statue's hand and rain immediately fell.

There are other legends showing how air-minded was this ingenious deity. It is told that at the age of 40 he journeyed alone to the sacred mountain of Li(歷山), near Tsinan, and there acquired various marvellous secrets, including the power to travel on a cloud. His final end was dramatically in keeping, for he was transported to heaven in broad daylight, presumably to live in retirement from his profession, for he left his axe and saw behind him.

Lu Pan, in the character of the junk builders' patron, is particularly popular in Szechwan, where his aid is invoked over the building of junks. The shrine to these gods is invariably to be found on the port side, for the left is the place of honour in China.

Although technically speaking the Chinese, or at any rate the Taoists, believe, or did originally, in some form of supreme god, yet in effect their religion consists of an enormous pantheon of gods. There are gods good and bad, powerful and weak, grave and gay, handsome and ugly, kindly and cruel. Many of these are sages, statesmen, and soldiers deified for some real or imagined service. From the following list it will be seen that there is a god to control nearly every department of Chinese life.

These gods all have their duly recognized functions and their own supporters and they enjoy a most complicated order of precedence among themselves. For the benefit of the mystically minded, among the most important are the gods of:

Fire-crackers, basket-makers, liver complaint, teeth, monkeys' lice, rain-clothes, skin, brush-makers, painters, hasteners of childbirth, shadows, frogs, beds, fishermen, incense merchants, smallpox marks, paper, cars, hearts, architecture, cruelty, candles, stomach-ache, strolling singers, midwives, centipedes, merchants, brigands, gamblers, manure, stones, fornication, corners, liver, clothing, perfumes,

Carpenter God.

Kitchen God.

measles, revenge, brothels, wig-makers, spectacle makers, cobblers, hands, luck, archery, literature, war, soil and crops, agriculture, cities, kitchens, silkworms, grasshoppers, goats, wine, barbers, tailors, jugglers, gold, tea, fortune tellers, dyers, butchers, furnishers, chemists, varnishers, pigs, theatres, horses, wind, locusts, compasses, bridges, snow, light, light of the eye, masons, carpenters, caves, flowers, tides, frost, cows, scorpions, dogs, longevity, serpents, wells, salt, sheep, happiness, wealth, doors, and many others. From the above, which makes no claim to being in any way complete, it would seem that there is considerable overcrowding in the Chinese celestial world.

Some gods have an additional eye in the forehead. This represents the faculty of seeing more than any other person or god, for the additional eye enables him to observe not only the innermost depth of the soul but the past, present, and future.

There is also a vast collection of supernatural creatures, beneficial or otherwise, such as devils, demons, dragons, fairies, and spirits of the air, sea, mountain, river, and earth. Each has a symbolic meaning to the initiated. For instance, the fish is a symbol of wealth, its sphere is regarded as the emblem of harmony. The phoenix stands for elegance and benevolence; it never harms herbs or insects, but lives in the highest regions of the air and only returns to earth when required to bring good news. The carp is the emblem of longevity; the parrot warns women to be faithful to their husbands; the stag is important as representing official honours and happiness, while the crane is celebrated throughout China for living hundreds of years, hence it has also been chosen as the emblem of longevity and endowed with many wonderful attributes. It always accompanies the Eight Immortals and serves them as transport whenever they wish to fly through the air. Ducks and geese typify conjugal happiness; quails are valued because of their fierceness in fighting; and the crow is the foreteller of evil.

One of the gods who has a special appeal to the junkmen of the Upper Yangtze is Lung Wang, the Dragon King, chief of the gods of water and rain,* ruler of the Universe, and moving spirit of the storms. Actually there are eight of these water spirits or dragons who give rain. Some authorities suggest that the dragons derive from the crocodile; whether this was so or not, it seems probable they were borrowed from Indian Buddhism where they were represented as Nagas, or Serpent Demons, but in China the dragon, being the symbol of rain and water, is a benevolent spirit of immense importance to the junkmen.

Usually only three of these mythological beings are considered. They are said to inhabit fabulously rich palaces under the sea or below lakes. The White Dragon, Peh-lung shen-miao, who lived five miles north-west of Soochow, was said to have had a miraculous birth, his mother being a young girl who thereby fell into disgrace. This gave rise to his popular name of the Bastard Dragon. Once a year this filial-minded monster visits his mother's tomb on his birthday, the 18th day of the 3rd moon, and for ten days before this the weather is said to be bleak and wet, although it always clears up for the event.

Then there are Chiang Lao Hsiang Kung who, with red face and black beard, stands with his retinue, ready like Charon to cross the Stygian waters that divide this world from the next; Chiang T'ai Kung, who, in remembrance of his early life as a poor fisherman, is now said to protect all who follow the same calling; and Hsiao Kung, the Kiangsi deity, who started life as a humble junkman during the Sung Dynasty A.D. 960–1280, and grew rich through his care and efficiency.

One of the most popular Chinese deities is Kwan Yin. Originally a Bodhisattva, he was worshipped in India and by his many deeds of mercy represented the personification of divine compassion. He was later, about the twelfth century, transformed into the female deity now known as Kuan Yin, a change which probably owes its origin to some deep-rooted desire for and reliance on maternal sympathy. The name of Kuan Yin, generally known in English as the Goddess of Mercy, literally means "Regard sound," and can be variously translated as "Helpful of prayer," or "She who hears the cries of men." While all other Chinese gods are feared and propitiated, she alone is loved, and is appealed to pity and save her worshippers, and is particularly the patron of the junkmen of the craft of the Lower Yangtze. It is curious that the Upper Yangtze junkmen do not specially venerate this gentle compassionate deity but have selected that rollicking old filibuster, Chen Chiang Wang Yeh.

Another feminine deity in high favour with the junkmen is Tien fei, the Queen, or as it may be translated, Concubine of Heaven, who acts as a protector from danger to the junkmen and blesses them with children. The curious title of Concubine of Heaven owes its origin to the following rather involved reasoning. As on earth the Emperor is lord of all, so in the celestial empire, heaven ranks first. Next to the Emperor comes the Empress, represented in the celestial sphere as the spirit of earth. Third in rank of honour are the feminine spirits of the waters, and these find their worldly analogy in the Royal Concubines.

* Once there was a serious drought at Chungking. Lung Wang had repeatedly refused to answer prayers and to send rain for the parched city. The Viceroy ordered him to be taken out and seated in the courtyard in the broiling sun. The god of rain sat there in complete silence. He never moved. He was wrapped in serious thought. No further argument was necessary, Lung Wang was convinced that the city was too dry and, we are told, heavy rain fell that night. Another method of obtaining rain is sometimes used. Believing that dragons are cousins of tadpoles, hundreds of the latter are put in a basin and placed in the sun. The rain-controlling dragons are thus given the alternative of giving rain or seeing their cousins die in the basin from the strong sun.

Tien fei is therefore a spirit of the waters. As in so many Chinese myths, there are varying versions of her earthly origin, but she is always said to have been a maiden of the name of Lin. In one version she is said to have been one of the three daughters of a Taoist priest named Lin Ling Sou of Chekiang who were all famous for their extravagances at the court of the Sung Emperor in the twelfth century.

In two cases she is said to have been a native of Fukien. One story says she was the daughter of a small mandarin named Lin Yuen, at P'ou-t'ien, about 960 A.D., while the other says she was born on a small island near the Fukien coast, being miraculously conceived after 14 months from a flower bestowed by Kuan Yin. This legend places her date at about 742 A.D. during the T'ang Dynasty. Precociously gifted and psychic, she fell into a trance one day. Her frightened parents aroused her, whereupon she complained at being checked in her efforts to aid her four sailor brothers. Three days later three of them returned home with the account of a frightful storm in which they had been helped by the appearance of a young girl who had taken over control and saved them and their three craft. The elder brother had, however, been drowned. Her parents then realized their daughter had supernatural powers, and they bitterly regretted recalling her from her trance before she could save her elder brother. She died young but her spirit continued to help the sailors.

During the Sung Dynasty, about 1119 A.D., an official named Lou yun ti, when returning from Korea, lost seven of his ships. His ship alone was saved thanks to Tien fei who, perched high on the mast, conned the junk to safety.

She was accordingly honoured with posthumous titles, a pagoda was raised to her memory on the island of Mei tcheou, and bullocks were sacrificed to her. She was termed spirit, and towards the end of the twelfth century received her present title.

Another favourite deity, though less well known, is Ngan-Kong, who calms the waves. He, too, is variously ascribed to either a period before the Three Kingdoms, or as late as the twelfth century. He is generally believed to have lived in Kiangsi and is credited with having performed miracles in connection with rivers and lakes.

The favourite legend is one which tells how, in the guise of an old fisherman, he vanquished a monster called the dragon pig which, by digging with its four feet beneath the waters, was undermining the bank of the Yangtze to a dangerous degree. Ngan-Kong prepared a bait of cooked pork suspended in a huge and bottomless earthen *kong*. When the monster ate the bait, the *kong* fell into the water and engulfed its head and neck and the fisherman then hauled it bodily out of the river. The story is unconfirmed and legend is silent as to how he disposed of his catch which must have furnished him with a supreme example of the fisherman's story.

For this very fine effort Ngan was honoured by the Emperor who following his own obscure line of reasoning made him Director, not of Conservancy or Natural History, but of Literature. He finally perished in a shipwreck while on his return to his home in Kiangsi. The peasants there saw him moving about his home premises dressed as usual. When they heard of his death they were convinced of his supernatural powers and this opinion was confirmed a month later when his coffin was brought home and, upon being opened, was found to be empty. He had become an immortal.

Money talks in China and so in many junks there is almost daily worship of the god of wealth. He was a great general who lived during the Shang period, 1766–1122 B.C., and was killed in action according to legend, in defence of the Emperor.

As a reward for this service he obtained the very desirable appointment as the god of wealth in the Celestial Empire despite the fact that he was not a financial expert.

Another very important personage in the spirit world is the kitchen god. One of these gods is stationed in each household as a supervisor to watch the affairs and general conduct of the members of the family to which he has been appointed. On every 23rd day of the 12th moon there is a mass flight of kitchen gods leaving for the Heavenly Empire to submit their reports. A bad report, of course, results in the Celestial Emperor's wrath and the imposition of bad omens to the particular family.

Kitchen gods are by nature talkative individuals and so in order to keep their wagging tongues from telling too much the worshippers buy a number of sticky sweetmeats which are served to the departing god. For their comfort during the ascent in the chilly weather, the families prepare various means of transport. The ancient sedan-chair and junk are still the most popular, but the modern prefer streamlined limousines and four-motored airliners. All are made of paper pasted on reed frames. These models, together with paper money and pictures of the god, are burnt by the family concerned and thus the god reaches the stratosphere. He is back again on duty by the last day of the year. During his few days of absence his wife does duty for him.

The Chinese do not commune with their deity as is done in the West. Their idea seems to be one of complete reciprocity. The petitioner does something that he hopes will please the god and the god in his turn is expected to do something which will please the petitioner.

The cautious junkman makes doubly sure of a propitious start of a voyage by a visit to a temple where advice can be obtained as regards any other important events such as a marriage, funeral, business deal, or a case of sickness.

At the season of the New Year especially, the junkman endeavours to make all comfortable with the gods. Those who have a vague dread that they will be overtaken by calamity for their misdeeds, make for their special temple to propitiate the gods by doing their worship in bulk at the end of the year.

Gods are notoriously inattentive and so in order to attract their attention to the petition offered, the priest, on behalf of the worshipper, sounds a bell, or beats a gong or drum made of wood or iron. If the god happens to be more than usually inattentive it may be necessary to use fire-crackers in addition.

A particularly pressing petition is usually accompanied by an offering of meat or other savory dishes. This is placed on the altar and subsequently taken home and eaten by the worshipper.

After the worshipper has lighted his candle and incense, the usual procedure takes the form of a type of casting lots. The petitioner selects a bamboo tally strip from a bamboo cylinder of many such, all numbered, and lays it aside. He then takes two concave pieces of wood polished by much handling. These he fits together so that they form a facsimile of a cow's hoof and after bowing before the altar, he throws them on the ground. If they fall with convex or both concave sides uppermost this is considered unlucky, but one convex and one concave is a good omen. The priest then interprets his numbered bamboo slip in conjunction with his lot casting and gives him a printed slip to correspond with his number drawn. This always bears a very ambiguous verse which requires the priest's skilled interpretation as applied to the matter in hand. He takes this to be an answer from the god and goes away happy or sad as the case may be.

The material from which an idol is made is not very important and covers a wide range from paper to gold. Wood and clay are perhaps the most common. The size is also immaterial. The one thing that matters is whether the spirit of the god has been introduced into the idol. This is done by painting the pupils of the eyes and inserting a living creature through the trap door in the middle of the back of the idol. This, in the larger idols, can be a bird, rat, or snake and in the case of the smaller idols, a fly or other insect.

From the earliest times the launching of a vessel has always been the occasion of considerable ceremony to the accompaniment of feasting and music. The ships of the ancients were often adorned with flowers as a happy omen for future prosperity. Neptune, Minerva, and other gods were appealed to by the Romans with prayers and appropriate sacrifices.

Similarly, on the Upper Yangtze once the junk is completed the ceremony of killing the cock takes place over the bow of the junk. A small, temporary altar is made of anchor chain on which stand cups of wine and joss sticks. Taking a live cock in his hands the junkmaster, or the carpenter who built the junk, performs the kowtow in the direction of the bow and to each side, and pours the wine on the deck as a libation. The cock's throat is then cut, and its blood is sprinkled on the bow. Blood is also daubed on each side of the front of the house and wherever deemed auspicious, and a feather or two is dipped in the blood and left adhering to the woodwork.

The bow where the ceremony takes place is regarded by the old junkmen as sacred to their peculiar chosen guardian deity. It would be a grave insult to sit down on the place where his incense sticks are burned, and profanatory even to walk ashore over the bow. This belief is dying out, though sticklers still continue to place their landing planks slightly to one side or the other.

A picturesque ancient custom is faithfully observed in Kwanhsien at the season of the New Year. This is, of course, the most important of all the festivals of China. The celebrations begin on the 23rd day of the 12th moon, when the kitchen god, after a year's hard work in the world, is given a royal send-off before he departs for heaven to make his annual report on the behaviour of the family during the year that is drawing to a close. The housewives give their homes a thorough cleanup, and all members of the family go to the bath houses and barbers' shops—where they pay double rates according to a time-honoured tradition—for the occasion demands that they make themselves entirely new and as presentable as possible. In addition the children, dressed in their best clothes, *k'o-t'ou* (literally, to knock the head) to their parents, the sons prostrating themselves three times with forehead touching the ground and giving thanks for wise counsel and training.

After the return of the kitchen god, it is time to welcome the god of wealth on the night of the 4th day. Being a Taoist god, he is not a vegetarian, and accordingly large slabs of pork figure prominently on the menu. This is a good night for enterprising beggars, who make house to house calls with a plate on which is an image of the god of wealth. They usually reap a rich harvest, as no one is prepared to incur the anger of this important god.

Not to be outdone, the god of Hell throws open the heavy gates of the inferno to give the spirits, good ones or evil ones, a holiday in this world, so that they may be able to visit their loved ones during the night and take part in the "spirit-pleasing" ceremonies.

On the 5th day the outdoor celebrations begin. Heralded by the inevitable band, privately organized troups of actors parade down the main street, followed by portable coloured cloth or paper arches carried by bearers in gay costumes.

High above the closely packed spectators who fill the street on either side of the clear central lane, are stilt walkers, fantastic figures, dipping and swaying grotesquely on their stilts, their bright brocades fluttering with each lunging step. From time to time these stilt walkers, of whom there are perhaps a dozen, stop at a street corner and perform a bizarre dance, stalking and circling round like vast and gaudy cranes, their strange headdresses bobbing, their arms flapping like wings to preserve their balance after each curtseying stride. The Chinese, perhaps, rank as the best stilt walkers in the world. Stilts, it is said, were invented as early as the days of the Emperor Shun, 2317 to 2208 B.C. Interspersed in the procession are companies of soldiers combining the double function of keeping order, if necessary, and of adding to the demonstration, which they often do by flying a small pennant from the muzzle of each slung rifle. A pair of fabulous green lions can often be seen; their paper bodies, each supported by two men, executing an absurd and pleasing dance, the strips of paper that form their ribs flickering and shivering in time to the bowing heads and lashing tails.

A rising volume of approbation from the crowd announces the approach of the ever popular dragon. First comes a man carrying a stick surmounted by a paper ball, then a man with a four-foot pole bearing the vast dragon's head, ingeniously fashioned out of paper, flat-topped, with horns and slanted ears, its huge gaping jaws fringed with fangs, displaying a curling red tongue. From this head a long looped cloth body is supported at each small barrel-shaped vertebra by a short pole wielded by a man, the last of whom carries the paper tail. Undulating and rocking high above the crowd, the monster proceeds slowly forward, until at a signal it is galvanized into an absolute frenzy of activity. Uttering wild cries and with the leader carrying the head to set the pace, the men supporting the dragon's body carry out the most intricate evolutions at an incredible speed. Winding and unwinding its enormous folds in ever higher and wilder circles, it whirls and spins in dizzy coils. Lower bows the terrifying head, higher cocks the tail, and a perfect fusillade of crackers marks the climax, leaving the air thick with smoke and the pungent smell of black powder. Temporarily exhausted, the dragon lapses into its stately rolling gait and passes slowly on.

A great feature of the procession is, of course, the paper boats. These make their appearance regularly twice a year: at the New Year and the Dragon Boat Festival. They are usually paid for by the junk guilds. War junks of a bygone age, for the protection of the city god, are by far the most popular. Sometimes these are quite large craft, all made of paper cunningly contrived round a bamboo framework. Paper shields line the gunwale and serve to hide the bearers below decks carrying the boat. The paper crews and even the muzzle-loading guns sway to the rhythm of the bearers and are not calculated to strike terror into the hearts of the enemy, but with the unfurled banners of coloured paper make a fine sight. The banners bear quite unbellicose sentiments, in gold lettering on a red ground, such as "The sea will not raise its waves"; "Grace flows over the kingdom of the sea"; "Protect within the four seas"; "Everlasting thanks for peaceful seas"; "The river is clear and the sea peaceful"; and many others.

The fleet makes majestic slow progress, the ships being given a not very realistic roll by the concealed bearers inside the hull, amid wild applause from the spectators. The boats are lighted up at night, and there is even more excitement when, due to a heavy roll or a burst of flying crackers, a boat catches fire, and the bearers have to abandon ship in great haste. This is regarded as great fun, especially when factional fights break out and give colour to the hostilities.

The "battle fleet," amid spluttering crackers and blue smoke, is followed by other craft; the Red Boats being, of course, well in evidence, while sampans and ferry boats, too, are featured in the procession.

In and out and round about dart other particularly interesting paper boats, usually operated by the children of the junkmen, each walking inside; these often take the form of sampans with turned-up bow and stern, on a wooden frame attached to braces over the wearers' shoulders. All but the bearers' feet and calves are hidden by the superstructure. These boats seem to be designed to catch fire, as they frequently do. Most of the celebrations take place after dark and, as the light begins to fail, the crowd becomes impatient and decides to seek points of vantage from which to view the lantern procession proper, which is always a part of the proceedings. The scene is soon dramatically outlined in coloured lights against the velvety darkness of the night sky; while across the river looms the inkier shadow of the ancient city wall, which dominates the town and surroundings.

Nodding and flickering to the throb of drums and the clash of cymbals, lighted lanterns are borne by countless small children, who pass by on silent cloth-soled feet, the only other sound being their subdued chatter and the rustle of their clothing, until the leaders call upon them for a song or slogan eulogizing the local officials, which is picked up and repeated in unison by different sections.

Youths and girls of all ages and sizes, each bearing a paper lantern, perhaps two or three, suspended on a small wand, file past in endless pairs, until the eye grows tired of travelling from face to face and from lantern to lantern in such rich and bewildering variety—red, green, or golden circles, stars, squares, diamonds, with Chinese characters written across their illuminated surfaces. Other lanterns, fashioned with crazy ingenuity, make their appearance in the shape of fans, clocks, baskets, vases or pots of flowers, aeroplanes, or cleverly joined fish with realistically waving tails, lucky bats, dragonflies with flapping wings, and birds with swaying heads in great profusion. After them prances a man, with set, staring eyes, who appears to be riding a lighted horse, for tied to him in two sections is the paper body of a horse with candles inside. A touch bearer lights up the next rider, a girl, her face expressionless under the high coroneted headdress. Her red satin-trousered legs paddle along quaintly below the swelling sides of the paper horse, already charred by the candle within. These lanterns make this the most picturesque part of the procession. It would be difficult to estimate how many take part in these gigantic festivities; but there are often ten or more bands, and the whole procession takes probably three hours to pass.

Preceded by torch bearers, interesting little plays are often enacted, partly in dumb show, partly in speech, dance and song, by strolling bands of actors. A man comically attired as a fisherman makes great play with his fishing net, as he dances intricate steps around the cleared space where two men lie on the ground, obviously impersonating fish and twitching their hands and feet like fins and tails. Another man dressed as a woman and enclosed within a large paper shell steps warily around with mincing gait just out of range of the fisherman; and, when one of the characters approaches too close, he sharply claps the sides of the shell together, imprisoning the intruder's hand, amidst the laughter of the onlookers. The fisherman finally casts his net over the "oyster," and the end of the little drama is indicated by the supers extinguishing their lights, while one throws up into the air a sort of silent bomb, which bursts into small particles and descends as a blazing red cloud. One may hazard a guess that it portrays some legend of a celestial fisherman securing pearls for the dragon's eternal game of ball. That is the end, as only the rabble brings up the rear.

The serpentine line of dipping and glancing lights winds its way through the narrow cobbled streets into the heart of the town. The beat of the drums and gongs grows less, until it becomes a very shadow of sound, and the shrill cries die away in the distance. The spectators, spellbound until now, stir, yawn, expectorate noisily, and shuffle off home.

Born within sound of the river, trained from boyhood in a junk, the junkmen live their lives in peril and uncertainty. For hundreds of years the junkmen and trackers of the Upper Yangtze have accepted suffering and adversity as just another fact of life, and although they are illiterate, overworked, and often hungry, they are not resentful of their hard lot. When a junkman dies, a letter announcing his departure to those realms where all good junkmen go is written to the King of Hades, in his famous temple at Fêngtu, the "Abundant Capital."

In the temple the skeleton of Pluto's bride, whom he is said to have abducted on her wedding day, is to be seen sitting beside him in her robes of state. Here, for the modest sum of $1, a passport to Heaven may be obtained. It consists of a large and impressive sheet of thin paper covered with characters. It is signed by the Chief Priest and the local Governor, and bears the seal of the King of Hades and the imprint of the seven stars of the Great Bear Constellation. This document has become an Upper Yangtze classic, and as such may herein be properly included:

A PASS FOR THE ROAD TO HADES FROM THE GREAT GOD
T'IEN-TZŬ (天 子), FENGTU MOUNTAIN.

The Great King of Hades is hereby respectfully requested by . . . ,* a believer in Buddha, favoured by the Great Sage of the Middle Heaven in charge of the Stars of the Northern Section, to issue a Pass.

When the Buddha was preaching with the monks in the Kudo Garden of She Wei Kingdom, the Heaven Folks attended and noticed that some of the men and women in the world died young and some lived long though they had not acted charitably nor considered the difficulty of being a human being in the Central Earth. Should they have disregarded the proper doctrine, they will be led astray and will discard the talents of "king and ministers," "parents and children," "husbands and wives," and will neglect the virtues of filial piety, respect to superiors, loyalty, faith, politeness, honesty, and shame. They will also become immoral. The result will be that their sins exceed their blessings, and when they come to the City of Hades they will have to be dealt with according to law by passing through 24 hells and the bankless sea of sin, and their spirits will be endlessly wandering in the roads of Hades and can never escape. But by the kindness of our Buddha this Pass is issued to help all souls to escape from hell. All men and women must clasp their hands and repeat 40,000 times "Hear us, O Buddha!" and with this Pass they will be protected by all other Gods and will finally arrive at the "Kingdom of Happiness." Any stations, etc., *en route*, after examination of this Pass, are to let the bearer pass without hindrance. Should any hindrance be met with, the God of Wei To will immediately despatch soldiers to bring the offenders to Fengtu so that action may be taken.

Hear us, O Buddha!

More about the Pass for Hades will be found in Part Four, page 522.

This certainly contains good news for sinners, and seemingly there have been no complaints from those who found the visa insufficient.

The letter is sent through the Celestial post by being burnt. In addition, food, imitation houses, paper furniture, boots, clothes, also paper boats for crossing the canals and lakes, together with land transport in the shape of horses and sedan chairs, are set alight. Even the half-consumed incense sticks are thrown into the flames. These serve as carrying poles for the spirits, who, after eating their fill, are thus able to take away with them what food is left.

* Name of applicant to be inserted here, together with his address and the time and date of birth.

RICE, FISH, AND SALT

CHINA probably leads the world in total agricultural production, and, although a considerable variety of crops are grown, rice remains the staple food of most of China's millions.*

The cultivation of rice must extend back into the very dim past, and its importance was fully recognized in the early capitals, for a royal ceremonial was said to have been inaugurated in the Chou dynasty (周 朝), 1122–255 B.C., in commemoration of the second of the Five Great Rulers, the Emperor Shên Nung Shih (神 農 氏), or the "Divine Husbandman," who is credited with having introduced the art of agriculture. At this annual ceremony the Emperor himself sowed the rice, whereas the four other important grains—millet, wheat, barley, and beans—were sown by the Princes of his family.

Rice will mature as far north as Vladivostock, but is little grown by the northerners, who subsist mostly on wheat and kaoliang (高 粱), while depending largely on import for such rice as they can obtain.

Wherever there is easy access to irrigation water, rice is grown. The Yangtze River may be described as the natural dividing line between the North and the rice-growing areas of the South.

The chief areas of production in the Yangtze Valley are in the Anhwei-Kiangsu belt, where the town of Wuhu holds an important position not only for production but for distribution because, situated as it is on the Yangtze in a district intersected by a network of creeks and canals, it has become one of the greatest grain-exporting centres of China.

In point of quality as well as productivity, Changshu (常 熟), in Kiangsu Province, ranks first. This city lies 60 miles north-west of Shanghai and is surrounded by a large tract of suitable alluvial land. The population of about 862,000 is composed of 80 per cent of farmers, with a leaven of *literati.*

The Yangtze Valley itself, prolific as it is, yields in the main only one crop of rice a year. In the extreme south of China two or even three crops may be reaped annually.

Rice produces more food value per acre than any other plant. Where one annual crop of rice alone may be looked for, wheat is then planted after the rice harvest and cut before the next year's rice is planted out in early summer, thus producing the largest possible yield. In the real rice regions, however, the farmer achieves a maximum return by growing two crops of rice. This is done by inter-planting, that is to say, planting late rice between the rows of early rice, or by double-cropping or planting late rice after the early rice has been harvested.

As the main national diet, the importance of rice can hardly be over-estimated, and it is not surprising that it is graded according to its quality, the district in which it is produced, and the time of year it is reaped. To the Westerner all Far Eastern rice may seem to vary little, but to the rice-eating Chinese there is an infinity of subtle differences marking one variety from another. Even the Chinese, however, find it rather a complicated matter to classify *tao* (稻), or rice plants. The farmers give different names to the plants according to their fancy,

* The technical information in this section is based largely on a voluminous semi-Government publication compiled under the auspices of the Shanghai Commercial and Savings Bank, Shanghai, and painstakingly translated for me by Mr. Whong Tze-yue. (Mr. Worcester's Chinese secretary).

but, generally speaking, *tao* may be divided into two main classes, the *no-mi* (糯米), or glutinous rice, and the *kêng-mi* (粳米), or non-glutinous rice. Glutinous rice is used for the making of cakes and wine. The non-glutinous, or "ordinary," rice is used for cooking and differs only in quality. It is again subdivided into two categories, *kêng* (粳), or *shui-mi* (水米), meaning water-rice; and *hsien*, or *han-mi* (秈或旱米), meaning upland rice. The best "ordinary" white rice comes from Changshu (常熟), already referred to, and the best *hsien* rice from Liyang (溧陽), Kunshan (崑山), Sungkiang (松江), and Ihing (宜興). There is, in addition, "foreign rice" of the ordinary upland class, known as *hsien-mi* (秈米), imported from Annam, Siam, and Rangoon.

In the "Rice Manual," published in 1931 by the Investigation Department of the Shanghai Commercial and Savings Bank, these types are classified under 100 different heads, together with an interesting description of the qualities which mark the superior rice. Each grain should be large, long, fat, of an even shining colour, and weighty, with a thin outer skin. It should, moreover, be dry enough to stand storage without deterioration. The taste should be sweet, and there should be no broken grains or rice powder.

An analysis of the food value shows that there is a difference of 1.65 in caloric content between the best and the worst types. The analysis goes on to show how, for better nourishment, the rice selected should have a high protein and fatty acid content and yield great heat, while the cellulose and ash content should be low. The interesting conclusion is reached that the coarse rice still in its outer husk is more nourishing than the finer white rice, as it contains a higher proportion of protein, vitamins, phosphorus, and iron.

Rice cultivation in the Shanghai area starts about April, when the seed is sown either in small beds or in boxes or tanks, which are perforated at the bottom. These are watered daily, and after about four weeks the sprouts appear. They are then pricked out into small plots and plentifully treated with liquid manure. Meanwhile the preparation of the rice fields has been progressing. These fields, which form the distinguishing feature of the Central and South China landscape, are of all sizes and shapes, for every square foot of land is utilized. The hillsides are patiently terraced, no small ledge or gradient being neglected.

The same simple, but effective, methods and implements for the cultivation of rice have been in use for centuries; but many authorities are of the opinion that the yield thereby obtained is insufficient and that human labour must in time be supplemented by the use of modern mechanism, though labour-saving devices are not popular with the farmers, particularly as their use must perforce introduce new problems of unemployment.

In anticipation of these innovations, therefore, and the consequent disappearance of the various age-old agricultural appliances still in use, scale plans of these are shown on the next two pages.

After being ploughed,* the fields are slightly flooded so as to soften the earth, and the harrow is used to break up the clods. The fields are then completely inundated and ploughed once more so as to ensure complete saturation.

When the rice plants have grown to about a foot in height, the women of the farmers' families settle down on low stools beside the nurseries to pull out the young seedlings. The soil is rinsed from the roots, and they are tied into bundles to facilitate transplanting into the fields now standing ready and flooded to receive them. The rice plants still continue to require attention, as they must be hoed, fertilized, and kept irrigated.

There are several ways of fertilizing. That most in favour in the Shanghai and Soochow districts is by means of the long ribbon-like aquatic grasses which

* The plough used is basically the same as that used all over the world. A plan of that used in the Shanghai area is shown on page 131.

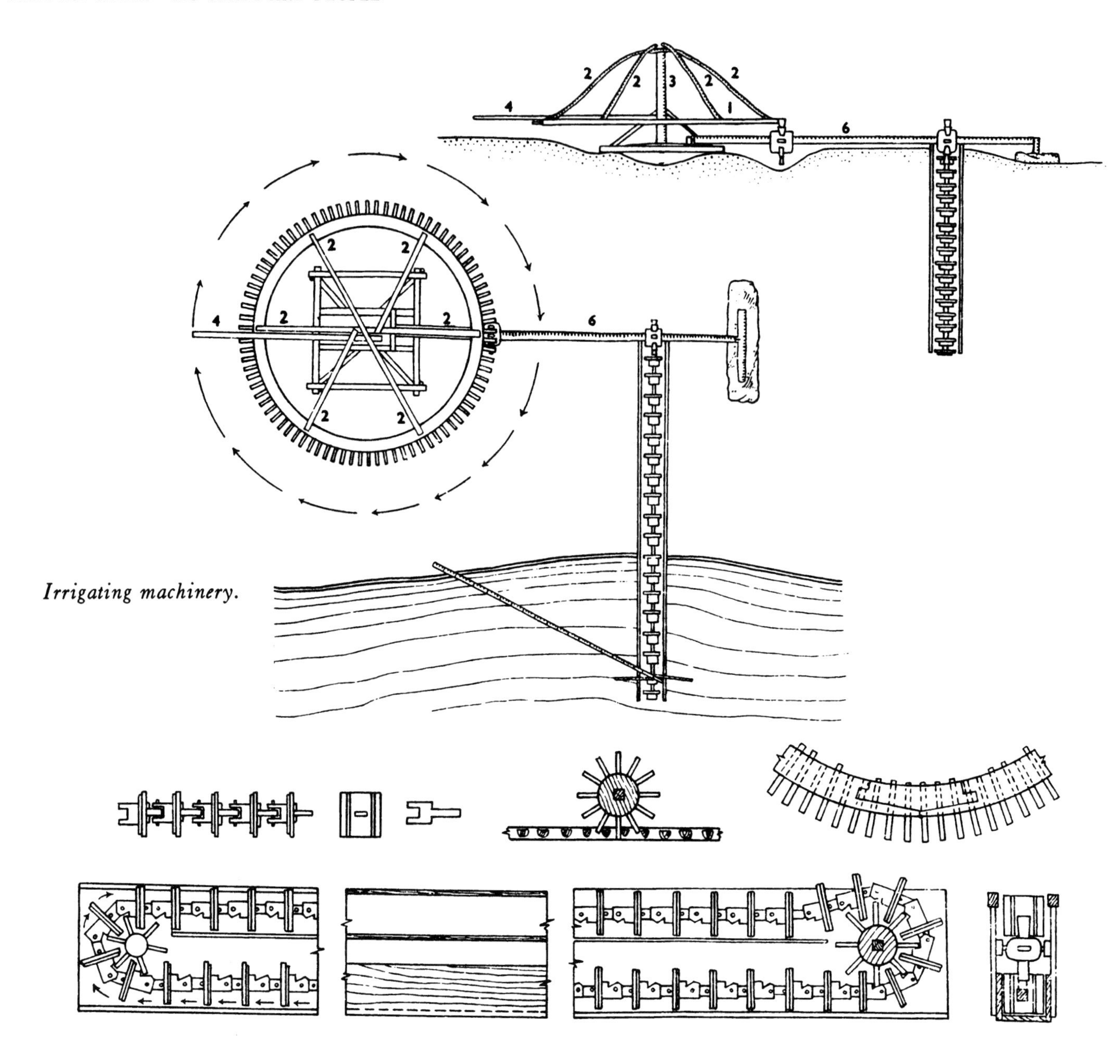

Irrigating machinery.

grow on the bottom of the canals and creeks. These are cut by men who work standing breast-deep in water and using a sickle (see Page No. 131, Fig. F) tied to the end of a 16-foot bamboo. This is pushed along the bottom and then drawn backwards, cutting across the stems of the grass, which rises to the surface, where it is gathered and stacked into small grass-boats similar to that illustrated in Plate No. 20. The grass is then worked into the moist mud of the rice fields.

In addition to these duties, there is the unending and enormous task of irrigation, to facilitate which all the fields have been levelled and the canals, ditches, and drains kept scoured and in good repair.

The irrigation gear consists of two parts, a large horizontal cog-wheel worked by a buffalo and an endless chain pump to raise the water.

The wooden cog-wheel is 7 feet in diameter and 3 inches thick. The component parts are scarfed at intervals as shown in the plate opposite, the teeth of the cogs serving also as pegs to strengthen the scarfing. There are 84 of these oval-shaped teeth in the wheel[1], which is slung from six bent hardwood spoke-spreaders[2] suspended from a central pivot-post[3], erected on a wooden framework bed with diagonal supports. Two of these spokes are in one continuous curved piece; the other four are joined at the apex.

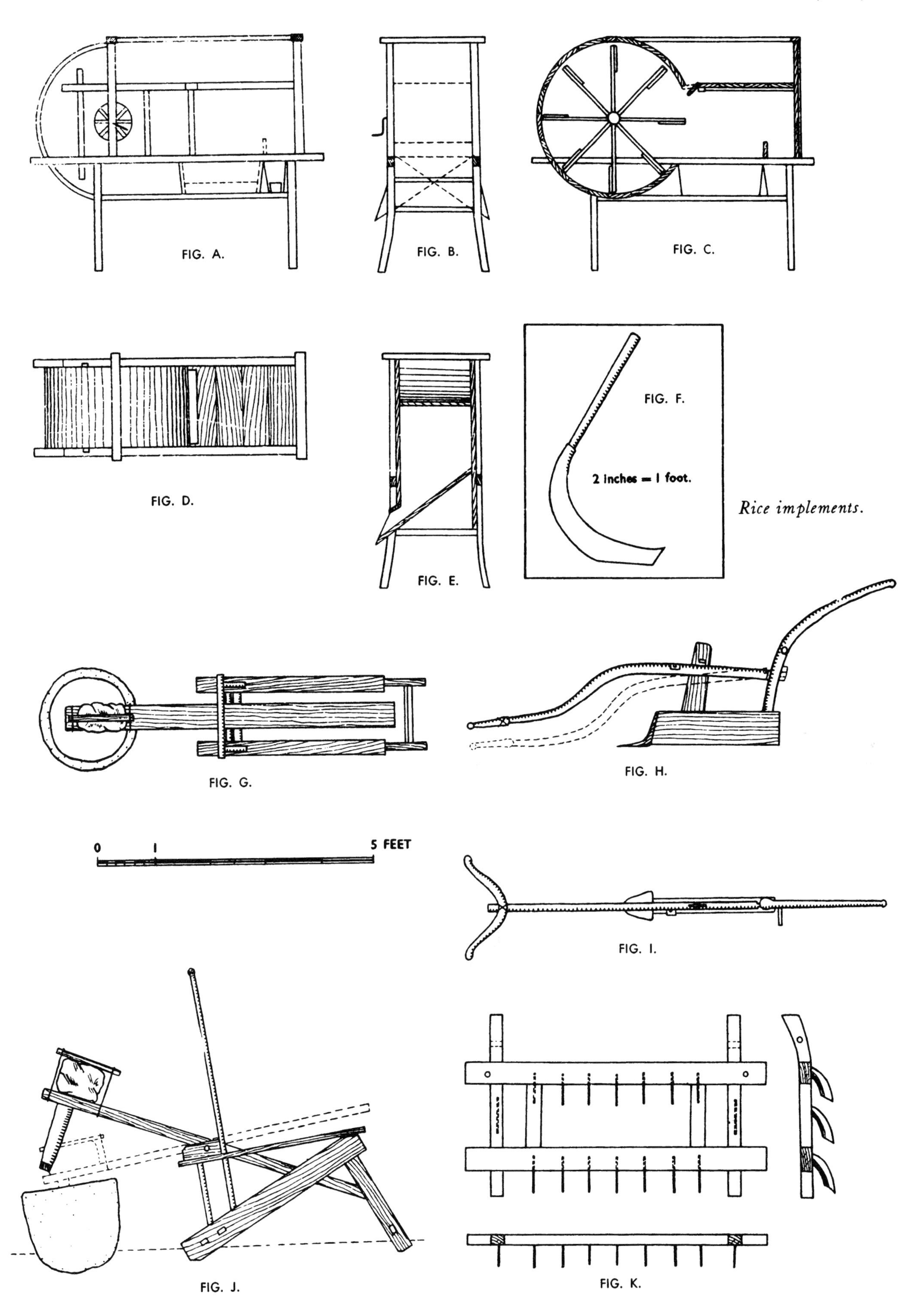

Rice implements.

A pole[4] is mortised into the central pivot-post and thence made fast to the wheel with rope. At the outer extremity of this pole the water-buffalo is harnessed by yoke and traces and, by walking round the beaten circle, turns the wheel.

Below the wheel on the framework bed[5] rests one end of a hardwood axle-beam[6], 10½ feet long, with a diameter of 4½ inches. The other end rests on a small upright projecting from a stone bed. A small vertical cog-wheel with 12 large teeth is shrunk on to this axle and in turn engages with the main horizontal cog-wheel. A similar small vertical cog-wheel is situated near the other extremity of the axle, and by these means an endless chain of wooden slats is worked in a trough.

The trough which forms the irrigation pump or elevator is a long three-sided box, 8 inches broad and 7½ inches deep, and varies in length according to requirements. One end connects with the second small cog-wheel on the axle-beam; the other end is placed at a gentle angle in the creek or irrigation canal, where it is secured by a bamboo driven into the mud bottom. Further support is provided by a spreader.

Through this trough revolves the endless chain of hardwood links carrying a series of loosely fitting *sha-mu* blades. These scoop the water into the lower portion of the trough and by pushing it before them finally discharge a fair percentage into the field above the creek-level.

One instance must be recorded of a progressively-minded farmer who introduced a motor pump into his village. The experiment, however, proved a failure in that no productive use could be made of the labour thereby saved, and the men usually employed on the irrigation troughs employed their months of idleness in gambling, with disastrous results.

The grain takes about 100 days to mature. When this stage is reached, the water is drained off and the land allowed to dry and harden. After cutting, which is done with a sickle,* the plants are laid out to dry, either on the banked edges of the paddy field or suspended, ears down, from bamboo posts. As with all harvests, a deluge at this stage can prove a calamity, and the successful amateur weather prophet has therefore an advantage over his less weather-wise brethren. After the rice is dried it is tied into sheaves and stacked with the heads inside. They are sometimes kept thus for several months, and marauding birds are kept away by a rather unusual form of scarecrow in the form of a sickle surmounted by a bunch of sesamum stalks.

The rice is threshed by drawing the heads through the teeth of a metal comb, after which the grain is hulled. The winnowing is carried out in different ways. One method is to toss the grain from great circular basket-sieves, but generally in the Shanghai district it is done by means of an ingenious box-device containing a hand-operated fan with eight blades. (See Page No. 131, Figs. **A-E.**)

The rice is fed into a hopper on the top of the winnowing-box and passes through a slot which can be regulated to suit the flow. The curve of the fan-casing gives a downward direction to the draught of air; and, as the rice comes into contact with it, the heavy grain falls into the sloping face and out through a chute into a basket on the ground outside the machine. The light chaff is blown farther along and alights against the end wall of the container, from which it, in like manner, falls down a chute and out into another basket.

While the rice is in the process of being husked, beggars are made very welcome and do not then beg in vain. For this good fortune they have to thank an old legend which describes how a beggar requested a farmer's son to give him the two loaves of bread he carried, undertaking in return that the boy's family

* Mr. P. L. Byrne, a Shanghai merchant, recounts the interesting fact that about 40 years ago there was an extensive market for worn-out horseshoes from England, which were imported into China for conversion into sickles. Horseshoes from Glasgow were in great request, for constant striking against the cobble stones further served to temper the iron.

would be rewarded for this charity by a plenitude of rice. As this promise was fulfilled, the farmers gamble on receiving similar results from a liberal outlay to importunate beggars.

The rice is next subjected to a treatment known as polishing, so as to remove any small scales of husk which may be clinging to it. There are various ways of achieving this result. In the delta area the usual procedure is to damp a quantity of rice and place it in a large mortar carved out of a rock (see Page No. 131, Figs. G and J). The pestle is in the form of a plunger with a heavy hardwood and iron-bound head, weighted with a stone and pivoted at its centre of gravity to a wooden framework. The operator stands with one foot on the trestle frame and the other on the haft of the hammer or plunger, which is thus automatically depressed to its full extent and then released. This drives the head deep into the rice kernels, forcing them to slide over each other until by continual abrasion they are worn smooth. There are the usual familiar handlebars provided for this, as for other treadle, or pedal, operators, upon which the elbows may be leaned for support (see Fig. J).

A very democratic system of land tenure obtains, which has become established by custom, whereby the peasant farmers become joint holders of the property with the landowners. It is popularly said that the landlords own the indestructible portion of the land, while the farmer rents the *fei-t'u* (肥 土), or fertility, including any such improvements as may be effected by development of the land. The whole of the winter crops are the tenants' sole property. One rice crop is raised annually in the Yangtze Valley, and rent in the form of 40 per cent of this yield is paid yearly to the landlord, who, if he can, usually stores it until a rise in market prices guarantees a good profit. If he has no storage room, he sends the rice by junk to be sold in the nearest town.

Every summer the landlord is invited to inspect the rice crops and arrange with the tenant the rent payable, which naturally varies with the harvest yields. Relations between both parties are nearly always cordial, and few farmers default in the rent. The rent is payable in three different ways, namely, by cash, crops, or a form of division. Sometimes the rent is paid partly in cash and partly in rice. Barley, beans, eggs, and poultry may also be used in part payment.

In cases of flood, drought, or plagues of locusts, the district government is requested to assist. By an ancient tradition, the District Magistrate was regarded as a sort of magician and was expected to produce beneficial results by interceding with the supernatural powers during times of distress. If the country-side was afflicted by a drought, he would adopt the time-honoured remedy of forbidding the slaughter of pigs. If a flood were the trouble, he would proceed with ceremony to the river or lake, and, sacrificing his official belongings by throwing them in, he would, like Canute and probably with equal success, call upon the waters to recede.

In the rarer case of a plague of locusts he would order a parade with Liu Mêng (劉 猛). This god, who was once an official of the Yüan dynasty, is sometimes known as Liu Chên Chün (劉 眞 君) and is credited with the power of being able to control these plagues.*

After all local requirements have been met the surplus rice harvest is marketed elsewhere.

The rice trade is exceedingly complicated. It is largely controlled by the rice hongs, through the agency of which the husked rice is collected from the farmers and, after milling, is either exported direct or sold to purchasers from other provinces.

* According to Mr. Hsiao Tung-fei, in "Peasant Life in China," Liu Mêng, who possessed supernatural powers, was as a boy much ill-treated by his step-mother—perhaps not without provocation—for he is said to have killed all the cattle belonging to his parents and invited all his friends to feast on the meat. He then buried the heads and tails of the animals, so that it appeared the whole bodies were attached under the covering soil. As the day began to break before this curious task was completed, he prevailed on the sun to remain below the horizon until he was ready for it. This uncomfortable youth then contrived to make the heads low and the tails wave. This astonishing trick incensed his step-mother, who redoubled her ill-treatment to such an extent that the unfortunate Liu Mêng finally threw himself into the river and was drowned.

The interior rice hongs, however, rarely export direct. These organizations serve as farmers' banks in a sense, for they will advance money, just before harvest, on the security of the crop. A farmer may contract with the hongs to buy his rice at the market price. Another method is for merchants from the nearest cities to buy the rice from the farms and transport it by junk to a central market for disposal to the rice hongs through intermediary rice brokers, called *mai-t'ou* (賣頭), or "sell-heads." When a cargo of rice arrives in Shanghai, these brokers send samples to the hongs, and the price settled upon is paid after the rice is measured and delivered.

The principal market for most surplus crops in the delta area is Shanghai. The towns of Wusih (無 錫), Chinkiang (鎮 江), Kiangning (江 甯), and Wutsin (武 進) follow in order of importance. Shanghai absorbs an enormous quantity, not only by virtue of her huge export trade to other provinces, but in order to feed her teeming millions. In 1930, with a population of over 4 millions, her consumption of rice was variously computed, but may be said to be nearly 4,000,000 piculs a year, with "ordinary" rice leading. A total amount, however, of over 7,000,000 piculs was imported, the surplus being exported again. The import of foreign rice from India and Annam is on the increase, particularly of late years, when, owing to military activities, the farmers have often had to abandon the export or even the cultivation of their "staff of life."

Normally there is more rice on the market at the end of the year, when the new crops of "ordinary" rice are brought in from the provinces. The import of foreign rice is mostly in the summer, before the new home-grown crops appear in the market.

The rice merchants of Shanghai fall into two categories. The Northern Group consists of merchants from Wuhsien, Kunshan, Changshu, Kiangyin, Wusih, Ihing, Liyang, and Kintan, and their junks usually congregate at the Sinza Road Bridge. The Southern Group of merchants hail from Sungkiang, Minhang, Tungli (同 里), Pingwang (平 望), Lutang (蘆 墟), Szeking (泗 涇), Tsingpu (青 浦), Changyen (張 堰), and Pachih (八 坼), while their junks are to be found at Wang-chia-ma-t'ou (王 家 碼 頭) at Nantao.

See rice-junks, Part Three, pages 314–323.

As is only to be expected with such an all-important commodity, there is a large class of junks exclusively given up to the carrying of rice. All these river craft are noticeably well kept and, as the rice is nearly always carried in bulk, are always well caulked and in good repair. In common with a good many junks used for a specific purpose, the rice-junks nearly always return empty. Doubtless this is due to the care that must be exercised not to carry any cargo likely to taint the wood and thus affect adversely the flavour of the rice.

It is, of course, quite impossible to say when fishing came to be practised in China first, but it is doubtless of very ancient origin. Fu Hsi (伏 羲), the earliest of the five legendary rulers, *circa* 2852, who are credited with the foundation of Chinese civilization, is said to have taught the people the art of fishing with nets for the purpose of procuring food.

There are many allusions to topics connected with fishing contained in the old Chinese classics, the most well-known being associated with T'ai Kung (太 公), the popular officer of state, also named Lü Shang (呂 尙), who broke his sword and went into voluntary retirement to escape the tyrannous rule of Chou Hsin (紂 辛), the wicked Emperor, 1122 B.C., the last of the Shang dynasty.

About this time a new leader appeared in the empire, Wên Wang (文 王), ruler of the feudal State of Chou and father of the founder of that dynasty. One day when he was going out hunting it was foretold that, although he would not bring back any such quarry as dragon or tiger, bear or black horse, yet he would meet with unusual success, for he would return with a great prince's counsellor. This prophecy was fulfilled, for Wên Wang came upon Lü Shang, who, now aged 80, was employing his retirement in literary pursuits, the study of nature, and the gentle art of fishing. This story furnishes a most outstanding example of competitive altruism, for Lü Shang would use only what is described in folklore as a "straight hook," so that no fish need be caught unawares or against its will, while the fish self-sacrificingly vied with one another in attaching themselves to the sage's line so that he might be supplied with food. Wên Wang was as much impressed as the fish by the wisdom and virtue of the old statesman and made him his chief counsellor.

Another interesting piscatorial reference occurs in the fourth century B.C., when an allegorical philosopher named Lieh Yü-k'ou (列御寇) is quoted as having described the way to obtain a good bag. "By taking a fishing-line made of a single silk cocoon, a hook of a minute needle, a rod of a branch of bramble, and using a portion of a grain as bait, Chan Ho, a famous fisherman in the Ts'o Kingdom, could catch a cartload of fish." (列子湯問篇詹何以獨繭絲爲綸芒鍼爲鈎荆篠爲竿剖粒爲餌引盈車之魚)

The Chinese are commonly credited with having been the first to turn their attention to fish culture* by collecting and disseminating the spawn and artificially rearing fry, which they employed for the purpose of stocking every available piece of water. T'ao Chu-kung, or Fan Li, to give his alternate name, who lived in the fifth century B.C., is credited with being the first to practise fish breeding. It is said that he dug a pond the size of an acre, leaving nine islands scattered about it; the nine islands were to deceive the fish, who innocently believed they were in the big ocean travelling round nine continents.† T'ao Chu-kung not only bred fish but wrote about them, notably in the "Yu Ching," some centuries before the Christian era. It is considered by modern fishermen, however, to be somewhat out of date.

The Egyptians likewise in times past must have taken considerable pains in this occupation, and under the Roman Republic fish culture was carried on for the purpose of augmenting the general food supply.

Pisciculture, therefore, not for any promotion of sport, as in the West, but for the strictly utilitarian motives of providing food for China's millions, is very extensively practised in the region of the delta and also throughout the Lower Yangtze areas.

Good results have been obtained by the inauguration of new organizations on modern lines, which raise fish according to scientific methods; yet in the main fish cultivation is still carried out in the traditional primitive way by whole communities of people who carry on the industry precisely as their fathers and grandfathers did before them.‡

In the early spring, fish ascend the rivers and canals to spawn, and some fish, such as the common carp and catfish, obligingly deposit their eggs among the under-water grass and weeds near the shore, thus rendering them easily accessible to the spawn-catchers. The other species, however, namely, the grass carp (草魚) (*Ctenopharyngodon idellus*), the big head (大頭) (*Aristichthys nobilis*), the black carp (青魚) (*Mylopharyngodon piceus*), and bream (鯿魚) (*Parabramis pekinensis*), whose fry are most important in pond culture, lay their eggs near the surface in swift water, and the eggs or spawn whilst drifting with the current hatch into minute fry after 24 hours. These are collected into the bag nets laid out by the spawn-catchers.

The season for gathering the spawn usually lasts no more than about two

* Monsieur Dabry de Thiersant, "La Pisciculture et la Pêche en Chine."

† The "Wu Yüeh Ch'un Ch'iu," or "Annals of the States of Wu and Yüeh."

‡ Mr. S. Wells Williams, LL.D., author of "Tonic and Syllabic Dictionaries of the Chinese Language," asserts on page 349 of the "Bulletin Universal" for 1829 "that in some parts of China spawn is carefully placed in an empty egg-shell and the hole closed; the egg is then replaced in the nest, and after the hen has sat a few days upon it is reopened and then placed in a vessel of water warmed in the sun, where it soon hatches." Perhaps this is only a fishing story.

months, beginning from the first week in May and closing at the Little Heat (小暑) in July.

When Kiukiang became the centre of this great industry is not known, but certain it is that for centuries now spawn-catchers have travelled from distant inland parts of the province to stake out their ingenious spawn-traps close to the river-banks in the curiously restricted area between Kiukiang, Erhtaokow (二套口), and Yükang (浴港).

The spawn-fishers follow traditional methods and work quite independently both in catching the spawn and in selling it to the *yü-hong* (魚行) (fish guild), which acts as commission agent.

A suitable and fairly shallow spot is chosen under the bank, and stout bamboo poles are driven into the mud bed of the river at intervals of a foot or more. Across these rough piles, which may extend out at right angles to the bank for a considerable number of feet, a long plank is laid for the convenience of those attending the nets. To these piles are attached the nets, which are made of extremely fine black mesh, wide at the mouth, which faces up stream, and tapering down to a point leading into an oblong fine-meshed box which floats on the surface of the water. Thus the spawn, entering at the broad end, are forced onward by the current and eventually collected in the netted box.

At Hankow the means employed are simpler in detail, though in the main the same as those described above. Instead of being attached to upright poles, the nets are fastened to floating spars, so lashed together as to form a triangle. This variation in method appears to be due to the shallow water, which enables the nets to be weighted at the bottom, whereas in deeper water they are attached to the upright poles under water. Every now and again the receivers are emptied into *kangs*, or earthenware jars,* and so clever do the spawn-gatherers become at their work that they can detect the different species among the almost invisible fry and sort them out after their kind. These aquatic nurseries are kept until the little fish have had a short start in life, and then the work of distribution begins.

Junks used in the fishing industry are described in Part Two. See the *liu-wang-ch'uan*, page 180; the *chenhai-ch'uan*, or ice-boat, page 174; the Chusan little fisherman, page 182; and the *yu-ch'uan*, or live-fish carrier, page 262. The fishing sampans are described in Part Two, pages 262–267.

A junk can carry as many as 2,500 baskets or *kangs* of spawn, and when this amount has been accumulated and embarked she proceeds at once with the catches.

It is customary for junks in this trade to be allowed to pay double clearance dues at one time: for the trip when passing through to collect the spawn, and also for the return journey with their cargo on board. This is to enable the spawn, a very perishable cargo, to be rushed to the fish farms as soon as possible.

On arrival at its destination the junk is unloaded and the fry is first deposited in tanks. They are fed with the yolk of egg. When they have grown a little larger they are transferred to the ponds, where they are kept until they grow to about 8 to 10 ounces in weight. Later they are removed to larger ponds, and after about a year they are ready for the market.

During the first period of their growth the fish require very great care and attention, and everything has to be avoided which might interfere with their development. Their food now consists of grass, which is cut from the borders of the ponds. Around the ponds no plants must be grown which might pollute the water, and the washing of vegetables or other articles in them must be carefully guarded against. The ponds are not stocked indiscriminately. Usually a pond 10 *mou* in area contains 3,000 grass-fish, 600 *lien-yü* (鰱魚), 200 white fish, 100 carp, 100 *pien-yü* (鯿魚), and about 30 *tsing-yü* (鯖魚).

The ponds are shallow—for a great depth is regarded as prejudicial to the growth of the fish—and are always dug in shady places. On the bottom a small excavation is made, where the fish can retreat in cold weather. The sides of the ponds are always rough, for it is the general belief among the owners that the fish

* Sometimes these containers consist of specially prepared waterproof baskets coated with the famous persimmon varnish (柿漆), which is a speciality of the province. It is made by pounding wild, unripe persimmons to a pulp and allowing the mass to decompose in an earthenware jar filled with water. This unattractive fluid is allowed to stand for about a month when, on skimming or straining off the pulp, a colourless gum varnish remains.

would not grow in a pond the sides of which were smooth. Around them trees having large foliage are generally grown, and rockeries are built within to afford hiding-places for the small fish.

The junk most used in this industry is the *sha-p'a-tzŭ* (沙扒子), or sand-scratching boat, or locally named the *p'ien-tou* (扁豆), so called from the similarity of its lines to a pea pod.

The various modes of catching and rearing fish exhibit, perhaps more than anything else, the skill and contrivance of the Chinese driven by necessity. In a country with so extensive a coast-line and so unusually well served with inland waterways and vast lakes, fish must necessarily play an important part in the diet of the people, many of whom depend largely, if not entirely, upon it to provide the necessary animal matter in their food, and great ingenuity is displayed in the innumerable methods of catching fish.

Catching fry for stocking fish farms is discussed in Part Two, pages 262–64.

All the implements used in Europe have their counterpart in China, but net fishing is the most common method. There is an infinite variety of types of nets, both large and worked by primitive machinery or small and worked direct by hand. There are square, triangular, and conical nets, drag-nets, and others with reinforced mesh. When the nets have ceased to be of use for catching fish they are sometimes suspended from the ceilings of houses for the purpose of warding off evil spirits. Sometimes they are spread over the beds on which sick men are laid for the same purpose. Lines are used with and without bait on the hooks. Fish are speared, dug for with a spade, scraped for with a form of dredge, ensnared in every sort of trap, frightened into nets by noise, or decoyed to jump

Refer to the drop-net fisherman and the *to-wang-ch'uan*, or drag-net boat, Part Two, pages 266 and 268.

Fishing with an otter at Ichang. The ingenious Chinese use a tamed otter to scare the fish into the net.
PAUL POPPER

into boats by painted boards. Finally, they are dived for by trained cormorants or otters. Naturally, different methods are used in the various provinces, but one important factor in the fishing industry is universal throughout China, and that is the care taken not to deplete the waters of the creeks and canals of fish.

The fishing cormorant, *Phalocrocorax carbo*, is found in many parts of China and is taught to catch fish. This bird is also called the black devil, a light in which the true followers of Izaak Walton regard him.

Cormorant fishing in China is too well known to need a detailed description herein, but the following account, written by E. Ysbrand Ides, Ambassador from the Czar to the Emperor of China, is interesting as being one of the first Europeans to describe the art:

> The inhabitants relate very strange things, many of which are found to be true. In this and other provinces is observed a sort of fishing bird, called *louwa*, which is somewhat less than a goose, and not unlike the raven, having also a very crooked bill towards the end. The manner of fishing with them is as follows. The fishers having rowed themselves in their boats to a proper place, throw these birds overboard, who immediately dive, and the very instant they have caught their game, dart up to the surface of the water when their masters immediately seize them, and very expeditiously pull the fish out of their crops. It is not possible for it to descend lower, by reason it is stopped by a ring fixed about the bird's neck, which is removed when the sport is over and the birds let loose, after which they go a-fish-stealing with open throats, and having satiated themselves return to their boats.

This account was written 237 years ago and ably describes the methods of cormorant fishing as carried out to this day.

Of the fresh-water fish of the Whangpoo, the eel fetches a very high price, as it is much sought after by Shanghai epicures, who regard it not only as a table delicacy but also as a tonic food.

The sea eel is much bigger in size than the fresh-water eel. The former also migrates to fresh streams in certain seasons of the year and is often caught in the Whangpoo. A large specimen measures over 3 feet in length.

The fresh-water eel of the Whangpoo is caught either by hooks or in a trap. The former method consists in throwing into the water a series of hooks tied to a line with earthworms as bait. The line is pulled from the water at intervals of every two or three hours in order to enable the fisherman to see if any eels have been caught. The latter method consists in digging a pool on the bank of the river, which is flooded at high tide. In the pool some bait is placed, and at ebb tide the pool is left above the high-water mark, and any unfortunate eels therein are captured.

Another method in the Whangpoo to catch eels and other fish that are in the mud is employed by men who appear to watch for air bubbles and then dig down. These fishermen are quick at their work and appear to catch a fair number.

Lime is sometimes used to aid the fisherman. It is thrown into the water, the fisherman having first enclosed a certain space with cone-shaped baskets into which the fish rush, not being able to live in the lime-impregnated water, and so are easily caught.

In Chinese books on Natural History, the "Êrh Ya" (爾雅) gives a list of 18 to 20 fish, and the "Pên Ts'ao Kang Mu (本草綱目) gives about 50 varieties with rough illustrations and descriptions of doubtful value.

The wide and interesting field of the fish of China has been dealt with at length by Western naturalists, notably A. de C. Sowerby, J. D. D. de la Touche, and others, who have probably enumerated and classified some few hundreds of species; but there seems good reason to suppose that this vast subject is by no means exhausted as regards both salt and fresh water fish.

The salt wells of Tzeliutsing.

There are various methods employed in the production of salt in China. In the Hwaipei (淮 北) district of Kiangsu, and in Chekiang, Fukien, and Kwangtung, salt pan evaporation (灘 晒) is used. In the Hwainan (淮 南) district of Kiangsu, in Sungkiang (松 江), and in Chekiang, both the board (板 晒) and fire evaporation methods are in general use, whilst the sun evaporation process prevails chiefly in Shansi, Shensi, and Mongolia. In Yunnan and Szechwan salt is produced chiefly by fire evaporation.

Szechwan, which, with 53 million inhabitants, has the largest population of any province and in size, 220,000 square miles, is second only to Sinkiang, or the New Dominion, produces not only sufficient salt for its own needs, but also supplies the neighbouring provinces of North-east Yunnan, Kweichow, Hupeh, and South Shensi. It is estimated that about 300,000 tons yearly, or more than half this vast amount of salt, comes from the wells of Tzeliutsing (自 流 井).

The specially constructed salt junks and sampans of this salt centre have, therefore, a peculiar interest of their own. So bound up are they with the life of the salt-producing district that no description of them would be really complete without an account of Tzeliutsing itself, and of the cumbrous, crude, and curious methods of obtaining the salt that is their cargo and the main—indeed, the only—cause of their existence.

In other parts of China the salt industry had provided one of the sources of Government revenue from as far back as the seventh century B.C. In Szechwan at that time the thickly wooded hills were inhabited by savage tribes as yet ignorant of the uses of salt and the luxury of salted meats, and it was not until after the province had been conquered by the Ch'in (秦) dynasty (255–206 B.C.) that the influx of Chinese settlers from the northern provinces of Shansi and Shensi made their civilising influence felt, for the Chinese must have been familiar with the production of salt from very ancient times.

The first written mention of salt is said to have been found in the annals of the Emperor Yü (禹 貢), 2205 to 2197 B.C., who ordered the court to be supplied with this commodity. The first actual reference to salt in Szechwan is in the "Hua Yang Kuo Chih" (華 陽 國 志). It is said that during the reign of Hsiao

Wên Wang (孝文王), 250 B.C., the opening of a salt well in the Kwangtu (廣都) district, south of the present Chengtu (成都), was attributed to the famous Li Ping (李冰), the Governor of the State of Shu (蜀), as Szechwan was then called. He is worshipped to-day as a Patron Saint, for he did more than anyone to develop the natural resources of the province, in addition to the main work of his career in devising the irrigation system to which the Chengtu plain owes its fertility.

Throughout the Han dynasty (漢朝) the salt industry in Szechwan made great advances. The Government inaugurated a monopoly of the evaporation pans and introduced the earliest form of salt-well tax, whereby the salt workers paid a proportion of the yield. Clandestine activities were punished by confiscation of all the implements as well as the salt, and every offender had his left great toe amputated.

Further historical mention of the wells of Tzeliutsing occurred during the Minor Han (蜀漢) dynasty, A.D. 221 to 265, and, in a reference dated about A.D. 347, it is stated that there were wells to a depth of 800 feet and that natural gas had also been discovered and was used then, as it is now, for the evaporation of the brine.

It is recorded in the biographies of the T'ien Shih (天師), who may be described as a line of Taoist popes of Lung Hu Shan (龍虎山), in the province of Kiangsi, that the first of these was requested to make a journey to Szechwan to cast out evil spirits from the salt wells. It is not certain that these are the wells referred to; but, from the fact that inflammable gas issues from some of the borings, it is quite probable that they are the identical wells, which thus earned an unpleasant supernatural reputation.

It is said that the Apostolic Missionary Imbert, in 1829, was probably the first foreigner to visit Tzeliutsing, and these ancient salt wells must be counted among the few centres of interest that the great mediæval traveller, Marco Polo, omitted to mention, although he spoke of salt in other parts of China. True, he passed through Chengtu, which, as the crow flies, is not far off; but his silence on the subject of Tzeliutsing is perhaps not surprising, for even now it lies well off the beaten track, away from a road to any important centre and therefore isolated. It is curious that even those very few inquisitive travellers who have succeeded in penetrating to Tzeliutsing have found so little to say about this unique centre of activity in their volumes of travels and have dismissed it with a mere paragraph or two.

The journey from Chungking to Tzeliutsing by river is indirect and tedious, necessitating changes from one uncomfortable form of craft to another, while overland from Chungking it takes almost two days by motor-bus over indifferent roads. The provincial highway is left at Neikiang (內江), some 468 *li* from Chungking, after which the branch road continues in a south-westerly direction for another 120 *li*.

Tzeliutsing (自流井), or Self-flowing Wells, is situated near the centre of the Red Basin of Szechwan on the Yentsingho (鹽井河), or Salt Well River, a small tributary of the T'o River (沱江), which is in turn a tributary of the Yangtze.

In this district there are an enormous number of salt wells, estimated by the local merchants to exceed 1,200,* surrounding a city, or what may be described as twin cities, known by the Chinese as the Upper Market and the Lower Market. The district covers an area of about 30 by 50 *li* (10 by 17 miles) with a population variously assessed at from 800,000 upwards. Some authorities assert that there are half a million workers alone, and that the sum total is nearly 4 million souls. Certainly the twin cities present all the bustle and alertness of prosperity and

* The number varies greatly; some authorities give a much higher figure.

enterprise to a marked degree. The huge derricks, which can be seen from 10 miles away, the myriads of ropes stretching from them in all directions, the bamboo aqueducts leading from hundreds of wells, the numerous low buildings sheltering the brine pans, all are the outward expression of one of the great industries in China.

In the crowded streets may be seen caravans of coolies and pack-animals laden not only with salt, but with food for the men, fodder for the beasts, and coal to supplement the natural gas used at the wells to evaporate the brine. Processions of water-buffaloes ceaselessly arrive to be drafted to the wells. A feature of the thronged streets is the prevalence of the white turban, or bandeau, wound round the head, or even round the ordinary black Chinese hat. For here in the heart of Western China this distinctly Szechwanese head-dress, known as the *Chu-ko-chin* (諸葛巾) or kerchief of Chu Ko Liang, has not yet given way to the unlovely head-gear adopted from foreign styles by the workers in the larger cities. The wearers assert that the bandeau is worn in perpetual memory of, and in mourning for, their great hero of the days of the Three Kingdoms, Chu Ko Liang (諸葛亮), who lived about 17 centuries ago.

The usual noise of a busy street is dominated by other sounds: the whining of the great drums of the capstans, the doleful creaking of the wheels on the derricks, the roaring of the flames of the natural gas, the yelling of the muleteers, the clatter of the ponies' shod feet on the hard road, and the bells of the caravans. All leave an ineffaceable impression.

The methods used in digging the wells have probably changed but little down the ages, and are still unbelievably primitive and equally ingenious. The selection of a site is determined by omens or portents, as interpreted by experts in Fêng Shui (風水). As these advisers are quite without geological knowledge, wells are often bored in unsuitable localities and not necessarily near existing gas supplies.

An auspicious start is secured by the usual ceremony of "Killing the Cock (殺雞)" and letting off fire-crackers, which in Szechwan accompanies every undertaking of importance.

After the geomancers have solved the problem of the precise spot, the well is sunk, being only from 9 inches to 1 foot in diameter. It is lined for the first 200 or 300 feet with cypress-wood in 6-foot lengths, and the long and expensive operation of deep-drilling then commences. The Chinese method is basically simple and makes use of a cutting tool suspended from a flexible line, which is alternatively raised and dropped, the percussion serving to cut and crumble the rock on the bottom of the hole. Scaffolding 10 to 12 feet high is erected nearby, on which is balanced a drill-beam, that is to say, a baulk of hardwood 12 feet or more in length and about 6 inches in diameter, which acts as a see-saw lever, the shorter end being over the well hole. When required, the axis about which the beam pivots is moved ever nearer the well, but despite this the suspension of a heavy drill from the shorter end serves to keep it depressed. As the boring deepens, and heavier lengths and rods are added, a considerable weight in the form of a large stone, or stones, is attached to the far end of the drill-beam to give it more lifting power. The drill, however, still remains in a depressed position in the well unless artificially raised.

The raising is effected by means of very ingeniously employed man-power. The scaffolding is so arranged that the beam rises and falls between parallel platforms on each side of which stand four men, who, with automatic precision, perform a continual simultaneous interchange of position. This performance consists of five steps. The second stride, using the beam as a stepping-stone, lands the weight of 8 feet together on the free end of the beam, or lever, which instantly sinks beneath them, raising the drill in the well. Instantly the men spring off the beam on to the opposite platform, thus again releasing the drill, and then turn ready for the next step back with the other foot. At each jump the drill is lifted and dropped about 2 feet, and in falling strikes a crushing blow of great force at the bottom of the well. An iron cross-piece at the far end of the scaffolding prevents the free end of the drill-beam from flying up too far. A man stationed at the well-mouth is employed in giving a quarter turn to the bamboo cable, which thereby imparts a rotary motion to the drill at the moment of its impact with the rock. The cable is so adjusted that, when the lever is horizontal, the drill rests easily on the bottom of the well.

The men's timing in jumping on and off the beam is perfect, as indeed it has to be, for the smallest error in judgment entails a serious accident, the man near the end of the beam being in the position of the greatest danger.

The initial drill used, an iron rod which ends in a sharp flange, can be as long as 14 feet with a weight varying from 150 pounds to more than double that amount. Various types of drills are used, some being roughened with incisions at the lower extremity. All have a ring at the upper end for attachment to the bamboo cable. As the boring goes deeper, other rods are bound tightly together so as to strike as one.

An average of 3 feet can be drilled in a 24-hour period, for the work is carried on day and night. Much delay is caused by the necessity of having to change the drills, which soon become blunted. The methods of removing the debris from the bottom of the well are varied and slow, for this operation takes longer than the drilling. Tins are lowered down in the hope of raking up the loose earth or rock, and iron rods with spikes and barbs, and other contrivances such as bamboo tubes fitted with suction valves, are also used. Sometimes the rope breaks and the drill falls down the well, and it then takes five or six months to crush the old drill and get it out piecemeal.

The men work in shifts, timed by means of incense-sticks hung from a beam. After 10 minutes the end man is changed and a new man comes on at the other end, while the others move down a place. It is a life-time occupation, and the men seem remarkably cheerful and contented despite the literally boring nature of their work.

The foreman, however, leads a life of comparative ease and comfort, for he reclines beneath the scaffolding in a long, specially designed bamboo chair, which is so tilted that he can watch and direct his gang at work above him.

The drilling of a well may take anything from 3 to 20 years, though in rare cases brine has been found after only a few months. Time is normally of small account to the Chinese, who will labour at an enterprise in the hope that it will be brought to a successful conclusion a generation or so hence. This patient anticipation is taxed to the uttermost at Tzeliutsing, where every irritating form of delay combines to retard progress. The work, too, is so expensive that a change of owners often occurs before it is completed, the originators having used up all their capital before striking brine or gas. Moreover, a well that flows to-day may be dry to-morrow, continue dry for days or years, and then mysteriously be renewed, for the quantity and length of time of the flow is erratic.

Brine boiling may sometimes be started while the drilling is still in progress. The first essential to the raising of the brine is the lofty derrick [1] (see Page No. 143) of a height varying from 60 to 175 feet over the well-mouth. This tripod is composed of a multitude of *sha-mu* (杉 木) poles lashed together to a considerable thickness, and so disposed that no two joins ever coincide. The lower sections

Detail of a supporting leg of a salt well tripod.

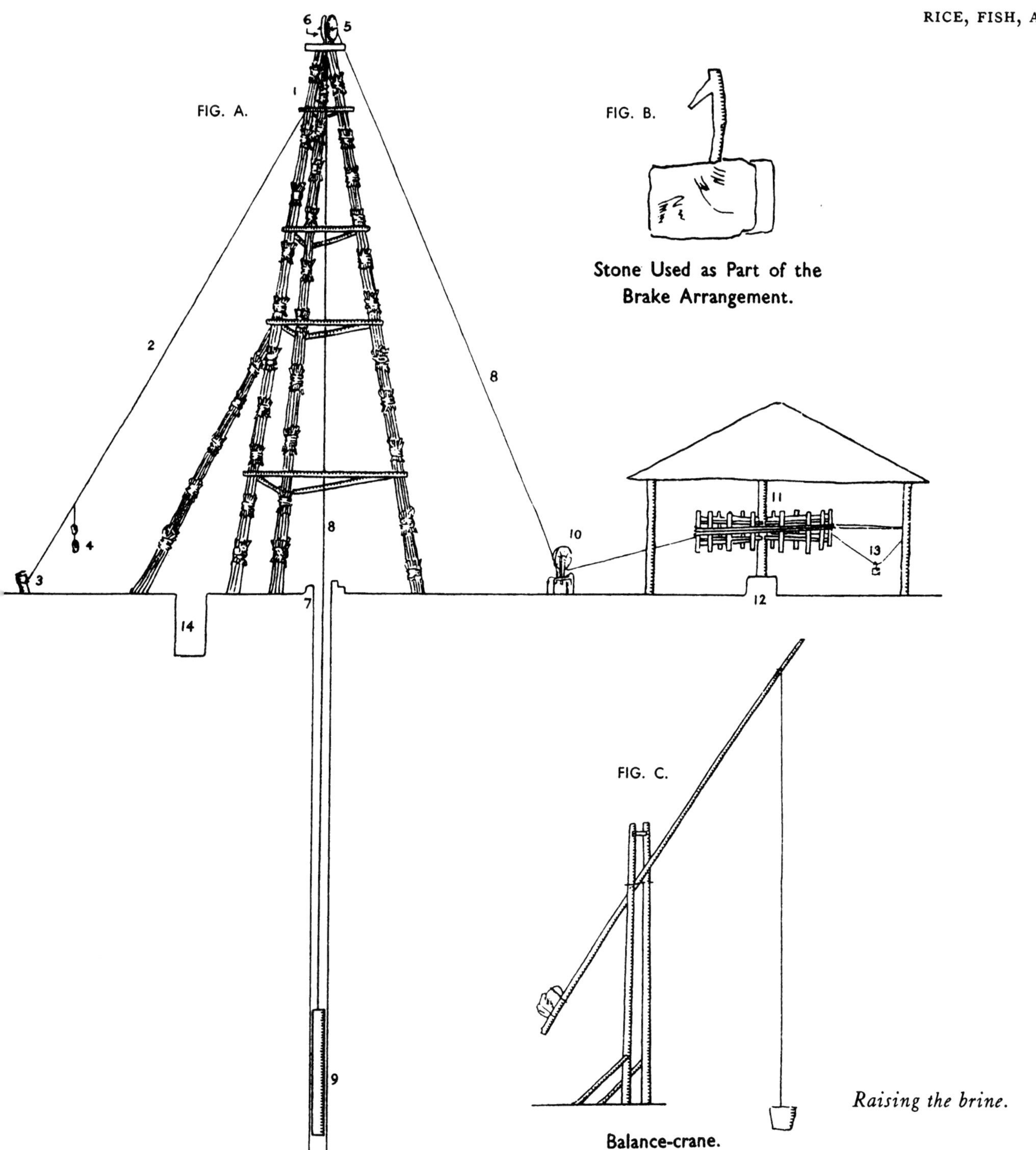

Raising the brine.

have five or more poles lashed together; the second, four; the third, three; and so on. The bamboo-rope lashings are tightened up by wedges, and additional support is provided by numerous cross-pieces and an extra leg.

The structure is stayed by the use of bamboo ropes[2] attached to buried stones,[3] often as many as 10 of these guys being used. When they get slack, adjustment is made by hanging heavy stones[4] to them near the ground. This dangerous practice seems to escape the nemesis it richly deserves.

At the derrick-head is a grooved wheel[5] about 2½ feet in diameter and running on a 1½-inch axle, which rests on heavy timbers mortised into the cross-beam.[6] This is situated directly over the well-head, which, when completed, is covered with a square stone[7] with a central aperture of less than 1 foot across. Over the central wheel[5] passes the cable[8] supporting the brine-pipe,[9] or bucket, which is made up of lengths of hollowed bamboo. A short distance from the derrick is a fair-lead,[10] * consisting of another wheel supported on an axle slung

* See Fig. B and Fig. A[13], on drawing above.

between two uprights, which in turn are wedged into a cross-beam resting on two more supports and heavily weighted with stones. The whole contrivance creaks and wobbles alarmingly, but nevertheless is astonishingly efficient.

The brine cable [8] passes under this wheel and thence to an enormous capstan [11] which supplies the motive power. The drum of the capstan, which is about 12 feet high and will wind about 60 feet of rope on its 16-sided circumference, is placed on a vertical axle tipped with iron on which it revolves in a hollow in a large stone [12] of hard consistency. The upper end of the axle engages in a hole in a heavy beam built into the structure of the shed, which covers the whole. The spokes of the capstan, which are about 8 feet long, are let into the rim, and all the component parts are lashed with bamboo rope.

Formerly mules and horses were used in considerable numbers to haul up the brine, but nowadays the well cable is wound round the capstan by means of water-buffaloes of any number up to five, harnessed to its circumference at equal intervals by means of a bamboo rope attached to a wooden yoke and pole. Each animal has its own driver, who controls it with a bamboo rope through its nose and a length of discarded cable used as a whip.

The work is arduous, and it is said that the animals are soon worn out, rarely lasting for more than four or five years at the most, after which they are sent to the butcher. During their reportedly brief lifetime these valuable workers are well fed and looked after. They are chiefly imported from Chungking, and it has been estimated that 10,000 are in use in the salt industry in Tzeliutsing alone. They are fed on hand-cut grass, rice straw in winter, and a daily ration of beans. Water baths are supplied for them to wallow in at least once daily, as it is found that this increases their powers of endurance. At a well-run well the buffaloes are changed every 25 minutes and do about 10 shifts in the 24 hours.

The height of the derrick varies according to the depth of the well and the length of the bamboo-tubing bucket in which the brine is raised. In a big well with a depth of 3,000 English feet* the derrick would be some 170 feet or more in height and the bucket as long as 130 feet. A bamboo rope 2 inches in diameter and 2½ *li* (over ¾ mile) in length would be used to draw the bucket to the surface. This rope has to be renewed every 10 days.

The process of raising and lowering the bucket takes 20 minutes or more, and 10,000 catties (5¾ tons) of brine are brought to the surface in the 24-hour period. This highly concentrated brine yields from one-fifth to one-fourth of its whole weight in salt. A total complement of 60 water-buffaloes and a staff of more than 30 men would be kept at an important well such as this.

The bucket, bound with hemp cord at the natural sections and with iron clamps at the telescoped joins, is a very ingenious device. Made from the giant bamboo (*Dendrocalamus giganteus*), it is fully 6 inches in diameter, with a wall ¾ inch thick. The outer skin is removed, and the bamboo is hollowed throughout its length. The base is provided with a buffalo-hide non-return valve, which on immersion opens to admit the brine and closes on leaving the level of the brine.

On reaching the surface a rope is thrown round the lower extremity of the bucket so as to draw it over an adjacent reservoir [14] sunk into the ground. Here a man is stationed with an iron rod, with which he forces open the leather valve, allowing the brine to gush out. A bucket of these dimensions is capable of holding about 350 pounds of dark, dirty-looking, and evil-smelling fluid.

The water-buffaloes are now unhitched and the bucket is placed back in the mouth of the well and let go. As it falls, the great lumbering capstan at first unwinds slowly, but after a few seconds it revolves at about 50 times a minute,

* The deepest well is said to be 4,200 feet.

and this high speed causes a tremendous current of air in the shed, which rocks with the vibration of the clumsy machinery while the bucket makes its 1½-minute descent. The revolutions are controlled by an improvised brake consisting of a band of split bamboo running round the upper end of the capstan. The standing part is made fast to a beam, while the other terminates in a bamboo rope. A large stone with a hole into which a wooden fork has been driven* rests on this rope and acts as a throttle, the operator moving the stone away from the capstan to obtain acceleration and towards the capstan when braking is necessary. This brake, although it is a most primitive device, is yet most efficient in the hands of an expert, and represents touch control developed to a nicety.

The buffaloes, meanwhile, with amazing agility and sagacity, step deftly aside and stand immovable not more than a foot away from the capstan, which unwinds with such force that a blow from it would have a most damaging effect even on these enormously strong beasts. There is food for speculation as to how the animals have learned their lesson so well.

The brine may be divided into three categories: black, which is the best and produces the most salt for its weight; yellow; and white, which is the thinnest. The average well produces enough brine to provide a steady supply for 10 boiling pans.

In cases where the gas and brine occur in the same locality there are no transport problems, but normally the transportation of the brine from the well-head to the boiling pans forms the second important and remarkable part of the industry.

After the brine has been run into a temporary reservoir some 25 feet from the well, it is allowed to settle. It is then necessary to raise it to a sufficient height so that gravity will convey it to the boiling pans. The general method is to hoist the brine by means of another capstan and team of buffaloes to the top of a derrick, whence it is decanted into a funnel, which feeds a system of bamboo pipes supported on high trestles. Another plan is to install a treadmill in a shed on poles some feet above the ground. Here men pedal the brine up into a tub, from which it flows down until lack of gravity requires a repetition of the operation. This is known as a dragon lift (龍 梯).

A third method is to carry up the brine in buckets by man-power. The coolies, who work in gangs, can take phenomenal weights, which they carry up wooden ramps to cisterns elevated so as to feed the brine-pipe system. Where possible, boats are also used to carry the brine to the boiling pans.

Yet another contrivance is the balance-crane † (a term used for want of a better). This device consists of a very long pole supported on two upright posts, on which the balance-beam pivots. The lower extremity is weighted with a stone, while the other end carries a bucket at the end of a rope—or sometimes a bamboo. This simple but eminently practical device is probably one of the oldest forms of leverage used in raising water.

In this connexion it is interesting to note that ancient Egyptian representations illustrated the use of the same device, which is still used in modern Egypt under the name of *shadóof*.

Any combination of all these methods may be used, for the outstanding and constant necessity is to elevate the brine so that it may run freely through the network of bamboo pipes. These primitive, rickety-looking aqueducts are a marked feature of the countryside, and they extend for many miles across hills and into valleys, over or under roads, and even through houses. The longest line is about 7 miles. The 6-inch pipes are made of the giant bamboo served

* See Fig. B, page 143.

† See Fig. C, page 143.

Brine evaporation pans.

with thin strips of bamboo tightened by the insertion of wedges. This frapping is usually converted into a strong outer casing by means of a liberal application of chunam, which hardens to a weather-proof consistency and preserves the pipes for a period of years. Joins are made in the usual manner by telescoping one bamboo length into another.

On arrival at the boiling site, the brine is diverted into various small reservoirs suspended on bamboo poles over the pans. When possible the natural gas is utilised to heat the pans, in which the brine crystallises in about 24 hours, whereupon the process is repeated. If gas is not available the evaporation is carried out by heating with coal brought in from neighbouring districts by junk and road, but the salt thus obtained, owing to the coal soot which discolours it, is not considered to be equal to that crystallised over a gas flame. Moreover, it takes about three times as long as when gas is used.

As the brine hardens it is removed and set in baskets to drip, the drippings being carefully collected and returned to the boiling pans. The boiling pans are of the usual shallow cast-iron type in use for various purposes all over China, but of extra large size, being about 5 to 6 feet in diameter and weighing sometimes over half a ton. Contrary to what one would expect, they are not manufactured locally. They can only be used for about 70 heatings, when they crack.

The ideal condition, of course, is to find brine and gas together. The gas is said to be deeper than the brine, and when a brine well runs dry and is dug again, it is not unusual to strike both brine and gas together, a combination which, with a steady output, ensures a fortune to the owner. Gas in a brine well is allowed to flow out from a side aperture into iron pipes, where it is set alight, burning with a bluish flame and very little odour. These pipes are increased as needed, each burner being sufficient to keep one pan boiling. The pans are arranged in parallel rows in ascending order, so as to permit the lighter-than-air gas to flow upwards. A large factory may have 100 pans in use. Flaring gas jets illuminate the working sheds, and as all the burners are more or less permanently alight, the waste of valuable gas is considerable.

The wells containing gas only are quite as valuable as the brine wells, since each can supply a number of factories with fuel. The gas is conserved in crude reservoirs and distributed by means of bamboo pipes, though a certain amount of difficulty is encountered in directing it downhill.

Many of these "fire wells" are of great antiquity and are said to have been in use since A.D. 347. The gas from a well, if directly ignited, will, it is said, throw up a flame 20 or 30 feet high, which can be readily extinguished by placing a piece of clay over the opening. The mouth of the well is then closed with a small bamboo tube through which the gas is led away as needed.

In 1826 one of the wells caught fire with a tremendous report, and the whole enclosure became a sea of flame swaying over the mouth of the well. A large, heavy stone was placed over the mouth, but was shot up into the air together with the men who had placed it there. The fire was finally extinguished by collecting a large amount of water high on a hillside and running it down the slope into the well.*

It would seem that there is still scope to exploit the numerous by-products of this great industry, for in addition to the residue from the salt, the wells undoubtedly contain other gases whose uses have not been developed. The carcasses of the worn-out buffaloes are, of course, marketable to the last ounce, from the flesh, which is eaten, to the hides, bones, horns, and hoofs. The dung of the live animal has a definite value and becomes the property of the driver, who dries the sweepings, and mixing them with earth, sells the cakes thus formed for fuel.

The expensive steam-engine is, in the long run, a much cheaper form of power than the necessary herds of buffaloes, even when it is aged before its time by being subjected to the rough and inexpert treatment which it receives at Tzeliutsing. The engineers, in true Szechwan fashion, contrive to extract the maximum power with the minimum expenditure from machines which would long since have been scrapped in other lands. The safety valves are tightly lashed down so that no ounce of energy may be lost. The gauge glasses are so encrusted with grime that no one could read them, even supposing they wished or were able to. Nevertheless, it is affirmed that explosions of the boilers are not of frequent occurrence.

With these innovations arrived that most inartistic of all products of Western culture, the kerosene tin, which even in Tzeliutsing threatens to become no mean rival to the bamboo as an article capable of almost universal use. It is found particularly serviceable as an alternative to the bamboo bucket. Nevertheless, despite the advent of up-to-date ideas, the main work of Tzeliutsing is carried on in the old picturesque way with its bamboos, buffaloes, and local customs, the methods and machinery used being in the main unchanged from ancient times; and it cannot be denied that, rude and clumsy as those methods may appear when compared with modern scientific devices, they have achieved remarkable results. True, the results are secured at the cost of much unnecessary expenditure of time, human labour, and potentially valuable gas, but there is always time to spare in China, and nature is prodigal of her resources of life and material in Szechwan.

It is interesting to note that 1,700 years ago the people in this far western province possessed sufficient skill and enterprise to bore down through rock for a depth of from 2,000 to 3,000 feet and the acumen to perceive that the brine was there to reward their efforts. The salt wells of Tzeliutsing deserve to be associated with the Great Wall and the Grand Canal as monuments to the industry and foresight of the ancient Chinese. Actually these wells are in a class apart, for the two other undertakings, prodigious as they were, required little engineering skill, whereas the wells stand out uniquely as evidence of Chinese ingenuity and perseverance.

* "China at Work." R. P. Hommel.

THE COMING OF THE STEAMER

HOW the steamer came to the Upper Yangtze and killed all the dragons and how the conservative junkmen, with a way of life unchanged for centuries, came to be introduced to the modern steamship make a fascinating story, particularly since the Chinese came eventually to adopt the steamship themselves, to their very great gain.

The idea of steam navigation on the Upper Yangtze occurred to many people: Admiral Lord Charles Beresford; the Reverend S. Chevalier, a French Jesuit priest; Thomas W. Blakiston; and others. Opposed to them were a number of famous Chinese authorities, who were just as determined that no new-fangled ideas should prevail.

The pioneer who, through persistent attempts, was eventually to break down this resistance was Mr. Archibald Little, whose name will always be associated with the Upper Yangtze and with steam navigation as far as Chungking, 1,350 miles from the sea.

Little, finding no support in China for his exciting ideas, took them to England, where in due course a small concern was formed under the name of the Upper Yangtze Steam Navigation Company. The *Kuling*, first steamer for the firm, was built on the Clyde. Specially designed to negotiate the rapids, she was a 500-ton stern-wheeler, 175 feet long, flat-bottomed, with a draught of 2½ feet when light. Her engines were amidships and drove the two paddles by piston rods 57 feet long. She was shipped out in sections, assembled in Shanghai, launched towards the end of 1887, and finally taken up to Ichang.

Mr. Little's difficulties then began; for from that date, for nearly two years, the Chinese officials exerted every artifice for delay that a clever people could devise. Innumerable despatches passed to and fro between the British Minister in Peking and the Tsung-li Yamen, detailing on the one hand the objections and obstructions that occurred in Ichang and, on the other, disclaiming all responsibility for these freshly contrived impediments.

One of the most ingenious, as well as the most famous, of these excuses was the plea put forward by the Ichang authorities that the cliffs of the gorges swarmed with fierce and uncontrolled monkeys, who would become so enraged by the noise and smoke emitted by the steamer that they would throw volleys of stones, whereby the ship would most certainly be disabled and the crew killed. Even that sage and enlightened statesman Li Hung-chang argued that it would be useless to attempt steam navigation of the Upper Yangtze, because when the great Emperor Yü had opened up the channels he had neglected to remove the rocks. The inference was that the far-sighted Yü, who over 2,000 years ago had traditionally laboured over improving China's waterways, had obviously not intended steamers to run there.

The negotiations broke down in 1889 and ended in a truly typical Chinese way, for the Chinese Government bought the ship they had refused permission to run and sold it to the China Merchants' Steam Navigation Company at a great profit. She continued to run for many years on the Ichang-Hankow section and finally became a hulk at Kiukiang.

Once the steamer was disposed of, the Chinese Government made concessions and Chungking was opened to foreign trade in 1890. American and British consulates were opened there.

Archibald Little was determined to be the first to take a steamer up to Chungking, but this time he was less ambitious. He designed a small 7-ton launch, which was built in Shanghai of teak and had a speed of 9 knots. Named the *Leechuan,* she measured 55 feet in length. The engine-room staff consisted of a middle-aged engineer from Ningpo and two stokers. With Little, who had some experience as a yachtsman, in command and two junkmen, the *Leechuan* finally set out from Ichang. Mrs. Little accompanied the expedition.

The Leechuan.

At some of the bad rapids 300 trackers had to be employed to help the launch up. After considerable strain, anxiety, and tragi-comic accidents and adventures, the *Leechuan* arrived safely ten miles below Chungking, and a runner was despatched to announce her arrival. Here, by request, she remained for the night to allow the Reception Committee to make due preparations.

Never before had the inhabitants of Chungking shown so much interest in things foreign as they evinced in the coming of the first steamer. The city officials warned all junks of the approach of an "iron plank ship, which moves very fast, and which it would be wise for all junks to avoid."

To the people of Chungking this launch, small as she was, was nevertheless a steamer and of immense importance as the first to surmount the obstacles presented by the most difficult part of the river.

On 9 March 1898, a party of seven men, one lady, and two children went down in a houseboat belonging to an American, Dr. McCartney, carrying flags and firecrackers. The Chinese also sent down six guard boats, decked with flags in honour of the occasion. The outbursts of cheering almost drowned the noise of the crackers.

The *Leechuan* then steamed up-river and made a triumphant entry into Chungking harbour. Amid fresh fusillades of crackers she anchored off the Chao T'ien Men, the Gate that looks to Heaven. The banks of the river were black with spectators. The Chinese guard boats fired salute after salute, and an address of welcome was read.

The *Leechuan* had successfully negotiated the passage up in the low-water season; but, as her own power was insufficient for her to surmount the worst rapids, she had had to be tracked over them like an ordinary junk. It may therefore be said that the journey, momentous enough as being that of the first steamer to pass through the waters of the Upper Yangtze, did little towards proving that those waters were really navigable for steamships. Nevertheless the *Leechuan* provided very real encouragement for future efforts, and the next attempt to invade the inviolable waters of the Upper Yangtze was to be made by a British man-of-war.

Chinese junks call on HMS Woodcock.

Admiral Lord Charles Beresford, while he was in China, had advocated the construction of specially built river gunboats and in this connexion had made inquiries into the possibilities of steam navigation on the Upper Yangtze. Lord Charles' recommendations were well received and carried out. The first British warships put together in the Far East had been shipped out from England in sections and assembled in Shanghai. They were HMS *Woodcock*, commanded by Lieutenant H. Watson, R.N., and HMS *Woodlark*, commanded by Lieutenant H. E. Hillman, R.N. These vessels measured 148 feet with a beam of 24 feet, a tonnage of 150, and had a speed of 13½ knots. They were constructed with nine watertight compartments, and their armament consisted of two 6-pounders and four machine guns.

Although not the best suited to the navigation of the rapids of the Upper Yangtze, they managed, with assistance, to get over all the rapids. At the Yeh T'an the gunboats, assisted by 400 trackers on the shore, a wire hawser to the steam capstan, and their engines steaming at full speed, succeeded in getting over the rapid. The *Woodlark* hung for a short time at the head of the rapid with her stern half-way down it, but all her men were sent at a run to the bows, the stern lifted slightly, and the ship got over the critical point.

Gunboats *Woodcock* and *Woodlark* arrived safely at Chungking on 7 May 1900, after an arduous and eventful journey of 31 days from Ichang. They were received with salutes by the Chinese war junks. The populace lined the city walls overlooking the river, but evinced no great measure of interest or excitement. Both vessels started their descent of the river towards the end of May 1900. Steaming by day and anchoring at night, they accomplished the journey in 24 steaming hours and arrived back in Ichang without mishap.

Not satisfied by his achievement in the *Leechuan* and deterred by the delays and frustrations of his adventure with the *Kuling*, Little maintained his fixed resolve to master the problem of steam navigation on the Upper Yangtze. He returned to England to form a new company and persuaded some of his friends to join him in the enterprise of building a more powerful ship than before.

At the Oriental Club in London he met Captain Cornell Plant, who had been master of a ship that had plied on two rivers well-known for their tricky navigation, the Tigris and the Euphrates. A common fascination for the navigation of rapids and dangerous waters eventually brought Plant out to China to study the rapids and to command Little's new ship, the *Pioneer*. She was built on the Clyde, came out in parts, and was assembled in Shanghai. Her tonnage was about double that of the gunboats. She measured about 178 feet long, was 60 feet broad over the paddles, and had a speed of 14 knots.

On 12 June 1900, with a load of 150 tons of cargo and many passengers, the *Pioneer* left Ichang.

When she arrived at the Hsin T'an, she hung for a time on the lip, but managed to get over. The greatest difficulty came at the Teh T'an, where she was delayed for three days before she could be got over the rushing torrent of water, with the aid of hawsers to the shore.

Finally she arrived at Chungking, having taken 73 steaming hours to make the ascent. The voyage was a great success; but unfortunately it was the only commercial trip she made, for owing to the repercussions from the Boxer troubles she was commandeered by the British Consul for use as an evacuation ship and eventually sold to the British Government. She served as a river gunboat under the name HMS *Kinsha* for more than 20 years, but was finally sold into Chinese hands and served to carry chickens from Ningpo to Shanghai.

The year 1900 was immensely important in the history of steam navigation on the Yangtze, for it saw a third assault on the hitherto impenetrable regions of Western China.

The SS Pioneer.

This was made by a German-built steamer, the *Suihsing*. She was larger and more powerful than the *Pioneer*, with a length of 210 feet and a speed of 14 knots. This extra length was probably her undoing, for it has now been accepted that in the winter the intricate channels cannot be navigated by a ship over 150 feet long.

She hit a rock on her maiden voyage and was a total loss. This so discouraged adventurous spirits that for some years no merchant ships attempted the ascent of the Upper Yangtze, and steam navigation in these waters was carried on only by vessels of the foreign navies and then only at the most favourable seasons of the year.

After relinquishing command of the *Pioneer*, Captain Plant built a junk-houseboat and, while trading profitably between Ichang and Chungking, made a thorough study of the rapids.

After a period of nine years of inactivity an attempt was made once more to build a suitable merchant ship, and Captain Plant was in this case the originator of

The German Steamer Suihsing.

the plan. His years of experience on the Upper River were embodied in a new steamer called the *Shutung*. Though lacking support from British firms, he managed to influence a number of rich and influential Chinese, and in 1908 the *Shutung* was built in England by Thornycroft. She represented quite a new approach to the problem, for she carried very little cargo herself and was more in the nature of a powerful tug designed to tow a 150-ton cargo lighter, the same length as herself, lashed alongside.

She measured 115 feet with a beam of 15 and had a speed of 13 knots—11 knots with a fully loaded barge alongside. She made her first trip on 19 October 1909, under Captain Plant, and surmounted every rapid under her own power. She soon settled down to regular runs of two trips a month loaded to capacity with freight and passengers. So popular was she that accommodation had to be booked weeks in advance. During the voyage the passengers were so crowded that they had to stand on deck all day and sleep in sampans alongside when the ship was anchored for the night. In the low-water season she was warped over the rapids that she could not surmount under her own power.

In 1926 there was an amalgamation of various United States shipping interests in the Yangtze Rapids Company, which functioned until 1935, when they were bought out by rival firms.

The influence of steamer competition on freights had a tendency to lower junk charges, and the junkmen had no cause to love the steamer. The disturbed internal condition of China at that time gave fresh grounds for their hostility. Bandits and armed robbers, high taxes and the army's habit of commandeering goods made life very difficult and confused.

Managing a steamer in a rapid is very much the same as handling a junk. In the case of a steamer with ample power her engines are usually sufficient to get her

The SS Shutung.

over the head of the rapid. When the rapid is running too strongly, a wire sometimes as much as 200 fathoms in length has to be passed ashore with the end made fast to a rock above the head of the rapid, and led in abreast of the bridge and so to the capstan. The ship is then eased out on the arc of a circle with the wire as a radius. As soon as the swing effect has ceased, the capstan heaves round at full speed, and, as the ship makes the bank again, a few feet of wire are "made."

Archibald Little, one of the two men who brought about these great changes was, like his famous ship, the true pioneer of the Upper Yangtze. His main life's work was embodied in the three steamers which he had worked for so indefatigably in the face of almost insuperable difficulties. He died at the age of 70, with the satisfaction of knowing that the problem so dear to him was being tackled again in the building of the *Shutung*.

Captain Plant carried on after Mr. Little. When he retired, the Chinese Government rewarded his services as River Inspector by building him a bungalow overlooking the Hsin T'an. Here, amid scenes familiar to him and his wife, he planned to live within sight and sound of the most spectacular and formidable of all the rapids. No steamship ever struggled up over the astonishing gradient, or careered down the roaring boiling reach unseen by the old sailor, who would watch their progress from his window. The custom grew up of saluting him in passing with a blast on the whistle, and he would reply with a wave of his handkerchief.

In the rapids.

Neither Plant nor his wife had been back to England since their first arrival in China, and in 1921 they decided to pay their own country a visit before returning to China to spend the remainder of their lives in the surroundings they loved best. He felt, moreover, a sense of responsibility towards the Chinese pilots whose training he had supervised, and in whom he felt such an interest that he was loath to leave them.

The Plants received a wonderful send off all down the river. They sailed from Shanghai in a Blue Funnel Steamer; but the old man died of pneumonia before the ship reached Hong Kong. The shock was overwhelming to his wife, and she too died as the ship was entering port. They were buried together in Happy Valley, Hong Kong.

More and more steamships came to the Upper Yangtze and proved a source of wealth for a time. In contrast with what might have been expected, the popularity of the steamer dealt no mortal blow to the junk traffic of the interior. Indeed quite the reverse—only their field of action was now more often off the beaten track and up the turbulent tributaries and creeks.

In the big cities, great changes in comfort and convenience have come to China: electric lights, plumbing, refrigerators, lipstick, wireless and the rest; and the town-dweller has changed with them.

Among the junkmen, however, life has changed their living standards hardly at all; they are as they were years and years ago; yet the junk pilots of the Upper Yangtze, in a decade, took to the art of piloting steamers, and the junkmen became seamen in the "iron plank ships" with the same degree of efficiency as they had shown for countless years in their own craft, and let it be said once more, to their very great gain.

PART TWO

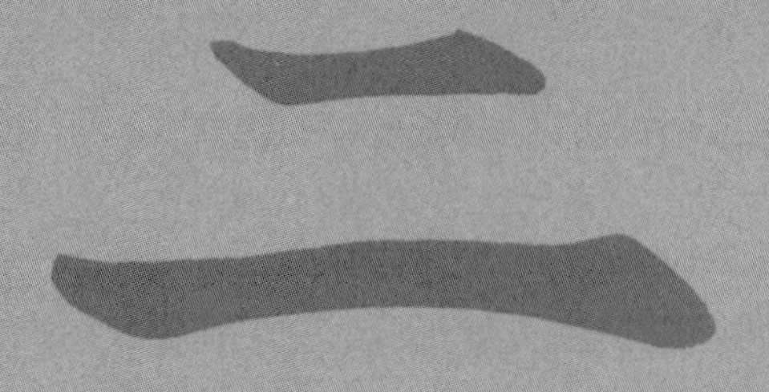

CRAFT OF THE ESTUARY & SHANGHAI AREA

Infomuch a man may fay there are two Empires of China, the one upon the water, and the other upon the land; and as many Venices as there are cities. For thefe veffels ferve inftead of houfes to them that are the makers of them. There they drefs their meat, there they are born, there they are bred, and there they dye.

THE NEW HISTORY OF CHINA, 1688
by Gabriel Magaillans,
Miffionary Apoftolick.

THE YANGTZE ESTUARY

IN ancient times the delta of the Yangtze extended very much farther inland, and the river found other alternative outlets to the sea by way of the T'aihu (太 湖), flowing, not through one broad channel, as it does to-day, but through three separate mouths.

Documentary evidence for this exists in an early chapter in the "Shu Ching" (書 經), known as the "Yü Kung" (禹 貢), which may be described as the most ancient of Chinese geographical works and is said to have been compiled 4,000 years ago by the Emperor Yü, the legendary conservancy expert. In this chapter appeared references to the three mouths of the river, and there are similar allusions in the latter chapters of the "Shu Ching."

References to the Emperor Yü will be found in Part One, pages 3, 5, and 7.

While there seems small room for doubt that these three mouths of the river existed, in the absence of any record defining their exact position any theories on the subject must be in the nature of conjecture.

In the "Yü Kung" the Emperor Yü is said to have so far described the three mouths as to name them the Peikiang, or North River; the Chungkiang, or middle or principal stream; and the Nankiang, or South River, which was the largest and entered the sea near Hangchow.

According to the "Cheng K'eng," the three rivers separated at the Poyang Lake. In the "Han Shu" it is said that at the beginning of the first century the waters of the great river entered the sea at Yüyao, about 30 miles west of Ningpo. This latter work states that the parting of the river occurred at Shihchêng, and that the southernmost branch passed near Chicheufu before entering the sea.

Basing their opinions on these ancient historical books, experts consider that the head of the delta was once at Wuhu, and that one arm traversed the lake south of the great plain and proceeded thence to the sea at the head of Hangchow Bay, while the other two started from the eastern side of the lake, one entering the sea at Kanp'u, the other at Woosung.

If one bears in mind the vagaries of this immense stream and the nature of the soft alluvial soil through which it cuts its imperious way, it seems not improbable that there may have been several changes in the position of its ancient mouths before it settled down to the more orthodox method of flowing through one embouchement into the sea. Certain it is that before this happened the configuration of the coast was very different, and a great part of the Shanghai plain was not yet reclaimed from the sea. Quinsan, which some 2,000 years ago was a seaport, is now 80 miles inland, and some 20 other cities have grown up on what was once a swampy waste.

In the latter part of its course the Yangtze flows through a wide alluvial plain, and the occasional hills resemble islands embedded in a loamy deposit of the river silt. This process is still continuing, and the Yangtze delta is said to be advancing at the rate of a mile in 60 years over a front of more than 80 miles. In 60 generations of the inhabitants it is said that 45,000 square miles of land have been reclaimed.

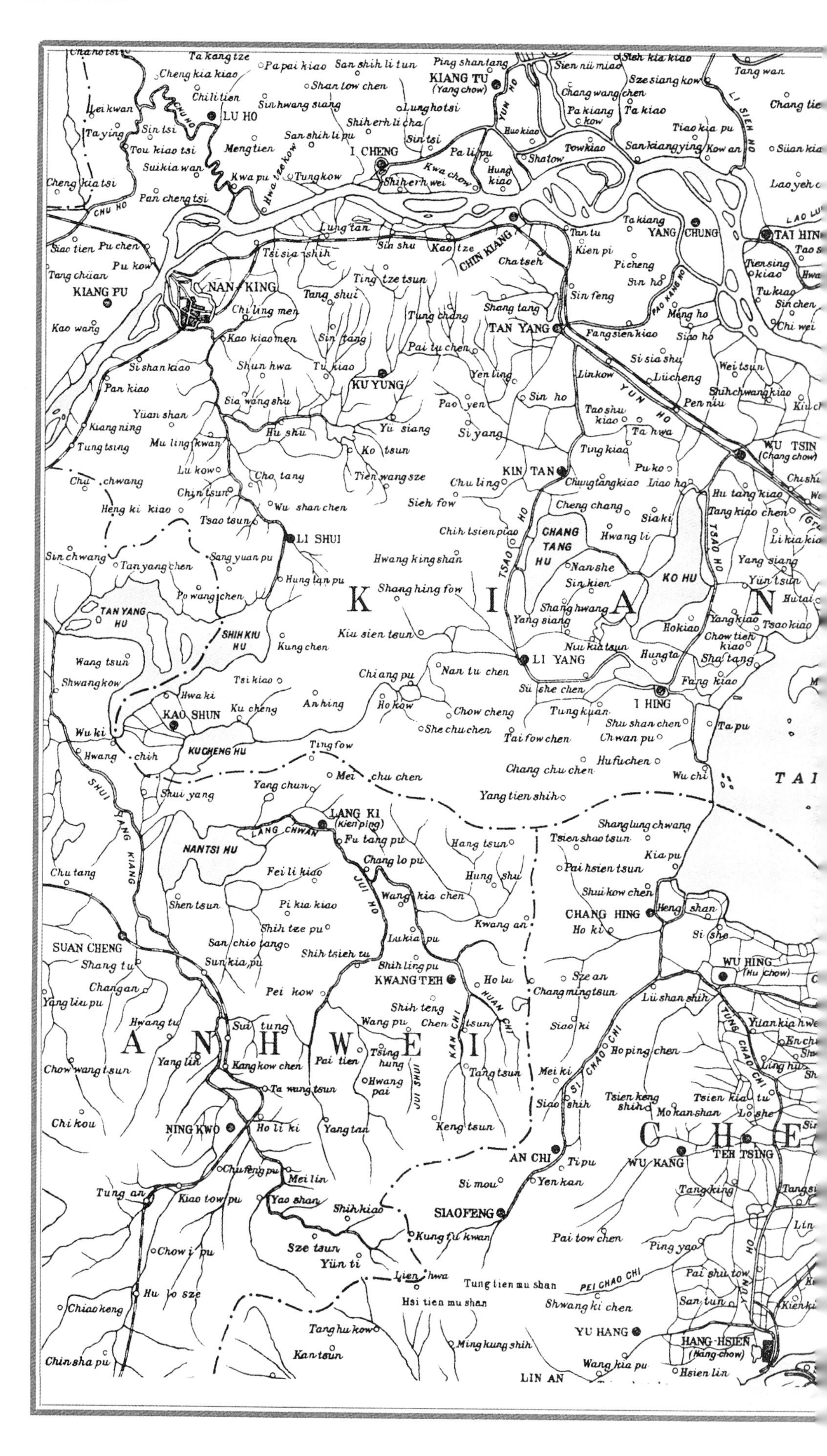
K I A N
A N H W E I
C H E
KIANG TU
(Yang chow)
LU HO
I CHENG
NAN KING
KIANG FU
CHIN KIANG
TAN YANG
YANG CHUNG
TAI HIN
KU YUNG
LI SHUI
KIN TAN
WU TSIN
(Chang chow)
CHANG TANG HU
KO HU
TAN YANG HU
SHIH KIU HU
LI YANG
I HING
KAO SHUN
KUCHENG HU
LANG KI
(Kien ping)
LANG CHWAN
NANTSI HU
CHANG HING
WU HING
(Hu chow)
SUAN CHENG
KWANG TEH
NING KWO
AN CHI
SIAOFENG
WU KANG
TEH TSING
YU HANG
HANG-HSIEN
(Hang chow)
LIN AN
CHU HO
YUN HO
LI SIEH HO
TSAO HO
JUI HO
SHUI YANG KIANG
HWANG CHI
SI CHAO CHI
PEI CHAO CHI
Lung tan
Chi ling men
Kao kiao men
Shun hwa
Tu kiao
Sia wang shu
Hu shu
Ko tsun
Pao yen
Yü siang
Si yang
Sin ho
Chu ling
Sieh fow
Chih tsien piao
Hwang king shan
Shang hing fow
Kiu sien tsun
Chiang pu
Nan tu chen
Ho kow
Chow cheng
She chu chen
Tai fow chen
Chang chu chen
Hufu chen
Yang tien shih
Mei chu chen
Yang chun
Ting fow
An hing
Ku cheng
Hwa ki
Tsi kiao
Kung chen
Wu ki
Hwang chih
Shui yang
Chu tang
Shang tu
Changan
Yang liu pu
Hwang tu
Sui tung
Yang lin
Kang kow chen
Chow wang tsun
Chi kou
Ta wang tsun
Ho li ki
Yang tan
Chu feng pu
Mei lin
Yao shan
Kiao tow pu
Tung an
Chow i pu
Hu lo sze
Chiao keng
Chin sha pu
Sze tsun
Yün ti
Shih kiao
Kung fu kwan
Lien hwa
Tung tien mu shan
Hsi tien mu shan
Tang hu kow
Kan tsun
Ming kung shih
Wang kia pu
Hsien lin
Shwang ki chen
Pai tow chen
Ping yao
Tang king
Yen kan
Ti pu
Si mou
Keng tsun
Tang tsun
Mei ki
Siao shih
Siao ki
Ho ping chen
Lü shan shih
Tsien keng shih
Mo kan shan
Tsien kia tu
Sze an
Chang ming tsun
Ho lu
Shih ling pu
Lu kia pu
Shih tsieh tu
Shih tze pu
Pi kia kiao
Fei li kiao
Shen tsun
San chio tang
Sun kia pu
Pei kow
Wang pu
Chen
Shih teng
Pai tien
Tsing hung
Hwang pai
Wang kia chen
Hung shu
Kwang an
Chang lo pu
Fu tang pu
Hang tsun
Tsien shao tsun
Shang lung chwang
Kia pu
Pai hsien tsun
Shui kow chen
Heng shan
Ho ki
Si she
Tung kuan
Shu shan chen
Chwan pu
Wu chi
Ta pu
Su she chen
Nui kia tsun
Hung ta
Fang kiao
Sha tang
Chow tien kiao
Hokiao
Yang kiao
Tsao kiao
Shang hwang
Yang siang
Nan she
Sin kien
Hwang li
Cheng chang
Siaki
Chwig tang kiao
Pu ko
Liao ha
Ting kiao
Tao shu kiao
Ta hwa
Lücheng
Pen niu
Si sia shu
Linkow
Fang sien kiao
Siao ho
Meng ho
Sin feng
Shang tang
Tung chang
Pai tu chen
Yen ling
Ting tze tsun
Tang shui
Sin fang
Chatseh
Kao tze
Sin shu
Tsi sia shih
Tan tu
Kien pi
Picheng
Sin ho
Ta kiang
Shatow
Towkiao
Hung kiao
Pa li pu
Kwa chow
Shih erh wei
Tungkow
Kwa pu
Mengtien
San shih li pu
Sin tsi
Shih erh li cha
Lunghotsi
Sin hwang siang
Shan tow chen
Papai kiao
San shih li tun
Ping shan tang
Ta kang tze
Cheng kia kiao
Chili tien
Lei kwan
Ta ying
Sin tsi
Tou kiao tsi
Suikia wan
Pan cheng tsi
Cheng kia tsi
Siao tien
Pu chen
Pu kow
Tang chüan
Kao wang
Si shan kiao
Pan kiao
Yüan shan
Kiang ning
Tung tsing
Mu ling kwan
Lu kow
Chu chwang
Chin tsun
Heng ki kiao
Cho tang
Wu shan chen
Tsao tsun
Tien wang sze
Sin chwang
Tan yang chen
Sang yuan pu
Hung lan pu
Po wang chen
Wang tsun
Shwang kow
Sien nü miao
Sieh kia kiao
Chang wang chen
Sze siang kow
Pa kiang kow
Ta kiao
Tiao kia pu
San kiang ying
Kow an
Tang wan
Chang tie
Siian kia
Lao yeh
Tien sing kiao
Tu kiao
Sin chen
Chi wei
Wei tsun
Shih chwang kiao
Hu tang kiao
Tang kiao chen
Li kia kiao
Yang siang
Yün tsun
Hu tai
Yüan kia hwe
Ling hu
TAI

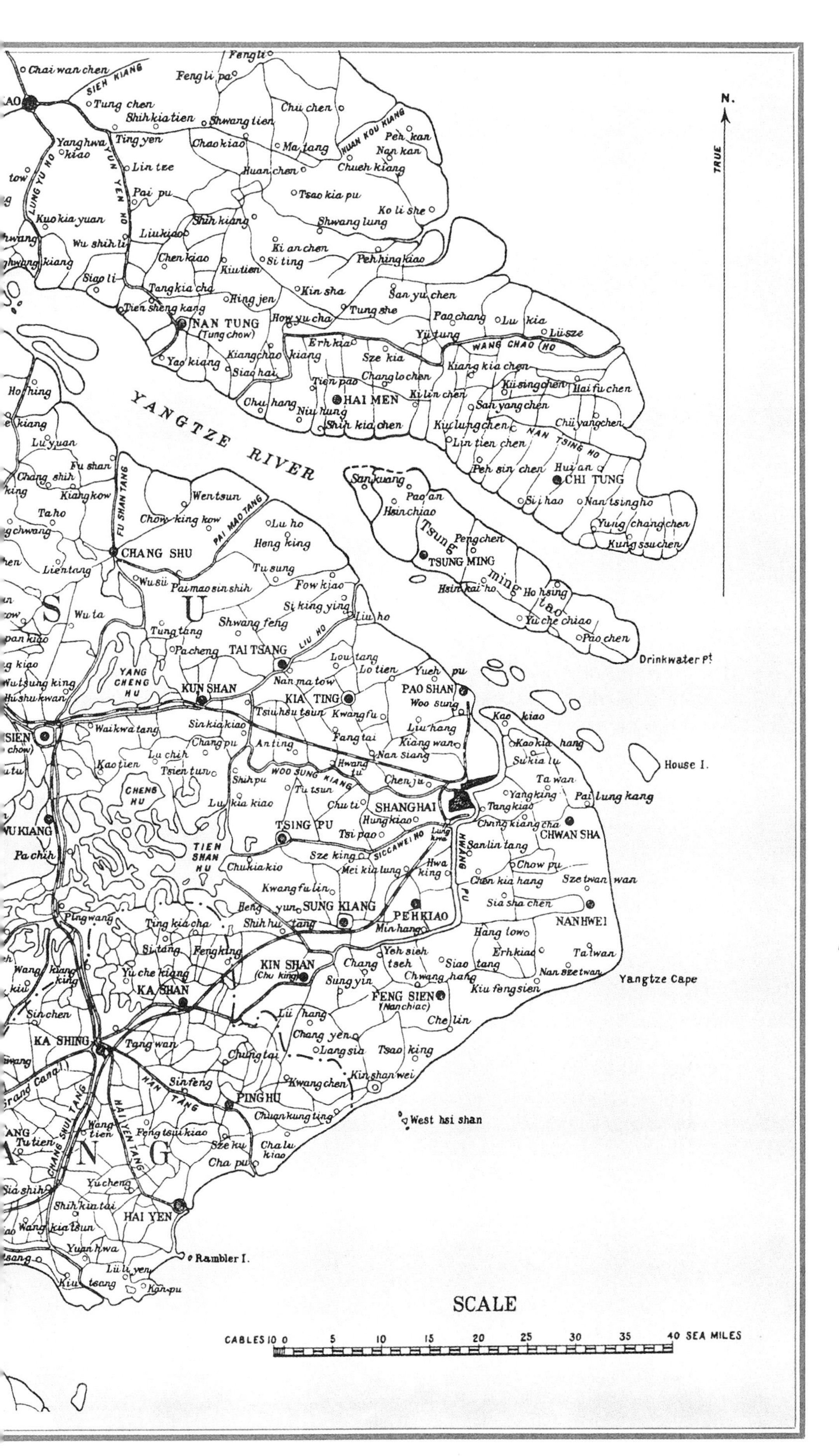

Shanghai waterways.

It is by no means improbable that the islands lying off the estuary may one day be joined to the mainland in the march forward of the alluvial plain, particularly as every yard of ground thus reclaimed is at once embanked and cultivated by the Chinese farmers. Mr. von Heidenstam* gives it as his opinion that in 1,200 years' time the present Yangtze cape will be at Gutzlaff, which rocky island will by then have become a hill upon a plain.

The China Sea off the mouth of the Yangtze River is open towards the north and east, with depths exceeding 10 fathoms at about 30 miles from the China coast. The effect of the muddy waters of the Yangtze is apparent many miles out to sea, where a more or less abrupt transition from clear to yellow water may be observed. To the reflective there is food for thought in this evidence of waters which have travelled over 3,000 miles from their source in the plateau of Tibet, close to the cradle of the great rivers of India.

The estuary, as it is to-day, presents no picturesque or beautiful features, and the lack of any natural landmarks adds an unsympathetic and inhospitable air to the dangers of its hidden sandbanks. Nevertheless, there is mystery and romance to the imaginative in the vast delta of this historic river as the deep blue of the outside limits of the estuary waters near the Saddles† thickens gradually till it becomes the turbid coffee-coloured flood associated with its name and the immense desolate stretches of water contract into the shape of the river at Tsungming.

The width of the estuary is about 60 miles, narrowing at Woosung to 20 miles. The fluctuating nature of the shoals and sandbanks extending far beyond the embouchement gives rise to navigational difficulties which begin over 50 miles from the land.

There are two main channels of approach. The North Channel, or Passage, which is not in use at the moment, is about 60 miles long from the 5-fathom line east of Shaweishan Island to Woosung. It has to make considerable bends to avoid a group of sandbanks and small islands. The South Channel is the better and more important. The length from the 5-fathom line is the same, but it runs practically straight. Both are subject to considerable fluctuations of tide and have strong tidal currents up to a maximum of 6 knots at springs. In the North Channel the current is rotary, but in the South Channel there is only a small lateral drift at the turn of the tide.

The land bordering the delta is low and cut by innumerable creek inlets and canals which spread inland, crossing and recrossing each other and forming a network of useful waterways to serve the dense population that thrives in this fertile area. The larger canals are laid out regularly, but there are many blind alleys.

The many streams and rivers, the great lakes, and the marshes of the mighty Yangtze Valley, while they impeded travel by land, offered unparalleled facilities for water transport, and the Chinese were not slow to take advantage of this. Not only did they use existing waterways, but they added to those by excavating countless canals.

Over extensive areas in the Yangtze Valley and southward, this served both to drain the swampy marsh land and to provide increased facilities for transport and travel by water. In some parts, especially on the great plain of Kiangsu and North Chekiang, until the advent of the modern motor road there was practically no transport except by boats. This area is an absolute network of rivers, canals, and creeks, many of the waterways being broad and deep enough to allow fast

* Engineer-in-Chief, Whangpoo Conservancy Board.

† The Saddle Islands consist of a group of islands lying about 30 miles east of the mouth of the Yangtze. They are inhabited during the fishing season by sailors from the mainland engaged in the cuttle-fish industry. The season lasts from April to June, when the islands present a busy scene, being crowded with fishermen from the Fukien coast. Thousands of fishing-boats are normally to be seen. The fish are dried and shipped to the mainland. The fish are split open and spread upon the rocks to dry under a bright, strong sun. When this short fishing season is over the fishermen disappear and the islands and their few inhabitants are left to themselves.

Waterways in the delta area. The dotted line encloses an area of one square mile and is illustrative of the manner in which the land of the delta is cut up into creeks and irrigational canals.

ferries of considerable size to ply between the large towns.

While designed primarily for transportation, the canals also serve countless indispensable functions, such as irrigation, drinking, fishing, and fish breeding, and the washing of food and clothes.

The Yangtze delta is now said to have a population of about 40 million, and it is interesting to note that in the opinion of some authorities the inhabitants of the Kiangsu–Chekiang plain approach more closely to the original indigenous stock of this area, for, with the exception of certain isolated south-western tribes of the interior, such as the Miaotzŭ and Lolo, these coastal folk alone have escaped being merged with the true Chinese who spread from the Yellow River Valley throughout the country. These more primitive people betray their aboriginal origin by their varied dialects and by their mode of subsistence, for they depend for a livelihood not on agriculture, but upon fishing, and are not altogether free from piratical tendencies.

THE SHA-CH'UAN OR KIANGSU TRADER*

Craft indigenous to the Whangpoo and Shanghai area, although they show a great variety, are in the main unadventurous in type, being built for quiet trading on the creeks of the vast surrounding system of waterways.

There are, however, two or three exceptions to these, for the Shanghai junkbuilding yards have produced a few examples of some of the large sea-going junks. The most notable of these is the Shanghai-built type of Kiangsu trader, a craft easily recognized by the two main distinctive features of five masts and the broad, flat stern, from which projects, at an upward angle, a stern gallery of 10 feet or more in length.

See Part One, pages 7–27.

As has been pointed out elsewhere in this book, particulars as to the dates of origin of Chinese riverine junks in general are totally absent, and this is just as true of the sea-going types; but it is at least known that one of the first sea-going junks was known as the bull-head ship (牛 頭 船), and this descriptive title is not inapt to the Kiangsu trader, which would appear to have evolved from the earliest of the bull-head types. The Kiangsu trader, therefore, may be classed with the Antung trader as one of the two fundamental types of sea-going craft of the north from which have evolved various other classes.

The large Kiangsu trader is seldom to be seen nowadays. It was often of considerable size, occasionally as long as 170 feet. This, large as it may seem in terms of junks, is nevertheless according to modern ideas very small for sea-going craft,† especially for those which have to beat up the northern waters of the China coast in any kind of weather.

Although the family of junks to which the bull-head, to be described later, and Kiangsu traders belong are commonly supposed to hail from the north, the latter junk having even been designated the Pechili trader, there seems very good reason to believe that they are really basically Yangtze estuary types which through constant intercourse with the north have become, as it were, naturalized there while still retaining their link with Shanghai. So it came about that types of this craft are built either at or near Shanghai or South Shantung.

Close observation strengthens this opinion, as these craft show none of the characteristics of the northern types; indeed, the main features are essentially those of the Yangtze estuary: for instance, the cut of the sails and the number of battens, the general lines and construction, the shape of the bow, and the projecting stern gallery.

The length of their passage north to Antung, Newchwang, Chefoo, and Tsingtao varies from under a week to as much as three weeks, according to weather and wind conditions. Many years ago they made four regular voyages a year, but this was later reduced to two trips owing to steamer competition.

The small type of craft is known by the Chinese as the *sha-ch'uan* (沙 船), or sand-boat, a generic name for the sea-going junks from Shanghai. A typical example is illustrated in Plate No. 1. It has an over-all length of only 85 feet, a beam of 18½ feet over-all, and 15 feet upper deck measurement. The depth from the main deck is 8 feet to water-line. The finer lines of this type will be appreciated by comparison with the measurement given above of the large Kiangsu trader.

Like its prototype, it is extremely strong in construction. This gives a clumsy appearance, especially in conjunction with the fact that the genuine turret-built hull is illustrated to a marked degree, that is to say, a barrel-shaped hull upon which is superimposed a relatively narrow deck.

* Sometimes known as the "Pechili trader."

† Drake's ship, the *Pelican*, which he renamed the *Golden Hind*, was not more than 66 feet long and of only about 100 tons burden. Yet in this small ship Drake successfully concluded a voyage of three years' duration and circumnavigated the world.

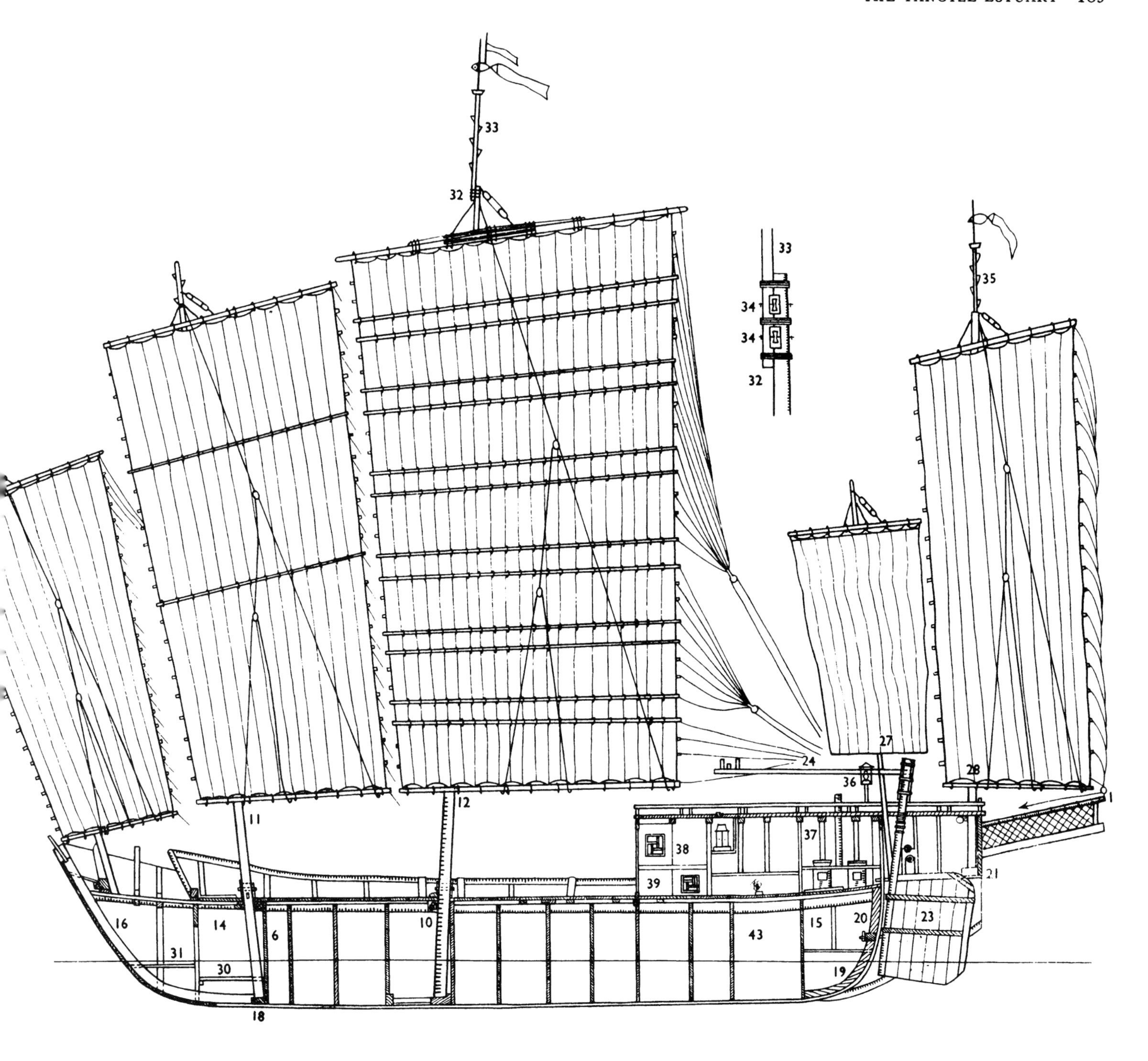
33
32
34
34
32
33
35
1
24
27
36
28
12
11
21
38
37
39
23
20
16
14
6
10
43
15
31
30
19
18

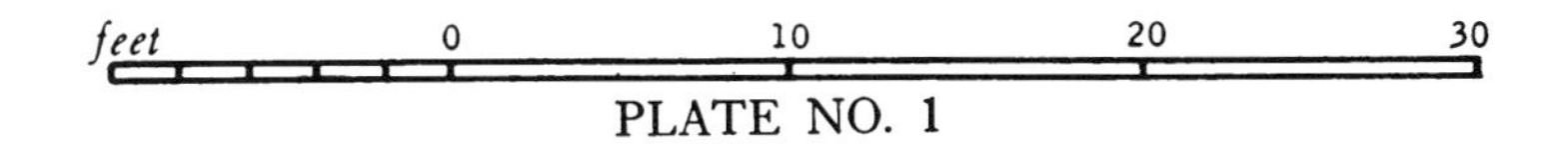
feet
0
10
20
30

PLATE NO. 1

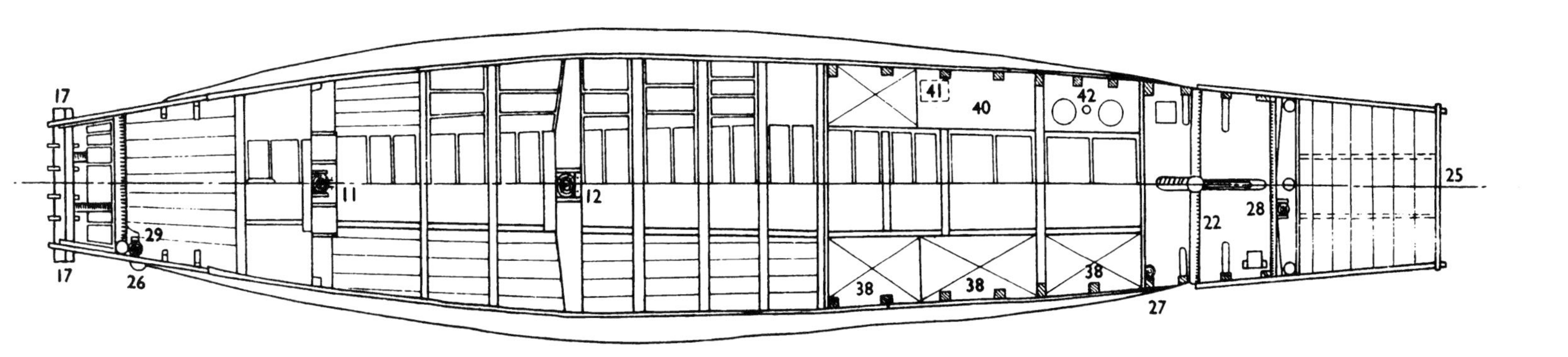
17
41
40
42
25
11
12
22
28
29
17
26
38
38
38
27

The pinewood hull is flat-bottomed, but the central one of the longitudinal planks, being thicker and heavier than the others and made of hardwood, serves as a keel. It measures 1 foot 2 inches in width and 4 inches in depth, and continues throughout the vessel. The planking from the turn of the bottom at bow and stern is laid athwartships. Much of the vessel's great strength is provided by 14 pinewood bulkheads. These are further strengthened by two vertical uprights amidships and by timbers across the bottom, joined to side timbers grown approximately to shape and roughly trimmed so as to fit to the sides and curves of the whale-back (see Plate No. 2).

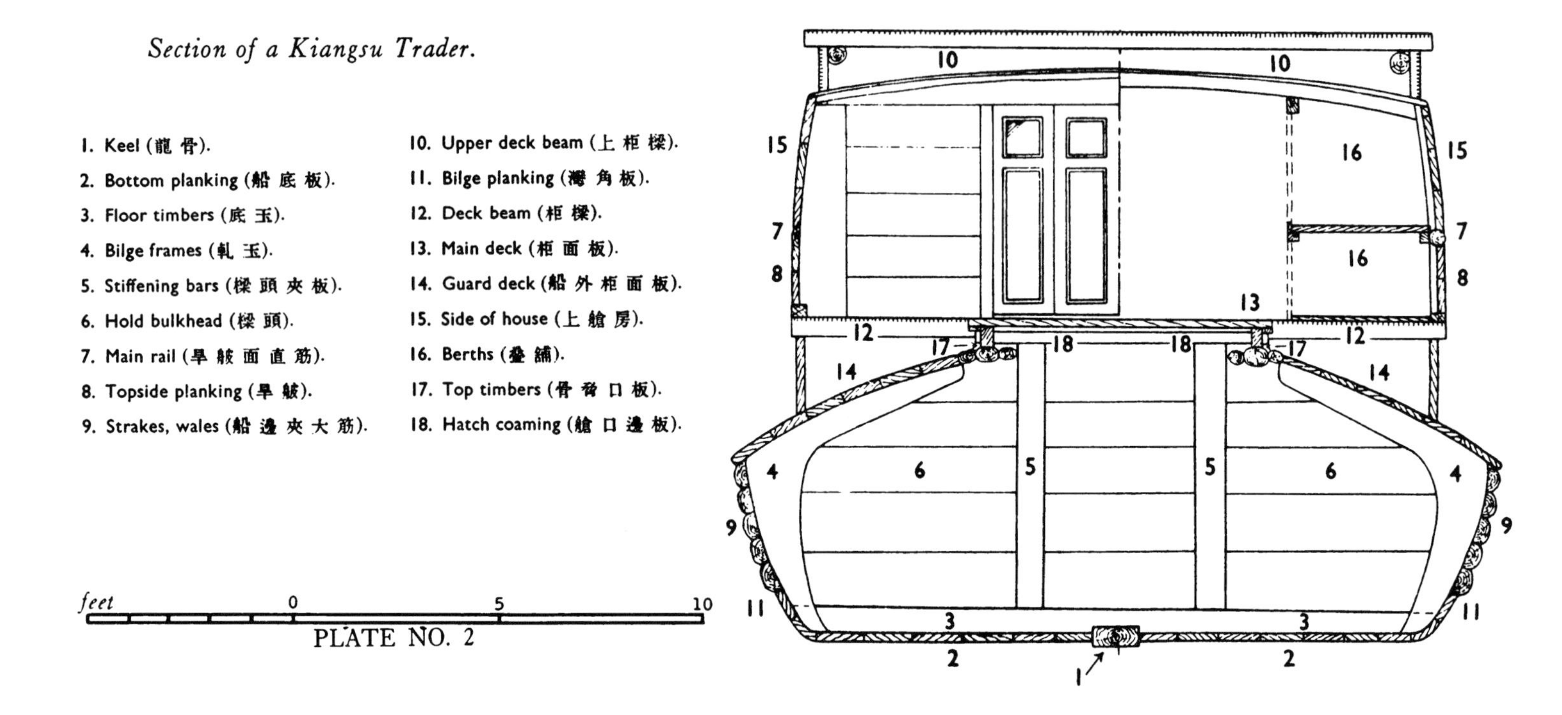

Section of a Kiangsu Trader.

PLATE NO. 2

The space between the first and second bulkheads is used for storing fresh water. Extra longitudinal strength is provided externally by five heavy wales, each being a split pole, and internally by three strong longitudinal members running from end to end of the vessel and situated just below the hatch coaming.

Transverse strength is derived from bulkheads and numerous deck beams[10], one on and above the second bulkhead, two especially large ones into which the fore[11] and main[12] masts enter, a fourth at the break of the house, and four smaller ones at appropriate intervals.

The beam of the vessel at the widest point of the whale-back is 18½ feet, while that of the deck proper itself is only 7¼ feet at the hatch coamings[9]. Additional deck space is provided over the curving whale-back[5] by filling in the interval between deck and bulwarks with removable planks so as to make a continuous, albeit temporary, flush deck.

As the curves of the turret-built hull converge more acutely at bow and stern, the foremost[14] and after compartments[15] are masterpieces of ship construction. This ingenuity is exercised to the full in the manner in which the curved deck beams are rabbeted into the curved frames of the hull. The strain is distributed in the bow by three fore and aft stem ribs[16] which are grown to shape, and following the line of the bottom extend from the stem cross-beam[17] to the heel of the foremast[18], which rests against the first bulkhead. The same method of construction, though to a lesser degree, is found in the after compartment[15], where a fore and aft stern timber[19] bears against the twelfth and last bulkhead.

The bluff, flaring bow rises high, and so long as it is kept to the sea the junk can, so it is claimed, weather anything. The stern proper[20] is bluff and rounded like the bow; a sort of false stern[21] is, however, built on by means of extending the sides of the hull 8 feet in a rising line, or curve, beyond the transom[20], where they are terminated in a shorter false transom[21] which ends 7 feet above the water-line. The deck surface of this serves as a prolongation of the house wherein is situated the windlass[22] for hoisting the rudder[23]. The rudder is slung within the enclosed space between the sides of the false stern[21]. The rudder is 16½ feet deep from the rudder head to the bottom edge and 7 feet at the lower band. It works in three open-jawed wooden gudgeons, which permit it to be raised or lowered as desired. When hoisted it is only a little more than a foot in the water, and the helmsman stands on top of the house. When the junk is under sail the rudder is nearly always lowered and is completely submerged, 5 feet or more being below the keel line. The helmsman then is stationed inside the house and has a rather restricted view ahead through it and a view of his sails through the skylight. The tiller[24] consists of a fine piece of highly-polished hardwood and is 16 feet long. There are always one or two spares kept at either level to facilitate the reshipping of the tiller after the rudder has been either hoisted or lowered to a new position.

False stern and projecting stern gallery of a Kiangsu Trader.
E. SIGAUT

Projecting beyond the false stern[21] and at an upward angle is one of the two most characteristic features of these junks, the 10-foot long stern-gallery[25]. The other distinguishing feature of the junks of this family is the number and arrangement of the masts. These, of which there are five, are staggered. They are named the *t'ou-wei* (頭 桅), or head mast, that is to say, the port foremast[26]; the *erh-wei* (二 桅), or second mast, that is to say, the foremast[11]; the *chung-ta-wei* (中 大 桅), or middle big mast, that is to say, the mainmast[12]; the *ssŭ-wei* (四 桅), or fourth mast, that is to say, the port mizzen[27]; and the *wei-wei* (尾 桅), the tail or last mast, that is to say, the mizzen[28].*

The port fore and fore masts are raked forward, the main has a slight rake aft, the port mizzen a forward rake, and the mizzen stands erect.† The port foremast is 31 feet high and is stepped inboard close to the port bulwarks which is between it and a single-winged tabernacle[29], the heel being stepped on a deck beam. The port foremast is not stepped on the outside of the bulwarks, as is popularly supposed, but inside, resting its heel on the beam and sometimes held by a small tabernacle which wedges it snugly against the inside of the bulwark. The other cheek, consisting of a curved piece of wood grown to shape, adds its support. The lower end of this baulk, which has the same forward rake as the mast itself, rests on the rising curve of the turret. That part which projects like a bit above the bulwark is vertical. The foremast, which is 46 feet in height, is in the true fore and aft line. It is housed in low tabernacles, the heel being fitted into a step on the keel, where it rests against the first bulkhead. This support, however, is not continuous upwards, as the foremast cants forward. Further strength is therefore rendered by a fore and aft baulk of timber bearing against the second frame[30]. A similar baulk of timber[31], though at a higher level and bearing against the first and second frames, serves still further to distribute the strain. The mainmast[12], which is 70 feet high, is a fine spar of *sha-mu* or Oregon pine, measuring 60 feet to the hounds[32] and iron bound at frequent intervals. It is practically the same length as the junk itself at deck level but without the stern gallery. It is in the same line as the foremast, and is similarly housed in a low tabernacle. As it is raked aft instead of forward, however, it rests at deck level against the upper portion of the fifth bulkhead instead of at its heel. A light top-mast[33] (see inset) is secured by three iron bands. The sheaves for the halyards are situated between the cheeks of the lower mast and the heel of the top-mast, and retained in place by the sheave pins[34] which pass through both masts. The port mizzen[27], 28 feet in height, and the after mizzen[28], 48 feet high, are stepped

* In the naming of the masts I have followed the suggestions of Monsieur Sigaut, who knows more about sea-going junks than any man.

† An individual variation is in the rake of the masts, which is peculiar to each junk. For instance, the foremast may have a rake forward or may be vertical, but, whichever it is, the invariable rule is that the mainmast will lean away from it, being vertical if the foremast has a forward rake, and raking aft when the foremast is vertical. Indeed, the general system followed is that all five masts diverge like the sticks of a half-opened fan.

at deck level in high tabernacles on the poop and are out of the fore and aft line. The port mizzen[27] is situated on the port side against the bulwarks and in a traverse line with the rudder-post. The mizzen[28] is stepped about 2 feet to port of the fore and aft line and carries a light top-mast[35] fitted with two halyard sheaves, similar to the mainmast. Each of these masts carries a square-headed brown canvas lug-sail, more or less of the type and pattern already described.

See Part One, pages 67–68.

Each mast has a light pole top-mast, the proportions in length of which are usually as follows (excluding the port mizzen). For the mainmast the total measurement to the truck is one-third of the height of the mast from deck level. The height of the mainsail when it is two blocks, that is to say, as high as it will go, reaches three-fourths of the way up the mast. In the case of the mizzen, the sail reaches up for four-fifths of the mast, five-sixths for the main foremast, and six-sevenths for the port foremast.

The reason for the staggering of this foremast is probably to allow more space for the handling of the anchors and cable. In the case of the mizzen-mast, it has obviously been so placed to be clear of the rudder hoisting gear. A study of the plan would indicate that this would also help to explain the staggered position of the port mizzen. An additional advantage to be gained from the position of both these masts is that the weather sail, whichever of the two that may happen to be, can be so set that it can never be becalmed by the main mizzen-sail. Their chief use is probably as steering sails, and this theory would seem to be borne out by the light method of housing.

A top-sail is occasionally fitted above the mainsail, in the ample space provided, and, more rarely, above the fore-sail. Staysails and triangular spinnakers are largely used. The vertical bonnet is not usual on this type of sail. The age of this class of junk would seem to justify the supposition that, as regards sails as well as design, it is probably the parent type for many kinds of junks. The sails are held to the mast in the usual way by parrels of bamboo, rope, or plaited cane.

See Part One, pages 57–73.

As has been pointed out in Part One, it seems fairly well substantiated that many junks in Marco Polo's day wore top-sails. They have now practically vanished from the China seas and are probably not to be found to-day except in the case of the large Kiangsu trader. They are never seen in the *sha-ch'uan.*

In a heavy sea-way the junk is hove to by means of a sea anchor or drogue. This consists of an oval basket 8 feet long and about 1 foot deep. It is veered to windward by a rope to which it is attached by a bridle. The basket acts as a kind of water parachute, and by the resistance offered by the water keeps the junk's head to the wind. When not in use it is stowed on top of the house.

There are two interesting fittings in this type of junk. One is the primitive navigation light[36]. It consists of a small kerosene-oil light enclosed in a crude glass box and secured by sundry string lashings to a short pole on the starboard quarter. The other is a very ingenious type of tin kettle on the samovar principle, except only that wood is used for fuel in the centre portion.

Masthead devices are described in Part One, pages 37–39. They are illustrated on the endpapers.

The masthead distinguishing device of the *sha-ch'uan* is sometimes one *tan* (蛋) or coloured wooden egg worn at the main and surmounted by a revolving framework carrying a series of pennants. The largest, which is red, is 6 feet or so in length, while above it are small pennants of varying lengths. The whole is topped by a tuft of palm fibre.

The roomy house measures 29 feet over-all, including the galley[37]. It consists of a 6-foot wide corridor flanked by six divisions, of which four are bunk cabins[38] with upper[38] and lower berths[39] and sliding doors. These are reserved for the more important members of the crew. In the sixth division on the starboard side is a cooking-stove[42]. The position aft of the transom proper, where

A familiar sight in the 1920s—a Pechili Trader.

the rudder-hoisting apparatus is kept, is devoted to various uses, such as fuel storage, vegetable cleaning, and so on. The fifth, on the starboard side, contains a large rice bin[40], and above it is a joss-house in miniature dedicated to the Chinese Stella Maris, Kuan Yin[41].

Stella Maris, Star of the Sea, an epithet of the Virgin Mary.

Kuan Yin, the Goddess of Mercy, is particularly the patron saint of the junkmen of the craft of the Lower Yangtze. The name literally means "regard sound," and can be translated as "helpful of prayer" or "she who hears the cries of men."

Below deck the two after compartments[43] are also used for living quarters for the crew, which may number over 20. Extra quarters are also to be found below decks forward of the first bulkhead[14]. Ropes and stores are also kept here. All the rest of the hull space is given up to cargo.

These junks are never painted but occasionally receive a coat of wood oil. There is little carving or ornament.

The large Kiangsu trader is now, alas, no longer built, and it is doubtful if any now remain afloat. There is consolation, however, in knowing that the *sha-ch'uan* still exists in appreciable numbers, for this craft follows its prototype so closely in all the main essentials as to preserve the memory and traditions of the craft of old that used to sail the seas from the far north to Hongkong and down to Singapore. Indeed, it is believed by some good authorities that these were the ships which originally traded to the Red Sea and East African ports before the Middle Ages.

There is another and more picturesque relation of the Kiangsu trader. It is known by the junkmen as the *ta-chi-ch'uan* (大 鷄 船), or big fowl-boat, from Shantung. It may, however, for convenience sake be called the bull-head, for it has just this appearance when seen end on.

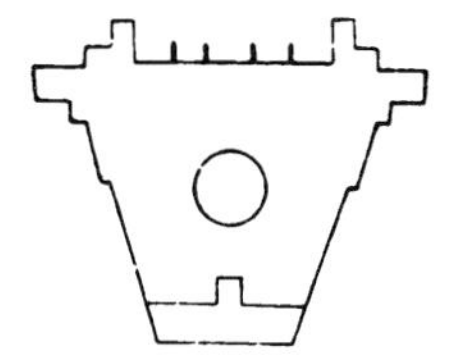

Ta-chi-chu'an, *or "bull-head," as seen from the stern.*

This type has five masts, and adheres very closely to the Kiangsu trader type in a general way; yet there are several individual variations as regards size of the hull, degree of turret build, height and proportional position of the masts, and most conspicuous of all, the style and extent of the ornamentation. This takes the form of a red-painted bow on which is depicted the character *fu* (福), meaning happiness, in black on a white circular ground. The presence of an oculus in this supposedly far-northern type is quite unusual.

The main distinguishing feature of the boat is the bold scheme of decoration; for instead of being plainly wood-oiled, the whole sweep of the bulwarks for a depth of about 1½ feet and a length of from 6 to 8 feet is painted dull green with a 3-inch border, top and bottom, of red. This band of colour terminates well aft of the oculus in four vertical stripes of white, red, green, and black.

The laodah, when questioned, affirmed with considerable pride that there were only three such craft in existence. The unsolved question remains. Is this an almost extinct type, is it an evolution, or is the pleasing colour scheme merely the artistic self-expression of some unusually æsthetic junkmaster?

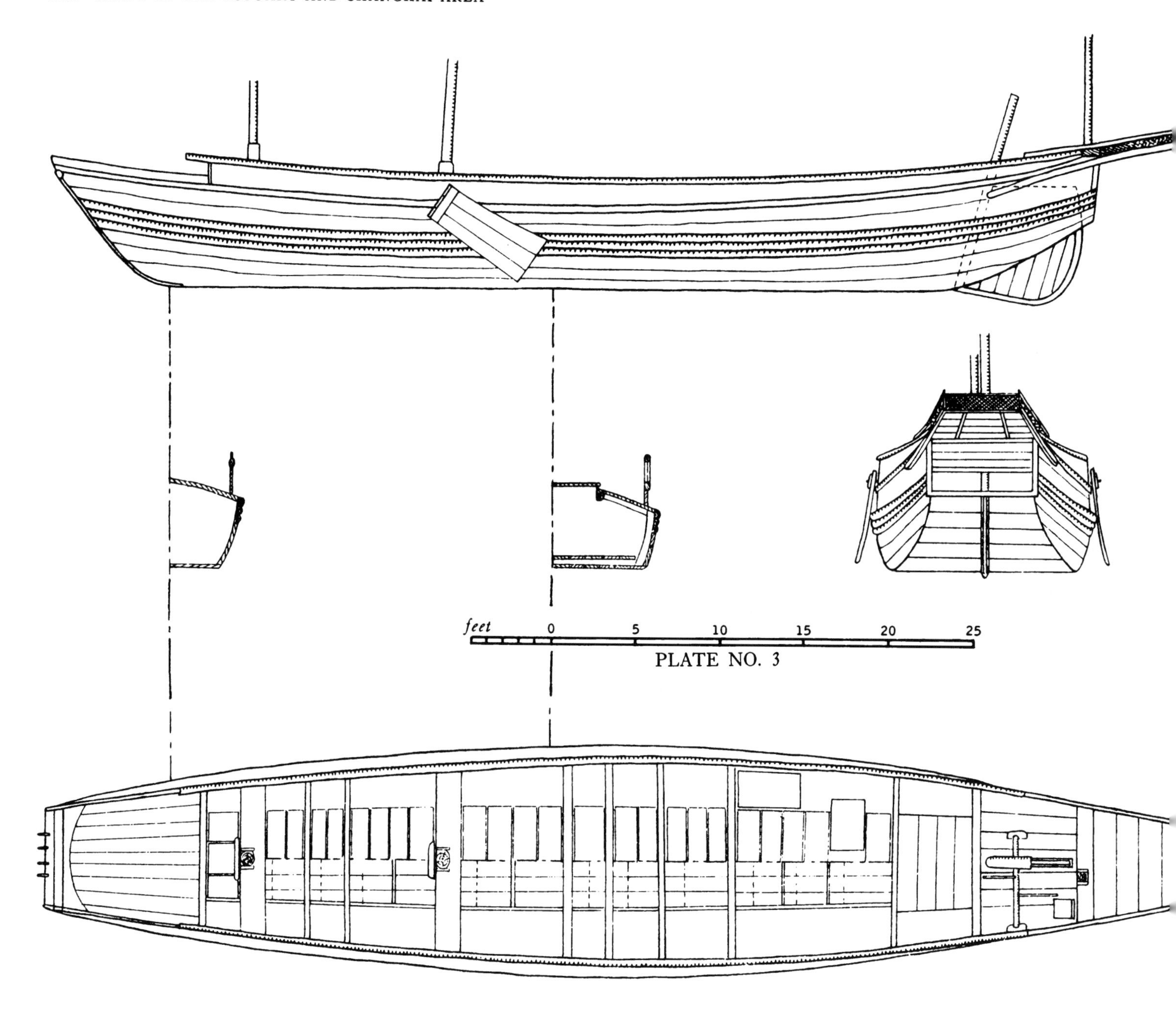

PLATE NO. 3

THE TSUNGMING COTTON-JUNK

Although cotton was not cultivated in China until the twelfth or, according to Hirth and Rockhill, the fourteenth century, it was of course known to the Chinese long before then. It is mentioned as such by Chinese historians as early as the sixth century A.D., and actually there are references in the "Shu Ching" to a kind of woven cloth being brought into China as tribute some 2,200 years before the Christian era.

Cotton first entered China from Central Asia, and was also imported from Hainan, Indo-China, and the Straits, India, Persia, and even as far afield as Asia Minor.

As the cultivation of the shrub spread from Chinese Turkestan into the north by way of Kansu and Shensi, the latter province was the first to go in for the industry; and the cotton from there, being later derived from American seed, was in about 1917 said to be the best in the country.

From these beginnings China has progressed until she is now the third greatest cotton producer in the world, ranking after the United States and India.

The first cotton mill project was started in 1878 by the Shanghai Cotton Manufacturing Company, but owing to official opposition it was not until 1890 that a factory was opened at Wuchang. The principal areas now under cultivation are in the Yangtze and Yellow River basins and in Chekiang, the smallest of the provinces, which has been very productive ever since the time of the Sung dynasty, about a thousand years ago. Kwangtung and Kiangsu are also important cotton-producing regions. Of these, the small province of Kiangsu is celebrated for the quantity and quality of its crop, the chief staple grown in the sandy alluvial soil of the flat country around Shanghai. The story of its introduction dates back to A.D. 1364, when an officer was appointed to encourage the cultivation of cotton in the provinces of Chekiang, Kiangsu, Kiangsi, Hupeh, Hunan, and Fukien. It was at about this time that the cotton plant was first grown in the district of Wuni, near Shanghai. The cultivators were deeply indebted to a certain old lady named Huang, who lived during the Ming dynasty. If she did not actually initiate the practice of cotton planting, she at least taught them how to make the crop most profitable by instruction in the use of the flocking bow and the loom, and in the weaving of fancy cloths with coloured threads worked into patterns. These arts she had brought with her from the cotton-producing regions of Kwangtung. So highly were her services appreciated that after her death she was apotheosized for her ingenuity, and a temple was erected to her memory in Shanghai.*

The old lady would be astonished to see how Kiangsu has now become the centre of the cotton spinning industry of China. There are 150,000 cotton mill workers in the province, of which 65 per cent are in Shanghai.

Cotton seed is sown about the end of April, or as soon after as the wheat crops are cleared. The ground is then broken up and manured, the ploughing being done with a three-pronged hoe or by a buffalo and plough. This plough is of the crudest construction, consisting of a crooked branch sometimes rudely shaped off, to which is attached a thin iron plate which can turn up the soil only to a depth of 5 or 6 inches. About a week after sowing the young plants show above the ground, and the first buds appear in about four or five weeks' time. A month later they expand into flowers. The flowers quickly drop off, and the formation of the pod begins, but the plants go on producing flowers and pods until the latter part of October. The pods are gathered as fast as they burst, this beginning about the end of August. The cotton, as it is gathered, is spread out daily in the sun on a platform of reeds raised a few feet from the ground until thoroughly dried, when the process of cleaning the cotton and separating it from the seed begins. The seed, save that which is kept for next year's planting, is sold to the oil-maker, who expresses the oil between two millstones, the upper one of which is turned by a buffalo.

The product of the cotton plant is now ready for transport to the markets. The raw cotton is usually packed in long bags of coarse white cloth, each being then bound with hemp rope. The packages, which vary in size, weigh about 250 lb. each.

The cotton-growing districts of Kiangsu fall into three separate zones, one lying to the north and the other two to the south of the Yangtze.

The Tsungming cotton-junks hereinafter described are concerned only with the trade between Shanghai and the first-named zone, which, with Nantungchow as its centre, extends to Tsungming, Haimên, and Jukao. Excluding the last-named place, this zone covers an area of about 100 by 50 miles, with a total

* The temple has been destroyed by fire on several occasions and rebuilt in different places, the last being in the city in 1826.

acreage of 3,600,000 *mou* under cotton and a yearly output of about 1,400,000 piculs, according to the Report of the Shanghai Cotton Millowners' Association in 1923.

Tsungming itself, with a population of about 1 million, is an alluvial island situated in the middle of the Yangtze estuary. As it has been formed from the silt deposited by the great river, it is very gradually extending in size year by year.

The Tsungming cotton-junks are built at their name-place, and their staple cargo is cotton, cotton yarn, cotton seed, and cotton cloth. They also fill up extra space with cereals, miscellaneous merchandise, and passengers for Shanghai.

These craft belong to the highly-respected Kiangsu trader family; but, sad to relate, they are rather careless about keeping up their dignity, for their only form of cargo on the return journey from Shanghai is night-soil in buckets.

They have a good deal in common with their very much larger prototype, the Kiangsu trader, and even more with a humbler member of the same family, the *yao-wang-chu'an* (搖網船). All three have the same bluff lines, upturned rounded bow, peculiar projecting gallery built out beyond the transom, and cambered fore deck.

In size the Tsungming cotton-junks are more or less standardized and surprisingly small. The specimen illustrated in Plate No. 3 measures 59 feet over-all, with a beam of 13 feet and a depth of 6½ feet; that is to say, she is deep and beamy for her length, and is very strongly constructed with 10 hardwood bulkheads and four frames. The flat-bottomed *sha-mu* hull is of modified turret build with three heavy wales to give longitudinal strength. Washboards extend from just forward of the first bulkhead to the stern. Removable planks are laid athwartships from the hatch coamings to these washboards so as to make the whole deck flush. The small space below is, in true Chinese fashion, utilized to the full for the stowage of ropes, fenders, etc. Deck planks are also sometimes fitted over the whale-backed fore deck.

The fourth bulkhead is 4 inches out of the perpendicular with a backward tilt, so that the housing of the raked mainmast may rest against it. There are three masts stepped in low tabernacles carrying square-headed lug-sails. The short mizzen-mast is stepped on deck right aft, against the transom and on the port side of the fore and aft line so as to be clear of the rudder trunk.

The rudder operates in a trunk and is slung from a point about 10 inches from the rudder-post. A wire pendant is rove round a windlass, which is fitted with two levers so as to hoist the rudder as need occurs. When fully raised it is just clear of the water when the junk is light. The range of travel is about 2 feet.

There is usually no deck house, and the crew live below decks in the foremost and after compartments in what would appear to be the utmost discomfort. Access is provided to these cramped quarters through a booby hatch on the forecastle and two removable hatches aft. The galley, such as it is, is on deck.

The cargo is normally stowed below decks, but in fine weather a deck cargo is carried in addition. In the early days of Shanghai's trade development it was said that if ever the Chinese could be induced to add an inch to the length of their short coats, the cotton mills of the world would be kept busy for years in supplying the increased demands. Now, however, China is fast becoming more self sufficient as regards manufactures, and a great proportion of cotton spinning is done in the Shanghai mills. Their increasing needs provide a steady and lucrative trade for the cotton-junks, and these craft are a well-known feature of the Whangpoo River.

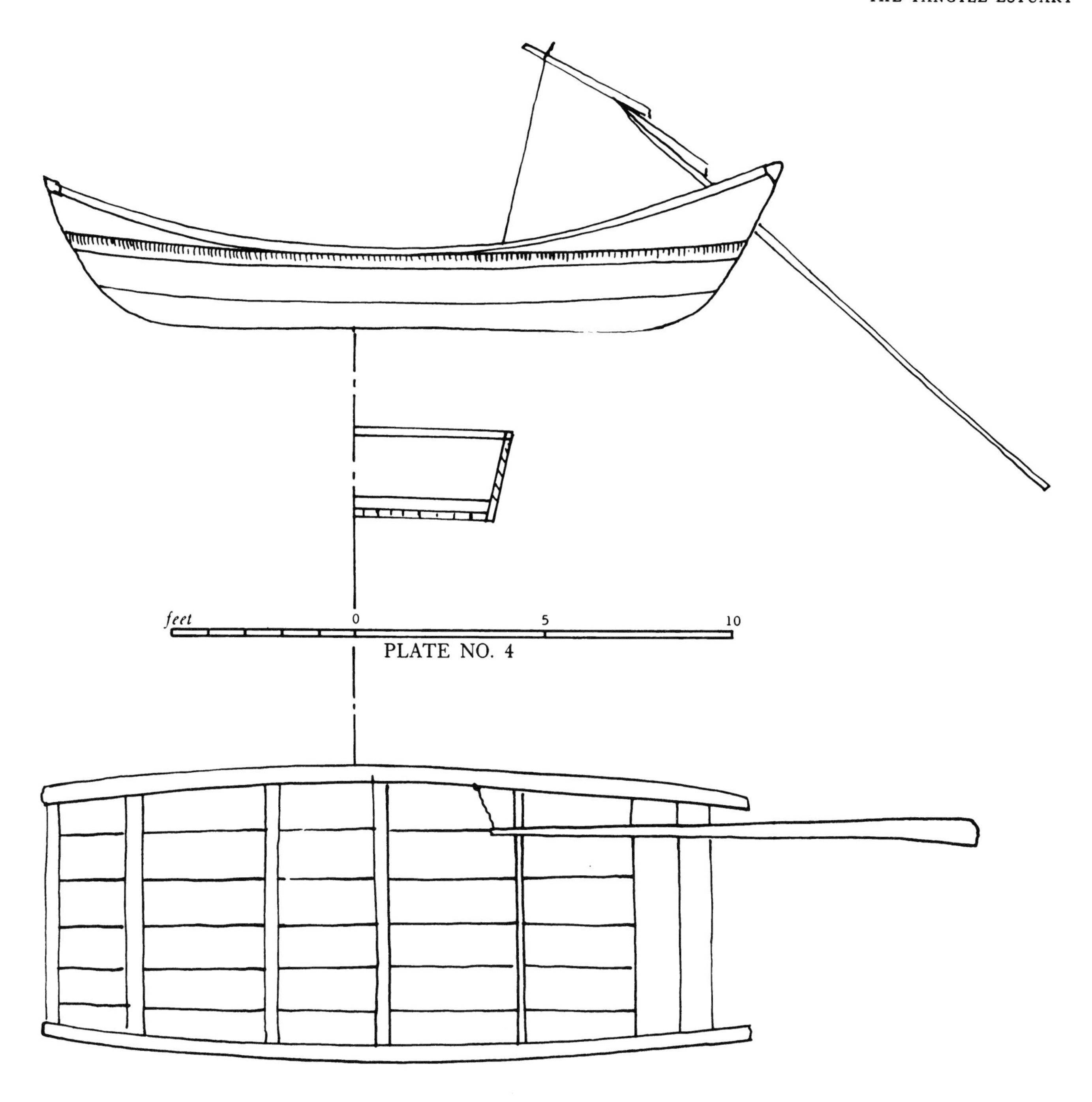

PLATE NO. 4

THE JUNK'S SAMPAN

This square-shaped little sampan may be aptly termed the dinghy of the Far East. With the exception of the *hu-ch'uan*, or kettle-boat, to be described later, it is certainly the smallest craft afloat in these waters.

Made of *sha-mu* on the simplest lines, she measures only 9 feet in length, with a beam of 3½ feet and a depth of 1 foot. Nevertheless, small as she is, she presents many of the distinguishing features of typical Shanghai craft in rounded bow, heavy rubbing-strake, yuloh in three sections, and, most notable of all, the winged stern joined by a plank so as to give the effect of a miniature gallery.

Her duties are to provide communication between ship and shore, and lay out lines. A child could propel these small boats, and indeed usually does.

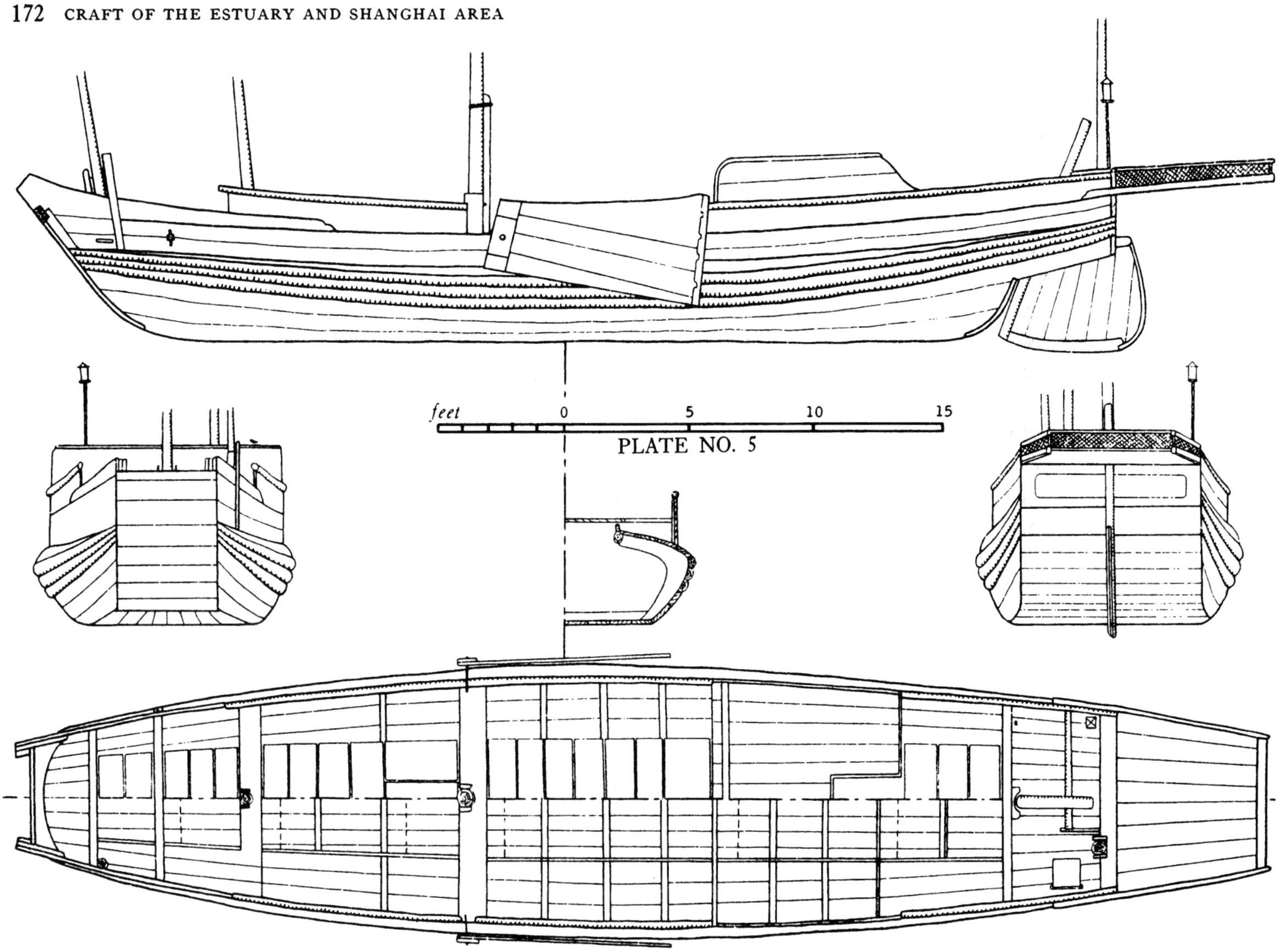

PLATE NO. 5

搖網船

THE YAO-WANG-CH'UAN OR PIG-BOAT

The *yao-wang-ch'uan* originally hailed from the north, being a Shantung fishing-junk, but a more fruitful field for her activities has been found in the pig trade from the delta ports to Shanghai, and more especially from Tsungming Island.

An offshoot of the Kiangsu trader family, it is interesting to compare this boat with her parent craft, already described. Structurally there is little difference between them. Both are turret-built and flat-bottomed, the foot-wide planking of the hull being laid carvel-fashion and longitudinally, except for the portions at the turn of the bottom at bluff, broad bow and flat, broad, overhanging stern, where it is laid athwartships.

These craft vary somewhat in size. That illustrated in Plate No. 5 is a medium-sized junk measuring 50 feet in length, with a beam of 10½ feet and a depth of 4 feet.

The *sha-mu* hull is divided into watertight compartments by six hardwood bulkheads and further strengthened by seven frames. These frames are in the larger compartments so as to assist in preserving the shape of the hull, and therefore the larger craft have eight or more frames. There is a small, low house between the fourth and fifth bulkheads which serves as quarters for the crew of six men, access being gained through a sliding door at the after end. The galley is inside the house. Some of these junks have no house, and the crew then live in the foremost and after compartments, the galley being then right aft. Considerable extra strength at the bow is provided by a heavy timber laid across it which takes into the longitudinals on either side.

The first deck beam is built into the structure of the hull, as is also the second, but the latter is in addition locked with a wooden pin into the side planking.

She is well protected by high weather-boarding from aft to the foremast, and again from abaft the foremast a new system rises to the bow. Being turret-built throughout, she is necessarily whale-backed, but the inconvenience of this cambered surface is remedied by extending the deck level by additional planking from the hatch coaming to the bulwarks.

There are four masts. Those at the two extremities are both on the port side and stepped on deck out of the centre line of the ship. The mizzen is situated just clear of the windlass, while the foremast is snugly tucked into the angle formed by the first deck beam and the ship's side and is further supported by tabernacles, the one inside the hull and the other outside, with the heel resting on the top of the wale. The fore and mizzen masts are very easily removed when required. The main and main-mizzen masts are stepped in the normal way amidships. All carry square-headed lug-sails.

The stern carries the traditional overhanging gallery of its family. The rudder is of the hoisting non-balance variety. Great numbers of these junks may be seen bringing their screaming cargo to the pig wharves of Woosung, whence they are transported to the slaughter-houses of Shanghai. Dishonest butchers have an ingenious trick of injecting water into the carcasses after they have been killed and bled, by which means the total weight is increased by several pounds. This deception has as detrimental an effect on the taste of the meat as it has a beneficial effect on the swindler's pocket.

Pigs are the principal domestic animals raised in Kiangsu, their number running to many millions. There are three different varieties of pigs in the province, each named after their port of origin. They are, in order of merit, the T'aihsing, Wusih, and the Haichow varieties. Two thousand five hundred of these unfortunates are slaughtered in Shanghai daily.

In ancient days the intestines of animals were used for making bow strings, but after the introduction of fire-arms to China the archer went out of fashion and there was no market for the intestines. Early in this century, however, an enterprising foreigner hit upon the idea of preserving this waste product and shipping it to Europe, chiefly Germany, to be used as casings for sausages. This has now become a very large and profitable industry.

Admirers of the sausage will, perhaps, be interested to learn how the casings are prepared for export. The intestines are first soaked in water for 24 hours, and after rinsing several times are again left in the water for another day, when they turn pink in colour. Three pieces are then fastened together, making about 13½ yards in length, and sprinkled with salt. The following day they are pressed to remove the water. Finally they are packed in wooden barrels, the insides of which are coated with wax and lined with cloth.*

The pig-boats carry human passengers back to Tsungming and the delta ports. Even the most prosaic of old sailors in the West believe that ships, and more particularly sailing ships, are real entities. There is therefore food for sad thought in the fact that it is a far cry from the Shantung fishing-grounds to the Yangtze delta pig trade, and the *yao-wang-ch'uan* is another instance of a northern aristocrat fallen from its high estate.

* The writer regards himself, if not a great authority, as at least having a very good working knowledge of this very disagreeable and noisome industry, for he had the misfortune to live next door to a casing factory while stationed at Chungking.

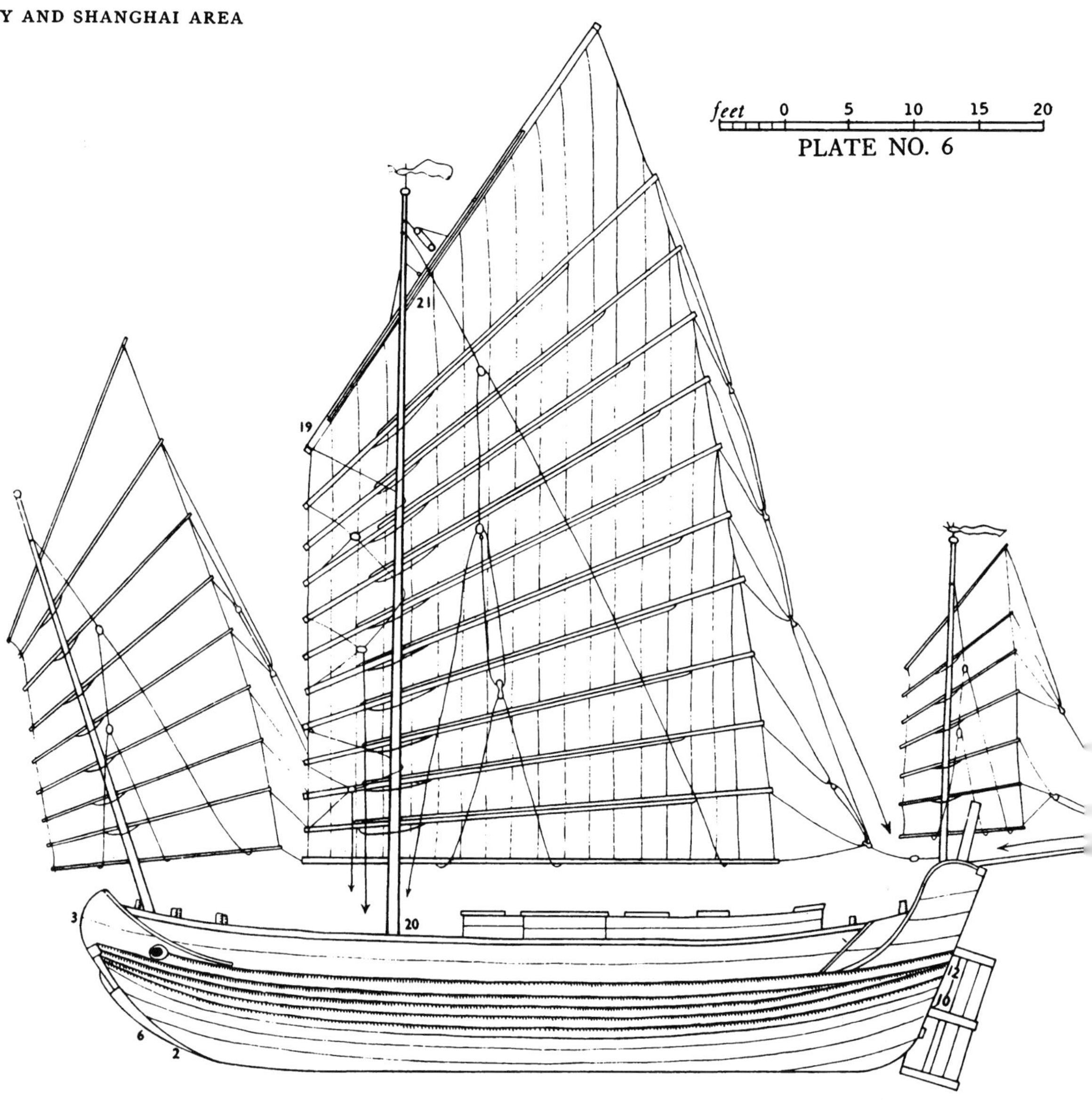

鎮海船

THE CHÊNHAI-CH'UAN OR ICE-BOAT

Ningpo (甯 波), or tranquil waves, is situated on the left bank of the Yungkiang, about 15 miles from the sea. It is said to have been founded just after the great deluge so successfully handled by the Emperor Yü.

In China nearly everyone fishes and everyone eats fish, but Ningpo is exceptionally busy in both respects and is one of the most important junk and fishing centres of Chekiang.*

It has been said of the Ningpo fishermen that "no people in the world apparently made so great an advance in the art of fishing; and for centuries past no people have made so little further progress." Certainly the modes of fishing and the gear used are apparently little changed from those of the remote past, and the simplicity of the former and the ingenious construction of the latter are as remarkable in these days of steam trawling as they were when they were first evolved.

The catches brought in from the great fishing-grounds are now ice-preserved and include many varieties of fish, including the very popular cuttle-fish.†

It is not proposed to deal with the fishing industry of Ningpo, for this engrossing subject would require a volume to itself; but two of the Ningpo

* According to the "Customs Trade Returns" for 1890, the Ningpo fishing industry, including that of the Chusan Archipelago, supported at least 10,000 fishing-boats and at least 80,000 fishermen.

† The Chinese use the fish only as food, and the valuable sepia is thrown away. This is the only instance I have come across in 33 years of any waste by Chinese.

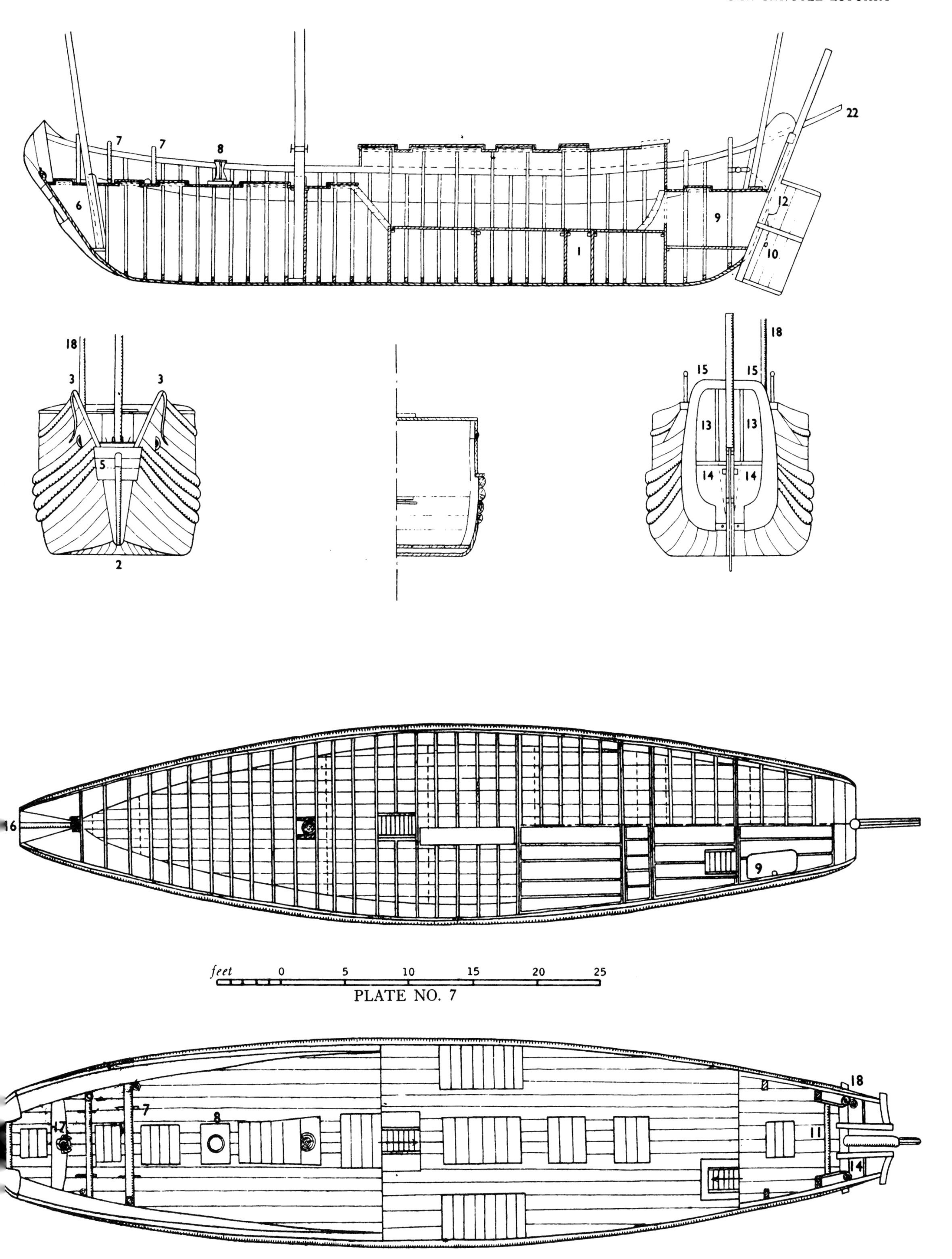

22
7
7
8
6
12
9
1
10
18
3
3
5
2
18
15
15
13
13
14
14
16
9
feet 0 5 10 15 20 25
17
7
8
18
11
14

PLATE NO. 7

fishing-boats are such constant visitors to the fish markets of Shanghai that they must be included in these pages.

The first of these craft is the *chênhai-ch'uan*, named after a town near Ningpo where this type is usually built. Another more colloquial name is the *ping-hsien-ch'uan* (冰 鮮 船), or the ice and fresh fish boat.

The *chênhai-ch'uan* is comparatively modern; for, as competition and the greater distances to be covered in search of fish forced the fishing fleets to go farther afield, a means had to be found to keep the fish fresh while it was being transported over the comparatively long distances to the markets of Ningpo and Shanghai. The duty of the ice-boat, therefore, is to follow the fishing fleets, to buy the catch, and to bring it back between layers of ice.

Native ice used to be preserved in ice houses. In 1884 there were 300 of these ice houses on the banks of the Yungkiang between Ningpo and the sea, and they are still quite a feature of the Ningpo landscape.

Ice houses are of very ancient origin, for it has been noted in his historical records that in the fifth century the first Sung Emperor, Kao Tsung (高 宗), built an ice house at the capital, which was then Nanking, so as to store ice for the summer.

The Shanghai ice houses used to be made of mud and reeds, but the ice house proper was a solid structure with very thick stone and mud walls and stood about 18 feet above the ground. The thick, high, thatched roof surmounting the whole rested on long bamboo rafters. A doorway, made in the roof and closed only by straw matting, was reached by means of two inclined planks or by steps. This was used for filling the ice house. A smaller door at ground level served for removing the ice.

In winter, when the temperature approaches freezing point, the rice fields surrounding the ice houses are dug down to a deeper level so as to keep the ice as free from mud as possible. Water is then pumped into the fields, and the ice which forms is gathered every morning and added to the store. Coarse bamboo matting is laid on the path and on the steps over which the ice is carried so as to ensure its cleanliness.

The ice is packed in the house in layers between straw matting, and when the house is full a thick filling of straw is laid over all. Below, in the floor of the ice reservoir, there are small gutters to drain off the water from the melting ice.

This simple system answered admirably, and it was remarkable how the ice survived the intense heat of the summer. Much if not the whole of the credit was due to the nature of the earthen walls, for they were made of the thick clayey loam which never really dries except on the surface and is practically impermeable to heat and water which in a lighter or more porous soil would penetrate to the ice and melt it. Ice stored in this manner would keep for years and was a boon to the people of Shanghai as well as to the fishing industry.

The pampered millions of Shanghai have now been introduced to the electric refrigerator, and modern science has invaded even the fishing industry, so that now, astonishing as it may seem, ice from the ice works is cheaper than that of the ice houses, and yet another old landmark is vanishing.

The specimen of the *chênhai-ch'uan* represented in Plate No. 6 is typical of her class. With a length of 70 feet, a beam of 15 feet, depth of 8 feet, and cargo capacity of 100 piculs, she is of exceptionally strong construction, being made with eight bulkheads and 28 frames. A feature is the number of these supports and the fact that the frames are of different shapes and sizes. Athough it is somewhat unusual, there is a coffer-dam measuring 2 feet across between the sixth and seventh bulkheads. Longitudinal strength is provided by five heavy wales merging into three or four at the stem-post and stern.

The flat bottom has a good lift[2] at the forefoot. The side planks of the hull meet at the typically Ningpo class of stem-post, which is a sort of elongated triangle in shape, widening as it rises to the characteristic bow of the Ningpo junks, which consists of a 3-foot wide aperture between the rising and diverging wings[3] of the bulwarks. There are twin stem-beams[4] running parallel 9 inches apart forward of the foremast.

There are two types of bow: the *ting-sung-t'ou* (頂 松 頭), or top pine head, and the *lu-mei-mao* (綠 眉 毛), or green eyebrow, the junk illustrated being fitted with the latter. The difference is so slight as to be scarcely noticeable to the untrained observer, though to the junkmen they remain as two distinct and recognized types. There appears to be no variation for these two types unless it is to be found in the lengths of timber available, for in the first-named type the top planking[5] extends farther forward.

There are two holes, 1 inch in diameter,* in the bottom planks of the foremost compartment to permit of free flooding. The reason for this given by the junkmen is so as to lessen the stresses sustained by the bluff-bowed junk when she encounters the head resistance from the sea. They claim that the flooding of a part of the fore-peak[6] through these holes, so that water communicates freely with the sea, balances the water pressure outside by that inside and thereby serves to reduce some of the pounding.

Two windlasses[7] and a foreign-type capstan[8] are situated on the forecastle. When rope cable is used for the anchors, as is the case in the smaller junks, it is "taken to" a windlass. When chain cable is used it is worked by the capstan.

The forecastle is protected as far aft as the break of the house by weather-boarding which is a continuation of the bow wings. In Plate No. 7 it starts at a height of 5 feet at the bow and diminishes to 1.6 feet at the house.

There are five hatches in the fore deck. Of these the after four give access to the fish holds. The ice used for packing the fish is prevented from melting by being laid between straw mats. Thick straw mats are also placed between it and the sides of the boat. The hatches are kept carefully closed, and straw mats are again made use of to cover them, water being frequently poured over them to keep them cool.

The large house is entered through sliding doors at deck level and down a ladder. There are five more hatches on the roof of the house, 3 feet above deck level. The small after deck abaft the house is for the use of the laodah in handling the ship. A hatch leads down to the galley[9] on the port side. Below is a storage room for firewood. The stern is typical of Ningpo. The rudder, which the junkmen describe as being like a hatchet, is slung in sockets, differing in this from the Foochow pole-junk. The hoisting gear consists of a bight of chain which, passing through a sheave[10] inset in the rudder and leading thence through two vertical knees on the transom, terminates with its standing parts travelling round the barrel of the windlass[11]. As the rudder rests on the top of the transom it cannot move back and is prevented from moving forward by a chock on the transom. When lowered the rudder extends 4 feet below the bottom of the junk and thus serves as a keel. The usual aperture[12] is cut in the top of the rudder so as to enable the helm to be put hard over in all positions without touching the transom. A noticeable feature of this, as of all Ningpo junks, is that the rudder-

* Sometimes these holes are triangular.

post and first plank of the bearding are carved out of one piece, a notable example of carpentry as of selection of material.

Two yulohs are used over the stern in calms. To facilitate this the planking[13] on either side of the oblong stern aperture is removed as far down as the cross-beam[14] at deck level. In addition, yulohs can be worked on both sides forward. They operate through holes in the bulwark, one man standing on the bumkin while another man stands at the yuloh inboard. The wings[15] on either side of the aperture rise to a height of 7 feet above the after deck level, and this makes it almost impossible for the junks to be pooped.

There are three masts. The foremast, 40 feet high from deck to truck, rakes slightly forward so that the sail may get a true wind. It is stepped in tabernacles and on a heel chock in the triangular fore-peak, where it is lodged against the first bulkhead and frame; the heel is prevented from coming forward by means of a baulk of timber[16] wedged into the bow. A heavy cross-beam[17] at deck level gives the main support. The mainmast, which is 55 feet above the deck, is almost vertical and iron bound at regular intervals. It is housed in the usual way in tabernacles against the bulkhead. The mizzen[18], which is 32 feet in height, is placed out of the centre line of the ship, being stepped on deck and in tabernacles against the starboard bulwarks and the transom. It is raked slightly aft. There are three balance lug-sails. These are hoisted by means of the capstan. An interesting feature is a large, loose bamboo cuff slipped over the iron holder for the belaying pin. This serves as a very efficient and smooth-running fair-lead. A small sampan is carried on davits over the stern[22].

The crew consists of 10 men: a laodah; assistant laodah; accountant; salesman; a bowman; a rating called *p'a-wei* (爬桅), or mast climber, who, as his name indicates, has to be able to climb the mast; one cook; and three seamen. They have comfortable accommodation, their box bunks being almost like small cabins wherein two men can comfortably sit and play cards.

Despite the crudest workmanship, for blend of colour and simple design the Ningpo fisherman as sailor-artist is hard to beat, and no one in the world takes more pride in his ship. In the matter of decoration the *chênhai-ch'uan* is a riot of colour when newly painted, though this is a luxury now seldom attainable. The predominant shades are red, green, and white, on a black hull. The head-ledges of the house are very often decorated with dragons and tigers disporting themselves in a countryside full of colour.

All the nets used in the industry are manufactured in only two or three places. The most important is the department of Taichow, 140 miles south of Ningpo. The work is done in the household, as there are no regular factories or workshops. Chênhai, at the entrance of the Yungkiang, is also a great *entrepôt*, and two hours from Ningpo to the north-east are two villages, called Shachi and Lute, where most of the nets used in this district are made. In the first-named place the whole population is employed in this industry. The village is well built, and the inhabitants seem comparatively well off. The visitor will find men, women, and children of both sexes busily engaged in spinning the hemp into thread and twine, making the nets, washing and dyeing them. The hemp used is obtained from China grass *(Urtica nivea)* by the tedious process of peeling its fibres with the finger-nails from the stem of the plant, which is generally cut three times in the year. The nails are the only instruments used to peel off the bark and separate the fibres into threads of the proper size. These long and fine strips are then made into a bundle, which is well washed and pounded with a wooden mallet. The material, being sufficiently bleached, is next made into a loose coil, and two such coils are placed in a shallow tub of water, which stands 50 feet distant from the spinning-wheel behind a bench, upon which sits the boy or girl who attends to the wheel. This wheel, simply constructed of bamboo and string, drives two small bamboo spinning-hooks, to each of which a thread of the hemp is attached. These threads are first twisted singly and then put together and twisted again, which completes the string, made of two strands.*

The instruments used by the net-makers are similar to those used in Europe. For the manufacture of the great net, so called, the workman sits at a small round table in the centre of which is fixed vertically a long bamboo on which the net is first fastened; as it grows longer it is suspended from the ceiling, and from there is coiled into a basket. This net is the largest of all, and is made in the shape of a pair of trousers. Most of the nets when finished are stretched by being simply hung on a wall and weighted with stones. This being found impracticable for the great net, another method is employed. The net is drawn over three benches, the middle one being the highest, and its ends are well fixed to the ground by pegs. Boards laden with heavy stones are then placed upon it between the benches, the result being a thorough stretching. It takes about 200 days to make this net, the makers working 12 hours per day.

Silk nets are a speciality of the city of Shaohing. They are made in long bands of some hundred feet or more, and of varying width, according to the size of the mesh. The material is fine threads of white silk. The floats consist of small lengths of reeds, and the nets are weighted with little pieces of lead or baked clay. They are dipped in boiling wood oil, which gives the silk a slight yellow colour and renders them invisible in the water, in which they float vertically. The fish strike against them and are caught by the gills. Some boats, especially certain very small ones which fish in the quiet bays, have a set of seven of these nets. They are often dried, and the floats and lines are dipped in pigs' blood.

The large nets of *Urtica nivea* are dyed on a stove, built of bricks, generally 2 feet in height; on it a wooden tub is placed, and a solution of mangrove bark is poured therein. The net is put into the tub and the fire is then lighted. The contents of the tub are kept boiling until the net is thoroughly saturated with the dye, when it is taken out and dried. Subsequently, in order to fix the colour and to give additional strength to the thread, the net is dipped in pigs' blood, and after it has been dried in the open air is ready for use. Nets so treated, if carefully used, dried monthly, and re-tanned, will last for three years. When old they are used with chunam to caulk the boats.

* "Customs Trade Returns" for 1880.

A junk beached for repairs.

溜

船

THE LIU-WANG-CH'UAN OR FISH-CARRIER

The second of the Ningpo fishing-junks which is a common visitor to Shanghai is that smaller relation of the *chênhai-ch'uan* the *liu-wang-ch'uan*, according to her local name, that is, the floating net boat.* This handy little junk shows practically all the characteristics of her larger sisters just described and is very similar in lines and build.

Despite her smaller size, however, she is the prototype, for she claims an older origin, and, indeed, the junkmen say she is one of the oldest kinds of fishing-junk working out of Ningpo.

If but half the legends which have grown up around this type of craft are true, she is of the greatest antiquity. The old sailors of Ningpo tell a naïvely broad story which throws an interesting light on the assumed age of the *liu-wang-ch'uan*. It is told how, in the days of the Chou dynasty, in the eleventh century B.C., these junks were never caulked but were still able to keep afloat. The great Emperor Wên Wang (文王), who had a wise and famous counsellor named Chiang T'ai-kung (姜太公) (who was, incidentally, supposed to have authority over the spirits of the unseen universe), is the subject of innumerable legends. On this occasion, however, the honours go to his wife. She once spent a night on board one of these junks and, being overcome by the demands of nature, retired into the bilges. From that day to this, so the junkmen solemnly affirm, though their reasoning is somewhat obscure, it has always been necessary to caulk these craft.

Another picturesque but utterly unauthenticated legend links the earliest fishing craft of Ningpo with the origin of the game of mah-jong. It is said that a fisherman named Sze, who lived by a lake near Ningpo, inaugurated the custom of fishing from boats instead of wading into the water with hand nets. He accordingly financed quite a fishing fleet. All went well until they encountered bad weather, when the newly-joined recruits to marine life fell victims to seasickness. All were mystified by this curious ailment and arrived at the very modern pronouncement that its cure must be effected through the power of the mind over the body. Sze and his nine brothers then invented the game of mah-jong, and the fishermen when playing it soon forgot their seasickness. History, however, does not relate what effect this had on their fishing.

The junks of Ningpo show a strange combination of clumsy serviceability and beauty, and the *liu-wang-ch'uan* is no exception. Built on slender lines, she is faster than most of the other types of Ningpo craft; and this quality of speed, linked with the ability to stand up to rough seas around the estuary, has resulted in this craft being diverted from her task of fishing so as to be used as a short-distance fish-carrier between the fishing fleet and the Shanghai market.

As has been said before, this craft varies very little from her larger relative the *chênhai-ch'uan*. The main difference is in size, for she measures only 57 feet in length, with a beam of $11\frac{3}{4}$ feet and a depth of $3\frac{1}{4}$ feet from the main deck, and has a cargo capacity of 50 tons.

The hull of *sung-mu*, a pine from Ningpo, is strengthened by seven hardwood bulkheads and 14 frames. There are only two masts. In place of the large, heavy, batten lug-sail she carries a spritsail measuring 25 by 50 feet and a fore staysail measuring 32 feet head to tack, 29 feet tack to clew, and 25 feet head to clew. A second spritsail is carried on the foremast.

* When boats fish in pairs, one vessel is used to carry food, water, and fuel, and is known as *wei-ch'uan* (喂船), or feeder, while the other does the fishing and handling of the nets and is known as *wang-ch'uan* (網船), or net-boat.

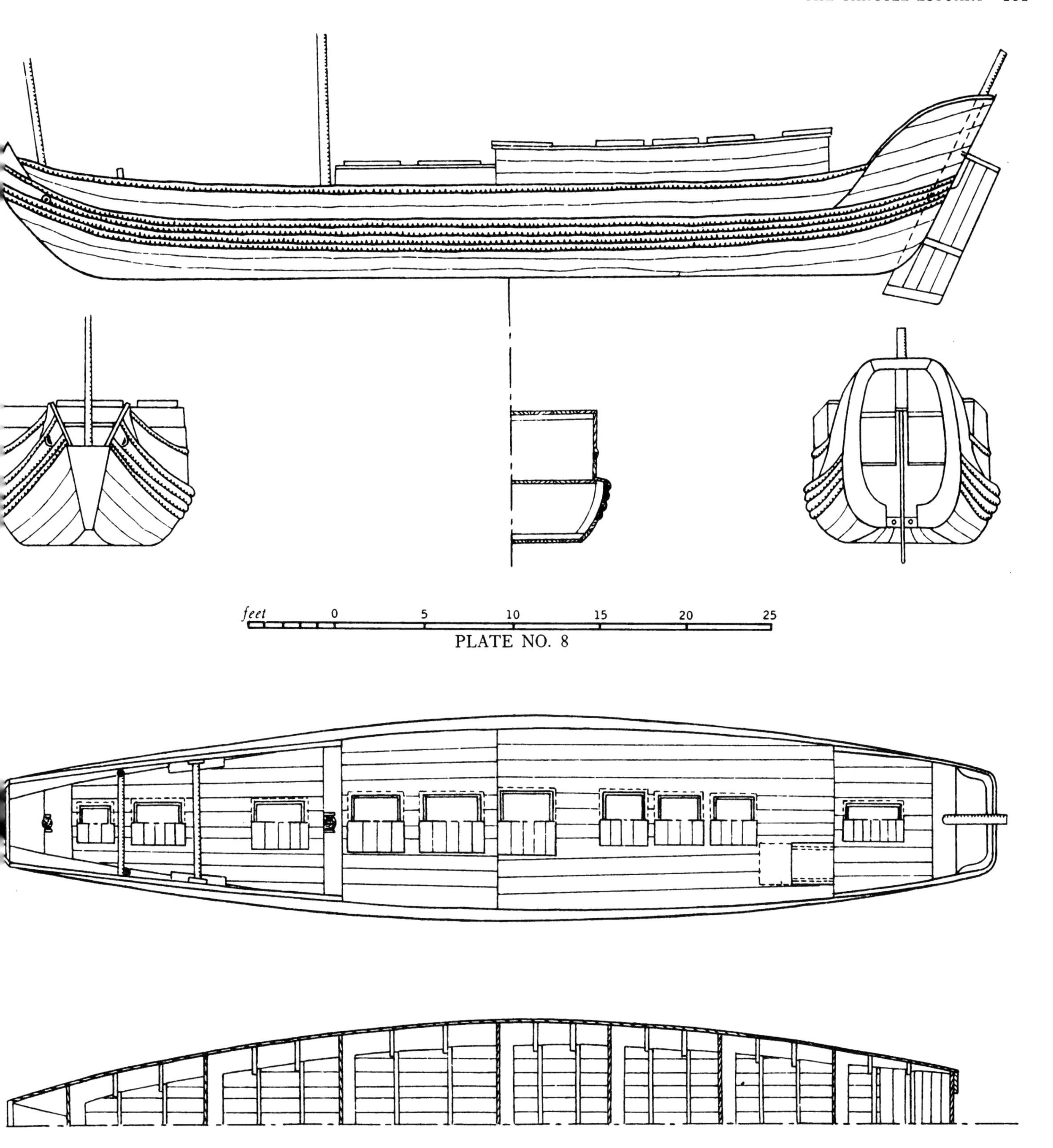

PLATE NO. 8

The crew of eight men have comparatively comfortable quarters in the after part of the house, which is longer in this type of junk, as it starts just abaft the mast. There is no foreign-style capstan, the two windlasses being used for the purpose. Yulohs over the stern are similarly used in calms.

The Ningpo junks and sailors have a wide reputation which is richly deserved.

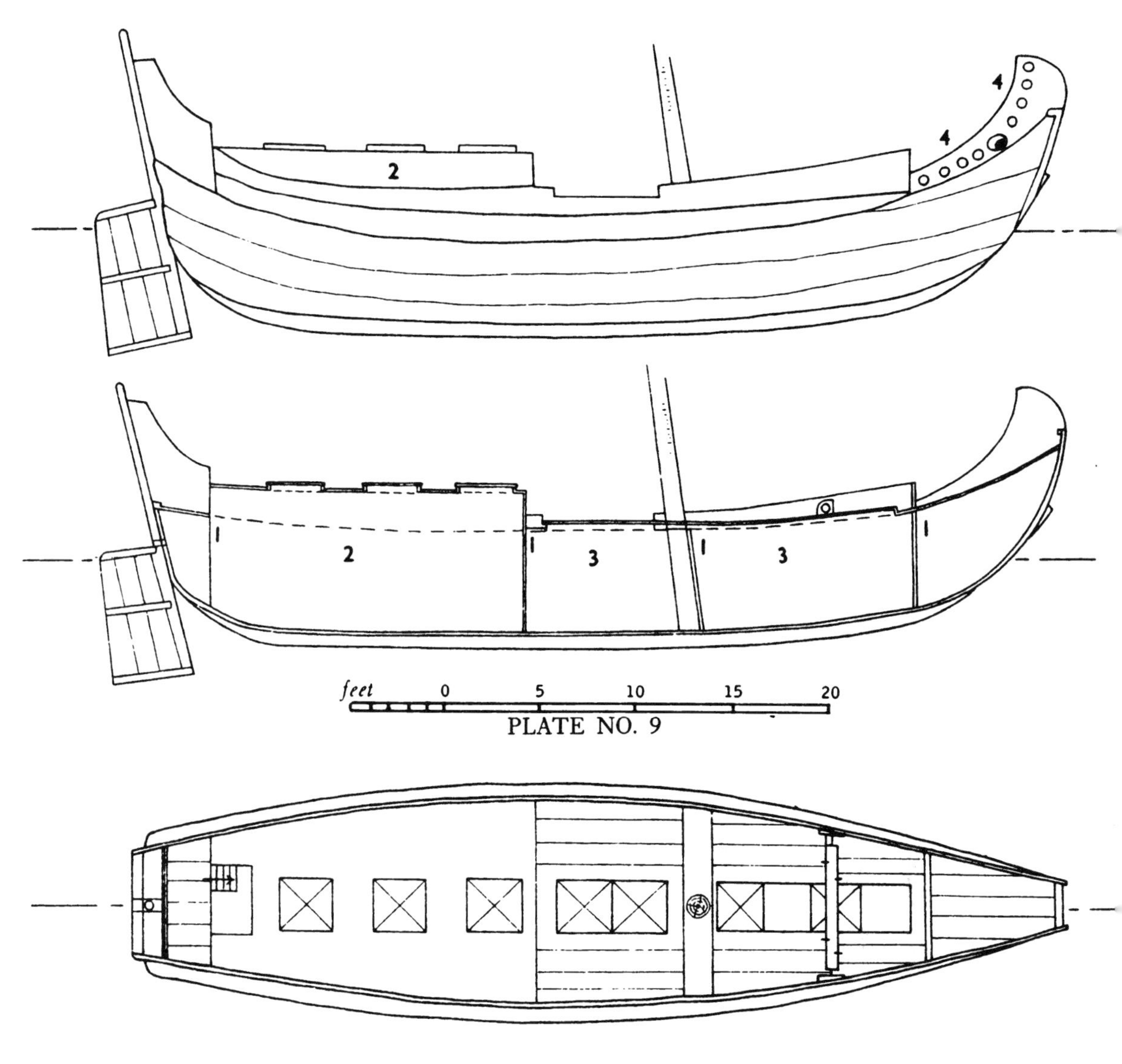

PLATE NO. 9

THE CHUSAN LITTLE FISHERMAN

To digress on the fascinating subject of the Chekiang fishing industry, tempting as it would be, is outside the geographical scope of this book, but as the Chusan fishermen are often to be seen in the estuary of the Yangtze and are always to be found in large numbers and varieties off the Shanghai fish market, passing mention must be made of these craft.

A representative type known as the Chusan little fisherman, or colloquially as the "small-pair" boat (小對船), is illustrated in Plate No. 9. Boats of this type are usually about 46 feet in length, with a beam of 12 feet and a depth of 6 feet. When at sea they usually go in pairs, hence the name. A larger variety of this type is known as the "large-pair" boat (大對船).

The island of Chusan, from which they hail, gives its name to the Archipelago and is the largest of the group. The main products of the soil are sweet potatoes, indian corn, and millet. On the low, muddy shore numerous saltworks are established. Here is the headquarters of the great Chusan fishing industry.

The fishermen who inhabit this island are, like their craft, rough and tough, and capable of enduring great hardship. Formerly they were pirates as well as fishermen, but the advent of steam navigation put a stop to this profitable sideline. To-day they are noted for being kind-hearted and hospitable.

Their wives do not accompany them to sea but stay at home and do the housework. Nets and lines are a handicraft of the island, and men, women, and children spin the hemp into twine, make and dye the nets. The nets are made from China grass *(Urtica nivea)* by peeling operations which are conducted entirely by old-style methods.

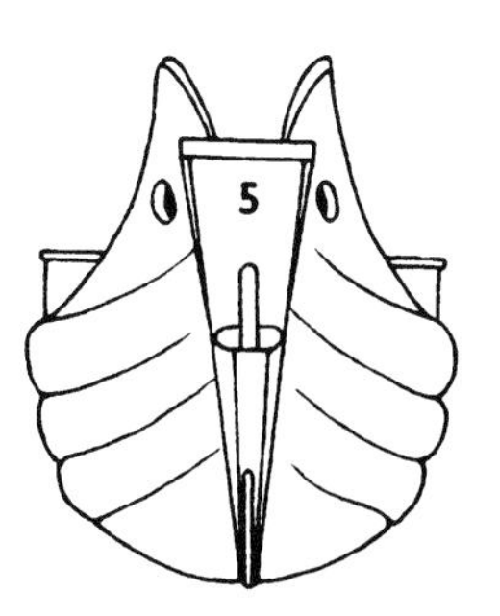

Bow.

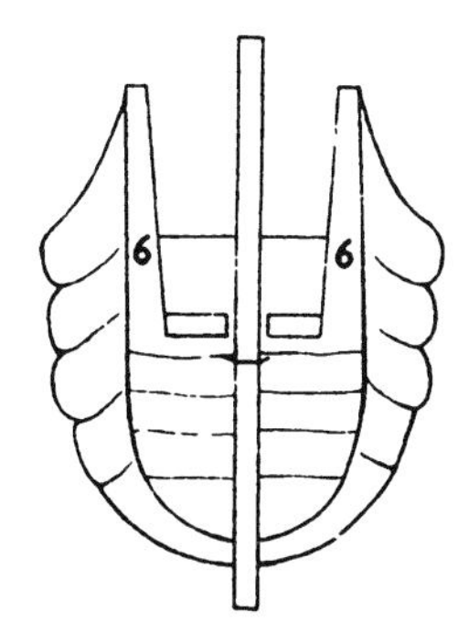

Stern.

Soon after March the fleet sets sail for the "first season" of fishing, the laodahs having selected an auspicious day for so important an event by the customary visit to their temple. This "first fishing" lasts for three months. The second or winter season is shorter.

The catch consists mainly of *wong-yü* and *chang-yü*. After the spring season has been concluded the boats are engaged in cuttle-fishing.

According to the "Customs Annual Report on Trade," there were in 1880 about 54,000 men engaged in the industry, and in 1935 there were said to be as many as "2,500 pairs of boats in the Chekiang fisheries, of which 240 pairs were concentrated in Chusan." It is disappointing that the numbers engaged in the fisheries quoted, being in the one case men and the other boats, do not permit of a comparison.

In times past each fishing-boat working out of the Chusan Islands used to pay a yearly sum of $2 towards the expenses of a number of guard-boats whose sole duty it was to accompany the fishing fleet to sea to protect them from pirates and to keep order among themselves. This volunteer fishing protection fleet consisted of 10 junks suitably armed.

No official restrictions are placed on the size of the mesh or the kind of gear used, but each convoy or fishing fleet has its own particular beat from which, according to local custom, it must not stray.

The crew consists of a laodah, who is sometimes the owner and who must be a good sailor and pilot, business man, and know the best fishing-grounds; his second in command, the cook, who is qualified to take command in case of need; and four or five hands. Usually she has one mast, 35 feet high, and carries a spritsail. Sometimes a very small sprit fore-sail is fitted as well with, in addition, a small staysail. And the laodah is quite as proud of the cut and set of his sails as any Cowes yachtsman.

Built of *sha-mu*, with hardwood frames and bulkheads, the main characteristics of these boats are their colourful decoration and crude but strong construction. They are fitted with four full bulkheads[1], and additional strength is provided by heavy wales. The crew live in the after house[2], while the two compartments forward of the house and up to the first bulkhead are the fish holds[3].

There are several varieties of this type, depending on the port of origin and duration of the cruises. There are, for instance, a long boat (長 船), a short boat (短 船), and a spring boat (春 船). All are colourful craft. The differences are usually to be found in the shape and build of the stern, and there are at least two different varieties of bow. Structurally these differences are small, being mostly in the decoration. One type follows the conventional Ningpo scheme, while that under review carries five white circles[4] on each side of the oculus. The wings of the bow are picked out in white in both cases, and both have a red-painted "water bruiser[5]."

The stern is of the horseshoe[6], open-stern type in contradistinction to the closed stern of the larger Ningpo and Chusan types. The stern-frame[6] is painted bright red, as is also the upper part of the house and the bulwarks.

紹

THE SHAOHING-CH'UAN OR HANGCHOW BAY TRADER

The old and renowned city of Hangchow has been famous for many things in its long and romantic history, but for none more in the eyes of the junk-lover than for having given its name to one of the most picturesque and ornamental junks in China—the Hangchow Bay trader.

The earliest notes we have of the site of Hangchow date back to the time of the great Emperor Yü (禹 王), 2198 B.C., who organized the river system of China and stopped the floods. In his travels he is said to have landed here, hence the original name of the city, Yühang, "the Place of the Boat-landing of Yü." About 255 B.C. the first Emperor of the Ch'in dynasty came to the foot of the hill where the Needle Pagoda now stands and moored his boat to the large rock now known as the Great Buddha. Marco Polo visited Hangchow, and his description of the city showed that much of its ancient grandeur had remained.

The "Chinese Repository" of July 1834, quoting Renaudot's "Ancient Accounts of India and China," by two Mohammedan travellers who went to these ports in the ninth century, says of Canfu, which is not Canton but Hangchow:—

> When a ship was got through the gates of China, she, with a tide of flood, goes into a fresh water gulf, and drops anchor in the chief port of China, which is that of Canfu, and here they have fresh water from both spring and rivers, as they have also in most other ports of China.

The seaport of Hangchow was situated at Kanpoo, its harbour now being blocked by sand. Here in the old days was the anchorage and the ordinary residence of the Arab merchants.

Probably little change was manifest in the appearance of the Hangchow Bay trader during the latter centuries of its existence. These vessels are usually three masted and have the symbolic *pa-kua* in place of the more usual eyes on the bow, and the hull and bow are both painted in bright colours. Nowadays the paint is usually the worse for wear.

These craft vary somewhat in size, the smallest types being about 60 feet over-all, while the largest attain a length of 85 feet. That illustrated in Plate No. 10 measures 84 by 23 feet, with a depth of 8 feet. There are 10 bulkheads and no ribs. These bulkheads share with the deck beams the responsibility for transversal strength.

As will be seen on the plan, longitudinal strength is provided by two massive fore and aft baulks of timber[1] which extend from the first bulkhead[2] to the stern[3] in a graceful curve. These travel practically parallel to the bottom planks[4]. The bow is set at an angle, and its athwartship planking rests on and slightly in rear of the rounded extremity of the ascending bottom planking[5], which, of course, runs fore and aft.

The deck is decidedly whale-backed, and the cambered deck planking is secured to the bulkheads in the usual manner and rises abruptly at bow and stern.

The foremost beam is pierced to receive the bitts[6]. These consist of a long, stout hardwood pole thrust through an aperture in the deck. On ordinary occasions the foot of the pole rests on the floor of the junk. In the event, however, of the fore part of the deck being piled high with cargo, the adjustable bitts are pulled up to any height required, so that any ropes secured to them shall be clear of the cargo. The strain on the snug-fitting bitts would seem to be sufficient to lock them in this new position.

The open stern, which is painted white and highly decorated, is flat, the

The junkmen say there are three wonders of the world in China: the third, they say, is the greatest of all—the Great Bore of Hangchow. The Hangchow Trader was specifically designed for riding the bore.

About 1,200 years ago a wall was built at Haining (26 miles from Hangchow), 120 miles long and 26 feet high, to protect the millions of people who live in the vicinity of Hangchow Bay. The sea-junks come in at high water and are secured to the top of the wall. As the tide goes out, they settle on shelves that project out from the wall. Facing the sea, Hangchow Bay, 60 miles wide, forms a funnel that narrows to 9 miles. Then in comes the bore. It can be seen as a thin white streak across the horizon. The incoming wave strikes the outer buttresses and rises to a height of some 15 to 30 feet. The white, roaring wave breaks into a crest which grows higher as it advances through the ever-narrowing funnel of Hangchow Bay.

Pandemonium breaks loose. The madly yelling junkmen fend off their boats from the stone wall and, smartly slipping their mooring lines, are afloat in an instant and are on their way to Hangchow in the wake of the bore. They usually do the 23 miles in about two hours. (Condensed from *The Junkman Smiles*, by G. R. G. Worcester, 1969.)

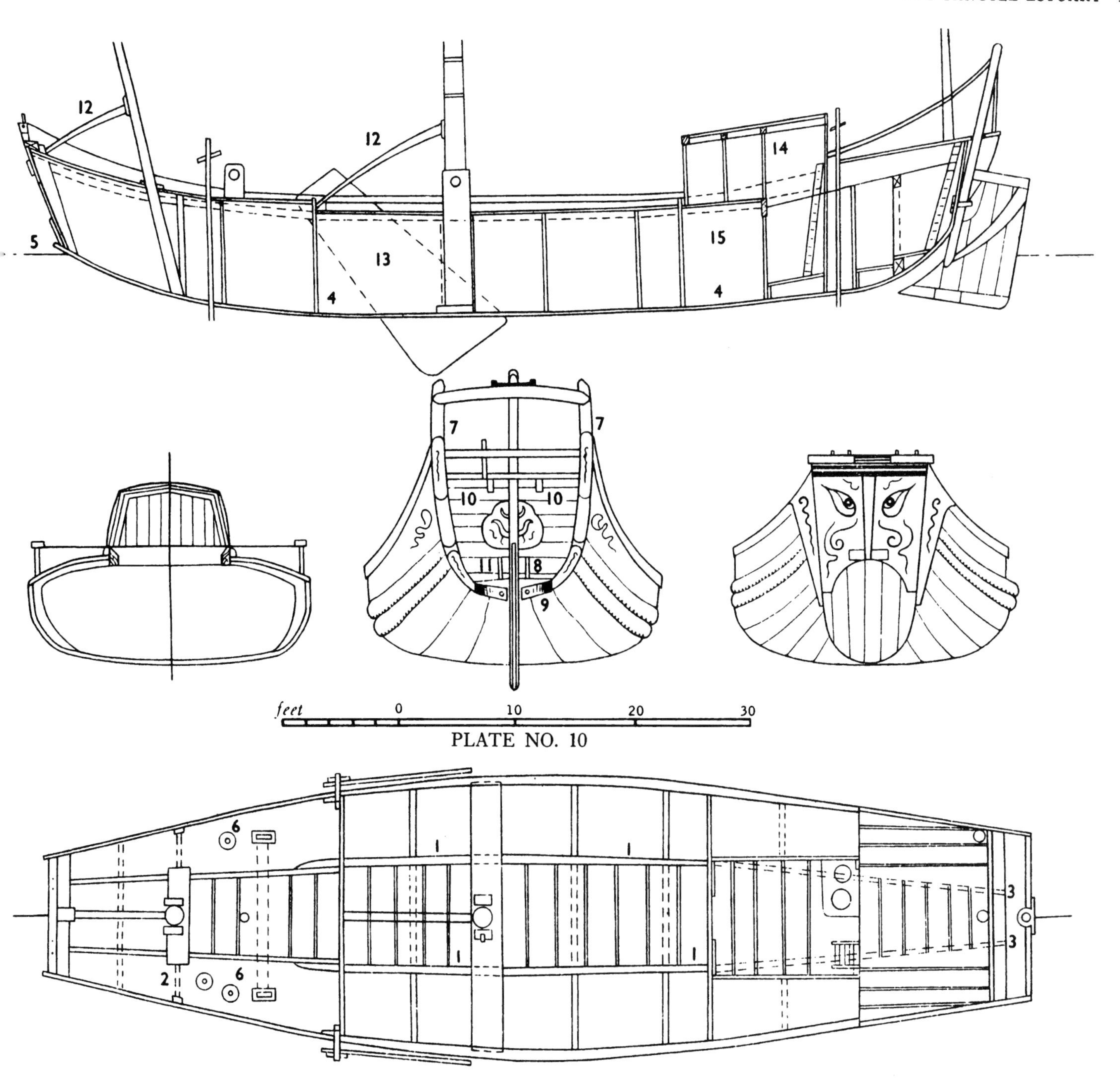

PLATE NO. 10

planking running athwartships, and is supported by red-painted wings[7], also decorated. The lower rudder chock[8] derives its support from resting on the ascending bottom planking[9], while the upper chock rests on the extremities of the fore and aft baulks already mentioned[10].

The heavy hardwood rudder is semi-balanced, crude in construction, but efficient in action. It rests between two red-painted knees[11] and is secured to the stern proper by a wire grummet fitted with a wooden chafing piece. The rudder chocks are cut to receive the post, which is raked at an angle of about 30° which makes her handy on her helm.

The mainmast stands erect, and is often "made" for about three-fourths of its length and is always iron bound. Wedges are sometimes driven between the iron bands and the mast to give greater rigidity. The halyards are usually double, both passing through sheave-holes in the mast. The mainsail is a well-peaked balance lug, generally with 12 battens; the foremast has a forward rake and carries a smaller, albeit similar, sail fitted with 10 battens. Both masts are supported

Bow of a Hangchow Trader

The Hangchow Trader, the junk that rides the bore.

longitudinally at deck level by a fore and aft prop[12]. The mizzen stands erect, stepped on deck. A most noticeable feature of the sails of these craft is that the foot of each sail is symmetrically on a line with that of the next, making a clean follow-through for all three sails at the foot.

For a detailed description of lee-boards, see note, page 238.

The lee-boards[13] consist of two or more strong frames of plank. These traverse on a stout bolt which passes through the bulwarks. The bolt is held to the ship's side by an iron chain which is made fast inboard to a ring-bolt on a deck beam. The position of the lee-boards is usually about 12 feet forward of the mast.

The deck house[14] is very small—usually it is little more than a galley and companion way to the quarters below[15]. It is often to be seen covered in with an additional mat roof.

The deck beams, of which there are three, are rough and irregular, unevenly spaced, and vary in size. For the most part they are split tree trunks in their natural state.

The surprising incongruity in the make-up of this interesting junk only adds to its attraction. For instance, the Hangchow shipwrights waste no time in superficial finish: the junks, though sturdily built, show crude workmanship, yet the daring colour scheme and originality of the painted decoration which covers the entire bow and many other parts of the vessel is executed with great finish and detail, and is always in excellent taste, however vivid.*

* The fascinating decoration of these junks is not carried out by the men themselves, but by artists who make a speciality of this type of work.

Not even the most ardent junk-lover could call the Hangchow Bay trader graceful, but this odd-looking craft possesses a nameless charm which probably derives a good deal from its faithful adherence to an old and well-tested design.

THE HUA-P'I-KU OR FOOCHOW POLE-JUNK

花屁股

The province of Fukien is well known for the forests which grow in its mountainous districts. Contrary to the custom in Hunan, these timber forests are not in the hands of any guild, but are usually owned by individual families. Timber merchants, therefore, send their representatives up country to make arrangements with the local landowners about a consignment of wood.

Probably the most widely-used varieties of wood are the Fukien fir, or *sha-mu (Cunninghamia lanceolate)*, and the Fukien pine, called the *sung-mu (Pinus massoniana)*, and both have been deservedly famous for centuries. The former provides what is known as Foochow softwood, while the latter supplies a superior and much stronger kind of timber, full of resin, which, besides being greatly in demand for making furniture, is very largely used in junkbuilding.

The trees are purchased in whole tracts or areas. The season for cutting them down is usually from March to June. First in the field is a gang of men with hoes, who clear the roots of earth and undergrowth so that the trees can be cut down as low as possible. Next come the axe-men, who are experts at their task. After felling, the trees are trimmed, peeled, and cut into logs and left throughout the summer months to dry so as to make them easier to handle in the early autumn, when they are ready to start their journey down to the river. Sometimes they have to be carried for many miles on men's shoulders, at others they travel on skidways down the hillsides or by creek or mountain stream. On arrival at the main tributary of the Min River they are built up into rafts by special raft-builders.

These rafts are long and narrow, being 100 feet in length by 10 feet only in width, and are made by fastening the logs or poles together with bamboo pegs and lashings of bamboo rope. Each raft has a crew of two men, who work the large, crude sweeps.

When the rafts finally arrive at Foochow *via* the Min River they either anchor or are dismantled, and the poles are stacked on shore while they await transhipment by junk to Shanghai and other parts of China.

The vessels which trade up and down the China coast carrying these timber cargoes from Fukien's rich interior are the picturesque and distinctive Foochow pole-junks, large, seaworthy craft which may be as long as 180 feet with a beam of 28 feet, the smaller junks being 60 feet shorter with a beam of 22 feet. The latter junks have no quarter-deck and usually no cabin on the poop.

The specimen illustrated in Plate No. 11 measures 148 feet with a beam of 30 feet. Built of the Fukien softwood she carries, she is of quite exceptionally strong construction, for there are at unusually close intervals 15 full bulkheads of hardwood,* extending from the bottom to the main deck in most cases. There are in addition 37 hardwood frames, some of which act as an extra strengthening to the bulkheads. The sides of the hull are composed of long and heavy planks laid on edge and secured to the bulkheads and timbers. Longitudinal strength is provided by three enormous hardwood wales[1] which, lying close together and following the curve of the bilge throughout, also serve as bilge keels, as they are placed so low on the hull that, except at bow and stern, they are at or below the water-line, according to whether the junk is light or loaded. Three lighter wales, or strakes[2], are situated at and above deck level at varying intervals. The bottom and bilges are gently curved transversely. Longitudinally the bottom is also

* The *Titanic*, a vessel of 45,000 tons, had the same number of watertight compartments.

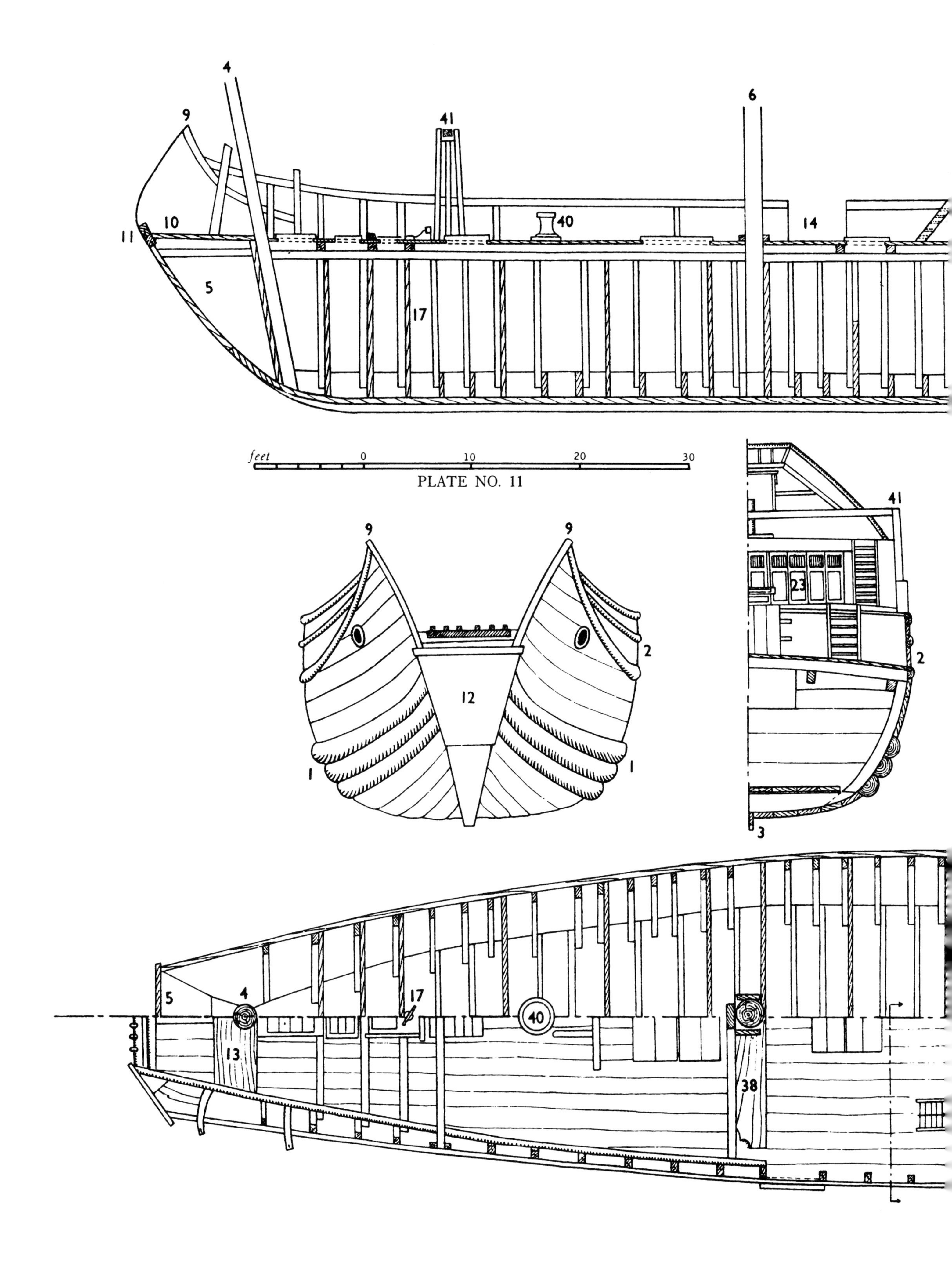
4
9
41
6
10
40
11
14
5
17
feet 0 10 20 30
9
9
41
23
2
2
12
1
1
3
5
4
17
40
13
38

PLATE NO. 11

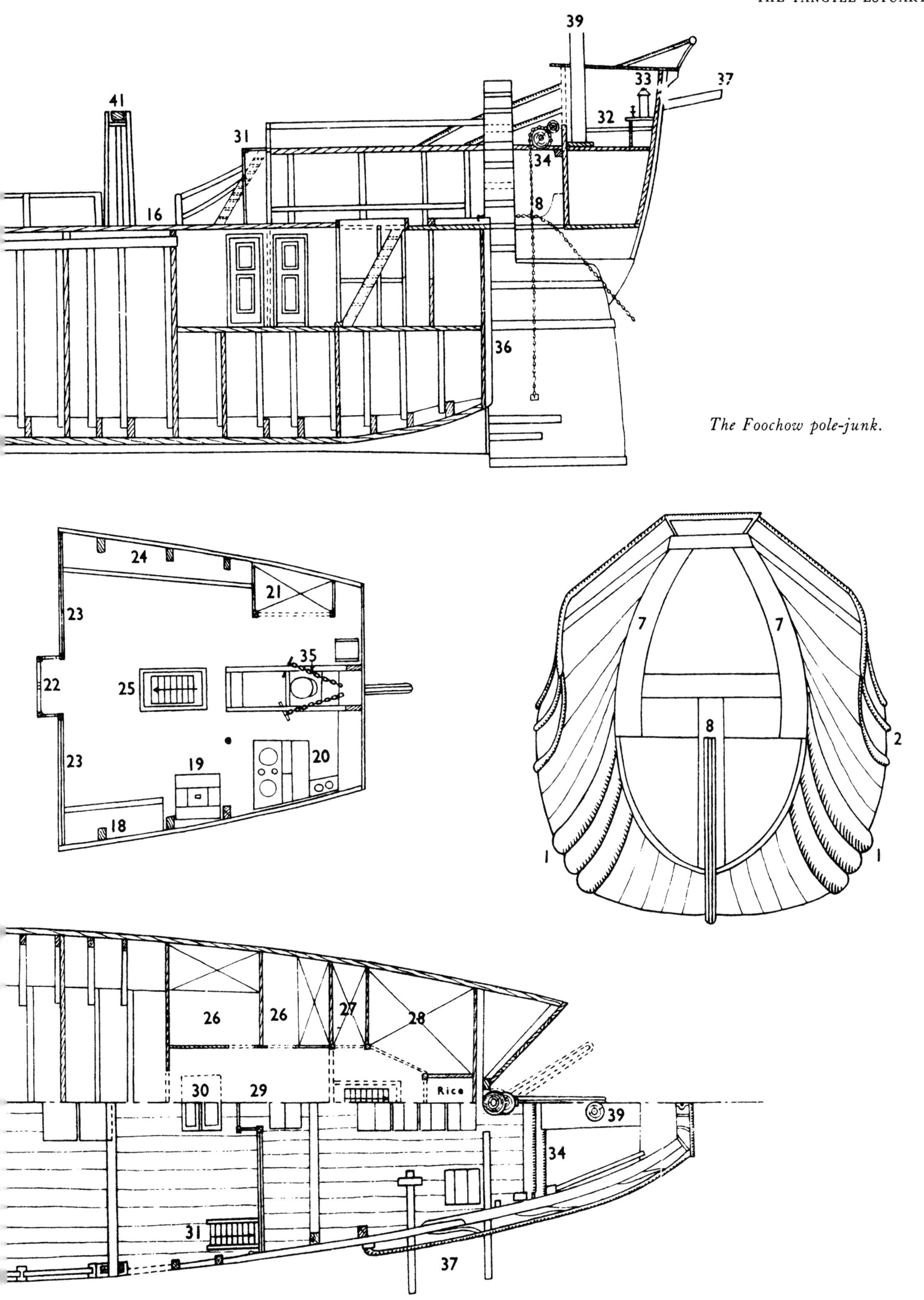

The Foochow pole-junk.

slightly curved throughout its length. This particular junk had a light keel[3], as one would expect from the type of sailing required of it.

These junks are necessarily of extremely strong construction, as they often carry as much as 5,000 piculs of timber. The shorter logs are stowed in the deep, broad holds which occupy all the hull from the foremast[4] to the orlop deck. The foremost triangular-shaped compartment is kept as a buoyancy chamber[5]. Timber is also carried on deck, and the longer poles are lashed in a fore and aft position alongside in the shape of gigantic bundles. The bamboo ropes securing them pass right round them under the junk and are secured to the mainmast[6]. The height of this outboard cargo serves to keep the deck cargo from shifting.

The distinctive features of these junks are the tall, oval sterns decorated with characteristic brightly-coloured paintings and the high, flaring bow. The decoration on the stern follows a conservative plan with only minor variations. Two long, narrow panels[7] border the sides of the oval-shaped stern facing. These

Decorated stern of the Foochow pole-junk.

contain different designs, the larger junks having a sprawling dragon on either hand. The upper panel between these borders invariably depicts a *yen* bird (燕 鳥) with outstretched wings on a rock in the midst of a troubled ocean. Its indifference to the tempest and its reputation for speed make it a most desirable emblem, for the junkmen consider that these qualities are thereby imparted to their vessel.

Next amongst conventional devices appear three characters 永 利 順, meaning permanent, profitable, and prosperous. The first signifies long life. In this case the presage has been amply fulfilled, for the laodah claims for his junk an age of 150 years. The second character is self-explanatory. The third has a bearing on prosperous—that is to say, fair—winds. Below, on a white ground, appears the registered number of the craft, in this case 1568, and under it, half-way down the design, the eight immortals extend in a row across the stern at its broadest part. Two large medallions usually complete the last panel of the decoration. These may contain floral designs or, in the case of the more important and elaborately-painted junks, a stag and a crane respectively, representing official honours and longevity. A square aperture[8] amongst this gay galaxy serves as a hawse-pipe for the stern moorings. Further decoration is to be seen on the quarter, where immediately below the rails colour is again introduced either in the form of a scroll pattern in the three cardinal colours or by green bulwarks adorned with red medallions. Below, on a black ground, is a crudely-drawn sea serpent in red or sometimes in green. This looks more like an enormous slug than a snake. At the bow there is further embellishment in the form of narrow bands of colours, white and others, but with green predominating, or a floral scroll pattern in red, blue, yellow, and green. The oculi are very conspicuous with large, glaring black eyeballs in white circles. The eyeball is in deep relief, and it projects 9 inches beyond the level of the ship's side. Even the white of the eye is embossed, and the whole measures 1 foot 8 inches in diameter. The characteristic bow consists of two wings which, converging sharply at the water-line, rise in a steep diverging curve to deck level, above which they curve abruptly back again. The horns[9] of the wings rise to a point 10 feet above the main deck[10]. This form of construction, viewed in profile, gives the bow of the junk a curious aspect not unlike the blunt nose of a fish, a similitude which is further heightened by the large oculi similarly placed below. The resemblance is obviously intentional, for the junkmen claim that the first inspiration for this craft was from a monstrous fish, the teeth being at the cut-water, while the wings, forming the armature of the head, carried the eyes. The masts and sails represented the fins, and the high stern the frisking tail.

The open space, measuring 9 feet at deck level, between the wide flare of the bow wings terminates in a heavy transverse stem-beam[11] laid over the deck planking and is iron covered. It is fitted with pin fair-leads for the cables for the anchors, of which four are carried.

Below this the triangular portion between the wings is fitted with a shaped piece[12] of hardwood timber laid transversely. Thirteen feet abaft the stem-beam[11] is a massive deck beam[13] which acts as additional support for the foremast[4]. The whole bow is of exceptionally strong construction so as to take the pounding of the seas. Some of the frames of the vessel are prolonged above deck level, and the horizontal planking forming the heavy bulwarks is laid outside them. These bulwarks are 6 feet high at the bows, where they merge into the spreading wings, and decrease to their lowest height of 3 feet at the cargo gangway[14] just abaft the mainmast. The longitudinal deck planking is continuous until the tenth bulkhead. Here the quarter-deck commences at an elevation of 4 feet and runs through to the stern. The bulwarks which now commence consist of a 3-foot high railing[15]

Looking forward on the Foochow pole-junk. Note the hatches, which provide access to the holds.
SIR FREDERICK MAZE, K.C.M.G.

which is pierced again just before the break of the house for the companion ladder[16]. Access to the capacious holds is provided by seven hatches. One compartment serves as a fresh-water tank[17], from which the water is obtained as required by means of a bamboo pump.

Over the after part of the quarter-deck a spacious house is built. It extends to the stern, and consists of one large compartment which serves as a living and mess room. It also accommodates the communal rice in a large bin[18], water in a butt[19], the galley, consisting of a large stove on the port side[20]; the cook, who sleeps in a bunk[21] on the starboard side; and the pilot, who cons the ship from a little bay[22] amidships between the two sliding doors leading on to the quarter-deck. A long locker[24] on the starboard side gives stowage space for clothes and gear. A ladder[25] in the centre gives access to the orlop deck, where quarters are reserved for the owner and important passengers, for the junk is owned by a joint stock trading company and some of the partners accompany her on her voyages. Four of the eight cabins on the lower deck are roomy and comfortable, and each contains two bunks[26]. The other four consist each of two small compartments[27] just large enough to hold two bunks and two larger ones[28] each designed to hold two tiers of men, who must necessarily be curled up in the triangular bunks provided. The last man in particular has the smallest and most awkward space in which to dispose himself, but all are compelled to lie in a ball like a hedgehog. The open space, or alleyway[29], between these cabins measures about 22 by 10 feet and provides extra accommodation for the crew of from 20 to 30 men, who may sleep here or in any other place not required for passengers or other purposes. A skylight[30] in the quarter-deck admits a limited amount of light and ventilation to the orlop deck.

Returning to the quarter-deck, a ladder[31] leads up to the poop above the house. The bulwarks slant up and terminate in a straight line in the side of the house, and their place on the poop is taken by an ornamental handrail which in its turn is crossed and superseded by the rising line of the three wales or strakes which finish off the line of the handrail right round the stern. The poop is flush throughout. The raised quarter-deck and high poop enable the junk to be worked in safety and comparative comfort during bad weather when every other part of the ship is awash. At the after part of the poop there is a small house in which is the laodah's bunk[32], but it serves another very important function, for here is housed the shrine containing an effigy of the sailors' patron saint, Kuan Yin, the Goddess of Mercy. Another very favourite guardian divinity is the Queen of Heaven (天 后), who was a young lady named Lin (林) in the province of Fukien, from which these junks hail. Her fame, however, spread far afield, for temples and shrines in her honour are to be met with along all the lines of communication throughout China.

Access to this temple-cum-laodah's cabin is impeded by the necessity of stepping over a massive baulk of timber[34] which, stretching from side to side of the poop, where it rests in uprights, forms the windlass for hoisting the rudder. The rudder, as is the case with all sea-going junks, appears to be large out of all proportion, but this disparity is explained by the necessity for holding the vessel against a drift to leeward. The rudder, which weighs some tons, measures 32½ feet in depth from the rudder head to the lower edge and 11½ feet in width at its broadest, which is at the bottom. The large and heavy rudder-post, 15 feet in length, is iron bound at intervals of a foot throughout. It is slung by a short tie[35], and is hoisted and lowered by a bight of chain passing through a sheave in the rudder with both standing parts of the chain passing round the barrel of the windlass. There are no gudgeons, and so it is kept in position by grass ropes attached to the bottom of the bearding and passed under the ship's bottom and over the bows. A wooden rudder when immersed is very little heavier than water, and, despite its size, the huge rudder of this type of junk can be hoisted with comparative ease by a few men who manipulate the windlass by means of two handspikes inserted into the holes provided.

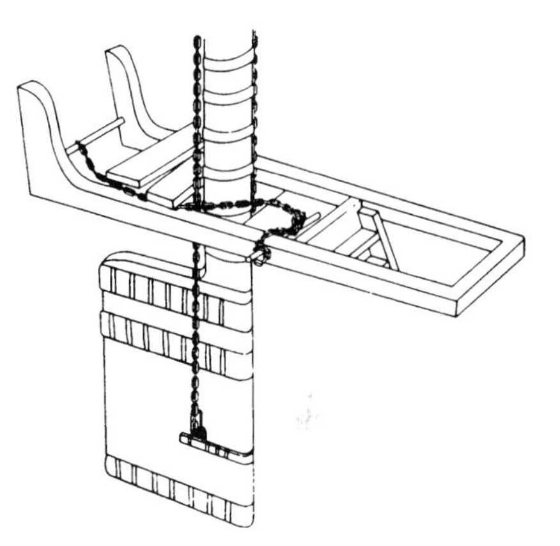

The rudder.

In harbour the rudder is kept in the raised position. When in use in the raised position, that is to say, if manœuvring in harbour or in very shallow water, it draws only 7 or 8 feet, or very little more than the junk itself. A short tiller is then fitted. When lowered the rudder draws as much as 11 feet, and a very long tiller is then used, which is operated by two luff tackles.

Three strongly-built sampans are carried, one on each quarter and a third over the stern. They are slung from spar davits[37].

There are three hardwood masts.* The foremast[4], which is 61 feet in height above the deck and hooped at frequent intervals, has a considerable rake forward. It is housed against the first bulkhead, which is similarly raked to afford continuous support. The deck beam[13], already alluded to, into which the foremast takes, measures 4 feet in width and is proportionately thick. The mainmast[6], which stands vertically 93 feet above the main deck, has a circumference of over 8 feet. It is stepped in the usual way, but as it is on such generous lines, great ingenuity is shown in the even distribution of the strain. The massive tabernacles stand 3 feet 5 inches above the deck and fit into an appropriately heavy transverse beam[38] which measures 2 feet 9 inches across by 8 inches in depth. There seems no adequate reason why this baulk of timber should not reach from bulwark to bulwark, but it invariably fails to extend the whole width of the deck. The mizzen mast[39], which is 54 feet in height above the deck, is stepped about a foot out of the centre line of the ship. The reason for this does not seem clear. All three masts carry balance lug-sails in their truest form. Until the end of the last

* This junk would seem to be under-sparred in proportion of length of mast to hull, for in the *king-yung-yu* (金永餘), another junk of the same type, with an over-all measurement of 134 feet, the masts measure 80, 120, and 60 feet respectively from deck to truck.

century these sails were made of matting, later cotton was used, and now they are made of foreign imported No. 2 canvas and often weigh several tons.

Masthead devices are illustrated in the Appendix.

Two masthead devices are carried, the principal one on the mainmast and another similar, but smaller, on the mizzen. The device consists of a gold leaf truck surmounting the masthead and carrying a wand surmounted by a red ball. Half way up the wand is a white-painted wooden fish with a long, broad, red cloth tail which, as the fish revolves in the wind, serves as a weather-vane. The fish has long, twisted wire antennæ ending in red balls. In the centre of its body is a mirror. As already explained, the idea is that any passing evil spirit which may stop to investigate it will be so alarmed by the reflection of its own hideous face that it will immediately sheer off.

A capstan[40] on the main deck midway between the fore and the main masts is used for hoisting the sails. The latter when lowered are stowed on gallows frames[41].

For ponderous dignity the Foochow pole-junks are unsurpassed, yet their manœuvrability is such that they need no outside assistance when entering and leaving Shanghai. The Chinese inventiveness and originality have reached their highest point in these craft, in which may be seen epitomized their ingenuity of ship design and the unique skill in seamanship of their crews.

The larger types are, unhappily, rapidly dying out. Indeed, it is said by the junkmen that there are only 10 of these magnificent vessels afloat to-day, and that of this number four are almost falling to pieces, while the remaining six are sadly in need of repair.

The fanciful may conjure up for themselves a pleasing picture of the Whangpoo at the time of the first settlers in Shanghai, when the river was crowded with sailing craft of all descriptions and the aristocrats of the East met those of the West. How intriguing must have been the contrast between the weighty age-old traditional junk and the light and graceful Clipper, the outcome of the most modern inspiration of the Western world of that day; and how curiously must the crews of each, masters of their own art, have surveyed each other.

Method of stowing poles on a Foochow pole-junk.

SHANGHAI AND THE WHANGPOO

THE port of Shanghai is situated some 75 miles from deep water, the approaches being by way of the Yangtze estuary as far as Woosung, and thence for about 12 to 15 miles up the Whangpoo.

In ancient days the original Shanghai was not considered of any great importance, for, unlike the neighbouring towns of Hangchow, Ningpo, and Foochow, it is rarely mentioned in Chinese history. One of the earliest references is in approximately 200 B.C., when it was spoken of as a prosperous fishing settlement named Hutuh, probably situated close to the present village of Whangtu.

It is believed to have been founded by Huang Hsieh (黃 歇), who was what might be termed an adviser to the young heir to the State of Ch'u. This kingdom embraced most of the Lower Yangtze Valley, including the provinces of Hunan, Hupeh, Kiangsi, Anhwei, and Kiangsu. When the Prince came to the throne towards the middle of the third century B.C., Huang Hsieh was made Governor of Soochow, which town was then said to be about 200 years old.

Huang Hsieh not only appreciated the potentiality of the present site of Shanghai and its waterways, but is credited with having laboured to make the shallows of the Whangpoo navigable with such success that the stream was named after him and Shanghai became the port for Soochow.

Soon after this the district embracing Shanghai was incorporated in a newly-made *hsien* named Lou (鄝), being in the principality of Kuaichi (會 稽). After the Christian era it became absorbed into the Three Kingdoms, celebrated in Chinese historical romance. The first time the present name occurs is said to have been in the time of the Sung dynasty, about A.D. 960, when the town was called Shanghai Chin, meaning out, or up, to the sea. It was formerly situated nearer the sea than now; but the accumulation of silt and sand gradually formed the plain of Pootung, or East of the Whangpoo, through which the Whangpoo scoured out a channel leading to Shanghai.

A Custom House was established in the eleventh century. The city walls, now demolished, were 3½ miles in circumference and were particularly useful in helping to repel marauding attacks from Japanese pirates.

Shanghai lies at the present confluence of the Soochow Creek with the Whangpoo. This fact has enormously increased the importance of the formerly insignificant little Whangpoo, which more than once in its history has almost ceased to exist. Its course has fluctuated considerably in position as well as navigability, which process of change still continues. From old records we learn that the tendency to silt has caused constant anxiety, and during the Sung dynasty the officials formed various plans for keeping it open, but by the fourteenth century it defeated them all by completely closing up. It was not until the Ming dynasty that navigation again became partially possible.

In the year 1560, however, matters worsened again, until finally the bed of the river once more became dry land. The Governor of the Province took the opportunity of straightening the bends in its course and cleared out the channel; but his efforts were not lasting, for in less than 50 years the reluctant stream had again ceased to flow.

In 1672 the local Lieutenant-Governor dug out the channel anew, and although troublesome it would seem that from that time the river has never again completely disappeared, and allowing for natural vagaries and various dredging operations, it has more or less kept to the same channel.

In recent years a Conservancy Board was formed. Since 1906 the whole river from Woosung to the Arsenal has been regulated, and, thanks to the operations of this organization, the bars which formerly impeded the reaches have been removed sufficiently to permit of a least depth at lowest low water of about 26 feet over a bottom width of 500 feet and a through navigational depth of 28 feet at low water.

After discounting the ingenuity of man, by which the Whangpoo has been deepened and enlarged, it is really in effect no more than a tidal channel which, penetrating for 40 miles into the interior, serves yet another important purpose by draining the waters from the interior lakes.

From old Chinese historical records of the provincial waterways it is clear that many and great changes have occurred throughout the centuries in connection with the important question of the main drainage from the Western Hills forming the local watershed.

About A.D. 400 this was said to have been carried out by the present Liu-ho, which enters the Yangtze 17 miles above Woosung. Later the main outlet for these inland waters was through the Soochow Creek, known as the Woosung-kiang, and recorded as being 20 *li* in width at its junction with the Whangpoo, than which it was then a very much larger and more important stream, its mouth being said to be in a different locality.

It would seem, therefore, that the depth and size of these streams depend on the volume of drainage they carry, and that their improvement or deterioration depends entirely on this factor. Captain Tyler,* formerly Coast Inspector, writing on this subject, stated that, as the Whangpoo is the latest agent of drainage without signs of any rival competitor, this fact of its functioning as a main drain tends towards naturally ameliorating its channel through scouring, though he added that efforts at conservancy should not be relaxed.

The hills of this watershed are 35 miles from Shanghai up the Whangpoo, near Sungkiangfu. Beyond this range lies a system of lakes artificially joined by canals, which in turn connect with the Grand Canal close to Soochow, about 90 miles from Shanghai.

Thus the Whangpoo fulfils another useful office in that it affords easy communication with the northern cities of Chekiang, with the trade centre of Hangchow, and also with Ningpo.

The first foreign connection with Shanghai and junks was in 1813, when the Rev. Charles Gutzlaff sailed in a trading junk from Canton to Tientsin, calling at various ports on the coast and visiting Shanghai in August of that year.

At the time of this first arrival of the foreigners, the Chinese city and its suburbs lay on the west or left bank of the river, here running north and south, and were separated from the Woosungkiang, or Soochow Creek, by an expanse of about 2 miles of reedy marsh land.

Owing to intercourse with the West and the volume of trade that thereby developed, the new Shanghai that has grown up on this marshy site is a vast city of such mushroom growth that many of the older inhabitants can still remember the time when the outer edge of the Settlement reached only as far as the present Race-course.

* "Customs Decennial Reports," 1892–1901.

In the seventies in Shanghai it was of quite common occurrence for batches of junks to be moored stem to stern with almost mathematical precision. As many as 24 of these rows, each consisting of about 20 large junks, could be seen in the harbour at the recognized anchorages for such craft. It used then to be said that there was hardly a type of junk in China without its representative in the Whangpoo.

Though this may be somewhat of an exaggeration, yet there was a good deal of truth in it, for junks from all over the China coast, as well as from the Yangtze and the communicating creeks and rivers, certainly congregated in large numbers at Shanghai; nor was there any very marked falling off in numbers or varieties until about the turn of the century.

The waterfront in those days must have presented a fascinating picture to the lover of sailing craft. There could be seen in casual juxtaposition the heavy Hainan junks with mat sails; the Fukien traders with their white-painted sides; the lorchas, which always seemed to present a deserted and uncared-for appearance; and finally the Ningpo junks, which, however they might vary in size, remained true to the unmistakable characteristics of their type, with their black hulls brightened by the oculi and the Ningpo sailor's love of colour in bright splashes. Junks from the north, from the south, from the Yangtze and its countless tributaries, and craft from the vast hinterland of waterways centring round the delta and the T'aihu could be seen.

The junk anchorages at Woosung were also closely packed with craft of all kinds: the heavy trading junks from the north; the cumbrous Foochow junks towering in unwieldy masses from the water or loaded down with immense masses of poles slung on each side; the fishing-junks, brightly painted; and the colourful craft of Wenchow; while all along the shore, as opportunity offered, were rows of boats and sampans banked-in.

The bulwarks of these junks used to be painted a standard colour prescribed by law and was very strictly enforced so as to indicate the port of origin. The bulwarks of junks from the province of Fukien were painted black with a green border; those from the ports of Chekiang were painted black with a white border; and those from Kwangtung, black with a red border. The junkmaster was, moreover, compelled to re-paint his junk every two years. By this means junks could be recognized at a distance.*

Many of these types have disappeared, a process which has been accelerated during the last few difficult years. It would be comforting to believe with the old junkmen that a proportion of these ancient types will return with the cessation of hostilities, but it is to be feared that there is little justification for this optimistic view and that the few remaining representatives of some of these junks are the last of their species. This is notably the case with the Foochow trader, of which there are now said to be only 11 left in Chinese waters, and even these are rapidly disintegrating. The Hainan and large Kiangsu traders would also appear to be doomed to complete extinction in the near future. The most recently-built of these craft is now said to be 20 years old; and, even if it were desired in future peaceful times to revive these types, the question of building them would present difficulties in that the old shipwrights who built by rule of thumb are passing away, if not already dead, and have left no records of any kind whereby their handicraft may be carried on. Nevertheless, leaving out these fast disappearing types, there is still a surprising richness of material in the Shanghai Harbour for the student of Chinese junks.

An interesting and unexpected feature is the presence of many kinds of craft whose prototypes hailed from far afield, either Ningpo or the north. Yet, for whatever reason, many of these junks have now as it were become naturalized

* "Customs Decennial Reports."

to Shanghai, even to the extent of being built here as a regular routine. Modified as these craft may be in small ways by a change of environment, they still retain their main original distinguishing characteristics and remain obstinately different in essential construction and appearance from the craft of the delta and Yangtze River, though by adoption they now fit in well with their new surroundings. Others of these varieties, even if they are not actually built in Shanghai, are such constant visitors to this terminal port that they may be said to be semi-indigenous. Some idea of the rapid development of this city may be gathered from the statistics compiled a few years ago by the Bureau of Agriculture, Industry, and Commerce, now called the Bureau of Social Affairs.

Workers.	Number Employed.	Workers.	Number Employed.
Sailors	167,375	Night-soil Coolies	2,079
Cotton Spinners	28,053	Shipbuilding Carpenters	1,445

Through Shanghai normally passes about 50 per cent of the imports and 35 per cent of the exports of China. In this modern *entrepôt* there are paper and cotton mills, shipbuilding yards, engineering plants, waterworks, skyscrapers, luxury hotels, and innumerable other commercial establishments. Ships from all over the world lie alongside and embark and discharge cargo at the extensive wharves or lie at the buoys in the Whangpoo, which from being a little stream of no account now serves the second largest city in the Far East and the fifth largest in the world.

Number of Junks Entered and Cleared at Shanghai during the Years 1902–41.*

Year.	Entered and Cleared.	Year.	Entered and Cleared.	Year.	Entered and Cleared.
1902	6,379	1916	9,288	1930	54,410
1903	7,642	1917	33,227	1931	28,098
1904	7,494	1918	36,230	1932	35,258
1905	8,454	1919	43,016	1933	61,401
1906	9,542	1920	58,092	1934	73,498
1907	10,112	1921	56,075	1935	77,420
1908	9,989	1922	57,422	1936	69,099
1909	10,430	1923	58,603	1937	44,420
1910	9,542	1924	52,469	1938	4,552
1911	9,714	1925	54,040	1939	19,624
1912	10,676	1926	51,582	1940	21,428
1913	10,385	1927	51,091	1941	8,724†
1914	10,213	1928	48,372		
1915	8,799	1929	49,134		

A general impression appears to prevail that the number of junks has been steadily decreasing. The above table, however, shows that, at least until 1935, this belief is erroneous. What appears to have happened is that while many of the large junks, such as the lorchas, Kiangsu traders, salt-junks, and others of this kind, if they did not completely disappear, lessened considerably in numbers, while other smaller types of junks greatly increased.

It is not clear why there was some decrease in junk shipping so long before the beginning of the Sino-Japanese War in 1937. With the outbreak of hostilities, however, the entrance and clearance figures decline most rapidly until they reach their nadir of 4,552 in 1938. With the end of hostilities, and especially the prohibition of foreign shipping on China's inland waterways, it seems reasonable to suppose that the figures will be very much on the up grade in the future.

* Kindly supplied by the Tidesurveyor's Office, Chinese Maritime Customs, Shanghai.

† January to May (inclusive).

It also seems reasonable to assume that as long as a crowded water-borne population remains dependent upon the navigation of their own craft for a livelihood, as long as there is cheap and bulky produce to be imported and exported to and from the hinterland *via* a vast network of creeks and canals, so long will junks be built and their owners find, if not a profit, at least a livelihood.

Unfortunately it seems as if the Japanese-sponsored practice of installing engines in junks has come to stay. From a strictly utilitarian viewpoint this habit may make for greater efficiency, safety, and, of course, speed; but it is to be feared that the result will inevitably be an alteration and perhaps blending of many of the well-known types.

Already the shadow of coming events is to be seen in the case of the Ningpo fishermen. In order to accommodate a foreign-style capstan, some of these craft have ruthlessly shorn off the graceful high wings of the bow, giving a strangely mutilated appearance. Another Ningpo type, as a concession to modernism, has completely altered the shape of its bow, and not for the better from an æsthetic point of view.

Most of the cargo for this huge industry of loading and discharging foreign ships is carried to and from them by junks. In 1919 more than 43,000 junks entered and cleared at Shanghai. Of this number, one-half plied between Shanghai and the province of Kiangsu, north of the Yangtze; 40 per cent traded with Chekiang Province, and about 5 per cent with Shantung. The main produce carried locally comprises poultry, eggs, firewood, vegetables, timber, vegetable oils, bricks, preserved eggs, flour, paper, straw hats, sugar, and tiles.

The Shanghai Harbour at all times presents an animated and interesting scene and, to the student of Oriental craft, an absorbing one. Hawkers in every type of small craft peddle their wares or vegetables; barbers or dentists will offer to cut your hair or draw your teeth; and sampans of many different types carry passengers, principally the gaily-coloured Shanghai sampans, to be seen deftly handled by the men of Ningpo or the women of Soochow.

Shanghai Harbour.

Daily large barges, heavily laden with all kinds of farm produce, make their way by canal or creek to the Shanghai markets, returning with ordure for the fields; and here will be seen at their best the handy-sailing cargo-boats of Shanghai and Ningpo.

Here may also be seen, after a little patient searching, many of the Chinese maritime inventions: the compass, the lee-board, the watertight compartment, the balance and hoisting rudders, the earliest types of fore and aft sails, and the art of reefing as first devised by these courageous and inventive Oriental seamen.

These inventions are described in Part One.

Finally there is, as always in Chinese waterside cities, the permanent floating population, estimated at about 18,000. These people live mainly afloat and rarely go ashore, even to buy food. They are mainly composed of Kiangpei, *i.e.*, north bank people, together with their wives and families; the Ningpo men, who rarely take their families about with them; and a considerable proportion of Tsungming Island men. In this connection it is interesting to note that the owners from Ningpo are the true shipping merchants of China and often own two or more junks, which is very rarely the case with other junkowners. In addition to this junk community proper of Shanghai, there is a transient floating population of about 80,000 which, according to Mr. Sowerby, are remarkably interesting biologically, since they probably represent the truest types of the original and indigenous races of the Kiangsu–Chekiang plain that remain to-day.

Arthur de Carle Sowerby, a naturalist who travelled extensively in China collecting specimens for the British Museum of Natural History; one of the founders of the China Society of Science and Arts; author of numerous books on the flora and fauna of China, and an expert on the culture of the Chinese people; editor of The China Journal until 1935.

碼
頭
船

THE MA-T'OU-CH'UAN OR NINGPO WHARF-BOAT

For sailing qualities and manœuvrability the Ningpo *ma-t'ou-ch'uan*, or wharf-boat, is the pride of the Whangpoo.

This heavy-draught type of craft, which renders invaluable lighterage service in all weathers, originated in the need for a medium-sized, short-distance cargo-carrier capable of operating in the rough tidal waters of the Whangpoo between Woosung and Shanghai.

It is also to be seen working the numerous creeks and waterways round Shanghai as far afield as Soochow on one side and Ningpo on the other. This type is largely built-in and takes its name from the latter town so as to satisfy the conservative watermen of Ningpo, who man this type of junk and feel at home only in the craft of their own district.

The junkmen say that the first Ming Emperor gave Ningpo its name, which means "Peaceful Wave."

More or less standard in size, this junk finds a typical representative in Plate No. 12. 60 feet in length, with a beam of 15 feet and a depth of 7 feet, she illustrates the ideal all-weather craft for going alongside ships lying in the stream. The strong hull is made of thick *sha-mu* planks, with three full hardwood bulkheads and 13 hardwood frames. Longitudinal strength is provided by four heavy wales 1 foot below the gunwale, running from bow to stern.

A marked characteristic is the box-like bluff bow with the planking lying horizontally. It terminates in the usual heavy transverse beam. The tapering stern is typical of all delta craft in that it ends in a built-out stern gallery fitted with removable planks which are more often out than in. The double-shaped end-on view of the transom is also distinctive of its class.

The large, deep main hold which occupies most of the central part of the vessel is covered with a tarpaulin only in bad weather. It is wall-sided and fitted with removable floor-boards, a 3½-inch iron pump, and a bamboo plunger.

The forward and after parts are always decked in and serve as quarters for the crew of five men and a cook. No families are kept on board. The living quarters are approached through booby hatches.

When new, if this phenomenon has ever been observed, this type would be easy to recognize, as they then receive their first and last baptismal coat of red paint over the entire hull. As this soon wears, or is rubbed, off there is generally very little evidence of this tribute to the artistic, so characteristic of the Ningpo sailor.

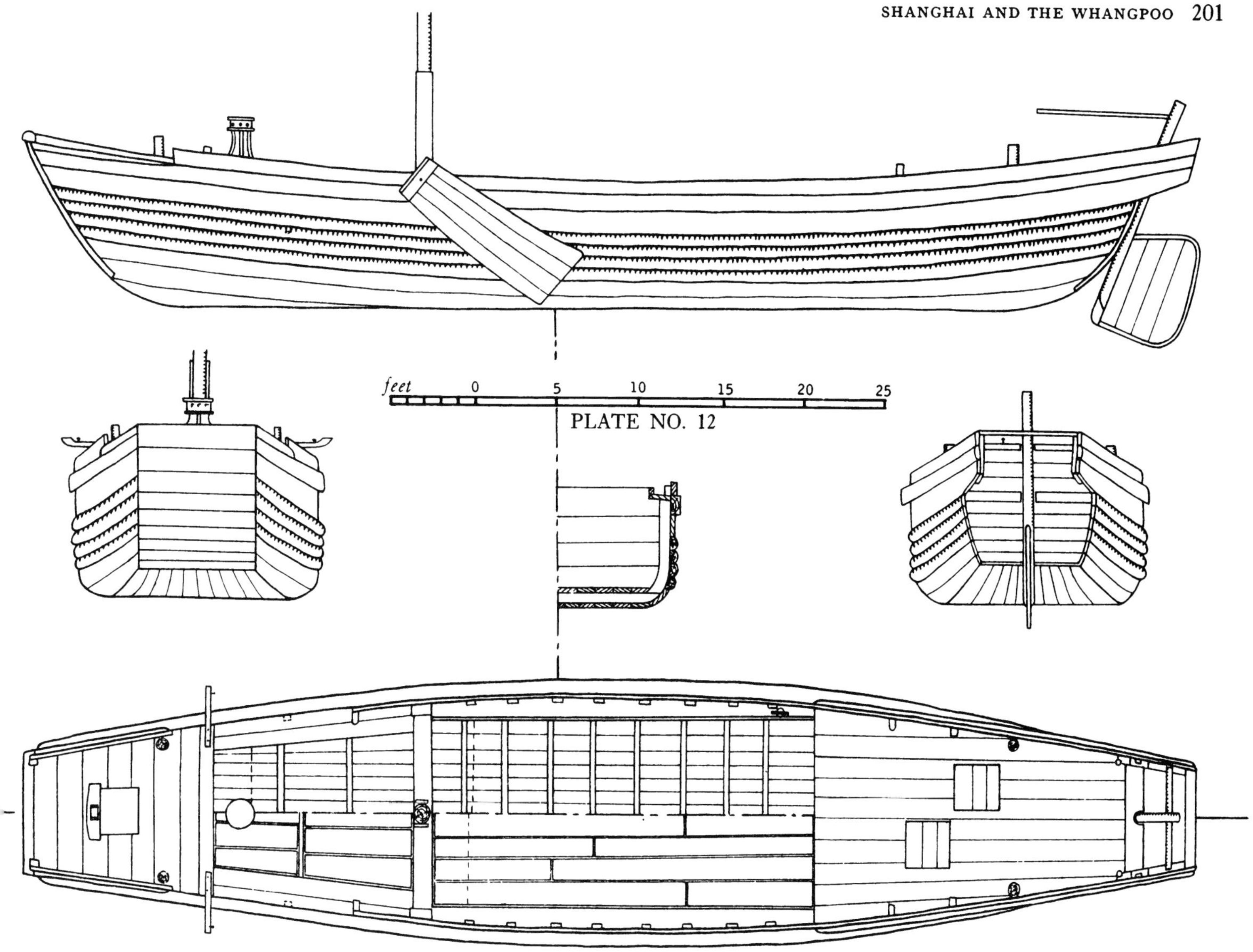

PLATE NO. 12

Propulsion is by means of two yulohs worked from bumkins on each bow and a third which can operate on the port side of the stern, the yuloh passing through the gaps left in the stern gallery by removing the planks. When sailing, a square-headed balance lug-sail is used, although a spritsail is sometimes fitted instead.

The gear and rigging, equipment and fittings are all of the simplest, yet these junks can be quickly and easily handled by their small crews, especially under the lug-sail. Time being of little object to the Whangpoo sailors, they are seldom to be seen beating against a head wind and seldom working otherwise than with the tide.

Although always a pleasure to watch under sail in the Whangpoo, these craft are to be seen at their best when manœuvring in the crowded waters of the Shanghai Harbour, where they provide a fascinating lesson in seamanship.*

As a matter of interest, the junkmen, owners, and carpenters of the wharf-boats frequent the Tea-house of Eternal Happiness (長 樂 茶 樓), in the Ssŭ Ma Lu (四 馬 路), or Four-horse Road, also known as Foochow Road. The official time for meeting and conducting business is between 4 and 5 p.m., and anyone interested in this boat should make a point of visiting this well-known tea-house. Here, it is said, the smokers are so opulent, and the brand of cigars smoked so good, that the collection of the cigar ends is keenly sought after and is let out to contract. The collections are sold to small stalls by the catty. There the salvaged ends are dried, rolled again, and resold as *k'ou-t'ou* (叩 頭) cigars.†

* Some 20 years ago a rich Australian saw these boats while he was visiting Shanghai. So impressed was he with their sailing qualities that, after a trial trip in one, he decided to buy her and have her shipped to Sydney. When the junk arrived the new owner, although he was a very experienced yachtsman, could do nothing with her. In desperation a laodah was sent for from Shanghai. Immediately the junk exhibited her old form and amazed the people of Sydney, but directly her laodah returned to China she reverted to her old sulky ways. This true story was told to me by an officer of the ship that carried the junk to Australia.

More about the tea-houses in Foochow Road can be found in Part One, pages 113–14.

† They derive their name from the fact that when reaching for butts the collector must bend, as if *k'ou-t'ouing*.

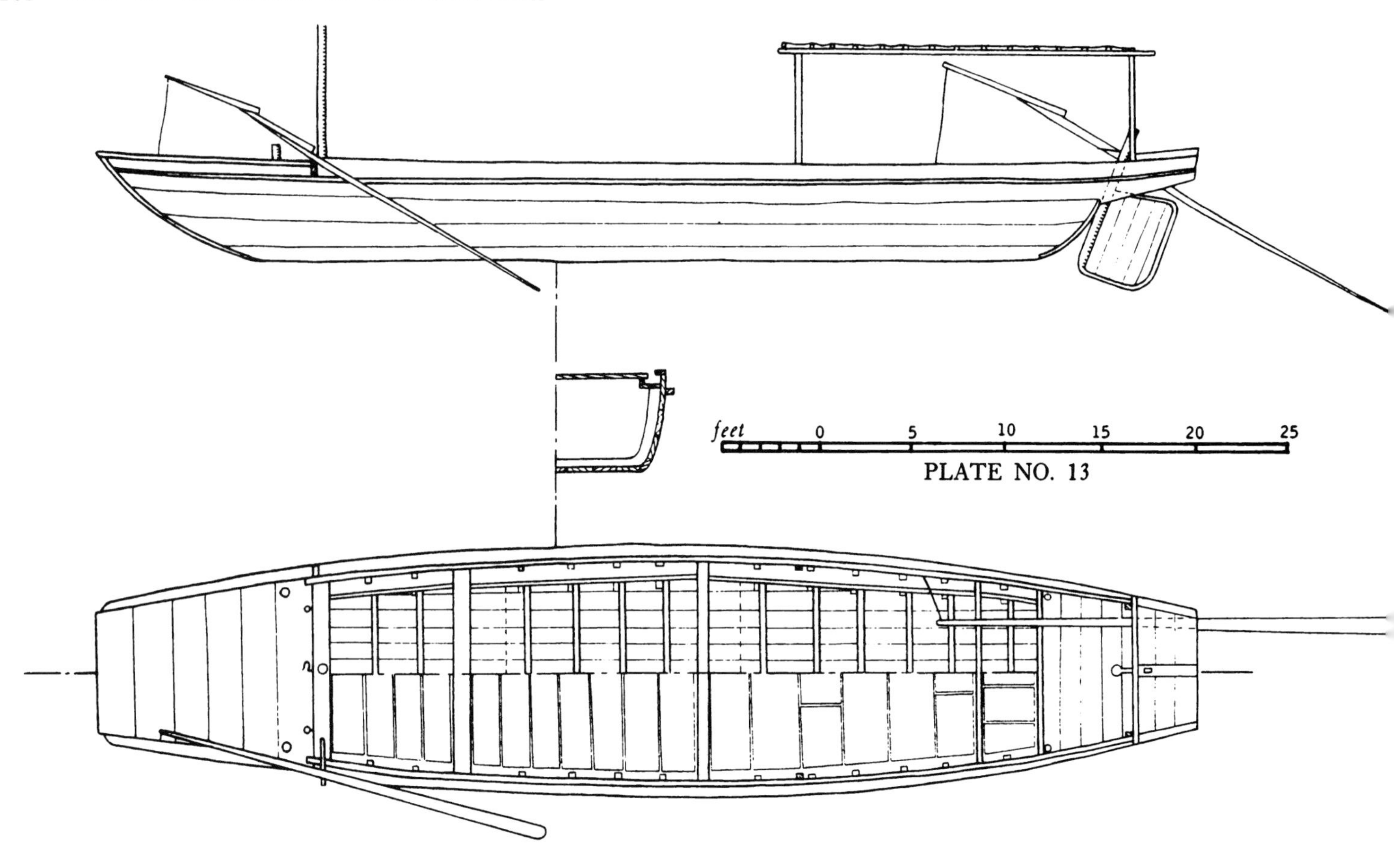

PLATE NO. 13

碼頭船 THE SHANGHAI MA-T'OU-CH'UAN

This type of craft, like the Ningpo wharf-boat, already described, is also equally designed to stand up to weather conditions of the Whangpoo when heavily laden. The two types are the most common in and around Shanghai, and both perform the same function of short-distance transport between ship and ship, and ship and shore. They are so similar in almost every respect that none but a very close observer can detect the slight differences. The most noticeable of these should be the fact that the Ningpo wharf-boat has a red-painted hull; but, as already noted, apparently this is seldom if ever renewed, and the weathering effect on poor quality pigment soon obliterates all traces of this adornment.

These craft vary considerably in size, the one illustrated in Plate No. 13 being one of the larger types. Broad, heavy, and square at bluff bow and stern, there is little worthy of notice in these useful weight-carriers.

She is very strongly built with four bulkheads, one having a sliding door, and 16 frames. The transom stern is half concealed by the overhanging stern gallery, a feature of these craft. The rudder is of the Shanghai type. The single mast is stepped rather far forward and carries a square-headed lug-sail. Very frequently, however, a supplementary bamboo mast is erected forward and carries an improvised spritsail. Two yulohs operate from bumkins in the fore part of the vessel and one over the stern on the port side.

Whether this utility type of lighter dates back only to the advent of foreign trading influence to Shanghai in the forties cannot be proved, though there is much to support such a theory. This is not to say they are of a comparatively new design, but to suggest they may be adaptations of other suitable local deep-draught sturdy junks, and at least it cannot be disputed that the expanding volume of shipping and trading facilities has enormously increased their numbers.

THE SHAOHING WINE-BOAT

In about 2205 B.C., the jade girl who, before her entry into the court of the Emperor Yü as an Imperial concubine, was the servant of a goddess in the distant western paradise, is said to have brought from there the formula for making wine. This important secret she imparted to one I Ti (儀狄) at the Emperor's court. The tradition is that when the Emperor Yü, whose fame is more commonly associated with water than with wine, tasted the new drink, he found it so attractive that he feared excessive indulgence would overpower his senses and cause him to become neglectful of the duties of his high office. He accordingly became a teetotaller and banished I Ti from his court.

More about the Emperor Yü appears in Part One, pages 3, 5, and 7.

It is more likely, however, that the Chinese had known the secret long before this.* The drinking of fermented liquor dates back to such remote times that there is no trace of its origin, and wine for sacrificial purposes has been used since time immemorial.

The chief wine centre of China lies to the south of Hangchow Bay and midway between Hangchow and Ningpo. This district of Eastern Chekiang, known as Shaohing, is so populous that there is a Chinese saying that "three things are to be met with everywhere under heaven: beancurd, sparrows, and Shaohing men." Here the industry is said to have originated, and it has been carried on throughout the centuries. The city has a long historical record. It is said that the great Emperor Yü used to meet his feudal princes there and that he derived his inspiration for the great work of draining the flood waters from studying a tablet erected to the memory of the Yellow Emperor near Shaohing. Later, in the time of Confucius, 551–479 B.C., Shaohing became the capital of the State of Yüeh. Under the Mongol dynasty the district acquired more importance, and in 1285 Kublai Khan decreed it should be exempted from the imposition of taxes. In the "Pên Ts'ao Kang Mu" (本草綱目) it is stated that distillation was first introduced into China during this, the Yüan, dynasty. The same authority mentions 64 kinds of *chiu* (酒) or fermented wine before coming to the distilled liquors or spirits known as *shao-chiu* (燒酒), burnt wine; *huo-chiu* (火酒), fire wine; samshu or *san-shao* (三燒), thrice fired, et cetera. According to the "Customs Trade Report" for 1909, 70 per cent of fermented wine as against 30 per cent of distilled products, generally called samshu, was drunk in China at that time.

Shaohing is also famous for its cormorants, which are skilfully trained to catch fish.

Rice, the principal grain of China, forms the basis of most of the alcoholic drinks of the country, wheat, millet, and kaoliang ranking next in importance. At Shaohing is produced the most popular of all brands, the "Yellow Wine," the flavour of which has never been surpassed or even equalled in any other district. The reason for the superiority is to be found in the quality of the water available. Shaohing lies in the middle of a network of streams and lakes of unusually clear water which, descending from the surrounding mountains, filters through many layers of sand and gravel. This physical formation has earned for Shaohing, as for Soochow, the title of the Venice of China from some writers. The nature of the water itself is also eminently suitable, containing as it does lime and salt in ideal proportions. The result, known as Shaohing, is justly famous throughout China. Similar beverages are made in nearly all the other provinces and are generally sold under the same name, which has become a generic term for the national drink of the country. Nevertheless, the genuine wines of Shaohing still hold the first place in public opinion.

William of Rubruck,† a Franciscan friar from French Flanders, who travelled to China in the thirteenth century, said of this wine that he "could not

* That the sages of old could take their drinks is evidenced by the "K'ung Tzŭ" (孔叢子). In the Chinese Encyclopædia (古今圖書集成), under heading of the history of wine, it is stated that "Yao (堯) and Shun (舜) could drink 1,000 *chung* (鍾) of wine, Confucius could drink 100 *ku* (觚), and Tzŭ Lu (子路), thought loquacious, could still drink 10 *ho* (榼)" (昔有遺諺堯舜千鍾孔子百觚子路嗑嗑尚飲十榼古之聖賢無不能飲也). No time is given, and therefore no comparison is possible.

† Spelt also Rubriquis, or Rubruquis. His travels are described in his "Itinerarium." Yule ranks this work with Marco Polo's writings, and says "it has few superiors in the whole library of travel."

distinguish it except by smell from the best wines of Auxerre." Friar Odoric, 1286–1331, called it "a noble drink." Evert Isbrand Ides, an emissary from Peter the Great in 1693–95, said that when kept for a year or two it very much resembled in colour, taste, and strength the very best Rhenish. Finally, the Abbé Huc has described how he dispatched some bottles of Shaohing to an English connoisseur. The latter not only found them excellent, but pronounced them to be "the product of a celebrated Spanish vintage," as he said the wine was distinguished by the true flavour and bouquet of Spanish wines. With great respect to the distinguished visitors, if these reports of theirs are true, the wines of Shaohing must have sadly deteriorated.

The wine is made in large earthenware vessels or vats known as *kangs*. The ingredients required to make a *kang* of the ordinary wine are 1.5 piculs of boiled rice of the large-grained glutinous variety produced at Chint'an, Liyang, and Tanyang in Kiangsu Province; 10 catties of "mother liquor," or wine base made from either wheat or barley, though preferably the latter; 36 catties of yeast; four buckets of water from a local lake called Chienhu; and three buckets of "rice soup," or the water in which the rice has been steeped. Twenty-four hours after fermentation the contents of the *kang* are inspected and stirred with a pair

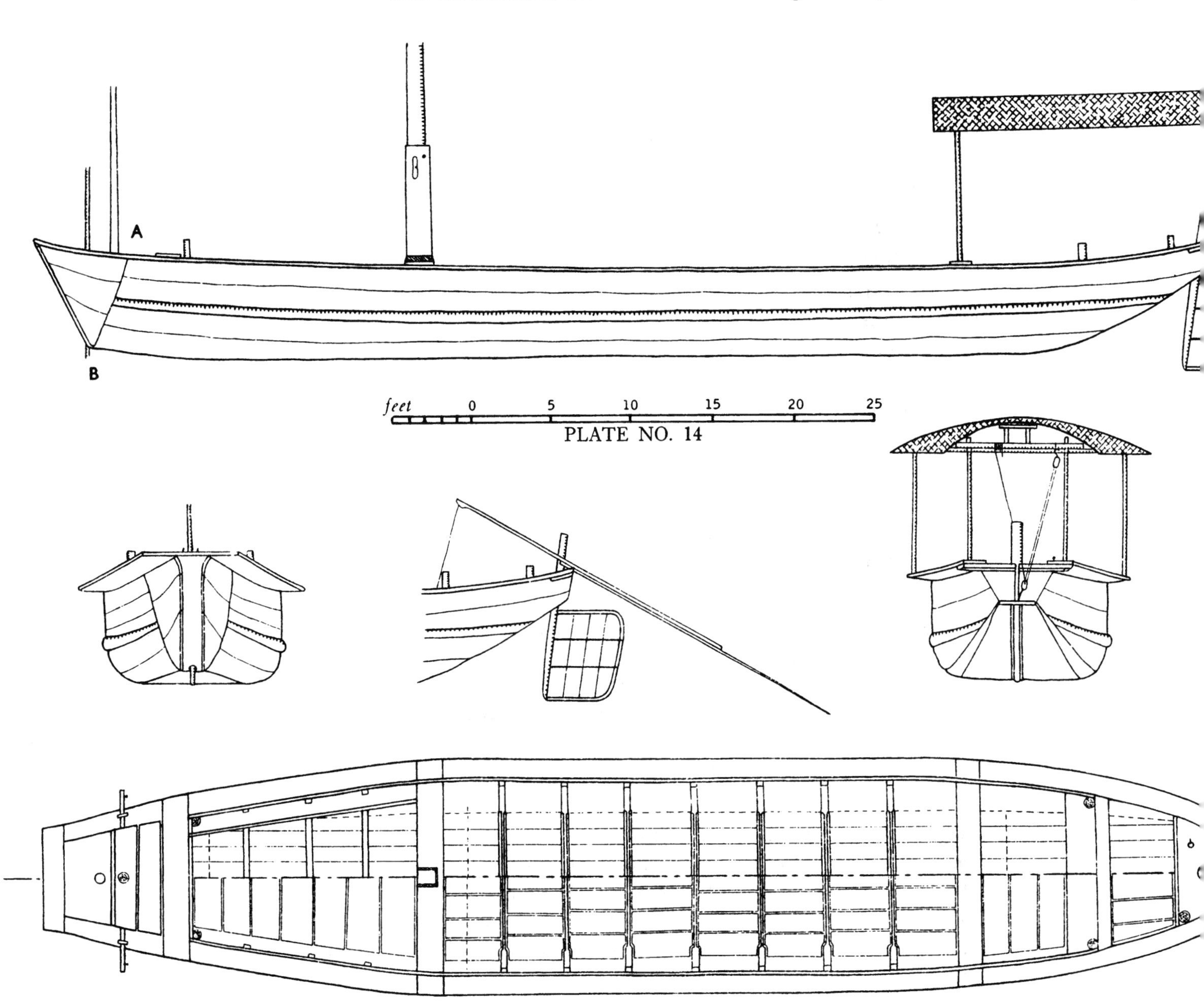

PLATE NO. 14

of long chopsticks. This stirring is repeated at intervals of two or three days until a week has elapsed, when the contents of the *kang* are poured into smaller earthenware pots and carefully stored. When the wine is 100 days old it is filtered through silk bags and then heated in a boiler to boiling point. The process is now complete. The wine is poured into earthenware pots or jars, sealed with lotus leaves or bamboo sheathing, and plastered with mud. It is now known as new wine and becomes marketable after six months or a year.

The "Customs Trade Report" for 1909, already quoted, makes an interesting comparison between the old-fashioned methods and the Pasteurian methods, and estimated that the latter would extract 112 catties of spirit from 1 picul of rice as against the former's 65 catties. This wastage is attributed to "ignorance of the laws of fermentation."

The "fermat" or, as it is termed, "medicine" in use for the saccharification of the rice always contains some paddy husk. This—only one out of as many as 40 or 50 ingredients and put in only to prevent the balls of "medicine" from sticking together—is, did they but know it, the only valuable ingredient of the lot. The people of Shaohing always distil many *kangs* of wine when a daughter is born in the family. The wine is then kept and only opened on her wedding day.

A prayer worthy of Omar Khayyam is recorded of an ardent connoisseur of those old days. "Bury me," he earnestly begged his relations when he was breathing his last, "near the kilns. Decades later they may use the soil my body has fertilized to make wine pots, and thus I shall again be united with wine."

Many stories are told of Shaohing wine. One tells how once the Emperor bestowed upon one of his princes a glass of wine. For whatever reason, he spat some out in a south-westerly direction with great force. Later, news came that there had been a terrible conflagration in Chengtu, but that it had been extinguished by a sudden rain squall from the north-east "which smelt strongly of wine."

The wine is exported to nearly every part of the country and also overseas for the use of the Chinese resident abroad. The craft which carry it to the Shanghai market are of a very distinctive type known as the Shaohing wine-boats. They are very much standardized as to size. The average specimen as illustrated in Plate No. 14 measures 73 feet in length, with a beam of 14 feet and a depth of 5½ feet, the greatest beam being just abaft the mainmast. Strongly constructed to carry the heavy jars which form her cargo, she has four hardwood bulkheads and 10 full frames. The large number and extra thickness of the frames counterbalance the small proportion of bulkheads.

There are several quite unusual features about this type of craft which are as inexplicable as they are strange, and the most interesting is the bow, which seems a sort of afterthought. The bow proper of the junk may be said to end at the line A B, which would, of course, give a very odd cut to the vessel. Although there is a heavy deck beam 1½ feet wide and over 6 feet long laid across the bow, it narrows below this to a comparatively sharp point. This false bow consists of three horizontal planks on each side measuring 2 feet in width and increasing in length as they ascend from the bottom plank, which is only a rough triangle, to the top plank, which measures 5½ feet at deck level. They are joined and faced in the centre line of the bow by a crudely-finished log in the form of a sort of false stem-post. The bottom of the junk lifts slightly at the bow and, when the vessel is light, is visible above the surface of the water. There is a "stick-in-the-mud" anchor which passes in through the decked-in portion of the false bow and out just forward of its junction with the hull proper. The "stick-in-the-mud" anchor has no boxed-in navel pipe, and the whole false bow is therefore free-flooding through the aperture in the bottom. The odd aspect of the bow is

"Stick-in-the-mud" anchors are described and illustrated in Part One, page 89.

heightened by the fact that the wale ceases abruptly at the join of the false bow with the hull, that is to say, at the line A B. No reasonable explanation is forthcoming for this form of construction or for the curious stern, details of which may be seen in the plan on Plate No. 14. It would be interesting to know why a hoisting variety of rudder is used and why it should, when lowered, project 2 feet below the bottom of the junk when the stern is so admirably suited to accommodate a balance rudder. Moreover, the method of securing the rudder is weak in the extreme, as there is a depth of only 2 feet of transom, to which is secured the open-jawed wooden gudgeon which has to bear all the weight.

A mat roof protects the conning position. The after stanchions are used as a Sampson post for the rudder hoisting gear, which consists of a single luff tackle.

Other notable features are the quanting platform, which projects 2 feet over the side throughout the length of the vessel, and the 7-foot tall tabernacle to support the mainmast, which is stepped on deck. The bamboo foremast, which is stepped very far forward and just over the false bow, is usually somewhat of an improvisation. It is fitted with a spritsail. The mainsail is the ordinary square-headed lug.

There are three yulohs of the straight variety, one over the stern on the starboard side and two working from bumkins on the fore deck. The latter are fitted very much farther forward than usual.

Sometimes there is a removable house 4 feet high which extends from the mainmast to the stern. There are, however, no deck planks inside it. Alternatively a deck cabin is fitted for the crew of six men.

This junk has much in common with the *wushan-ch'uan* next described, and is together with the *pa-kua-ch'uan* (八卦船), dealt with hereafter, of the same family.

烏

THE WUSHAN-CH'UAN

The *wushan-ch'uan* may be said to belong to the Hangchow Bay trader family navigating the creeks between Shanghai and Hangchow.

The numerous intersecting waterways of Chekiang are served by junks of varying size and draught so as to utilize water transport to the utmost.

As always in the case of the best traditional sailors of China, the Ningpo men, they insist on using their own types of craft. This preference is quite understandable in view of the justifiable fame of the Ningpo carpenters.

The Wushan junks, though built in Shanghai, are built by Ningpo men after the plan of their home types of inland waters craft, which have stood the tests of time. They are named after a town on the Yungkiang (甬江), at the mouth of which Ningpo itself is situated.

The junk illustrated in Plate No. 15 is 56 feet long, with a beam of 14 feet and a depth of 5½ feet. There are two bulkheads and 11 frames, all of hardwood, in the *sha-mu* hull.

More tapered at bow and stern than the usual run of delta craft, it narrows to the low stern, where there is a projecting and raked rudder.

The bow, which is quite sharp, is laid with horizontal planking and measures 2 feet across at deck level, decreasing to only 10 inches at the water-line. A vertical strengthening piece and bow fender bisects it. A curious feature is the upward slope of the flat bottom towards the bow in order to ensure very light

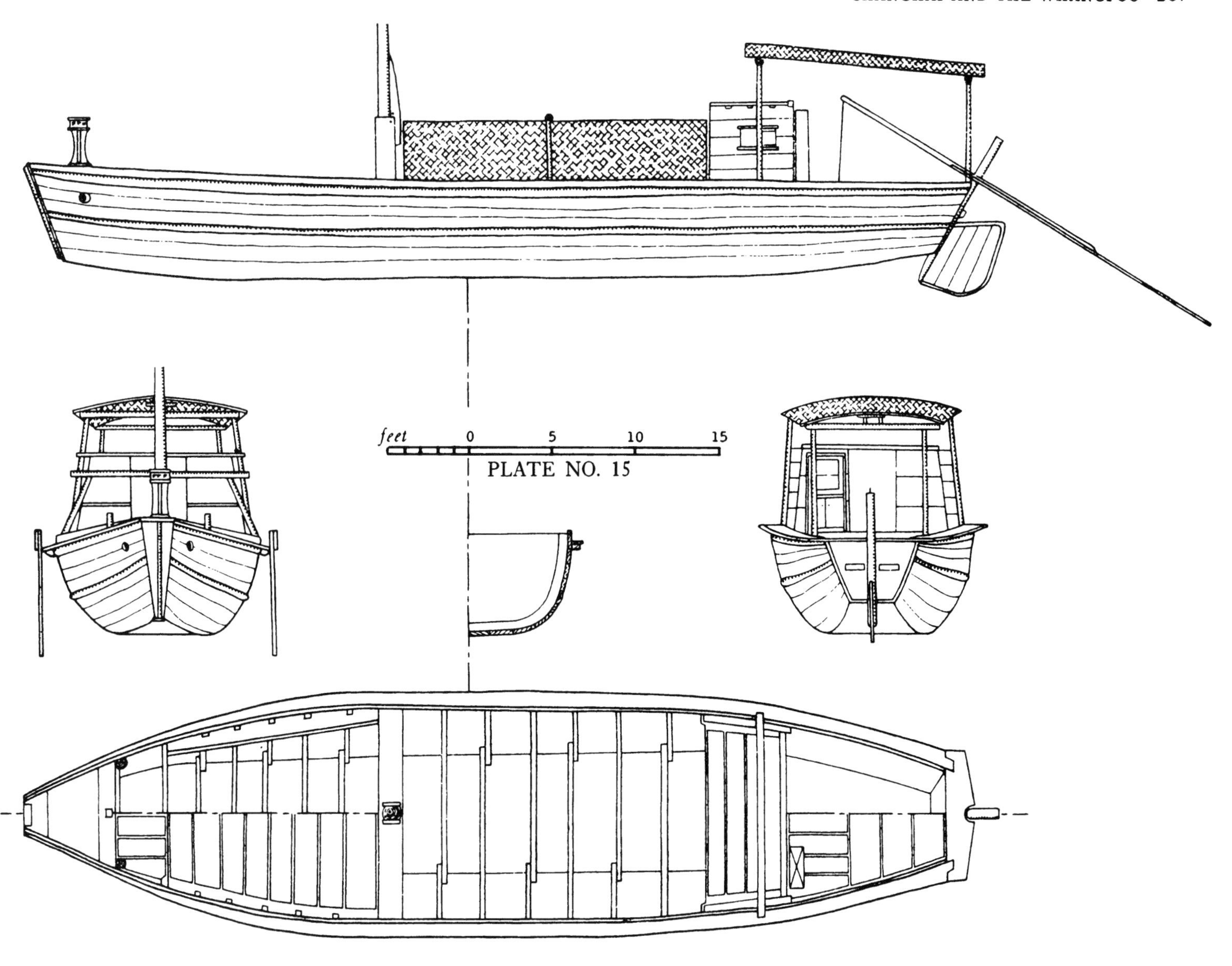

draught forward. The rising fore-foot gives a very peculiar appearance when the junk is light.

This form of construction necessitates placing the centre of effort of the sail area comparatively far aft. The junk is decked in fore and aft of the main hold. There is a small flat-topped wooden house measuring 5 by 10 feet situated aft. Shelter can be extended forward to the mast by means of a removable mat roof over the hold, and aft from house to stern there is a standing awning.

The junk may be propelled by spritsails, generally two, but when navigating the creeks, depends chiefly on her yulohs or on quanting. There is a narrow quanters' platform running the length of the vessel and built out over the side.

There are two yulohs, one over the stern on the port side and the other forward on the starboard side. Each yuloh is worked by two men; one works the rope, while the other operates the loom. This he does from a small removable platform measuring 3 feet by 8 inches, projecting from the starboard bow and pivoting on a pin, so that it can be turned in out of the way when not required. A diagram of this device will be found as an inset on Page No. 48. The yulohs, it should be noted, are both of the straight variety, in three sections, and fitted with a cheek-piece.

The Ningpo sailor's love of adornment for his craft finds expression in the eye on the bow.

快板船 THE K'UAI-PAN OR SPEED BOAT

The *k'uai-pan*, or quick plank boat, is, as its name indicates, a speed boat. More or less standard in size, this boat is usually 35 feet in length with a beam of only 6½ feet, which for a Chinese craft is very fine-lined indeed, and the long, narrow craft terminates abruptly in a sharp bow and high, sloping, and slightly-tapered stern. Extra beam is provided, however, for the crew to work the ship by a quanters' gangway[1] at deck level, built out from the ship's side[2], as may be seen in the section plan on Plate No. 16. A long, rounded mat house[3] encloses most of the boat. It is surmounted by three strongbacks[4] to accommodate the yulohs when not in use.

The junk, which is neatly finished and well kept, is built of *sha-mu* throughout. There are three bulkheads[5], five full frames[6], and six half-frames[7] disposed alternately. The extra number of frames is necessary because of the small number of bulkheads.

An interesting feature is the "stick-in-the-mud" anchor[8] so rarely to be seen in the Shanghai area, although common enough on the Yangtze.

All the features of the quick plank boat—the pointed bow[9], rising stern[10], stick-in-the-mud anchor[8], projecting quanting gangway[2], and absence of deck planks inside the house—are characteristics of the Shaohing family of junks. This adherence to type is quite remarkable and shows how conservative the old junk-builders still can be.

The construction of yulohs and the art of skulling with yulohs is discussed in Part One, page 48.

The turn of speed for which these junks are renowned is provided by no less than four yulohs[10], two operating over the stern and two more from projecting bumkins[11] on either quarter, and two primitive spritsails. The yulohs, which are made in two parts—the loom and the gradually broadening blade,—are perfectly straight and measure 19 feet, a sizable length for the craft they propel. One man is stationed at each yuloh, and one of the men in the stern also steers by kicking the tiller in the direction required. Skill, good timing, and neat, contained movements are essential to enable four men to scull together, standing in so small an area. Additional power is provided by quanters, who, from the bow, drive their poles into the bed of the creek and, tucking the upper ends into their shoulders, bend almost double as they walk in succession down the length of the quanters' gangway. A speed of 12 *li* an hour is claimed for this craft by the junkmen.

The K'uai-pan. *Note the yulohs and spritsails.*

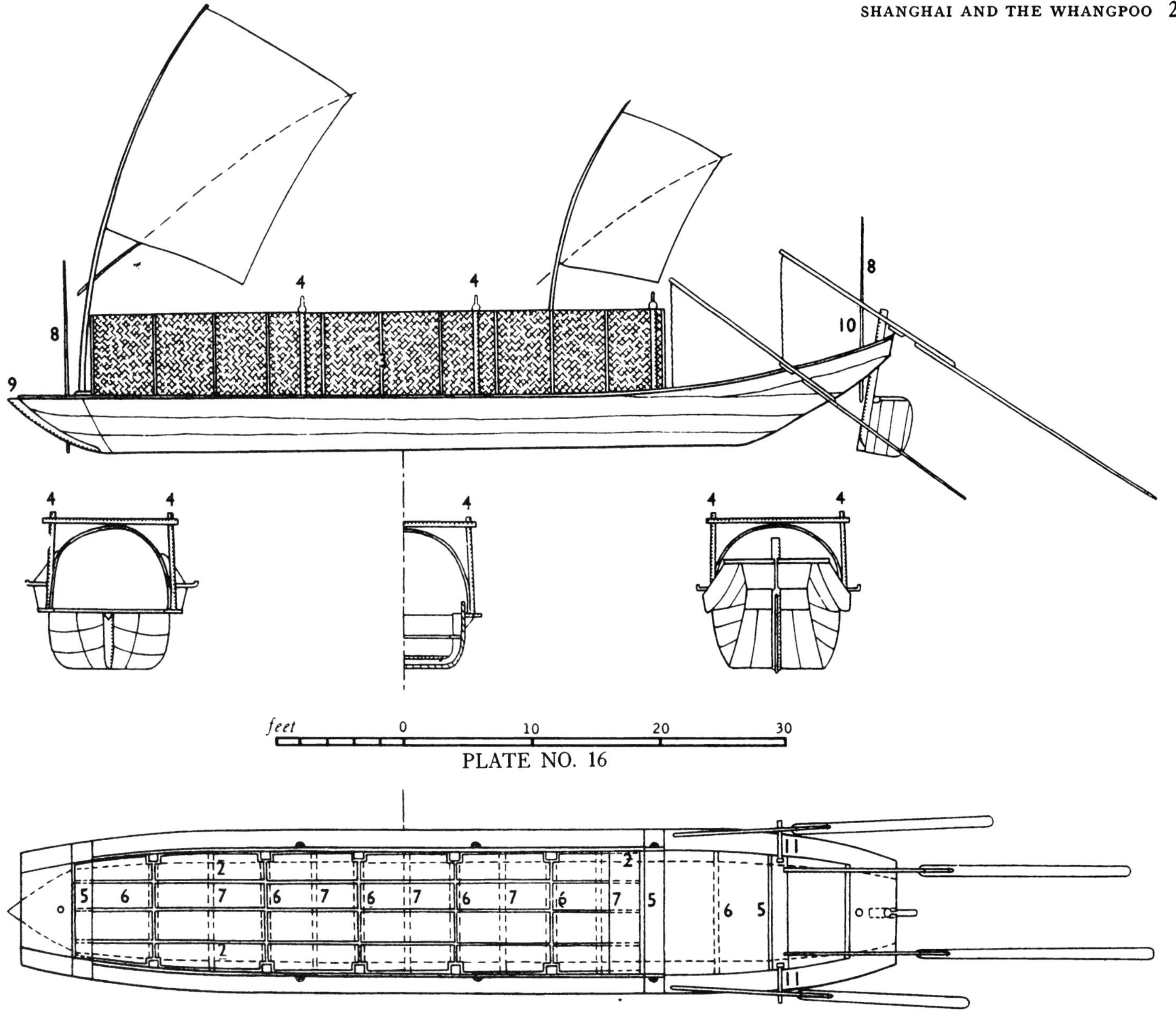

PLATE NO. 16

There is a small, light rudder which fits into a circular aperture in the transom. When it is not in use, the crew, to their shame as sailors, instead of hoisting the rudder or lifting it clear of the water, adopt the almost universal practice of removing it bodily and inserting it back in the aperture upside down, which unseamanlike practice gives the boat a most odd appearance.

These craft operate mainly on the creeks inland from Pootung and rarely appear in the Whangpoo. They carry passengers usually on a fixed run. A slightly larger type of the same junk carries cargo instead of passengers, and for this purpose is built on broader and less graceful lines.

To the peasant-traveller time is no object, and the *k'uai-pan* makes small appeal to him; but to the richer country gentry, hurrying to a wedding or a funeral, this humble form of speed boat is very welcome, and they readily pay the higher fare to shorten an otherwise tedious journey.

Modern progress and a desire for even greater speed has played havoc with these beautiful little junks in that many of them now are propelled by condemned motor-car engines, ingeniously adapted to burn kerosene oil. They are fitted with a crude form of balance rudder of iron which replaces their former graceful one, and they are extensively painted in grotesque colours.

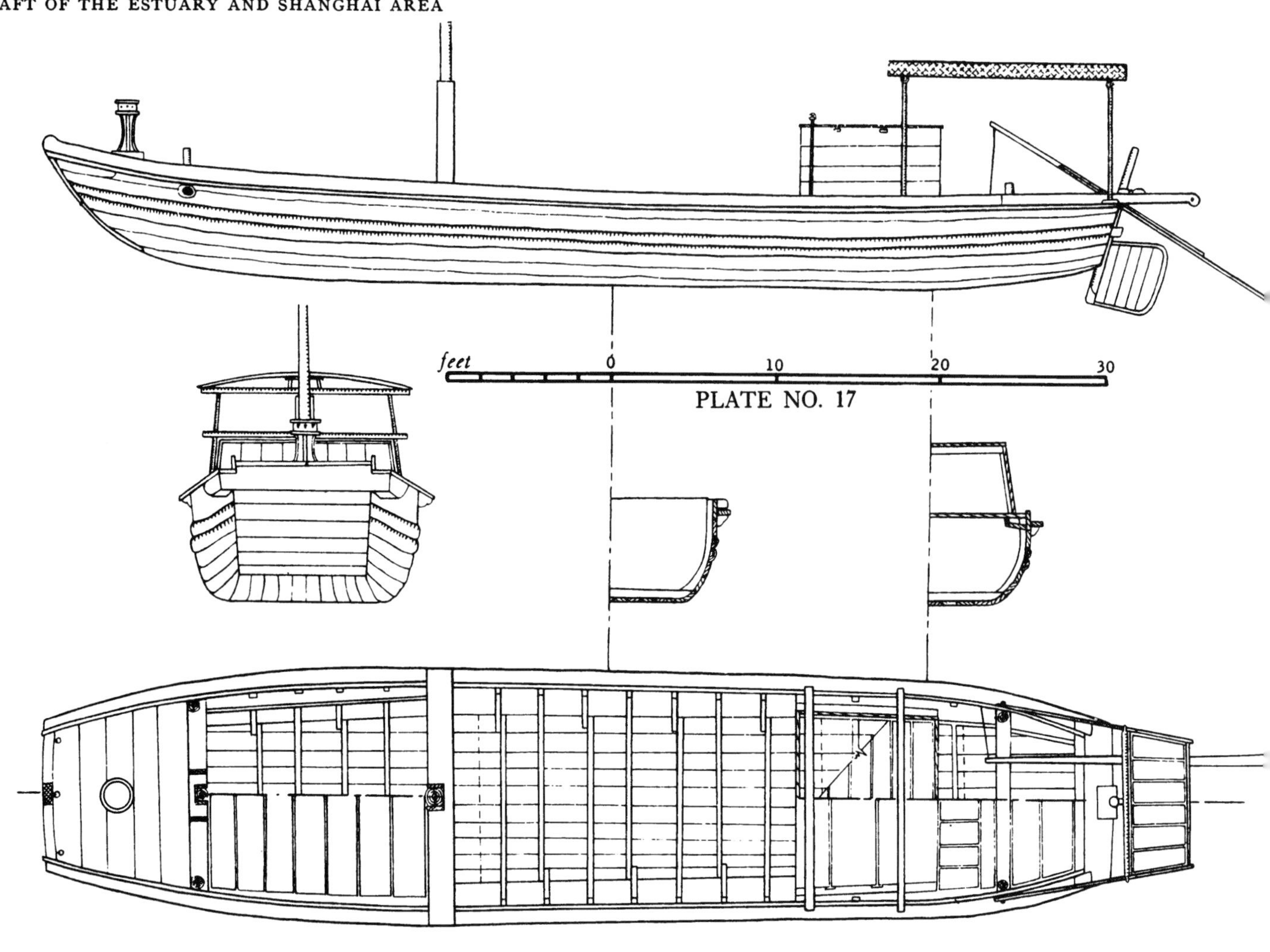

八卦船

THE PA-KUA-CH'UAN

This craft may be termed a half-sister to the *wushan-ch'uan* and is therefore of the same family as the *shaohing-ch'uan*.

Many of the main characteristics are the same for all these craft, which originated at Ningpo, notably the solid, heavy construction with the massive bulkheads, the small house aft with standing awning, and mat house capable of extension forward.

Other features in common are the type of rudder, the high tabernacle, and the straight yuloh over the stern.

In like manner also the *pa-kua-ch'uan* navigates the narrow winding canals and creeks of Chekiang Province, though occasionally it may be seen on the Yangtze.

The principal difference from the other members of this family is in the shape of the bluff bow, tapering to the stern, which latter terminates in the gallery so typical of Shanghai craft.

More about Fu Hsi appears in Part One.

These junks are named after the magic talisman the *pa-kua*, or eight diagrams, said to have been devised by Fu Hsi, the legendary monarch, nearly 3,000 years B.C. It is a particularly favourite emblem with the junkmen. Sometimes the boat is painted red.

The craft illustrated measures 60 feet, with a beam of 15 feet and a depth of 6 feet. It is built of *sha-mu*, with two hardwood bulkheads and 14 hardwood frames spaced 40 inches apart.

THE SHANGHAI CARGO-BOAT

The *hsiao-ma-t'ou-ch'uan*, or small Shanghai cargo-boat, is built in Shanghai and exclusively used for harbour work.* These craft vary considerably in size from those capable of carrying 28 tons to others with a capacity of 70 tons.

The boat illustrated in Plate No. 18 measures 57 feet in length, with a beam of 120 feet and a depth of 5 feet, and is of heavy and exceedingly strong construction. Designed as she is for the accommodation of cargo which is usually, though not always, stowed below decks, she has only two bulkheads, but the extra necessary strength is provided by 11 full frames at 2-foot intervals.

The low, bluff bow has a considerable overhang, as has the typical Shanghai-type stern. The Shanghai variety of non-balance rudder can be hoisted and slung from the after cross-beam. There is no house but a more than usually elaborate standing awning aft, made of wood and covered with oiled canvas. The crew of three to five live below decks either forward or aft of the second bulkhead, the galley being in the after compartment.

There is one removable mast, usually of bamboo, which is stepped, when needed, very far forward. The sail is nearly always an improvised form of spritsail, and in a breeze the bamboo mast is often bent nearly double. The main method of propulsion is by means of yulohs over the starboard side of the stern. Additional power is provided by two further yulohs if the craft is of the larger type. These are operated from bumkins, one on each bow.

As is so often the case with what is in common daily use, it is impossible to trace the origin of these craft, but it would appear probable that they date back no further than the *ma-t'ou-ch'uan*, which they closely resemble, that is to say, the Clipper days.

* In addition to the regular lighters, in 1935 there were 297 Chinese cargo-boats of a capacity up to 60 tons serving as lighters and 295 lighters of 100 to 600 tons. Of these, about one-half are in use at any one time, the remainder mooring in the shallow parts of the river or, in the case of about 25 per cent, at the owners' wharves. Most of the unloading is performed by the ship's derricks and hand labour on the lighters. Only a few of the lighters are fitted with cranes.

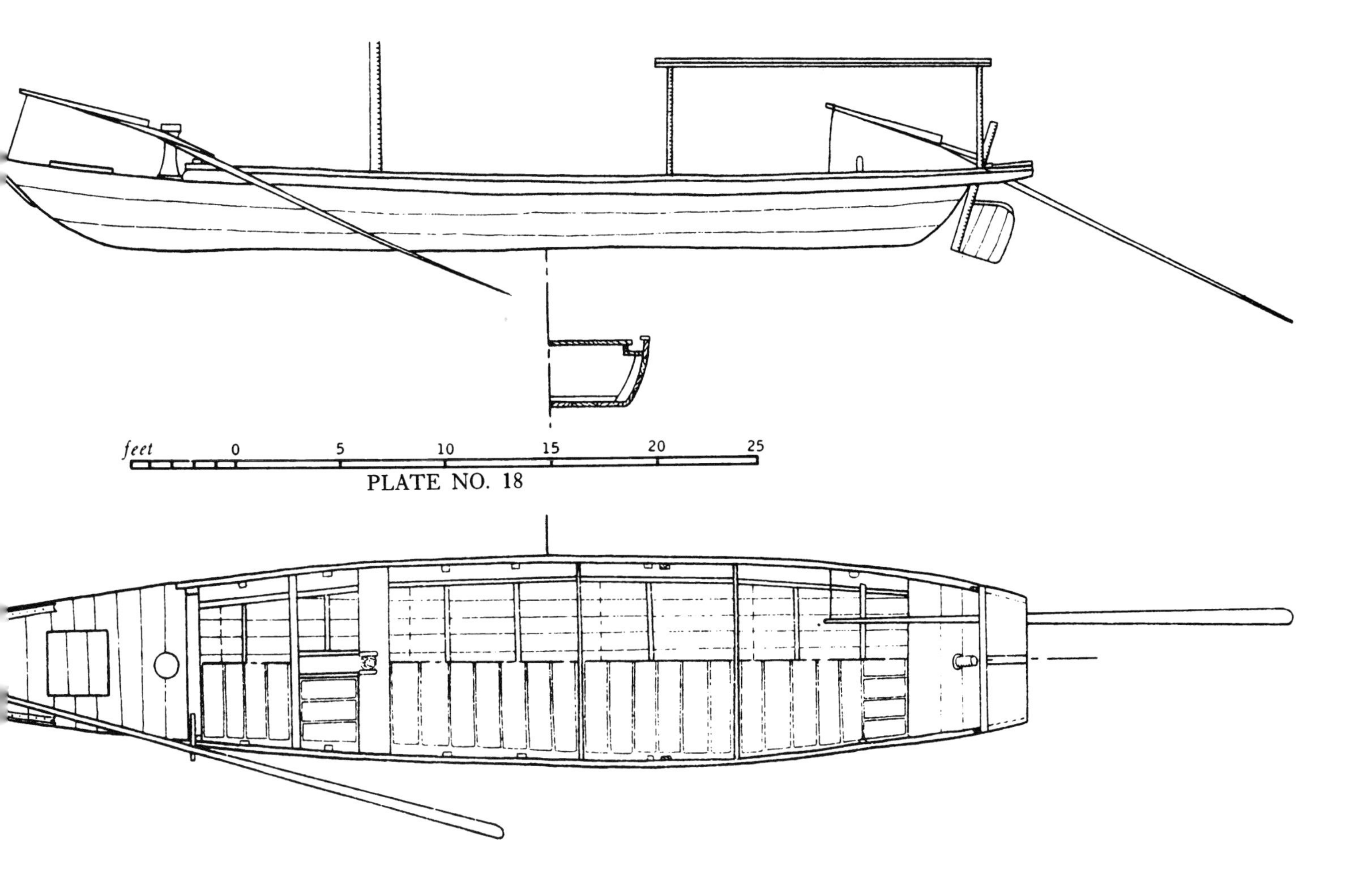

PLATE NO. 18

Broad and solid, there is little outstanding about these dull but useful boats except that for their size and outlay they are probably the best of their kind in the world. This is sufficient to commend them to any sailor, and makes them well worthy of the high standard of seamanship displayed by their crews.

Such general interest as is possessed by these lighters centres in the widely varied nature of their cargoes, for they can be seen making their way through the harbour loaded down to the gunwales almost with anything from a locomotive to a cargo of flimsy baskets of eggs, or from sycee, transported in bulk, to garbage.

Actually the disposal of garbage is one of the major problems of a large town. In a city as large as Shanghai the statistics are staggering. House refuse and street sweepings, for instance, amount to 1,000 tons per day, of which the house refuse accounts for less than one-half. A percentage of this, roughly one-fourth, is destroyed by incinerators; rather more is used in land reclamation or to fill up low-lying sites; while nearly one-half of the total amount is barged away under contract to riverside dumps for final utilization as manure.

Western civilization spends enormous sums to destroy waste matter which to the practical, if unsqueamish, Chinese is of supreme value agriculturally. Quite a feature, if an unsavoury one, in the early morning on the Whangpoo is the large number of garbage-boats which may be seen on their way to the waste dumps.

Another of the important functions of the Shanghai cargo-boat is the transportation of coal, a service for which she is unsurpassed. Shanghai absorbs about 4,000,000 tons per annum from all sources, Kailan coal heading the list, with Fushun second. Roughly more than two-thirds of the total supplies come from these centres. Along the banks of the Whangpoo River are to be seen about a dozen coal wharves, and there are in addition many storage yards piled high with coal.

Shanghai has probably a larger and more important hinterland than any other Asiatic port. In addition to serving as an outlet to the vast Yangtze Valley with its population of some 200 millions, it is the distributing centre for a coast-line some 800 miles in length.

Practically all the merchandise that comes and goes is water borne, and a very large proportion of this vast traffic in imports and exports is handled by the Shanghai cargo-boat.

The owner, with the help of his wife, a number of children, and a crew of three men, and perhaps a "wonk" dog, with no more appliances than two or three yulohs and an improvised and usually ragged spritsail on a bamboo-pole mast, safely negotiates the perils of the harbour, which, with its swift current and teeming craft, presents a series of hazards which would make the London Board of Underwriters shudder; yet, thanks to incomparable seamanship, cargoes of tremendous value are safely carried every day to and from the shore with surprisingly few accidents.

THE HAINING-CH'UAN OR HANGCHOW LIGHTER

The *haining-ch'uan* is, as happens so often with Chinese craft in the Shanghai area, named after the place where it is built, in this case a town near Hangchow. It navigates the Whangpoo and creeks between its port of origin and Shanghai.

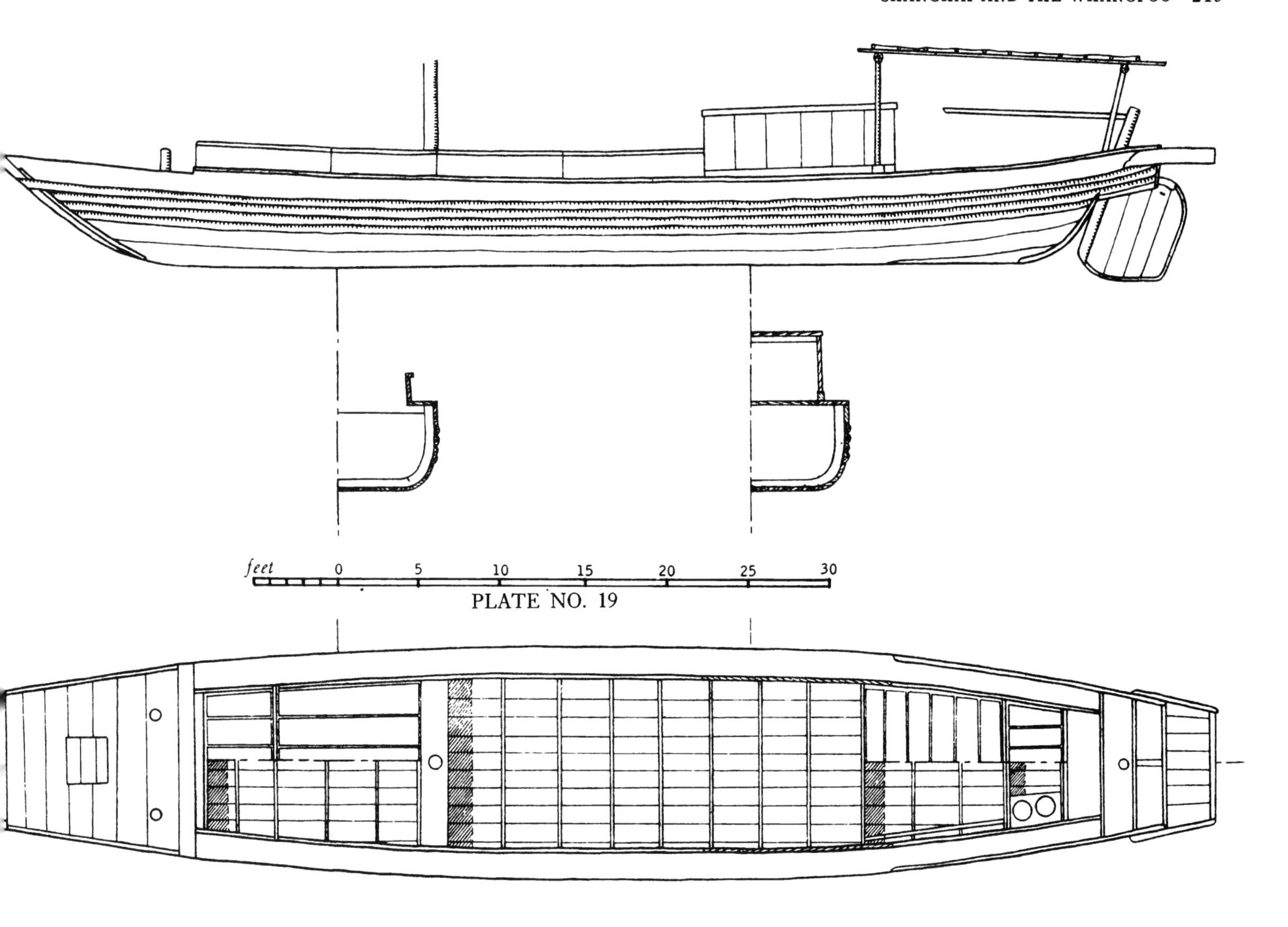

PLATE NO. 19

Built of *sha-mu*, this junk, as shown in Plate No. 19, measures 72 feet, with a beam of 13½ feet and a depth of 5 feet. There are four hardwood bulkheads, one half-bulkhead, and 12 frames, making a very strongly-constructed general cargo-carrier with a capacity of 60 tons.

Extra strength is provided by a heavy double wale and another wale above it, also by the double planking of the gently curved bow, which ends squarely at deck level in a heavy transverse beam. Most of the usual Shanghai features are present: the stern gallery and hoisting type of non-balance rudder, the standing awning, and the weather boarding. There is one mast and sail. Propulsion in the narrow creeks is by means of two bow yulohs operating from short bumkins.

From the mast forward the junk is decked in. Abaft the mast, as far as the house, is the main hold. This is not decked in but is covered with a tarpaulin. The very small house measures only 12 feet and 3½ feet in height, but is nevertheless divided into two small compartments with access through sliding doors for the owner and his family. The galley is in the space between the fourth bulkhead and the stern, the cooking-stove being on the port side. The crew of five men live in incredibly cramped quarters below decks in the foremost compartment, entrance being through a booby-hatch.

This comparatively modern type of junk is really little more than a glorified lighter and may be described as the Hangchow counterpart of the Shanghai and Ningpo wharf-boats, both of which, of course, come under the same heading. All three are very frequently to be seen in the Shanghai Harbour.

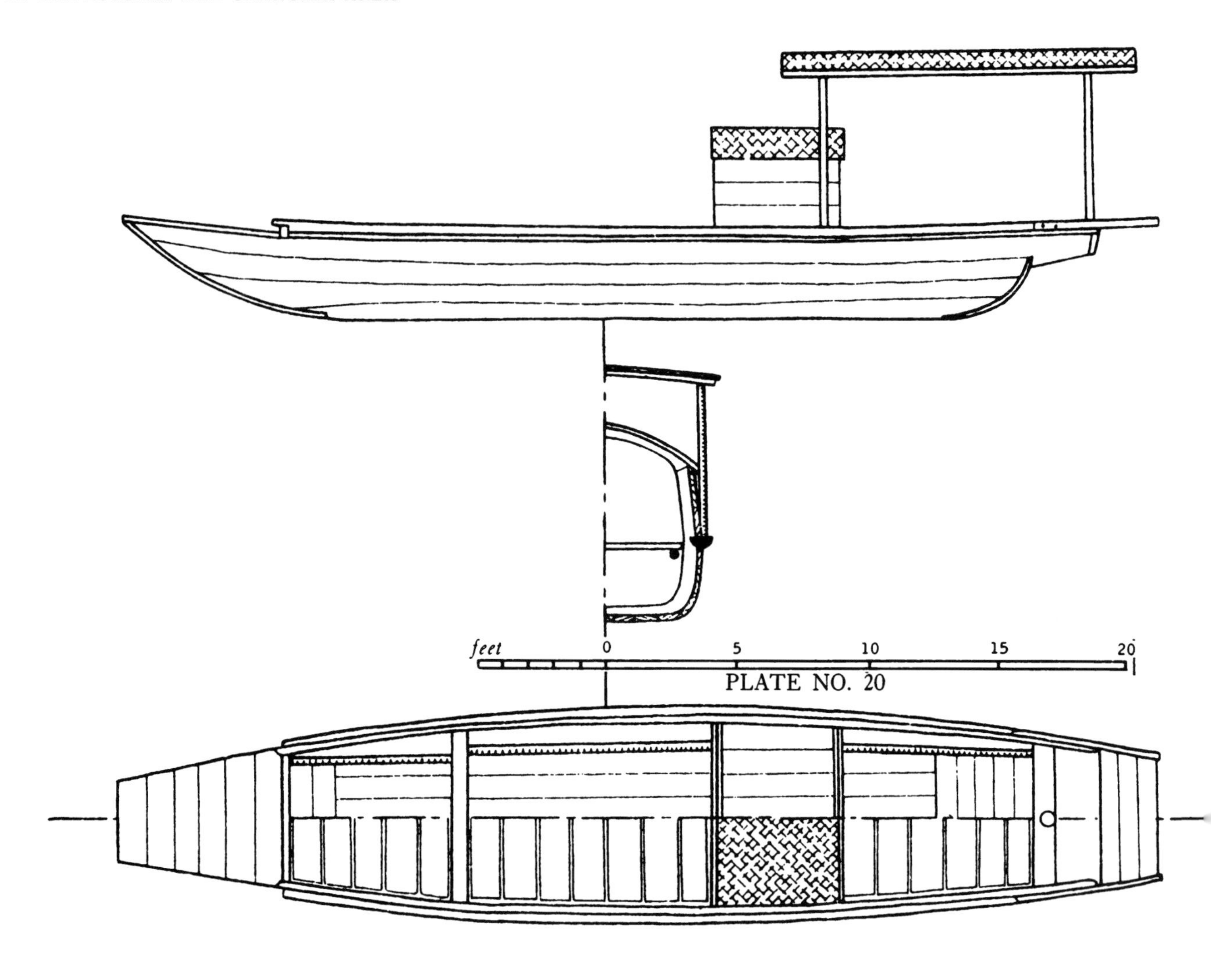

PLATE NO. 20

小鄉下船

THE HSIAO-HSIANG-HSIA-CH'UAN OR COUNTRY-BOAT

This craft, the name of which being translated means the small country-boat, is built on the Pootung side of the Whangpoo and serves as a fuel-boat for all the creeks around Shanghai. Made of *sha-mu*, a typical specimen (as illustrated in Plate No. 20) measures 39½ feet by 8 feet beam and a depth of 3½ feet. She follows the usual fashion of Shanghai craft in her general lines, having a long, low bow, in this case tapering somewhat, a gallery stern, and standing wood awning abaft the small house.

In construction she is light, with three bulkheads and three frames, but this provides ample strength for the light cargo carried. There is no mast or sail, propulsion being by means of a single yuloh. A rudder is sometimes fitted.

The crew of two live in the small house, which measures only 5 by 8 feet. This craft is also used for conveying vegetables from the Pootung side to Shanghai, but its main purpose is to carry the light vegetable fuel grown on the farms around the delta. This fuel consists of the stems of all agricultural crops which are not required for any other purpose. Beanstalks, cotton plants, rape, millet, and rice, all are pulled up by the roots and tied into bundles for the market. They are bought for domestic use, and also for the burning of lime and for the firing of tiles and earthenware.

When this light, bulky fuel is used for cooking, one of the family, usually a child, is deputed to feed the fire with one hand while working a bellows with the other so as to ensure sufficient draught.

THE HUNG-T'OU OR SHANGHAI HARBOUR SAMPAN

紅頭三板

This quaint and colourful little craft is a distinctive feature of the Shanghai Harbour. It is called the *hung-t'ou* (紅 頭), or red head, because of its painted bow, but is more commonly referred to as the *mu-chi* (母 雞), or hen boat, for its supposed resemblance to that fowl. Actually, if one were to liken it to a bird, a duck would be a better choice, for it is squat in appearance, with a turned-up tail, and rides the river like a duck.

These boats are entirely Chinese in design and construction. It would seem that they owe something to Amoy influence. Their history is obscure, but the fact that they have no guild would seem to point to a comparatively recent origin.

They are preferably built of Foochow pine, but if this is unavailable, softwood from Ningpo is used. The bulkheads are made of *hsiang-chang* (香 樟), a hardwood from Kiangsi. The timber is supplied by the merchants in the form of *chang-pa-t'ung* (丈 八 筒), that is to say, poles of 1 *chang* 8 *ch'ih* (一 丈 八 尺). These sampans are all built in or near Shanghai.

The sampan illustrated in Plate No. 21 is 18 feet over-all, with a beam of 5 feet and depth of 2 feet. It draws only a few inches unless loaded to capacity, when there is the minimum of freeboard.

There are three bulkheads, forming four compartments. In addition, there are two half-bulkheads and four frames. The fore part is decked, leaving a cockpit amidships which is covered with a small house made of closely woven matting arranged in three overlapping sections and painted white. In this portion the passengers are accommodated, and actually as many as five can be carried and even more; nine, however, is about the limit. In the after compartment is the galley, that is to say, a cooking-stove. Here, too, is the oarsman, who acts in the capacity of "owner-driver." He can, therefore, keep an eye on the meal that is cooking while he yulohs, if he is alone. If his family live on board, they also stow themselves away in this small space during working hours. In the fore compartment are stored the bedding, clothing, provisions, oil, charcoal, and extra cooking utensils.

Propulsion is by means of a single yuloh, or *lu* (櫓), a quite original and extremely efficient implement which has already been described in detail. 13 feet in length, it is scarfed in three pieces, thus forming a gentle curve. The loom measures 2 feet 8 inches, the neck 2 feet 2 inches, and the blade 9 feet 8 inches, the overlapping portions being never less than 10 inches in length. When in operation the blade is kept very deep in the water, that is to say, 3½ feet, or more than one-third of its length being below the surface, and as the face of the blade is 6 inches in width, this combination gives much increased leverage and power.

The word *yuloh* evolved from the words *lu* and *yao*. See Part One, pages 44–50.

The yuloh pirots on a 3-inch bearing-pin which ends in a knob. This pin is situated on the transom, and the loom is held in place by a coir lanyard, 5½ feet long, attached to a ring-bolt in the deck.

The hand holding the yuloh is held at head level and rather behind, while the hand on the lanyard works across the breast. It is interesting to record that the sculler can average 41 strokes to the minute under favourable weather conditions, yielding the satisfactory speed of 8 *li* per hour.* This type of boat is sometimes called the Ningpo sampan, and has many features in common with the Ningpo junk, such as the shape of the bow and stern, the free-flooding foremost compartment, the standard pattern of gaudy design, and, sometimes, the oculus. With the exception of the eye, which may or may not be present, these sampans are most markedly uniform in every particular, for all are of identical construction

* In 1927 the officers of the Coldstream Guards took home with them a Shanghai Harbour sampan for the June Regatta at Henley. History does not relate what success it met with.

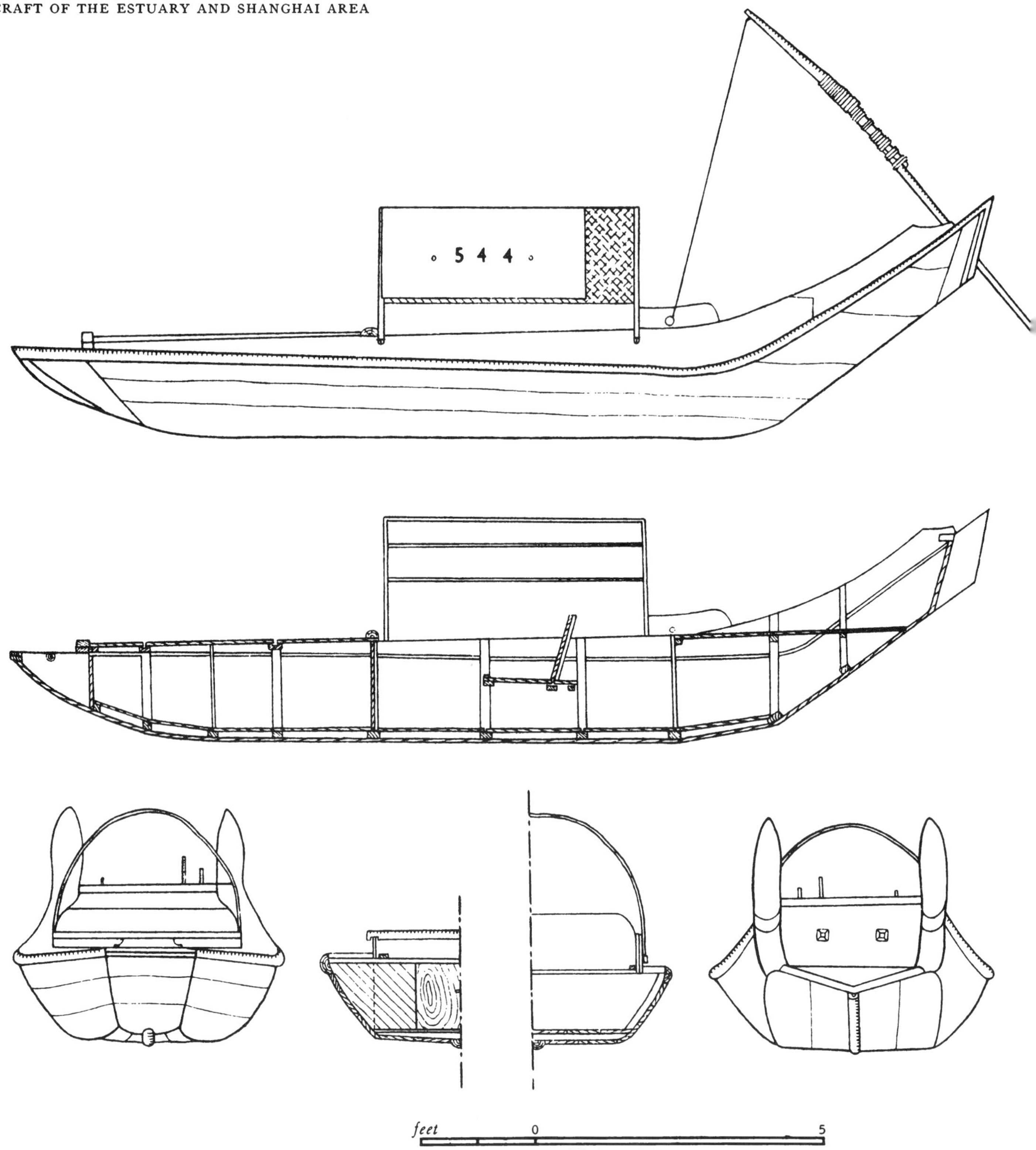

544

feet 0 5

PLATE NO. 21

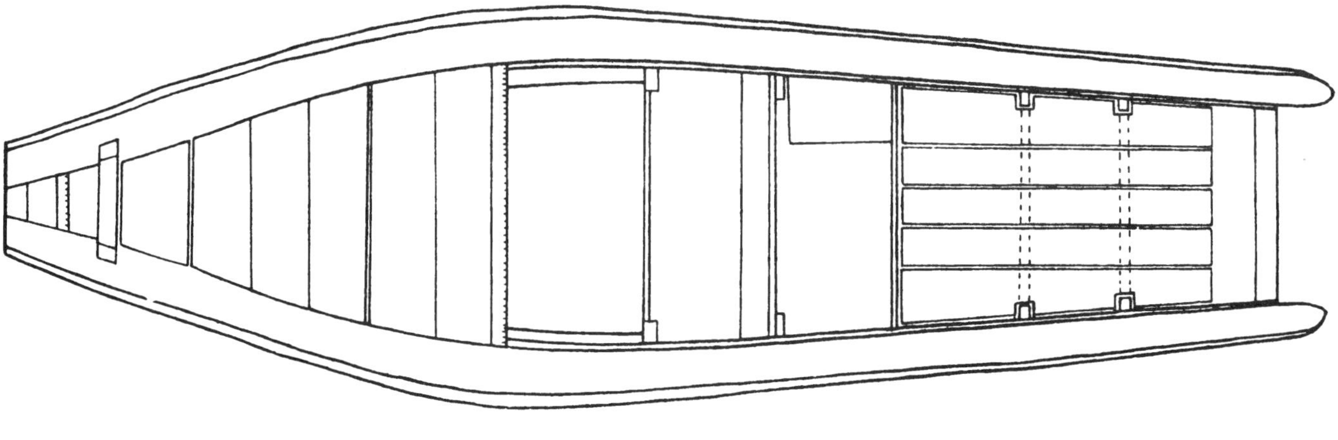

and size. Even the painted ornamentation on bow and stern hardly varies. Nevertheless, these boats fall into two definite categories, known as *pang* (幫), or groups. These are the *ning-pang* (寧幫), or group manned by Ningpo men, and the *soo-pang* (蘇幫), or group manned by either Soochow men, men of Shanghai, or men from Kiangyin, a small town some 80 miles up the Yangtze.

Even the experienced observer finds it hard to detect any difference between these two types of craft. Actually the distinguishing feature is that in the Ningpo-owned craft the bearing-pin for the yuloh is situated on the port side, which necessitates the sculler using his left hand on the oar; while in the boats operated by Soochow, Shanghai, and Kiangyin men the bearing-pin is on the starboard side and the sculler operates the yuloh with his right hand. The exponents of both methods maintain that theirs is the only reasonable mode of propulsion. The only other differences are that Ningpo men never take their wives and families afloat, as do the sampanmen from the three other localities, and that the former also, when living on board, are content to sleep in the confined space between the first half-bulkhead and the third bulkhead, which compels them to lie more or less doubled up. These Ningpo people would seem to be rather a free translation of which is to the effect that "it is preferable to quarrel with a Soochow man than to have a friendly conversation with a man from Ningpo (情願與蘇州人相罵不願與寧波人白話)."

The Soochow people, on the other hand, are universally popular, the women having a reputation for beauty and the men for an easy and graceful bearing. They must, moreover, have either more ingenuity or longer legs than the Ningpo men, for the sampan-dwellers sleep in pairs between the second and third bulkheads, which gives a space of 5 feet 4 inches. In the winter all the various groups sleep in the space between the first half-bulkhead and the first frame. Two sliding sections can be withdrawn from the first bulkhead to enable them to lie at full length.

As already mentioned, the men of the *soo-pang* live in these small boats accompanied by their families. It is astonishing that so small an area can constitute a permanent home for two adults and several children while functioning in addition as a passenger-carrier. The wives and even the children of these sampan-dwellers can take their turn at the yuloh. They scornfully maintain that one reason why the women of Ningpo do not live afloat is that they suffer from seasickness and are unhandy in a boat.

These sampans, of which there are to-day the record low figure of 813, are required to register with the Harbour Police of the Chinese Maritime Customs. This is done annually, usually in April. No fee is charged for registration, but the sampanmen are required each to pay 40 cents towards the cost of the paint used in numbering the boats. On the hood, on each side of the registered number of the sampan, a coloured dot will be noticed. The colour is changed each year and shows at a glance when the boat was last registered. The Harbour Police record the names, addresses, and other particulars of the boatmen and insist on the boats being kept seaworthy and clean. The sampanmen claim that they belong to the Customs and are very proud of this association.

For the men of the other group, the *ning-pang*, the Shanghai sampan forms probably as clever an adaptation of a very limited space as it is possible to find, and combines the dual purpose of a passenger-boat and a two-roomed floating dwelling with a degree of seaworthiness surprising for its size. It has, in addition, the charm of pleasing lines and bright colours.

It seems not improbable that this beautiful little craft will at no distant date vanish completely from the Whangpoo, and with it much of the romance and charm of the waterfront.

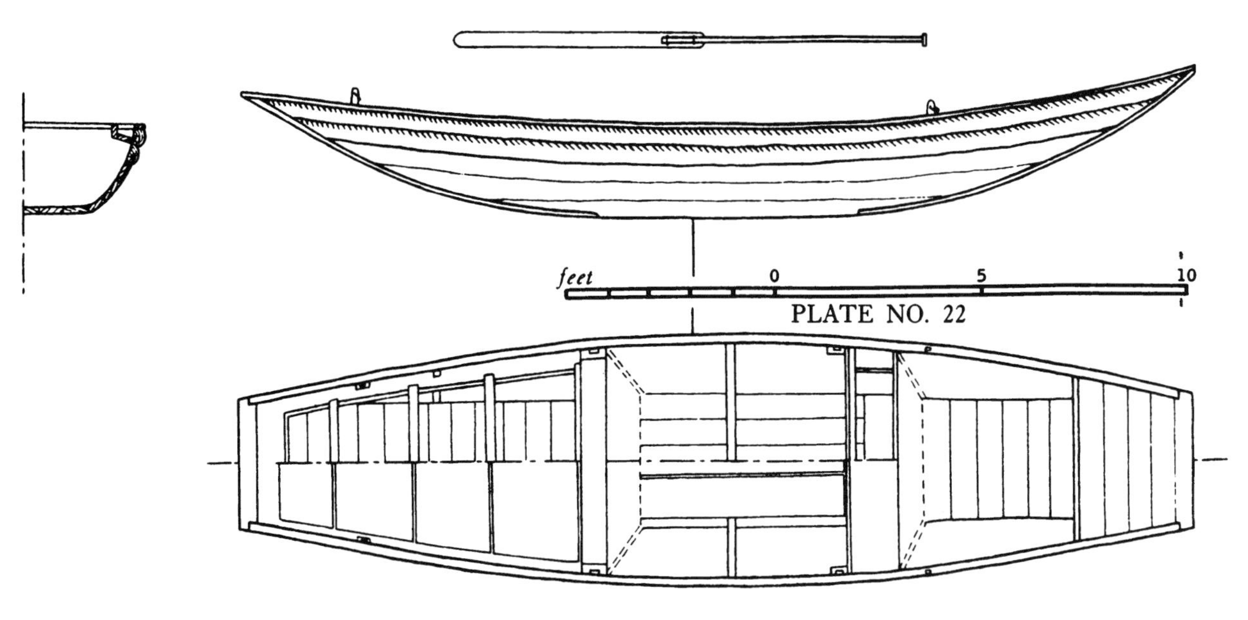

PLATE NO. 22

淌

划

THE T'ANG-CHIANG-HUA-TZŬ OR LANNITU SAMPAN

Every river and tributary, almost every district, has its own peculiar kind of small boat, and the craft frequenting any one town differ in greater or lesser degree from those of other places. Sampans are extensively used for long-distance traffic, and indeed all kinds of transportation, and in the delta region there is hardly a household without a boat of its own to facilitate the main industries of agriculture and fishing.

A surprising number of types, or variations from types, is to be found in the Pootung area. Notwithstanding local differences of detail, these small boats vary very little as a class, and all approximate fairly closely to the type illustrated in Plate No. 22, which has been selected as generally representative of the class of small dual-purpose boat propelled by oars.

Popularly known among foreigners as the Lannitu sampan, after her district of origin, the junkmen call her the *t'ang-chiang-hua-tzŭ*, which means an oar-drifting small boat.

This sturdy craft is merely an open boat designed to carry 30 piculs of cargo. She is shorter than the ordinary sampan, more beamy, and higher in the side, the measurements being 23 feet in length, with a beam of 6 feet and a depth of 2 feet 5 inches. There are two bulkheads and four frames, and the fore deck is decked in. Stem and stern are alike, and rise in a long, shallow flare from the water.

Propulsion is by two oars. The boatman stands facing the bow, and in rowing pushes the oars so that the looms cross each other in the form of a St. Andrew's cross. Normally no rudder is fitted, but when the boat is working under sail a foreign-pattern rudder with iron pintles and gudgeons is used.

These craft were recently suspected of being engaged in doubtful lucrative commerce. In order, therefore, to assist the authorities in watching their activities they were required to register with the Customs Harbour Police.

Figures now available show an enormous increase in their numbers, for it is a lamentable fact that these serviceable, albeit dull, little craft are rapidly superseding the picturesquely-painted harbour sampan, which cannot accommodate the same amount of cargo and/or passengers. A few years ago there were 1,300 harbour sampans as compared with 1,200 of the Lannitu type. In 1940 there were 836 of the harbour type, compared with 2,789 Lannitu sampans.

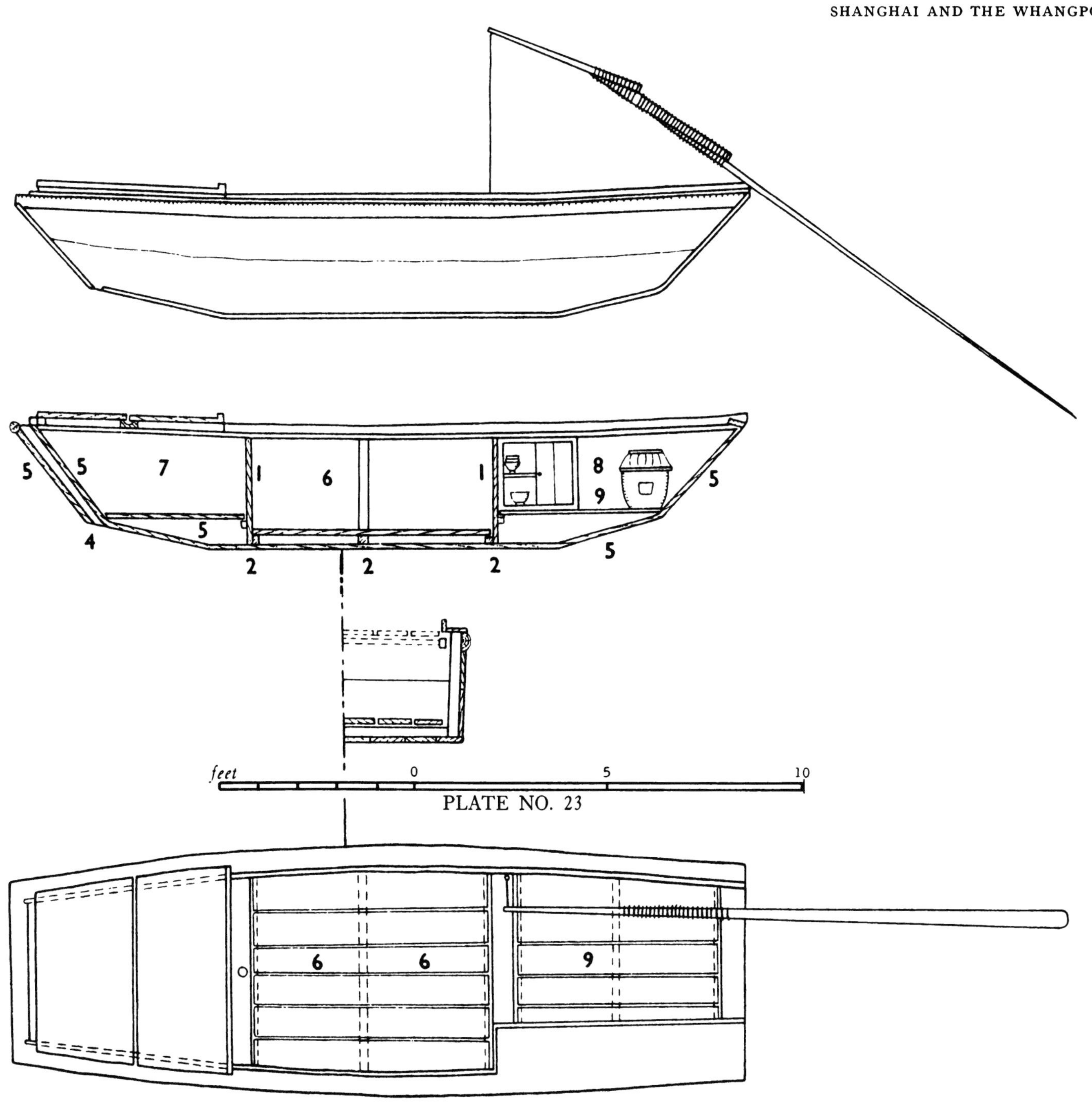

PLATE NO. 23

THE WOOSUNG FANG-T'OU OR SQUARE-HEAD BOAT

This seaworthy and beamy sampan is ideally described by its name, *fang-t'ou* (方 頭), or square-head. Designed primarily for work at Woosung or on the Whangpoo, where it stands up well to rough weather, it does not compete with the Shanghai sampan recently described and is rarely to be seen in the harbour. Plying as they do in less populated areas, there are only 221 of these craft registered with the Customs Harbour Police.

Somewhat ungainly in appearance, it nevertheless furnishes proof of good constructive skill. It varies in length from 12 feet, with a beam of 4 feet, up to 18 feet with a beam of 6½ feet. It is built throughout of *sha-mu*, its square proportions being divided into two full bulkheads[1] with three frames[2]. There is in addition a *chia-t'ou* (假 頭), or false bow[3], which small compartment is free-flooding by means of the usual hole in the bottom at the turn of the bow[4].

The four angles[5] in the under-water line are rather unusual. The deck planks and bottom boards are interchangeable, and the whole boat can be decked in completely if need be; but the larger midship section[6] is usually in the form of a cockpit for the accommodation of the passengers by day and the crew by night. The forward[7] and after compartments[8] have their bottom boards at a higher level and are used for the stowage of personal effects and cooking respectively. The oarswoman stands on this raised bottom board[9], the spaces below being utilized to store gear and fuel. A removable awning on stanchions is fitted.

Sometimes these craft are to be seen under an improvised sail of the spritsail variety, with a thin bamboo mast so flexible that the clew of the sail is almost in the water. The normal means of propulsion, as of steering, for there is no rudder, is by yuloh. The single yuloh is proportionally long and heavy, being as a rule the same length as the sampan. It is made in three pieces, being very similar to that used by the Shanghai sampan except that, for the same-sized boat, there is about double the length of yuloh working below the surface, that is to say, 7 feet instead of 3½ feet as in the Shanghai sampan. This leverage gives the extra power required for this clumsier craft.

Two people are more often than not at the yuloh, while a third, usually a youngster, assists by pulling on the cord. The synchronization displayed in this task is worthy of special notice in view of the fact that the crew are mostly Woosung women who employ their time in this way while their husbands are working in larger junks.

The women are wonderful "seamen," and so thoroughly competent to train the young sons who help them that these smart-looking and well-kept craft are the nursery of some of China's best sailors.

小江北船

THE HSIAO-KIANGPEI-CH'UAN OR KOMPO BOAT

This small craft, known as the *hsiao-kiangpei-ch'uan*, or small Kiangpei boat, is a vegetable-pedlar's sampan, and is so named after a district on the Pootung side of the Whangpoo. It is also commonly known as the Kompo boat, though this annoyingly loose description is by no means confined only to this craft.

Kompo (江北), in Shanghai dialect, means "of or belonging to the north bank." Anything unfamiliar or of uncertain origin is therefore liable to be termed Kompo, including even the people who hail from some far-off or little-known area.

Built in the town of its own name, this craft peddles vegetables up and down the creeks and waterways around Shanghai and also in the vicinity of the T'aihu, where large quantities of vegetables are produced and find a ready market amongst the adjacent villagers, whose own allotments may happen to be insufficient for their needs.

The craft vary somewhat in size. A typical specimen is illustrated in Plate No. 24 and measures 21½ feet in length, with a beam of 5 feet 9 inches and a depth

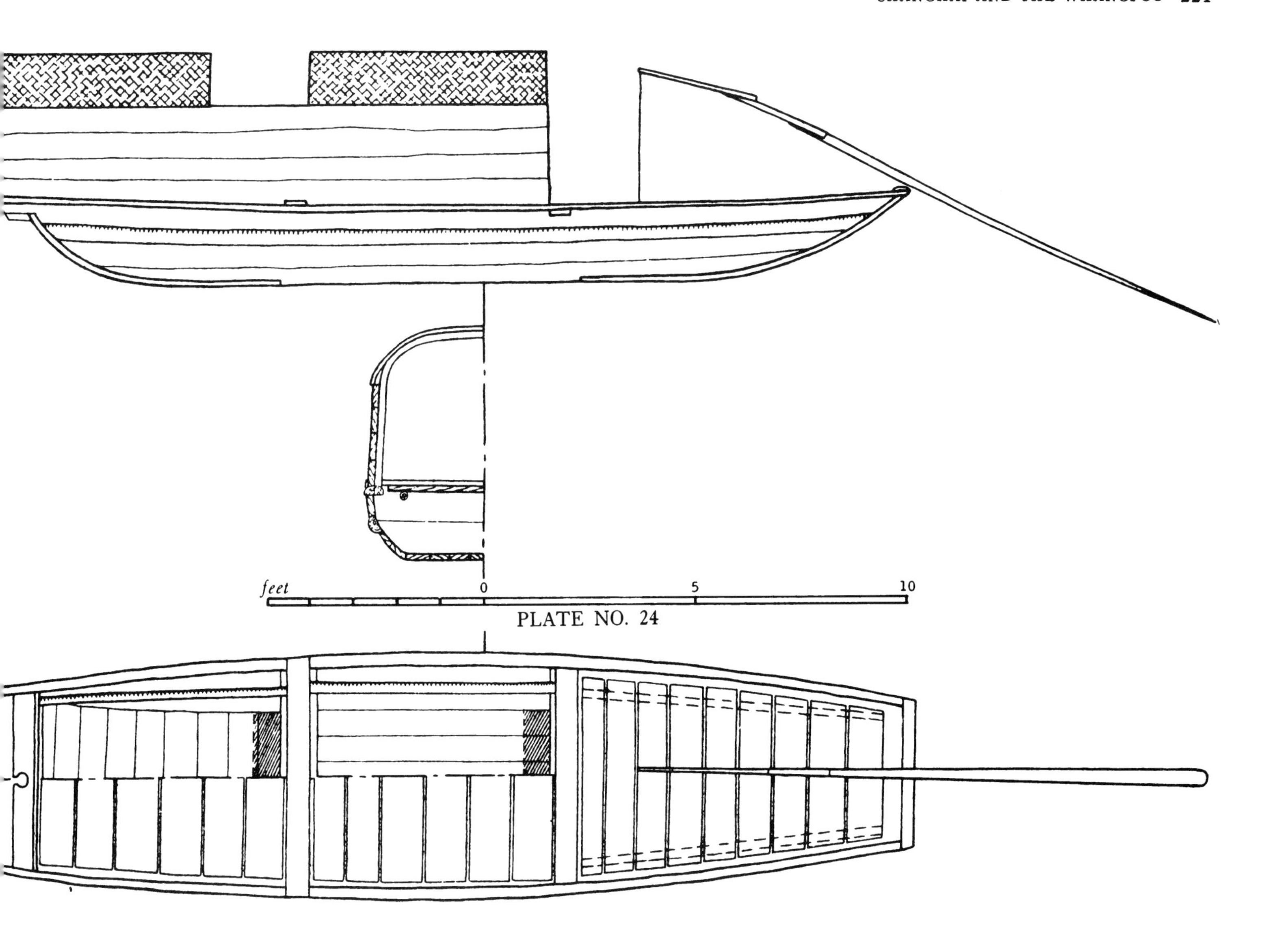

PLATE NO. 24

of 1 foot 10 inches. Her light construction matches her light but bulky cargo, for there are only two bulkheads and one half-frame. A distinguishing feature is the very small overhanging stern gallery, which in the smaller sampans projects 6 inches and in the larger ones never exceeds 10 inches.

The low bow, which is decked in back to the first bulkhead, has a long overhang. Both bow and stern have athwartship planking which extends over the bottom of the hull below the water to the forward and after bulkheads respectively.

It is not clear why the two supporting deck beams above the two bulkheads should rest the one below and the other above the gunwale.

A disproportionately large built-up wooden house with a mat roof extends from aft of the first bulkhead right to the end of the small stern gallery. This comfortable accommodation for the owner and his family makes it quite impossible to work the yuloh—the only means of propulsion—over the stern in the usual manner.

A *modus operandi* can always be improvised by the practical junkmen. In this case, without regard to appearance, precedent, or tradition, which decrees that a boat should move forward bow first, the yuloh is shipped over the bow, and, to a sailor, the astonishing spectacle may be seen of a craft habitually proceeding backwards.

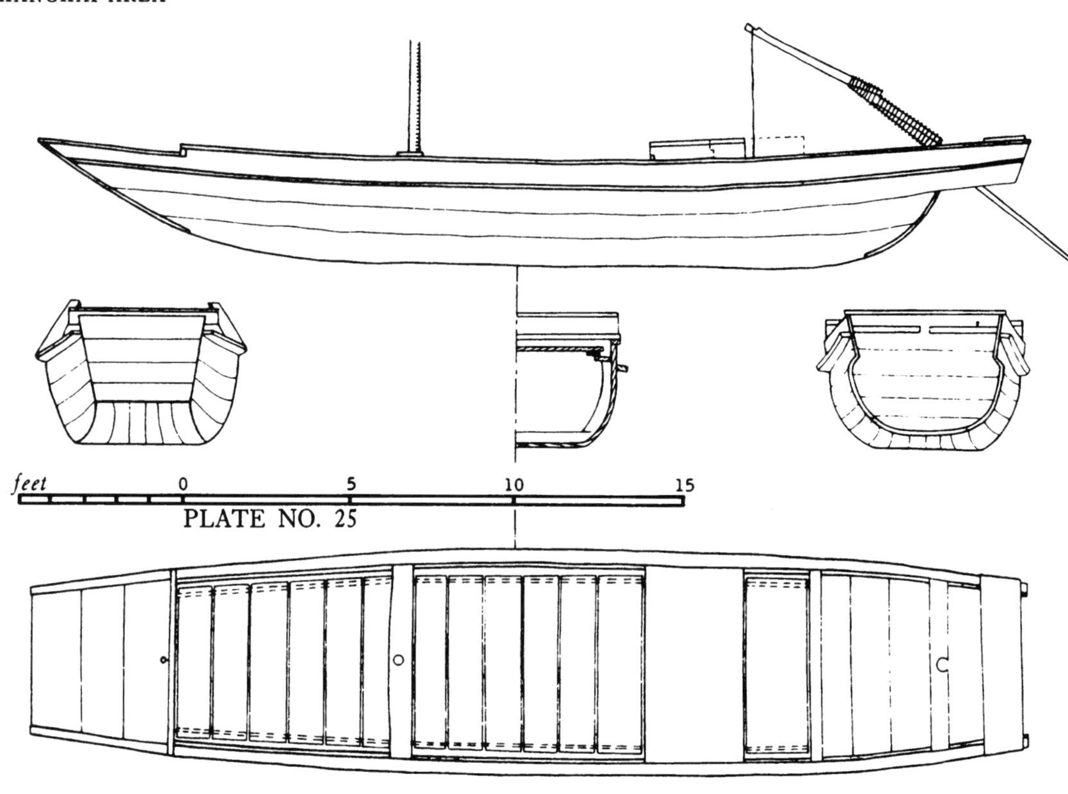

PLATE NO. 25

灘船

THE T'AN-CH'UAN OR SANDBANK BOAT

Besides the ordinary junk routes there are numerous lesser creeks navigable by craft of 2½ to 3 inches draught, and in addition there is a perfect network of still smaller creeks on which small junks and sampans of very light draught can ply. To such an extent is the Yangtze delta cut up into creeks and canals that every villager can almost, if not quite, reach his door by boat.

T'an-ch'uan is the local name given to the craft here described. The literal translation of the word *t'an* (灘) is sandbank or foreshore. These small junks are collected together in *ch'uan-ch'ang* (船廠), or boat yards, situated at various focal points on the creeks inland from the Whangpoo on the Pootung side. When a farmer has collected sufficient produce to fill a boat, he hires it for a fixed sum (50 cents a day a few years ago) and carries his wares to market by one of the numerous creek routes. With long practice the farmers and their wives and children have become expert "watermen."

There are frequently branch canals leading to the outlying farmhouses. On these waterways the farm boat takes the place of the farm waggon, and heavily-laden boats may be seen plying in all directions carrying farm produce.

A medium-sized craft, such as is illustrated in Plate No. 25, is 30 feet long, with a beam of 6½ feet and a draught of 3 inches. The largest craft may measure 50 feet in length.

The boat is strongly built with two bulkheads and six frames, and is decked throughout with removable planks, the cargo being stowed in the two foremost compartments while the third has a sliding hatch reaching from gunwale to gunwale for the accommodation of the crew below decks.

The characteristic overhang of the stern provides increased deck space, and there is an aperture for a rudder, though one is seldom used. The boat is propelled by means of a yuloh 15 feet long, of which 3 feet alone operate below the water-line in the shallow creeks. Sails are never used, although a small tracking mast is sometimes stepped.

THE YAO-LU-HUA-TZŬ OR OAR-BOAT

The *yao-lu-hua-tzŭ*, or oar-boat, is to all outward appearances remarkably like the Woosung *fang-t'ou*; but, unlike the latter, she carries cargo almost exclusively instead of passengers, and indeed may be described as the cargo-carrying sampan of the Whangpoo, with a capacity of about 40 piculs.

The junkmen themselves, of course, would never confuse the two types, and actually there are several differences in their construction. The *yao-lu-hua-tzŭ* has no false bow and the boat is decked in throughout, for in place of a single midship section awning there are two awnings covering the whole length. The after awning may be raised about 1½ feet, if necessary, into the strongback in the stern.

A curious feature of the construction is that the bottom measurement of the stern is wider than at deck level, while the galley is forward instead of aft. Another notable distinguishing feature is a long *sha-mu* pole suspended as a fender on each side. These serve to protect the hull but detract from the smartly-kept air customary to these boats.

There is considerably more room and comfort for the crew which, like those of the Woosung *fang-t'ou*, consist, generally, of the wives and families of junkmen.

Propulsion is by the same type of yuloh, which is also situated on the starboard side. This yuloh extends 7 feet below the surface of the water. There is no rudder, but masts and sail may sometimes be seen.

The *yao-lu-hua-tzŭ* has two bulkheads and three frames, and is somewhat larger than her sister the *fang-t'ou*, measuring as she does 23 by 7 feet. The people on board go about their domestic duties as unconcernedly as if they had the privacy and safety of four walls.

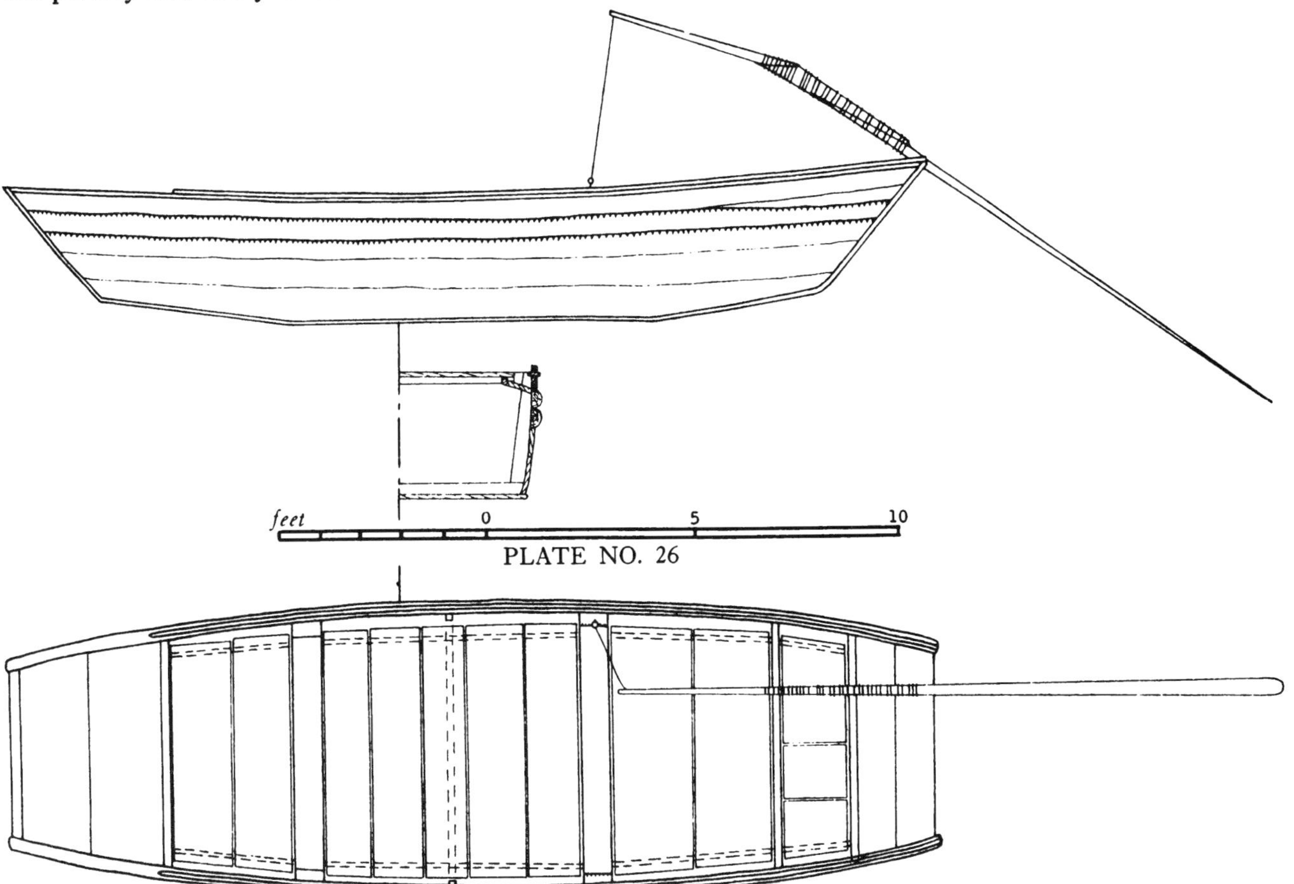

PLATE NO. 26

THE MUD-BOAT

No plans were available for the following seven boats. The information, according to Mr. Worcester's notes, was obtained from reliable sources, but in some cases relates to craft that were already obsolete at the time of writing.

The mud-boat is really only the Shanghai cargo-boat when it has reached such a stage of disintegration as to be obliged to step down in the social scale.

The little-known mud trade of Shanghai is a thriving industry, and presumably amply remunerative. The mud is sold by the *fang*, that is to say, in blocks of 10 square feet and 1 foot in depth. Previously this cost $2, but it has now risen to the phenomenal price of $30 per *fang*.

Mud from the Whangpoo is used for plaster work inside Chinese houses and, it is said, even finds its way into Shanghai luxury flats, where it serves the same purpose when mixed with lime and paper. A cheap substitute for the paper is chopped straw.

It is not clear why the Whangpoo mud should be so much in demand, but apparently it possesses valuable properties absent from the mud of the near creeks and waterways, for boats will travel long distances to obtain the more precious brand of mother earth.

The happy hunting-ground for the industrious crews of the mud-boats is off the Shanghai Waterworks; and in addition to being specialists in mud assessing, the crew are also experts in tidal matters, for, directly the mud banks commence to dry, the empty mud-boats make their appearance as if from nowhere. When the water falls the boats are left high and dry, whereupon the men jump into the soft mud and shovel the precious substance into their boat.

When the river rises again the mud-boats, loaded to the gunwales, laboriously yuloh their way home, and disappear into the hinterland with their uninteresting cargo.

THE SALVAGE BOAT

About 20 years ago an enterprising drag-boat man conceived the idea of forming a salvage co-operative. From that day to this, these experts in recovering lost property from the bottom of the river have kept it as a family concern, the number of the relatives so engaged being now about 300. It is purely socialistic in outlook, in that all share and share alike, the women and children each counting individually in the division of the prize money.

The gangs have divided themselves up into watertight compartments, each attending to a certain section of the river, although under certain conditions it is allowable to work in another section. The craft used are the small Shanghai cargo-boats which also form the family residences. The unwritten laws are very complex; the headman of the clan is elected by popular vote, and they appear to give him unquestioning obedience. When a salvage undertaking presents itself he assesses the number of boats that will be required and proceeds with them to the scene of action, where he directs operations. Individual boats, however, are permitted to "pick up jobs on the side."

As in the case of the drag-boats, every possible device of Chinese ingenuity is made use of to retrieve any lost article from the muddy bed of the Whangpoo; but when such means fail the men of the salvage-boats are prepared to dive for it. Evidence of their skill is shown by the fact that they have even been known to recover wrist watches, but such small jobs are as a rule left for the humbler, cheaper drag-boat. The salvage crews are mostly employed on larger jobs, such as raising lost anchors and cables. There are countless interesting stories of their successful activities, which are occasionally of a rather shady nature. On one occasion a salvage crew with an urge to acquire an anchor tied up their boat exactly over the site of one of the anchors of a moored ship. As the tide fell the salvage-boat settled down on to the anchor, and a diver passed a rope round it while at the same time sawing through the cable. When the tide rose again the boat made off with the anchor to a quiet reach and slipped it there to be recovered later. Their plans, however, were frustrated by a small launch which ran on to the cache and holed herself. The ownership of the anchor was easily discovered by the fact that the steamer, on starting to drift, hove up and discovered her anchor cable cut and anchor gone.

There are, however, far more stories on the credit side; for instance, the case of a box containing $5,000 which, while being loaded on to a ship, broke and let fall a shower of silver into the river. $4,900 of the total amount was recovered by the salvage-boats.

The fee charged is 10 per cent of the value on the "no cure, no pay" basis.

Some five years ago the salvage organization subscribed together and brought their equipment up to date by the acquisition of a condemned foreign-style diving-suit and a locally-made pump. This is a great success, and is let out on hire to any individual boat in their community for a small fee.

THE WHANGPOO LIFE-BOAT

There is always something very romantic about a life-boat. Of all the benevolent institutions in China, the Life-boat Association may be ranked among the foremost. As there are no records of any such organizations on the coast, it would seem that it was at first solely confined to the Yangtze, where its establishment dates back some centuries.

The red, or life-boat, of the Lower Yangtze is described in Part Three, page 372.
The hung-ch'uan, or life-boat, used on the Upper Yangtze is described in Part Four, page 528 and illustrated in Plate No. 145.

The first evidence of any life-saving boats in operation in Shanghai was in 1871, when a set of rules was sanctioned by Imperial edict to give protection to shipwrecked persons and property on that part of the Whangpoo which extends from Woosung to Minp'u, about 70 *li*. It would appear that the first boats designed and built for the purpose were a steam launch, a house-boat, and a foreign-type gig, with a complement of 13 men all told. From this beginning grew the Life-boat Service. It was under the patronage of the Taotai, while the salaries of the staff and expenses of maintenance were borne by the Pu-tao Chü, police officials, and the Kuo-yu T'ang, a benevolent institution. The combined salaries in those days, it may be mentioned, were not a considerable amount, for they came to no more than 82,000 cash per month, or between £8 and £11 10*s*., for the cash of that day had a variable value of from one-thirtieth to one-fortieth of an English penny.

Officers in charge were required by the regulations to remain day and night in their respective boats and not to go ashore without leave, so that they should be ready for any emergency.

The life-boats were most in demand in bad weather, and cruised from daylight to dusk within the defined limits. They were equipped with long bamboo poles, ropes, and other articles necessary for saving life. If required, the sailors were instructed to tie one end of the rope to the launch and the other to their own bodies and "dive under the water to render whatever service may be necessary."

The launch carried a small cannon and four muskets to summon help, and, as the institution cared for the drowning not only before but after their rescue, two sets of mattresses and coverlets were provided, together with 10 suits of wadded coats and trousers for the use of the rescued until such time as their own clothes could be dried and returned to them. The instructions for restoring the apparently drowned are interesting:

> On rescuing a drowning man, the crew are to lose no time in changing the patient's clothes for the dry ones of the Society, after which a tisane of ginger is to be administered. The boatmen are on no account to give up the patient for dead because he may be perfectly insensible, and they are to be careful not to place the patient near a fire, as such a measure would force the cold inwards and lessen the chances of recovery.

The duties of the life-boatmen, in addition to saving life, were to be on the look-out for bad characters, and "in the event of meeting with any committing illegal acts, to seize them and bring them to the station to be handed over to the magistrate for punishment."

The Chinese authorities legislated against any propensity to exercise any undue ingenuity in a new field of exploitation. Rules were drawn up to deal with dishonest individuals who might throw people into the river so as to rescue them and "claim the reward," or with swimmers who would conspire together to sham drowning for the same purpose. Boatmen, too, were forbidden to claim for work done by others, or to intimidate the rescued by demanding rewards from them.

The Superintendent of Customs appointed officials, known as Weiyüan, regularly to inspect and register all classes of ferry-boat on the river, and to fix the limit of passengers allowed to each boat for the prevention of accidents by overcrowding. The most dire penalties were laid down for rescuers who "gazed at accidents when prompt action on their part would save life," and particularly against those who "robbed those in peril on the pretext of saving them."

The Service thus commenced continued until in the nature of things much of its work was carried out by the Customs Harbour Police.

THE BEGGAR-BOAT

Every visitor to Shanghai knows the small craft which appear as if by magic from nowhere whenever a large liner makes fast to the buoys, and no record of Shanghai craft would be complete that ignored this feature of harbour life.

These beggar-boats may be any variety of sampan, and descend to these social depths only when they are too decrepit to serve their normal purpose. They often seem to be literally hanging together, but nevertheless provide a shelter for whole families.

On the small fore deck may be witnessed the full scope of their domestic life, such as it is, of which the only really important function is the preparing, cooking, and eating of meals. There is always the inexhaustible supply of small children, who wear an assortment of patched garments. This makeshift clothing is usually completely discarded in the summer. In spite of the cramped quarters there is more often than not a dog or two and a fowl, and sometimes a duck is

The beggar-boat, a familiar sight in Shanghai Harbour.

swimming close by, tethered to the boat by a string which considerably restricts its pleasure cruising.

Every boat is supplied with a net on the end of a very long pole, which is waved about expectantly under the eyes of lounging tourists, for whose benefit is staged a pathetic picture of an unhappy, destitute family. A ceaseless whining gabble is kept up, by which means it is hoped to charm, threaten, or weary the listener into a charitable frame of mind.

No trifle is counted inconsiderable by the beggar crews, and no floating debris escapes their sharp eyes. A favourite point of vantage is near the waste chutes of steamers, and these sampans swarm there as eagerly as seagulls and are scarcely more discriminating.* They continue to eke out a meagre living with commendable cheerfulness. If they occasionally supplement it in illicit ways by a little pilfering of cargo or any other commodity at all when opportunity offers it is perhaps hardly surprising, and those more comfortably situated would do well to pause and imagine themselves in these poor folks' ragged shoes before passing too severe a judgment.

After the day's work is done the beggar-boats retire to snug anchorages off Pootung Point or up the Soochow Creek to count their takings and plan a new campaign of importunity for the morrow.

* Carl Crow, in "400 Million Customers," a book which should be read by all interested in China, suggests that the Shanghai Harbour is the cleanest in the world because the scavenger-boats do their work so thoroughly, and even goes so far as to suggest that this accounts for the absence of seagulls in the Whangpoo.

THE FLOATING HUT-BOAT

No study of the craft of Shanghai would be complete without reference to the local floating-hut boats, the poor and stunted relations of the floating dwellings.

The inhabitants, although of a lower stratum of society, are, similarly, mostly those who cannot afford house-rent ashore. The hut-boat is usually some small derelict craft lying in a canal or creek; or, if it is too old to float, it is shored up on the bank with oddments of wood. The sides are decked in with matting in all stages of decrepitude, old bits of boarding, tin or sacking in various stages of antiquity, and straw even is used to fill up the larger holes.

Many thousands of the very poor of Shanghai live in this way, and sometimes two or three families may be seen sharing these diminutive dwellings, divided from each other by a mere mat partition. Nearly all of them keep chickens or ducks under the beds and, if funds permit of the capital outlay, a pig.

Miserable as conditions are, these people seem neither unhappy nor uncomfortable. Some have existed in the same slowly-decaying boat for years and, in favour of their mode of living, point out that life ashore is often worse, for they are spared the demands of a rapacious landlord, as of the tax collector, and the overcrowding makes for extra warmth in the winter.

An interesting feature in connection with these craft is that the majority of the inhabitants are Kiangpei (江 北) or Kompo people from the north bank of the Yangtze and are " not nice to know." Although not junkmen, they might perhaps be described as a clan of longshore men and women. They have earned their rather shady reputation from their quarrelsome and thievish propensities, which they probably owe to their pirate ancestry. Being tough, therefore, as well as rough, they are doubtless not sensitive, and manage not only to live happily in the disapproving atmosphere of their more law-abiding neighbours but to bring up their families in the same gipsy traditions.

棺材船

THE COFFIN-BOAT

It is a truism, of course, to state that any Chinese, whatever his station in life or the state of his finances, considers it essential to be buried near his ancestral home.

Wherever he dies, his body must be sent back to his native place; and China being so well and universally served by waterways, this is usually done by boat.

This cargo-boat is illustrated in Plate No. 18, page 211.

The craft that carry out this melancholy but honourable duty are not specially built for the task; but, in the Shanghai district, they are nearly always of a particular class of strong, heavy cargo-boat which is too old for the heavier work for which it was designed.

They are in no way structurally altered or adapted for this work, and when not loaded with coffins, may be recognized only by their air of neglect and antiquity; for mouldy growths appear where the chunam has fallen out, and it is obvious that no attempt is ever made to smarten or polish up their derelict appearance. This may be due to the work being poorly paid for or to a sense of fitting the instrument to the deed.

For many reasons the body of a Chinese who dies in another district may not be conveniently sent home at once. Floods, civil wars, bandits, or lack of funds may delay, and in any case it often takes some time for the geomancers to settle on an auspicious site for the grave. In the case of a poor man, whose small capacity for payment is soon exhausted, the matter is put through quickly; but the richer the family, the longer it takes the priests to decide on a suitable spot.

While the bodies are waiting, for whatever reason, safe custody has to be provided all over China for the thousands of coffins before they are shipped home.

As Shanghai is a centre to which Chinese from all provinces collect, its mortuaries are the largest and most numerous. Some 40 years ago the mortuaries of Sinza and other districts were famous. There could be seen hundreds of temporary brick graves, each with a stone bearing the name of the occupant in red letters. The much-travelled Cantonese supported two such mortuaries, while the people of Nanking, Huchow, and Soochow had one each.

In Canton, a special type of junk called the Fy T'eng, or quick boat, is used for the coffin-carrying trade only. It is constructed on slender lines, and built of soft wood with hardwood frames. The planks of the fore deck are removable, to permit the coffin to be lowered into the hold. The midship compartment consists of a comfortable cabin, where the relatives of the deceased may be housed during the voyage. (From *The Junkman Smiles*.)

To-day, now that the price of building land has soared to unprecedented heights, the dead are housed in coffin repositories, which are merely enormous bamboo sheds and can be readily moved to another vacant lot if ground rents are high or the plot sold.

Here may be seen whole battalions of coffins in every stage and condition: good coffins, bad coffins, broken coffins. The rich lie in beautifully carved or lacquered state, embellished with red, black, or gold, while the poor efface themselves within humble *sha-mu* planks.

Here the comprador of some princely hong may be the neighbour of a lowly junkman; and both alike bear the same levelling label of the Shanghai Municipal Council, giving the bald particulars and grade. This strange and oppressive sight of row upon row of coffins demonstrates how strong is the hold the dead have on the living in China.

The Chinese are very particular about their coffins. The men of the old school take their coffins with them wherever they go, and make them their constant companions in life, until in death they become their homes.

THE FLOATING STRAW-STACK

The desperate need for cheap fuel has resulted in a very profitable trade on the Whangpoo River in the floating straw-stacks which block the waterways for miles around Shanghai.

This straw fuel is much favoured by the Chinese, even when economy is no object, for it provides a quick blaze. Cooking by straw has one disadvantage, however, as it requires the whole-time service of a stoker as well as a cook. Straw is also used to roof cottages, and even to build the cheaper types, the interstices being filled in with mud. The same methods are used to make fences.

There is nothing remarkable about the actual junks so used, but there is much of interest in the manner in which their cargo is stowed. A number of baulks of timber, usually five, is laid athwartships on the boat at deck level. From the outboard extremities of these is suspended below them on each side a form of shelf lying horizontally only a few inches above the water and composed of five parallel bamboo poles running the whole length of the boat. These bamboos are lashed together and slung from a wire becket.

Bundles of straw are then packed on the shelves below the athwartship timbers; and, once this level is reached, the whole area with the outriggers is stacked up with straw to a height of 18 feet or more until scarcely any portion of the vessel remains visible.

At the bow a plank laid in the fore and aft line projects a few feet ahead of the cargo, providing just sufficient space for working cables. The top of the straw stack is more or less flat and is covered with matting secured by ropes.

The living quarters in the stern occupy about one-fifth of the deck surface, and a hatch gives access to a lower level of rather cramped accommodation. Holes are cut in the straw walls to allow water to be drawn up into the kitchen or galley. The cooking-stove is situated within a foot of the inflammable cargo, and, as no precautions are taken against fire, accidents are not infrequent. Cooking in a powder magazine could hardly be more dangerous, particularly in hot weather, when the straw is dry and tindery.

In the stern an oblong section of the top portion of the straw is cut away, and a temporary wooden bridge is erected above the level of the roof, temporary planking forming the roof of the living quarters below. Access is, of course, on either side, and the living quarters are inside the straw. Two men stationed on the bridge operate the two yulohs and steer by means of a very long tiller, which consists of a ragged, unshaped branch of a tree.

These craft, which travel through the narrow creeks and canals between highly cultivated areas, appear, when seen from inland, like slowly-moving hay-stacks on wheels.

THE SOOCHOW CREEK

THE Soochow Creek, so called by the foreigners after Shanghai was opened as a Treaty Port, was known to the Chinese in ancient times as the Sungkiang. Its first appearance in Chinese history dates back to the third century A.D., when it is mentioned in the "Hou Han Shu" (後漢書), the "History of the Later Han Dynasty."

In the "History of Ch'ên," A.D. 557–589, it is mentioned under the name of Woosungkiang, and doubtless owes the origin of this latter name to the fact that this area was once included in the Kingdom of Wu, about 513 B.C.

The creek, which is very largely a canalized river, has sadly dwindled in size from its reputed 20 *li* in breadth during the T'ang dynasty to 9 *li* during that of the Sung, until it finally reached its present modest dimensions.

The story of its origin is that in A.D. 446 the Yangchow Viceroy ordered a canal to be cut from Soochow to the mouth of the Yangtze. The work was rendered easier by using and developing an existing stream; and, when it was completed, it followed the present course of the Soochow Creek but was many miles wide at its mouth. In those days it flowed independently of the Whangpoo into the sea near Woosung, and the fishing craft and salt-junks of Southern Kiangsu could sail direct from the sea up the Woosungkiang, that is to say, the Soochow Creek, to a mart called Ch'inglung or Ts'inglung.

Later a canal was dug, called the Fanchiapang, uniting the waters of those two rivers. Under the Ming dynasty, about A.D. 1400, this was deepened and widened to the eventual detriment of the Woosungkiang, which, being unable to scour itself out, started to silt up. The canal became a continuation of the Whangpoo and lost its original name. It is said that this section, which was once the old canal, is that portion of the Whangpoo which flows past Shanghai from a point near the Arsenal to Pootung Point.

To the junkmen the Soochow Creek is still the Laokiang or Old River. Those who are interested in tracing it to its source should follow the Grand Canal.

A journey up the Soochow Creek, as it soon came to be called, takes the traveller past Whangtu to T'aits'ang, 38 miles up. Another stretch of 17 miles leads to Quinsan, or, as the name is written of old, K'unshan, famous as the headquarters of General Gordon in his victorious campaign against the Taiping rebels. Twenty miles farther up is the town of Soochow, and 10 miles up again lies the lake known as the T'aihu, measuring 25 by 330 miles.

Across the lake from Soochow is the place where the so-called Soochow tubs are made. Ihsing, the seat of this industry, has been noted for its pottery products from time immemorial. The ruins of some of the kilns are said to date from 473 B.C. Large articles, such as *kangs*, wash-tubs, and earthenware seats, are loaded direct on to junks, but fine articles, such as teapots and flower vases, are packed in baskets lined with straw. Extensive silk cultivation is carried on by the shores of this small inland sea.

Kangs are the large earthenware vessels or vats used in winemaking.

A least depth of 4 feet extends all the way up the creek to Soochow and

Hangchow *via* the Grand Canal, which also connects with Chinkiang and in favourable circumstances thence with Tientsin.

In 1843 the mouth of the Soochow Creek was wide enough to accommodate some of the British fleet at anchor. The silting up of this waterway has continued unceasingly since then. It was further hastened in 1866 by the foundering of a British sailing ship at the junction of the creek with the Whangpoo on the site now occupied by the bandstand in the Public Gardens. The barque *Hotspur*, coming up to her anchorage off the Bund on the 27th January, stood too close to the Bund, got caught in the chowchow water and drifted ashore on the mud in front of the British Consulate. At low water she heeled over and became a total loss within a ship's length of her destination.

The accumulation of silt that formed round the wreck soon produced the Consular mud flat, so called from its proximity to the British Consulate. This area was, in 1868, handed over to the Council, who transformed it into a public garden, to be extended later, when the present embankment was built.

At certain stages of the tide the creek can claim the distinction of being unsurpassed for the strength and variety of its smells, and an oar will stand erect without extraneous help. When the creek reaches this stage even the hardy junkmen cannot drink the water, and a highly efficient service for the supply of cleaner water has been evolved, whereby 100 bamboo tokens could at one time be purchased for a dollar. At intervals along the bank of the creek and inland among the mat settlements are water shops where, in exchange for a token, a kettle may be filled with a more palatable brand of water.

Shrunk as it is now to a mere 40 yards in width, the Soochow Creek presents all the aspects of a busy thoroughfare, with floating craft of all sizes and types taking the place of vehicles. The congestion in a waterway, however, can be many times more acute than on a road, and the Harbour Police of the Customs have to cope with apparently insuperable problems in traffic regulation. Tightly-wedged vessels often cover the creek from bank to bank, and it would appear that it was impossible in some places for progress to be made in either direction; but by deft manœuvring and stealthy encroachment, encouraged by the maximum amount of "walla walla," disentanglement is achieved and progress is finally made.*

Most of the old landmarks of the Shanghai and neighbouring waterfronts have vanished; but one interesting and historic temple still remains on the Hongkew side of the Soochow Creek, on the North Honan Road, next to the bridge. This temple was very popular with the junkmen. Now, although the building still stands, the only relics of its former glories are the stone lions beside the entrance door, which are reputed to come to life each night and act as the guardians they represent by day. A few scattered fragments of granite bear evidence to the pillars that used to adorn the entrance.

The temple housed two important and very accomplished gods, for the one, Ching Tsiang-ching, could hear anything that occurred within 1,000 *li* of Shanghai, while the other, Liu Tsiang-ching, equally gifted, could see for the same distance. He had an eye carved in the forehead called the 1,000-*li* eye (千 里 眼). These deities were the chief assistants of the Queen of Heaven, who herself when alive on earth was distinguished by the gift of prophecy. A local junkmen's legend tells how, when her four brothers were out at sea, she fell into a trance until she was aroused by the lamentations of her parents, who supposed her dead.

On awakening she told them in her dreams she had seen her brother in a typhoon. Later her youngest brother alone returned, reporting the loss of his brothers at sea and how during the storm a lady appeared in mid-heaven and

* The writer has seen five large boilers towed by a launch pass a timber raft with complete safety, albeit with much shouting and gratuitous advice from the longshoremen. Nevertheless, there were at times acute traffic jams, to quote from the "Shanghai Customs Trade Returns" for 1927: "on 13 different occasions a block-up occurred, the periods of time being mostly of two or three hours duration, excepting on three occasions when the times were 8, 15, and 16 hours." In former days affairs on the Soochow Creek were controlled by the Customs, who maintained Harbour Police patrols and directed the traffic. To-day things are not so simple, for the Municipal Police Bureau, the Social Affairs Bureau, the Public Works Bureau, the Navigation Bureau, the Whangpoo Conservancy Board, the Port Commission's Garrison Section, the Inland Shipping Companies Guild, and the Sixth District Wharf Labour Union all have an interest and say in the matter.

The water gate, Soochow.
E. SIGAUT

dragged the ship to safety by a rope. The sister related how in her vision she had hastened to help her brothers, but in the act of rescue was awakened by the cries of her parents. Soon after this the father of this seafaring family was drowned, and in despair his daughter cast herself into the sea. She was deified and became an Oriental Stella Maris, known as the Queen of Heaven, with shrines and temples in her honour.

Tien fei, Queen of Heaven.

In after years an official travelling to Korea told how he was saved in a typhoon by a supernatural light guiding his junk to an island whereon was one of her shrines. She is looked upon as the guardian of all sailors, over whom she watches, particularly when they are at sea, and hence this temple was built amongst the busy shipping centres of the creek. Once famous and prosperous, it is now inhabited by the poorest refugees. The gods have departed—where, no man knows.

The true junkmen's temple, however, still survives with its full complement of heavenly guardians. This is also situated on the Soochow Creek, but a good deal higher up and on the right or south bank. It is close to the waterfront, at the east corner of the Chekiang Road, and is well worth a visit. It is of particular interest to those interested in junks, for various models are suspended from the roof in the time-honoured fashion of sailors, just as ship models may be seen in English and Breton fishing-town churches. The Temple of Tranquil Repose, for such is its name, has many sentences hung up in gold lettering on long, oblong boards. Outside the temple one says "stiff winds and settled waves," others read "grace flows over the kingdom of the sea," "the sea will not raise its waves," "protection within the four seas," "the river is clear and the sea peaceful," "everlasting thanks for peaceful seas." There is a shrine to the four great kings of the golden dragon, and there are two junks suspended from the high roof, both of which have been there for "more than 50 years," that is to say, a very long time.

That a temple has been on this site for about a thousand years is evidenced by a sentence from a prayer made in A.D. 1038 by the Governor of the Liang-chê Province while making his sacrifice to the Dragon King. He said:

> "As it was told by the people, there was a temple built in the river shore in worship of the river god during the last century by the Kings of the Wu-yüeh Kingdoms (A.D. 907–979), but owing to the change of dynasties it was destroyed."

The temple was rebuilt soon after, and again about the middle of the sixteenth century, when it was dedicated to the memory of Hsieh Hsü, who lived in 1270. As nephew of the last Queen of the Sung dynasty, he had refused to take office under the invading Mongols, but lived as a recluse in his native province. Later, on learning that his aunt had been taken to Peking by the Mongols, in his grief he threw himself into the river. His body, as in the case of several famous suicides in China, it is said, would not sink, but floated up river against the current.

The first Emperor of the Ming dynasty, Chu Yüan-chang, who rose against the Mongol rulers, won a great battle on the Yellow River and attributed much of his success to the appearance of Hsieh's spirit with a band of demon fighters. He accordingly canonized the patriot Hsieh under the title of Chin Lung Ssŭ Ta Wang, or Fourth Great King of the Golden Dragon. The temple is said to have been rebuilt again at the beginning of the nineteenth century.

Yet another temple situated on the south bank of the creek lies at the end of the Chengtu Road and is said to have been built in about 1818 with the funds raised by a considerable subscription from the junkmen, whose various associations still make its maintenance their charge.* In former more colourful years an elaborate musical procession was held annually on the 28th day of the 3rd moon of the lunar calendar. This was discontinued after the establishment of the Republic. The temple is still held in high repute, and the Dragon King's assistance is continually sought by those suffering from sickness, poverty, or misfortune.

On the Soochow Creek.
E. SIGAUT

* Large subscriptions were made by the rice transportation junks.

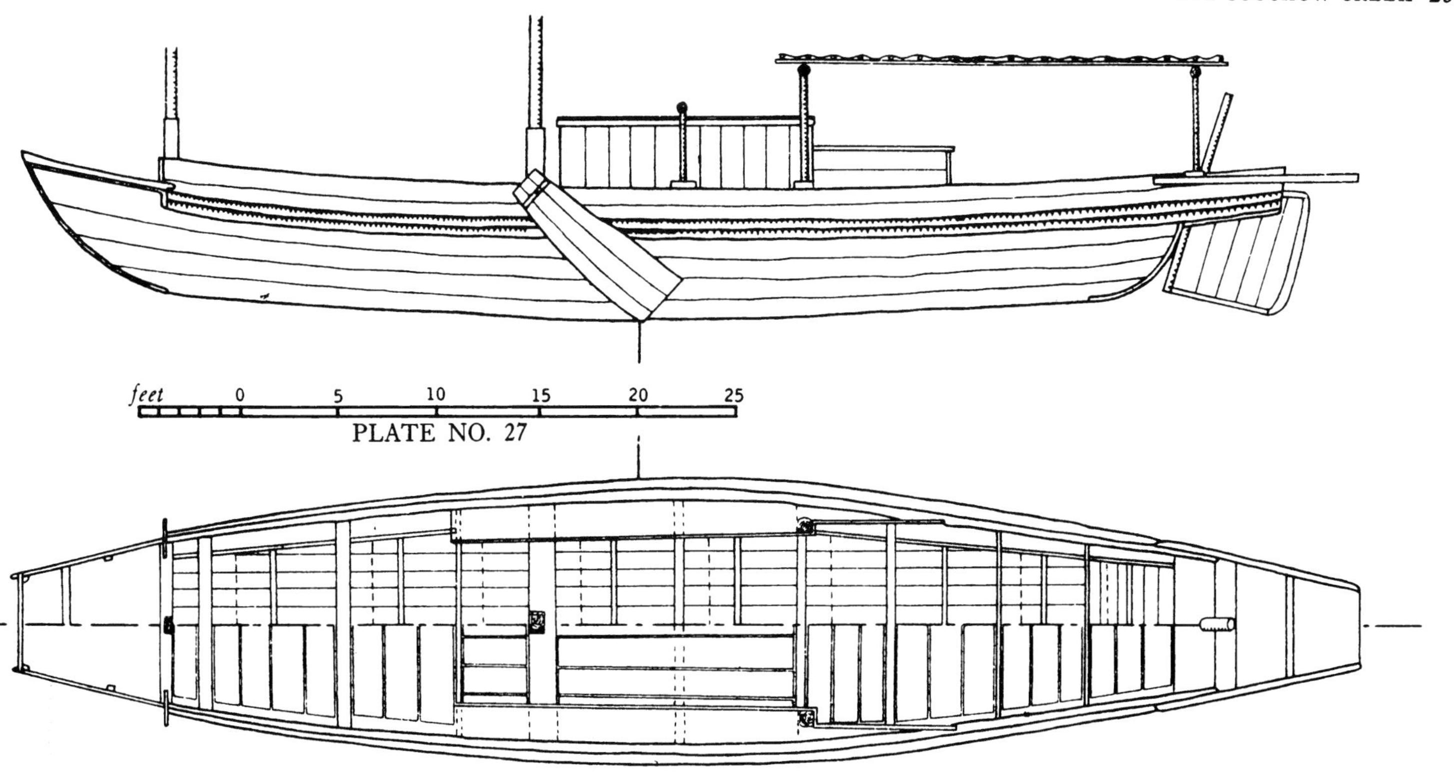

THE FU-CH'UAN OR OFFICIAL BOAT

The *fu-ch'uan* (府 船) is built at Changchow (常 州), a city lying north-west of Wusih, where the Grand Canal runs north to Chinkiang parallel with the Shanghai–Nanking Railway. This junk serves the waterways leading from the T'aihu to Shanghai, though it is occasionally to be seen on the Yangtze. It would appear that this craft, or its prototype, was used originally in some form or other for official purposes; but now, despite the impressive title, she has degenerated into a cargo-junk which carries stones to Shanghai and returns empty.

Made of *sha-mu* and measuring 66 feet, with a beam of 13½ feet and a depth of 6 feet, she is of exceptionally strong construction, as indeed she needs to be, with nine hardwood bulkheads and eight frames, and a carrying capacity of 42 tons. Built on pleasing lines, tapering gracefully to the stern, and with the very narrow bow characteristic of the T'aihu, she displays some unusual features in her construction, notably the double strengthening of planks in the "turnover" below the quanting gangway which runs throughout the length of the vessel on either side. This peculiarity of hull is illustrated in the sectional plan (*in margin*).

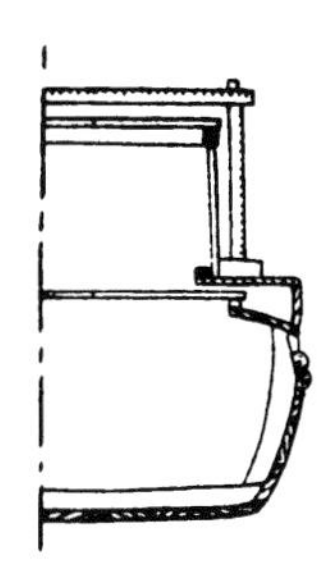

The small, low house, which is removable, is amidships and accommodates the crew of six. The owner and his family live below decks aft, between the seventh and eighth bulkheads, while the galley, also below decks, is abaft the ninth bulkhead.

There are two masts, both fitted with tabernacles and situated well forward; indeed, the foremast is abnormally far forward for this type of junk. The rudder is of the Shanghai non-hoisting variety. Alternative or auxiliary propulsion is effected by two bow yulohs operating from bumkins.

Stone-junks which, by reason of their dead weight of heavy cargo, should rigorously avoid overloading are actually notorious offenders in this respect, their margin of safety being reduced to the minimum possible. The serious dangers of swamping are slightly offset by the use of washboards, upon which the crew rely, almost entirely, to save them from swamping.

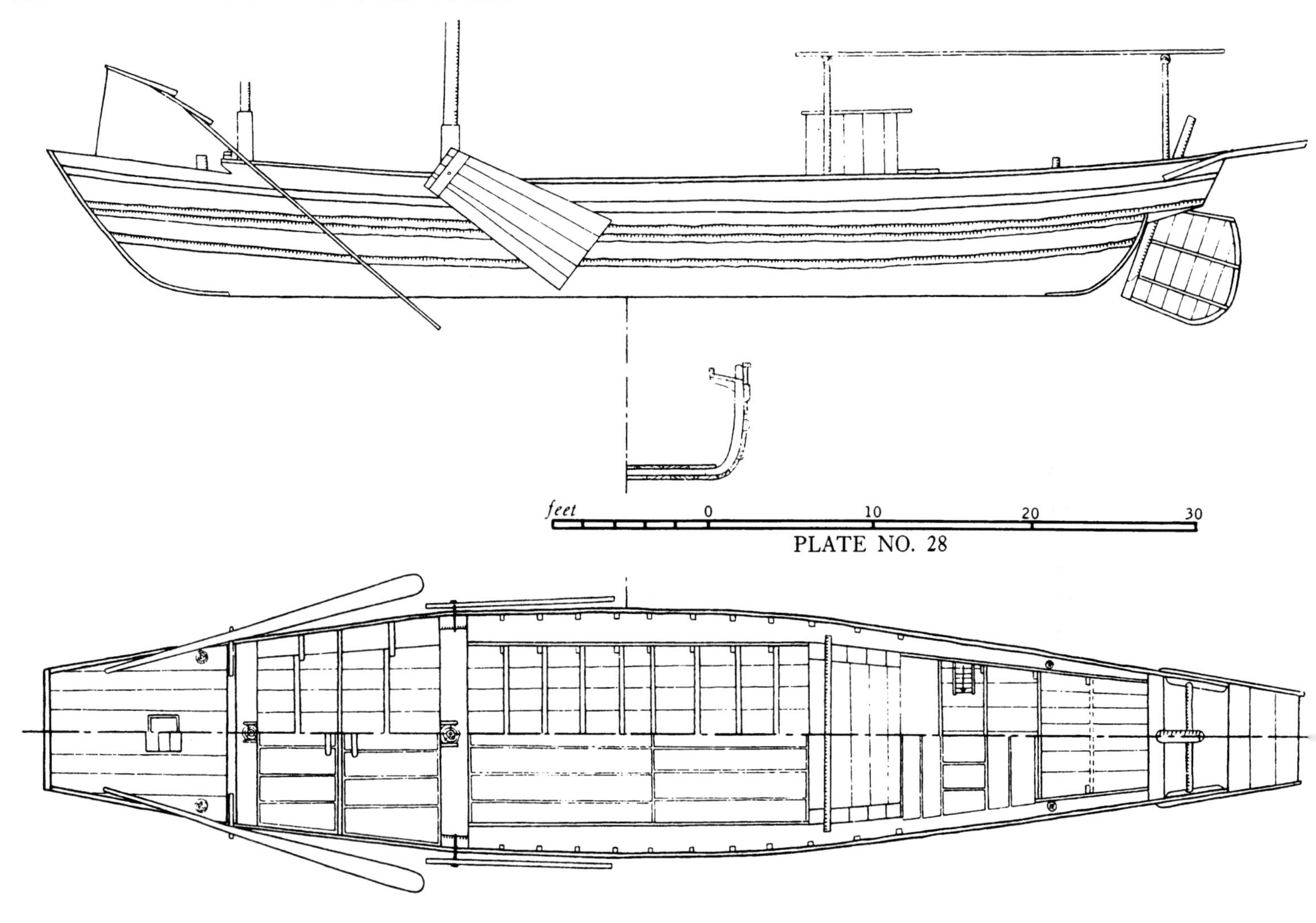

窑貨船

THE YAO-HUO-CH'UAN OR BRICK-BOAT

Bricks and tiles play an important and interesting part in the study of ancient civilizations, not only from an historical viewpoint, but also artistically. Their invention dates back to very ancient times, and excavations at Ur of the Chaldees has produced bricks made 6,000 years ago.

According to the oldest Chinese records, the people first lived in caves in winter and "nest dwellings" in summer. Mention of this and of the unknown benefactor who first inaugurated house-building is made by Confucius in the "I Hsi Tz'ü" (易繫辭); and the "Li Yün" (禮運), a record of old rites said to have been compiled by the followers of Confucius, describes how the people "utilized the power of fire for melting metals and cementing clays to build walls, houses, and pavilions." During the Shang and Chou dynasties, however, cave dwellings were still in use.

There is no knowing how the first homes were built, whether stones were used, as in the West, or if brick-making was almost contemporaneous with the new activities; but bricks and tiles in China are certainly of very ancient origin. There are no authentic records as to dates of this invention. Ch'iao Chou (譙周),* in compiling his "Reviews of Ancient History" (古史考), in the third century A.D., claimed that bricks and tiles were first made by Wu Ts'ao during the Hsia dynasty, about 2205–1766 B.C., but this must be regarded as pure supposition.

The word for brick in ancient times was *p'i* (坯), and is first mentioned in a poem written about 650 B.C. Another reference is that of Mao Ch'ang (毛萇)

* A noted scholar of the Minor Han dynasty, it is recorded of him that he used to sit up all night studying the classics. He would have a lighted twist of hemp arranged in such a way as to burn his hair if he began to nod from drowsiness.

during the Han dynasty, who, in a review of old poetry known as the "Shih Mao Chuan" (詩 毛 傳), states:

As there are bricks in the yards, so there is fine grass on the mounds. (中 唐 有 甓 邛 有 旨 鷊)

Some 300 years later a new word, *chuan* (塼), made its appearance in a philosophical writing of Hsün Ch'ing (荀 卿) and is still in use to-day. A third word, *chi* (墼), was used in the "Shuo Wên" (說 文), a dictionary written in A.D. 100; but this, it would seem, designated bricks which were not fired and were probably sun dried.

The oldest known ancient Chinese bricks as portrayed in illustrated books of old art treasures date back to the Ch'in dynasty, 255–206 B.C. These specimens were said to have been excavated from ruins and bore records of their date of origin stamped upon them. The most monumental example of brick-building is, of course, to be found in the Great Wall of China, which was built during the same Ch'in dynasty. The bricks used in its construction vary considerably in size, but the most common measure 15 inches long, 7½ inches wide, and 3½ inches in thickness. After all these centuries the mortar still binds the masonry. The art of mixing it seems to have been lost, though the Chinese believe rice flour was mixed with the lime. The method of making the earliest of Chinese bricks is that still used throughout the country districts, that is to say, they are moulded by hand between boards and then sun dried.

It is not, however, these bricks, or those of the Great Wall, which are carried by the craft hereinafter described, but their modern counterpart which is brought to the Shanghai market from the brick-making centres of Kashing and Soochow.

The more elaborate process begins with the drying and grinding of the clay, which, after being pulverized, is sifted and tempered with water and plugged to a certain degree of consistency before being pressed in a mould into bricks. The wet bricks are placed in a yard to dry for four or five days. When ready for firing they are packed into the kiln, which then has all openings sealed up and an iron lid placed on the top. The amount of air introduced through a ventilating shaft at the base of the kiln is regulated by a valve. As soon as the fire begins to show white flames the burning ceases and the bricks are left, still sealed up, to cool off slowly. The red colour of bricks or tiles is due to the presence of an iron oxide in the clay.

The brick-burners sell their stock to dealers either on order or for spot cash. In the latter case the burners ship their bricks to Shanghai themselves.

There are nearly 100 dealers in bricks and tiles in Shanghai, divided into two groups having a common guild. The yearly sales of a large dealer exceed $100,000, which is hardly surprising in view of a total annual expenditure of $3,000,000 in Shanghai on these commodities.

The business negotiations between the dealers and the house-building contractors are almost always conducted in a tea-house named the Ssŭ Hai Shêng P'ing Lou (四 海 昇 平 樓), or "Four Seas Peace House." The words Ssŭ Hai, in local dialect, have also the meaning of "broad minded." This tea-house is situated in Foochow Road.

Often a junkowner, if he has sufficient enterprise or capital, or both, will purchase a cargo of bricks and tiles direct from the burners and bring it down to sell in Shanghai at a good profit.

The craft which carry this cargo are known as the *yao-huo* (窰 貨), or kiln-product boats, of which a typical example is shown in Plate No. 28. Designed, as the name implies, to bring the products of this industry down the Soochow

Creek, they are built in Shanghai and measure 77 feet in length, with a beam of 14.6 feet and a depth of 7 feet.

This type of junk is of exceptionally strong construction so as to accommodate the 60 tons of dead-weight cargo she carries, for her *sha-mu* hull is strengthened by five hardwood bulkheads and 16 full frames. There is, moreover, a strong double wale with a single wale below, while above is a square-shaped gunwale, stronger and more substantial than the other wales, which serves also as a fender. This is surmounted by low, fixed weather-boarding running from the foremast aft.

Despite her solidity, this brick-carrier has remarkably graceful lines, and tapers to quite a narrow stern with the usual Shanghai-type stern gallery fitted with an extension.

The rudder-hoisting gear is rather more elaborate than usual, consisting of a small windlass resting in heavy chocks, and is operated by means of two short handspikes.

From Mr. Worcester's notes:
The lee-board is a marked feature of all riverine craft and acts to a certain extent as a removable keel. The lee-board is usually composed of three or more planks joined together to make a wing of varying shapes, the most usual being an elongated and truncated triangle. Two lee-boards are carried, one on either side. When it is required to give the vessel greater draught, the lee-board on the lee side is lowered so as to present a vertical plane of resistance to the water, the pressure of which retains it in position when beating to windward. By this means the drift is reduced. The Chinese lee-board, which varies in size, is generally about one-sixth the length of the boat and at its broadest part about two-thirds of its own length. At its narrowest part it is approximately one-fourth its length.

Propulsion is by sail and yuloh. Of the latter there are two, of the curved variety operating from short bumkins disposed on each bow. There are two masts, both very far forward. The fore and aft planks of the deck in a line with and between the masts are fitted with a cross batten to enable them to be readily removed when the masts are struck. Each mast is supported by a pair of tabernacles strengthened with an iron bar. There are two lee-boards, and the two pairs of bitts, according to a fairly general Shanghai custom, are situated close to the gunwales.

The weight is carried well forward, for the cargo is stowed in the forward and broader portion of the vessel in the two holds which lie between the first and fourth bulkheads.

The owner and his family live in a small house, and also below in a cabin measuring 8 by 13 feet. Entry to this is through a sliding doorway and down a ladder. The crew of eight men live forward in quarters below deck, reached through a booby hatch. The galley, which measures 8 by 10 feet, is also below decks and aft of the owner's cabin.

THE FÊN-CH'UAN OR FU-FU BOAT

China is essentially an agricultural country, and, according to their historical records, the Chinese from a very early period have been masters of agriculture. The great mass of the people are farmers, who spend their lives in the cultivation of the countless farms that cover the face of the whole country.

One of the most remarkable customs to be practised by a civilized country is their method of utilizing all human waste to maintain the fertility of the land. The Chinese farmer wastes nothing. While the ultra-civilized Westerner turns sewage into the sea, the Chinese use it for manure. For more than 30 centuries this practice has been carried out, and it is estimated that, to-day, the 400 millions of China's population send back to their fields an annual weight of 150,000 tons of phosphorus, 376,000 tons of potassium, and 1,158,000 tons of nitrogen comprised in a gross weight exceeding 182 million tons of these valuable salts and chemicals.* The conservation and use of this form of fertilizer has been

* The student desirous of following up this noisome subject should consult "Farmers of Forty Centuries," by F. H. King.

carefully worked out. It is deposited in a shady place, in a concrete container or earthenware vat, partly buried and kept tightly covered for 10 days until ready for use. It should not be kept longer, or the nitrogen content becomes lost. It is then diluted with three or four times its own volume of water and applied to the plants or vegetables. Without any chemical knowledge, the Chinese farmers have apparently, by the usual trial-and-error methods, arrived at a scientific fact.

Before the advent of modern plumbing to a large proportion of the houses in Shanghai, the disposal of the sewage of the city was a source of no inconsiderable revenue, ranging from a monthly payment by a Chinese contractor of $3,200 in 1899 to $5,300 in 1905. By 1920 a Chinese contractor paid the immense sum of *U.S.* $26,640 for the privilege of collecting 78,000 tons—or a daily average of 26,640 gallons—for distribution to the farmers.* The main problem of sanitation is to cleanse the city: if this can be done at a profit, so much the better.

The collection and distribution of night-soil in the country is a simple matter, but in dealing with the vast accumulations still to be had from the big cities a good deal of organization is necessary, and a considerable industry has grown up around it.

In China, of course, the cheapest, easiest, and most usual form of transport is, as always, by water. It is therefore not surprising to find craft specially designed for the malodorous cargo and that the flotilla engaged in the trade is enormous.

These boats vary in capacity from about 35 cartloads to 150 cartloads, these being the technical form of measure.

The craft under description measures 50 feet in length with a beam of 9½ feet, and is divided into five compartments. The three amidship compartments are used for the cargo. The foremost compartment, which is approached through a hatch, is used to accommodate the crew of four men, and the fifth and sixth after compartments beneath a standing awning form the living quarters of the owner and his family, for, amazing as it may seem, human beings can, and do, live aboard these craft and appear in no way overwhelmed by the atmosphere

* "Shanghai Municipal Gazette."

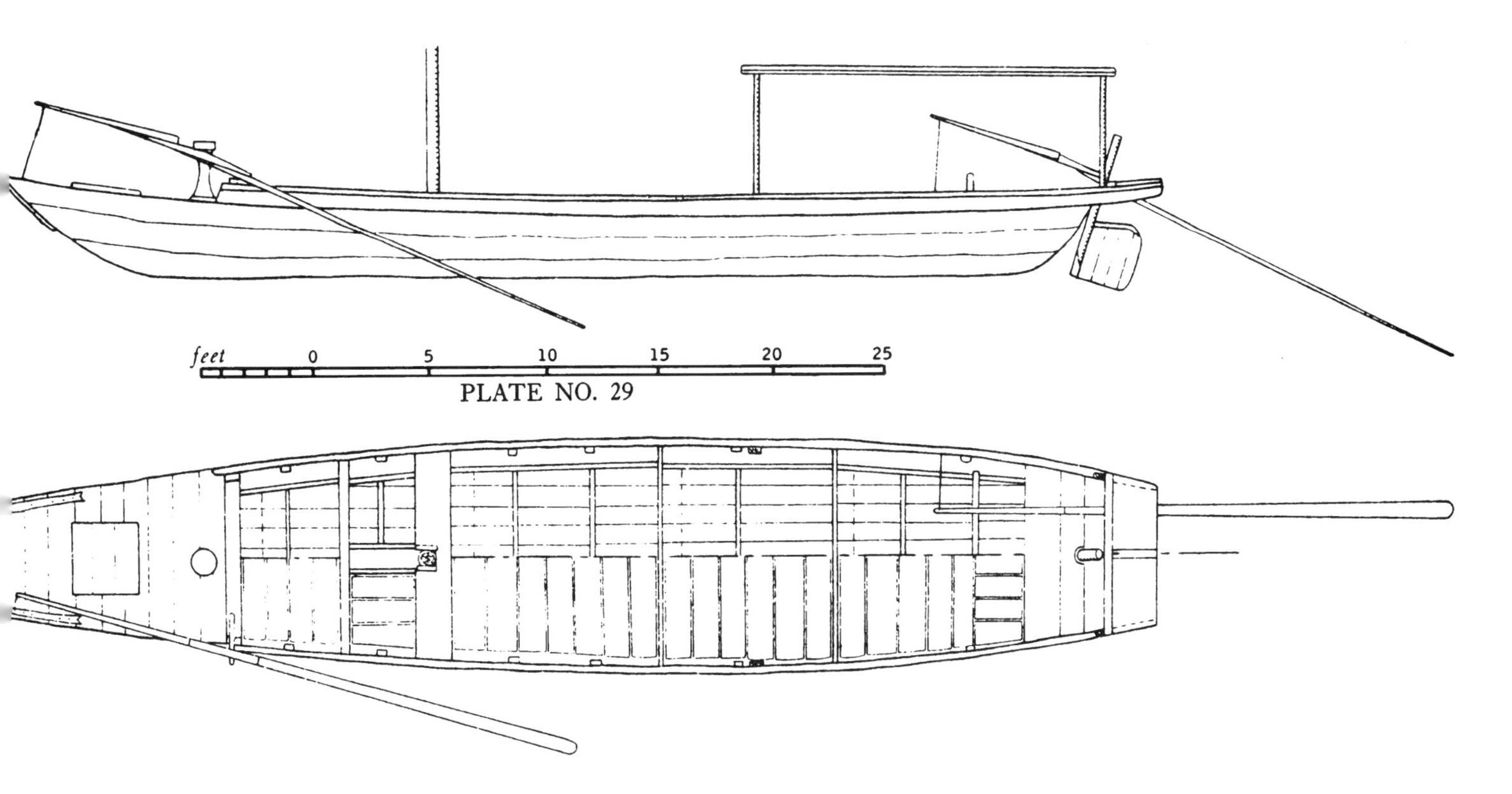

PLATE NO. 29

of their unattractive trade. Indeed, they all prepare and eat their meals on board, for there is a community galley in the sixth compartment, while in close proximity to it, in the next or last compartment of all, the buckets and bailers for the cargo are stored.

A high coaming extends aft from the capstan to the overhanging gallery in the stern, where a small, sloping rudder is fitted. The square bow is reinforced at deck level with iron strengtheners.

Propulsion is by means of a sail and a tall mast, which can be struck for passage under bridges. There are sheer-legs to accelerate the sending up of the mast when required for use. Two yulohs are used, one over the stern on the starboard side and the other on the port bow. This last operates from a bumkin situated on the foremost bulkhead.

The cargo is embarked from one of the ordure stations, of which there are as many as 37 on the Soochow Creek alone. It arrives in small decked-in handcarts—resembling a sea chest on wheels—with a primitive pipe at the fore end. This is connected to a bamboo pipe, and the cargo runs down into the waiting boat.

The men who pushed the carts in 1937 received a flat rate of $20 a month from the contractor, with a bonus according to the number of trips—over five—per day. The bonus mounted up to as much as $100 a month. In addition, a gratuity was collected on the house-to-house visits of a minimum of 50 cents per month.

A junkowner buys a book of tickets, a leaf of which he delivers up to the cart man on receipt of each cartload. This is exchanged at the ordure station for a more durable bamboo token, and after 10 days the accumulated bamboo tokens are exchanged in turn for cash.

No love is lost between the cart men and the junkmen. The former are keen business men bent on the immemorial landsman's habit—and delight—of outwitting the simple sailor.

A favourite dodge is to receive the paper ticket, which is valued at $1.42 for a cartload of night-soil, and then decamp with the cart only half empty. It must be admitted that in this case the simple sailorman is not always so simple as his brothers in the West, for, when he discovers a deficiency between the cargo received and the tickets paid out, he makes this good by the easy expedient of bailing in water from over the side.

Meanwhile the cart man has also resorted to illicit dilution and, after filling up his half-empty cart with water, delivers the contents to another unsuspecting junkowner and saves himself an extra trip.

The junkmen too, in making sure of having full measure, often overdo their extra intake over the side, with the result that their overloaded craft, on encountering any sort of sea in the Whangpoo or the wash of a passing steamer, not infrequently gets swamped, involving a most unpleasant death. A study of the profession gives one the impression that to be a success in the ordure trade of Shanghai one has to have one's wits about one.

Two trips a month are usually made by these craft, which journey as far afield as Soochow or even more distant inland centres.

There is food for thought to the fastidious in the knowledge that these boats return from the country with their three central cargo-carrying compartments filled with vegetables.

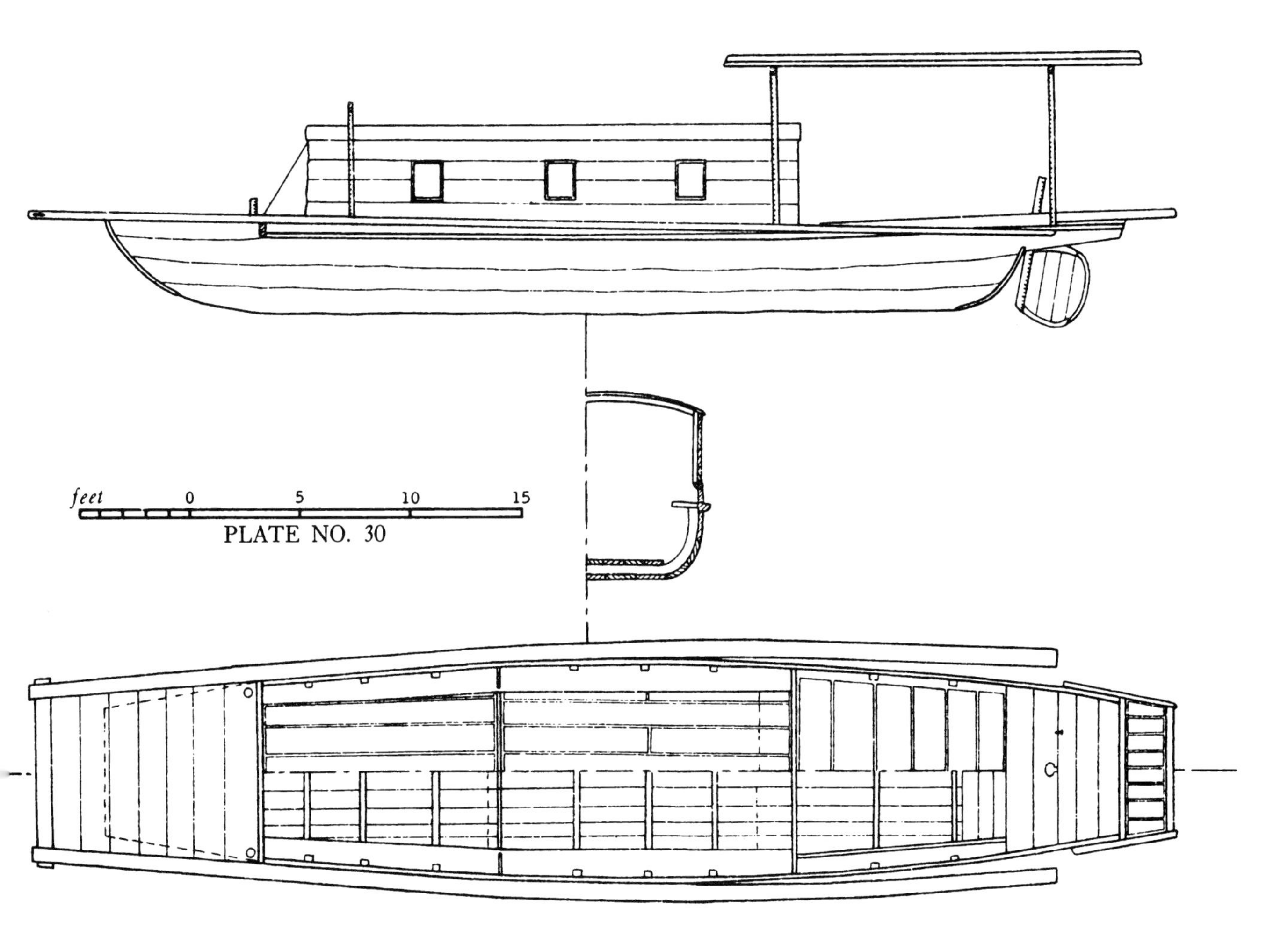

THE NEI-HO-HANG-CH'UAN OR CREEK PASSENGER-BOAT

The *nei-ho-hang-ch'uan*, which is usually built at Pootung, is to be found on any of the creeks in which there is sufficient water for it to navigate. It serves a very useful purpose in connecting the various small towns with each other and with Shanghai.

In size these craft vary from 30 feet in length, with a beam of 7 feet, up to 65 feet in length and a beam of 15 feet. The one selected for illustration in Plate No. 30 is 50 feet long and 9 feet in beam, with a depth of 4 feet.

Of necessity light in draught, they are also lightly built of *sha-mu* with one bulkhead of hardwood and 10 frames. Bow and stern are both provided with extension galleries. A narrow platform runs on either side from the bow almost the length of the junk, resting most of the way on a light wale. Shelter from the weather is provided by the standing awning and by a house disproportionately large and fitted with three sliding windows. The aft part of the junk is used as a galley. The interior of the house is free of deck planks so as to give more head room, and seating accommodation is along the ship's side. There are no bunks for such long-distance travellers as may have to spend a night or two on board banked in at the side of the creeks when night falls.

The number of passengers varies according to the amount of luggage they require transported with them. Propulsion is by the large yuloh in the stern and sometimes by tracking. The owner and his family usually act as the crew.

In normal times these craft could be hired for a few dollars a day each and were therefore much in demand by travellers of the middle class.

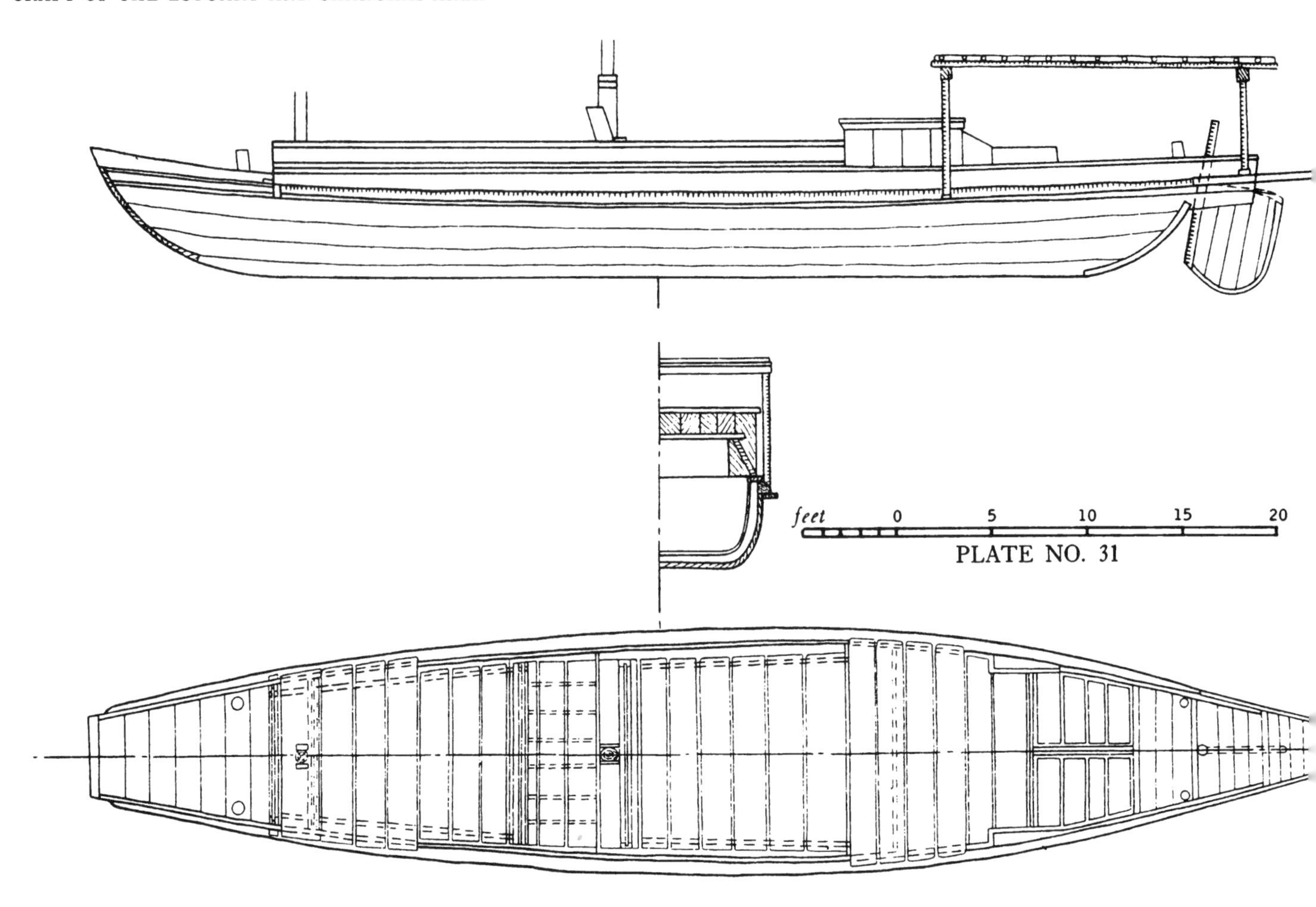

石灰船

THE SHIH-HUI-CH'UAN OR LIME-BOAT

From limestone, which is found practically throughout the country, quicklime is produced by means of heating in kilns. This industrial product is very largely used in a variety of ways, such as for mixing mortar and cement; in making bleaching powder and soap; as a fertilizer; in refining sugar; in preparing coal gas; in the preparation of leather and of various chemicals; in making glass; as a disinfectant; in metallurgical operations; and for many other purposes.

So long as lime is kept dry it is safe enough; but if it becomes wet it generates a considerable amount of heat and is liable to set fire to any adjacent combustible material.

It is therefore hardly surprising to find that a special type of junk is used exclusively for carrying this rather dangerous form of cargo. These craft are known as the *shih-hui-ch'uan*, or lime-boats, or sometimes as the *p'ing-p'êng-ch'uan* (平 棚 船), or flat-roofed boats. They are built at Luch'ü (蘆 墟), a town on the T'aihu. Another centre for building these junks is Soochow. Shanghai, which is, of course, a most profitable and practically inexhaustible market for this commodity, draws its supply chiefly from the T'aihu district, where the two important towns in the lime trade are Ch'ênmu (陳 墓) and Luch'ü (蘆 墟), south-east of Soochow. The direct route to Shanghai and that generally used is therefore down the Soochow Creek.

This craft, which measures 65 feet in length, with a beam of 12 feet, a depth of 4½ feet, and a capacity of 700 piculs, is of very strong construction, being provided with six bulkheads and eight frames. She tapers gently to bow and stern, though, by reason of the long, narrowing stern gallery, she gives the impression of even finer lines aft than she has in reality. There are two masts and square-headed lug-sails. The rudder is of the hoisting non-balance Shanghai type. Additional propulsion is effected by means of a curved yuloh operating aft on the starboard side of the stern. The crew of six live in a small house. The main interest in this type of junk lies in the insulating device used in the two cargo holds which extend from the first to the second bulkhead and from the third to the fourth bulkheads, the two holds being divided by a coffer-dam between the second and third bulkheads. These two main holds are ingeniously and inexpensively insulated by a surface covering consisting of four layers of oiled paper sandwiched between bamboo matting. The whole is nailed to the frames, which arrangement permits a current of air to circulate round and beneath the cargo of lime. The bulkheads are also covered in the same way to prevent any seepage of water.

As a further precaution against unwelcome entry of water, not only is there a high weather-boarding extending from the second frame to the house and continuing past it as far as the sixth bulkhead, but additional protection against any chance wash from passing ships is provided by a 6-inch high coaming on either side of the bow.

Despite excessive care, accidents occasionally occur, due to the cargo getting damp. It is said that one junk in the Soochow Creek recently exploded with a loud report and became a total loss, bits of wreckage being blown for some distance in all directions.

THE KOMPO FLOATING DWELLING

The Kiangpei, or, more popularly, "Kompo floating dwellings," may be built up on any type of junk or sampan which is past its normal work, they can therefore be of any size. That illustrated in Plate No. 32 measures 42 feet, with a beam of 8 feet and a depth of 3½ feet. The Kompo floating dwellings may be described as the aristocrats of their class, for, although the craft of the Yangtze are usually considerably larger, those of the Whangpoo are more comfortable, and the style of living is better.

Anything unfamiliar or of uncertain origin is liable to be termed "Kompo." See the Kompo boat on page 220.

The element of over-crowding is, however, still present. Eight people in a small floating dwelling is not uncommon; and usually there are many more, including grandparents, father and mother, possibly an uncle and aunt and two or three children, and almost invariably a baby. The latter is tied to its mother's back. Pigs, dogs, and hens add congestion to the small available space. However many children there are, all seem to be wanted, for the parents fit them out with a sort of life-belt made from bamboo, which is attached to any convenient hold-fast by a short piece of rope, so that if a child falls overboard it can be readily hauled back. Some parents add a bell to the life-saving device, which accelerates salvage operations considerably.

Although the standard of cleanliness is, perforce, not high, the women on board seem to spend most of their time washing clothes, since they can obtain an unlimited supply of water from over the side, which is not often the case on shore.

These boats are not necessarily inhabited by junk folk, but very often by ordinary working-class families who cannot afford to pay the high rents obtaining

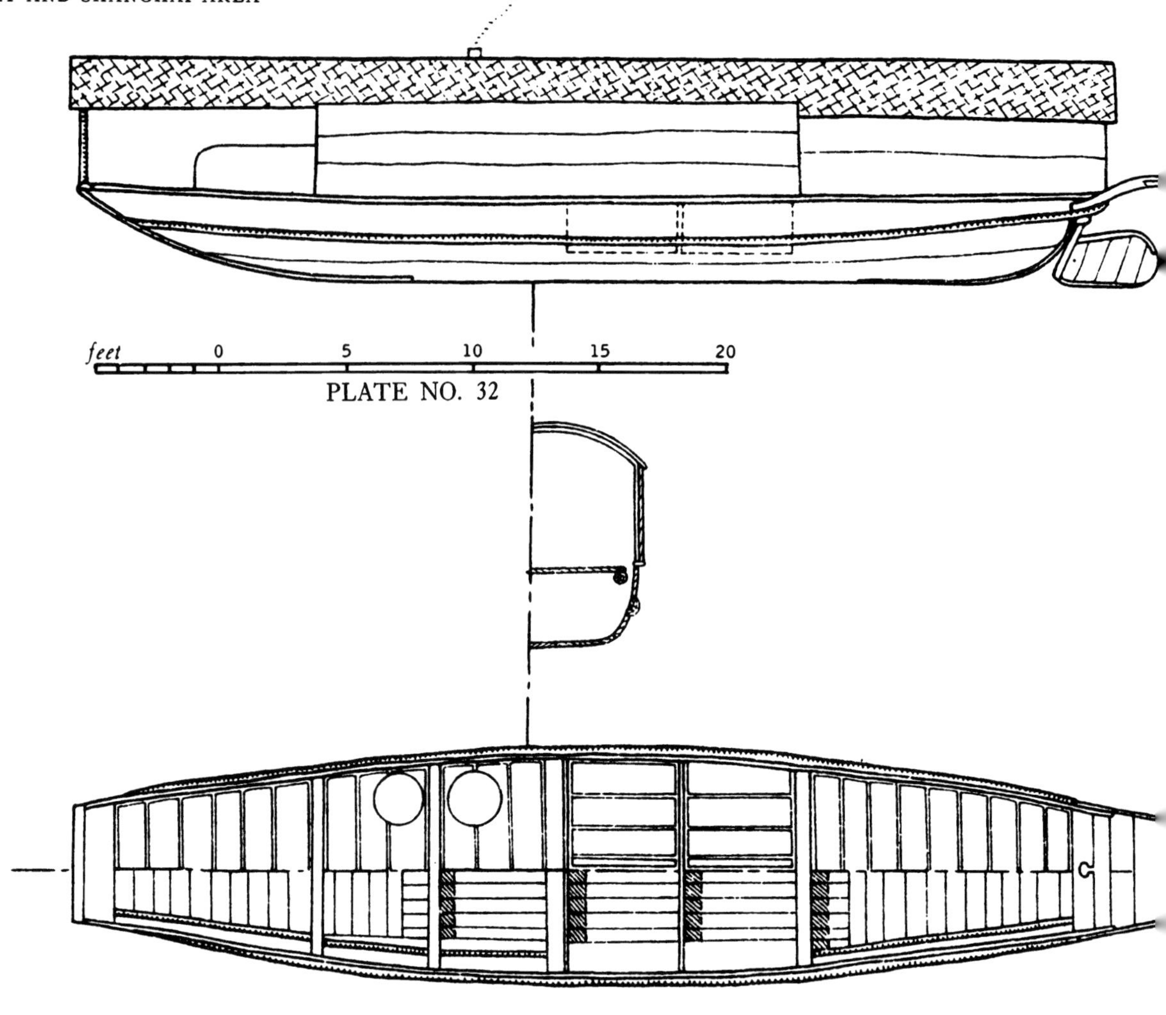

PLATE NO. 32

ashore. Hardworking factory workers, ricsha coolies, and the like find peace—if not quiet—surrounded by their families, who have probably been out all day on the equally tiring duty of peddling small articles in the streets or rummaging in the rubbish heaps for inconsiderable but welcome trifles. Much of the fuel for cooking is obtained in this way. The cramped living quarters may be dark and dreary, but the galley, or kitchen, the most important part of the boat, is kept bright, so that, as it is said, the kitchen god may see the good points of the family.

The kitchen god, to whom an altar is dedicated above the stove, ascends to heaven annually on the 24th day of the 12th moon to report on the behaviour of the family. On this day he receives offerings of rice and sweets to make his lips sticky and his mouth sweet, so that he may be prevented from repeating any of the bad deeds of the family.

The boat-houses of China are of very ancient origin. It is interesting to note that the Dominican Friar John de Cora,* writing about 1330, says:

> A good half of the realm of Cathay and its territory is water. And on these waters dwell great multitudes of people because of the vast population that there is in the said realm. They build wooden houses upon boats, and so their houses go up and down with the waters; and the people go trafficking in their houses from one province to another; whilst they dwell in these houses with all their families, with their wives and children, and all their household utensils and necessities. And so they live upon the waters all the days of their life . . . And if you ask of these folk where they were born ? they can reply nought else that they were born upon the waters, as I told you.

When their boats become unseaworthy they are still considered landworthy and are transformed into houses by being set bodily upon four stones above the reach of the water.

* Quoted by Yule: "Cathay, and the Way Thither."

THE FOREIGN-TYPE HOUSE-BOAT

There are two types of house-boats, the Chinese house-boat proper and the foreign adaptation thereof, known as the *wusih-k'uai*, or Wusih fast-boat, after a town of that name on the Grand Canal, where they are usually built.

The latter type of house-boat, selected for illustration in Plate No. 33, is on generous lines, being 67 feet in length, with a beam of 14 feet and a depth of 4 feet. As there is no great weight or strain involved, the hull is not outstandingly strong, and three full bulkheads and 14 half-frames are ample for strengthening purposes.

The unusual features in construction are the wide, square, overhanging bow in conjunction with the tapering, narrow stern. The latter ends in the usual Shanghai type of winged stern gallery, which is decked in and encloses the upper part of the Shanghai-type hoisting rudder, beyond which it projects as a flat platform extending far beyond the stern. The bow is also fitted with a small projecting platform. Two long planks run the length of the boat on either side for the quanters. These quanting gangways do not follow the tapering lines of the stern from the second bulkhead aft but diverge to form a square outline. The house, which occupies the whole central space between the first and second bulkheads, is elaborately made with two rows of removable windows, of which the upper ones are fixed while the lower ones tip outwards if required. Three steps down from the after deck give access to the house-boat down an alleyway with three cabins on the port side. In the saloon there is a divan with a table to seat eight persons, though there is actual bunk accommodation for only five passengers,

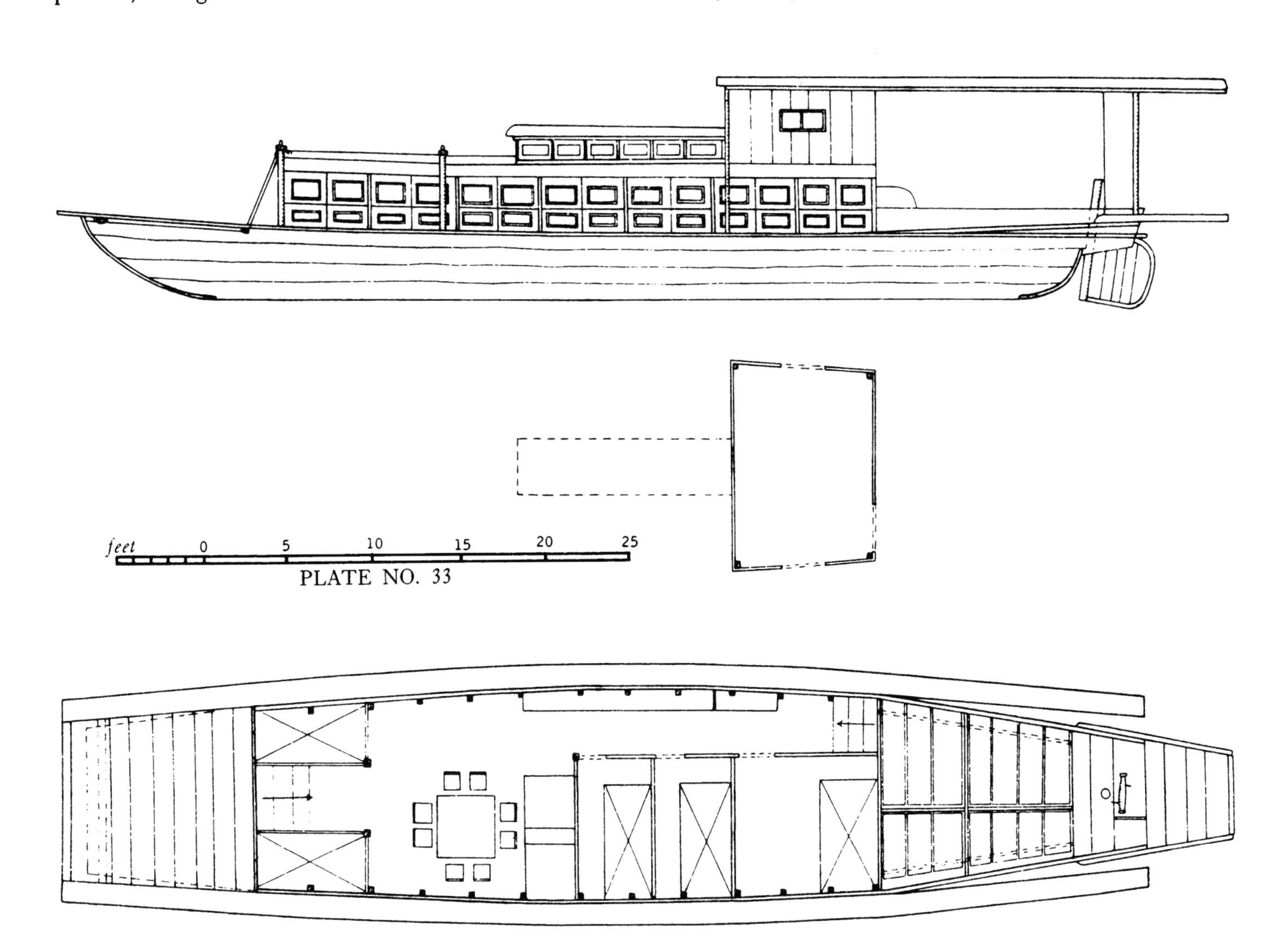

PLATE NO. 33

including two servants, whose bunks are forward on either side of the three steps up to the fore deck.

The owner, who hires out the junk, lives in the upper cabin, while the large crew of eight find what shelter they can aft under such protection as is afforded by the wooden standing awning and the weather-boards. The galley is aft, below decks.

A noticeable feature of all these house-boats of whatever size is in the odd sloping lines of the front of the house, including the doorway, as it rises from the fore deck. A completely Western introduction is the skylight extending along one-half the roof—probably due to the foreign mania for fresh air.

These house-boats may be, and often were, very luxuriously fitted up, yet they could formerly be hired complete with crew for about $5 a day, while the total daily expenses of such an outing would not exceed $12 daily. A Chinese-style house-boat could be hired for much less.

In the far-off days when Shanghai society drove down the tow-path that is now the Bund and the ladies wore bustle skirts, possibly the house-boat was nothing more than the Shanghai *ma-t'ou-ch'uan*, or wharf-boat.

The *ma-t'ou-ch'uan*, page 200.

Gradually the Western desire for comfort and speed were incorporated under foreign direction by the Chinese junk carpenters accustomed to build the majestic boats used to transport the Imperial officials on their tours of inspection.

The *man-kiang-hung*, described on page 424.

The Wusih type of house-boat is a direct descendant of the official boat described in Part Three. The latter has, unfortunately, ceased to exist, and the house-boat is now threatened with extinction. She will, however, long be remembered, for she has been immortalized in J. O. P. Bland's classic "House-boat Days in China." In the pages of that well-known book she lives again, so aptly described as the "embodiment of European ideas adapted to Chinese ways and byways, ideas of accommodation, water craft, and common humanity."

Time there was when not only the members of the "princely hongs" but nearly all Shanghai sportsmen owned house-boats and would make their way up the Soochow Creek to the happy hunting-grounds on the T'aihu, and indeed as far afield up the great river as Wuhu, that paradise for small game; and the compensation for accidentally-bagged larger game, such as a farmer peppered by mistake, was only a bottle of beer.

In the early days the house-boat was tracked up stream by four to six men, but later on the trackers could not be procured and it became customary to join up in a boat-train towed by a small Chinese launch with a laodah and crew of three to six men. The boat-trains left for Soochow, Wusih, Huchow, and Chinsa, the launch towing up as many as six craft. A ticket for a foreign-type house-boat to be towed to Soochow could be bought for $10 in 1913. For Easter and special holiday seasons space in the boat-train had to be booked well ahead. Leaving Shanghai at 4 p.m., the launch would steam all night and arrive at Soochow at 8 p.m. the next day. The return journey would be so timed as to return the holiday-maker in time to go to the office in the morning.

Conditions, however, have changed. The shooting-grounds of Kiangsu to-day are not what they were in the days so charmingly written of by Wade and Bland and Sowerby. The sportsman has farther to travel. The high cost of living and the increase in wages and materials have gradually reduced the number of house-boats, and the unsettled political conditions of the past difficult years have sounded their knell. The few that remain may now be seen on the Soochow Creek, being used as crowded living quarters or makeshift offices, and are gradually falling to pieces.

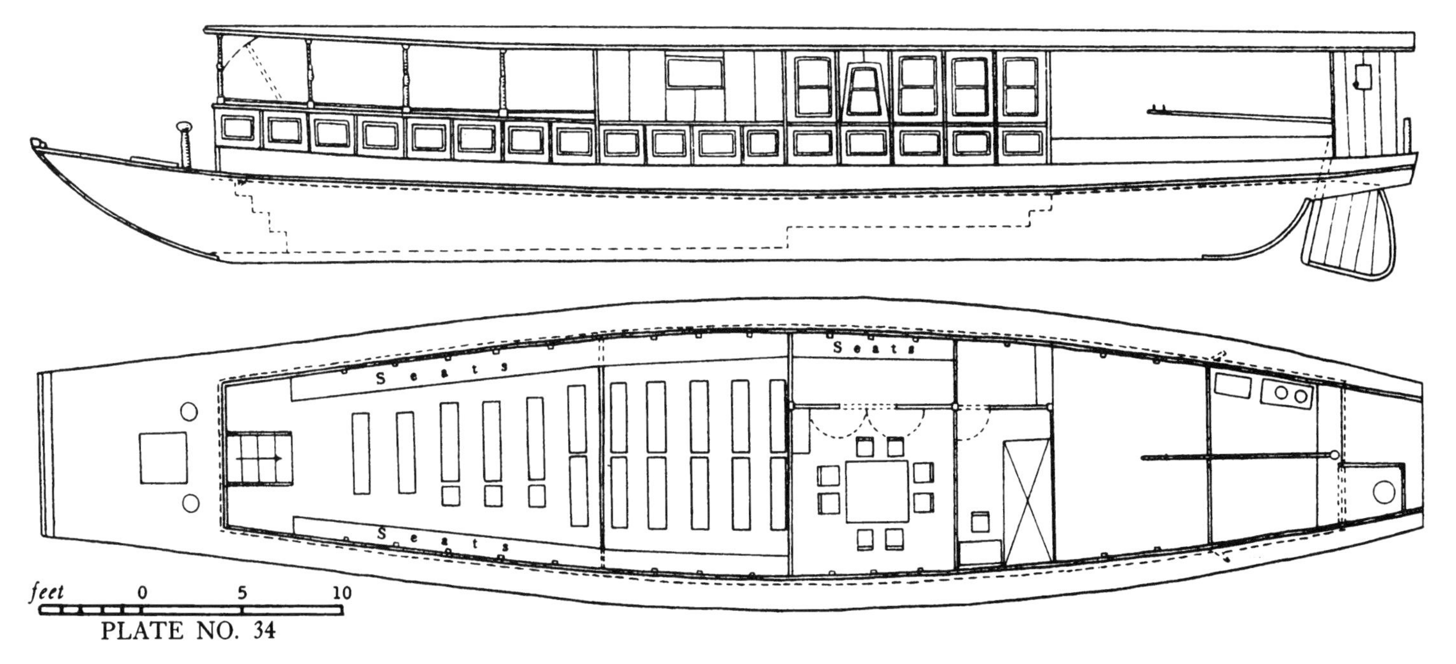

PLATE NO. 34

THE T'O-CH'UAN OR BOAT-TRAIN

拖船

The *t'o-ch'uan*, or, as it is known to the foreigners of Shanghai, the "boat-train," takes its name from the word *t'o* (拖), which oddly enough has exactly the same significance in Chinese as "tow" in English.

Built at Shanghai, these passenger-craft operate up the Soochow Creek and also up the Whangpoo, penetrating as far afield as into Chekiang Province. They are, however, most largely used for intercommunication between the T'aihu ports.

The size of these craft is more or less standard, but there are large differences in detail of fittings and superstructure. In the interests of increased accommodation and consequently higher return on capital outlay, some boat-owners take greater liberties with stability.

The craft represented in Plate No. 34 measures 68 feet, with a beam of 13½ feet and a depth of 4½ feet. As will be seen, she is nothing more or less than a house-boat. She is very stoutly built in order to stand up to the weight of 200 passengers with their not inconsiderable luggage, which can be, and usually is, carried; for, although there are only two bulkheads and three half-bulkheads, there are no less than 15 closely-spaced full frames affording the necessary strength.

The rudder is of the Shanghai non-balance hoisting variety. There is no mast or sail, and progress is dependent entirely on a towing launch. The towing wire runs under the fender gangway, under the counter, right round the length of the boat, and finally up through two holes on the forecastle, where two towing-hooks are situated. It is said that this method of towing prevents hogging.

A pair of oars can operate from two thole-pins aft on the last half-bulkhead. These are used only for manœuvring when the boat has cast off from the towing launch.

In former days much more attempt was made to provide comfort for the passengers, and there was often a certain number of cabins. The bunks consisted of flat wooden shelves less than 30 inches wide, without any rail or front and separated from the next bunk or shelf by a partition head-board 6 inches high. The travellers brought their own bedding. The cabins had each a small table for meals. A lamp set in the opening in the partition would light two cabins.

The top deck portion above the cabins was roofed with an awning and divided crosswise into two lines of bunks. Here the less wealthy spread their beds and slept head to head, divided from each other by a 6-inch high head-board. The awning was just high enough to permit a passenger to sit upright. The ventilation, it is needless to add, was ample, but privacy did not exist. Forty years ago such a passage to Soochow cost 25 cents, while a cabin could be obtained for $1.

For the most part the boat-trains were patronized by the poorer classes, for a small private boat could always be engaged at a very low figure. The company on board now, as then, is not of the most select order but is characterized by an abounding and uncomplaining good humour.

Meals were served free as a matter of course to all classes of passenger, and at frequent intervals a tea-boy walked the deck with hot water for everybody to have an extra cup of tea.

Such happy conditions have long since ceased to exist. The comparatively spacious cabins have been sacrificed so as to accommodate up to 200 passengers, of which 60 are on the upper deck and 140 elsewhere. Free meals are no longer provided. Meals of a sort can be had at a price, and tea and even plain hot water are also sold at a very handsome profit. The latter is heated on a special tea stove on the starboard side of the after deck. Below the main deck is the galley proper for the use of the owner, his family, and the crew, or anyone rash or rich enough to incur the expense of an ordered meal.

The one remaining cabin is reserved for the family of the owner and himself. He steers the vessel, for he is laodah and owner, and hires his craft out to the launch company who arrange for the towage.

The ship's complement consists of two deck-hands,* two ticket collectors, and two tea-boys. They all live in the baggage-room, where they camp out in apparent comfort on the passengers' boxes and bundles.

The normal passenger traffic between Shanghai and the outlying ports is very heavy. Various companies operate their boat-trains of large house-boats, each towed by a launch. Occasionally a launch will tow a second boat, though this practice is not at all general as it is on the Middle Yangtze.

However many are scheduled to leave daily, they are always full. Their daily departures are controlled by the Police Regulations. The Hangchow boat-train leaves Shanghai daily at 4.30 p.m. and reaches its destination at 5.30 the next afternoon, taking 25 hours to cover the distance of 117 miles. They tie up at nightfall and proceed again before dawn.

The Soochow boat-train leaves in the afternoon. Nothing could more strongly demonstrate the activity of the Chinese internal traffic than the number of these boat-trains, always consistently crowded, which in normal times continually navigate the creeks and canals of the vast hinterland behind Shanghai.

The departure of one of these trains from the Soochow Creek is well worth watching. It is rich in human interest and presents an unrivalled scene of confusion. Hawkers, coolies, loafers, and tea-boys crowd round the prospective passengers and offer free advice or highly-priced service. Everyone seems to be struggling with one or more pieces of unhandy luggage. But the chief interest centres in the mass of craft of all kinds with which the creek appears to be completely blocked, so that the question occurs, how did the boat-train worm its way in among this congestion of junks, sampans, launches, and pontoons; and, having got there, how will it ever extricate itself?

* Large numbers of Chinese sailors belonging to these boats are Roman Catholics, particularly the laodahs, whose loyalty to their foreign co-religionists prompted them to act with courage and devotion towards them even during the Chinese war with France in 1884–85.

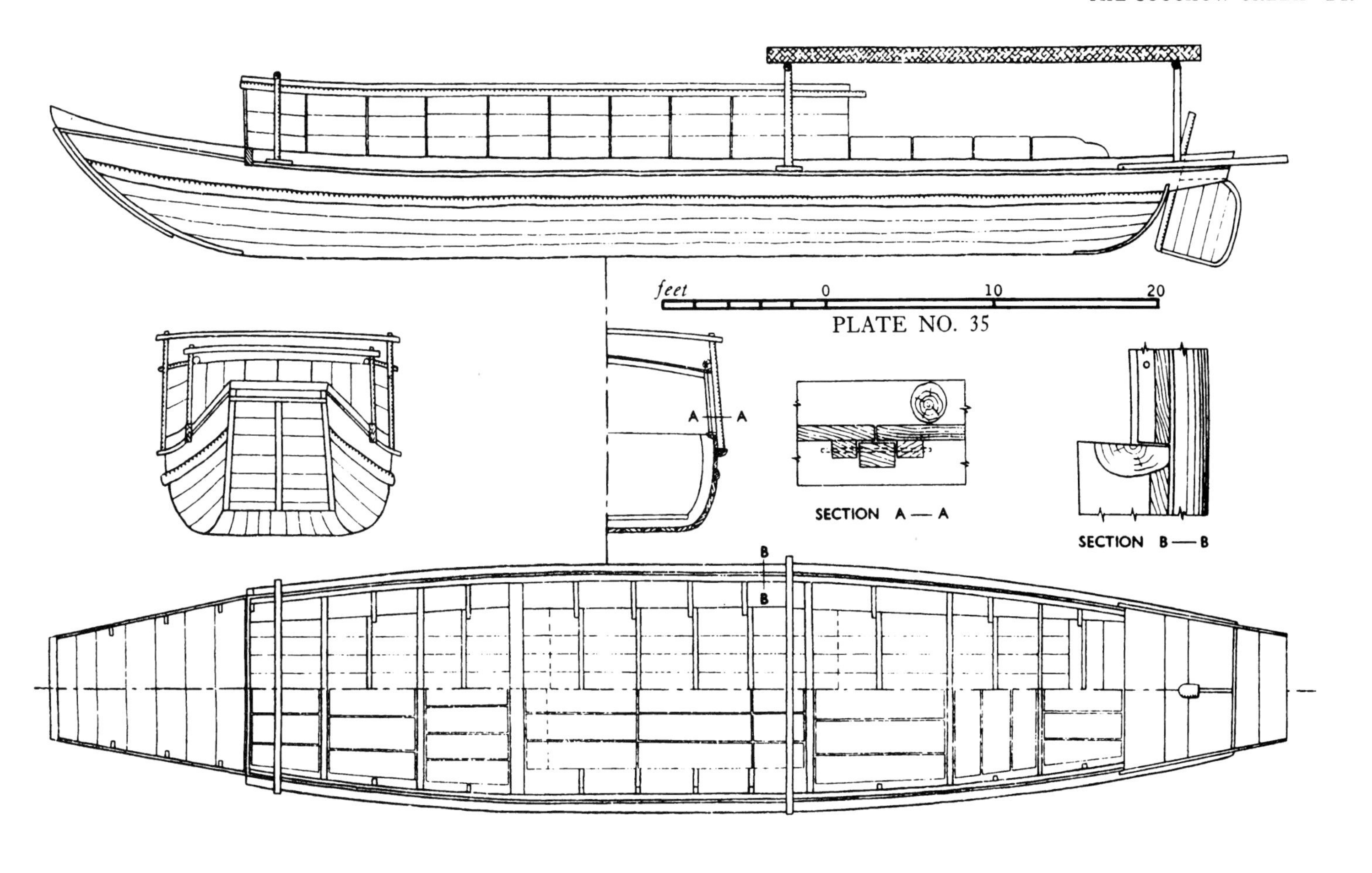

PLATE NO. 35

THE HSICHUANG-CH'UAN OR TOWED CARGO-BOAT

The *hsichuang-ch'uan*, called after a village of that name, is built at Wusih, a town on the Grand Canal situated at its junction with the Tsaoho, which joins the Yangtze at Kiangyin.

Just as the *t'o-ch'uan*, or boat-train, just described, is the towed passenger-boat, so this craft is the towed cargo-carrier on very much the same creek routes.

There are no outstanding points of interest in the general design (as illustrated in Plate No. 35), which represents what is in effect a decked-in lighter. Made of *sha-mu*, with the usual hardwood frames, of which there are 13, and six bulkheads, the usual measurements are 73 feet in length, 14 feet beam, and 5½ feet in depth. She shows three of the main Shanghai characteristics, namely, the overhanging stern gallery, the standing wooden awning, and horizontal bow planking. The rudder, also typical of Shanghai, is of the hoisting non-balance variety. Two long poles are slung along the ship's side just above the water to act as fenders. The only detail in the construction worthy of mention is the method of securing the removable house by means of iron pins engaging in the opposing portions of woodwork (see inset plans on Plate No. 35). The extra large house measures 36 feet in length and 4 feet in height, and is roofed with matting, the sides being continued aft by lower wash-boards. The house, which is divided into quarters for the crew of six between the first and fourth bulkheads and the owner's cabin from the fifth to the sixth bulkheads, is cramped for head room, as it is decked throughout. The after portion from the last bulkhead to the stern is used as galley and is then kept free from deck-boards. There are no masts, sails, or lee-boards, and even no yulohs, for these craft rely entirely on being towed by a launch and thereby lose much of their interest. The carrying capacity is 56 tons, and the cargo carried to Shanghai is usually grain in bags.

THE FERRY

According to Mr. Worcester's notation, no plans were available or necessary for the following types. The information in some cases relates to craft obsolete at the time of writing.

The earliest types of craft to be made must undoubtedly have been to serve as ferries; for man has always been filled with the desire to get to the other side of the water.

As ferries in the Far East are usually of the simplest construction, there seems good reason to presume that they have mostly preserved their ancient form more or less unchanged.

Ferry craft figure very often in ancient Chinese history and literature, and although these references are no help as regards scientific research or in tracing the origin of existing types, they are of sufficient general and historic interest to be included here.

One of the earliest known of these references is in the "Shih Ching," (詩 經), an anthology said to have been compiled by Confucius. It occurs in a poem, "Ku Feng," by an unknown writer in the year A.D. 1100. It says:

"To cross a deep river you may use either boats or *fang*." (就其深矣方之舟之)

These alternatives are further explained in an ancient dictionary, the "Erh Ya" (爾 雅), which probably dates back to the second century B.C.

Apparently in those days the manner of a man's crossing the river was entirely dependent upon his rank in life. The humble peasant got across by the tedious *fu* (浮), or raft. The literati were honoured by being given transport in a *t'ê-chou* (特 舟), or special boat, *chou* being the ancient equivalent of the modern *ch'uan* (船).

Next in the social scale came the officials, who were provided with two boats lashed together and called *fang-chou* (方 舟). The lords and barons used the *wei-chou* (維 舟), meaning four boats lashed together, while the Emperor himself, if he desired to cross a river, did so over a pontoon bridge known as a *ts'ao-chou* (造 舟).

When a fee is normally charged, beggars are allowed free transit. The custom of the delta, however, is that the owner of a ferry need take only one beggar at a time, who must not sit beneath the mat-house when such is provided. The indulgence which the proprietors of ferry-boats show towards beggars is regarded by the Buddhists as highly meritorious.

Ferries in so well-watered an area as the Shanghai delta are extremely numerous, especially on the wider waterways where bridges are comparatively few. Any village without a bridge over its adjacent creek almost invariably runs its own ferry service.

The ferry services between Shanghai and Pootung are very highly organized. They consist of separate fleets which operate in strictly prescribed sections from various wharves, each being under a central control which enforces the unwritten law of the Whangpoo.

Entry amongst the ranks of the ferrymen is not easily effected, and once admitted to one section, they cannot transfer to another without a good deal of trouble. There is always a long waiting list of applicants to join each fleet or section, and the new-comer, complete with family, has to pay "key money" for the job by taking on his predecessor's boat.

The main objective of the controlling bodies is to provide a living for as many persons as possible, and the number of boats allowed to operate is so adapted to the traffic as to secure sufficient remuneration to feed a family. To achieve this end various means are resorted to, the most astonishing being the pact whereby ferries carry passengers only one way and return light so as not to prejudice the custom of their opposite numbers—the ferries on the other bank of the river.

All the boats load passengers in strict rotation and carry only a fixed number. A certain amount of cheating does obtain, and if a big row on the waterfront is in progress it is usually because someone has been discovered crossing out of turn or carrying a passenger more than allowed.

The ferry-boats are each manned by any number up to four men or, more often, women. When plying for hire the large and small sampans lie close to each other, and at suitable vantage points runners are stationed to direct the flow of passengers to the advantage of the ferry-boats. Space being at a premium, the runners endeavour to persuade the carriers of light luggage to enter their own boats, while deftly directing those with bulky possessions to enter the boat of a competitor. A passenger with a baby lashed to her back and carrying a small, delicate piece of pork on the end of a string is greatly to be preferred from a stowage point of view to one who insists on embarking a full-sized paper chest of drawers to be burnt for the use of a departed ancestor in the next world.

The bicycle has become the universal means of transporting every form of commodity from milk to coal in ingenious side-carriers devised from kerosene tins; it is hardly surprising, therefore, that these new-fangled machines should be charged for in the ferry as a single person.

In fine weather and foul, in the heat of the summer and the depths of winter, the Shanghai ferry service continues to operate uninterruptedly and provides quite an education to any sailor in the correct handling of boats.

About 2 miles farther down the Whangpoo another ferry service runs from the Asiatic Petroleum Company's wharf to the Shanghai side. Formerly 3 coppers was the fare charged per person, but later the cost, like everything else, rose as high as 10 cents in the rush hour. At other times the charge is from 15 to 20 cents, according to the time of day. To-day the price runs into astronomical figures. The ferry is for the convenience of the factory girls and does a very thriving trade.

At certain times of the day the boats are so liable to be over-crowded that regulations are enforced by the Customs Harbour Police limiting the number of persons to be carried at one time to 34 in the small boats and 67 in the large ones. The mill girls are forced to sit down in the boat and take other sailor-like precautions. The crew consists of three men, and the trip across the river occupies half an hour or more.

Left to themselves, the sampanmen would load their boats down to the gunwale without regard to safety, and in the interests of economy or of the saving of a few minutes of time, the passengers would accept the risk. Regulations are therefore enforced by the Customs Harbour Police limiting the number of persons that may be carried to eight for the Lannitu sampan, 10 and 20 for the small and large Woosung sampans respectively, 20 for the square sampan, and six for the Harbour sampans.

Ferries, of course, vary very largely in size and capacity, from the large boats capable of carrying 40 and more passengers, 10 wheelbarrows, and several water buffaloes, to the smaller boats for foot passengers only, or sampans which hold half a dozen or so people.

There are, of course, no special sampans built solely for the purpose of ferrying. Any type may be pressed into service, and it is not unusual to see even small cargo-boats engaged in the trade.

Ferries in the Shanghai Harbour, however, are nearly always served by either the Lannitu or, sometimes, the *fang-t'ou* type of sampan. As the latter are ordinarily used for cargo and have three times the carrying capacity of the former, they run in accordance with the number of passengers embarked, that is to say, the one with the smaller capacity puts in a larger number of trips. The Lannitu and Woosung *fang-t'ou* sampans may be said on the whole to do more organized ferry work in the Whangpoo than any other type.

THE MEETING-BOAT

The "meeting-boat," as it is called, is used only on the few brief occasions when it plays its part in the ritual of a peasant wedding ceremony in and around the Soochow area and also on the Soochow Creek after it leaves the populous suburbs of Shanghai.

In the absence of any reliable information about the boat itself no statement can be made as to its type. It seems, however, not unlikely that no particular class of boat is used for this office, but that any handy available craft is pressed into service for the purpose. One thing seems to be fairly clear, that this interesting custom is confined purely to the region mentioned.

The meeting-boat is used to convey the bridegroom to his prospective father-in-law's home to meet his bride and bring her home.

Innumerable rules are laid down as to the bridegroom's behaviour under the ordeal of facing the lady's relatives, who are often very numerous and usually appear rather unfriendly. He is required to adopt a humble and modest air, and is prompted by experts in etiquette who accompany him. Any major mistake on his part may cause the whole affair to be postponed.

The ceremony may last throughout the night. The final scene is when the bride makes a great show of reluctance and tears at leaving her ancestral home.

Then follows the ritual known as "throwing the bride," when her father puts her into the bridal sedan-chair in the meeting-boat. After this the bridegroom's party leaves and, once clear of the village, starts up the music of gongs and flutes as they journey back to the bridegroom's home.

THE PEDLAR'S BOAT

The pedlar's boat is a genuine name describing a form of traffic or industry, for no special type of craft is built or exclusively used in this activity, which may be carried out by any variety of small suitable boat. The Lannitu sampan is perhaps the most commonly used.

In a district so intersected by waterways, which are still the main highways for the country people of the Shanghai hinterland, it follows logically that salesmen should peddle their wares in boats, and they do a thriving trade in the outlying villages. The busy housewife who has little time or money to spare for outings to the nearest town is a constant customer for the stock-in-trade of the pedlar's boat, which includes candles, matches, sweets, paper, cigarettes, and various religious articles such as paper money, incense sticks, and crackers.

Bargaining is usually carried out not by offering a lower price but by demanding more for the sum stated.

Each pedlar's boat has its own beat comprising several villages, the distance being decided by the time it takes to do the round and the profit to be gained therefrom.

These craft also do a brisk trade in the Shanghai Harbour, where they may be seen peddling their goods round the junks. In the case of selling foodstuffs, a boat usually sells one variety alone. For instance, one sampan will sell meat only, while another deals exclusively in vegetables.

As has been pointed out elsewhere in this book, the water-borne population of Shanghai goes ashore as little as possible, and these small floating shops therefore more than justify their existence.

THE POST-BOAT

The plan of introducing a postal service on Western lines very early found a place among the constructive ideas in Sir Robert Hart's mind. As early as 1861 he made the suggestion to Li Hung-chang, but he had to wait 30 years for the scheme to mature and develop into the National Post Office as he had visualized it.*

Sir Robert Hart was the Inspector General of the Chinese Customs Service. The Chinese postal system was organized and administered for many years by the Customs.

Previous to this, of course, the Chinese, like other civilizations, such as the Egyptians, the Assyrians, the Persians, and the Arabs, had very early in their history installed a system of Government posts known in China as the I Chan (驛站), or couriers, said to date back to the Chou dynasty, 1122–255 B.C.

We have no very clear description of this postal system in China until the thirteenth century, when a most efficient overland organization was maintained under Genghis Khan whereby a direct and uninterrupted service was maintained over various parts of China. A vivid picture of these posts was given by Marco Polo. There were two types of courier service: overland by means of horses or post chariots, and by water in boats.

Post-boats, though they must have been in use in China from very early times, make their appearance in history only under the T'ang dynasty (唐朝), A.D. 618–907, but that they were very extensively used is incontestable. To come to more modern times, until the advent of steamers in China the principal method of transmitting correspondence for foreigners and Chinese alike was by means of couriers and boats.

Deservedly famous among the latter and much used as post-boats were the *chiao-hua-ch'uan* (脚划船), or foot-paddling boats, which were gaily painted, both inside and out, with elaborate scenes of Chinese life. The propulsion was effected by foot and not hand power. These sampans, which during the last decade or so have completely vanished off the face of China's waterways, were built on long, slender lines. Judging from photographs, they must have measured somewhere in the neighbourhood of 25 feet in length. There was a large house amidships, occupying most of the boat.

The novel form of rowing was carried out by the sampanman-owner, who sat in the stern against a back rest and with both feet manipulated the single oar

* The well-known device of the flying goose used on the postal flag, and which figured on some of the earlier stamps, owes its origin to the fact that fish and geese passing to and fro mean epistolary communications. The Governor of Yuchang, in Kiangsi, during the first century B.C., used to throw his letters into the river to be carried with the stream or by the fish. Su Wu (蘇武), of the same period, tied a letter to the leg of a goose.

The chiao-hua-ch'uan, or foot-paddling boat.

on the starboard side. The oar was made in two parts, and seems to have been about 8 feet long, with a short loom and long, broad blade. The inboard end of the loom was fitted with a solid wooden pedal, and on this the left foot rested, providing the main motive power. The right foot grasped the loom with similar dexterity and drew it back to the body. The feathering was actually done by both feet. Both hands were thus left free to use the paddle, with which the oarsman steered, holding it under his left arm. By this means he could, with his single oar, make the sampan travel twice as fast as any other type and with apparently the minimum exertion. So expert did these men become that, while rowing, they could cook, eat, smoke, or play the flute without relaxing speed. An additional standard fitting was the paper umbrella stepped in the after beam of the transom. These craft were so fast that they made record passages on the routes they served. In addition, the very light draught enabled them to negotiate the shallow canals and creeks denied to other craft, which made them in still greater demand, for they could convey letters to otherwise inaccessible towns and villages and moreover take a chance with cross-country short cuts. This was not in any way a Government enterprise. Mails were carried for the Hsin Chü (信 局), or letter-hongs, and later, when it was inaugurated, for the Express Letter Service. The fact that they were used to transport silver caused them to be frequently robbed, but by means of a system of insurance the senders were, in such an event, indemnified to the full amount. If a bank draft was sent, the amount was inscribed on the outside of the envelope; and, in return for double postage, the Post Service undertook to pay compensation for the loss of the sum involved. The mail service between Shanghai and Hangchow was both regular and reliable, with two deliveries and two collections per day.

Although these novel craft are now, unhappily, obsolete in the Shanghai area, there is a type of similarly-propelled speed-boat still in use on the canals of Eastern Chekiang. They are used for swift passenger transport, and will carry four persons with light luggage.

While on the subject of the Postal Service of China it seems relevant here to mention postage stamps.

Although the literati of China have so neglected the important subject of junks, yet, happily, almost from the beginning of modern postal organization of China the junk has figured pictorially on the stamps of the country they have served so well.

Mr. Archibald Little was determined to be the first to navigate the Upper Yangtze by steamer. See "The Coming of the Steamer," Part One, pages 148–53.

The first stamp to carry the junk as a motif in the design of a postage stamp was in 1893 and came from Chungking. To Mr. Archibald Little belongs the credit for having taken the initiative in establishing a local post. The rapids and races of the Upper Yangtze, the only highway to Szechwan, did not lend themselves to such a scheme, and the mails had to be carried by fast post-boats which took five days down and 17 upward bound.

The Chungking design, value 2 candareens, was engraved and printed by Messrs. Kelly & Walsh in Shanghai, and shows a sampan of the type familiar on the Lower Yangtze, under very doubtful circumstances below the pagoda on the left bank of the river.

The next stamp to incorporate the junk as part of its design was the 24-cent rose red in the commemorative issue of H.I.M. the Empress Dowager in 1894. This is a very well-balanced design and shows a well-drawn and accurate sea-going junk of the Ningpo type.

Not satisfied with the chop "paid" which had hitherto been used on all correspondence, the Municipality of Chinkiang, under the chairmanship of the British Consul, issued a set of local stamps. Much artistic licence has been taken with this design, which shows an incredibly large sampan down-bound passing Golden Island. The issue was lithographed and printed in Shanghai in 1894.

In 1895 the foreign residents of Foochow decided to establish a local post. Many designs were submitted, and the final decision was to place an order with Messrs. Waterloo & Sons, London. The set, which consisted of values from ½-cent blue to 40-cent red-brown, is admirably engraved and printed, and is probably the most attractive, to foreign eyes at least, of the Chinese designs. It has additional charm in that it is completely accurate, and shows a "dragon" boat with an attractive background.

Perhaps the best known and the most artistically satisfying as well as the longest in circulation was the junk and reaper design which remained in current issue—albeit with slight modifications—from 1913 to 1933. It is a great pity that this charming stamp should have been marred by the many inaccuracies which appear in the junk—which purports to be a Kiangsu trader.

The thrift issue of 1941, printed in Hongkong, is, artistically, far behind any of the other designs of the series, and although it does include two small junks and a lightship amid a holocaust of modern inventions, the junks are too small to be worthy representations of China's first merchant navy.

THE AGENT-BOAT

The agent-boat must not be confused with the pedlar's boat, but fulfils rather the function of a carrier-cart in European country districts. It plays a large part in village economy, for it offers a free daily service to all the regions of the hinterland of Shanghai, being especially prevalent round the T'aihu.

In the absence of any authentic information as to the type of craft used, it may be surmised that, as with the meeting and pedlar's boats, any sort of suitable boat may be used. In this case a rather large sampan would be the most serviceable, and the evidence would appear to be more in favour of using the country-boat than any other type.

An agent-boat is run not only by each village, but even by separate sections of a large village, and the owners of the various craft are on friendly competitive terms. Early every morning each boat moves slowly down stream, collecting orders from the neighbours in the shape of wine or oil, sugar, salt, or any other article required. The necessary money is delivered to the agent with the orders and is thrown into the stern sheets. Passengers from the village are taken on board free provided they keep to their own special agent-boat, and the younger men work their passage by helping to row the boat.

On arrival at the town, the agent executes all the commissions he has been entrusted with. He deals with the various shops with which he has formed connections and derives his income from the commission given him by the dealers on such cash purchases as he makes on behalf of his clients.

The agent-boat usually takes all day to reach the trading centre, carry out all its commissions, and return home to its own village, which is reached just before dark. As it passes each home on the banks of the stream it hands out the packets and bottles with unfailing accuracy. No shopping list is ever made, but there are no mistakes in purchases or change.

THE "DRAGON" BOAT

Disgraced and banished by his relative, King Huai of Ch'u (楚懷王), whom he had faithfully served, Ch'ü Yüan (屈原), who lived in 400 B.C., sought out the court diviner for advice. "Will I," said he, "remain pure and honest, or will I follow the world drift? Will I speak frankly at the peril of my life, or will I lie basely to my own profit? Will I be firm as a pillar, or unctuous as ointment? Will I make for my object like a proud charger, or allow myself to drift like a duck? Will I champ my bit like a battle horse, or will I walk like a hackney with ears down? Will I struggle on the wing with free swans, or will I dispute with poultry for a mouthful? The corrupted principality," he continued, "resembles a stagnant pool. The culminators have the ear of the Prince, the sages vegetate in oblivion. What shall I do; what shall I not do?"

The diviner excused himself by saying "there are things larger than can be measured by the foot, and there are incalculable numbers, insoluble problems, irremediable situations; I am afraid I can do nothing in your case."

Ch'ü Yüan then wandered on the banks of the river and encountered a fisherman, who asked him why he should be so haggard in feature. "The world," replied Ch'ü Yüan, "is like a muddy pond; I alone am clean. All men are drunk; I alone am sober; and that is why I am exiled." The fisherman said, "the sage does not quarrel, he adapts himself. If all are drunk, do as they do. Of what use are abstruse principles and sublime aspirations?"

"Never will I consent to soil myself by contact with the world," said Ch'ü Yüan. "Rather than sink in the mud of the world I will seek a grave in the stomach of the fishes."

The fisherman smiled, hoisted his sail and left, singing as he did so, "when the waters of the Ts'ang Lang (滄浪) are clear, I wash my hat-strings in them; when they are muddy, I wash my feet in them."* (滄浪之水清兮可以濯我纓滄浪之水濁兮可以濯我足)

No more was heard of Ch'ü Yüan, for in his despair he jumped into the waters of the Milo River (汨羅江) and was drowned. Such is one version of the legend of the "dragon" boats which set out to search for the body of the dishonoured but honourable statesman.

The Dragon Boat Festival as observed on the Upper Yangtze is described in Part Four, pages 531–35. Plans for the boat are shown on pages 530–31.

In most of the outlying districts of Shanghai, as in other ports in China, boat races are one of the chief features of the Dragon Boat Festival, which takes place on the 5th day of the 5th moon. In Shanghai itself, however, this is not the case. The local people prefer rather to take an æsthetic view, and it is customary to build up ordinary sampans with grotesque structures of coloured paper, cloth, and wood, and multitudes of spectators line both banks of the Soochow Creek to watch the various highly-decorated boats which pass out of the creek into the Whangpoo.

Crowds cross to the north bank of the Whangpoo to watch the regatta which is held on the Pailienching Creek. A similar meeting ground is at the Pan Sung Gardens near the South Railway Station, and a roaring trade is done by presenting various entertainments for the visitors who crowd to see the boat races. The craft used here conform to no particular design, but are merely decorated so as to appear as huge dragons with open mouths. They are manned by six to eight men dressed in richly embroidered coats, who paddle vigorously to the accompaniment of the band of musicians carried on board, who beat gongs and drums in the usual way. In Shanghai and other areas, when, together with other holidays of the lunar calendar, the observance of the Dragon Boat Festival was officially banned by the Government, it was kept under the title of the Mid-Summer Festival.

* Extracted from Chapters VI and VII of the "Ch'u Tz'u," written by Ch'ü Yüan (摘引屈原所著楚辭 第六第七兩卷).

Care for children figures largely among the customs peculiar to this time, when it is believed that the five noxious insects are abroad and many evil spirits are on the prowl. In the country districts the children wear a little embroidered bag containing musk, which, it is believed, acts as a safeguard against trouble.

There is an ancient legend telling how a man was once watching a "dragon" boat race with his young grandchild in his arms. Tightly wedged in the crowds, he was mindful only of the contest and moved his arms convulsively in time with the paddles of the rival crews. As a result the child was squeezed to death, and the incident has been commemorated by a proverb in the Kwangtung dialect, thus:

Paddling a "dragon" boat on the water,
Squeezing a child to death on shore;
Why should it be in such a hurry?
(水上扒龍船岸上挾死仔使乜咁着緊)

THE BAMBOO RAFT AND BAMBOO-CARRYING JUNK

Most of the bamboo offered for sale in the Shanghai market comes from Kiangsu and Chekiang. In the former province the chief districts are in the central and southern parts, cultivation being concentrated around Sungkiang, Shanghai, Quinsan, Soochow, Wusih, along the Grand Canal to Yangchow, and up the Yangtze as far as Nanking. In Chekiang the bamboo grows abundantly in the districts of Huchow, Mokanshan, Hangchow, up the Ch'ient'ang River, Shaohing, Chenghsien, Ningpo, and Haimen. The Shanghai wholesale dealers have resident agents in most of the producing districts, especially at Huchow and Hangchow.

Streams and rivers offer the easiest egress from the bamboo-producing areas, and, by their very structure, the bamboos are eminently suited to such shallow water transportation, which has the additional advantage of being far cheaper than transport by rail or road.

The streams adjacent to the bamboo-growing centres are seldom large enough for junk traffic, so that transportation by raft is a necessity as well as a convenient and inexpensive method of marketing the cut poles. Even on the larger canals and rivers rafts are still used, though for short distances only, as the culms, if allowed to soak in water too long, deteriorate, are liable to mildew, and may even become waterlogged.

At the bamboo centres the poles are cut down by the local growers and collected into piles. The rafts are made from bundles of the culms tied together and often take the form of long serpentine rafts extending sometimes for 100 feet. They are an interesting feature of the Soochow Creek as they snake their way in and out of the water traffic.

Whenever possible, the better quality bamboos are loaded direct on to a junk so as to obviate any lowering of their quality or value by prolonged immersion in the water. Junking, that is to say, transporting bamboos by junk, is a distinct trade, and some boatmen handle nothing else. The junkowners accept all responsibility for delivering the cargo safely to its destination, even to the extent of paying transit taxes. Freight is usually paid according to the number of poles, but in the case of bundles cut from the bamboo tops, charges are by agreement and depend upon the size of the bundles.

Two hundred bamboo chairs on their way to market.

On arrival in Shanghai the poles are graded by the dealers and stacked in their yards in cones, with the thicker or bottom ends on the ground. The unit of sale is a *ti* or bundle, which consists of 15 of the largest size of poles, 30 of medium size, and 50 of the smallest, each bundle containing approximately the same amount of wood. Formerly buying was by weight, but this method became unpopular with the dealers and was discontinued, as the farmers soaked their bamboos in the creeks for weeks so as to render them heavier.

Although there are many small hongs in Shanghai which retail bamboos, most of the trade is done through seven large wholesale dealers. It is estimated that each of these does a yearly business of more than $300,000, making an aggregate turnover of more than 2 million dollars a year in raw bamboo alone.

It should be remembered that Shanghai is only one out of many large towns, and as the use of bamboo is also very extensive throughout all rural as well as urban districts, some idea may be gained of the universal use of this essential necessity of life throughout China.

In the "Chu Pu," or "Treatise on Bamboo," published in the third or fourth century, there is a fairly complete account of the varieties of this plant and its uses, which have altered little despite the passage of centuries.

No other plant in the world has ever been so generally made use of in so many ways.* Not only are innumerable objects of common daily use made from bamboos, but the shoots are prized as food, either fresh or salted, and the root stock, the sap, the thin outer skin, and the leaves have their value as medicines, tonics, or remedies against worms. To no one perhaps is the bamboo more indispensable than the junkman or fisherman. The following list, which makes no claim to being exhaustive, is an indication of some of the nautical uses to which it can be put: boats, rope, thole-pins, masts, sails, net-floats, basket fish-traps, awnings, food baskets, beds, blinds, bottles, bridges, brooms, foot-rules, food, lanterns, umbrellas, fans, brushes, buckets, chairs, chopsticks, combs, cooking gear, cups, drogues, dust-pans, pens, nails, pillows, tobacco pipes, water pipes, carrying-poles, boat-hooks, fishing-nets, fishing-rods, flagpoles, fuel, hats, ladders,

* That the Chinese appreciate the value of the bamboo is evidenced by the old proverb "it is better to have no meat to eat than to live in a place without bamboos." (寧可食無肉不可居無竹)

ladles, lamps, musical instruments, mah-jong sets, tiles, mats, tubs, rafts, caulking material, scoops, shoes, sieves, stools, tables, tallies, tokens, torches, rat-traps, flea-traps, back-scratchers, medicine, walking-sticks, paper, joss sticks.

If China was suddenly denuded of bamboos, the interruption and disorganization of daily life would be tremendous, although few probably recognize the importance of this apparently humble and common staple.

THE PADDLE-WHEEL CRAFT

The Chinese do not claim to have invented steamers, but to them can with justice be conceded the honour of inventing paddle-wheels. The first use of them is attributed to a skilful General named Li Kao (李 皐), who lived between A.D. 733–792. Of him it is recorded that he built "fighting ships with two paddle-wheels on each side so that the boats ran as fast as horses."

The war-junks are described at length in Part Three, pages 334–42.

Later, in the Sung dynasty, in A.D. 1135, a rebel General named Yang Yao (楊 么) used paddle-wheel boats in the Tungting Lake, without much success, it would appear, for he was captured by the famous General Yo Fei (岳 飛).*

It seems difficult, if not impossible, to trace when they were first used in Shanghai, but the earliest historical mention would seem to be in connection with the paddle-wheeled war-junks which took part in the naval operations at Woosung in June 1842.

Another type was that operating a passenger-boat service to Soochow. These craft were stern-wheelers, the motive power being provided by a machine like a treadmill situated at the stern and worked by from six to a score of men at a time. They are described as larger and more roomy than the ordinary boats and carried between 60 and 70 passengers. In the nineties there was little traffic on the Soochow Creek. Steam-launches were unknown, and these craft had what was practically a monopoly of the passenger traffic. The stern-wheel flotilla was owned by a company which maintained about 14 boats worth $2,000 each. For a fare ranging from 8 cents to $1.20 or $2, according to the accommodation, they made a quick passage to Soochow in about 30 hours. The laodah, instead of a whistle, blew a conch at each bend to warn other craft to get out of the way.

THE FLOATING HOTEL

Formerly floating hotels were often to be found by the banks of rivers and creeks. These were large boats specially constructed for the purpose. As the waterways of China were, and still are, the main highways of the country, these institutions were of the greatest convenience to travellers, the more particularly in that a passenger arriving in the evening at a town, even at a comparatively early hour, would find the city gates shut and would be otherwise unable to disembark until the next morning. The floating hotels, being made fast outside the walls of the town, provided welcome accommodation for this type of traveller and also for the passengers in transit only who merely wished for a meal and a few hours' rest before transhipping to other passenger-boats.

Doubtless the disappearance of the city walls and gates is responsible for the discontinuance of this nautical form of hostelry.

* The junkmen claim the invention to be the work of Chên Chiang Wang Yeh, the River-guarding King, or patron saint of the Upper Yangtze junkmen. He is supposed to have lived in the Sung dynasty, A.D. 960–1280.

A small floating kitchen.

A junkman's wife in her galley.

THE FLOATING KITCHEN BOAT

A variation of the floating hotel and tea-house is a craft which is a floating kitchen wherein meals are served to the passengers and/or crew of other junks. In the old days quite large floating kitchens of a special type were built, but those in use now are merely medium-sized sampans fitted with a more extensive galley than usual and covered over with a mat roof. The stern section is often used as a simple eating-house for junkmen.

THE FLOATING GARDEN

The "China Review" of 1889 describes a very curious system of floating gardens and fields in the Yangtze delta districts. In the spring, usually in the month of April, a bamboo raft was made measuring about 10 or 12 feet in length and half that in breadth, the poles being lashed together with interstices of an inch between them. A layer of straw, an inch thick, was then spread over the raft, over which was put a coating, 2 inches deep, of adhesive mud from the bed of a canal or pond. Seeds were then sown on the artificial vegetable plot. The rafts were made fast, in still water, to the nearest bank and needed no more attention until the seed germinated. First the straw disintegrated, and the soil also disappeared, until finally the roots of the plants drew support exclusively from the water. After about three weeks the raft became covered with the creeper *shui-ch'in-ts'ai* (水 芹 菜), water convolvulus (*Ipomœa reptans*), of which both stems and roots are gathered for cooking.

Even more ambitious was the fabrication of what were known as frame fields or water vegetable fields for growing rice. These are described by Hsü Kuang-ch'i (徐 光 啟), the famous scholar, in his "Treatise on Agriculture" (農 政 全 書) in 1663, where he speaks of rows of these rice fields tied up to trees on river, creek, or lake banks.

These were similarly made from bamboo rafts, upon which weeds and their adherent clods of earth were placed as a seed bed. Into this soil the young rice shoots were transplanted, and the adhesive nature of the soaked soil of the floating field, bound by the roots of the weeds, kept the plants in position throughout the season. The rice thus grown and known as fire grain ripened in from 60 to 70 days instead of the normal time of 90 to 100 days or more.

For this form of aquatic husbandry it was claimed that it served to avert famines due either to drought or to floods. Whether the real fields were submerged and their crops rendered sodden or rotten, or whether they were burnt up by a rainless summer, the rice produced by these artificial fields always attained to uninterrupted maturity.

Without personal exploration of the hinterland of the delta and estuary regions it is impossible to make any definite statement, but the closest questioning fails to produce evidence of any survival of this early art of *aqua*-horticulture.

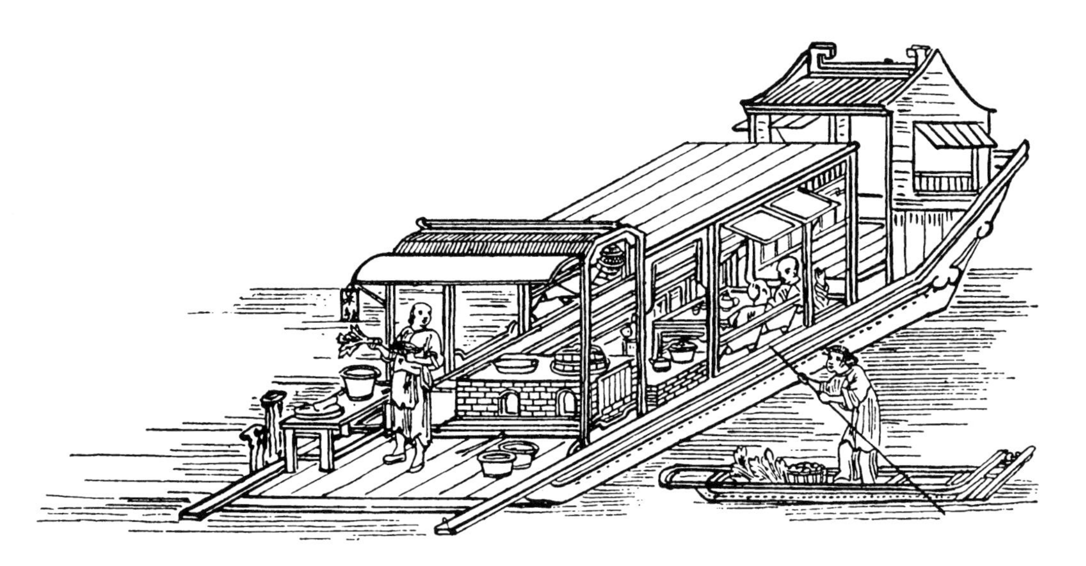

The floating-kitchen boat.
FROM A CHINESE WOODCUT

THE LIVE FISH CARRIER

Fresh-water fish migrate every spring far up the Yangtze to spawn in the quiet waters of the great Poyang or Tungting Lakes. There are two methods of dealing with the spawn. In the first case, men trained to the work gather the eggs into a place of safety and tend the small fry when they hatch out. As an alternative, after the fry have hatched and are descending the river in the spring freshets, a fine-meshed net is set against the current to catch them at and below the mouth of the Poyang Lake or at Kiukiang. The season for catching the fry lasts from the "beginning of summer" (立 夏), in early May, to the "little heat" (小 暑), in early July, or a month earlier south of the Yangtze.

In either case, after they are caught, the fry are carefully stored in bamboo baskets covered with thick oiled paper. Not the least remarkable feature is that this oiled paper can stand the dead weight of the fry and the water containing them.

Mr. Worcester has noted that the fishing craft of the Shanghai area are very numerous, but the differences are slight. A selection has been made of the types illustrating the principal varieties which work in the creeks and waterways connecting with the Whangpoo.

These *shui-chi* (水 雞), or water chickens, as they are termed, are then transported by boat. Sometimes they may be marketed cheaply to the owners of any suitable piece of water, but more often they are sent to Linghu (菱 湖), in Huchow, Chekiang Province, the distributing centre. During the voyage they are carefully tended and fed with powdered yolk of egg. They are kept for about two weeks at Linghu, and from there the dealers export them to the various fish farms, where the ratio of distribution is about 600 to the *mou* of water.

They are stocked either in a *ch'ih* (池), or artificial pond, or in a *t'ang* (塘), which is a section of a stream or lake fenced round with bamboo to prevent the fish from escaping, though losses from this cause are nevertheless excessive. The fish thus reared, however, are less liable to disease than those kept in the stagnant waters of a pond and also require less artificial food, as such waters provide a proportion of their natural diet of weeds and snails.

Where ponds are used, once every three years they are drained; the silt and dredgings are used on the fields for manure, and they are refilled with fresh water and new fry.

Fish culture and fishing is also discussed in Part One, pages 134–38.

For the first few weeks the young fry are fed with bean juice until they are old enough to be fed as adult fishes with grass, crushed snails, beans, or rape seed-cake for the "grass fish," and distillers' grain and kitchen refuse for other varieties. Care must be taken to avoid disease through over-feeding in midsummer.

By the end of the Chinese year the larger fish are caught and sold, while the smaller ones are left for another year or two to mature. In the more cheaply run fish farms the fish are not artificially fed and the results are necessarily not nearly so good.

Of the varieties of fish so raised, the first in quality is the *ch'ing-yü* (青 魚), or green fish, and the *ts'ao-yü* (草 魚), or grass fish; the *pien-yü* (鯿 魚) is second, the *lien-yü* (鰱 魚) third, and the carp last. The greatest quantity produced are the grass fish, with the *lien-yü* next in order of production.

The bream is a very common article of food, as is the silver carp. The common carp is not so popular, but serves well enough for a sacrificial dish

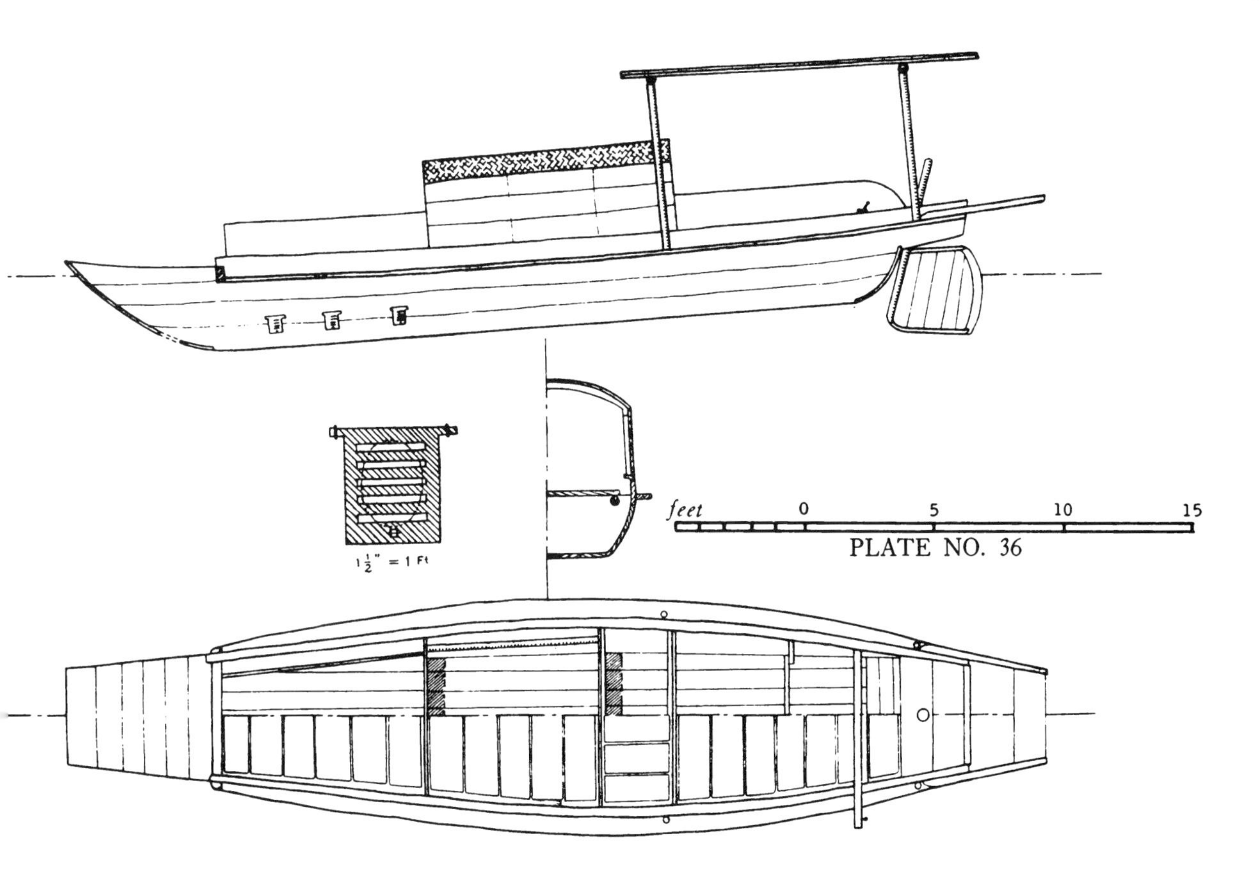

PLATE NO. 36

to those spirits who presumably are too rarefied to be discriminating over the pleasures of the table.

These artificially-raised fish are known as *chia-yü* (家 魚), or domesticated fish, in contradistinction to the "wild fish" (野 魚) caught in their natural habitat.

Statistics are not available as to the number of fish farms in the delta areas, but south of the Yangtze the fish-raising zone stretches from the Chekiang–Kiangsu border down to Soochow, Wusih, and neighbouring districts with, according to the fish dealers' estimates, 15,000 ponds covering 70,000 *mou*. North of the Yangtze is another large area engaged in the same industry in the region of Taichow (泰 州) and Kaoyu (高 郵).

The fish, when mature, are taken to the market either by dealers or by the fish farmers themselves and sold to the *yü* hong or commission agents. The fish are always bought alive, and if the *yü* hong cannot dispose of them immediately they are kept in bamboo baskets in a stream.

In the case of the Shanghai market, as the fish farms are situated some hundreds of *li* away, the fish are always handled by dealers, who export direct to the Shanghai *yü* hong. There are eleven such organizations, of which the two largest are the Chu Chang Shun and the Tung Jên Chang, each with an enormous yearly turnover. These *yü* hong have their own Fresh-water Fish Guild.

The specially-constructed cargo-craft which bring the fish down to Shanghai are so designed as to permit free flooding of the compartment containing their live cargo.

One such craft is illustrated in Plate No. 36. It is known as the *yü-ch'uan* (魚 船), or live fish carrier, and is built at Nansha, up the Soochow Creek.

A most noteworthy feature of the boat is the fact that there are only two frames and two bulkheads, which are sufficient to carry the light load, although it makes her weak in construction. This craft measures 37 feet, with a beam of 8½ feet and a depth of 3 feet, and tapers gently to long, low, flat bow and the

characteristically Shanghai type of stern and stern gallery with a hoisting variety of rudder.

There are two bulkheads and two frames. The main distinguishing feature of this sampan is the free-flooding device whereby all the fore hold right up to the first bulkhead may be converted into an aquarium so as to deliver the live cargo in a marketable condition after a three days' journey from the fish farms. During the trip the fish are fed with egg powder to keep them in good condition. The self-flooding is achieved by means of three square apertures spaced between the first frame and the first bulkhead on each side of the hull below the water-line, and one more forward on the under side of the horizontally-planked bow just before its turn.

When it is desired to fill the fish tank, these apertures are fitted with hinged flaps in the form of wooden gratings (see inset on Plate No. 36), which are secured by a peg at the bottom. When the boat is returning empty after discharging its lively cargo, these gratings are replaced by leak-stoppers in the form of close-fitting blocks of wood set in cushions of cloth, making the tank quite watertight. When the tank is full this naturally puts the sampan down by the head, so much so indeed as to leave only a very few inches of freeboard, and in the wash from passing vessels water is frequently taken in over the bow. In order to prevent this water from running back over the top of the tank and, by floating off the fore-deck hatches, inadvertently releasing the fish, a 4-inch high athwartship weather-board is affixed across the bow above the first frame and high weather-boards run throughout the length of the boat on either side of the small house amidships.

Two very large stones are carried as portable ballast and are placed in varying parts of the vessel so as to adjust the trim as required. There is a short mast which carries a square-headed lug-sail. Additional or alternative propulsion is provided by the single yuloh, which operates from a bumkin on a beam on the port quarter. This yuloh is of an unusual type in that the broad blade is iron bound round the edges. According to the crew, this is to withstand the wear and tear of contact with the stony bottom of some of the creeks on their journey down. This, however, does not explain why these iron edges should extend so far up the blade, and another reason therefore may be found in the better cutting edge thus provided when feathering.

The boats never travel down by the quicker route of the crowded Soochow Creek, as the strong meat provided by its polluted waters would prove too much for even fish hardened by being fed from the refuse of the kitchens of the fish farmers. A more leisurely course is therefore followed through the winding channels of less frequented and cleaner waterways. This knowledge will doubtless be welcome to Shanghai housewives, as is the fact that these craft are clean and well kept.*

The crew of five men live inside the house, some of them below decks in the narrow space between their live and dead cargo. The all-pervading smell of fish must here be at its strongest, particularly in hot weather. In the summer 5 or 6 piculs of fish are carried, but the amount can be doubled in winter.

When the fish-carriers reach the Whangpoo River they are met by a launch and towed in three rows of three abreast to the fish market. A marked feature of the whole proceeding is the leisurely manner in which everybody concerned moves, for, despite the ingenious methods used for "bringing them back alive," the cargo is still of a more or less perishable nature.

On arrival at the fish wharves in Shanghai the fish are ladled out from their tank with a long-handled landing-net, and the boat proceeds back to the fish farms *via* the Soochow Creek for another cargo.

* Not so acceptable is the information that the fish which may happen to die en route are lifted out from the tank and deposited in a large tub. This serves as a mortuary for the casualties, which are sold off at cheaper rates on arrival.

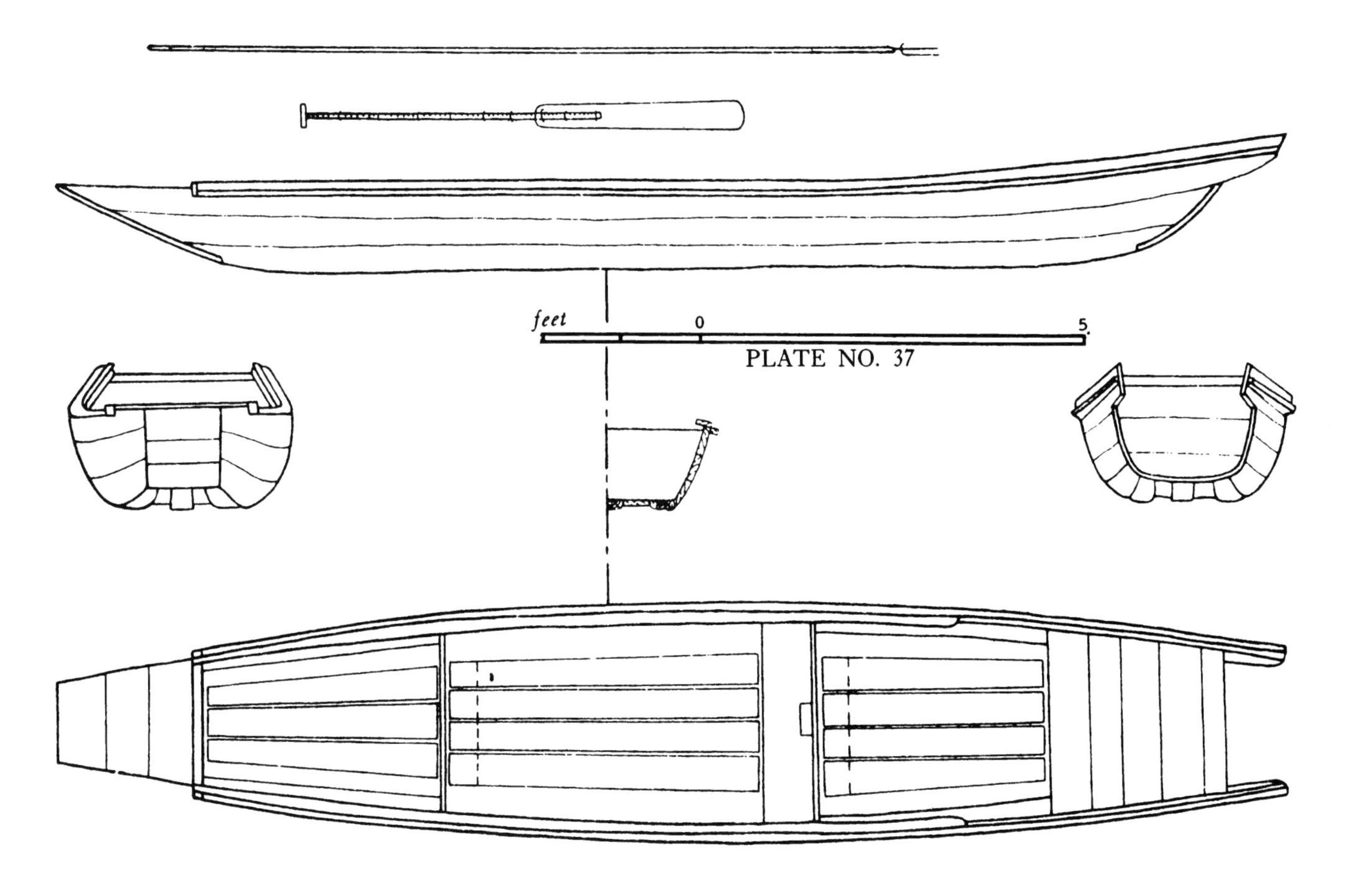

THE CREEK FISHING-BOAT

小漁船

The sampan illustrated in Plate No. 37 is known as the *hsiao-yü-ch'uan*, the generic name for any small sampan. The boat measures 15 feet, with a beam of 2 feet 10 inches and a depth of 1 foot 2 inches, and is used for shallow water net-fishing. This occupation, so patiently persisted in up and down the creeks, usually yields only fish of a kind which in the West would not be considered worth eating.

The boat is quite uninteresting from a structural point of view; but the Chinese methods of fishing, even if a study of them is unlikely to prove of much service to the practical fisherman, are notable for their simplicity and for the ingenuity of the primitive gear, which probably is little changed from that used in the remote past.

The framework[1] of the net is not unlike a large, round dish-cover in shape, with a netted oblong base[2] 4 feet by 1 foot and three netted sides only[3], extending upwards for about 1½ feet and leaving one side open. The bamboos forming the frame[4] at the four corners bend over to form a conical top[5]. A vertical bamboo runs from the bottom of the net through the apex of the top, above which it projects as a handle.

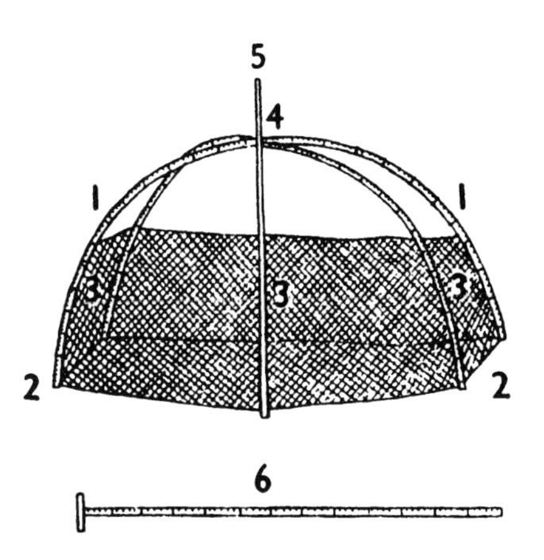

Holding the end of this vertical bamboo[5], the fisherman lowers the net slowly to the bed of the creek, while with the other hand he scoops any unsuspecting fish towards the net, using a pusher[6] or persuader, a bamboo with a wooden cross-piece at the bottom. As the net is only 4 feet wide, any agile fish can very easily evade capture. A fish spear made of bamboo, with iron prongs, is also part of the equipment.

To achieve success at this type of fishing, unlimited time and exceptional perseverance are absolutely essential.

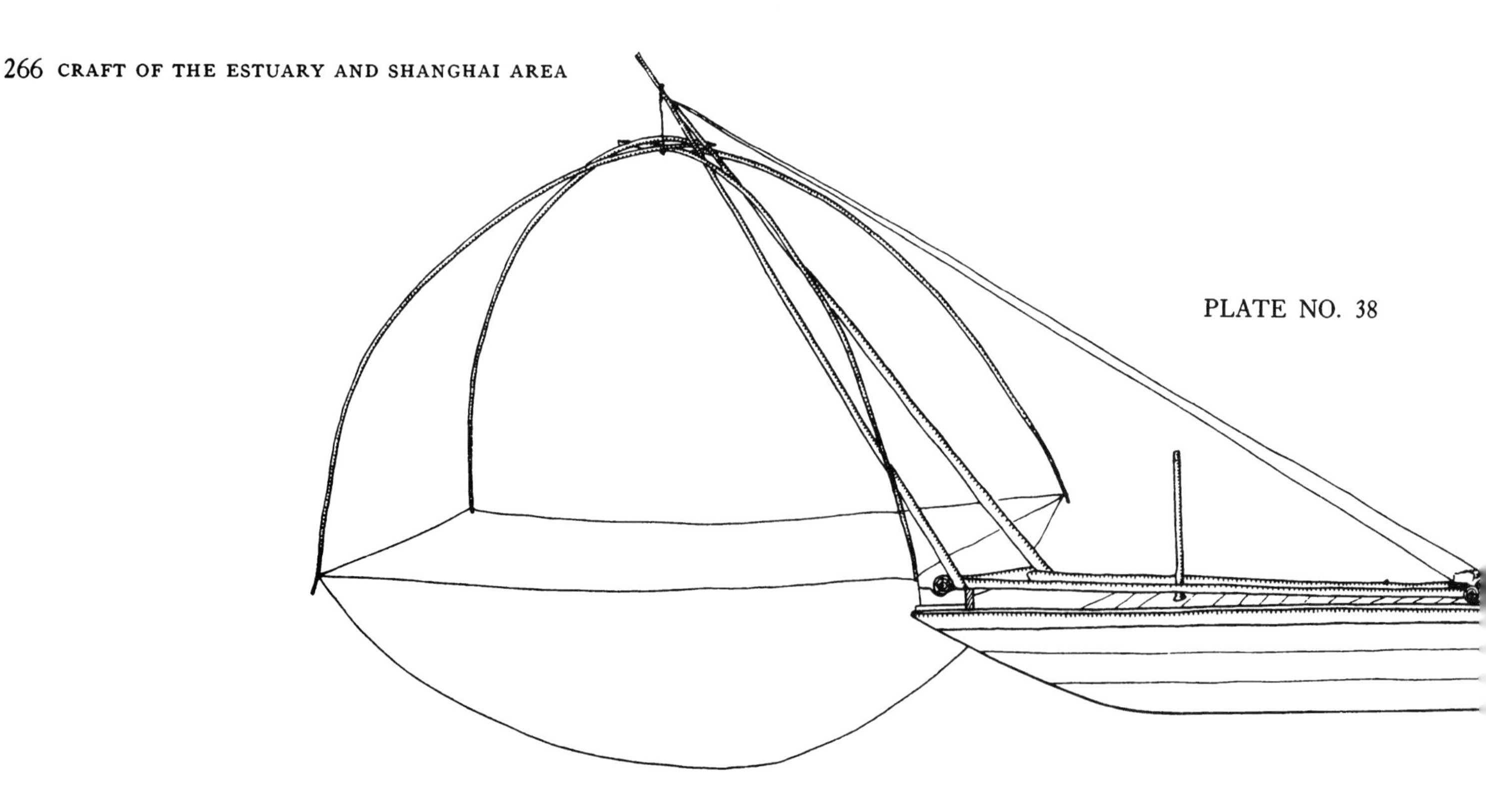

PLATE NO. 38

THE DROP-NET FISHERMAN

Drop-net fishing is very common in the waterways of the delta. Fishermen, with remarkable perseverance, comb the waters of the river from the shore and from sampans and small junks.

The structure for the purpose is a framework consisting of two pairs of bamboo poles joined together at an angle of about 120°, the central portion resting in a bed and forming a pivot. One pair of bamboos supports the net while the other acts as a lever. Stones are placed at strategic points to adjust the balance.

The whole affair is very ingeniously contrived so that it can be lowered into the water, where it remains until the operator thinks there may be a fish over the net. He then hauls on a rope attached to the apex of the lever pair of bamboos, which brings the net to the surface, when, if there should happen to be a luckless fish in it, it is scooped out with a long bamboo landing-net.

This form of net is also rigged on a staging or on the river bank itself, but the apparatus when fitted in sampans or small junks is more efficient, as the fishing-grounds can be frequently changed.

There is a pocket in the centre of the net for the reception of the captives.

Fishing with drop-nets.

THE WUSIH-PANG CHO-YÜ-CH'UAN OR WUSIH FISH-SAMPAN

The *wusih-pang cho-yü-ch'uan*, or Wusih fish-sampan, takes its name from its port of origin, a town on the Grand Canal; but despite this it usually is to be seen fishing the waters of the Whangpoo between Woosung and Lunghwa (龍 華).

A distinguishing feature of this craft is that it is built of *pai-mu* (柏 木), cypress, instead of the almost universal *sha-mu*. There are three hardwood bulkheads and four frames.

More or less uniform in size, these sampans are represented by the one selected for illustration in Plate No. 39, which measures 26 feet long, with a beam of 5½ feet and a depth of 2 feet 10 inches.

Although not particularly strong in construction, this well-built and handy little craft is eminently seaworthy; and full advantage is taken of this, for she remains out on the fishing-grounds when other and larger craft are scudding for shelter. The high weather-boards[1] running almost the length of the hull serve to prevent her from being swamped by the wash of passing vessels, and the sloping gunwale[2] also helps by permitting the water to run off.

There is a stern gallery[3]. The rudder is very rarely used, being usually kept unshipped in the house. These boats are designed to be propelled by their single long yuloh, but an improvised spritsail is often set on a bamboo mast which may or may not combine that office with that of boat-hook. It is suspected that the improvised spritsail, when not thus used, serves as a bed-cover. There are four lumber irons[4] to hold the boat-hooks, landing-nets, spars, etc. The house, which measures 8 by 4½ feet, accommodates the fisherman-owner and his family. The galley is right aft.

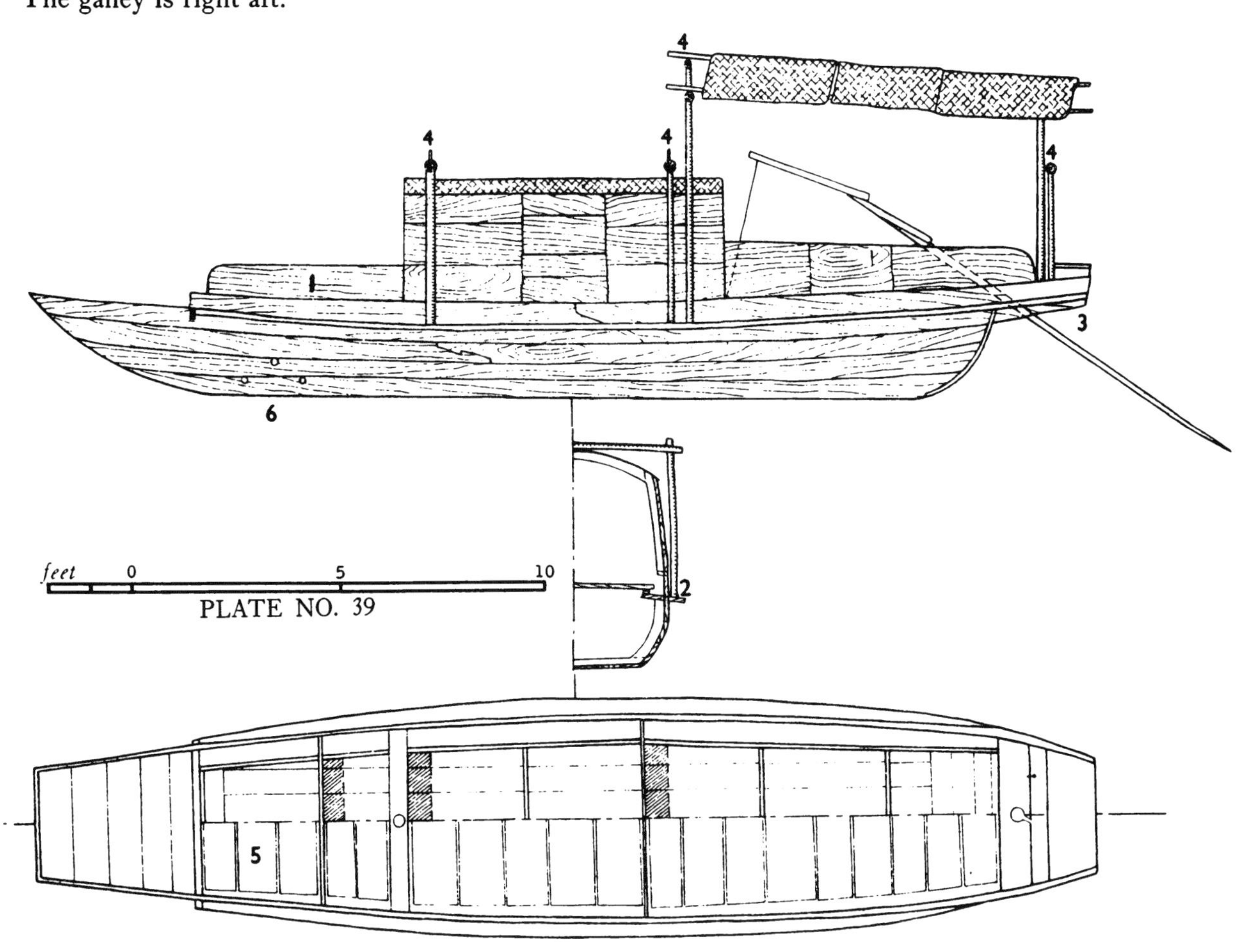

PLATE NO. 39

The fish when caught are stowed in the compartment[5] between the bow and the first bulkhead. This compartment is transformed into a reservoir by the drilling of three holes[6] in the hull on each side below the water-line, thus permitting free flooding.

The method of fishing is with a cast-net, 26 feet in diameter. There are two main fishing-grounds. In that up river, off Lunghwa, small fish are caught and a close mesh is used. The same type of net, with a larger mesh, is used between Pootung Point and Woosung. The fish often congregate close to the wharf. The winter provides the best fishing, particularly just after rain.

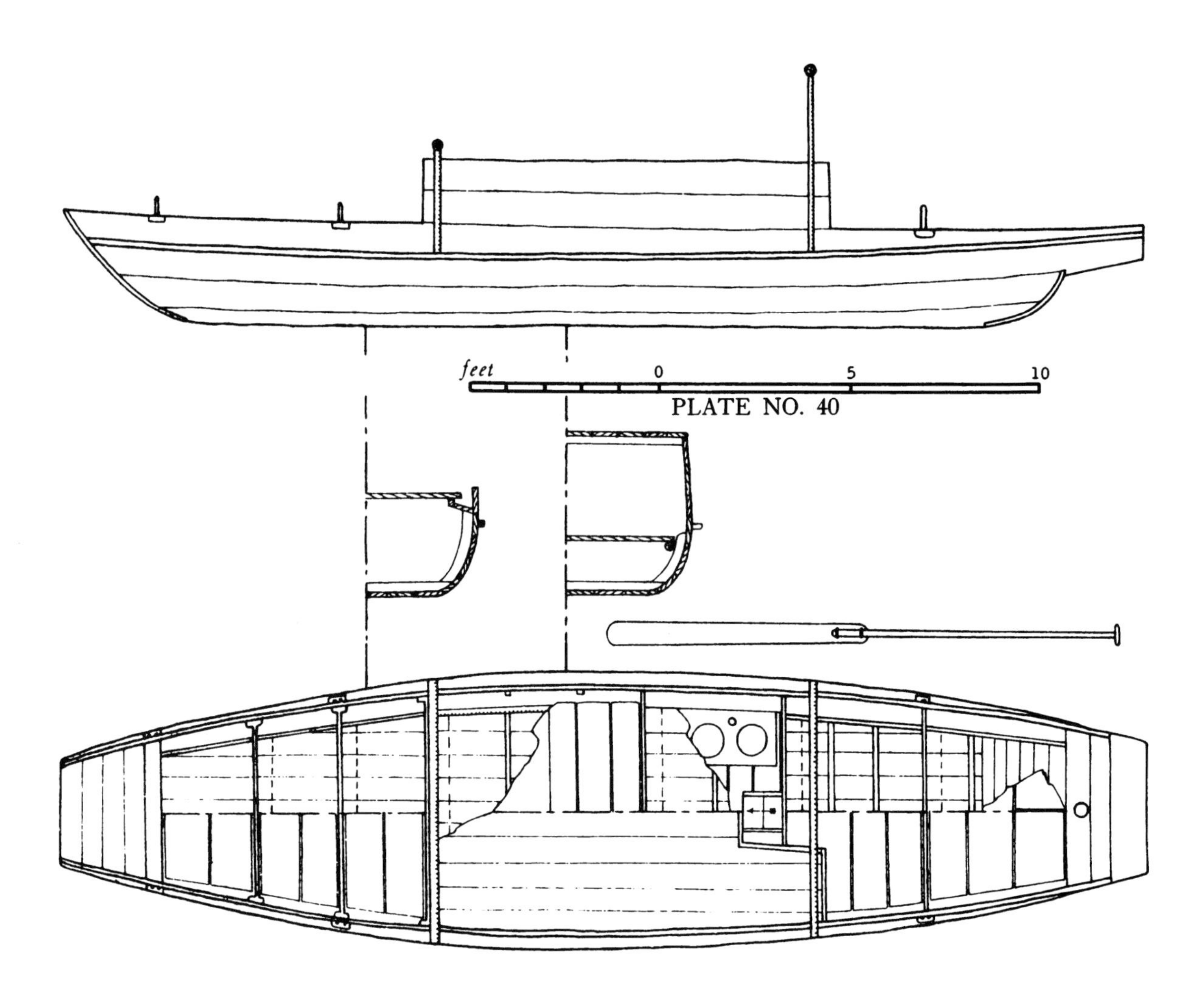

PLATE NO. 40

拖網船 THE T'O-WANG-CH'UAN OR DRAG-NET BOAT

The men of these craft, as the name implies, literally pick up a living in the creeks and canals of Kiangsu, and may be seen in their hundreds in the Whangpoo and the waterways surrounding Shanghai.

Lightly constructed of *sha-mu*, with six bulkheads and eight hardwood frames, their boats are very much standardized as regards shape and size. The boat here illustrated measures 28 feet in length, 7 feet in beam, and has a depth of 2½ feet. A rudder is seldom used, and there is no mast, though a spritsail is sometimes improvised. Propulsion is commonly by the three oars, two in the bow, always together on the same side, and one in the stern. The owner's family, which form the crew, live in the midship house, which measures 9 by 6 feet. The galley is also in the house, down two steps and situated on the bottom of the boat. Above the house, at either end of it, are two lumber irons to accommodate boat-hooks, spars, and so forth.

Quite one of the most remarkable things about these sampans is the very limited space in which a family of six or more are content to be cramped. The wonder, indeed, is how they are to be accommodated—where they will eat and, most important of all, where they will sleep. When the boat is under weigh the problem is less difficult to solve, for the various members of the family are scattered about at their various duties—poling, yulohing, dragging, cooking, and so on.

These water gypsies may be best described as professional scavengers, the riverine prototypes of the less fortunate classes on land who spend so much of their time foraging in dust-bins and spearing cigarette ends skilfully out of the gutters on a long fork. In like manner the drag-boats pick over the refuse at the garbage wharves awaiting shipment to the dumps.

Occasionally, if they get the opportunity, the drag-boat men carry cargo or are hired to drag for lost property. Another activity is that of catching crabs, although not in a nautical sense. This industry is carried out in the creeks around Shanghai and lasts from the 8th to the 10th moon. In the main, however, they are dependent for their living on dragging the river or creek beds for any articles that may reward their labours, and even such weighty rubbish as old tins has its market value. The most lucrative field for this branch of their work is dragging for coal; and when Shanghai was a port of call for the great ocean liners the drag-boats could count on a fair return, qualified only by the number of competitors.

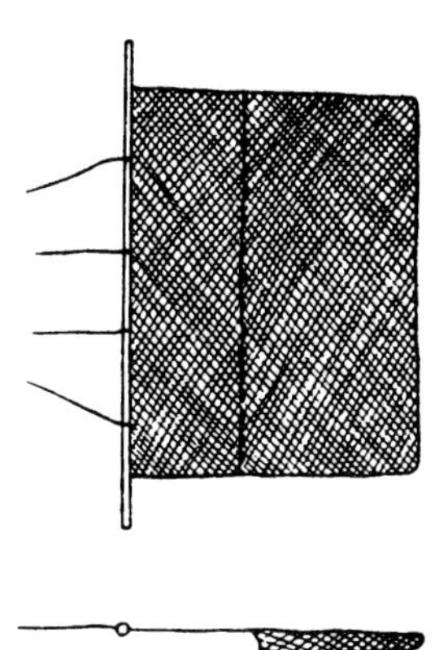

The drag used is a "pocket net" in the shape of a rectangular bag made of 1-inch mesh hemp string and measuring 5½ by 4½ feet. A number of iron hoops keep the mouth of the bag open, and their weight also serves to keep the net in the correct position. The net, which is attached by a bridle to a bamboo rope, heavily weighted, is lowered over the side and, as the boat moves, is deftly manœuvred, mouth downwards, over the site expected to yield coal or crabs. So expert are the drag-men that they can work in depths up to 30 or 40 feet. The excitement of the chase runs high, for occasionally great prizes are recovered. For example, while dragging for coal near where the luxury liners embark their fuel they might (as actually happened on one occasion) fish up a passenger's false teeth, for which service they were suitably rewarded.

Drag-boat fishers sometimes penetrate far up the creeks into the hinterland, where groups of these craft may be seen working over the shallow agricultural canals gathering anything which may serve as food, even including bulbs or the fleshy roots of edible aquatic plants.

There is yet another branch of their activities which must be touched on here, albeit lightly. The detectives of the Customs Harbour Police will tell you that if there is anything missing from a cargo-boat, if a boat loses its anchor, if hats are snatched from crowded ferries, there is sure to be a drag-boat somewhere in the case. Thieving, like other professions in Shanghai, is very highly organized, and is, moreover, strictly controlled so as to benefit the majority. The water thieves are therefore allocated to definite spheres of influence.

A thief from one wharf is not permitted to practise on another but must confine his activities to his own beat. Nothing movable is safe from the Shanghai wharf thief, and so the merchant has recourse to the Thieves' Guild, which will, for a retaining fee, guarantee that nothing is stolen. Setting a thief to catch a thief is thus literally true.

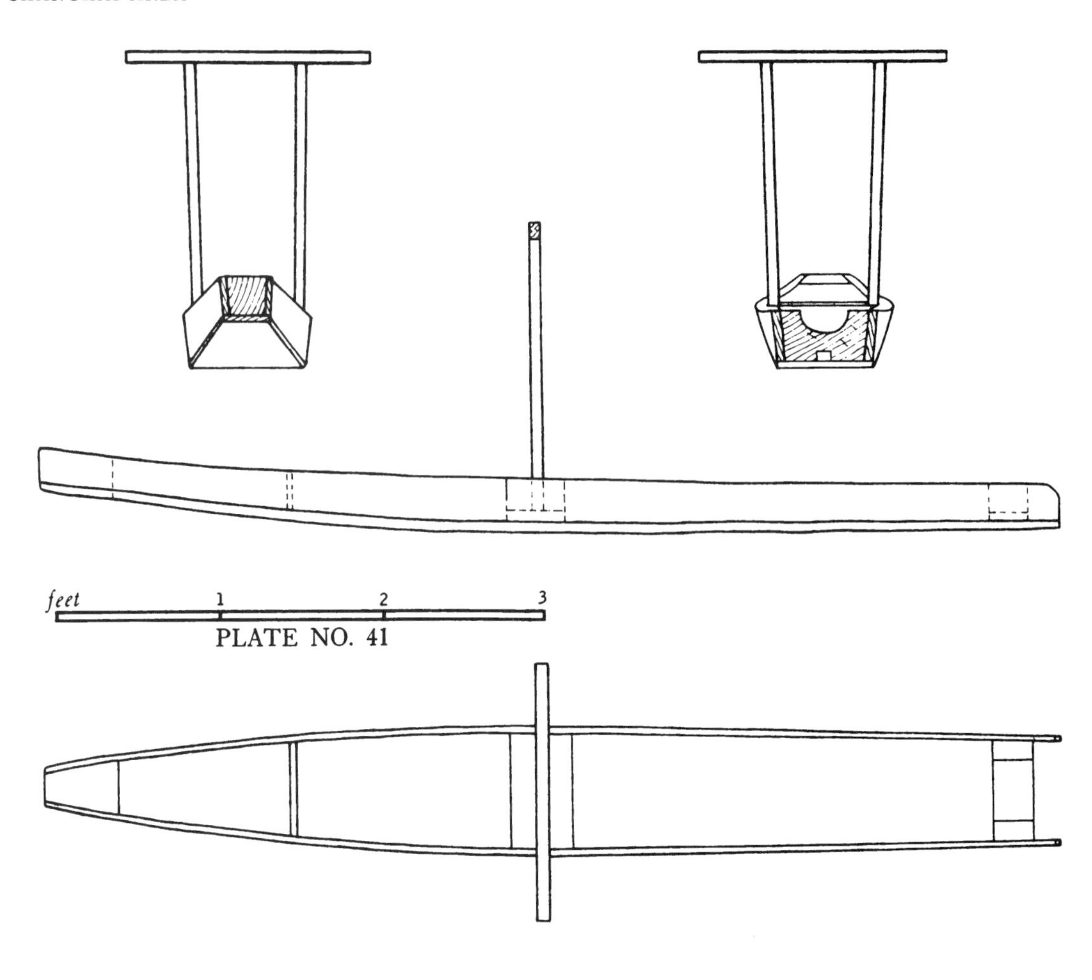

PLATE NO. 41

泥模船

THE NI-MO-CH'UAN

This strange little craft, known as the *ni-mo-ch'uan*, or mud-touching boat, is the next to be herein recorded, and is uniquely interesting as being the only type that is so accurately described in Chinese history as to enable its identity and origin to be traced beyond question.

Its invention is ascribed to the Emperor Yü (禹 王), 2205 B.C. In the "Shih Chi" (史 記), an ancient history written in 90 B.C., it is stated that the great Yü crossed a mud flat on a *ch'iao* (橇), as it was then called. The next link connecting the *ch'iao* with the *ni-mo-ch'uan* occurs in the third century A.D., when scholars spoke of the *ch'iao* as a mud-sledge made in the form of a dust-pan (箕).

Later, under the T'ang dynasty (唐 朝), there is a more detailed description of it as a small, short boat with rising bow and stern in which the user knelt on one knee while using the other leg to propel himself over the soft mud flats. This description holds good of the craft to-day, for it has remained absolutely unchanged except for its name. It is probably the smallest fishing vessel, if such it can be called, in the world.

In addition to its royal descent as an Imperial brain-wave, it has the distinction of having been used as a warship in the Ch'ing dynasty. It is recorded that a town on Hangchow Bay was once attacked by pirates whose boats had grounded on the mud flats by the falling tide. A certain enterprising and warlike villager called together all the owners of the mud-touching boats and at night proceeded out to the stranded pirates, who, being taken completely by surprise, were all either killed or captured.

When the mud flats are exposed at low water, the *ni-mo-ch'uan* goes out in search of a slender mollusc. This creature, which is known as the *ni-lo*

(泥 螺), or mud screw, inhabits a thin and fragile white shell. It is sold as a delicacy in the confectioners' shops and held in the greatest esteem by Chinese gourmets, being preserved in wine and served on small saucers by the side of each guest's bowl at a banquet.

Although not perhaps, properly speaking, a sampan, the *ni-mo-ch'uan* is in actuality just that, for it is composed of three small ½-inch planks. The bottom board, square at the stern and tapering to the raised box-shaped bow, measures 6 feet by 9½ inches. The two side planks each measure 3½ inches high. The whole structure is strengthened by three bulkheads a few inches high. The square transom has a semicircular cut-out portion to accommodate the shin of the leg on which the owner kneels. He supports himself in this rather cramped position by holding with both hands to a transverse bar which crosses and projects beyond the sledge amidships, where it rests on two uprights 18 inches high. Progress is achieved quite rapidly by pushing with the other leg over the mud. A small limber in the transom permits the escape of any water that may come in over the bow. A basket in the fore part of the craft holds the captured snails.

Although the type here described is indigenous to the Shanghai area, similar craft are used in most of the shallow lakes and in the Tungting Lake, being diverted from their ordinary purpose and used for duck shooting.

As has been pointed out, a clear continuity in design has been proved for the *ni-mo-ch'uan*, definitely establishing it as the same craft as that in use over 4,000 years ago.

There is an added interest in the fact that so old a survival should exist in the hinterland of Shanghai, a city where East and West, the old and the most modern, meet, mingle, and overlap in a manner probably unequalled anywhere in the Far East.

THE LO-SHIH-CH'UAN OR SNAIL-BOAT 螺螄船

The *lo-shih-ch'uan*, or snail-boat, is designed solely for the purpose of catching snails, for which there is a very large market.

There are numerous kinds of land molluscs or snails, of the class *Gastropoda*, which are in demand for the table in China. Fresh-water snails are also largely eaten. The chief varieties in the order of popular snail appeal are the *lo-shih* (螺 螄), the *hsiang-shih* (香 螄), and the largest of all, the *t'ien-lo* (田 螺). The *hsiang-shih* is eaten by the country people at the Ch'ing Ming (清 明), the Festival of Pure Brightness.

The *lo-shih* is very popular in the winter and, despite the fact that it is cooked in wine, is regarded as being quite an inexpensive dish. It hails from the Pootung side of the Whangpoo and is to be found mainly in the Shanghai Harbour and up the Soochow Creek.

The boat illustrated in Plate No. 42 is 24 feet in length, with a beam of 7 feet and a depth of 2½ feet. There are three frames and three bulkheads, the last two of which are situated near together almost like a coffer-dam. She is light in construction, as befits her light duties, and tapers abruptly at the low bow and even narrower stern. Both bow and stern have athwartship planking, and the bow has an additional short doubling plank. There is neither mast nor rudder.

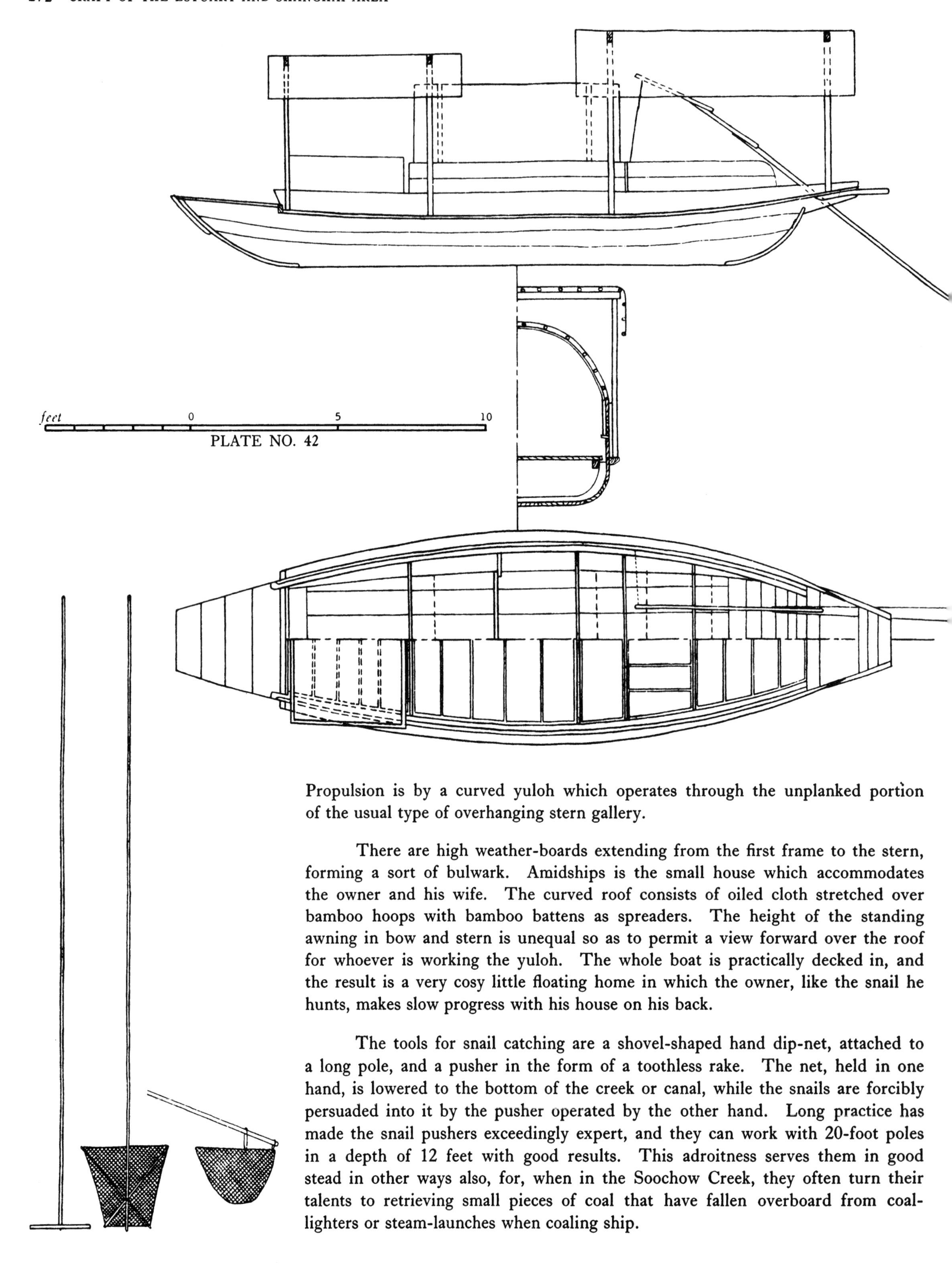

PLATE NO. 42

Propulsion is by a curved yuloh which operates through the unplanked portion of the usual type of overhanging stern gallery.

There are high weather-boards extending from the first frame to the stern, forming a sort of bulwark. Amidships is the small house which accommodates the owner and his wife. The curved roof consists of oiled cloth stretched over bamboo hoops with bamboo battens as spreaders. The height of the standing awning in bow and stern is unequal so as to permit a view forward over the roof for whoever is working the yuloh. The whole boat is practically decked in, and the result is a very cosy little floating home in which the owner, like the snail he hunts, makes slow progress with his house on his back.

The tools for snail catching are a shovel-shaped hand dip-net, attached to a long pole, and a pusher in the form of a toothless rake. The net, held in one hand, is lowered to the bottom of the creek or canal, while the snails are forcibly persuaded into it by the pusher operated by the other hand. Long practice has made the snail pushers exceedingly expert, and they can work with 20-foot poles in a depth of 12 feet with good results. This adroitness serves them in good stead in other ways also, for, when in the Soochow Creek, they often turn their talents to retrieving small pieces of coal that have fallen overboard from coal-lighters or steam-launches when coaling ship.

HOUSE-BOAT FISHERS

Families living in house-boats are said sometimes to make a business of fishing for shrimps. They trail behind the house-boat one or two other boats carrying hundreds of shrimp traps, cleverly constructed in such a manner that when they are dragged along the bottom the shrimps dart into holes in the trap, mistaking them for safe hiding-places.

It will be of interest to the epicure of the West to learn what his colleague in China considers to be one of the most succulent ways of cooking the shrimp. They are usually eaten raw—if not actually alive. There is, however, an alternative method. The shrimps are put into a mixture of soya-bean sauce and Shaohing rice wine with minced ginger. They are left in this solution for 15 to 20 minutes, after which they are ready for eating.

PART THREE

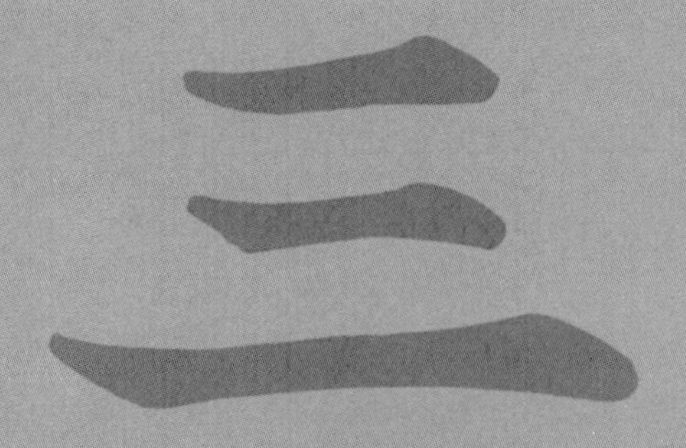

THE LOWER & MIDDLE RIVER & TRIBUTARIES

Certainly there is no Kingdom in the world ſo vaſt as this is, that enjoys the like advantage. Neverthleleſs what I am now going to relate will indeed ſeem to be yet more incredible; and, indeed, I should hardly have believed it my ſelf, had I not ſeen it my ſelf.

The New History of China, 1688
by Gabriel Magaillans,
Miſſionary Apoſtolick.

THE LOWER YANGTZE: THE ESTUARY TO WUHU

THE embouchement of the Yangtze is about 20 miles wide at the head of Tsungming Island (崇明島). This island is an alluvial formation dating back at least 500 years and is 37 miles long, with a width varying from 5 to 10 miles. The old name for it was Chiangshê (江舌), or Tongue of the River, a most apt description, for the long slightly-tapering island lies like a tongue in the mighty mouth of the Yangtze, which it divides into the two branches of the estuary, which follow the lines, so to speak, of the upper and lower jaw. On this latter, that is to say, the right bank, the Whangpoo enters the Yangtze at Woosung. Formerly Tsungming Island was used as a place of banishment for criminals, who were employed in building dikes. From a sandy desert the place gradually became fertile, and finally in A.D. 1369 it was established as a *hsien* (縣治), or district magistracy, with a population of over half a million.

For the first 80 miles above Woosung the river has a considerable breadth, varying from 3 to 9 miles, but above this point it contracts in width. As a consequence the channels are subject to continual change, caused partly by the annual floods and partly by the ebb and flood of tidal streams flowing in different channels, the effect of which is to form vast flats, shoals, and middle grounds which are frequently altering both in extent and position, so that the river may be said to be in a continual state of change for 50 miles above Woosung.

In enormous rivers like the Yangtze, sandbanks often change with great rapidity and suddenness. This is particularly true of Langshan (狼 山).

Whole islands are gradually shifted, washing away at their upper ends and making ground at their lower ends. Other islands disappear altogether, and new ones are formed from the matter which is held in suspension while the water is in motion but deposited when the stream slackens or is obstructed in any way. The volume of water is affected from both up and down stream; for rains, flooded tributaries, and melting snows bring down water from the upper reaches, while the tidal streams from the sea ascend. This tidal fluctuation is perceptible as high up river as Tatung, 350 miles from the sea, although it ceases to be of any practical importance above Wuhu, 289 miles from the sea.

On ascending the river navigational difficulties are soon encountered, beginning only 15 miles above Woosung, where middle grounds divide the river into two branches. About 37 miles above Woosung is Hsüluchinkow (徐 六 涇 口), near which is a valuable anchorage for junks to wait overnight before attempting the famous Langshan Crossing, where the channel crosses from the right to the left bank of the river.

At Kiangyin (江 陰) hills first come into view. Here, too, will be seen fortifications, and the river narrows down to a width of only three-quarters of a mile. A creek, usually crowded with junks, leads inland to the town of Kiangyin, which has a tall pagoda and is surrounded by a moat, which connects with the waterways leading south-west to the Grand Canal and back again circuitously to the Yangtze.

From this point to Chiao Shan* (焦 山), or Hill of Sorrows, better known as Silver Island, no navigational difficulties are experienced. Here the river

* Called after Chiao Hsien (焦先), a hermit who lived in the Han dynasty.

divides and meets again to the westward of the island, which is the first above the entrance to the Yangtze that is not altogether alluvial in character.

The river below Silver Island is upward of a mile in breadth and is swept by a current of such unusual depth and velocity that salt-junks and others bound for Kwachow (瓜 州), the salt port opposite Chinkiang, make use of a system of inland waters commencing on the left bank about 15 miles below Chinkiang and, by an extensive loop, join the northern mouth of the Grand Canal.

Chinkiang was the first Yangtze port to be opened to foreign trade. In its early days, curious as it may seem to-day, it had been expected to outvie Shanghai as a trading centre, chiefly on account of its commanding position at the junction of the Grand Canal and because it was situated where all the year round sea navigation may be said to cease and the difficulties of river navigation begin in earnest. On the north bank there are several cuttings or creeks leading into the northern section of the canal. Chinkiang, moreover, is in water communication by the Grand Canal and natural watercourses with Shanghai, Hangchow, and Ningpo to the south, to the north with the Yellow River and the Peiho, and by these means with Tientsin and Peiping. The Hwai and Kwei Rivers also communicate with the south of Honan and the north of Hupeh.

The port is first mentioned in history in the third century A.D. during the period of the Three Kingdoms, when for a time it functioned as capital of the Kingdom of Wu (吳). It is one of the few Yangtze ports that has had many changes of name but has always reverted to its original one.

It was here in 1275 that Marco Polo crossed the Yangtze. His reporter, Rusticiano, who wrote down Marco's experiences at his dictation, says of the river here:

> "There pass and repass on its waters a great number of vessels, and more wealth and merchandise than all the rivers and the seas of Christendom put together. It seems more like a sea than a river."

The swiftly changing nature of the river-bed is well illustrated by the fact that Golden Island or Hill was formerly on the left bank of the river, but owing to the erosion of the bank, the navigable channel moved to the north, until by 1842 Golden Island had reached mid-stream. In 1802 it was joined to the right bank by a spit, and by 1907 was well inside the low-water coast-line of the right bank. It is surmounted by a five-storied pagoda and several temples.

In days of old there used to be a great rush of junk traffic occurring at the New Year owing to the custom of allowing cargoes to be carried duty free. This practice is said to owe its origin to a misunderstanding. According to popular tradition, the Emperor K'ang Hsi (康 熙), while spending the New Year holidays in the Golden Island Monastery, was disturbed by the continuous squealing of pigs. On learning that the pigs were brought there to pay Customs dues, he decided on the spot that "the duty on pigs must not be levied at New Year" (免 徵 猪 稅). The Prime Minister in attendance misunderstood the word *chu* (猪), "pigs," as meaning *chu* (諸), that is to say, "all," or "any," and in his memorial, which was approved in due course, proposed that "at the New Year no duties should be levied on any goods."

Through this fortunate misunderstanding, therefore, junks were allowed the privilege of landing and shipping any quantity of cargo duty free on the last day of the Old Year and the first of the New, until the caprice of the changing river directed its course so far to the north that Golden Island ceased to be by the waterside and became Golden Hill several miles inland. The mudbank which formed on its north was left for years undeveloped, for it was one of the prerogatives of the monks, to whom this little island was given as an Imperial bounty many centuries ago, that Buddhist feelings must not be offended by the casting of nets in its front.

The distance from Chinkiang to Nanking is 45 miles. The hills stretching to the westward, some 3 or 4 miles inland, are about 800 feet high.

Nanking, or Southern Capital, owes its title to the fact of its having figured at intervals until the commencement of the fifteenth century as the seat of the Chinese Court and to the maintenance of three important offices of the Chinese Government for centuries after the removal of the capital to Shunt'ienfu (順天府), and later to Peking (Northern Capital), which is now renamed Peiping.

Some 50 miles above Nanking the "Pillars" are reached, a narrow cleft between two towering walls of rock, through which the river sweeps with a velocity and depth notably increased by the confinement of its current. The cliffs rise precipitously on either hand to a height of from 300 to 400 feet. Beyond the Pillars, at a distance of about 1½ miles inland, lies the city of Wuhu.

Between Tatung (大通) and Wuhu (蕪湖) a three-storied pagoda stands on the river-bank. It is told among the junkmen that there was once a far from virtuous widow who was over friendly with the monk of a temple on the site of the present pagoda. She was drowned, however, when attempting to cross the river in a storm to keep an assignation. Her bereaved son, in an access of filial piety, built a seven-storied pagoda onto the temple in memory of his mother. On completion it was found to the great astonishment of the country-side that the top four stories of the pagoda had mysteriously vanished. By this miracle it was made clear that the supernatural powers could not permit the whole structure to stand; but the first three stories remained as a monument, not to the undeserving widow, but to her dutiful son. History is silent as to the monk's reactions to this astonishing event.

The city of Wuhu (蕪湖), which name may be translated Weedy Lake, is situated on a creek about 1½ miles inland from the right bank of the river. This navigable stream, the Changho (長河), is connected with a network of waterways serving an extensive grain-growing hinterland and joining up with the Grand Canal system.

Near-by is the place associated with the tragic death of the famous poet Li T'ai-po (李太白), who lived in the eighth century A.D. After a convivial dinner he was crossing the stream in a sampan one moonlight night. On seeing the reflection of the moon in the river he tried to embrace it, with the distressing result that he fell overboard and was drowned.

Another reference to the poet Li T'ai-po will be found in Part One, page 16.

This district is rich in junkmen's legends, for it is believed that on this section of the river an evil spirit with a large appetite claimed a yearly ration of a junk laden with rice. Its place of abode was about a mile above Wuhu, and the spot was marked by swirls on the face of the water. The spirit's greed, however, was tempered with mercy, for, although a rice-carrying junk was sunk or capsized near this spot each year, no lives were ever lost.

Interesting ground for this superstition is provided by a discovery made by the River Inspectorate of the Chinese Customs. Surveys of the locality showed the Wuhu Reach to be deep and free from dangers to navigation, but in 1928 an ocean steamer passing the place reported striking a submerged object. Closer lines of soundings made by the Customs revealed an isolated pinnacle rock as being a hidden menace to all shipping. Its situation in mid-channel made it all the more remarkable that more accidents had not occurred, probably owing to the fact that shipping instinctively tended to avoid the heavy swirls that circled the region of the rock. The obstruction was thereafter marked with a light-boat named the *Chingyun* Light-boat, and the evil spirit has been deprived of its annual meal.

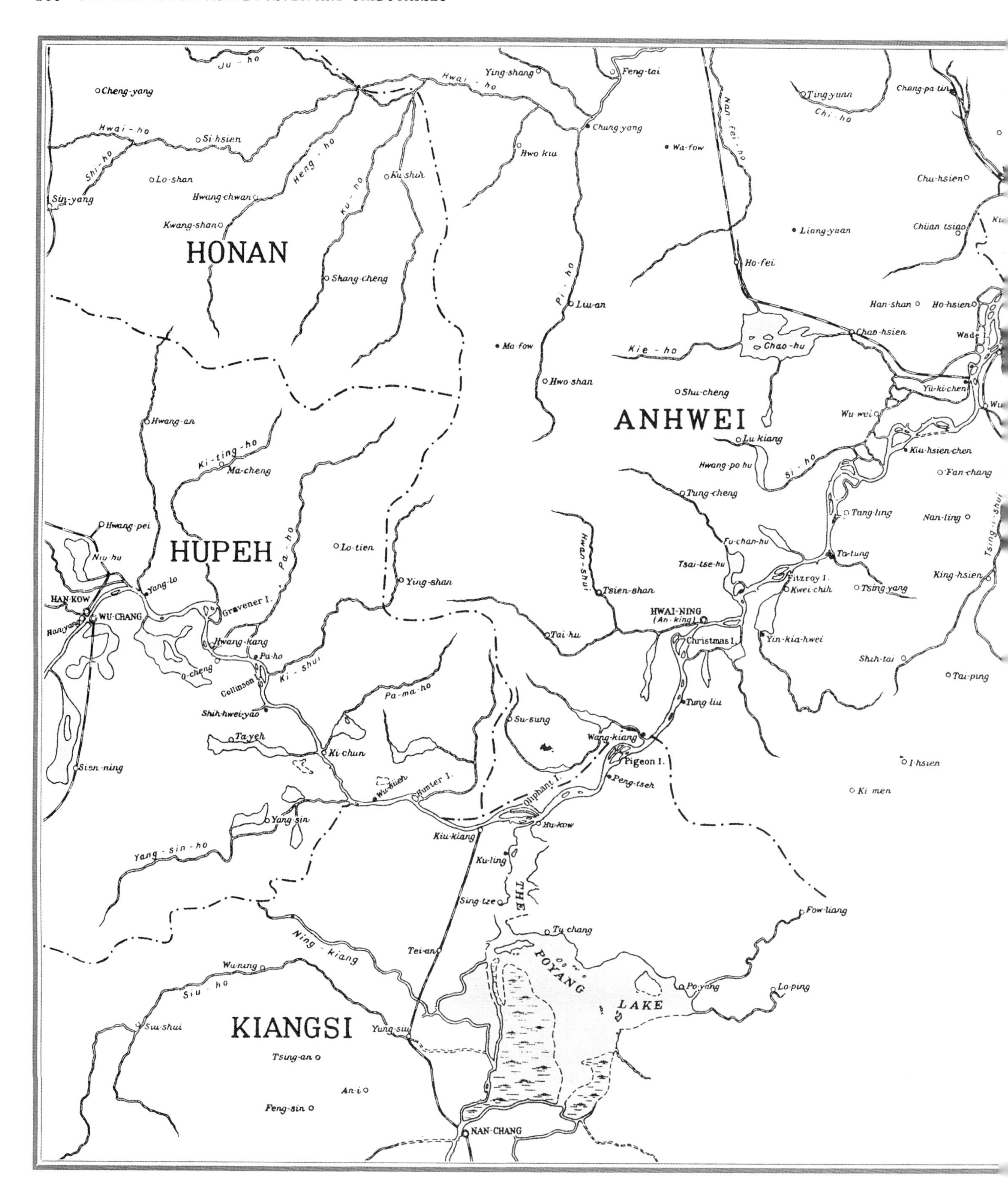
HONAN
HUPEH
ANHWEI
KIANGSI
Ju - ho
Cheng-yang
Hwai - ho
Si-hsien
Shi-ho
Lo-shan
Sin-yang
Hwang-chwan
Kwang-shan
Heng - ho
Ku - ho
Ku-shih
Ying-shang
Feng-tai
Chung-yang
Hwo-kiu
Shang-cheng
Pi - ho
Liu-an
Ma-fow
Hwo-shan
Wa-fow
Nan-fei-ho
Ting-yuan
Chi - ho
Cheng-pa-tin
Chu-hsien
Liang-yuan
Chüan-tsiao
Ho-fei
Han-shan
Ho-hsien
Chao-hsien
Chao-hu
Kie - ho
Shu-cheng
Wade
Yü-ki-chen
Wu-wei
Lu-kiang
Hwang-po-hu
Si - ho
Kiu-hsien-chen
Fan-chang
Tang-ling
Nan-ling
Tung-cheng
Hwan-shui
Fu-chan-hu
Tsai-tse-hu
Ta-tung
Fitzroy I.
Kwei-chih
Tsing-yang
King-hsien
Tsien-shan
HWAI-NING
(An-king)
Christmas I.
Yin-kia-hwei
Shih-tai
Tai-ping
Tai-hu
Tung-liu
Hwang-an
Ki-ting-ho
Ma-cheng
Hwang-pei
Niu-hu
Yang-lo
HAN-KOW
WU-CHANG
Hanyang
Gravener I.
Hwang-kang
Pa-ho
Pa - ho
Lo-tien
Ying-shan
Ki - shui
Collinson
Shih-hwei-yao
Ta-yeh
Pa-ma-ho
Ki-chun
Su-sung
Wang-kiang
Pigeon I.
Peng-tseh
I-hsien
Ki-men
Sien-ning
Wu-süeh
Hunter I.
Olphant I.
Hu-kow
Kiu-kiang
Ku-ling
Yang-sin
Yang - sin - ho
Sing-tze
THE
Fow-liang
Tu-chang
POYANG
LAKE
Po-yang
Lo-ping
Tei-an
Ning - kiang
Wu-ning
Siu - ho
Suu-shui
Yung-siu
Tsing-an
An-i
Feng-sin
NAN-CHANG

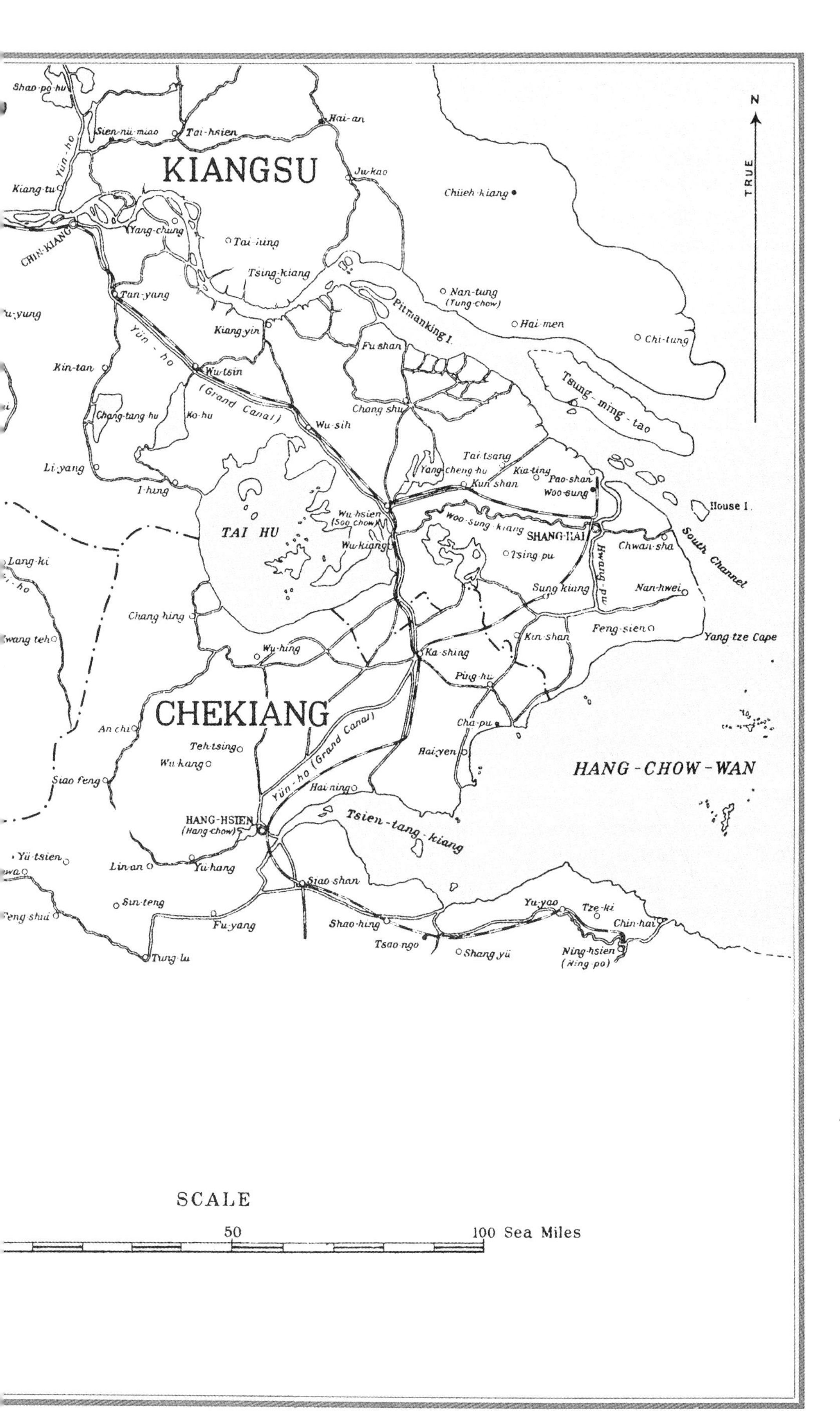

The lower Yangtze River and adjacent waterways from the sea to Hankow.

鹽
城

THE YENCHENG-CH'UAN OR SALT CITY BOAT

The Salt City boat is not noteworthy for speed or for grace of line, but, being a half-sister of the Kiangsu trader, she can justly lay claim to a distinguished and ancient ancestry. Her port of origin is Liuho (劉 河).

Junks of this type are quite admirable in design and construction, for they are capable of navigating shoal water with a minimum draught and maximum carrying capacity, while at the same time possessing sea-going qualities of a high order.

Made of *sha-mu*, with camphor-wood bulkheads and frames, its over-all measurement is 104 feet, with a beam of 22 feet and a depth of 7 feet. The main deck is continuous from bow to stern, and the square-shaped abrupt stem terminates in a heavy transverse beam[1] fitted with pin fair-leads.

The 32-foot house[2] fitted with sliding hatches[3] is built on the main deck. It is very low. An attempt at adornment is here seen in the varnished and carved doors. The house is divided into two parts. The foremost end includes the living quarters of some of the crew and box bunk-cabins for the laodah and second hand, while the after-end, including the cockpit, is given up to the galley. Abaft this, through a "moon door," the space at the stern is available for the stowage of pots and pans, washing tubs, and so forth[4].

There are 16 transverse bulkheads[5] made up of planks laid horizontally on edge. Ribs[6], less the futtocks, are built into each bulkhead.

Of the five masts, none is vertical and only two are stepped in the median line. The sails are of the square-headed lug variety and differ little except as regards size from those illustrated for the Kiangsu trader.

The description and plan drawing of the Kiangsu Trader are in Part Two, page 162.

A couple of four-fluked anchors are stowed forward. The rope cable is faked on deck, some turns being passed round the upper rail of the bulwarks. A pair of yulohs are carried, and are used in the ordinary standing-up position common in all estuary craft.

The housing of the foremast is a masterpiece of ingenuity (*illustrated*). It is stepped, inboard, on the port side, against the bulwarks[1] on the one side and on the other to the single wing of a tabernacle[2]-cum-deck beam[3], grown to shape. It is lashed[4] to another tabernacle[5] wing of similar design and construction outside

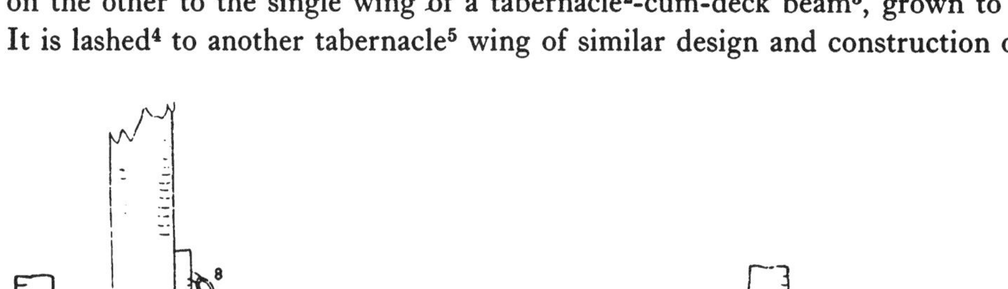

Method of housing the foremast.

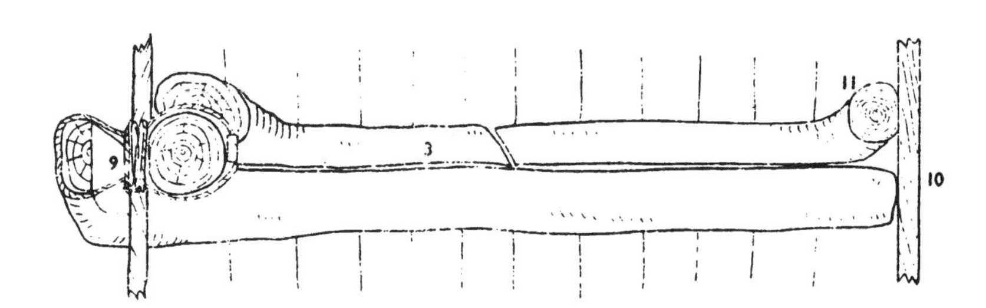

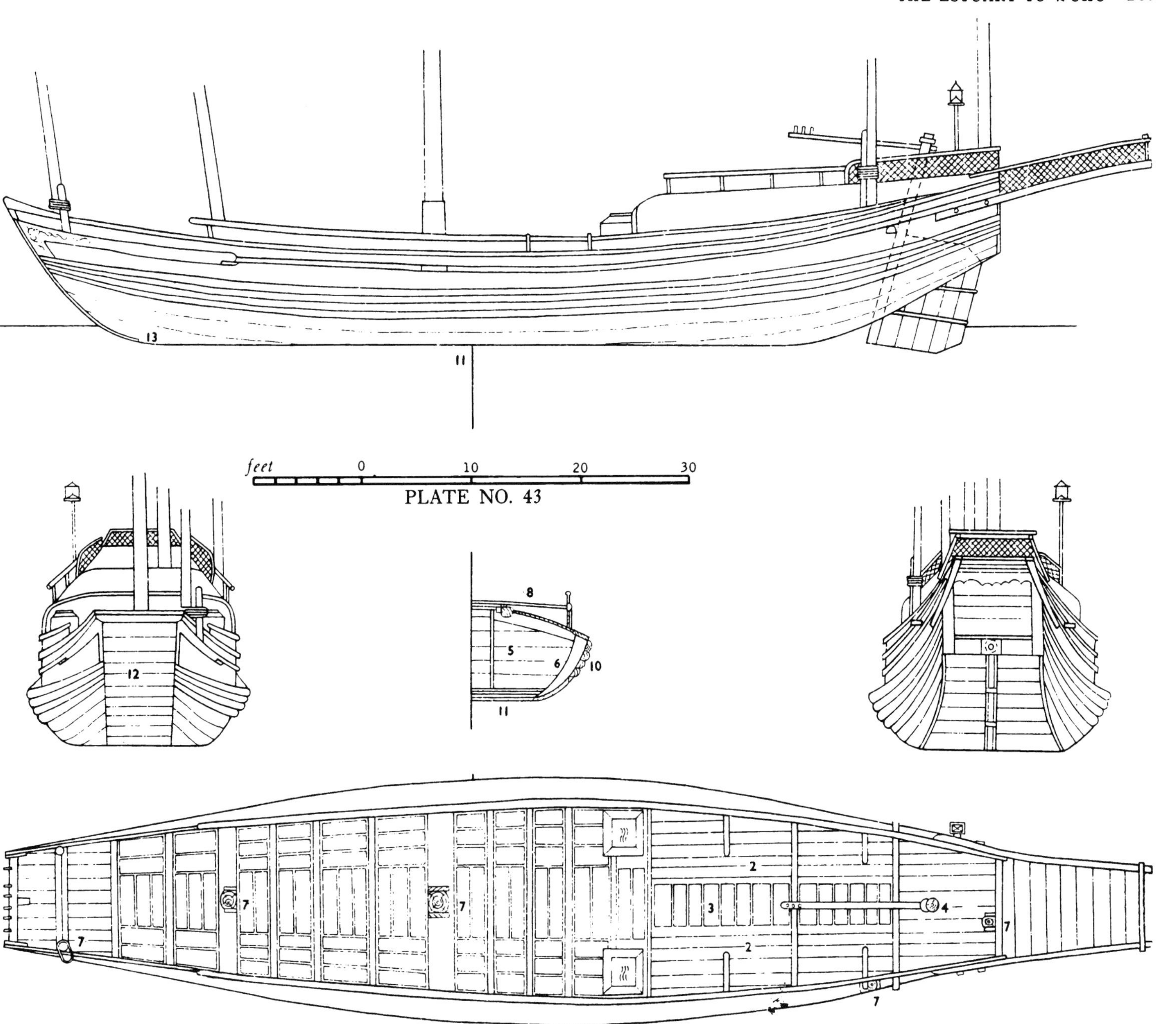

PLATE NO. 43

the port bulwarks.[1] There being no space available for a pin-rail, a moving cleat[6] of novel design is secured to the mast by means of a ring-bolt at top and bottom.[8] The sail, when furled, lodges in the aperture[9] between the mast and the tabernacle. The inboard wing of the tabernacle terminates against the starboard bulwarks[10] and forms a bitt.[11]

The junk is turret-built, with a broad deck[8] superimposed upon it, and derives her main strength from two heavy longitudinals[9] running from bow to stern laid across the bulkheads[5] as well as from four heavy wales[10]. The hull is completely flat-bottomed[11]. The planks run fore and aft except for the bow planking[12], which runs athwartships to a point well below the water-line, where it meets the bottom planks[13].

The method by which the deck planking is secured to the whale-back may be seen from the section on Plate No. 43.

This particular junk is of outstanding interest. She was built since the Sino-Japanese War and abundantly proves that the Kiangsu shipwrights have lost none of their skill and have not forgotten how to build these wonderful junks.

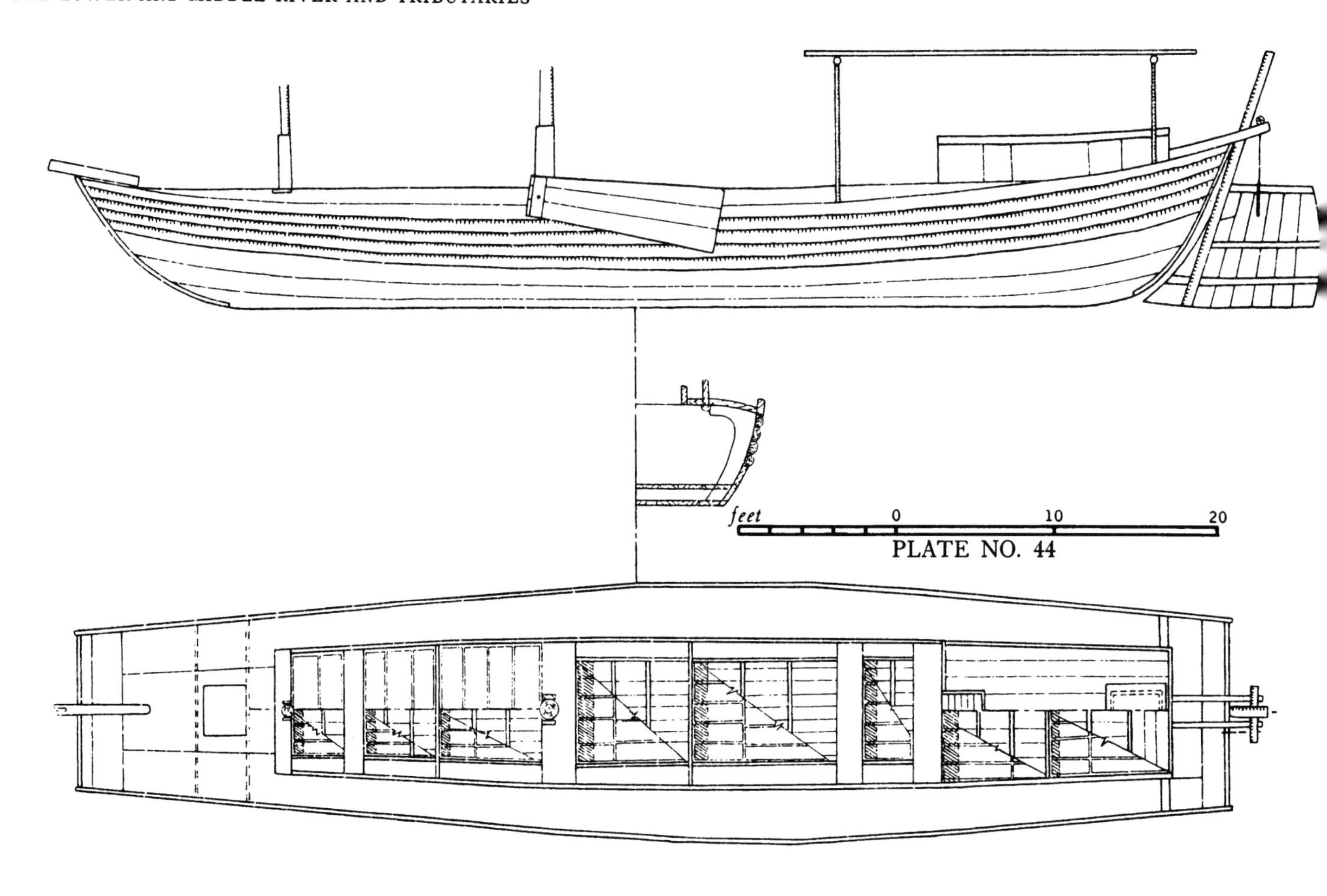

PLATE NO. 44

THE LOWER YANGTZE "HEAVY-LIFT" CARGO-BOAT

These craft, which are for the most part built at Shanghai, have a very wide radius of action, for they serve the whole of the Lower Yangtze from Hankow down to Shanghai. They are also to be met with on the Poyang Lake, but are too large to navigate the creeks and inland waterways. This type does not vary much in size. The specimen illustrated in Plate No. 44 measures 83 feet in length, with a beam of 15 feet, a depth of 7½ feet, and a cargo capacity of 100 tons.

Made of *sha-mu* with hardwood frames, the main characteristic of these boats is their exceptional strength, supplied by 15 full frames and eight bulkheads of massive proportions, the latter being built up to the shape of the hull. The hull planking, which measures 1 foot wide, is from 2 to 3 inches thick and is laid longitudinally as far as the round of the bow and stern, that is to say, about as far as the foremost and aftermost bulkheads respectively. From thence the bottom boards of the hull are laid transversely and continue upwards to form the gently curving bow and stern. Additional strength is given by four heavy wales. There is a hatch-coaming about a foot high, which extends from the house to the foremast. The owner lives in the house, which is roomier than in most junks, for steps lead down to the level of the bottom boards. Extra shelter is provided by a wooden standing awning. The crew of eight live forward in quarters reached by means of a booby hatch.

The cat-head for the anchor, which extends over the bow, is secured to the deck. There are two masts with square-headed lug-sails, but these craft are more often than not towed by a small launch. The two lee-boards when down extend 4½ feet below the bottom of the junk. The rudder is of the embryo semi-balance variety and has a slot cut out to allow of the helm being put hard over.

These sturdy weight-carriers are capable of transporting cargo of almost incredible weight and dimensions.

Their capacity may be judged by the following instance. Two of these craft were lashed together abreast and kept at an even distance by means of spars lashed at bow and stern. Railway lines and sleepers were then laid transversely across, projecting rather beyond both junks amidships. Onto these rails was then run a tank locomotive weighing 76 tons. Onto a similar pair of temporarily joined boats were loaded three sets of rails, two 8-ton goods wagons, and a 30-foot 20-ton passenger coach. The whole cargo of rolling stock contained on four cargo-boats was then towed by a small launch from Nanking up the Yangtze and *via* the shallows of the Poyang Lake to Nanchang. A red flag on a bamboo stick down the funnel of the locomotive struck a typically Chinese note.

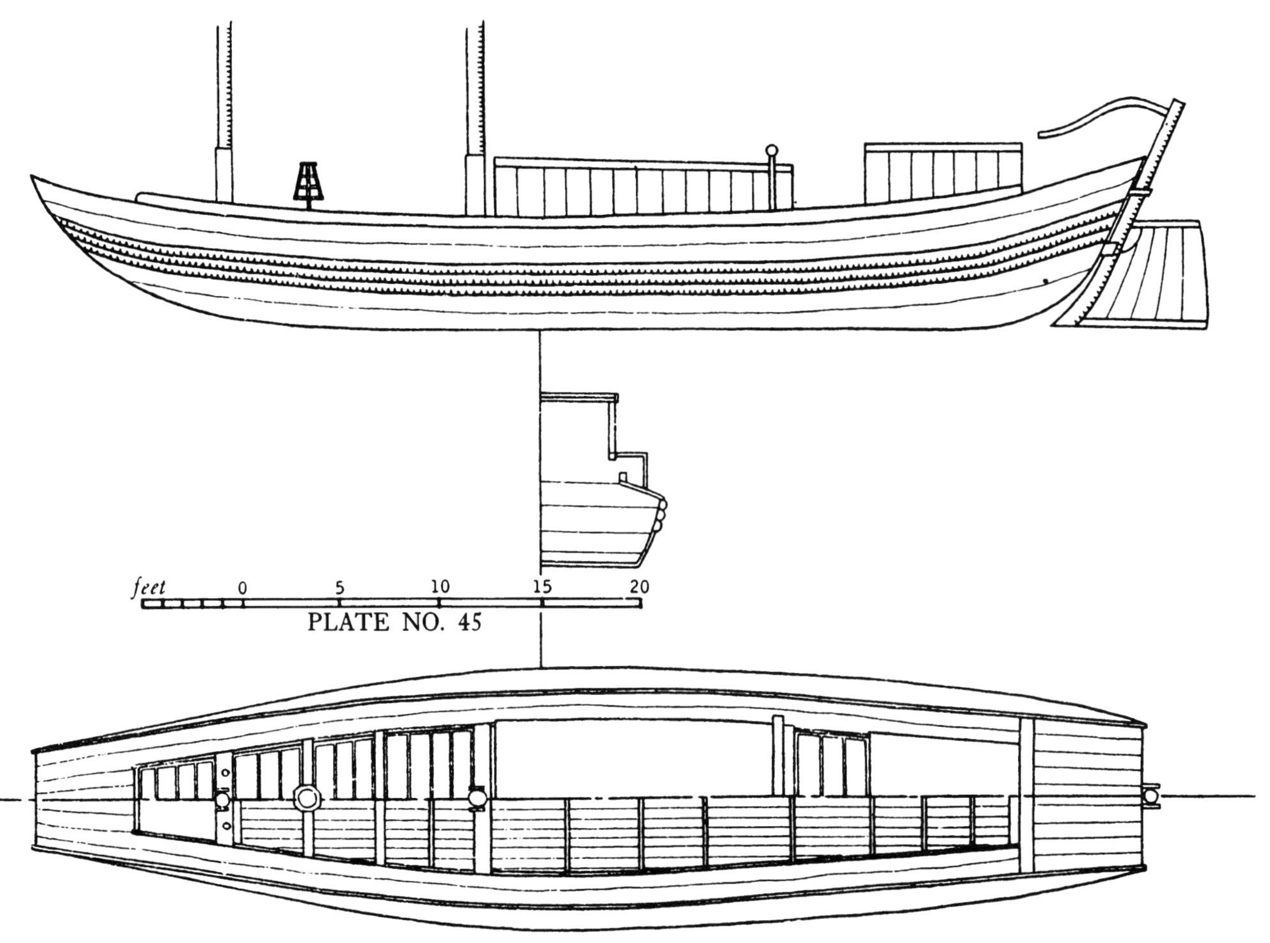

PLATE NO. 45

THE CHIH-SHAO-TZŬ OR STRAIGHT-STERN BOAT

The *chih-shao-tzŭ*, or straight-stern junk, illustrated in Plate No. 45, is the second cousin of the cargo-boat, with which she has much in common.

Designed for open-water work on the river between the estuary and Wuhu, this type of craft usually measures 54 feet, with a beam of 12½ feet and a depth of 5½ feet.

The main characteristics of this broad and powerful junk are the exceptionally square and sloping stern (it can hardly be called straight) and the box-like shape of the hull.

Of simple construction, she is built of *sha-mu* and has seven frames and seven bulkheads, that farthest aft being fitted with a sliding door.

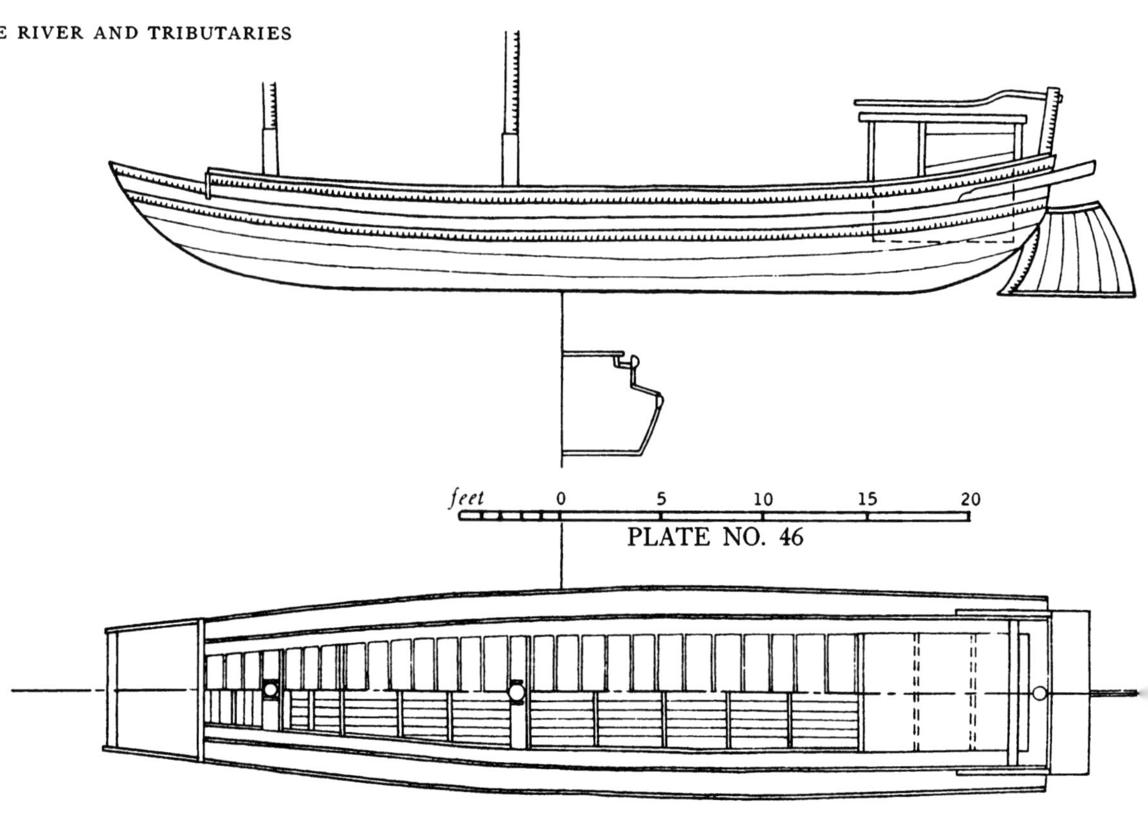

PLATE NO. 46

武梁舟子

THE WULIANG CHOU-TZŬ OR WULIANG BOAT

The Wuliang *chou-tzŭ*, or Wuliang boat, is of pure Wuhu descent and belongs to the dull but useful cargo-boat family.

The craft illustrated in Plate No. 46 shows a characteristic junk of this type, which is designed chiefly for work in the creeks and waterways in the Wuhu hinterland. She measures 48 feet, with a beam of 10 feet 10 inches and a depth of 4 feet 9 inches. Her capacity is about 200 piculs.

The Wuliang *chou-tzŭ* is strongly built and is fitted with four traverse bulkheads and 10 frames. The flush-deck has a low coaming. The stern, which is wide in shape, has a considerable rise and a small part is decked-in. The house is very small.

江蘇鹽船

THE KIANGSU YEN-CH'UAN OR KIANGSU SALT-JUNK

Salt is of the greatest importance to any largely vegetarian diet, and it is therefore not surprising that there are in China many varieties of junks primarily designed for carrying the vast amount of salt which is produced.

Of the salt-producing provinces, Kiangsu heads the list; and the actual salt districts within its borders are three in number: Hwaipei (淮 北) and Hwainan (淮 南), both under the administration of the Lianghwai Salt Bureau, and Sungkiang (松 江), under the Liangchê Salt Bureau. In all, these comprise 19 salt-fields, of which that nearest to Shanghai is the Tsungming salt-field on the island of that name.

The *yen-ch'uan*, or, to give its local name, the *changan-ch'uan* (長 安 船), so named after a town near Hangchow, is a typical short-distance salt-carrier of the Yangtze estuary and normally operates between Liuho (劉 河), a town at the mouth

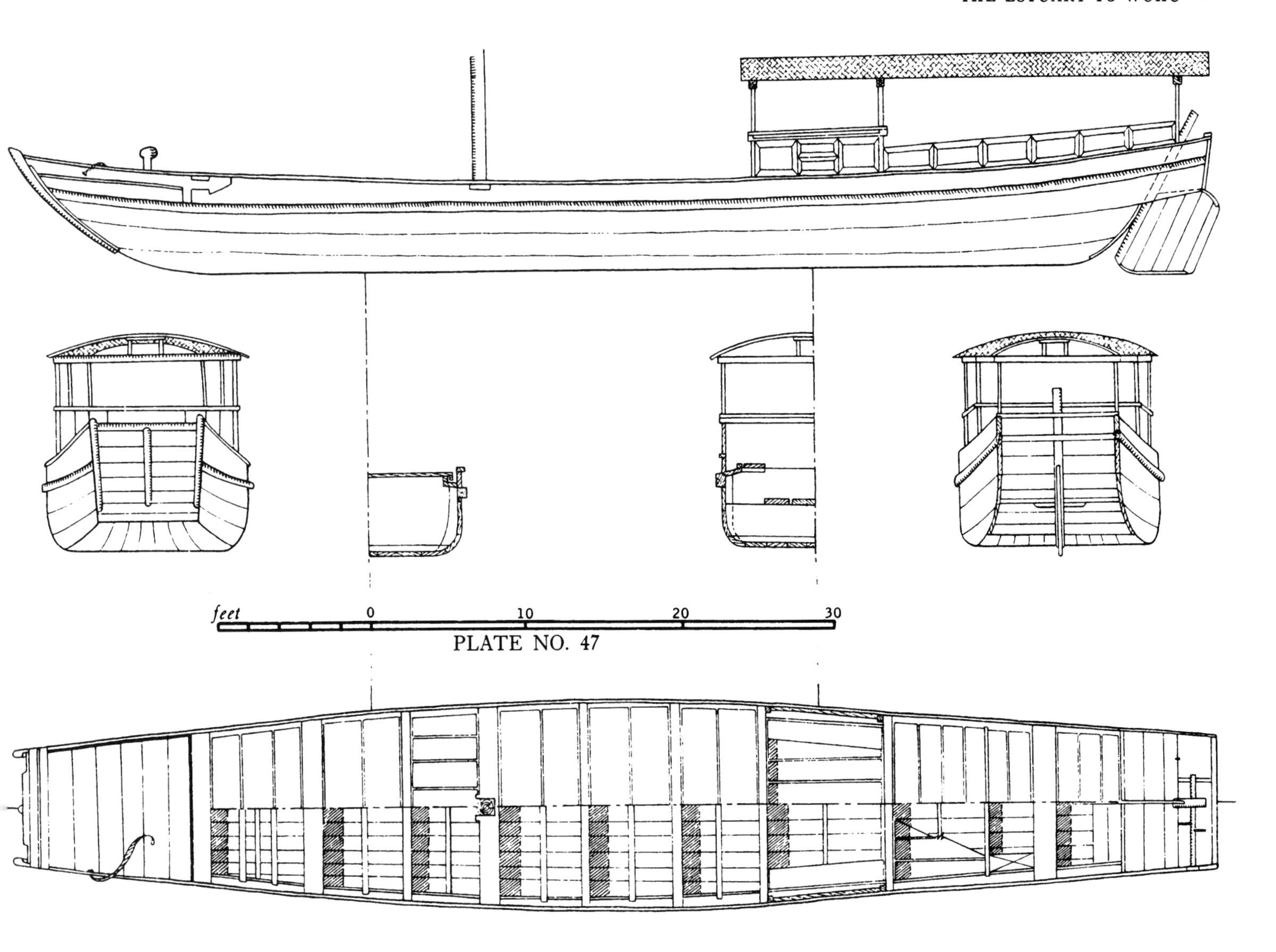

PLATE NO. 47

of a creek on the right bank of the Yangtze, and Shanghai, *via* the river.

Built of *sha-mu*, with 10 hardwood bulkheads and one half-bulkhead inside the house, she has in addition seven frames to give extra strength. The junk is longer than the usual delta craft and measures 78 feet, with a beam of 13 feet and a depth of 5½ feet, so that, despite her length, she is not a heavy-draught craft.

She is, like most salt-junks, in all respects superior to the usual run of cargo-boats in design, finish, and accommodation. The crew, for instance, occupy a compartment measuring 8½ by 12 feet, with the luxury of 5 feet of headroom. Well-made removable panels fitted from abaft the small house to the stern act as bulwarks as necessary. A long heavy wale runs from bow to stern, which latter ends in a more elaborate and deeper overhanging gallery than usual. The bow, which follows graceful lines, has the usual horizontal planking; but this is bisected by a vertical strengthening timber flanked by another similar vertical on either side. A curious feature is the graving piece let in on either side of the bow and extending aft to the first bulkhead. It consists of a newly-scraped portion of *sha-mu*, nicely wood-oiled. Its only use, it appears, is for ornament.

The fore-deck is slightly sunk for reasons undiscernible, and from this position the two bow yulohs are operated from bumkins. A third yuloh is worked from the starboard side of the stern. A windlass is situated on the port side in the stern for hoisting the rudder when in shallow reaches or when not required for use. The boat has the characteristic overhang of the Shanghai district and carries a sloping rudder.

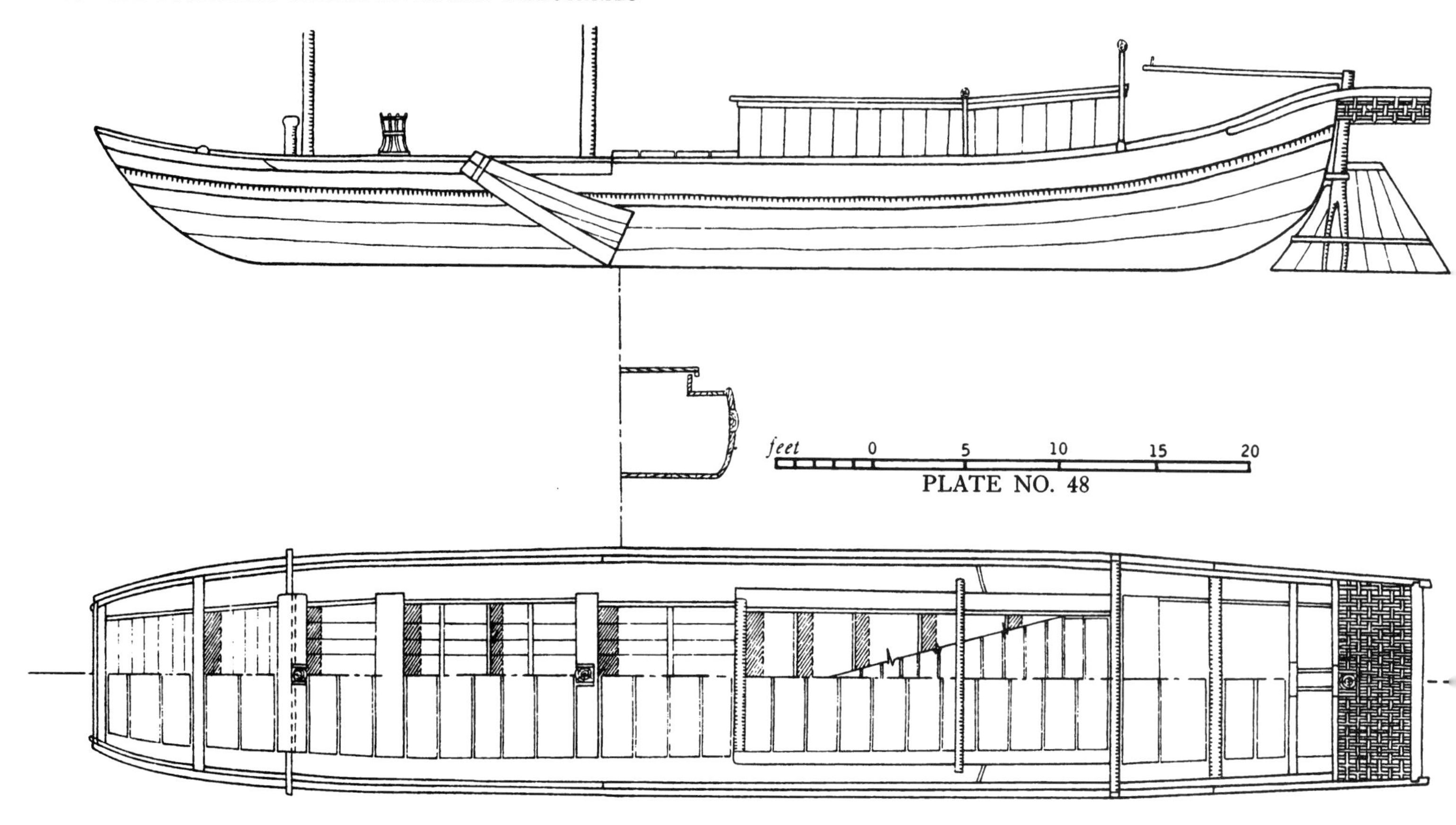

PLATE NO. 48

江北船

THE KIANGPEI-CH'UAN

The *kiangpei-ch'uan*, or "north bank of the river" boat, hails from Taichow (泰州), a town on the north bank of the Yangtze, which river it mainly serves, linking it up with the adjacent creeks, though sometimes the *kiangpei-ch'uan* may be seen as far afield as the Grand Canal.

Made of *sha-mu*, with hardwood frames, this all-purpose craft normally measures 59 feet in length, with a beam of 12 feet and a depth of 5 feet 9 inches—that is to say, it is a narrow deep-draught type with a capacity of 40 tons. The extra strength necessary for this type of construction is provided by seven full bulkheads, five half-bulkheads, and four frames. A raised hatch-coaming runs the length of the vessel. The bluff box-like bow narrows as it ascends from the water-line. The stern is an interesting example of adaptation of the Shanghai type of gallery stern, which has been raised and rounded to accommodate a balance rudder. The heavy rudder itself has perforce been reduced in area and weight, and this sacrifice is particularly noticeable in the fore-part of the rudder, as a considerable portion of the area is in this case placed abaft the turning axis. The result, although inelegant, achieves its purpose well. The rudder is non-hoisting, and the method of slinging employed is the *kiangpei* type. It is suspended from two fore and aft partners engaging into the after cross-beam. The overhanging stern gallery, which projects about 4½ feet, is floored with bamboo slats and serves as a convenient storage space for firewood and lumber.

The low house, which permits of passage fore and aft outside, measures 20 feet, is divided into a living-room for the owner and his family and a galley aft, which is on the port side, and is fitted with a galley-funnel. The planks forming the roof of the house are fitted with a flange to prevent the entry of water and are all removable, as indeed is every deck-plank in the junk, even those usually found fixed in the extreme bow and stern.

The crew of five live below deck in an area measuring 9 by 10 feet in the fore-part of the junk.

Two yulohs of the curved variety are worked as necessary from the bumkins fitted in the bow.

These junks, clumsy and roughly built as they may look, are yet full of interest, for their very crudeness points to a more ancient and unchanged origin than that of many others of the delta craft.

THE FLOWER-BOATS OF NANKING

南京花船

For very many centuries it has been the custom in China for the gentleman of leisure to find amusement on a warm summer evening by chartering a boat for himself and his friends to be rowed about the placid waters of the lake or river to the accompaniment of music provided by singing girls. They sang, read, played the lute, drank wine, and composed poems.

This practice is said to have started in the time of the Liu Ch'ao (六 朝), or Six Dynasties, A.D. 265–589, a period prolific in literature and verse, when the *literati* and poets sought inspiration in this manner, with the stimulus of wine, women, and song added to the age-old romance of idly floating on the moon-lit waters.

The denizens of "flower streets" and "willow lanes" in these ancient days were not only trained to accompany themselves on various musical instruments and to sing in their highly complicated falsetto style, but also were girls of education versed in literature. Many of them, indeed, were able to write poetry themselves as well as being qualified to criticize that of their employers.

Gradually the custom of hiring boats and singing girls became more general, and the boatmen named their craft *hua-ch'uan*, or "flower-boats."

The picturesque imagery of the Chinese language is well exemplified by the titles given to the frail little singers, a great many of the names being taken from characters in that most celebrated of all Chinese romantic novels, "Hung Lou Mêng" (紅 樓 夢), "The Dream of the Red Chamber," by Ts'ao Hsüeh-ch'in (曹 雪 芹), such as Tai Yü (Black Jade), Pao Ch'ai (Precious Hairpins), Hsi Fêng (Glorious Phœnix), Yüan Ying (Mandarin Duck), Tzŭ Chuan (Purple Cuckoo), Pao Ch'in (Precious Lute), Ch'ing Wên (Lovable Cloud), Ying Ch'un (to Welcome the Spring), and many others.

The present-day sing-song girls, as they have been so expressively named in English, are far below their early prototypes in education, but illiterate though they may be, they have a word-perfect repertoire of between 20 and 30 different songs, each having sometimes as many as 100 verses, and they are as much in request as ever as an additional attraction to the flower-boats of Nanking.

These craft used to ply on the Chinhwaiho (秦 淮 河), a name literally translated as the "River opened during the Ch'in dynasty" (秦 朝), which flowed into the Yangtze at Nanking. The Fu Tzŭ Miao (夫 子 廟), or Confucius Temple, used to be the centre of the trade, and here the flower-boats used to be seen in great numbers. In course of time, however, this waterway became silted up and the boats moved to the Hsüanwuhu (玄 武 湖), or Lotus Lake, now a public park and beauty spot. It is a large lake, several miles in circumference, situated

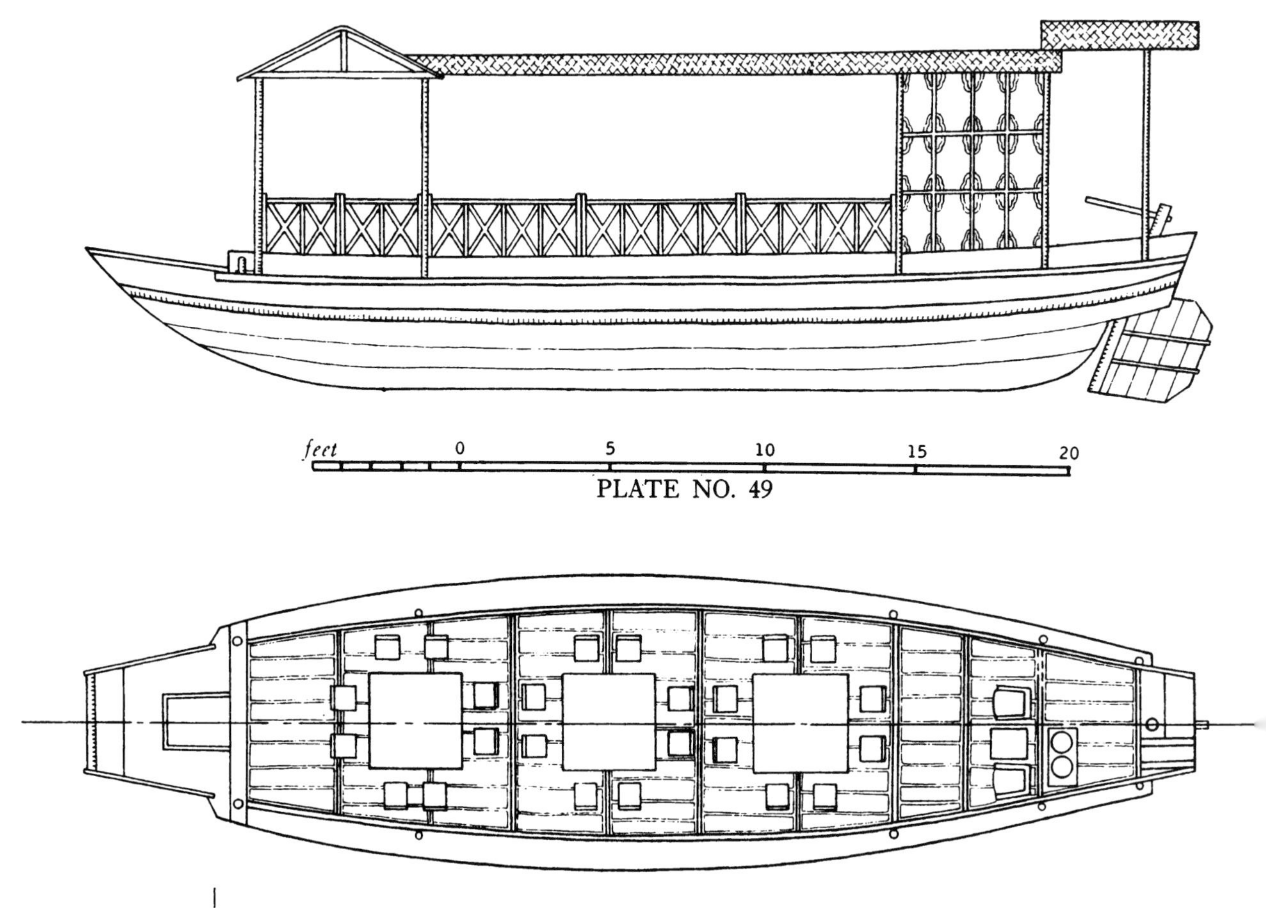

PLATE NO. 49

immediately north of Nanking. In course of time houses were built round the lake and the water became polluted.

The large flower-boats (see Plate No. 49), with an over-all measurement of 35 feet, are called *lou-tzŭ* (樓子), or "boat with a gallery," and are big enough to accommodate three tables of guests. These craft are decorated with polished lattice-work sides, windows with gay paint of various colours, and are well furnished with tables and chairs. A large wooden bed, or *k'ang* (炕), which has a small low table placed in the middle of it so that a guest may sit or lie on either side, used to be part of the equipment, but this has now been disallowed in recent times.

The smaller boats, with an over-all measurement of 18 feet, have room for one table of eight only. These are called *hsiao-ch'i-pan* (小七板), or "small seven planks." Sing-song girls are also carried in still smaller flower-boats measuring about 10 feet, which are merely sampans with a steeply arched awning amidships. Under the mat roof in the light of a paper lantern sit the girls, who are dressed in bright silks. Kuan Niang (Lady Sincerity), Hsiao Chun-hung (Laughing Peach Blossom), Chih Ting (Iris Pavilion), Chiao Yun (Elevated Clouds), and Yin Hsiang (Singing Fragrance) sing by turns in a shrill voice to the accompaniment of the two-stringed fiddle played by an elderly man, while a second man in the bow beats time with a pair of bamboo clappers in his left hand and a drumstick in his right with which he hammers away at the drum on his knees. Sometimes one of the girls may play on a sort of guitar.

One hundred cash was once the modest cost for this entertainment, and for this sum three songs could be selected from a list inscribed on a paper fan. The price for hiring a whole flower-boat was once $4 per day, unless competition was keen owing to a spell of hot weather or the presence of a specially talented singer. The times, however, have changed considerably as regards price, and now only the rich reserve the fair.

THE NANKING CARGO-BOAT

南京駁船

These craft are built at the town from which they take their name and function mainly in the harbour at Nanking, where they are employed in transporting cargo from ship to ship, from ship to shore, or *vice versa*.

Lighter in construction than most cargo-carriers, they are typical craft for light short-distance work and might very well be described as huge sampans. Indeed, it is interesting to compare them with the Lower Yangtze type of sampans with which they have much in common, notably the double-wing variety of stern.

The boat illustrated in Plate No. 50 measures 57 feet in length, with a beam of 12 feet and a depth of 5 feet. The *sha-mu* hull is divided by five hardwood bulkheads and five full frames. There is nothing remarkable about her lines, which gradually widen from the broad, low, square bow until the widest part of the boat is reached at the sixth bulkhead, and are only very slightly reduced at the stern. The bow is reinforced by a heavy transverse stem-beam. Both bow and stern are decked in. A heavy wale runs from end to end of the vessel. The rudder is of the true balance-rudder variety. The mainmast carries a square-headed lug-sail. The crew of four live below deck in the after compartment. A removable mat awning extends from abaft the mast to the stern.

As a point of interest, it may be noted that the particular boat here depicted was "measured up" at Chungking. She had left Nanking in the face of the Japanese advance up river, and, with a cargo of machinery, travelled 1,100 miles up the Yangtze, successfully negotiating all the rapids of the Upper Yangtze in what must have been quite an epic voyage for a light cargo-boat.

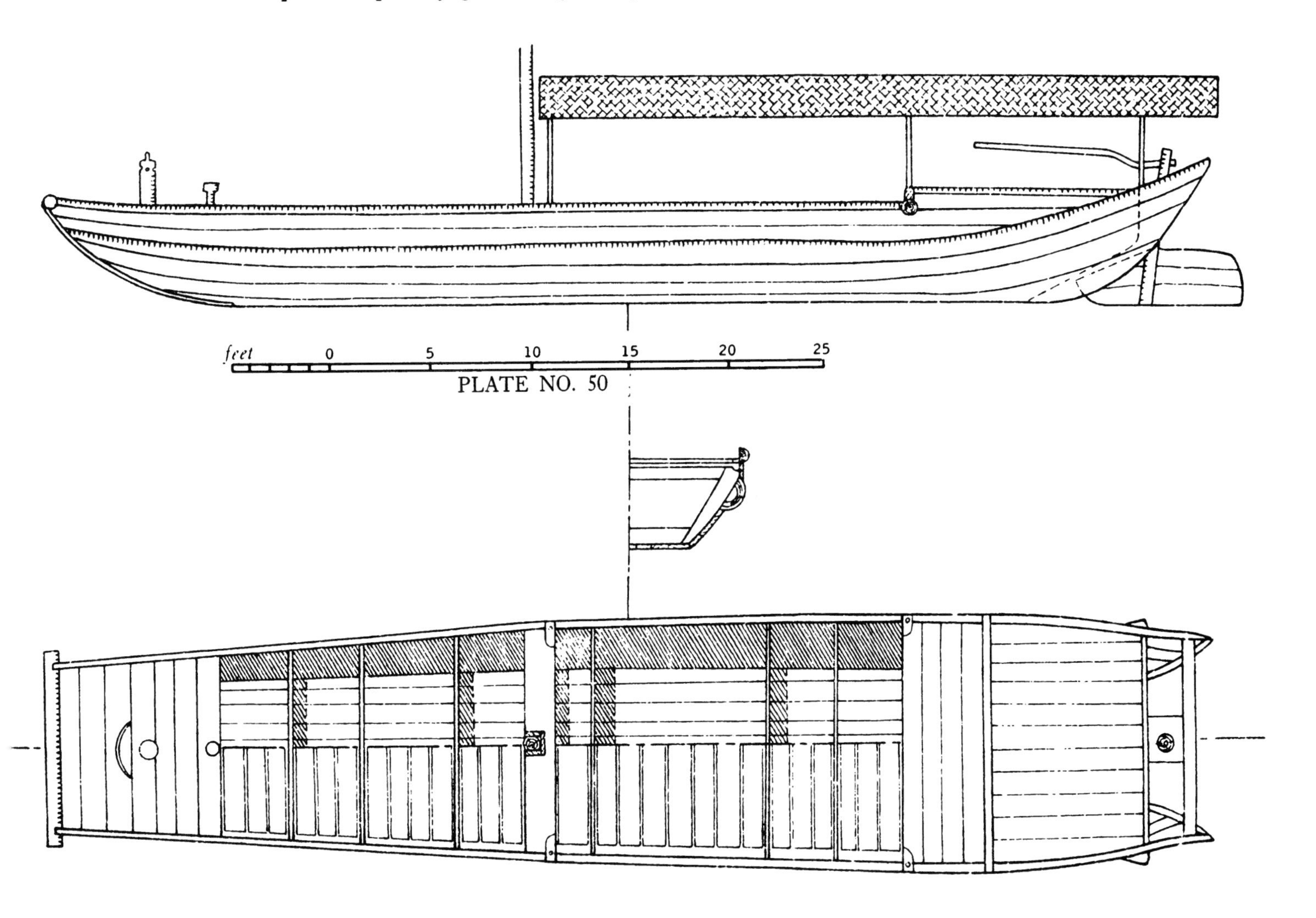

PLATE NO. 50

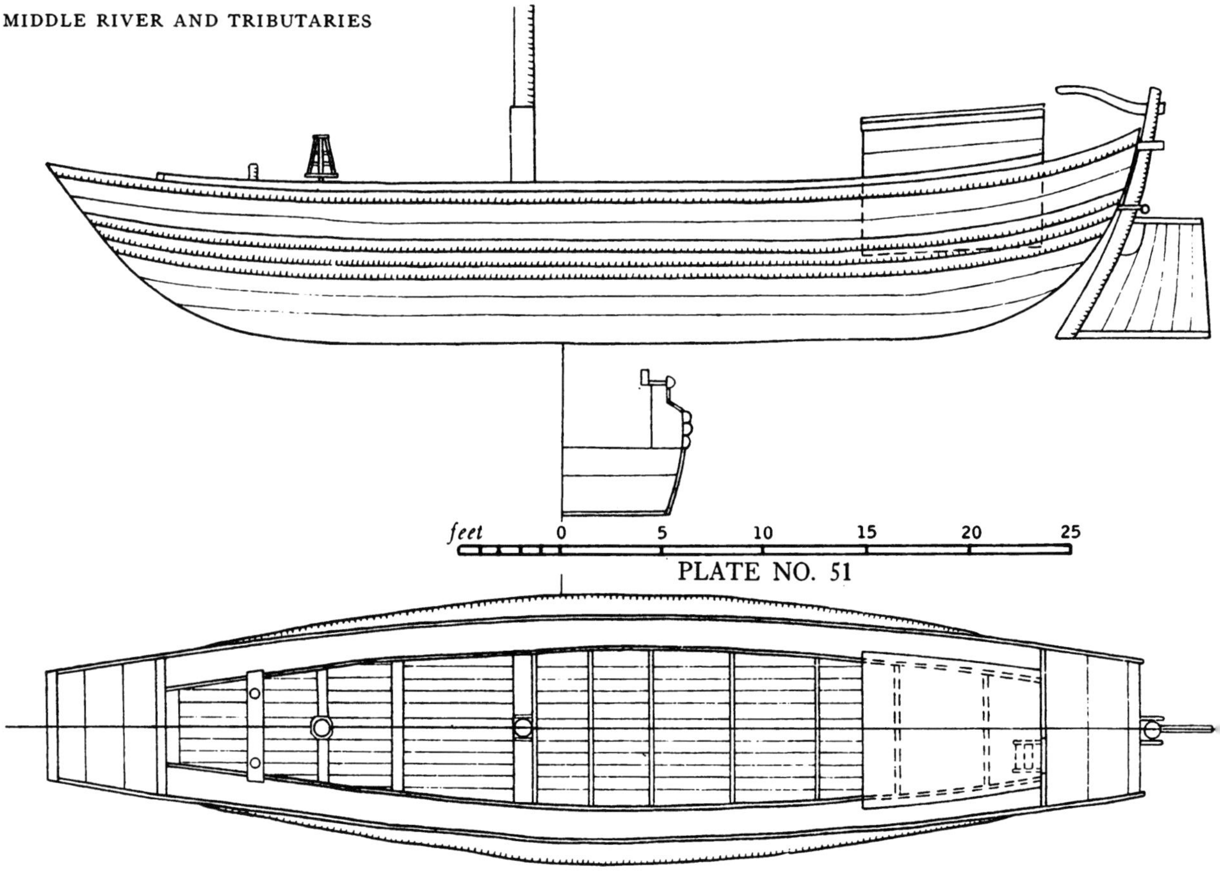

feet 0 5 10 15 20 25

PLATE NO. 51

横梢子

THE HÊNG-SHAO-TZŬ

A typical cargo-boat, which has much in common with the Wuhu cargo-boats to be described later, is the *hêng-shao-tzŭ*, or curved-stern junk.

This boat, which is illustrated in Plate No. 51, is remarkable for its square box-like appearance, and measures 53 feet in length, with a beam of 12½ feet and a depth of 7 feet.

The curved rudder-post is secured to the stern in the customary manner.

These cargo-boat types, which bear a strong family likeness, are rather dull craft.

THE "WALKEE WALKEE" DUCKS OF NANKING

Although they cannot come under any nautical category, the travelling flocks of Nanking ducks, or "walkee walkee" ducks as they are known to foreigners, are such a feature of the district that no book dealing with this section of the river would be complete without a description of them.

The utilization of small streams, canals, and ponds for raising ducks is practised everywhere on the river, especially in the Yangtze Delta. Beginning from the latter part of spring, thousands of ducklings are to be seen paddling along the banks of the canals.

Because of the excellent feeding grounds around the many lakes in the vicinity, Wuhu has become the recognized centre of the duck-breeding industry, which is divided into various branches. Thus, some see to the hatching of the eggs and the selling of them or of the ducklings, others fatten the young birds for eating, and some deal in the feathers only. Birds from Tatung (大 通), near Fitzroy Island, and Kiangpei (江 北), opposite Wuhu, are much sought after by the epicures of Nanking and Shanghai.

Although some of them are disposed of locally at Wuhu, the majority go down river to Nanking where, despite their place of origin, they become Nanking *ya-tzŭ* (南 京 鴨 子), or Nanking ducks.

They usually swim down in convoys of between 2,000 and 3,000 birds, although occasionally a gigantic flock of 10,000 may be seen. They are accompanied by three sampans to guide, collect, and urge them forward. One sampan is stationed on each beam of the convoy, and a larger one astern carries a bowman who monotonously beats the water with a long bamboo pole to hurry on the stragglers in the rear.

The distance to be covered from the feeding grounds down to Nanking varies from 50 to 100 miles. The normal speed of the convoy is at most 1 knot, but it is helped considerably, especially during the summer and autumn months, by the existence of down-river current in this portion of the Lower Yangtze, so that as much as 4 knots may be achieved at times. Rests are, of course, necessary; but, with good luck and good weather, the ducks are probably brought to market in two days, before they lose much weight from over-driving.

At night the convoy comes ashore. During the passage the ducks feed on fallen rice in the fields along the way. In exchange for the rice picked up the farmers get the manure that is left behind.

If, however, a breeze should spring up, the choppy waves set up in the long open reaches are too much for the domestically-reared ducks, who are "flying fish sailors," accustomed to sheltered ponds and small lakes. In such an event a halt must be called, sometimes for as long as a week; and the drivers, or duckherds, build temporary straw huts on the river-bank as shelters to keep their charges from straying.

Once they have arrived at Nanking their nautical career is over and their "expectation of life" is practically non-existent.

A convoy of "Walkee Walkee" ducks en route to Nanking.

The ducks are not considered fit to eat if over a year old, and this short lifetime is divided into four specialized periods from a feeding point of view. Firstly, they are fed on coarse cooked rice and allowed to pick up a living from worms and duckweed. Secondly, they are given a cooked mixture of shellfish and bran, supplemented by the shrimps and small fish they can find in the waters of the lakes. Thirdly, about the 7th moon, after the harvest, they are driven into the fields to glean what remains from the reaping, and flocks of 100 or more may be seen being shepherded from field to field by men with two long bamboo driving-poles. As they grow older they find more of their feed from the water than the pail, but during the final period the ducks are fed more intensively, being given three cooked meals a day of rice and bran, and after 10 days of such fattening fare, are ready for the Nanking market.

Ducklings as young as "100 days" may be eaten, but they are considered more desirable for the table after eight months or a year. In Nanking eight months' birds are termed *kuei-hua-ya* (桂 花 鴨), or "ducks with the delicious fragrance of the *Olea*, or cassia tree." The year-old ducks are called *pan-ya* (板 鴨), or "plank ducks"—that is to say, they have been dried until they are literally as "stiff as a board." Both these varieties are famous along the Yangtze Valley.

It is said by the Chinese that Mohammed was very fond of eating ducks and that, therefore, the birds are always specially palatable when cooked by Mohammedans, who, as they are denied by their religion the succulent ham and pork, have developed the cooking of poultry to a fine art. Nine out of every 10 shops in Nanking, where tastily cooked ducks are a speciality, therefore, are owned by Mohammedans. The two most celebrated are the Hêng Yüan (恆 源) and Han Fu Hsing (韓 復 興), whose cooked ducks fulfil the four demands of the Chinese gourmet, that is to say, that they are nicely fattened, correctly coloured, pleasant to the smell, and delicious to the taste.

I am indebted to Mr. Chang Ch'i-tung (張 啓 棟), the noted cook and owner of the Hung Hsing Shop at Nanking, for the following recipe. After the duck has been plucked and cleaned, it is stuffed with 2 ounces of salt in the case of a *kuei-hua-ya*, or 4 ounces for the larger *pan-ya*, and put to soak in a solution of brine, known as *lao-lu* (老 滷), which is not thrown away after use but kept for a succession of birds.

The younger and more tender *kuei-hua-ya* is soaked for four hours and dried before a fire and is then ready for cooking. The *pan-ya* remains in the brine overnight and is then hung up to dry in a current of air for at least three months.

Both are then cooked in the following manner. A pan of fresh water is brought to the boil and removed from the fire. The duck is then immersed in it together with some *chiang* (薑), or fresh ginger, *ts'ung* (葱), or Chinese onions, *ping-t'ang* (冰 糖), or sugar candy, and *pa-chio* (八 角), or aniseed. Cold water is then added so as to reduce the surface temperature of the bird, while the inside remains nearly at boiling point. After an hour the bird is removed, and the water is again boiled, the pan removed from the fire, the bird soaked as before, and again cold water* is added. Another hour is allowed to elapse, and then the bird is boiled in the same water over the fire until tender. When cooked, the ducks are varnished with *ma-yu* (蔴 油), or sesamum-seed oil, which colours them a rich red-brown and also serves to keep away insects and flies. The *pan-ya* has a more salty flavour than the *kuei-hua-ya*.

The mandarin duck is to the Chinese symbolic of connubial happiness. The Nanking duck, albeit on a lower plane, also plays an important *rôle*, for in the Yangtze Valley it stands for the best the table has to offer.

* In the case of the *pan-ya*, an additional boiling is required.

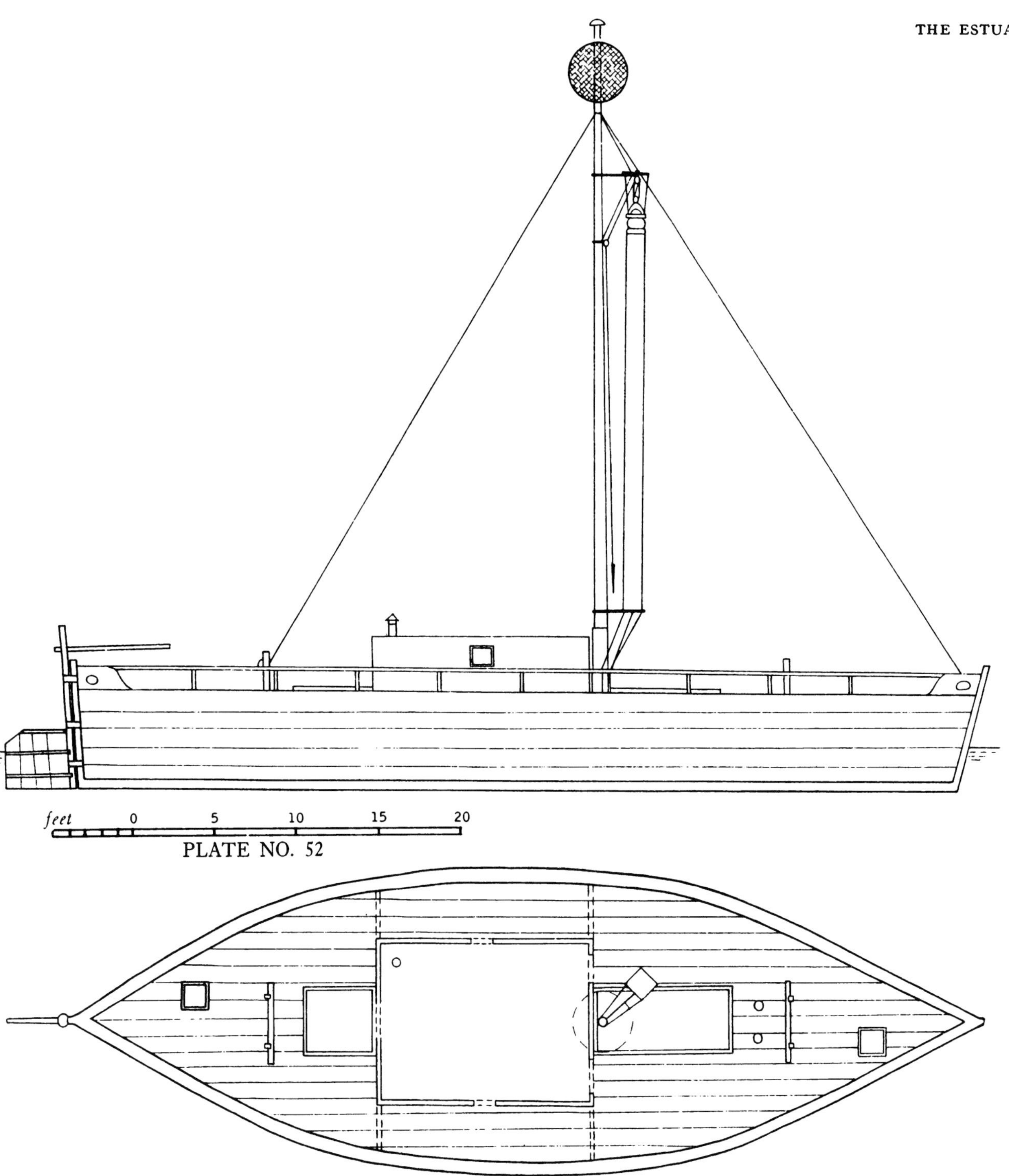

PLATE NO. 52

THE CUSTOMS LIGHT-BOAT

The Customs wooden light-boat played so important a part in the safe navigation of the Yangtze that any account of the craft of the river must include a description of this rather unusual type of light-vessel, which is now obsolete, as it was decided some years ago to replace these craft by those of steel construction so as to obviate expensive overhauls.

Built on the river by Chinese carpenters, the design of these wooden boats kept close to the accepted form of junk construction except that they were provided with a sharp bow and stern, enabling them to ride at anchor in all weathers. The principal feature of the light-boat was, of course, its great proportionate breadth of beam. This was necessitated by the dangerous sea that rises in some of the exposed reaches of the Yangtze.

Their chief function, as their name suggests, was to carry a light; but they also acted as aids to daylight navigation. As the light-boat had no means of self-propulsion, she was towed into the position where she was to be anchored to mark an important turning point. Usually stationed in narrow and tortuous channels and unable to manœuvre, she was particularly liable to suffer collision, an additional reason why she should be strongly built. Generally these boats measured 56 feet in length, with a beam of 18 feet, tapering at bow and stern, and were built of *sha-mu* throughout, except for four camphor-wood frames and 15 watertight bulkheads. The bitts, tabernacles, davits, and so forth were built and fitted in the same manner as in junks of similar size. A small sampan was always carried.

The boats, which were painted a conspicuous red with a white house, carried a sixth order or one or two unclassed lanterns. One or two lights were exhibited, either red or white, or any combination thereof, hoisted vertically or horizontally at the yard. The pole-mast was surmounted by a spherical bamboo daymark, painted black.

When a light-boat was run down or driven out of position by a gale, she exhibited signals to this effect. By day two red flags were hoisted at one yard-arm and at the other the International Code Signal "PC," meaning "I am not in my correct position." By night a system of lights was used.

The greatest hazard the light-boat had to face was the timber rafts. These enormous floating islands, sometimes 280 feet long and more or less out of control, travelled down river with the current, often sweeping all floating aids to navigation before them. In such a case the light-boat is in theory supposed to slip her cable, buoy the end, and drift clear; but in practice the raft almost invariably fouled the anchor buoy and the expensive cable was lost.

River navigation is exceptional in a number of ways: for instance, in the 600-mile stretch from Shanghai to Hankow, large portions of the distance consist of intricate channels, sometimes with very little water, at other times exceptionally deep, when even the banks are flooded. In addition, the dangers from fog, snow, and ice are greater than at sea; and, as a further hazard, an occasional dust-storm has to be faced at certain seasons of the year.

The importance of navigation on the Yangtze led to the adoption of an extensive system of lights and other marks. In normal times there are on the Lower Yangtze 47 light-boats and 104 light-beacons controlled by the River Inspectorate of the Chinese Customs. These aids to navigation, primarily designed to assist steam navigation and paid for from the tonnage dues of vessels, are also of great benefit to junks, particularly during the winter, when their draught is sometimes as much as or more than that of steamers.

The Middle Yangtze wooden light-boats, or mark-boats as they came to be known, were never a success and were the first to be superseded by boats of steel construction. They were still more true to the junk type in that they had square bows and typical junk sterns and were, moreover, provided with two masts and lug-sails. They were also very much larger than the Lower Yangtze types.

It is difficult to leave this section without yielding to the temptation at least to mention the bamboo buoys which marked the critical channels for daylight navigation in the low-water season. These buoys, as used in the Lower Yangtze channels, were strongly constructed of large bamboos, averaging 6 inches in diameter. They consisted of triangular rafts. Each raft had equilateral 10-foot sides with an additional bamboo laid across the centre and extending a foot beyond into the apex. At the after end, in the three places where the bamboos crossed, half of each was cut away so as to make a dovetailing fit. At the fore end, or apex, the side bamboos were tapered to fit snugly against the main central one, and a large bamboo pin passed through the three sections to give rigidity to the raft.

A little forward of the centre of the main bamboo a hole was cut in the upper surface to take a bamboo mast of about $1\frac{1}{2}$ inches in diameter and 5 to 6 feet in height. The three angles of the triangular raft were lashed firmly with wire, and three spun-yarn stays set up the mast also to these three angles. The mast carried a red flag about 18 inches square, or a black kerosene tin or black basketwork ball, according to the side of the channel on which it was placed. The former marked the starboard side and the latter the port side of the channel for vessels bound up river.

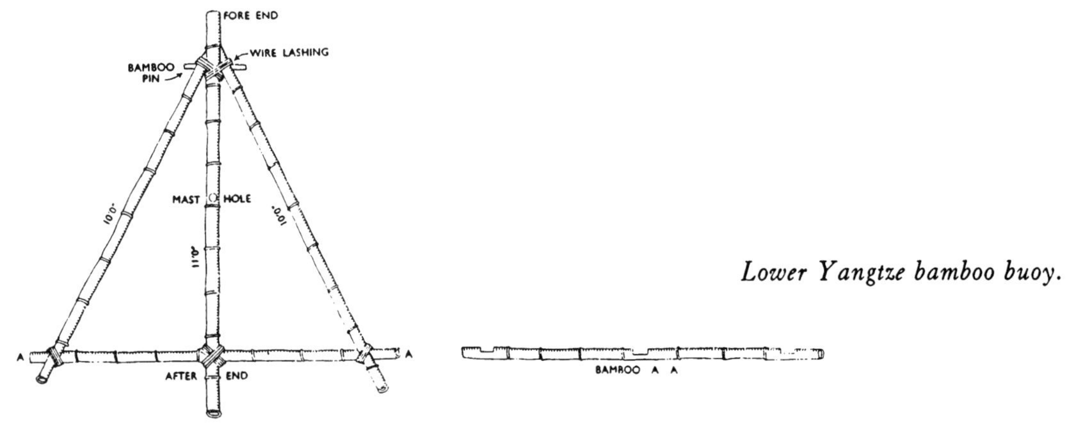

Lower Yangtze bamboo buoy.

Moorings for this type of strong triangular buoy consisted usually of an iron anchor of junk pattern, having four flukes and weighing about 30 catties, and $1\frac{1}{4}$-inch iron wire, usually 15 fathoms in length. Long experience has shown that the best results were obtained by making this wire fast to the centre bamboo by a clove hitch, half the hitch being on the fore side of the mast and half on the after side, the end being seized to another part to prevent the clove hitch from working loose. This apparently minor detail of placing the hitch is actually of great importance, as is also the fact that the mast-hole should be just forward of the half-way mark, for the buoy will then ride truly and steadily in the strong current often found in the narrow winter channels. A less careful arrangement would cause the buoy to dip at the head and eventually to be carried under, the current then breaking away the mast and topmark, or else it might cause the buoy to yaw from side to side, breaking out the anchor and setting all adrift, perhaps to bring up at, and mark falsely, a dangerous place farther down river.

Stowed flat, many of these buoys could be carried by the River Inspectorate launches, the mast and topmark being fitted at the last moment just before the buoy was laid, the moorings being attached at the same time. The launch crews were very expert at this work; and with men standing by to stream the buoy and the coils of mooring wire and, as the wire tightens, the anchor, a succession of buoys could be laid to mark the complete side of a channel as fast as the launch could steam against the current.

Each light-boat on the Lower Yangtze was manned by a crew of three Chinese Lightkeepers. Through summer heat and winter gales these men maintained a constant watch on the riverine lights of China, despite all disturbances from civil wars, bandits, armed robberies, political upheavals, floods, and famines.

The Chinese Lightkeepers have traditions of service of which any Government department could be proud; and if at some future date the history of the River Inspectorate comes to be written, the story of how the Chinese Lightkeepers kept their lights burning will provide many examples of heroism and devotion to duty.

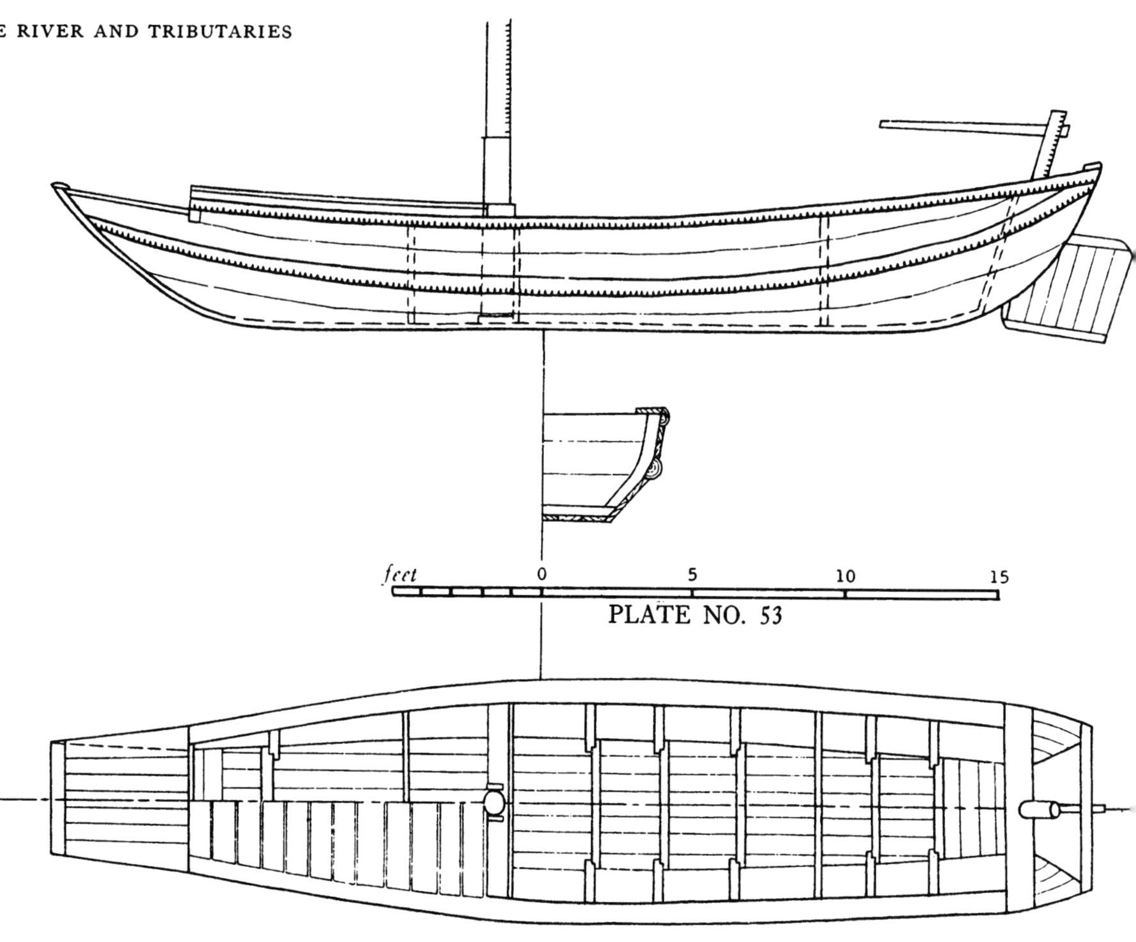

蕪湖擺江划子

THE WUHU FERRY

The Wuhu ferry-boat is a rather dull, commonplace little craft measuring 34 feet in length, 7 feet 10 inches beam, and 4 feet in depth. Although she is not much to look at and is of the roughest in material and appearance, she has a most distinguished ancestry in that she is descended from the "Wuhu Free Ferry" and can, therefore, claim lineage with the famous Wuhu Life-boat Service.

Free ferries are sometimes established by benevolent persons of charitable institutions. In such a category was the Wuhu Free Ferry, a branch of the Wuhu Life Saving Service, which was supported by voluntary contributions. Its fame travelled far beyond its port of origin.

It had a constitution and code of rules. These required that the boats' crews must be "strong in body, quiet in disposition, and well acquainted with the river." Rule 3 provided that "persons using the ferry should obtain tickets, and the boat was not allowed to wait for a passenger who, after obtaining a ticket, found himself delayed." Drinking and quarrelling were strictly forbidden. Finally, it was laid down that, when the boat was not needed as a ferry, it should "put out to the assistance of ships in distress and also pick up any floating corpses." Moreover, when a boat was required to take over a funeral party, a wedding chair, or a doctor engaged in a critical case, the crew, on presentation of a special pass, must at once get under weigh "without making trouble."

The accounts were audited once a year, one copy of the statement being forwarded to the local god.* At the religious service at which all the officers of the Association were compelled to be present, the following joint declaration was made:

> We, the Officers of the Life Saving Society, venture to come before thee, O God, and humbly represent that owing to the vastness of the waters and the raging of the billows in the rivers of Wuhu, a sudden squall striking the passing craft and taking the sailors unawares will cause shipwreck and loss of life. Though we are aware that the term of a man's life is always decreed and that Heaven's power may not be opposed, yet such sights grieve the

* The statement was written on inflammable material and burned; the smoke ascending to heaven carried the message.

heart. Thus it is that we have sought means of saving life, and that persons have come together to form a Life Saving Society supported entirely by voluntary contributions. Premises have been erected and boats built with the object of affording security from danger and ensuring a safe passage in stormy weather. A public cemetery has been opened for the burial of the dead and coffins are kept ready for use. Thus are good deeds done afloat and ashore. A statement of receipts and disbursements has been prepared, and in this work of humanity we have been faithful. We pray thee, O God, to examine our conduct and to mete out justice to us. May we be punished if we have sacrificed the public good to our private ends, and if we have been labourers unworthy of our hire, if we have misappropriated public funds, or if we have caused subscriptions to fall off by spreading false reports. While, on the other hand, may we be recompensed if we have discharged our duty with all fidelity, sparing neither trouble nor fatigue. This we pray to the end that good deeds may endure for ever. Humbly we submit our statement of accounts for the year now ended.

This excellent service, like many other good things in China, has passed away and travellers now have to pay when crossing the river.

THE WUHU TUB

Floods, droughts, famines, civil wars, and other disasters carrying widespread poverty and distress in their train have brought begging to a fine art in certain parts of the Yangtze Valley.

Normally this is by no means a highly skilled profession, but at Wuhu its followers require to have a knowledge of nautical matters quite out of the ordinary. Here swarms of beggars in tubs cluster round ships made fast to the pontoons and occasionally venture to those at anchor some distance out.

It is interesting to compare the beggars of Wuhu with those of the Shanghai area, Part Two, page 226.

This economical and ingenious custom originated as a practice with two old ladies some 30 or more years ago. Noting that sampanmen were often fortunate in begging from the passengers of ships making a call at the port, and not having the necessary capital to own or even to hire a sampan, they, nothing daunted, took to the water in the one available craft they did possess, a large wash-tub.

Instant success attended the introduction of this novel form of craft, a success dependent largely on human nature, for the idle passengers on deck are only too ready to be amused by the vociferous and heated competition between the rival crews as they scramble for coins or morsels of food, with all the attendant risks of colliding or capsizing.

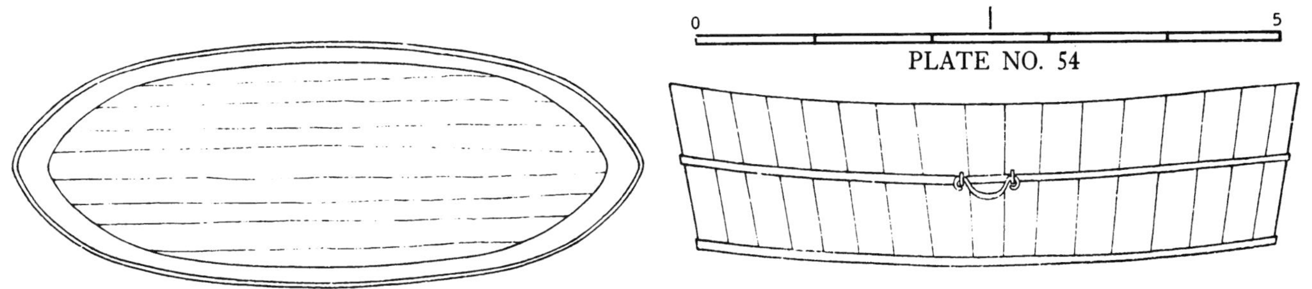

PLATE NO. 54

As soon as one of the Yangtze passenger-steamers has made fast, several of these elliptical tubs, ranging from 3 to 5 feet across the major axis and sometimes as large as 8 by 6 feet, will appear as from nowhere off the outer side of the ship, varying from the "single seater" variety, paddled with the hands over the side, to one holding a complete family progressing in style with home-made paddles.

The crew in this case usually consists of a woman who, with the inevitable child lashed to her back, acts as navigator and helmsman, and as many children as the craft will accommodate to paddle. There may be a supercargo in the shape of a baby in a cradle. All the children of an age to do so are trained to hold out their hands in whining supplication.

The tubs travel up and down the ship from bow to stern, retrieving anything that may be thrown overboard. They present a small target for casual pot-shots from a high deck, and to the frugally minded it must be a distressing feature of the profession that so much largesse misses its mark and is for ever lost in the muddy waters of Mother Yangtze.

A young beggar in a Wuhu tub.

A billet under the waste chutes discharging refuse into the river is much sought after, and here tubs are to be seen jockeying for position. No piece of jetsam is too worthless for inspection, and very little is again discarded.

Owing to the originality of the craft, the risks they appear to run, and the human interest which attaches to the seemingly distressed children belonging to a large family, the profession is a comparatively lucrative one.

A high degree of dexterity is required to navigate these over-crowded and clumsy tubs in the swift running current of the harbour, where a local knowledge of up-currents and swirls is essential. The steering is also of a very specialized order, as it entails avoiding many obstacles, such as hulk moorings, and the ability to get to a piece of floating garbage or other similar desirable object by the shortest route ahead of a competitor.

It is a standing wonder and a tribute to their skill that with only a few inches of freeboard there are not more serious accidents and losses of life among the floating beggars of Wuhu.

THE EMPEROR'S BOAT

No plans or photographs are available for this type of craft, and research in this case has perforce to rely on a Chinese woodcut taken from the "K'ao Kung Chi" (考 工 記) together with descriptions from foreign sources, which are of a perfunctory nature, and models found in temples.

From contemporary writers, however, it is clear that the junks used by the Emperor, the mandarins, and other opulent persons in comparatively recent times showed a degree of comfort unknown in boats of the same type in use elsewhere.

According to one writer, there seems to have been three sizes of Imperial barges or house-boats which plied on the Grand Canal. One was "equal in bigness to a third-rate man-of-war, painted and embellished with dragons and japanned both within and without." The size most in demand seems to have been a medium type of 64 feet in length, 16 feet beam, and a depth of about 9 feet, and "square and flat" in form. Besides the cabin of the master of the bark, who has his family, his kitchen, and two large rooms, there seems to have been in the fore-part of the vessel an ante-chamber to the "audience hall," or officials' saloon, and two or three other rooms abaft. Oyster shells or waxed paper were used instead of glass for the ports. The deck was fitted with projecting galleries for the junkmen to quant through shallow water and also to allow the servants and bodyguards to pass from bow to stern without incommoding the inmates. Cooking was carried out in the over-hanging stern, where some of the crew also slept, the rest being accommodated forward.

The Emperor's Boat.
WOODCUT FROM THE "K'AO KUNG CHI."

The officials and less illustrious passengers travelled in craft called *poo-ya-tow*, after a town near Chinkiang, where they were usually built, being adjacent to the Grand Canal and where they were mainly used. They were hired only by the wealthy, for, as an early foreign writer in 1873 pointed out, the expense of hiring such boats at a fee of from $2 to $3 per day " placed them beyond the means of any but the rich gentry or important officials."

The average size of these boats was 70 feet long, with a beam of 18 feet and a draught of 3 feet.

The accommodation varied according to the boat, but usually it contained a reception or dining room for the use of the chief traveller. The small glassed-in house above accommodated his attendants of the higher class, while those of the lower class found sleeping room along the sides and in the house forward. Luggage was stored below the bottom boards, and the space abaft the house was given up to the crew and the general galley. The boat was sometimes propelled by sail, under which she was an indifferent performer, but was generally sculled with yulohs. Thirty miles a day was very good going.

The shape and construction from which they derived their comfort and safety rendered them extremely slow in the most favourable circumstances; indeed, with the exception of the snake or smuggling junks, the Chinese may be said to be anything but economists of time on the water.

Models of these types of officials' boats are still to be met with hanging from the rafters or standing on trestles in such temples as have an interest for the junkmen.* In the same way as the dishes of food set out on the altars are for the consumption of the gods, so are these model junks hung up in the temples so that the god in whose honour they are placed there may have a ready means of transport at hand when it becomes necessary to go out in a boat to safeguard the junkmen under his care.

The models are usually donations from men who have escaped from a shipwreck and wish to testify to their gratitude for what is regarded as divine intervention. Sometimes a man suspends in a neighbouring temple the actual garment in which he was saved.

* An exceptionally fine model of a junk of this description is to be found in the Kuan Yin Temple (觀音廟) in the Dragon Street at Soochow. This model, which measures about 17 feet long, has a crew of some 30 or more men dressed in the costume of the period. Two junkmen are shown in the act of hoisting the sheer-legs of the "A" type tracking-mast. The model is well supplied with chairs, tables, lanterns, cooking stoves, and so forth, all more or less to scale.

Many of the models are of the official type of craft, complete with the high-sounding title boards. When hung from the rafters they are never taken down from one year's end to another. There is, however, a tale which is told on the Soochow Creek, which shows that, in at least one case, a boat was absent on one particular night.

It seems that in ancient times a Chinese lady in Shanghai fell ill and summoned her son from Yangchow. The youth, who was a pattern of filial virtue, on finding no boat available for hire, set out to walk the whole way, a distance of some 500 *li*. He had not, however, gone more than 80 *li* when to his surprise a boat loomed mysteriously out of the night apparently from nowhere, and, on being hailed, the boatman offered a passage to Shanghai on condition that the young man sat throughout the journey in the stern sheets with closed eyes. This he gladly agreed to do.

Although there was nothing about the boat to indicate any supernatural agency, Shanghai was reached in an unbelievably short time. Whether through carelessness or destitution the young man had no money on him, and as on his stepping out of the boat the man asked for payment, he yielded up instead his umbrella which he much valued.

His premature arrival home caused as much surprise as joy, for his mother's letter had been so recently dispatched that they had not counted on seeing him for some days to come.

On hearing the strange circumstances of his journey his mother at once realized that the junkman was no ordinary mortal and urged her son to go and return thanks at the junkmen's temple for his miraculous journey by the supernatural express.

The cream of the story is its climax. As the youth dutifully performed his obeisance before the altar, he happened to glance up and, to his astonishment, saw his humble umbrella in the model of an official boat which hung from the rafters. The priest when questioned denied any possibility that it could be his umbrella, as the junk had been in that position and untouched for a great number of years. The youth pressed for further investigation, and the fact that his name was carved on the umbrella-handle proved his story and demonstrated how a kindly deity had used the model junk to go on an errand of mercy to bring a filial son to his sick mother's bed-side. The scene of this story is at the temple of Hsieh Hsü, one of the last of the real junkmen's temples in Shanghai, situated on the north bank of the Soochow Creek. Here the curious and sceptical may view two handsome large models of the official boat perched high among the rafters, and any old junkman will vouch for the truth of the strangest adventure that ever befell any umbrella.

THE SPIRIT BOAT

The boat illustrated (*following page*) is not the kind of craft that one would choose for a voyage of any length. Actually it is designed not for this world but the next, for it is a spirit boat and is one of the few types of junks which are not being superseded by power craft.

Its function is to figure in funeral processions together with the various other paper and pasteboard models of worldly possessions, which are eventually ceremoniously burned so as to be transported to the other world for the use of the deceased.

Paper money and a Spirit boat, designed to be burned for the benefit of the deceased in the next world.

The spirit boat is built entirely of paper except for the framework, which is of reeds tied together with cotton string, and measures usually from 7 to 9 feet in length, although, for the rich or for special occasions, it is often much bigger. That built for the funeral of the Empress Dowager, for instance, was very many times greater than full size.

While the body lies in state in the house, the relatives, if they can afford it, call in the assistance of the priests, and those who are rich enough expend large sums for them to recite prayers. Altars are erected in the house, hired musicians keep up a ceaseless clamour of gongs and conches, and finally paper models of various kinds are burned in honour of, and for the use of, the dead. Chief amongst these models is the spirit boat.

Chinese beliefs and superstitions are related in Part One, pages 118–27.

In many lands the number seven and the multiples of seven have a mystic significance, and this also holds good in China, for the boat again figures on the forty-ninth day after death. During this interval the soul is supposed to be going through the various judgment halls, being judged for the deeds done in the body. This completed, it now has to travel by a way in the course of which two rivers must be crossed—the Gold River, for the crossing of which paper models of bridges are supplied, and the Yin Yang, or Death and Life River, which, like the Styx, is wide enough to require a ferry. However, there is no obliging Charon to ferry the soul across, as in the classical myth.

On this day a tablet bearing the names of the deceased is put up on a table whereon food is also laid out for the soul's refreshment. This tablet and three kinds of paper money are all put into the boat and burned, together with the bridges, outside the street door at 4 o'clock in the afternoon.

During elaborate funeral ceremonies paper models of all kinds, such as houses,* are carried in procession through the streets. Among them are often groups of figures representing ladies in gay attire. These are also burned with the other models and are thus transported into the spirit world, where they become companions or servants of the dead.

This practice of burning paper models of any commodity of daily life is rather falling into desuetude, chiefly because few families can afford the cost in addition to the heavy expense of the ordinary funeral, and also because those who are wealthy enough have usually acquired sufficient education to arouse scepticism in them as to the efficacy of the practice.

The burning of paper money called *cheu-ling*, or " providing for old age," is still very general, as it is an inexpensive way of ensuring that the soul will be enabled to meet all its liabilities in the next world, with something over.

The boat illustrated (*preceding page*) was made in a shop solely employed in the making of such paper models, and it is an excellent example of the ingenuity and deftness of the workers at this curious trade.

The shop is situated in the temple precincts of the Bubbling Well Road (靜 安 寺 路), which is one of the few authentic local sites known to, and mentioned in, Chinese history. It is claimed that it dates back to A.D. 250, being contemporaneous with the middle of the Roman period in Britain. It stands close to the Bubbling Well (湧 泉), to which it doubtless owes its popularity and the wealth it enjoyed in former times. This well, the " Sixth Spring in the Empire," stands in the middle of a busy thoroughfare and is still somewhat of a curiosity to idle passers-by. Its thick waters are stirred by slow gaseous bubbles due to a mixture of marsh and carbonic-acid gas. The low surrounding parapet is carved and bears an inscription to the effect that one of the priests of the near-by temple was so expert at chanting Buddhist liturgies that even the frogs were enthralled and stopped to listen.

The paper-model shop is well worth a visit. Here may be seen a rich selection of every sort of luxurious device for the comfort of the inhabitants of the next world.

There are splendid paper houses built upon a frail framework of reeds. These are about 4 feet high and adhere closely to the Chinese form of architecture. The open back or side reveals complete furnishings, including tables with paper dishes of food. On the floor a paper pig and chicken feed from a bowl. In another room a paper servant may be seen sweeping or carrying baskets by means of the usual carrying-pole. Yet a third room shows a shrine with miniature models of the gods and all the appropriate appurtenances.

Outside the small shop may be seen a headless troop of paper cavalry, their cane structures still imperfectly concealed and their featureless heads lying in a row on the counter waiting to be painted and assembled.

Exploration of the dingy shelves and two glass show-cases shows a bizarre touch of realism in portraying the estimated needs of that army of silent clients

* It seems probable that the custom of burning paper houses for the benefit of the dead has been correlative with the burning of mock money, paper horsemen, etc. The latter began under the T'ang dynasty, A.D. 618–907. People fancied that since it was sufficient to burn paper money, they could also through the same process send other things. Why stop at houses? It sometimes happens that an old man has no surviving children and that his next of kin are already dead. As he will thus have nobody to offer him a paper house after death, he anticipates the event and burns one for his own use, having taken care to forward it to one of his relatives in the nether world, begging him to keep it in store for him until the day when he shall come to enjoy it. The Chinese are far-seeing, whatever people may say to the contrary.

who have lived long enough in this modern China to acquire a taste for the products of science.* For, in addition to sedan chairs and bowls of paper fruit, trunks, suitcases, and incredibly life-like imitations of the bamboo double-tiered food carriers, there are such exotic articles as motor-cars, aeroplanes, electric-light fittings, gramophones, wireless sets, whose open backs disclose five valves, and telephones so cunningly contrived as to tempt one to dial in on a long-distance call to Hades. Black and brown shoes, complete with laces and imitation rubber heels, cosmetic sets of powder, cream and lipstick, and scent. Clocks to tell the time in an existence where one imagines all time stands still, even a neatly rolled "Chamberlain" umbrella to be burned by some confirmed pessimist who cannot picture the perfect climate of the Elysian Fields. For the latter too, no doubt, was designed an exact paper replica of a three-switch G.E.C. electric heater.

* The manufacturers of paper articles, ever up to date, have now introduced among their attractions a facsimile of a modern jeep. One cannot but wonder why the model selected for portrayal should be the American police patrol car, which is painted white throughout, but perhaps the mourning colour of white provides the attraction.

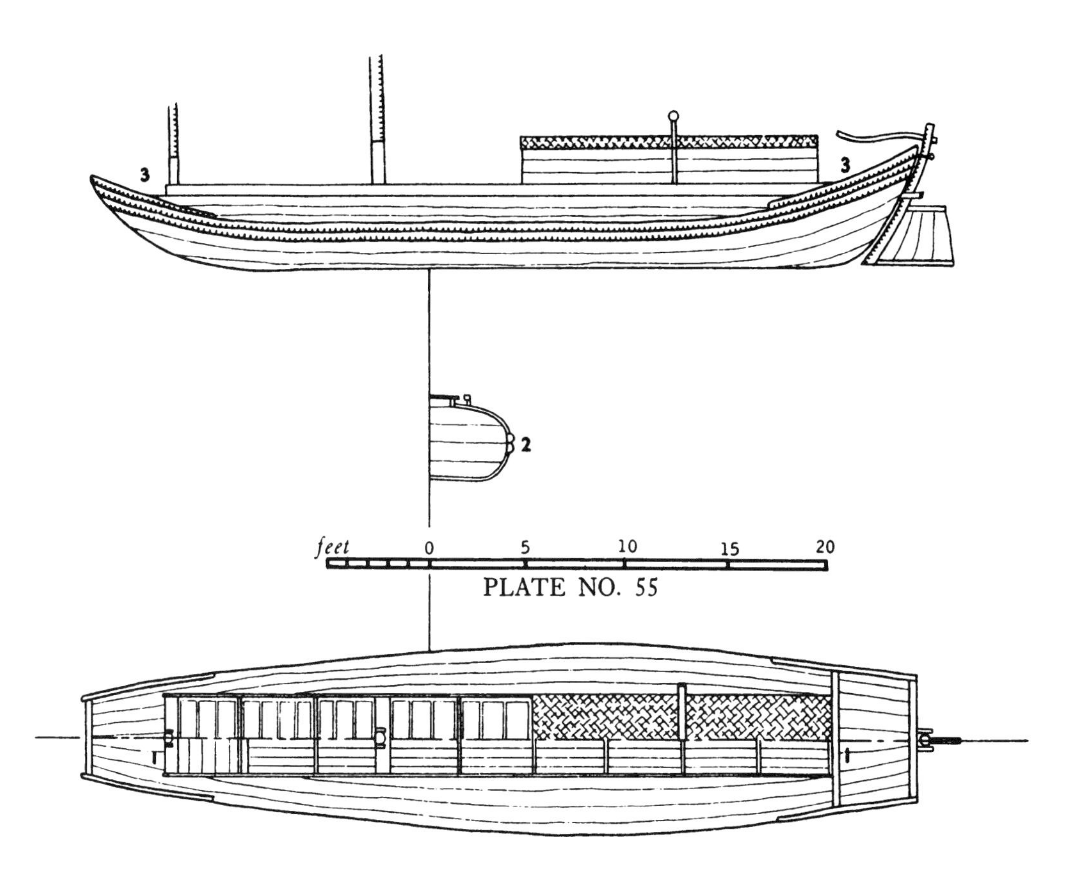

PLATE NO. 55

THE MA-YU-HU-TZŬ OR SEED-OIL BOTTLE

The *ma-yu-hu-tzŭ*, or "seed-oil bottle," so called from its supposed likeness thereto, forms an exception to the usual run of craft working waters inland from the Yangtze in that she is turret-built.

The type of craft illustrated in Plate No. 55 is built at Sanho (三河), a small town on the Chaohu, and is to be found on any of the creeks and canals of Anhwei and Honan. This particular craft, which has a crew of three, measures 41 feet, a beam of 9 feet, and a depth of 4 feet.

This type of junk is designed for carrying grain in bulk and requires to be strongly built so as to accommodate the 160 piculs of deadweight cargo she carries. The hull is strengthened by eight full bulkheads and two frames[1]. There is, moreover, a double wale[2] and strengthening pieces at bow and stern[3].

Grain is carried in seven compartments.

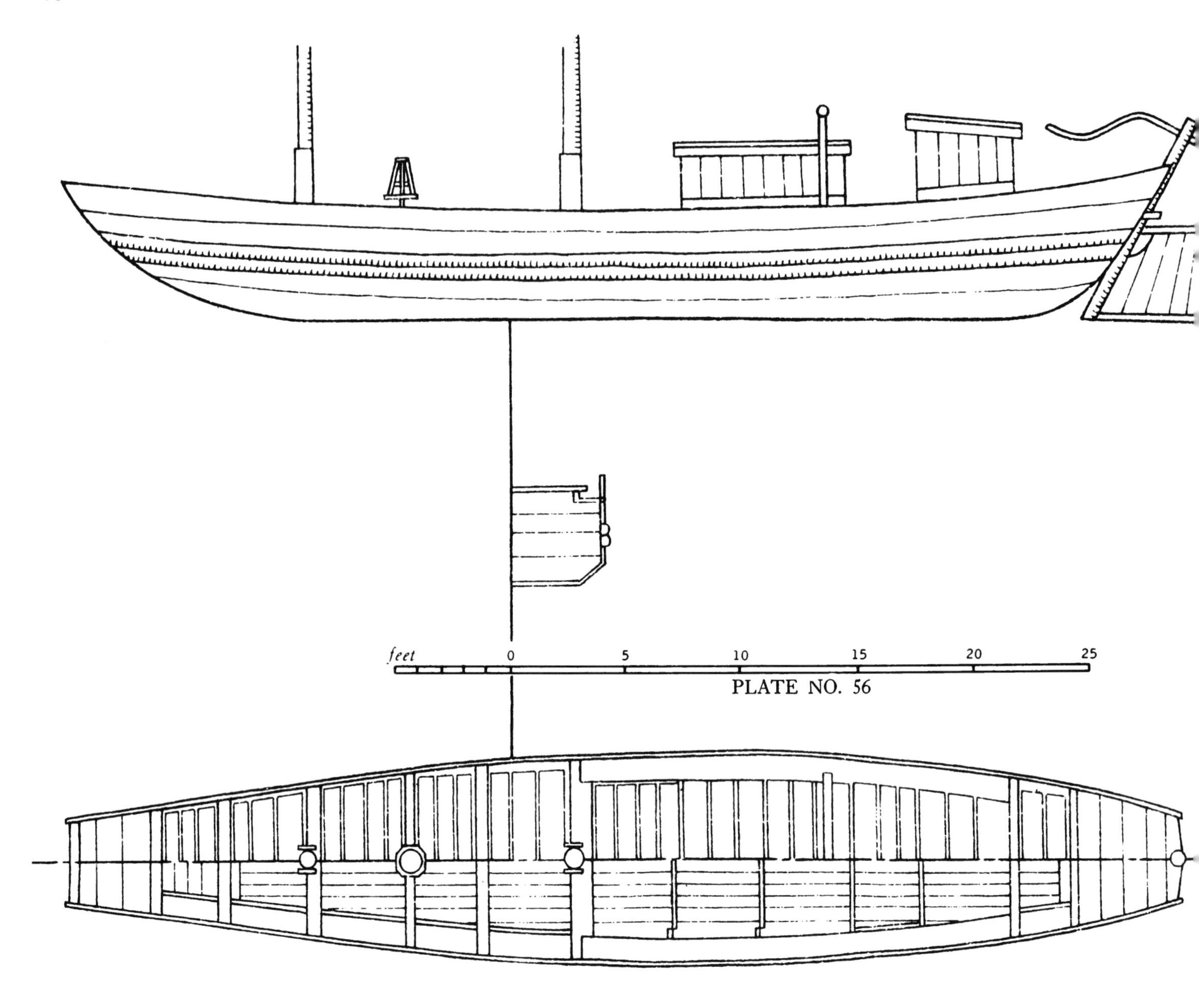

PLATE NO. 56

黃化子

THE HUANG-HUA-TZŬ OR YELLOW BOAT

The *huang-hua-tzŭ*, or yellow boat, is a fairly common, medium-sized, short-distance trader on the Lower Yangtze. These craft are usually to be seen on the river between Wuhu and Nanking.

The craft illustrated in Plate No. 56 measures 49 feet, with a beam of 9 feet and a depth of 4 feet. She has a capacity of 250 piculs.

These junks are strongly built; usually they have nine bulkheads and three frames.

The crew of four men live in the comparatively comfortable quarters in the fore-house. The after-house, just forward of the conning position, is used as a galley. The stern is of the transom variety and the rudder of the non-balance type.

Two masts are usual. They set the classic, high, square-headed lug-sail of the Lower Yangtze. A pair of lumber irons support the sail when lowered.

At a distance this boat can be easily confused with the *pai-chiang-tzŭ*, described later.

See Part Three, page 358.

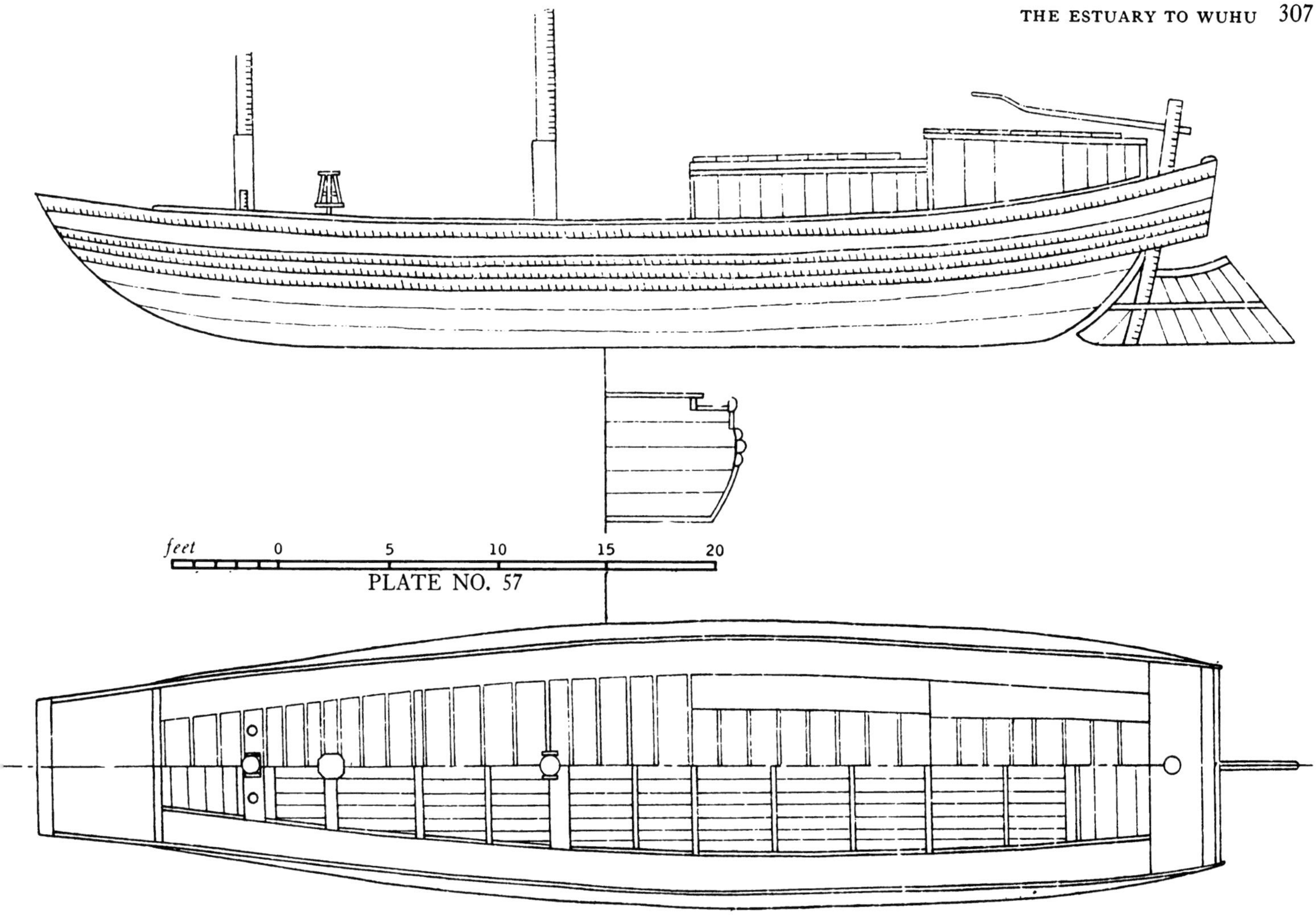

feet 0 5 10 15 20

PLATE NO. 57

THE TOU-CH'UAN OR RICE-MEASURE BOAT

To the junkmen of Anhwei goes the honour of having provided one of the four deities of the province. They are, in order of seniority, Chang T'ien-shih (張天師), the Taoist Pope, Hsü Chên-chün (徐珍君), Hsiao Kung (蕭公), and Yen Kung (嚴公), the junkmen's candidate. Yen Kung, who lived *circa* A.D. 25, was a junkman who ran his boat so carefully that he never had an accident. For this reason he had many patrons anxious to give him business. Later he retired from the sea; was made an official; of course, became very rich, and in course of time a great friend of the Emperor. Yen, however, preferred a life in the country, devoted to fishing and agriculture. The junkmen of the *tou-ch'uan* claim him as their especial patron, for he is supposed to have designed this type of junk.

The *tou-ch'uan*, or rice-measure boat, is so named from its supposed similarity to that article. These junks, which are usually grain-carriers, are fairly uniform in size. That illustrated in Plate No. 57 measures 54 feet in length, with a beam of 12½ feet and a depth of 5½ feet, and a capacity of 500 piculs. The port of origin of these junks is Tungcheng (銅城), north of the Yangtze, and they are usually to be found working the river between Tatung and Anking.

They are very strongly built and are fitted with seven bulkheads, three frames, and four half-bulkheads.

The main characteristics of these junks are the markedly square stern, the wide strakes of great thickness, and their great beam.

Yen Kung, referred to above, certainly possessed a good eye for form as well as efficiency.

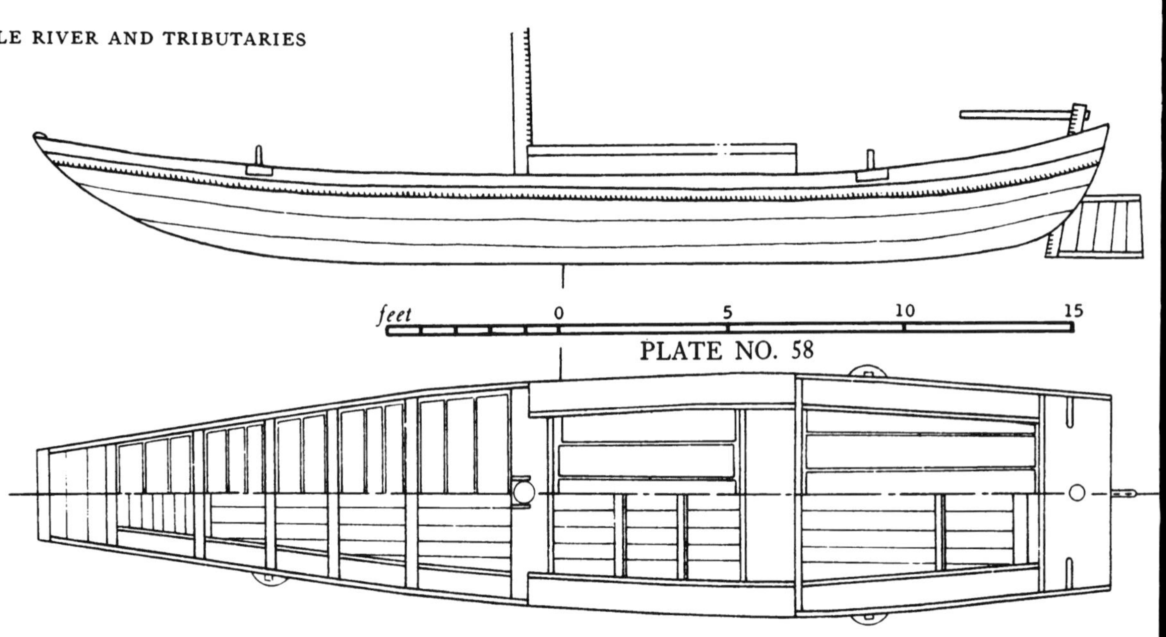

PLATE NO. 58

THE T'AIHU CRABBER

From the earliest times crabs have always been a favourite dish with Chinese poets and writers. Famous men of letters of ancient days claimed that a dish of crabs nicely cooked with a dash of Shaohing wine could be guaranteed to coax inspiration to its highest pitch. While wine heats the blood, crab meat, it is said, has the opposite effect, and this is the reason why, to obtain the best results, a liberal sprinkling of vinegar, ginger, and pepper is necessary to add zest.

To the Chinese gourmet, crabs fall into two classes: those from the Yangtze, distinguished by the deeper hue of the shell, and those from the inland streams, but the most sought-after crabs come from the T'aihu. Unlike their poorer relations of the Yangtze, they have a lighter-coloured shell and are white on the under-carriage. Those which show reddish brown hair on their legs are especially popular with the culinary expert and command high prices.

Mud crabs are caught in their burrows in two ways. In summer a spikelet of flowering grass is presented at the entrance of the burrow, and, as the crab seizes it, it is jerked out, its retreat being cut off by the simultaneous insertion of a small spade across the hole. In winter the same spade is used to open the hole, into which a two-pronged fork, with teeth directed upwards, is thrust. With this the crab, which lies dormant at a depth of 2 or 3 feet, is dexterously drawn out.

The crab season is from late autumn to the middle of winter, and it is during this period that stalls selling crabs spring up like mushrooms. Some of the stalls display attractive lanterns to advertise their goods; others more prosaically depend on the modern electric light bulb. Doubtless Neon lights will soon be used, as they already are in the more expensive emporiums.

Before the Japanese War the best inland-water crabs were selling at $1 a catty; to-day, however, in common with other foodstuffs, they are changing hands at the unprecedented high figure of $40,000. Lovers of this, the greatest shell delicacy, however, are paying it unflinchingly and may be seen triumphantly wending their way home carrying a few bubbling crabs on the end of a string.

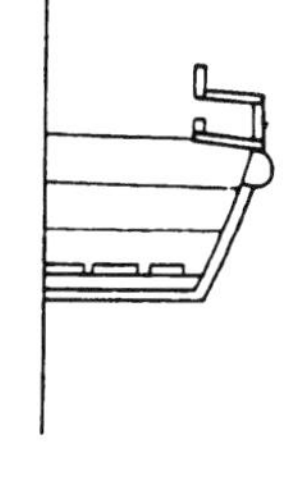

The type of craft which carries out the duty of providing Shanghai with crab meat is illustrated in Plate No. 58. She is a rather drab little boat, 31½ feet in length, with a beam of 6¾ feet and a depth of 2½ feet.

She is strengthened by no less than six bulkheads, four frames, and one half-bulkhead. From the bow to the mast the deck is flush with the gunwale. There is a well from the mast to the stern.

The methods of propulsion include the use of three oars, poling in shallow reaches, and sailing.

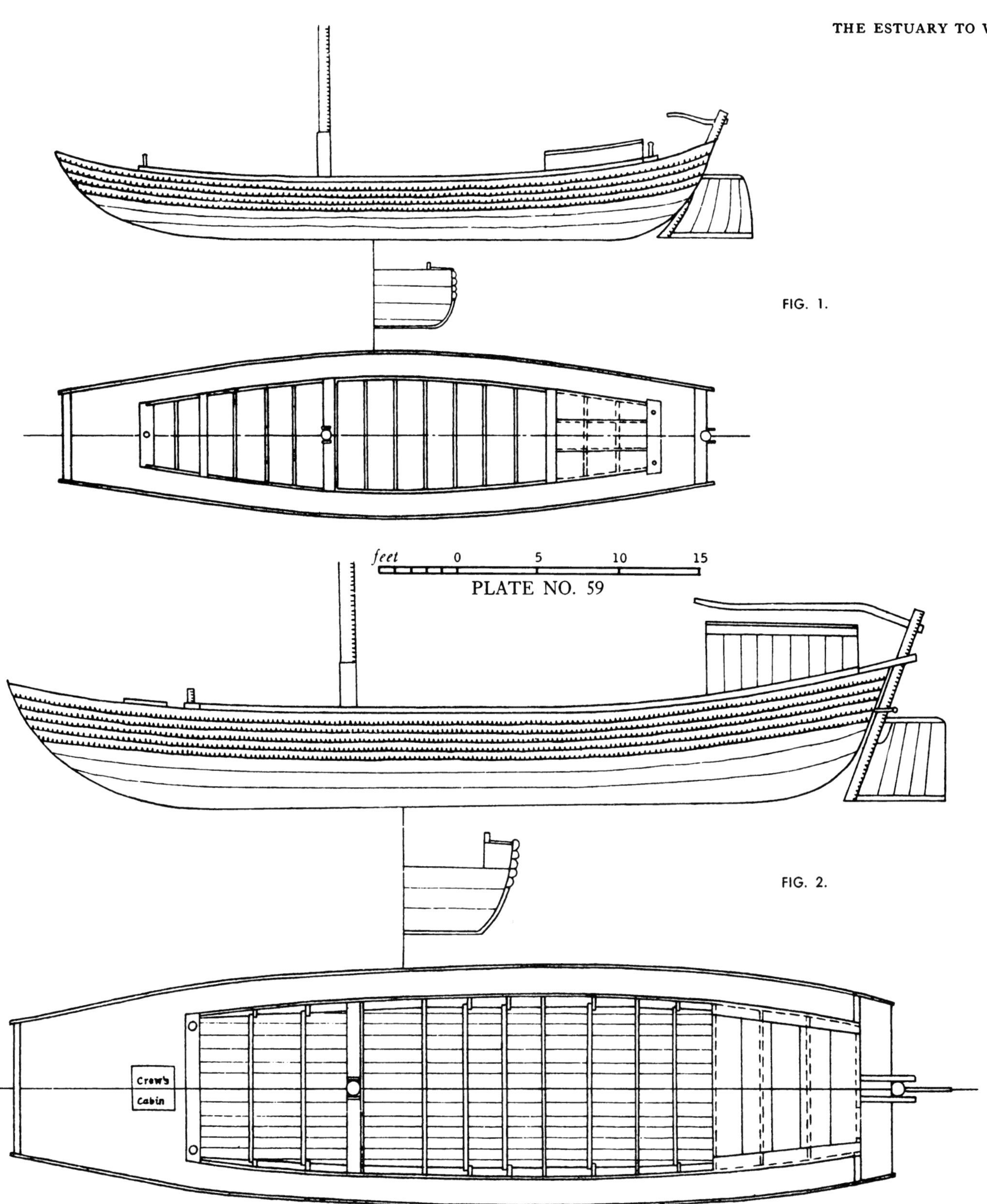

PLATE NO. 59

THE WUHU CARGO-BOAT

Wuhu is the home of the cargo-boat. Two examples of the cargo-boat design are shown in Plate No. 59, both plotted to the same scale.

Fig. 1 shows the small type which is generally used for inland waters, where boats of this variety are to be found trading up the numerous small creeks and canals in the hinterland of Wuhu. It measures 41 feet, with a beam of $10\frac{1}{2}$ feet and a depth of $3\frac{1}{2}$ feet. As these boats are designed primarily for light-draught work, they are not noted for the strength of their construction. They have a capacity of 120 piculs, that is to say, about 5 tons, and are fitted with 14 frames and three bulkheads.

Fig. 2 shows a heavy-draught cargo-boat of simple construction, measuring 56 feet, with a beam of 15 feet and a depth of 6 feet. The depth of the hold at its deepest is about 6 feet, and this permits a carrying capacity of about 50 tons.

The solidly built hull is made of *sha-mu*, and is fitted with six frames, five bulkheads, and four half-bulkheads, all of *ch'un-mu*. Two heavy hardwood bitts are firmly secured to the first bulkhead.

The flush-deck has a low coaming. The stern, which is wide in shape, has a slight rise, and a small portion of it is decked-in to form a cabin for the laodah and his family. Under the fore-deck there is a cabin, reached through a manhole, and a removable hatch gives access to the crew's quarters.

The broad flaring bow, the transom stern, and the non-balance rudder hung from the stern outside the vessel are characteristics of these as well as most cargo-boats. From an artistic point of view these boats have little to recommend them, but for simplicity, economy, and efficiency, as well as for speed in building, they are not excelled.

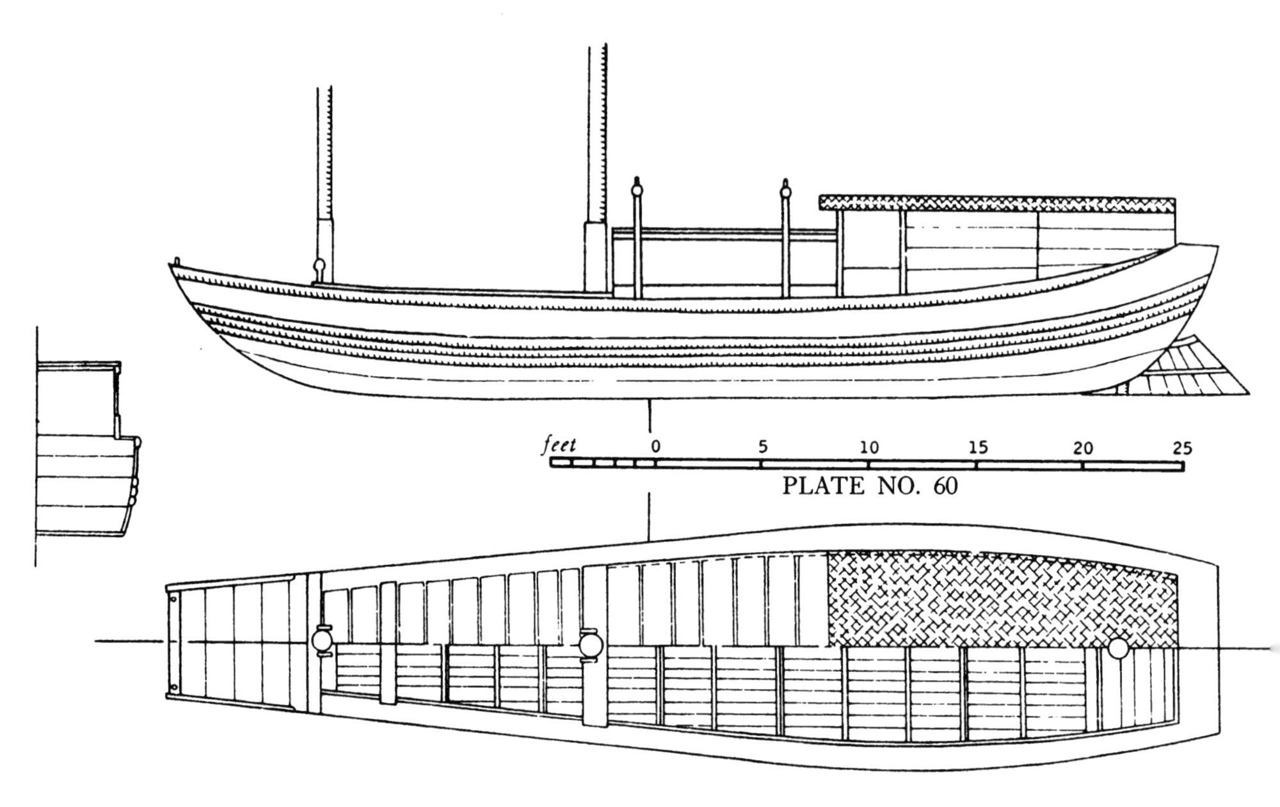

PLATE NO. 60

鹽船 THE YEN-CH'UAN OR SALT-BOAT

The craft illustrated in Plate No. 60 is but a poor example of a true Lower Yangtze salt-junk. Unfortunately, however, it is the only one available.

The huge, majestic salt-junks, with their enormous sails, are unhappily a thing of the past, for salt to-day is carried by steamers.

The craft illustrated is a typical example of a creek salt-junk, measuring 50 feet in length, with a beam of 11½ feet and a depth of 5 feet.

Very box-like in design, she has a capacity of 400 piculs. The crew consists of five men under a laodah.

THE HSIHO RAFTS

No plans of the Hsiho raft are available.

A primitive means of conveyance popular on the small streams and the headwaters of the small rivers in the interior of Anhwei Province is the bamboo raft, which is designed to negotiate shallows and rapids in the upper reaches of those waterways which would defy any other kind of vessel. This light structure is built by binding bamboo poles together with rattan ropes. The bottom is reinforced by saplings fastened to the bamboo poles. On the bamboo poles another row of wooden slats is fastened crosswise. Planks are laid on the poles to provide space for passengers and cargo. The bow of the raft is bent by heating so as to enable it to surmount half-submerged rocks. On the planks a matshed is erected for the passengers or raftsmen. Quanting is the usual form of propulsion, although tracking is often employed.

There are several types of rafts all made of bamboo of the *man-chu* (*Phyllostachus pubescens*) variety. The Tungho raft (東 河 筏) is made of a number of bamboo poles laid together in rows and securely lashed. As the poles are uneven, only the thicker part is used for raft-making. A single pole so cut is too short for building the hull, so two are fastened together on end. The Hsiho raft (西 河 筏) is smaller and made of about 50 poles. It cost $4,500 in 1927 to make a raft, the work being done by the owner himself. Such a raft will last for two or three years. Regular overhauls are carried out and rotten bamboo poles are replaced as necessary. The owner generally has two such rafts which he operates at the same time, each being managed by four or five men.

The work of the raftsmen is very hard, particularly in the winter when it is necessary to work all day barefooted in water, for a fully loaded raft is always partly submerged.

CHINKIANG LIFE-BOATS

The Chinkiang Association for the Saving of Life (京 口 救 生 會) was established in 1708 by a committee of benefactors, whose names have been handed down to posterity in a laudatory tablet which is still to be seen at Tantu. Little was done apparently beyond the supply of coffins to corpses recovered from the river. In 1796, however, local subscriptions enabled life-boats to be built, the maintenance of which was defrayed by their plying for hire when disengaged. This appears to have lasted until the Taiping Rebellion, when the life-boats were destroyed. The service was then practically extinct until its resuscitation in 1862 under the Emperor T'ung Chih (同 治).

No plans are available for the Chinkiang life-boats. Details of the Upper Yangtze life-boat, or *hung-ch'uan*, will be found in Part Four, page 528.

The life-boats of Chinkiang were of two sizes: the larger, called *hung-ch'uan* (紅 船), were of about 20 tons capacity and cost about $1,200 in 1892, while the smaller were called *hsün-ch'uan* (巡 船), or cruisers, and of 12 tons capacity and cost $600. They were built of pine, and each boat had two masts. The deck-house, built for shelter in rough weather, occupied less than one-third of the length of the boat.

Between the years 1889 and 1891 the boats saved no less than 2,281 souls, a most creditable performance.

Other riparian cities have similar life-boats, such as Nanking and Ichang. The boats of the last-named city are known as "red boats" on account of the colour of their paint. Here the boats were first managed by a co-operative society, but were later taken over by the Government on account of the importance of their work.

An old-time Hunan four-master.

THE SALT-JUNKS OF THE LOWER YANGTZE

The town of Kwachow (瓜州) (map, pages 158–9) is now the central station on the river at which salt brought from the coast is transhipped. The transport of this article into the interior was stated, in 1867, to give employment to some 1,800 junks manned by 30,000 sailors. The first notice of evaporation of sea-water to obtain salt was in the year 686 B.C. A tax on salt was, it is known, levied as early as the seventh century B.C. and is one of the oldest sources of revenue in China. Whenever a deficit occurred in the public treasury, the salt tax put the Government back in funds again.

Marco Polo mentions salt-junks in the following words:

> And all these ships carry wares to this city of Sinju or from it to other cities. And the principal commodity traded along the river is salt. The merchants load the boats with it in this city and then they carry it to all the regions along the banks of the river: and they also go into the interior, leaving the river and sailing up the tributaries, thus furnishing all the surrounding districts with salt. Hence from all places on the seacoast where salt is made it is carried to the same city of Sinju. Here it is loaded on boats and carried to the aforesaid places.

The salt trade on the Yangtze, owing to the peculiar conditions involved, has from about 1864 placed it upon a different footing as regards the Government monopoly of this staple. Throughout China the production and sale of salt were alike controlled by special functionaries of the Government for the purpose of securing the revenue derivable from its consumption, dealings in this article being usually restricted to privileged monopolists. In the provinces bordering the Great River, however, later regulations permitted all Chinese willing to undertake the transport of salt up the river to do so, with the restriction that purchases must be made under the supervision of officials deputed by the Commissioner of the Salt Revenue residing at Yangchow, near Chinkiang.

It may reasonably be supposed that salt-junks are one of the oldest classes of junks trading in China. They are generally three-masted, but, in the case of such big salt-junks as the *ta-fu-ch'uan* (大 撫 船) from Kiangsi, one more mast is stepped in front of the foremast and raked well forward over the bow. The large number of masts, due to the enormous carrying capacity of between two and three *p'iao** (票), make these junks seem rather unwieldy. The crew consists of as many as 14. Sweeps and boat-hooks, though provided, are very seldom used, the junks being entirely dependent on their sails.

These junks are built in Hunan and Kiangsi and occasionally in Shiherhwei (十 二 圩). There is an invariable tradition that the length of the junk should be the same as that of the mainmast.

Inside the deck-house there is usually a shrine for the worship of Yang Ssŭ (楊 四), who is held to be the deity that governs all floating craft in the salt trade. Before departure the laodah always burns a considerable amount of joss paper in the hope that the trip will be profitable.

They make only two trips a year to Hankow and Hunan ports with salt from Shiherhwei, taking about three months. On the downward trip they often carry softwood poles, gypsum, and cow bones for Chinkiang or other ports on the Lower Yangtze.

The best-known types from Hunan and Hupeh are called *man-kiang-hung* (滿 江 紅) and *t'o-kou-tzŭ* (拖 鈎 子), and the Kiangsi types *ta-fu-ch'uan* (大 撫 船) and *kiang-tu-tzŭ* (江 都 子).

The Taichow *chuang-yen-kuan-po* (泰 州 裝 鹽 關 駁), or salt-junks, bring salt from Haichow, Hwaian, Jukao, and other places in the north and north-east of the province as far as Kwachow by canal and thence a few miles up the river to a place on the north bank called Shiherhwei (十 二 圩) where salt is stored. Sometimes they go to Shiherhwei direct by another branch of the canal. At this salt depot may often be seen a large fleet of junks anchored in rows, consisting of those mentioned and of another, larger, kind which carry the salt up river. The latter junks were said once to number as many as 1,800 and were manned by some 30,000 Hupeh men. It is a matter of infinite regret that these beautiful craft are very seldom to be seen on the river to-day.

* A *p'iao* is 4,000 straw bags, approximately 2,700 quintals.

THE LUHÜ RICE-BOAT

This rice-carrying junk is called after a town on the Tienshan Lake (澱山湖) on the southern boundary of the Province of Kiangsu and is usually built in the place from which she derives her name. She trades between Luhü (蘆墟) and Shanghai *via* Tsingpu (青浦).

Made of *sha-mu*, she measures 41 feet in length and 7 feet in beam, with a depth of 3½ feet. She is of strong construction, with five hardwood bulkheads and seven frames, and a cargo capacity of 90 piculs.

Her lines are pleasing, with a long, low, narrow bow and still more tapered stern of the open-wing type and Shanghai style of gallery. The typical bulge of the hull of rice-carrying craft is present to a lesser degree than usual. The planking of the deck runs athwartships. There is a small mast, which carries a square-headed lug-sail. A curved type of yuloh is used.

The story of rice cultivation in the Yangtze Valley is told in Part One, pages 128–34.

Although this junk is quite small, she is curiously enough provided with lee-boards for the reason that she has to pass through several open lakes and down the broad reaches of the Whangpoo.

The crew of three live in the small house amidships. An unusual feature and one illustrating how lucrative is the rice trade is that the whole of the compartment between the fourth and fifth bulkheads is used as a "strong room," wherein the rice merchants who travel with their cargo can stow their money and valuables. The deck-planks in this compartment lie fore and aft, and the primitive built-in safe below is secured by means of a wooden batten travelling across the deck and fastened with a Chinese lock.

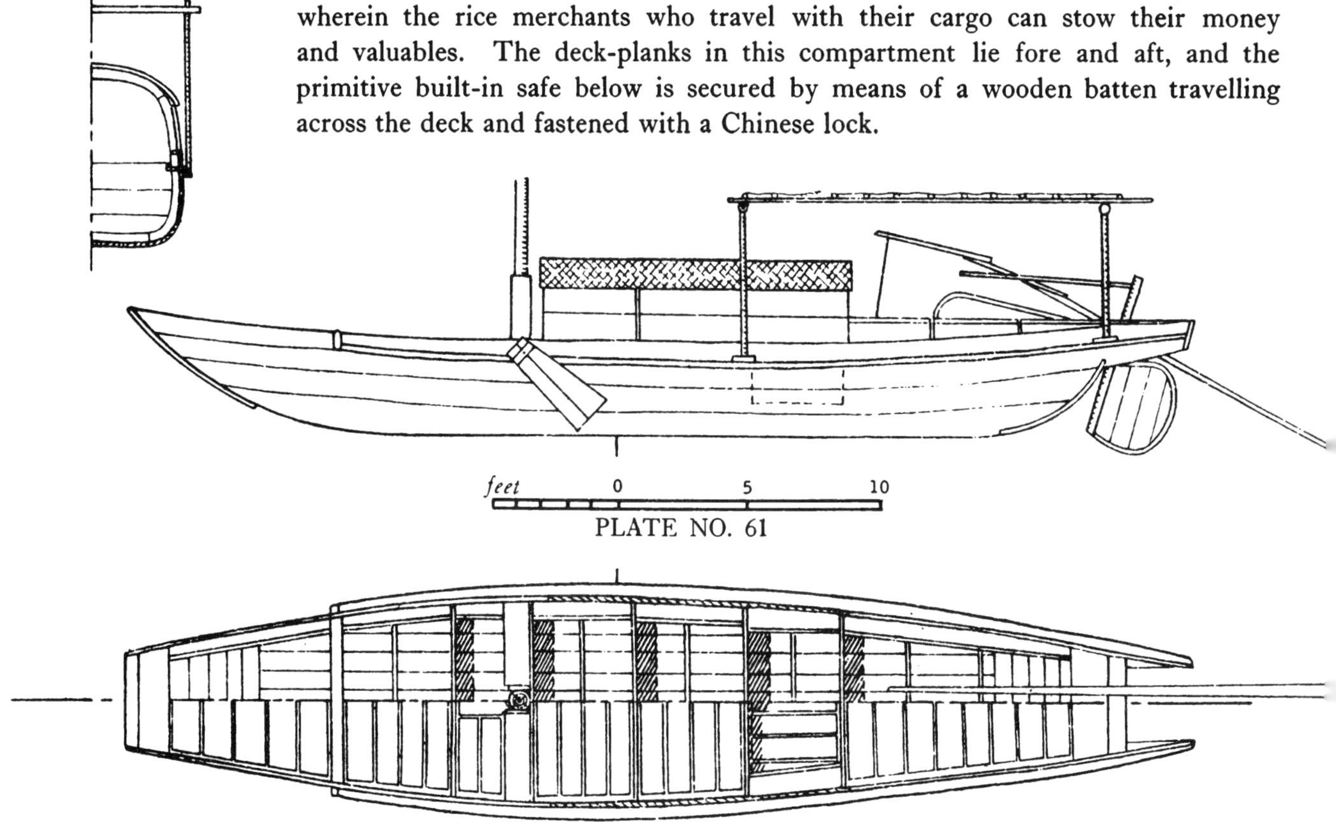

PLATE NO. 61

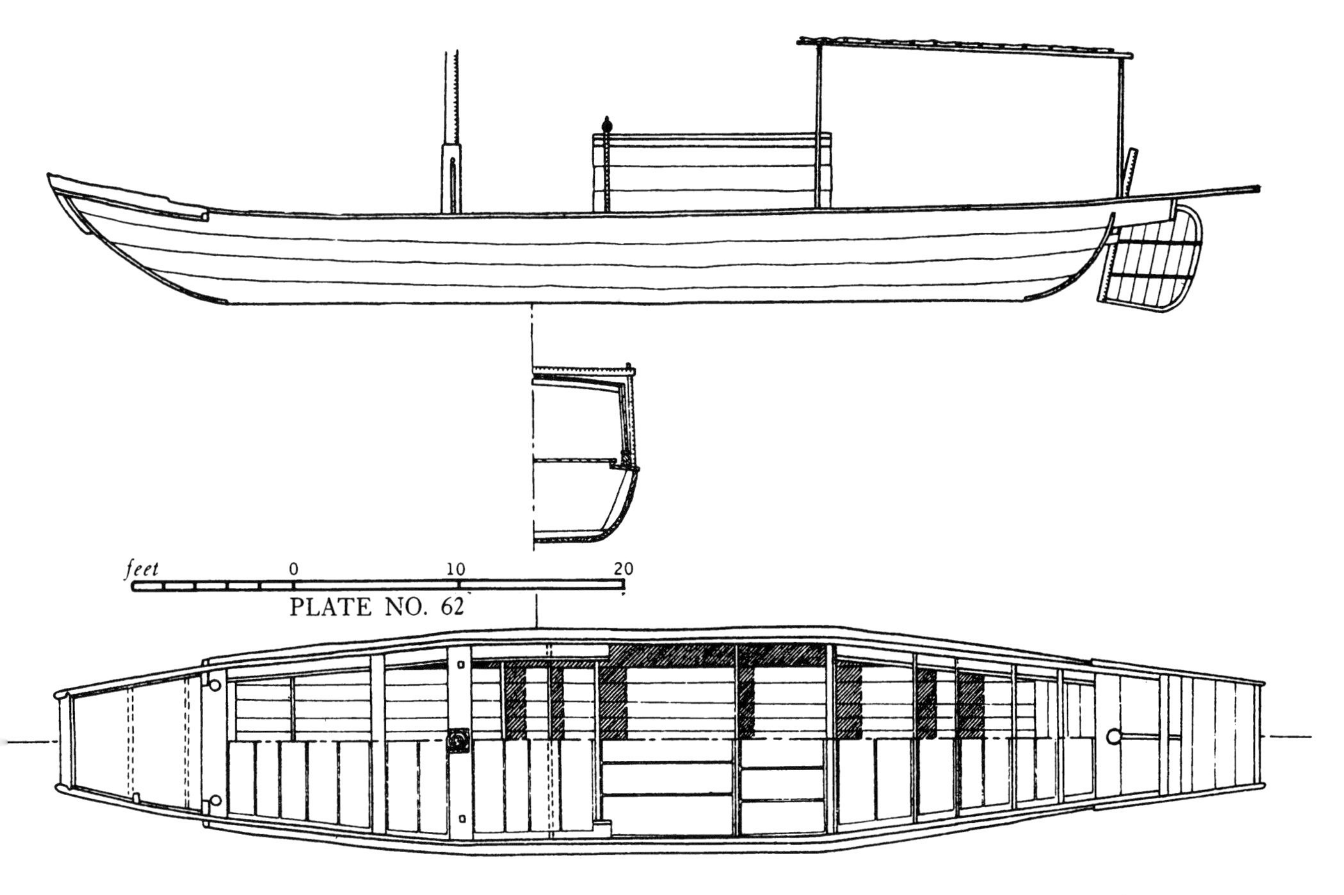

THE LINGHU-CH'UAN 菱湖船

One of the larger rice-junks navigating the Whangpoo and adjacent inland creeks is the *linghu-ch'uan*, so named after a village where it is built, near Huchow (湖 州), on the upper reaches of the Whangpoo. This craft, with a carrying capacity of 200 piculs of rice in bulk, is moderately strong in construction, being made of *sha-mu*, with six hardwood bulkheads, two half-bulkheads, and seven frames. It measures 71 feet in length, with a beam of 13 feet and a depth of 5 feet, and shows pleasing and graceful lines, tapering gently at either extremity. The square narrow bow shows a doubling plank rabbeted in from just below the athwartship cross-beam to a depth of about 2 feet. The rounded flare, widening as it rises, is rather an unusual feature of the hull, as is the fact that the first bulkhead is so far aft.

The rudder is of the hoisting variety, slung in the Shanghai fashion from the after cross-beam and fitted with a block and tackle. There is one mast, which carries a square-headed lug-sail.

The small 4-foot high removable house accommodates the owner and his family. For additional protection, removable washboards can be fitted to extend from the two bitts right forward back to the house. The usual standing awning covers the after-portion of the junk.

The small crew of two live in quarters forward of the mast, in an area measuring 7 by 7½ feet. In this type of craft they always keep their clothes, personal effects, and bedding between the fourth and fifth bulkheads. The galley, which consists of two pans on two stoves, is situated right aft and fills the width of the vessel.

Propulsion is by sailing or yulohs, one on the bow and one on the starboard side of the stern.

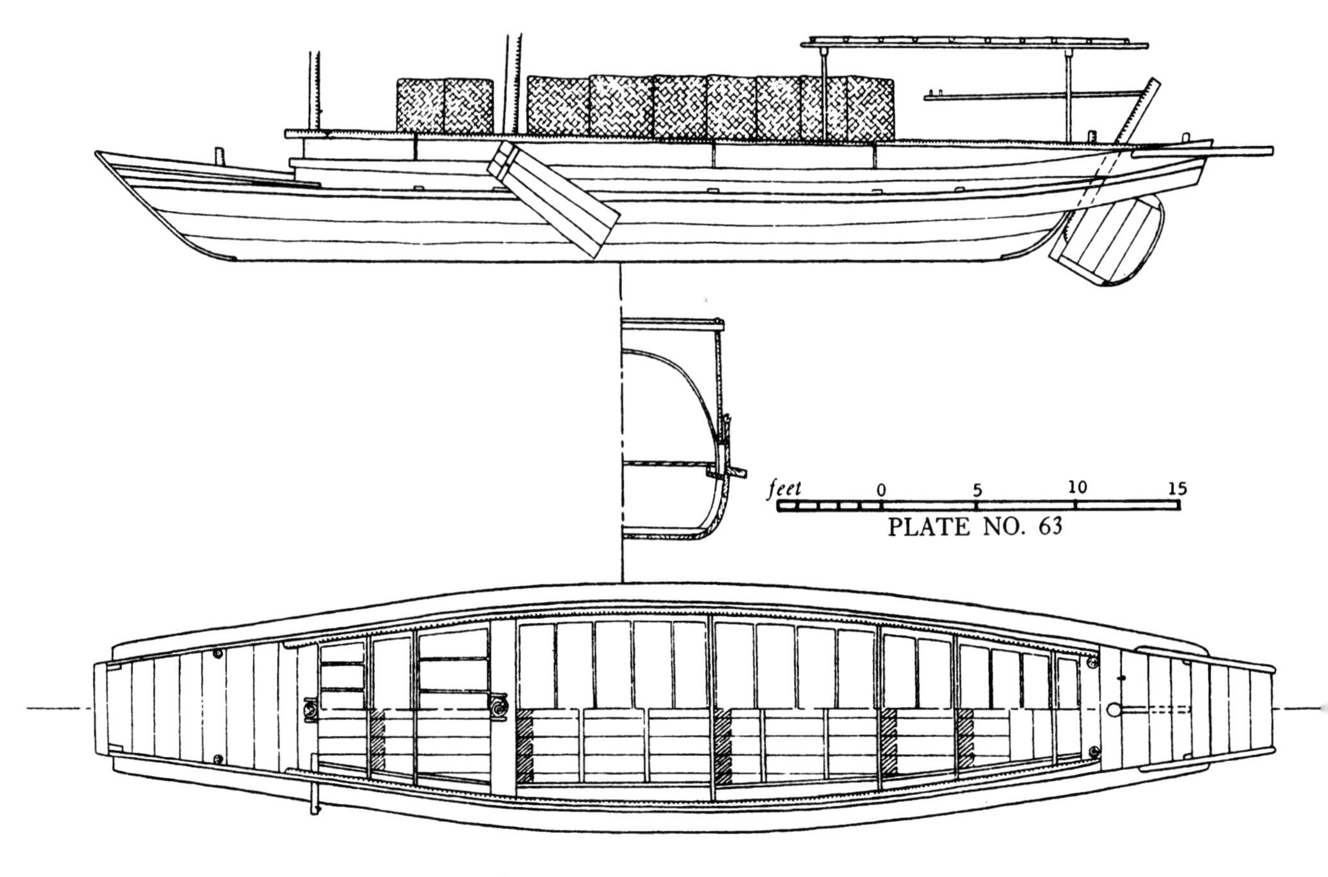

出門船

THE CH'U-MÊN-CH'UAN

This rice-junk is known as the *ch'u-mên-ch'uan*, which literally means the " go-out junk," more freely translated as the " outport junk."

Built at Pootung of *sha-mu*, with five hardwood bulkheads and seven frames, these junks are more or less standard. The specimen here illustrated in Plate No. 63 measures 58 feet, with a beam of 12 feet and a depth of 3½ feet.

An unusual feature in the construction is the presence of two hardwood top-beams near either extremity which do not rest, as is usual, on bulkheads. Also uncommon is the fact that all the deck-beams are mortised into the structure of the hull, as may be seen in the plan. This is probably to afford extra strength to a hull which, though adequate for carrying the cargo of 300 piculs of rice, is yet not outstandingly sturdy.

The junk carries rice from the Pootung hinterland to Shanghai and also brings its cargo of grain down the Whangpoo from river ports.

High removable washboards extending from the foremast until they merge in the structure at the stern serve to prevent the wash from passing vessels reaching the perishable cargo.

The raked rudder of the non-balance hoisting variety is at a more than normally acute angle and has a long straight tiller. There are two masts, situated far forward and close together, and two lee-boards. The propulsion is supplemented or alternated by the three yulohs, two of which are in the bow, operating on short bumkins, and the third over the stern. A temporary house can be formed of any size desired by means of a succession of removable arched bamboo mats, the surplus of which, when not in use, can be stowed on the top of the others. The ends of the mats are fitted inside the washboards, so that the rain running down the smooth waterproof mat surface may find an exit through apertures cut in the weather-boarding at regular intervals.

The owner and crew of four men live in the commodious house, the galley being between the fifth bulkhead and the stern.

Like all rice-junks, these are well found, clean, and particularly well kept, and the crew obviously take a pride in their craft.

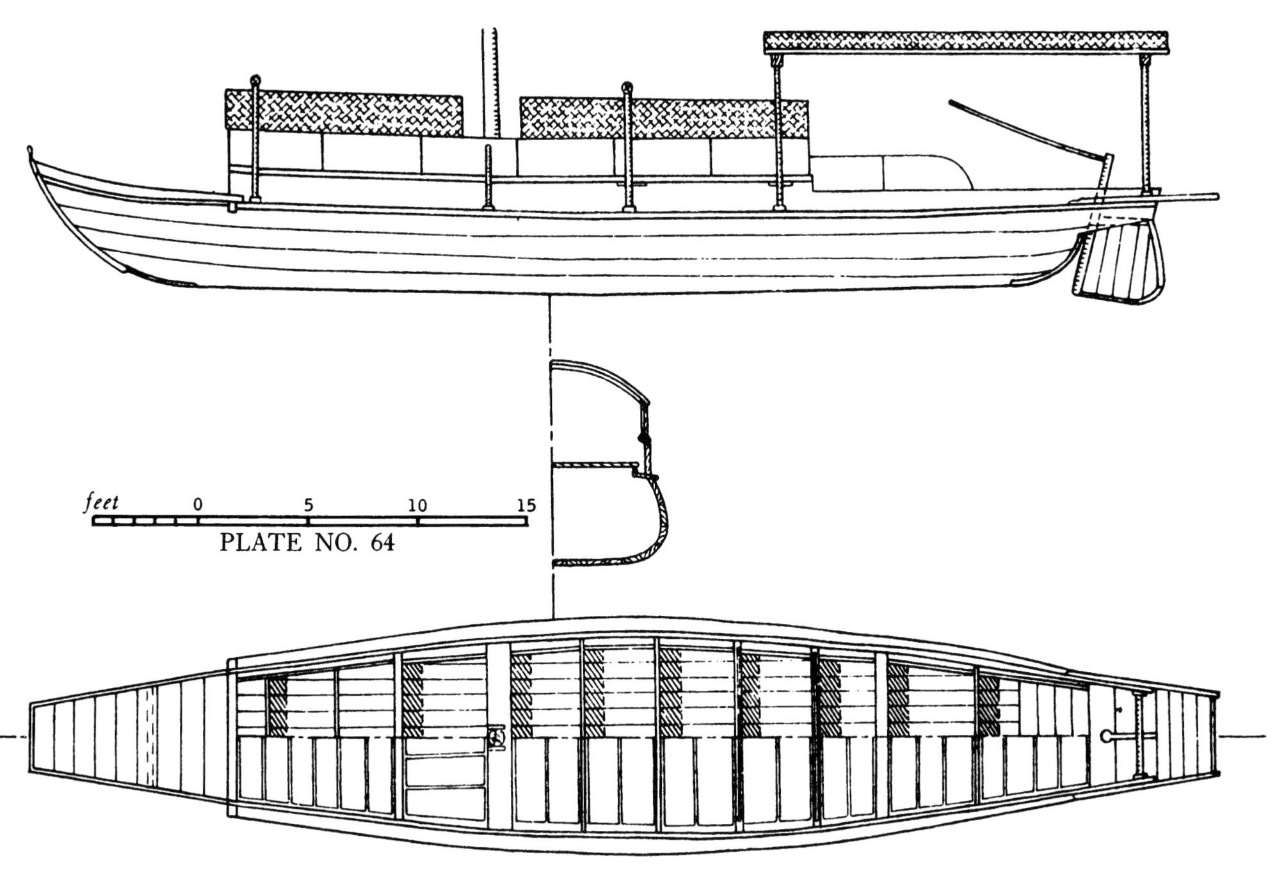

PLATE NO. 64

THE CHANGSHU-CH'UAN

This small rice-junk is also named after the place where it is built, a town on a tributary of the Soochow Creek. An alternative name, however, is the *mi-pao-tzŭ* (米 包 子), or " packet of rice." It navigates direct to Shanghai down the Soochow Creek, a distance of about 100 *li*.

Built of *sha-mu*, she is a nice-looking craft measuring 54 feet, with a beam of $10\frac{1}{2}$ feet, a depth of $4\frac{1}{2}$ feet, and a capacity of 180 piculs of rice in bulk. These junks vary in size, the largest having a carrying capacity of as much as 500 piculs.

There are nine bulkheads and three frames. The sixth and seventh bulkheads are fitted with sliding doors. Tapering considerably to the narrow 3-foot bow and stern, this type is distinguished by the bulky shape of the midship section, both laterally and vertically, for the swelling of the typical rice-junk is so marked as to present what is almost a modified form of turret-built hull.

The house, which is entirely removable down to the washboards, is bisected by the mast. In rainy weather the gaps between the fore and aft portions of the house are covered with a tarpaulin. The owner lives in the after-portion of the house between the sixth and seventh bulkheads, where the deck is sunk about a foot below deck-level.

The rest of the crew of three live in the forward part of the house in a section measuring 10 by 8 feet. The galley is in the stern abaft the ninth bulkhead.

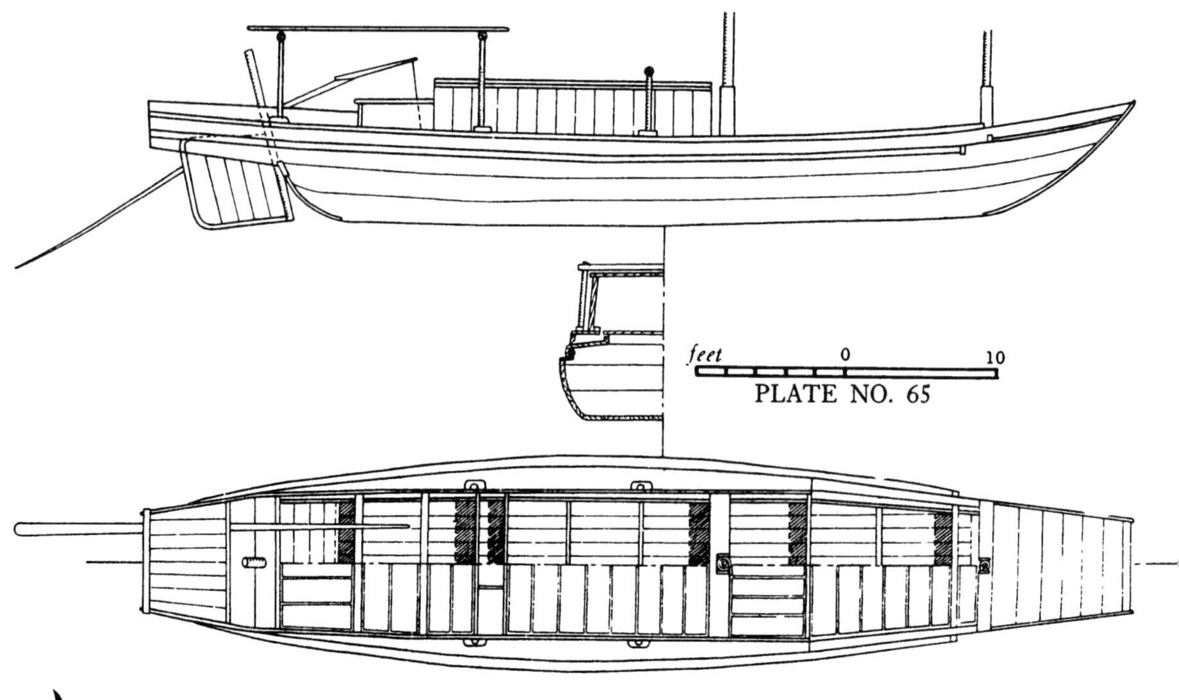

THE T'AIHU HSI-HU-CH'UAN

太湖西湖船

The T'aihu *hsi-hu-ch'uan*, or T'ai Lake boat, is, like the *fu-ch'uan*, also built at Changchow and serves the T'aihu, navigating as far as Shanghai.

Built of *sha-mu*, with six hardwood bulkheads and five frames, she measures 64½ feet long, with a beam of 13½ feet and a depth of 5½ feet. Except for slight differences in measurements and bulkheads and consequent diminishing strength and cargo capacity, there is very little indeed whereby to distinguish this type from the *fu-ch'uan*, except perhaps the rather blunter bow and stern and the fact that she is a carrier of rice instead of stones.

The unusual features of hull construction, quanting gangway, number and disposition of crew, and masts and sails are all identical. Nevertheless, this craft must be included here as a separate type to illustrate the junkmen's insistence that it is not only easy to recognize her as a totally different craft, but that it would be quite unpardonable to confuse her with the *fu-ch'uan*.

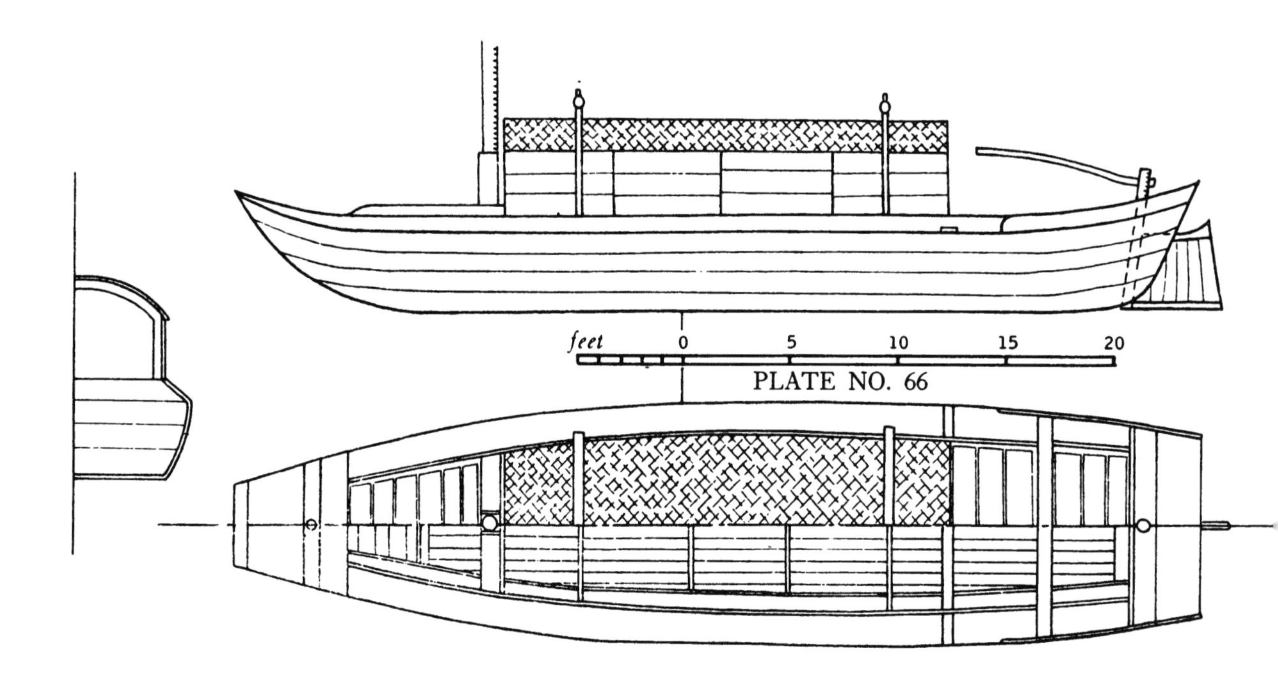

THE WU-TS'ANG-TZŬ OR FIVE-COMPARTMENT BOAT

A typical example of the junks engaged in inland water rice trade is provided by the *wu-ts'ang-tzŭ*, or five-compartment boat. This is quite an inappropriate name, as they are invariably fitted with six compartments.

The craft illustrated in Plate No. 66 measures 45 feet, with a beam of 10½ feet, a depth of 4 feet, and a capacity of 60 piculs. In construction they are light, with five bulkheads and four frames. The sides meet the bottom at a sharp angle, and amidships especially they are of box-like proportions tapering to a gently curving bow and fairly wide transom stern.

These junks operate mainly on the Chao Lake (巢 湖) and the many creeks which spread inland forming a network of waterways serving the rich rice-growing areas.

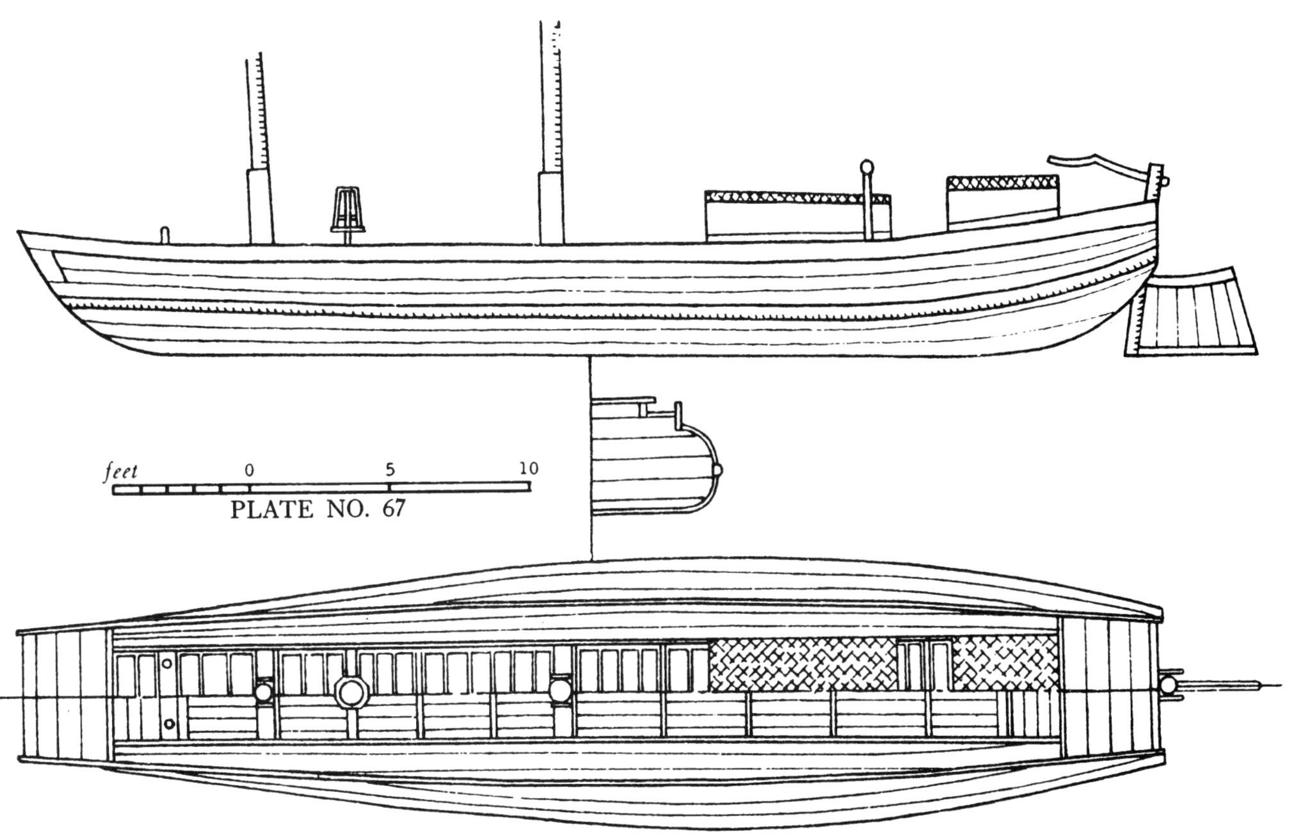

PLATE NO. 67

THE CHAOHU HUA-TZŬ OR CHAO BOAT

The Chaohu lies in the very heart of one of the very best rice-growing districts in China, and so it is not surprising to find a great number of very interesting and distinctive types of junk in the Chaohu–Wuhu rice trade.

The Chaohu *hua-tzŭ*, illustrated in Plate No. 67, is turret-built on very full lines and is fitted with one frame, seven bulkheads, and five half-bulkheads. The carrying capacity is about 150 piculs.

Although this junk is primarily designed for the transport of rice to Wuhu, the return journey is made with a general cargo on board.

The mainmast is stepped against the fifth bulkhead and carries the customary fairly flat-headed lug-sail. In addition, a smaller mast is stepped against the second bulkhead.

These junks carry a crew of four men.

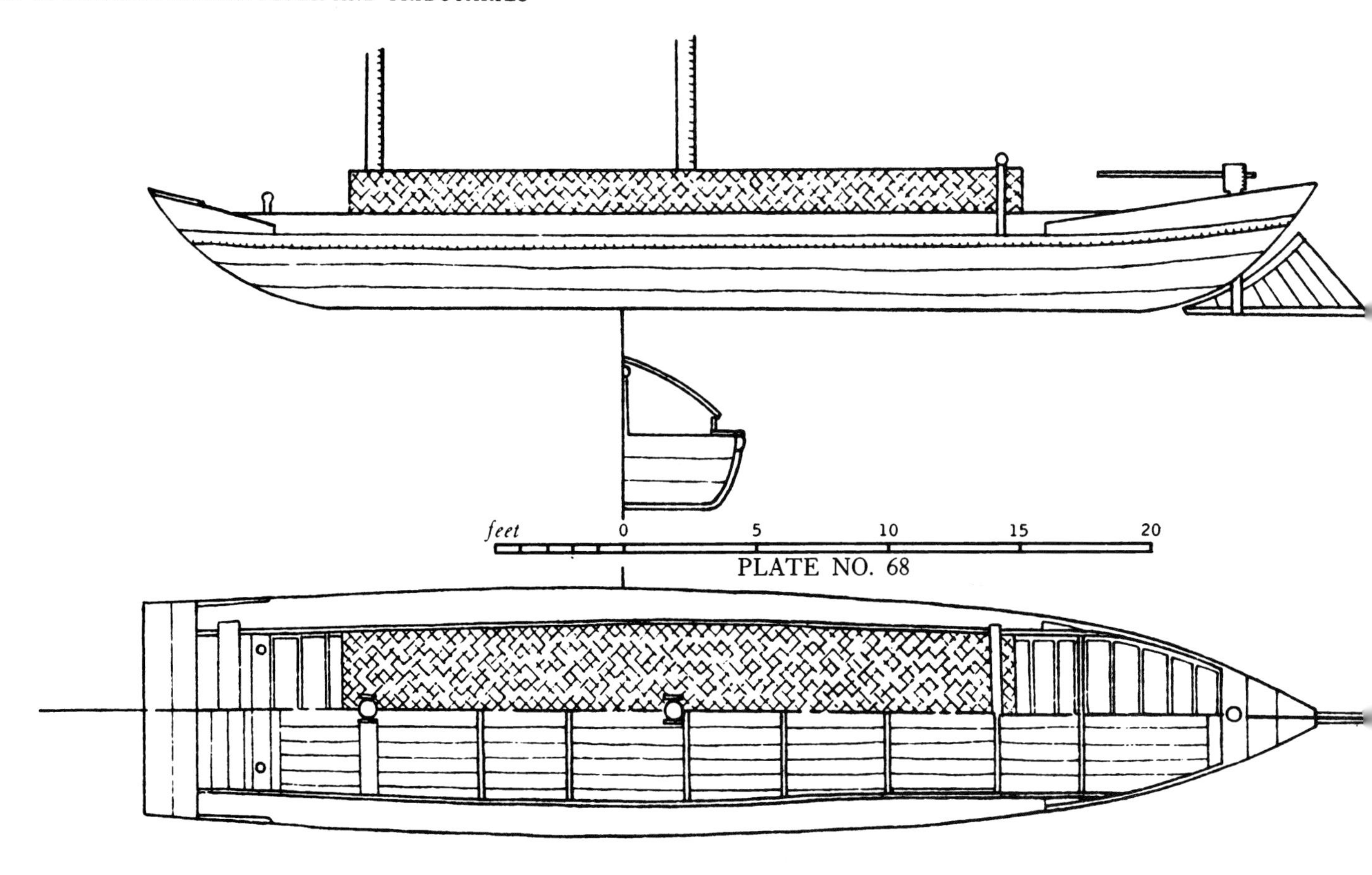

PLATE NO. 68

THE T'IAO-PO-TZŬ OR BAMBOO POLE

The *t'iao-po-tzŭ*, meaning bamboo pole, is another variety of rice-boat working the creek routes between Wuhu and the Chaohu (巢 湖), *via* Yüntsao (運 漕) and Yükikou (裕 溪 口).

These queer craft, which are very uniform in design, are quite common in the vicinity of Wuhu. They have an over-all measurement of 44 feet, a beam of 9 feet, and a depth of 3½ feet.

They have a capacity of about 130 piculs of rice, which is always carried in bulk. The main characteristics of this broad and stoutly-built junk are the sharp stern and the markedly square bow, which makes them quite unique among junks.

See Part One, pages 118–19, for the story of Lu Pan, the carpenter god.

The origin of the build of stern in these boats is said by the junkmen to be due to the influence of Lu Pan, the carpenter god, who lived as far back as 506 B.C.*

These junks are sometimes known by the purely local name of *shu-ch'uan* (舒 船), after a small town on a creek west of the Chaohu.

THE GRAIN TRIBUTE-JUNKS

It is a matter for regret that, although there are innumerable accounts of this strange service, there are apparently no plans, photographs, or reliable drawings extant of the craft which for so many years carried the tribute rice from almost all parts of the Empire to the Imperial Court at Peking.

* Opinions differ as to the actual date when he lived, some placing it some hundreds of years later.

It has not, unfortunately, been recorded where the grain tribute-junks were built or under whose control the building yards, which must have been very extensive, were placed. Yet the rules for the building and repairing of these craft were carefully laid down by statute. The size varied slightly according to the district of origin. The smallest types of junk hailed from Kiangnan (江 南), with a uniform size of 80 Chinese feet in length, a beam of 15 feet, and a depth of 6 feet. The junks of Kiangsi, Hupeh, and Hunan, having to pass through several large lakes and rivers before they reached the Grand Canal, were of slightly larger and heavier build, but all were of standard size, that is, 90 feet in length and 15½ feet beam, with a depth of 6½ Chinese feet. Each vessel carried on an average 300 piculs of grain. The sizes had to conform strictly to regulations, even down to the standard height of the awning. Inspectors examined the junks at regular intervals, and should they be found to have transgressed the dimensions laid down, the laodah was subject to heavy penalties, while the Intendant responsible was liable to be denounced to the Throne. As this had only one unhappy result, there is little doubt that the Inspectors had an easy task. The junks were regularly inspected and repaired, and, when passed for service, were stamped with the official seal.

Each junk had a 10 years' commission. If at the end of that time she was fit for service, she continued to operate, but if not, the Transport Intendant would send in a requisition for the necessary materials, and the repairs would be proceeded with. The cost of the overhaul of the junks which had completed their 10 years' service was a charge on the Government; but when repairs were necessary after a shorter period, it was presumed that the officials were to blame and they had to pay the cost.

In the "Ta Ch'ing Hui Tien" (大 淸 會 典), which is a collection of the rules which governed the administration of every Government department under the Manchu dynasty, is to be found a detailed description of the organization and working of the Grain Transport System, perhaps one of the most highly organized services in China. The original rules date from 1684, but they were revised from time to time to meet the needs of the Service. The latest were dated 1818 and are extremely interesting as showing what the system once was.

The administration was entrusted to a board consisting of nine members, of which six were Manchus and three Chinese, the executive power being vested in a Director General, an official of equal rank with a Viceroy.* Under him were Intendants of the eight Intendancies of Shantung, Honan, Kiangnan, Susung (宿 松), Chekiang, Kiangsi, Hupeh, and Hunan.

The Grain Transport Brigade was a military police organization numbering 240 Lieutenants, 120 Escorting Officers, and 66,000 Flagmen. The latter were in charge of individual transports and were so named because a flag was officially issued to each transport.

The selection of the Flagmen was conducted on principles bearing a strong resemblance to the European feudal system, for under the Ming dynasty certain lands were set apart and the tenants were bound to render service to the State in the transportation of grain. A census of these Crown-tenants, as they might be called, was made every year, and from these men the required number of hands was selected by the subordinate officers of the garrisons established at intervals along the Grand Canal. The annual list of conscripts was finally laid before the Emperor for his approval. Rewards were given for good service. For instance, a Flagman after 12 years' service, during which no short weight

* The office of Director General of Grain Transport was abolished in January 1905.

had been found in the grain under his charge, would be awarded a button of the Ninth Grade.

Over every 10 junks a Decurion was in charge. These men were drawn from the class of substantial householders, their duty being to receive the cargo and accompany it to its destination. Each junk carried a crew of 7 to 11 men, specially selected by the garrison and transport officers.

The regulations governing the supply of tribute were extremely complex, but they seem to have been designed to facilitate the system of "squeeze" so essential to the officials of that day. None but the initiated could understand the endless wheels within wheels on which it was constructed and the unending provisions to meet every possible case. Theoretically, the tribute was all delivered in grain, but in practice one-sixth was commuted in silver, which was sent along with the ordinary money contributions.

The supply of grain required from the eight Intendancies depended on the varieties each district produced, and the regulations in this respect were very strict and exacting in respect of the grade of rice. It was laid down that "each separate grain must be round, clean, and dry." Any shortage had to be made up according to a fixed scale, which was further complicated quite unnecessarily by the minuteness of detail characterizing the regulations on the subject. In addition, each Intendancy had to supply one mat measuring 6.4 by 3.6 Chinese feet for each picul of tribute proper. The mats were used to cover the grain when stored in Old Peking, and for the same purpose during the voyage of the junks. Nine deal planks and one log had also to be provided for each 2,000 piculs of tribute. Finally, a quantity of large hollowed-out bamboos had to be provided. These were inserted at intervals among the heaps of stored grain to permit the circulation of air.

The rice used for the Emperor, which was naturally of the highest grade, was known as "white rice," and the Intendancies of Susung and Chekiang, which produced the best rice, had the honour of supplying his needs. The Imperial Princes were also provided with this grade of rice, as was the Banqueting Office, and the total of 164,180 piculs would seem to indicate fairly healthy appetites for the Imperial families and their guests.

In an average year tribute consisted of 4,217,978 piculs of rice of all grades, *Tls*. 780,963 in silver, and bamboos, mats, and deal boards in proportion, according to the regulations.

The accounts given show the cost of transporting this grain to the capital to have been almost incredible. The number of junks annually employed varied. In Volume XVII of the "Chinese Repository," the number for 1848 was placed at 6,318, but it more often amounted to nearly 8,000 junks, each of which was allowed from *Tls*. 160 to *Tls*. 260 to cover expenses.

The junks were divided up into 114 fleets with a staff of about 71,000 officers and men of all ranks. The vessels assembled at certain points, from which they sailed in convoys, starting off at different times so as to avoid confusion and congestion.

There is apparently no record to show when the Grain Transport Service ceased to exist, and, as already stated, authorities differ very considerably in the figures they have given as to the number of tribute grain-junks which proceeded to the capital each year. All are agreed, however, in recording a marked diminution in the yearly figure. By 1873 Chekiang and Kiangsu were sending large quantities of grain by sea to the capital, and one estimate gives only 670 grain-junks in operation in the Grand Canal. The China Merchants Steam Navigation Company were officially recognized and therefore carried one-third of the tribute grain to the North by sea.

This served to accelerate the break-up of the Grain Tribute Service, which was already disintegrating owing to internal deterioration resulting from rebellions at home and wars with the Western powers. Whether as a cause or as a result, another contributing factor was the failure of the responsible organizations to conserve the Grand Canal. This neglect and inefficiency has not only rendered nearly useless an important waterway that could have been of lasting benefit to the trade of both North and South, but, by allowing the canal to degenerate into a stagnant ditch, has developed an active menace to the drainage of the surrounding country.

THE GRAND CANAL

THE Chinese call the Grand Canal either Yüho (御 河), Imperial River; Yünho (運 河), Transport River; or Chaho (閘 河), River of Locks. It has also been termed the Tribute-bearing River (漕 河). In these names are epitomized in brief the history of that great artificial waterway, its principal reasons for existence, and a description of its main physical features.

The Grand Canal, like most canals of China, was made to serve a double purpose, primarily to supply an easy means of communication but also to provide a system of drainage and irrigation.

It runs for a distance of about 1,000 miles or more from its southern terminus, Hangchow, the provincial capital of Chekiang, across Kiangsu, traversing the whole province from south to north in a line parallel to the seacoast, through Shantung and Hopeh to its northern terminus at Tientsin. From here the Peiho serves to link it up with Peiping.

This great artificial waterway is not the result of one well-thought out scheme but of numerous experiments carried out through many centuries and brought to a successful issue after many failures, for canals in China were amongst the first public works to be attempted, and it is known that there was a fairly extensive canal system in Kiangsu at an early date. In the sixth century B.C. the State of Wu for the first time linked up the Yangtze and Hwai Rivers and continued the connecting canal still farther north so as to give access to the southern and central part of what is now known as Shantung. The section from Hangchow to Chinkiang on the Yangtze was built early in the seventh century A.D. The northern part, extending from the old Yellow River bed to Tientsin, was completed by Kublai Khan within the three years A.D. 1280–83. By this means the transport of tribute rice to the capital for the use of the troops in the less fertile northern provinces was ensured.

The transport had previously been slow and uncertain, but with the opening of the canal, which was utilized as it was being completed, the supplies of rice reached their destination with increasing regularity.

This northern and most recent portion has always presented the greatest navigational difficulties, owing to the less efficient construction and the silting up of the Yellow River, and further complicated by the neglect which has, throughout its length, served to lessen the utility of the Grand Canal.

In its course the canal crosses the two greatest rivers of China. The first, in the north, is the Yellow River, and the strange and remarkable feature of this crossing is that, as the river has been for so long imprisoned between high banks, its bed is here actually 16 feet above the level of the canal and is, of course, correspondingly higher than the surrounding country. This state of affairs is due to the facts that waterways silt up rapidly in China and that the Chinese, instead of dredging the beds, prefer to raise the embankments of the canals.* The strain thrown on the earthworks is enormous, and it is not surprising that they should, from time to time, give way and cause the terrible floods that have earned for the Yellow River the name of " China's Sorrow." The difference in the level of the bed of the river and that of the canal makes navigation at their junction

* An exception to this rule is to be found at Kwanhsien, on the Chengtu Plain. Here, since the third century B.C., the river has been dammed and cleared each year.

difficult, for if the water is too low the junks cannot cross the bar, and if it is too high the current becomes too strong.

The central and oldest portion of the Grand Canal lies between Chinkiang and Tsingkiangpu. Fed by the Hwaiho and the drainage from several adjacent lakes, it runs through a thickly populated and fertile alluvial plain situated north of the Yangtze and east of the canal and lying for the most part at, or very little above, sea-level. In this region the country west of the canal lies above the level of the canal-bed, but that to the east lies below it, so that the volume of water in the canal may rise from 7 to 22 feet above the neighbouring plain.

On this part of the canal most of the craft used are modifications of the *yen-ch'uan*, or salt-boat; or of the *nan-wan-tzŭ* (南灣子), or passenger-boat.

The *yen-ch'uan* is described in Part Three, page 310.

The numerous instances of differences of water-level on the canal, as it is crossed by or utilizes the channels of other streams, are controlled by a species of lock known as *chah*. This consists of an artificially constructed narrow neck with a dam or weir built across it, and fitted with a removable central part made of beams slipped one above the other into sockets of masonry.

When the beams are removed they provide an opening of about 22 feet in width. The difference in level above and below the lock is often considerable, as much as 2 feet. Ascending boats have to be lightened and dragged up "haul-overs" by means of capstans and cables, requiring the services of hundreds of coolies. Needless to say, these locks are a great impediment to navigation.

A haul-over on the Grand Canal.

There are four of them in Kiangsu: one in Tsingkiangpu and three others a few miles above it. They become more frequent as one goes north, but they are less formidable.

The southernmost portion of the canal begins where it crosses another great stream, this time the Yangtze. Here, on the south bank of the river at Chinkiang, the original course of the canal runs under the southern wall of the city, its entrance being near the ex-British Concession. In winter, however, the channel silts up completely, and traffic from the Yangtze has to proceed down the river for about 10 miles below Chinkiang to another channel at Tantu, where, by following the tortuous course of a small river or creek, the Grand Canal may be reached at a spot where, after leaving Chinkiang, it curves to the north-east in a loop towards the Yangtze. At other points also navigation becomes difficult owing to the shallowness of the water: this is particularly the case at Tanyang, some 20 miles south of Tantu. Some of the shoals can be avoided by following side canals. The depth is usually sufficient for a draught of 4½ feet and in most places is far greater than this. The canal now runs in long straight reaches and is of a fairly uniform width of about 40 yards. Of the total distance of 200 miles from Chinkiang to Hangchow, the first 135 miles lie in the Province of Kiangsu. Skirting round the great stretch of the T'aihu, the canal, some 40 miles south of the Yangtze, passes the famous city of Soochow. From here on it passes through a network of lakes into Chekiang until it terminates at Hangchow.

The waters of the Grand Canal and those of the Ch'ient'ang River at Hangchow are not connected owing to the difference of water-level. This forms a great obstacle to navigation and necessitates transhipment of cargo or passengers, or even, in some cases, transport of the junks overland.

In Southern Kiangsu and Chekiang there is a vast network of numerous rivers, lakes, creeks, canals, and even navigable ditches. This inland-water system is, by means of the Grand Canal, also linked not only with the basin of the Ch'ient'ang River extending west from Hangchow, but with the vast alluvial basins of the Yangtze and Yellow Rivers and the basins of the Hwaiho and even the Peiho in the far north.

Intercommunication is also available through the Provinces of Anhwei, Kiangsi, and Fukien, and farther west *via* the Tungting Lake with the Siang, Kwei, and Si, or West, Rivers, providing at certain seasons of the year an uninterrupted waterway stretching from Peiping to Canton.

THE LIANG-CHIEH-T'OU

The *liang-chieh-t'ou* (兩 節 頭), or two-section junk, although, properly speaking, a native of the North, plies a regular trade down the Grand Canal and is therefore often to be met with crossing the Yangtze at Chinkiang or lying up in the harbour awaiting favourable water-levels.

Up to the month of June the Grand Canal is so shallow that it is navigable only by small junks or these specially designed craft. When the Yellow River is swollen, the current rapidly increases until the canal is deep enough by July for large weight-carrying craft.

The *liang-chieh-t'ou* also proceeds as far afield as Shanghai by way of the Grand Canal and the Soochow Creek and may sometimes be seen banked-in in its two separate sections on the crowded waterfront in Shanghai. The principal cargo carried is grain, beans, or fresh vegetables.

The unique character of the construction of this curious junk may be traced to the shallowness of its main thoroughfare, the Grand Canal, at certain parts and during certain seasons. These conditions, combined with the many sharp and narrow bends, have been countered by the ingenious junk-builders by developing an extremely long, narrow craft, which can be divided in the middle so as to allow separate handling of the bow and stern halves. By this means a sufficient pay load is ensured for the junk in normal waters, while retaining, by means of the separation arrangement, the advantage of being divisible into two mobile small craft so as to negotiate channels where clumsier junks would be forced to await a rising water-level. Another obvious advantage is that the junk when separated occupies less space when banked-in.

Although it is said that these boats may attain a length of 150 feet, the usual length on the Soochow Creek is about 110 feet, with a beam of 14½ feet and a depth of 5 feet. Boats of the largest size are decked-in throughout and have spacious houses.

A common size is that of the craft here illustrated, that is to say, about 90 feet in length with a beam of 11½ feet. Like all these craft, it is unusually narrow in proportion to the length, for the hull is about eight times as long over-all as it is wide, while the beam is about three times the depth in the hold.

Constructed with nine bulkheads and 14 frames of quite exceptional strength, as will be seen from the sectional drawing, everything about these craft demonstrates that they are built for shallow inland waters. The bottom is slightly curved transversely, but the curve is so gentle as to be hardly noticeable. Longitudinally the bottom is also curved throughout its entire length, but this becomes more marked at bow and stern, which sweep up in a long deep curve and meet the transverse stem-beam and transom respectively. Both bow and stern facing are horizontally planked. There are no hatch-covers, but the cargo is sheltered by a series of matting covers[1] resting on a detachable strongback and extending from the mast to just short of the after-house. The bottom ends of the matting extend over the high hatch-coaming[2], which runs nearly the whole length of the junk at a distance of 2 feet inboard.

When the wind is fair, the junk proceeds under sail, but is otherwise tracked by one or two of the crew, the mast and sail being lowered so as to rest on the lumber irons[3]. The mast is retained in place by a fore and aft plank fitting snugly between two bulkheads, thus distributing the weight. It depends for its support upon a short tabernacle, a fid at deck-level giving additional rigidity. The mast[4] is so arranged that it can be struck with ease and speed so as to enable the junk to shoot under bridges. For this purpose a pair of sheer-legs[5] are fitted, the heel being connected by a rope becket to ring-bolts in the deck. There is a topping-lift to the mast, which can be sent down in a surprisingly short time. Once through the bridge the mast can be sent up and the sail made nearly as speedily. Before either operation it is necessary to remove some of the matting of the house abaft the capstan[6]. The lee-boards[7] are situated unusually far forward and are small for the size of the junk; for instance, in the craft measuring 110 feet in length, the lee-boards are 7½ feet in length. They are secured by a chain stopper terminating in a hook taking into a ring-bolt on the deck.

The balance rudder furnishes an example of the shoal-water variety in its truest form. The rudder-post is held to the stern by an athwartship beam running parallel to the transom. Assistance in negotiating the difficult bends is provided by the crude bow-sweeps, which also, of course, are of use when the boat is divided and the two sections operate independently. The bow-sweep,

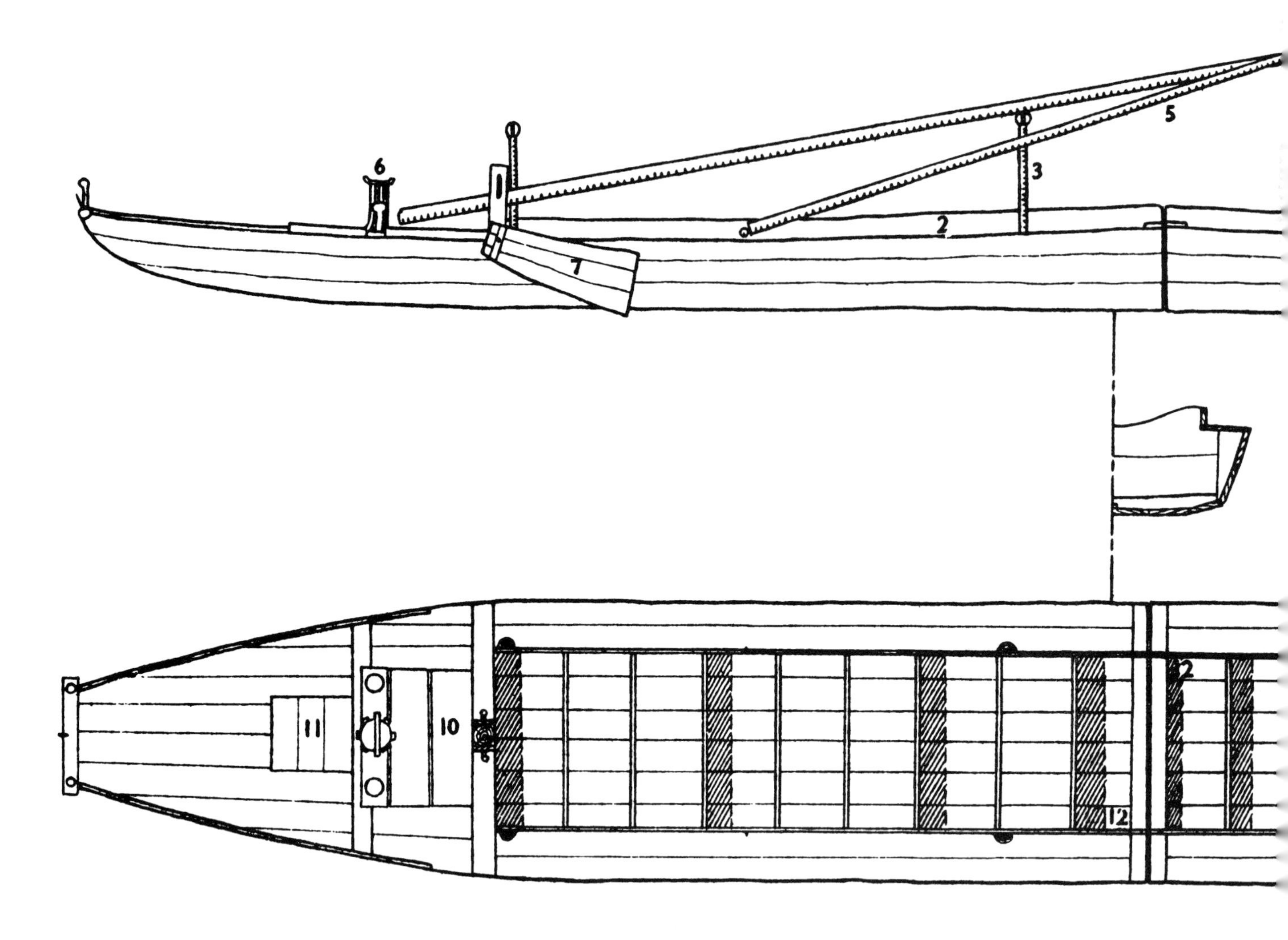

which is straight, is formed of two poles lashed together, while the blade is a short, pointed, oval board secured by wire to the extremity of the shaft. The whole measures 45 feet, or precisely the same as one of the sections of the boat. The cheek-piece is slotted to receive, and to pivot on, the bearing-pin which is situated on the stem-beam.

The stern-sweep, which is very much larger, measures about 62 feet and is composed of two pieces, a very long straight loom made from an irregular tree trunk and a wavy blade. The cheek-piece, which is rather large and clumsy, has a hole in the centre to take into the thick iron bearing-pin on the transom; the rudder and the after-house strongback[8] are necessarily removed when the sweep is in use. The bearing-pin is of sufficient height to give the sweep about an inch clearance over the after-house[9]. The sweep is worked from a temporary bridge amidships, which usually consists of a plank resting on the high coaming. A large stone is suspended from the loom of the stern-sweep to adjust the balance as desired.

The crew of Northerners, up to 10 in number, according to the size of the junk, are accommodated below decks forward, the quarters being entered down a large booby hatch[11]. A large hatch[10] abaft this leads to a storeroom for ropes and sails not in use. Others of the crew also sleep in the exceedingly small wooden house situated right aft. Small ports on each side provide ventilation and light. Although there is no lock or any sort of device to secure these sliding wooden panels, a small bell is sometimes fitted in such a manner as to cause a warning tinkle when the window is slid back, thus furnishing an interesting, if not very effective, burglar alarm.

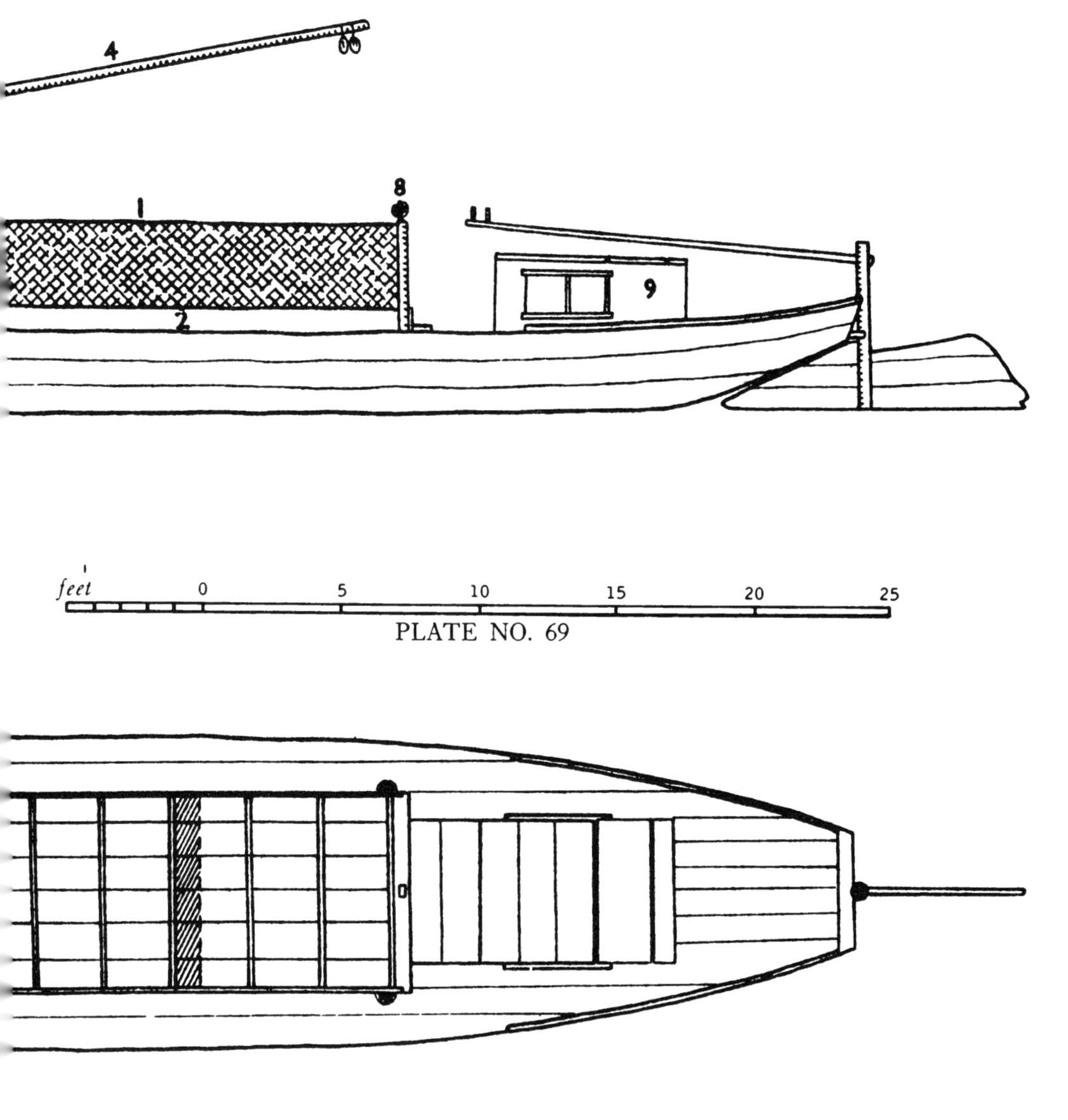

PLATE NO. 69

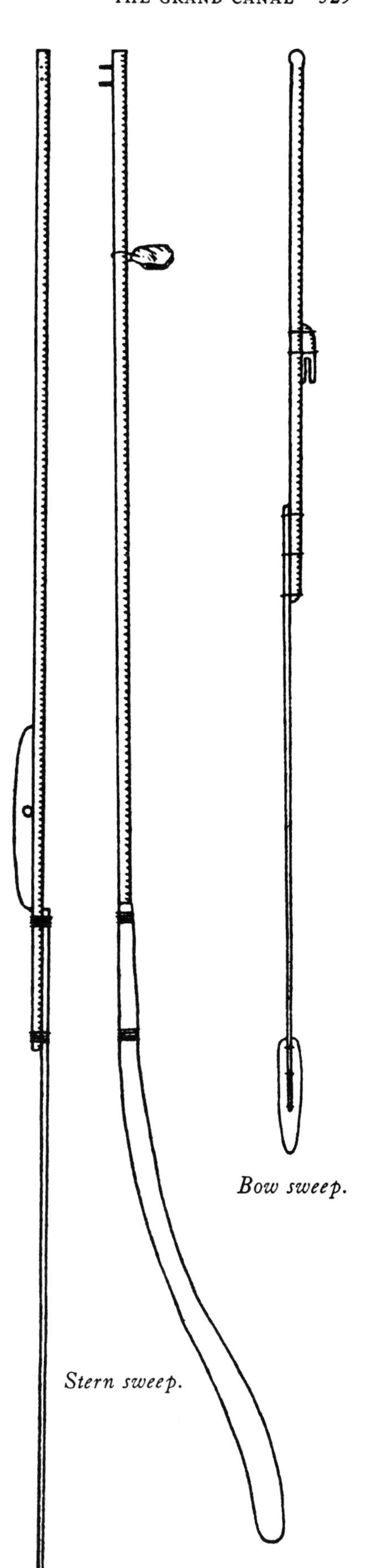

Bow sweep.

Stern sweep.

The junkmen always carry with them their wives and children. This arrangement is much to the advantage of the owner—usually the laodah,—as by this means he increases his complement of hands considerably without a corresponding addition to the portage bill. Even the children lend a hand about the ship.

Cooking is down below decks in the foremost part of the after-section. The connection or severing of the two component sections of this junk is very easily performed, for they are joined by a supremely simple device consisting of a wire becket, into the bights of which two short handspikes have been inserted, one on each section of the junk. One end of each handspike is held down under the covering board[12], while the other end is secured at its extremity by a rope. When it is desired to disconnect the sections, this rope is slipped, whereupon the handspikes fall out, releasing the wire becket, and the two sections of the junk drift apart. To secure additional rigidity a circular chock passes over the join between the two parts of the boat, and a condemned shoe does duty as a chafing mat. The junks are connected by reversing the process. The trim of the two sections of the junk is rarely the same, and so it is necessary when connecting up for men to bear down on the high section until they are even, when the handspikes are inserted. So simple and convenient is this arrangement that the whole operation can be accomplished in a few minutes.

When loaded with not less than 37 tons and with lee-boards down, these strange, but efficient, junks draw about 3 feet, but when light can float in a few inches of water only. They probably represent the handiest and certainly one of the most unusual types of cargo-carriers in the Far East.

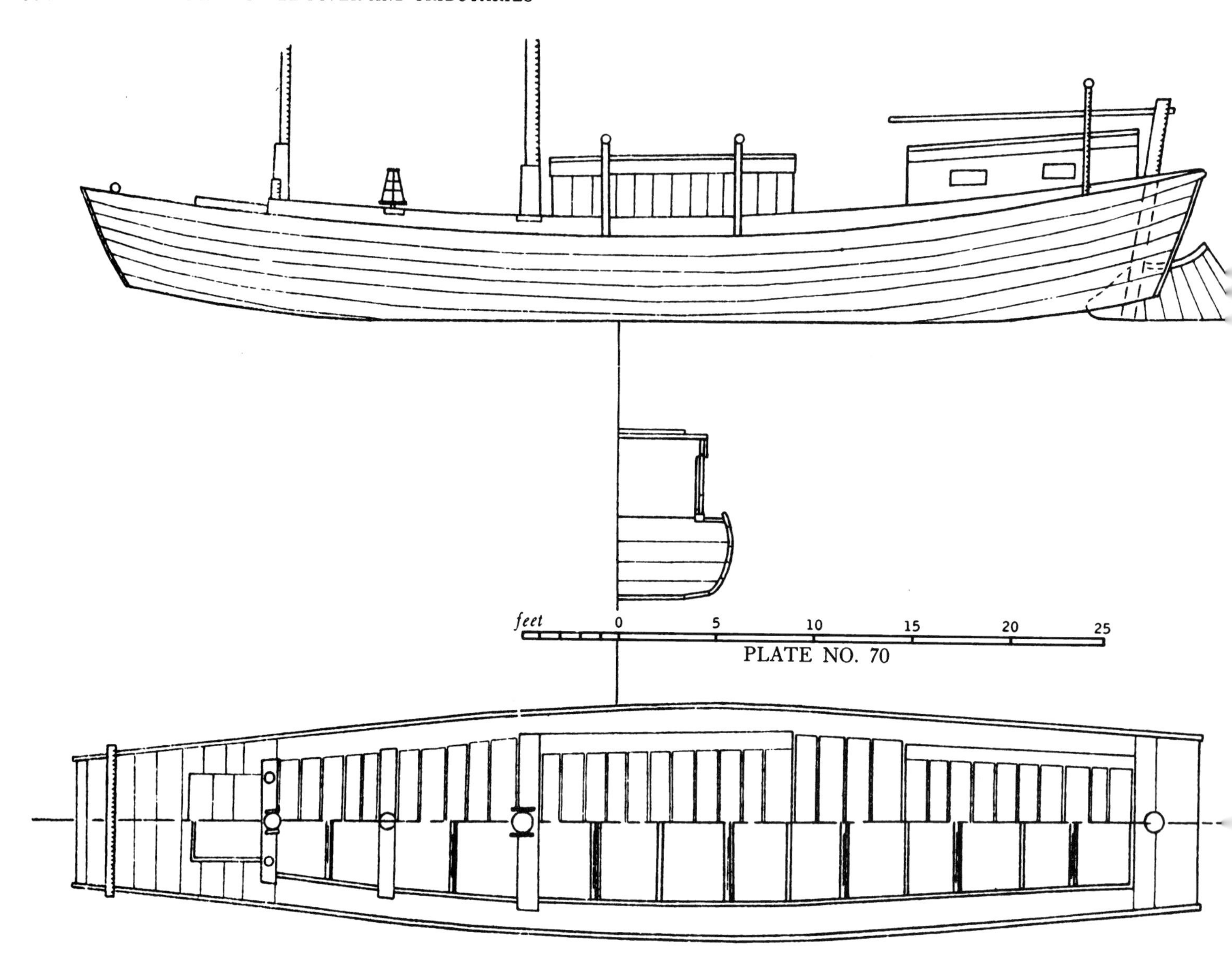

PLATE NO. 70

THE LIANG-HUA OR FOODSTUFF-JUNK

There is nothing particularly noteworthy or of interest about the *liang-hua*, illustrated in Plate No. 70. As her name implies, she is a food-carrier, usually grain, from Wuhu up the Grand Canal.

Her over-all measurements are 58 feet in length, with a beam of 12 feet and a depth of 4 feet.

Lighter in construction than the usual run of grain-carriers, she has seven bulkheads and seven frames.

The lofty and very narrow form of sails shows she is accustomed to inland waters. The tall *sha-mu* masts are stepped in the ordinary way, and immediately abaft the mainmast is the central deck-house. The roof is of wood and quite flat, the side planking being removable to give light and air. The crew of six men live in the after-house, the fore-part of which is used as a galley.

There is a great bluffness about the bow which ends in a light cross-beam, abaft which is a removable cross-beam. The heavy balance-rudder has a long curved tiller leading to the conning position just forward of the house.

Notwithstanding local differences of detail, these cargo-lighter types vary very little as a class.

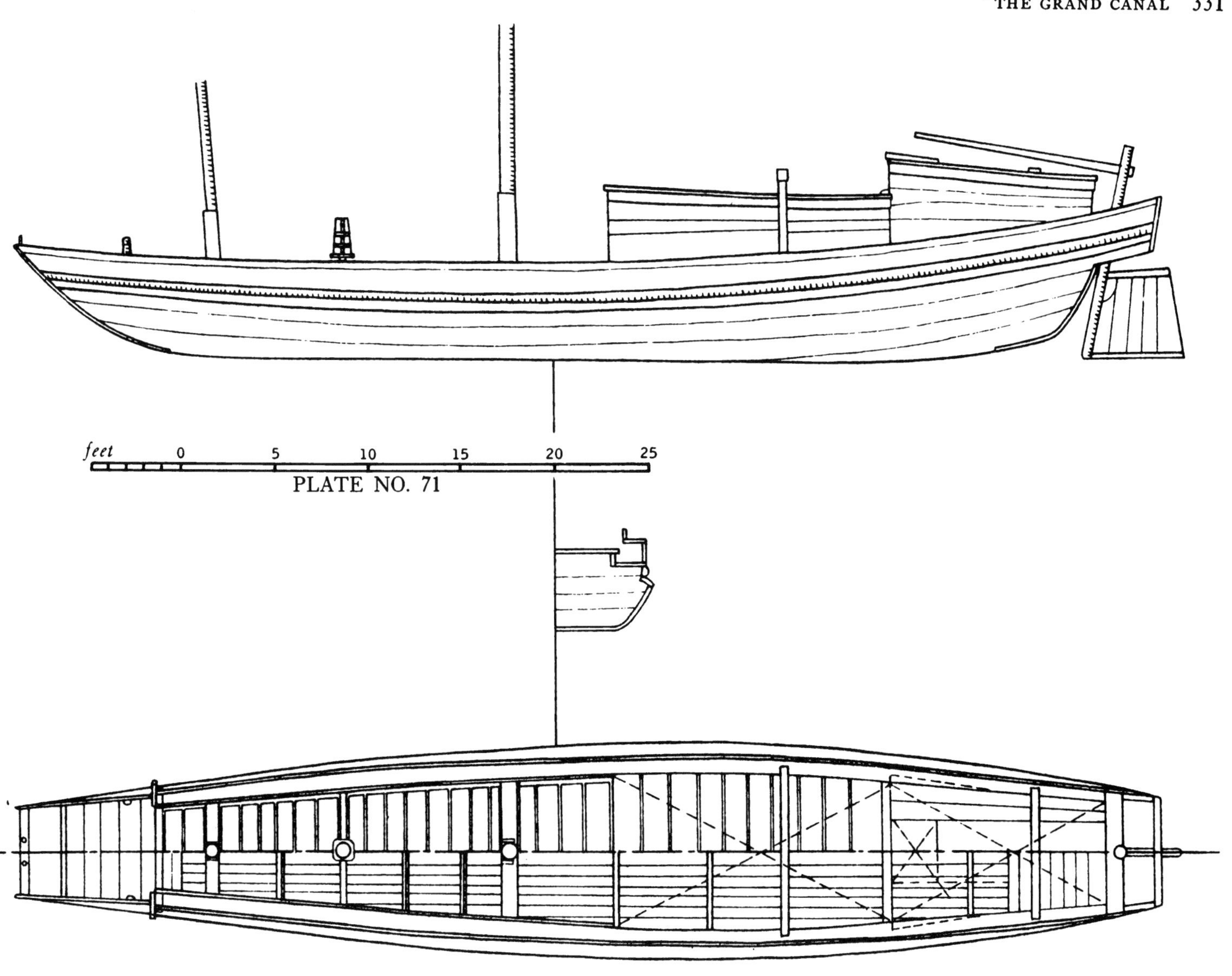

PLATE NO. 71

THE SSŬ-WANG-TZŬ OR SSŬ TRADER 泗網子

A craft which is frequently to be seen on the Grand Canal is the *ssŭ-wang-tzŭ*, literally " river net," or the Ssŭ trader.

This junk is illustrated in Plate No. 71 and measures 59 feet in length, with a beam of 11 feet and a depth of 5 feet.

This junk is built on well-proportioned lines tapering at bow and stern. There are nine bulkheads, one half-bulkhead, and three frames. Three deck-beams are laid across those bulkheads accommodating the masts and capstan.

The fore-part of the house is used for the stowage of cargo, while the after-part is used as living quarters. The house is supported by two heavy roof-beams. The helmsman stands inside the after-house, his head protruding through a hatch which is fitted with a sliding door.

Although these junks are, of course, equipped with masts and sails, they rely to a large extent on yulohs which are worked from bumkins on each bow. Two bollards are situated forward of the foremast.

The rudder is of the hoisting non-balance variety, the planks being laid vertically except at the top and bottom edges. A grapnel type of anchor is used in lieu of the more usual stick-in-the-mud variety.

THE EMPEROR'S "LITTLE RED" BOAT

According to Mr. Worcester's notes, no plans were available for this or the following boat.

The Emperor Yang Ti (煬 帝), A.D. 580–618, was a man of violence and luxury, with a hobby for making gardens and waterways. He caused a huge lake to be dug, measuring 40 square *li*. It was modelled on the imaginary forms of the islands where the immortals lived in the " sea of heaven."

Sixteen islands stood in the lake, on each side of which was a mansion well stocked with rare food and inhabited by young girls of ravishing beauty. On still, star-lit nights the Emperor was often to be seen carrying out visits of inspection.

To facilitate a royal sight-seeing tour throughout his domains, he constructed an elaborate system of canals connecting the Yellow River with the Yangtze. These canals were said to be 40 paces wide, lined with stone and embellished with willow trees along their banks. Fully half of the workmen employed died from the rigours of the forced labour.

He was also interested in boat-building and naval architecture, and is reported to have made 30,000 to 40,000 craft, called "dragon" boats, for his private use. When the canals were ready, he made a journey from Loyang to Nanking, the boats being guarded by 80,000 troops.

From a nautical research point of view it is a great pity that no illustrations have come down to us of the royal barge, which was somewhat inappropriately known as " the little red," for she was said to be 40 feet high and 2,000 feet in length, with four decks. This amazing vessel was fitted with a throne room, a miniature private palace, 120 sumptuous cabins for the use of members of his harem, as well as other " luxury liner " apartments.

The Empress, who accompanied him, travelled in her own barge in similar style. The royal pair were followed by nine other craft described as " floating landscapes," together with 50 small craft with names such as *Flying Feather*, *Green Shelldrake*, *Crimson Bird*, *Shimmering Light*, *White Tiger*, and so forth. These latter craft carried princes and princesses, priests, court officials, eunuchs, concubines, and other entertainers. Provision was thoughtfully made for the resident ambassadors of other nations.

The Emperor employed his leisure in devising new court dresses and inventing feathered head-dresses for the luscious birds of his enormous harem. As a result of his profound sartorial inspiration, on his return from one of his trips, he instructed his highest court officials to wear violet robes; the next grade, red; the lower officers, green; and the populace, white. Merchants were ordered to wear black, and soldiers yellow.

Another favourite recreation of his was gambling. Lovers of games of chance will be interested to know that dice were probably invented by the Chinese. The invention is claimed for Ch'ên Ssŭ-wang (陳 思 王), a royal member of the Kingdom of Wei, who lived in the third century A.D. The Chinese dice are peculiar in that the ace and the four are always red, all others being black. A story is recounted by Giles, the great sinologue (which is not confirmed in the " Shih Fu Chi Yüan " (詩 賦 紀 源), and may be apocryphal), of how the Emperor during one of his famous house-boat trips was playing dice with his favourite concubine and wanted only three " fours " to win. As the dice rolled out, one of them settled down at once showing the desired number, while the others went on spinning round. " Four! four! four! " cried His Majesty, much excited, and the dice immediately settled in obedience to the Imperial call. A eunuch standing by suggested that something should be done to mark this extraordinary event, and orders were immediately issued that in future the "four" should be coloured red. And so it is to this day.

The craft were propelled by trackers dressed in silk, while hundreds of young girls especially chosen for their beauty assisted by gently pulling on brightly coloured cords. The fleet, it is recorded, stretched for nearly 1,000 *li*, and after it had passed the smell of perfumes lingered for "tens of miles."

In A.D. 617 the Emperor surpassed himself by ordering a "travelling town" to be built. Unhappily for him he did not live to see this nautical dream come true. The inhabitants of the places he honoured with these visits soon wearied of his overwhelming attentions and gradually a revolt sprang up, which culminated in his assassination.

SERPENT-BOATS

In "An Embassy from the East India Company of the United Provinces to the Emperor of China," ingeniously described by Mr. John Nievhoff, Steward to the Ambassadors, dated 1669, the following description is given of boats designated as serpent-boats:

> "We found a great number of all manner of ſtrange built veſſels: but the moſt to be admired at were two barques, or ſloops, which by the Chineſe were called Long chon, which ſignifies Serpent Boat. Theſe two veſſels are built after a peculiar faſhion, very curiouſly painted with all manner of colours that they ſeemed much to exceed thoſe boats which carry the fiſh from Nanking to Peking for the Emperor's uſe: and becauſe of the more ſtrange contrivance of this boat, I thought it good to make a draught thereof which you have in the annexed cut.
>
> "The mould or caſt of this fair bottom ſeems much like the form of our water ſnake. The ſtern hung full of ſtrange ſerpents so faſtened with ribbons of ſeveral colours, which made a gallant ſhow: at the ſtern of this veſſel, hung likewise two nimble boys, who played tricks and gambols to delight the ſpectators both above, and diving under water. Upon the top of each maſt, which were three in all, ſtood an idol, very curiouſly adorned with ſilk flags and pennants. In like manner on the poop, an image dreſſed with ducks and drakes, the ſtern was also ſtacked with numbers of ſtandards, ſet out with taſſels of hair, ſilk flags and long feathers: the boat covered round with rich ſilk.
>
> "Under an upper raiſed deck, full of flags and ſtandards ſate twelve luſty ſeamen, with gild crowns upon their heads, clothed in ſilk, their arms naked: theſe were ſo dexterous at rowing that the boat went at an extraordinary rate."

THE WAR-JUNK

THE war-junk, in some form or other, is probably as old as the nation itself, and even a brief study of Chinese history will show that nowhere in the Empire did the war-junk play a more important part than on the Yangtze.

A serious obstacle to the satisfactory reconstruction of the ancient Chinese fighting-ship is the total absence of any plans or dependable descriptions. It was never the custom in China, as in some countries of the West, for a chieftain to be buried in his ship, nor did the ship-model figure in Chinese tombs as in those of the early Egyptians. Nautical research in China is therefore the poorer for the absence of such relics.

China, probably more than any other country in the world, holds scholarship in high honour, and the country has produced a goodly company of historians, philosophers, and scientific writers; but apparently they did not concern themselves with naval history or nautical lore.

In the sixth century B.C. warfare in China became a science through the work of Sun Wu (孫 武), sometimes known as Sun Tzŭ (孫 子), and author of the "Art of War" (兵 法). This book was revised by Wu Ch'i (吳 起) about the beginning of the Christian era. Although it is somewhat out of date, it still influences Chinese military tactics, even to-day.* Actually there is so much good sense in it that, although it was written more than 2,000 years ago, it may yet furnish many useful hints even in these days of atomic warfare.

Probably the most famous Chinese naval action was the Battle of the Crimson Cliff, fought on the Yangtze *circa* A.D. 208. The leader of the men of Wei, who was the famous traitor Ts'ao Ts'ao (曹 操), had seized the person of the Emperor and thereby constituted himself supreme ruler. He was faced by the two united armies of Liu Pei (劉 備) and Sun Ch'üan (孫 權).

Liu Pei had an adviser, named Chu-ko Liang (諸 葛 亮), of great sagacity, while Sun Ch'üan was aided by Chou Yü (周 瑜), in command of the fleet. Ts'ao Ts'ao had established himself on the south bank of the Yangtze with a large army and a huge flotilla. As his Northern troops, being unused to large stretches of, water, suffered considerably from seasickness, the junks were lashed together to lessen the distressing movement of the vessels. This plan is supposed to have been adopted on the suggestion of a traitor from the enemy's camp, the latter's idea being to float down fire-rafts on them when they were thus secured.

The only objection to this very excellent scheme was that the wind was in the opposite direction to that required to carry out the manœuvre. Chu-ko Liang, however, undertook to produce the necessary easterly gale. Accordingly he built what was called "the Seven-star Altar," 9 feet high. On the three lower stories soldiers were grouped in mythical formation in accordance with the seven stars of the *pa-kua* (八 卦); Chu-ko Liang, who had prepared himself for the ceremony by "abstaining from garlic," prayed before the altar thrice a day, reciting magic spells.

Sceptical, but co-operative, the Admiral had prepared boats loaded with oil

* Prince Ho Lu (闔 廬), of the Wu State, once asked Sun Wu if he could apply the principles of this book to women. Sun replied that he could. Accordingly the Prince took 180 girls out of his harem and told Sun to submit them to military discipline. He divided them into companies and at the head of each placed a favourite concubine of the Prince. When the drums sounded for the first drill to commence all the girls laughed, whereupon Sun immediately ordered the concubines in command of the sections to be beheaded and order was restored. Ultimately he raised this corps to a high standard of efficiency without prejudice to their other duties in the palace.

and firewood ready for the attack, if the wind should rise in the south-east as Chu-ko Liang affirmed it would. Punctually at the hour appointed the wind blew. Immediately the fire-ships set sail and, on getting within a mile of the enemy, were burning fiercely, there being nothing that could prevent their rapid and disastrous descent on Ts'ao Ts'ao's helpless fleet. In a desperate attempt to save themselves the crew ran their ships ashore, but their defeat was complete. The casualty list was a heavy one. It is said that of the whole 830,000 men only 23, including the traitor Ts'ao Ts'ao, were able to make good their escape.

There are extant woodcuts of Chinese warships of a bygone age in the "San Ts'ai T'u Hui" (三才圖會), a book of 100 volumes written by Wang Ch'i (王圻), who lived during the Ming dynasty, 1368–1644. These pictures were later reproduced in the "Ku Chin T'u Shu Chi Ch'êng" (古今圖書集成). A selection of these highly interesting woodcuts is given (*following page*).

From these representations it would seem that these astonishing ships were as uncomfortable to live in as they must have been dangerous to fight in. The descriptions which accompany them bear out the slight resemblance that may be traced in the woodcuts to the fighting craft of the ancient Egyptians, and a likeness may also be traced to the warships of the Venetians of A.D. 1200, who constructed their craft with towers of wood and machines for attacking the enemy.

According to Colonel Yule, the Chinese methods of sea warfare were not unlike those adopted by the Venetians, for they both relied a good deal on flags and banners and the stirring noise of trumpets and gongs and drums* to hearten their own men and strike terror into the enemy. Another common method of building up morale and giving an appearance of bravery was to paint a tiger's head on the bows of the war-junks, and the warriors were given hats and uniforms to produce the illusion that they were tigers too.

The text accompanying the woodcuts of the four war-junks shown (*following page*) gives a graphic, if fanciful, description of these obsolete men-of-war. In the case of the red "dragon" boat, we learn that it derived its name from its appearance, the fore-part of the boat being formed like the head of a dragon with open mouth, in which a soldier was posted to watch the enemy's movements. The sides of the hull were adorned with imitation scales fastened with bamboo nails. A small aperture with an iron door was made in the "breast of the dragon." We are told that there were two hardwood frames and a keel, on which was set a machine, which was presumably a form of catapult. She was further fitted with a mast and sail and also a cabin. Apparently only two men were employed at the yulohs. It was claimed that several hundreds of these craft would patrol the river in company ready to launch fire, "poison smoke," or arrows from their "invisible machine" on an unsuspecting enemy.

As regards the wheel-boat, the fore-deck measured 8 feet, the midship section 27 feet, and the after-part 7 feet, making an over-all measurement of 42 feet, with a beam of 13 feet. Under the 1-foot wide projecting gunwale were suspended two wooden wheels on each side, the blade being submerged for about 1 foot in depth. These paddles were operated by man-power. The midship house was roofed with two sloping planks, which could be opened to permit the men behind its protection to shoot arrows, fire, or even sand. The junk was armoured with cow hide so as to give added protection to the archers. The remaining illustrations (*on next page*) show two typical war-junks. These types, we are told, could carry 100 soldiers and were "bulky and lofty like a storied house," for there were three decks built up with protecting sides reinforced with armour formed from bamboo slats. We are told the midship section had a fourth deck, which is further explained by the fact that the lower

* The drum has always been held in high honour in China. Sacrificing to the regimental drum before a fight was a very ancient custom. The most famous exponent on this instrument was Ni Hêng (禰衡), who lived in the second century A.D. and was chief drummer to the ill-famed Ts'ao Ts'ao (曹操). In order to impress some visiting officials he was ordered to put on a new uniform. Ni Hêng waited until all the great men had assembled and then played a tune on his drum which drew tears from those present. He spoilt the good impression he had made by stripping himself naked and then donning his new uniform. Later this eccentric musician further misconducted himself and was executed.

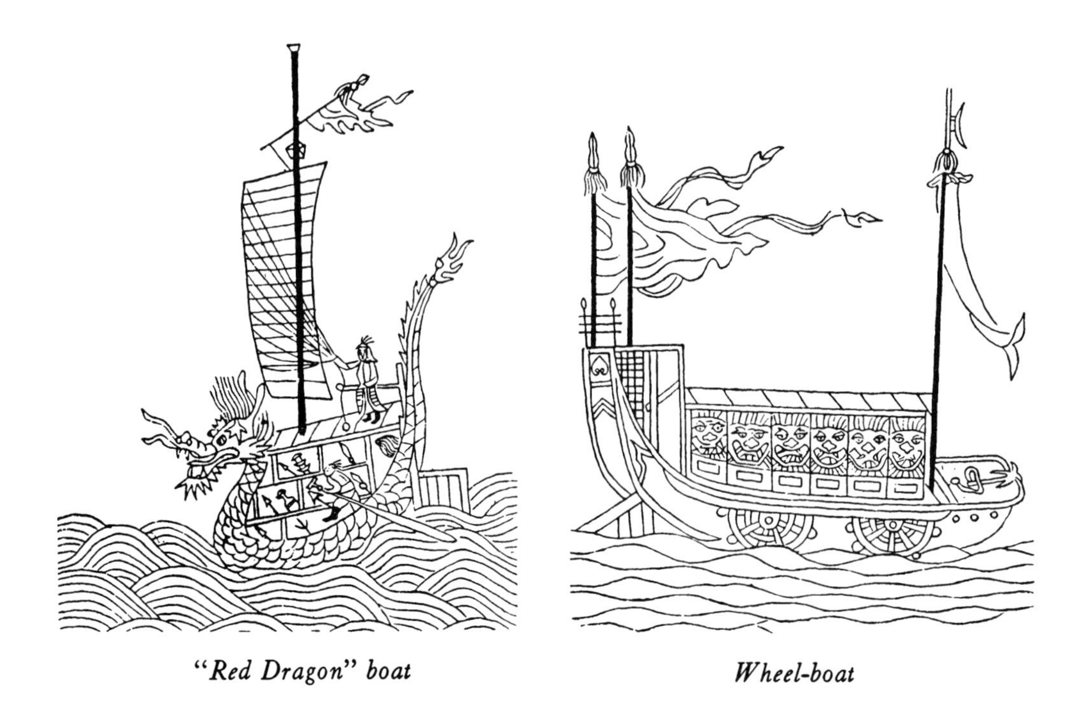

"Red Dragon" boat *Wheel-boat*

hold was uninhabited, being used only for "mud and stone" ballast. The main deck was "floored" and used as sleeping quarters by the soldiers, who approached it down a ladder. The upper deck contained a water *kang* and the galley, and bow and stern anchors were stowed here with coir-rope cables. The bridge, as one might term the fourth deck, was reached by a ladder through a manhole. It was protected by a bulwark, from behind which the soldiers fired their volleys of assorted missiles.

If an enemy junk of small size was encountered, it is said that the ram was used to sink her. Altogether these men-of-war were considered to be very powerful and effective fighting units—although they may not have looked it—and calculated to give a good account of themselves in the numberless naval battles that were continually being waged by the rival warlords of the Yangtze Valley.

Chinese naval history of the period, if we are to believe the "History of the Three Kingdoms,"* was both heroic and romantic. A naval commander-in-chief at the beginning of the Christian era was supposed to be able to deal with fairies, dragons, devils, evil spirits, mothers-in-law, and miracles, and each problem required a different technique. Naval strategy, therefore, resolved itself into the ability of the commander-in-chief of the fleet to trick the opposing side, and naval actions were both remarkable and piquant.

A leader in war, according to Chu-ko Liang (諸葛亮), probably China's most famous soldier, should "be able to come and go, be facile and obdurate, be able to advance and retire, to show himself weak or strong, be immovable as mountains, inscrutable as the operations of nature, infinite as the universe, everlasting as the blue void, vast as the ocean, and dazzling as the lights of heaven. Moreover, he should be able to foresee droughts and floods, know the nature of the ground, understand the possibilities of battle arrays, and conjecture the excellences and defects of the enemy."†

Chu-ko Liang would often appear in difficult situations dressed in a simple white robe, sitting in a chariot and holding a feather fan; sometimes a lute was added to his equipment.

* The sceptical should consult "The Three Kingdoms," written by Lo Kuan-chung, who lived some time in the thirteenth century, translated by C. H. Brewitt-Taylor, published by Kelly and Walsh, Shanghai.

† The battle arrays were of the greatest importance. The formations were according to stereotyped rules, the *pa-kua* being the favourite model, wherein would be eight gates. The enemy would then enter into the attack as in a maze. They were called by various names, such as Heaven, Earth, Wind, Cloud, Bird, Serpent, Dragon, and Tiger. There were varieties such as the "Serpents Coil." Indeed, it is said there were 365 different variations, corresponding to the circuit of the heavens. One was the "Nine Nines." This was a very complicated manœuvre, and only the most experienced generals ever attempted it.

War-junk

War-junk

Woodcuts of old Chinese warships.
FROM "SAN TS'AI T'U HUI"

Astrology and divination were important factors in ancient Chinese warfare on sea and land. For instance, when Chu-ko Liang contemplated attacking the Kingdom of Wei, the Court astrologer warned him it would be a failure, as several flights of golden orioles had plunged into the river and been drowned, moreover, " the cypress trees were moaning at night."

An interesting trait in these military men of iron was that even the strongest would always faint on learning of the death of a valued general, or commander, and often " spit blood " or " weep blood " in addition. They also almost invariably wept over any traitors they executed.

Great care had to be exercised not to supersede or slight an army leader, for if he "lost face" he would instantly desert to the enemy. A leader with a dash of the magician in him, who could invoke or imitate supernatural aid, was a made man and almost certain of victory. A reluctant enemy could sometimes be stung into coming out and joining battle by sending him a woman's head-dress and robe of white silk in a box as a suitable gift.

More or less the same tactics were employed in land operations. The strategy of the Emperor Kao Tsu (高 祖), of the Han dynasty, is a classical example of this form of warfare in the second century B.C. It occurred when Mao Tun (冒 頓) was attacking the Emperor's forces. The Emperor's military commander happened to know that Mao Tun's wife, who was in command on one side of the city, was a slave to jealousy; he therefore caused a number of wooden figures of beautiful women to be exhibited on the city-walls, at which sight the lady's fears for her husband's fidelity were aroused, and she drew off her troops and the Emperor was thus enabled to escape.

As already stated, the famous Chinese historical and classical novel, " The Three Kingdoms," gives innumerable examples of the tactics of that romantic period. All up and down the banks of the Yangtze wandering story-tellers take up their stands on village streets or in the junkmen's tea-houses and recount the ever-fresh stories and legends of this age of Chinese chivalry. The most popular deal with the unending exploits of the statesman Chu-ko Liang (諸 葛 亮). He was the hero of the two most famous naval actions, the Battle of the Crimson Cliff and the Battle of 100,000 Arrows, both of which took place on the Yangtze.

The latter engagement, it is thought by the junkmen, probably took place in the vicinity of Nanking, after Liu Pei, the King of the Shu Kingdom (蜀國), had joined forces with Sun Ch'üan (孫權), of the Kingdom of Wu (吳國). Sun Ch'üan's naval leader, or Admiral, Chou Yü (周瑜), was jealous of Liu Pei's Minister, Chu-ko Liang, and plotted to procure his downfall by discrediting him in the eyes of his master. Chou Yü, therefore, invited his rival to a council of war against their common enemy, Ts'ao Ts'ao (曹操), and, while they were seated drinking tea together, asked for his opinion on the best weapons in a sea fight. As Chu-ko Liang replied that he believed the bow and arrow to be the most effective weapons, Chou Yü commissioned him to obtain 100,000 arrows within 10 days' time. Chu-ko Liang, realizing he would be disgraced if he failed to achieve this apparently impossible task, nevertheless declared he would accomplish it within three days or suffer any punishment meted out to him.

He then fitted out 20 junks, each with 1,000 bundles of straw stacked in an upright position and with men concealed inside them. They advanced on the enemy on the morning of the third day, the hidden men beating on drums and gongs to attract attention. The enemy let fly showers of arrows, which lodged in the piled-up stacks of straw.

After sufficient arrows had been acquired in this manner, Chu-ko Liang shouted out: "Thanks for the loan of the arrows," and the decoy junks withdrew from the danger zone to count the arrows they plucked from the straw. These arrows, which numbered 100,000 precisely, were laid before Chou Yü, much to his chagrin, as his rival by means of his resource had settled himself more firmly in the saddle than ever.

There are many instances to show how Chu-ko Liang was equal to any emergency and could turn defeat to his advantage. On one occasion he suffered reverses owing to the fact that the enemy were equipped with bamboo armour through which the swords of his troops could not penetrate. Chu-ko Liang's answer to this problem was to provide each soldier with a lighted torch—a brilliant solution in every sense of the word, and one which led to victory, for it was not long before the whole enemy army was alight, and the soldiers perished in the flames of their own armour.

Ts'ao Ts'ao's forces of the Kingdom of Wei did not appear at their best in marine warfare and were again defeated in A.D. 223 whilst trying to cross the Yangtze near Nanking to invade Sun Ch'üan's territory. A storm arose, and the large waves not only terrified the inland troops, but made them so seasick as to be helpless in the management of their junks. Consequently they were compelled to return to Loyang without having accomplished what to-day would be known as an act of aggression.

Chinese history abounds with references to the use of war-junks throughout the centuries when tribal and civil wars were the rule and periods of peace the exception. Mostly these allusions to the fighting craft in use then are vague and unilluminating and provide a monotonous repetition of the tactics of the period. Feints and ruses, mass attacks of huge fleets of ships lashed together with chains, fire-junks used in small or greater numbers, and the unexpected results when nature took a hand and lent aid to one side or the other in the form of gales and high seas.

There is one interesting passage which occurs in an abridgment of Chinese history, which shows the early use of paddle-wheels and describes a rebellion which broke out near the T'aihu under a leader named Yang Yao (楊么). The Emperor Kao Tsung, 1127–62, of the Southern Sung dynasty, sent out an army and a large fleet under Yo Fei (岳飛) to defeat the rebels. The historian says:

The vessels of Yang, striking the water with wheels, went along as if they were flying; they carried poles on the sides to strike and break up any vessels they might run against.

Yo Fei * was equal to the occasion and scattered rotten straw and wood on the water so as to obstruct the paddle-wheels,† thereby winning a great victory, whereupon the disappointed Yang jumped into the water and was drowned.

The Poyang Lake is not without its naval history. The most important naval engagement there took place in the year 1363, when Chu Yüan-chang (朱元璋), ex-Buddhist monk and founder of the Ming dynasty, had to face a formidable rival. Chu set sail from Nanking, bound for the Poyang Lake, where the enemy had concentrated two large armies of 11 divisions, supported by a huge fleet, disposed in a most advantageous position. The ships were lashed together with chains, and Chu's fleet, unable to break the line, may be said to have lost the first phase of the action. A north-west gale and high sea came to the rescue. Profiting by the weather, Chu sent his fire-ships into action, which made the situation extremely serious for the enemy's ships, which were not only anchored but chained together. Regardless of the storm which was raging, the war-junks of Chu bore down on the enemy and won a most notable victory.

Fire-ships had been in use from the very earliest times. The usual tactics were to chain a number together, so that in drifting down stream they would hang across the bows of a ship and could be cleared only with great difficulty and danger. There were other curious engines of war used by the Chinese, and their weapons, technique, and strategy certainly had the merit of novelty and ingenuity. As early as the seventh century it is recorded that machines called *p'ao* (砲) were used for casting stones at the enemy and that they had a range of from 100 to 200 paces.

In ancient China, as in Europe until the days of Drake, the personnel of a warship consisted of two distinct parts: the seamen who actually handled the ship, and soldiers sent on board who did the actual fighting.

China produced many such amphibious soldiers, one of the most famous being Chou Yü (周瑜), who lived A.D. 174–218. Although Ts'ao Ts'ao's forces were estimated at 830,000 men, his warships were said to "stretch stem to stern for a thousand *li* and his banners darkened the sky," Chou Yü had such confidence in himself that, against this formidable force, he only asked for 30,000 men and won a considerable victory. In addition to his military prowess, he is said to have possessed such an exquisite ear for music that if any one played a false note he "would immediately look up, even though tipsy."

Another equally famous soldier was Chang Hsün (張巡), A.D. 709–757, a native of Nanyang in Honan, who as a youth was very fond of military studies. He graduated as Chin-shih about 735 and entered upon a public career. Employed in military operations against hostile tribes, he departed from all time-honoured tactics, complaining that it was impossible to fight these barbarians according to fixed rules, since they would persist in attacking him when he was unprepared. His discipline, however, was so perfect that one of his officers, named Wan Ch'un (萬春), is said to have received six arrows in his face without budging from the post which had been assigned to him. In 756 the rebellion of An Lu-shan (安祿山) brought Chang to the front. He fought many battles and performed prodigies of valour, not without receiving many wounds. The climax was reached by his heroic defence of Suiyang (睢陽) against An Lu-shan's son. Hemmed in on all sides, provisions ran short, but he would not yield. He even sacrificed his favourite concubine, without avail. At length the enemy broke in upon his enfeebled garrison, and as he scorned to own allegiance to the conqueror, he was at once put to death. During the siege his patriotic rage had caused him to grind

* General Yo Fei may be regarded as China's national hero. He was murdered by Ch'in Kuei (秦檜), whose name to-day is popularly used for a spittoon.

† The paddle-wheel junk, so it is claimed, was invented by Wang Yeh, a pirate in the Tungting Lake, who was later deified and became the junkmen's god.

his teeth with such fury that after his death all but three or four were found to be worn down to the very gums.

The arms used in a war-junk consisted largely of swords of various kinds, such as the cutting-sword (割 刀), the phœnix-sword (鸞 刀), the gem-cutting sword (割 玉 刀), and so on. In addition there were a great selection of halberds (戟) and spears (槍). But the arm most generally used was the bow. In ancient times archery became a science and always formed a part of the official examinations. One of China's most famous bowmen was Chi Ch'ang (紀 昌), who studied the art under Fei Wei (飛 衛). He began his career as an archer by lying for three years under his wife's loom in order to learn not to blink. He then hung up a louse and gazed at it for three years, until at length it appeared to him as big as a cart-wheel. After this his skill is said to have been so great that he was able to pierce a louse through the heart with an arrow.

One of the most famous expeditions of the Chinese Navy was that made in the third year of Yung-lo (永 樂), or A.D. 1406, under the famous eunuch Cheng Ho (鄭 和), who distinguished himself as a military officer in the rebellion which placed the Emperor Cheng Tsu (成 祖) on the throne. Cheng Ho collected troops to the number of 28,786 and a great quantity of silver and treasure. He then built 62 ships (some authorities say 100), each measuring 44 *chang* in length with a beam of 18 *chang*.*

His squadron set sail from Soochow (some authorities say from Woosung), and, with a grand display, came first to Foochow, and afterwards cruised along the coasts of Cambodia and Siam to manifest to the world the wealth and prowess of the Middle Kingdom. It would be out of place here to narrate in detail the wonderful exploits and victories which Cheng Ho achieved with his astonishing ships at Ceylon, Sumatra, and many other places whose names cannot to-day be identified.

Opinions vary as to the invention of gunpowder, called by the Chinese *huo-yueh* (火 藥), or fire-drug. The indication of a foreign origin in the Chinese characters seems to bear out the claim that it was not a Chinese invention, but was introduced from India about the fifth century. Authorities agree in the view that the first Chinese guns appeared about the middle of the thirteenth century. Certainly a form of fire-engine was used by the Tartars about 1275. Lime and sulphur enclosed in paper bags were thrown by the besieged into the ditches surrounding the walled towns, and these surprise packets, which exploded upon contact with the water, had a definite nuisance value. At the commencement of the Ming dynasty, in 1368, other devices in use were fire-chariots, fire-umbrellas (whatever they may have been), and a kind of musket known as *shên-chi-huo-ch'iang* (神 機 火 槍). Leaden bullets, it is said, were introduced in the 43rd year of Chia Ching (嘉 靖), that is, in 1564.

To leave the realms of more or less legendary history and come down to more modern times, the war-junk played a considerable, if not very successful, part in the various hostilities between China and various foreign Powers. It is unfortunate that these interesting and curious old craft passed into oblivion before the days of photography. The drawings of contemporary artists are not very convincing and therefore yield little evidence of value, but we have many detailed descriptions provided by writers of that time.

The Chinese had not made great advances in the destructive sciences since the Middle Ages until, under the tuition of those paradoxical men of God, the Jesuits, they had acquired the art of making guns and muskets. Theoretically, the Chinese armament differed little from that of the British save in respect of quality, care in manufacture, and, of course, consequent accuracy of fire. Nevertheless, these exceptions were in reality essentials and made all the difference

* Reckoning the *chang* as no more than 10 English feet, the ships were 440 feet in length with a beam of 180 feet. If these figures were correct, Cheng Ho's ships were precisely the same beam as the *Queen Mary*, and roughly half her length.

between two articles of approximately similar design. Robert Morrison, the great sinologue, described the powder as being very inferior and the cannons as being as badly made as possible.

Earthen jars, called stink-pots (火 藥 煲 or 雷 石), charged with materials having an offensive and suffocating smell, were a recognized weapon in Chinese warfare. The jars, portions of which held about half a gallon, were filled with powder, sulphur, small nails, and shot. Another compartment contained materials calculated to produce an offensive and suffocating smell. The whole was covered with clay and rendered gas-tight with chunam and placed in a calico bag closed at the mouth with a stout string. Three or four of these primitive bombs were then placed in a basket and hoisted to the masthead, whence they were fired by a man who climbed up and threw in a handful of lighted joss sticks, finally cutting the halyards attaching the "Molotoff's bread-baskets" to the mast. The best results were obtained when this curious contraption fell on the enemy's deck, smashing the earthen jar and thereby igniting the contents by means of the smouldering joss sticks. The ensuing explosion was intended to knock down, blind, and suffocate the bystanders.*

Bernard † also describes another device used against that famous little ship the *Nemesis*, in the campaigns of 1842. It was a kind of boarding-net, formed from a number of strong fishing-nets and made fast all round the sides of the war-junk. These were not extended on booms so as to hang clear of the hull and prevent boarding, but were triced up outboard over each gun, so that, as the enemy's boats came alongside, the nets could be thrown over them.

It is hardly relevant, but certainly interesting, to note that China may probably be credited with the invention of the submarine mine, named by them the "water thunder." A contemporary writer, describing the invention in 1858, says it was a "mere tub, with a false bottom capable of containing a charge of powder at the base and other combustibles above." One, he continued, exploding "close to one of our ships, was charged with some filthy mess, which was blown up all over the rigging." ‡

Fire-junks were also extensively used against the western Powers. On one occasion nearly a hundred were used.

A large number of war-junks opposed the British fleet in the action at Woosung in 1842. Among them were several paddle-wheel junks, each commanded by a high mandarin, showing the importance attached to these craft. At first they attacked the British fleet with great bravery; but, finding the odds so much against them, they paddled away out of danger at a speed of about 3 knots, until they were finally overtaken, boarded, and captured by the *Nemesis*. On examination it was found that these craft were operated by two paddles on each side turned by a capstan which interlocked its cogs with those upon a shaft connected to the paddle-wheels. The capstan was turned by relays of men who "walked it round." It was believed at the time by the foreigners that these junks were built in imitation of steamers by the Chinese, who had received reports of the British "fire-wheel boats." Actually, as we have already seen, the man-propelled paddle-junk was an ancient Chinese device, although it is possible there was some vague attempt to modernize these craft, for it was said that a junk designer from Chusan endeavoured to propel them "by means of a smoke made in the hold"; but, as the paddles declined to co-operate, the ancient methods were reverted to. §

During the Second China War, 1857–60, improvements inspired by European craft were made in the types of war-junks; and, towards the end of the war, one or two particularly large craft were built with gun ports and 36 guns, many of them being 9 or 12 pounders.

* Junkmen used to defend themselves against this weapon by spreading a fishing-net tightly drawn about 7 feet above the deck. When the stink-pots struck the net, its elasticity caused them to rebound and fall overboard before exploding.

† "Narrative of the Voyages and Services of the *Nemesis*," by W. D. Bernard.

‡ "Personal Narrative of Three Years' Service in China." Lieutenant-Colonel Fisher.

§ As a point of general interest it may be worth recording that the Captain of H.M.S. *Galatea*, in 1829, had his ship fitted with paddles actuated by winches. With two-thirds of the crew working, it is recorded that a speed of 3 knots in a dead calm was achieved.

As in the Army there were hereditary Tartar soldiers, so in the Navy there were hereditary Tartar sailors. These came chiefly from the Liaotung Province and were given their uniforms, though they had to provide their own food. The punishment for desertion was decapitation.

The modern Chinese Navy owes its inception to Li Hung-chang (李 鴻 章). This great statesman moved with the times, and a foreign-style navy was begun in 1880 with the purchase, through the London Office of the Chinese Maritime Customs, of the two fast cruisers the *Ch'aoyung* (超 勇) and *Yangwei* (揚 威), together with a flotilla of gunboats. These were built at Newcastle by Sir William Armstrong.

This gave an impetus to the study of foreign shipbuilding and the manufacture of guns. Arsenals were established at Anking, then at Nanking, and later at Kiangnan, near Shanghai.

These changes soon resulted in the disappearance for ever of the picturesque war-junks from the waters they had sailed for so many centuries.

THE TA-PING-CH'UAN SOLDIER BOAT OR SEA-GOING WAR-JUNK

The *ta-ping-ch'uan* (大 兵 船), or large soldier-boat, illustrated in Plate No. 72 is of the greatest interest as showing a typical sea-going war-junk of the early nineteenth century. This contemporary plan, probably the only one of its kind, was made in 1842 by Lieutenant Paris, later Admiral Paris, the celebrated French naval writer. It shows a vessel with a length of 120 feet, a beam of 25.6 feet, and a depth of 12 feet.

Although piracy was a vocation of long standing, probably the first record of it in China was from a Chinese—Fa Hsien (法 顯), who lived in the fifth century A.D. The account of his voyage shows us not only the dangers from perils of the sea but from pirates, who were the terror of seafarers. " The sea," said Fa Hsien, " was infested with them; to meet them meant death." Indeed, for decades in the fifth century, the Lin-I (林 邑) pirates of south-eastern Indo-China were such a menace that the Emperor Wên of Sung (宋 文 帝) had to send a punitive expedition which in 446 effectively stopped piracy, at least for some years. Piracy appeals strongly to an adventurous imagination. As a profession it went out of fashion in Europe at the close of the sixteenth century. In China, however, it can be said to be still in high favour.

As piracy was very prevalent along the China coast and in the estuary of the Yangtze during the last century, a considerable force of sea-going war-junks patrolled the infested areas.

This junk navy was divided into the "inner and outer water squadrons" and, in addition to combating the pirates and " bad characters," was required to prevent the people from the islands immigrating in large numbers to the mainland. A high-ranking general usually had command of both fleet and land troops, and the ranks of officers afloat were the same as in the army.

Operations against pirates were not always successful. Indeed, in the " Peking Gazette " of the 17th day, 9th moon, 13th year of the reign of the Emperor Tao Kuang (道 光), there is a document of six pages devoted to the sea-going navy of that day.

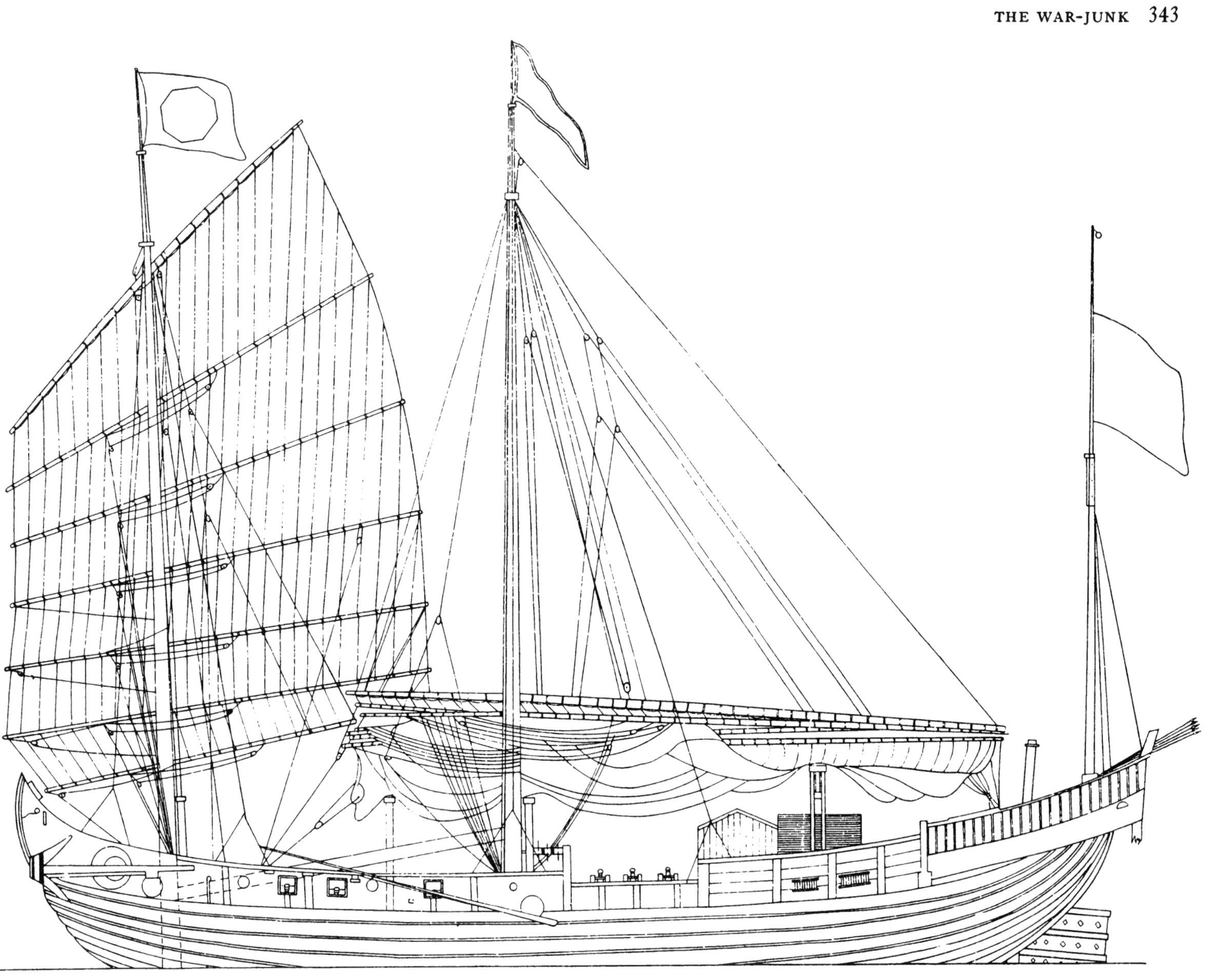

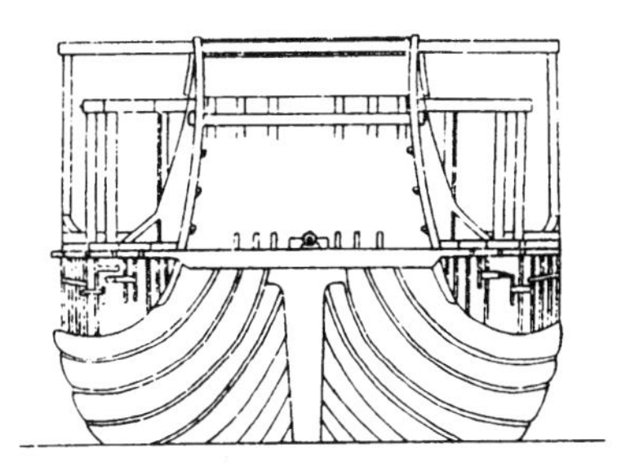

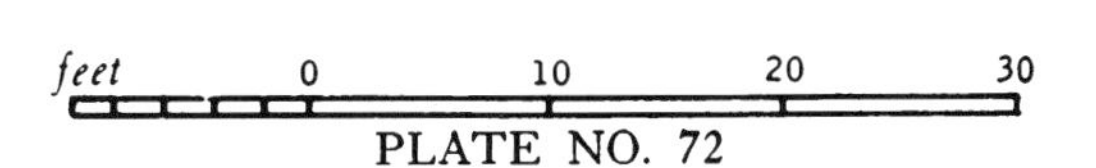

PLATE NO. 72

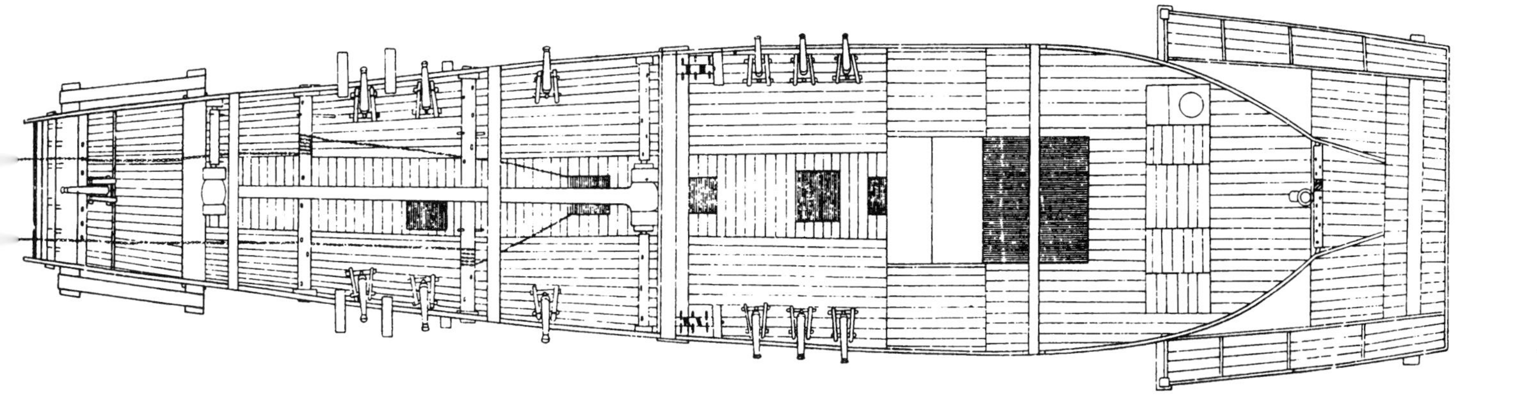

The Emperor's attention being called to the failure of the war-junks in an operation against pirates, he took the occasion to animadvert in rather severe terms on the state of the Chinese Navy. He began his paper by saying in effect that the Government appointed soldiers for the protection of the people; and naval captains are no less important than dry land soldiers. But the Navy had fallen off, as appeared by many cases of failure on the high seas. And he continued:

"On shore a man's ability is measured by his archery and his horsemanship, but a sailor's talent by his ability to fight with and on the water. A sailor must know the winds and the clouds, and the lands and the lines (or passages among the sands). He must be thoroughly versed in breaking a spear with (or beating against) the wind. He must know, like a god, how to break through the billows, handle his ship, and be all in regular order for action. Then, when his spears are thrown, they will pierce, and his guns will follow to give them effect. The spitting tornadoes of the fire-physic (gunpowder) will all reach truly their mark; and whenever pirates are met with, they will be vanquished wonderously. No aim will miss its mark. The pirate bandits will be impoverished and crippled, and even on the high seas, when they take to flight, they will be followed and caught and slaughtered. Thus the monsters of the deep, and the waves will be still, and the sea become a perfect calm, not a ripple will be raised.

"But, far different from this has of late been the case. The Navy is a nonentity. There is the report of going to sea; but there is no going to sea in reality. Cases of piracy are perpetually occurring, and even barbarian barks anchor in our inner seas without the least notice being taken of them. I, the Emperor, consider . . . "

and here His Majesty looks back on the past, and has rather dismal forebodings for the future. After advising and threatening his naval servants, the Emperor concludes, "Do not hereafter say that you were not early warned."

Eyewitnesses, writing in the "Chinese Repository," have described the war-junks of the period as "large, unwieldy-looking masses of timber of shallow draught and with a displacement of 250 to 350 tons at most." Other notable features were the flat upright stems and considerable sheer of the hull, the wooden anchors, rattan cables, and mat sails. The junks were flush-decked vessels and had large quarter-galleries and look-out houses on deck. The whole was painted black and red and adorned with large eyes in the bows. They usually carried from two to 14 guns, some of foreign manufacture, mounted on wooden carriages. The guns varied considerably in calibre.

Another description by Bernard in 1842 uses the same adjective of "unwieldy" to describe the large war-junks and estimates them to have been about 800 tons. He alludes to the rattan shields, which he describes as being from 2 to 3 feet in diameter and so closely woven and elastic in consistency that they were not only impossible to cut through with a sword but were even proof against a long-range musket shot.

The crews, who, as far as personal bravery were concerned, formed an enemy by no means to be despised, were armed with spears, swords, matchlocks, and frequently large gingalls fitted with a rest on the bulwarks.

War-junks of this type flew a flag bearing the "Yin" and "Yang" (陰 陽) from a short staff and a triangular flag with the name of the officer, under whose supervision she was, in large red characters.

The war-junk in the closing days of her career was, no doubt, practically identical with that of the sixteenth century, which in turn, except perhaps for the armament, had altered nothing from the vessels in vogue centuries earlier.

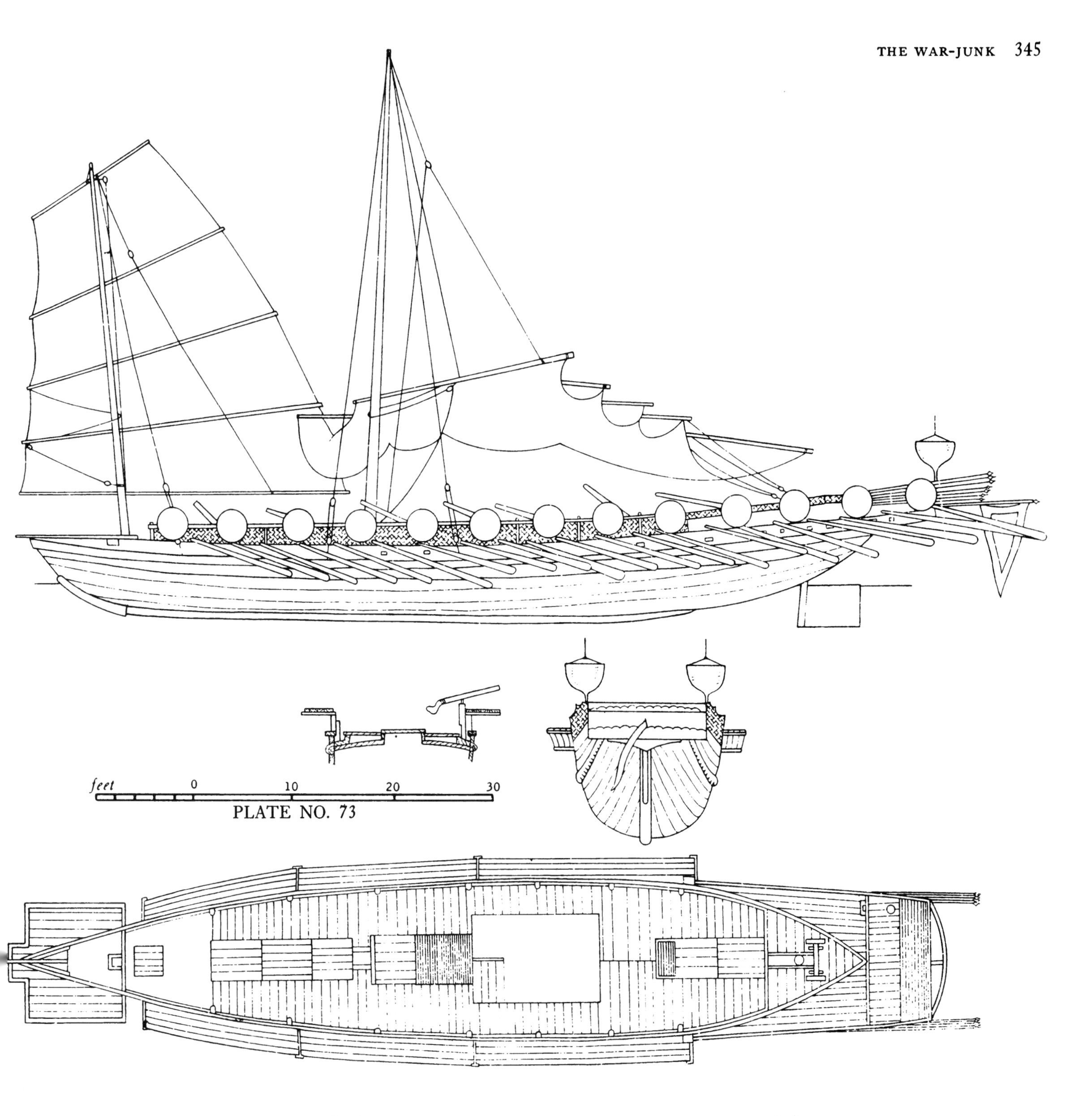

PLATE NO. 73

THE K'UAI-TU OR SMALL WAR-JUNK

The ocean-going war-junks just described did not form the bulk of the Imperial Navy. This consisted of vessels of much smaller dimensions, capable, in consequence of their light draught, of navigating shallow rivers and creeks.

The type of craft illustrated in Plate No. 73 was known as the *k'uai-tu*, or " quick leaping." This vessel measured 72 feet in length, with a beam of 15 feet and a depth of 6 feet. They were painted green and yellow.*

The number of hands serving in a junk of this type varied from 40 to 60 men, who were described by foreign observers as being exceedingly brave, albeit not very expert, fighters. All were agreed that they were excellent in the handling of their junks.

* A fine model of this type of junk is to be seen in the National Maritime Museum, London.

Contemporary writers speak of these small craft as being " less shapeless " and in fact as showing neat lines. They were very fast vessels and pulled from 10 to 20 oars a side. They were sometimes armed with one or two guns (2, 3, or 4 pounders) mounted in the bow, and five or six gingalls in the waist,* while over the sides of the junk were hung shields of rattan painted with tigers' heads to discourage and repel attack.

After the Taiping Rebellion a new naval force was instituted to guard river and sea navigation and placed under an " Admiral " of the Yangtze, whose jurisdiction extended over the five Provinces of Kiangsu, Anhwei, Kiangsi, Hupeh, and Hunan. This fleet was more in the nature of a constabulary force and was highly organized and efficiently run, with a strict code of honour and regulations for all contingencies.

Eminently sensible methods of overhaul of softwood craft were carried out, for they were "slightly repaired" after three years, "completely repaired" after six years, and finally " condemned " after nine years.

Additional types or variations of war vessels for which no plans were available are listed in the Appendix.

Some of the Chinese names of these vessels are still on record, such as *chui-ch'uan* (追 船), or chasers; *sha-ch'uan* (沙 船), or flat-bottomed; *hsiang-yüan-ch'uan* (享 元 船), vessels to cross; and *k'uai-ma* (快 馬), fast horse.

THE RIVER POLICE BOAT

In the 1860s . . .

In the sixties, before the coming of the Chinese Maritime Customs as we know it to-day, junk gunboats were employed on preventive duties.

One boat would be stationed above or below every Customs station, ready, nominally, to give chase to any junk that might attempt to run past without paying the legal and illegal duties imposed. Actually, although they were used thus against smuggling, they did a certain amount of illicit trade for the Imperial mandarins.

These police junks were known as the *fei-hsieh* (飛 蟹), or " fast crabs." A certain number of them were apportioned to each of the Eighteen Provinces of China Proper, the number varying, of course, according to the size and requirements of the province. There were, it is recorded, no fewer than 161 always in commission, divided into three divisions. Each in the first division cost *Tls.* 4,378, in the second division, *Tls.* 3,620, and in the third, *Tls.* 2,677. The crew consisted of a helmsman in command and 46 seamen. In calms they were propelled by oars.

The River Police, Shui-pao-chia (水 保 甲), were revived and reorganized in 1892. In addition to the supression of maritime crime, they were required to keep a daily record of the movements of boats, showing both the absence during the night of any boat belonging to the anchorage and the presence and destination of other craft temporarily at anchor. The River Police were also required to co-operate with the benevolent societies in rescue work.

These gunboats carried a gun, a bow chaser. When under weigh they carried a striped, blue and white, cotton lug-sail, and when at anchor a tent of the same material and colour scheme was rigged amidships, which made them look bright and cheerful.

This interesting and picturesque force has now ceased to exist and nothing has taken its place.

* Gingalls were long tapering guns, 6 to 14 feet long. When employed afloat they were mounted on a tripod or more usually set in the bulwarks. This type of arm was considered to be less liable to burst than cannon and consequently the most effective gun the Chinese possessed. Indeed, it is claimed that it conquered China, being invented by the Manchus. The charge was "a good handful of black powder" and the shot two or more 2½-ounce bullets.

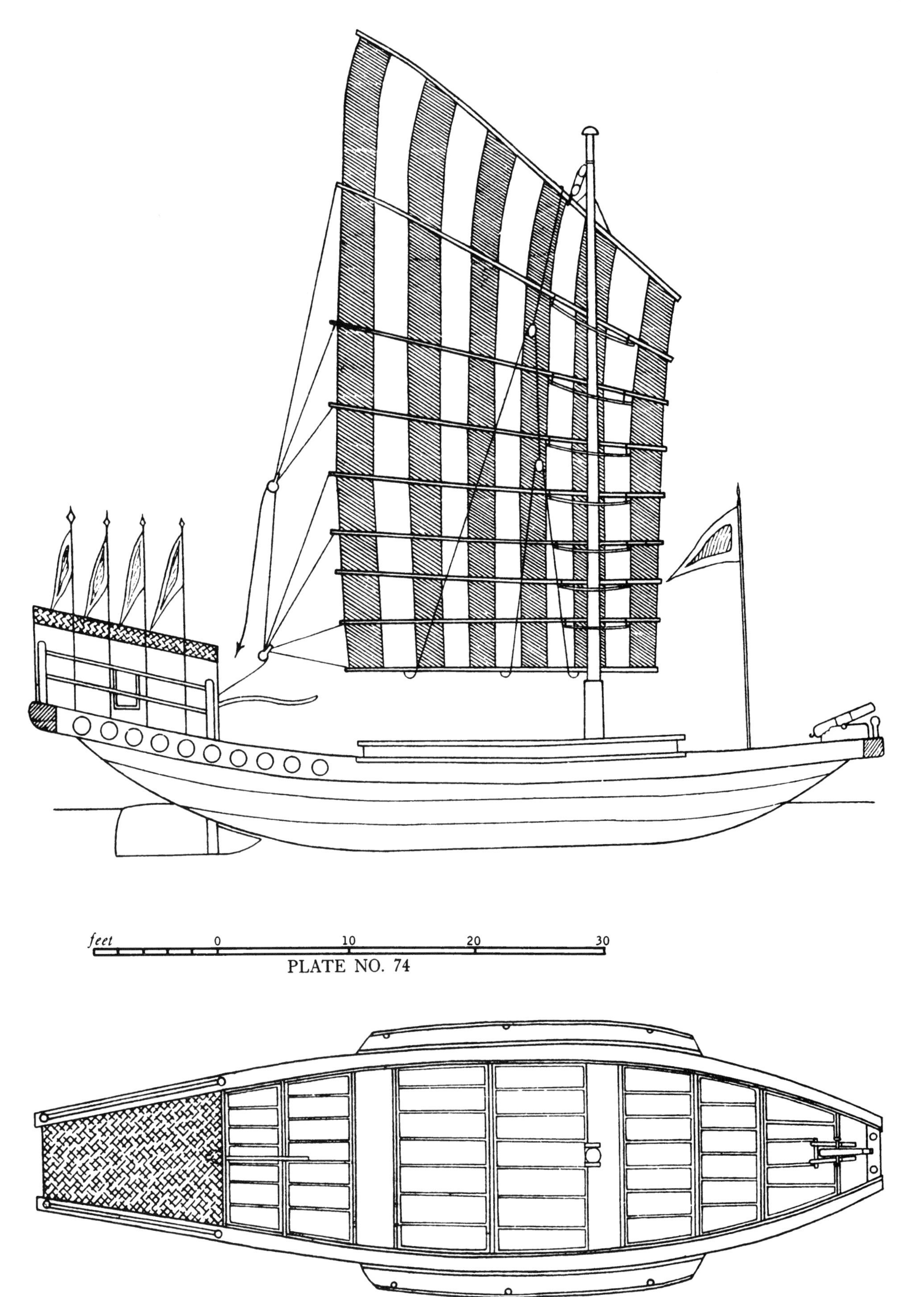

PLATE NO. 74

THE LOWER YANGTZE: WUHU-HANKOW

BETWEEN Wuhu and Anking (安慶) the broad expanse of the river is broken by low islands, the navigable channel crossing over from one bank of the river to the other with monotonous regularity.

Inland from the left bank of the river, 60 miles above Wuhu, stand the town and pagodas of Chihchowfu (池州府). Hereabouts, it will be remembered, it is alleged that the southern and principal stream of the Yangtze in ancient days branched and finally emptied itself into Hangchow Bay. The river-bank here is very low and is subject to much inundation in the summer.

The river now approaches from a south-westerly direction and is accompanied for several miles by a long lagoon separated from the river by only a narrow strip of land. This is known as Muken Lake and is backed by a low range of hills. Twenty-four miles above Wuhu is the picturesque isolated rock of Taitzechi (太子磯), rising abruptly to a height of 30 feet above the surrounding river and surmounted by a temple.

At Lankiangki (攔江磯), or Hen Point, a dangerous barrier of rocks, which dry at low water, is known as the Hen and Chicks and extends in a westerly direction almost to mid-river. Between this danger and the left bank of the river lies a narrow rocky ledge 37 feet long by 20 feet broad, and thereon are two close-set isolated pinnacle rocks, each 1 foot square at the summit and surrounded by very deep water. The river here is very narrow, and the navigable channel is reduced to little more than 300 feet. These pinnacle rocks have been responsible for many accidents to junks and one to the *Kiangloong*, a river steamer after which the rock is named. So that junks may avoid these dangers and the strong current hereabouts, a passage has been cut through Lankiangki, which is generally used except at dead low water. This cutting is a very creditable engineering feat.

There are, as may be expected, several legends connected with this spot. The most exhaustive version describes how a priest in a near-by temple once saw in a dream a titanic struggle between the beneficent spirits of the air and the vindictive spirits of the rocks which already blocked half the river. The latter, under the presiding spirit, which took the form of a rock shaped like a hen, ill-naturedly determined to block up the whole of the river. The Hen Rock, therefore, started off across the stream with all the small rocks in her train. The priest at this moment awoke from his trance and, realizing swift action was required, commenced with great presence of mind to crow like a cock. This immediately arrested the evil spirit of the Hen Rock, who stopped in mid-channel and, enthralled by the priest's melodious crowing, turned to look, and the spell was immediately broken. The country people who had assembled immediately cut off the Hen Rock's head, and she and her attendant rocks were checked in their progress and may be seen there to this day in the form of the dangerous barrier to which they have given their name, the Hen and Chicks.

Another explanation of the hen's motive for crossing the river is the time-honoured Western one that she wished to get to the other side, the incentive being the desire to take possession of a plot of good land there. A temple still stands on the opposite bank.

The Anking Pagoda during the flood of 1931.

Anking, which means peace and happiness, or peaceful congratulations, is the capital of the Province of Anhwei and claims to have the best, as well as the most conspicuous, pagoda on the river. Its official name is Chên Fêng (振 風), or Wind Mover, and this is not an inappropriate name, for the pagoda is supposed to sway with the wind.

Here in the temple is a great bronze bell which, when struck, is said to reverberate for a full minute. Before the repercussion completely dies away, another stroke carries on the sound so as to represent perpetual prayer. It is claimed that the bell has been constantly tended in this way for very many years. There is said to be a marble obelisk on the basement floor of the pagoda in which is enshrined the heart of a famous Chinese warrior.

The pagoda itself is eight-sided and eight stories high, rather an unusual number, for pagodas are usually built in an uneven number of stories. It towers to a considerable height and has whitewashed walls, but the balconies and turned-up eaves are coloured a yellow brown. Inside, on each story, there is a labyrinth of small rooms leading one out of the other, the stairway to the floor above being never direct of access. The pinnacle of the conical roof is surmounted by six huge coloured balls, diminishing in size in their ascending order. Between each ball is a circular iron framework. The last ball is surmounted by a slender rod, and iron guys stretch from its tip down to the roof corners. Small bells are strung on the roof rod, and guys and larger ones suspended from every projecting corner of the carved ornamental beams and eaves. The lightest breeze keeps these multitudinous bells swinging to a very pleasant aerial tune.

The view from the topmost balcony is fine and extensive both of the country round and of the town itself and of the clustering buildings round its own foot, which in themselves rise in terraces above the river-banks, their red or whitewashed walls being topped with what appears from above to be a sea of ornamental tiled roofs with tip-tilted eaves. Outside the city-walls, on the long foreshore, can be seen the busy life of the river, a marked feature being the traffic in reeds, which are continually being unloaded here.

The pagoda was built many hundreds of years ago, and is essentially a shrine for the junkmen, who affirm that the city of Anking is laid out in the form of a junk, the pagoda representing the mast. On each side of the gate leading into the temple of the pagoda the flukes of two gigantic grapnel anchors project from the walls, showing that Anking is at anchor. The junkmen believe that if these anchors are removed the city will drift up stream and be no more.

The priests declare that all the other pagodas in the world recognize the Anking Pagoda as their King. On the 15th day of the 8th, or harvest, moon, when the Yin (陰), or watery element, takes the upper hand, is celebrated the festival of the Moon's Birthday, and moon-cakes, *yüeh-ping* (月 餅), are arranged in batches of 13, one for each lunar month. At this time only in the year it is said that the moon is completely round. Services commence as soon as it clears the tree tops, and it is believed at Anking that by its light millions of shadowy pagodas of all sorts, sizes, and shapes may be seen mirrored in the river. These are the reflections of all the pagodas throughout the world, who come to Anking to have audience with their King, and on this particular night no junk or craft dares to cross this section of the river.

The general trend of the river after leaving Anking is from a direction between south-west and south for 33 miles. This portion is known as Tungliu Reach (東 流). There are hills and red sandstone bluffs to be seen on, or inland from, the right bank of the river, but on the left bank the well-cultivated land lies low and flat. The town of Tungliu is set on undulating ground some miles inland from the right bank. It is a picturesque spot with rambling city-wall skirted on the east by a lake edged with trees and—guarding it to the north and south—two pagodas, one being eight-storied.

A short distance above the town of Tungliu and some 400 miles from Shanghai the Little Orphan is passed. At this point the channel of the river is compressed within a narrow gorge, leaving a width of barely 400 yards from the cliff. This remarkable rock stands in bold relief, like a guardian of the pass, almost perpendicularly out of the river to a height of 300 feet, and is surmounted by a pavilion and temple. It is a great resort for cormorants, which perch on the ledges in immense numbers. Opposite is a rocky bluff, 400 feet high, known as Ching Tzŭ Shan (鏡 子 山), or Mirror Mountain.

As might be supposed, the junkmen have many legends regarding the Little Orphan. All attribute it to various individuals who fell or threw themselves into the river at this point and subsequently turned into the island. The most popular version centres round a wholesale drowning of all concerned, and relates how, in bygone days, a man, his wife, and their two children were crossing the river when their boat capsized in a sudden squall. The parents immediately sank and were seen no more, but an obliging turtle, suddenly rising to the surface, took the children on his back and, instead of making for the shore, appears to have swum up stream. One of the children slipped off and was drowned, and there arose the rock known as the Little Orphan. The turtle, still heading up stream, made for the Poyang Lake with his remaining charge, but, before he was able to reach the shore, the other child fell off at the spot where rose out of the water the rock called the Big Orphan. The benevolent, if inefficient, turtle then died too, and his broken heart formed a huge rock now known as Kuei Shan (龜 山).

In this connection it is noteworthy that an interesting recurring feature in many of the junkmen's legends is the peculiarity whereby the subject of the story is enabled to drift up stream against the current.

A short distance above the Little Orphan is Hukow (湖 口), or Lake Mouth, where the clear waters of the Poyang Lake flow into the muddy waters of the Yangtze. The walled city is perched on the steep side of a precipitous rocky hillside commanding the passage.

Outside the entrance to the Poyang Lake in the Yangtze is an island which is some 10 miles in length and 2 miles in breadth. A few miles above this the city of Kiukiang lies on the right bank of the river some 447 miles above the Whangpoo. Like many other Yangtze ports, the town was desolated between 1850 and 1864 by the Taiping rebels. About 8 miles inland, at the foot of the Lushan Range, was one of the largest and finest monasteries in China, known as the T'ai P'ing Kung. The unique feature of this pilgrim centre was the pair of strongly constructed octagonal towers on either side of the gateway, rather after the fashion of the entrance to a Norman castle. The ruins of these, decorated with rather unusual designs in red brickwork, alone remain of all the great mass of temples and houses which once marked the site.

The name Kiukiang, meaning Nine Rivers, seems to have no justification, for, besides the Yangtze, the only immediately adjacent waterway is the Lungkai Creek, which borders the former British Concession on the west.

On account of the extraordinary rise and fall of the river during the year, most of the river ports have a bund-wall of great strength, and Kiukiang presents a good example of this type of river frontage. The level of the river can be, and sometimes is, as much as 37 feet below the bund-wall during the winter, while during the summer it sometimes rises as much as 2 feet over the bund itself. During floods it is considerably higher.

Before 1842, tea for export from the interior went *via* the Kan River down to Canton. With the opening of Kiukiang, so favourably placed close to one of the principal tea-growing districts, the city became an important tea-collecting centre with a season lasting four months—from April to July. The peak was reached in 1914-15, but the high hopes entertained for the port's future prosperity were never realized, and after the Russian Revolution the Kiukiang tea trade dwindled and died. The important trade in porcelain, however, still continues, for Kiukiang is the clearing station for the Kingtehchen ware. The town has been much modernized of late. The 5 miles of city-walls, topped by picturesque gate-houses, have been pulled down and the ancient bricks used for building.

The Kiukiang Reach of 16 miles extends up to Hunter Island, the trend up river being between west and north-west. Twenty-five miles above Kiukiang is the passenger station of Wusüeh, an important port in the salt trade.

From this point the grandest scenery of the Lower Yangtze is to be found. At first, opposite Wusüeh, the hills on the right bank are low, a large group of them lying together with deep ravines between. Behind these small hills a higher range is seen, and behind it again still higher peaks rise boldly against the blue and cloudless sky. A large hill, with a steep slope full of gullies, descends down to the water's edge, and on it stands the white-painted house once used as a Customs light station at Li Yü Shan (鯉 魚 山). These groups and ranges of hills extend for 9 miles until Pan Pi Shan (半 壁 山), or Split Hill, is reached. While on the right bank there is this extensive and varied mountain range, on the left bank of the river the scenery is also imposing. For the first few miles above Wusüeh the land is low-lying, and a bold range of hills is seen inland, rolling onwards until it closes in on the river farther ahead.

A large amount of limestone rock is in these hills, and along the bank of the river there are numerous lime kilns, the kilns being formed of huge baskets of bamboo wicker-work.

Split Hill is of remarkable appearance. The face of it is a sheer precipice of rock at a point where the river makes a sharp bend, and the side of the hill first seen is terraced from base to summit with patches of cultivation. After passing Split Hill the trend up river is to the north-west until it is like a semicircular bay and the right bank a sandy beach. Up from the bay there is a beautiful expanse

The waterfront at Kichow.

of green and yellow fields, and the farther side of the valley is closed in with a small hemispherical hill.

The wall of the city of Kichow is quite close to the river-bank, mounting over a rocky knoll at a corner opposite Ruined Fort, then extending up the river-bank for some distance and sweeping round two or three small hills which are included in the city boundary of moss-grown brick and mortar.

A series of small hills extends along the left bank, beginning several miles above Kichow (蘄 州) and terminating in a bend of the river opposite Cock's Head, which is a bold rocky eminence standing on the right bank of the Yangtze at a point where the river takes a sharp turn. When viewed from a distance the outline of the rock resembles a cock's comb. The face of the rock, as seen when coming up the reach, is a sharp rugged line descending to the water. The summit of the rock, about 300 feet high, is covered with foliage.

From Cock's Head the trend is westerly, then north, then west again, and the country-side is flat once more. Three miles up is the town of Tayeh, and 2½ miles on, that of Hwangshihkang (黃 石 港), or Yellow Stone. These towns are linked, along the river front, by an extensive bunding providing facilities for loading iron ore, coal, and cement.

This area may be described as the start of one of the great coal regions of China, which centres in the Lower and Middle Yangtze Valley. For many decades Hunan coal has reached Hankow by junk, as has the anthracite from the Lei River in that province, where these seams are said to be 3 feet thick. Bituminous coal from the near-by district of the Siang is equally richly distributed. The modern mine at Pingsiang in Western Kiangsi also sends much of its coal to Hankow.

The river now becomes more liable to violent fluctuations. The channels passing Poole and Collinson Islands and at or near Gravener Island are probably the most critical on the river and constitute the greatest obstacle to shipping *en route* to Hankow at certain seasons of the year.

From the earliest times China's great waterways have given rise to endless trouble from having either too much or too little water. Ever since the days of the great Emperor Yü of the first specified dynasty, the channels of the rivers have been subject to constant change. Summer after summer, when the mountain snows melt and add their quota to the floods due to rain, the streams have burst their banks and spread death and destruction over the huge fertile plains. The lesser troubles due to navigational difficulties in the Yangtze also present their problems, which are acute enough to disturb the mariner. The many draught-limiting channels are liable to constant change. Exceptionally heavy inundations cause an excessive amount of alluvial matter to be deposited in the bed of the river, rendering it shallower as the water recedes. Although the river is enormously broad here, nearly 460 miles frôm its mouth, the channel used by shipping, at certain stages of the river, is often as narrow as 300 feet.

No estimate can be formed of the probable depth from what may have been reported a week ago: first, because from the shifting nature of the bottom the depth does not decrease uniformly with the fall of the surface, and, next, because the level can never be assumed as rising or falling steadily.

The bottom in all these shallows is in the nature of quicksand, and vessels taking the ground, as frequently happens in the low-water season, find a bank rapidly thrown up to leeward of them, which sometimes dries in the course of a few hours, but by continued motion the ship and sandbank work down stream together, and the channel is again clear.

During the latter part of the last century, before the days of the River Inspectorate, the approach to Hankow was made very difficult, during the low-water season, by a bar at the Hukwang Flats, about 80 miles below Hankow. Steamers had to be lightened, and special pilots were stationed there to sound and mark the channels. This caused delay and inconvenience to the shippers and great expense to the companies. Large junks, some drawing as much as 10 feet, however, suffered no such inconvenience, as they passed up and down the right bank hugging the shore.

For over 20 years this lightening of vessels was of yearly occurrence until in January 1885 Captain W. Smith, of the *Cores de Vries*, determined to attempt the junk channel. He followed a junk and found a deep, though narrow, channel carrying a depth of 30 feet. Although, unfortunately, he damaged his ship slightly by touching a pinnacle rock, he managed to reach Hankow in safety. This feat caused a considerable stir in shipping circles, and the channel is used to this day when, as often happens, the Hukwang Flats limit the draught of vessels to Hankow.

Hankow, 137 miles above Kiukiang and over 600 miles from the sea, is in reality composed of three towns known as the Wu-Han cities, namely, Wuchang, the seat of the provincial government, lying opposite on the right bank; Hanyang, up-river on the left bank; and Hankow, which is divided from Hanyang only by the River Han, which here, at its mouth, is little more than a cable wide. This bottle-neck, however, opens out on its upper reaches, and the Han, which is 1,250 miles long, is navigable by small launches for some 300 miles, and much farther by small junks.

The Yangtze and the Yellow River, so widely diverging in their courses, approach to their nearest point to each other north of Hankow, and the area of about 300 miles between these two giant streams is tapped by the Han River.

Hankow, therefore, by virtue of its position at the junction of the Han with the Yangtze, and lying midway between the two great lake systems of Poyang and Tungting, occupies a unique trade position as a centre of innumerable converging inland waterways covering a hinterland equal in area to that of Europe, with a population of more than 140 millions.

Hankow stands out as the most important city in the interior of China and is, of course, a great junk centre. The river swarms with craft of every kind. One-third of China's cow hides, buffalo hides, and goat skins (the latter making, it may be observed, the best "lizard-skin" hand-bags) come from, or pass through, the Hankow district, some part at least being carried by junks. Two-thirds of the total export of sesamum seed and six-sevenths of the trade in wood oil centre at Hankow from the neighbouring provinces.

It is estimated that at least 25,000 junks are engaged in traffic with the Wu-Han cities. They lie 10 or 12 abreast on both banks of the Han River for a distance of 5 miles back and are packed so close that the Chinese expression "like scales of a fish" is not inappropriate. When there would seem to be no room for a single other boat, two or three will come poling along and finally, edging their bows into the angle formed by two boats already in position, force them apart and so make a berth for themselves.

Other names for the Yangtze are given in Part One, pages 3–6.

As already stated, down the centuries and throughout its varied course the Yangtze has been, and is, known by many varied names. Of all these the truest and most descriptive is one which, alas, is scarcely recognized, or even known, by the Chinese themselves, though it has been much quoted by many of the pioneer foreign writers on China. This name, "The Son of the Sea," it will be remembered, derives from a mistaken translation of the characters 揚子. It is not known who first made this charming error, but it is indeed a pity that the latter-day sinologues have proved it to be wrong.

通進香船

THE TATUNG-CH'UAN OR PILGRIM-BOAT

A type of ferry, in vogue on the Yangtze, which comes under a general rather than a specialized classification, is represented by the enormous number of boats of all kinds which are used to ferry pilgrims about. The boat most commonly used in the pilgrim trade is the sampan illustrated in Plate No. 75.

One of the most famous of these pilgrimages is to the foot of the mountain of Chiu Hua Shan (九華山), in Anhwei Province. This hill is one of a high range of mountains on the south bank of the Yangtze, a little west of Chihchowfu (池州府), and is easy of access from the port of Tatung (大通). There is a succession of shrines up the slopes of the hill, particularly on its northern side overlooking the river. The personage so venerated here is the Buddhist monk Chin Ch'iao-chio (金喬覺), heir to a small kingdom in Korea called Hsinlo (新羅), which became extinct in the tenth century. Some writers name him Fu Lo-pu (傅羅卜) and say he came from Western China. In religion he is known as Mu Lien (目蓮).

Wherever he hailed from, the royal hermit began his ascetic life in China under the T'ang dynasty, A.D. 618–907, and lived on his mountain retreat on an economical, if indigestible, diet of "white clay and boiled millet," which was nevertheless sufficient to maintain life in him for 90 years. On learning through a vision that his mother was suffering tortures in the nether world through her backsliding from the Buddhist law of vegetarianism into the vice of meat-eating, he managed by dint of a personal visit to Buddha to redeem his errant parent from her punishment.

The filial and holy monk is worshipped as one of the incarnations of Ti Ts'ang Wang (地 藏 王), God of the Underworld. Because of his kindly rescue of his mother, his protection is sought by the pilgrims, and like Kuan Yin (觀 音), the Goddess of Mercy, he is hailed as a saviour and deliverer, who can be induced to go down into Hades on errands of mercy. He is one of the most popular deities in Anhwei and Kiangsu, and in the pilgrim season, from September to November, a million or more pilgrims are annually conveyed across the river in thousands of boats, which are gaily ornamented with banners and coloured paper lanterns. Each boat carries a Buddhist priest, who prays for his passengers and offers incense on their behalf.

The monks cultivate a special kind of tea, which grows in the adjacent valleys and is said to have been introduced by the royal monk himself. Canisters of this tea are sold to the pilgrims to take home as souvenirs. A more peculiar form of trophy is that taken home by men who dress themselves up as women and, so it is said, get the monks to mark their clothes with the seal of the God of the Underworld. These garments are then presented to their parents with the pledge of protection for them from the perils of the nether world by this filial-minded deity.

Ti Ts'ang Wang is further linked with the Yangtze by a legend connecting him with the beauty-loving and wine-bibbing poet Li T'ai-po (李 太 白), who lived in the eighth century A.D. The story goes, according to the junkmen, that, when Ti Ts'ang Wang was crossing the Yangtze on the way to the site of the present shrine a storm imperilled his life. At once the poet, who had previously himself been drowned in the Yangtze,* literally and figuratively rose to the occasion and transported the god safely to the shore. The two then struck up an eternal friendship.

More about Li T'ai-po in Part One, page 16.

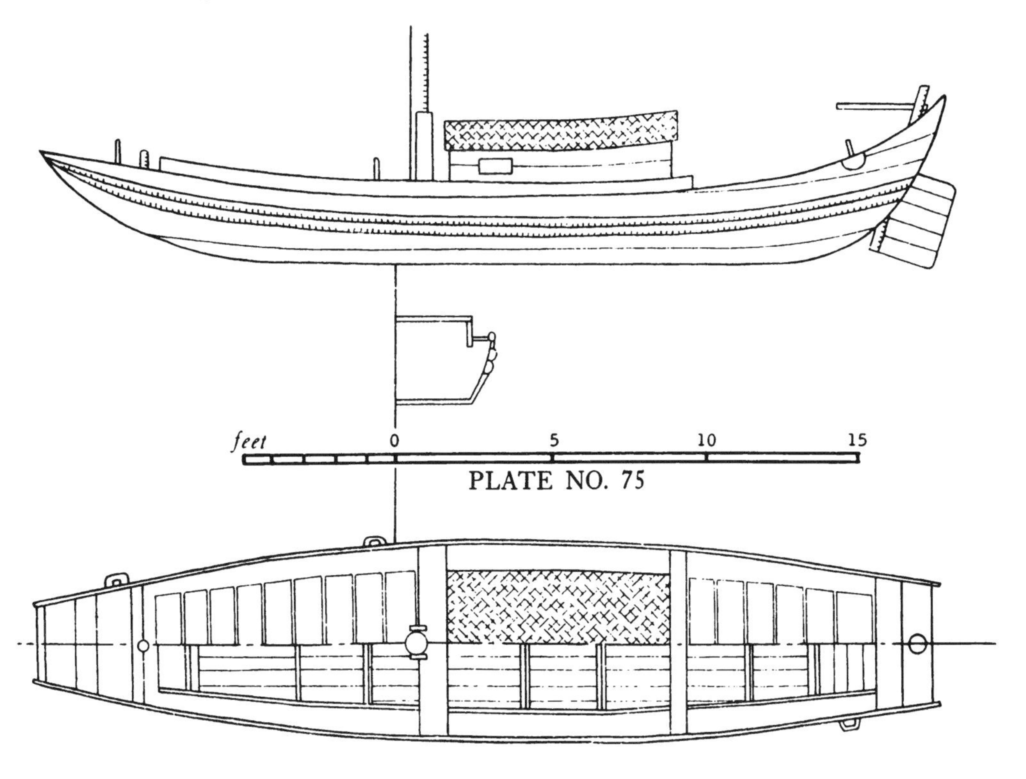

PLATE NO. 75

* Li T'ai-po had met his watery death through his endeavours to lean from a boat and embrace the reflection of the moon on the waters. From his condition at the time it seems probable that he saw the object of his affection in duplicate. Actually this legend constitutes a glaring anachronism, for Li T'ai-po was reputedly drowned after the time that Ti Ts'ang Wang was said to have reached Chiu Hua Shan in A.D. 756.

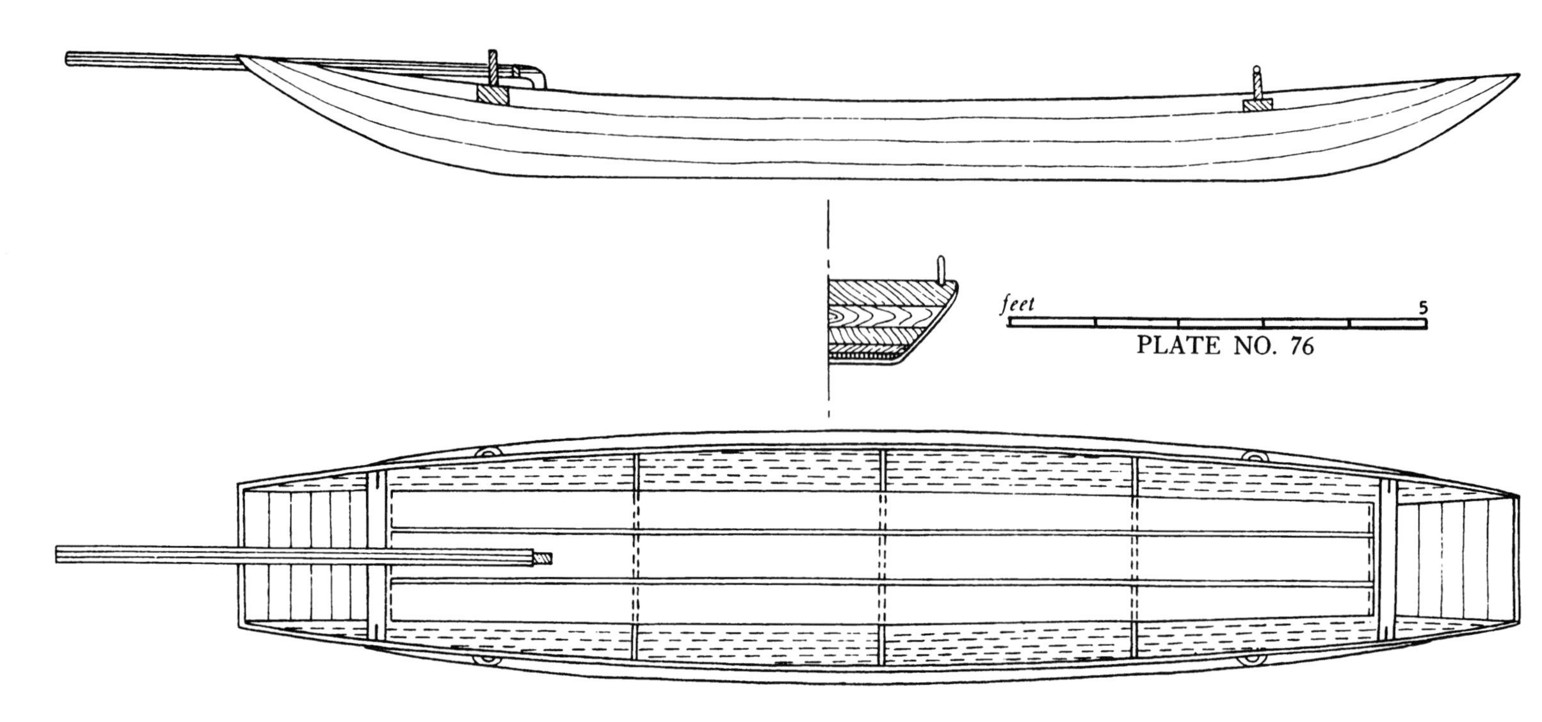

PLATE NO. 76

THE CH'IANG-HUA-TZŬ OR GUN-SAMPAN

The Yangtze River, which forms the dividing line between the two great zoological regions of China, flows through the valley named after it, an area which, flat, dry, and cold in the north and, in the south, warm, humid, and intersected with swift-running, slow, and stagnant waters, is eminently suited to a large and varied fauna.

At the beginning of December the wildfowl, swans, geese, and swarms of duck arrive from the Amur lands. The duck alone are the object of the native wildfowler, who is to be found all up and down the Lower and Middle Yangtze as well as in some places on the Upper River. Large flights of wild duck usually congregate on the quiet stretches of water at the up-river extremities of spits extending from islands in mid-river.

The wildfowlers, who become fishermen during the summer months, work in a small and quite uninteresting type of little sampan measuring 14½ feet, with a beam of 3 feet and a depth of less than a foot, illustrated in Plate No. 76.

Built on punt-like lines, it has two bulkheads at either extremity, is flat-bottomed, and, when fully loaded, has a mere few inches of freeboard. Over the bow projects a long primitive gun, which rests supported on the foremost bulkhead, a groove being cut in the woodwork of the bow so as to allow of its being trained. The gingall, or jingall, as this formidable weapon is called in China, is 6 feet long and consists of a length of 1½-inch pipe onto which a short wooden pistol-grip butt is fitted.

The use of gunpowder by the Chinese dates back to very remote times, but their not very warlike inclinations applied the invention to fire-crackers until the advent of the Jesuits, who taught them the use of guns.

Gunpowder is made by the wildfowlers themselves. At Wuhu the ingredients consist of 2 catties of ground charcoal, 3 catties of saltpetre, and 10 catties of sulphur. After being placed in a pan over a low charcoal fire, a jar of kaoliang spirits is poured over them and the mixture well stirred with a stick until it becomes of the consistency of paste. It is then laid in the sun to dry. About half an ounce is the ordinary charge.

The shot is made by melting a quantity of iron and pouring the liquid metal from a height onto a stone laid in a tub of water. When cool the pellets are collected and sorted according to size by hand; for whatever reason, they are not passed through a sieve.

The gun is usually loaded on shore by a man who stands on a stool and pours powder down through the muzzle. The butt end is then thumped on the ground and the powder rammed home with the inevitable bamboo rod until the charge occupies about 6 inches depth in the barrel. One and a half ounces of coarse shot mixed with dried peas are then loaded, and the gun, now ready for action, is lifted into its place in the boat.

The sampan is first manœuvred into position by the oarsman in the stern, the object being to drift down with the current so as to get within range of the sleeping or unsuspecting birds. The crew, consisting of a gunlayer and an oarsman, lie prone in the bottom of the boat, the former manning the gun and the latter keeping the boat heading in the right direction by paddling with his hands over the side or using, in lieu, one of the long balers.

When the quarry is neared a primer[1] is put in position. This ingenious and simple device consists of a small quantity of gunpowder contained in a rolled spill of paper[1] inserted through the vent[2], which is on the side of the barrel. An iron oblong plate[3], projecting horizontally about an inch from the wooden stock below the vent[2], acts as a platform to hold the spill.

The gun is fired by pressing the trigger[4], which releases a hammer[5]. This takes the form of an S-shaped piece of metal divided at its apex[6] so as exactly to receive the thickness of the end of an incense stick[7], which has previously been lit from a flint. The smouldering slow-match[7], on striking the gunpowder-filled spill[2], ignites it, and the sparks entering the vent fire the gun, both the noise and the recoil being very considerable. The range is said to be as much as about 200 Chinese feet, and the gunlayer claims that the spread of shot is 6 feet soon after leaving the muzzle.

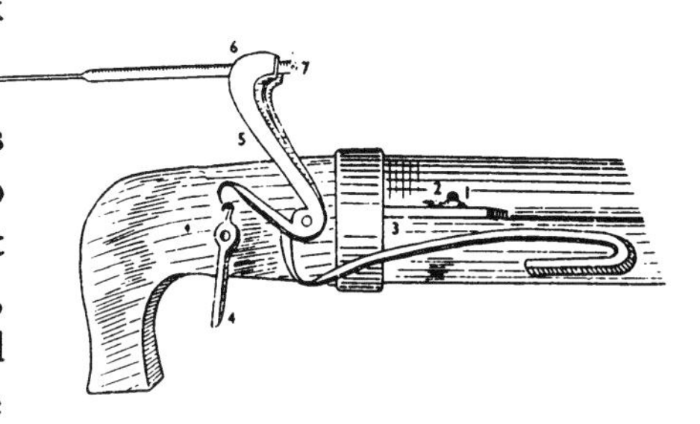

Chinese shotgun.

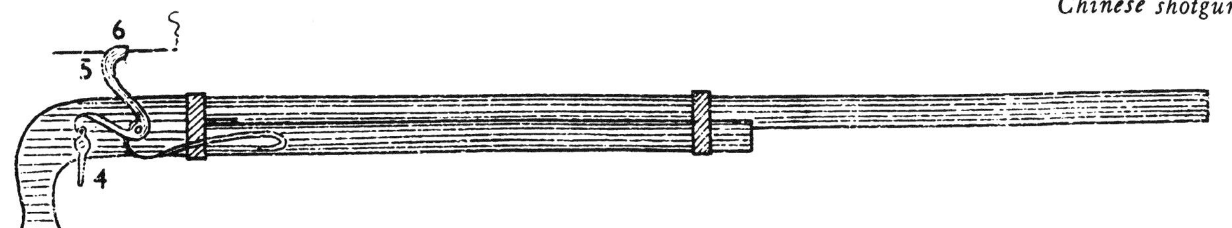

Having recovered somewhat from the shock of the discharge, the gunlayer blows down the vent to clear the barrel.

After the one-sided engagement, supporting sampans on either side close in to assist in picking up the dead or wounded birds. Not every attack is successful, for the ducks are often warned of the approach of the sampans and get up out of range.

Good results for the most part depend on luck, for the aim is a matter of judgment. Promptitude in firing is dependent on the whim of the incense stick and the primer, and the path of the peas and shot is difficult to predict with complete, or indeed any, accuracy. Under ideal conditions, and provided the gun goes off when required, which is problematical—for misfires are not uncommon,—the fowlers may expect to wing, wound, or kill at least 10 to 20 birds at a single discharge.

When there is success, the casualty list is always a heavy one and is increased by the gunlayer's assistant, who, armed with a smaller but similar gun, fires another shot at the wounded and dying birds or those late in taking off.

The attack has a distinctly adverse effect on the morale of the duck, who usually do not return for 24 hours, so that the fowlers may have only one shot in the day.

To the casual observer it would appear that the gunlayer runs nearly as many risks as the duck.

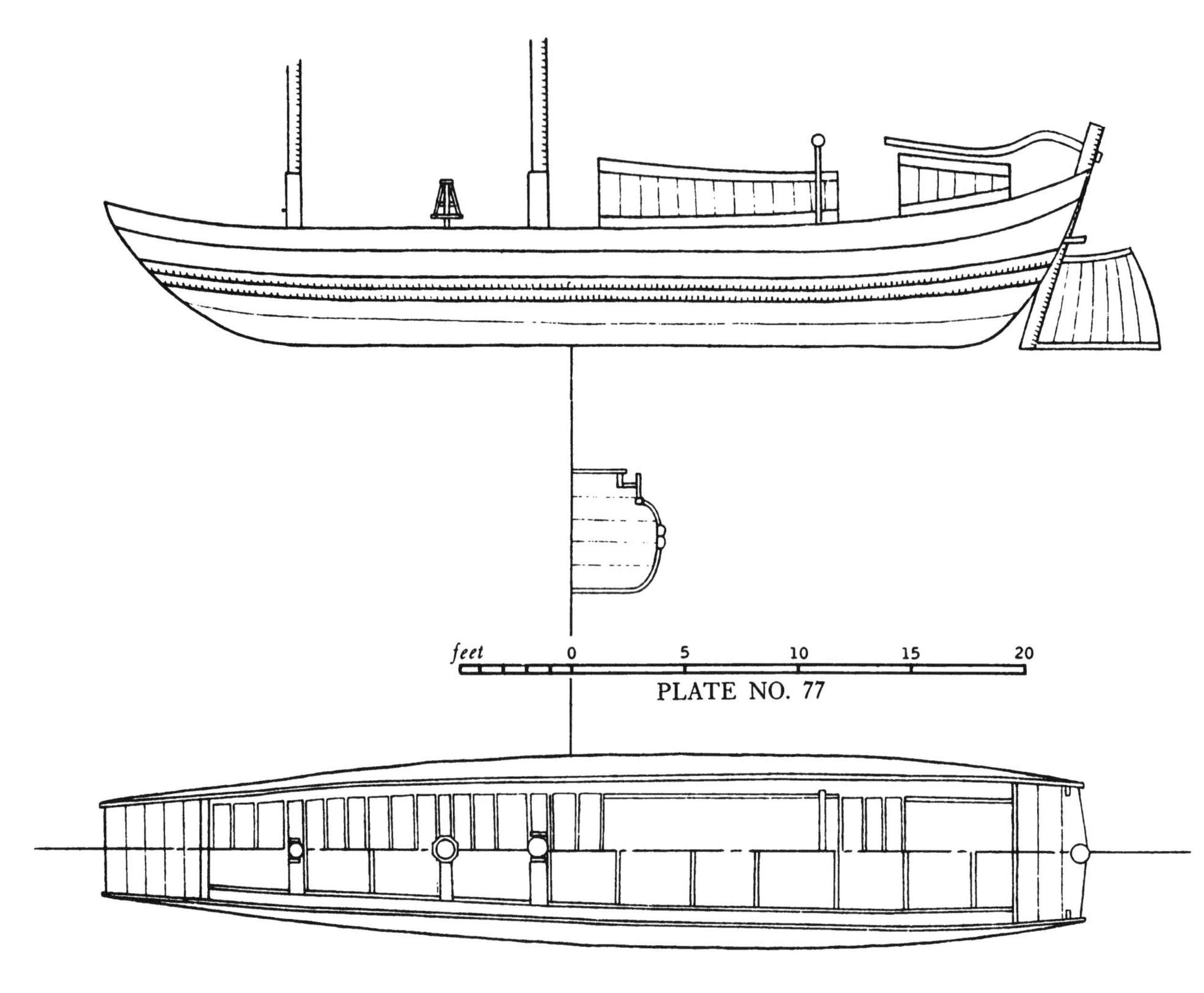

PLATE NO. 77

THE PAI-CHIANG-TZŬ OR CARGO-FERRY

擺江子

The *pai-chiang-tzŭ*, or cargo-ferry, has a good deal in common with the *huang-hua-tzŭ* types of junk; indeed, they may be said to be distant relations.

The *pai-chiang-tzŭ* is a flat-bottomed, medium-draught cargo-carrier used at Wuhu and the vicinity for the transport of cargo across the river.

Normally measuring about 43 feet in length, with a beam of 8 feet and a depth of 4 feet 10 inches, this type is sturdily built. The cross section on Plate No. 77 shows the method of combining the essential light-draught quality demanded with the additional cargo space. This is provided by a sudden increase in beam with a sharp tumble home below the water-line.

The house and galley both have flat roofs. The rudder is of the non-balance variety. The crew consists of two men besides the laodah, who is usually also the owner.

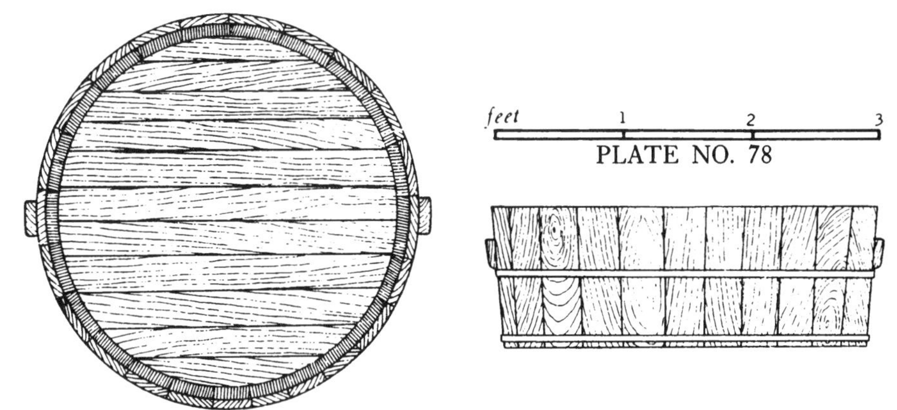

PLATE NO. 78

THE HU-CH'UAN OR KETTLE-BOAT

The reason for the designation seems obscure, for translated it signifies the kettle-boat. In point of fact it resembles neither kettle nor boat, being nothing more or less than a wide, shallow wash-tub, which, besides fulfilling its normal functions, serves to tend the crops when the fields are flooded. Nevertheless, this humble contrivance also has its legend, for it is told of General Yo Fei (岳 飛) that, when he was a few weeks old, his mother used one of these tubs wherein to cross the Yellow River with him in her arms during a flood and thus escaped to safety with the child that was later to become one of China's most celebrated commanders under the Emperor Sung Kao Tsung (宋 高 宗), in the early twelfth century wars against the Chins, or " Golden Hordes."

In construction there is nothing to distinguish this craft from its less adventurous stay-at-home brethren, except that any such tub selected for use would necessarily be large enough—say, 3 feet—in diameter to accommodate the farmer and sufficiently stoutly built to take the weight. Propulsion is by means of the hands paddling over the side. Its use is illustrative of the Chinese genius for practical and economical ingenuity.

The cultivation of edible plants grown in water is, probably, nowhere in the world so extensively carried out as in China. There are four main varieties of these plants, the most generally grown is the perennial *p'o-chi* (荸 薺), or water chestnut (*Trapa natans*), popularly known as the tail-pear. The root, which is edible, is a small, fleshy, onion-shaped, brown bulb. These, when peeled and spitted together on thin bamboo sticks, are hawked as sweetmeats all over China. Sometimes they are dipped in a red sugary syrup. They are also used in cooking, and Chinese doctors prescribe their juice as a cure for measles; indeed, during an epidemic of this complaint the price of water chestnuts jumps up 30 per cent. The Chinese botanical work "Pen Ts'ao" (本 草) describes it as follows:

> Its taste is sweetish, and it possesses cooling properties; taken as food or medicine, it is a stimulant and produces a soothing effect on the bowels. It promotes appetite and assists digestion, especially when taken after meals. As a febrifuge it is of value; and it dispels dyspepsia and obstructions of the alimentary canal, quenches thirst, and has the power of dissolving brass or copper; hence it is a food remedy in cases of copper cash swallowed accidentally by children.

Lien-hua (蓮 花), or the lotus lily (*Nelumbium speciosum*), is also very extensively used for food. It is grown in permanent ponds. Now and then these are drained, and for the fastidious all appetite for this delicacy would be lost after seeing the lily-roots dug out of the dark, slimy, and evil-smelling recesses of a muddy pond-bed.

Another aquatic plant is the water caltrop (菱), which is grown in canals and creeks and produces a fruit resembling a horny nut, some with three horns and some with four, a shape which has inspired the name of *niu-chiao* (牛 角), " buffalo horn." It is used in cooking to flavour fish and meat.

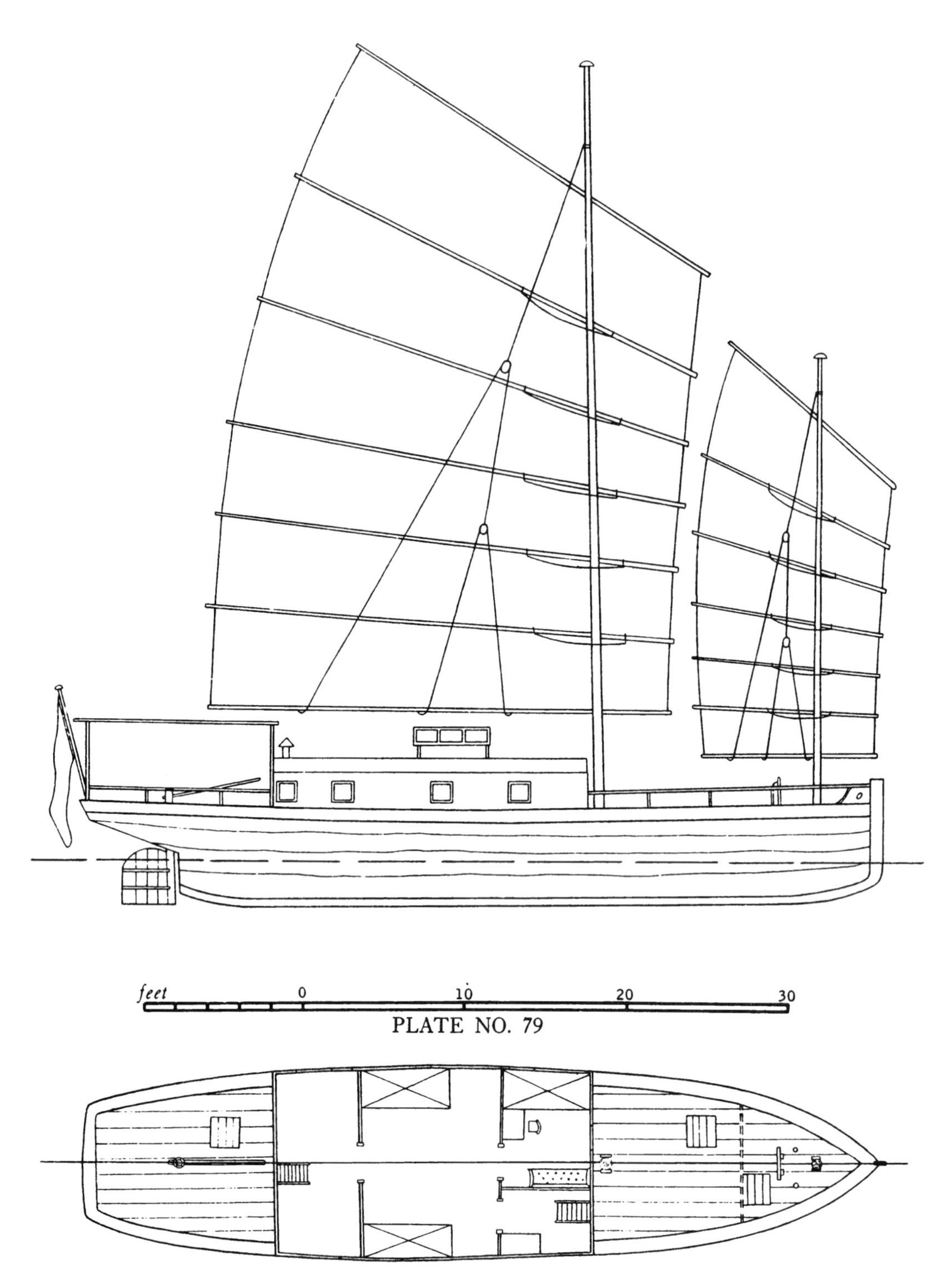

PLATE NO. 79

THE CUSTOMS WOODEN LIGHTS TENDER

Any exhaustive description of the craft of the Yangtze must, of necessity, include mention of the work of that youngest branch of the Marine Department of the Chinese Maritime Customs, the River Inspectorate, whose lights and aids to navigation served to safeguard the junks no less than the steamers that passed incessantly up and down its waters.

Prior to the formation of the River Inspectorate, the aids to navigation on the river were administered by the various port Harbour Masters, who detailed a Tidewaiter to visit the lights in a sailing tender to pay the staff and issue stores.

Plate No. 79 illustrates the first Yangtze lights tender of this type, the

Lushan (廬山), which for many years did yeoman service. She was built by Chinese carpenters in semi-foreign style; but the sails remain typically Chinese, being of the balance-lug variety fitted with battens. With a length over-all of 54 feet and maximum beam of 13 feet, she appears to have been a strong and comfortable cruiser.

Her log book for the year 1893 now reposes in the Customs archives, and its 572 pages tell in laconic phrases the story of a bygone age. In the neat sloping handwriting of the period is recorded the monotonous routine of lights-tending. Nothing unusual appears ever to have happened on these uneventful voyages, which often took as long as six weeks to accomplish. The sounding of the channels was carried out by the Foreign Pilots' Association independently of the Customs, and they used to station one of their members at the various critical channels to assist navigation.

This unsatisfactory condition could not continue, and therefore, in 1903, a special launch, the *Chianghsing*, was built, and in 1906 a River Inspector was appointed together with a Launch Officer. The River Inspector had no executive control, but carried out occasional surveys, acted as adviser, and inspected the lights.

In May 1911 a reorganization took place, and the River Inspector was placed in executive control of the Kiukiang and Hankow districts. For the next few years the new Department functioned in a very modest way with quite a small staff, never exceeding five foreign officers. Three Marine Department Officers returned from active service in the Great War, 1914–18, and were absorbed into the growing River Inspectorate together with many other recruits, until by the end of 1920 the River Inspectorate executive control of the Lower Yangtze was completed by the appointment of a District River Inspector to take charge of the Wuhu district and another to assist the River Inspector. From this date the activities of the Department may be said to have started in earnest.

The River Inspectorate of the Chinese Maritime Customs was a highly efficient service. In the brief space of time bounded roughly by the two World Wars, it rose and, despite many vicissitudes, flourished.

It is the youngest child of the Customs; the River Inspectorate, despite its immaturity,—perhaps, indeed, because of its youth and vigour—displayed an energy and devotion to duty of a very high order from which grew up traditions of loyalty to the Service and of service to the public. This loyalty was inextricably bound up with interest in the capricious river, every mood and whim of which it was their business to study in circumstances calculated to strain the resources of the toughest.

Looking back over the last 21 years, one incident after another stands out, each deserving of praise, and wonder is again excited that both Officers and men could stand the incredible hardships of sounding and surveying in the winter, when the lead lines had to be soaked at intervals in boiling water to keep them from freezing, and the leadsmen's hands were often cracked and bleeding. Conversely, in the summer the Yangtze Valley is sultry and trying to a degree which must be experienced to be realized. Yet long hours of triangulation were put in, until the effect of the dazzle of the sunlight on the water tried the strongest eyes to the point when the vernier on the sextant could hardly be deciphered—yet the day's work would be plotted after dark in defiance of all fatigue. Besides long hours of work there were not infrequent dangers from bullets, bandits, bombs, mines, and the natural hazards of fog and sudden treacherous storms blowing up in a long reach or wide lake. All these things were cheerfully and uncomplainingly borne by Chinese and foreigners alike.

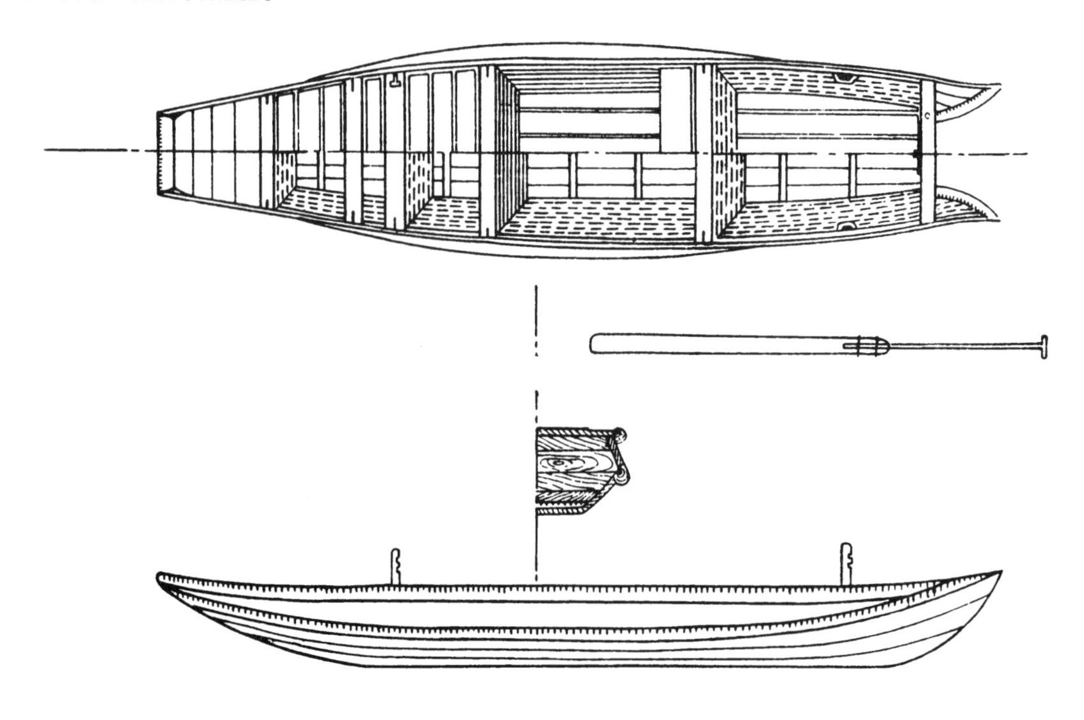

湖北舢板

LOWER YANGTZE SAMPANS

The type of Lower Yangtze sampan illustrated in Plate No. 80 has a capacity of 20 to 50 piculs, that is to say, 1 to 2½ tons. The hull is usually built of softwood, with hardwood frames. One mast is stepped amidships, and the sail is of the usual lug type, made of cotton cloth. The midship portion is often covered with a mat roof for the convenience of the passengers. The craft, although it is a typical Hankow sampan, is nevertheless to be found in great numbers throughout the Yangtze. It measures 21 feet over-all, with a beam of 5 feet and a depth of 2 feet. It is built with three bulkheads and six frames, and is of very strong construction. Although they are often used for transporting live stock, perishable goods, and so forth from inland places, the boats are more often used for carrying passengers. For the most part they are family-owned, being worked by the father and his sons. The boat is usually fitted with two oars operated in the stern sheets and one in the bow. A smaller type is used within the harbour limits or, less frequently, in the immediate outskirts of Wu-Han. Although it may be carried, the mast is seldom stepped. The chief business of this craft, which is known as the *hua-tzŭ* (划 子), is to carry passengers from Hankow to Wuchang and *vice versa*. One man is sufficient to work this small craft.

The chief communications of the Yangtze Valley are by means of its rivers and canals, the Yangtze itself being the main artery. Not only are there junks plying up and down the great river, but nearly the whole of the bordering provinces is interlaced with canals and small rivers on which sampans do a thriving trade carrying passengers.

Boat travel is much cheaper than by donkey, wheelbarrow, or the modern motor-bus.* In the good old days, before inflation came to China, travelling by small sampans cost 120 cash a *ch'êng* (程) for each person, a water *ch'êng* being 100 *li*, or 33 miles. In large sampans, called three-*ts'ang* boats (三 艙 船), each passenger paid about 185 cash per *ch'êng*. On routes where there was competition with small launches the cost was reduced to 133 cash per *ch'êng* for long distances. In addition to the fare the passenger was required to pay wine money for the sampanmen and incense money for propitiating the gods and securing fine weather. Food on the boats was extra and cost, in those far-off days, 35 cash a meal.

* Long-distance travel by boat has another advantage in that the passengers may sleep therein, whereas those who proceed by all other means of transport must seek lodging for the night.

Sampans, of all sizes, are also used to carry cargo for short or long distances. Prices vary, of course, but at the beginning of the century it was possible to engage boats at 1,000 cash a *ch'êng*. For long distances the cost would be reduced to about 800 cash a *ch'êng*, or by the day for 600 cash per day.

Quite large sampans or small junks are still available with a carrying capacity of 10 tons; the hirer is required to pay all dues, plus extra charges for wine money and for writing the contract. Another type, much lighter in construction, hails from the inland waters around Wuhu. This craft, named the Wuhu country-boat, which is illustrated in Plate No. 81, is fitted with six frames and three half-bulkheads.

The ordure-boat illustrated in Plate No. 81 is a typical example of the craft used in the night-soil trade on the inland waters of Anhwei. The ramifications of this noisome industry have already been described,* and so there will, happily, be no necessity to enter into any further description of the trade. The craft depicted measures 35½ feet in length, with a beam of 5 feet 8 inches and a depth of 1½ feet, and is divided into five cargo compartments, all of which are used for cargo.

North, south, south-east, and south-west from Hankow, waterways link up with the roads of the Provinces of Shensi, Honan, Shantung, Kweichow, Kwangsi, and Kwangtung. The ubiquitous sampan is, therefore, not only the common means of conveyance but also a bond of union between the five provinces.

* Part Two, page 239, the Fên-ch'uan, or Fu-fu boat.

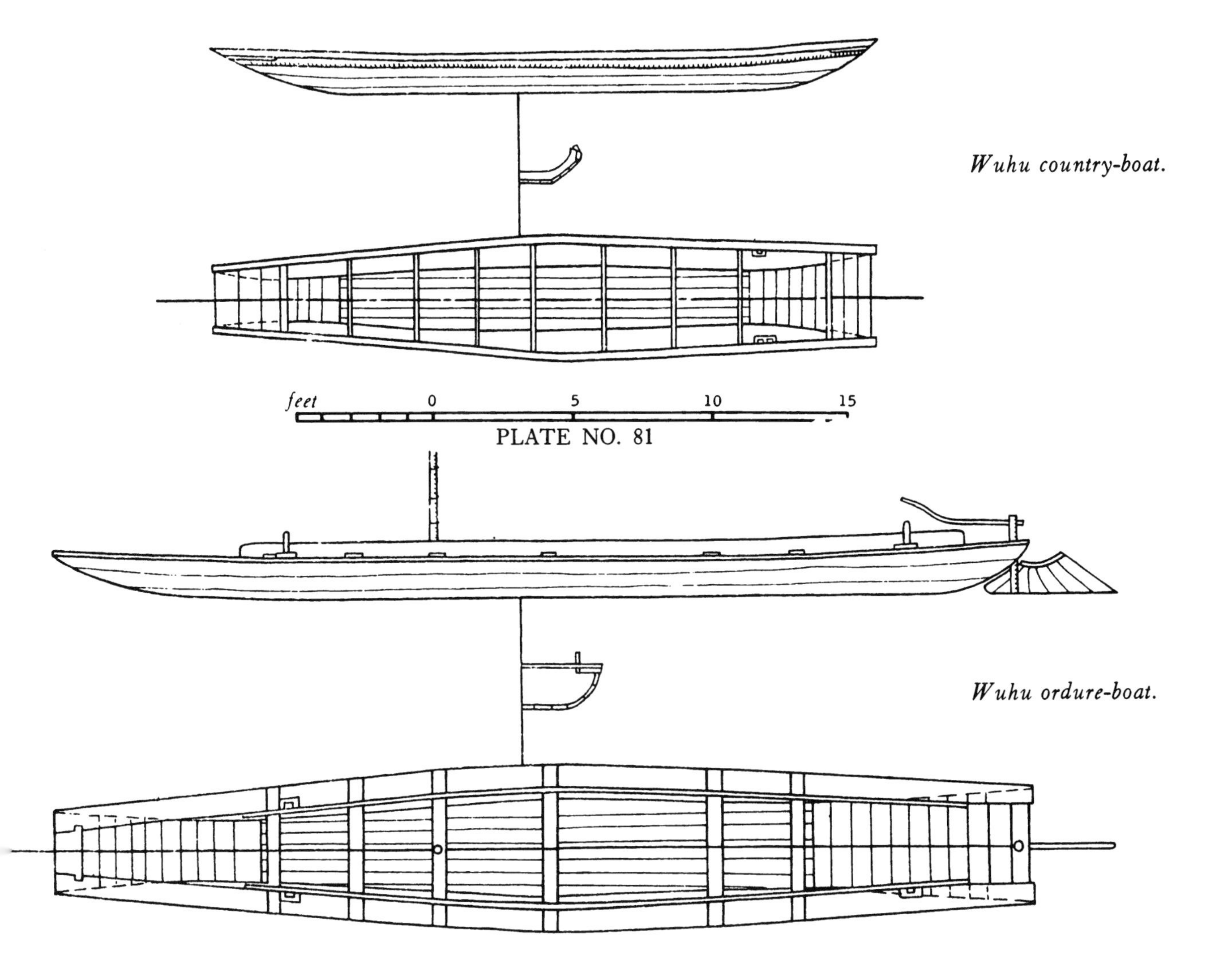

Wuhu country-boat.

Wuhu ordure-boat.

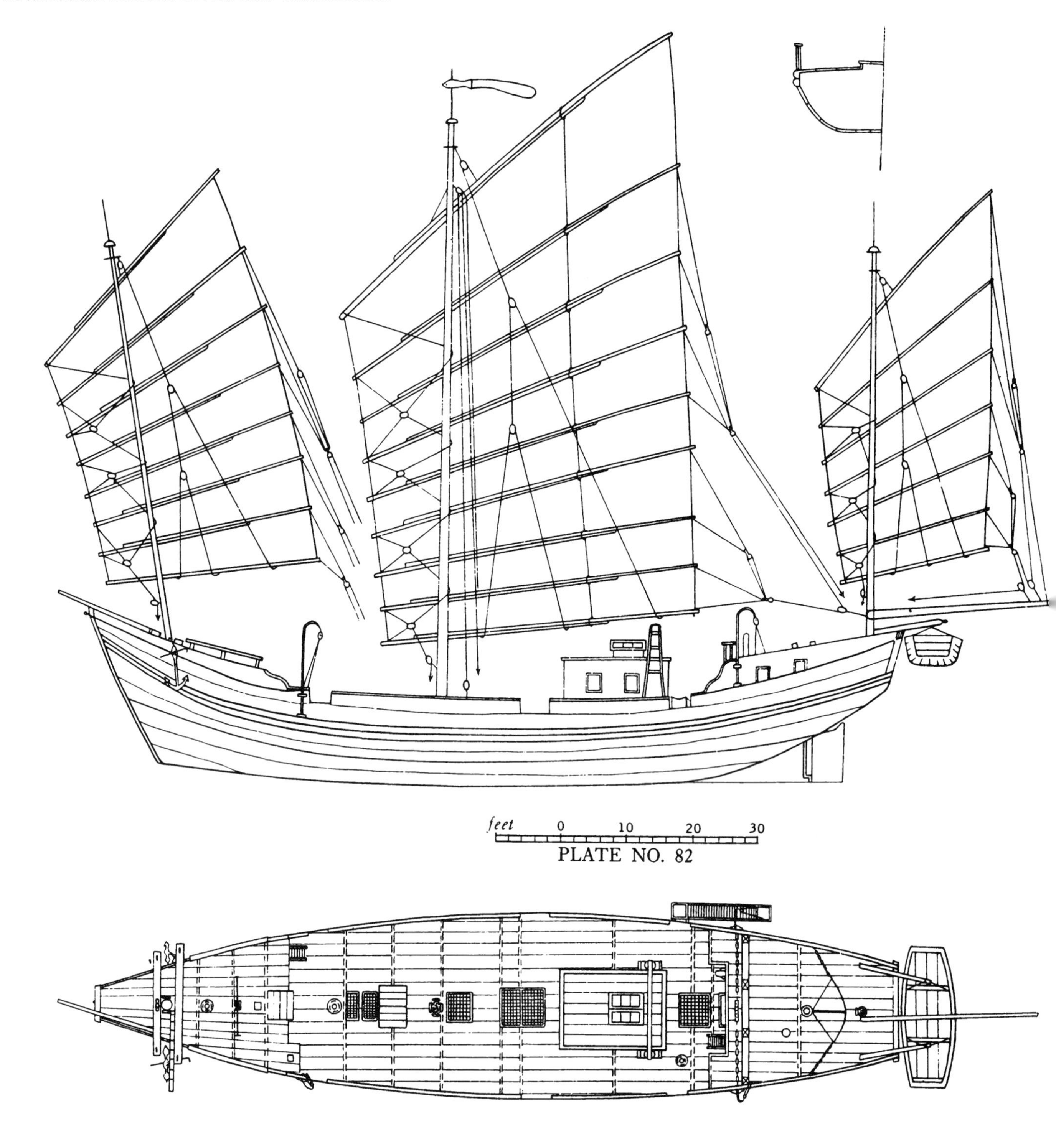

PLATE NO. 82

THE LORCHA

The term " lorcha," or " lorch," is from the Portuguese, but it is of obscure derivation. The Oxford Dictionary defines it as being " a fast sailing craft built in China with the hull after a European model, but rigged in Chinese fashion, usually carrying guns."

Although it is commonly believed that the lorcha was first built in Macao, all available evidence points to a much earlier origin; for Macao was only a dangerous pirates' lair until 1540, whereas in an account of his wanderings the Portuguese adventurer Pinto* writes of a "lorch" in connection with his travels in 1553, that is to say, some years before Macao was occupied by his countrymen. Previous to the colonization of Macao the early Portuguese settlers had in 1517

* Ferdinand Mendez Pinto (*circa* 1509–83). His "Perigrinacio" was first published in Lisbon in 1614 and translated by H. Cogan in 1653.

arrived first at the port of Tamou on an island adjacent to that of San Chuan or St. John, south-west of Macao, and later at Liampo, or Ningpo, where they established themselves in such force that it became their wealthiest settlement in Asia with a community of 1,200 Portuguese. Allusions to "Portuguese trading junks" of this period make it seem feasible to suppose that the new-comers had at this time, and probably at Ningpo, built for themselves speedier adaptations of the useful and seaworthy Chinese junk which, while retaining the handy Chinese style of rig, would by means of its finer Western lines expedite the delivery of the merchandise, which was the basis of the flourishing trade carried on by the Portuguese with Japan, Malacca, India, and the China coast. This supposition is rather supported by contemporary references to "Portuguese trading junks."

Alternative suggestions for the origin of the lorcha are either that it was first built at one of the other adjacent Portuguese settlements of Chincheo or Lampacao,* or that it may have originated even earlier still at Malacca as an adaptation of the junks found in those waters, for Malacca was conquered in 1511 by the great Portuguese empire-builder and administrator Alphonso d'Albuquerque, who there immediately established excellent relations with the Chinese traders. In his commentaries he says that he noticed more kindness and politeness in the Chinese junkmasters than in the aristocrats from the West. Albuquerque despatched well-known officers, including Raphael Perestrello, from Malacca to China, and it is of the greatest interest to note that these first voyages were undertaken in junks; and even when in 1517 a mission in a Portuguese fleet of five ships, under the command of Fernaõ Peres de Andrade, appeared in the China Seas, it was accompanied by four junks.

Where, and whenever, the lorcha originated, it played such a notable part in the destinies of Macao that no account of the vessel would be adequate without reference to that historic centre of early Western intercourse with China.

As has already been pointed out, Macao was, until past the middle of the sixteenth century, a rocky waste and the headquarters of the swarms of pirates who, joining with the Japanese desperadoes, terrorized the China coast so successfully that their leader, Chang Si-lao, even aspired to capture Canton. The Chinese, knowing the Portuguese prowess against corsairs, invited them to assist in raising the piratical siege of Canton and in stamping out piracy in the China Seas.

The Portuguese started off in six galleons and, though greatly outnumbered, managed by their superior tactics and artillery to rout the pirates utterly. Portuguese historians, notably C. A. Montalto de Jesus,† claim that the Portuguese were permitted to colonize Macao as a reward for driving away the pirates from their lair on that peninsula. Others suggest that the Portuguese were allowed to settle there as it was merely a barren rock for which the Chinese had no use themselves. There is apparently no documentary evidence to support either theory.

Nevertheless, by whatever means obtained, Macao has been continuously occupied by the Portuguese ever since 1557, and its history has been intermittently linked with the story of the lorchas as well as with that of the pirates against whom these gallant craft waged war so successfully. This nautical flavour to Macao's history finds a fitting complement in the fact that as a port it is closely associated with the T'ien Hou (天后), or Queen of Heaven, and the name in Chinese signifies "Harbour of the Goddess A-Ma."

The legend from which the name sprang concerns a Fukien junk and a young girl who sought and was refused a passage in it, as it was already full. The

* According to Ferdinand Pinto, a wholesale massacre of the Portuguese in Ningpo wiped out the colony, and a similar disaster befell Chincheo, but the indomitable Portuguese then settled in Lampacao in 1842 until about 1860. This island, near Macao, is not identifiable. The Chinese officials themselves were ultimately responsible for the fact that the Japanese traders took to piracy; for China's officially anti-foreign attitude was inimical to the trading concessions which the Japanese, like other foreigners, wanted from China. C. A. Montalto de Jesus in "Historic Macao" contradicts the statements by Pinto.

† "Historic Macao," by C. A. Montalto de Jesus, a book which should certainly be consulted by all serious students of Macao and the lorcha.

junkmaster at length listened to her entreaties and allowed her to occupy a seat in the fore-part. Later, a storm arose and blew with such violence that the laodah tried to return to port, but the mysterious passenger called to him from her position in the bow and told him not to fear but to continue on his course. The vessel drifted along until she found a sheltered place in which to anchor. As the lady passenger had by now vanished, a search was made for her on shore. All that was found, however, was a carved goddess, believed to be the same that is now to be seen at the Ma Ko Pagoda. Near-by is the representation of the junk, said to have been cut out of the rock by the search-party, together with a banner on which is inscribed her sailing orders to the laodah. The place is now known as Amagao, and, whenever there is a storm, the junkmen of that locality call on the goddess for aid.

The Portuguese settlement of Macao soon became the most flourishing western trade centre of the Far East. This era of prosperity was accompanied by intermittent naval activity occasioned by the trade jealousy of Japanese or Dutch rivals.

The end of the eighteenth century saw a marked recrudescence of the pirate menace. It was said that the pirate fleet numbered over 600 junks, divided into two squadrons, and about 1,000 auxiliary craft, while the total personnel was estimated at some 60,000 strong.

It was decided to employ a guardship at Macao, and a sloop, the *Princeza Carlota*, 120 tons and 16 guns, was ordered and built in 28 days at Calcutta. A galley, the *Ulysses*, renamed the *Arriaga*, was also equipped, and with them was associated one of the first lorchas to be specifically mentioned by name, a 10-ton craft called the *Leao* and armed with a revolving howitzer and four swivel guns. She was commanded by a Macanese pilot, Antonio Gonçalves Carocha, and her task, at which she excelled, was to convoy the provision vessels.

On the 6th May 1807 a small Portuguese force achieved a remarkable victory over the marauders, and the action deserves mention in these pages, because the lorcha *Leao* took part in it.

The Portuguese, commanded by Pereira Barreto in the *Princeza Carlota*, found themselves, when not far from Macao, faced by 50 junks, and 30 of these engaged the Portuguese ships. After an hour's exchange of shots the enemy withdrew with the exception of the pirate flagship, a large junk armed with 20 guns and 300 men. Barreto drew in and boarded the vessel, which fought to the last man. The pirate commander finally killed his wife and jumped with her body in his arms into the sea.

In a later action, when the *Leao* was carrying provisions to the fleet, she was assailed by 16 pirate junks and continued to give such a good account of herself that half her Chinese crew were killed or wounded. The eight survivors, in a final bid for life, seized and bound the intrepid Carocha, since that was the only way by which he could be persuaded to stop fighting, and fled back to Macao with him. On arrival at Macao their indignant captive had them dismissed, but doubtless they felt their lives had been purchased cheaply at the expense of their jobs.

The Portuguese successes had not passed unnoticed, and the Imperial Government negotiated a convention on the 23rd November 1809, whereby a coast guard of six Portuguese ships and a fleet of 60 Imperial junks was to cruise for six months between the Bogue and Macao to wage war against the pirates. The Chinese agreed to pay *Tls.* 80,000 towards the equipment of the foreign ships, and all spoils were to be equally divided. As the Imperial fleet proved unreliable, the Portuguese worked alone and soon established such an ascendency over the pirates that the leader of the Black Flag Squadron surrendered with 180 junks.

A final action took place on 21st January 1810, when the six Portuguese ships with only 730 men engaged 300 junks manned by 20,000 Chinese. The fight ended in complete victory for the Portuguese and the capitulation of 270 junks.

The suppression of the pirates was, however, not permanent. The disruption caused by the First China War afforded an opportunity for lawless depredations to break out again. Once again the ever useful lorchas of Macao were pressed into service as leaders of convoys of trading or Imperial junks, for guarding fisheries, as coast guards, and as flagships for such Chinese Admirals as cared or dared to go to sea in command of their fleets of war-junks.

Again the lorchas proved their value and valour in numberless encounters with the sea-raiders, often in conjunction with British gunboats. When there were only a few Portuguese on board, the Chinese lorchamen were dressed as Europeans so as to intimidate the pirates. The pirate junks were often disguised as fishing vessels. In such cases the nets were folded and reinforced with leather, which made such a useful means of defence that the Portuguese adopted the same practice for the lorchas.

When on convoy duty, half the captured booty of a pirate junk was distributed to the victorious lorcha, as well as rewards for every pirate dead or alive. The returning lorchas were greeted with gongs and cheers on arrival at Macao. One of the most famous of these lorchas was the *Amazona* under Captain Silva Carvalho.

The value of these craft was fully appreciated, and the Macao authorities increased their numbers. In 1847 disaster had overtaken 12 lorchas which were wrecked in a typhoon. Twenty were built in their place the following spring. The number of foreign-type ships available at Macao, which had been only 18 in 1835, dwindled to seven in 1851. More and more lorchas were accordingly built until their number, which was 60 in 1853, rose to 180 in 1855.

So, sadly enough, an interesting, historic, and gallant type of craft fell upon evil days and lost its well-deserved prestige.

Nevertheless, although they had fallen from their high estate as naval auxiliaries, if not actual warships, these seaworthy and handy craft were to continue in use for many decades to come, albeit only in a trading capacity. They were now, for the most part, Chinese-owned, though in order to facilitate trade under foreign tariff and treaty conditions they sailed under a foreign flag and therefore necessarily a foreign captain. Sometimes this was a purely honorary function, and the vessel was navigated by the Chinese laodah, the supercargo being also a Chinese.

After the opening of the Yangtze to foreign shipping, they ran from Ningpo to Shanghai with native cargoes of wine, gypsum, cow bones, and medicines, and thence carried hardware and sundries up the river to the ports. They then sailed direct from Hankow to Ningpo with wood oil, hemp, hides, tobacco, fungus, vegetable tallow, etc.

They were not at first affected by steam competition, for the cargo they carried, both native and foreign, was either of commodities that made speedy delivery unimportant, of a bulk, such as sugar or metals, as to render shipment by steamer too expensive, or else of a nature that rendered insurance unprofitable.

Captain Blakiston in his book "Five Months on the Yangtze," published in 1861, writes of seeing three or four lorchas off Wuhu. They belonged, he said, to Shanghai business firms and were sent up to purchase tea from Southern Anhwei.

In 1877 the "Customs Trade Report" recorded two lorchas under the American flag, three British, four German, and seven Spanish. The latter flag was popular, as Spanish natives of Manila could be hired cheaply to sleep on board as captains; and, in addition, there were no Spanish Consulates at which fees would have to be paid at Ningpo or at the Yangtze ports.

In 1889, 14 lorchas, with an average tonnage of 131 tons, were trading regularly on the river. A frequent change of flag made it difficult to be sure of figures, but in a "Customs Trade Report" of 1880 it is recorded that as many as 272 lorchas entered and cleared from Hankow, with a total tonnage of 43,158 tons. Of this number 125 were American, 68 British, 40 Dutch, 35 German, and 4 Spanish. This yearly clearance, of course, gives only a rough indication of the number of lorchas making this regular run, for it is impossible to estimate how many trips each lorcha made per year.

The increase in steam navigation at length had its effect, and the number of lorchas decreased. Many of them were placed under the Chinese flag on the Northern routes in serious competition with the heavier, slower junks. In 1874, 30 were on this run to Newchwang.

Those still on the river carried arms and munitions, kerosene oil, and bulky native produce.

C. A. Montalto de Jesus gives a description of the early lorchas of Macao. Built at the Inner Praya, they were usually made of camphor-wood or teak. Flat-bottomed and of shallow draught, they varied in size from 40 to 150 tons, the majority being between 50 and 100 tons. The number of guns, according to the size of the craft, ranged from 4 to 20 and were of from 1 to 24 pounds calibre. The larger guns were mounted on swivels. The crew, half Portuguese, half Chinese, were armed with muskets, swords, hatchets, and spears.

These hybrid craft, designed as they were to do the work of the clumsier junk but with more speed and efficiency, were not only faster, but for their size had a greater cargo capacity. These advantages were achieved with no sacrifice of strength; indeed, they were probably stronger than the junk. Planned more or less on the lines of European small craft, they were fitted with an adaptation of the Chinese type of stern and rudder. The two masts and rigging also owed something to the West as well as the East.

The standard rig of the early lorchas has not been authenticated. Some pictures of the middle of the nineteenth century show one or more top-sails and sometimes a jib. It may be argued that the representation of top-sails was a flight of fancy on the part of the artist so as to differentiate more clearly between the junks and lorchas in their pictures, but would so many artists have used the same artistic licence? One Jesuit observer writes of "lateen as well as round sails, of matting in some." This claim, if true, is extremely interesting. The lateen sail, though essentially Moorish or Arabian in origin, is in common use throughout the Mediterranean and also on the Atlantic coast of Spain and Portugal. It seems by no means unlikely, therefore, that the Portuguese should have introduced a type of rig so familiar to them. If this were so, the innovation did not in any way influence the Chinese craft, nor is this surprising, for there is no more conservative seaman in the world than the junkman, to whom all change is repugnant and who is always satisfied with what has served his father before him.

After the industry of building lorchas died out in Macao, these craft were still built on the same lines when made elsewhere. The "Customs Trade Returns" of

1881 quotes the cost of the lorcha as being $16 to $25 per ton when built in China and from $25 to $30 when made at Singapore. This raises an interesting point indeed as to the number of these craft that hailed from Malaya, and might seem to some degree to confirm a supposition that the lorcha originated in those waters.

Warington Smyth writes in 1906 of a fleet of about 60 foreign-owned lorchas in Bangkok. Built of local teak-wood, these vessels were of the usual Chinese three-masted rig so as to facilitate management by the Chinese crew.

The lorcha is the only Chinese vessel which has not only a European character but a stirring history bound up with the development of Western trade in China. They are unhappily now seldom to be seen. A few are laid up in out-of-the-way ports; others are used as hulks. Their final disappearance was surprisingly rapid. Twelve years ago 10 or more of these craft could be seen on the Yangtze awaiting a fair wind at one of the intricate and narrow river crossings, but within five years they had vanished completely from the river.

The specimen illustrated in Plate No. 82,* therefore, has a peculiar interest, for it shows a type of craft which has passed from the China waters. She was found at Ningpo, laid up and fast disintegrating, probably the last lorcha remaining to-day.†

Like her ancient prototypes, she has her name *Yuansing* (源 興), or "Prosperous Origin," painted in English and Chinese on bow and stern. Three varieties of wood were used in her construction, camphor-wood being used where hardwood was necessary and Oregon pine and fir elsewhere. Her over-all length is 136 feet (including the bowsprit), with a beam of 24 feet, a depth of 7 feet, and a burden of about 300 tons. That is to say, she is of the standard size as formerly built in Macao, but considerably smaller than the Siamese-built lorchas, which were said to have an over-all measurement of 200 feet.

There are nine watertight compartments divided by eight camphor-wood bulkheads, and with frames spaced at appropriate intervals, but not necessarily in the centre of each watertight compartment. The bulkheads vary slightly in thickness from 4 to 5 inches. The frames are 7 inches in thickness. The vessel is of light draught and with a flat bottom, though with a light keel.

The foreign-type long slender hull is not graceful, but eminently practical, and displays a quite unusual manœuvrability. Proof of this was formerly frequently to be seen on the Yangtze, when down-bound lorchas would negotiate the narrow and winding "flagged channels" of Matung and Oliphant Island with surprisingly few groundings. When up bound they would use their own tugs stationed at these points to assist them for only a very short distance.

Longitudinal strength is provided by three strong wales which follow a gentle curve from bow and stern, dipping amidships nearly to the water-line. In this instance there is a more or less swan bow, but a straight bow was on the whole much more usual in these craft. The bow is always sharp and ends in a heavy stem-piece, on the port side of which projects the 7-foot capped bowsprit. When the vessel is light, the bowsprit is about 15 feet above the water. These spars, although still present in the lorchas, are not used in any way, nor are they rigged at all. If, as seems likely, they were originally used by their foreign designers to carry a jib, this is an instance, frequently met with, of the conservative Chinese who, having once adopted a fitting or method of construction, perpetuates it in all later shipbuilding even when the use for which it was intended has utterly lapsed.

The deck, which is of very much better construction than is usual in Chinese craft, serves to lend additional support to the vessel. The small house, measuring 16½ by 11½ feet, is situated abaft the mainmast. There are four cargo hatches, varying in size from 4½ to 7 feet across.

* This plan was made from measurements painstakingly taken for me by Mr. Tao Ting Sing, Second Class Tidewaiter.

† In 1937–38, one or two very old lorchas, without masts, but with auxiliary motor engines, locally known as "puff-puff motors," ran between Shanghai and Ningpo.

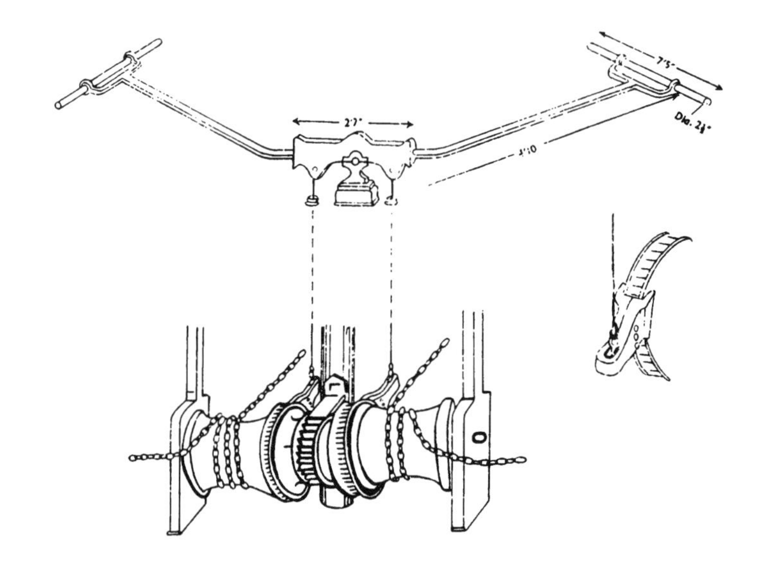

The windlass.

The bulwarks on the high forecastle, as on the poop, measure 1½ feet in height, but increase to 2½ feet on the main deck. The square overhanging stern measures 16 feet from the poop to the water-level when the vessel is light. The flat angular counter, as viewed broadside on, takes a semicircular aspect when seen from astern, while the bottom planks of the hull ascend in a gradual curve to meet it.

The small Chinese-type rudder measures 8 feet 2 inches by 5 feet. The tiller, consisting of three 5-foot 8-inch iron rods, is situated abaft the rudder-post. This position, of course, is unknown in the average junk. Steering is by means of wheel and chains, the standing parts of the chain being secured to the ship's side, while the bight, travelling first through blocks attached to the after-end of the tiller rods, returns to the ship's side, passing through more blocks for further purchase, and thence round the barrel of the steering wheel.

There are three masts stepped in the usual Chinese manner, and the cotton twill sails are of the ordinary balance-lug variety. Stay-sails, if such they can be called, for they are completely unconnected by stays, are sometimes set between the fore and main masts. The modern variety of this sail is jib-shaped, that is to say, triangular. There would therefore seem to be an historic interest in the fact that the stay-sails as used by lorchas were usually of the oblong shape common to old ships in the West. The odd appearance of this type of sail was enhanced by its being frequently roached at the foot. When so set the halyards travel through blocks at the fore and main trucks.

There is a foreign-type capstan on the forecastle and another on the break of the poop for hoisting sails. Below the forecastle is a windlass of the most primitive type for heaving up the anchors. The cable is brought directly to the barrel of the windlass, which is 4½ feet in circumference. The device is operated by pump handles situated on the forecastle. Two Admiralty-pattern anchors with wooden stocks are slung, one from each bow, from a cat-davit beam which runs from side to side across the forecastle.

The traditional picturesque manner of painting the lorchas has been preserved in this case, for the hull is a dark red-brown, the deck-house white, and the poop and forecastle a bright shade of yellow.

The crew numbered 20. The cost of the vessel was about $20,000 when new some decades ago. The normal run for this craft years ago was from Ningpo to Hankow with samshu, medicines, and beancurd; while on the downward trip wood oil, ramie, gypsum, and bones were carried. With a favourable wind a voyage could be completed in 10 days, but bad weather could prolong it to two months.

These craft are alternatively known by the junkmen as *chia-pan-ch'uan* (夾板船), or *ya-p'i-ku* (鴨屁股), "duck's buttock."

It is a matter for congratulation that, although the lorcha is passing, if it has not by now already passed completely away from the Far Eastern waters where it played so great a part, yet a realistic representation of it has been preserved for posterity in the Maze Collection* of Junks in the Science Museum at South Kensington. It is both suitable and gratifying that the most satisfying and meticulously accurate of all these models should be that of the lorcha, one of the most interesting and historic of the craft of China and the one most intimately bound up with the fortunes of the foreigners in their first adventurous endeavours in these far-off seas.

* The "Maze Collection" consists, according to the "Times," dated 27th October 1938, of "10 model Chinese junks each built to seale, complete and accurate in every detail, beautiful specimens of the Chinese modelmaker's art." The collection was presented by Sir Frederick Maze, K.C.M.G., K.B.E., when Inspector General of the Chinese Maritime Customs, to the Science Museum, South Kensington.

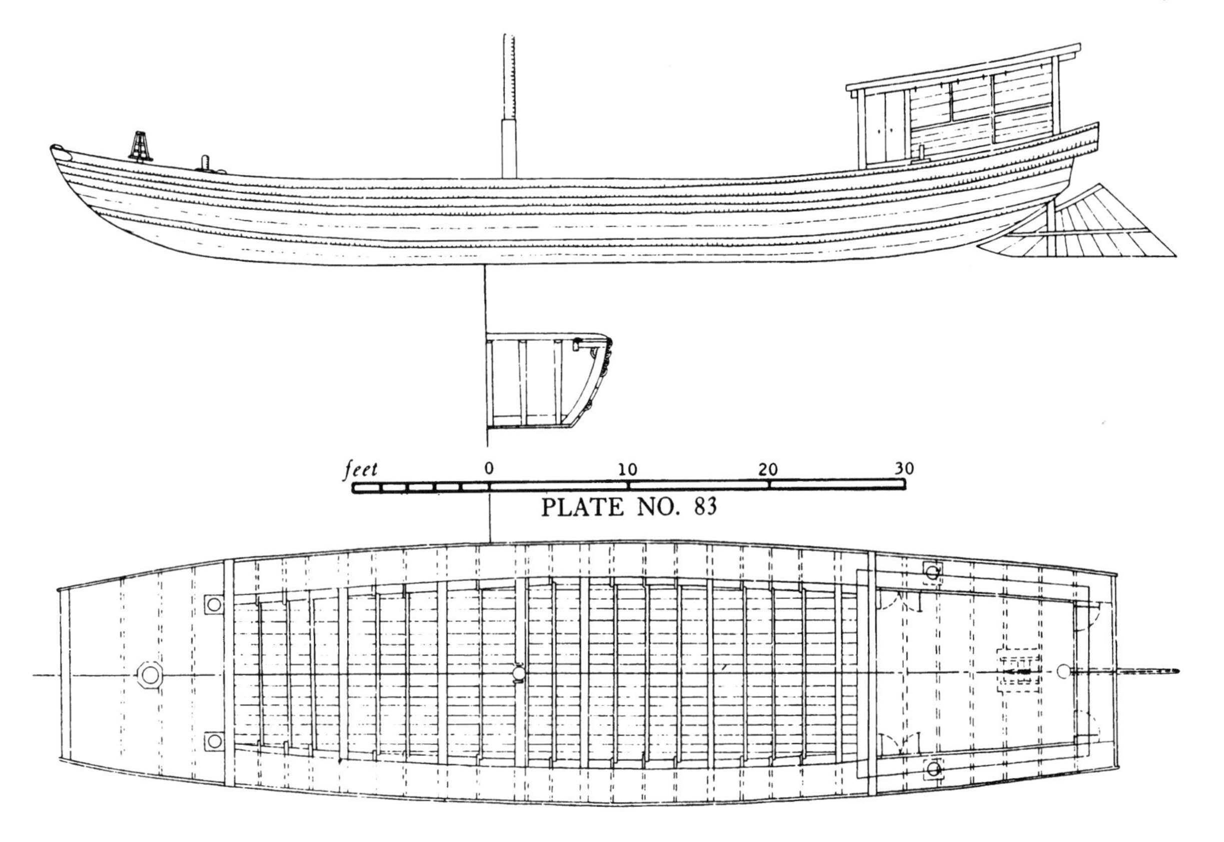

PLATE NO. 83

THE HANKOW CARGO-BOAT

The Hankow cargo-boats are used chiefly in connection with steamers. They carry cargo of all kinds from ship to shore and *vice versa*. At times, however, they make trips to various ports on the river under charter.

When working in the harbour they are paid according to a tariff which varies with the size of the package, distance carried, and so forth.

These craft are comparatively few in number and are usually to be found operating at the mouth of the Han River.

The cargo-boat illustrated in Plate No. 83 measures 74 feet and has a beam of 18 feet, a depth of 6 feet, and a capacity of 120 tons.

The Chinese shipwright is a master at the art of cargo-boat construction. As is natural, these vessels are built on massive proportions, plenty of beam being a desideratum. In build and lines they are somewhat similar to other cargo-boats, notably those of Wuhu, which are also about four beams to length. The stem and arrangements generally are almost identical.

THE RED, OR LIFE, BOATS OF THE LOWER YANGTZE

Only a few life-boat institutions (救生會) remain on the Yangtze to-day, and these are fast disappearing. Until comparatively recent times, however, life-saving junks could be seen stationed at many dangerous points on the river. These boats were strongly built and of great beam, and, with their wood-oiled sides and gaily uniformed crews, were remarkably smart-looking.

See also the Whangpoo life-boat, Part Two, page 225, and the *hung-ch'uan*, or Upper Yangtze life-boat, described in Part Four, page 528.

At Chinkiang there used to be a Life-saving Society with three branches, one at Silver Island, one near Golden Island, and a third on the north bank. The two former were under the management of a paid official selected by the Society but appointed by the Prefect of Chinkiang. This Society possessed 22 boats, large and small, chiefly hired, some of which were distinguished by being painted red, but all having characters denoting their purpose and station painted on their quarter and also on the flags.

Their duty was to assist any boat in distress. For saving a man's life they received a reward of 2,000 cash and 500 cash for the recovery of a corpse. If the body was unclaimed, half this amount was paid to the boat's crew and the balance used to defray burial expenses.

The crews of the boats stationed at Golden Island received no wages but were allowed to make use of the boats in carrying passengers and goods across the river when others would not venture out. To anyone with a knowledge of the Yangtze, it must be startling to read of a life-boat station on Golden Island, which is now a precipitous rocky hill a few miles inland, but it was, as its name implies, and as we have already seen, once an island in mid-stream.

The crew of the large boat of the Silver Island institution used to receive an allowance of 1,320 cash a day and the smaller boats 450 cash, neither being permitted to trade.

At Kiukiang a humane society, known as the I-tu Ch'u (義渡處), was formed in 1872 with the object of saving lives and recovering corpses from the river. It possessed four life-boats.

The Wuhu Life-saving Association was revived about 1873 and amalgamated with an association formed to provide coffins gratuitously. The offices of the Association were prominent on the bank of the river, just below the mouth of the creek. The three life-saving boats were well found, well manned, well handled, and able to face any weather. The crews were under very strict rules. When there was danger, they cruised up and down the river, aiding vessels in distress, rescuing the drowning or recovering bodies for burial, and saving property, for which they received small rewards in addition to their pay. If the rescued was a stranger and left destitute, he was lent dry clothes and given shelter for three days and a gratuity of 200 cash for each 100 *li* of his journey home. A free ferry was established in 1875. Four large ferry-boats used to ply at all times, but were chiefly valuable for those who would otherwise have risked their lives by trying to cross the river in ordinary sampans in bad weather.

The Chinese solicitude for the victims of shipwreck and especially in connection with the recovery of the corpses of the drowned has its roots in the cult of ancestral worship; for as it is always of the utmost importance to a man to know where his forbears are buried, it becomes a double disaster if, in addition to his being drowned, his body is not recovered.

These unfortunates are especially remembered on the Chinese All Souls' Day, Yü Lan P'ên Hui (盂蘭盆會), *i.e.*, the Festival of the Hungry Ghosts (餓鬼), or " Relief Mission to Ghosts," to give its modern equivalent, which begins on the 15th day of the 7th moon and lasts until the 30th.

On the 1st day of the moon the gates of purgatory are opened, and the hungry ghosts troop forth for a month of enjoyment of the good things provided for them by the devout. On the night of the 15th food is set out for them, and temporary altars are established at various points whereat the priests chant liturgies summoning the "hungry ghosts" from the " ten directions of space." The image of the Ti Ts'ang Wang (地藏王), or God of the Underworld, always figures largely at all feasts of the dead. Bags of imitation money are laid on the altar, and paper money is burned everywhere for the enrichment of the needy spirits. All the offerings bear strips of red paper with the name of the deceased and date of his death, and that of the contributor who has remembered him, who hopes to acquire merit and protection in return.

The particular protection provided on the night of the 15th for the souls of the drowned takes the form of launching little red paper lanterns to float down the rivers, so that by their light the disconsolate spirits of the drowned may be led to that place whence they may be born again or, more fortunate still, attain supreme enlightenment. These little lamps are made in the shape of the sacred Buddhist lotus flower and are called *ho-hua-têng* (荷花燈), or *lien-hua-têng* (蓮花燈), both signifying " water-lily lamp." *

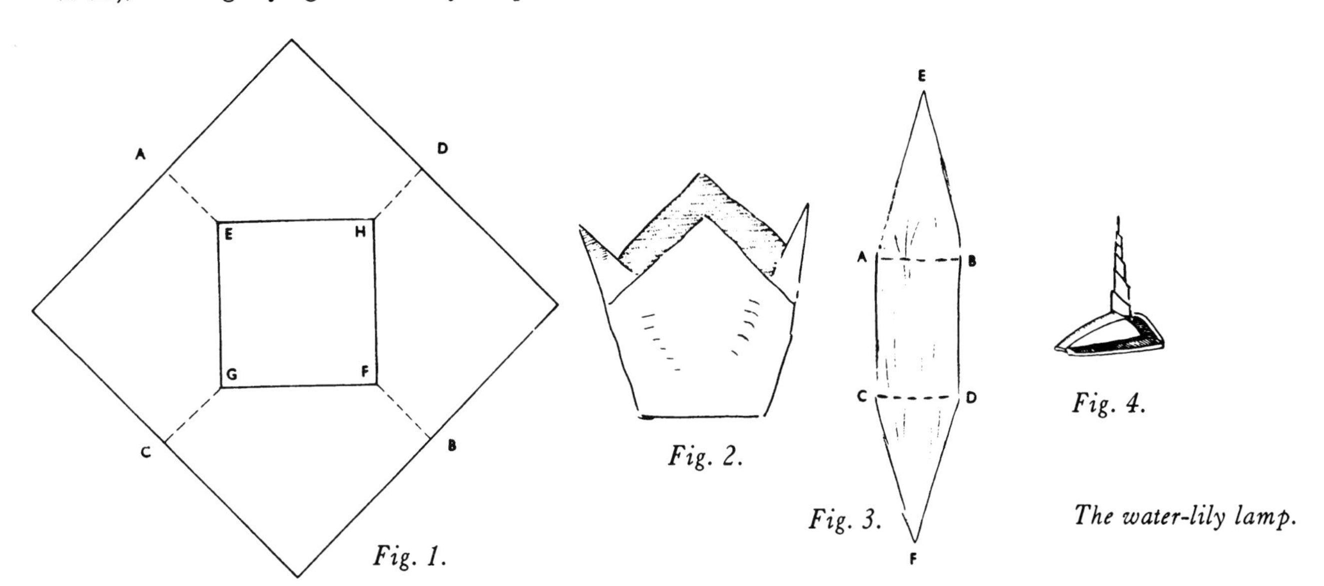

Fig. 1. *Fig. 2.* *Fig. 3.* *Fig. 4.*

The water-lily lamp.

As will be seen (*illustration above*), they are fashioned of 8½-inch squares of red paper soaked in the resinous oil of the pine tree to make them waterproof. The outer square is cut along the lines AE, DH, BF, and CG. The paper is then folded on the lines EH, HF, FG, and GE, and gummed at the cardinal points of the inner square so as to form a four-petalled container as shown in Fig. 2. The wick, which is made of a kind of parchment, is cut to the shape shown in Fig. 3 and folded along the lines AB and CD, the extremes E and F being screwed together into a point as shown in Fig. 4. It is then soaked in vegetable oil, lighted at the tapered end and placed in the paper container. These frail little lanterns, under favourable conditions, may be counted upon to float down river for a distance of 10 *li*, or over three miles, before burning out. When this lighted lantern is finally extinguished the junkmen believe that it is because a water spirit has swallowed it.

* My friend, Mr. A. C. H. Lay, tells me that this is the same idea as that behind the big Bon Matsuri festival of 15th July at Nagasaki, Japan, where, after a long, colourful procession, thousands of boats of all sizes made of paper are launched and float away.

THE MU-P'AI OR LOWER YANGTZE TIMBER RAFTS

Some Western writers of the early seventeenth century affirm that the rafts on the Yangtze were said to be a mile long. This is hard to believe, for the difficulty in negotiating the bends in the channels alone would discredit so fantastic a claim.

Sir George Staunton, the observant Secretary of the Macartney Mission, writing of the Yangtze timber rafts in 1822, says:

> "The river swarmed with rafts of timber, chiefly of the larch and camphor trees, destined for middle and northern provinces. These rafts were supplied with masts and sails by which in fair winds they would stem the current; otherwise they were trailed by persons who lived on board in cabins built expressly for them."

The *mu-p'ai*, or timber rafts, are still a characteristic feature of the Lower Yangtze to-day. They vary considerably in size. The larger ones have the appearance of floating villages, for small matshed huts, often as many as a dozen, are erected on them in two or more rows, so as to accommodate the raftsmen and their families for the long passage down river.

Rafts vary widely in build, the differences in construction being due to the traditions of the locality in which the raft is built, to the idiosyncrasies of the various timber guilds, to the depth of water likely to prevail in river or lake when the raft is *en route*, and to the ingenuity of the builders in devising forms, more especially as regards depth, which will, if possible, baffle the Customs.

The Lower Yangtze rafts may be divided into two classes: the Hunan rafts, from the vast tracts of forest surrounding the north-western shores of the Tungting Lake, and the Kiangsi rafts, from the regions around and beyond the Poyang Lake.

The logs, or poles, which make up the former class, are floated down in large but shallow rafts, which are described in the section of this book which deals with the Middle Yangtze.

This section begins on page 447.

Ten miles above the mouth of the Han River where it debouches at Hankow,

and on the left bank of the Yangtze River, there are timber yards, and here the Hunan rafts are assembled and rebuilt into great rafts varying in size from 300 to 500 feet in length, with a breadth of from 50 to 70 feet and a depth of 8 or 10 feet. Page No. 377 shows this rebuilt deep-draught type. Made, as a rule, in 8 or 10 sections, they comprise on an average from 10,000 to 15,000 spars of all sizes from 20 to 30 feet and with an additional thousand or more planks laid down as a deck. Some of the planks are 10 to 12 feet long, 24 to 27 inches wide, and 3 to 4 inches thick.

More often than not each raft is double, that is to say, it consists in reality of two rafts of different sizes, a secondary raft being attached and lashed end to end onto the main structure by means of stout bamboo cables. When such is the case the fore, or leading, section usually has a greater beam than the rear section. Typical measurements of such a raft are: fore section: length 236 feet, beam 80 feet, draught 18 feet; rear section: length 99 feet, beam 52 feet, draught 17 feet. The intervening space varies from 1 to 4 feet according to the extent of the projection of the submerged poles at the ends of the rafts.

In the autumn, with falling water, three-fold rafts are often to be met with, but they are invariably of much shallower draught than their spring and summer forerunners. The sides and bottom do not present the smooth and symmetrical surfaces one would expect. On the contrary, they are rough and uneven and show countless crevices and interstices. The crafty ingenuity of the lumbermen and timber merchants has been set to the problem of constructing rafts the true depth of which it is almost impossible to determine. Hence they are built much deeper down the centre than at the sides.

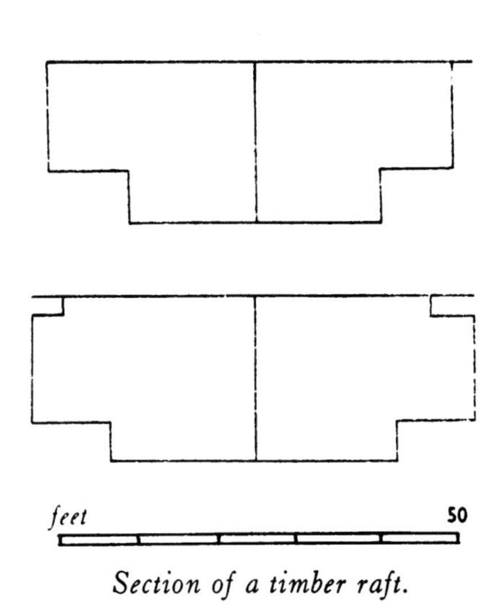

Section of a timber raft.

The widely projecting *fu-mu*, or side timbers, below the water-level are built out in such a fashion as to prevent, if possible, a measuring rod from reaching the true bottom of the raft beneath the centre portion. In a few cases the top of the *fu-mu* may be level with the water, but in others it is deeply submerged;

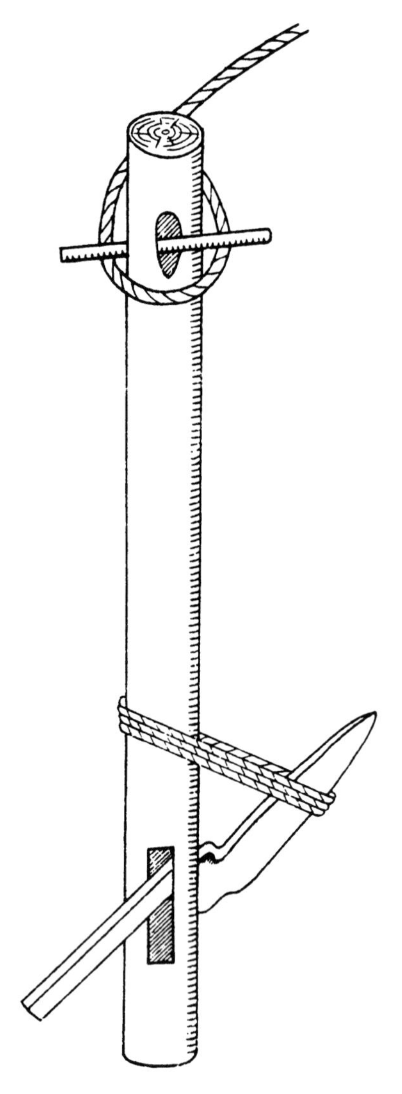

A long, wooden anchor used for rafts.

usually the top is from 2 to 5 feet below the water-line. This lateral projection may extend for 10 to 11 feet, its length being conterminous with the raft, while in depth or thickness it would measure from 4 to 9 feet. The Tayeh rafts are shining examples of the art of *fu-mu* construction.

A long, narrow, shallow bridge of rafts is used at the mooring places to connect the main structure with the shore. The mooring ropes are made of bamboo secured to a wooden anchor 7 feet long which is buried on the foreshore. Such an anchor is illustrated.

Down each side of the deck on every large or average-sized raft runs a double row of living quarters and shops to house the complement of from 120 to 200 men, who consist of crew, supercargoes, lumbermen, cooks, watchmen, barbers, butchers, and all their families. The owner, or his deputy, has a slightly better house with kitchen and reception room, the last two being nearly always provided with a small built-out veranda. Bamboo rope alone is always used for hawsers, mooring, binding the structure, or steering purposes; and spare coils of this tough cable are stowed in the alleyway between the huts of the "village street." At various points deck cargo in the shape of poles, and sometimes firewood or brushwood, is built up to a height of 10 or more feet in such a way as to leave alleyways and living quarters in the structure of the stacking.

As before stated, the rafts are nearly always constructed so as to circumvent the Customs duty. Before the days of Maritime Customs control of the Native Customs, taxes on a raft were assessed according to the breadth immediately in front of the capstan, and rafts in those days were in consequence built on a bottle-shaped plan, with the capstan at the neck of the bottle. This interesting shape immediately vanished when the Maritime Customs took over and duty had to be paid according to cubic capacity.

The masts and sails Sir George Staunton spoke of at the end of the eighteenth century are never to be seen now. The raft's rate of progress down stream is entirely at the caprice of the current, although small launches are sometimes used to accelerate the passage of the raft and to assist in steering through difficult channels.

The bow of every raft or, where there are two or more joined together, of the main section consists of an open platform. In the middle of it is situated an enormous capstan about 12 to 14 feet high. Round this huge drum, which is really a many-sided framework, the bamboo cable revolves. Comparatively short capstan-bars are fitted at breast height. The centre pivot consists of a well-turned baulk of camphor-wood. The cross-bars supporting the pivot are themselves in turn supported by four trestles. The function of this capstan is to heave the large drogues, or sea anchors, by which means the raft is kept heading in the desired direction.

The ancient Egyptians were past masters at this art of drifting, and Herodotus gives an account of what is, probably, the earliest form of drogue, made of matting on a wooden frame. By this means the boat's head was kept heading down stream, and even to-day this same method is used by the timber rafts of the Yangtze.

This drogue consists of a huge rectangular wooden frame. Over this is stretched matting strengthened by battens. A cross-bar through the centre permits it to pivot from the horizontal position across the attendant sampan into the submerged vertical position, where the resistance offered by its surface to the water enables the men to haul the raft in the direction required by the aid of the great capstan, round which they walk to the beat of a drum and gong.

When it is decided to make use of the drogue, it is sent out in the sampan

Capstan on a timber raft.

with a large coil of bamboo rope in the stern. This is cast out as the sampan leaves the raft. When the boat has reached a distance of about 200 feet away, the laodah beats a loud tattoo on his drum. At this signal the boat's crew lowers the drogue into the water so that it rests in a vertical position against the side of the boat nearest to the raft. The capstan crew on board the raft then heaves in on the bamboo cable. This, though it effects no progress towards the sampan and drogue, yet succeeds in checking an undesirable drift in the opposite direction, and so by means of patient repetition of the laborious process enables these huge clumsy rafts to negotiate bends in the river that are almost at right angles. The same method is employed to clear a shoal or round a point.

The voyage down river, a distance of some 500 miles, can usually be completed in from two to four months. Grounding in the shallows, however, and other accidents may render it necessary to take the raft to pieces and rebuild it again several times before it reaches it's destination, and the passage under adverse conditions may take as long as a year. During the greater part of the time there is little for the men to do; but occasionally their work is arduous, as when warping their unwieldy craft round the various bends or over the crossings on the river.

A few of the rafts go as far as Shanghai, but more often they are broken up at Chinkiang, whence the wood is taken by river or canal to the various centres.

It is recorded that in 1867 there was an extensive trade in the transport of timber from Hankow and Chinkiang. Vast quantities of wood for buildings were required upon the expulsion of the Taipings from the country adjacent to Soochow and Nanking, as also in the north-bank districts. The rafts, often with foreign financial backing, and even sometimes with foreigners in charge, were floated down river in large numbers to fill these needs.

Needless to say, the Yangtze rafts are a menace to other craft and the bane of the River Inspectorate of the Chinese Maritime Customs.

The main structural differences that distinguish the Kiangsi rafts from the Hunan variety is that the former are more symmetrically built and are rarely to be found with the widely projecting *fu-mu*. The pontoon raft-bridge connection with the shore is much more rare, and there is little attempt at planking. Such planks as there are, are insignificant in size, and the deck is covered instead with short lengths of small poles roughly planed and battened together in groups of three or four. Another typical variation is in the nature of the deck cargo. Some of the Kiangsi rafts carry piles of neatly stacked coffin logs, others heaps of firewood, or some may carry both.

There is naturally a wide range in length and breadth, but a fair average would be 180 feet in length, with a beam of 50 feet. In the Kiukiang Customs records for the past 15 years, the largest reported single raft was some 280 feet in length, with a beam of 110 feet and a draught of 22 feet. Closely lashed to this, however, and registered in the same owner's name was a secondary raft of about 200 feet in length and of slightly less beam and draught.

A small proportion of the Kiangsi rafts are made up of camphor-wood, but the bulk of both this type and the Hunan rafts is made up of fir (*Cunninghamia sinensis*), the residue being mostly pine. Oak and cedar are rarely to be seen; occasionally layers of bamboo are incorporated, and they naturally add much to the buoyancy of the structure. The camphor tree is an innovation in Kiangsi. Originally, Formosa was the main source of the world's supply of camphor-wood. After the cession of the island to Japan, traders sought for new supplies. These were first found in Fukien, but were so recklessly drawn upon that they were soon exhausted. The growth of camphor trees was then fostered in the interior of Kiangsi in the forests at Kanchow and Kian and farther afield still in Yunnan. Of late years the Chinese Government has become alive to the dangers of thoughtless exploitation of the timber forests without due regard to the future or replacement of the trees cut down. A Ministry of Agriculture was accordingly inaugurated in August 1912, including a Department of Forestry, to remedy the losses incurred through wholesale destruction of the forests. This Forestry Department was of a purely nominal character until January 1916, from which time a real beginning was made in the science of keeping up the supply of timber.

THE YA-SHAO

鴨梢

Probably the most common type of junk in Hupeh is the *ya-shao*, or "duck's tail," so called from its shape, which somewhat resembles a duck's tail. This generic name is qualified by the name of one of their many home ports, for they hail from Hwangpei (黃陂), Siaokan (孝感), Wusüeh (武穴), Kichun (蘄春), Yangsin (陽新), Simakow (繫馬口), Ocheng (鄂城), Tsaitien (蔡甸), Sinti (新隄), Hanyang (漢陽), and Hwangchow (黃州). The variations in the 11 different types are not very noticeable to the foreign eye, although easily recognized by every junkman.

These junks vary considerably in size. The largest variety, illustrated in Plate No. 85, is 64 feet in length, 12 feet in beam, and 6 feet in depth, while the smallest type, illustrated in Plate No. 84, measures 52 feet in length and has a beam of 9 feet and a depth of 4 feet. The former are, as a general rule, built with nine bulkheads and five frames, while the latter have 14 bulkheads and two frames. In some types a small open staging, which projects for 2 or 3 feet over the stern, is fitted.

The hull is usually built of Hunan softwood, while the frames, beams, knees, and the wales are made of hardwood, such as camphor-wood (樟木) or *ch'un-mu* (椿木).

These junks are almost invariably two-masted. Both the foremast and mainmast are made of *sha-mu* and are stepped between two partners through a hole in the deck in the customary manner. The sails are of the usual balance-lug type, with straight luff, extended and stiffened by bamboo battens. The deck is flush throughout. A deck-house is usually built amidships with a bamboo mat

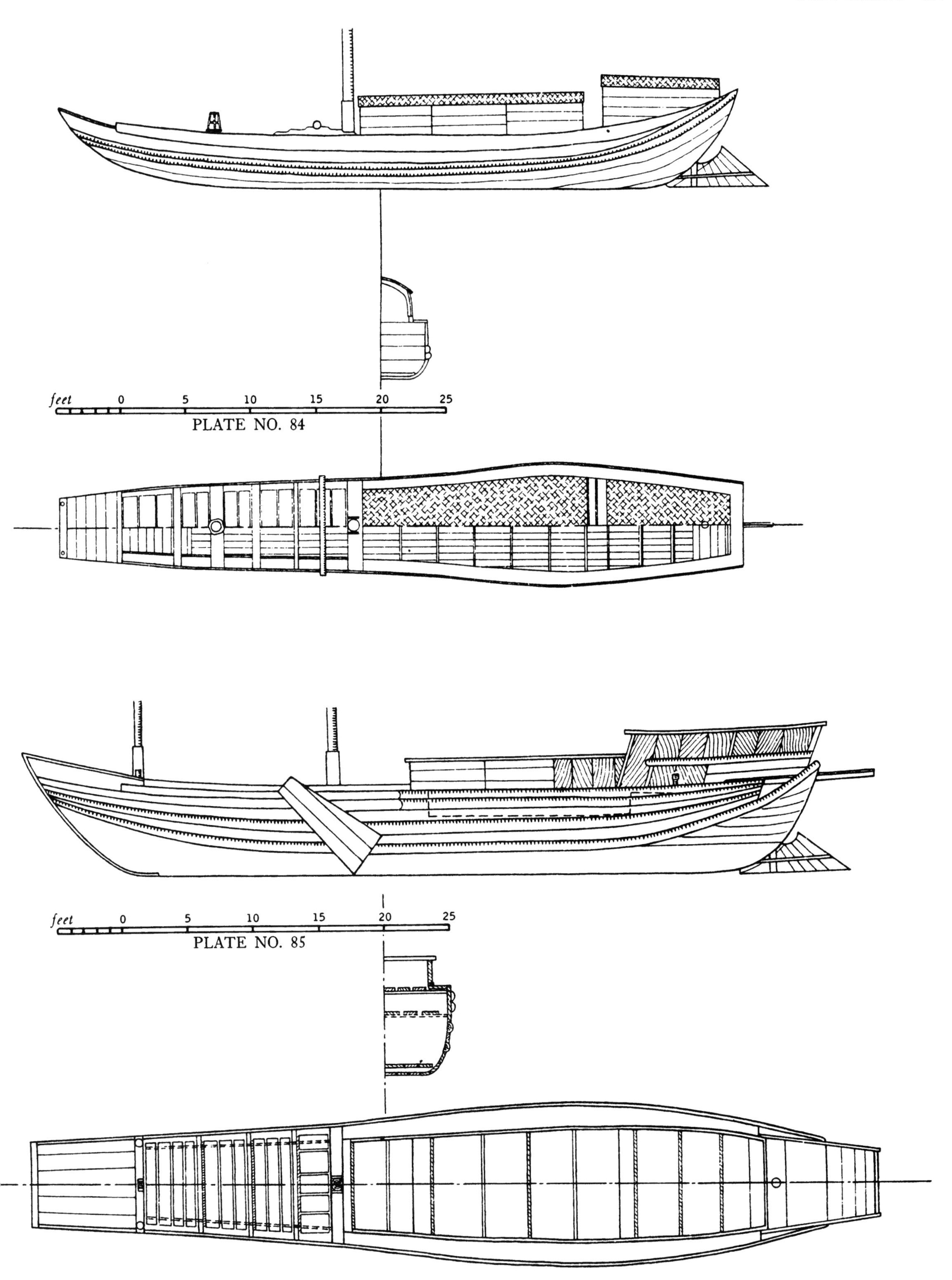
feet 0 5 10 15 20 25
PLATE NO. 84
feet 0 5 10 15 20 25
PLATE NO. 85

or wooden roofing, the sides being built up of softwood planks. The after-deck is nearly all covered in the same way, but leaving a cockpit for the helmsman, which also serves as a galley. The anchors are of the usual four-fluke variety, made of cast iron, the ground tackle generally consisting of 1 fathom of chain and 3 to 4 fathoms of rope. A large, low cat-davit, between primitive knight-heads, is often used for working cables. The bitts are usually in line with the foremast, and the capstan, which is used for hoisting the sails and heaving up the anchor, is conveniently placed between the masts. The crew consists of six or seven men under a laodah.

These craft, which have a capacity ranging from 50 to 800 piculs, are chiefly engaged in bringing native produce to Hankow and returning with foreign imports, factory products, and so forth. The local produce brought to the Hankow market is as follows. The Hwangpei and Siaokan *ya-shao*, with a capacity of 80 to 800 piculs, usually carry beans, rice, and raw cotton. The Wusüeh *ya-shao* carries ramie, hemp, sesamum-seed oil, roots, and rice. The Kichun *ya-shao* brings softwood planks, roots, firewood, vegetable tallow, chestnuts, and sugar cane. The Yangsin *ya-shao* carries tea, corn, kaoliang, and paper, and usually proceeds through Fuchihkow (富池口), a small inlet of the Yangtze River, taking some three days to Hankow. The Shakow *ya-shao* carries cotton cloth, raw cotton, rape seed-cake, and cow hides to Hankow and also sundries to Tsangtzefow (倉子埠), a town in the interior of Hupeh Province. The Ocheng (鄂城) *ya-shao* carries raw silk, cow hides, and other native produce, while the Kotien (葛店) and the Sinchow (新洲) *ya-shao* carry raw cotton, cotton cloth, groundnuts, roots, charcoal, and tobacco leaf.

The Puchi *ya-shao*, curiously enough, is not often found near its home port, but is mostly to be seen between Hwangshihkang (黃石港) and Hankow, bringing up lime and coal. The Sientaochen and the Tsaitien *ya-shao* are chiefly raw cotton carriers.

Generally speaking, the Chingshan and the Makow *ya-shao* are the largest among this type of junk; the former has a capacity of 400 to 800 piculs, while the latter runs from 300 to 700 piculs and formerly traded with ports beyond the borders of the province. This type is known for its good sailing qualities and can be counted upon to sail 40 miles a day up, and 70 to 80 miles down, river with a favourable breeze.

THE KIUKIANG LIFE-BOAT SERVICE

According to Mr. Worcester's notes, no plans were available for the following types, some of which were obsolete at the time of writing.

The Kiukiang Life-boat Service was established in 1886 by the tea and opium merchants to replace a small service of two boats controlled by the Tehwa-hsien (德化), and this society was managed by a board of which the principal members were the Hung Mei-hsi (洪梅熙) of China Merchants Steam Navigation Company. It operated four life-boats. One was stationed near the West Gate, one in the Lungkai Creek (龍開河), and two boats were used to ferry poor people across the river free of charge. The first two vessels used to cruise for a distance of 5 miles only above and below their respective stations. No statistics are available, but Customs reports of the day stated that, during the first six years of its existence, 63 lives were saved and four corpses were recovered. The boats' crews received a bounty of 1,000 cash for every life saved and 500 cash for every corpse recovered.

The Kiukiang life-boats differed only from the "ordinary junks," say the Customs reports, in having dark brown sails, a raised poop, and a small house amidships. They were of about 200 to 300 piculs burden. In addition, they carried their names and numbers written in a diamond on the bow, and an inscription painted on the stern giving the name of the location to which they belonged.

Taiping Road, Hankow, during the flood of 1931.

MAKESHIFT FLOOD CRAFT

We learn of numerous instances of extensive floods on the Yangtze referring back, we are told, to 922 B.C.; but not for hundreds of .years has so destructive an inundation ravaged the central districts as that which occurred during the summer of 1931, when 25 million people, inhabiting an area of 70,000 square miles, were affected in various ways by this the greatest flood in the recorded history of China.

Approximately 140,000 persons were drowned and a crop worth $900,000,000 was lost. The streets of the Wu-Han cities were flooded in some places to a depth of 9 feet, while the surrounding country was 30 feet under water.

Under these circumstances it is not surprising that the inhabitants used any sort of contrivance that would float. At first the cyclist could negotiate the streets, motor-cars could dash through the flooded thoroughfares, putting up a huge bow wave, and the ricsha could still make a rich harvest in carrying those unwilling to get their feet wet. But still the water rose, and boats made their appearance in the streets far from their true sphere. The taipans (大 班) used to go to their offices in sampans, sitting in state in arm-chairs. The police patrolled the streets in sampans fitted with outboard motors, a machine gun in the bows, and as many men in the stern-sheets as possible. The Fire Brigade boat was painted red and carried a portable hand-pump and many lengths of hose, while a bugler sat in the bow to blow a warning blast to the half-submerged carriages, ricshas, boats, tubs, and rafts of all kinds, that they might get out of the way in time.

Policemen on traffic duty sat on stools on the tops of pillar boxes or in trees. Overhead cables, some of them live wires, soon came within dangerous reach of the boat-hooks of sampans. There was a regular service of boats to the Race Club from the Bund in Hankow. Once out of that vicinity, the depth of water increased alarmingly, as is evidenced by the rule forbidding sampans to make fast to the chimneys of the houses on the Jardine's estate.

Even 50-ton lighters were used on the Bund, and with still rising water junks came blundering up the flooded and crowded streets to remove cargo from the godowns. The quanters fastened their boat-hooks onto the nearest object, such as telephone or electric light poles, some of which, with their bases undermined by the water, fell down.

The interesting feature of these abnormal conditions was the variety of curious and ingenious substitutes for boats that was pressed into service. Anything that could float took to the water. Tubs, planks, dismantled doors, wooden bedsteads, caulked boxes, and even coffins were to be seen paddling about the streets. The Post Office rose to the occasion and instituted a service of floating post offices housed in small junks which patrolled the streets, collecting and delivering mail, and selling stamps and postal orders. These floating post offices used a special cancellation on the stamps.

A junk, too, played a part in the culminating disaster. While the devastating flood waters continued a stranglehold on the city and the horrors of famine and disease mounted daily, a conflagration, probably the most destructive and spectacular ever seen on the Yangtze, broke out on the 27th August 1931 on the Texas Oil Company's property at Hankow. The fire originated in the cooking stove of a junk which was unloading benzine and which burst into flames. The burning spirit, which ran along the top of the water, was carried by the current into the Texas Oil Company's godown, and, before anything could be done to avert the tragedy, a blaze was started which, in a few seconds, had reached serious proportions. Smoke and flames from the burning oil rose up high into the sky to the accompaniment of continuous explosions as the heated steel drums of oil were shot up 100 feet into the air, there to burst with a loud report.

The flood at length receded, and it is interesting and fitting that the record of the maximum height reached by the water in the ex-Concession areas of Hankow was preserved by the presence of a sampan in the Hankow Club gardens. The sampan was mounted on four concrete pillars so as to represent the level at which she would have floated during the flood.

The inquisitive observer might well wonder why the craft, instead of being of a local type, should be one of the very distinctive Shanghai Harbour sampans. The presence of this stranger to Hankow waters was due to a Hankow taipan's desire to further the prestige of his hong by importing this gaudy little craft to carry him about his business in the flooded streets. This harmless piece of vanity was never gratified, for the Hankow sampanmen were quite unable to acquire the necessary technique to propel it. Hence its immolation as a bench mark to preserve to posterity the flood height of 1931.*

* Unfortunately it was removed during the vicissitudes of the Sino-Japanese War.

THE PA-TOU

The *pa-tou* is usually built in such a manner that her midship section bulges, and accordingly derives her name from the resemblance to a *pa-tou* (巴 斗), or " grain measure."

The hull is built of softwood, with hardwood frames and beams. These junks are generally two-masted, with balance lug-sails and straight luff. Hailing from Wusüeh (武 穴), they carry sesamum-seed oil, ramie, hemp, rice, tobacco leaf, china-root, and other native produce to Hankow and return with a general cargo.

THE PA-TUNG-TZŬ 巴東子

This junk is said also to resemble a *pa-tou*, or bamboo measure for rice, and is built of camphor-wood at Shiherhwei, at Nanking, and at Wuhu. In length it may be found as long as 125 feet, with a beam of 25 feet and a depth of 12 feet. The smaller varieties measure 90 feet, with a beam of 18 feet and 7 feet depth. Their carrying capacity varies from 300 to 600 piculs. The usual cargo up river is salt. The junk is a regular trader between Shiherhwei and Yochow. It has a crew of 24 men.

THE HUANG-KU-TZŬ 黄鼓子

This type of junk has a very small capacity of 100 to 200 piculs. They usually make one trip to Hankow in August, September, or October, bringing sugar cane, water chestnuts, and other perishable goods from Kiangsi and taking back gypsum and sundries.

THE MONK'S BOAT

Finally, mention must be made of one more boat well known indeed to the Yangtze junkmen. Although all believe in its existence, none can claim to have seen this mysterious craft, which is reserved for supernatural passengers only.

The craft in question is the begging bowl of the legendary monk called Pei Tu Ch'an-shih (杯 渡 禪 師), who frequently crossed all manner of rivers and streams in this novel conveyance, a singularly creditable feat of seamanship. There is something typically Chinese in the choice of a rice-bowl. In addition to this unusual habit, he was given to taking cold baths and would even break the ice in order to do so. The Chinese instinctive aversion to cold water, whether internally or externally applied, would account for the monk's being regarded as quite eccentric, even in China. He is commonly depicted as crossing the rivers and streams on a banana leaf or a reed.

THE POYANG LAKE

THE Poyang Lake is about 90 miles in length and almost 20 miles in breadth, but its condition, like that of the Tungting Lake, differs widely at various seasons of the year. Its waters are comparatively clear as contrasted with the Yangtze River.

Incidentally, the province owes its inappropriate name of Kiangsi, or West of the River, to the ancient division of all the country from Kweichow to the sea into one *tao*, or circuit, called Kiangnan, or South of the River. In the Sung dynasty, 960–1280, this was subdivided into six *lu*, two of which retained their names of Kiangnan Tung and Kiangnan Hsi, or South River East and South River West. From this the shortened form of Kiangsi derives.

For fully 30 miles from its entrance to the Yangtze the Poyang Lake has the appearance rather of a river than of an actual lake, in some places the navigable channel being only a few hundred yards in width and in no place more than a mile. It is finally, however, found to expand to an average width of some 15 miles with a total length of about 50 miles, though only a narrow channel in the centre is available for deeply laden junks.

Although it is said to be gradually silting up, junks are able to ascend at all seasons to Wuchengchen (吳 城 鎮), the chief port and commercial city. The provincial capital, Nanchang, on the Kan River, originally stood on the shores of the lake, but its waters have since receded some 35 miles to the north.

The lake is surrounded by a vast system of canals, which serve the treble purpose of communication, irrigation, and drainage. So numerous are the waterways of Kiangsi, both natural and artificial, that it is possible at certain seasons of the year to go from one large city of the province to any other entirely by water; but towards the end of the summer the water is often so thoroughly drained from the canals by irrigation channels to the rice fields as to leave their beds dry.

During the winter the greater part of the lake consists of sandbanks, more or less uncovered, through which passes a meandering channel of about 3 cables width. This channel is navigable for junks drawing 2 to 3 feet at all seasons of the year. In the summer, however, the whole area is covered.

About 6½ miles above Hukow, in the channel connecting the Yangtze with the lake, is a remarkable rock which much resembles that known as the Little Orphan in the river. It rises like a guardian of the passage and is usually known as the Big Orphan. It is also named the Hsieh Shan (鞋 山), or Shoe Rock, owing to its resemblance to a shoe, and has given rise to the legend that in ancient times the daughter of a king lost her shoe while fleeing with her lover across the lake and that the present island rose on the spot where the shoe sank. There are innumerable legends attached to the locality, and most of them associate the rocky islands known as Orphans.

The Chinese Classics state that the Emperor Yü of the Hsia dynasty, 2205 B.C., retired to the Big Orphan during the time of the great flood, the island being the only dry spot in the country.

T'ien Hou is the patron goddess of the island and is worshipped by sailors

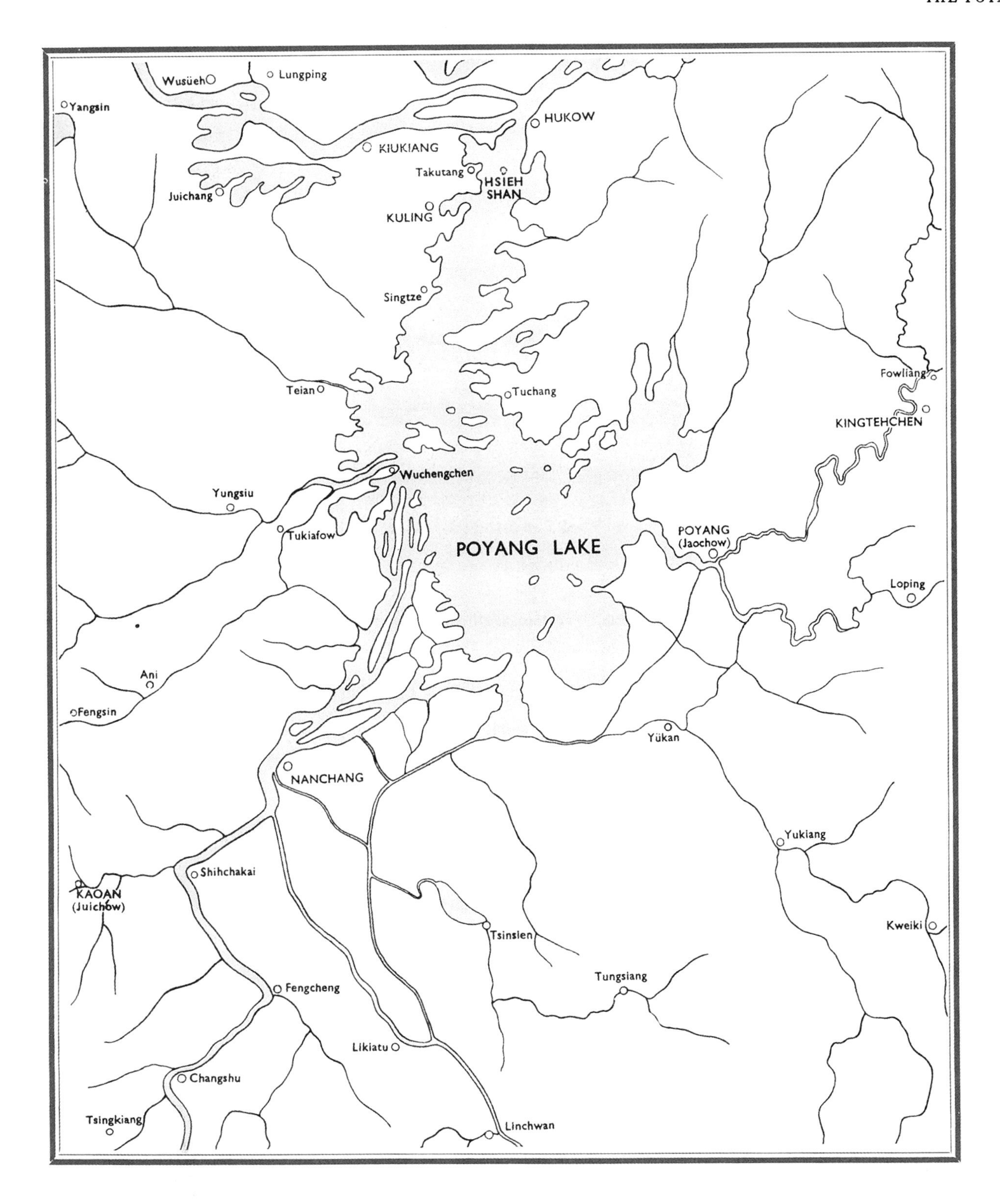

and fishermen. She has the reputation of being able to guide ships in peril across the lake at night, and women regard her as the last resort when praying for sons. The pagoda on the summit, which bears the name of Ling Yün Pao T'a (凌雲寶塔), or Glistening Cloud Pagoda, was built in the year 1681 and is supposed to be the guardian of the *fêng-shui** (風水) of the whole neighbourhood.

Another Poyang Lake legend concerns a well-known temple where the turtle is worshipped by boatmen, for according to their ideas the creature is capable of raising a storm when it " gets its back up." Instances are recorded and firmly believed in, in which many boats have been capsized and the occupants drowned owing to the latter's having been guilty of levity and disrespect towards the power and temper of the turtle.

* *Fêng-shui*, literally, "wind and water," or "that which cannot be grasped," or "that which cannot be seen." The great geomantic system of the Chinese, by the science of which it is possible to determine the desirability of sites, whether of tombs, houses, or cities, from the configuration of such natural objects as rivers, trees, and hills, and to foretell with certainty the fortunes of any family, community, or individual, according to the spot selected.

There are several places of interest in the lake, among others, Nankang (南康), at the base of the lofty Lu Shan Range, celebrated as the resort of literary men. Near here a renowned philosopher and interpreter of the Confucian doctrine resided about A.D. 1200. The town of Takutang lies 14 miles from Hukow, and as it is the last place affording a good anchorage that is reached on leaving the lake before arriving in Kiukiang, large numbers of junks are to be seen at anchor laden with produce from the interior, which includes tea, rice, cotton, silk, and, of course, porcelain from the kilns of Kingtehchen on the Ch'ang River.

The principal waterway feeding the Poyang Lake is the Kan River (贛江). It travels from south to north and cuts the province roughly in half. And down the river and its tributaries come junks carrying ramie, sesamum, rape, oranges, sugar cane, and cotton from the deep and fertile valleys of the province. Tributaries of the Kan are the Ch'ang (章江), draining the forest lands of South-western Kiangsi, the Jung (袁水), the Hsiu (修水), and the Jui (瑞江), from whence come tobacco, coal, and paper. Another tributary is the Fu (撫水). The Loan (樂安江) and the Ch'ang unite just below the city of Jaochow (饒州), the latter river being famous for its connection with the renowned porcelain industry at Kingtehchen* (景德鎮) and the no less celebrated Keemun tea.

In addition to the above rivers there are a great many small affluents, creeks, and canals which explain why the people of Kiangsi have never worried—until recently—about roads. This vast network of waterways served to bind the province together and make boat communication a matter of comparative ease. Indeed, this water-borne transport is not only confined to the province. So widely do these creeks and canals serve the country-side that junk transport obtains on the eastern border between Kiangsi and its neighbouring Province of Anhwei, while the land barriers that separate the water routes of Chekiang, Fukien, and Kwangtung Provinces from those of Kiangsi can be traversed on foot in a few hours.

The entire carrying trade of the Poyang Lake was, until comparatively recently, in the hands of the junks. There are several types specially constructed to negotiate the shallows and rapids. The *fu-shao-tzŭ* (富梢子), plying between Kingtehchen and Fowliang, is a long, lightly built vessel incapable of navigating the lake in bad weather. The Tuchang (都昌) junk, sailing between Tuchang and Kingtehchen, is engaged chiefly in importing foodstuffs and exporting porcelain on its return trip. The Hsikwang junk always carries coal and firewood to the Kingtehchen kiln burners.† The *shao-yah-tzŭ*, hailing from Jaochow, visits the town only in the high-water season. The *jao-hua-tzŭ*, a comparatively deep-draught junk, carries both goods and passengers between Kaoan and Kingtehchen.

The Poyang Lake is the home of craft that have elegant sterns. These junks vary greatly in size and type, their variety depending mainly on the depth of water and the nature of the waterway to be negotiated. Each type has some distinctive feature designed to suit some particular need.

The Poyang Lake was opened to steam navigation in 1896. At first the few invading launches contented themselves with the passenger trade and towing cargo-boats, while at the same time cargo continued to come in by junk. In 1911, however, the foreign-type wooden cargo-boat developed rapidly and later a dozen or more steel lighters began to make their appearance, and the number of launches rose from 11 in 1901 to 49 in 1917. The climax came with the appearance of motor-launches in considerable numbers and oil-tank lighters.

In addition, it is sad to relate, railway competition and the products of Mr. Dodge have had the effect of driving whole classes of junks out of existence, and others are fast following.

* English readers will be interested to learn that President and Madame Chiang Kai-shek gave a dinner set especially made at Kingtehchen to Princess Elizabeth as a wedding present.

† Every year more than 4 million piculs of firewood and 1½ million piculs of brushwood are required by the porcelain factories.

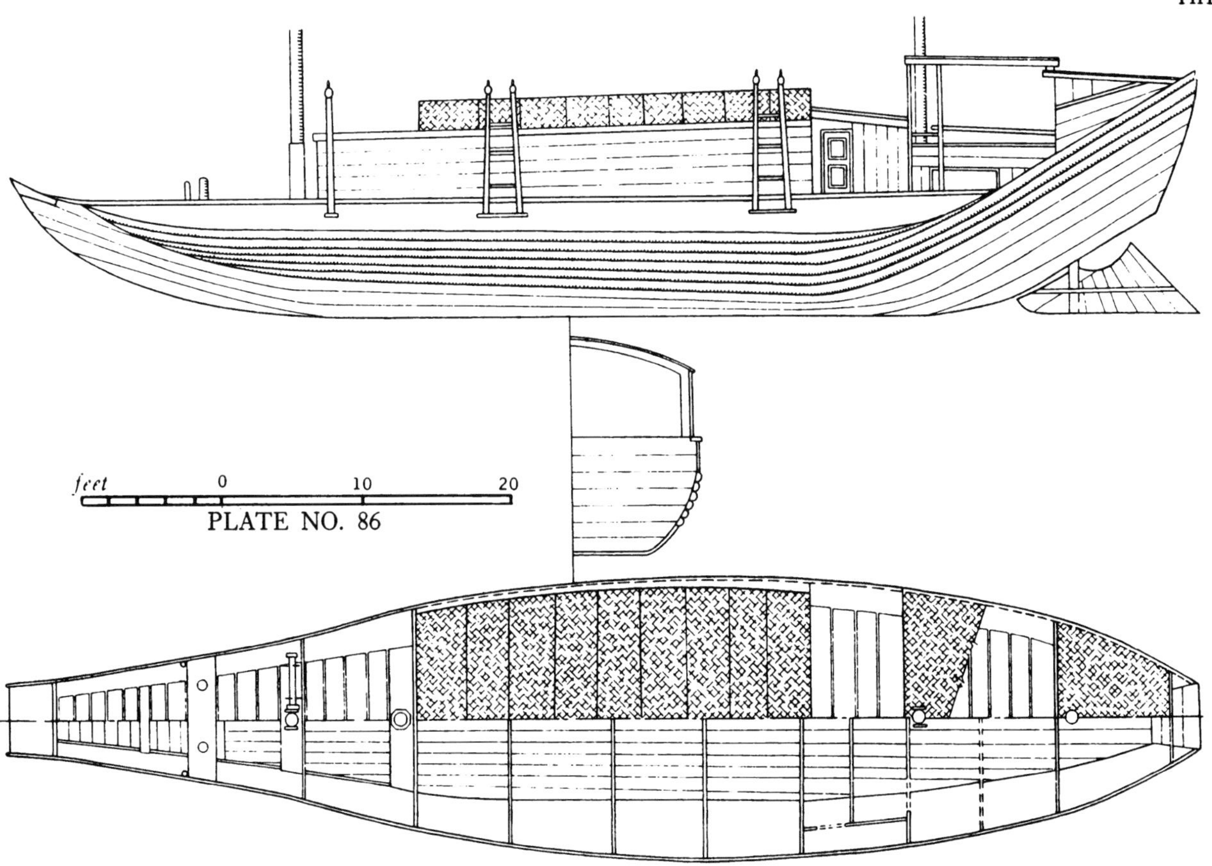

PLATE NO. 86

THE FU-TIAO-TZŬ OR RED SLIPPER JUNK

府凋子

The *fu-tiao-tzŭ*, or, to give its more common name, the *hung-hsiu-hsieh* (紅繡鞋), meaning the " lady's red embroidered slipper," hails from the Poyang Lake and is usually a large and heavy craft. They are of uncommon build, being very broad amidships and tapering sharply at bow and stern. This makes them appear somewhat unwieldy.

Another surprising and interesting feature of this type is the fact that the foremast is higher than the mainmast. The reason commonly given for this peculiarity is embodied in a legend connected with the Little Orphan Rock. This isolated pinnacle, 300 feet high, and surmounted by a temple and small monastery, is for the greater part of the year an island in the Yangtze River. During the Yüan dynasty, 1260–1368, a junk anchored one evening at the Little Orphan. On board was a rather notorious character, one Chang T'ien-shih (張天師), the chief of a Taoist sect well versed in the secret and occult arts. On their attempting to weigh the next morning it was found that the anchor would not come home. Chang ordered the crew to jump overboard to discover the obstruction, and the divers reported that the anchor was firmly entangled in a pair of lady's red embroidered slippers of the bound-foot variety lying on the bed of the river. All efforts to weigh being fruitless, Chang had perforce to make use of his extensive knowledge of magic, which he did with complete success, for not only was the anchor recovered, but the pair of red slippers as well. The shoes, however, belonged to Hsiao Ku Niang Niang (小姑娘娘), the goddess of the Little Orphan, who was one of the nine Niang Niangs, or Lady Healers. She had removed them before retiring and, not unreasonably, was exceedingly annoyed the next morning to find they had vanished. Suspicion naturally rested on the junk carrying Chang, who, in the meantime, had made sail and disappeared. The goddess, highly incensed, immediately gave chase. In his efforts to elude the angry goddess, Chang in his junk had turned aside into the Poyang Lake; and when it became clear that he was facing capture, he jettisoned the shoes, which became transformed into the hill known as Hsieh Shan (鞋 山), or Hill of Shoes. Notwithstanding, the chase still continued until Chang conceived the brilliant idea of deluding the goddess by reversing the positions of the masts, so that the foremast, now being taller than the mainmast, gave the impression that he was closing, while in actual fact he was still making off at a good speed in the opposite direction. Whether this was to alarm his pursuer by showing he had turned at bay again, or whether it was to make her think it was quite another innocent junk approaching, history does not relate; but, as the goddess appears to have lacked any knowledge of seamanship, the primitive camouflage was completely successful, and Chang made good his escape.

As a monument to this famous chase, the masts of the *fu-tiao-tzŭ* are always stepped in the unconventional order instituted by Chang T'ien-shih. Or that is what the junkmen will have one believe.

A "Custom House" was functioning at Kiukiang in the 4th year of the Emperor Hsüan Tê (宣 德), of the Ming dynasty, in 1429. We also know that there was a very old-established rule that measurements for calculating a junk's capacity allowed depth and beam measurements to be made only at the tallest mast, in this case, the foremast which, as will be seen from the plan, secures for this type of junk very preferential treatment. The consensus of opinion among the junkmen is that the rule was not made in order to benefit this type of junk in particular, but that the type was built to take full advantage of the rule.

If the rule was established at the time of the Customs first functioning at Kiukiang and if this type was built soon after, this class of junk could very reasonably be supposed to date back nearly 500 years.

These junks, which are the product of Kiangsi Province, are built at Kanchow (贛 州) and Nanchang (南 昌), and serve the Lower Yangtze, its tributaries and lakes. Made of camphor-wood throughout, the types vary in size from 60 feet in length, with a beam of 14 feet and 3 feet depth, to the great dimensions of 100 feet, with a beam of 28 feet and 9 feet depth.

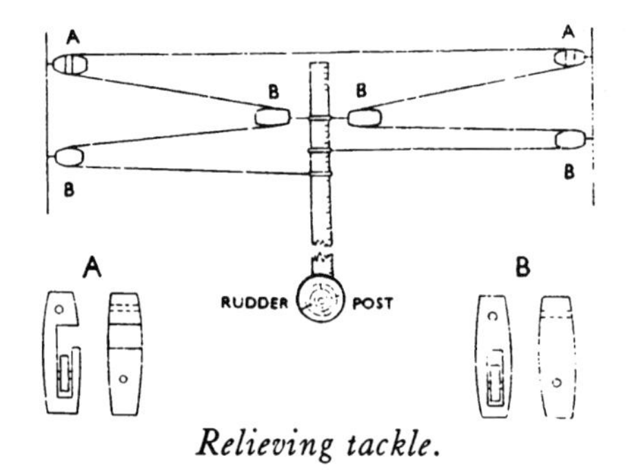

Relieving tackle.

The craft illustrated in Plate No. 86 is of medium size, measuring 84½ feet, 19 feet beam, and a depth of 7½ feet.

The number of masts varies according to the size. The smallest type sometimes has only one mast, while the largest can have as many as four. When three masts are fitted, the foremast is stepped between the windlasses, the mainmast forward of the centre deck-house, and the mizzen-mast abaft the house.

The carrying capacity ranges from 100 to 200 tons, and the cargo usually consists of salt, rice, paper, grain, and fruit. The smaller types trade through the Provinces of Kiangsi, Hupeh, Anhwei, and Hunan, the larger ones voyaging from Shiherhwei (十 二 圩) to Yochow.

The sails are of the common balance-lug variety with a slightly curving leech. The fore-sail has 32 battens, the mainsail 24. This is an unusual number. The sail stows on lumber irons. The height of the foremast in the craft illustrated is 75 feet, while the mainmast is 50 feet. A roller fair-lead is fitted to the foremast.

The crew vary from 16 to 24 men, according to the size of the craft, and are accommodated in the after-house, which is entered through a door. The conning position is situated just abaft the mainmast, the tiller being low and controlled by fibre rope rove as illustrated. A capstan is situated inside the house for hoisting the sails and weighing the anchors.

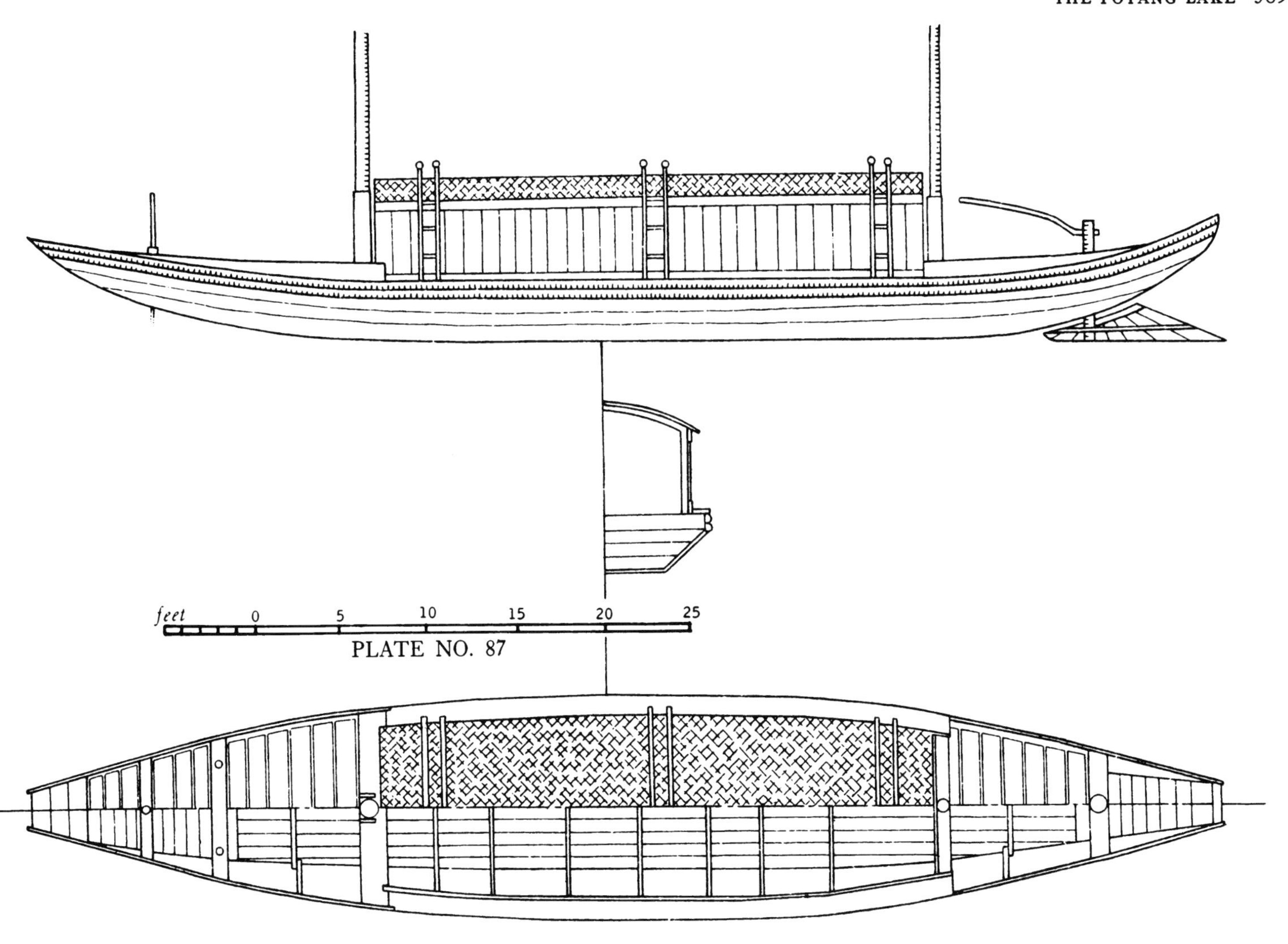

PLATE NO. 87

THE T'O-KOU-TZŬ OR LIGHT-DRAUGHT POYANG TRADER

拖鉤子

Another tale which preserves the same theory of a woman's shoe as inspiration for the design of a junk is to be found in the legend associated with the *t'o-kou-tzŭ*.

In very ancient days, so runs the old junkman's story, the shipwrights of the Poyang Lake, anxious to improve the design of their craft, appealed to the Emperor for ideas. The Empress, who was present at the time, anxious to end the audience, impatiently kicked off her red slipper, demanding what better pattern they could have than that.

The *t'o-kou-tzŭ* is a flat-bottomed, shallow-draught, mud-larking type of about 5½ beams to length. The craft illustrated in Plate No. 87 has a length of 66 feet, a beam of 12 feet, and a depth of 3 feet, with a carrying capacity of 120 piculs, about 7 tons.

Although light in construction, she is strongly built, having 12 bulkheads and three frames. On the ninth, tenth, and eleventh bulkheads partitions are built up to form two compartments. The foremost one serves as the galley, while the after compartment, which is fitted with a bunk, is the owner's cabin.

A "stick-in-the-mud" anchor is situated on the first bulkhead and a pair of small bollards on the second bulkhead. The usual lumber irons are secured to the house to accommodate the sail when not in use.

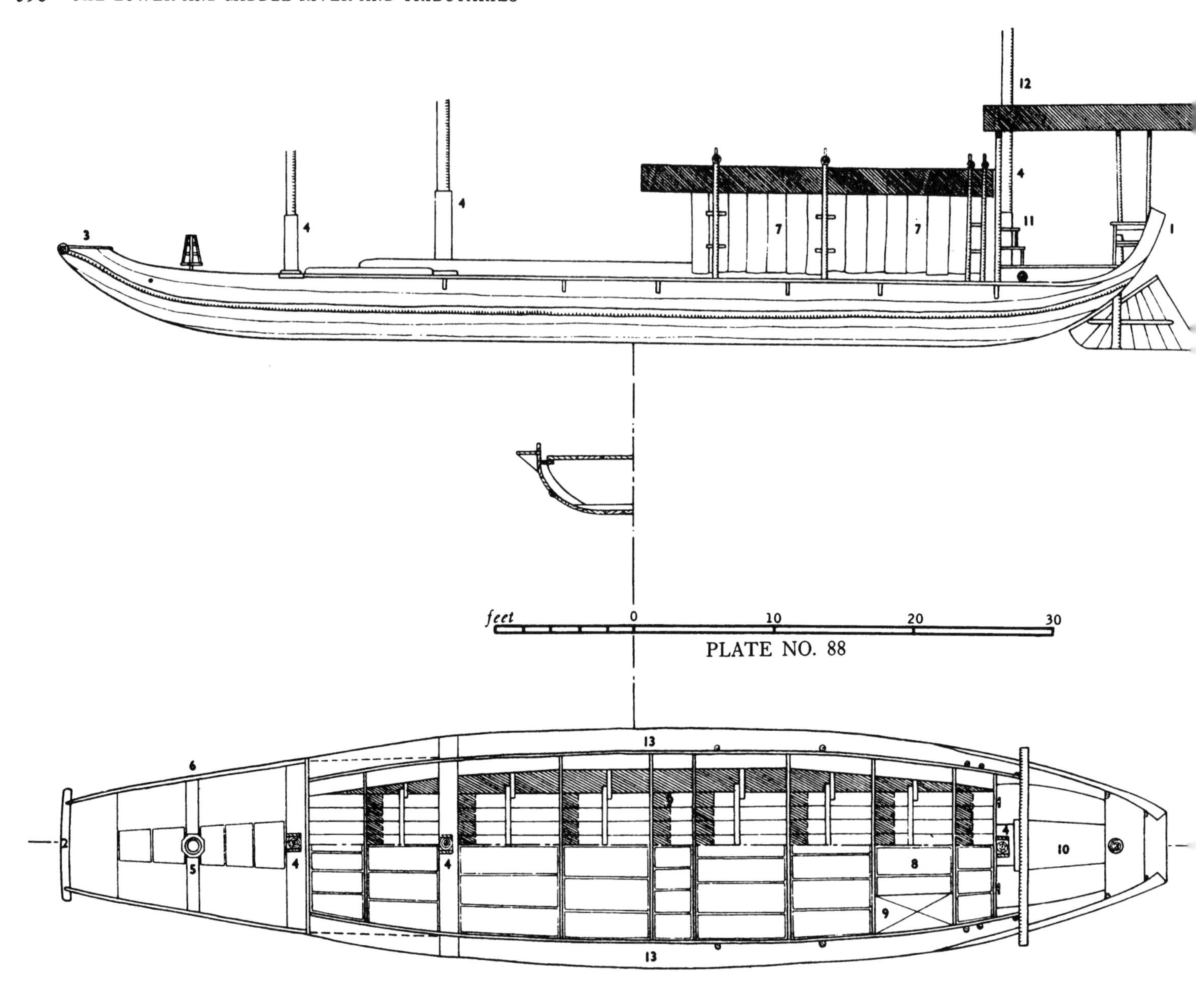

PLATE NO. 88

羅籠子 THE LO-LUNG-TZŬ OR PORCELAIN-TRADER

Chinese porcelain and pottery, its history and all the wealth of information concerning it, is probably one of the most written-up topics. Here it is not proposed to treat with this huge and interesting subject in any save a very superficial way; but to appreciate the importance of the industry it is essential to outline the manner in which the porcelain is produced in Kingtehchen (景德鎮), the great kilns of Kiangsi, and, above all, to describe how this fragile cargo is dealt with.

It is to China that the world owes the invention of porcelain. The date of its first appearance seems uncertain; but, according to Chinese tradition, pottery was being produced in the time of Huang Ti (黃帝), about 2800 B.C. There is evidence that porcelain was being manufactured in the T'ang dynasty, A.D. 618–907.

The ancient porcelain factory of Kingtehchen, or Mart of Brilliant Virtue, which dates back to the Sung dynasty, derives its name from the Emperor Chên Tsung (眞宗), 997–1022, who founded it in 1004. The best work produced was known as "tribute porcelain," which was baked in special furnaces called *yu-yao*, or *kuan-yao*, Imperial or official, as against *wai-yao* (外 窰), or *min-yao*, " outside," or popular furnaces. Only perfect pieces were sent to Kaifeng, the capital at that time.

Two kinds of earth, *pai-tun-tzŭ* (白 不 子), a hard, white, fusible quartz, and *kao-ling* (高 嶺), a decomposed felspar of granite, are imported from other places in Kiangsi and from Anhwei. Other ingredients have from time to time been tried, principally soapstone. Glaze is made by mixing the ashes of a fern which grows near the town with pounded *pai-tun-tzŭ*, forming thus a silicate of flint and alkali.

Artists and artificers are rated low, almost as labourers, hence lack of development in the painting and decoration of this porcelain. One man painted flowers, another circles, and so forth, and so individuality was stifled.

One of the chief difficulties in connection with this industry has been the problem of water transport, involving to some extent the importation of the necessary clays, but concerned principally with the exportation of the finished wares to the outside world, *via* the port of Kiukiang. The most difficult part of the journey is at Hungkiang, about 60 *li* down-stream from Kingtehchen. Here there are numerous rapids, and on the other portions of the river the level of the bed has been raised by an accumulation of the debris of broken porcelain which, for hundreds of years, has been thrown into the river with the mistaken idea that it would be washed away in the flood season. In some places there are only a few inches of water, and junks are continually grounding. In such an event the crew jump into the water and lever the craft along with poles through the shoal water. When, as often happens, even this method fails, the cargo is removed, and the vessel is partly lifted and partly pulled along. The sound produced by the rubbing of the bottom of the boat over the broken porcelain underneath is quite loud. This section of the river, although only 60 *li* long, takes a junk two days to get over. In the low-water season only small craft can be used in these reaches.

Between 20 and 30 shipping agents are concerned in this trade. A consigner hands one of these agents his invoice, and the latter charters the junk and loads the cargo. All responsibility devolves on the laodah for accident or pilfering. The freight charges are based on the *tan* system, a flexible term which may apply to six, four, or even only two pieces of porcelain, according to size and value.

Plate No. 88 shows a typical example of a shallow-draught porcelain-trader working the Poyang Lake. This type of craft is easily recognized by the high interrupted wing-stern[1].

The deck terminates in the bow in a heavy stem-timber[2], abaft of which is a raised platform[3] for the bow-man with his boat-hook. The fore-deck consists of outstandingly broad camphor-wood planks. The three masts[4] are made of *sha-mu*, and a wooden capstan[5], stepped in a strong beam[6], is used to hoist the three sails and to work the cables.

A deck-house[7] is situated at the after-end of the vessel and is used for stowing cargo as well as sleeping quarters for the crew. The after-end of the house is fitted up as a cabin[8] with two bunks[9]. The after-hold[10] is reached through a manhole.

The laodah stands on a raised plank[11], which is cut to receive the mizzen[12]. The conning position is fitted with a mat awning and in bad weather can be completely matted-in.

A projecting gangway[13] extends from the foremast to the conning position to facilitate the poling of the vessel in shoal water.

THE CH'A-CH'UAN OR TEA-BOAT

On the Poyang Lake there is a class of boat to which the name *ch'a-ch'uan*, or tea-boat, is more especially applied. Junks of this class are about 79 feet in length, with a beam of 12 feet. Though called tea-boats, they are frequently engaged to carry all kinds of cargo. This craft is illustrated in Plate No. 89.

The tea plant, a native of Southern China, was known from very early times to Chinese botany and medicine. It is alluded to in the classics under various names: *t'u* (荼), *shê* (蔎), *ch'uan* (荈), and *ming* (茗), and was highly prized for "possessing the virtues of relieving fatigue, delighting the soul, strengthening the will, and repairing the eyesight." Not only was it taken internally but was often applied externally in the form of a paste to alleviate rheumatic pains. The Taoists claimed it as an important ingredient of the elixir of immortality, and the Buddhists used it extensively to prevent drowsiness during their long hours of meditation.

The method of preparing tea in those early days was primitive. The leaves were steamed and crushed in a mortar, made into a cake, and boiled with rice, ginger, salt, orange peel, spices, and sometimes with onions.

It needed the genius of the T'ang dynasty, A.D. 618–907, to emancipate tea from its crude use and lead it to its final idealization, and tea then became a favourite beverage among the inhabitants of the Yangtze Valley.

The poets of China have left us some fragments of their adoration of the "froth of the liquid jade." Wang Yü-cheng (王 禹 偁), for example, eulogized tea as "flooding his soul like a direct appeal, so that its delicate bitterness reminded of the after-taste of good council," whatever that may mean.

In those days the preparation of tea needed the hand of a master to bring out its noblest qualities. Each preparation of the leaves had to have its own individuality, its "special affinity with water and heat." The "truly beautiful" had always to be in it. Like painting, tea-making had its changing cults. There were, for example, the classic, the romantic, and the naturalistic periods in the history of tea. In course of time tea began to be, in the words of a Chinese master, "not a poetic pastime but one of the methods of self-realization."

The Emperors used to bestow some rare preparation of the leaves on their high ministers as a reward for eminent services; and tea-drinking used, even until comparatively recent times, to be an important phase of the refined scholarly life. Every scholar had to be able to drink tea artistically, and was supposed to be able to tell not only the type of tea used but also the quality of the water used in brewing it.

Among the modern Chinese, sad to relate, the art of preparing tea and the appreciation of it are on the wane. The romance of the T'ang and Sung ceremonies is not to be found in the modern cup. Tea to-day is a beverage, not an ideal; indeed, tea-drinking has become little more than "watering the ox." Iced water, coca-cola, and the products of Mr. Lipton are possibly responsible for this mournful decline in the elegant national custom.

Nevertheless, the destiny of the China tea trade is one that touches Kiangsi very closely. For centuries now the province has held a leading place among the tea-producing districts.

The climate best adapted for tea is that which is warm, moist, and equitable throughout the year. The presence of iron in the soil is believed to be

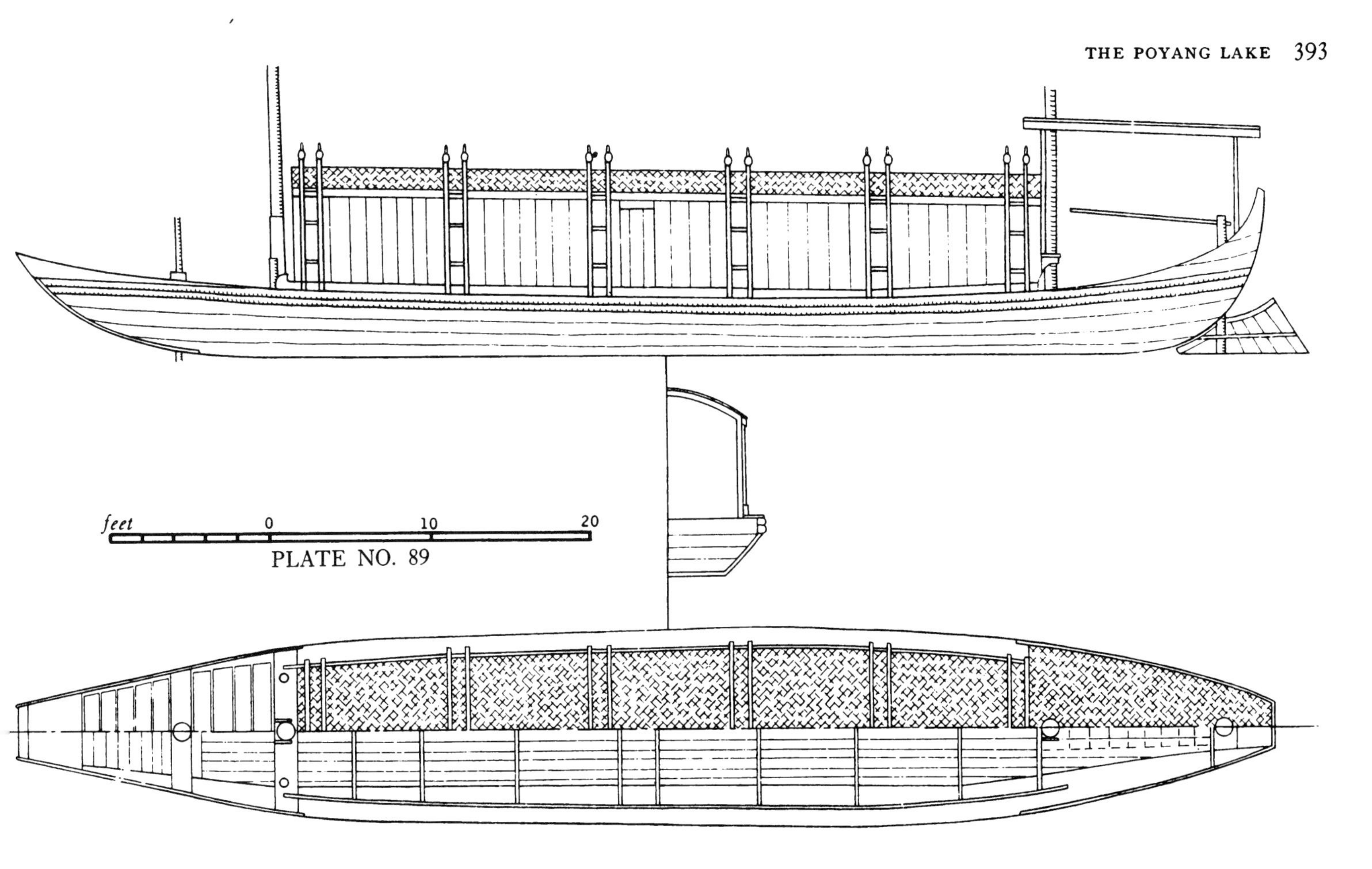

PLATE NO. 89

desirable, and hence red soils are preferable to others. All these conditions make the Chinese tea gardens well distributed on the slopes of hilly country, south of the Tsin Ling Range (秦 嶺 山 脈). The tea plant in China seldom exceeds 3 feet in height. The leaves are dull dark green in colour. About four crops are obtained each year, the first in April, the second in May, the third in July, and the fourth in September, each successive crop being less fragrant and consequently less valuable than the previous one. Green tea and black tea come from the same plant, the difference in colour being produced by different processes in the manufacture.

In the tea districts of the Yangtze Valley large tea gardens are unknown. Farmers originally grew merely what each needed, gradually adding plants as demands promised profits. They had, and still have, no scientific knowledge but followed the rough-and-ready methods of local tradition.

To trace the origin, growth, and the much to be regretted lapse of the China tea trade would be out of place here; suffice it to say that since the days of Robert Fortune there has been little or no change in China's methods of tea cultivation and manufacture.

Although most of the tea coming from the world-renowned gardens of Kiangsi is transported by land, there is still a considerable junk traffic in the trade on the Kuanghsin (廣 信), while the Ch'ang River is the natural outlet for much of the celebrated Keemun tea.

The junk most in demand for carrying tea is the *sha-pa-ch'uan*, a handsome craft usually measuring 79 feet in length, with a beam of 12 feet and a depth of 3½ feet.

The deck-house is larger and considerably higher than in most junks, and it is here that most of the perishable cargo of tea is stowed. The house is covered with a mat roof. The short decks at either end are connected by quanting gangways on each side.

The sails used are the classic balance variety, the mainsail being particularly large. When not in use it stows on six lumber irons.

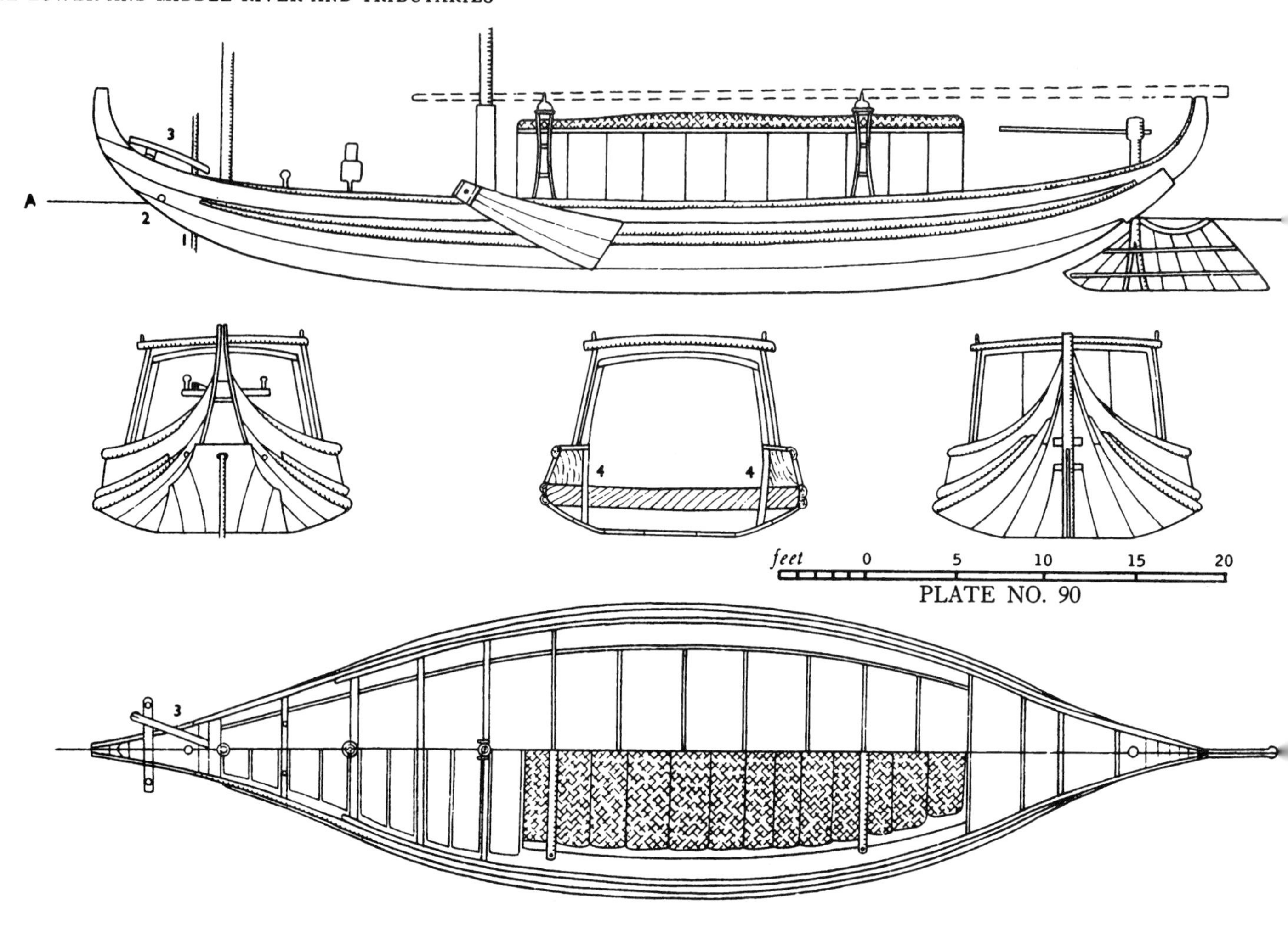

PLATE NO. 90

THE TO-LUNG-FU-CH'UAN OR GONDOLA-BOW JUNK

It is probable that tobacco was introduced into China by the Portuguese or the Spaniards during the sixteenth century.

The Emperor Ch'ung Chên (崇 禎) attempted to suppress the habit of tobacco-smoking by his subjects at about the same time as James I was doing the same thing in England, and with no better success.

Before the advent of the cigarette the Chinese were essentially a nation of pipe-smokers. They made their pipes of metal, cane, bone, bamboo, and many varieties of wood. The stick type of pipe is often elongated so as to form the double function of pipe and walking-stick, but the most characteristic is the hookah variety, as it is often necessary to purify the smoke by passing it through water.

It may come as something of a surprise and a shock to the connoisseur to learn that no tobacco is grown in Egypt and that 30 per cent of the raw material that goes to the make-up of the famous high-class Egyptian cigarettes of Mr. Simon Artz comes (or at least used to come) from China, possibly from Kiukiang. Indeed, so popular did it at one time become that Chinese tobacco threatened to drive the other brands out of the market altogether. Since the last war, however, this trade with China has dwindled.

Tobacco leaf is abundantly produced in the Poyang Lake area, and the river and creek routes in the hinterland provide adequate facilities for transport. The craft most commonly used in the tobacco trade is the far-famed *to-lung-fu-ch'uan*, or gondola-bow junk.

This double-ended type of junk, which hails from the Poyang Lake, is one of the most easily recognized on the Lower Yangtze because of the characteristically tapered bow and stern, with a graceful sheer down low between them, suggestive of a Mediterranean influence. The sharp lift to the overhanging bow is also typical.

Although there is little to justify it, the junkmen claim that this type belongs to the *lo-lung-tzŭ* (羅 龍 子) family, which is also of pure Poyang Lake descent. It is therefore known by the hybrid name of *to-lung-fu-ch'uan* and is locally known as the *lo-yüan*, or "round basket," a very appropriate name.

This type of junk is one of the most curious and interesting to be seen on the Poyang Lake. The foremost compartment is free flooding from the "stick-in-the-mud" anchor hole[1] and also from the two apertures[2], one on each side of the bow. The latter holes are to take a bamboo, which is inserted right through the fore-part of the vessel when it is desired to lift the bow of the junk by man-power over boulders in shallow water. The crew, of course, when performing this operation, stand in the water and, with the aid of the bamboo, lift the bow of the junk supported on their shoulders.

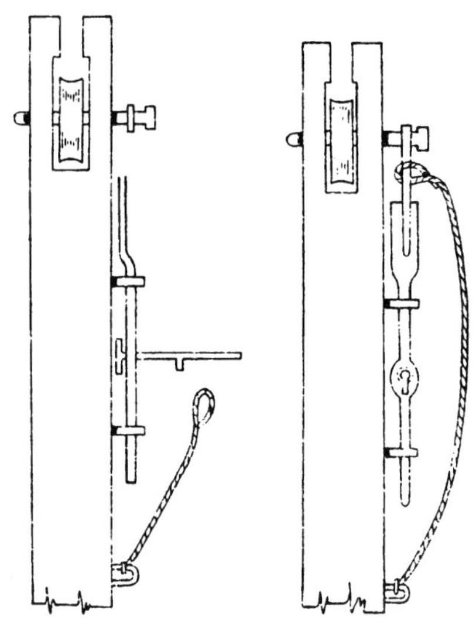

Releasing gear.

The formation of the bow does not lend itself to ease in working cables, and for this reason a primitive form of cat-head[3] is fitted. This is permanently fixed on the starboard bow. The simple but efficient arrangement of the releasing gear fitted to the cat-head is illustrated.

The craft illustrated in Plate No. 90 is 63½ feet long, with a beam of 15½ feet and a depth of 5 feet. It is surprising how uniform these craft are in size and type.

The athwartship strength is derived from the nine bulkheads and the seven half-bulkheads. As will be seen from the section, the half-frames are strengthened by two verticals[4] secured to the after-part.

The rudder is of the non-hoisting balance type and is fitted with a forked rudder-post grown to shape.

No risks are too great for the Poyang Lake sailor. Their well-known habit of overloading is well illustrated in the *to-lung-fu-ch'uan*. Sometimes the freeboard is no more than an inch or so. The full load-line is marked AB in Plate No. 90.

The *to-lung-fu-ch'uan*, with their high flaring bows, are to be seen in considerable numbers in the Lungkaiho at Kiukiang, and it is pleasing to be able to record that these handsome and distinctive craft show no signs of dying out.

THE KAN-PAN-TZŬ

This junk, which is built at Kanchow (贛 州) on the Poyang Lake, may sometimes be seen on the Yangtze, between Kiukiang and Hankow, carrying grain and fruit.

The size of these junks is about 100 feet in length, with a beam of 18 feet and a depth of 5 feet. The smallest variety is about 75 feet, 12 feet beam, and 2½ feet depth.

They can be easily recognized by their very high, broad, flaring bow, so essential for work in steep rapids, and the original type of cat-heads which project over the bow.

An additional type for which no plans are available.

THE HAN RIVER

HISTORICALLY, the Han River has been associated with the great Emperor Yü, who died in 2198 B.C. and may be described as the first experimenter in river conservancy, as it was he who canalized the Hankiang.

The first important reference to the craft of this stream, according to popular legend, was about 1001 B.C. The Emperor Chao (昭 王) had come down, so the story goes, from the North to inspect the remote parts of his empire and had encountered disaster while crossing the Han. It is said that the riverine people showed their contempt for him by rowing him over in a boat of which the planks were merely glued together, and, the glue melting in mid-stream, he and his whole party of officials were drowned.

The Han, which has some considerable value among the secondary waterways of China, rises in the mountains of Shensi, between the parallels of 33° and 34° N. and the meridians of 106° and 107° E. It runs at first in an easterly direction parallel to, and not very far from, the borders of Szechwan. In this portion of its length it travels through rugged gorges, and its course is interrupted by rocks and rapids until it leaves Shensi. At Fancheng (樊 城), after entering Hupeh, it takes a southerly turn and finally turns east again.

Just before reaching Laohokow* (老 河 口) the river leaves its rocky bed, taking a southerly turn and bending east to Siangyang. Thence the trend is in a southerly direction, and the river enters the southern half of Hupeh, consisting of a large alluvial plain which, in prehistoric times, was an inland sea and even now is largely made up of lakes and swamps and their connecting waterways. At Shayang (沙 洋) the stream again turns east before emptying itself into the Yangtze at Hankow.

It is navigable by large junks, small steamers, and launches for a distance of 300 miles up to Siangyang and, during the high-water season, can be navigated by small junks and sampans for a farther 600 miles up to Hanchung (漢 中) in Shensi, a trip requiring two or three months or more to go up and only two weeks to come down.

A curious feature of this river is that, for the latter part of its course, its bed is higher than the surrounding plain, and, were it not for the artificially constructed banks, the country would be flooded every year. This system of making dikes instead of digging out or dredging the bed has had the inevitable result of raising the river-bed still further. The elevation of the plain is only 1 foot above low-water level, and the summer rise presents an ever-present danger of inundation, and floods occur with uncomfortable frequency. As a protection, dikes have been raised on both banks of the river but some 50 to 100 feet inland. This permits the intervening space to be flooded, and the yearly deposits of silt and sand serve to strengthen the existing earthworks. Neglect of these precautions has, of late years, led to disastrous flooding, the worst being in 1931. Another unusual feature of the Han is that it narrows abruptly at its mouth to a mere 200 feet.

The annual number of junks visiting the Han, or the mouth of the Han, according to Customs records was, in 1891, as already stated, estimated to be

* Laohokow is the usual transhipment port where merchandise is transferred to Upper Han boats. The stream is here about 85 yards broad. Beyond this point rapids are numerous and navigation attended with danger.

about 23,000, with a total tonnage of about 1 million, and it was further estimated that they carried 165,000 men.

The craft vary from vessels of 7 feet beam, with a carrying capacity of 150 piculs and a crew of three men, to vessels of 15½ feet beam, with 1,100 piculs carrying capacity and a crew of 12 men. About 14 different types of junks are to be found navigating the Han, of which four types come from other sections of the Yangtze. These latter are the *ma-yang* (麻 陽) from Changteh (常 德), in Hunan, carrying oil, paper, coal, rice, and grasscloth; the *ma-ch'iao-wei* (麻 雀 尾), which is seldom to be seen now; the *pai-mu* (栢 木), a cotton-junk from Szechwan; and the *t'ien-mên* (天 門) from Teian (德 安), with tallow, gypsum, and sesamum-seed oil.

The junks on the lower part of the river are propelled by oars, using a sail when the wind is fair. On the upper section of the river tracking is the more usual mode of propulsion.

The navigation of the Upper Han is very difficult at all times of the year. This is due to rapids and races, shifting sandbanks, narrow and winding channels, and, between April and August, to freshets. The work of a laodah on the Han is a job for which only the courageous need apply.

There are two very important tributaries to the Han, the Tankiang (丹 江), which, rising in Eastern Shensi, joins the parent stream above Laohokow, and the Paiho (白 河), previously joined by the T'angho, the waters of both merging in the Han at Siangyang. All three are navigable, though the first is only so at high water.

In the fertile regions of the Han River Valley the farmers can get as much as two harvests a year. The land can not only be utilized for crop production but also for cattle-raising. The different crops grown are cotton, rice, beans, wheat, barley, millet, sesamum seed, peanuts, tea, tobacco, and *t'ung* oil.

Hankow, therefore, by reason of its position on the Yangtze and at the mouth of the Han River, is enabled to tap a vast hinterland equal in area to the size of Europe and with an aggregate population of more than 150 million souls.

Formerly, all this produce came to Hankow by junks, which enjoyed a very prosperous trade; but since the Hupeh motor roads have linked up Laohokow with Hankow this mechanized competition has caused a sad diminution in the Han River junk traffic.

THE WAI-CH'IU-TZŬ OR CROOKED JUNK

These pleasing and interesting junks vary slightly in size. A typical example is illustrated in Plate No. 91 and measures 73 feet in length, with a beam of 12 feet and a depth of 4 feet. They are, of course, designed for the shallow rapids of the Upper Han River, and are built at Sichwan (淅 川), a town on the Tankiang (丹 江), a tributary of the Upper Han.

As a general rule, the Chinese shipwrights, when building craft for use in deep rapids, favour a more or less rounded under-water line, as this makes for greater stability in broken water, whereas in shallow and narrow rapids they almost invariably build their vessels flat-bottomed, square in the bilge, and about 5½ to 6 beams to length. In this the *wai-ch'iu-tzŭ* conforms to general practice, but what places her in a category by herself is the high and recurving bow and the raked, crooked, and elevated stern.

In China there is generally a reason for everything, although the reason

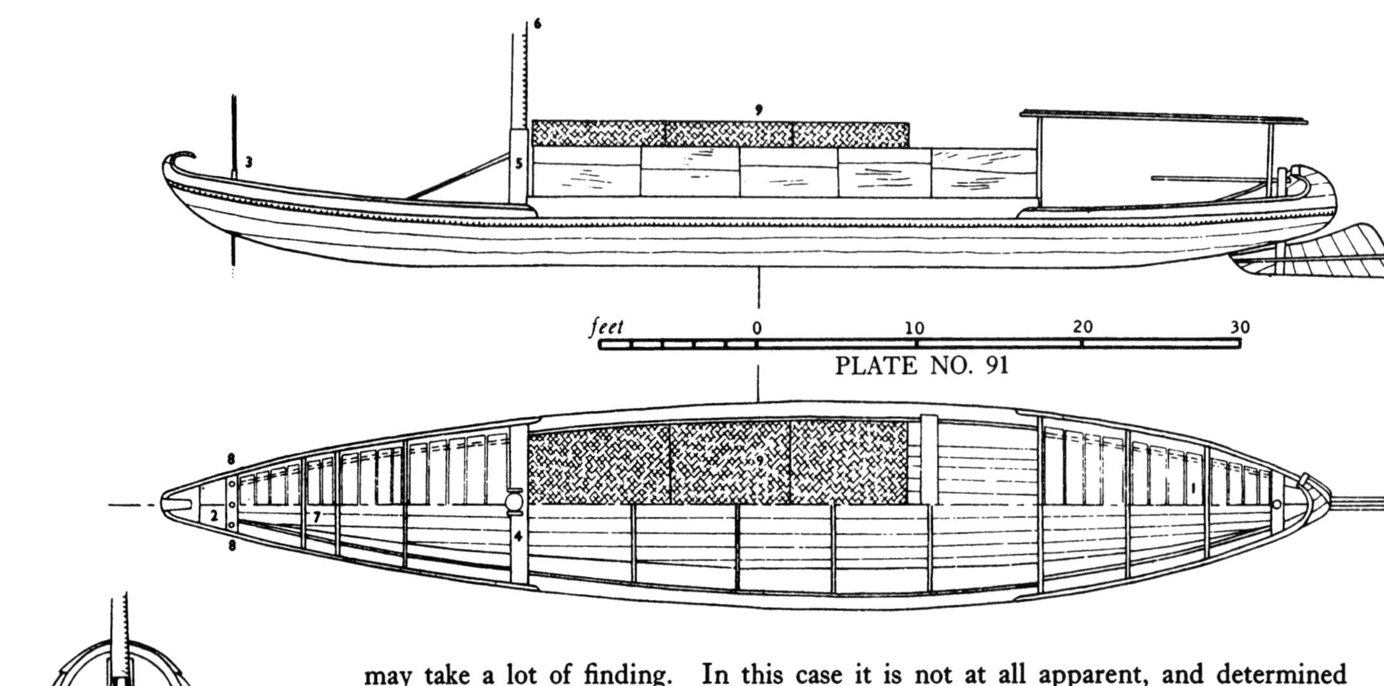

PLATE NO. 91

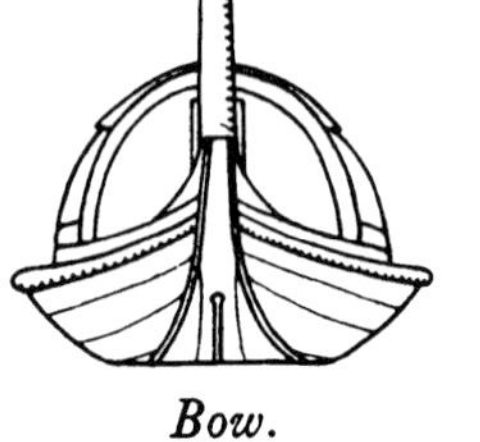

Bow.

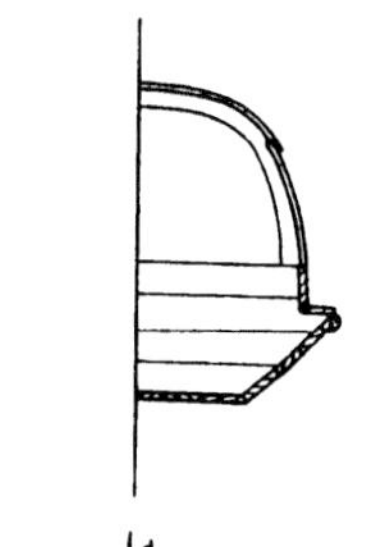

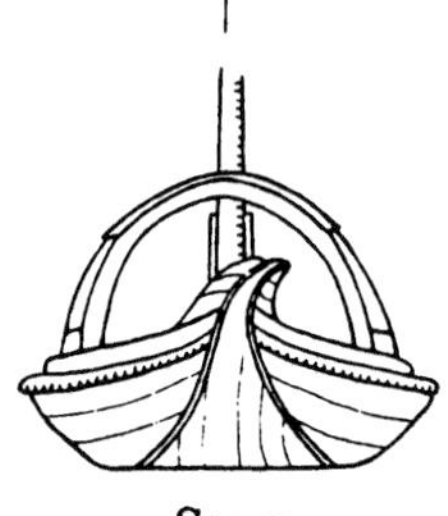

Stern.

may take a lot of finding. In this case it is not at all apparent, and determined research and close questioning of the junkmen has brought to light no practical reason whatever for this curious form of construction.

A local legend of the Han River junkmen, however, affirms that the origin of the crooked stern is to be found in a story connected with the early days of the Three Kingdoms, which relates how a junk was peacefully sailing the waters of the Upper Han River in the year A.D. 222 when it was commandeered by no less a personage than the famous General Kuan Yü (關羽) of the State of Shu (蜀國), while on his way to Fancheng (樊城).

The General, who is always depicted with a red face and is described as having "eyes like a phœnix" and "eyebrows like sleeping silkworms," a long black beard, and enormous proportions, carried with him on this occasion his long curved sword, called Green Dragon (青龍偃月刀), or Cold Beauty, which is almost as famous as himself. Representations of this sword are to be found in all temples dedicated to the God of War and show that the sword must have been some 15 feet long, with a blade of 6 feet, and is said to have weighed 150 pounds. In any case, both the General and his sword were outsizes of their kind.

Kuan Yü entered the boat and threw down his sword with such careless disregard of its weight and size and the manner in which it fell that the stern of the junk became twisted in the form it is to-day.

Tradition embroiders the story by adding that the General, later to become the God of War,* being a kindly soul, was greatly distressed at the damage his thoughtlessness had caused. No "cumshaw" did the great man give to the poor boatman, but a promise to all good Han sailormen that junks of this type should, in future, and for all time, be exempt from paying taxes, provided they all had crooked sterns. A hard-hearted government has rescinded the privilege, but the crooked sterns of the junks hopefully remain.

As will be seen in Plate No. 91, there are 10 bulkheads, one half-bulkhead[1], and no frames. There are two deck-beams. The foremost one[2] is pierced to take the stick-in-the-mud anchor[3] and that amidships[4] is used in conjunction with the tabernacles[5] to support the mast[6]. A coffer-dam[7] is situated abaft the second bulkhead. There are two small forward bollards[8] on the first bulkhead.

The mat house[9] begins at the fifth bulkhead and extends to the tenth. There

* Kuan Yü, the God of War, is celebrated as the most renowned of China's military heroes. On one occasion, as a young officer, he was captured by Ts'ao Ts'ao, the famous traitor, together with the ladies Kan (甘夫人) and Mi (糜夫人), two of the wives of his commanding officer Liu Pei (劉備). In order to test his fidelity, his captor allotted only one sleeping apartment to his prisoners. Thereupon Kuan Yü remained standing all night at the door of the room with a lighted candle in his hand. His birthday is on the 13th day of the 5th moon, and is observed throughout the country with religious services. It usually rains on that day, because, it is said, the god showers a few drops of water on the grindstone to sharpen his sword.

is little comfort in the house. The crew of seven men live in any convenient space not occupied by the cargo.

All the compartments are decked-in with athwartship planking. The hull and bottom are made of *sha-mu* and the bulkheads of *pai-mu*.

The serious student of Oriental naval architecture would do well to compare this craft with the "fan-tail" junks of the Tanningho and the crooked-bow junks of the Yentsingho.

The fan-tail junks of the Tanningho, Part Four, page 503. The crooked-bow junks of the Yentsingho, Part Four, page 564.

The *wai-ch'iu-tzŭ* with her curiously shaped extremities may certainly claim precedence among the curious craft of the Han River and probably of the Yangtze.

THE SIANG-WO-TZŬ OR SIANGYANG BOAT

The *siang-wo-tzŭ*, so named after the town of Siangyang, is the largest type of craft to be found operating on the Lower Han section.

Built on pleasing lines, and rising gently at bow and stern, the craft illustrated in Plate No. 92 measures 76 feet, with a beam of 14½ feet and a depth of 5 feet. As may be seen on the plan, there are 10 full bulkheads and four frames[1]. The bottom planking[2] is of *sha-mu*, while the hull[3] and bulkheads[4] are of camphor-wood.

There are several unusual features about these craft. In the first place, the wales[5] are conterminus 9 feet from bow and stern[6]. The bottom planking, too, is very narrow, with a very abrupt ascent[7]. The fore-part of the house has a square roof[8] with an attempt at ornamentation[9], while the after-part is rounded[10]. The foremast rakes well forward, and the sail stows on lumber irons when not in use[11].

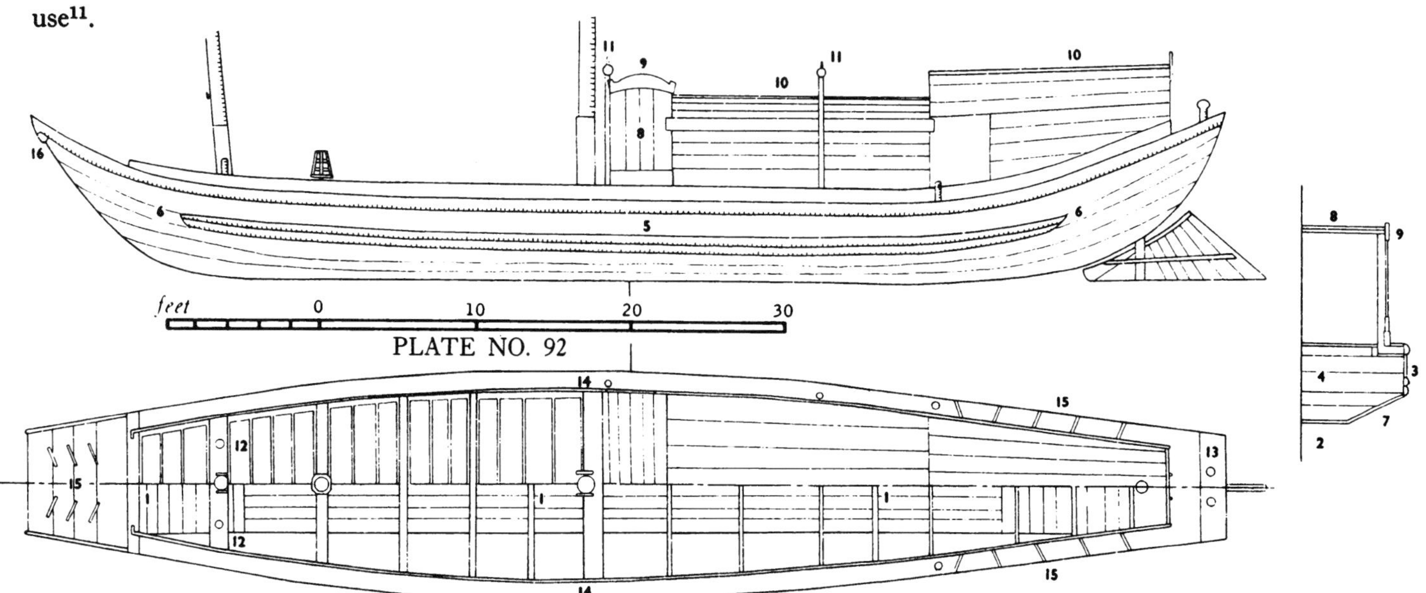

PLATE NO. 92

There are two small forward bollards[12] on the first bulkhead and two of similar size and design on the transom[13], considerably farther aft than is usual.

The wider section of the gunwale forms a convenient gangway outside the house for quanting[14]. Wooden treads are placed on the rising deck at bow and stern[15] to prevent the quanters from slipping.

The high bow, so desirable for work in rapids, terminates in a transverse beam laid below the ascending gunwale[16].

襄陽邱子

THE SIANGYANG CH'IU-TZŬ OR WOOD-ROOFED BOAT

The Siangyang *ch'iu-tzŭ* hails from a town of that name, 283 miles from the mouth of the Han River, and is to be found working that section between Laohokow (老 河 口) and Hankow as a deep-draught cargo-carrier.

The specimen illustrated in Plate No. 93 is a typical double-ender, measuring 64 feet, with a beam of 14 feet, a depth of 4½ feet, and a capacity of 30 tons on a maximum draught of 3 feet.

The stern is almost elliptical in shape. The hull is constructed of *sha-mu* and divided into 10 compartments by hardwood bulkheads.

These junks trade throughout the year with Hankow, carrying down sesamum-seed oil, groundnut oil, watermelon seeds, cow hides, animal bones, bristles, and other local produce, and returning to Siangyang or Laohokow with general cargo.

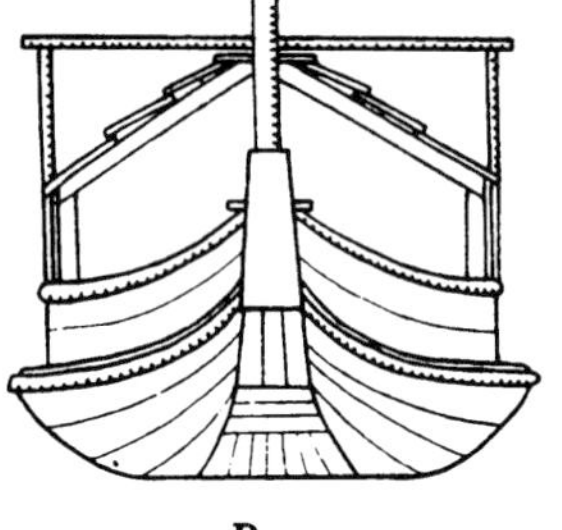

Bow.

There are two masts carrying a classic low-peaked square-headed lug-sail. Iron anchors are used, and a capstan is mounted abaft the foremast.

These junks are often to be found navigating the tributaries which in parts are narrow with sharp turns. In certain reaches these waterways are very crowded, and so, in order to protect the bow from damage, "bumpers"[1] are fitted. This original contraption is also a protection against the iron-shod quant of a rival ahead.

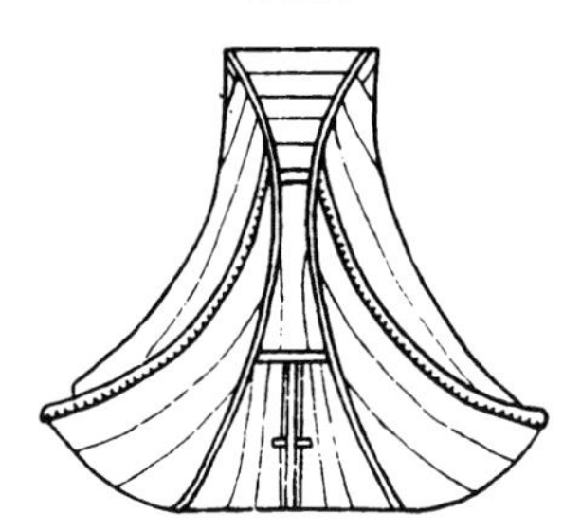

Stern.

The roof of the house[2] is clinker-built. Cargo is stowed in the fore-part[3], while the after-end is used as a galley[4]. The annex[5] is used for the accommodation of the crew and their wives and children. Lumber irons[6] are fitted to the house to take the sail when not in use.

The stern[7] is, as usual, very raked and, above the water-line, makes the curious, albeit pleasing, elbow which is so characteristic of craft navigating the shallow channels of the Yangtze and its tributaries.

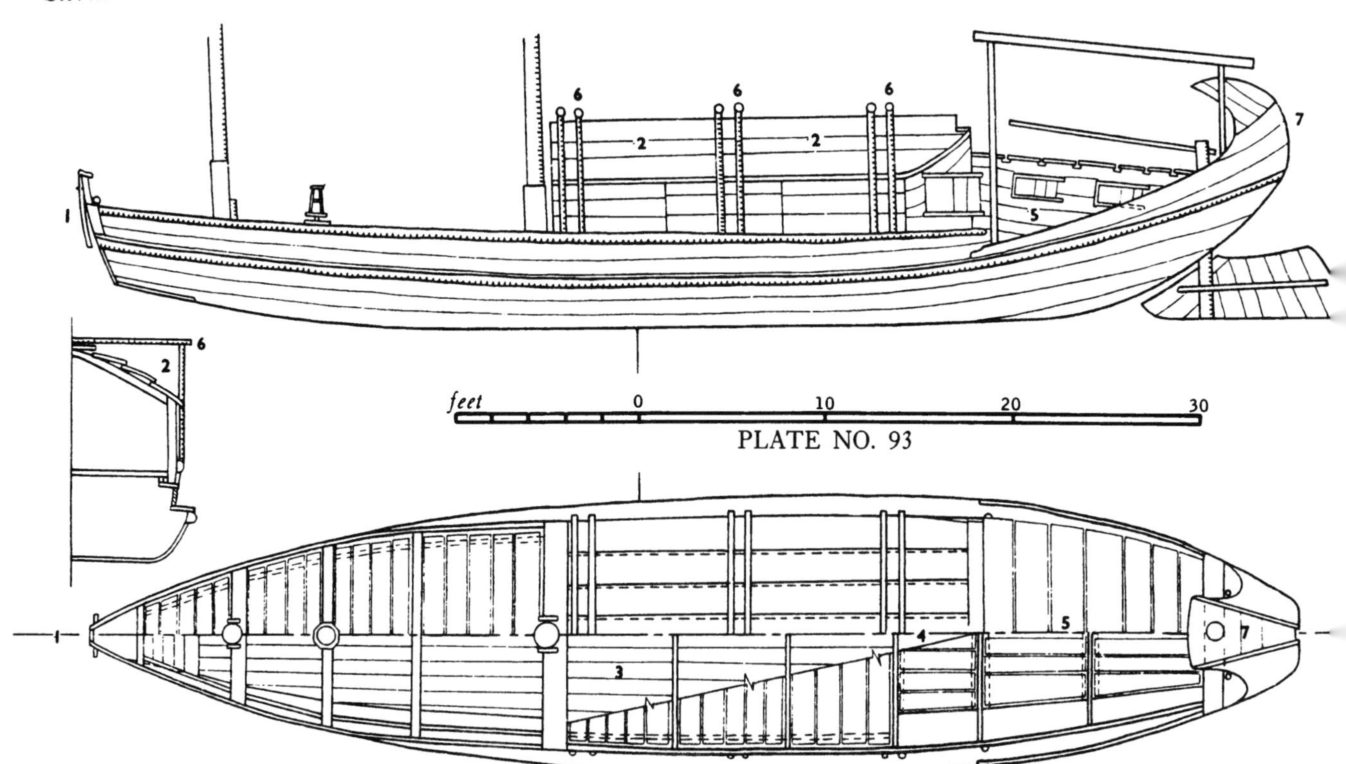

PLATE NO. 93

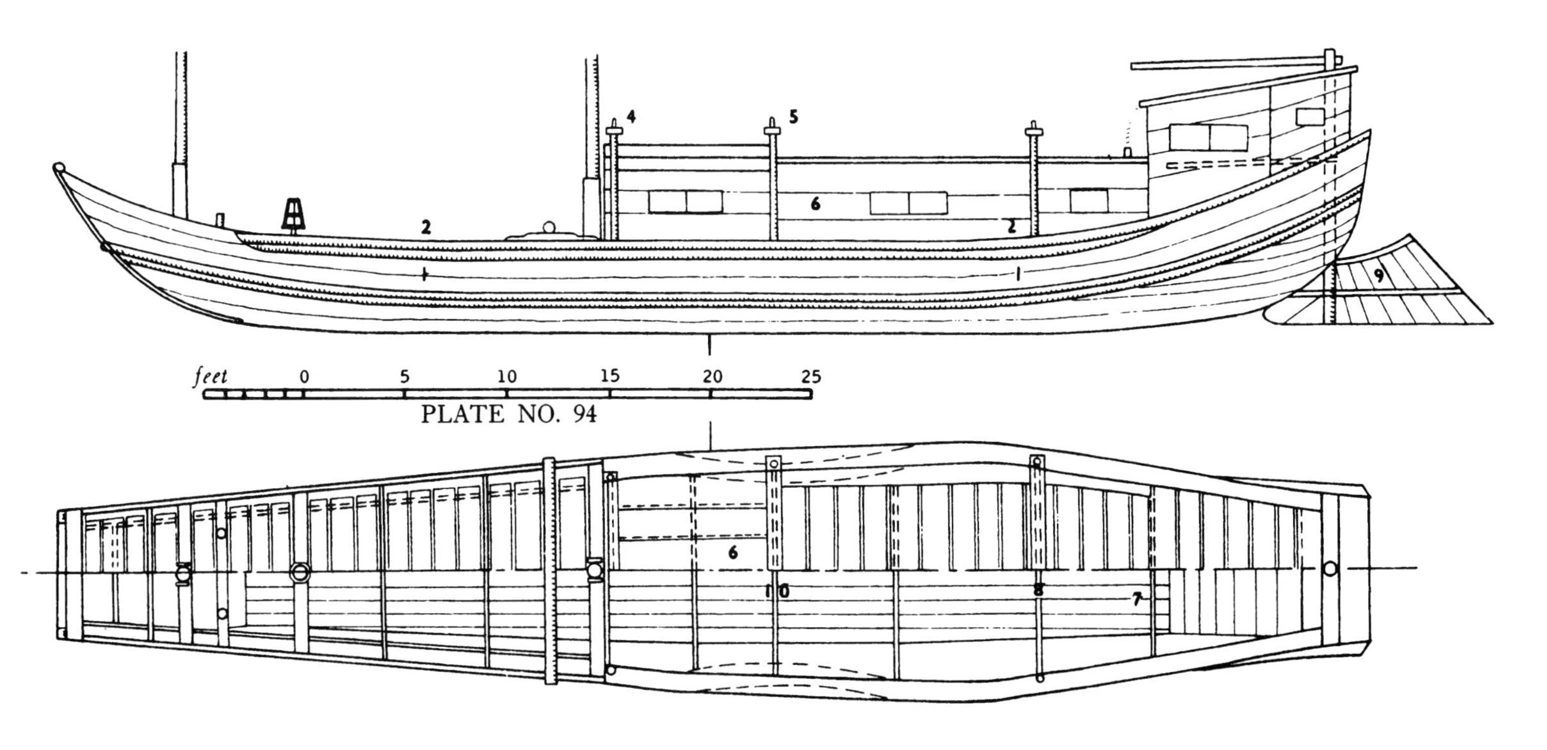

PLATE NO. 94

THE P'AI-TZŬ OR DUMB-BELL JUNK

Another junk very similar in most respects to the types just mentioned, except for the curious indentation amidships, may be referred to here as hailing from Laohokow.

This junk, the *p'ai-tzŭ*, is a medium-draught junk capable of working the Lower and parts of the Upper Han River.

This type of craft is exceptionally strong in construction, especially in the bow. There are two double-wales[1], while above is a double gunwale[2] stronger and more substantial than the others. There is considerable rise forward, and the wales are connected across the bow by a strengthening piece[3] about 3 feet below the heavy projecting cross-beam.

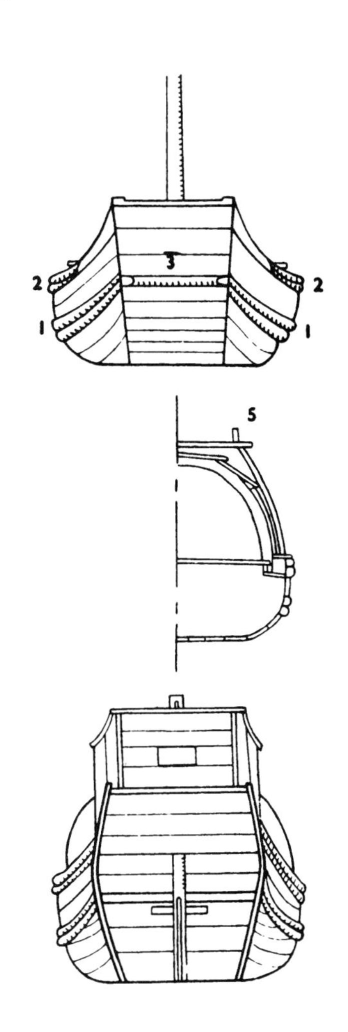

The craft illustrated in Plate No. 94 measures 64 feet, with a beam of 12 feet and a depth of 4 feet. There are 10 bulkheads and one frame.

The capacious house extends from the mainmast to the stern. The roof between the first[4] and second[5] lumber irons is clinker-built, and from there aft it is flat and can be used as a deck. The after-part of the house is also flat. The fore-part[6] is used for the stowage of cargo, abaft the tenth bulkhead[7] is the galley, and the after-part, or tiller-room[8], is used as living quarters by the crew and their families. The balance rudder[9] can be operated from either inside or outside the house.

The flat-surfaced high stern widens as it rises to a gentle curve above the water. The planking of the stern facing is laid horizontally. A small square port with sliding door looks out over the stern.

The chief distinguishing characteristic of the *p'ai-tzŭ* is the curious indentation (marked on the plan by pecked lines) which is present always at the eighth bulkhead[10]. This peculiarity is rigidly adhered to. This type of craft is quite common on the Han River and all have the same curious feature. Painstaking research has produced no reason; the only explanation offered by the junkmen is 這 種 船 就 是 這 樣 釘, which means "the junks of this type are always built like that."

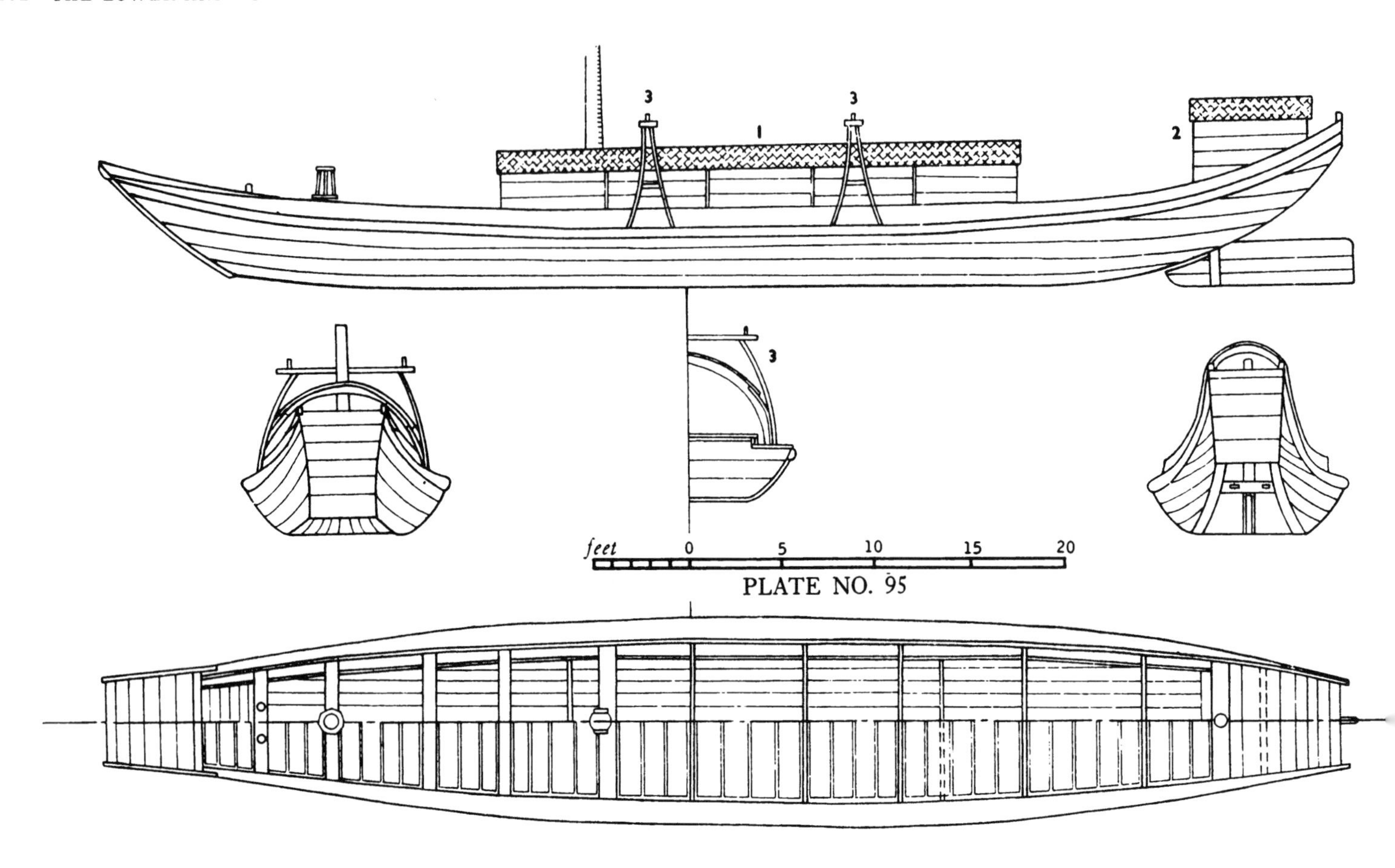

PLATE NO. 95

THE T'AN-HO-CH'UAN OR RAPID-BOAT

灘河船

For creek work the Honan shipwrights have succeeded in developing a very strong type of craft, considering the draught and size to which they are limited by the restrictions imposed on them by the shallow rapids and the very narrow waterways of the Upper Han River.

The junk illustrated in Plate No. 95 measures 65 feet in length, with a beam of 10½ feet and a depth of 3½ feet. She is fitted with 10 camphor-wood bulkheads, and one half-bulkhead which supports the mast and serves as an extra strengthening to the bulkhead.

The local name of this craft is the *t'an-ho-ch'uan* (灘 河 船), or rapid creek boat, but is also known as the *nanyang-ch'uan* (南 陽 船), after a town of that name standing on a tributary of the Han River, which it joins at Fancheng (樊 城).

The junk is flush throughout, with a low mat-covered house amidships[1] and a galley[2] in the stern. All the mats are removable. Cargo is stowed below decks and also in the fore-part of the house. The after-part of the house is used by the crew of three hands and their wives and families as living quarters.

The single sail is a balance lug of which little need be said, since it is only used as an auxiliary in fair winds. The sail, when not in use, lies on the lumber irons[3] resting against the house.

The bow, stern, rudder, and lines generally all indicate that the *t'an-ho-ch'uan* is primarily designed for use in swift waters, and it is useful to compare her with the *to-lung-tzŭ* (鮀 龍 子), a more powerful cousin on the Upper Yangtze.

The plans and a description of the *to-lung-tzŭ* are in Part Four, page 548.

THE TUNGTING LAKE AND SIANG RIVER

THREE rivers, the Siangkiang, the Yüankiang, and the Tzŭkiang, run in a northerly direction through the Province of Hunan into a huge depression known as the Tungting Lake.

This lake, about 75 miles long by 60 miles broad, is the largest in China. In summer its area is enormously extended, but in winter it empties until it is little more than a marsh, intersected by several streams and channels, and is the home of countless wildfowl.

The lake performs a very important function in that it is a reservoir for the drainage of the province. In the summer it receives the surplus waters of the Yangtze through the various channels and creeks above and below Shasi, as well as those of the rivers of Hunan, and its waters sometimes rise to as much as 40 feet above winter levels.

Junk traffic may be detained for weeks on either side of the lake awaiting a favourable wind, as a full day is needed to cross it, during which time a vessel is without benefit of good anchorages to shelter from the sudden squalls and the nasty sea, which are such a feature of the lake at certain seasons of the year. The lake route, therefore, is never attempted except during fine weather, the junkmen preferring the safer, albeit longer, routes by the canals and creeks through the delta land south and west of the lake.

Ever since the time of the Emperor K'ang Hsi in the years 1662–1723, the lake inhabitants have been reclaiming the lake and converting the fertile banks into farmland, and this has resulted in a gradual lessening of the lake's surface. The lake is connected with the Yangtze by a short waterway at Yochow and a number of other canals or creeks, and is the centre of a very active movement of junks. The city of Yochow is situated on high ground at the entrance to the Tungting Lake.

Just past Yochow and standing guard at the entrance to the lake is the island of Pien Shan (扁 山). The god who is supposed to control the weather in the lake has his headquarters in the temple, which crowns the summit of the island. Many propitiatory models of junks are hung from the roof of this temple as evidence of the belief in his powers. At certain seasons of the year, when subscriptions are due, the accommodating priests, anxious to give the passing junkmen as little trouble as possible, collect tribute from them by means of nets suspended from long bamboos.

The Siang is the largest of the four rivers which empty themselves into the lake. It rises in the Nan Ling Mountains in Kwangsi, near the town of Hingan (興 安), from which a canal joins the waters of the Siang to the waters of the Kweikiang (桂 江), so that it is possible to travel by boat from Canton to Wuchow (梧 州), thence up the Kweikiang to this canal and then up the Siang River to the Yangtze.

The Siang is navigable for small junks to the southernmost part of the province. During the low-water season, however, large junks cannot get beyond Siangtan (湘 潭), although small junks drawing a foot or so can reach Yunghing (永 興) at all times of the year.

The junkman's legend relates how a graduate named Liu Hsiu-ts'ai (柳秀才), not being able to pass his examination, went one day to amuse himself beside the island, and there came to him a female dragon who asked him to remain in her company, to which he consented and was made the spirit of the neighbouring mountain. Ever since, when boats go to the lake for recreation and then anchor, the spirits weigh the anchor. The boats, the junkmen affirm, drift about the lake, and music is heard; yet none dares to look at what is passing round the boat. After one round the boats are brought back to their anchorages, but those containing graduates are exempted from this exhibition tour.

Across the lake is another famous island, that of Chün Shan (君山), celebrated for its rare green tea. Here is to be seen a memorial tablet in honour of the two concubines of the Emperor Shun, 2205 B.C., who drowned themselves for grief at the news of their royal master's death. Some say that they threw themselves into the lake in the fashionable manner, for the number of China's legendary characters who have sought their death in this way must be very great. According to the junkmen, however, the sisters drowned themselves in their own tears. That their weeping was fairly excessive is evidenced, so says the famous story, by the fact that the bamboos growing there near their memorial stone have ever since been spotted by the marks of their tears. The island tea used to be sent by the priests to the Viceroy at Changsha, who forwarded it to Peking. The very excellent bamboos grown on the hills behind Yochow were also cultivated for the use of the Emperor in Peking.

Another reference to Emperor Shun and his two faithful concubines is given on page 440.

Another famous suicide in the lake was that of Chiang Wang Yeh, the patron saint, or god, of the Upper Yangtze junkmen, who was a pirate before he was deified. He commanded a fortress in the lake during the time of the Emperor Kao Tsung, as late as 1127–62, and therefore is probably the most junior of the gods.

One of the many historic spots is Yingtien (營田) on the south-eastern corner of the lake, where Tso Tsung-t'ang (左宗棠), one of the famous generals of the Ch'ing dynasty, trained his navy.

The Milo River (汨羅江) is really a tributary of the Siang, yet appears to enter the lake owing to its watery confines being so widely extended. This is the stream that is the scene of the "dragon" boat legend which owes its origin to yet another historic suicide, that of Ch'ü Yüan (屈原).

More about Ch'ü Yüan and the Dragon boat legend will be found in Part Three, page 459, and Part Four, page 531.

At its south-western end the lake runs into a bay between Lungyang and Yüankiang, called the Tienhsihu. The canals connecting it with the Yüan River to the west, and the Tzŭ and Siang Rivers on the east, are here intersected by this bay. Large rafts are often to be seen drifting down the Yüan River from the forests of Kweichow.

Changsha is the capital of the Province of Hunan. It is one of the great trading centres of inland China. Among some of the local industries for which the city is famous are embroidered linen, white brassware, bamboo articles, and fire-crackers, which all find a ready market all over China.

The Province of Hunan is sometimes described as being one huge coal-field with from 16,200 to 27,700 square miles of coal deposits, and so it is not surprising to find innumerable types of junks in the coal trade, and, curious as it may seem, they are, as a class, among the most numerous, graceful, and the smartest and cleanest to be found on the Yangtze. Indeed, it is hardly too much to say that in any Hunan creekside village or town with a couple of feet of water, there, sure enough, will be found a coal-junk adding colour and grace to the scene.

The first reference to coal in China is said to be found in the "Chou

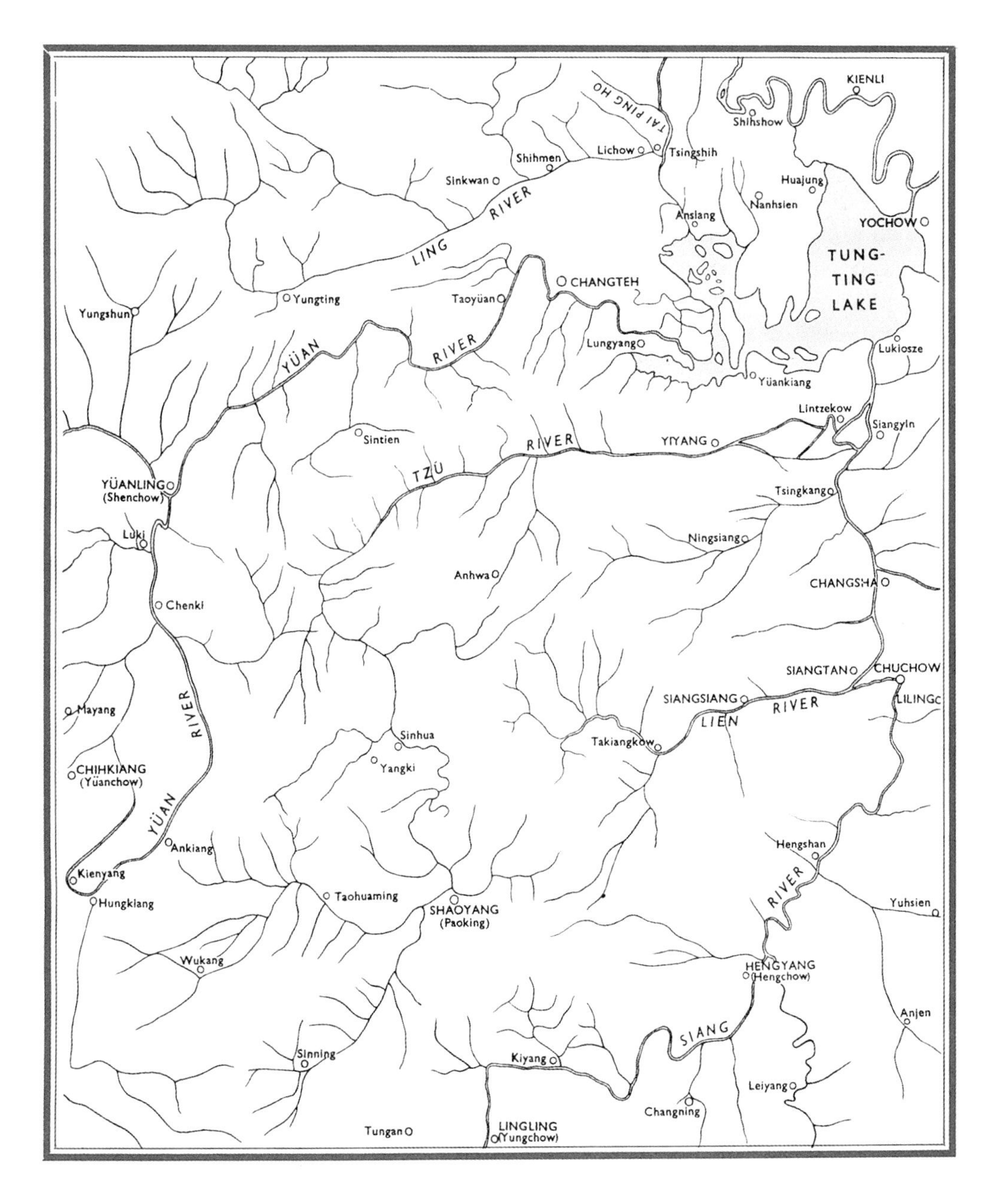

The Hunan Waterways.

Ritual " (周 禮), a book written in the eleventh century B.C. by the Duke of Chou. Coal is again mentioned in a descriptive geography dating from the Han dynasty, 206 B.C.–A.D. 25, which makes reference to a " kind of stone," which was produced in the present Province of Kiangsi, " which could be burned like fuel." It was not until some 1,300 years later that Marco Polo, in the latter part of the thirteenth century, gave Europe the first authentic account of the use of coal in China.

Nevertheless, although coal mining has been in operation in China from these remote times, it was not until the reign of K'ang Hsi in 1662–1723 that coal came to attain its present importance.

Extensive coal deposits, of excellent quality, are known to exist in the mountainous regions, and in some places surface deposits are so conveniently situated that the coal-junks can go alongside the river-bank where the crew go ashore and dig out a boatload themselves.

The coal, which thousands of junks are engaged in shipping to Hankow and ports beyond, affords employment to countless people. The " Customs Decennial Reports " estimate that between 4,000,000 and 5,000,000 tons of coal are annually exported by junks in normal times.

Other industries of the province include tea, rice, cotton, timber, mining, and fishing. Salt alone is lacking. There is a Hunan saying that "with a full harvest in Hunan there is enough for the whole world," for there are three crops of rice which ripen in the 5th, 7th, and 10th moons.

The old junkmen say "when you reach the Tungting Lake, keep very still and do not laugh. There are many spirits in the lake, and you must sacrifice a cock and burn incense to them." It is said that a magistrate while crossing the lake with his wife once laughed at this old superstition. His wife, alarmed at his foolhardiness, secretly dropped her ring in the lake as appeasement. Not long afterwards, when a large fish caught in the lake was served up at the magistrate's table, the missing ring was found inside in token of the water spirits' acceptance of the offering.

Here is to be seen the inland commerce of China at its best. Between the ports on the Yangtze, the Tungting Lake, and the Siang, trade employs thousands of small craft. The boats are among the smartest and cleanest in China, and this great waterway may well claim precedence as the junk-lover's paradise.

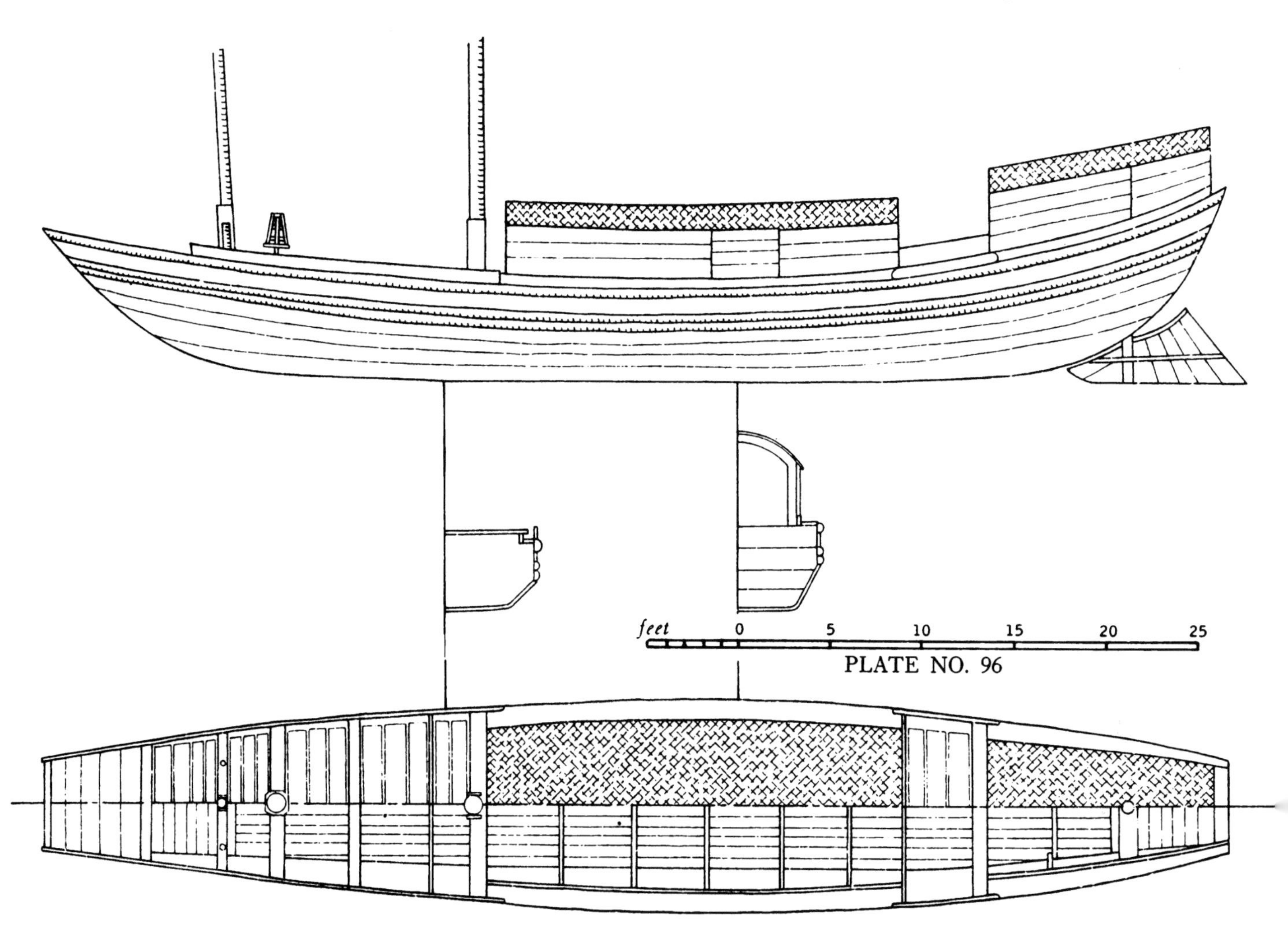

PLATE NO. 96

THE PIEN-TZŬ OR BAMBOO CARRYING-POLE JUNK

The *pien-tzŭ*, literally, "flat boat," is usually slightly larger than the usual run of Siang craft. It is comparatively narrow, shallow, long, and has a slight sheer, and for this reason, probably, it gets its name *pien-tan* (扁 担), or bamboo carrying-pole. The junk illustrated in Plate No. 96 is a typical shallow-draught design and measures 65 feet, with a beam of 11 feet and a depth of 4½ feet.

The wood used in its construction is exactly the same as that for the *ya-shao*, already described; and the boat is also nearly always two-masted, the foremast having a slight forward rake.

The hull is usually divided into 13 watertight compartments; and, like the small *ya-shao*, the midship and after-deck is covered with a mat-roofed house. The capacity is about 150 piculs, and the crew numbers six men, including the laodah.

The *ya-shao* is described on page 378.

These junks, which are noted for their manœuvrability, hail from Hwangpei (黃陂), Siaokan (孝感), Yangsin (陽新), Sinchow (新州), Tsungyang (崇陽), Siangho (湘河), and Fuho (府河), and there are consequently seven slightly different varieties.

The cargo carried to Hankow usually consists of beans, rice, and raw cotton from Hwangpei and Siaokan; tea leaf, kaoliang, corn, ramie, hemp, and paper from Yangsin; raw cotton, native cloth, china-root, charcoal, and tobacco leaf from Sinchow. The junks return home with miscellaneous loads.

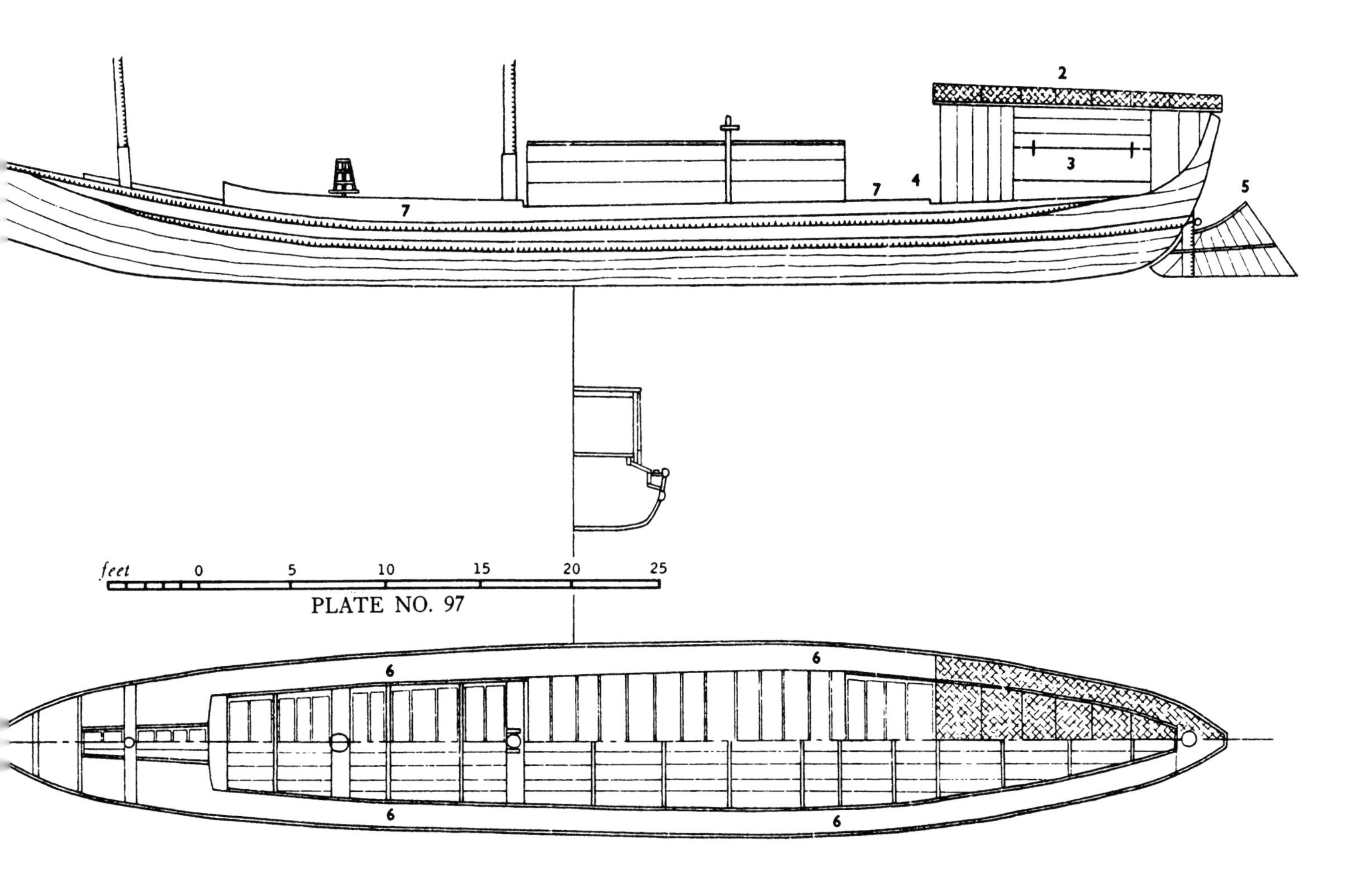

PLATE NO. 97

THE HSIAO-PO OR SMALL LIGHTER

The *hsiao-po* is known as the small lighter and is one of the commonest types working the Siang and Tungting Lake. It can be easily recognized by its characteristic and unusually tapering bow, terminating in an elongated upright[1] which sometimes stands as much as 2 feet above the deck. This unaccountable timber, which is not a stem-piece in the true sense of the word, is called the *ling-p'ai* (靈牌) and is reverenced in place of the junk god, hereabout known as the Tungting Wang Yeh (洞庭王爺). It is therefore highly important that in the event of shipwreck every endeavour should be made to save this emblem, so that it may be set up in its proper position in a new junk.

The stern of this craft is also characteristic. It is bluntly round from the water-line up and, rising somewhat, terminates in a narrow, forked timber, like a fish tail. Here is situated the owner's cabin, tiller-room, and galley[2]. It is fitted with a flap-window for air and light[3]. In the summer the galley stove is placed on deck[4].

The junks vary in size from about 60 feet,* with a beam of 7 feet, a draught of 2 feet, and a capacity of 20 tons, to 100 feet, with a beam of 18 feet and a draught of 3 feet. The largest types are said to have a capacity of 30 tons. The type illustrated in Plate No. 97 is 68 feet in length, and has a beam of 10 feet and a depth of 4½ feet. They usually have a freeboard of 5 inches or less.

These roomy cargo-carriers have the typical deep-draught rudder with the triangular top which projects out of the water[5], not unlike a shark's fin. The hull is almost invariably built of hardwood, mostly of *pai-mu*, while the bottom is of *sha-mu*. There are 17 bulkheads.

Normally these junks have two masts, the mainmast being only a few feet shorter than the junk itself. The larger types may, however, have three masts, all being placed well forward and rising in steps from the foremast, which is markedly short, to the mizzen, which is the tallest. In exceptional cases there are four masts.

The upper deck, close to the ship's side, is free of all obstacles from bow to stern when poling in shoal water[6]. These junks are great offenders in the manner in which they overload and would make the late Mr. Samuel Plimsoll turn in his grave. For instance, when carrying a cargo of stones, 1 inch of freeboard[7] is considered quite safe. Washboards[7] are often fitted.

These junks hail from the Siang River and the Tungting Lake, their home ports being Changning (常寧), Leiyang (耒陽), Hengshan (衡山), Chüanhsien (全縣), Hengyang (衡陽), Yuhsien (攸縣), and Liuyang (瀏陽). Types built at these places all differ in non-essentials.

The large junks have as many as 20 men in the crew, and carry salt up river, from as far afield as Kiangsu (江蘇), and charcoal, plaster, and wood down river; while the smaller craft with four men carry imported foreign goods up river from Hupeh ports and bring down stones, coal, grain, and rice.

* Although they are not common, some types of *hsiao-po* are to be found as small as 30 feet over-all.

白河船 THE PAIHO-CH'UAN OR PAIHO BOAT

The *paiho-ch'uan*, although a native of the Siang River, belongs to the *nanho-ch'uan* family, whose home port is on the Middle Yangtze.

So famous are the Hunan shipwrights that it is possible, as they claim, this is the parent craft. It is, however, more probable that this type of junk is not of ancient ancestry, for a comprehensive list of the names of Siang River craft was compiled by the Customs in 1901 and its name does not appear therein. It would seem, therefore, that its introduction can only date back to comparatively recent times. Be this as it may, the *paiho-ch'uan* is to-day one of the favourite types of craft to be seen on the Siang River.

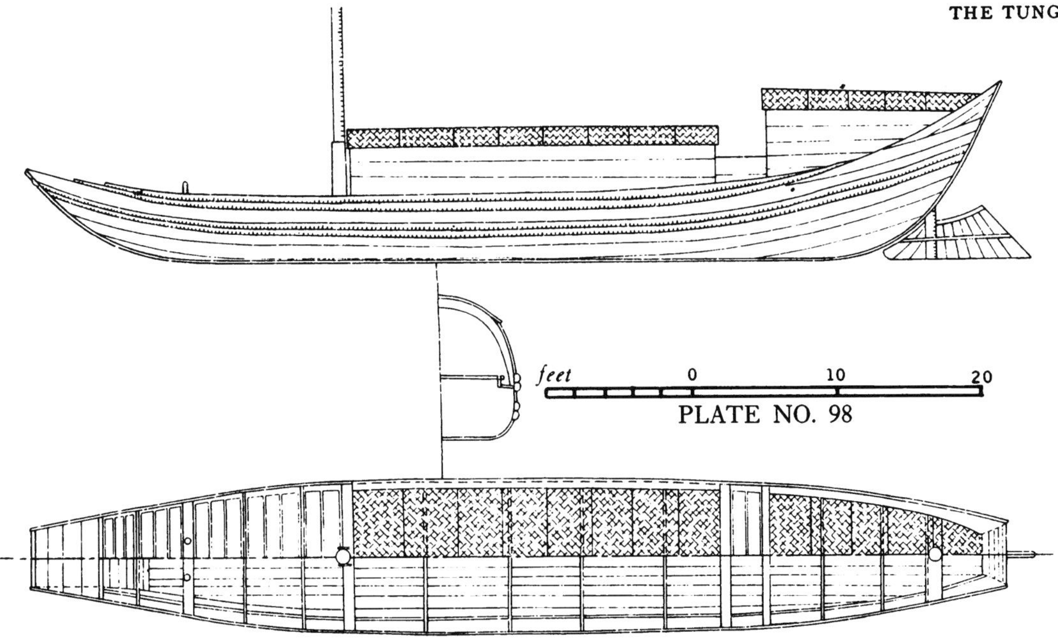

PLATE NO. 98

Plate No. 98 shows a typical example of the class, which measures 66 by 10 feet, with a depth of 4 feet and a carrying capacity of about 25 tons.

The house, which is of exceptionally large dimensions, is used as well as the holds for the stowage of cargo. The after-house provides accommodation for the laodah and his family. A removable washboard connects the two houses.

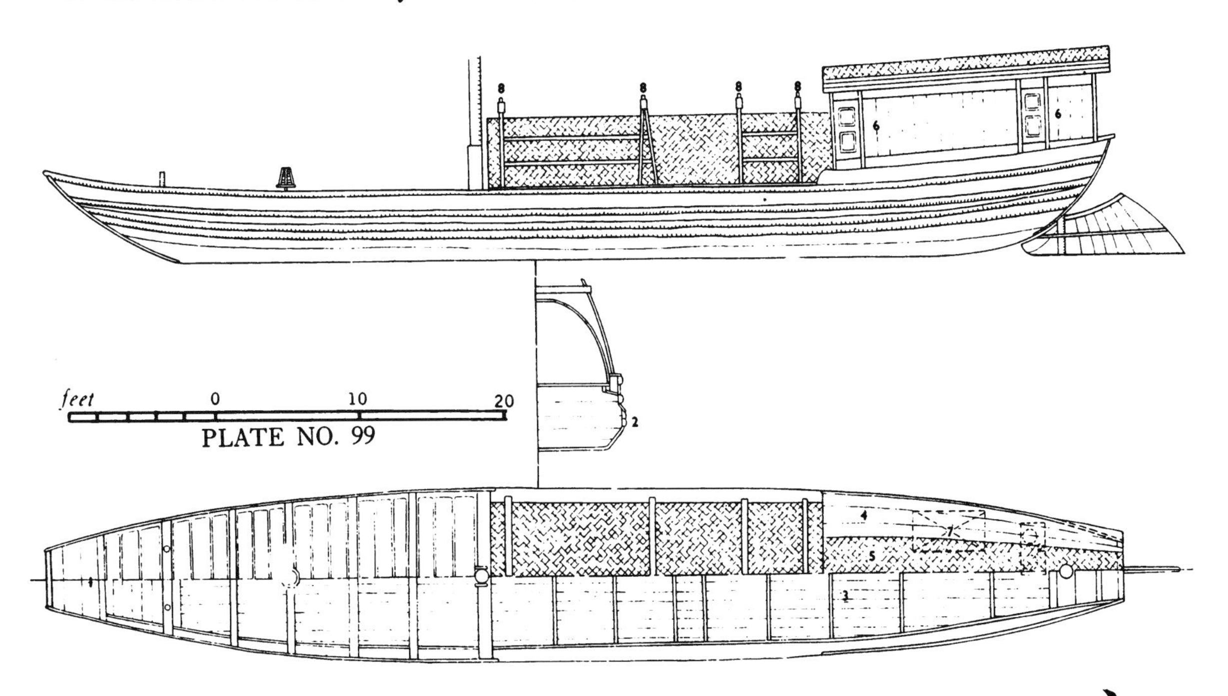

PLATE NO. 99

THE PAOKING CH'IU-TZŬ

Heavy, cumbrous, bluff of bow and stern, but perhaps one of the smartest and most luxurious craft on the river above Hankow, is the Paoking *ch'iu-tzŭ*, so named after a town on a tributary of the Siang River.

The type illustrated in Plate No. 99 measures 73 feet in length, has a beam of $11\frac{1}{2}$ feet and a depth of $4\frac{1}{2}$ feet, and is fitted with 15 full bulkheads and one frame[1]. Longitudinal strength is provided by heavy wales built in as side planks[2].

The house, which occupies more than half of the upper deck, is divided into two parts. The fore-part from the mast aft to the twelfth bulkhead[3] is matted-in, and is used for cargo and living quarters for the crew. The after-part from the twelfth bulkhead[3] to the stern has a clinker-built plank roof[4] with a mat centre[5]. The sides of this part of the house are of wood and fitted with two doors[6]. The foremost one gives access to the owner's cabin, which is fitted with a bunk[7], and the after one to the galley. The usual lumber irons[8] are fitted to the house in the customary manner.

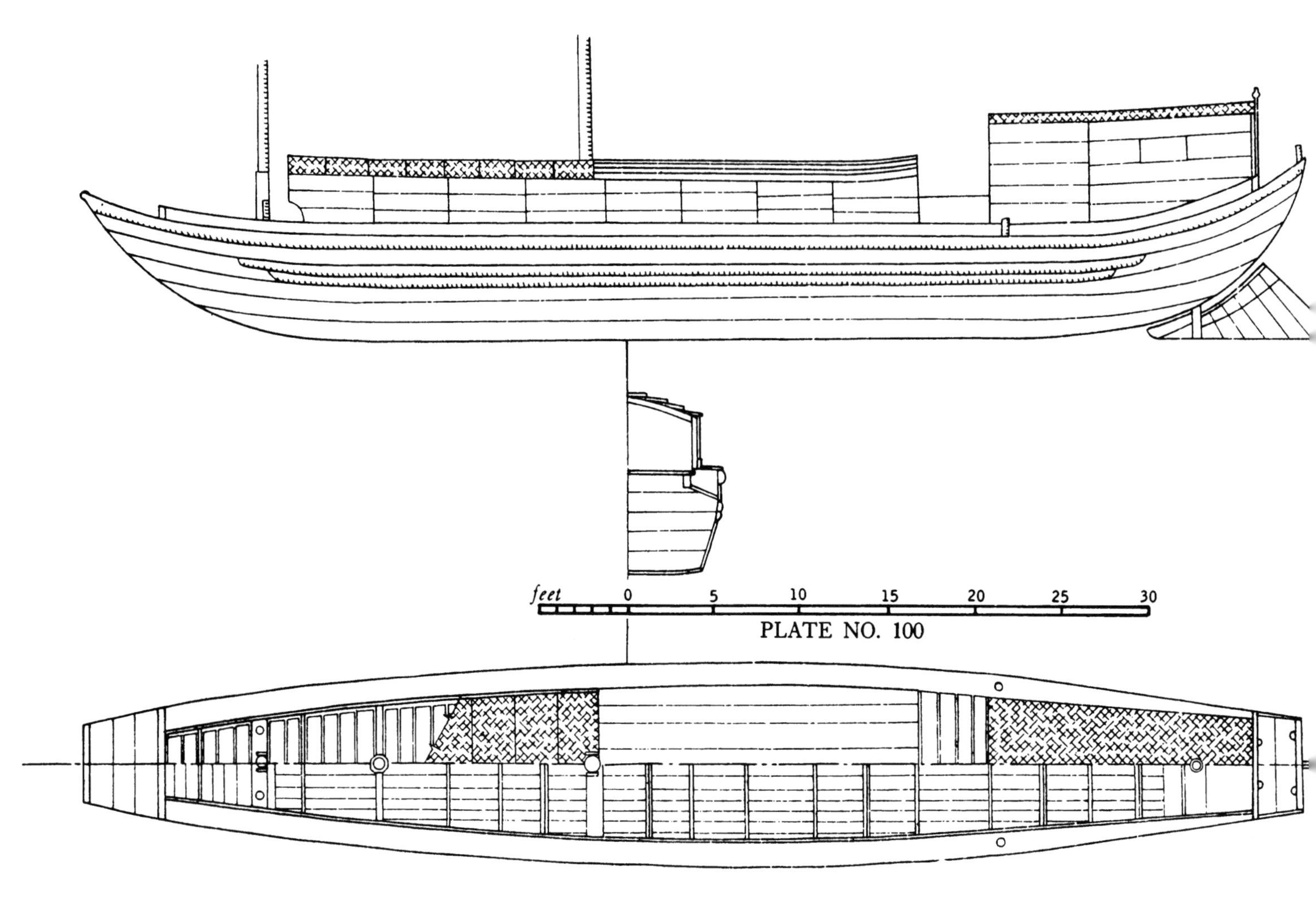

PLATE NO. 100

倒把子 THE TAO-PA-TZŬ OR SCRATCH BACK BOAT

The *tao-pa*, meaning " to scratch back," that is to say, to get something back, embodies an omen of prosperity. They hail mostly from Siangyin (湘 陰), Siangtan (湘 潭), Changsha (長 沙), Siangsiang (湘 鄉), Ningsiang (寧 鄉), and Hengshan (衡 山), and are usually to be seen on the many small rivers and creeks of Hunan and Hupeh. These junks are built for the most part of *pai-mu*, *chang-mu*, and *sha-mu*, and vary in size from 70 feet in length, 12 feet beam, and 5 feet in depth in the largest types down to 60 feet in length, 8 feet beam, and 1½ feet in depth. This class of junk carries paper, wood oil, bambooware, coarse porcelain, rice, and beans to Hankow, returning with a general cargo.

The craft illustrated in Plate No. 100 measures 70 feet, with a beam of 11 feet and a depth of 5½ feet, the capacity being about 60 tons. There are 14 bulkheads, mostly in the fore-part of the vessel, and five frames.

The amidship part of the house is roofed with wood, the foremost and after ends with matting.

The junk is by no means the most handsome on the Siang River.

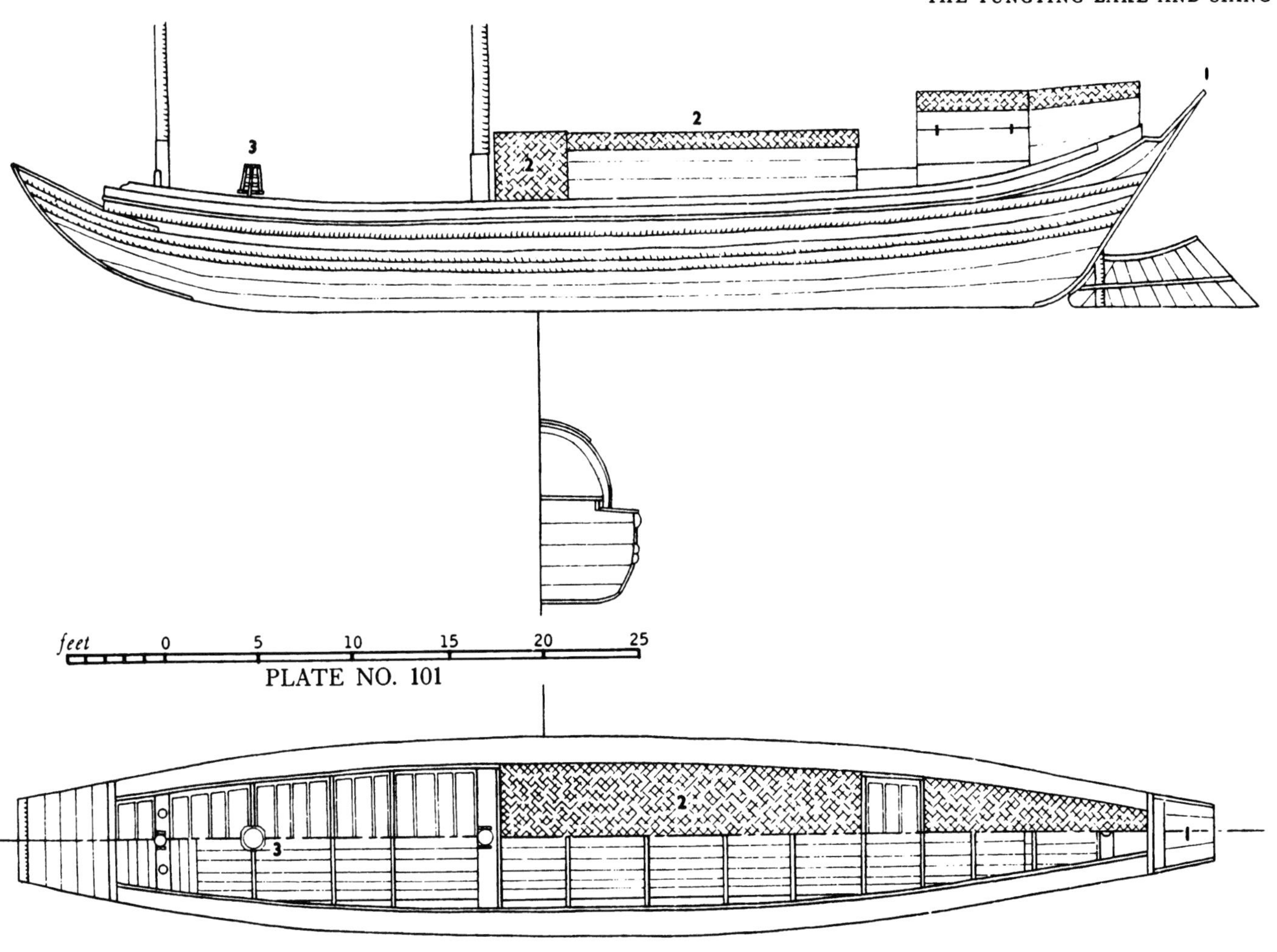

PLATE NO. 101

THE YOCHOW CH'AN-TZŬ OR YOCHOW SPADE

岳州鏟子

A very fine junk, which suggests its good qualities by its looks, is the Yochow *ch'an-tzŭ*, so called from the shape of the upper part of the stern[1], which has the appearance of a spade.

These junks are used almost exclusively in the pig-carrying trade between Hunan ports and Hankow. The number of pigs carried per trip varies from 20 animals in the smaller types to as many as 60 or more in the largest, which is illustrated in Plate No. 101. This craft measures 61 feet in length, and has a beam of 10 feet and a depth of 4 feet 6 inches. It is fitted with 11 bulkheads and three half-bulkheads.

The roof of the house consists of a number of removable mats[2]. The fore-part of the house is also of mat and can be unshipped to give air to the pigs in the hold. The deck-house covers all the portion abaft the mast, being interrupted by an aperture to enable the helmsman to obtain a clear view from the conning position when the junk is under weigh.

The windlass[3], which is situated midway between the masts, is of the old-fashioned type, made of wood and worked by crude handspikes. It is used for hoisting the sails and weighing the anchor.

These junks are usually built in Yochow (岳 州), Pingkiang (平 江), and Paotsing (保 靖), and are usually 60 feet or so in length, the smaller types being 40 feet. The crew consists of not more than five men, including the swineherds. The Hunan pig trade may not be a very inspiring one, but its craft have great beauty of line.

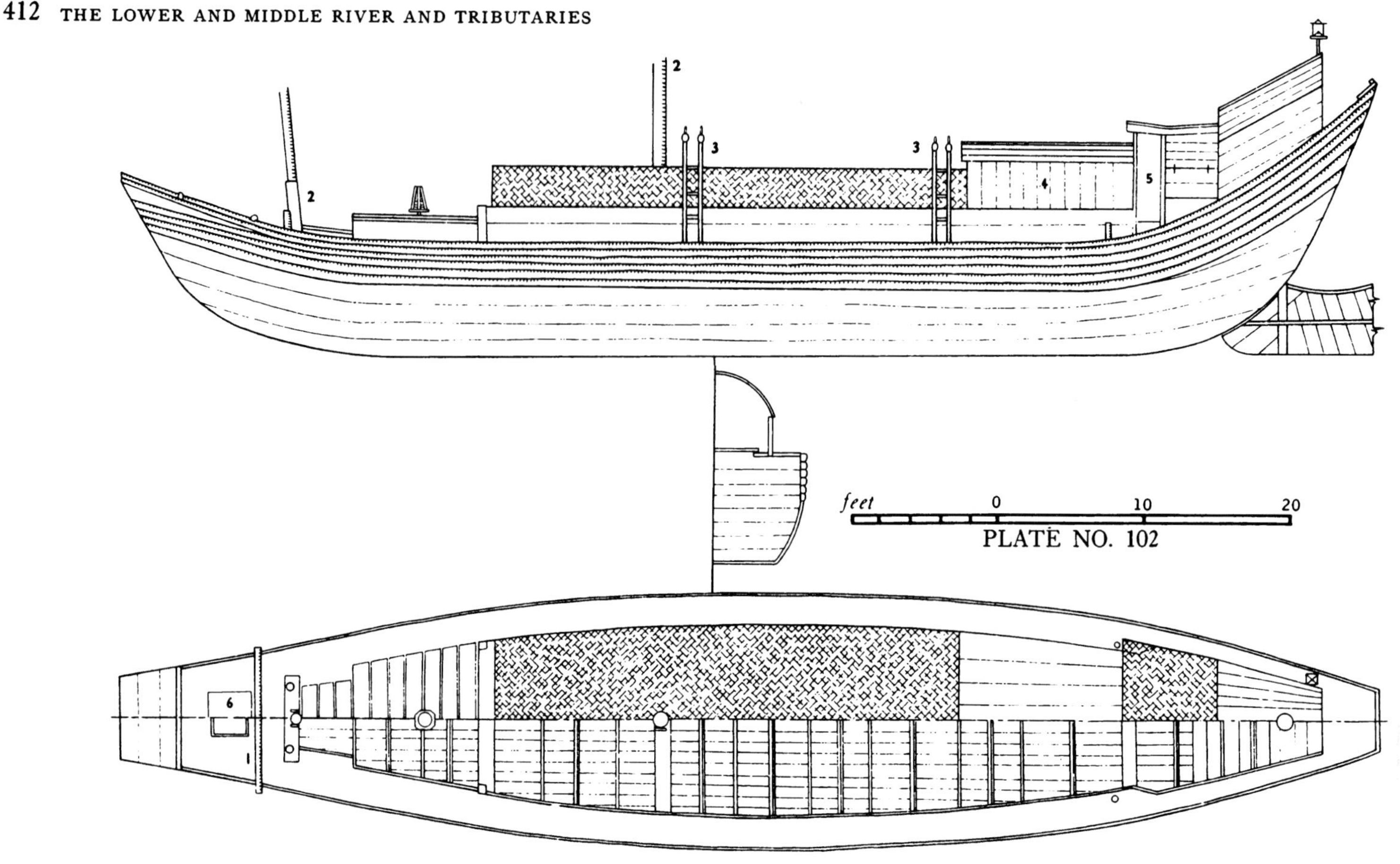

桐子殼

THE T'UNG-TZŬ-K'O OR HULL OF POLES

The *t'ung-tzŭ-k'o*, or hull of poles, derives its name from the fact that its hull above the water-line is nearly all made of split poles. It is usually to be found in two sizes. The largest, illustrated in Plate No. 102, measures 80 to 90 feet, with a beam of 16½ feet and a depth of 7½ feet, while the smaller size is usually about 60 feet, with a beam of 10 feet and a depth of 3 feet. The largest types are credited with a capacity of 200 to 300 tons. They are built at Kiyang (祁陽), Paishui (白水), and Kweiyang (桂陽).

Normally these junks ply throughout the year between Hankow and their home ports. They load Hengchow (衡州) and Paoking (寶慶) coal, rice, paper, or other produce on the downward voyage, and raw cotton, hardware, and sundries on the upward trip. The downward voyage to Hankow usually takes about a week, but the return trip takes a month or more owing to the current.

They are of quite exceptionally strong construction, the craft under description having 15 bulkheads and 11 half-bulkheads. On the fore-deck is a heavy projecting cross-beam[1].

Two tall *sha-mu* pole-masts[2], setting high-peaked, cotton balance lug-sails laced to a boom at its foot, is the rig of these craft; sometimes as many as four masts are carried. The sails stow on lumber irons[3].

Eight compartments and the fore-part of the house are given up to cargo. The after deck-houses are larger and higher than the usual run of Siang craft. The owner's cabin[4] is particularly spacious and is provided with two bunks. On deck abaft this cabin there is a living room, reached through a door[5]. A removable hatchway[6] gives access to the crews' quarters in the forecastle.

The usual method of navigation in very shoal waters is by poling, and so plenty of accommodation along the sides of the junk is provided for quanters.

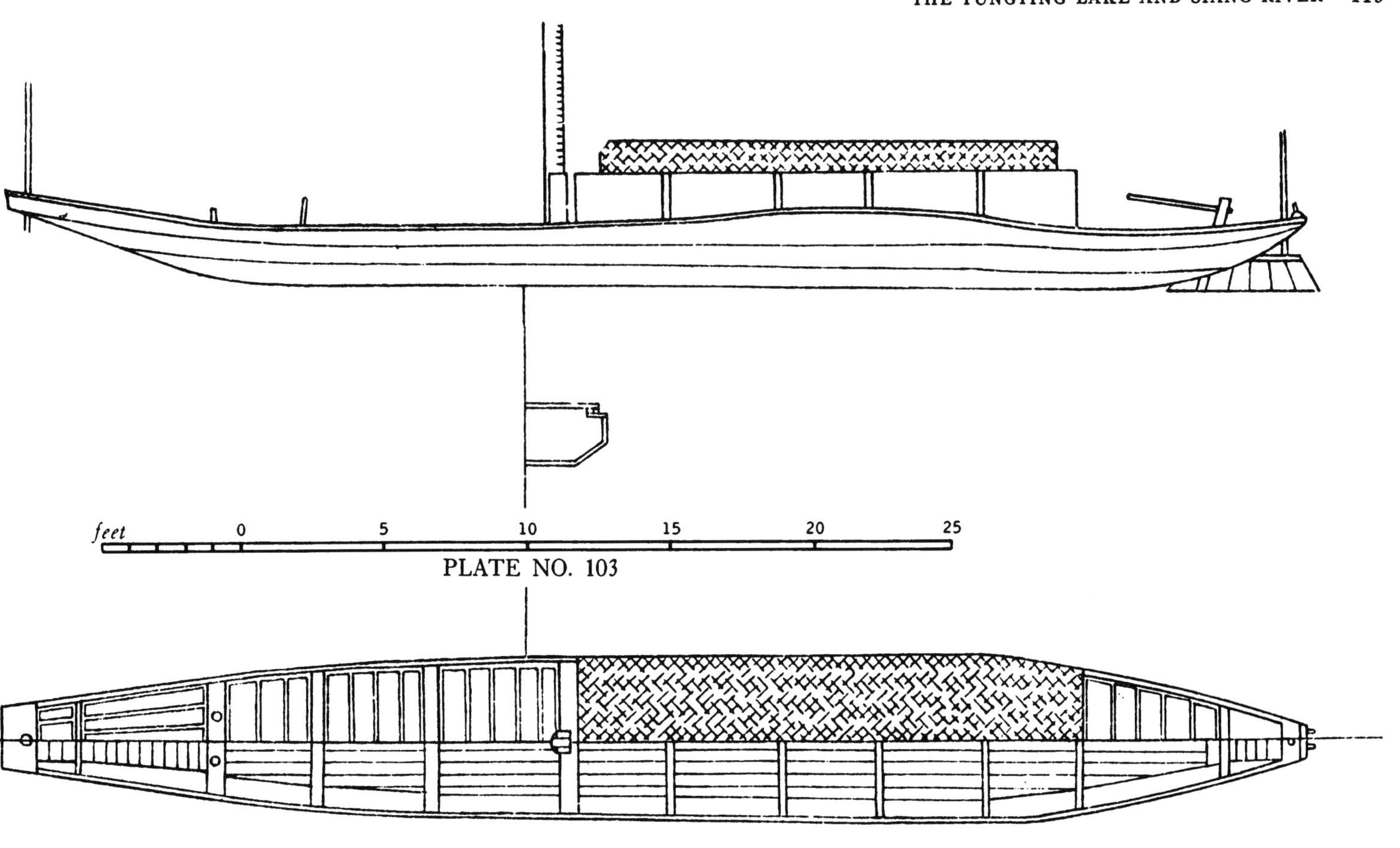

PLATE NO. 103

THE CHANGSHA TAO-PA-TZŬ OR HUMPBACK JUNK

長沙倒把子

The name of *tao-pa-tzŭ* is applied in Hunan to a vast family of junks which often have little in common. This family is divided into a number of types, which are again subdivided into various classes. So fine are the distinctions that at Changsha, for instance (the ancestral home of the *tao-pa-tzŭ*), the type is divided into "Changsha Upper" and "Changsha Lower."

Except to the Hunan junkmen, the classification of these junks is most confusing, for many of the types bear not the slightest family likeness.

The craft illustrated in Plate No. 103 measures 45 feet, with a beam of 5½ feet and a depth of 2 feet, which is a fairly typical example of this particular type.

This class of vessel is designed as a high-speed, light-draught coal-carrier working the river between the coal ports on the Upper Siang and Changsha.

The *tao-pa-tzŭ* is lightly built with slender lines, and for speed she is second to none on the Siang River. The sails are of the Siang type, high-peaked, with 17 battens. The Changsha variety of *tao-pa-tzŭ* is remarkable for the marked hump amidships, which is designed to assist in keeping the water out when the junk is deeply laden and listing with perhaps only an inch or two of freeboard. As a further precaution against the wash of passing vessels, sectional washboards are also fitted.

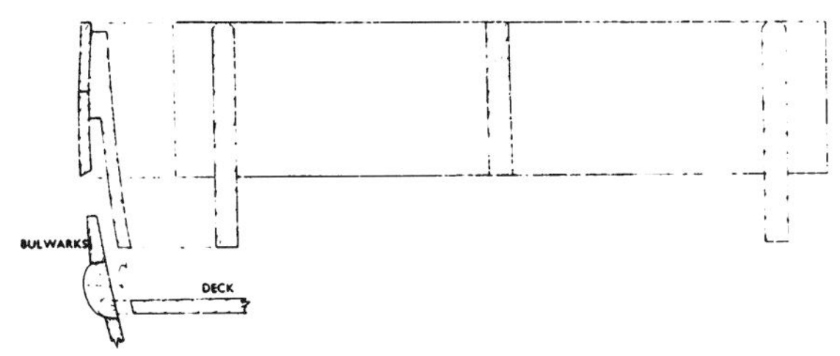

Washboards.

To the Western sailor the junkmen of the Siang seem to take great chances; but in most cases they reach their destination just the same.

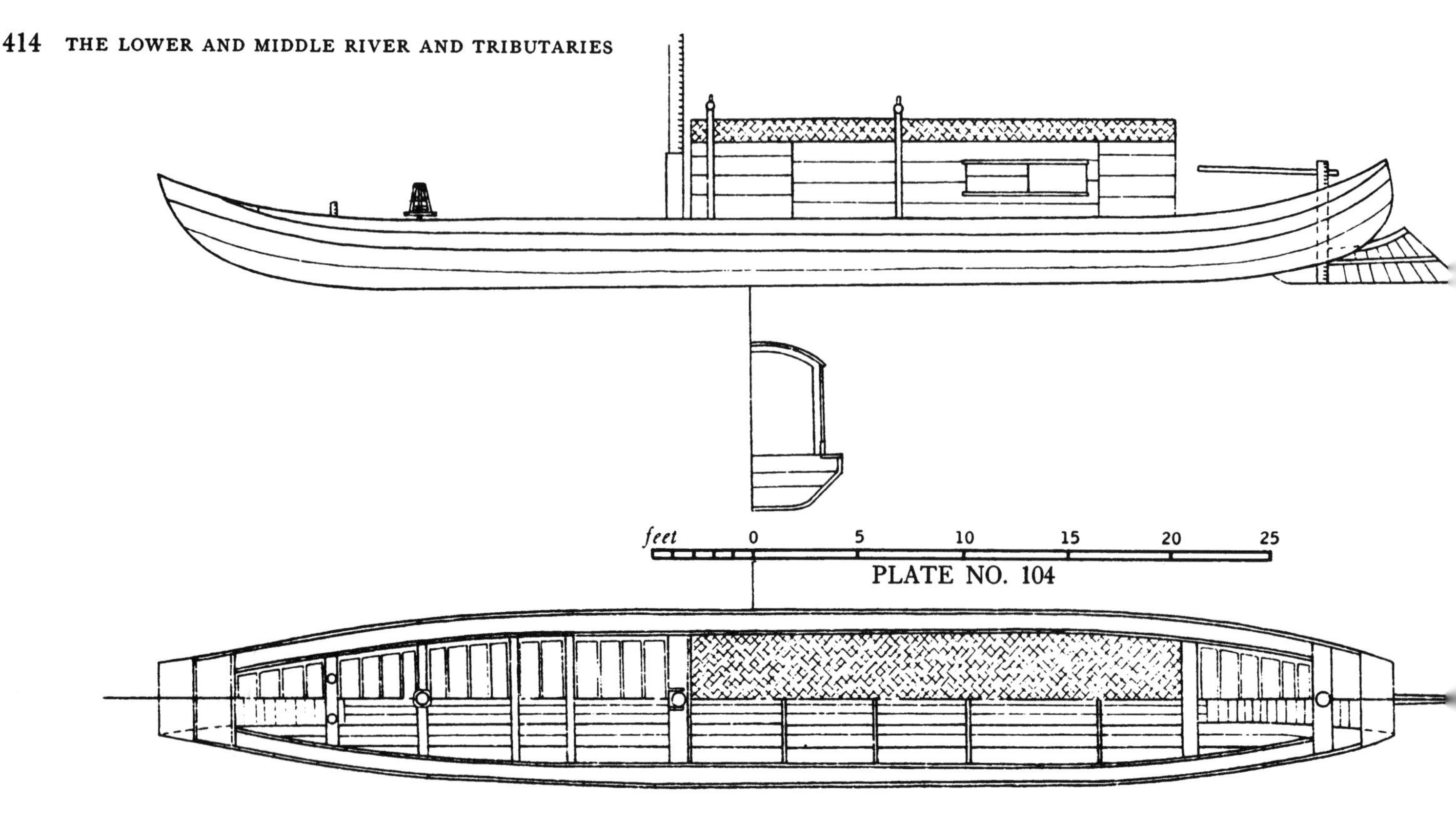

PLATE NO. 104

醴陵倒把子

THE LILING TAO-PA-TZŬ OR LO RIVER JUNK

The Liling *tao-pa-tzŭ*, belonging to the *tao-pa-tzŭ* family, is a comparatively light-draught wide-beamed native of Kiangsi well designed for the requirements of the coal trade on the Lo River. Liling (醴陵) is a town on the left bank of the Lo River about 50 miles above Siangtan. Although normally these craft stay in their own district, they are often to be seen on the Tungting Lake, the Yangtze, and, indeed, as far abroad as Hankow during certain seasons of the year.

These junks carry the coal which comes from the mines at Pingsiang (萍鄉) in Kiangsi across the Hunan border and pass down through this province *via* Liling (醴陵). Excellent coking coal is found here, and the Hangyang Iron Works are largely dependent upon coke from these mines, which are said to be capable of turning out 300,000 tons per year.

Plate No. 104 shows a typical example of this class of vessel, measuring 61 feet, with a beam of 8 feet 4 inches, a depth of 3 feet 3 inches, and a carrying capacity of 200 piculs. The crew numbers four men.

湘鄉倒把子

SIANGSIANG TAO-PA-TZŬ OR LIEN RIVER COAL-BOAT

Another type of *tao-pa-tzŭ* is that hailing from the Lien River (漣水), an affluent of the Siang, which enters the river about 2 miles above Siangtan (湘潭). This is the antimony and zinc country.

Perhaps the most typical craft of this river is the Siangsiang *tao-pa-tzŭ*, or Lien River coal-boat, which hails from Siangsiang (湘鄉).

This junk is an exceptionally graceful and sturdy long-distance trader. The type illustrated in Plate No. 105 measures 80 feet in length, with a beam of 12 feet and a depth of $5\frac{1}{2}$ feet. She is fitted with 11 full bulkheads and three frames. Junks of this type usually have a very large cargo capacity ranging from

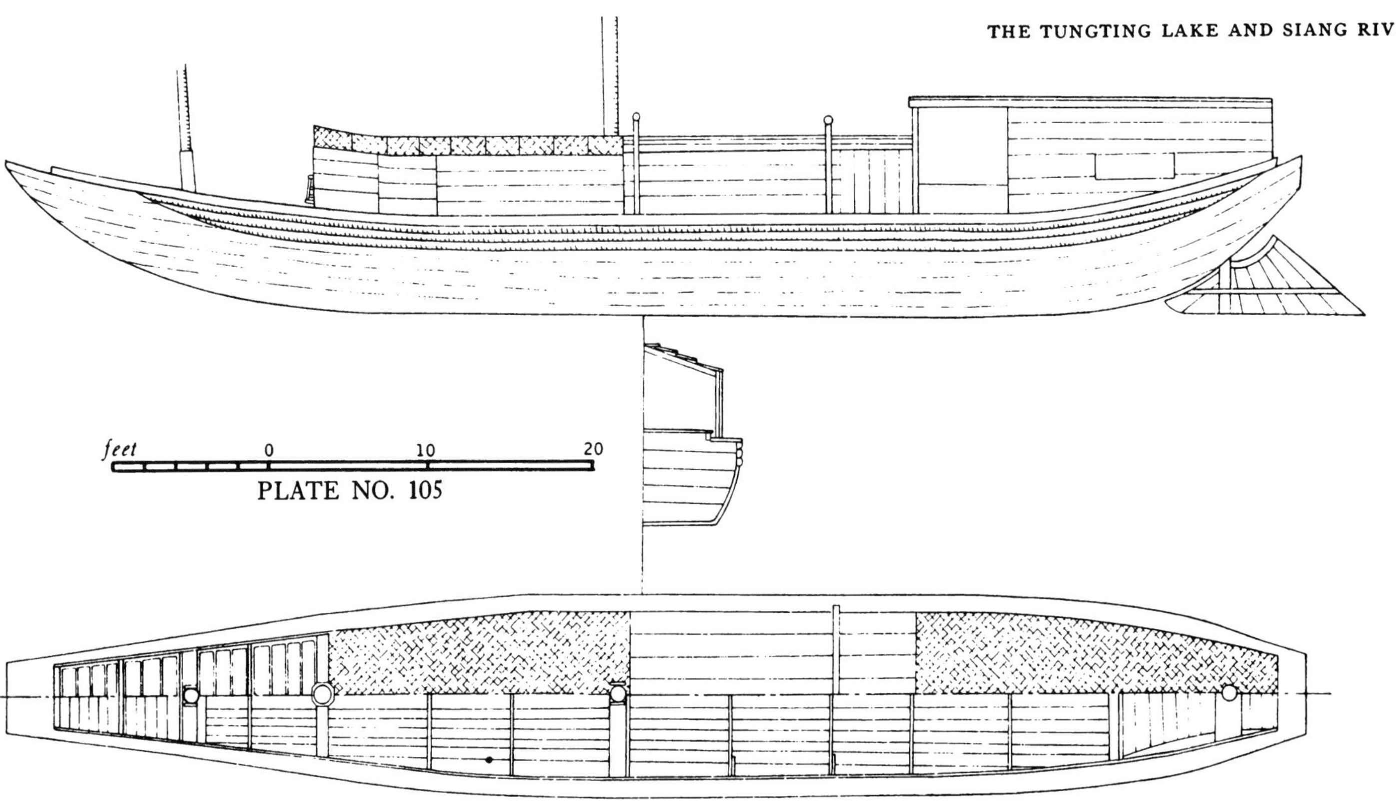

PLATE NO. 105

800 to 1,500 piculs. Often they are to be found transporting coal and minerals from Siang River ports to Hankow, returning with a general cargo.

The main characteristics of this long and slimly built craft are the markedly square stern with practically no overhang, the large after-cabin, and the very distinctive wales which cease before reaching the bow and stern.

The crew consists of seven men.

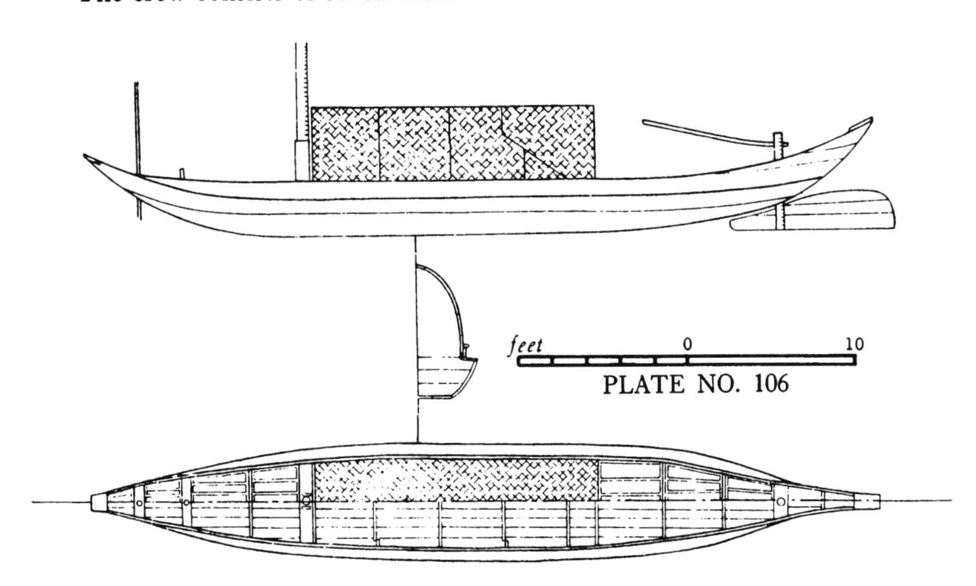

PLATE NO. 106

THE TUNG-PO-TZŬ OR HOLLOW BOAT

The *tung-po-tzŭ*, or hollow boat, is principally intended for work in shallow water and narrow rapids on the Upper Siang River.

This craft, which is illustrated in Plate No. 106, is a very light-draught cargo-carrier, with an over-all length of 46 feet, a beam of 7 feet, and a depth of 3 feet. The *pai-mu* hull is divided by 10 bulkheads and has four frames. The boat has a carrying capacity of 5 tons.

They are sharp-sterned boats, double-ended, with a great fineness about the bow which is generally much curved. This is a peculiarity of many junks built for swift waters, but seldom is it more accentuated than in the *tung-po-tzŭ*. Both bow and stern are almost the same in breadth.

The shallow-draught type of rudder projects slightly beyond the overhang of the stern. The crew consists of two men.

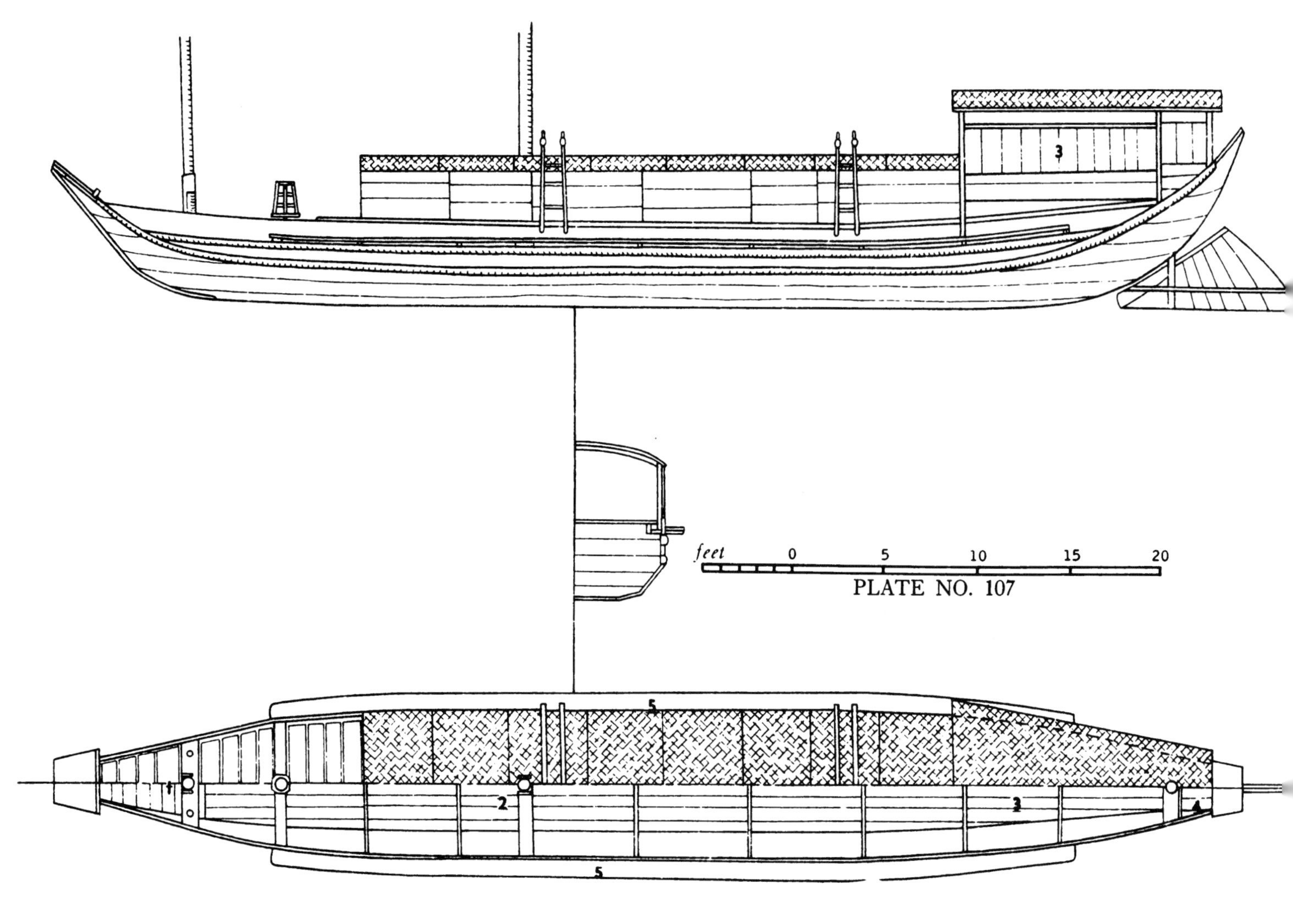

PLATE NO. 107

THE KIYANG PA-KAN-TZŬ OR POLE-BOAT

祁陽巴杆子

On the Siang, and as far down river as Hankow, a medium-sized light-draught junk is often to be met with which has a curious high stem and a rising pointed stern. This is the Kiyang *pa-kan-tzŭ*, or pole-boat, so named from her long and narrow lines.

Her true home is Lingling (零陵), a small town on the Upper Siang River. This type is designed especially for work in narrow and very shallow rapids. A typical example, illustrated in Plate No. 107, measures $64\frac{1}{2}$ feet, with a beam of $7\frac{3}{4}$ feet and a depth of $4\frac{1}{2}$ feet. Her cargo capacity is about 22 tons.

As will be seen from the plan, there are 11 full bulkheads. Additional strength is imparted to the first[1] and fifth[2] compartments by means of the mast-partners.

The low, rounded mat house, fitted with removable panels, begins at the third bulkhead and extends to the ninth. Abaft this is the owner's cabin[3], where there is ample headroom. The galley[4], which is fitted with a built-in stove, is right aft.

The most outstanding feature of these craft is the high tapering bow, so desirable for work in rapids.

A "parodos[5]," if such it may be called, or poling gangway, is built out on each side wide enough to leave a walk on either side of the vessel for the quanters.

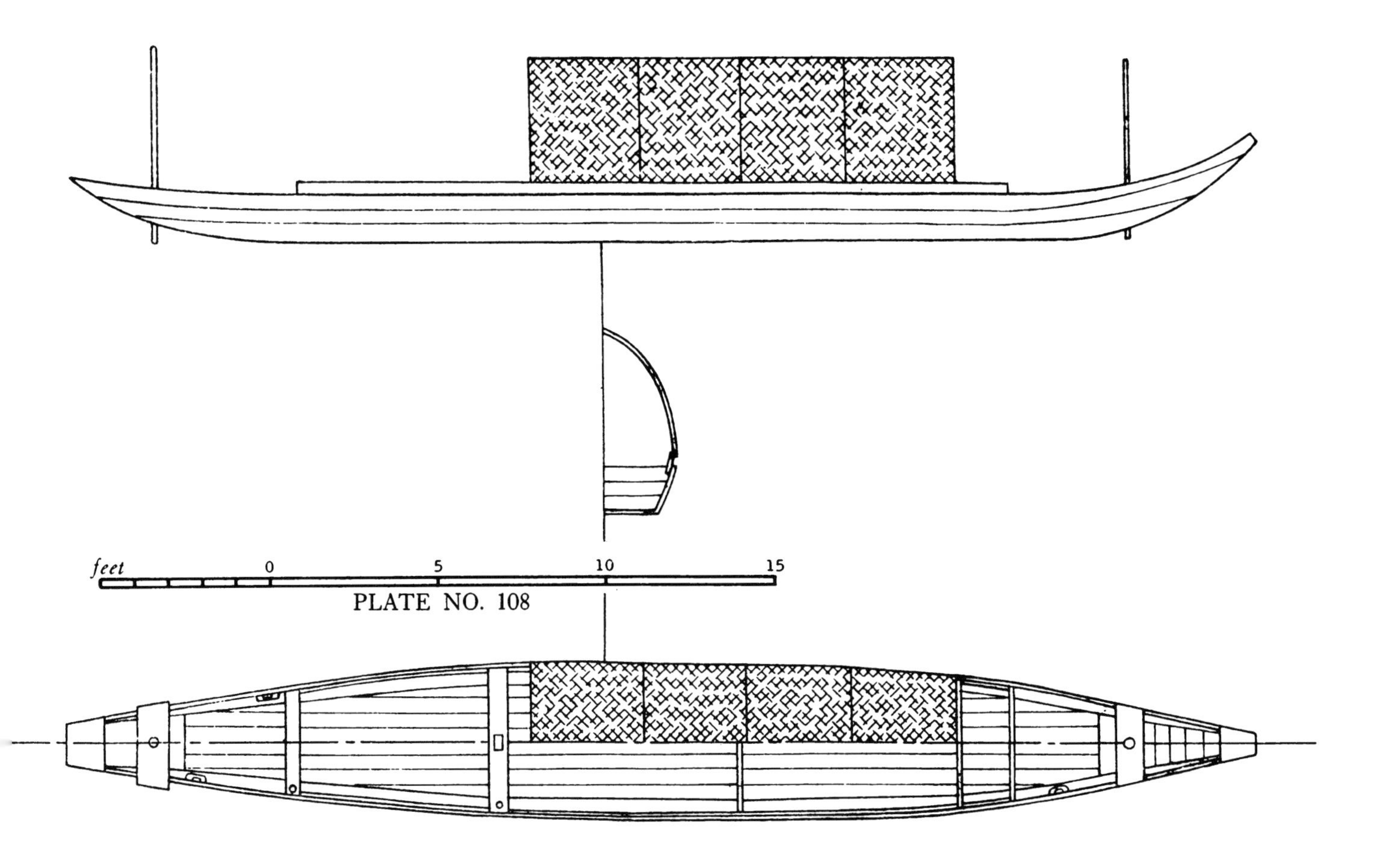

PLATE NO. 108

THE TUNGTING LAKE FISHERMAN

Although the rivers of Hunan, like the Yangtze, abound in fish, the industry is not of any great significance, the market being generally limited to local sales. The principal catches are carp (鯉), *lien-yü* (鰱魚), and *pien-yü* (鯿魚).

According to the "Chinese Economic Journal," there are only 22 districts in Hunan producing fish, of which 17 produced statistics showing the number of fishing families to be 21,900, representing only 0.36 per cent of the total number of families in the province. Most of them, it is said, live around the Tungting Lake, especially at Hanshow (漢壽), where there are somewhat less than 7,000 families engaged in fishing. At Nanhsien (南縣) there are 5,000 fishing families.

The total number of fishing-boats in the 17 districts in 1933 was about 14,250, of which 6,000 were in Nanhsien, 4,300 in Hanshow, and 1,000 in Lihsien (澧縣).

The boats used are all of the sampan variety, a typical example being illustrated in Plate No. 108. This craft measures 35½ feet, and has a beam of 4 feet 8 inches and a depth of 1 foot 6 inches. These boats usually fish with a cast or dip net.

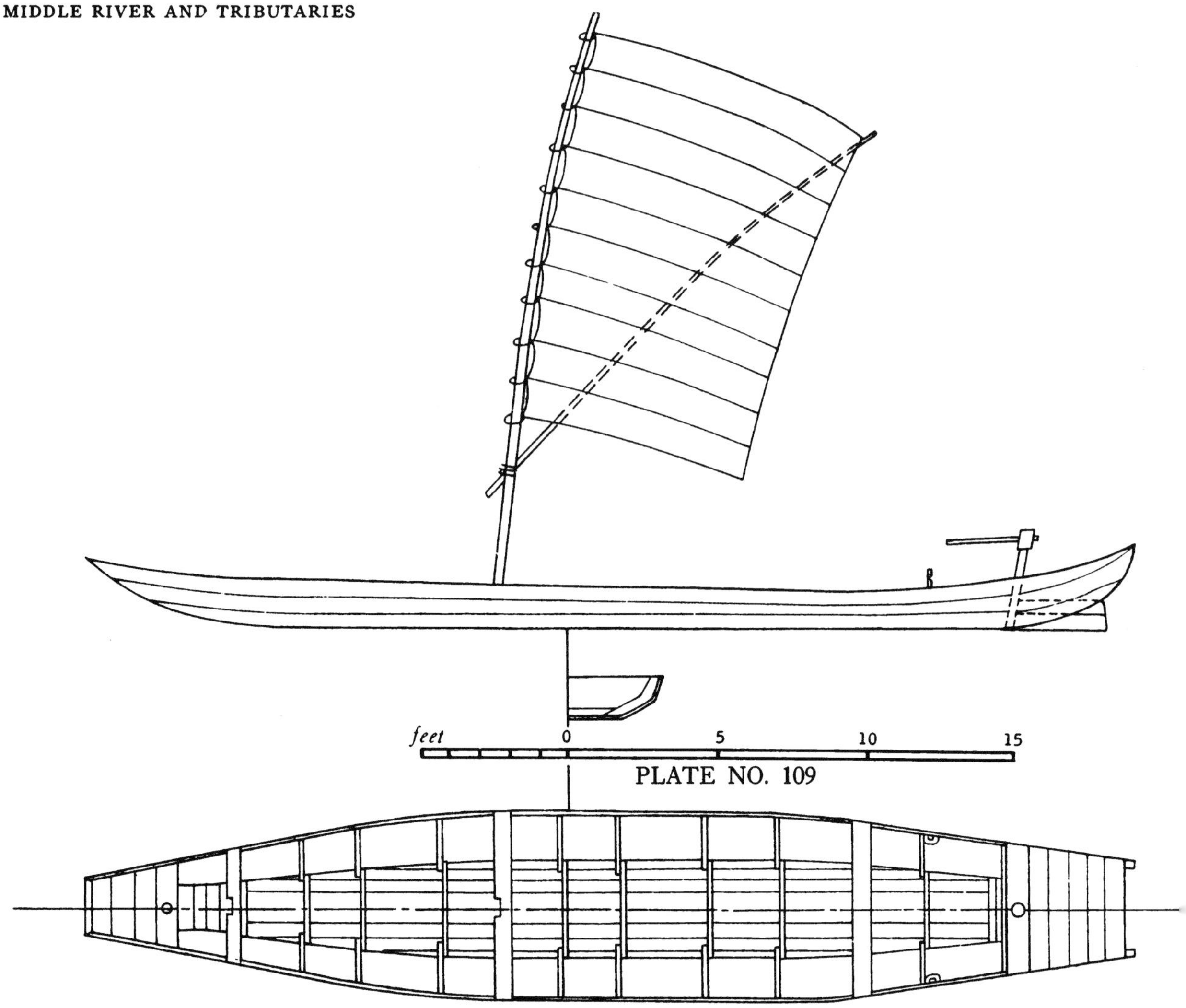

feet 0 5 10 15

PLATE NO. 109

THE CHANGSHA SAMPAN

The Changsha sampan differs little from other sampans found in the Middle Yangtze area.

The craft illustrated in Plate No. 109 is sturdily built and measures 45 by 6½ feet, with a depth of 1½ feet, and is fitted with five bulkheads and seven frames. The bow and stern are slightly raked. A large rudder and tiller are fitted in the customary manner. This is a very common type which is used for many purposes, such as fishing, transport of light cargo and passengers. Its cargo-carrying capacity is small.

竹簰

THE CHU-P'AI OR BAMBOO RAFT

Much interest attaches to bamboo rafts in China, for here we probably have the Chinese ship in its most primitive form. From it, doubtless, evolved the various types of junks as we know them to-day.

The raft shown in Plate No. 110 is to be found wherever a strong and inexpensive craft is required for work in very shallow rapids. These craft are also used as tenders to wood rafts or for ferrying passengers and cargo from place to place.

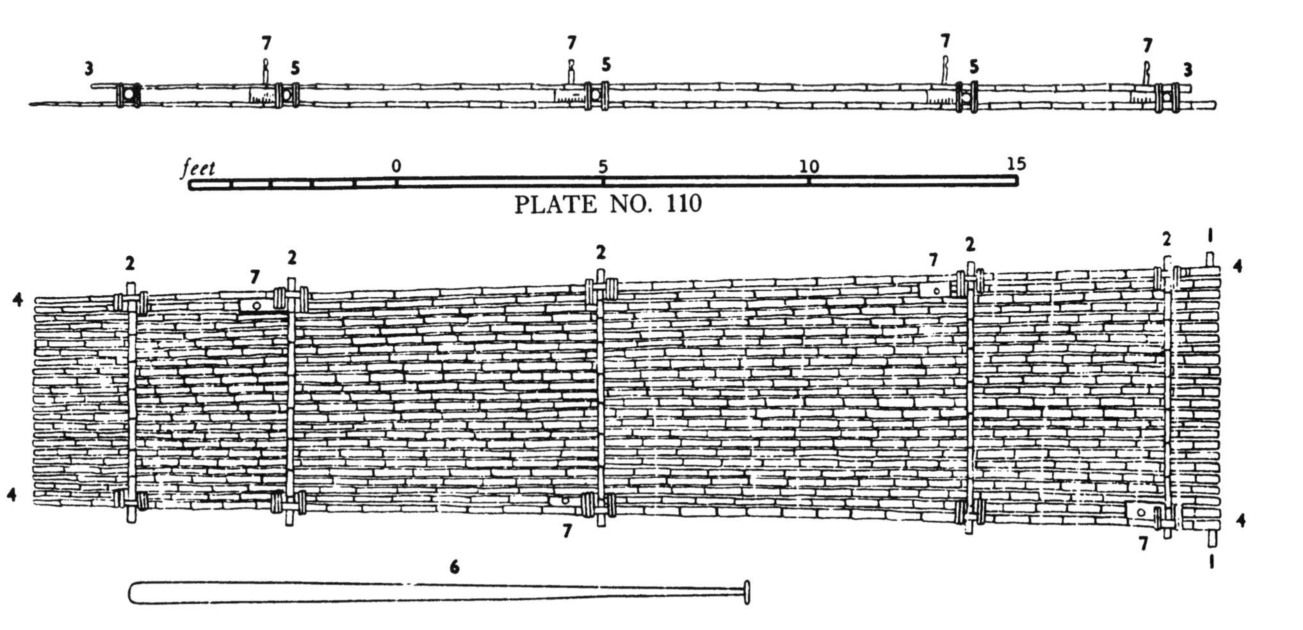

PLATE NO. 110

The raft illustrated is constructed of 24 bamboo poles, 6 inches in circumference at their thickest part, laid side by side and pinned together at the bow by a slat of wood[1] passing through a slot cut in each bamboo. In addition there are five frames[2] lashed across the raft by strips of bamboo. Along each side a bamboo strengthening piece[3] running fore and aft is fitted on top of the extremities of the frames to give further rigidity to the whole structure. This strengthening piece is lashed to the two outside bamboos on each side of the raft[4] by bamboo ropes[5]. Four crude, 15-foot oars[6], each in one piece, are used for normal propulsion, and thole-pins[7], 2 feet high, are placed as shown in Plate No. 110. They are embedded in logs[8] which are lashed to the strengthening piece on the raft itself. This type of raft carries from two to four men.

THE TIMBER-CARRYING JUNK

No plans are available for the following types.

Junks are often used for transporting certain kinds of timber on the waterways between Changteh and Hankow. This method has an advantage in that the timber is not lost in bad weather, as is sometimes the case with rafts.

The timber thus transported by junk is stowed in a number of ways, the most common being to use two junks joined together by a spar at bow and stern, leaving an interval of 15 feet between the two craft. The poles are laid fore and aft on the spars and securely lashed with bamboo ropes.

THE TIMBER RAFTS OF HUNAN

Much of the wealth of the west of the Province of Hunan is in the form of forests, and the principal timber rafts hail from those parts. The trade used to be a monopoly in the control of three guilds which sent their own *fu-shou* (斧 手), or axe hands, to the forest regions.

With the advent of the spring and summer freshets the timber is floated down the mountain streams to the nearest deep water. Here it is formed into small rafts to be later enlarged at the chief timber marts of the Siang, Tzŭ, and Yüan Rivers.

The timber from which the rafts are made is chiefly fir and pine; but other varieties are also included, such as cypress, cedar, redwood, camphor, and willow. The rafts from the upper reaches of the Siang River above Yungchow (永州) and over the border are somewhat different from the Hunan type in that they are less "built up." At Lokcheung in Kwangsi they are made in a simple rectangular form just big enough to accommodate two large sweeps at each end. Farther down the Siang River, at and below Siangtan, these rafts are considerably enlarged.

On the Tzŭ River the shallow-draught rafts are similarly enlarged in size as they progress down stream—that is to say, those that survive intact, for 20 per cent are said to be wrecked in the rapids on their way to Yiyang. From here they follow the tortuous waterway leading from the Tzŭ River to the Siang. On arrival at Lintzekow or at Lulintan on the latter river, the enlargement is effected, and their size is increased to some 80 feet in length, with a breadth of 60 feet and a draught of from 6 to 8 feet.

From two to five of these sections are then connected together in line ahead with an interval of a few feet between each. In this form they proceed down to Hankow, sometimes taking months to get there.

The Yüan River rafts, which are sometimes known as the West Lake rafts, cannot always navigate the shallows of the western portion of the lake, which becomes a mere marsh in the autumn and winter. It is then necessary for them to travel *via* the winding creeks and canals connecting the Yüan, Tzŭ, and Siang Rivers. While proceeding east on this route between Changteh and Lintzekow, they are permitted to move only on the 3rd, 6th, 9th, 13th, 16th, 19th, 23rd, 24th, and 29th of each month, so as to avoid collision with the considerable traffic of junks, which are forbidden to travel in the opposite direction on those days.

The rafts in their newly enlarged state have a few matsheds built on them to house the crew, which vary in number from 16 to 60, the number being on the basis of four men for every hundred *liang* (樑) of measurement. Their wives, children, and live stock accompany them, and their home life carries on undisturbed.

If, owing to bad weather, the voyage occupies more than 80 days, the crew receive a gratuity. The headman is responsible for the navigation and safety, and any loss of poles must be made good by him. He is known as the *ta-ku-lao* (打鼓老), or drum-beater, for he controls his men by the beat of a drum.

Steering is effected in the same manner as on the Lower Yangtze rafts already described. The greatest danger lies in grounding during falling water on the submerged banks of the narrow channels through the lake and the risk of consequent exposure to bad weather in these unsheltered expanses of water, where sudden gales may blow up with disconcerting rapidity.

The wrecking of a raft under such conditions is not unusual, and even if it remains intact, it is often necessary to break it up so as to refloat it, after which it must be again assembled. This, of course, means a delay of from two to three months.

Among other annoyances which the raft-owners have to put up with are the not infrequent collisions which, although the raft remains unscathed, entail disbursement for damage to the craft collided with. This applies particularly to the River Inspectorate aids to navigation, for damage to a light-boat or buoy and the loss of the anchor cables is an expensive accident for the raft-owners. Loss of the poles by petty pilfering is another hazard, for the inhabitants adjacent to the river down which the rafts float are always on the look-out for some fortunate mishap whereby a pole may break adrift. By the unwritten law of the

Yangtze it then becomes the property of the first person to find it and is then sold back to the owners for a third of its value. Such an easy method of gain arouses all their most predatory instincts, and these villagers may be described as confirmed "wreckers." If a whole raft catches temporarily on a rock or runs ashore, they will sometimes assist matters by cutting the bamboo retaining ropes, so that they can put in the stereotyped claim of one-third of the value on the maximum amount of timber.

The patron god of rafts is "General Yang," or to give him his full name, Yang Sze Tsiang Kuin, one of the mythical Generals of the Naga King, Lung Wang (the Dragon King). He heads a big staff of immortals and is in charge of the policing of the waters. For this reason he is worshipped by lumbermen on rafts. His symbol is a dragon, showing that he also controls and stills storms. He carries an axe as an emblem suggestive of a wood-cutter.

THE TOWED PASSENGER-BOATS OF HUNAN

湖南乘客拖船

Time was when travel by junk or sampan in the bewildering and intricate network of waterways of Hunan was the only means of long-distance cross-country transport—and nobody was in a hurry.

But about the turn of the present century things began to change, and there came into being a service composed of a few small launches running between Changsha and Changteh during the high-water season. These instantly became popular, and each year saw more and more boats on the run. Finally a variety of dumb-lighter carrying passengers was added, and the service was extended to other runs. And so the Hunan "boat-train" service was born.

The following is a list showing the various main towns and districts which are now connected with Changsha by launch traffic:

	Approximate Distance.		Route.
	Kilometres.	*Sea Miles.*	
Siangtan (湘潭)	48	26	*Via* Ikiawan (易家灣).
Chuchow (株州)	80	43	„ Siangtan.
Hengshan (衡山)	209	113	„ Siangtan, Chuchow.
Hengyang (衡陽)	262	141	„ Siangtan, Chuchow, and Hengshan.
Kiyang (祁陽)	450	245	„ Siangtan, Chuchow, Hengshan, and Hengyang.
Yungchow (永州)	530	285	„ Siangtan, Chuchow, and Hengshan.
Changteh (常德)	322	174	„ Yüankiang.
Yiyang (益陽)	136	73	„ Lintzekow (臨資口).
Tsingshih (津市)	375	202	„ Yüankiang and Ansiang (安鄉).
Yüankiang (沅江)	128	69	„ Lintzekow.
Nanhsien (南縣)	209	113	„ Yüankiang.
Siangyin (湘陰)	64	35	„ Tsingkang (靖港).
Taoyüan (桃源)	342	185	„ Changteh.
Tzehukow (茈湖口)	85	46	„ Lintzekow.

The escorting launch tows a number of clumsy built-up lighters, the actual number being dependent on the power of the launch and the winding of the creeks. As many as five may sometimes be seen towed in a long line, with a total tow length of 140 yards, at a speed of about 3 knots, with accompanying sampans to take the overflow, trailing along too, made fast to any vantage point that offers. More usually, however, the tow-ropes are kept a few feet in length, so that the procession looks more akin to the coaches of a train than the usual lengthy water-borne tow. This practice has earned for the procession the name of the "boat-train." Whilst the launch itself may carry as many as 100 passengers, the passenger-boats will carry double that number with perhaps some concealed cargo in addition. The passenger-boats are built with square bows as a rule, to give the maximum capacity, and have a mast and sail for use in a fair wind, which otherwise is lowered.

Heath Robinson —a British "Rube Goldberg."

These craft consist basically of wooden lighters built up in a manner which would make instant appeal to Mr. Heath Robinson. Often they have two decks, and sometimes there are cabins—if they can be dignified by the name—on the upper deck; one cabin, with one or two shelf type of bunks, is reserved for any distinguished traveller, and when not occupied is filled with seemingly useless gear.

Everything possible is left to chance. The deck is usually unsafe and leaks; the deck-house is composed of every sort of wood, patched as often as not with rusty tin; but this was in the days when tins were cheap. The hand-rails are liable to give way at any moment, and the whole pantechnicon, for such it may be described, is over-crowded to a degree beyond description. Like so many things Chinese, however, it serves its purpose very well, and seafaring accidents are rare owing to the skill of the lake laodahs, with their uncanny ability to gauge the weather on the Lake Crossing.

The Chinese are always on the move. For the number that proceed down river to buy rice, an equal number will be found travelling up river for the same purpose. All have produce to sell, and all seem to travel the longest distance to dispose of it. Fortunately for them they are born travellers; that is to say, they will put up with the greatest possible discomfort, inconvenience, and even risk, without appearing to notice it. Passengers are huddled together in such numbers that there is barely room to sit, still less to lie down, and ventilation and privacy are alike lacking. No other nation in the world would tolerate such conditions.

The "boat-train" starts early. Before dawn the passengers swarm on board. The soldier with his tin mug, tooth-brush, and paper umbrella; the old woman with her bundle of chickens tied together by the legs like a bouquet; old men, young men; old women, young women; children, innumerable children, of all ages. Country people going to town, and town people going to the country, each with their merchandise, their luggage, and their live stock.

Hawkers, the only people on board able to move, try to avoid stepping on the passengers as they sell sweets, groundnuts, oranges, and sunflower seed. The shells and orange peel in quite a short time form a thick carpet. Hour succeeds hour, while the launch pants on with just sufficient steerage way. Amidst the unending clamour of crying babies, protesting live stock, and the clatter and noisy expectoration of the wakeful, many of the passengers manage miraculously to sleep while lying, sitting, and even standing, their heads swaying in oblivion.

A hat may fall overboard from the foremost boat, and attempts are made from each lighter as it passes the spot to retrieve it with a boat-hook by men leaning dangerously over the side. The passengers instantly wake up and struggle to reach the side to see the result or find out what has happened. The boat's list becomes greater, and there has been no inconsiderable number of accidents to various types of craft through just this kind of occurrence.

But, generally speaking, the lighter maintains its stability under the most awful odds. It would seem that a special providence watches over the passengers in the boat-train.

At each passenger-stage stowage is broken and out they pour, while an equal number of new-comers press forward in an attempt to get on board before the detraining passengers have left. Pushing, shoving, spitting, and shouting, they wriggle and elbow their way in or out, until almost simultaneously the outgoing and incoming passengers reach their objectives. The launch whistles to recall most of the crew who have gone to the village to buy food, and after a long delay the voyage is resumed.

At the end of the voyage it would probably be found that not one passenger who embarked at the commencement of the trip remained on board at its destination, and yet the density of the human cargo has remained always the same.

THE TUNGTING LIFE-BOATS

The *hung-ch'uan*, or life-boat, of the Tungting Lake measures about 40 feet, and there is little to distinguish it from the ordinary junks of the same class save the white-painted discs with red characters setting forth the name and character of the boat's work.

A description of the Chinkiang life-boats appears in Part Three, page 311. Details of the Upper Yangtze *hung-ch'uan* are in Part Four, page 528.

In former times the traffic on the lake must have been very great. A stone tower, 60 feet high, "the pinnacle of which was 200 feet above the level of the water," was built on Tokan Island (舵桿洲) in 1732, by Imperial command, at a cost of *Hk.Tls.* 200,000 (at that time the equivalent of £70,000) as an aid to navigation. The natural harbour there was furthermore improved and 16 life-boats stationed on the island; this number was some six years afterwards increased to 28. The number of junks passing the island, says the "Customs Decennial Report" for 1892–1901, was very great and attracted large numbers of pirates, with whom the lake was then infested. In course of time the lighthouse fell into disrepair; the route, owing to silting in the vicinity, became little used; and finally, in 1841, the lighthouse and life-boat station were abolished, the materials being used for building purposes elsewhere.

Up to the outbreak of the "China Incident" in 1937 there were 11 life-boats in service between Yochow and Lokia. The boats were not painted red, as one might suppose from their name, but were treated with wood oil. Their sails were dyed brown or more often blue. They had two masts and a crew of six men including the laodah. The institution was operated by the Junk Guilds, the money being supplied by the local merchants.

釣鈎子

THE TIAO-KOU-TZŬ

The *tiao-kou-tzŭ* is a salt-junk working the Siang River, usually running between Shiherhwei and Changsha. These junks are usually large, being 120 feet in length, with a beam of 18 feet, a depth of 9 feet, and a carrying capacity of 450 tons. They usually make two trips a year. The crew consists of 12 men. They are built at Siangtan, of *sha-mu* bottom and camphor-wood sides.

江東子

THE KIANG-TUNG-TZŬ

This junk is said to resemble a coffin, and is a regular salt-trader between Shiherhwei and Yochow. It makes two round trips a year, returning with lumber and charcoal. The crew consists of 24 men. The size varies from 80 feet in length, 18 feet beam, and 7 feet depth, to 100 feet in length, 22 feet beam, and 12 feet depth, with a carrying capacity of 300 to 600 piculs. Usually they have four masts and are built of camphor-wood at Shiherhwei, though sometimes at Wuhu and Nanking.

長船子

THE CH'ANG-CH'UAN-TZŬ

These junks are built at Yiyang and serve the Siang and the Tungting Lake; they may sometimes be seen on the Yangtze carrying paper to Hankow, their terminal port. In size they are usually 60 feet long, with a beam of 13 feet, a draught of 5 feet, and a capacity of about 80 tons.

滿江紅

THE MAN-KIANG-HUNG

The *man-kiang-hung*, or official boat, is so named because under the Ming or Ch'ing dynasty it was specially built for the purpose of carrying high officials from port to port. For this reason it has a special cabin, usually beautifully polished and decorated with dragons and flowers. The bottom is made of *sha-mu* and the sides of camphor-wood. This craft is also known as the *kuan-ch'uan* or *hung-ch'uan*, and is now used for carrying salt from Shiherhwei to Changsha, about two trips being made each year. They are built at Siangtan, and the length is usually 120 feet, with a beam of 18 feet and 10 feet draught. The carrying capacity can, it is said, be as much as 450 tons. The crew consists of 18 men.

THE TZŬKIANG

THE Tzŭkiang (資 江), or T'ankiang (灘 江), River of Rapids, as it is sometimes called, has its source near the Kwangsi-Hunan borders.

It has two branches, the true Tzŭkiang and the Lokiang, which unite at Tangtukow (塘 渡 口). The river pursues a steep and tortuous course in a general north-westerly direction for the first part of its course to Mapeishih (馬 轡 市), afterwards turning north-eastward and then eastward to Yiyang (益 陽), which is situated on the left bank of the river, 94½ miles from Yochow. It is a large distributing centre for timber, which is rafted down from the upper reaches. It has also some considerable coal trade, the coal being loaded into especially built junks for transport to Hankow.

The river from Yiyang upwards is very narrow in parts and runs between steep hills. It is said to be one long succession of rapids, some of them being very difficult to negotiate. Junks double their crews for the journey between Yiyang and Paoking, yet accidents are said to be frequent. Rain causes a sudden swelling of the river, for which the down-bound junks often wait, when they will shoot the rapids from Paoking to Yiyang, a distance of 500 *li*, in two days.

Yüankiang (沅 江), an important town, is situated at the entrance of the river to the Tungting Lake. It is a large port of call for tugs and lighters and a stopping-place for junks, which usually moor alongside the river-bank at the town.

The junks which ply on this river are unusually large for a small tributary, being on the average 66½ feet long, with a beam of 10 feet and a maximum draught of 2 feet. They are strongly built to withstand the series of difficult rapids which exist above Yiyang.

The method of propulsion is the usual laborious tracking on the up-bound journey, when the junks carry loads up to 15 tons. The sail is seldom used, even when down bound.

The Tzŭ, which is navigable by junks as far as Paoking (寶 慶), is an important waterway, as it taps the rich hinterland of Central Hunan.

THE MAO-PAN-TZŬ OR UNPLANED BOAT

On the route between the Tzŭ River ports and Hankow there exists the unusual case of a junk type which plies in only one direction—down river. This is the *mao-pan-tzŭ*, or unplaned boat, so named from her rough construction, and is quite different from any other of the Hunan junks in that its short life consists of one trip only. Here, as in so many types of junks, the special circumstances have given rise to a peculiar type, and " necessity has been the mother of invention." Hankow is a large market for coal, and Hunan can supply it. Wood is cheap, extremely cheap, on the Tungting Lake borders, but labour for handling junks, especially upwards against the current, is expensive.

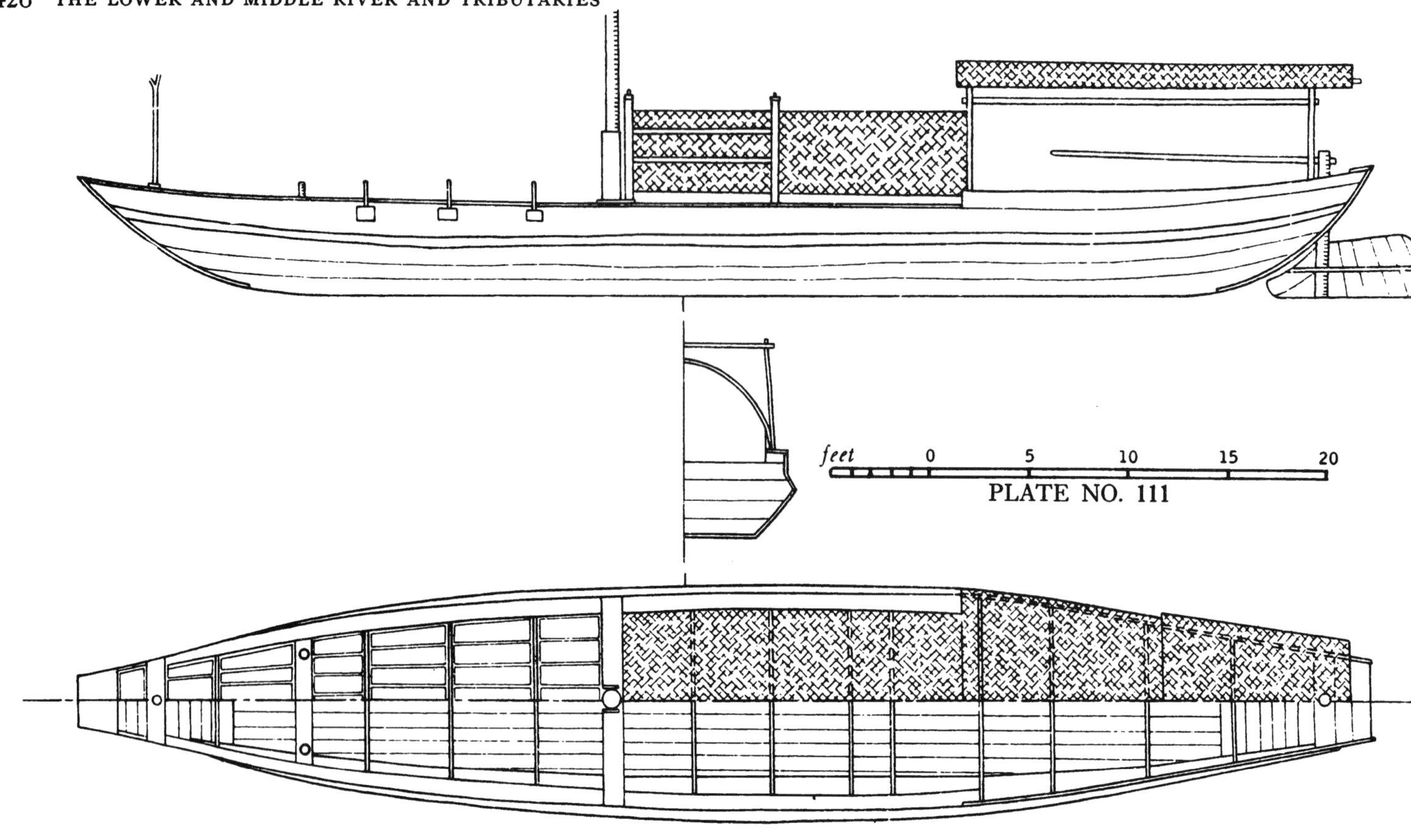

PLATE NO. 111

Such a set of circumstances has produced the Tzŭ and the Siang River coal-junk, carrying 50 to 60 tons of coal from Anhwa (安化) and other ports in Central Hunan to Hankow.

The junks are made of *sung-mu* (松木), or pine, and, as the name suggests, are very roughly constructed of very thin planking, butted edge to edge with bamboo pegs* but not caulked above the water-line. They are just sufficiently seaworthy to reach Hankow under favourable conditions. The strictest economy obtains throughout. They take perhaps a month for the journey, lying up for shelter at any sign of rough weather and bailing continuously to counteract the shortcomings of their very leaky seams.

The craft illustrated in Plate No. 111 is 65 feet in length, and has a beam of 11 feet and a depth of 4 feet, although sometimes they are much larger. These junks are not strongly built, are not much to look at, and are of the roughest in material and appearance. The plan gives a far too flattering representation of what is in fact a sorry piece of naval architecture.

On arrival at Hankow, which, improbable as it may seem, the crews manage to achieve with a fair percentage of success, their cargo is discharged, and the hulls are sold on the spot. Certain planking can be used as such, and the more inferior is just broken up for firewood. The yulohs, sweeps, and sails are returned with the crew by other types of Siang coal-junks, but the masts seldom, on account of their bulk. In preference they are sold as masts or special poles to Hankow boat-builders. Sometimes the sails are made of bamboo, being cheaper than cotton cloth in the interior, in which case, of course, they are not returned up river.

Propulsion is by oars or under sail according to the exigencies of the moment.

In the old days of likin tax the *mao-pan-tzŭ* successfully claimed exemption from this levy because of the likelihood of the craft's being damaged and sunk in moving amidst the usual busy traffic at the stations. This must have been an enormous advantage.

* In recent years iron nails have been substituted for bamboo pegs. According to the "Mariner's Mirror" for January 1941, the binding of planks by pegs obliquely driven in is unusual, paralleled only in four other localities, namely, the Upper Nile, the Gujarat Coast of India, in some craft in Northern Russia and in the Lamu Archipelago. To this list may be added a canoe of the Island of Botel Tobago off the south-east coast of Formosa, and the famous medicine-boats of the Upper Yangtze. (See page 552.)

A likin tax was a Chinese provincial tax levied at inland stations on imports or articles in transit.

As is only to be expected, these craft are very unsafe, and many are sunk; indeed, 20 per cent are said to be wrecked before reaching Yiyang. But it is said that the junkmen claim that if only one out of 10 junks reaches Hankow in safety the owners can still make a profit.

The crew consists of eight men, and all of them are, as they may well need to be, very strong swimmers.

The other types of Siang River coal-junks are usually smaller than the *mao-pan-tzŭ:* they are the *pao-ch'ing* (寶 慶), the *shên-pao-tzŭ* (神 保 子), and the *hsiao-po* (小 駁). There seems to be a mutual understanding that the crews of the *mao-pan-tzŭ*, having witnessed their own craft reduced to firewood—a sad moment for any sailor,—are given a free return passage to the Tzŭ River by any of the three other permanent types; but it should be noted that this mutual understanding does not preclude the "passengers" being required to assist at the yulohs for some hundreds of weary miles up against the current.

The practice of breaking up boats after arrival at their destination is not uncommon and is of very ancient origin, for precisely the same thing was done on the Euphrates centuries before the Christian era. Armenian boats, constructed for the downward voyage only, after bringing down cargo to Babylon, were broken up and the materials disposed of while the merchants and the crew returned by land.*

* This is mentioned by Herodotus.

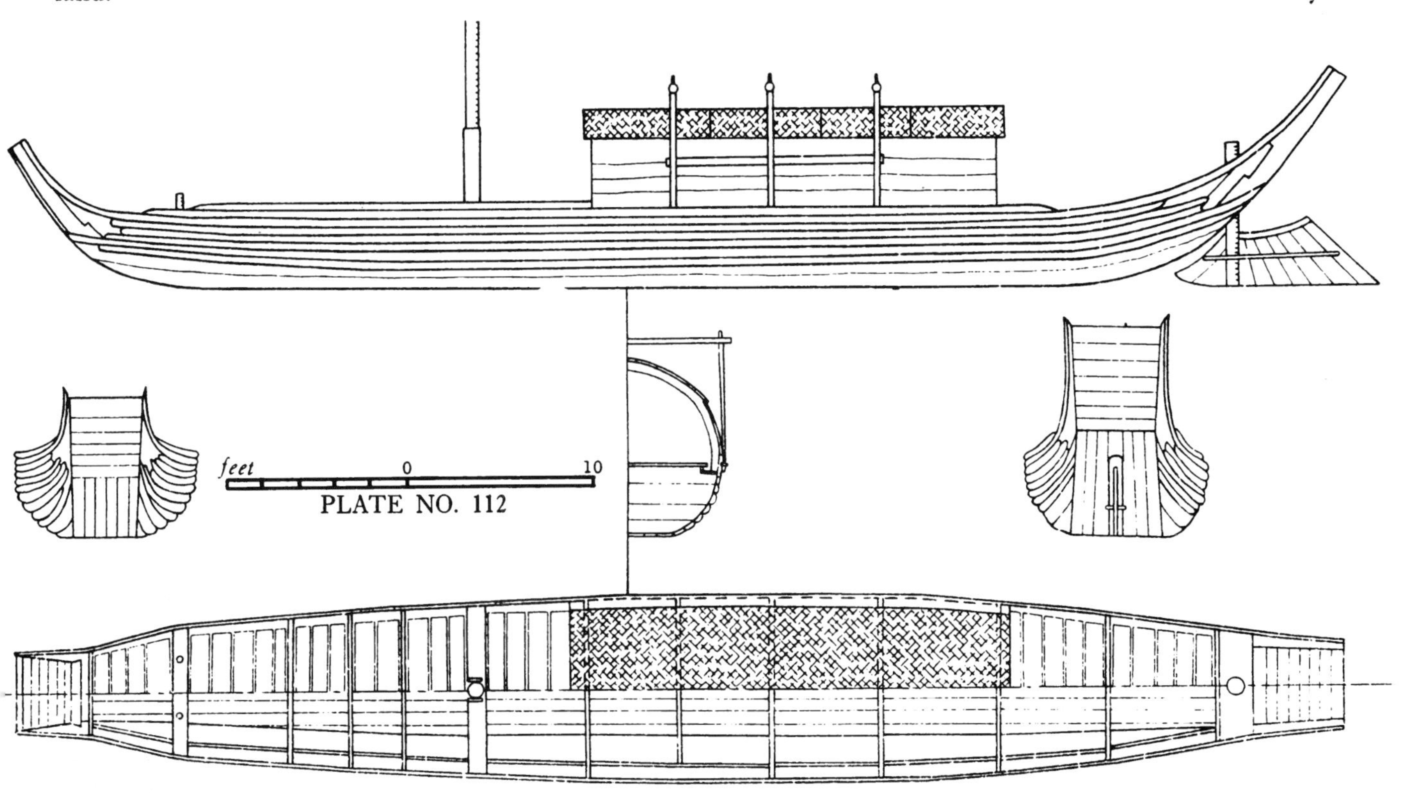

PLATE NO. 112

THE SHÊN-CH'UAN OR COAL-BOAT

This type of junk is of very shallow draught and is especially built for the navigation of the dangerous rapids on the Tzŭ River, where she functions as a coal-carrier.

Unlike the square box-like shapes of the usual run of Hunan and Hupeh junks, the craft illustrated in Plate No. 112 has a considerable sheer at both bow and stern, rising in a semicircle. Their main dimensions are 72 feet long, 9 feet beam, 3 feet 9 inches in depth, and a capacity of 30 tons.

The hull planking consists for the most part of long, heavy, unplaned, natural *pai-mu* poles, 2 inches thick, laid on edge and secured to the bulkheads, of which there are 13. At the turn of the bottom, *sha-mu* planks 1 to 1½ inches thick are used. These are continued up to form the bluff bow and broad stern to deck-level, where they are joined by the descending athwartship planking.

Their port of origin is Sinhwa (新 化), about 150 miles above Yiyang. Generally speaking, these interesting craft are dilapidated and are wood-oiled once in a lifetime.

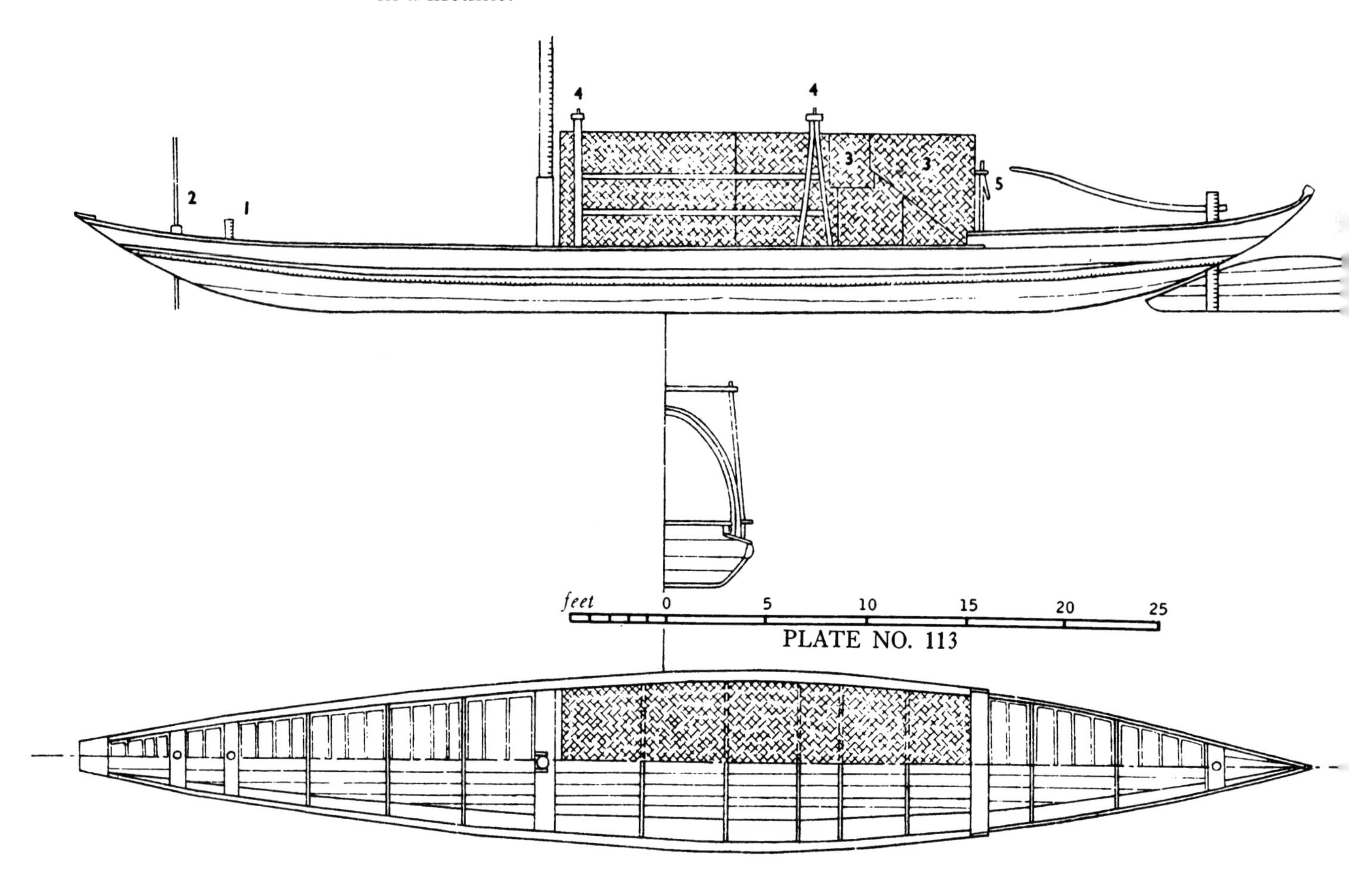

PLATE NO. 113

陽氣鼓 THE YANG-CH'I-KU OR SUN-LIT DRUM-BOAT

Few craft of the Tungting Lake area can equal in charm and gracefulness the *yang-ch'i-ku*, or sun-lit drum-boat.

By reason of its narrow bow and sharp stern this type of junk is one of the most distinctive classes to be found in Hunan. The sun-lit drum-boat is especially designed to carry coal from the mines on the Tzŭ River and usually returns light. These craft are often to be seen in considerable numbers as far afield as Hankow.

Built long of bow, low in the waist, square in the bilge, and with a gradually ascending stern, they vary very little as a class. That illustrated in Plate No. 113 has a length of 64 feet, a beam of 9 feet, a depth of 3¼ feet, and a capacity of 18 tons. The crew consists of four men.

The bottom is made of *sha-mu* and the sides and bulkheads of *pai-mu*. There are 15 bulkheads and no frames. The shallow-draught rudder projects beyond the stern and is 10 feet in length at its foot; it has a greatest depth of 2½ feet and is of the balance variety. A single bollard[1] is placed just abaft the stick-in-the-mud anchor[2] on the first bulkhead.

The house, which starts abaft the mast, is made entirely of matting. The irregular-shaped sections[3] are used to mat-in the after-part of the junk. When not in use they are stowed in piles on the after-end of the house. Lumber irons are situated on the fore-end of the house[4]. Abaft the house is a light pin-rail[5] carrying one or more belaying pins for the use of the sheet of the sail.

It is quite a noticeable and curious fact that nearly all junks on the middle river carrying coal, or some equally uninspiring cargo, have graceful lines or some artistic feature of interest.

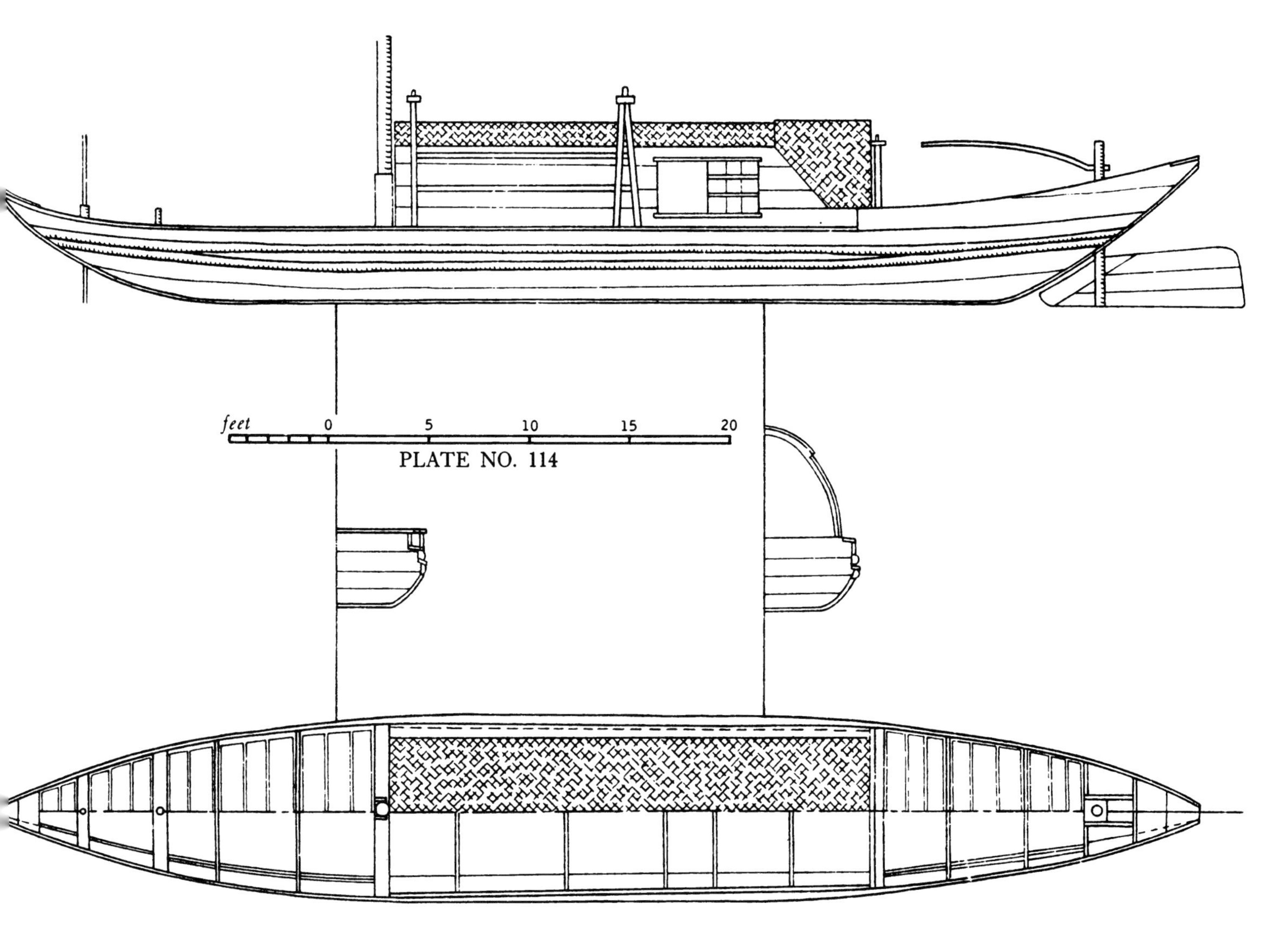

PLATE NO. 114

THE ANHWA CH'IU-TZŬ OR ANHWA BOAT

Another craft well known on the Tzŭ River is the less graceful Anhwa *ch'iu-tzŭ*, a light-draught cargo-carrier designed for the shoal-water reaches of the Ishui (伊 水), a tributary of the Tzŭ.

Flat-bottomed and about seven beams to length, she has the same general features of build as the *yang-ch'i-ku*, just described, notably the slightly raised deck abaft the house.

The craft illustrated in Plate No. 114 is a double-ender, and measures about 61 feet, with a beam of 8½ feet and a depth of 3½ feet. This type of craft is strongly, if lightly, built and, for its size, is admirably adapted to carry a maximum load on a minimum draught in a locality where deep channels are few and far between.

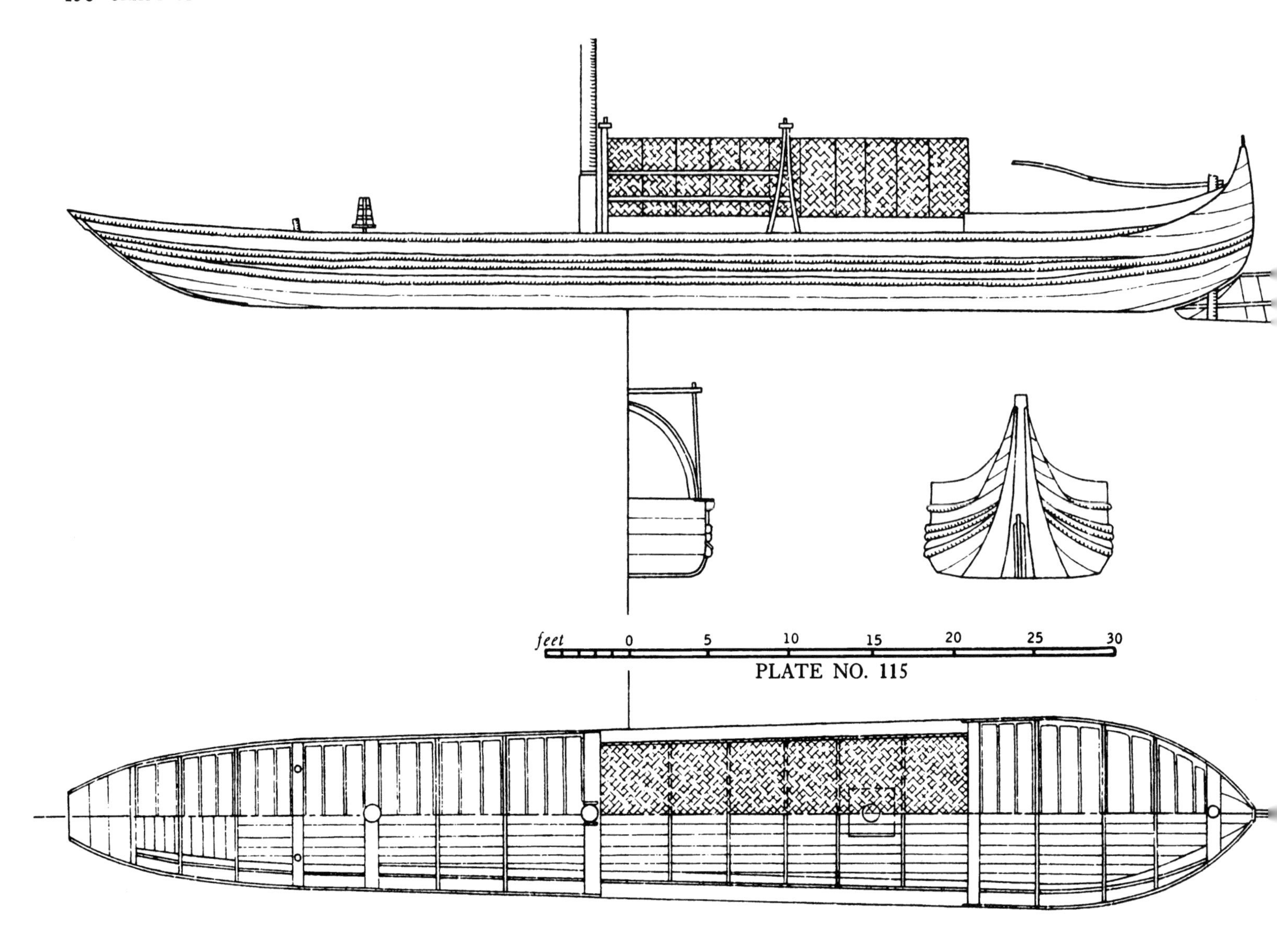

PLATE NO. 115

平條子

THE P'ING-T'IAO-TZŬ OR LONG AND NARROW BOAT

The craft as illustrated in Plate No. 115 is an altogether different example of coal-carrier on the Tzŭ River. It is called the *p'ing-t'iao-tzŭ*, a free translation of which is " something long and narrow." Unlike the sun-lit drum-boat just described, she is not exclusively engaged in the coal trade.

The most distinguishing feature of this type of junk is that the greatest beam measurement is aft—actually as far aft as the thirteenth bulkhead. Another unusual feature is that the deck of this portion is raised 1 foot higher than the rest of the vessel.

They are stout boats and, with a length of 71 feet, a beam of 11 feet, and a depth of 4 feet, are the largest type of craft to be found navigating the Tzŭ River. Great strength is provided by the long and comparatively heavy wales running the whole length of the vessel.

There are 17 bulkheads forming 18 compartments and no frames. The bulkheads and sides are of *pai-mu*, while the bottom is of *sha-mu*. The house is entirely of matting. Inside is to be found a fixed table-cum-stove. A high coaming extends from the mast to the break of the poop.

The craft of the Tzŭ River have a strange combination of awkwardness and beauty, and in simplicity and efficiency they are not excelled.

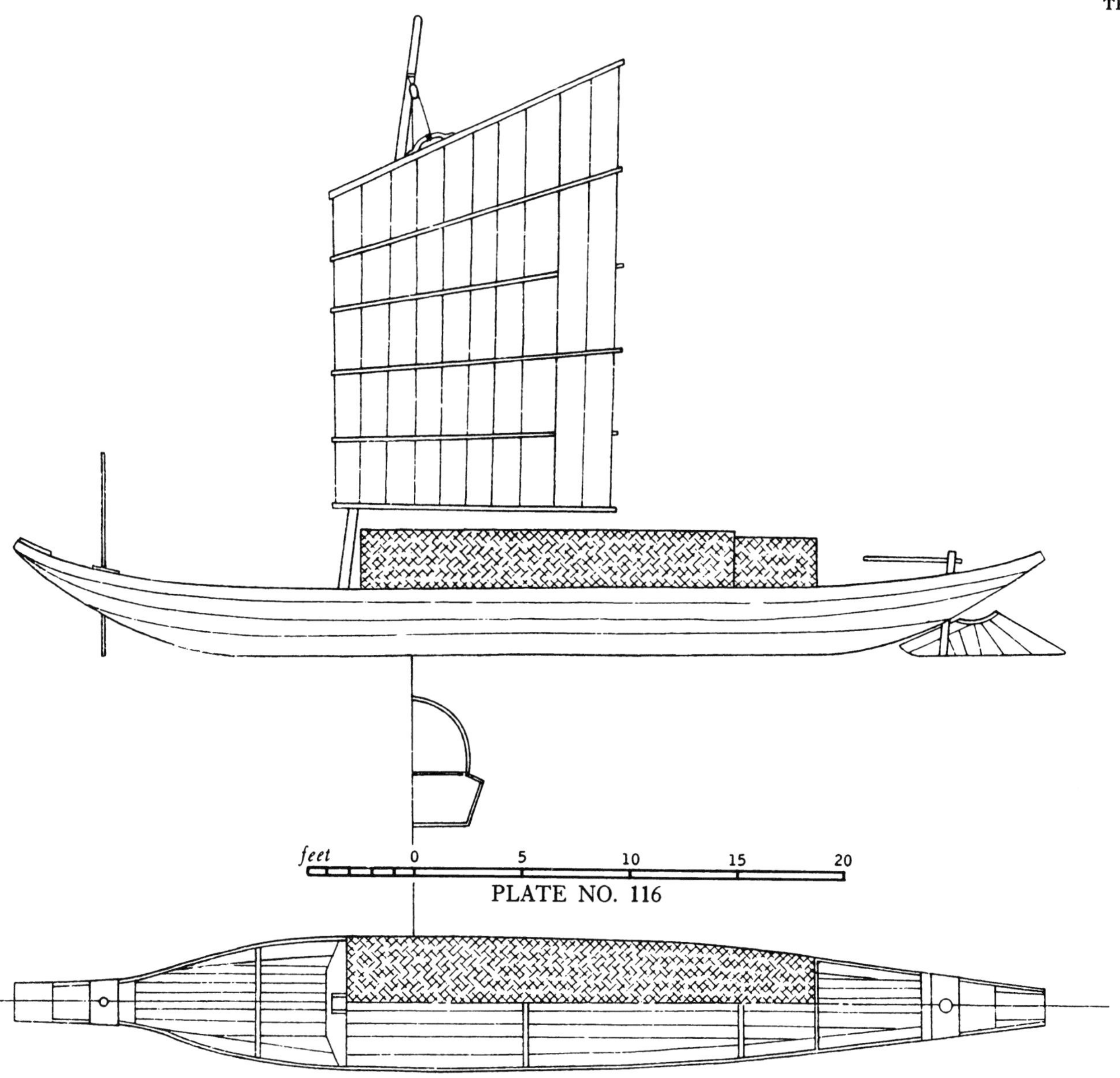

PLATE NO. 116

THE YIYANG SAMPAN

The Yiyang sampan is one of the most distinctive types of craft to be found on the Tzŭ River.

These open and curiously shaped boats do not vary much in size. That illustrated in Plate No. 116 measures 37 feet in length, with a beam of 5 feet and a depth of 2 feet.

They are chiefly used for transporting passengers across the river.

THE YÜAN RIVER

FROM ancient times the Province of Hunan has been one of the chief sources of the timber supply of China. The logical outcome of this profusion of wood is that there has always been a traditional high standard of boat-building in the types peculiar to this region.

The Yüan River has its source in Kweichow Province, and passes the ports of Yüanchow (沅 州) and Shenchow (辰 州) before it reaches the important town of Changteh, on its northern bank, and finally joins the Tungting Lake.

Changteh, the port for transhipment for traffic with Western Hunan and Kweichow, is reached mainly by creeks through the delta land south of the lake and by the Taipingho (太 平 河) joining the Yangtze above Shasi or the Owchihho (藕 池 河) below Shasi and near Sunday Island. The latter is the best in winter. These all form a huge network of waterways, natural and artificial, intersecting the country between the Yangtze and the lake and also west and south of the lake. The creeks are intricate and bewildering. The direction of flow changes in sympathy with water-levels in the Yangtze and the lake. None, however, flows with great velocity.

As a means of communication between the Yangtze and the Provinces of Kweichow and Yunnan, the Yüan River offers a short cut and is therefore of very great value. The junk traffic on it is very large.

Unfortunately, however, it suffers from two very grave navigational difficulties: firstly, a number of large and formidable rapids; and secondly, numerous shoal-water channels situated at the entrance to the river and on the West Tungting Lake Crossing. These obstacles necessarily restrict navigation for the most part to the high-water season, although some junks drawing 2 feet of water ply between Changteh and Hungkiang (洪 江) during the major portion of the year.

The river is navigable during the summer for small sampans as far as Hwangping, while navigation for junks of 150 piculs capacity ceases at Chenyüan (鎮 遠), from which town cargo is carried by coolies into the interior.

According to the junkmen, there are 28 difficult rapids between Chenyüan in Kweichow and Changteh. Of this number, 16 are above Yüanchow, three between Yüanchow and Hungkiang, two between the latter town and Shenchow, and, finally, seven between Shenchow and Changteh. These rapids are at their worst in November, December, and during the greater part of January. At this time junks with a cargo of 3½ tons can approach within 200 miles of Yüanchow. The cargo is then transferred to boats limited to a cargo of 1½ tons. These smaller vessels can reach Yüanchow and ascend even higher into Kweichow Province. Only sampans drawing less than a foot are able to ply above Hungkiang. During the autumn and spring the junks draw no more than 3 feet, but when the river is high in the summer they can load to their full capacity, sometimes to as much as 5 feet in the case of Lower Yangtze junks visiting the Yüan.

The first freshets make their unwelcome appearance in April, when the river rises rapidly. Obviously, for the navigation of this swift and difficult river special types of junk are required. The type most to be met with is the famous *ma-yang-tzŭ*, the size most in demand being a junk with a carrying capacity of

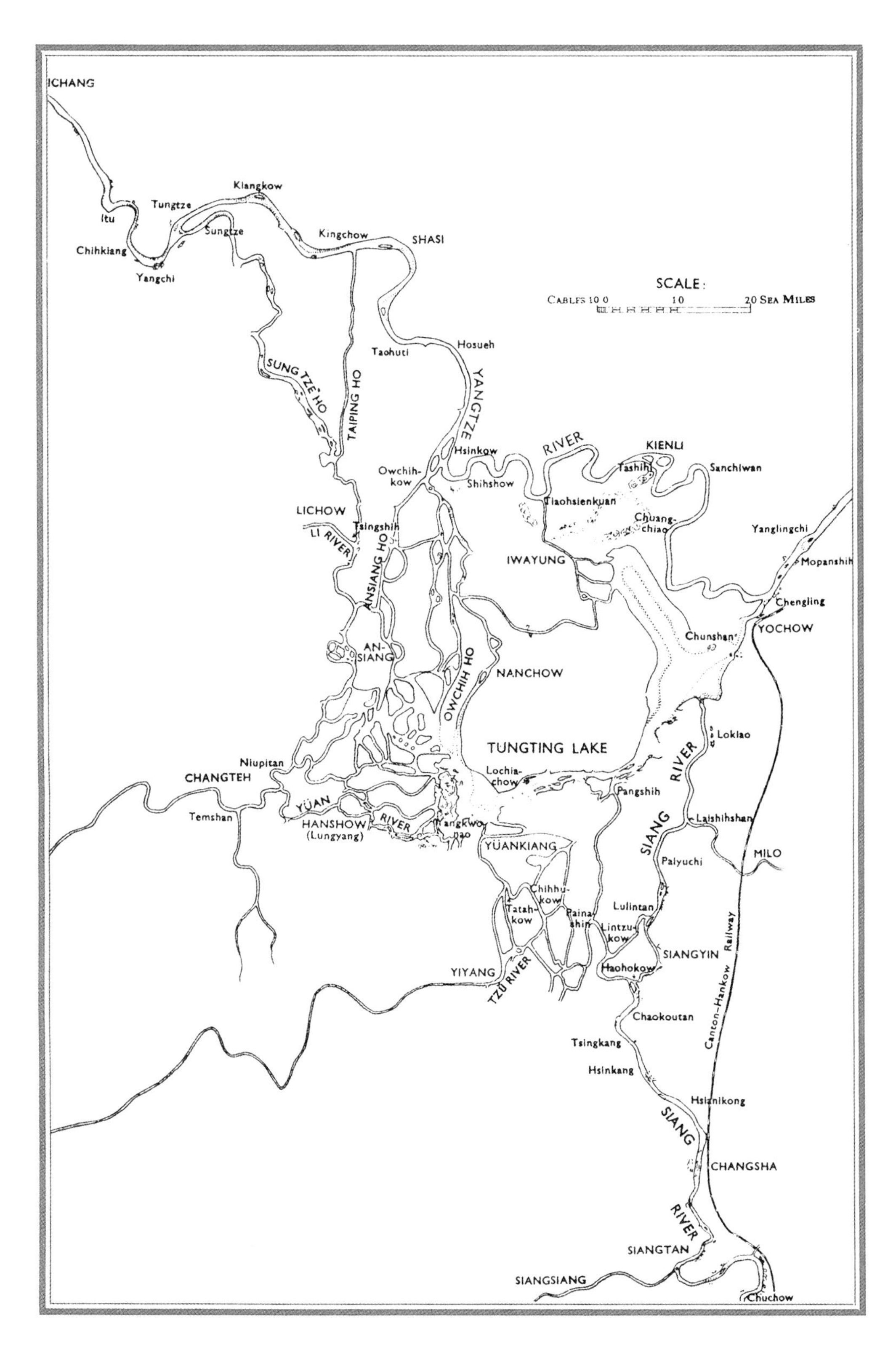

Tungting Lake.

150 piculs on a draught of little more than 15 inches.

These craft, which will be described in detail later, when not under sail are tracked up river and proceed under six-man yulohs when down bound. The sails of the Yüan River junks are the lofty and narrow variety. There is usually a fine, rounded shoulder to the upper part of the leech.

The *ma-yang-tzŭ* are described on pages 434–35, 437, 438, and 464 in Part Three; in Part Four, page 498.

In 1908 the number of junks coming to Changteh from Hankow, Changsha, and other down-river ports was estimated at 5,000 to 6,000 per annum and those trading farther up river at 4,000 per annum.*

The cargo usually consists of wood oil, tea oil, tea, varnish, indigo, hemp,

* "Customs Trade Reports."

china grass, gypsum, vegetable dyes, timber, and various metal ores, such as antimony, iron, and copper.

There are seven tributaries of the Yüan—all navigable by junks—which give access to a wide tract of country. Produce from Yunnan, Kweichow, and the borders of Kwangsi and Szechwan find a market in Changteh, which owes its importance to the necessity for transhipment at that point from deep to shallow draught junks at certain times of the year. Junks require to renew their bamboo tracking-ropes each trip, and so Changteh is also a great centre for the making of bamboo cable.

Freight charges from Hankow vary according to the season of the year. During the low-water period, when lightening is necessary, they are considerably higher than during the high-water season. Junks usually take 15 to 20 days to reach Hankow and usually 7 to 10 days to reach Yochow from Changteh.

The Yüan River is famous not only for its value as a means of communication between the Yangtze and the Provinces of Kweichow and Yunnan, but also for being the scene of some of the exploits of that famous statesman and warrior Chu-ko Liang in his operations against the Mantzŭ. In the eyes of the junk-lover, however, it is scarcely less renowned for the admirable quality of the work turned out by the shipwrights of Hunan, who supply distant ports with some of their finest craft.

The narrow creeks and tributaries of the rivers of Hunan form a vital link in the system of inland communications. The boatmen of the Yüan take kindly to navigation of all sorts; they can negotiate the smallest stream in which a bamboo can float; and on the lower reaches these simple, hospitable sailors have for centuries been bold and skilled navigators in swift waters.

THE CHANG-K'OU MA-YANG-TZŬ

Mayang (麻 陽), a town in Hunan, situated on a small tributary of the Yüankiang (沅 江), has given its name to the large and important family of *ma-yang-tzŭ* junks, which were first designed to navigate the quite formidable rapids of the Yüan River. Several varieties of this junk have evolved, but the *chang-k'ou* (張 口), or "open mouth," *ma-yang-tzŭ* is said by the junkmen to be the prototype from which they all have sprung and is therefore a highly important link in the history of junk-building on the Upper and Middle Yangtze and has probably changed little in appearance and construction throughout the centuries.

The only known alteration that can be traced with any certainty is the addition some hundreds of years ago of a house to the original type, which at first had no superstructure above the deck.

All the *ma-yang-tzŭ* types are heavy, cumbersome, deep-draught cargo-carriers, strongly built to negotiate the long-distance voyages required of them. The size varies greatly in range from a length of 110 feet down to only 38 feet, but invariably the main characteristics are faithfully adhered to.

The junk illustrated in Plate No. 117 is 91 feet long, with a beam of 18½ feet and a depth of 7 feet. She is divided into 13 compartments, which include two coffer-dams.

The foremast, which is stepped in the usual manner, rests against the after-end of the second bulkhead, while the mainmast rests between the seventh and eighth frames in the after coffer-dam.

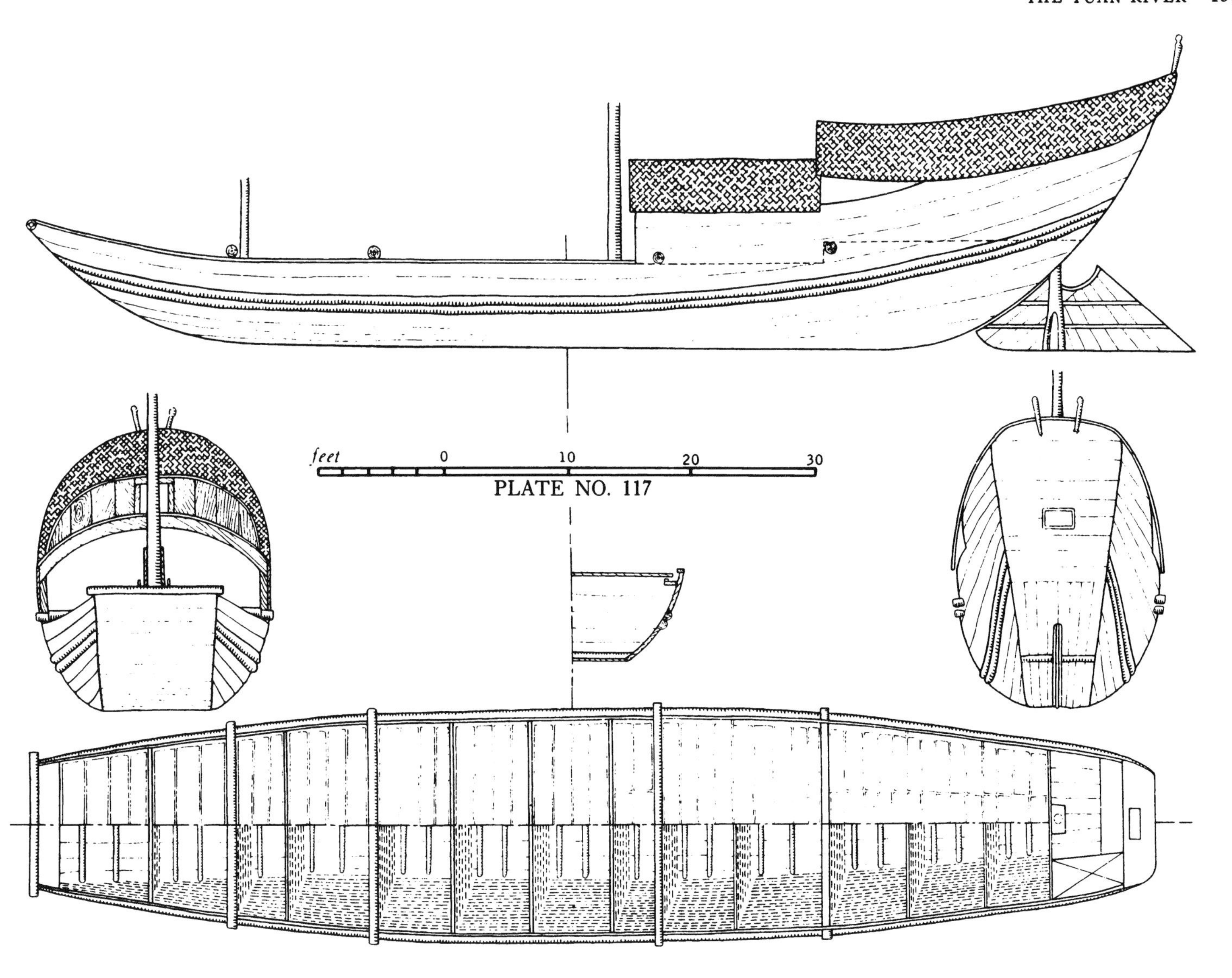

PLATE NO. 117

Typical of some *ma-yang-tzŭ* types are the heavy beams, of which there are, in this case, five, built into the structure of the vessel. Longitudinal strength is provided by two heavy wales or strakes, which run side by side throughout the length of the junk just below the sheer line, rising in a definite curve towards the blunt bow and a still sharper lift to the characteristically high stern. The deck is flush from the bow to the tenth frame, where a 1-foot step leads up to the stern, indicated on the plan by the dotted line. The deck-house covers all of the junk abaft the mainmast. She is fitted with the true balance rudder so typical of Upper Yangtze craft. The reason for this is, of course, to be found in the fact that she is designed to negotiate rapids. Yulohs of over 35 feet in length are used to propel the vessel during calms. When negotiating a rapid a bow sweep is employed to assist the steering.

These junks mostly ply from Hunan ports to Hankow and are also largely used to transport wood oil transhipped from Ichang down river in large oil-proof baskets.

This most serviceable type of junk very soon proved its worth and became deservedly popular beyond the confines of the Yüanho, its river of origin.

Its fame spread to the Middle Yangtze, when is not known, on which section of the river it became the recognized cargo-carrier. Later it found its way into Szechwan, in which province the first of its type to be built was constructed by a Hunan merchant who took up business in Chungking. It soon demonstrated its superiority over other craft as the basic type best suited to the navigation of the rapids above Ichang, though retaining the old generic name of *ma-yang-tzŭ*, which explains why the Hunanese name is still in general use in Szechwan for the most representative craft of the gorges, which is a modified and adapted form* of the old prototype. This also accounts for the popular saying that none but a Hunan carpenter can build a true *ma-yang-tzŭ*.

It is interesting that these wonderful Yüan River craft so favourably impress the people of the ports they visit that there are few places to which they have found their way between Chungking and Hankow which do not now own some *ma-yang* boats of their own.

* This modified form in use on the Upper Yangtze is the turret-built *shou-k'ou ma-yang-tzŭ*.

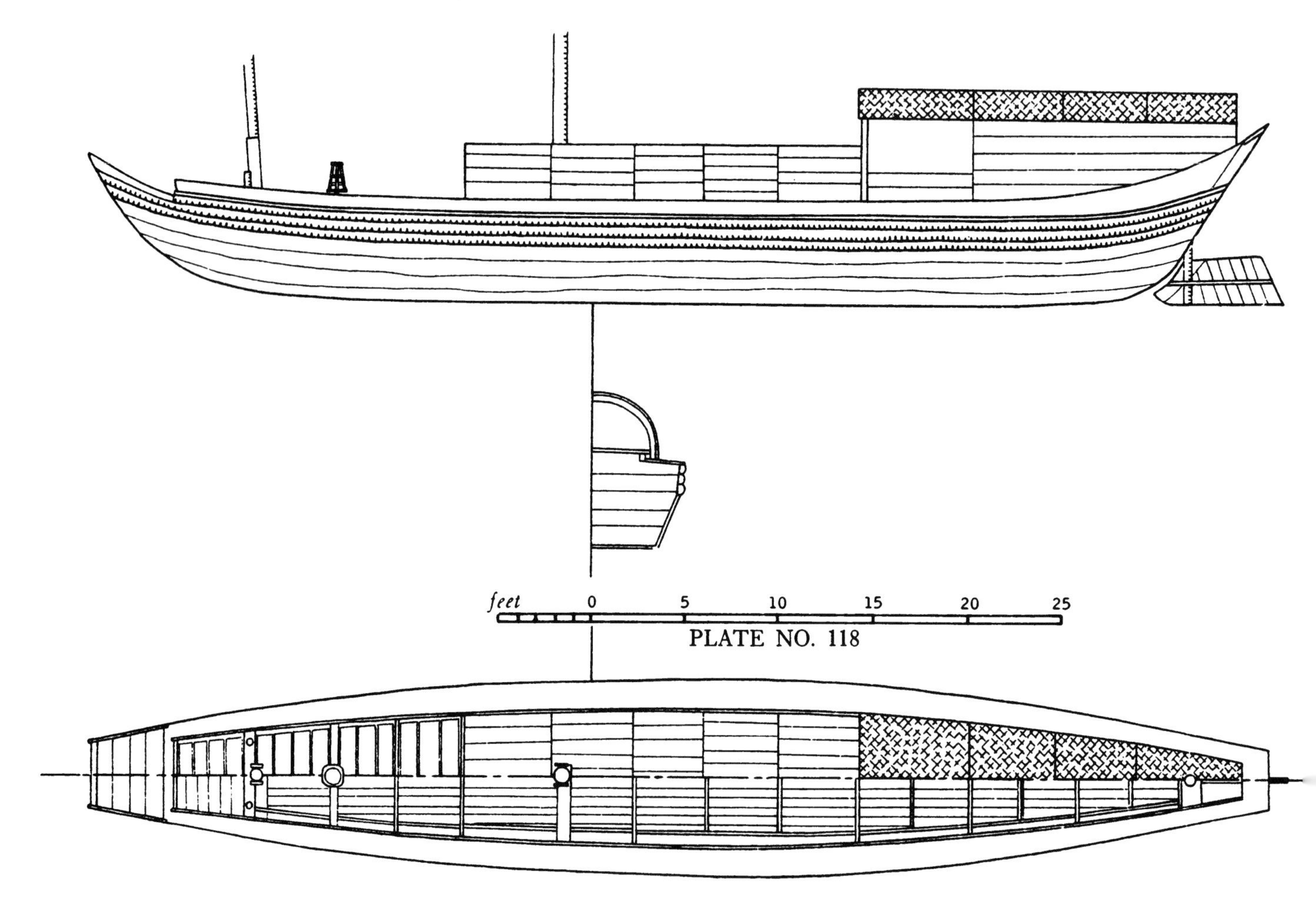

益陽鏟子

THE YIYANG CH'AN-TZŬ OR YIYANG SPADE

The main distinguishing characteristic of the *ch'an-tzŭ* and that which has earned for them the name of spade-boats is the formation of the raised stern. They belong to a large family of junks; indeed, there are few riverside towns of any importance in Hunan which have no *ch'an-tzŭ* of their own.

The hull, which is strengthened by 10 bulkheads, five half-bulkheads, and one frame, is very sturdily built. There are also three wales running from bow to stern.

The deck-house is larger than normal and extends from 5 feet before the mast to the stern, that part forward of the after-house being removable. The after-part, as usual, provides accommodation for the owner and his family. The crew of five men sleep in any space not occupied by cargo.

This type of junk is perhaps one of the most standardized of all types plying on the river above Hankow. Making allowances for different builders, they are surprisingly uniform in design, though not always in size.

The serious student of Oriental naval architecture will do well to compare the craft illustrated in Plate No. 118 with that in Plate No. 101. Both plans are of the same type of junk but built at different ports—about 80 miles apart as the crow flies. It will be noticed that they differ in length by 2 feet, while in beam and depth they are identical. Another similarity is that the masts in both cases are placed precisely 12 feet apart.

Mr. Worcester is referring to the Yochow *ch'an-tzŭ* illustrated on page 411.

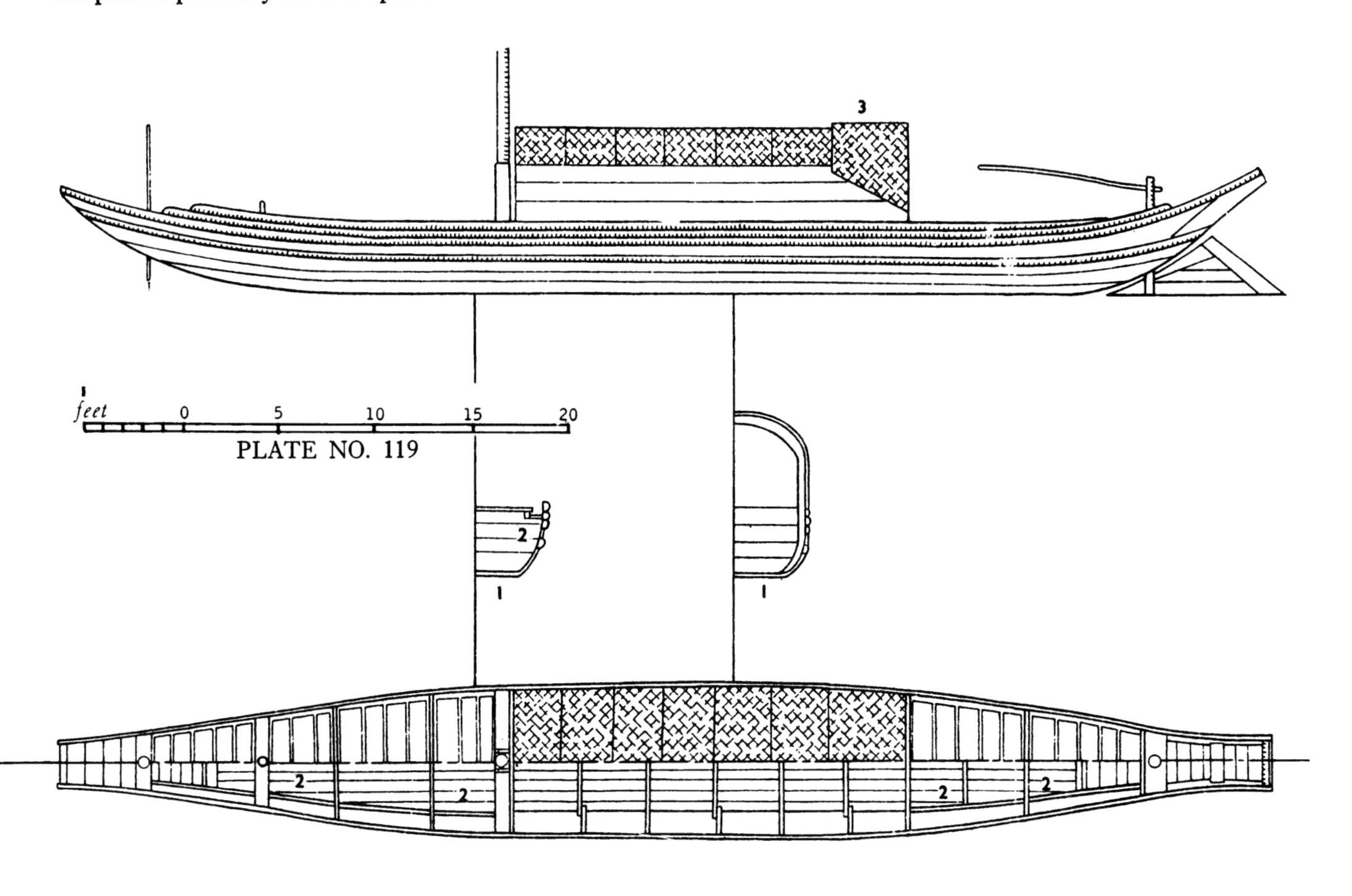

PLATE NO. 119

THE YÜANCHOW MA-YANG-TZŬ 沅州麻陽子

Of all the junks that sail the Hunan waterways, few are more handsome than the Yüanchow *ma-yang-tzŭ*. She has much in common with several types to be found on the Upper Yangtze, notably the *pa-wan-ch'uan*.

The craft illustrated in Plate No. 119 is a medium-sized cargo-carrier designed for the upper reaches of the Yüan River, where narrow and swiftly running streams abound. Her over-all measurements are 61 feet in length, with a beam of 7½ feet, a depth of 3½ feet, and a capacity of 15 tons. This type of junk is lightly built, there being nine full bulkheads and seven frames.

The bottom[1] is made of *sha-mu*; the hull and bulkheads of *pai-mu*. Between the stick-in-the-mud anchor and the mast, and between the after-part of the house and the after-bulkhead, interrupted longitudinals[2] are built in below the deck-beams to provide extra strength.

The after-part of the junk can be matted-in. For this purpose additional mats[3] are provided, and when not in use are stowed in piles on the after-end of the house.

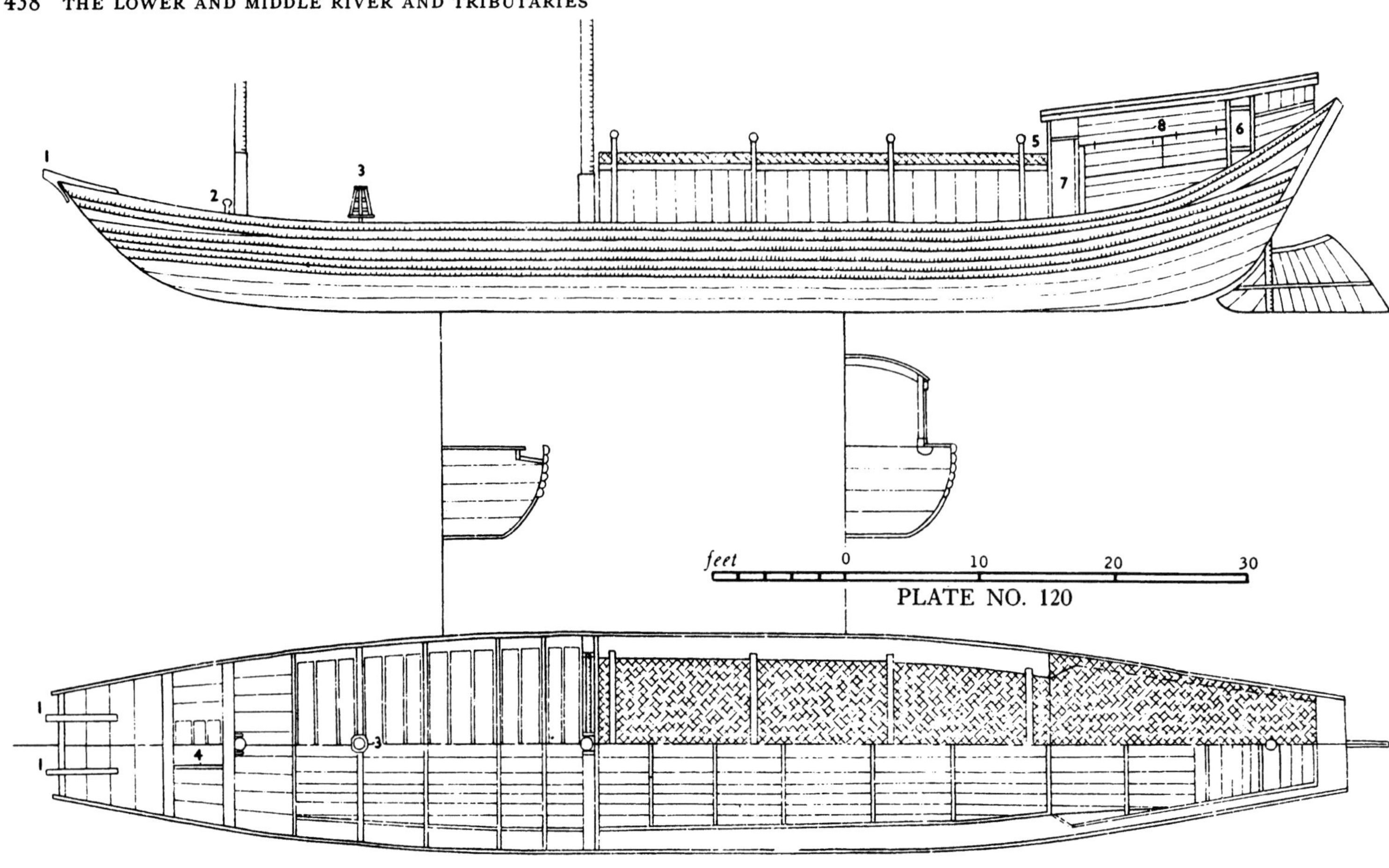

PLATE NO. 120

州

THE SHENCHOW MA-YANG-TZŬ

A type which worthily upholds the traditions of the famous *ma-yang-tzŭ* family is illustrated in Plate No. 120.

The Shenchow *ma-yang-tzŭ* measures 98 feet in length, has a beam of 16 feet and a depth of 6½ feet, and is therefore the largest type to be seen on the Yüan River.

These very strong craft are one of the most standard of all types to be found in the Middle Yangtze area. The bulkheads and the hull are built of *pai-mu*, while the bottom is made of *sha-mu*. The hull is strengthened by 16 full bulkheads and is very sturdily built, there being no less than six wales built into the hull of the vessel.

These craft are normally employed on the lower reaches of the Yüan River and are said to carry as much as 110 tons of cargo. The square bow rises hardly at all and is fitted with removable cat-heads[1] for the heavy grapnel-type anchors.

On the fore-deck a pair of bollards[2] are situated on the first bulkhead and a capstan on the third bulkhead[3]. The storeroom[4] is entered through a hatch just forward of the mast.

The mat-roofed house is typical of the class. The deck inside the owner's cabin is 2 feet higher than the main deck and this permits the helmsman to see out of the aperture[5] on the fore-part of the house. Abaft the deck-house is the galley fitted with a square port[6]. Access to the deck-house is obtained through a door[7], while light and ventilation are provided by means of two flaps[8]. The crew of nine men are accommodated in the fore-part of the house.

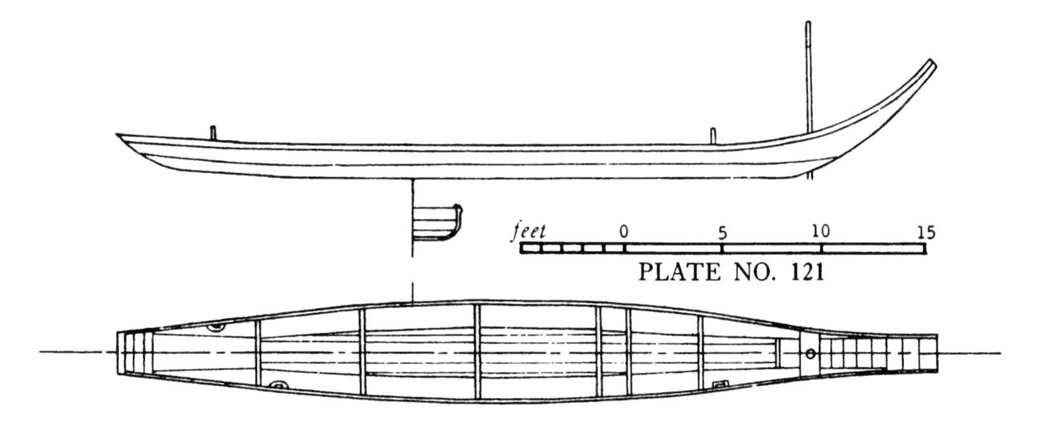

PLATE NO. 121

THE CHENKI SAMPAN 辰谿划子

The sampan illustrated in Plate No. 121 is designed for use in ferrying passengers and their effects across the Yüan at Chenki, where the river is about half a mile broad in summer and runs very swiftly.

This little craft is a strongly built open boat of simple construction. The floor boards are removable and serve as seats for the passengers when required.

The crew consists of three men, who row or pole according to circumstances.

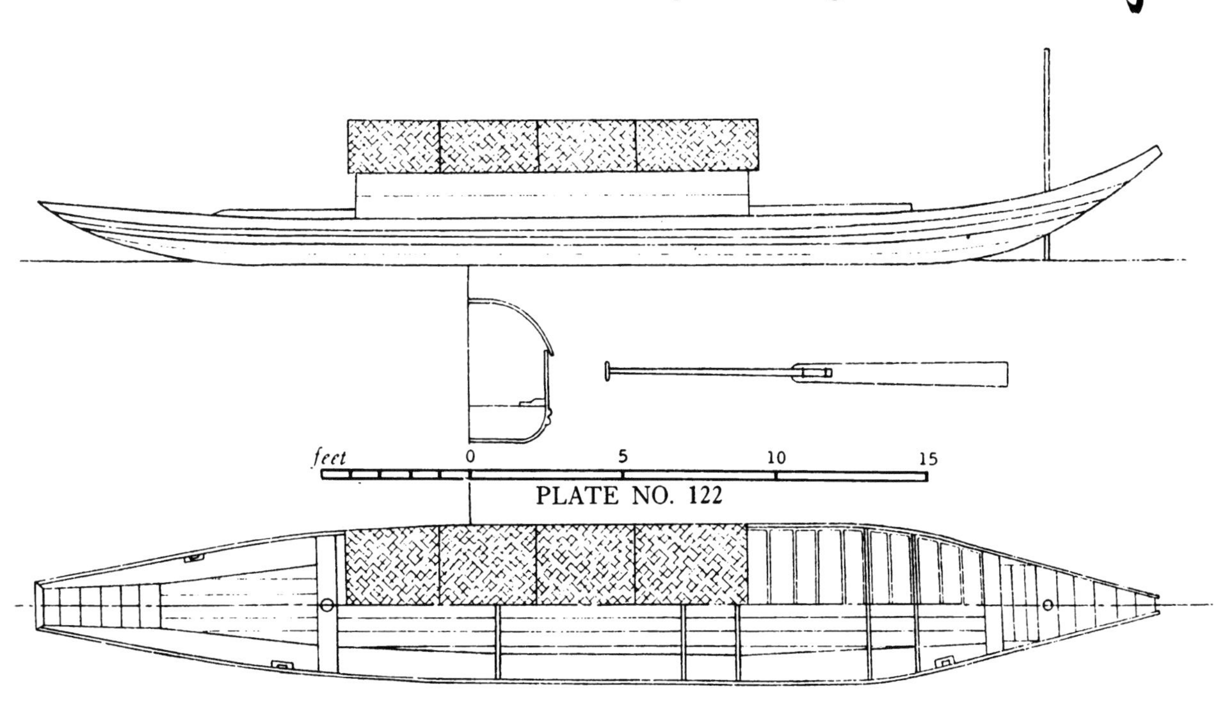

PLATE NO. 122

THE YÜANLING SAMPAN 沅陵划子

The Yüanling sampan is in universal use on the lower and middle section of the Yüan River.

The craft illustrated in Plate No. 122 measures 36 feet in length, has a beam of 5 feet 3 inches and a depth of 1 foot 8 inches, and is constructed on the same sort of general lines as other Hunan sampans.

Propulsion is by oars, two being in the bow and one aft, which is used by the laodah.

The house and mat roof are removable, the latter markedly so, for a section of it is often to be seen hoisted as a sail on a light bamboo mast or boat-hook.

THE KAILI RIVER AND CRAFT OF THE MIAO TRIBESMEN

THE name Miao is given to a collection of about 70 aboriginal tribes living in West China who are not Chinese in speech or customs.

Although from early days to comparatively recent times they have fought with varying success against the encroaching Chinese, yet intermarriage has taken place and in many areas to-day the process of assimilation with the Chinese can be observed. As a rule they inhabit the hills and mountains, apparently because the Chinese have, over the centuries, driven them out of the more fertile valleys and plains.

Long before the dawn of the Christian era these races were known to the Chinese in other parts of what is now the Chinese Republic. Indeed, they were mentioned in the "Canon of Shun" (舜 典), written more than 4,000 years ago, wherein it is stated Shun drove the San Miao into Sanwei (竄 三 苗 於 三 危), a district to the south of Tunwang (敦 煌) in Kansu. As the Miao continued to resist, for they were a warlike race, Yü (禹) was sent later at Shun's command to subdue them. He tried moral suasion and recalled his troops. In 70 days the Prince of Miao capitulated.

Shun did not live to see the successful conclusion of the expedition, for he died of the hardships he had undergone during the campaign. His death provides the immortal story of the suicide of the two faithful concubines, O Huang (娥 皇) and Nü Ying (女 英). Tradition tells how, on learning of his illness, they rushed to his side. The news of his death reached them as they were crossing the Tungting Lake, and, distracted with grief, they immediately jumped overboard and were drowned.

Emperor Shun and his two faithful concubines are also referred to on page 404.

Their burial place, at Chün Shan, opposite Yochow, has since been recognized as the "most celebrated of all famous places in Hunan." Temples have been erected in their honour, and poets have written and bards have sung innumerable elegies to the faithfulness of these two ladies.

Unfortunately little is known of the ancient history of the Miao, for they have no written language and the tribesmen to-day are almost as illiterate as their ancestors thousands of years ago. The Chinese account for this lack of a language by whimsically suggesting that during the course of their wanderings they came to the edge of the Tungting Lake and, having no boats, were unable to cross. As some of them stood perplexed by the edge of the lake, so the famous old story goes, they noticed some water spiders moving with great agility on its surface. They attempted to emulate them with poor success, and before they could manage to get back to the bank and safety they had absorbed so much water that they had swallowed all the characters they knew and as a result have been without them ever since.

The process of assimilating or pushing back the original inhabitants of the country—the descendants of whom, in a direct line, are known at the present time as the Yaohu (猺 戶)—of the mountainous regions in the south-west of Hunan, or Miaotzŭ of Kweichow and other places, has been going on for more than 3,000 years, attended by many fiercely contested combats. Indeed, the last page of the interesting history of the heroic fight for independence of these tribes, the Miaotzŭ Rebellion in Kweichow, occurred no more than about 80 years ago.

Some of the Miao tribes claim to be the original inhabitants of the land and to have always from time immemorial lived where they now are, while others claim to have come from the East. They have been struggling with the Chinese, a struggle in which the more civilized, better organized, and more industrious Chinese have invariably prevailed. Gradually, therefore, they have been absorbed among the Chinese or driven from the fertile plains to the mountains and less fertile regions.

Of the various tribes, the only one which comes within the geographical scope of this book is the *hei*, or black, Miao. They suit their name, for their women wear a dark chocolate-coloured embroidered costume, and the men also wear a dark brown calico. They are the more manly of the Miao tribes. Another tribe is called the *hsia*, or shrimp, Miao, as they catch and sell shrimps.

Until very recently the Miaos were, while really subject to the Chinese, ruled by their own hereditary chiefs. The *hei* Miao call themselves M'peo, which probably means embroidery. They are the most intelligent and self-reliant of the Miao tribes, though their artisans are not as skilful or as honest as the Chinese. Most of them own lands and are well-to-do. Some raise pigs and cultivate beans, rice, and other commodities and carry them in their own boats to Hungkiang (洪 江), their ancient capital, in Hunan.

Although they have no literature or records, they have a large stock of legends, some of which are sung or recited at their festivals. Not the least interesting of their folklore is an account of the Deluge. In this story of the flood only two persons were saved in a large bottle-gourd, or calabash, used as a boat.

The Province of Kweichow, where they live, means Precious and Honourable Region, although as originally written the character *kuei* (鬼) meant demon, or devil.

The greater part of the area is over 3,000 feet above sea-level, is mountainous, and composed of a labyrinth of hills and valleys. In some places streams, only fordable in certain parts, disappear into the bowels of the earth and come out again a considerable distance away.

Kweichow, therefore, is not noted for its waterways or navigational interests. Indeed, of its streams none are navigable, even for small boats, until they leave the province. This, together with the fact that there are few roads, makes the conveyance of products a costly undertaking.

Miao boatmen, however, are to be seen working the Changki in Hunan, which is a tributary of the Yüan River. This stream, which flows through a region occupied for the most part by *hei* Miao, is navigable when in flood almost to Tuyün (都 匀), in longitude 107°.25 E. and latitude 26°.15 N., and all the year round as far as Kaili (凱 里).

Everywhere in this beautiful and little-known part of China there is a rich field for antiquarian as well as nautical research, and hardly any district promises a richer reward than in the home of this picturesque race of farmer-sailors. Nor should such research be long delayed, for the processes of extermination, expulsion, and assimilation over countless years have already caused the disappearance of the vast majority of these interesting people.

The missionaries say the tribesmen are sad tipplers and lead immoral lives. Be this as it may, they are brave and fearless in the handling of their boats and rafts and show fine qualities as sailors.

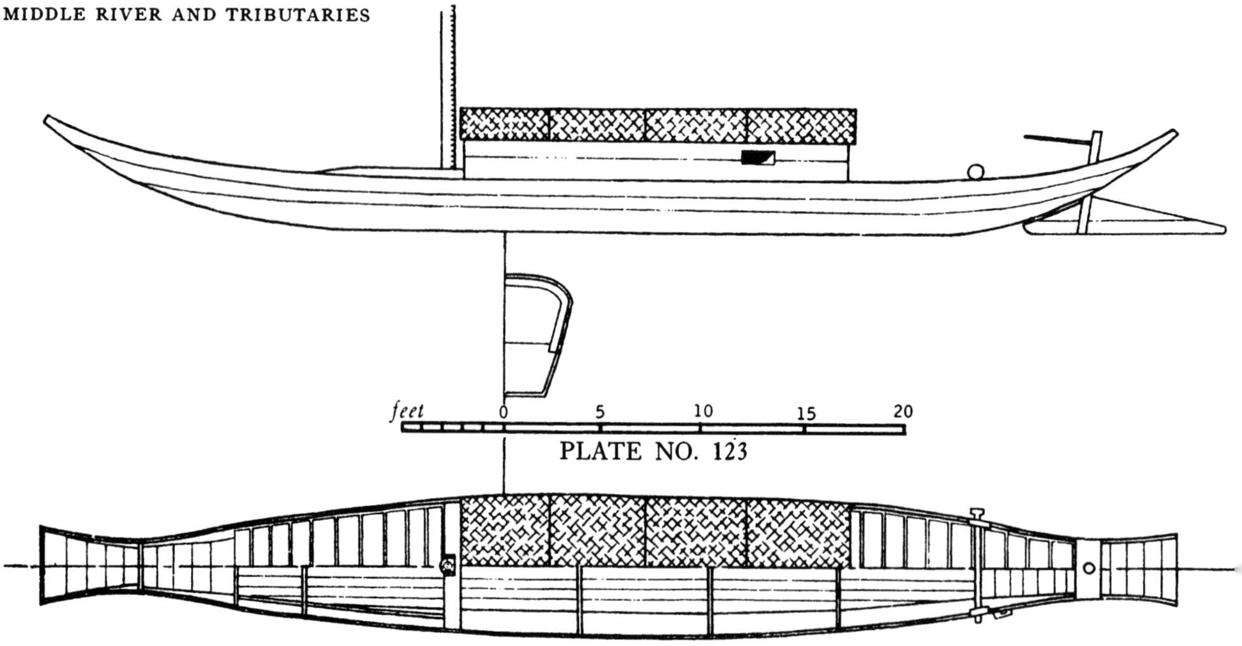

feet 0 5 10 15 20

PLATE NO. 123

THE KWEICHOW-CH'UAN OR KWEICHOW BOAT

The *kweichow-ch'uan* is of Miao descent and consequently its origin is lost in the mists of time. It is not, however, exclusively used by the tribesmen to-day.

Its main interest lies in the fact that it is the only type of boat used on the upper reaches of the Yüan River. Here a craft of strong build and very light draught is absolutely essential.

The junk illustrated in Plate No. *123* is 56 feet in length and has a beam of 6 feet 7 inches and a depth of 2 feet 5 inches.

A light tracking-mast is fitted against the third bulkhead, the inboard end of the tracking-line being made fast to a removable horse in the stern-sheets.

This interesting craft preserves the main characteristics of Yüan River design in that it has the distinctive bow and stern for work in swift waters.

THE WOOD RAFTS OF THE MIAO

Timber plays an important part in the lives of the Miao tribesmen; indeed, formerly timber-cutting was their exclusive occupation, as they were most familiar with the mountainous regions. In recent years, however, the Chinese have penetrated these parts and the wooded areas of the mountains now form part of their lumber estates.

Timber is to be found in almost every district; indeed, the Province of Hunan, traversed by many mountain ranges and served by many large streams, is one of China's principal lumber regions.

Trees are usually felled in the autumn. The buyers, after examining the forests and bargaining with the owner, send lumbermen to cut down all the trees over a certain size in a definite area. The branches are next lopped off and the poles slid down the mountain-side into the streams below, where they are made into log rafts by the Miao raftsmen and floated down with the swift current to Hungkiang, which is the main transhipment port for the timber coming from West Hunan and North Kweichow.

The method of assessing the value of the timber is exceedingly complicated. That most commonly used in Hunan, which has been in use for hundreds of years, is known locally as *lung-ch'üan-ma-tzŭ* (龍 泉 碼 子), or "dragon spring measurement." The lumbermen cut a *pi* (鼻), or "nose," through each pole at a point 5 inches from the heel. The uppermost side of this hole is the datum from which measurements for the circumference are taken to determine the tael worth in *lung-ch'üan-ma-tzŭ*. There are many different systems of measuring the poles, which vary according to local conditions in each district. For instance, at Kinping (錦 屏), in the Miao region, where timber is cheap, the measurement of the circumference is taken 8 feet from the heel. When the wood reaches Hankow, however, the price has gone up and so the measurement for circumference is taken 5 feet 5 inches from the heel. At Nanking, where the price has again risen, the measurement is taken at a point 5 feet from the upper part of the *pi* (鼻).

Transportation of the timber is entirely by waterways, the raftsmen being for the most part Miaos. Their rafts are to be seen in great numbers making their way down the swiftly descending mountain streams, which empty themselves into the various tributaries.

The raft illustrated in Plate No. 124 consists of 10 small or seven large *sha-mu* poles held together by a thin lath[1] passing through the *pi* and pinned by a wooden peg. Further rigidity is secured by means of a cross-piece of wood[2] lashed athwart the other end of the raft by strands of bamboo rope.

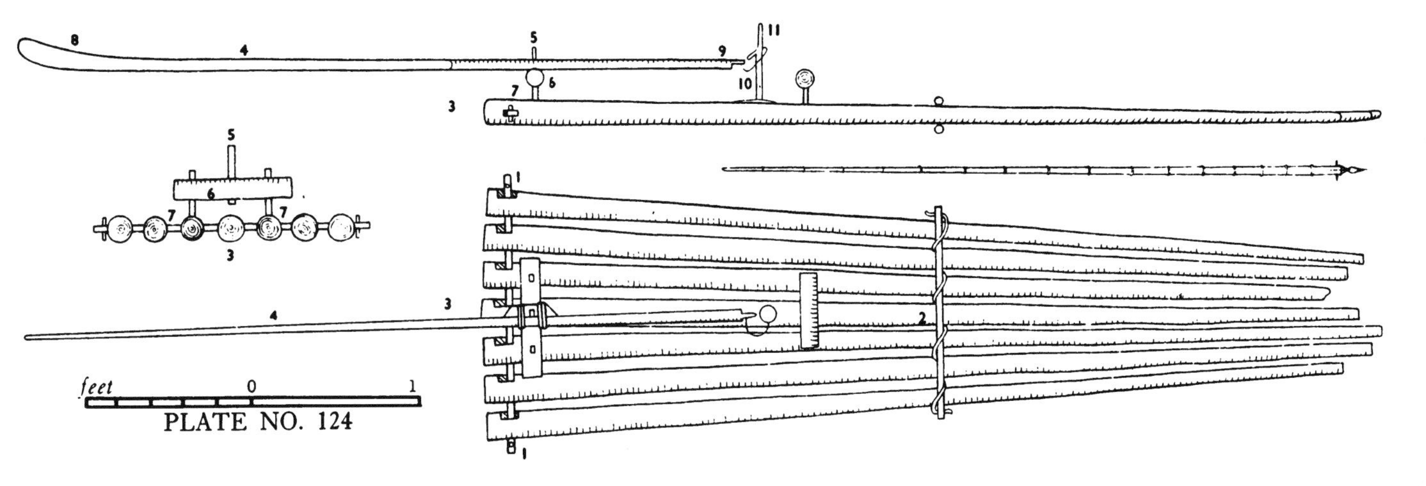

PLATE NO. 124

The poles composing the raft vary in age, from the smaller ones, which are about 15 years old with a circumference of about 1 foot, to the larger variety, which have a circumference of about 2 feet with an age of over 20 years. In both cases the length is about the same, the average being about 40 feet. The greatest length handled is about 80 feet.

A pole usually takes about a year to travel from its mountain home to Hankow, where it is marketed and sold in the Lower Yangtze Valley for use in making coffins, building houses, and for junk construction, in that order of importance.

The raft travels down stream stern first[3], that is to say, with the broadest part leading. The lumbermen say that although it takes more force to start it, yet it requires less to maintain it in motion than with the small end foremost, and it is steered by means of a long sweep[4] mounted on a wooden bearing-pin[5] which is set into a short length of wood[6] secured to the raft on short legs[7]. This sweep is a medium-sized *sha-mu* pole about 35 feet or more in length, curved at the heel. The blade is formed by trimming this heel[8] with an axe. The loom is formed by trimming the narrow end[9]. When not in use the sweep is kept out of the water by a becket[10] on the loom, which is slipped over a short forked branch[11] of a tree driven into one of the logs.

When negotiating a rapid the helmsman has a good deal to do, for he also operates a quant, which he uses with great dexterity to assist the steering. Work of this nature is a speciality, and the Miao boatmen are experts. In smooth waters between rapids, however, he usually sits down on an improvised seat, smokes a long bamboo pipe, and allows the swiftly moving current to provide the necessary locomotion.

The Miao handle their rafts with great skill, and it is an interesting lesson in the art of poling to watch several rafts jockeying for position while attempting to overtake each other in a narrow rapid with an abrupt drop of 2 to 3 feet.

THE MIAO-CH'UAN OR MIAO BOAT

Much interest attaches to the *miao-ch'uan*, for it is probably the same to-day as it was centuries ago.

These junks hail from Lushan (鑪 山) and Chungankiang (重 安 江) in Kweichow. The craft illustrated in Plate No. 125 is a typical one of the class and measures 47 feet in length, with a beam of 5 feet and a depth of 2 feet, the standard size of these craft, which are to be found in great numbers on the lovely but dangerous stretch of river between Kienyang (黔 陽) and Hungkiang (洪 江). Occasionally they are to be seen at Changteh.

These boats of the Miao are built on slender and graceful lines, tapering gently to bow and stern. They are, however, strongly built, for in the rapids and races in which they operate the boatmen need to have strong craft under them.

As will be seen in Plate No. 125, there are eight bulkheads, which divide the boat into seven compartments. The foremost compartment is not decked-in and forms a convenient well for working the bow sweep when down bound and for the bow-oarsman or polers when ascending the river. The next compartment, that between the first and second bulkheads, is given up to the galley. The rounded mat house begins at the third bulkhead and is in three sections. The central part[1] is fixed and rigid, while the foremost[2] and the after[3] ones are free to travel in the fore and aft line as required.

The tracking-mast[4] is a light spar stepped well forward of the midship section. The inboard end of the tracking-line, which is always made of 1½-inch bamboo rope, is made fast to a ring-bolt in the after-end of the boat[5]. Thence the tracking-line travels to the mast, where it passes through a dumb-block[6] which is hoisted on halyards[7] to suit the conditions obtaining and the height of the tracking-path. The halyards are kept to the mast by a bamboo grummet[8].

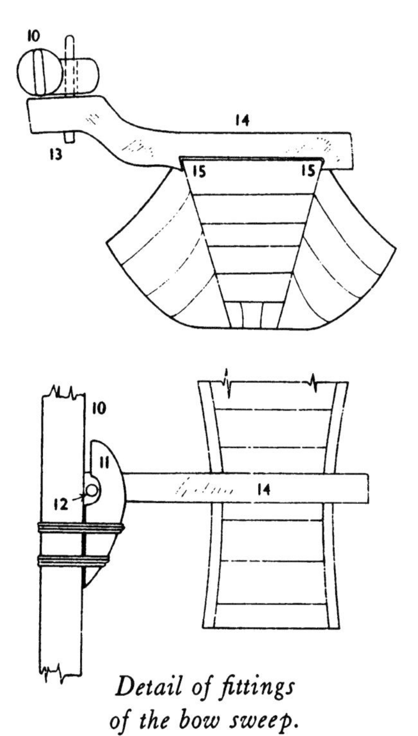

Detail of fittings of the bow sweep.

There are no bitts, but a ring-bolt[9], situated some 6 feet from the bow, serves the purpose equally well. The bow sweep[10], which is appropriately known as the *chao* (爪), or claw, measures about 22 feet over-all and consists of a medium-sized crooked-grown *sha-mu* pole trimmed to form a blade with an upturned bend at the thick and crooked end and to form a loom at the thin and straight end. At the centre of balance a cheek-piece[11] is securely lashed with bamboo rope and set up with wooden wedges. There is an aperture[12] in the cheek-piece to take the wooden bearing-pin[13], which is carried by a baulk of timber[14], 3 feet 7 inches over-all, which is grooved[15] and fits snugly over the bow, where it is lashed by bamboo rope.

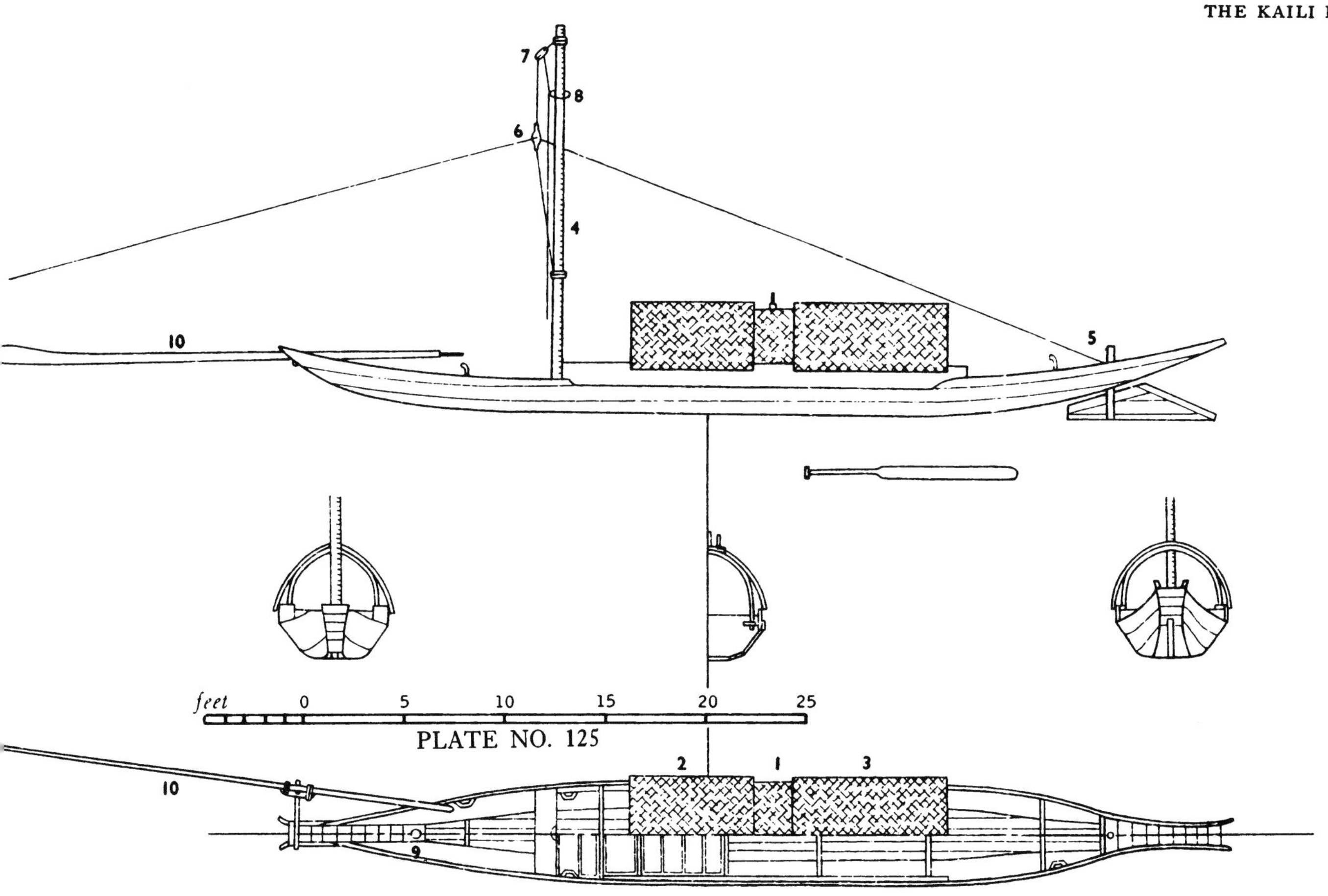

PLATE NO. 125

The compartments from the second to the fifth bulkheads are devoted to the cargo, which is stowed below deck and usually consists of beans, cotton, cotton yarn, and gypsum.

Pig-raising is a very important side-line among the Miao farmers. These animals are kept not only to provide meat, but also for bristles and bones, while the manure is used as fertilizer. For this reason most of these boats are to be found in the pig trade between their home ports and Yüanling (沅 陵), which, before they were driven out by the encroaching Chinese, was one of the Miaos' most important towns.

The crew, consisting of from three to five men, live inside the house. At night the whole junk can be matted-in.

The sail is seldom used on the Yüan River, but for occasional use the Miao boatman hoists a section of its awning or mat roof, which is fitted with the necessary beckets for this economical purpose.

When descending the river the junk relies on the swift current to carry her down. For ascending the river tracking is the most general method of progress. Poling is also very extensively employed. The Miao boatmen are probably the most skilled quanters in the whole of China.

Although a rudder is carried and sometimes fitted, it is seldom used. The junks are steered by the after-oar, which also does duty as a sweep, according to circumstances. At times when all the men are required to pole or track and the after-oar has to be left unattended a dumb-rudder is shipped, usually on the port side. This is nothing more than a narrow plank measuring about 3 feet by 6 inches, which is supported on the gunwale.

The interest of these strange craft and the beauty of the Yüan River exercise a peculiar fascination, no less than the kindly ways of the hardy people who live upon its shores and navigate its dangerous and turbulent waters.

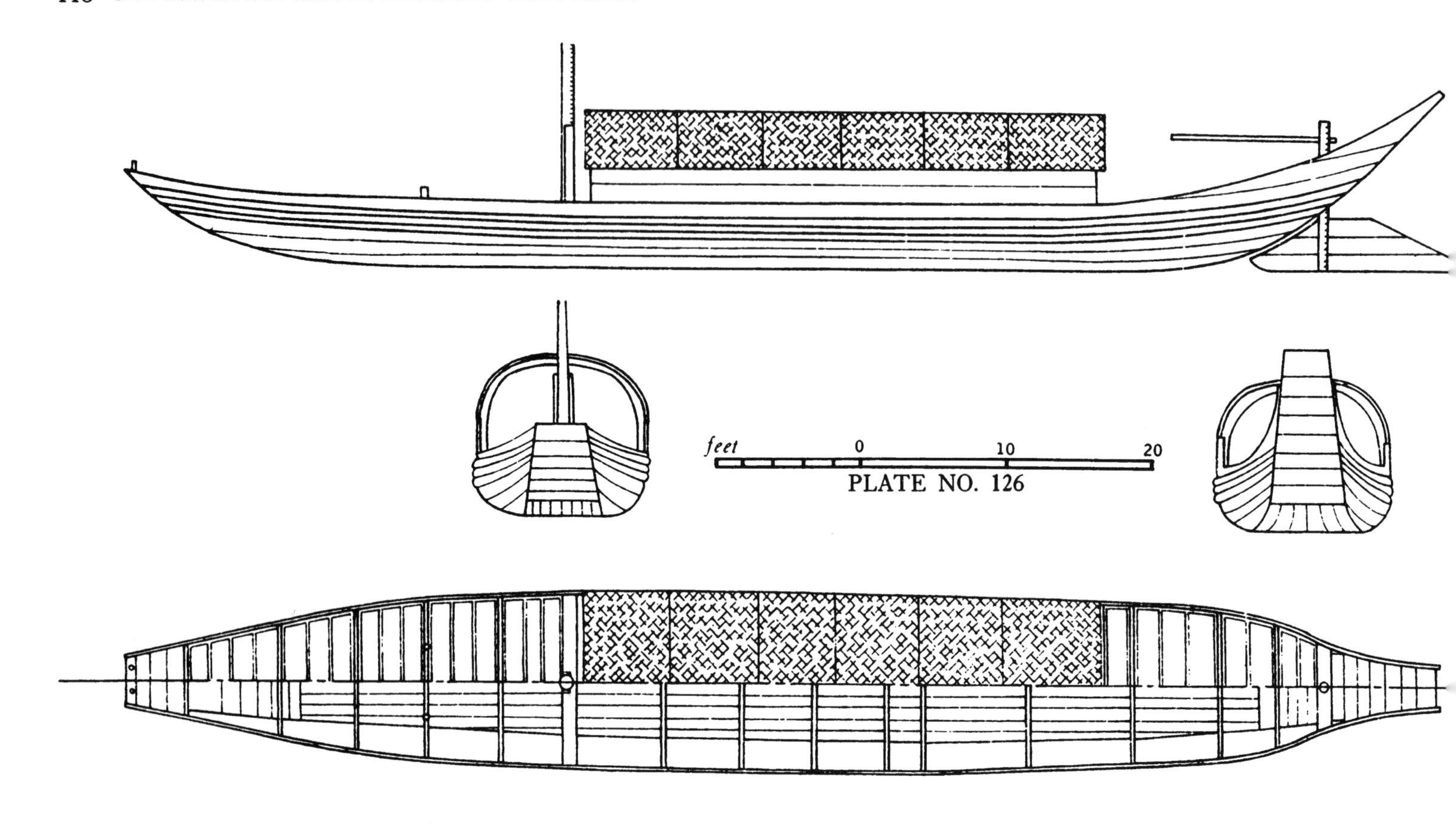

PLATE NO. 126

馬雀尾

THE MA-CH'IAO-WEI OR SPARROW TAIL

Another of the Miao craft somewhat similar in general design to the type just mentioned, except that she is much larger, may be referred to here as hailing from Hungkiang (洪 江), at one time the chief trading city of these aboriginal people.

This junk is the far-famed *ma-ch'iao-wei*, or " sparrow tail," so called from the similarity of its stern to that part of a sparrow.

Although they are no longer built by the tribesmen, these craft are unmistakably Miao in appearance. Because of their very fine qualities in rapids, the design has been copied by the Chinese, and these junks are now being built in large numbers by the Hunan shipwrights. Indeed, it is hardly too much to say that they are probably the most popular and certainly the most typical junks on the Yüan River to-day.

The *ma-ch'iao-wei*, as illustrated in Plate No. 126, is quite typical of the class and measures 91 feet in length, with a beam of 12 feet and a depth of 4 feet. They are built on fine and pleasing lines, being about 7½ beams to length and are fitted with 15 full bulkheads and one half-bulkhead. The three bulkheads forward of the mast are cut so as to enable the heel to come up when the mast is being sent down.

The boldness of the curves of the sterns of these junks forms one of their most handsome features and gives them an easily recognized appearance. The high stern formation probably serves as some protection against being "pooped" in a rapid. In some junks the stern is very exaggerated. Indeed, it is not unusual to find the top of the transom as much as 15 feet above the water.

These boats have, no doubt, a long and interesting history behind them, and the early Miao shipwrights are certainly to be congratulated on producing a craft possessing beauty of form as well as efficiency of design.

THE MIDDLE YANGTZE

THAT portion of the river called the Middle Yangtze begins, for all practical purposes, just above Hankow and extends up the Yangtze for nearly 400 miles to the port of Ichang.

Above Hankow the river takes a south-westerly trend for the 119 miles to Yochow, running fairly straight for the most part. The scenery is still typical of the Lower Yangtze, with flat country on the north or left bank and low hills on the right bank. The great dike, the Wancheng Ti (萬 城 隄), designed to control the country, and especially Hankow, when the river floods its normal banks, begins in the shape of small earthworks, advancing to, and retreating from, the river according to the nature of the intervening ground.

About 17 miles above Hankow is the town of Kinkow (金 口) at the mouth of the Kin River, on the right bank. About 10 miles farther up at Meitanchui is the one great exception to the river's direct course, the huge loop known as Farmer's Bend, where the stream makes an enormous detour of about 26 miles round a pear-shaped peninsula, doubling back to a point only 2 miles from where it started. If the river could therefore break through this narrow neck, a saving of about 25 miles could be effected on the whole journey.

In summer, when the river rises above the level of its banks, the junks make a short cut across the flooded isthmus. About half-way round Farmer's Bend is an inland waterway known as the Pienho, a canal which, avoiding the snake-like windings of the Yangtze above Yochow, as well as its strong down-current, affords a shorter passage to the town of Shasi.

After Farmer's Bend a straight reach runs for 17 miles past rising hills to the village of Kiayü (嘉 魚), which stands on a red earth bluff on the right bank. Some say it was here, in the days of the romantic Three Kingdoms, that the naval action of the Crimson Cliff took place.

One hundred and one miles above Hankow is the rather important trade centre of Sinti (新 隄), on the left bank. On the opposite bank is a stream linking up with the Hwangkai Lake (黃 蓋 湖), a few miles inland.

Except for one or two bluffs there is little worthy of note until, at Yanglingtsi, the river narrows to half a mile and runs between red sandstone cliffs, which follow the river for about 1½ miles on the right bank, which now shows broken ground all the way to Yochow.

From the entrance to the Tungting Lake at Yochow the Yangtze curves round to the north, past the sandy point called Kwanyinchow (觀 音 洲), which marks the elbow of the junction, and narrows to less than half a mile in width. The great Hupeh 200-mile plain through which the river flows extends from Hankow nearly up to Ichang. This plain is alluvial, except where in the south it touches on the Province of Hunan and the Tungting Lake, when it is edged by mountains. The country bordering the banks of the Middle Yangtze is dead flat and so low-lying that an extensive dike system is necessary to keep the water within bounds. As is only to be expected, it is poorly drained, and there are great expanses of standing water. These large shallow lakes play a useful part, however, for they act as reservoirs, absorbing much of the embarrassing summer overflow and serving in winter to feed the river and to help it to maintain a more

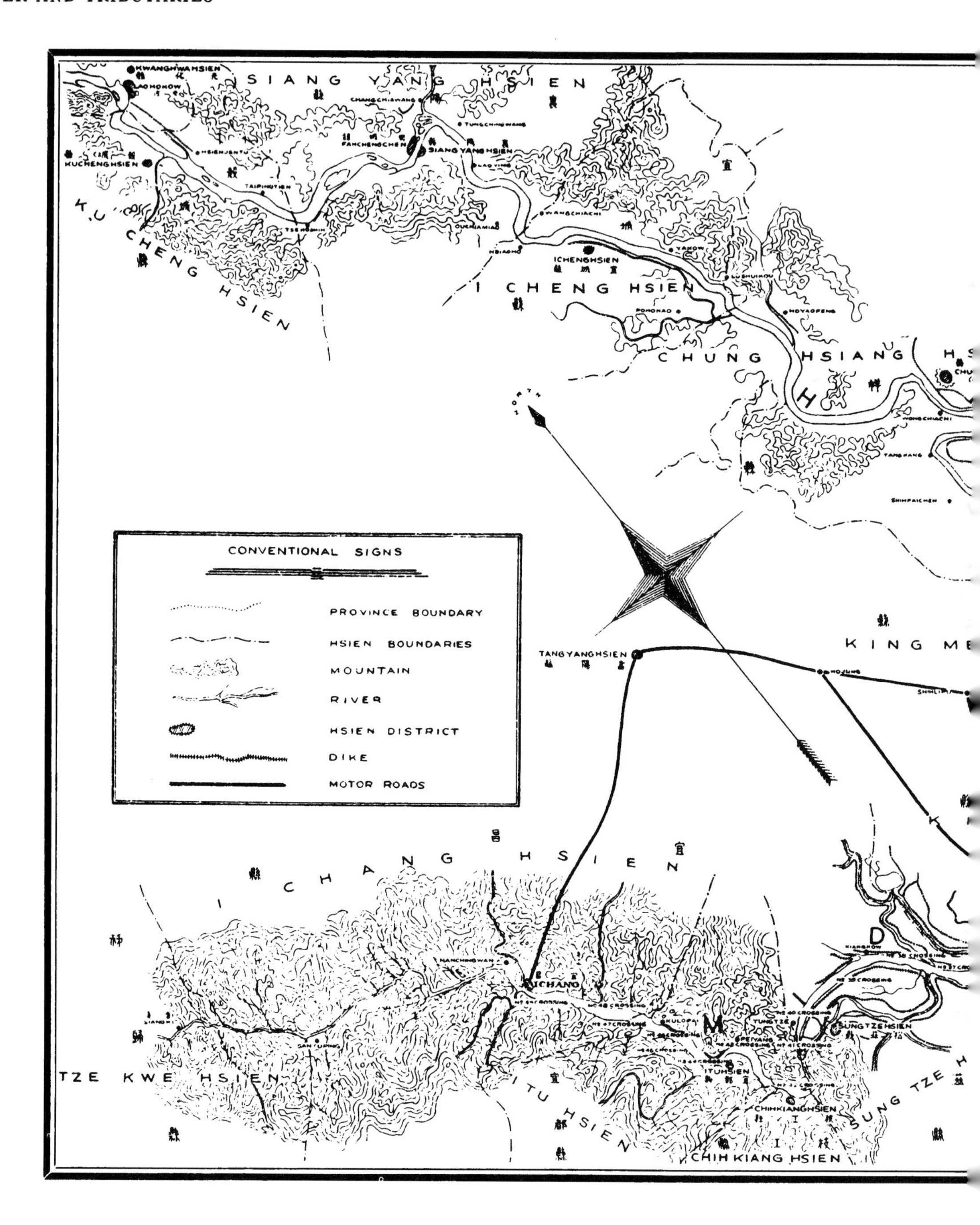

even level. To the existence of these safety valves may be attributed the fact that the Yangtze floods are on the whole less sudden and disastrous than those of the Yellow River, which has no such similar adjacent reservoirs.

From the Tungting Lake entrance up to Sunday Island the Yangtze enters a new phase and winds a tortuous course covering 119 miles between these two points, although the direct distance is no more than 48 miles. Formerly these loops and curls measured 130 miles, but the navigable route appears to be shortening. The effect of this random circuitous progress is bewildering, for a landmark such as Temple Hill, appearing on the port bow for an hour or so, will suddenly shift to starboard, then abeam, and finally move astern, only, after some hours, to reappear ahead in its old position.

The alluvial banks show strata mixed with sand. They are about 20 feet above the water in the spring. It is noticeable that they are always steep-to on the concave side of the river, while on the other bank they shelve gradually to the muddy foreshore, the outline of which is here and there broken by long sandy

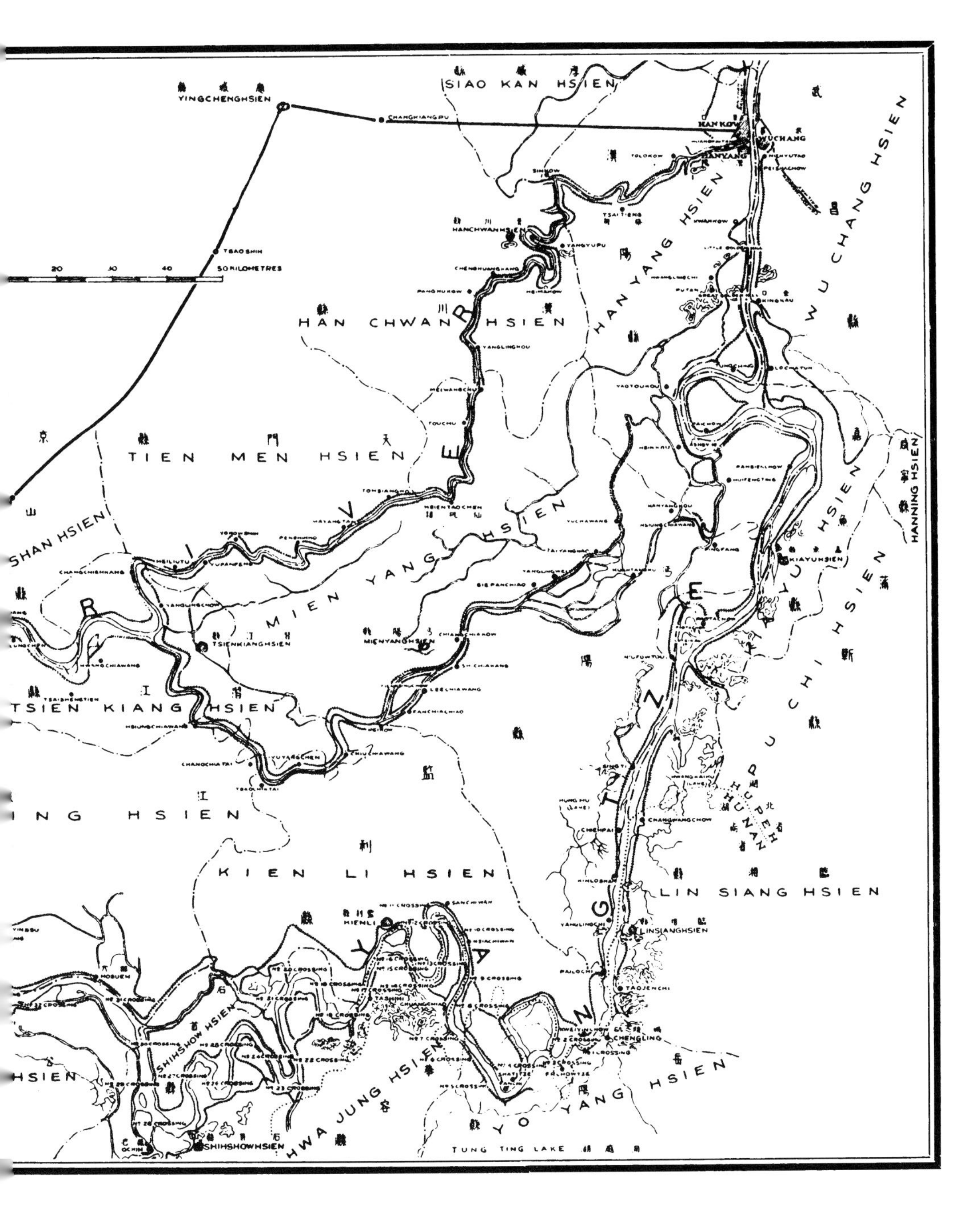

Middle Yangtze and Han Rivers. Hankow to Ichang and Hankow to Kwang-Hwa-Hsien.

spits. There is little of outstanding interest in the monotonous flat country dotted with farms and clumps of trees.

As on the Lower Yangtze, much of the land is under rice and illustrates the farmers' ingenuity in irrigation. Cotton-growing is also very largely carried on, being one of the main industries of the Middle Yangtze.

A horseshoe-shaped bend leads to Temple Hill Bend, so named from a conspicuous hill 400 feet high, crowned with a temple. Near-by is the small walled town of Shihshow (石 首) lying between two other hills; at the foot of this, the only rising ground for miles around and the first place since the Tungting Lake where hills touch the river-bank, the Yangtze has broken through the right bank and flooded the land beyond.

Here the character of the river changes; it loses its serpentine nature. The width averages about half a mile, though now and then it opens out to nearly a mile across. Flat islands rise in the stream, and shoal water is found in places. In the high-water season the scenery is even more monotonous, for with the summer floods, which happen inevitably each year, the general view is of a great inland sea, the only available landmarks for the navigators being the roofs of the inundated hamlets or unusually shaped tree tops.

At the large village of Hosüeh (郝 穴) the river narrows to only 700 yards in width. In this region it is said that the river-banks are receding at the rate of 30 yards a year. The great dike here approaches near to the river and follows its banks more or less closely as far as Shasi.

As Shasi is neared, the country appears flatter and more low-lying than ever, some portions being under water or more or less swampy during most seasons of the year. In and around the town all the built-up area not on raised ground lies below the summer level of the river. In order to safeguard the town as far as possible from inundation a strong limestone-faced bunding has been built. A fine seven-storied pagoda stands at the western end of the point where it projects into the river, which here narrows somewhat.

Shasi, meaning in Chinese "sand market," probably derived its name from the fact that it may first have functioned as a matshed colony or mart, established on the sandbanks.

Situated on the left bank, where it straggles along for some 4 miles or so, this unwalled and uninspiring-looking town is nevertheless highly important, not only as a cotton-growing district and transhipment port, but because of its strategic position at the centre of a network of canals and waterways and at the crossing point of the two most important commercial water routes of Central China running from east to west and from north to south.

The Han River approaches to within 30 miles of the Yangtze near Shasi, though the latter town lies 273 miles from Hankow, where the two rivers eventually join. The distance to Hankow by road is, however, much less, and the inland water routes are also considerably shorter, although they carry considerably less water and are therefore suitable only for small craft.

There are two main canals affording communication with Hankow. One runs towards Kingchow, through a lake, Changhu (長 湖), north of Shasi, and thence to Shayang (沙 洋) on the Han River, a distance of 160 miles or so. The second route is by the Pienho, which, running east and west through several small lakes, enters the Yangtze at the points Tsintungkow, already mentioned, south of Ashby Island (a low-water route), and Kwankow, only 7 miles above Hankow. This latter waterway is said to carry insufficient depths at winter levels.

A few miles above Shasi the cross-country water-borne traffic from Hankow can proceed through the Taipingho to the western portion of the Tungting Lake and thence in almost any direction. Intercommunication with the Province of Kweichow and thence with the south is provided by the Yüan River. There were originally three great trade routes linking Hupeh with Szechwan: firstly, the northern, now fallen into disuse, which followed the Chuho (渠 河) to Suiting (綏 定), meeting the Han River at Sinyang; secondly, the central route, overland to Itu (宜 都), and thence to Shasi by water; and, finally, the southern route, mainly water-borne, *via* the Fowling River (涪 陵 河) at Fowchow (涪 州) (about 60 miles below Chungking) across the divide and down the Yüan River to Changteh and the Tungting Lake. This was once the main roûte to the south until the advent of steam navigation gave the lead to the central route.

These routes, however, old as they may be, are not so very ancient from the Chinese historical viewpoint. The Rev. Warren of Changsha notes how, in the "Tribute of Yü," written about 600 B.C., which deals with all the then known waterways of China, there are no descriptions of any river or tributary south of the Yangtze, and the whole water system of Hunan is ignored, which would seem to indicate that that province was as yet unknown territory.

Although Shasi, from the Chinese historical point of view, is of little interest, it is quite otherwise with its sister city of Kiangling (江 陵), or Kingchow, a large walled town, half Chinese, half Tartar, situated 3 or 4 miles to the north-west, with its south wall running parallel to, but 1½ miles in from, the river's edge. It has three times figured as a capital: once of the Kingdom of Ch'u (楚), 722–481 B.C., once of the Kingdom of Liang (後 梁) in A.D. 552, and again it was proclaimed the capital by the rebel General Kao Chi-hsing (高 季 興) at the beginning of the tenth century. In this neighbourhood innumerable battles have raged between war lords struggling for supremacy. In A.D. 201, before he conquered Szechwan, the famous Liu Pei annexed it from the Kingdom of Wu, and both kingdoms warred and negotiated ceaselessly for its possession. The Chinese military hero, Kuan Yü, later promoted to be the God of War, was the garrison commander in the great war zone, a triangular area comprising the country within the points Siangyang (襄 陽), Fancheng (樊 城), Tanyang (丹 陽), Ichang (宜 昌), Kiangling (江 陵), and Shasi (沙 市). He won his greatest victory by drowning seven attacking armies of the Wei Kingdom in the waters of the Han at Fancheng. When armed war-junks were fighting along the Yangtze or up the Han River, troops including cavalry would march through, bound up or down, according to whichever side had the attacking advantage, on the Tangyang–Kingmen line, the overland gateway to Ichang. Bitter fighting has far more recently raged over the same ancient battle-field during the "War of Greater East Asia."

Shasi, as has been indicated, lies in a great plain which stretches without any kind of eminence or hill for 50 miles to the south and west and 100 miles to the east, after which, for as far again, the plain still extends, broken only here and there by an occasional hill. Such being the nature of the country, it is not surprising that the inhabitants are sadly accustomed to flood conditions during the summer, when the river level frequently tops the embankment. One of the most extensive inundations was in 1909, when it was attacked on both sides, for the Han as well as the Yangtze broke its banks, the one at Shayang and the other at Shasi. The water rose to the eaves of the houses, and destitution and misery were widespread.

North of Shasi the plain extends for about 15 miles only. On proceeding up river there is a bend to the west into Kingchow Reach, in the south-east of which the mouth of the Taipingho forms a sort of delta. The next town is Kiangkow (江 口), about 20 miles beyond Shasi, and next is the large village of Tungshih (董 市), on the left bank of the river west of a creek, marked by a conspicuous temple. At Spring Reach, above here, the first change in the alluvial plain occurs. Shingle beaches and rising ground demonstrate the new character of the river basin, the bed of which is now stony in parts, while the soil of the adjacent country is clay or gravel. The first hills appear; and farther on, above Grant Point, the right bank is steep, rising in places to a height of 200 feet. At the village of Yangki, or Yangchi (洋 溪), on the same side, lime is quarried, and red brick tiles and bricks are made. About 3 miles above Yangki is the attractive-looking walled city of Chihkiang (枝 江) with a pagoda on a hill to the south-east.

A pinkish limestone can now be seen in the low bluffs on the east side. From here onwards the Yangtze skirts the edge of mountainous country, passing at times through vertical walls of very coarse conglomerate containing quartz and limestone. To the west the country is of much the same character, split into gorges and chasms and very much broken up. A tributary called the Ch'ingkiang (清 江), or Clear River, breaks through this west chain and joins the Yangtze at the walled town of Itu (宜都). The southern trade route from Szechwan Province here strikes the Yangtze. Down this ancient road used to come the salt, sugar and tobacco, hemp, spices and opium, drugs, silk, wax, wood oil, and gold which represent but a portion of the great and unlimited wealth of that rich province. The junction of the Ch'ingkiang with the Yangtze, meeting as they do at right angles, has caused unusual disturbance of the river-bed, and a bar has formed consisting of a shingle bank covered with mud deposit. The bar, which lies in mid-stream, has shallow water on either side between it and the river-banks.

Ten miles above Itu and the same distance below Ichang is the first gorge of the Yangtze, known as the Tiger's Teeth Gorge (虎牙峡). It is about 2 miles long and 800 to 900 yards wide and lined with sheer walls of coarse conglomerate. As there is no tow-path, tracking for junks is impossible, and they are obliged to sail or row their way through. Fortunately for them the wind is nearly always blowing from the south-east.

The gorge gets its name from a rock said to be shaped like a tiger's tooth. It used to be said that foreigners would never be able to pass that point, for they would be eaten like sheep by the tiger. This is a play on words such as the Chinese delight in, for the sound *yang* applies to the character 羊 for "sheep" as well as that 洋 for " foreign."

Above this gorge the river runs through the Ichang Reach and Ichang Gorge, the right bank being lined with hills the whole way.

Ichang, the gateway between the vast Hupeh plain and the rich and rugged grandeur of Szechwan, is 363 miles above Hankow and some 1,000 miles from the sea. It lies on the left bank of the river, and the slender pagoda below the town and the wreaths of smoke from the harbour shipping are in view for some time whilst ascending the last straight reach of 17 odd miles. The banks rise higher and show a porous blend of coarse conglomerate with sandstone. On the right bank there is mountainous country right to the river's edge. The climate here is one of the most equable on the Yangtze, being dry and pleasantly warmer than in most other ports in winter, and favoured in summer by welcome breezes. The vegetation is temperate and sub-tropical and shows a wide range, from cotton, winter wheat, barley, peas and beans, to rice, poppies, and *t'ung* oil nuts. The fruit supply is good, particularly of oranges. Nevertheless, there is no local trade or noteworthy production, and the place derives its undoubted importance solely from its geographical position as an ideal junction for transhipment of cargo from junks or steamers built for the leisurely navigation of the Lower or Middle River into other craft specially constructed to negotiate the perils and currents of the Upper River.

The harbour accommodation is good, and the proximity of an island, known as Hsiapa (下壩), near the left bank and just above the former walled part of the city serves for eight months of the year to protect it from the force of the current, which runs strong and deep past the other bank. For most of the year this island is connected with the shore by a narrow isthmus.

Ichang, which occupies a blunt point of the Yangtze, is built on a more or less level site, but it lies in a basin, surrounded by hills rising in all directions. Immediately behind the town these are low and consist of red clay. An enormous area of these rolling hills is covered by grave mounds. Every road and path leading from the city skirts or passes through this vast necropolis, and the living are ever ringed by a quiet army of the dead.

The hills on the opposite or right bank take the form of a series of pyramids varying from 500 to 600 feet in height, rising sheer from the water's edge and connected by ridges and ravines emerging finally into the extensive ranges that lie behind. The triangular-shaped hill exactly facing Ichang, which rises to a height of 572 feet, is called by the Chinese Mo Chi Shan, the Mountain of Lonely Evening, or sometimes less poetically as Kotaochow, Mount of the Taoist. A small temple built at its base used to house an ingenious priest who acquired alms with the minimum trouble to all concerned by extending a long bamboo with a small basket hanging from its tip to passing junks. The peculiar position and form of this hill were believed by the local geomancers to have such a malevolent effect on that great guiding principle of China, the *fêng-shui*, as to react unfavourably on the prosperity of the town of Ichang, and to these evil influences was attributed the ill success of the Ichang candidates at the triennial examinations. The local trading community likewise suffered from a tendency to throw the profits of their business into the hands of strangers.

A subscription of 10,000 dollars was accordingly raised to build a Buddhist temple and monastery on the 1,200-foot high hill behind the town, to be equal in height to the pyramid across the river and thus oppose its baneful influences. Even so, there were those who maintained that the site was on the wrong hill or that the spacious three-storied pavilion was still not high enough to achieve the best results.

Ichang is said to have been originally built during the Han dynasty, 206 B.C.–A.D. 25. Its early names were Siling (西 陵), Iling (夷 陵), or Yiling, and Tunghu (東 湖). It finally received its present name and rank of prefecture under a Taotai under the Emperor Yung Chêng (雍 正) in 1736.

War-junks and armies have passed and repassed and fought over and around the vicinity. The greatest battle in ancient days was in A.D. 222, when King Liu Pei of the Kingdom of Shu, or Szechwan, was defeated in a fruitless attempt to avenge the death of his brother in arms and sworn friend, Kuan Yü, who was killed by the army of the Wu Kingdom.

Liu Pei's men, numbering about a million, were stationed along the Yangtze for some considerable distance; but by a clever flanking movement and an attack by fire-ships, the men of Wu burned his camps and routed his armies. Liu Pei died soon afterwards at Paiticheng (白 帝 城), the White King City, by the Yangtze, on the borders of Szechwan and Hupeh.

Except for its striking position and the attractive irregular line of its roofs crowded together by the waterside, there is little that remains of interest in Ichang, now that the crenellated wall with its six or seven picturesque gates has been pulled down. There are a few local craftsmen who produce articles that have a great appeal to the tourist, notably the famous Ichang model junks, the equally well-known Ichang thorn walking-sticks, and the filigree silverware, which also shows delicate and intricate craftsmanship.

As has been pointed out, Ichang is the transhipment centre for the journey through the Upper Yangtze. The river here has narrowed to only a quarter of a mile. In the shallow and comparatively slack water the river steamers lie at anchor, and the Upper Yangtze junks tie up to the shore and prepare at their leisure for their long and perilous voyage to Chungking.

Ichang.

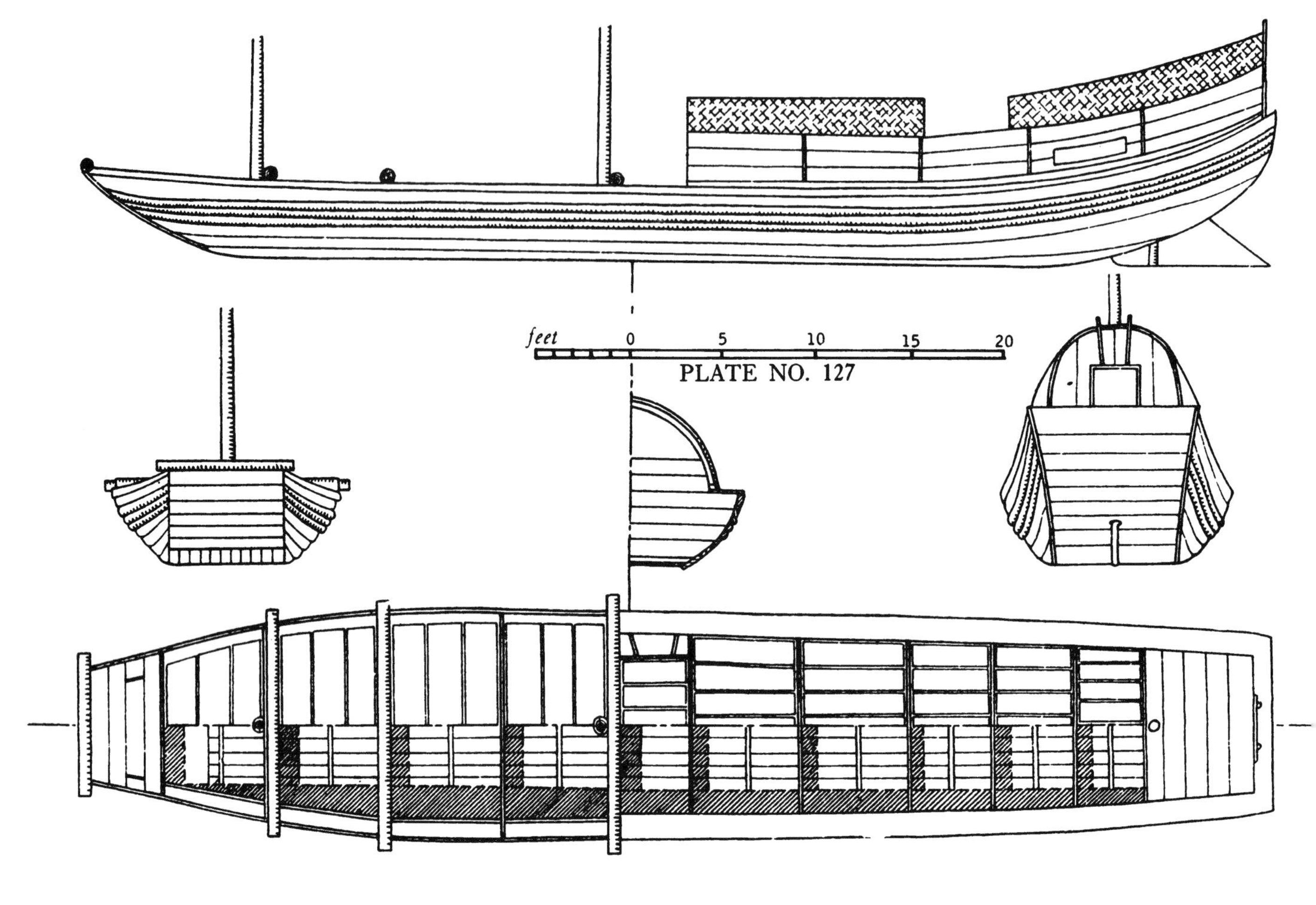

荆幫船

Descriptions of *ma-yang-tzŭ* types can be found on pages 434–35, 437, 438, and 464 in Part Three. The Upper Yangtze *ma-yang-tzŭ* is described in Part Four, page 498.

THE CHING-PANG-CH'UAN

The Yangtze between Ichang and Kwanyinchow (觀 音 洲) is known by the junkmen as the Kingho (荆 河), so named from the important town of Kingchow (荆 州), near Shasi, and famous in the time of the Three Kingdoms; hence the name *ching-pang-ch'uan*, which may be translated as Kingchow River group junk.

It belongs to the *ma-yang-tzŭ* family; and, as it is often to be seen working the same areas, that is, from Shasi, or even Hankow, to Ichang and sometimes beyond to Chungking, it is not surprising that they have several features common to the Middle Yangtze as well as the Upper Yangtze, notably the broad high bow, with its heavy transverse stem-beam, and, among other arrangements for work in the rapids of the Upper Yangtze, the poling gangway, which is essentially a Middle Yangtze characteristic.

These junks are usually built in Itu (宜 都). The bottom is made of *sha-mu* and the hull of cypress. A very usual size is 63 feet, with a beam of 11 feet, as illustrated in Plate No. 127, which gives a carrying capacity of about 500 piculs. The junk is shown with the cross-beams laid over the deck-beams, to which they are lashed. They are removable and are in position only when the junk is operating in the rapids of the Upper Yangtze.

The galley is situated on the port side, sunk 9 inches in a well over the coffer-dam, and is fitted with a waste chute. A small bin, extending athwartships across the junk and 1½ feet high, is so situated as to enable the laodah at the conning position to use it as a bridge. With these small exceptions the junk is flush throughout, and the deck-line rises in a gentle curve from 4 feet at the bow to the considerable height of 8 feet at the stern.

The deck-house is light in construction and consists of a roof of matting and sloping sides of thin wood, carried on ribs fitted to the deck cross-beams, giving a headroom of 4½ feet. Down each side of the house and across the transom is a wide gangway.

This class of craft is very popular with the junkmen, who assert that her ability to operate in rapids is quite remarkable for so small a junk, while her shallow draught and handiness make her an ideal type for use in the creek waterways.

In construction the *ching-pang-ch'uan* combines strength with simplicity.

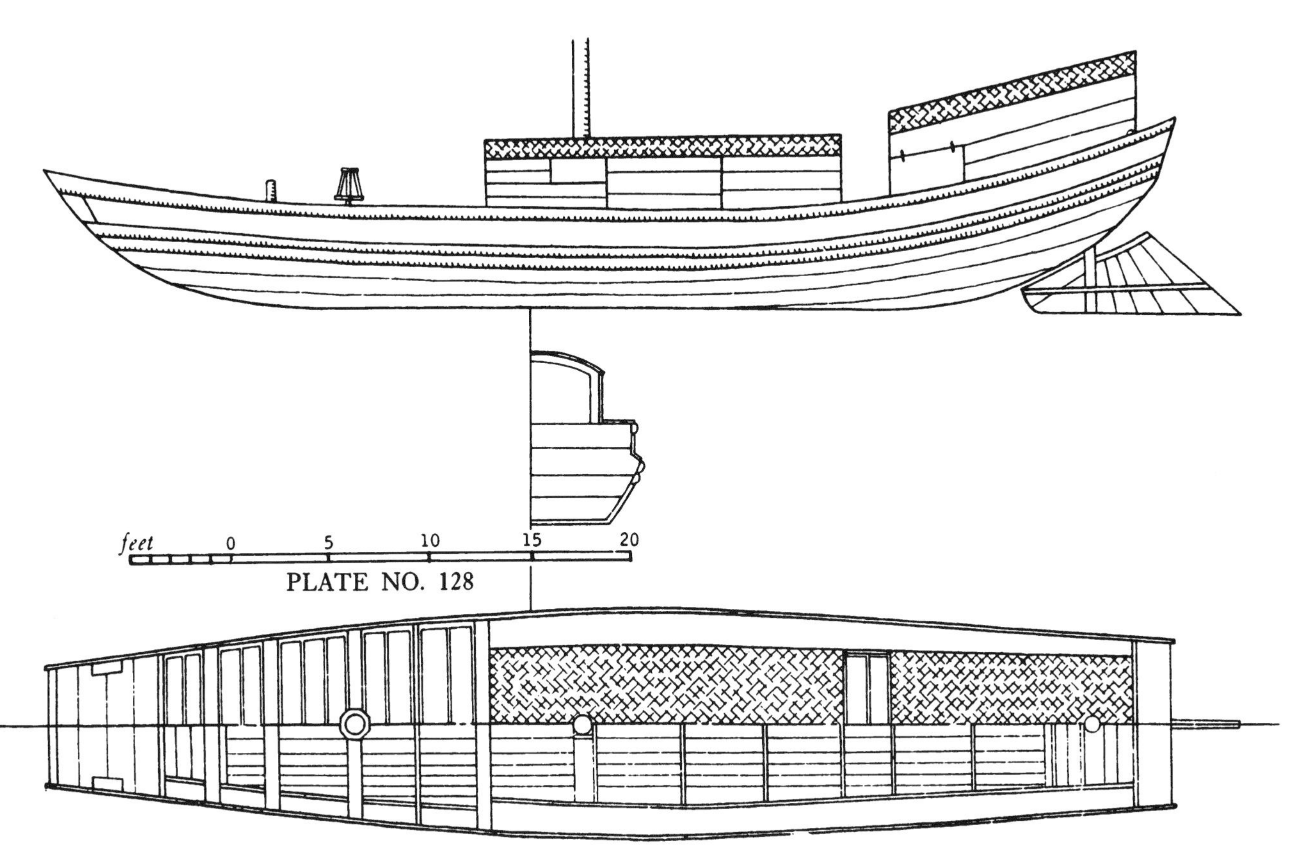

PLATE NO. 128

THE CHING-PANG-HUA-TZŬ OR SHASI TRADER

The *ching-pang-hua-tzŭ*, or Shasi trader, is, according to the junkmen, the offspring of the *pien-tzŭ* and the *ma-yang-tzŭ*, both of which hail from the Siang River area. It has also very much in common with the *ching-pang-ch'uan.*

The Shasi trader has high sides, about five beams to length, bluff bows with considerable overhang, and a transom stern. There is plenty of room along the sides of the vessel for poling, which is often resorted to when navigating the shallow inland waters between Hankow and Shasi.

The vessels are often single-masted and appear to obtain the balance of sail by placing the mast almost amidships.

The craft illustrated in Plate No. 128 measures 55 feet and has a beam of 11 feet, a depth of 4½ feet, and a capacity of about 20 tons.

The hull is strengthened by 10 bulkheads and four half-bulkheads, and is very sturdily built throughout. The foremost compartment between the bow and the first half-bulkhead is used as a chain-locker.

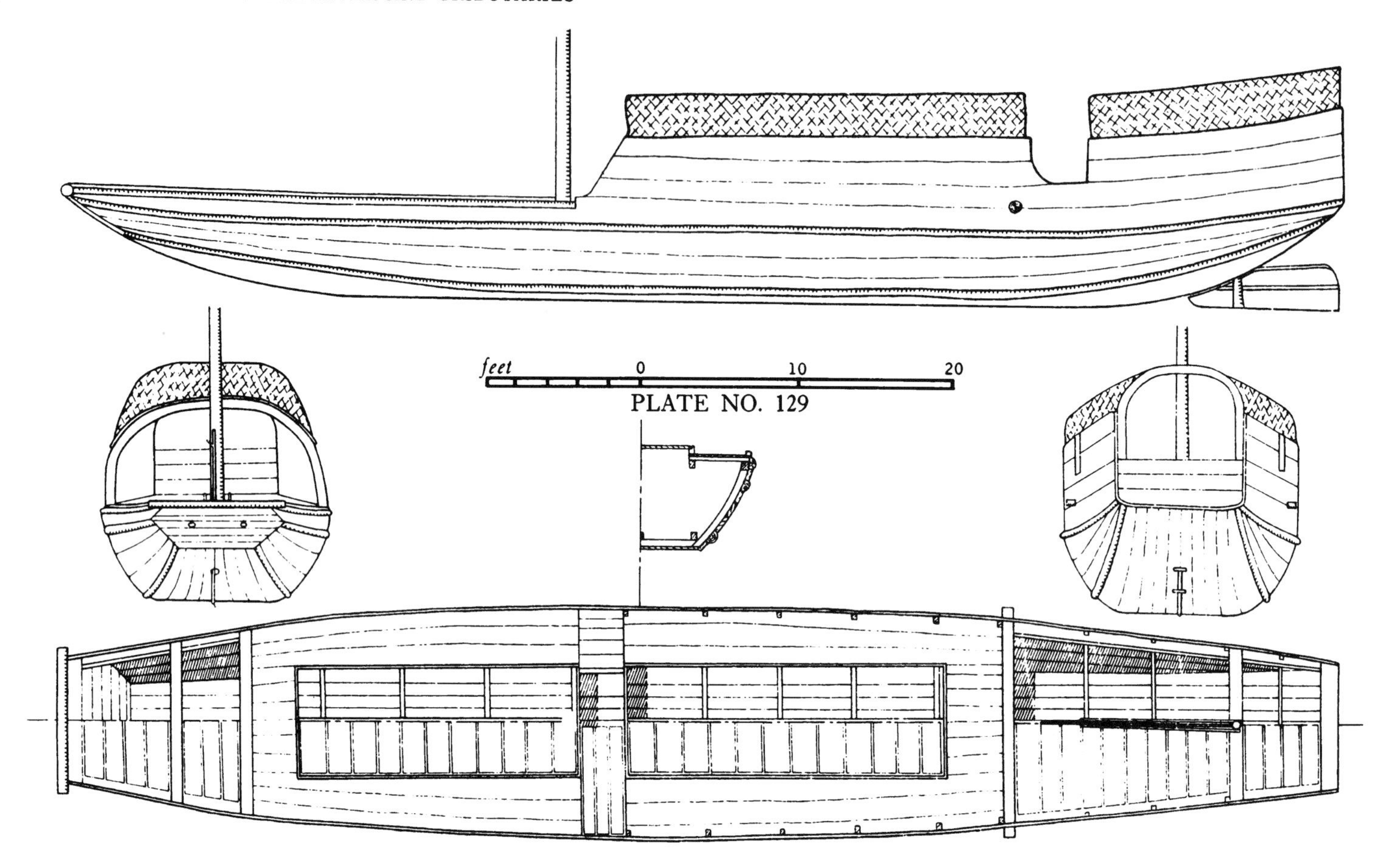

PLATE NO. 129

内

THE NEI-HO-CH'UAN

Broadside on, in outward appearance the *nei-ho-ch'uan* is very like the *shao-ma-yang* and the Upper Yangtze *nan-ho-ch'uan* (南 河 船). Closer inspection, however, reveals a most characteristic bow and stern.

The *nei-ho-ch'uan* is a beamy, cumbrous vessel designed to carry a maximum load on a minimum draught. The junk illustrated in Plate No. 129 measures 80 feet, with a beam of 14 feet. Two large holds are divided by a coffer-dam. In the waist, access to the holds is provided by two central hatches, edged with a low coaming. The hatch covers are removable in sections.

The solidly-built hull of *pai-mu* is decked-in and strengthened by a keelson and by two side-keelsons at the turn of the bilge, which makes four bulkheads, sufficient for the strength required. From this flat bottom the bilges curve up traversely and longitudinally.

Additional strength is provided by the two heavy strakes. The lower garboard strake is considerably curved and sweeps up to meet the bluff box-like bow at one extremity and the exceptionally wide stern at the other.

The bow terminates in a heavy transverse stem-beam built into the structure of the junk. Below is an apron or doubling planks affixed over the upper portion of the rising bottom planks. Two ring-bolts are fitted to carry grass-line pennants for use in conjunction with a boat-hook to assist in snubbing-to. There is a "stick-in-the-mud" anchor situated between the two bitts.

The stern is comparatively wide and has only a slight rise. An unusual feature is its termination in horizontal planking. The after-house is decked-in at the sides and is fitted with mats at its after-end. The *nei-ho-ch'uan* is a very good example of a strongly built shoal-water cargo-carrier.

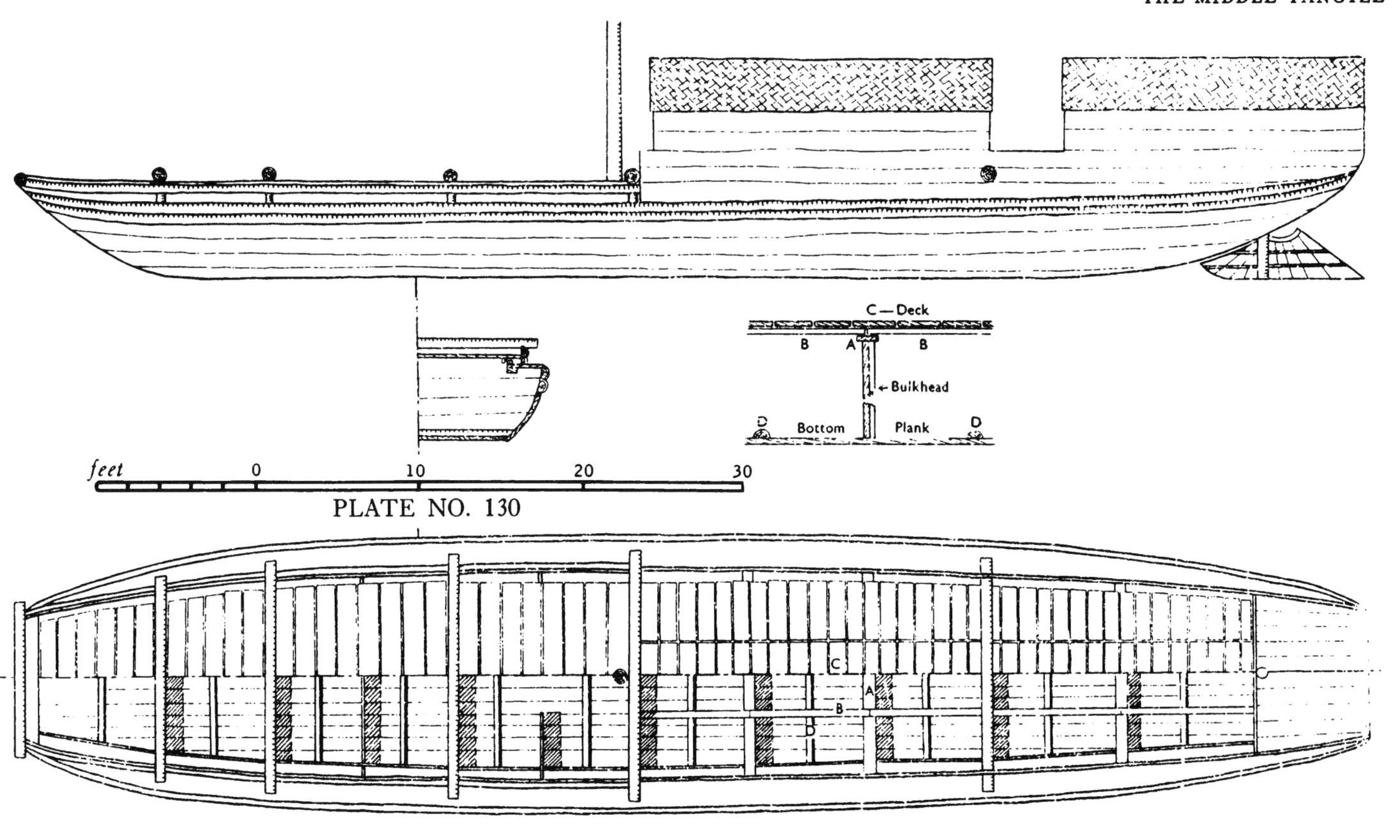

PLATE NO. 130

THE SHAO-MA-YANG

The *shao-ma-yang* (梢 麻 陽), a medium-draught cargo-carrier, while normally trading between Ichang and Shasi, is to be found as far down river as Hankow and even up river at Chungking.

The very representative type illustrated in Plate No. 130 measures 85 by 16 feet. When viewed broadside on, it may easily be mistaken for the *nei-ho-ch'uan* (內 河 船) of Changsha; and it also bears a very strong resemblance to an Upper Yangtze craft, the *nan-ho-ch'uan* (南 河 船), the difference being in the shape of the whale-back, which in the *shao-ma-yang* is rounded instead of angular and provides a clear gangway from bow to stern, so as to facilitate poling in the shoal waters of the Middle Yangtze.

The *nan-ho-ch'uan*, Part Four, page 579.

This is an interesting type in that it is a compromise as regards its build. The general arrangements and medium draught are designed not only to operate in the shallow-water channels between Ichang and Shasi, where light draught is desirable, but also sometimes to navigate the swirls and rapids of the Upper Yangtze, where deep draught is often an advantage.

THE FLOATING REED-STACK

As there are very few wooded districts on the Middle Yangtze, the peasants depend to a great extent on dried reeds for fuel, matting, and house-building; but the transport of reeds is by no means confined to this district, for the commodity is a notable product of the whole Yangtze Valley. From where the river emerges from the mountains below Ichang down to its mouth, the marshy banks and extensive flats through which it flows are overgrown by reeds, which often grow to a height of 15 or 20 feet and are of the utmost use to a vast population.

There are two kinds of reeds. One is called *kan-ch'ai* (乾 柴), or strong reeds, and the other *lu-ch'ai* (蘆 柴), or weak reeds. The former are used for fuel, making sun-blinds, and the like, while the latter are used for making mats.

Various methods of carrying the reeds to the waterside are employed, one of the more common being a type of wooden trolley not unlike a crude model of a modern railway truck, the four solid wheels of which revolve, with the axles being situated below the truck and inside the protecting framework.* In the Kiukiang district the reed bundles are loaded onto a double-decker type of sledge pushed by men or drawn by buffaloes across the flats. On arrival at the water's edge the reeds are built up on pairs of junks which, when loaded, look like floating haystacks.

The considerable industry in reeds on the Middle Yangtze is carried on between Linsiang (臨 湘), Paotachow (寶 塔 洲), Paichow (簰 洲), and Kiayü (嘉 魚), and the terminal ports of Sinti (新 隄) and Hankow. On the Siang River reeds come from the West Tungting Lake to Tsingshih (津 市), Nanhsien (南 縣), and Yüankiang (沅 江). The pairs of junks which carry the reeds are known as *ch'ai-pan-tzŭ* (柴 板 子), or reed plank boats.

They are joined together by a spar at bow and stern, leaving a space of about 6 feet between the two craft, whereby a comparatively large area is provided upon which to stack the reeds. The junks vary in size from 30 feet up to 70 feet in length. Various types of old or even condemned junks are used in the reed-carrying trade, but the most favoured are the *yao-shao* and the *pien-tzŭ* on the Middle Yangtze and the *shên-po-tzŭ* and the *ma-yang-tzŭ* on the Siang.

When the junks are of the larger types and approximately the same size, they both use sails, their masts being generally, though not invariably, parallel to each other; if, as quite often happens, the two junks are of markedly different sizes, the large junk only carries a sail.

The sails are of the ordinary type and size, but the mast used is always much taller than usual. As a rule the extra height is obtained by fitting a topmast. Additional aid to propulsion when up bound is provided by oars, if there is room to wield them.

The reed-stack, which practically envelops the whole of the two junks and the intervening space, is built up on poles so that it projects well over the sides of both craft with a width of anything up to or over 50 feet. It is also built up high, nearly to the masthead in some cases. As the mast is thus buried in reeds, only a very much reefed sail can be used.

Usually the reeds are carried down stream, and little sail is then required; for, as the junks drift with the current, they present such a broad surface to the wind that they are thereby enabled to travel at a good speed.

* The axles are large and circular and this permits the cart to move even when embedded in mud up to the axles.

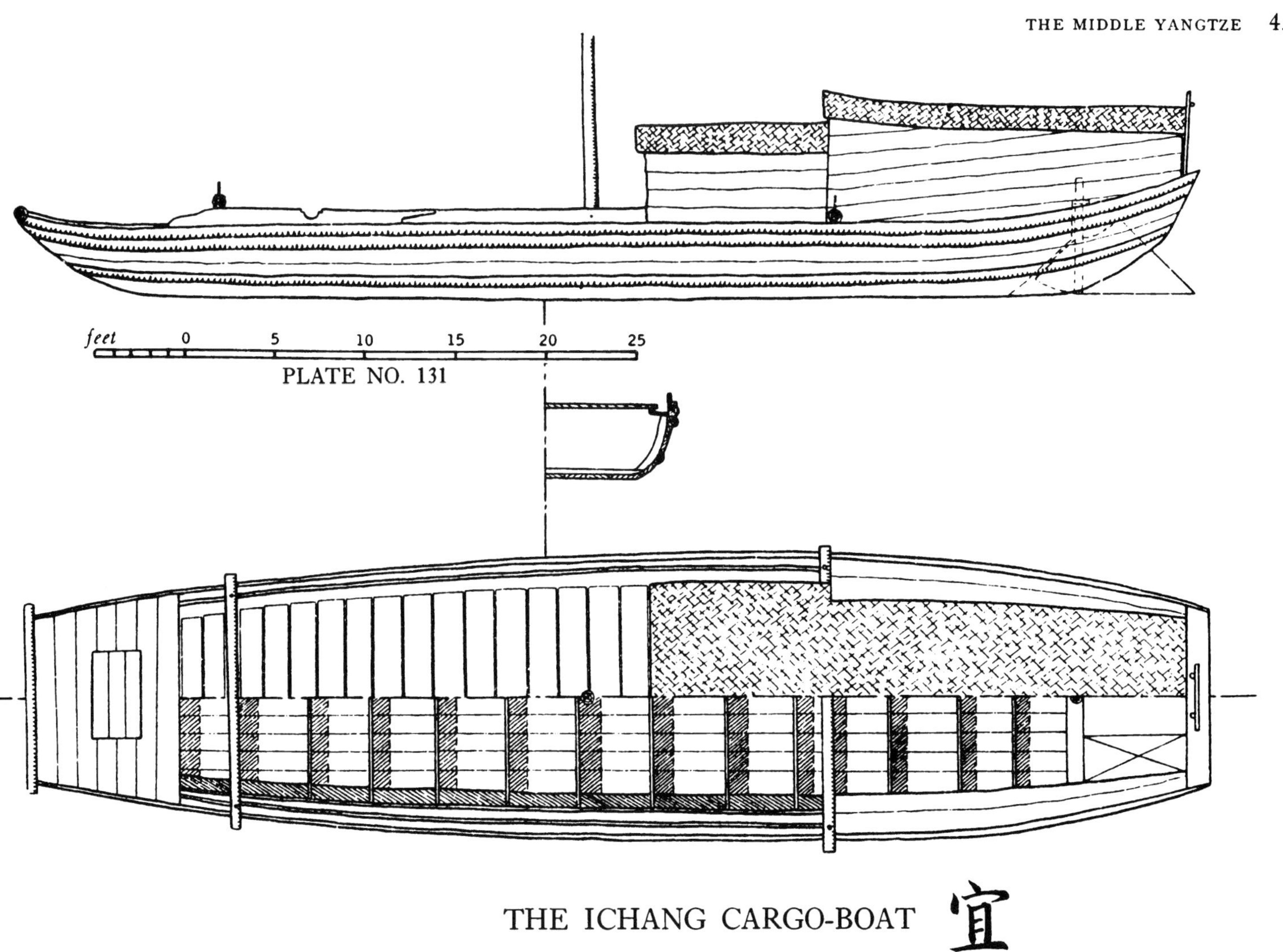

PLATE NO. 131

THE ICHANG CARGO-BOAT 宜昌駁船

There is little of interest and nothing original in the cargo-boats of Ichang. They are usually employed to transport cargo from the steamers anchored in the stream to the shore. That illustrated in Plate No. 131 shows a towed cargo-boat. These uninspiring craft are used to carry cargo from Ichang down to Itu and thence down the creek routes; they are usually towed by an old and decrepit launch.

A mast carries a sail, which is used with a fair wind, and the junk is fitted with yulohs to propel her for short distances.

The crew live in a small deck-house, the laodah being supplied with a bunk.

The junk depicted is fitted with 15 bulkheads and is of great strength, as indeed all cargo-boats have to be. Additional strength is provided by three heavy wales.

THE ICHANG "DRAGON" BOAT 宜昌龍舟

The Milo River runs into the Tungting Lake in the vicinity of Lei Shih Shan (磊石山). It was here in the fourth century B.C. that Ch'ü Yüan (屈原), a political critic, poet, and official of the Kingdom of Ch'u, committed suicide by drowning himself. He was not the first historical person to do so, for the Tungting Lake has always been popular with historical and legendary personages as a desirable site at which to end their lives. Nevertheless, Ch'ü Yüan is by far the most famous, and the Tungting Lake is always associated with him.

According to the legend, Ch'ü Yüan was an official under the ruler Huai (懷 王) in the Kingdom of Ch'u in the period of the warring Kingdoms, about 22 centuries ago. Through the slander of a treacherous official, Ch'ü Yüan was dismissed. He then lived a solitary and disgruntled life, during which he composed the famous "Li Sao" (離 騷), an elegy on "encountering sorrow." This famous poem, which has been translated into English, best represents the austere and ascetic purity of its author, who stood out as a beacon in the darkness of political corruption at the time.

Ch'ü Yüan was readmitted into the court by Siang (頃 襄 王), successor to Huai, only to be again slandered, persecuted, and disappointed. He then wrote "Chiu Ko" (九 歌), the "Nine Songs," after which he jumped into the Milo River in Hunan Province and was drowned.

Although his worth was not realized at the time, Ch'ü Yüan was later remembered by every Chinese as a lofty, faithful, righteous, and talented man. Thereafter, in honour of his death, the people on that day threw offerings of pyramid-shaped rice dumplings into the water until the tradition became universal, and the 5th and 15th days of the 5th moon are always observed by racing boats in mimic attempts to recover the poet's body.

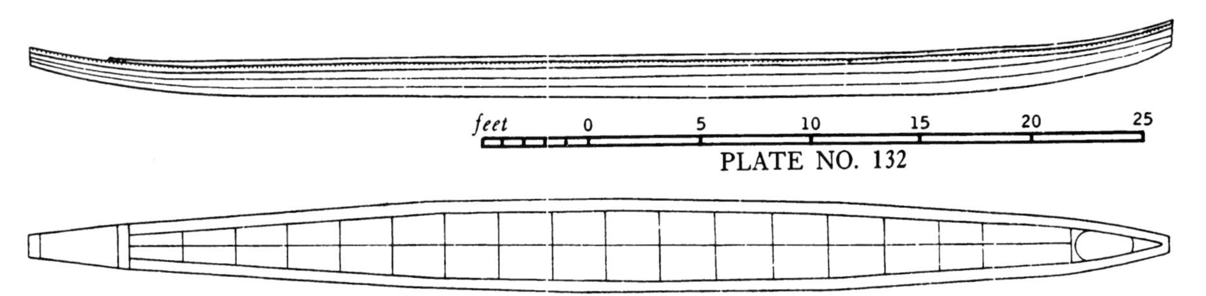

PLATE NO. 132

These boats vary considerably in the different widely separated riverine ports of China. At Ichang they take the form of long, slender racing boats. Although the "dragon" boat may be said to have originated in the Tungting Lake, the lakeside people are not particularly interested in "dragon" boat races. The type, therefore, taken as representative of the Middle Yangtze is the Ichang "dragon" boat.

This boat, illustrated in Plate No. 132, is interesting in that it represents the smallest type of "dragon" boat used in Chinese long boat racing. It measures 4 *chang* 4 *ch'ih*, that is to say, 44 Chinese feet. The largest-sized boats used are of 10 *chang* 10 *ch'ih*. It is a convention that all "dragon" boats, which may be of any intermediate size, must contain the same number of *chang* as of *ch'ih*.

For more information on "Dragon" boats, see Part Three, page 404 and Part Four, page 531.

Most of the usual conventions with respect to "dragon" boats obtain at Ichang, such as naming them after the colours of the dragons of the four winds: red, black, yellow, and white. The crew, stripped to the waist, all wear gaily coloured short trousers to match. A distinctive feature of the Ichang ceremonies is that before the race the crews parade through the streets with broad, red sashes across their bodies and a black handkerchief tied round their heads, with a large bow in front, and carrying the head and tail of a dragon, which are subsequently fixed to the bow and stern of the boat.

The man who beats the gong (鑼) usually stands in the bow. The local custom is that, if there is any official or prominent person whom it is wished to honour, he is invited to take a place in the boat during a practice trip. For this he is expected to "pay his footing," however small the sum.

The boats hailing from the vicinity of the north gate, or from small villages near-by, are red or yellow in colour, while those from the districts of the other city gates are black or white. The popularity of the event is shown by the fact that the "dragon" boat from the little town of Tzekwei (秭 歸), 46 miles above Ichang, travels yearly down to Ichang to participate in the race.

The boat shown in Plate No. 132 is the Ichang Customs "dragon" boat, called the black boat. Contrary to the usual procedure, this craft is not broken up after use, but is kept for service year after year, this particular boat being 25 years old. It is maintained and kept in repair by the sampanmen and the boatmen of the Customs, who seldom fail to enter for the race.

At Ichang the Dragon Boat Festival comes during a period of usually good weather and is one of the most universally popular of the year. It arouses widespread interest on the part of the supporters of the various competing crews, who watch with practised and critical eye the racing of the boats in their mad search for the body of Ch'ü Yüan.

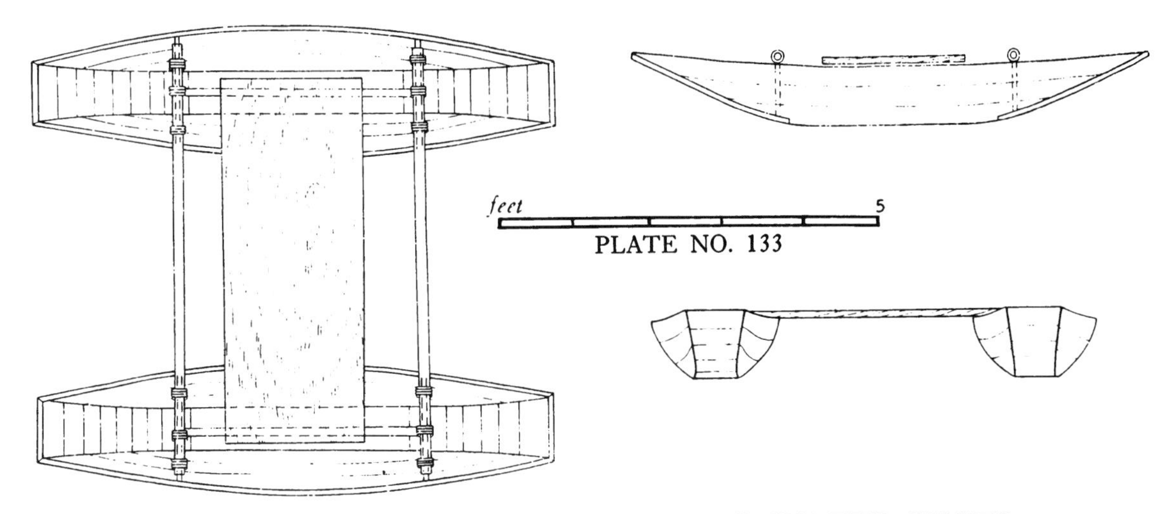

PLATE NO. 133

THE ICHANG WATER-SHOES

This peculiar form of craft is the smallest sampan, or rather pair of sampans, in use in China.

It has been devised for dip-net fishing in very shallow ponds of flooded tracts of land and also in any other still water where the depth is not too great for convenient poling, which is the only form of propulsion.

This craft is largely in use in and around Ichang on the lakes and ponds. It may be likened to a pair of snow-shoes, for it consists of twin miniature sampans of the conventional double-ended square-bowed type which measure only about 5½ feet in length, with a beam of 9 inches and a depth of about 7 inches. They are placed about 5 or 6 inches apart and are joined together by two connecting pieces of wood.

The operator standing on these cross-pieces, by exercising a highly developed sense of balance only to be compared with that of a tight-rope walker, contrives not only to keep in an upright position, but to punt himself about in search of the fish he so deftly manages to collect in his hand-net. When his fishing is over he can carry the water-shoes home across his shoulder.

On the Wei River (渭 水), in Shensi, where this type of craft is also widely used, the fisherman stands on a single board joining the two sampans and in place of a net employs cormorants to do his fishing for him.

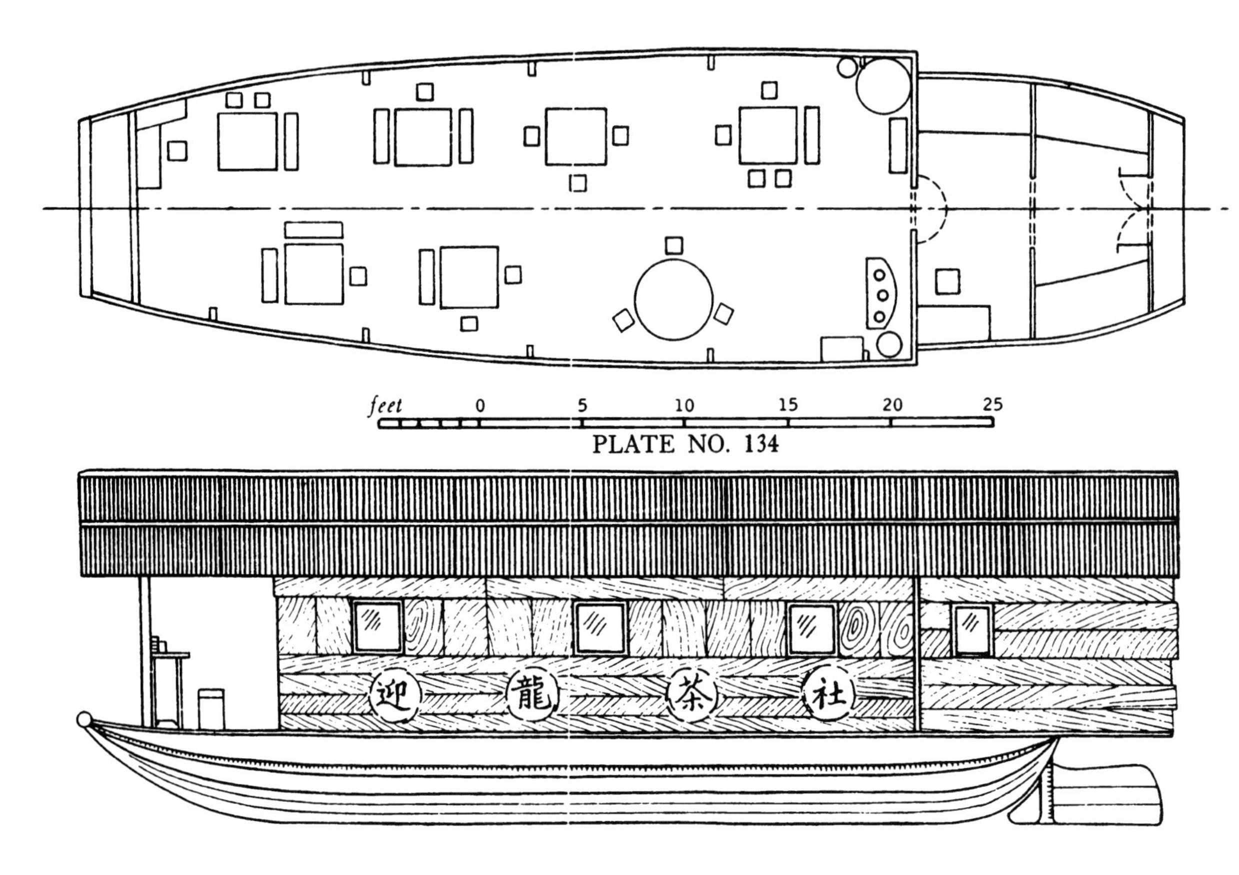

PLATE NO. 134

FLOATING DWELLING AND TEA-HOUSES OF ICHANG

Ichang stands on a conglomerate rise which is only just above the average high level of the river. In winter the long, low sandspit disclosed below by the receding waters occupies nearly one-third of the river's breadth in summer.

Colonies of matshed huts spring up on this extensive sandbank when it appears; and rows of house-boats of all sizes and shapes tie up to the mudbanks during the winter months, forming a migratory suburb of floating villas. In common with those of the Upper Yangtze, which they closely resemble, these consist of any condemned junk or sampan built up with every sort, size, and description of wood in every sort of condition. As only the comparatively rich can afford bits of packing cases, timber no longer serviceable for junks is generally used. The wood is sometimes bought, though much is often acquired. A neighbour's house may have caught fire and may yield a plank or two. Floating wood from accidents to craft forms a welcome windfall, for it is the unwritten law of the Yangtze that floating wood is never returned to the owner if it can be avoided.

A favourite type of house-boat is a sampan with a patchwork dwelling superimposed upon it, and in countless of these craft live many thousands of Ichang residents who know no other home. Ducks, chickens, cats, dogs, and pigs often live on board on terms of equality with the owners.

Actually this floating population is rather to be envied than pitied. Instead of being condemned to the narrow restrictions of drab streets and mean houses, they enjoy a roving life in the open air with constant variations of scene. The question of water supply need present no problem, neither need floods nor civil disasters concern them, for they may profit from the former by collecting flotsam and can always remove themselves and their property bodily from the vicinity of the latter.

Among the clusters of these humble homes, larger craft may be seen towering above the others. These are the tea-house boats—the aristocrats of the floating suburbia of Middle Yangtze River ports. On the arrival of a river steamer these unwieldy craft make their way out from the shore under crude oars, aided by poling, when shoal water permits, or even tracking up the bank far ahead of all shipping in port. Then, leaving the shelter of the river-bank, they sheer out into the swift current and progress with it crab-wise down stream until, by a miracle of fine judgment and to the accompaniment of a pandemonium of shouting and noise, they manage to secure a hold to the steamer's stern. The tea-house bow being then almost alongside the ship's fender, an easy access is assured to thirsty passengers when the whole doorway across the bows is thrown open.

The floating tea-house selected for description here is known as the Tea House of the Welcome Dragon (迎 龍 茶 社) (Plate No. 134). It is built up on a condemned Upper Yangtze junk of the *pao-wan-ch'uan* type, which, for whatever reason, is much in favour for the purpose. This specimen had, no doubt, served for many years among the rapids and races of the gorges, but, despite this, was in very fair condition.

It measures 52 feet, with a beam of 15 feet, and, as regards the hull, presents no variation from the *pao-wan-ch'uan* in construction. The superstructure, which projects laterally for 6 inches on either side over the junk deck, is supported by cross-beams. About one-third of the after-portion is completely built up to form a space for two quite roomy and comfortable cabins for the owner and his large family.

The remaining part of the craft has breast-high bulwarks of irregular planking along both sides terminating in a large entrance door right across the bow. The whole junk is covered by a mat roof. In this semi-open café are distributed seven small tables, while close to the entrance on the starboard side is a counter where the owner's wife sells cigarettes, sweets, peanuts, and sunflower seed.

Behind the tea tables are a serving table, a stove, and a water *kang*. Before each customer is placed a covered bowl without handles, a few tea leaves being sprinkled in the bottom. A servant then moves, swiftly and inquisitively, from table to table, filling these bowls from a tin kettle of boiling water with a spout over 2 feet long. From an elevation of about a foot and at a distance of nearly a yard, he fills each bowl to the brim with the greatest dexterity and without a drop going astray, and passes on to the next table, moving nonchalantly among the crowded clients, who have such faith in his skill that no one flinches when the formidable kettle is balanced within a few inches of his shoulder.

The tea-bowls are filled and refilled. A very modest sum entitles a man to stay all day if he should so desire. Deck-chairs are often provided as an extra lure, and it sometimes happens that a floating-kitchen junk will tie up alongside and serve ready cooked meals to hand up to the tea-drinking clients in the tea-house. In the winter the sides of the boat are closed in with bamboo matting to keep out the cold wind and the rain.

An additional source of income is provided by allowing passengers from the over-crowded decks of the adjacent river steamer to lay out their rolls of bedding on the floor of the floating tea-house and spend the night there after the tea-drinking clients have gone.

However old and however rickety the craft may be, the visitor may always count on his money's worth in welcome, warm weak tea, and the amusement to be gained by watching unaffected human nature in the raw taking its ease.

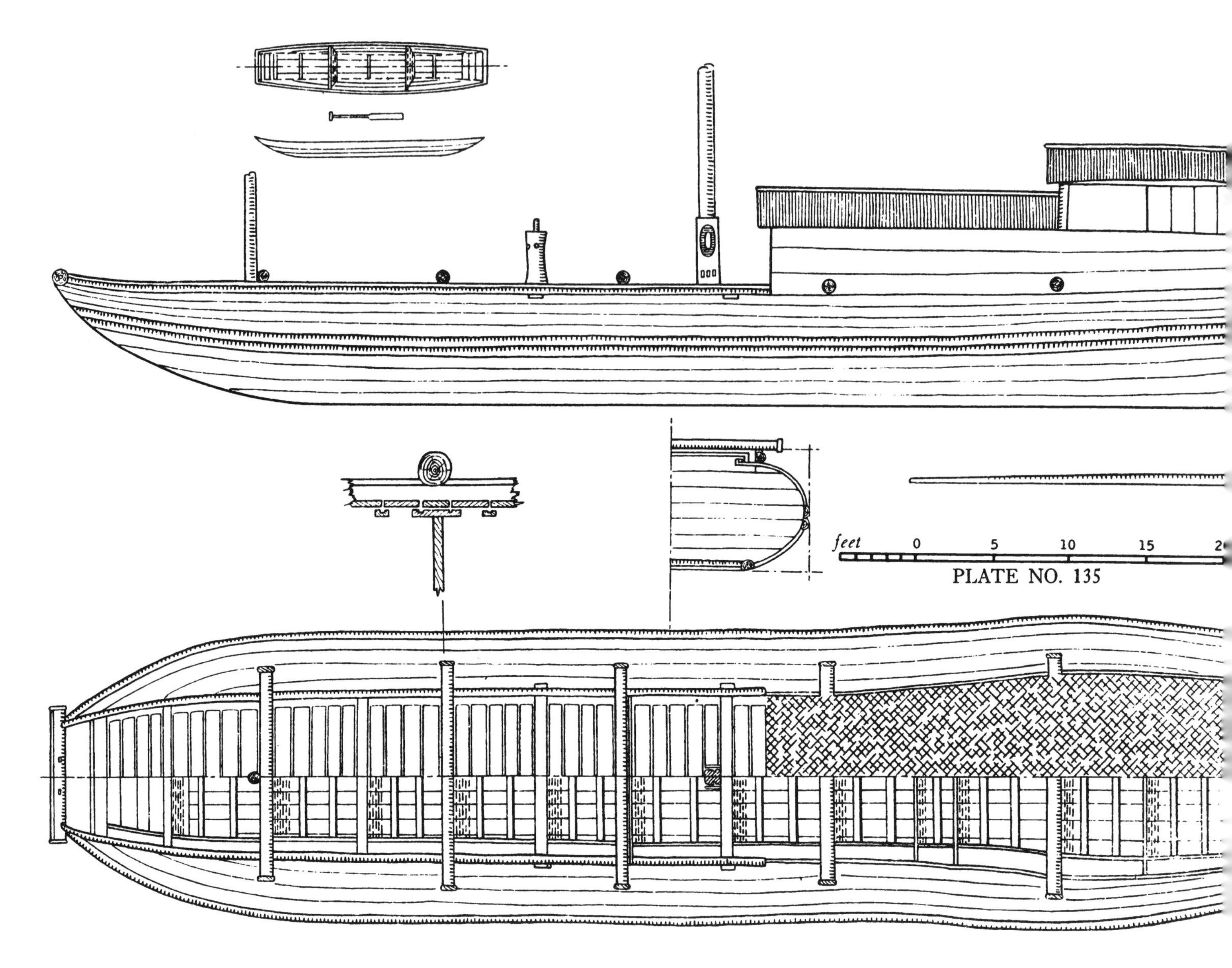

PLATE NO. 135

收口麻陽子 THE SHOU-K'OU MA-YANG-TZŬ

Most of the variations of the *ma-yang-tzŭ* have unfortunately become obsolete, leaving no authentic records behind them, but from the *chang-k'ou ma-yang-tzŭ* already described evolved a very distinctive type known as the *shou-k'ou* (收 口), or " closed mouth," *ma-yang-tzŭ*, being modified to carry specified heavy cargoes through the strong currents and dangerous rapids of the Upper Yangtze, for these craft are more often to be seen in those waters than in or around their true place of origin.

Like the great proportion of the deviations from the main type, the *shou-k'ou* is turret-built. The structural alteration was made so as to render the deck more watertight for the cargoes of grain and wood oil. This form of construction, for which the junkmen offer many fallacious reasons, also gives extra strength and protection in the rapids of the Upper Yangtze on the principle that a barrel is stronger than a box.

The *shou-k'ou ma-yang-tzŭ* has, therefore, strictly speaking, become an Upper Yangtze craft, but as they are so often to be seen proceeding down as far as Shasi to collect cargoes of cotton for Szechwan, a short description is justified in the pages of this section.

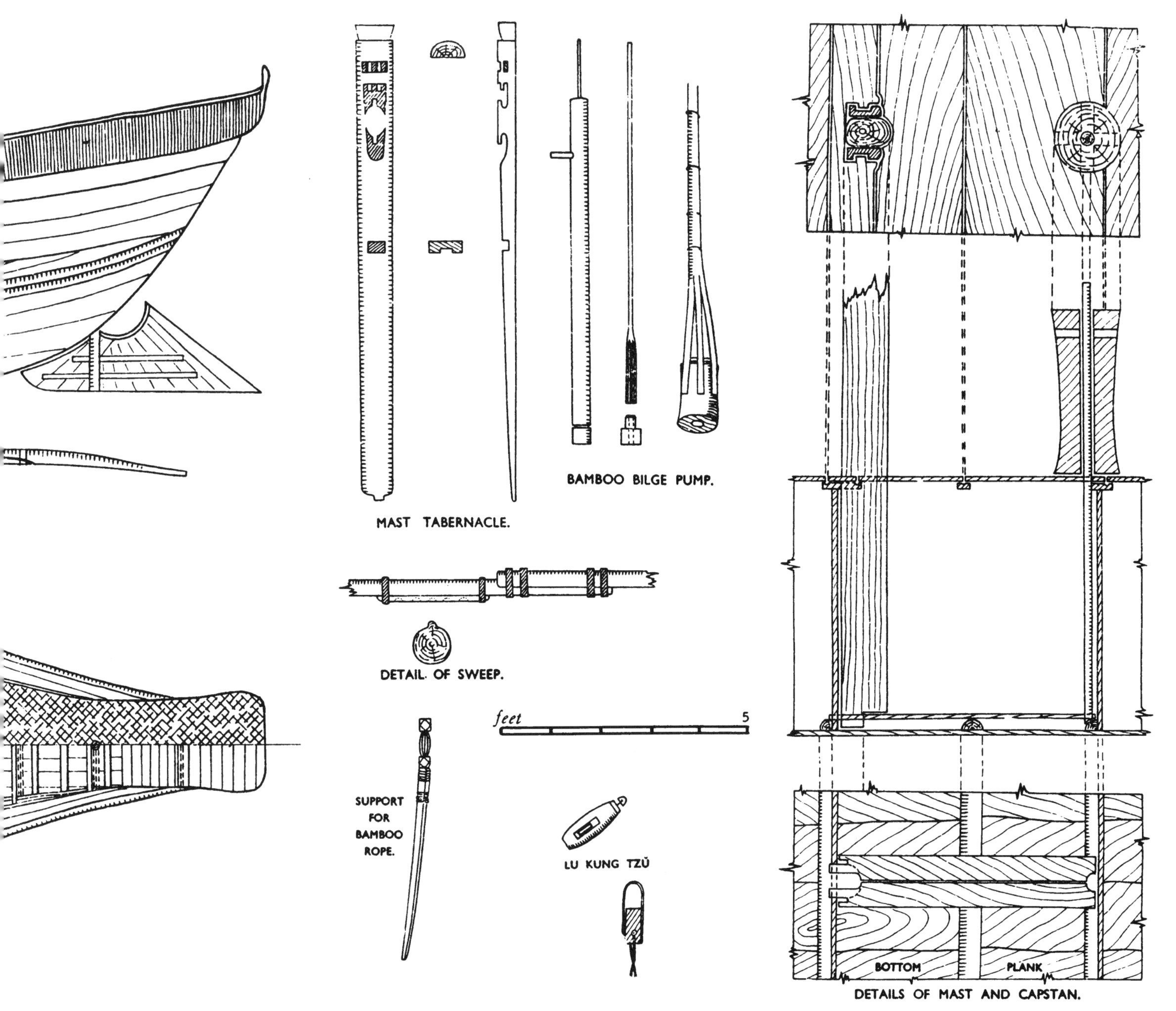

Briefly, the *shou-k'ou ma-yang-tzŭ*, which hails from Wanhsien, is a turret-built variation of the *chang-k'ou ma-yang-tzŭ* and is built on similar lines to the *ma-yang-tzŭ* proper of the Upper Yangtze.

Before the coming of steamers to the Upper Yangtze these junks were the chief cargo-carriers and reached considerable size, some being, it is said, as long as 150 feet. The usual lengths at the present time vary from as small as 36 feet to as long as 110 feet. It is interesting that even the miniature types follow the same lines and characteristics of the larger varieties.

The specimen selected for representation in Plate No. 135 measures 102 feet in length, with a beam of 19 feet and a depth of 8½ feet. Made of cypress, she is pre-eminently designed for hard service. There are 28 half-frames of exceptional strength and seven of the massive cross-beams which constitute so marked a characteristic of the *ma-yang-tzŭ* craft as a whole. These cross-beams come into use when the junk is navigating the rapids, for the tracking-lines are secured to them. The heaviest and strongest is in the bow. It is built into the structure, firstly, by having the skirting board let into it, secondly, by being secured by three iron clamps or dogs, and lastly, it is iron-bound on either side from well behind the bow at deck-level, over the bow and cross-beam, and then under the bow to below the water-line. On Plate No. 135 will be seen details of mast fittings, capstan, and other appurtenances of this type of craft. Such fittings are typical of most classes of Middle Yangtze craft.

Model-making is covered in the Appendix.

This class and others, such as the *ma-yang-tzŭ*, which are so closely akin as to be indistinguishable save to the eye of a junkman, are probably the best known of all the many Yangtze types. More models are made of this kind of junk than of any other, and curiously enough, difficult as they must be to make, they are nearly always as completely accurate as any model not made to scale can be, that is to say, if they originate from the Ichang model-makers.

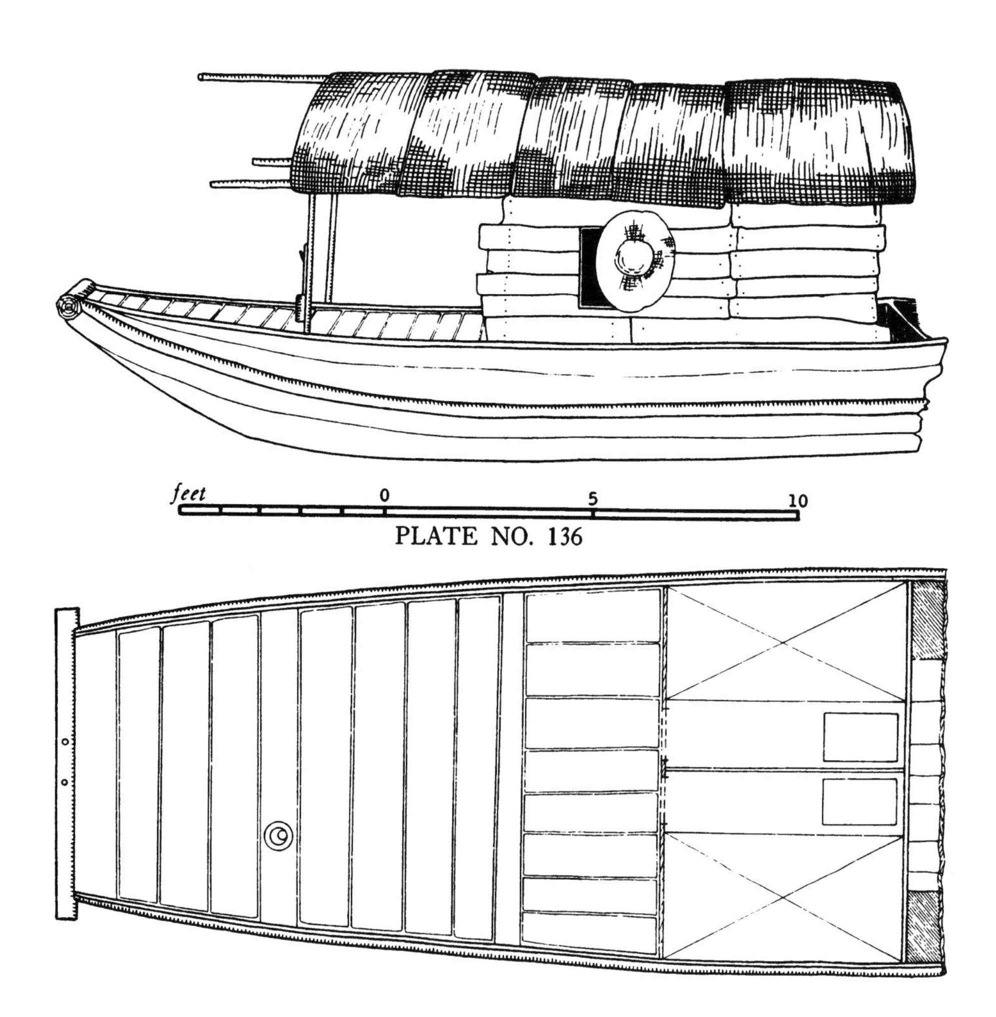

PLATE NO. 136

THE HALF-BOAT

Quite one of the most interesting types of floating dwelling is the half-boat, illustrated in Plate No. 136. This consists of a junk cut in two athwartships, thus forming foundations for two separate dwellings. The trim of the boat is adjusted by a careful distribution of the furniture, such as *kangs* of water or large stones used in the usual hammering process so indispensable in the washing of clothes.

In the smaller types such as this, it is astonishing how restricted an amount of space is allowed for sleeping and living as compared with the area devoted to the kitchen and its utensils; and, as may be expected, the larger the floating dwelling, the more tubs, baskets, pots, and pans are in use, out of all proportion to the needs of the family and its live stock.

The "house" selected for description here is about 21 feet long and is more spacious and more luxurious than usual. The after-end contains two bunks with a partition between (a privacy undreamt of in other dwellings), and accommodates two families with their children.

When more children arrive, and/or poor relations have to be supported, the floating dwelling can be extended by planking in the sides until the whole boat is finally covered in. Alternatively, a flimsy stern gallery extension may be built on to provide the extra space required.

The fore-deck is given up to cooking and living quarters for the live stock. A hole is cut in one side of the house, and a straw hat tied at the top with string may often act as a shutter to this improvised window.

Land taxes, high rents, and key money are evaded, and a scarcity of dwellings is felt not at all.

There is one more type of half-boat which serves as a moral reminder to those junkmen who have strayed from paths of rectitude. When a junk has been caught by the Yangtze Water Police in illegal practices, such as slipping past tax stations, smuggling, or other offences, it sometimes suffers the extreme penalty, which is to be sawn in half and exposed, erected on end, on the river-bank, where it serves as a mournful object lesson to others.

THE WALKING-BOATS OF ICHANG

According to Mr. Worcester's notes, no plans were available for the following types.

A frail and transient craft is that which makes its appearance on one day of the year only, Têng Chieh (燈節), or the Feast of Lanterns, celebrated on the evening of the 15th day of the 1st moon, that is to say, at the end of the lunar New Year holidays.

These are the walking-boats of Ichang. They are made of paper pasted on to a cane foundation or framework and are fairly standard as to size and design. They are carried at waist height by a man who walks inside the structure, below which his feet and legs appear; and, as he adopts a rolling gait, the craft appears to be in a heavy seaway. The boats appear only at night, when they are lighted from the inside by a candle; and, as is not surprising, the paper hull often catches fire, when the crew has to "abandon ship" or rather step out of the ship with some alacrity.

Paper boats and the Chinese New Year celebrations are extensively described in Part One, in the chapter on Beliefs and Superstitions.

Owing to the Government having banned the observance of any holidays of the lunar calendar, celebrations of the old-style Chinese New Year have been officially forbidden; yet in Ichang, at a safe distance from the seat of Government, the Feast of Lanterns on the last day of the lunar New Year holidays is still observed in a perfect frenzy of fantastic celebrations exactly as it has been since its inception under the Han dynasty 2,000 years ago.

Fir branches and coloured paper lanterns are hung above the doorways. Large quantities of little round moon-cakes, so named after the full moon and made of glutinous rice, are consumed.

Models of dragons, which since the revolution have been proclaimed to be of the old Imperial regime and therefore taboo, and which a more enlightened Government has further proclaimed to be relics of ancient and ridiculous superstitions, are carried round the country districts in the daylight; but it is after dark that the real fun commences, and the dragons, now lighted up, pursue their way down the main streets of the city precisely as they have always done at this season.

The entire city goes on holiday and the streets are full of beggars, blind fortune-tellers, gamblers, acrobats, and so forth.

The dragon procession consists of men stripped to the waist, who carry the dragon through the enormous crowds of spectators. The immensely long body, made of paper or sometimes coloured cloth streamers, sways and heaves along the street, supported every few feet by a carrier who holds up a section on a short pole. Each section is of paper on a light wooden frame and is lit up inside like a Chinese lantern. The leading man carries the huge dragon's head most cunningly fashioned out of paper on a wood or bamboo frame and also lit up within.

Attendant dragons caper about, waving huge flaring torches from which the smoke and fumes, wreathing together in the still night air, add a yet more sinister aspect to the scene. From time to time the dragon pauses in its bobbing progress and, halting outside some generous patron's door or prominent merchant's shop, performs a special extravaganza for the benefit of the household. This is the signal for a renewed outbreak of fire-crackers, for bursts of shouting and appreciative laughter from the crowds; and the applause and excitement goads the leading two men, on whom the chief responsibility falls, to further contortions. The foremost man starts off in a wild and curtsying dance, causing the huge ferocious head to swirl and dip in a grotesque semblance of reality. The rest of the dragon crew become worked up into a state of wild hysteria and whirl their sections in great circles, so that the whole body is undulating and writhing. The banging of gongs and the incessant explosions of fire-crackers which snap and hiss in addition form an infernal accompaniment to the performance, while the mob surges round and presses closer so as to miss nothing of the show.

The dragon, which, it is believed, derives from the crocodile once so common in China, is regarded as a benign deity with none of the malevolent associations of the West, hence it was an Imperial symbol of dignity. The fecund properties of this "rain-giver" and god of the waters is demonstrated by the fact that the candle ends from the illuminated dragons are in great demand by childless women, and it is said that the dragon's eyes will give complete success to a brooding hen.

When the dragons have passed on there is a respite, and the people stroll about waiting for the next item of interest. In the distance can be heard a beating of gongs and more fire-crackers, and then come youths carrying large red lanterns, followed by others riding paper horses with lighted candles inside. These horses are in two sections and are tied to the riders. Torch-bearers light up a flotilla of walking-boats, always a feature of the procession, which tails off into a succession of children of all ages carrying paper lanterns of all sorts and sizes, fashioned with crazy ingenuity into shapes of fish, flowers, squares, circles, and triangles.

A modern flavour is introduced sometimes when a child, more belligerently minded than its fellows, is seen carrying a tank or an aeroplane lighted up from the inside.

THE SHASI PAI-CH'UAN OR BUNDLE-BOAT

The first craft of the ancient Egyptians were simple floats of reeds tied together in bundles. Such floats have been used by all types of primitive peoples, and their origin must date back to prehistoric times. To take a most famous instance, Moses was found in an "ark of bulrushes."

Reed boats were made in widely different parts of the world and are still to be found on Lake Tzana in Abyssinia, in parts of the west coast of South America and on Lake Titicaca, in use by the Shilluk and Dinka tribes, and even in Europe on the Oristano Lagoon of Sardinia.

Boats made from bundles of reeds must be of very early origin in China also, where their use has survived to this day, for bundle-boats are not uncommon in parts of the Middle Yangtze, notably in the hinterland of Shasi, where they are used on the ponds and flooded fields and marsh lands in the search for edible fish.

This type of craft is known as *pai-ch'uan* (白 船), or white boat, for they are treated with lime, because the fishermen believe that the *lien* (鰱) or *huan* (鯇) fish are attracted by the sight of white objects. Indeed, the fishermen affirm that on moonlight nights these fish obligingly jump out of the water into the boat and are thus caught.

In shape the *pai-ch'uan* is a crude oval with pointed bow and stern. The bottom of the craft is composed of bundles of reeds, while the sides are formed of mats of woven reeds called *lu-hsi* (蘆 蓆). These bundle-boats measure some 4 by 2 feet across at the broadest part. Comfort or convenience has been in no way studied in the design of these craft, nor are they to be recommended to those who dislike getting wet, for the fisherman has to lie prone, with his feet in the air, while propelling himself with his hands.

The bundle-boats of Shasi are light, their construction is simple, and their cost low, but for obvious reasons they do not last long in service, for the reeds soon become waterlogged and heavy, making progress slow. When in daily use they last for little more than a month. Nevertheless, they probably are the most economical fishing craft in the world.

THE CHOLERA-BOAT

One very strange superstition is connected with a ceremony which takes place if an epidemic of cholera should break out. Such a visitation on a city is said to show supernatural anger, which has prompted evil spirits to take possession of the town. Appeasement is resorted to and takes the form of feasts, gifts, and especially the following strange ceremony, which is prompted by the citizens' desire to speed the unwelcome guests with all despatch by the curious custom known as "sending a boat." This religious observance, which costs thousands of dollars, is usually contributed by the rich. With part of the subscription a huge full-sized boat of bamboos is built. Into this are put the offerings of the people in the shape of models of chairs, tables, cooking stoves, besides clothes, cash, and copper money. Even an opium-pipe used to be added for the delectation of the spirit. These objects remain in the boat for seven days, during which the boat stands in one of the chief temples. Everything is of paper, boat and contents, except the framework. Gods from other temples are sometimes invited to come and view the boat; the gods are carried through the streets. Finally the boat is carried through the streets, which means that the evil spirits are being escorted out of the city in state. When the outside of the city is reached the people cry "We, the people of this city, are a poor, wretched, and miserable lot not worthy of attention."

PART FOUR

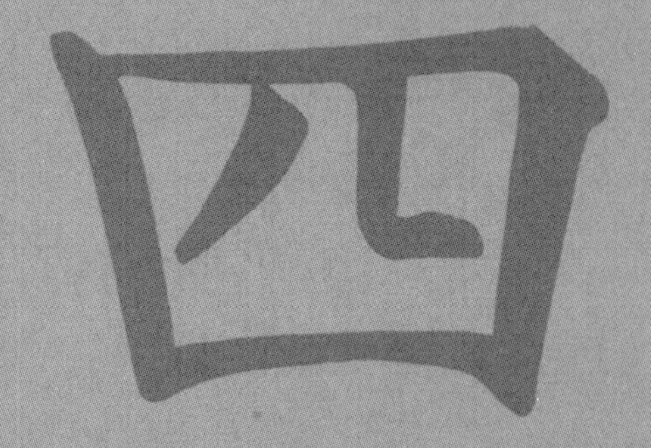

CRAFT OF THE UPPER YANGTZE & TRIBUTARIES

The river runs as ſwift as an arrow from a bow, and is full of banks, rocks, and ſhoals which require much care and experiance in the Mariners.

THE NEW HISTORY OF CHINA, 1688
by Gabriel Magaillans,
Miſſionary Apoſtolick.

THE CRAFT

Most of the material in this section of the book was taken from Mr. Worcester's first volume, *Junks and Sampans of the Upper Yangtze*, and from his small volume on *Notes on the Crooked-bow and Crooked-stern Junks of Szechwan*. The material used in Parts One, Two, and Three of this book was written later. Therefore, some duplication has resulted, especially on the history of junk-building, means of propulsion, tracking, anchors, sails and rigging, which are covered extensively in Part One.

OF the five legendary and illustrious rulers who were supposed to have laid the foundations of Chinese civilisation, the third, Huang Ti (黃帝), 2697–2595 B.C., is credited, amongst other things, with the development of the junk. It is probable, however, that the origin of this craft, which is lost in antiquity, dates back very much further than that.

Another historical reference to shipbuilding in China is that made by Confucius (孔子) in the "Book of History," the "Shu Ching (書經)," wherein he records that the industry was fostered and encouraged by the great Emperor Yü (禹王) of the Golden Age.

The first important mention of junks on the Upper Yangtze was when the troops of General Mêng Liang (孟良), who lived during the period of the Sung dynasty (宋朝), A.D. 976–997, on finding themselves trapped in the canyon now known as the Wind Box Gorge (風箱峽), cut a stairway in the vertical cliff, 526 feet high, and, destroying their junks, climbed to safety.

Rivers and waterways have always played a very large part in the life of China, where, with junk, sampan, or raft, the shallowest reaches, the most perilous rapids, and the narrowest gutters of channels have been utilised to the full.

The earliest of these methods of conveyance by water was the raft, which in its simplest form consists of a small number of natural logs, tree trunks, or bamboo poles fastened together. The next advance was to build up the sides and turn up the ends, and from this crude beginning all the varieties of flat-bottomed craft have evolved.

In China, where so much that is ancient still remains in common usage, there is a surprising variety in type and size of the many rafts that ply on her inland waterways. They range from the great Lower Yangtze rafts, which carry a small street of temporary houses, to the small, narrow bamboo rafts to be seen at Chungking (重慶).

The reason for the persistence of these craft is to be found in the nature of the upper reaches of the various affluents of the Yangtze for which they were built, for they have to negotiate almost impassable rapids and shallows requiring the very minimum draught. Only in this way are some of the rivers navigable at all. With the exception of the Ya River (雅江或青衣江) raft, all are designed for descending rivers only. Even with the additional safety which a raft affords, the navigation of these dangerous stretches is perilous and demands ceaseless vigilance and indefatigable energy; moreover, a particular skill and technique are required in the handling of such cumbersome craft.

One of the earliest important references to rafts in Chinese history is that describing how, before he became the first emperor of the Mongol dynasty, Kublai Khan (忽必烈漢) commenced his campaigns by the conquest of Yunnan (雲南), so as to cut the communications of the troops of the Sung Empire in the west and south. In 1252, therefore, he marched through Szechwan (四川) with a large army and, on his way to Talifu (大理府) and future successes, crossed the Upper Yangtze on rafts. It would, indeed, be interesting to know which type he employed.

The name "Szechwan" is derived from four rivers, the Yangtze, the Min-

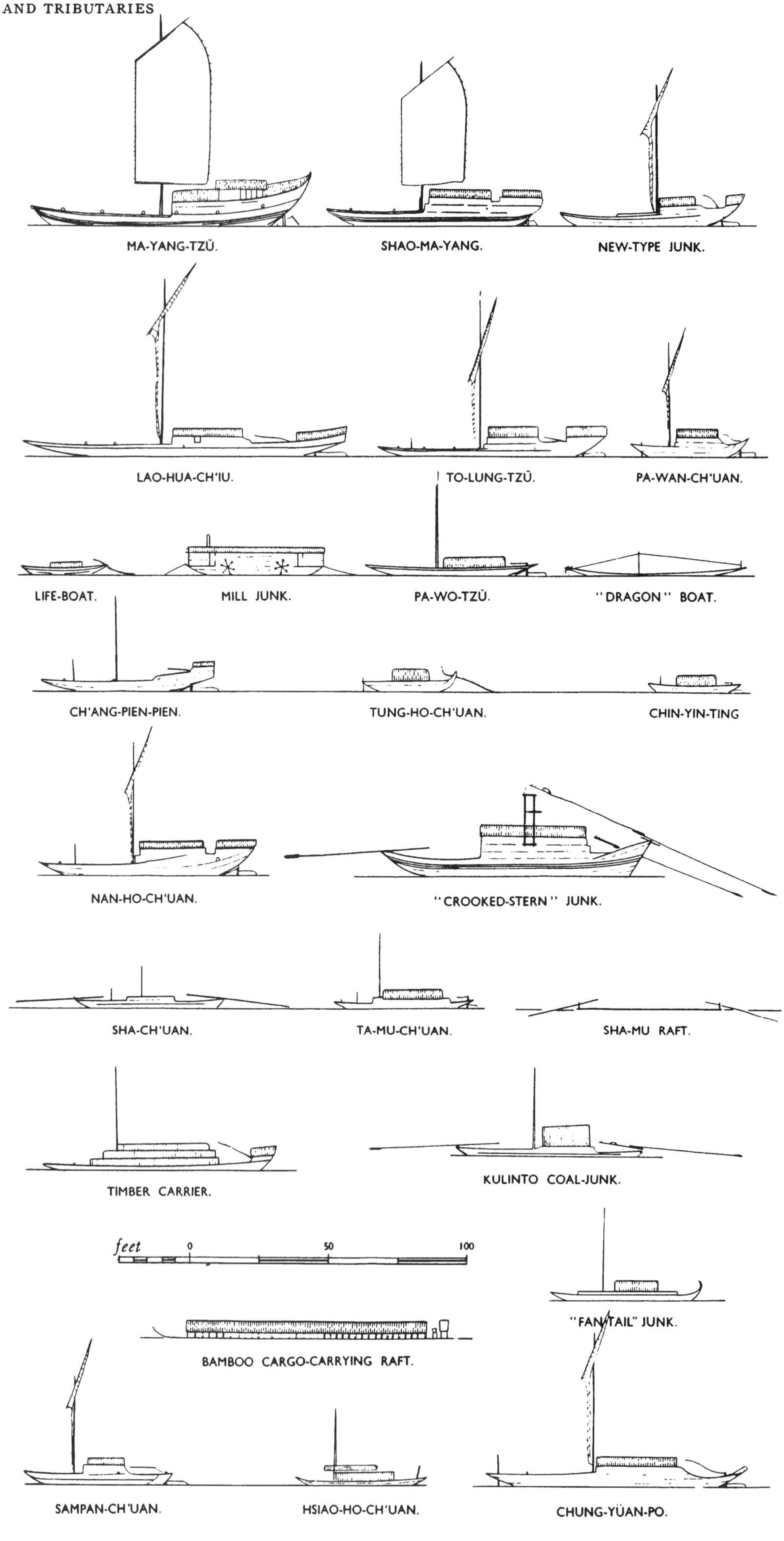

MA-YANG-TZŬ.
SHAO-MA-YANG.
NEW-TYPE JUNK.
LAO-HUA-CH'IU.
TO-LUNG-TZŬ.
PA-WAN-CH'UAN.
LIFE-BOAT.
MILL JUNK.
PA-WO-TZŬ.
"DRAGON" BOAT.
CH'ANG-PIEN-PIEN.
TUNG-HO-CH'UAN.
CHIN-YIN-TING
NAN-HO-CH'UAN.
"CROOKED-STERN" JUNK.
SHA-CH'UAN.
TA-MU-CH'UAN.
SHA-MU RAFT.
TIMBER CARRIER.
KULINTO COAL-JUNK.
feet 0 50 100
"FAN-TAIL" JUNK.
BAMBOO CARGO-CARRYING RAFT.
SAMPAN-CH'UAN.
HSIAO-HO-CH'UAN.
CHUNG-YÜAN-PO.

The main types of Upper Yangtze craft.

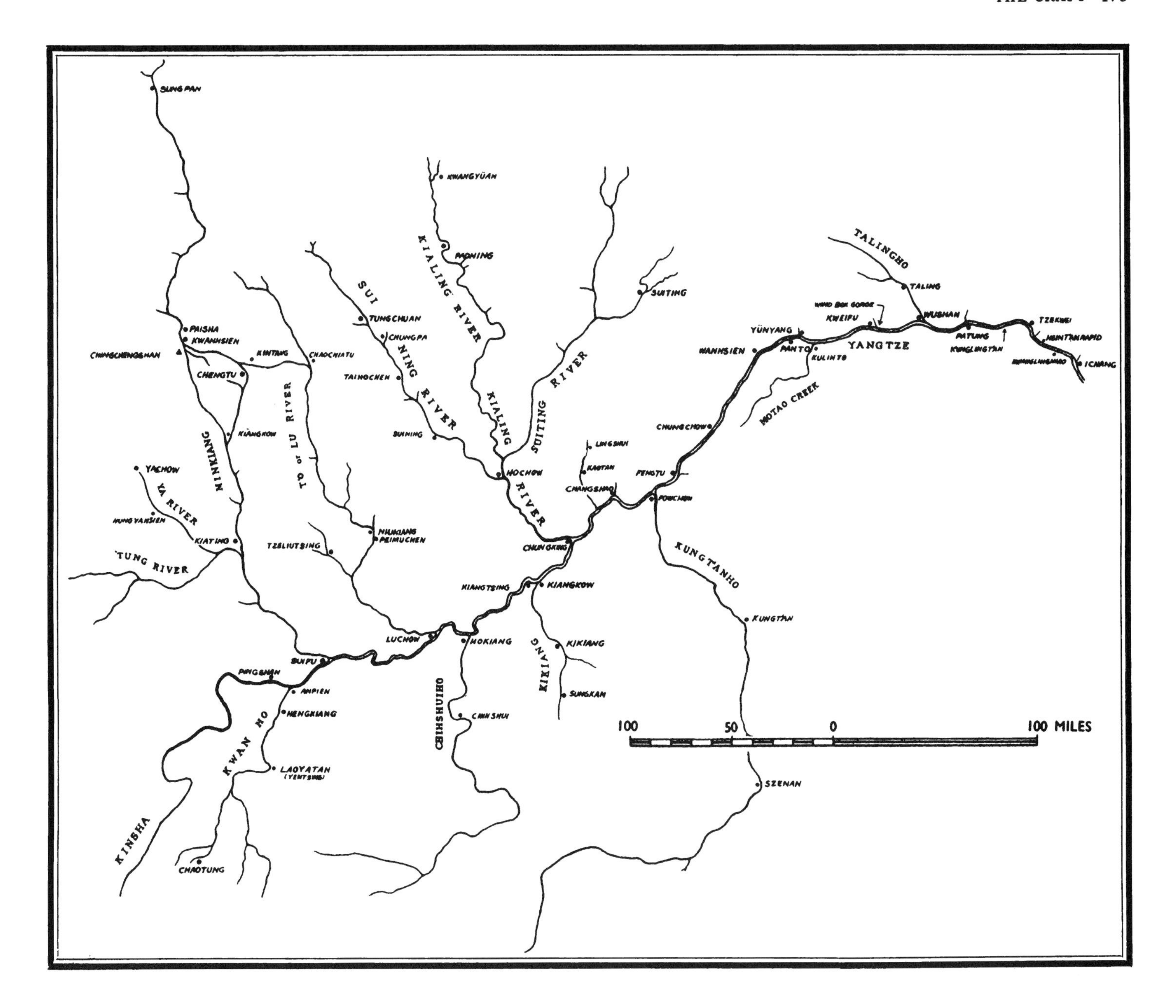

Sketch map of the Upper Yangtze.

kiang (岷 江), the T'o or Lu River (沱 江), and the Kialing River (嘉 陵 江), the three latter flowing from north to south into the Red Basin of Szechwan, where they meet the Yangtze.

The pages which follow deal with the junks and sampans to be met with in these waters, for each river has its own craft, and those familiar with them can identify their district of origin by their design. The dividing line between sampan and junk has yet to be defined, but a local acceptance of the latter term is a vessel capable of accommodating a water-buffalo athwartships.

Nearly all the types of Upper Yangtze junks and sampans are built to negotiate rapids of some sort, and therefore are strongly constructed.

Chungking and Wanhsien (萬 縣) have always been acknowledged as the two great centres of junkbuilding in Szechwan. Other centres are Yünyang (雲 陽); Luchow (瀘 州), for the types above Chungking; and Linshih (陵 石), Lochih (樂 至), and Hochwan (合 川), for the Kialing River craft; junkbuilding, however, can be, and is, carried out anywhere on a convenient foreshore.

The main kinds of wood employed in the construction of junks are *ch'ing-kang* (青 杠), or oak, in the form of planking for the bottom; *nan-mu* (楠 木),

an evergreen of the laurel family; and *pai-mu* (栢 木), a fir, or cypress; these two latter are used for the lower part of the hull and for bulkheads and cross-beams.

The common China fir (*Cunninghamia*), known as *sha-mu* (杉 木), is utilised for masts and deck-houses. Rudder posts are usually made from *huang-lien-mu* (黃 連 木), a tree which grows at high altitudes.

Many kinds of wood are used, some junks being made almost exclusively of one or the other. Those in most general use are *nan-mu* and *pai-mu*, or cypress; this latter, which is a hard, white, heavy, and exceedingly tough wood, grows plentifully everywhere, being usually planted over tombs and in temple grounds. *Chang-mu* (樟 木), or camphor-wood, which is so extensively used in the junks of the Lower River, is very rarely employed in Szechwan.

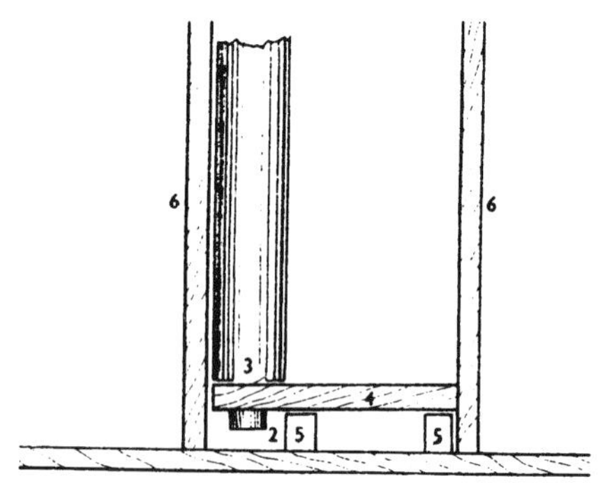

The method for housing the mast.

As a general rule, it may be accepted that most junks built above Chungking are made largely, if not exclusively, of *nan-mu*, while those built below Chungking and on the Kialing River are made of *pai-mu*.

The one tall mast is always a *sha-mu* pole, as long and straight as can be procured, and is usually housed against a bulkhead.[6] A tenon [2] on the heel [3] fits into a socket in a movable timber [4] of considerable strength, bearing on the ribs [5] and fitting snugly against the sides of the bulkheads.[6] This prevents the heel of the mast from moving forward, and also serves to distribute the thrust.

The junk itself is a ship in its simplest and most primitive form, that is to say, it dispenses with all but the barest necessities, while yet contriving to be strong and always entirely suitable for the work for which it was designed. The chief strength lies in the considerable number of watertight bulkheads, which vary according to the size and purpose of the junk. These bulkheads are thick, solid, hardwood timbers, mortised together and secured either to the frames or, as is more commonly done, to the half-frames, as they may be termed; that is to say, a frame or timber which extends across the bottom, ceasing at the turn of the bilge. When, however, full frames are used, these are of the usual type, one timber crossing the floors with wings mortised in on either side at the turn of the bottom, the junction being overlapped for extra strength. Longitudinal strength is added by a varying number of heavy wales, either as part of the structure or superimposed. Generally there is no keel, and the flat bottom facilitates overhauls, repairs, etc.

The hull planks are joined together on the inner face by frequent wrought-iron staples, consisting of two sharp nail-points joined by a longer ribbon of the metal. The seams are payed with a mixture of coarse dried grass * (粗 麻) and a putty-like substance called chunam (油 石 灰), which is composed of wood oil and lime pounded together in a mortar. This caulking is done in the usual Chinese manner; that is to say, it is pressed in with a blunt chisel, which is hammered with the back of an axe. The Chinese carpenters do not take kindly to a caulking hammer. In some districts, in order to prevent the caulking from splaying out on the reverse side, necessitating subsequent trimming, a plank is placed against the inner side of the seam as a basis upon which to caulk. The chunam sets hard and white in about 48 hours, and not only makes a good watertight join, but serves to fill up many deficiencies in the irregular and sometimes crudely cut planks.

The finished Upper River junk is never painted, but receives about three or more coats of wood oil, with an interval of about three days between each. In course of time this dries a dark brown.

The main timbers of the deck, that is to say, the heavy cross-beams, made

* Bamboo shavings are sometimes used.

from a single timber and built into the structure of the hull, are laid across the longitudinals above the bulkheads.

A marked feature of all such junks is that these cross-beams, which vary in number, often extend 6 inches to 1 foot outboard on either side. These projections give a very characteristic appearance and, besides adding considerable additional strength to the hull, have many uses. Those amidships form a bed to support the bumkins which carry the bearing-pins for the yulohs, while the after ones serve to secure the inboard end of the tracking-lines and what is called the *chuan-chio-lan-tzŭ* (轉角纜子), or heel lashing of the mast, universally used by all up-bound junks to give additional support to the mast when tracking. This lashing varies considerably, but generally commences at the mast at house-height; thence it leads direct to the after cross-beam, round which it makes a turn, and then travels under the counter, sometimes tightly round the rudder post, and up to the cross-beam on the farther side, from whence it returns to the mast. The two parts are then securely frapped about 4 feet abaft the mast. In order to distribute the strain, an additional lashing connects the two cross-beams on one side, and sometimes another lashing travels from the after cross-beam, under the counter, and joins the corresponding cross-beam on the other side.

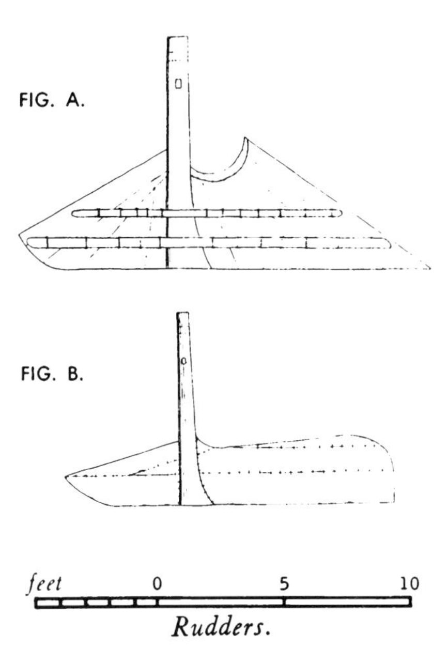

Rudders.

The rudder (*see margin*), which is almost invariably of the balance variety,* is slung from a transom forming part of the after bulkhead, where it is retained in place by a long, heavy, wooden fid which fits into a slot in the rudder-head. The long tiller, which is often reinforced by two poles lashed one on each side of it, curves upwards to the helmsman at his conning position, where he stands perched on a raised plank and commanding a view over the top of the mat roof of the house or central portion of the house. With his right hand he holds the tiller, and with the other maintains his rather precarious balance by a form of strap-hanging to a long loop of rope attached to the centre beam of the house in front of him. This rope is also used to secure the tiller in any desired position. In some junks, in a strong current, two men may be needed to work the rudder.

Figure A shows the type of rudder used by the *ma-yang-tzŭ* (麻秧子) and similar classes working in comparatively deep water. Figure B, drawn to the same scale, shows a typical rudder as fitted to shallow-draught junks of about the same size.

When it is impracticable to use a rudder, owing to shoal water or other reasons, steering is carried out by a stern-sweep, known as *hou-shao* (後梢), which may be any length from the 98-foot sweep of the "crooked-stern" junk to the 29-foot sweep of the Chungking sampan. Some are made in two parts and some in one; some are straight and some are curved; and there are many varieties. They are also used to hold to a course in an emergency. Two types are illustrated in Plate No. 169, the *sha-ch'uan* (沙船), and Plate No. 147, the Chungking sampan. The bow-sweep, or *ch'ien-shao* (前梢), which is exclusively used to keep the bow heading in the right direction, is in some junks very similar in its arrangement to the stern-sweep, but no very rigid rule can be laid down about either, except that, as a rough guide, it may be said that both bow and stern sweeps are in length approximately one-tenth less than the water-line measurement of the junk, and both, it should be borne in mind, are only used to supplement or replace the rudder.

The junk is propelled by sail, oars, yulohs, tracking, and any combination of these methods. Despite the Chinese flavour about the word "yuloh," which is loosely employed by foreigners to describe all types of propelling oar, the Chinese themselves never use the word, but have classified the two varieties of oar as *chiang* (槳) and *lu* (櫓). The derivation of the word "yuloh" seems obscure, but it is probably of pidgin-English origin. A Chinese suggestion is that it is an onomatopœic word describing the rhythm of the motion of rowing.

See Part One, "Methods of Propulsion."

* By extending the rudder on either side of the rudder post, the weight is balanced, making the work of steering easier—a device subsequently adopted in Europe.

Moving down river towards rapids on the Upper Yangtze.

The *chiang*, or *nao* (槳 或 橈), as it is locally termed in Chungking, is a crude oar composed of two parts, that is to say, the loom and the blade, these being joined together by iron bands, the join being designed to give elasticity. The loom always ends in a small wooden cross-piece. The oar is attached to a thole pin by a grummet of hemp rope or pigskin. Cargo is sometimes stowed on the fore-deck. When this is the case and the junk is under oars, an exceptionally tall thole pin, with slots at different heights for the grummet, enables the men to row while poised at different levels on the cargo. Rowing is always performed while standing, though the oar is sometimes pushed * and at other times pulled, possibly in order to provide a change after long spells at one or the other position. When the oar is pulled, a short, jerky, ineffectual movement is the result.

The *lu*, which for convenience will hereinafter be referred to as a yuloh, is a long, tapering member, composed, like the oar, of two parts, the loom and the blade. Its distinguishing characteristic is the fact that the loom, which is usually one-third of its total length, is set at an angle of 150° with the rest. It is joined at both extremities of the overlap by iron bands or a seizing, or both. A foot or more down the blade from this join, and at the centre of gravity, is a wooden block on the underside, secured by two more iron bands or seizing. The wooden bearing-pin takes into a hold in this block, which can be readily replaced without damage to the yuloh when the tremendous amount of friction wears it down, and the system of balance permits the yuloh to be worked over the side of the junk with a species of screw motion, the blade being always in the water. The inboard end of the loom is secured by a light rope made fast to a ring-bolt in the deck.

The galley, which varies in size from a small charcoal brazier to an elaborate cement coal-stove, is almost invariably placed on the port side and usually just abaft the mast.

A diagram of a "stick-in-the-mud" anchor is shown in Part One, page 89.

The smaller Upper Yangtze junks invariably bank in and adopt the universal "stick in the mud" form of anchoring; that is to say, a sort of square, boxed-in, navel pipe going right through the foremost compartment, through which a pole is driven into the bed of the river. This pole has a small cross-haft from which a stone is sometimes suspended. The Chinese apparently have no prejudice against putting a round peg in a square hole. The antiquity of this form of anchoring is borne out by the fact that in an early Chinese painting called "Drinking to the Moon on a Deserted Mountain Lake," by an unidentified Sung artist, a "stick in the mud" anchor is clearly depicted, denoting that it was in use about 1,000 years ago.

* When the oar is pushed the loom of the oar is sometimes actually above the head of the standing oarsman.

Large junks always spar-moor when lying near the bank. This very ingenious and efficient method of making fast is carried out as follows. Depending on current conditions, two or three strong, heavy spars, usually of oak, are used, 4 or 5 inches in diameter and 20 to 25 feet long. When the depth of water permits the junk to lie close enough to the bank, two spars are put out on the beam from the forward and after cross-beams with their outer ends resting on the shore. If shallow water prohibits this, the spars are dug obliquely into the mud or shingle bottom of the river. In both cases ropes are secured to pegs or rocks on the shore, and the tension on the ropes against an outward pull, together with the rigidity of the spars against an inward drift or wash, maintains the junks in position. The third or forward spar is used to give extra rigidity. This spar, which rests on the bottom of the river, is rigged over the inboard bow and directed up stream in the fore and aft line of the junk. At least two head ropes are used.

The crew of the Upper Yangtze junks are a tough and manly lot, usually descended from generations of junkmen. The permanent staff is small, being from five to ten, and additional men are engaged as required according to the size of the craft, its load, and destination.

When tracking they attach themselves fanwise to the bamboo tracking-line by a simple but practical form of harness, consisting of a loop of rope, or more often white cloth, passed over one shoulder and round the body, and joined to a short length of square sennit which takes into a bone, or wooden button, terminating through it in a wale knot. A half-hitch is made with this round the bamboo rope, which bears against the button when the strain is on but loosens directly the tension relaxes, forming a safety device whereby the tracker can easily release himself in an emergency.

For a fuller description of tracking on the Upper Yangtze see Part One, pages 51–55.

Once harnessed to the junk the men display perfect discipline and teamwork and are controlled by the rhythmic beat of the drum from the junk, the note being varied from the signal "Stop," denoted by a short sharp beat; "Slow," indicated by a slow and even rhythm; and "Full speed," denoted by a rapid, constant drumming. The sound of the throb of the drum is a marked characteristic of the Upper Yangtze waters.

Most up-bound junks are accompanied by a sampan to land the trackers and the bamboo hawsers. Failing this they have to bank in to do so. In the ordinary way, about a dozen men track a large junk and two or more follow behind to clear the line, which may extend for 800 yards in a difficult rapid. When such a length of rope is out, it has to be supported by a sampan ahead in the slack water above the rapid.

The word "sampan" has come to be accepted as the generic name for that most ubiquitous of craft in Chinese waters. In point of fact, in the province of Szechwan the Chinese name of sampan (三 板), or "three planks," indicates a small junk, while the type of craft commonly misnamed "sampan" by foreigners is called by the Chinese *hua-tzŭ* (划 子), although locally it is known as *mu-ch'uan* (木 船), or "wooden boat."

The types of *mu-ch'uan*, henceforward herein called sampan, in use on the upper reaches of the Yangtze and its tributaries differ completely from those on the Lower River. All are admirably designed for their work, and the sampanmen are probably the best of their kind on the River. The Ichang (宜 昌) sampan is reminiscent of the Lower River in the forked wings of the stern, for this type is very rare on the Upper River above Ichang.

There are, in addition, other local variations which differ so slightly as not to merit the inclusion of any plans or detailed description. These types include the Panto (盤 沱) sampan, the Wanhsien officials' sampan, the Wanhsien bum-boat, and an odd little craft which may be seen 10 miles above and below Wanhsien which may be called the "double master," as it has a pair of masts set close together at an acute angle, leaning forward, almost like a pair of sheer legs. There are, moreover, many small coal and fruit boats—such as the Kweifu (夔府) "fan-tail" sampan—which navigate obscure little tributaries.

The craft of the Upper Yangtze are admirably designed for their work, and although it must be admitted a good deal is often left to chance, they are, nevertheless, handled with consummate skill and dexterity by men whose knowledge is the outcome of generations of experience.

The sailing equipment of the Upper Yangtze junks is rather rudimentary and may be classified in two main groups:

(*a*) A standard single lug-sail of cloth stiffened with bamboo battens, and multiple sheets, common throughout China; and

(*b*) A single square sail of cloth extended upon a yard, with a foot batten.

The former type, though heavy and unwieldy, is more efficient and is used in large junks which travel as far down as Shasi (沙市) or even below, while the latter type is most generally used in all junks plying above Wanhsien. As a general rule, it may be said that in both types the sail from head to foot measures about one-tenth less than the length of the junk. No definite rule can be laid down as to which type of sail is used exclusively by any one type of junk.

The illustration (*following page*) shows a typical lug-sail as used by a small-type *ma-yang-tzŭ* junk. The sail, which is roped at the head and foot, consists of a number of 1-foot 3-inch wide sailcloths sewn together and is laced to a hardwood yard and also to a light bamboo boom at the foot. The sail is stiffened with a number of battens. On to each of these is lashed a split bamboo, which extends from about the middle of the sail across the mast towards the luff [1] and acts as a parrel. The multiple sheets are worthy of special notice. They consist of a lower crow's-foot,[2] the component parts of which lead fanwise from each batten on the lower part of the leech [3] of the sail to a block at the apex of the crow's-foot, which is the standing part. From this the main sheet leads through a block [5] on the deck-house, and up through another which forms the apex of a second upper crow's-foot [6] rigged in the same manner. Thence the sheet leads down again to the conning position.[7] In this manner the set of the sail uniformly adjusts itself to receive an equal distribution of wind pressure down its entire length. The lug-sail has one extremely useful attribute in that it is self-reefing. Until comparatively recent times, when the superiority of the modern flat-sail became apparent in the United States and Europe, it should be considered that the Chinese were unquestionably ahead of others in their conception of the principles of scientific fore and aft sails, as evidenced by the design of their lug-sail.

In light airs, with a favouring breeze, a form of spinnaker is often used. This is by no means standard, but usually consists of a triangular sail, the foot of which is extended upon a light bamboo boom, the halyards being made fast to the apex or head of the sail. The boom is usually—though not always—secured to the mast.

The square sail (*opposite*), however, is the rig most employed by junks, not only on the Upper Yangtze, but on its many tributaries, and is almost exclusively used by all small and medium sized junks with small crews, for it can be handled with ease and speed in all weathers, and when furled takes up no space, which is a considerable advantage.

Like the lug-sail, it is made of vertical cotton sailcloths, sewn together and

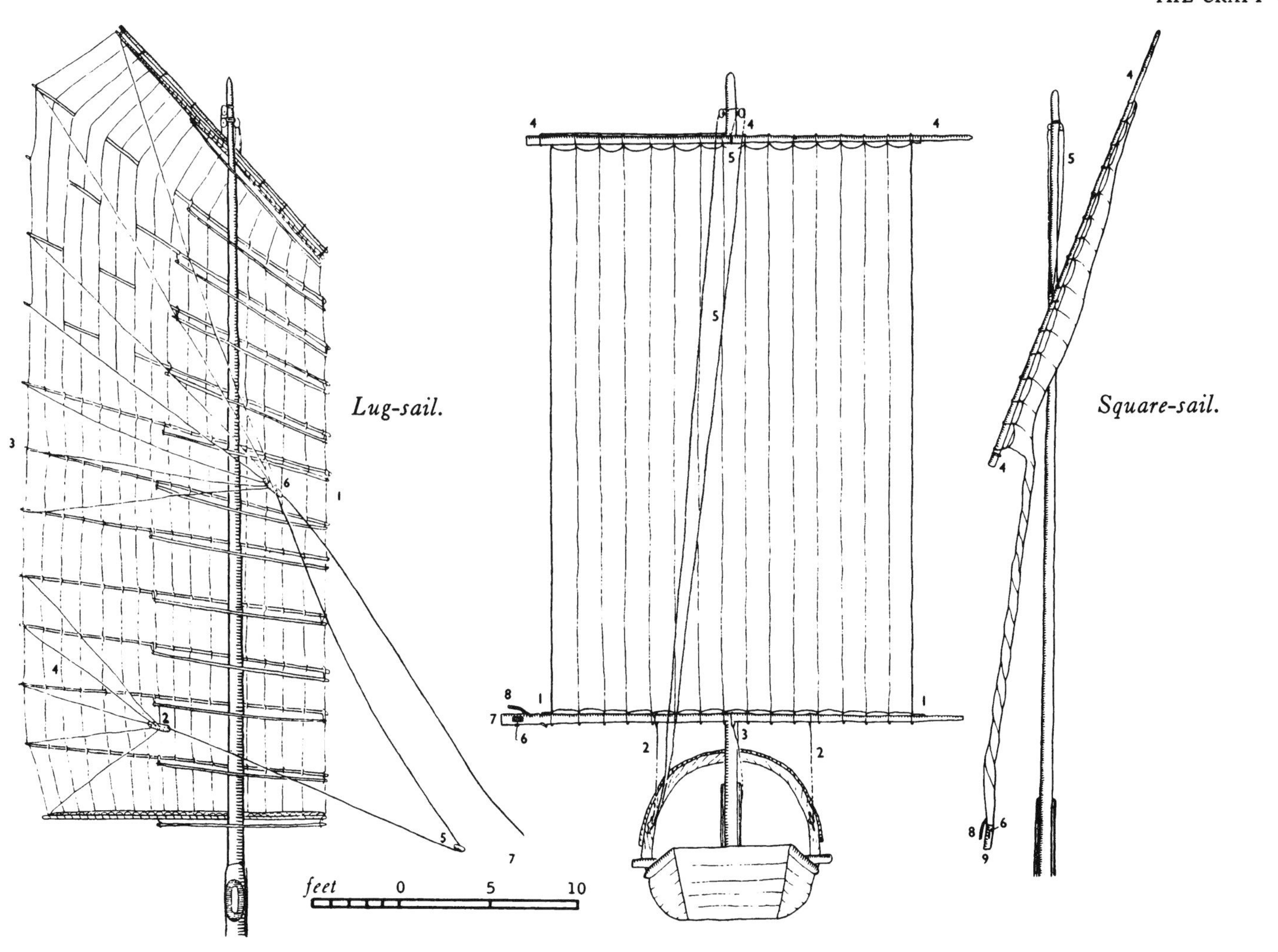

roped at head and foot. The head also is extended upon a yard, to which it is laced in the manner illustrated.

The stiffening, however, is vertical instead of horizontal, and consists of a light rope sewn up each seam. The sail is not loose-footed as one might suppose, for it is laced to a lower yard, or boom, which also acts as an extension for the tacks [1] of the sail. Light ropes attached to the inner part of the boom,[2] and secured to the deck, hold down the sail. The boom is hauled close to the mast by a truss, consisting of a rope secured near the bunt [3] and led round the mast. The upper yard [4] is sustained by the halyards,[5] which are also used on the rare occasions when the sail is lowered, for when it is not in use it is furled in the following way.*

One man tends the halyards, while another inserts his left hand in a slot [6] cut in the end of the starboard side of the boom [7] and grasps with his right hand the lower end of a wooden peg,[8] driven obliquely through the bamboo boom a few inches inboard from the slot. He then spills the sail by jerking the boom over into its centre, and still holding the now nearly vertical boom well above his head, he gyrates smartly two or three times. The sail being by now half-furled at the lower end, he finishes the winding process with more deliberation. The result is a long, neat cylinder of sail, the boom [9] being concealed in the lower part of the roll, while the yard lies nearly parallel above on the outside. The original starboard tack is then made fast to the starboard side. The whole operation can be accomplished by two men in about a minute. Two backstays, which are set up when the junk is under way, are the only standing rigging. They lead from the masthead and are made fast as far aft as possible. Reefing is carried out by lowering the yard to the requisite distance, according to the wind. This allows the sail to belly out and thus exposes less surface to the wind.

* This square rig represents a sail in its very simplest form; indeed, it is interesting to note that this type of sail and its rigging is practically the same as that of the Egyptian galley of 1600 B.C., from which it differs in only one essential, that is to say, in the method of furling. In the galley the yard was lowered instead of, as in the junk, being twisted round the boom.

ICHANG TO WANHSIEN

AT Ichang, in Hupeh, a city of approximately 60,000 inhabitants, there is little that is noteworthy except that it marks the commencement of that portion of the river known as the Upper Yangtze. The town is mainly important in that it is ideally placed geographically as a transhipment centre for cargo from junks or steamers built for the leisurely navigation of the Lower and Middle River into those especially constructed for the perils and dangers of the rapids of the Upper Yangtze.

Here, 1,000 miles from the sea, the Yangtze ceases to flow between monotonous level banks and the mountainous area wherein it is confined is sometimes little more than a ravine. It may now be sub-divided into four sections:

Ichang to Hu T'an;
Hu T'an to Chungking;
Chungking to Suifu; and
Suifu to Pingshan.

The first section of about 200 miles presents the greatest difficulties and hazards to navigation of the entire river. The second section is not fraught with nearly so many risks; in the third section also, although the fall of the river is steeper, there are no dangerous rapids, and it is therefore navigable to steamers and, of course, junks except during freshets or at low water. The last section is only 36 miles in length, and although there are gorges and rapids the whole way, they are not particularly dangerous, the main drawback to navigation being shallow water. At Pingshan the elevation is 1,000 feet, and above this point it rises so sharply that the river becomes a swift and impassable mountain torrent.

The boundary line of the province of Hupeh lies 90 miles above Ichang. Here the Yangtze traverses the mountainous region of Szechwan, the largest of the 18 provinces, which, roughly triangular in shape, is guarded on all its frontiers by inhospitable ranges. The western border line is the most inaccessible, formed as it is by the 12,000-foot-high plateau of Tibet; other ranges running down on a north eastern line meet the Kweichow plateau composing the southern boundary, and at this converging point the Yangtze forces its way out from the region of the gorges into the vast alluvial plain of central China. Although the mountains are considerably lower at the eastern end of the province, that is to say, not more than 5,000 feet above sea level, they still render it hard of access. As the Chinese proverb expresses it: "It is more difficult to ascend to Szechwan than to ascend to heaven."

It is noticeable that where the river runs parallel to the adjacent mountains the reaches are long and straight. When on the other hand the stream runs athwart the ranges, its course is tortuous, with short winding reaches.

With rising water the up-river junk traffic dwindles, finally ceasing by mid-June for about three months. In these summer months the aspect of the river changes completely. A tawny torrent sweeps down, completely filling its bed and almost devoid of craft save for an occasional junk crawling slowly up with greatly increased numbers of trackers to haul her against the swollen, swift current. The expense involved in hiring these additional crews is a much more decided factor in the diminished traffic than any consideration for the increased danger from the rapids. In the other seasons of the year, however, the river reverts more to normal. The water is clearer and flows in a marked and more numerous series of decided drops or rapids, with long reaches between. Craft of all sorts are active, and the river presents a busy scene.

Formerly the officials and rich gentry, as well as the few foreigners who penetrated so far into the interior, travelled by *k'ua-tzu*, or house boat. Now they travel by high-powered steamers. Then the upward journey took 30 days with a favourable wind at low water and anything up to 60 days at the summer level. Now it can be accomplished in five days at most by steamer and in a few hours by aeroplane.

But the coming of steam and the aeroplane have by no means ousted the native craft, which have remained practically unaltered for hundreds of years in design, as in methods of handling and type of personnel. Manned by a hardy and cheerful breed of junkmen inured to hardships and risks, they navigate the most perilous rapids and the most difficult channels of the Upper Yangtze, despite casualties which are estimated as being about 10 per cent.

From Ichang, the trend up river is in a northerly direction until after a few miles, when the transition from a broad stream with low-graded channels is dramatically abrupt, for it vanishes into the rocky walls of the Ichang Gorge.

Just below the entrance to the gorge and on the left bank is a narrow ravine where a stream under an old stone bridge falls into the Yangtze. This is San Yu Tung, or Cave of the Three Travellers, also known as Wild Goat Glen, a deep valley some 220 yards wide and overgrown with scrub and plants, which winds into the mountains. Wild goats are said to live or have lived on the ledges on the steep rocky walls. The clear stream which flows along the rocky floor of this glen forms pools which used to attract bathing-picnic parties on day-long trips from Ichang.

A short distance above this spot is a yellow rock on the south bank with a long narrow crack known as the Shih Mên, or Stone Door. It is said that gold was hidden therein, and this treasure was known of by a man who sought far and wide for it. When he eventually secured the key, it was found to be made not of metal, but of a particular kind of melon. Shouldering this melon, he stood before the rock and called "Open," whereupon the rock fell open, and he removed all the gold, but neglected to shut the door again, for it stands there now—a long narrow crack in the stone.

From here a sharp turn to the west leads into the Ichang Gorge. Mussulman Point, so named by Blakiston * in honour of his Indian guards, a large high rock standing out into the stream from the left bank, marks the entrance, which is here little more than 100 yards wide. The 15-mile long gorge extends from Nanchinkuan to Tenshanto and actually consists of two gorges, the Huang Mao Hsia, or Yellow Cat Gorge, running west for six miles to Shihpai, and the Têng Ying Hsia, or Lampshine Gorge.

At first the Ichang Gorge is composed of conglomerate and sandstone, which soon change to the characteristic limestone of the gorges proper. From here comes much of the limestone which is extensively used in the plains for building and for facing embankments, and this industry provides work for a great number of stone workers. Some dress the huge blocks, while others split them into squares by means of iron wedges and huge iron hammers weighing about 30 pounds. The usual procedure for the stone splitters is to bore small holes about three inches deep and 18 inches apart, marking the outline of the required block. A wedge-shaped piece of iron is then inserted into each hole and struck in rotation until the stone splits.

* Thomas W. Blakiston was the leader of the "Yangtze Expedition," a private venture. The party accompanied Vice Admiral James Hope in his trip to open the Yangtze to foreign trade in 1861. Blakiston and his expedition left Admiral Hope at Yochow and continued up the Yangtze. It was planned to travel through China into Tibet and then across the Himalayas into China. The disturbed condition of the country made it necessary for the expedition to turn back at Pingshan. Blakiston surveyed more than 900 miles of river above Yochow.

The towpath for trackers of upbound junks is on the right or south bank. Two villages are passed; the second, P'ing Shan Pa, is in a wooded ravine and is marked by a pagoda. A little above is a Customs barrier station, and nearby is the celebrated waterworn Dragon's Cave, called by the Chinese Shên K'an Tzŭ and said by them to extend many miles—the junkmen say as far as Ningpo. The entrance to the cave is four feet wide. No one living nearby will venture in far, as they fear they will never come out alive; but the country folk have frequently used it as a form of safe deposit for their valuables when the province was being overrun by the "Red-haired Barbarians" from the interior.

The western extremity of the Lampshine Gorge is marked on the east side by a lonely pinnacle, 1,250 feet high, called T'ien Chu Shan, or Pillar of Heaven; and here, after a bend to the west, is the village of Nanto. One and a half miles beyond is Toushanto at the upper end of the Ichang Gorge. The cliff-bound river then broadens out and runs for some 14 miles through a mile-wide valley known as Yao Chan Ho, or Crooked River, the entrance being marked by the first race of the Upper River, sometimes called a rapid and named Wuit'an. At this point, on the north or left bank and east of an affluent which here enters the Yangtze, is a temple to the River God Wang Yeh and adjoining a village named Cha Po T'an. The rather curious derivation of this name is from *cha*, meaning sediment which subsides to the bottom; *po*, a wave; and *t'an*, a sandy beach or rapid; and the whole may be translated as a Rapid without Ripples, or the Still Rapid.

There is an equally curious legend attached to the locality. During the time of the Sung Dynasty (A.D. 960–1280), one of the civil officials named K'ou Tsun, who had been degraded and banished to Pa Tung, was passing here in a junk, when he heard a voice speaking from the river and was astonished to see a stark naked man helping to haul his boat up through the water. When questioned the man disclosed that he was Huang Mo Shên, or the Yellow Demon, and foretold that K'ou would later be received back into favour by the Emperor. Although the Demon had good-naturedly come to his assistance, he expressed himself as feeling embarrassed at his lack of clothes. K'ou immediately threw him an embroidered robe, whereupon the demon grasped it and disappeared. One wonders why he felt this access of modesty, for it is customary for the trackers to work naked in the summer months without evincing any signs of embarrassment. It seems not unlikely that this ancient legend has some bearing on this custom of theirs; and they may be merely offering the sincerest form of flattery in emulating the nakedness of their illustrious prototype, the Demon Tracker.

About three miles above Cha-po on the south or right bank of the river is a village known as Huang Ling Miao, which is famous for producing good pilots and stout bamboo rope. Every port of call of any size along the banks of the Upper Yangtze has a temple to the River God Wang Yeh, but that at Huang Ling Miao is one of the four most famous of them all. Around the village bamboo groves cover the red sandstone foothills, behind which rises a striking feature of this reach, the 1,000-foot, sheer ochre-coloured rock wall known as Huang Niu Hsia or Yellow Cow Cliff.

Junks when tracked up are kept in the slack water over the shingle as much as possible, but even so the going is very laborious. Fishing with cormorants or with otters is common in the bays and pools left over from high water. The latter practice probably accounts for the name of the next rapid of interest, the Ta Tung T'an or Great Otter Rapid. This, the first real rapid on the river, disappears at high river, giving place to the Pai Tung Tzŭ Rapid in the same spot, a mile below the village of Taipingchi; they are caused one by a large reef in mid-stream and the other by huge reefs extending out from both banks.

The rapids of the Upper Yangtze are periodical, that is to say, they wax or wane in violence at certain times of the year and in accordance with the varying heights of the river. They differ greatly in their natural characteristics owing to the different conditions which affect them, as for instance a ledge across the river; ledges projecting from both banks; a boulder, bank, or rock extending from one side of the river; an obstruction in the middle of the river; or a narrow gorge contracting the fairway. Most of the rapids of the Upper Yangtze are formed by a combination of these obstructions, and each presents its own problems. Again, each rapid varies with the water level.

Each rapid displays a number of features. The "lip" is the glassy, smooth bank of water right across the top of the rapid. From the bank at either side, that is, from the obstructions that cause the constriction, runs a "frill" of distinct, though small, breakers into a V-shaped point. Within this V is a prolongation of the glassy smooth water of the lip. This is the "head" or "tongue." On either side of this, between the frill and the bank, are the back eddies. Immediately below the end of the head the axis, or main channel, becomes a confused mass of whirlpools and eddies, usually spinning in opposite directions. This is the "tail." The axis may be nearly straight, but is often curved, sometimes highly so.

It is not generally appreciated that the greatest strength of a rapid is almost invariably at its lip, the area of maximum velocity, where the water runs down an inclined plane, being usually little more than a few yards wide.

The curving course of the river contains numerous other hazards, such as isolated pinnacles, deadly projecting shelves, rocky points and "steep-to" or shelving banks. The rise and fall of the water in the gorges is, as may be expected, very considerable. It is lowest in February and highest towards early August. Flood levels due to freshets show a violent fluctuation, there being often over 100 feet in difference between high and low water. In abnormal cases, such as that of a flood level, it may reach 150 feet in the gorge district. During freshets even the peaceful gorges, not normally the scene of "rapid" character, become a gyrating mass of turbulent waters, filled with whirlpools, eddies, vertical "boils" and backwashes. These various peculiarities in the flow of the river often present quite an alarming appearance. The whirlpools, caused by the ragged nature of the banks, which deflect the water at an angle, are to be seen in the vicinity of the rapids and also with rising water, when they attain their maximum violence. A dangerous variation of this feature is the running whirlpool, or *pao hsüan* which, while rapidly revolving, at the same time moves across the stream. This, if of any size and strength, constitutes a menace to all shipping.

Another phenomenon is the Chinese *fa-shui*, or "boil" of water, which occurs at intervals at many of the rapids and races at mid or high level. The water will at a particular spot suddenly become very swift and angry. This activity is immediately followed by a sort of quiet miniature tidal wave, succeeded by slack water or sometimes an eddy or backwater. After a considerable space of time, when the rapid returns to normal, the whole performance is regularly repeated. Another odd characteristic of these waters is of rarer occurrence, fortunately, for it presents an alarming form of hazard. This consists of a strange globular up-rising of water, like a vast air bubble rising to the surface, which, after forming, collapses as if it had been sucked down by a vacuum pump, leaving a deep cavity, into which the surrounding water rushes with a crashing sound.

Yet one more unpleasant feature is the formation of quicksands or *sha-shui*, sand water, which owe their origin to huge silt deposits appearing during high water, when some form of check blocks a free exit from the channel. This, too, is infrequent and occurs mainly in the autumn.

A down-bound junk negotiating the Hsin T'an at low level.
CAPTAIN CHOW HAI CHING

The depth of water varies enormously, from places shallow enough to cause a rapid, to quiet reaches where soundings of 60 to 70 fathoms have been obtained. The rapids are situated in belts of soft shale and sandstone, and the rocky walls of the gorges have been carved out by the river from the vertical limestone cliffs. The river bed in the shallow parts is then of similar nature. In the deeper gorges, however, when the water at the lower levels is nearly still, fine sand brought down from the upper reaches, which is held in suspension while in rapid motion, is deposited on the bottom. Innumerable are beds of shingle and large stones, either in the river or lining its banks, which owe their origin either to landslips or to the washing away of all the smaller particles, leaving only pebbles and boulders behind.

The rate of the current on the Upper Yangtze varies with different water levels, from 1½ to 3 knots in winter to 4 to 8 in summer. At special points, however, this is augmented, sometimes reaching 13 knots at a rapid where, at low water, the level of the river alters by several feet in a few yards. Again the pace is often reduced in some of the gorges to as little as 2 knots, when, at low water, the upper part of the river moves smoothly over the deep water beneath without much friction.

As the rapids run at these high speeds, it can be readily understood that they cannot be surmounted by junks without much additional help being afforded to the ordinary crews.

Ahead now lies the famous rapid of K'ung Ling at the foot of Tong Ling Hsia, or Pierced Mountain Gorge, which is the grand gateway to the Niu Kan Ma Fei Hsia, or Ox Liver and Horse Lung Gorge. This rapid has been the cause of many accidents at low water.

In midstream a long black rock, called the Huang Chien, rises some 50 feet above low water level and divides it into two channels, that towards the left bank being known as the "Pearls" because of the submerged rocks scattered nearby. Special pilots for this locality live in the attractive hamlet of Miao Ho, which is situated above the rapid and rises in terraces set in groves of cypress and bamboo and poplars. Nearby on a rise is a Taoist temple called Ch'ing Kiang Szŭ, Pure Stream Temple, in front of which may be seen a very ancient cast iron bell, the inspiration of many local stories and folklore. The Upper River Inspectorate of the Customs has of late years effected a notable improvement to the hitherto impracticable channel between the rock and the right bank by blasting away certain pinnacles.

A westerly trend of the river now leads towards what appears to be a massive mountain wall, in which is a huge cleft through which the river emerges as from a funnel. This is the second, or Ox Liver and Horse Lung Gorge, which derives its unromantic name from some oddly shaped stalactites which, hanging high up in a crevice of the cliffs, are supposed to resemble these internal organs. The rocky walls confining the narrow channel tower vertically up for 800 or 900 feet, with here and there huge flat slabs of stone overhanging at strange and perilous angles, the strata showing a definite dip towards the north-west. Trees which at that height appear little more than shrubs wind their roots round every projection in the struggle for existence.

The shutting off of all direct light lends to the water a dark, uncanny aspect which is intensified by its deep quiet flow through the four-mile-long canyon. About a mile into the gorge it takes a turn to the north-west, and an affluent named the Chiu yüan chi, or Nine Cornered Stream, runs down through a deep ravine to meet the river. Above, on the right bank, is a high plateau, behind which rise mountains of 3,000 feet.

Above the gorge a short reach with villages on both banks divides it from the third, or Mit'an Gorge. The valley here is some three or four miles wide between steep mountains of hard grey sandstone, and the river is banked by long jagged rocks which, being submerged from May to November, make navigation difficult; while at the low water season there is a very bad rapid there known as the Hsin T'an, or New Rapid. Actually, the fall of rocks from the steep cliff in the right bank to which the rapid owes its existence occurred about 1640. This dangerous rapid is at its worst in the low water season and consists of three distinct steps: the T'ou T'an, or Head Rapid; the Erh T'an, or Second Rapid; and the San T'an, or Third Rapid. At the head rapid the fall of masses of rock into the stream has formed a series of dams. Through the gaps between, the river rushes as through sluice gates, the largest being close to the right bank, 70 yards in width and at dead low water about 150 in length with a drop of six feet. When the river rises the rapid disappears.

During the low water season local pilots are engaged to navigate Chinese craft through this danger, and it is an unique and awe-inspiring sight to see a junk descending. The junk is eased down the right bank into a little bay, above the head of the rapid, and, when certain marks are on, she is slipped and heads as far as possible for the left bank, though she often travels, with accumulating velocity, broadside on or even stern first, over the head of the rushing foaming rapid, until by a combination of skill and good fortune she reaches the slack water below. Should she fail to reach the centre of the axis of the current, she may get shot out into a whirlpool or eddy and as likely as not turn aimlessly in all directions despite the efforts of all the men on the huge bow sweep. This is by no means an uncommon occurrence and need not necessarily spell disaster. For piloting a junk through these three incredibly dangerous steps of the Hsin T'an at dead low water the local pilot risks his life for a couple of dollars a trip; and if business is good he makes about ten trips a day. With luck the upward trip passage should be accomplished in an hour and a half with the aid of 100 or more trackers.

Overlooking the middle rapid at the Hsin T'an is the Temple of the Double Dragon, offering an extensive and impressive view. The village below is newly built, as the old one was swept away when in the flood of 1870 the river rose more than 200 feet above low level.

Just ahead lies the Mit'an, or Rice Granary Gorge, also known as the Ping Shu Pao Chien Hsia, or Gorge of the Military Code and Precious Blade, which extends for two miles through sheer vertical walls of cliff rising 1500 feet above the water. The strata is much inclined, dipping to the north-west. Inland the mountains ascend to 3,000 feet. There is no foothold for trackers in this gorge, and up-bound junks are entirely dependent on a favourable wind.* A kindly providence has, however, arranged that on nine out of ten days there is an up-river breeze. The finest and most dramatic view of this gorge is from up-river, looking back into the mysterious and gloomy depths.

Immediately above the gorge the little village of Hsiang Chi shows up on the left bank. Inland, about a mile and a half is a cave called Yü Shih Tung, or Pure Jade Cave. Access is down through a hole in the hillside which opens out into an immense cavern. From it, legend reports, is a narrow passage leading to the earth's centre.

Two miles further on are two great rocks nearly 60 feet above low-water level forming a gateway for the river. These are named Shih Mên, or Stone Gate. Just above them is the hamlet of Lao Kwei Chow on the right bank; and opposite, on the foreshore of Ma Whang To, is a temple named after Ch'ü Yüan, the official of Dragon Boat fame, who lived in the 4th century B.C. He fell into disgrace with the Emperor and, adopting the usual practice of such unfortunates, threw himself into the river. A local variation of this legend is that he was swallowed by a huge dragon or fish which threw him up, but, with commendable consideration or else by an astonishing coincidence, selected his native village of Ma Wang for the operation. There the sister of the deceased performed his funeral rites and built his tomb. The local people say that his body remains intact and that the large fish is still at liberty in the regions around and is responsible for the three bad whirlpools which at certain water levels are to be seen near the temple.

Above this, also on the left bank and four and a half miles above the upper end of the Mit'an, is the walled city of Kweichow with a conspicuous white temple at its east gate. This picturesque little town is built at a sufficient height to avoid flooding when the freshets come down, the houses being attractively set amongst trees and gardens or in small ravines. The foreshore presents an unapproachable aspect, for the inclination of the strata has caused the formation of a number of forked ledges extending out into the stream. These, together with the rapids and races due to these obstructions, are a formidable obstacle to up-bound junks, which, if there is no fair wind, need a whole day's work for the trackers to haul them round Roller Point, where rollers may be seen on the surface of the rock over which the long bamboo tow ropes run. In this locality flights of steps and paths are carved for the trackers out of the rocky cliffs.

The trend of the river from Kweichow is westerly. On the right bank are high mountains with foothills coming down to the river. A rocky mound, named Liulaikuan, with a pagoda on its leafy summit, heralds the approach to the Yeh T'an. This rapid is caused by a fan-shaped deposit of detritus from a tributary flowing in from the mouth at right angles to the Yangtze. A jutting rocky point on the opposite bank plays its part in narrowing the river to less than half its normal breadth. At low water there is not enough water to pile up at the narrow neck, but, with rising levels or spring freshets, it becomes a sort of sluice through which the water descends at a pronounced slope against which only high-powered engines

* It is interesting to old sailors to hear the junkmen whistling for the wind in the gorges. There are said to be only two winds, the *hsia-fêng*, or down-river wind, and the prevailing *shang-fêng*, or up-river wind, which may at times be so strong that down-bound junks have to use their oars to make any headway against it. This wind blows steadily from September to May, during the period of the north-east monsoon on the China coast, and, like most easterly breezes, begins in the forenoon and drops at sunset.

can make any headway unaided: for the fall at this short steep smooth rapid is about 8 feet.

An outstanding feature of the Upper Yangtze is that the navigational channel will often follow one bank or the other so closely that the proverbial biscuit can frequently be thrown ashore, and the uninitiated wonders at the closeness with which rocks are approached.

In other places are quiet reaches where the current flows swift and still, reflecting the sheer cliffs in its placid surface. There is nowhere a square foot of cultivated ground that has not been utilized. The hillsides, laid out in terraces from foot to summit, are irrigated laboriously from the streams below. Farms and temples, each with its small bunding, sheltered by trees or groves, cling to the cliffs in seemingly inaccessible places and raise the inevitable question, why should anyone require or desire to live so high?

Two miles above Yeh t'an village is Shangshihmen, or Upper Gateway, which, like the lower Shihmen below Kweichow, consists of rocky cliffs standing guard on either side of the river. There are two more rapids in the next few miles, the Ta Patou T'an, or Great Eight Start Rapid, and the Niu T'ou T'an, or Ox Head Rapid, the largest of all, which like the Yeh T'an owes its being to a narrowing of the river bed due to a rocky boulder shelf on the north bank. At the head of the rapid a white pagoda and the last town in Hupeh, that of Pa-Tung Hsien, face each other from opposite sides of the river, among desolate surroundings. A red temple and crazily built huts on piles make this town recognizable; it is the last of any note before the Wushan Gorge and possesses the negative fame of being one of the worst anchorages on the Upper Yangtze.

Next comes the Ching Chu Piao Rapid, which is at its most turbulent at mid-river level. On the north bank just below the entrance to the gorge is a ravine with the village of Kuan-to-ku on the one side and on the other one more of the four celebrated temples to Wang Yeh, the River King. It stands like a white sentinel on a pinnacle, guarding the entrance to the longest of all the gorges, the Wushan or Witches' Mountain Great Gorge, which winds through the mountain walls for almost 30 miles. The witch after whom the gorge is named was Wu O Nü, the enchantress of Mount Wu.

Even in bright sunlight the entrance to this gorge gives an impression of sombre gloom. There is a bend very soon after entering, and it seems like the end of a fiord with no way round, until, through a narrow aperture, a straight stretch appears. The white and yellow limestone cliffs soar up, with peaks 2,000 feet above, which seem even higher owing to their steepness.

The first reach extends for about a mile and is known as T'iehkwan ts'ai hsia, or Iron Coffin Gorge, wherein, so the legend runs, Chu Ko Liang buried his magic sword and mystic war books. Judging by the occult methods of warfare employed by that strategist, if these ancient text books could only be unearthed, new and even more terrible secret weapons could be made use of by the war-greedy nations of the world.

At Huo-yen-shih the river becomes very narrow, and there are masses of pock-marked reefs. A marked feature of the Gorges is the immense number of holes along the surface of the sheer cliffs and rocks bordering the river. These have been made by the iron points of the boat hooks used by the junkmen to haul their craft along at different points. The pock-marked appearance of the surface of the rocks is very curious. The number and depth of these holes and the fact that they are not in soft sandstone, but in hard conglomerate rocks, points to their having been gradually worn away over a period of some hundreds of years. From here the canyon is known as the Fire Smoke Gorge, so named for its blackened and smoked appearance. An interesting feature is the difference in fertility between the left bank, which is shaded, steep and barren, and the right bank, with its slopes wooded because of the rays of the sun.

During the high-water season or in a freshet, the Wushan Gorge presents an awe-inspiring sight when the stormy yellow flood rages down through the majestic gloom of its confining ramparts, cannoning from side to side and churning itself into deadly whirlpools.

Before the last turn of the gorge is Kong Min Pei, or the Dynasty Stone, on the left bank. Here the recessed face of the cliff is covered with characters. Legend says that with each new dynasty a layer of rock falls away, disclosing a new face with engraved characters describing the coming dynasty.

Finally, the river rounds the last curve of the Wushan Gorge under a curious, steep mountain peak about 1,500 feet high, on the apex of which is the Wên fêng shan, or Temple of Literature, in a grove of trees. Behind soar mountain ranges. A small affluent, the Ta Ling or Tanningho, here joins the Yangtze from the north. On it plies a peculiar type of junk with a fan-tail stern suggestive of the early craft of the Nile. It brings down brine from the tempestuous upper reaches of the Tanningho. The town of Wushan stands at the junction of this stream and the Yangtze, its curved grey roofs and temples clustering behind its ancient walls with picturesque gatehouses at the corners. It is the easternmost city in the province of Szechwan.

This is the commencement of the wood-oil tree-growing area. There are two varieties of this tree. The *aleurites Fordii* is peculiar to Szechwan, where it thrives in thin-soiled rocky ground. Reaching a height of about 20 feet, it grows in a compact shape not unlike a small walnut tree with large leaves and small pink and white flowers. The fruit, shaped like an apple, only slightly pointed, is gathered in August and September; and the oil is extracted from the large seeds by primitive wooden presses. The oil is then boiled for two hours with earth pellets and powdered quartz, and the finished product is sent to the market in wooden tubs and sometimes in wood-oil baskets lined with paper.

Its uses are manifold. It serves for caulking and oiling junks; for varnishing furniture or wood of all kinds. It is the basic ingredient in the making of paint, varnish, and waterproof paper. Latterly it has been used for lighting and even for fuel.

Above Wushan the ravine opens out into a valley; and, during the next 13 miles, several rapids occur. The Hsia Ma T'an, or "Get Down From Horse Rapid," is about three miles above Wushan. It is formed, like the Yeh T'an, by a boulder bank deposit from a right-angled affluent. Up the ravine through which it flows down to the Yangtze is a cave called Lao Lung Tung, or Old Dragon Cave; and, as any passing rider is required here to dismount and pay his respects to the occupant, the rapid has been so named in commemoration of this act of courtesy or careful tact.

After some minor rapids, the Pao Tzŭ T'an, or Precious Son Rapid, is encountered. This rapid is at its most unpleasant at mid-level.

Two miles higher up is a deep cleft in the 3,000-foot mountains named the Tso kia hsia, or False Gorge. Legend claims that all the gorges were cut by the Emperor Yü, 2208 B.C., but that he overestimated his capacity in attempting to cut through at this spot and so had to abandon the attempt. The Wizard Wu Tzŭ, who is said to have aided him in cutting out the Wushan Gorge, also came to his

The Windbox Gorge.
R. B. DENT

help in this dilemma and, taking on the appearance of an ape, blew a great trumpeting blast from his nostrils which cut through the mountains to the west, so forming the Bellows, or Windbox Gorge.

Below the entrance is the Li Kuan T'an with its guardian "Cat Rock," Mao-tzŭ-shih, which is the extension of the Ichang shê hang, or Snake Reef. This causes a cross-set which is a menace to all down-bound junks. A sandy bay leads round to the signal station at Chin yin ho, or Gold and Silver River. Above this is a curious fall of limestone. The softer portions have eroded, leaving what looks like giant sponges.

The fifth and last gorge is now at hand, the Fenghsiang, or Windbox. It is short, not over four miles in length, but is the grandest and most striking of all. At first no aperture appears in the 3,000-foot-high wall of solid mountain, but a sharp turn reveals the entrance dominated by a curious shaped peak named by some the Frog Mountain. This gorge, like that of Wushan, is solemnly impressive and justifies its alternative Chinese name of the Gorge of the Fearsome Pool. The cliffs rise in sheer walls of 800 to 900 feet in height, hemming in the river in a mighty corridor that averages 300 yards in width, narrowing to half that in two or three places. The Chinese say that not even a monkey could find a foothold or a bird a resting place in these inhospitable walls. Certainly there is little bird life to be seen in any of the gorges.

On the left bank half a mile inland, the mountains rise to nearly 5,000 feet. At high water foaming whirlpools swirl or surge in the constricted area, and the level of the stream is almost unbelievably heightened. There is a watermark painted on the rock which runs up to 190 feet above the low river level. Large caverns have been scooped out by the wash of the current, so roomy that fishing sampans can shelter there from bad weather. In winter with a fair wind a junk may sail up through the whole gorge in under an hour, but in summer the rising water piles up above and pours through the narrow confines like a sluice.

Half a mile inland lies a village that is a favourite stop for retired junk owners. The name of the village is Tai Chi.

During the last century it was decided that the provinces of Hupeh and Szechwan would combine to make a road or trackers' path. But Szechwan, in 1888, alone fulfilled its part of the undertaking. The path is in some places literally hollowed out of the live rock, leaving a roof of cliff above.

A mile from the entrance is the Heishih T'an, or Black Stone Rapid. About half way through the gorge caverns and chimneys appear on the side of the yellow cliff. Above one of these caves on the left bank is a rock bearing some resemblance to a box-bellows; hence the name of the gorge. Close by is an inscription and not far off a long fissure in which, wedged high under the over-hanging cliff, are three boxes or coffins, said by some to be Chinese bellows. Whatever these boxes may be, the remarkable thing about them is how they got put into their present inaccessible position some 600 feet above the river.

On the right bank of the western outlet, where the river narrows again to 150 yards, is a Chinese inscription, and here may be seen a number of 14-inch square holes chiselled into the limestone rock to a depth of two feet. Tradition has it that the troops of General Mêng Liang, who lived during the romantic period of the Three Kingdoms, A.D. 221 to 265, on finding themselves trapped in the gorge by their enemies, cut this stairway in the vertical cliff 526 feet high and, destroying their junks, climbed to safety. A toll of 10 lives was said to be the price of every hole cut in the rock.

General Mêng's normal sphere of influence was in the far north, but no reasons are given by historians to explain the presence of himself and his troops in Szechwan. This astonishing journey so far west is even more remarkable than their spectacular escape.

There is another less war-like version of the story of General Mêng's Ladder. This says that he made a bet with another General, Chiao Tsian, who was encamped on the hill, that he could cross the bluff and enter his camp before daybreak. In spite of his excavating the holes in the cliff, the cock crew before Mêng was able to install his ladders; and, disappointed at his failure, he returned by the way he had come. To his astonishment it was long before morning broke; and he found, on investigation, that the false cock crowing that had induced him to give up his attempted climb had proceeded from a monk who had been sent by General Chiao to trick him according to the best traditions of Chinese strategy of the time. This enraged Mêng so much that he kicked the crowing monk over the cliff, where he still lies in the form of a rock known as the "Upside Down Hanging Monk," near Mêng Liang's Ladder.

A few hundred yards from the General's cliff, a flat rock projects from the left bank, on which stand two iron posts called Tei chu hsi, to which it is said chains were attached and stretched across the gorge in the reign of Tai-kung, Emperor of Shu, in the Ch'ing Dynasty, 1821–1851, to prevent the junks carrying salt into Hupeh. This is comparatively modern history, and it is not true that the chains were stolen during the night and that they turned into snakes before daylight.

Marking the western entrance to the Windbox Gorge is the Yen Wei Shih, or Goosetail Rock, which in the low water season stands 60 feet above the water, dividing it into two channels, the north being the wider. In summer it is awash; and when it is covered it is considered too dangerous for downbound junks to proceed.

There is a belief among the junkmen that this rock stands above a famous Dragon Castle. The legend says one day Lung Wang, the Dragon King, was disposed to leave his palace, which was deep under this rock, and go out and see the submarine world over which he ruled. His ministers protested, but Lung Wang was resolute.

Accordingly he transformed himself into a little fish and went abroad, much delighted with all the strange things which he saw. But, as his curiosity was much in excess of his experience, he was soon entangled in a fisherman's net, from which escape was impossible.

He was taken out by the fisherman, sold in the market, bought by a housewife, who took him to her house, split him in two and fried him in a skillet before he had time to recover himself. As soon as he could disengage himself he hastened to the Palace of Ya Hwang, the Chief Ruler of the gods, to complain of his ill treatment. Yu Hwang inquired how Lung Wang came to be personating a little fish and decided he had left his proper station for a sphere in which he had no business to be; he had only himself to thank for his misfortune.

The moral, the junkmen say, is "Do not enter a business you do not understand or leave one with which you are familiar."

Near the Goosetail Rock on the starboard side of the channel going up is a semi-foreign style house on the top of a hill, once the home of the former Tu chün, or poet war lord of the "twenties," Wu P'ei Fu.

Just above the gorge, east of the city of K'wei fu, is a small river called the Jangchi. The usual shingle bank was formed at its mouth, but in this case it extends more than half way across the Yangtze. It is known as Ch'ou yen chi and from it arise dense clouds of white smoke, giving the impression of a large village undergoing an air raid. Actually this is a temporary matshed colony which springs up anew each year on that site as soon as the shingle bank is uncovered, to condense the natural brine which wells up there. The smoke and steam which rise proceed from innumerable large iron pans heating over furnaces stoked with coal from a neighbouring source up the affluent east of K'wei fu. The wells are sunk about 12 feet and then boarded to form a kind of shaft, from the bottom of which men hand up water to others standing halfway up, who in turn hand it to others on the bank, whence it is carried to small mud reservoirs conveniently placed near the burning pans which are balanced over mud-built fire places. The water finds its way into the pits through the soil and becomes in its passage impregnated with salt, but not strongly, for the taste is scarcely perceptible.

Legend says that the salt spring was first discovered by a beggar in the reign of the Emperor Hsien Fêng and was named Ch'ou yen chi, or Stinking Salt Stream —which actually is quite an accurate description.

Above the shingle bank lies the ancient town of K'wei chou fu, formerly known as Fong Chi hsieng, now more commonly called K'wei fu, picturesquely situated in an amphitheatre of hills. The town, which has a high wall, is on a steep slope bunded in four terraces and with a small pagoda behind. Facing the river is the imposing main gate with a curved tiled roof to the double-storied pavilion above the gate. On the face of the wall above the gate itself is the inscription "Slow" written in vast letters. This refers not, as might be surmised, to the character of the inhabitants or the trade of the place, but to the speed at which it is desired ships shall pass the town so as to avoid inflicting damage from their wash to junks banked in.

This is one of the few places on the Upper Yangtze where the river silts up badly each autumn and then suddenly scours itself out, opening the south channel.

On leaving K'wei fu the trend of the river is westerly as far as Yün Yang, and the rock formation is, as is usual among coal fields, grey sandstone; and the north bank, where it lies thicker, is noticeably less fertile than the south bank. The coal in this neighbourhood is said to be anthracite. Extensive shingle flats are worked for gold, but with poor results.

The valley now opens out, and the hills withdraw. The river is about 400 yards wide, sometimes reduced to half by rocky points or boulder banks. A number of rapids follow each other in quick succession. The Lai Pa T'an or "Trumpet Rapid" or Lao Ma T'an, "Old Horse Rapid," as it is more commonly called, at the village of An Ping, is the first. Here the steep cliffs have sloping heaps of sandstone piled at their feet. Two miles above An Ping a ravine on the left bank naturally bridged by the rock heralds the village of Huang shih Tsui, with a rapid of the same name, meaning "Mouth of Yellow Stones Rapid" after the mass of stones in the mouth of the ravine.

About nine miles up are the white temple and the village of Ku Ling Tu, or Spiritual Ferry, followed by the Miao Chi Tzŭ T'an, or Temple Stairs Rapid, formed by a boulder shoal on the left bank with ledges on the right bank. Three miles farther up is the village of Tung Yang Tzŭ lying athwart a ravine on the left bank. The usual rapid has formed at the mouth of this stream, and about 60 years ago the Chinese built a dam or break-water with a broad flat top so as to divert the stream and lessen the amount of detritus deposited at its mouth. On the face of the masonry there are four graven characters meaning "To still the waters is a perpetual boon." Several such places have inscriptions of the same type, such as "By chiselling away the rocks one stills the waves." This would seem to point to the continual influence of the Emperor Yü's efforts at conservancy.

Above Tung Yang Tzŭ another ravine on the left bank is arched by a bridge of the natural rock. There are two pagodas in commanding positions three miles apart from each other with rapids between. A bend to the north-west leads round to the walled town of Yün Yang, or Clouded Sun City, on the left bank of the river at its junction with a small affluent, and on the western side of this small gorge there are a fine Kung Kwan, or Guildhall, several temples, and a three-storied pagoda with a green roof which is said to be coppered. The extensive suburbs seem to have escaped the old walls which extend up the mountainside behind. On the opposite side of the river is the well kept and attractive temple of the Ethereal Bell of Ten Thousand Ages, also sometimes known as the Willow Prince Temple and built to commemorate Chang Fei, a hero of the time of the Three Kingdoms. It stands on a large mound of talus from an old landslide of the hill behind it. Chang Fei's head is reputed to be buried here, and a mysterious tradition amongst the junkmen says that if the oil tank in the temple is filled with oil, the General's head will float to the surface. There is no record of the experiment's having been successfully carried out or what became of the head when the original temple was washed away by a 200-foot rise in the river in 1870. His body is buried at Lang Chung. It is said that when a fire breaks out in the District the magical bell rings of its own accord. Junks when passing are supposed to burn incense and candles and let off fire-crackers in homage to Chang Fei, who in return always guarantees them a fair wind up-stream for about 10 miles, thereby living up to the inscription on the temple "Gentle wind on the river."

Above Yün Yang the river bank becomes steeper and more barren-looking, with many landslips to mar the smooth contours of the hillsides and a series of waterfalls. The upward tilt of the sandstone beds has caused many underwater caverns, particularly at Panto. The succession of terraces through which the river has carved its way down deeper and deeper can be clearly seen. Their silted soil is very fertile and produces several crops a year.

Ten miles above Yün Yang is the Hsin Lung T'an, or New Dragon Rapid. This low-level rapid is due to an immense landslide which occurred on 30 September 1896, when, after 40 days of incessant rain, a large portion of the hill on the north bank, measuring 700 yards by 30 yards, slipped 150 yards forward into the bay and built up a projecting spit composed of clay and rock debris. In one night the river narrowed from 400 to 150 yards, the high spit converting a quiet reach into a boiling rapid, with a fall of nearly a dozen feet in 100 yards and with vicious whirlpools below the rapid. Many junks and junkmen are lost here, some say as many as a thousand in a year.

This rapid is at its worst during the months of February and March, when it certainly deserves its more usual name of Glorious Dragon Rapid, for at this time the river presents a never to be forgotten sight as it sweeps downwards at an incredible speed and with a roar that can be heard throughout the gorge. Happily, however, with rising water, the rapid improves and disappears completely when the river rises towards mid-level.

Tremendous efforts were made to improve the condition of this rapid. An army of 2,000 men chipped away at the point, the produce of their excavations being emptied into the huge whirlpool which formed in the remains of the bay below the rapid. In January 1898, Captain Tyler, of the Marine Department of the Chinese Maritime Customs, and two assistants were detailed to supervise the work. In

The upper end of the Hsin T'an at summer level.
KELLY & WALSH, LTD.

On the Upper Yangtze.
KELLY & WALSH, LTD.

spite of limited materials and appliances, much debris was removed and was used to build up a tracker's path on the south bank. A new temple was also built nearby to the patron saint of the junkmen, Wang Yeh. The texture of the debris that fell in this landslide is much less intractable than the tough reefs of the other rapid due to the same cause, the Hsin T'an; and here at the New Dragon Rapid much of the material has broken up and disintegrated, so that even in the comparatively short time since it occurred (as against 300 years at the Hsin T'an) the passage shows quite an improvement.

Despite its youth this, the most recent addition to the rapids of the river, has already acquired a suitable legend attributing its origin to supernatural agency and, as usual, connecting it with an official, in this case one named P'an Pin, who, on retiring from office at P'êng Shan, commenced his return journey to his native province of Kiangsi by junk with his family and a hired wet nurse. P'an Pin had words with this woman over some quite trivial cause; but nevertheless that night, when the junk anchored at the spot now marked by the Hsin Lung T'an, the nurse resigned and departed to the nearest village, despite all efforts to placate her.

She certainly had the last word, for that night a tremendous storm raged, the rocks fell from the left bank, and the junk, complete with the whole family of P'an Pin, had vanished by the morning.

The moral value of this story is doubtful, for had not the wet nurse let the sun go down upon her wrath she would never have lived to see another sunset.

In this vicinity and that of the next village and anchorage of Panto there are various picturesque temples, including one built by the junkmen to Wang Yeh and another with two gilded buddhas mounting guard over it. Above Panto on a hill is another of the cities of refuge built during one of the endless wars.

The strata still lie mostly horizontal, which accounts for the curious flat-topped hills. The rapids proper are now left behind together with the vast ranges which divide Hupeh from Szechwan. The river, which has widened, however, suddenly narrows to enter the curious reach of Pa yai hsia.

At its entrance there are three Guardians of the Water, named Shiu fu san kwan, carved out of the cliff face and painted and gilded. They, very properly, are opposed to night navigation, for they are supposed to guard the waterway for the day only.

This is a tricky place for navigators at mid-level season, as the ledges, together with the three gilded Guardians of the Water, become submerged, and the channel is then hard to find. These shrines and images, so common on the Upper Yangtze, are usually situated close to some recognized danger and more often than not owe their existence to some junkmaster desirous of commemorating the preservation of his vessel or his life. The temple or figure is therefore mostly to be found so placed that the supernatural being it humours can keep an eye on the danger to navigation and also serve the more prosaic, but no less useful, function of navigational landmark.

The four-mile defile of Pa yai hsia, or Eight Cliff Gorge, runs through a wide valley which is floored with horizontal sandstone strata through which the river has carved a clean-cut, low water channel which never exceeds 150 yards in width. The hard, grey sandstone walls of this natural canal range in height from 30 to 60 feet and have been worn by the action of the water into strange fantastic shapes and ridges. These are also, as in other places on the Upper Yangtze, numerous indentations, like pock marks, in the hard rock made by countless generations of junkmen poling themselves along or pushing themselves off the banks with their sharp-pointed boathook, which is no hook, but an iron-shod bamboo. Here and there are tablets with characters cut out of the stone, and scoop-fishermen with nets are busy in this reach. Halfway up the corridor, as it has been called, is the village of Huang pei chi chang with two streams, a temple, and a four-storied pagoda in the vicinity. When the river rises the stone ledges that border it become submerged, and navigation is correspondingly difficult.

The gorge ends where a pair of good-sized affluents enter the river from either side at a bend. It takes three hours for a junk to pass through this reach. Once it is left behind the river widens again, and a new feature presents itself, flat of sand as well as shingle. From here nearly all the way up to Chungking gold washing is carried out in rockers—shallow bamboo baskets set on pointed wooden structures. The gold washers sometimes mark out their claim with whitened stones or lines. When they have selected their site, the load from the digging is poured bodily into the basket, water is then added and the whole rocked to and fro until the sand is washed out. The shingle is then discarded and the sand run down a wooden ramp into a receptacle. The particles of gold are later smelted out of the sand. There is very little gold to be found, and the gold diggers barely make a living by their labours. The presence of a good deal of gold mica in the sand must raise many false hopes.

A straight-forward run of under ten miles leads from the Eight Cliff Gorge to

Wanhsien. Here after a sharp turn to the south the approach to this, the Myriad City, is heralded by a nine-storied white pagoda on a 1,000-foot conical hill on the right bank of the river and a five-storied one on the left bank.

This important centre, 1,100 sea miles up the Yangtze, is situated almost exactly halfway between Ichang and Chungking in picturesque surroundings, backed by hills and forest. To the north of the town is another picturesque 3-storied pavilion capping a fine temple. Behind the city is an unusual rock formation rising for 1,200 feet and reached by stone steps cut out of the cliff. The plateau at the top, which is said to cover about 30 acres, is fortified with battlements and walls enclosing a small city of refuge named the Celestial City.

These refuge cities are common in Szechwan and have been built by various communities or rich families to provide "funkholes" in case of trouble from bandits or civil commotion.

The *fêng-shui* of the town is said to be almost perfect, for a distant range affords protection from the evil influences of the *Yin* or darkness; a lower range on the opposite bank of the river screens it from the south, yet is low enough to allow the benign influence of the *Yang* or light to penetrate. Finally, a smooth point of rock juts out into the harbour just above the city, thus providing the indispensable Lung or Dragon; known as the Pan Lung Shih, it is said to contain a deep pot hole extending right down to its base. Nearby is another great sandstone reef, the Tsaopan shih. They rise about 75 feet above low level, but are flooded at high water. The river here is about 550 yards wide, but increases when the shingle bank opposite the town is submerged.

The town is a celebrated junk-building centre, as the *pai-mu* or cypress trees grow in profusion round about. It is also famous for its bamboo, paper, and pretty girls, although this last is not so apparent. From here a highway known as the Great East Road connects with Chengtu.

THE MA-YANG-TZŬ

子

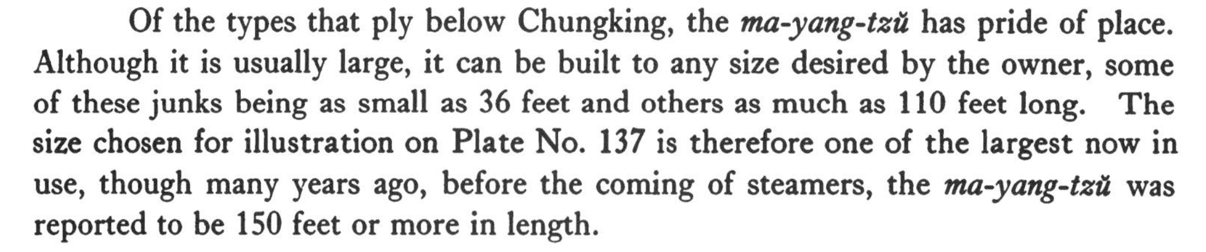

Of the types that ply below Chungking, the *ma-yang-tzŭ* has pride of place. Although it is usually large, it can be built to any size desired by the owner, some of these junks being as small as 36 feet and others as much as 110 feet long. The size chosen for illustration on Plate No. 137 is therefore one of the largest now in use, though many years ago, before the coming of steamers, the *ma-yang-tzŭ* was reported to be 150 feet or more in length.

This junk, which is 102 feet long, 19 feet beam, and with a depth of 8½ feet, is made throughout of the tough cypress of Wanhsien, and gives the appearance of tremendous strength, which is primarily supplied by 14 bulkheads. This heaviness of construction necessarily detracts from grace, but this lack is counterbalanced by a certain sturdy symmetry.

The solid hull is turret-built with a comparatively narrow deck superimposed upon it. Additional strength is provided by long and heavy wales [1] running the whole length of the vessel. The square bow ends in a heavy projecting cross-beam [2]; indeed, these massive cross-beams are a marked feature throughout its length, as there are seven in all. A low 4-inch wide coaming [3] extends from the bow to the house.

On the whale-back the planking runs fore and aft, as also does that below the rubbing strake. The bow planking runs athwartships to a point well below

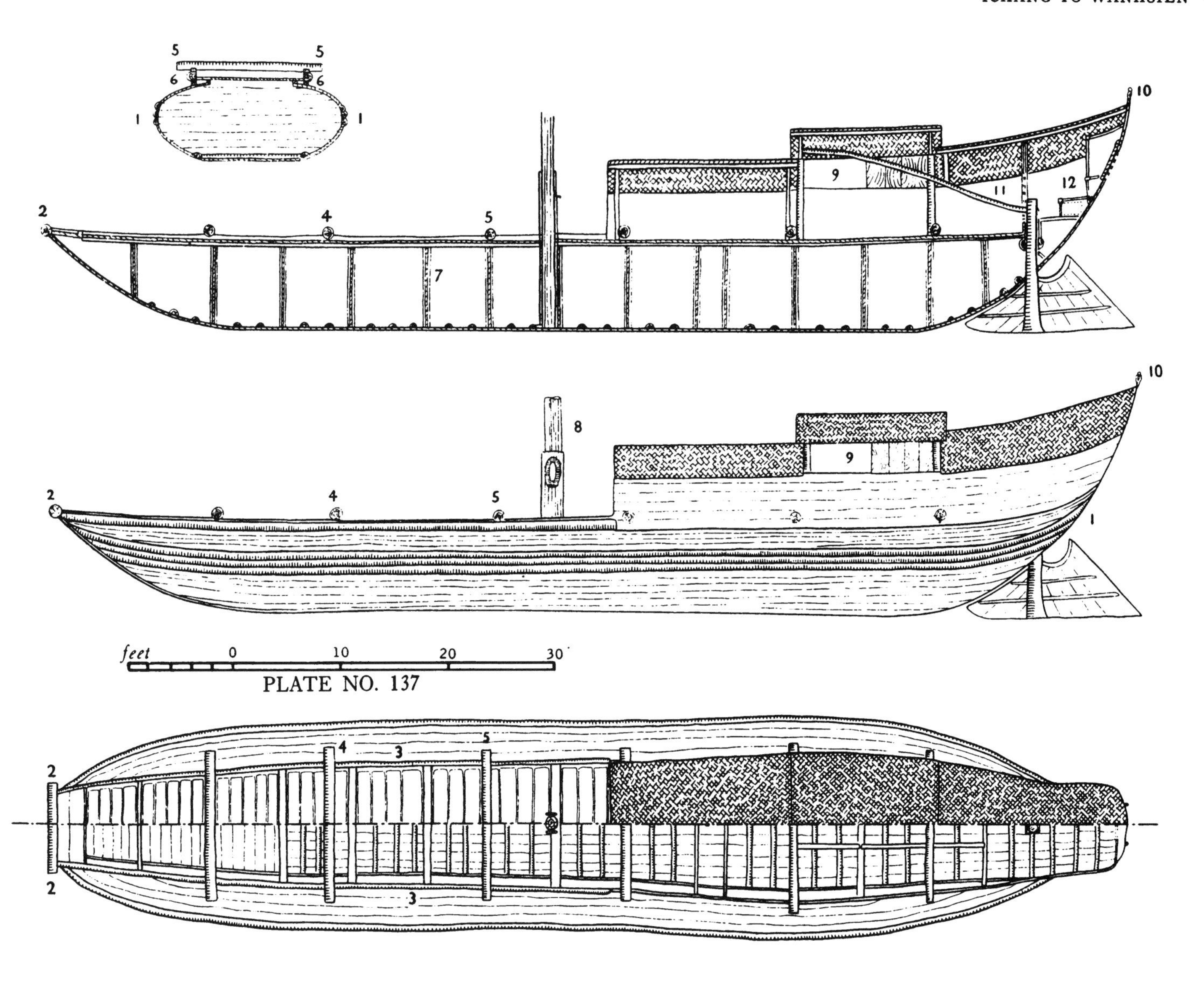

PLATE NO. 137

the water-line, where it meets the bottom planks, which lie longitudinally. In lieu of frames, 28 half-frames, that is to say, thick balks of timber, occur at intervals, laterally across the bottom only, between the traverse bulkheads, which are built up to the shape of the hull. The flat-surfaced high stern widens as it rises in a gentle curve from the water. The planking of the stern facing, which ascends vertically from the bottom, is laid horizontally on the top portion. A small square port with a sliding door looks out over the stern.

The flush-deck removable planking is laid athwartships and follows the sheer of the hull continuously. The second[4] and third[5] large foremost cross-beams are lashed to the transoms [6] and serve for the working of the yulohs.

A solid truncated capstan of hardwood, iron-bound at the base, can be fitted into a transom on the fifth bulkhead[7] on the fore-deck. The *sha-mu* mast of over 80 feet in height is stepped in tall tabernacles[8] which terminate 6 feet above deck-level. Each tabernacle near its summit has a deep cleat carved out to take the halyards for the lug-sail.

The short, low deck-house starts about 5 feet abaft the mast, and a charcoal galley-stove is on the port side in this open space. An overhead shelf under the arched beam of the deck-house and a few lockers provide space for stowing cooking gear.

The hold at its deepest is about 8 feet or more, and this permits a carrying capacity of 100 tons down river and 80 tons up river. A portable bamboo pump is used to empty the bilges.

The tiller-room,[9] abaft the deck-house, is decked-in and has a higher roof level than the rest of the junk, though the roof of the after-house rises gently to its apex at the stern, where it terminates in two tall pins[10] on which the spare bamboo rope is coiled.

The 25-foot tiller[11] curves gently up to the conning position over the eleventh bulkhead and requires three men to handle it in a difficult rapid.

The after-house may be divided into one or two cabins, the last one being approached by a steep step.[12] The niche above the plain cabin door is prolonged on either side into a small gallery, which contains mirrors, pictures, and ornaments.

The crew varies with the size, but a junk of about 90 feet in length with a permanent crew of eight men engages for the trip up a total of 60 men and 50 for the trip down. Twelve men are required at each of the four yulohs and 13 on the bow-sweep on the downward trip, though 16 are required to work the latter on the way up as well as 50 on the tracking-line.

At the rapids extra trackers are engaged, and at the Hsint'an as many as 300 or 400 coolies may be required on the tow-rope to haul her over the rapid. This operation costs on an average $30 irrespective of the number of trackers employed.

梢

秧

THE SHAO-MA-YANG

This junk, as illustrated in Plate No. 130, is very rarely seen at Chungking; indeed, it can hardly be called an Upper Yangtze junk, as its normal trade is between Ichang and Shasi and other Middle Yangtze ports. The type usually measures about 85 feet by 16 feet with a depth of 8 feet, and, like her opposite number the *ma-yang-tzŭ*, is a turret-built, heavy-draught vessel. Nearly identical in size with the *nan-ho-ch'uan* (南河船), she also follows very much the same lines, except for the whale-back,[1] the top surface of which acts as a clear gangway from bow to stern when poling in shoal water.

The scale drawing of the *shao-ma-yang* is shown in Part Three, page 457.

This method of progress is entirely alien to normal Upper Yangtze junk practice and rather marks the *shao-ma-yang* as a "down-river" craft (下游船). Moreover, the gangway for poling gives her an unfamiliar appearance.

This poling is carried out by one or more men, each with a long iron-shod bamboo. Standing in turns at the bow, each poler allows his bamboo to slip through his two hands into the shallow water until securely lodged on the bed of the river. Tucking the end of the pole in the fleshy front part of his shoulder, he then bends to his task, sometimes at such an angle as to be almost prone, and walks thus down the gangway. Having traversed the whole length of the junk, he returns to the bow and repeats the process.

The square bow tapers hardly at all, and the heavy stern is bluntly rounded and contains the owner's cabin.[2] Sturdy wales[3] run the whole length of the hull, just beneath the poling gangway.

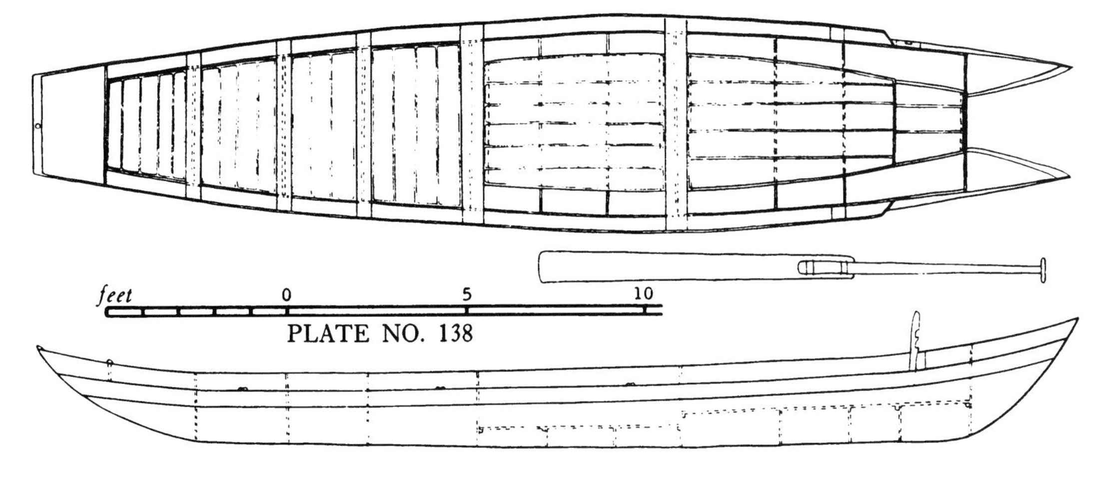

PLATE NO. 138

THE ICHANG SAMPAN

昌

There is nothing original nor outstandingly interesting about this craft, Plate No. 138, which is, except for the forecastle, an open boat, measuring 29 feet by 6 feet beam.

It is propelled by two or three oars, one of which is worked by a bowman who also uses a boat-hook, while one or two oars, and sometimes a rudder, are operated by the laodah. How he manages to push two heavy 14-foot oars, the looms of which cross in front of him, steer by placing his foot on the tiller, and still retain his balance on the other foot, is one of the mysteries of the Yangtze. Equally amazing is the fact that he knows the exact position of the tiller, though his back is towards it, and the "sleight-of-foot" that enables him to find it without having to look down or round.

Like the bowman, he is a master with the boat-hook, which, when in use, is usually gripped close under his arm, while a foot and hand alternate on the tiller. His difficulties are greatly increased by the presence of a matting awning used in the summer to give shelter from the sun and in winter from the rain. It is usually dilapidated and gives little protection from either, but obscures most of his view.

A good illustration of the prowess of these men is displayed by their courage and judgment in boarding a ship going at full speed. As soon as a steamer approaches Ichang, a fleet of these sampans put out to meet her and converge almost simultaneously.

The technique is, briefly, to approach with the current until some hold presents itself for the boat-hook, either on the ship's side or on to a sampan of a fortunate colleague nearer than himself. Immediately on perceiving this opening the laodah turns his boat short round. The bowman has meanwhile taken hold well up the boat-hook so that he has spare length of the pole to pay out when the strain comes on, and as soon as possible he secures the sampan with a short painter having a hook at its end.

No rancour is ever displayed by the crew of one boat when hauled on to, and sometimes hauled off, by those of another. It is not unusual to see five or six of these boats abreast, each hanging on to the other, the whole strain being taken by the one nearest the steamer.

The astonishing risks taken seem in no way commensurate to the few minutes in time thereby saved, and the casualty list is quite heavy amongst the impatient passengers or hotel touts, who leap on or off the steamer over a yawning chasm of swiftly running current.

The luggage they carry in their headlong leap is embarrassing and unhandy in the extreme, consisting as it generally does of bulky baskets of food, kerosene-oil tins, unwieldy bundles, babies, chickens, etc.

This practice of boarding, which is as often as not carried out at night, is developed to a fine though dangerous art in Ichang and is frequently attended with loss of life.

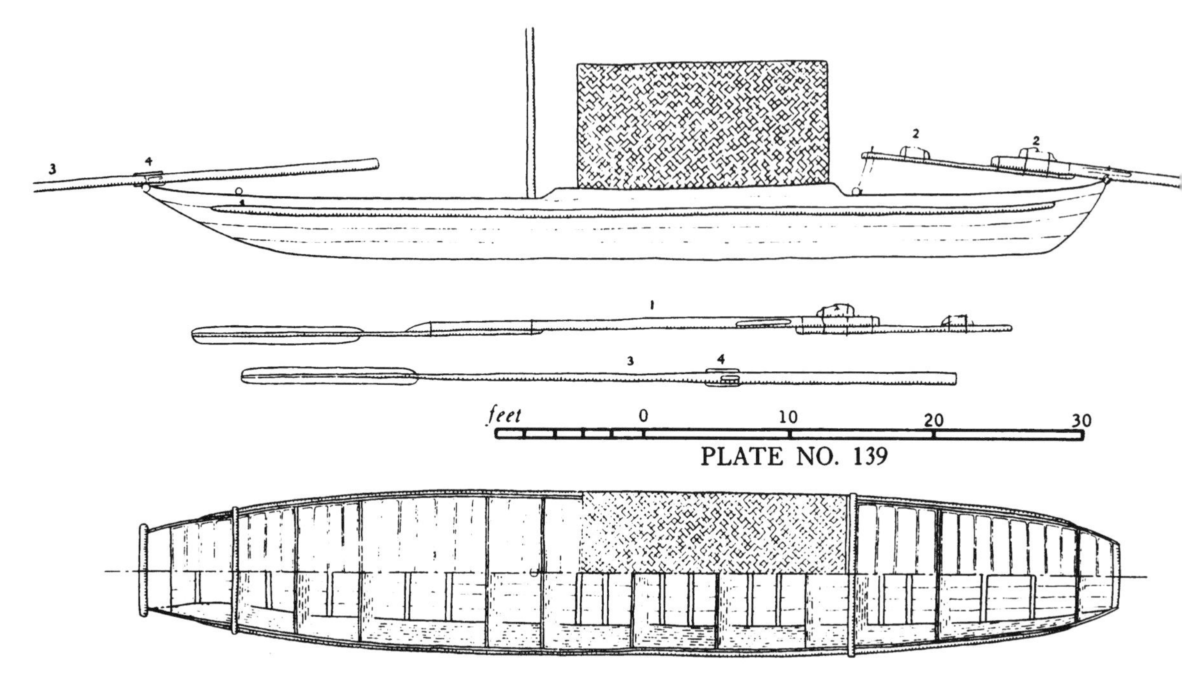

PLATE NO. 139

古林陀煤船

THE KULINTO COAL-JUNK

On the right bank of the Yangtze, 134 miles above Ichang, is Kulinto (古林陀), which is the market town and distributing centre for the coal produced in the valley of the Motao Creek (磨刀溪). This tortuous little stream enters the Yangtze just below the Shihpan Rapid (石板灘), near Kulinto, and junks ascend it for about 8 miles in summer to embark the coal. In the winter, when the creek is no longer navigable, the coal is transported from the mines by mules and ponies and is embarked at the mouth of the creek.

The Kulinto coal-junks, which carry the coal down as far as Wushan (巫山), are fairly uniform in size. That illustrated in Plate No. 139 measures 67 feet in length with a beam of 10 feet, and is of extra strong construction so as to accommodate the weight of its cargo.

The main characteristics of this long and slimly built craft are the markedly square stern with practically no overhang, the curiously tall house, usually set rather far aft, and the very distinctive stern-sweep.[1] This sweep is exceptionally long, being only 11 feet shorter than the over-all length of the junk and actually longer than the water-line measurement. The sweep is formed of three poles, the middle section being much the longest, and joined to the loom and the blade by deep overlaps. The balance is nicely, if crudely, adjusted by means of stones[2] lashed on the upper surface of the loom end. The bow-sweep[3] shows nothing out of the ordinary, and has the usual chafing piece[4] where it engages in the thole-pin fair-lead.

In common with most craft operating below Wanhsien, the Kulinto coal-junk uses a lug-sail.

THE TANNINGHO (大寧河)

NINETY miles above Ichang is Wushan, the easternmost city of the province of Szechwan. This walled town is situated on the left, or north, bank of the Yangtze, at its junction with a small affluent, the Taling, or Tanningho, although it is usually called Hsiaoho, or Little River, the generic name for nearly all the Upper River tributaries. Entering the Yangtze at right angles, as it does, there is a large bank of shingle and sand at its mouth, formed by the action of the main stream.

The Tanningho is navigable up to Taling, or Taningt'an (大寧灘), which is a distance of about 60 miles, estimated by the local inhabitants as 240 *li*. The stream is shallow and contains many rapids, and a special type of small junk has evolved to negotiate the difficulties to be encountered.

THE FAN-TAIL JUNK

This is the *shên-po-tzŭ* (神駁子), or boat of the god, but is better known among foreigners as the "fan-tail" junk, Plate No. 140. The story of its design, which is said to date back 1,000 years or more, is that it was originally built by a priest at a place named Hsint'anhsia (新灘峽), 180 *li* up the Tanningho.

The priest was subsequently deified, and seems to have merged his personality in that of the Chief River God of the junkmen, for an image in the temple at Hsint'anhsia, which is reputed to be his, is worshipped under the familiar name of Wang Yeh (王爺).

Fan-tail junks of the Tanningho.

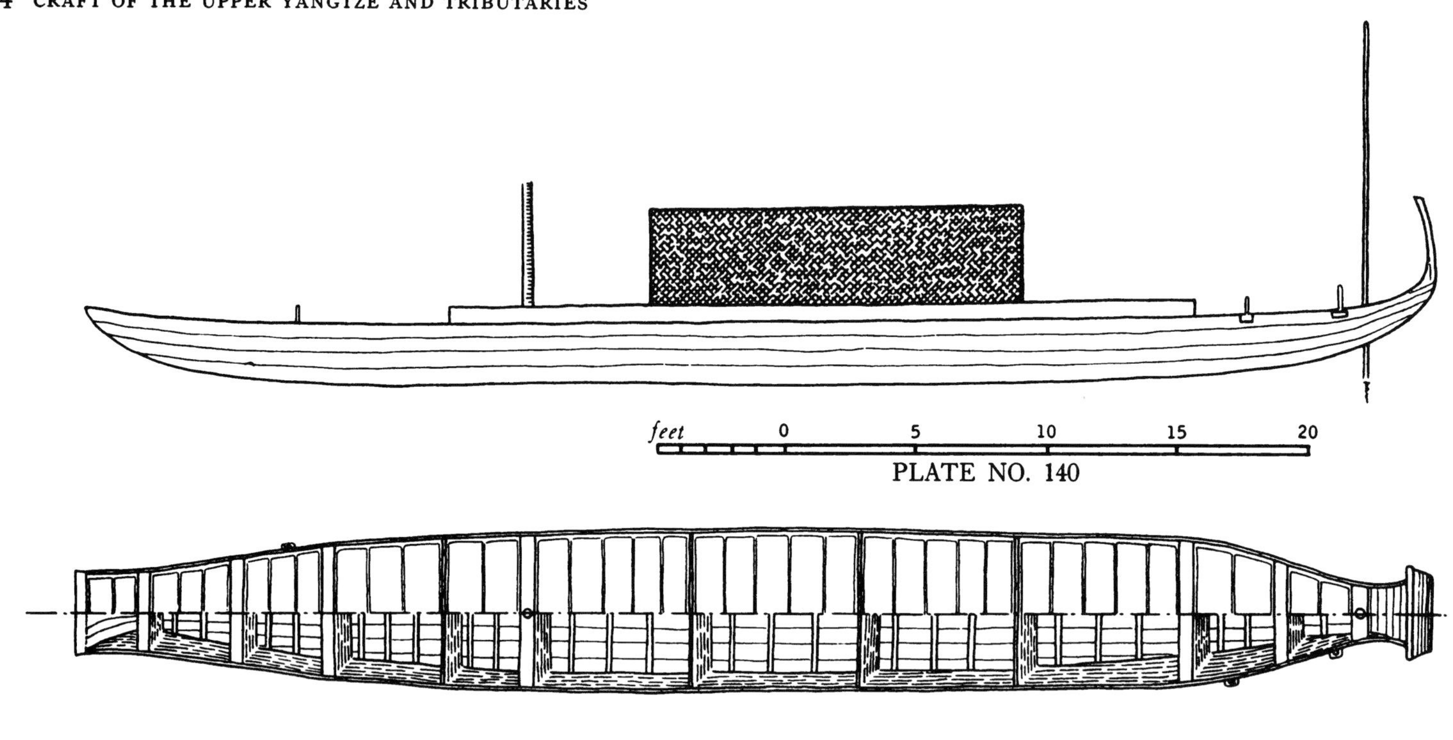

PLATE NO. 140

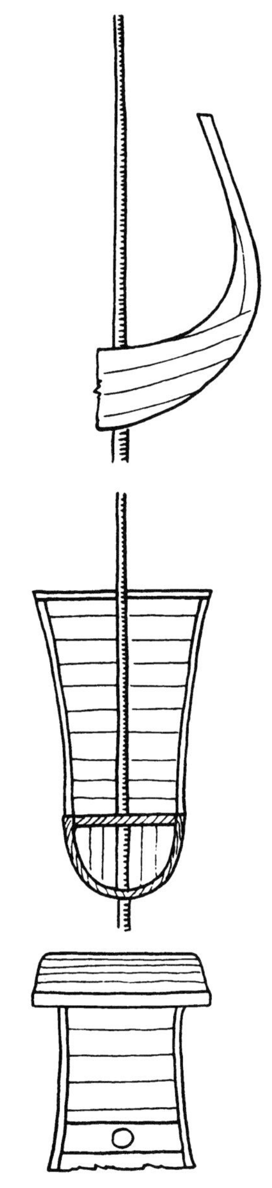

Fan-tail, showing "stick-in-the-mud" anchor.

The original measurements are 36 feet 8 inches in length, 5 feet 8 inches in breadth, narrowing to 3 feet 8 inches at the bottom boards, and 3 feet 6 inches in depth (Chinese feet). The size of the boats varies somewhat, but the original designed is faithfully adhered to. The specimen illustrated in Plate No. 140 is 51½ feet in length with a beam of 6 feet. The draught when loaded to capacity with 2,500 catties of cargo is 1 foot 3 inches, and when light is only actually 5 inches. These draughts give a good indication of the local river conditions. There are 11 compartments, and 11 bulkheads each 1 inch thick. The bow tapers to 2 feet 11 inches. Owing to the shallow waters to be traversed, there is no rudder. No sail is used for navigation on the Tanningho, where propulsion is by tracking, and by three oars, and a large stern-sweep fitted to the port side at the break of the fan-tail. This is operated by a man with his left hand while manipulating an oar with his right.

The early Chinese naval architect, referred to above, must have possessed a good eye for form as well as suitability, for these craft are built on very fine and pleasing lines. Their most distinguishing feature is the high gondola-like stern, which contracts to a narrow waist and then, spreading fanlike to a width of 2 feet 8 inches, curves gracefully over inboard, the planks composing the fan-tail running athwartships. The stern formation is attributed by the junkmen to a whim of the original designer, but like most things Chinese, there is undoubtedly some good solid reason for it. Probably this formation serves as some protection against being "pooped" in the rapids and races of the river, where water may very easily be shipped over the stern. Another reason which suggests itself is that the design provides a convenient hand-fast for at least two men on the frequent occasions when it becomes necessary for some of the crew to enter the water and, by wading and pushing, to assist in manœuvring over a shallow reach.

Various experiments are said to have been made with larger junks, but these never seem to have survived a maiden voyage, and a superstitious aura now surrounds the priest-cum-god's pattern, the efficiency of which has been proved by long experience.

A crew of three or four men is usually carried, but these are augmented by one or two more when the current is stronger. The junks travel in convoys of six to ten for protection. At night they bank in and secure alongside each other. A curious and unusual characteristic is the fact that the "stick in the mud" anchor is situated in the stern, as in the case of the *hsiao-ho-ch'uan* (小 河 船) on the Ki River (綦 江). The reason is to be found in the fluctuations in the level of the Tanningho, due to the holding up of the water in the bottle-neck above a gorge. This causes a lull, or even sometimes an up-current below, until the banked-up water forces an outlet. The resultant down rush of the stream raises the level of the river again, and the process is repeated every two or three hours in the vicinity of all the five gorges of the navigable portion of the river. As the convoy of junks all lies alongside each other when tied up, this ingenious system of anchoring obviates any of the unpleasant bumping and banging which would be inevitable with the fluctuating level of the stream. This very well illustrates the efficiency of the "stick in the mud" method of anchoring, for as the water rises or falls, so the boat travels up or down the stick, which itself remains stationary.

See page 558.

The junks cover an average distance of 30 *li* per day either up or down bound, and 10 trackers are required to take the boat the whole way to Taling. In the middle of the high-water season these junks do not venture to navigate for about two months.

The cargo carried up to Taling consists of rice, wine, tobacco, and sugar, while Chinese sauce, medicines, lacquer, wood oil, fruit, and salt from the brine wells at Taling, or Taningchang (大 寧 廠), are brought down.

It has been said that a trip down through the rapids and gorges of the Tanningho is an exciting and interesting experience.

THE KUNGT'ANHO (龔 灘 河)

This river, which was always marked as Pei on the old maps, is also known as the Kung T'an Ho or Hsiao Ho, Little River. The first large-sized tributary to join the Yangtze above the Tungting Lake, it provides inter-communication with the south.

THE Kungt'anho, or Hsiaoho, known in its upper reaches as the Wukiang (烏 江), or Crow River, is a clear-water stream which rises in the north-west of the province of Kweichow (貴 州) and joins the Upper Yangtze at Fowchow, about 65 miles below Chungking.

Fowchow, on the right bank of the Yangtze, is a very picturesque town, rising 70 feet in terraces above the high water-level, and backed by hills of about 1,000 feet in height. Both rivers are at first separated by a shingle bank at the mouth of the Kungt'anho, but even after this ceases they run side by side in two separate bands of colour until at last they merge. This is, of course, not so apparent at high water.

Navigation is said to be possible for about 360 miles, but the current is so swift and the rapids are so formidable that this has to be accomplished in five stages, and cargo is transhipped from junk to junk as each can only navigate to the limit of its own section.

The first and longest section, from Fowchow to Kungt'an (龔 灘), is 200 miles long, or more than one-half the whole navigable stretch. As Kungt'an is situated at a level some 1,200 feet higher than Fowchow, this accounts for the existence between these points of 71 difficult rapids, said to be the most dangerous ever navigated by junks. The remainder of the river from Kungt'an to a point above Szenan (思 南) is divided into four sections, namely, Kungt'an to Yenho (沿 河), 60 miles; Yenho to Hsint'an, 40 miles; Hsint'an to Tsaoti (漕 地), 20 miles; Tsaoti to Szenan, 20 miles.

The Kungt'anho is celebrated for the unusual types of "crooked-stern" junks which negotiate its many and violent rapids, and numbers of these peculiar craft may always be seen clustered in convoys together, and banked in along both sides of the mouth of the Kungt'an at Fowchow and for about half a mile above.

The river is placid enough in midsummer for some miles up from its mouth, and flows between low green slopes rendered still more picturesque by a profusion of wild flowers. Higher up, rapid succeeds rapid in so dangerous and turbulent a fashion that the local legend says that the control of the river was regarded as a very pleasant sinecure for a retired Dragon, since there could not possibly be any junk traffic with which to concern himself. However, Lu Pan (魯 班), the Carpenter god, was so much moved by the boasted lightness of the Dragon's labours that he proposed to provide some work for him by building a junk that would navigate the Kungt'anho. He accordingly devised the crooked-stern junk, which by its peculiar formation was able to employ two sweeps instead of only one, and so negotiate even the dreaded Yangchiot'an (羊 角 灘), or Goat Horn Rapid.

The Dragon, being greatly concerned at the presence of these craft, which increased his responsibilities, begged the Carpenter god to build no more. Eventually they came to an understanding whereby, if the Carpenter god could build a wooden pagoda without employing any nails, the Dragon would acknowledge himself worsted and perforce agree to the building of more junks.

On the Kungt'anho.
REV. A. E. OWEN

The Carpenter god performed this miracle of cabinet making without difficulty, and a small wooden pagoda is supposed to have stood for many years on the left bank of the Yangtze River opposite Fowchow, a monument to his skill and a sign that the Dragon had henceforward to resign himself to the task of caring for the mariners of the Kungt'anho.

THE CROOKED-STERN SALT JUNK

歪屁股

These junks are called *wai-p'i-ku* (歪屁股) by the inhabitants of Fowchow, meaning crooked-stern junks; the junkmen and carpenters, however, refer to them as the *hou-pan-ch'uan* (厚板船), or thick-plank boats—or, more shortly, *hou-pan.*

They are constructed either wholly or in part of *hung-ch'un* (紅椿), a wood possessing some of the character of the English elm, though in colour resembling mahogany. *Fêng-hsiang* (楓香), or maple, is also in favour, but the bulkheads are always made of *pai-mu* (柏木), or cypress.

The first process in the building of a *wai-p'i-ku* is to lay five or more planks of varying lengths, but rarely exceeding 30 feet, side by side on the ground. These are the bottom planks, to which others are joined by scarfing so as to extend from the stern to as far forward as the first bulkhead, and provide much of the longitudinal strength of the junk. They are secured to each other by long, square clincher nails which are driven in obliquely, a hole being first provided for each by a primitive auger. The bottom of the vessel is thus formed, and one end is now hoisted up about 5 feet clear of the ground on to a crutch, the under side receiving a thick coating of mud, while the top is soaked with water. A large fire is kindled beneath the raised end and so adjusted that the greatest heat is along the line AB obliquely across the bottom planks (*next page*).

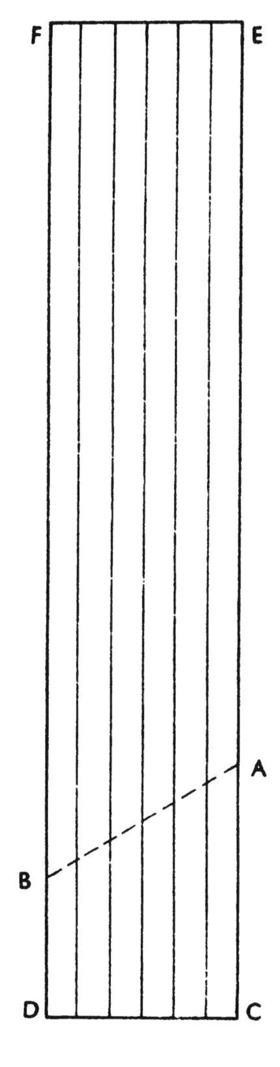

Large quantities of stones are placed over the extremity CD, and in about two hours the whole area ABCD is bent over along the line AB. Very often the wood splits, but this is not objected to unless it is likely to permit the entry of water, and the scars of this burning can always be seen in the junks.

The bottom planks when cooled are turned over bodily, and the bulkheads or half bulkheads, which may total as many as 13 in number and consist of *pai-mu* planks laid horizontally on edge, are assembled in position and gradually built up. These provide the primary athwartship strength. It is a convention that no iron clamps, or dogs, are ever used in the bottom planking except to join it to the bilge planks. The first and second bulkheads,[1] together with one just abaft the house, are stiffened with two rather ineffectual verticals, or knee-pieces, extending from the bulwarks down to the turn of the bilge and are secured by nails.

The angle that the line AB makes with the line EA determines the angle of the crooked stern, for the planks forming the upper portion of the stern are then built up horizontally, parallel, and on edge on the line CD, point C becoming the higher side of the stern.

The bilge planks are next placed in position beneath and overlapping the bottom planks, a long channel about 4 feet wide being thus formed along the outside of the bottom.

Plank succeeds plank, carvel fashion, each being nailed in the middle, and the two ends of these shaped timbers are hove down into position by a form of Spanish windlass. Nails are driven into the hull in all directions in great profusion and equal carelessness, until the whole hull is a mass of protruding nails, which are subsequently clinched, and the considerable holes filled with chunam. Three wales, the highest being the stoutest, are built-in as side planks.[2]

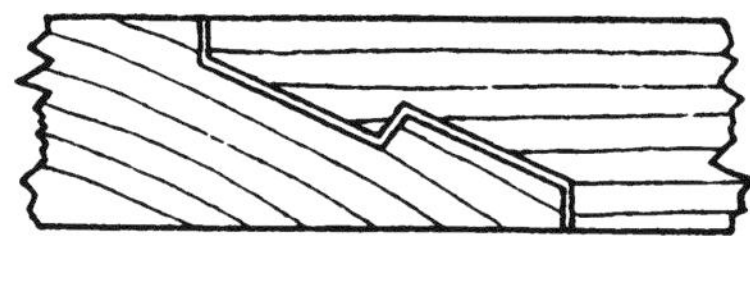

FIG. A.

The method of joining two planks or wales together so that they make one continuous timber of uniform size throughout is illustrated (*left*). Figure A shows the manner adopted when scarfing a large and heavy timber, while Figure B shows the usual method employed in dealing with planks and similar members.

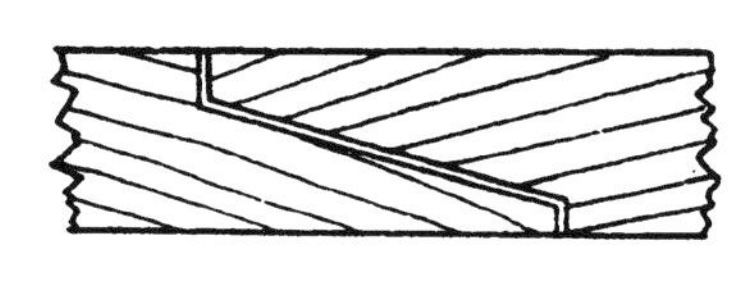

FIG. B.

The join is rarely finely adjusted, and gaps of nearly half an inch in width are quite common, the aperture being filled with chunam.

The general method of joining planks and timbers is by means of wrought-iron clamps, or dogs, and spikes, which are illustrated on Page No. 509. Type A is used to secure a built-in wale to a side plank. The long slender point is first hammered home as far as the waist from the inside of the plank lying immediately below the wale and is then clinched downward, while the two-pronged fork left protruding on the inner side is then hammered home in the opposite, or upward, direction, the turned-over prongs being buried deeply into the thickness of the wale (*left*).

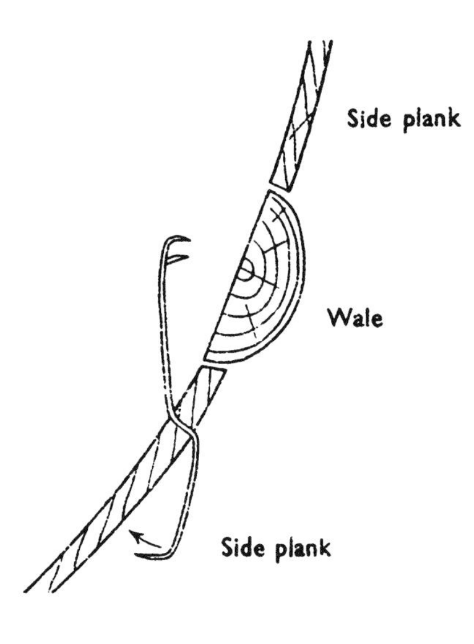

Type C is used in a similar manner, but to connect timbers at right angles, such as side planks to a bulkhead, while types B and E are ordinary connecting clamps. Type D represents a standard-pattern nail with square shanks. For convenience these nails are made in pairs head to head, the portion joining them being so thin that they can be separated by hand.

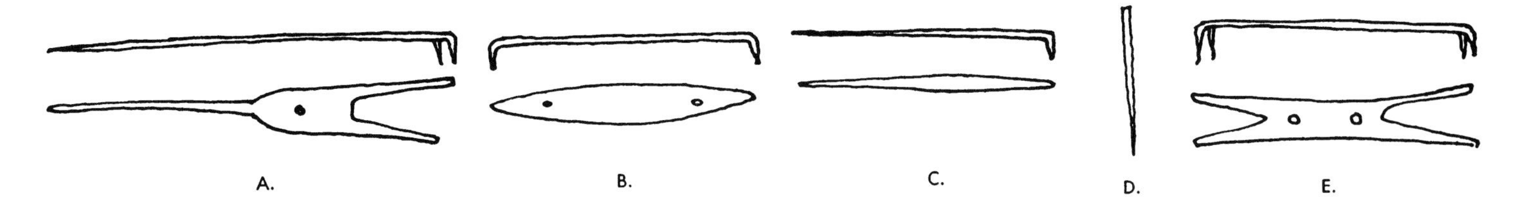

The square bow, rising steeply to a much higher elevation from the water than is usual, is reinforced by two, three, and sometimes as many as five parallel fore and aft strengthening pieces, known as *lung-ku* (龍 骨), or dragon's ribs.[3] Additional thickness and strength is also provided for along the bottom by the fitting of an apron, or doubling-planks, from a point 29 feet from the bow back as far as the coffer-dam.[4] This double skin [5] enables the vessel to withstand frequent contact with rocks, and invariably shows the scars of such impacts. Two grass-line pennants[6] are suspended from each bow for use in conjunction with a boat-hook to assist in snubbing-to.

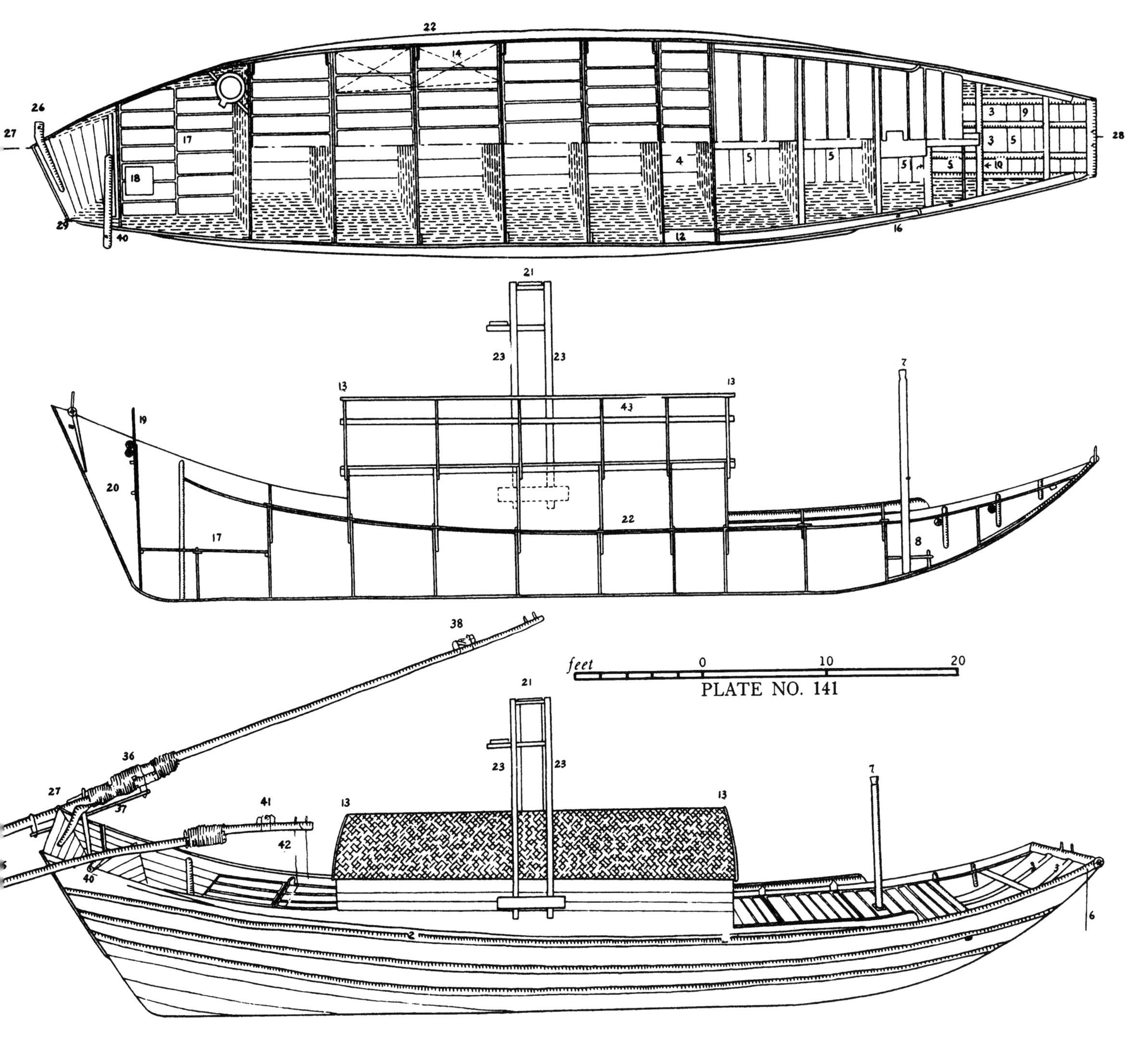

PLATE NO. 141

On the fore-deck is a tall, hardwood, removable timber [7] standing 8 feet above the deck. It is stepped in a shoe [8] at the bottom of the boat and bears against a bulkhead and half bulkhead. At deck-level it rests in a similar shoe. This contrivance has several uses. It can be used as a bollard, or to assist the trackers when the tracking-lines are made fast ashore. Its chief function, however, is as a Spanish windlass, or capstan, and in this it is astonishingly efficient when used to heave a rapid. When not in use it is stowed on the house deck-head beams.

The foremost compartment,[9] known as *chien-tzŭ* (尖 子), contrary to usual junk custom, is never decked-in. This departure from convention is in order to leave free the foremost towing-beam,[10] to which three bamboo tracking-lines are secured. The second compartment, *ch'ien-chia-chia* (前 夾 夾), is kept free from deck planks when the junk is proceeding, so as to expose a second towing-beam [11] which accommodates three more tracking-lines, so that six in all are available for use in a difficult rapid.

Seven compartments are given up to cargo and are dunnaged with split bamboos joined together. Limber holes, that is to say, apertures to permit the bilge water to flow freely to the coffer-dam, are cut through each bulkhead. On the starboard side of the coffer-dam a trough-scupper is fitted [12] in which is a large square wooden bailer obviously designed to deal with large quantities of water. This bailer usually lies in the water at the bottom of the compartment and swims aimlessly about with the roll of the vessel.

The deck-house [13] is larger and higher than in other types of junks, and contains two or four bunks,[14] and in some junks what may pass as a cabin. These primitive bunks consist merely of softwood uprights nailed to the deck-head beams, with a cross-piece at each extremity supporting rough and uneven planks. A log of wood roughly nailed into the ship's side acts as a shelf above the bunk. Sometimes these bunks are improvised out of bamboos.

The design of the matshed roof is not standard. It is sometimes made in one piece, often in two, and more rarely in several smaller portions. It always consists of two skins of bamboo matting with a layer of dried grass and another

The wai-p'i-ku, *or "crooked-stern" junk.*
REV. A. E. OWEN

of bamboo leaves between. When out of commission or banked-in at night the fore-deck is matted-in. For this purpose small mats are provided, and when not in use are stowed in piles on the fore and also on the after ends of the house. Sockets [16] in the bulwarks are provided, but the awning stanchions are nearly always improvised from stray spars or boat-hooks.

The whole of the after compartment [17] is given up to the galley. It contains a cooking-stove,[18] innumerable tubs, baskets containing food, and other utensils inseparable from Chinese cooking, littered in great profusion, and is always black from the smoke of the stove. Usually, even when under way, this compartment is covered with matting. A strongback from an upright [19] on the after bulkhead travels to the after end of the deck-house and rests on a deck-head beam. When this strongback is being used elsewhere or has been cut up for firewood, an oar, boat-hook, or any available pole or spar is used. The last, small, after compartment [20] is used for nothing at all and is the only part of the junk, or its equipment, which comes under this heading. Naturally, it is full of rubbish, and often has water in it.

In 1941, Mr. Worcester was commissioned by Sir Frederick Maze to supervise the building of a model of this junk for President Roosevelt. It was six feet in length, built to scale; correct in every detail, it included such items as clothing, bamboo hawsers, tracking gear, kitchen utensils, etc. The model left China in the USS *Houston*, flagship of the U. S. Asiatic Fleet, which took part in the operations against the Japanese in the Philippines and Netherlands East Indies. The model, however, was transferred to another U. S. ship before the *Houston* was sunk. It reached the White House two months before the President died and is now in the Franklin D. Roosevelt Museum, Hyde Park, New York.

A structure, which may best be described as a flying-bridge,[21] crosses the vessel amidships at some feet above the top of the house. This bridge is commonly 20 feet above the water and may be considerably more. It is almost invariably unbelievably rickety and unsafe. The uprights are often crudely fished, sometimes at most dangerous points, and the whole is saved from complete collapse by bamboo-rope lashings from each wing to the foot of the stanchion on the opposite side. Even under ideal conditions it sways gently. There are no facilities for reaching this conning position except outside the house along the cat's walk [22] (a term employed for want of a better) to the bridge uprights [23] or supports, and thence by swarming up the side rungs when such are fitted.

The stern is not the only thing that is crooked about the *wai-p'i-ku*. Bulkheads out of alignment are not uncommon. Planks running thereon are seldom parallel, and a great many junks have been noticed to possess slightly crooked bows. This may arise from a variety of reasons, such as faulty workmanship, or sagging, or even possibly be due not to accident but to design.

But, of course, the main characteristic of these craft, and that which has earned for them their name of "crooked-stern junks," is the distinctive distortion of the after part of the vessel. This section is full of interest, is exceedingly intricate, and raises innumerable questions for the inquirer.

A great many reasons have been advanced for this form of construction, mostly fallacious. It is said that the crooked stern permits the junk to negotiate the sharp right-handed bends in the river, but this argument, even if permissible, would hold good only for one direction. Another explanation claims that the peculiarity is due to the fact that a junk once fashioned by a master-builder suffered from warping timbers, and, so as not to cause him to "lose face," all builders subsequently copied his example.

Actually this peculiar construction follows a carefully thought out plan, which is probably the outcome of centuries of trial and error. Study of the plan on Page No. 512 makes the reason clear and demonstrates the efficiency of the novel method employed, for the necessary requirements could, it seems, be achieved in no other way.

The crooked-stern junk has no rudder and is steered by a gigantic stern-sweep.[24] The main purpose, therefore, of the twisted and uneven taffrail is to permit the use both of this stern-sweep and of a second, smaller, sweep [25] on the starboard quarter.

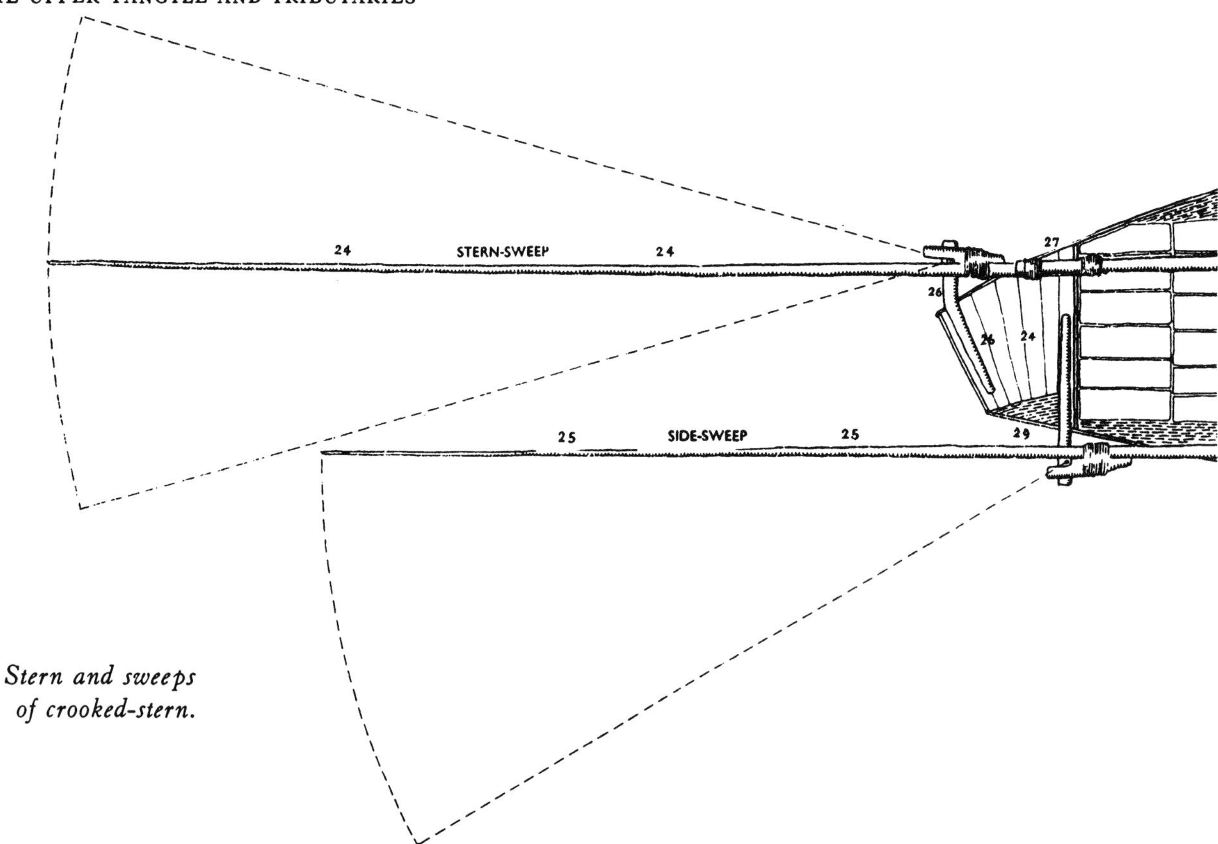

Stern and sweeps of crooked-stern.

Both sweeps, though working from different planes, have nearly the same radius of action, namely, 28 feet in the case of the large sweep and 36 feet in the smaller, and can be operated simultaneously if need be. Parallel as they are to each other and able to be used in a small compact area, there is nevertheless not the slightest danger of fouling, which would be so disastrous in a rapid.

The position of the large sweep,[24] more or less amidships, is nicely calculated to give the maximum amount of play in the minimum time, and finally the situation of a huge bumkin [26] on the tilted construction provides considerable additional strength and leverage for the large and heavy stern-sweep,[24] which may measure 90 feet and more. It seems rather a paradox to say that the stern yields extra strength, for the after portion of the junk is as weak in construction as the rest of the craft is sturdy; this nevertheless is the case.

As has been stressed, it is essential to have the stern-sweep running down the centre line of the junk so as to provide an equal control area for the blade on either side of the fore and aft line. The height and position of the bridge [21] and the length of the great sweep itself are accordingly subject to this necessity. In order to achieve this, the square taffrail of the stern is raised on the port side [27] so as to bring the bumkin [26] for the sweep, and its bearing-pin situated on the outer end, or corner, almost precisely into the centre fore and aft line [28] of the junk. The word "precisely" is used with intention, for even the breadth of the man on the bridge in control of the sweep is taken into consideration. The starboard corner of the taffrail is correspondingly depressed,[29] and this gives the impression that the after part of the junk has a heavy list to starboard.

There are a number of very strict conventions regarding the crooked sterns. As has been described in the building process, the planks on the high section of the stern run horizontally, while those below run vertically. A cross-piece,[30] probably a strengthening device, runs across the stern, but this never under any circumstances crosses at the point of junction,[31] as would naturally be supposed. Another odd custom is that the upper section [32] is never caulked. If the planks do not happen to fit, large gaps are left between them. For no apparent reason also, the Fowchow carpenters aim at achieving an extra twist, or wave, to the upper part of the stern.

There are two distinct types of crooked-stern junks, known as the *hou-pan* (厚 板), or thick plank, and the *huang-shan* (黃 鱔), or yellow eel, both of which are shown in the drawing below. The former type is always true to form, and there is, moreover, a very strict convention that two conspicuous vertical slats [33] should be affixed to the outer surface of the stern. The carpenters could give no reason for this peculiarity except that it was the custom. The yellow eel type is distinctive in that the high, or port, side of the stern is finished in a fourth wale,[34] or portion of a wale, which, after travelling a short distance, merges in the wale immediately below it.[35] This type varies considerably in the curve and extent of this wale—or yellow eel.

Types of crooked sterns.

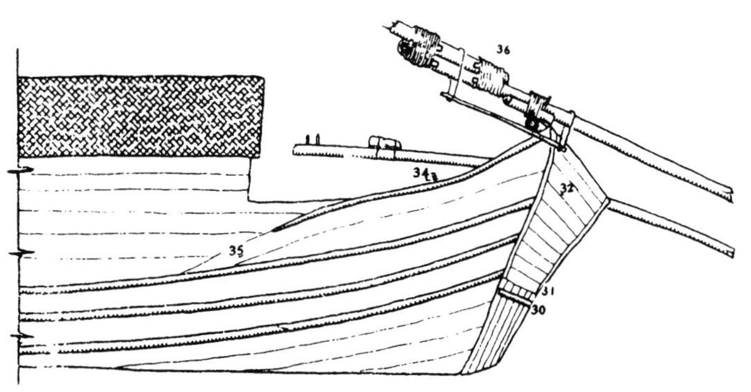

Yellow Eel (黃鱔屁股)

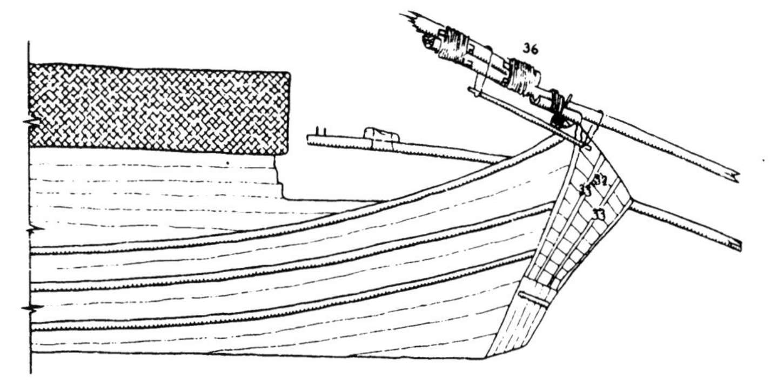

Thick Plank (厚板屁股)

The *hou-shao* (後 梢), or stern-sweep,[24] is made of two, and in the case of the larger ones, sometimes three, hardwood tree trunks, the overlapping ends being lashed together with bamboo rope [36] in the customary manner, but rendered taut and firm by the introduction of wedges of varying shapes and sizes, a wedge being driven in between the turns of the rope over the first and last turns of the lashing, which can be further tightened at will by more wedges. This very efficient device deserves to be better known. At the centre of gravity of the sweep is a cheek-piece with a slot 1½ feet deep cut in its projecting side, with which the bearing-pin on the heavy bumkin engages, and which, while allowing the maximum amount of play, holds the sweep firmly in position. The cheek-piece is secured with the usual wedge and rope lashings.

There seems to be no rule as to the size of this stern-sweep, which approximates in length to that of the junk itself, although it may be a few feet longer or shorter. The bumkin [26] on which it rests consists of a hardwood tree grown to shape, which projects outboard from the apex of the raised side of the taffrail, and as it is liable to get unshipped in a rapid, it is locked by means of a heavy wooden batten [37] fitting snugly to the under side of the bumkin. Heavy stones,[38] resting on a featherway, are lashed to the sweep so as to maintain the centre of gravity in the correct place. When used for the blade section of the sweep, a hole is bored through the stones, which are then suspended from a short strop.[39] Despite its enormous size and weight, the stern-sweep is balanced with such meticulous care and skill that it is surprisingly easy to handle, and is operated by one man, the laodah (老 大), literally the "old great one," who normally stands on the top rung of the flying-bridge [21] and preserves his precarious footing and balance by means of the sweep he holds. As the sweep is always head-heavy, he is easily able to elevate the blade about 1 foot out of the water by depressing the loom, although to achieve this he has to bend nearly double until the handle of the sweep is only a few inches above the bridge-deck.

The side-sweep, known as the *hsiao-shao* [25] (小 梢), is used to supplement the steering. Fashioned similarly of two or more tree trunks lashed and wedged in the same manner, this member is about half the length of the big stern-sweep.

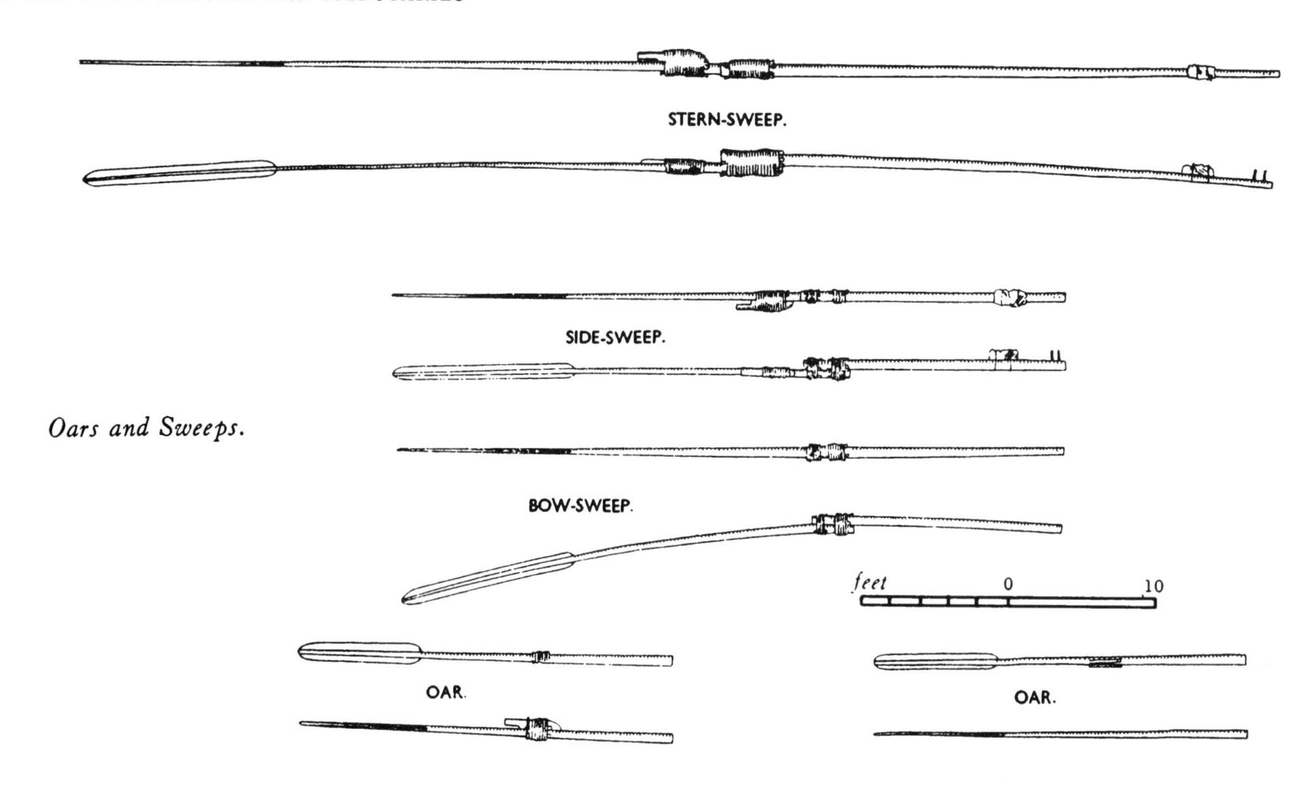

Oars and Sweeps.

It, too, is fitted with a large cheek-piece and, like the large sweep, rests on a heavy bumkin [40] composed of a section of a tree trunk. Large stones [41] are also used to correct the balance, which is very nicely adjusted to the control of one man alone. As the side-sweep is situated near the galley, the duty of tending it is assigned to the cook, who has also to attend to various ropes, which are sometimes run out from the stern and secured to one or other of the sweep-bumkins. A rope [42] rove through the bulwarks, where it terminates in a knot, runs from one side of the vessel to the other and is used to keep the sweep in the required position. These two sweeps, as may be imagined, when used in conjunction, afford a manœuvring power unequalled in any other type of junk.

When descending the river the junk relies upon the swift current to carry her down, but for occasional use, as for instance in quiet reaches or when moving short distances, the boat is propelled by two types of primitive oar, if such they can be called. These crude, heavy members are also formed of tree trunks with roughly fitted blades, and both types of oar are operated by eight men, who stand in two groups facing each other, four pushing and four pulling on the loom. The only difference in the two varieties of oar lies in their method of attachment. One type functions between two thole-pins and is protected at the fulcrum by a chafing-piece, while the other has a cheek-piece of the usual pattern, which engages against one thole-pin only. In addition to the two sweeps already mentioned, a bow-sweep is also used when descending the river to assist in keeping the bow heading in the right direction. True to Kungt'anho tradition, this is usually formed of two tree trunks lashed together, although it may sometimes be in one piece. The length seems to vary considerably. A bow-sweep with a downward bend is much in demand. It is seldom employed when bound up river except when it is desired to sheer out so as to clear outlying rocks, small headlands, and so forth, which the helmsman unaided would be unable to avoid, and also to assist in keeping the junk at the required distance from the bank.

The crew consists of the laodah, or junkmaster, already mentioned, who also acts as the pilot as well as being in control of the large sweep. Next in rank comes the bowman, called the *t'ai-kung* (太 公), who is in charge of the forecastle. He directs the men on the bow-sweep, and, when it is not in use, he stands on a beam on the fore part of the junk with a large boat-hook, indicating to the laodah the depth of water, which he frequently sounds with his pole. A good bowman is of the greatest importance. The next two men, named the *hsien-ch'üeh* (開 缺), translated freely as the man of all work, and the *pa-liang-chia-ti* (爬 樑 架 的), the man who has to climb or ascend, are, as their names imply, general helpers, as is the *shao-huo-ti* (燒 火 的), or cook.

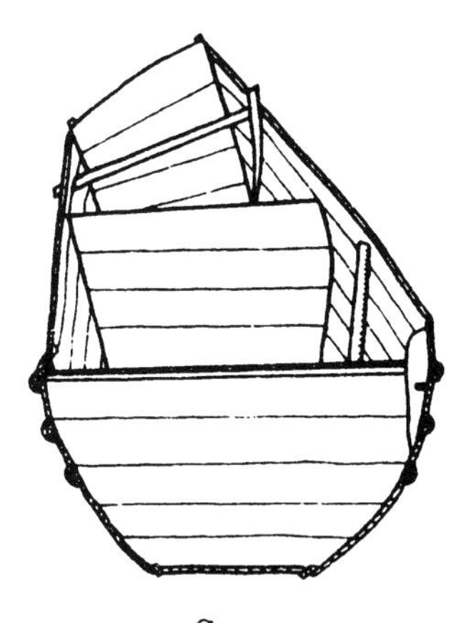

Stern.
(View from forward.)

The hired trackers live under the shelter of the main house and sleep on the deck below the coiled tracking-lines, which are slung round poles stowed on the beams [43] of the deck-house. About 10,000 feet of bamboo rope is stowed in this manner so that it can be readily run out to the shore or hauled in. Coiling and uncoiling the heavy bamboo rope—as thick as a man's wrist—requires great skill. This paying out and hauling in is an incessant duty, as the necessities of the route require the use of a longer or a shorter tracking-line.

With increasing age the junk takes on a number of strengthening beams, and very early in her career bow and stern lashings are adopted to give greater strength. Another very common "old-age" lashing is that between the two bumkins, a handspike being inserted between the strands so that additional tension may be secured when the rope ages and stretches.

Three kinds of rope are used, all made from bamboo. That used for mooring, instead of being plaited as usual, has the strands laid as in hemp rope. A lighter type of rope is used to lash the joins in sweeps and oars, and for the bow and stern "old-age lashings," as they might be termed.

The tracking-line, upon which so much depends, is eight-stranded and has a double heart. Sometimes six tracking-lines are used, three from each towing beam, but it is more usual to employ three tracking-lines from the foremost towing horse.

The crooked-stern junks when up-bound always move in convoys of seven or eight so that they can pool all their trackers at a particularly difficult rapid. As 16 trackers are engaged for each junk, if necessary, the junks do not move from convoy to convoy, but always remain associated with that which they originally joined. In this connexion it is interesting to note that the name *hou-pan*, or thick-plank junk, is the homonymic name for "wait for company."

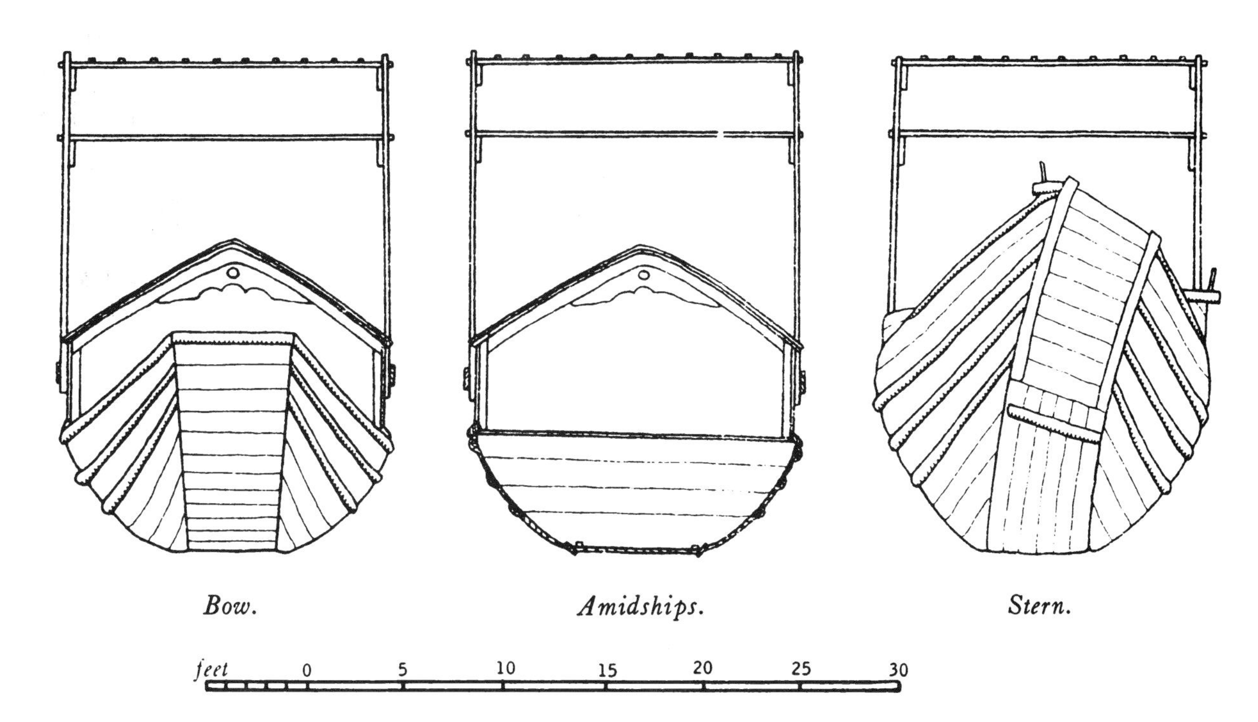

Bow. *Amidships.* *Stern.*

The diamond-shaped device is only used on the junk's stern, and means "fair winds escort you."

梯航南來定獲萬頃波金

樓船東下預卜一帆風順

Parallel sentences.

The junks take their turn in strict rotation for loading their cargo, of which there is no lack, though there is said to be a shortage of trained men and trackers. The Crooked-stern Junk Guild, which has its headquarters at Fowchow, estimates that there are only 250 of these craft functioning on the Kungt'anho. An 80-foot junk can be built by 20 carpenters in three weeks at a cost, in 1940, of $7,000.

The junkmen of the Kungt'anho are, like most old sailors, a superstitious folk, and therefore before each voyage a ceremony known as "Killing the Cock (殺雞)" is always performed by the carpenter who built the boat. The bow and parts of the house are sprinkled with blood, and while it is wet a few feathers are left adhering to the woodwork.

Although few of the Kungt'anho junkmen can read, they make a point of adorning their craft with *tui-tzŭ* (對子), or parallel sentences. Seldom is a junk to be found on this river that has not at least one pair of these sentences displayed on the fore part of the house. A *tui-tzŭ*, or couplet, as it might be termed, has the same number of characters in each half, each character belonging more or less to the same class of word as its opposite number, with either a similar, complementary, or entirely opposite meaning. Thus:

1.	樓 Upper story.	1.	梯 Staircase.
2.	船 Ship.	2.	航 Boat.
3.	東 East.	3.	南 South.
4.	下 Go.	4.	來 Come.
5.	預 } Foretells.	5.	定 } Promises.
6.	卜 }	6.	獲 }
7.	一 One—implying the whole.	7.	萬 10,000—implying all *or* the whole.
8.	帆 Sail.	8.	頃 100 acres—implying wealth.
9.	風 Wind.	9.	波 Wave.
10.	順 Favourable.	10.	金 Gold.

A free translation of this would be:

"Southward as the good ship moves,
Boundless wealth her coming hails;
If the course be eastward set,
Favo'ring winds shall fill her sails."

To compose an original couplet requires considerable literary ability. The many varieties to be found on the junks of the Kungt'anho are more or less stereotyped. They are always written on red paper, which is reserved for happy occasions. In the above couplet considerable poetic licence has been taken, for at no time can the junk travel east on the Kungt'anho, and very seldom south.

The laodahs, their crews, and the trackers, descended from generations of such junkmen, are tough, hardy, efficient, and courageous, as befits men who have to brave the perils of this dangerous river and struggle at such odds with rocks, races, and rapids.

The Fowchow carpenters are not noted for their symmetrical or finished craftsmanship, but, crude as it is, there is a great appeal in their direct, if slipshod, workmanship, a charm which grows and is difficult to describe unless under the heading of "utilitarian." The only tools they know are the axe and an ancient type of auger. Few understand the use of the saw and still fewer the plane, and yet, despite their primitive instruments, it is an astonishing fact that these simple, unlettered folk should for generations have been able to pass on the tradition of building these curious craft which are so admirably designed and adapted to withstand the formidable torrents of the Kungt'anho.

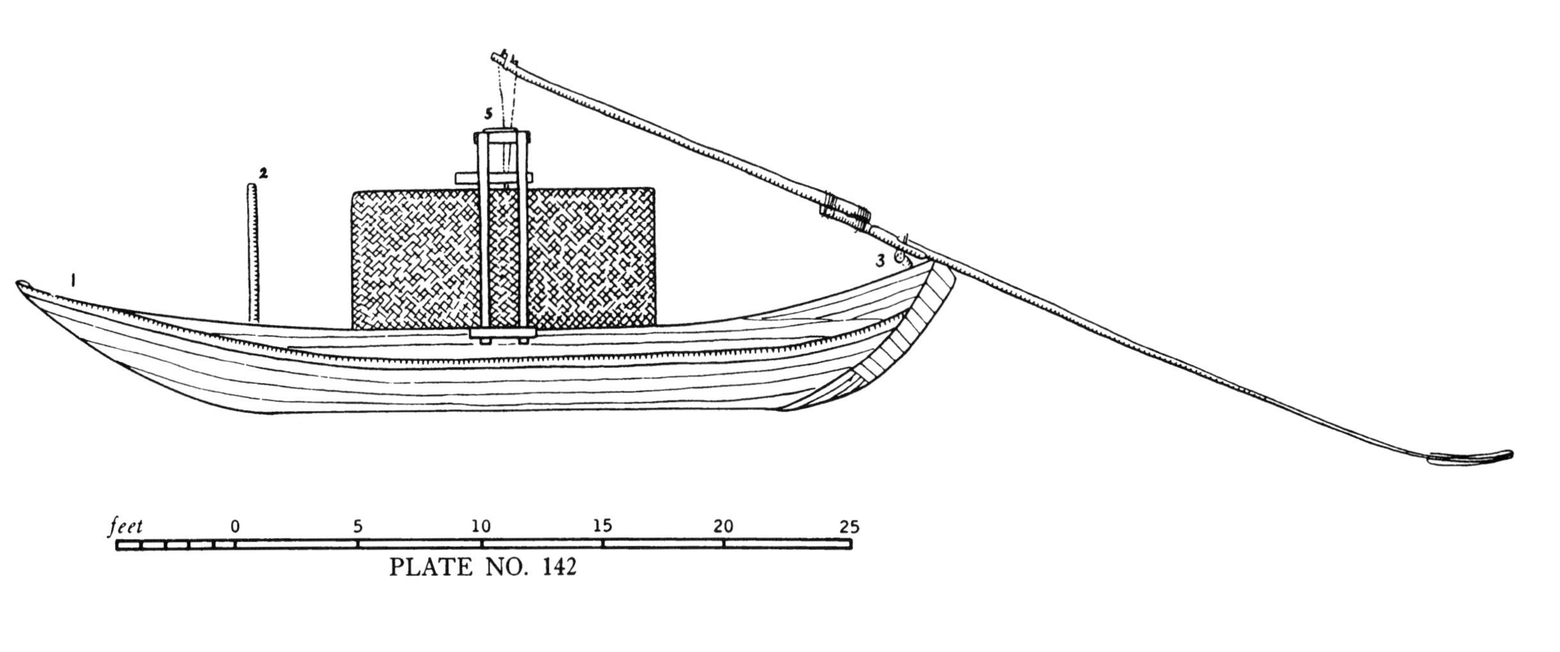

PLATE NO. 142

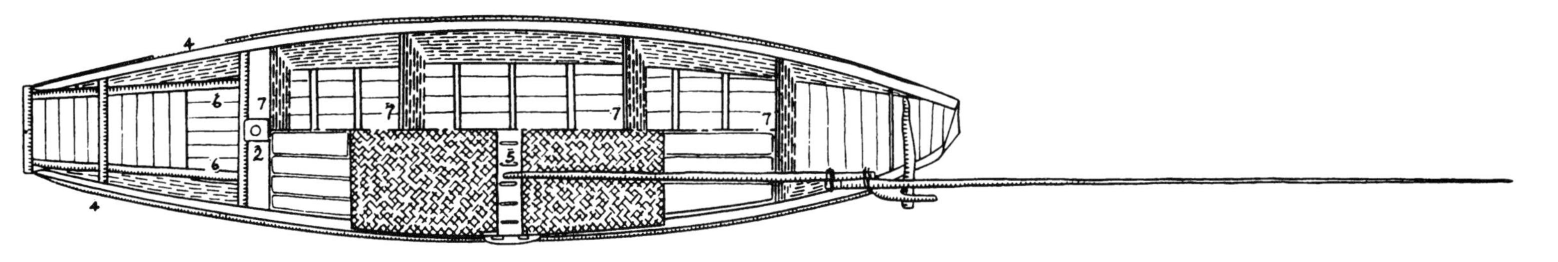

THE SMALL CROOKED-STERN JUNK

This type of junk is about one-third of the length of the heavy salt junks just described, and is quite as rickety and ill-found as its prototype.

It conforms with all the principles of the larger junk except that it has no built-up wooden house and no bow and side sweeps. It is difficult to believe that these comparatively frail craft are capable of navigating so dangerous a river. They are credited with being able to reach Kungt'an, and if so, it may safely be assumed that they can do so only when the river is at its best. The high bow[1] and large towing bollard[2] suggest work in difficult rapids, as does the enormous stern-sweep which rests on the usual bumkin.[3]

As previously stated, the boats have no bow-sweep but are fitted with thole pins to take two oars.[4] The men operating these actually stand on the inch-wide gunwale of the boat, a miracle of equilibrium only surpassed by the laodah, who stands on the insecure and swaying bridge[5] of narrow planks 7 feet above the water and controls the sweep.

This sweep, which measures 44 feet, or 6 feet longer than the junk itself, is beautifully balanced, but even so it requires much practice and considerable skill and agility to operate it. The laodah stands amidship, but, as is noticeable in the plan, the sweep is not in the centre line of the junk.

In construction these craft closely resemble the larger junks, albeit in miniature. The fore and aft parallel strengthening pieces on the bow,[6] the number of bulkheads,[7] the crooked stern, and the flying bridge[5] differ not at all.

These boats never carry salt, but are the general cargo carriers of the Kungt'anho.

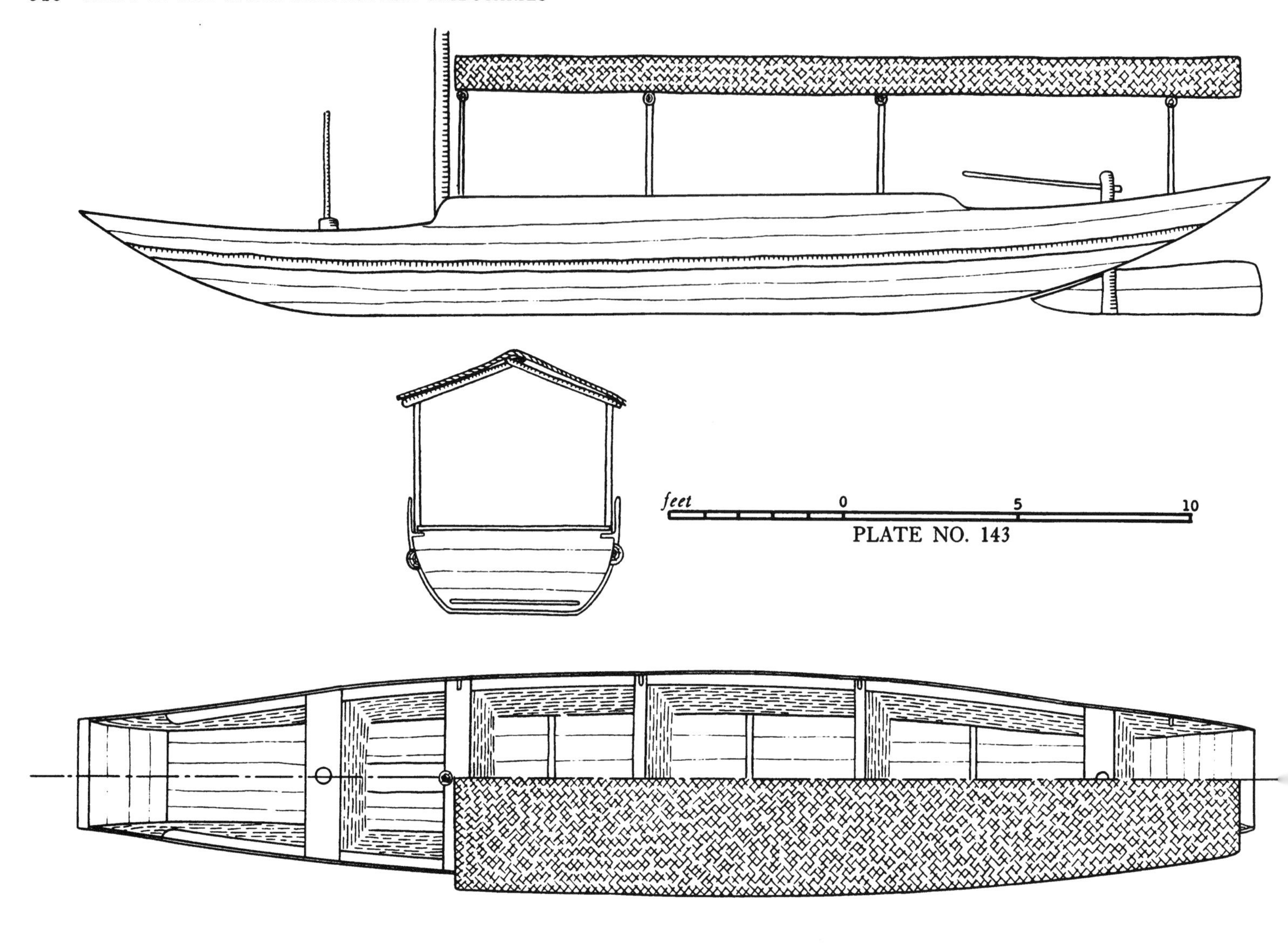

PLATE NO. 143

涪州過

THE FOWCHOW FERRY-BOAT

Although the Fowchow ferry-boat should not perhaps, strictly speaking, be included as a denizen of the Kungt'anho, yet it is often to be seen crossing this tributary, is always built at Fowchow, and regards that town as its headquarters.

Made of *pai-mu* and measuring 34 feet by 6½ feet, it is constructed on the same sort of general lines as the Chungking sampan, only with a permanent mat roof supported by stanchions, on which luggage of all sorts is stowed out of the way. The maximum load consists of 40 passengers with their gear, and the crew numbering five men.

Propulsion is by oars, tracking, or under sail according to the exigencies of the moment. It carries passengers as far up river as Litu (李 渡), 6 miles above Fowchow, and to all the small towns and villages for 28 miles down the Yangtze.

The boat has nothing remarkable about it except that its lower terminal port is Fengtu, the Abundant Capital and headquarters of the Emperor of the *Yin* (陰), or Dead, or King of Hades, where in the temple the skeleton of Pluto's bride, whom he is said to have abducted on her wedding day, is to be seen sitting beside him in her robes of state. Here, too, for the modest sum of $1 a passport to Heaven may be obtained. It consists of a large and impressive sheet of thin paper covered with characters. It is signed by the Chief Priest and the local Governor, and bears the seal of the King of Hades and the imprint of the seven stars of the Great Bear Constellation.

More about the Emperor of the *Yin* and his bride on page 522.

See Part One, page 127 for the contents of the passport to Heaven.

THE SHÊ-CH'UAN 蛇船

The *shê-ch'uan*, or snake boat, operates for the most part on the lower reaches of the Kungt'anho. There is perhaps some slight resemblance to a snake in the appearance of its bow, but none respecting its progress, which appears unhandy and clumsy in the extreme. For all this, however, they have the name of being the speed boats *par excellence* of the Kungt'anho.

This type, which is essentially a passenger carrier, is built of *pai-mu*, or *hung-ch'un*, a wood found extensively on the Kungt'anho. Propulsion is by oars, two being in the bow [1] and one aft [2] in rear of the laodah, who controls the long 31-foot sweep from a slightly raised platform.[3] Tracking by 12 men is, however, the more usual means of ascending the river. The boats are surprisingly uniform, a feature of all the craft on this river, and usually measure 45 feet, with a beam of 6½ feet. In construction this type is unique in that it has no bulkheads of any sort, and only five frames.[4] It is strengthened longitudinally by three fore and aft planks [5] running from the tall, towing bollard [6] to the after thwart.[7] These are arranged with a slight lift to the centre, giving the bottom a concave formation.[8]

These boats are never built at Fowchow, although this is a great building centre, but are said to be built at Kungt'an and Pengshui (彭 水). It is difficult to believe that they can stand up to the dangerous rapids of these portions of the river, unless they only once make the initial downward trip to Yangkiohtsi (羊 角 磧), a town just below the first difficult rapid, from which town they maintain a passenger service with Fowchow.

The high rising bow is typical of craft on this river, and secured thereto is a small plank,[9] through which a line and toggle is fitted.[10] This is used in conjunction with the boat-hook to round-to in an emergency, the pole being forced into the river bottom and the line secured to it by two or three turns. The operator stands on a specially constructed platform.[11]

The boats carry a crew of five men, and, when no passengers are embarked, convey general cargo, such as tobacco, rice, wine, and sugar.

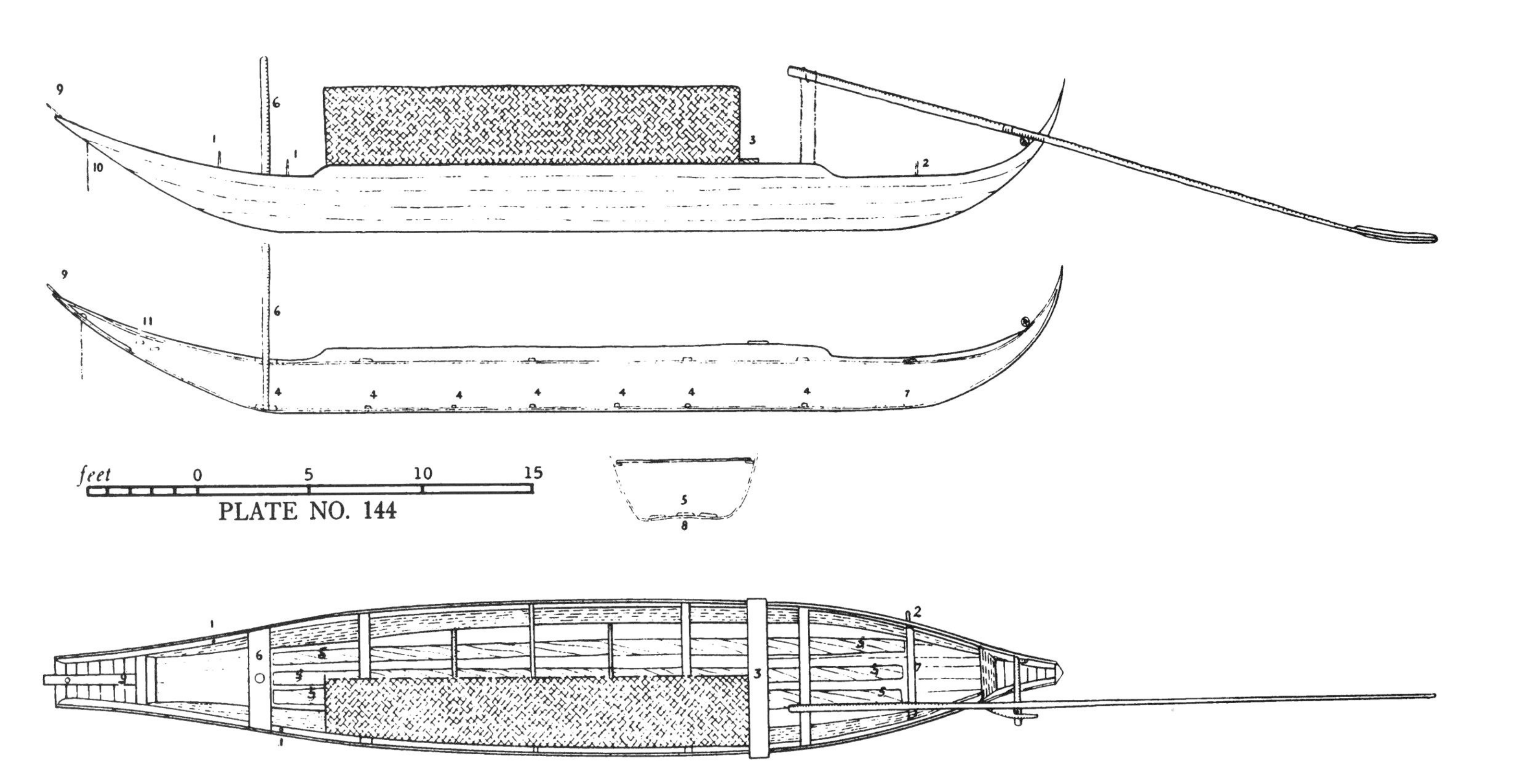

PLATE NO. 144

WANHSIEN TO CHUNGKING

THE trend of the river after leaving Wanhsien is south-south-west for about four miles. It is edged with 100-foot-high wooded cliffs. The country then becomes more open; and, after rounding a shingle bank, one of the few remaining rapids of any consequence is reached. This is the Hu T'an or Fu T'an, the Tiger or, as some translate it, Fox Rapid. It is situated at the bend at Paishuchi and owes its existence to massive sandstone reefs projecting from the left bank and two boulder points opposite. The heaps of detritus that lie on the bank here look like ruined masonry, and the pot holes of the gorges are to be seen again. The approach to the Fu T'an is marked by a signal station, and immediately above it a small affluent runs into the Yangtze under a picturesque bridge. During the low water season the river streams calmly down the Fu T'an, giving no indication of the boiling race that appears in the summer in this short, but violent, rapid.

The river now opens out considerably and assumes a softer aspect. Red sandstone hills, well cultivated, lie on the right bank. The left bank retains a more austere and rocky outline, and a few cliff dwellings may be seen in high and inaccessible spots below a wall of cliff. The temples, too, are hollowed out of the cliff or in some way utilize the material of the hillside on which they may be situated. In the case of a temple the door is high on a cliff 60 or 70 feet up a vertical ladder over the rock face.

Great shingle banks extend from either bank and, in midstream, the patient gold washer is busy again with his primitive "cradle." One shingle flat, off the right bank, has the curious name of Niupaochi or Knotted Parcel Beach. Other characteristic names are Ta Sin Chang, Great Prosperous Fields; Shuangyützu, a rocky plateau, the name meaning Sons of the Two Fish; Wu Lin Chi, Beach of the Five Forests; and Laokuanchi, Beach of the Old Heron. The size of the stones in the shingle banks is dependent on the current. When uninfluenced by side streams, they are a flattish oval in shape and about a foot or less in length. There is always a proportion of sand and fine mud. The foundation of the bank itself is nearly always a reef or rocky ledge which has led to the shingle bank formation thereon. Debris from landslides is constantly to be seen in this neighbourhood.

Four miles above Wu Lin Chi is a line of cliffs along the left bank about 30 feet high known as Shihku Hsia, or Stone Drum Gorge.

After a rambling course and a westward turn of the river, a remarkable rock formation appears on the left bank, 22 miles above the Fu T'an. This is the rock temple and pagoda of Shih pao chi, or Precious Stone Castle, sometimes translated as the House of the Precious Stone.

It consists of a yellowish detached mass of rock of irregular rectangular shape about 65 feet in height which is itself set upon a 200-foot platform of rock, the whole towering some 300 feet above the village at the river's edge. A nine-storied pagoda, claimed to be 1,500 years old, is built up against the east side of the cliff and encloses a staircase which leads up to the temple and monastery buildings on the summit; this measures about 50 by 30 yards across. Beyond these buildings lies a small city of refuge reached by a bridge.

The Precious Stone Castle.

One of the shrines was originally erected to the memory of a famous Amazon of the Ming Dynasty days. Ch'ing Liang Yu was the wife of a general of Shih Chu under the Emperor Chung Chang, 1573–1620. On his death during a campaign, she took over the leadership of his troops. She fought so valiantly against the rebel Chang Hsien Chung that through her efforts he was defeated, and many towns were saved from his depredations, including Wanhsien, Fêngtu and Fu Ling. The Emperor, no doubt banking on her femininity, rewarded her only, legend says, with embroidered robes and by writing verses in her praise.

But the most famous legend connected with the Precious Stone Castle is that of the Miraculous Supply of Rice. The scene was laid in the top story of the monastery.

Authorities differ as to the details; but it would appear that if a priest put a handful of rice into a hole in the floor, all of the inmates of the monastery were able to take out as much as they could eat, irrespective of the number of the holy men who partook of it.

The rest of the story is soon told. In the time of Chia Ch'ing, 1796–1821, a wicked and avaricious monk was appointed to the temple. Some say that he sold the heaven-sent food, others that he enlarged the hole so as to increase the dole. Whichever his crime the result was the same, for the offended deities immediately stopped the supply. The truth of the story is proved to the satisfaction of the local people by the fact that, although the hole remains, there is a complete lack of any supply of rice therefrom.

Just above this spot there is said to be a place where for many years no efforts of the industrious Chinese had availed to produce rice, but on the cessation of the miracle in the monastery just mentioned the gods compensated the country by fructifying this unfertile spot, since when rice has always been produced there.

An 18-mile stretch of the river, now more tortuous and beset with small rapids and a few islands, follows with here and there a hazard such as the reef Yenchiutzŭ, Mist of the Little Hills, extending from the left bank; another Cat Rock; and then Pochitzŭ, Chaff from the Winnower's Fan: a maze of reefs with a rock lying in midstream. Another corner, Chu Wei Tzŭ, has the significant meaning of Broken Mast Place. The Bay of Lanniwan, or Overflowing Mud, now takes a great curve and from heading due east loops round to the west, the river being here at one point over a mile wide at summer level; and finally, round a bend, Chungchou, or Faithful District, comes into sight, a large shingle bank and a reef dividing the river into two channels just opposite. This walled town, set on a sandstone cliff 100 feet above the river and with a circle of hills covered with bamboos and other trees, is situated on the left bank 222 miles above Ichang. The walls, as so often happens, ramble away from the town and enclose a large area of open ground. The temples and a pagoda add to its interest and opposite, two pagodas, one conspicuously white, and a red temple add to the charm of the scene.

The river now winds for about 16 miles through rich country to the unromantically named village of Yangtuchi, or Sheep's Stomach, from where on for about 20 miles the course is more or less directly south-south-west to Fêngtu. A race called Huhsutzŭ or Fuhsŭtzŭ, Thing with the Tiger's Whiskers, is produced by a pile of boulders projecting from the left bank to meet a rocky shelf from the opposite side, leaving only a narrow pass; and one and a half miles further on is Lanchupa, or Bamboo Basket Island. At low water the current is noticeably less strong than it is a few feet below, dropping to almost nothing at the river bed. During high water, however, there is so much disturbance that the whole river is on the move.

Steep hills on the left bank and sloping fields on the other lead up to Fêngtu, or Affluent City, on the left bank. The site of this city is much lower than most Upper Yangtze river-side towns, and the error of so building was demonstrated in 1870, when a great flood washed the whole city away. A grand new city named Sin Chang was built on a neighbouring bluff for the people by their magistrate. But in spite of its cost and attractions, the people refused to leave their old site. The reasons given were varied. Some objected to have to carry water up 200 feet from the river; others claimed the new site was haunted.

North of the city is T'ien-tzŭ shan, the Son of Heaven Mountain, an isolated mound rising about 500 feet above the river and joined to the city by a bridge. It is thickly wooded with many varieties of trees: poplars, cedars, palms, bananas, bamboo, and the strange and beautiful "false banyan" tree, which twines its tortuous roots fantastically about the rocks and surface of the ground. This hill is surmounted by ancient temples, and there are stone tablets lining the broad sandstone pathway leading up to it which are said to be over 1,000 years old.

The most noticeable of these temples is that to the chief local celestial dignitary, Yen Lo Wang, King of Hades, or Emperor of the *Yin*, or the Dead.* By his side sits the skeleton of his wife, richly dressed and masked.

The legend of this sinister bride begins with her journey down from Chungking to worship at his shrine. While at her devotions she lost a pearl and gold earring and despite prolonged search had to leave the mountain without it. The priest then discovered the missing jewel in the hand of the god, who seems to have been a connoisseur of feminine charms. The girl's parents were duly informed of this indication that she had been selected for the high but barren honour of being a spiritual bride to Yen Lo Wang. To accomplish her destiny she was to die, and as the date fixed drew near, preparations were made for her wedding. Gradually she seemed to fail in health until, after a nerve-shattering storm, it was found she had vanished. Her dead body was later found in the temple at Fêngtu.

Her awed parents brought richly embroidered garments for the "Spiritualized Flesh" and gilded her face so as to preserve it. The descendants of the family

* At a Chinese death, the Taoist priest writes a letter to the King of Hades, addressed to Fêngtu, and dispatches it through the terrestial post by burning it to ashes.

of Chen in commemoration of this macabre occurrence bring their ancestress offerings every year consisting of a silk robe, bundles of incense sticks, and so enormous a wax candle that "two men are needed to carry it."

The myth that Fêngtu is on or near the site of the entrance to Hell probably owes its origin to the presence of large caverns which penetrate some miles into the heart of the mountain. Another contributing factor to this belief is the report of "fire wells" nearby, that is to say, of escapes of natural gas which when ignited will burn continually.

In accordance with the tolerant Chinese custom various shrines, both Buddhist and Taoist, have been raised to other deities. The ever popular Kuan Yin, Goddess of Mercy, is here represented with 1,000 heads and eyes. The temple is topped with a pavilion containing images of two Taoist worthies who lived 2,000 years ago in the days of the Han Dynasty; these are Wang Fan Pin and Yin Chang Sên playing their favourite game of chess. There is a piquant legend of how a boy who stopped to watch them was so enthralled that he lost all sense of time, a process which was, one feels, rather unkindly hastened by the gift of a magic datestone made for him by one of the players. When the boy finally bethought himself and went home, it was to find that he had outlived his generation; there were none left who knew him. He accordingly returned to the site of the game of chess, which had lasted so much longer than even modern international chess contests, and spent the rest of his days as a famous recluse.

Two miles above Fêngtu the left bank opens out into a bay called Peishato. Above this a head of Buddha and three Chinese characters are so carved on a spur of the rock as to face westwards. The characters signify Ta Fu Mien, or Buddha Face Reef, and there is a high, level rapid of the same name. This and a rapid just beyond are caused by two big reefs extending the one above the other from the left bank, while another reef and a bluff on the opposite side narrow the fairway down to less than a cable's width. With an increase in water the violence of these rapids with a speed of ten knots and waves six feet deep becomes dangerous, particularly as the actual Fu Mien T'an rapid sets obliquely on the Buddha Face Reef.

It is said that when the water rises over its mouth the Buddha can see, but can no longer voice a warning, and that, when the river rises still further so as to cover his head, he can neither see nor warn the junkmen, who must proceed at their own risk. There is no junkman of the old school who does not believe that it is the reappearance of the Buddha which again stills the rapid.

The second rapid immediately above the Fu Mien T'an is the Kuan Yin T'an, or Goddess of Mercy Rapid, which also exists only at high water, when it is dangerous enough to justify the junkmen's prayers to that most gentle and attractive of all the Chinese heavenly hierarchy.

When the Buddha's face is quite submerged together with the extremity of the Kuan Yin Reef, the volume of the flooded river pent into a narrow channel is such that the upward slope of the gradient of the water surface is most marked; high-powered engines only can negotiate the passage.

For the next 26 miles the river curves through a wider valley, past rocks and villages, hills and ravines, until a tall white pagoda on a hill is seen, mounting guard over the nearby town. This is Fowchow situated on the right bank, where the Kung T'an Ho, a clear green-blue water stream 250 to 300 yards wide at the mouth, flows in from the south to join the muddy waters of the Yangtze.

The river now soon broadens very considerably by Shanto Bay and then suddenly narrows into a rocky defile only 200 yards wide called Huang tsao hsia, or

Yellow Flower Gorge, with sheer banks 1,000 feet high. In this reach may be seen lime kilns, coal mines and a 7-storied pagoda which, as usual, mounts distant guard over a town. This is the little walled city of Ch'angshou, hidden almost out of sight on the left bank high on a hill with a riverside suburb at its feet at the mouth of a ravine. The stream running through the ravine has a fine stone bridge across it. The chief industry is the making of flexible bamboo matting for packing purposes.

There is a legend connecting the town and the stream in the ravine, which is called Mo yu chi. The town is named after a feudal warlord who ruled it for over a century. He had a very marriagable daughter, but in spite of many offers her proud father would not accept any of her suitors as a fit son-in-law. In the course of time it became obvious that all was not well with the girl who seemed ill and showed signs of distress. After a time she confessed she had a constant midnight visitor in the shape of a fairy named Mo Yu. The irate father made a prolonged and fruitless search for any man of that name. Finally the mother after many visits to the temples came to the conclusion that the disturber of their household was the Yin Mo Yu who lived in a remarkable rock in the ravine. Determined to break the spell or the jinn, the father hired stone masons, who split the rock down with hammer and chisel, whereupon blood poured out, and presumably all that remains of the unfortunate Mo Yu is a memory and the stream that now bears his name. The girl's reactions to this drastic punishment of her midnight lover are not recorded.

On leaving Ch'angshou the river bends to the south-west past the hilly banks for 20 miles to Mu Tung and from thence 20 more, winding in a westerly direction to Chungking.

Junks approaching a rapid.

About a mile above Ch'angshou a single island named Shashih separates the river into two arms. The low-water channel between the island and the left bank is called Tai pan tzŭ. It is both narrow and twisted, and there is an awkward corner to be negotiated between the shoal water off the upper end of the island and the reefs extending from the left bank. A very short distance beyond is a large rock called Yang tsan tui, with a watermark painted on its side, standing in midstream. Another island, one and one-quarter miles long, Nan ping pa, is passed, as well as a fair-sized tributary, the Ta hung kiang, said to be navigable for 60 miles by small craft; and the trading centre of Mu Tung is reached, which derives its importance from its situation not only as a port on the great river, but as a stage on the main road between Chungking and Fuchou.

More islands are passed; a particularly large one is Kuangyüanpa, two and a half miles long and three-quarters of a mile broad at high water. It is joined to the right bank at low level by reefs and shingle flats. The rest of the journey up to Chungking has little of outstanding interest except for the varying panorama of mountainous scenery and occasional islands or isolated rocks in the stream.

There is a story told of one part of the river here where it opens out into a bay in which it was said a malevolent dragon lived whose usual practice it was, when hungry, to lash the water into a whirlpool with his tail and then feed off the inevitable wrecked junk and men. The junkmen instituted a search for some public-spirited man who would rid them of this menace. Finally one named Wang came down from Peking and brought with him the body of his son and buried it on the hill that stood above the bay. This proved a master stroke in the obscure art of *fêng-shui*, for the disgruntled dragon departed almost immediately in the midst of noise and flame and a thunderstorm.

A few miles below Chungking the river closes in again to a width of only 250 yards and runs for a mile or more through a defile known as T'unglohsia, or Brass Gong Gorge. The hills on either side rise in tiers from 800 feet to nearly double that height, and the cedars and bamboos add to the attraction of the scene. At its upper end is a bay with the village of Tangchiato on the north-west bank.

Eight or nine miles on, round a horseshoe bend past the village of Tsuntan and a three-arched bridge over a stream, and Ta jossŭ is reached, a temple in a walled garden set about with trees. The striking gateway shows a figure riding on an elephant and two large guardian spirits of red plaster.

In an open pavilion, facing the river, and up a flight of steps, is an enormous gilded Buddha, often locally alluded to by the foreigners as the Harbour Master. It was formerly the custom for junks to anchor here while the laodah went ashore to pay his respects and offer thanks for the blessings of a safe voyage.

From here Chungking can be seen and below it on the left bank its suburb of Kiang pei, or North of the River, situated at the junction of the Yangtze and one of its largest tributaries, the Kialing.

This river is 130 yards wide at its mouth and enters the Yangtze with a slow current; and its comparatively clear waters may be plainly distinguished running down stream beside the Yangtze until they finally merge and are lost in the yellow flood. This important affluent, known also as the Little River, is fed by two tributaries, the Sui Ning, which enters it at or near Hochow, and the Sui Ting Ho, 52 miles from its mouth. The Kialing itself rises in the high mountain ranges in Southern Kansu and, passing through Shensi, enters northern Szechwan; together with its affluents, it waters and provides means of communication for a large area which yields an immense amount of produce, agricultural and mineral, yet which, like the whole province, has as yet unfolded only a small proportion of its potential wealth.

The Gate of Peace, Chungking, 1940.

As the catchment basins of the Yangtze and Kialing are so widely separated, their water levels rise and fall independently of each other. When the Kialing is in flood due to a freshet or any other cause, it occasionally runs out so strongly as to act as a temporary dam and check the Yangtze's downward flow. This causes a race at the watersmeet and sometimes extends right across the Yangtze, which here, at Chungking, is about 800 yards wide.

Chungking, 750 feet above sea level and 1,400 miles from the sea, stands, a grey, close-huddled city sprawling over two hills which rise about 300 feet sheer from the water, at the point of a rugged peninsula which runs like a tongue down between the two rivers. Despite the red sandstone nature of the rocky promontory, it presents the same uniform grey aspect as the buildings upon it, an aspect largely due to the atmospheric effect of constant mists and cloudy, lowering skies as much as to the nondescript walls and slate roofs of the houses.

The origin of Chungking is as indeterminate as that of any of the older Chinese cities. It has certainly stood on that site for a period computed by the Chinese historians to be about 4,000 years, and therefore it is older than Rome. The earliest classical references link it up to the semi-legendary Hsia Dynasty, 2,200 B.C. In 375 B.C. it was incorporated in the Kingdom of Pa, the capital being situated about 30 miles away.

Soon after this it must have gained in importance and been recognized as a town, under the name of Chiangchow, or River Prefecture, for the first wall was built around it. The town has had a change of name 13 times, six of them making use of the word Pa. The name of Pahsien, which is still sometimes used as an alternative title, was adopted in the 5th or 6th century, while the present name of Chungking, or Repeated Good Luck, dates back to 1188 in the Southern Sung Dynasty.

Of the several city gates which lead down to the river's edge by long broad flights of steps worn by the passage of countless feet, the chief is the T'ai P'ing Mên, or Gate of Peace. Two hundred and forty steps fully twenty feet broad lead up past the Post Office and Custom House to the main street. The results of bombing and street planning have served to clear and widen this flight of steps, but it is still closely bordered by houses which seemed to stand on one another's roof as they climb the long flight of steps to the city.

These streets of steps, filthy to start with and continually wet from the drippings from the water carriers, were then, as now, thronged with teeming life. Something or other is always being carried up or down, buying and selling goes on in the open-fronted shops which are little more than stalls, and the inhabitants live out their meagre lives within sight and sound of the street, where most of their toilet and the daily routine of their lives is carried on in the public eye with an almost complete lack of privacy. In the light of this fact the modest bearing and, in the main, neat and clean appearance of the Chinese women with small means of existence is most praiseworthy. Slatterns, of course, are to be seen, as in all countries; but, considering that it costs money to be clean and tidy, an amazing proportion of these people who live on the edge of starvation are neat and approximately clean with hair well-oiled and smoothed with the old-fashioned intricate coils or kept short and trim in the new fashion. Any small wave of prosperity will result in a crop of the heavy black curls produced by an incredibly cheap permanent wave.

Outside the walls and overlooking the river, haphazard dwellings cling to the cliff sides of the promontory, precariously supported one above the other and at all levels, on stilts of varying length and uneven distribution, and approached by crazy stairways. These houses on piles are as notable a feature of Chungking as the winding streets of steps.

Below the steps of the various gates the falling water level of autumn and winter discloses an extensive foreshore, sometimes of rock but mostly of shelving mud. Here on both banks of the river flimsy matshed houses spring up, until quite a village forms with streets and shops, yet with rising water the little town is pulled down in an unbelievably short time, and the whole community migrates to a higher level.

A relic of old feudal times found everywhere in Szechwan is the white turban, or bandeau, which is more in the nature of a scarf or kerchief, which the inhabitants, especially the junkmen, wear tied round their heads. This is in perpetual memory of and mourning for that favourite of all Chinese heroes of the period of the Three Kingdoms, Chu Ko Liang. He it was who, 17 centuries ago, by his skill and cunning set Liu Pei on the throne of Shu, as the Kingdom of Szechwan was then called, and advised and aided Liu Pei in his endless struggle against his enemies.

The difficulties and dangers on the Yangtze between Chungking and Ichang, particularly in that formidable stretch known as the Gorges, necessitated the building of special types of junks which do not normally operate above Chungking. It cannot be said that there are any particular types of craft designed for the upper reaches of the main river above Chungking, where there are no very dangerous rapids, and these waters are navigated by all the various types of junks belonging to the tributaries which join the Yangtze above Chungking. There are in all some 1,400 odd miles of Szechwan affluents of the Yangtze which are navigable for junks.

紅船或救生船

THE HUNG-CH'UAN OR LIFE-BOAT

Perhaps one of the most interesting types of craft was that comparatively modern invention the red boat. Interesting, not on account of its design, which was simple, but for its purpose, which was humane, for it was a life-boat. All must regret the passing of this great service, which has been instrumental in saving so many lives.

In 1854 a prosperous merchant named Li Yung-kuei (李榮貴), who lived near the dreaded Hsint'an, conceived the idea of collecting subscriptions from the traders whose junks had to face this danger. With this money he built three life-saving craft. To distinguish them they were painted red, from which their general name of red boats, *hung-ch'uan*, originated, though these particular ones were known as *kan-ssŭ-tang* (敢死黨)—the "dare to die" service.

Some years later the great statesman, Li Hung-chang (李鴻章), on his return down river from a mission to Szechwan, was so impressed with the splendid work done by these boats that he took the merchant, his namesake, Li, down to Ichang with him and there obtained for him additional subscriptions from the likin and salt bureaux. Three new boats were built.

Li later fell on evil days; his fields were flooded and funds became insufficient to maintain the boats, two of which were dispensed with. It is an interesting piece of evidence attesting to the strength of the boats and the skill of the men that one of the original craft (numbered 1) was to be seen at the Hsint'an up to the year 1901.

In 1875 the Shantung Hsün-fu (山東巡撫), Ting Pao-chêng (丁寶楨), after personally experiencing the hazards of the rapids while returning from Chungking, subscribed *Tls.* 4,000 to augment the numbers of the life-boats. Thirteen new red boats were built and stationed at different rapids, and from this time no dangerous rapid was without at least one red boat. Eight years later a high official of Hunan (湖南), Tai Pao-ch'ao (戴寶超), on his way up to Szechwan, was wrecked in his junk near Kweichow (夔州) and received valuable help from the red boats, though his son was unfortunately drowned.

The Whangpoo Life-boat is described in Part Two, page 225; see also the Red or Life-boat of the Lower Yangtze, Part Three, page 372.

In recognition of their excellent work, he petitioned the Emperor that the number of red boats might be increased and that they should become a Government institution under the Chêntai (鎮臺) of Ichang. This was granted, and a special department was set aside in the Ichang Yamên (宜昌衙門) and known as the Chiu-shêng Chü (救生局), or Life-saving Office.

In the year 1899 they were instrumental in saving 1,473 lives from 49 wrecked junks, and 1,235 from 37 junks in 1900. That year was also remarkable for the first total wreck of a foreign steamer, the German s.s. *Suihsing*, on her maiden voyage up from Ichang. Unskilfully handled against the advice of the pilot, she ran on a rock in the K'ungling Rapid and drifted down in a sinking condition. The crew had commandeered the ship's two boats and lowered them, and one was sunk by the ship's wash, but the red boats played their part and made trip after trip to the shore with rescued Chinese passengers. In this way considerable loss of life was avoided, though many, including the captain, who had generously parted with his life-belt, were drowned. Thirty-three foreign passengers and 285 Chinese were rescued in all, and a collection of $300 was made by the British Consul at Ichang for the crews of the red boats in recognition of their services. Moreover, a subscription was kept open for visitors to contribute to after making use of the life-boats, which were available, when not on duty, as escort for officials or tourists. Captain Blunt of H.M.S. *Esk*, then stationed at Ichang, accompanied by the Commissioner of Customs, proceeded to the scene

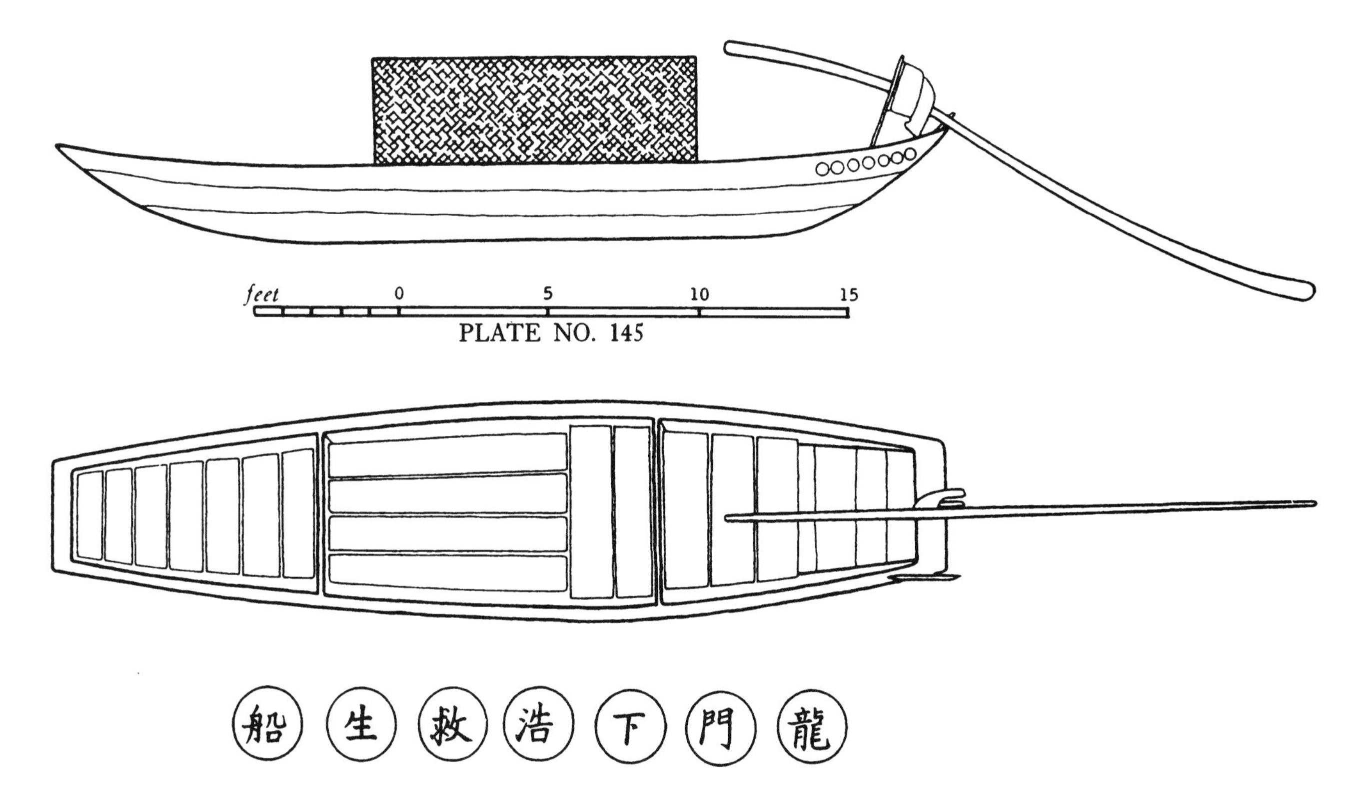

of the disaster in a steam pinnace and rendered assistance. He subsequently surveyed the K'ungling Rapid and located the position of the wreck, which had moved some few miles down stream and lay in 21 fathoms at dead low water.

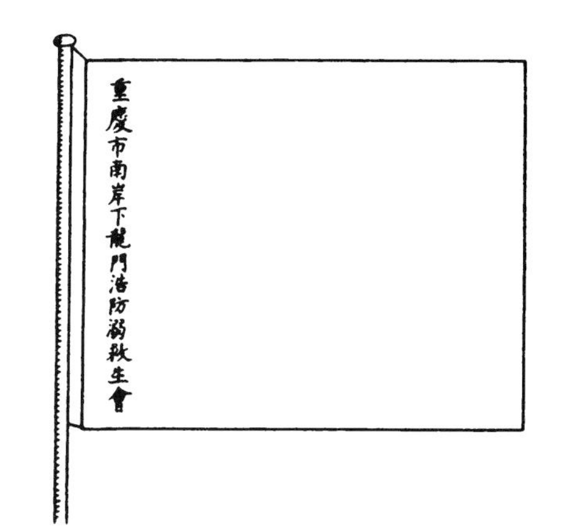

By 1901 there were 44 of these boats in commission. They had undergone several modifications, and in type were shallow vessels on the lines of a fishing-sampan, steered by a stern-sweep—often supplemented by a bow-sweep, which ensured perfect control. The crew consisted of a helmsman and four boatmen, and the cost of the yearly upkeep was $200 for each boat.

The service, which was maintained by public subscription, was admirably organised. The river was divided into districts, each patrolled by one of five small guard-boats or gunboats of similar design, though larger, and in charge of a minor official called a Shao-kuan (哨 官). These acted as river police and generally supervised the work. The boats stationed on the rapids constantly cruised up the eddies and down the rapids, keenly on the watch for accidents or for the cry of *chiu-ming* (救 命), " save life," when a junk capsized.

Regulations were drawn up. Plots of ground were bought for burial of the dead bodies found in the river, and matsheds were erected on the banks for the crews and for the rescued.

As the rapids varied in danger according to the level of the water, the patrol areas of the red boats changed. Every up-bound junk being tracked through a rapid had its attendant red boat. Down-bound craft, having less to fear while kept on a middle course, were not so attended unless seen to be standing into danger. When a wreck occurred, a gun was fired to summon all boats to help. After the rescue work the circumstances of the disaster, the name of the junkmaster, and number of the crew were reported, and the red boats' crews received 1,200 cash for each life saved and 400 cash for every body recovered.

The salvaging of cargo was expressly forbidden. The duty was undertaken by specially registered fishing-boats from the nearest village, the salvaged cargoes being removed to safe custody, usually in a temple, there to await identification by the owner, who rewarded the fishermen according to a fixed scale. Theft or false declaration was severely punished.

Later, a larger type of red boat was introduced, but with the same number of crew. In 1921 Captain Plant speaks of no less than six of these vessels at the more dangerous rapids in the high-water season, displaying their traditional courage and skill.

It is a matter for regret that this noble service has seemingly disappeared, except for an odd survival here and there. The specimen illustrated in Plate No. 145 is manned by two ancient mariners and is stationed at Chungking, 100 yards distant from the entrance to the Dragon's Mouth at Lungmenhao (龍門浩). This is a tortuous entry into a narrow and shallow lagoon, much sought after as a shelter and formed at low water by a high, jagged ridge of wicked rock, which rears itself out of the water half a cable from the south bank. A dangerous race runs past the entrance which is just wide enough to permit a junk to pass. Many lives are lost here, and more would be lost but for the presence of the red boat.

The red boat as shown measures 30 feet in length, with a maximum beam of 7 feet, and is a well built and seaworthy little craft, rather smaller than the Chungking sampan and on much the same lines, though considerably easier to handle. On its side it bears the typical seven characters 龍門下浩救生船, meaning "The Lungmenhao Lower Section Life-boat," each character being enclosed in a white circle. The boat flies the life-boat flag on the port quarter, adorned with an upright line of characters in black on a red ground 重慶市南岸下龍門浩防溺救生會, meaning "The Society for Rescuing Drowning People, Lower Section, Lungmenhao, South Bank, Chungking." A removable mat cover serves as shelter for the two old men who operate the boat with an oar and a 20-foot stern-sweep.

It may be anticipated that the demise of these two veteran survivors will mean the end of the life-boat service.

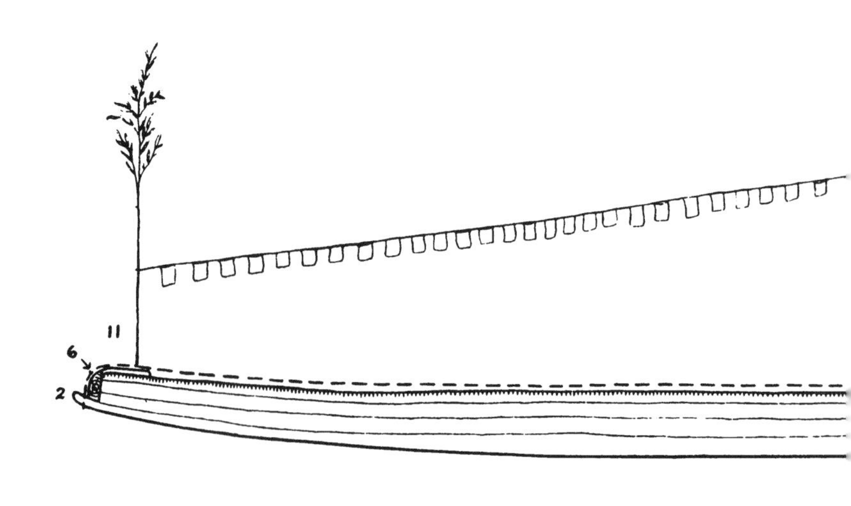

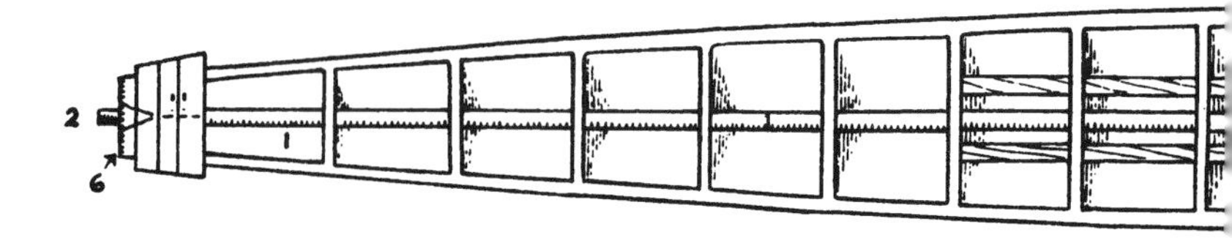

THE "DRAGON" BOAT 龍船

The gradual adoption of Western forms of civilisation is tending towards the elimination of the ancient picturesque customs. This is unfortunately particularly true of the Dragon Boat Festival, *Tuan-wu-chieh* (端午節), which provides a holiday of more than ordinary gaiety and liveliness, despite the fact that the tradition from which it originated was a historical tragedy.

The event commemorated is the death of the famous poet and statesman, Ch'ü Yüan (屈原), who lived in the fourth century, B.C., in the Chou dynasty (周朝). On being denounced by a jealous rival he had ventured to point out the faults of his master, he lost the confidence of his ruler, Prince Huai of Ch'u (楚懷王), by whom he was degraded.

He fell into a melancholy state, and, resolving to end his life, announced his decision in a celebrated sonnet named the "Li Sao" (離騷). While lamenting on the banks of the Milo River (汨羅江), which runs into the Tungting Lake, a passing fisherman asked how the great Minister had fallen so low. Ch'ü Yüan replied: "The world is foul, and I alone am clean. They are all drunk, and I alone am sober. So am I dismissed." The fisherman, who seems to have possessed a singularly odd form of philosophy, replied: "The true sage does not quarrel with his environment, but adapts himself to it. If the world is foul, leap into the tide and make it clean; if all men are drunk, drink with them and avoid excess."

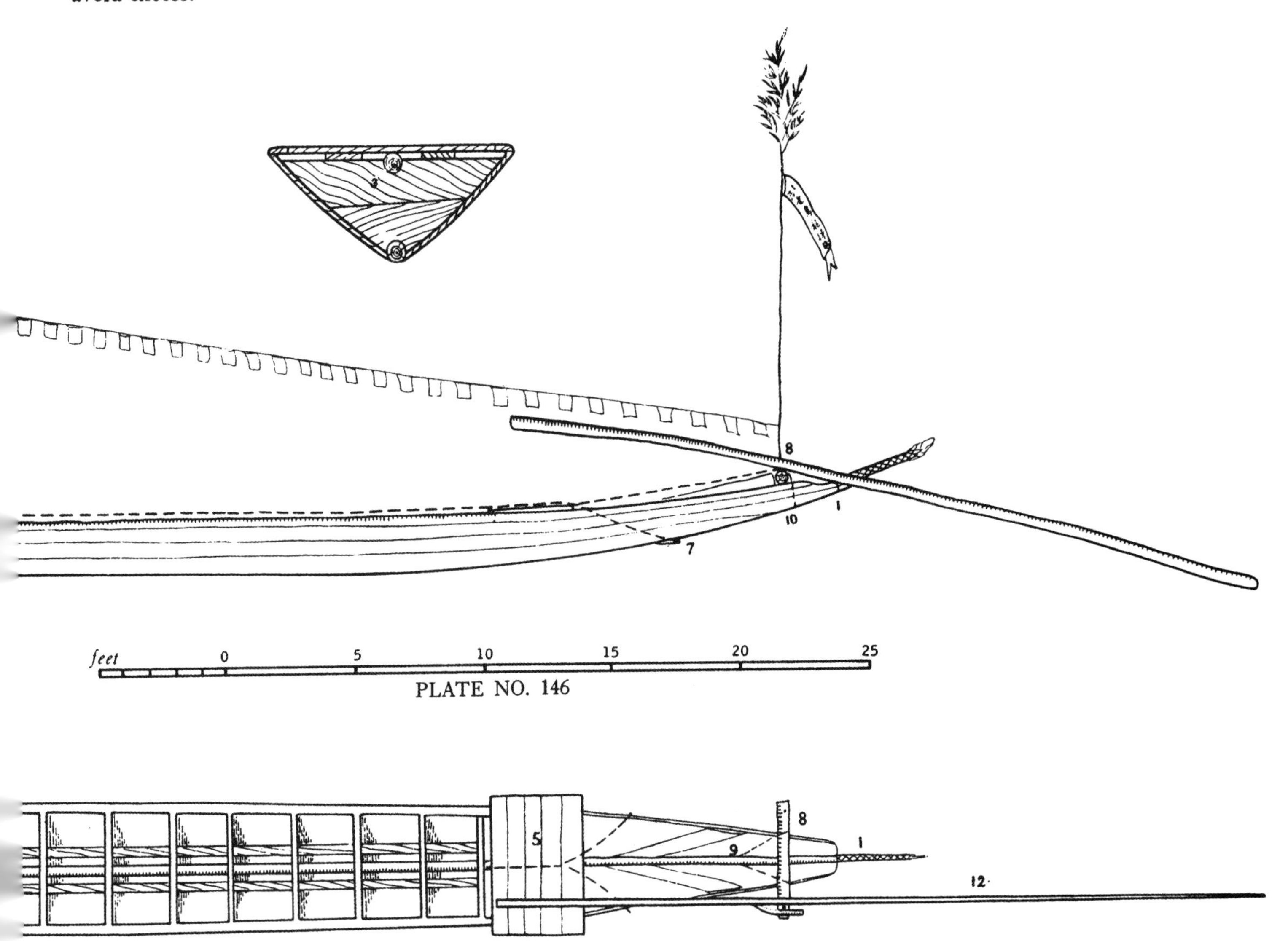

PLATE NO. 146

As soon as he had left, Ch'ü Yüan clasped a large stone in his arms, and, plunging into the river, added one more to the list of romantic suicides in the vicinity of the Tungting Lake in Hunan.

His song of sorrow had brought many sympathisers to seek him, and, finding him gone, they searched for him in boats. The tragedy took place on the 5th day of the 5th moon, and ever after the people of that district of Chingch'u (秦 楚) held an annual festival on that date, and used to throw offerings of boiled rice in bamboo tubes into the river to appease his spirit.

One day his apparition presented itself and complained that he had been unable to partake of these sacrifices, as they were all devoured by an ill-natured reptile. He suggested that the rice should be wrapped in silk and tied with five-coloured threads so as to frighten the dragon. After this plan was adopted the spirit appeared once more to praise its success.

Silks and coloured threads being expensive commodities, the ever practical Chinese eventually substituted bamboo leaves tied with string, seemingly with equal success. The parcels of rice thus rolled up are known as *tsung-tzŭ* (粽 子), and the custom of throwing them into the river was continued with the additional purpose of appeasing the spirits of all those who had been drowned. This practice was finally discontinued in favour of that of eating the rice.

The cone-shaped packets are still wrapped in bamboo leaves and steamed, which gives a peculiar flavour to the sweet rice, and if expense is no object, chopped ham is also added. This delicacy, which is eaten at the midday meal, remains in season for several weeks.

Gradually the boats which put out in the symbolic search for the poet's body came to take part in races, until the Dragon Boat Festival evolved in its present form and is celebrated all over China on the 5th and 15th days of the 5th moon, wherever there is sufficient water on which to race the boats.

It is customary for debts to be settled at this festival, which also coincides with that of the Last Sowing of Corn (芒 種) and with the Summer Solstice, *Hsia-chih* (夏 至).

Many superstitions have grown up around this season, for the 5th moon is regarded as so dangerous and pestilential that no new undertakings are willingly embarked upon in this month. At noon on the 5th day the five venomous creatures appear: the snake, the scorpion, the lizard, the toad, and the centipede. A concoction called *hsiung-huang* (雄 黃) is applied to the lips, ears, eyes, and nose, to keep insects and odours away. For the same purpose the talisman plant of the mugwort, *ai-hao* (艾 蒿), and the long sword-shaped leaves of the flag, acorus, *ch'ang-p'u* (菖 蒲), are hung up together over the door-way or on the door-posts. Sometimes a Taoist charm is added to them. Mothers write the character "*wang* (王)" on their sons' foreheads, as it is said to resemble the wrinkles on a tiger's head. Little girls used to have paper flowers tied in their hair, but this custom seems to be dying out. Formerly, also, baskets of paper dolls, "substitutes for the body," which were designed to collect the evil influences, were burned.

At this season of the year the cult of the old River Gods revives strongly, and prayers are offered to the various dragons, of which there are said to be eight varieties, Lung Wang (龍 王), or the Dragon King, being the chief. A man in search of health may achieve his purpose by the donation of a "dragon" boat, or, to a lesser degree, of money to defray some of the expenses connected therewith.

About 10 days before the race the prospective crews of the competing "dragon" boats may be seen practising in ordinary sampans in the harbour. Poles are set up at various points to mark the headquarters of the different boats and carry banners with the appropriate colours. The boats are each named after the colour selected, which is also used for the men's turbans, sashes, and sleeveless coats. These colours are probably taken from the four dragons of the points of the compass, blue or green signifying the spring and the dragon of the east; red and yellow for summer and the dragon of the south; similarly, white for the autumn and the west; and black for winter and the north.

If there is a temple to the Dragon King in the vicinity, the dragon's head and tail designed for use on the bow and stern of the boat are kept therein. Failing this, they lie in state on the foreshore, side by side, on a trestle supported on a high platform covered by a matshed roof, the whole being decorated with pine foliage. The crews, too, often wear pine wreaths round their heads while they are gathering at the boats for practice.

Before the platform a table is arranged with a drum on the right, a bunch of flowers, cymbals of different kinds and sizes, and a variety of gongs and clappers. Incense sticks and paper money, an oil lamp, bread, and a bottle of wine complete the properties.

Five days before the festival the building of the "dragon" boats is commenced. About 15 carpenters assemble and caulk the boat in about three days. They are expected to give their services rather below the current rates obtaining. The process of building, which is carried out on the foreshore, acts as a magnet for the crowds of interested spectators, who proffer much gratuitous advice.

The first operation is the shaping of the kelson,[1] which takes the form of a *sha-mu* pole the length of the boat. The tapering end projects a few inches over the stern, where it serves as a support for the dragon's tail. The remainder of the pole, which is dressed down to a more or less uniform measurement of 6 inches, projects also in the bow,[2] where it carries the dragon's head. This kelson lies on two joined, hardwood, *ch'ing-kang* planks, 6 inches broad. The bulkheads, varying in number from 12 to 18 according to the size of the boat and diminishing in size at bow and stern, are placed in position and slotted so as to engage into the kelson.

The sides, each consisting of three *sha-mu* planks, are assembled and nailed together and lifted bodily into position, where they are secured to the *ch'ing-kang* bottom. Ropes are then passed round under the bottom of the boat from gunwale to gunwale at spaced intervals, and hove down by means of a Spanish windlass, whereby the sides of the boat are forced tightly home against the many bulkheads, and thus the boat is shaped.

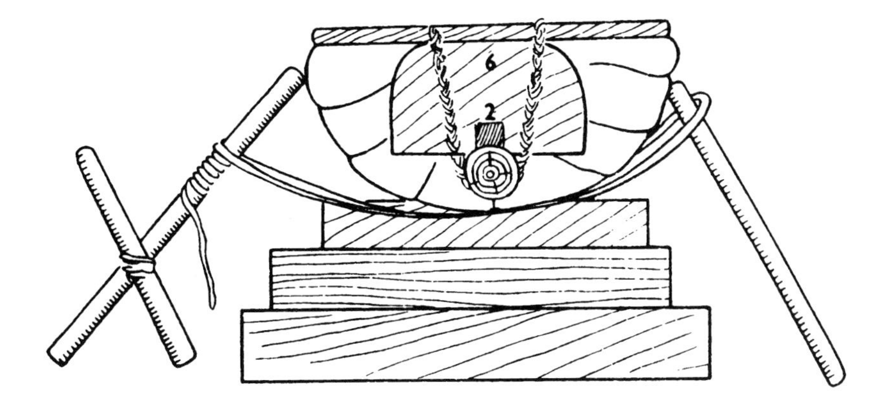

For further strength a stringer[3] in the shape of another pole, similar to the kelson but shorter, is slotted through the top of all the bulkheads from aft to the sixth bulkhead. Two separate 6-inch planks[4] also run from aft, along over the top of the bulkheads, and also cease at the sixth bulkhead. These serve as a gangway for the various officials and a site to carry the drum, and terminate in a platform[5] for the coxswain and his assistant.

The weight of the crew is approximately as much as 3 tons, and to support this, further strengthening is provided by long bamboo slats laid up into the form of flat rope. This passes under the projecting low stump of the kelson at the bow,[2] above which rests a large, rounded wooden chock,[6] and travels along the top of the bulkheads down the fore and aft line of the boat. At the coxswain's platform[5] this rope divides and passes round under the boat, where it is secured by a chock,[7] while the main rope continues on to the after transom,[8] over which it passes in the form of a bridle[9] and thence under the counter.[10] This rope can be set up to any degree of tension by twisting various small poles which are inserted between the strands in much the same way as a tourniquet. Economical and efficient chafing mats are provided for these ropes wherever they lie against the hull by inserting grass sandals.

Before launching the boat, a ceremony known as *Kuan-shou* (觀 首) takes place, in the course of which the head carpenter places the dragon's head in a propitious position for the success of the race.

The maximum size of the boats is 10 *chang* 10 *ch'ih*, that is to say, 110 Chinese feet, while the minimum is 4 *chang* 4 *ch'ih*, or 44 Chinese feet. They can be any intermediate size, provided there are an equal number of *chang* as of *ch'ih*. The crew of a 5 *chang* 5 *ch'ih* "dragon" boat of 18 bulkheads consists of 36 paddlers (all sampanmen, who sit in pairs on the bulkheads) and eight officials.

Each boat carries a *shou-shao* (首 梢), or man in charge of the rowers, and he stands across the dragon's head in the bow on a small platform. In the stern, where the dragon's tail is fixed,[1] the *chang-shao* (掌 梢), or coxswain, takes charge at the stern-sweep. The *mo-shou* (摸 手), or instructor, is stationed right aft and directs the rhythm of the paddlers through his instructions to those sounding the gong and beating the large drum. He holds, moreover, a bamboo flying a pennant, which conforms to the colour of the boat. The number of instructors may be increased according to the size of the boat, but not more than three are ever employed.

These instructors hold a coloured handkerchief in each hand, which they wave in the air, twisting themselves into the most astounding contortions and allowing themselves, the drummer, the men at the gongs, and the paddlers to get worked up into a frenzy of excitement. The antics of the man in the bow, who has his back to the way the boat is travelling, seem to foreign eyes to have no relation to those of the instructor or instructors, who are also, or seem to be, out of rhythm with the paddlers, while the drummer and the men at the gongs appear to be equally out of time. It is suggested that the men with the handkerchiefs serve to keep the paddlers in time, while the drummer and gongmen control the speed of the boat.

The paddles have coloured scales painted on one side and the name of the boat on the other. The drummer who officiates amidships often stands under a canopy or umbrella of flowers. The boat has three or more short masts of thin bamboo terminating in their natural feathery tops. The main mast supports two dressing-lines with paper flags.

The actual length of the race differs in various localities. A distance of about ½ mile obliquely across the river is a very usual course.

The boat when under way and fully loaded has a free-board of no more than 3 inches, and the paddlers frequently scoop large quantities of water into the boat. When this becomes an embarrassment the boat stops, and bailing with special wooden bailers is energetically carried out.

The boats are very easily capsized, and accidents frequently occur. Moreover, feeling is apt to run high, resulting in clashes and unfortunate incidents between rival crews. For this reason the "dragon" boat races are often not encouraged by the authorities.

After the race some of the boats are kept for next season while those built as a special offering to the Dragon King are dismantled and used as firewood. The dragon's head and tail are always stored for future use, preferably in a temple to the Dragon King.

After an interval of four years the authorities at Chungking revived the "dragon" boat races in 1940, under the auspices of the New Life Movement, for the encouragement of physical culture. Twenty-two boats took part in the races, which were run on the Kialing River amidst scenes of the greatest enthusiasm. Every boat received a prize, and *tsung-tzŭ* were distributed to the paddlers. The boat illustrated in Plate No. 146 is the Black Dragon of Lungmenhao, which came in third in the race.

In the "Encyclopædia Britannica" the claim is made for the Chinese that in their "dragon" boat races they were the earliest exponents of long boat racing in the world. The "dragon" boats, moreover, are compared to the Greek trireme in that there were "27 thwarts and rowers in both."

THE CHUNGKING SAMPAN

The Chungking sampan, Plate No. 147, a craft designed for use in the rapids and strong currents of the Upper Yangtze, is a solid and strongly built double-ender of almost uniform dimensions, that is to say, 40 feet long, with a beam of 8 feet at its broadest part.

It is strengthened by three bulkheads, the centre one [1] being exactly amidships and the other two [2] being 7 feet on each side of it. From the after bulkhead to the stern the deck is flush with the gunwale and is exclusively used by the helmsman. The corresponding forward portion, also flush with the gunwale, is reserved for the man or men at the forward oars.[3] The two remaining midship wells [4] serve for passengers and cargo. All floor-boards are loose and serve as seats when required. There is no rudder, as the enormous sweep,[5] two-thirds of the length of the boat, performs this function.

When ferrying, the sampan can carry as many as 25 persons besides the crew of two or three, and even as many as 40 can be accommodated—without safety. The laodah, or helmsman, stands aft and controls the boat with a small oar [6] on the port side, which he uses with his right hand, a large stern-sweep being operated with his left. This sweep,[5] which is long and curved, is reinforced at its centre of gravity by a cheek-piece,[7] which has a long slot [8] cut in its projecting side, into which the bearing-pin [9] engages and which, while allowing the maximum of play, holds the sweep firmly in place. The bearing-pin [9] lies at an angle, and this facilitates the movements of the heavy sweep and enables it to be more easily unshipped. The cheek-piece [7] is secured with wire lashings, and the loom [10] is

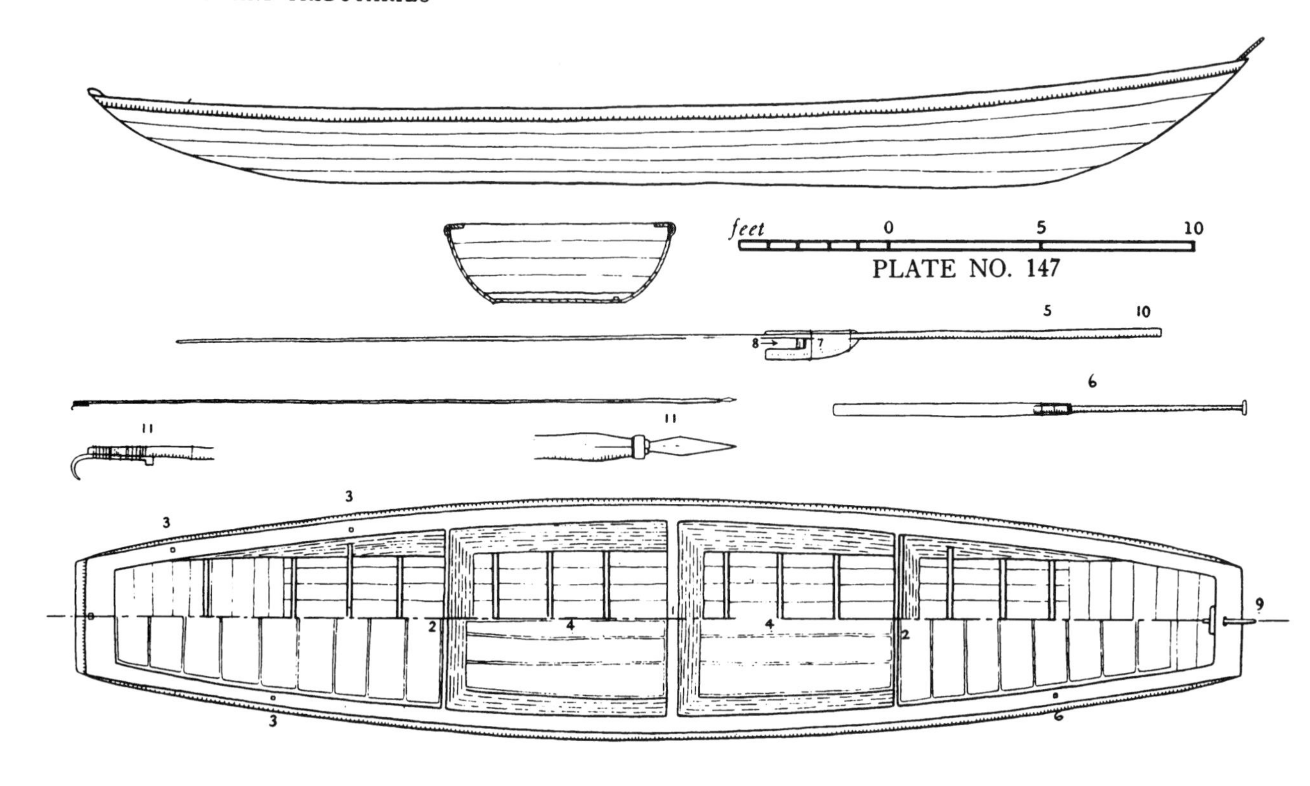

PLATE NO. 147

curved to fit the hand. The blade is also curved and shaped so as to ensure that the maximum amount shall be under water, but not too deep.

Forward stands the bowman, upon whom falls the duty of propelling the boat either with an oar or with the universal boat-hook,[11] which is ready for instant use. The skill shown by these men in the use of boat-hooks is amazing. Any smallest possible advantage within their radius is exploited with uncanny dexterity. The rocky banks of the Yangtze are pitted with holes worn down by the action of boat-hooks in all types and sizes of craft.

There is, however, a variation from the above sampan in that it is fitted with a rudder and carries no sweep. The dimensions and appearance are much the same, though it is often a little smaller. It is used exclusively for transporting cargo about the harbour.

THE FLOATING DWELLING

Characteristic of the Upper Yangtze is a floating population who live in all shapes, types, and sizes of floating houses which line the banks of some of the riverside cities. These dwellings are mainly inhabited by people brought up in the tradition of this mode of living and who pursue a vocation connected in some manner with the river.

The house-boats vary according to the means and tastes of the owners, from a five to six roomed dwelling of comparative comfort to that which is merely a miserable matshed hovel erected on some derelict sampan. They all have one thing in common, and that is the haphazard patchwork type of the superstructure, for which all manner of material is pressed into service. Kerosene-oil boxes, condemned pieces of rusty tin, odd boards from packing cases, matting in all stages of decay, discarded doors, or planks from wrecked junks all have their uses even in the superior types of floating dwellings. A coolie's straw hat is a favourite means of blocking up an unwelcome air-hole.

Where the junk nature of the boat is still in evidence, some of the same customs still obtain, such as keeping the galley on the port side and anchoring in the "stick in the mud" method. One most noticeable feature is the vast accumulation of odd bits of furniture, rubbish, and all the paraphernalia of living, which in the true junk is reduced to the barest workmanlike necessities and neatly arranged in the minimum of space.

The smallest floating house seems elastic enough to accommodate at least two families of a total of eight or nine persons, with additional live stock in the shape of a dog or two, the inevitable chicken hobbled or tied to the leg of a table, and the noisy Chungking cat either caged or tethered by a large collar and chain. In some cases ducks, and even pigs, live on board. The pigs go ashore in search of food and variety by day and return at night when called to their quarters afloat. The ducks enjoy the same freedom, and are often provided with a miniature gang-plank of their own, up which they waddle home with the solemnity of their kind.

The anchor-buoy or mark-buoy in use. Note the bell to indicate the whereabouts of the child.

E. SIGAUT

Children from the earliest age stroll about the floating dwellings, as, indeed, they also do in junks. Apparently they rarely fall overboard, for precautions are never taken to protect them from this fate—or hardly ever. Very occasionally an anchor-buoy may be noticed attached with a small rope round a child's waist, so that it can be retrieved with the minimum time and trouble. A child not brought up in a junk would probably fall overboard within the first 15 minutes of arrival on board. A child of the same age brought up in a junk, sampan, or floating dwelling would not only be expected not to fall overboard but would have a younger brother or sister strapped to its back.

From Mr. Worcester's notes: Very few deaths occur from drowning. Children often are attached by long ropes to the junk so that if they fall overboard they can readily be hauled up again. It is popularly supposed that the Chinese are, on superstitious grounds, reluctant to rescue a person from drowning, but the author had never seen anything to substantiate this belief.

Other forms of these boats are the floating bath-houses and eating-houses, which go off and lie alongside incoming ships, with which they do a good trade. There are also floating shops which supply grain and rice.

One of the more spacious dwelling-boats has been selected for description here. The owner was a junkbuilder, and he had given his naval architectural fancy full play. The result was a spacious four-roomed structure approached by a wide gang-plank, which led to a small, square, roofed-in veranda-cum-forecastle entrance. The living-room was furnished with a table, a garden seat, and a high shelf altar, with bronze candlesticks and an incense-burner before a scroll bearing the names of the River-guarding God and the Money God. A narrow ladder led from here to an attic, which raised the level of the matting roof amidships and was provided with upper windows.

Abaft the saloon, or living-room, was a large bedroom, furnished with a four-poster bed, a cupboard, a table, and an old-fashioned foreign-style dressing table, littered with hats, food, a Laughing Buddha, and a variety of other objects. A smaller bedroom farther aft led into an outside alleyway running from there the whole length on the starboard side forward. The galley, or kitchen, was situated in the stern. The coal-stove smoke escaped through a tall, square, brick chimney covered with plaster. Eight adults and a servant occupied this dwelling.

These boats move from time to time according to river conditions. They are always spar-moored in the traditional Upper Yangtze style.

Floating dwellings.

THE FOWCHOW PADDLE-WHEEL MILL JUNK

A record of Upper Yangtze craft would be incomplete without a description of the Fowchow paddlers, the river steamer captain's delight, for they cannot resist telling their inquisitive passengers that these are a new species of junk paddling their way to Chungking. This illusion is heightened when smoke is seen passing out of the high galley funnel.

No craft on the Upper Yangtze owes more to Yang Yao (楊么), the Patron Saint, or God, of the junkmen, than these, for he is credited with the invention of paddle-wheels in the twelfth century.

Actually these floating mills consist of an old junk, on which is superimposed a large house of the traditional, haphazard, patchwork design with a matting roof. The two pairs of paddles, which can be raised at will, are, once the junk is moored, lowered so that they can be revolved by the swift current.

The whole arrangement, though it would greatly appeal to Mr. Heath Robinson, is nevertheless extremely efficient, cannot get out of order, and the running costs are reduced to a minimum. Any junk can be used for the purpose, but the *to-lung-tzŭ* (舵籠子) is the type most favoured.

The junk, Plate No. 148, is usually divided into three compartments, the foremost [1] one on the forecastle being used as a storeroom and galley. The midship compartment has the deck removed and is given up to the milling machinery, which is housed on the bottom of the junk. The after compartment [2] is also used as a storeroom for the finished product and as living quarters for the ship's company, comprising two millers and two sampanmen, whose pay varies from $10 to $16 per month according to length of service and ability.

The milling gear consists of a grindstone,[6] worked by the action of the water on the paddles,[4] and a sieve,[16] which is worked by foot.

The grinding gear comprises a wooden shaft [3] carrying a paddle [4] at each extremity, and, between, a wooden cog-wheel,[5] not unlike a ship's steering wheel and fitted with 18 large wooden teeth which engage in 16 wooden teeth driven into a grindstone [6] below. These grinding arrangements are exactly duplicated for the second pair of paddles. Occasionally three sets of paddles may be found. The ponderous machinery revolves with a jerky, hesitating action and the maximum amount of backlash.

The shafting [3] rests on two pairs of strong uprights [7] on either hand, close to the ship's side, and secured to the bottom and roof of the junk. Additional strength is provided by two cross-pieces between the uprights, one against the roof and the other [9] 2½ feet from the bottom.

When the machinery is not in use, the shafting [3] is lifted bodily, with paddle-wheels and cog-wheel attached, and rests on a heavy wooden fid [8] thrust through the uprights, 4 feet above the bottom of the junk. When the fid is removed the shafting [3] is eased down with a light whip, and, travelling between the uprights,[7] comes to rest on the lower cross-piece,[9] which is curved to reduce friction. The paddles in this position are in the water, and the machinery starts working.

The grindstone [6] is nailed to the bottom of the junk and is in two parts, the lower [10] being the standing part, while the upper, which carries the teeth, revolves. A saucer-like top to the upper grindstone contains the wheat, which feeds through two holes, when the current is swift, to the grinding face. When the current is not so strong one hole is plugged. The flour is forced out at the junction of the two stones.

The sieving gear consists of four parts. The foot pedals [11] are secured at right angles to the connecting piece,[12] which rests on two blocks of wood [13] and carries an upright,[14] to which it is attached by a rocking-bar. This is in turn attached by another rocking-bar to the framework [15] leading to the sieve,[16] which is slung from the roof by means of a thin rope [17] secured to each of the corners. Below is a large bin [18] against the ship's side into which the sieved flour falls.

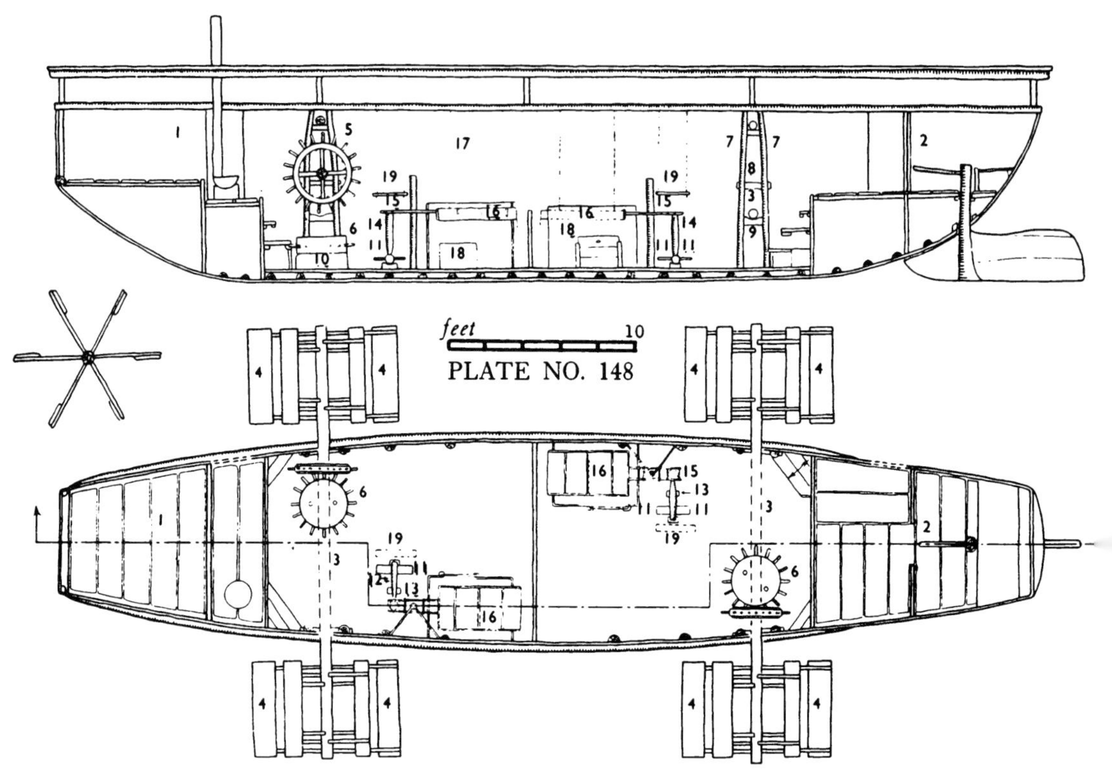

PLATE NO. 148

The operator stands on the pedals,[11] facing inboard, and rests his elbows on a wooden support [19]—not unlike the handle-bars of a bicycle—slung from the roof. The action of pedalling cants the connecting piece from one side to the other, and this alternately pulls and pushes the framework, and thereby the sieve, backwards and forwards at right angles to him.

The men work in shifts so that the mill may be kept going for long continuous periods. The machinery as illustrated is capable of dealing with 840 catties of wheat in a 24-hour period. The wheat passes through the mill and the sieve five times and produces 720 catties of flour. It seems curious that the sieving gear should not be connected up to the water-power so as to obviate man-power altogether.

It has been pointed out earlier in this chapter that the number of teeth on the driving gear is not the same as those on the grindstone. This system of gearing is therefore in keeping with modern engineering practice, for an unequal number of teeth in the meshing arrangements ensures even wear. This principle of marine engineering is comparatively new, in that it did not come into regular use before the introduction of geared turbines.

It may reasonably be assumed that the practice has been in use in China—not only in the Fowchow paddlers but in all machinery requiring the meshing of cogs—for centuries, and the question arises whether the Western nations owe the discovery of the principle to China.

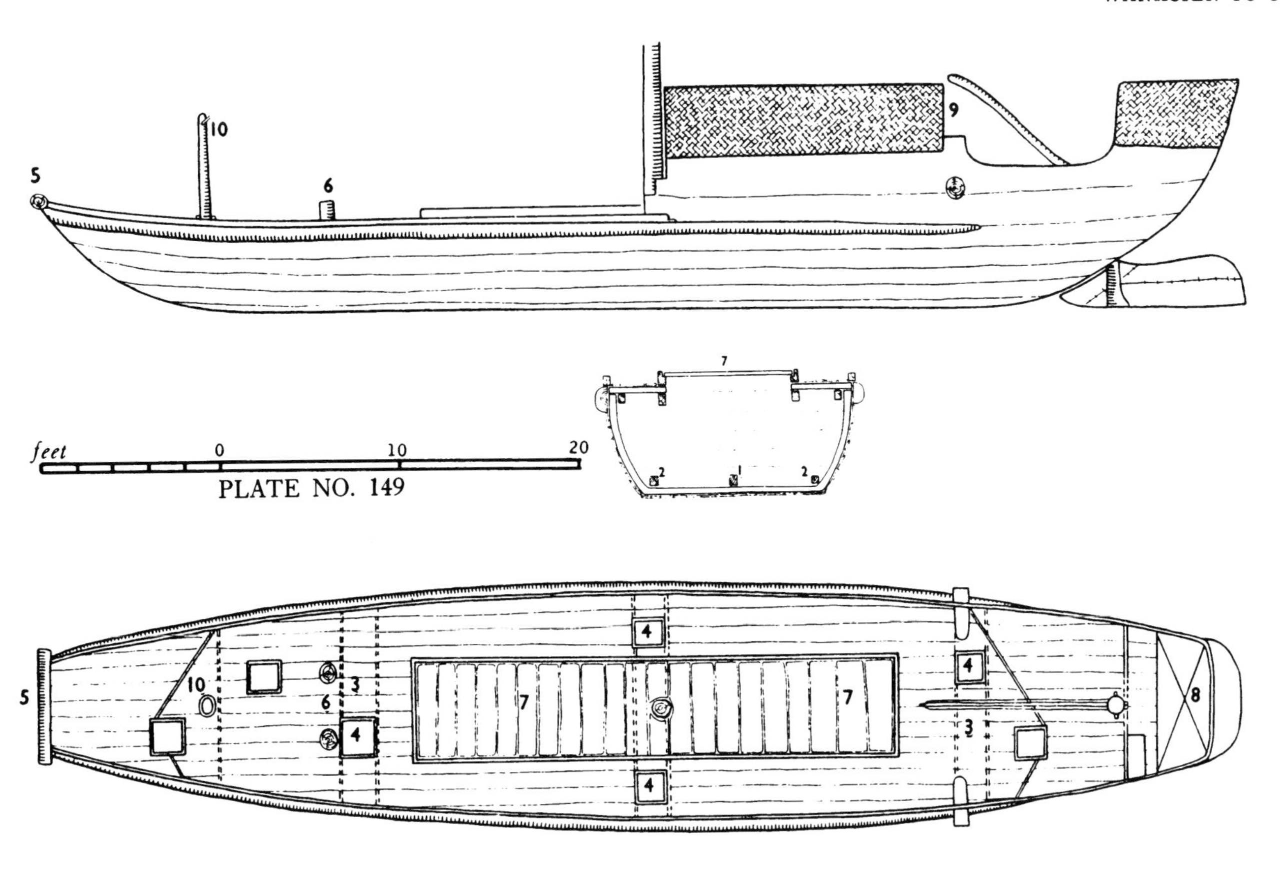

PLATE NO. 149

THE NEW TYPE OR ALL-PURPOSE JUNK

This serviceable junk, which is to be found in three classes, of a carrying capacity of 20, 40, and 60 tons, is probably the first really new design to be made for a very long time; indeed, one might surmise, for centuries.

It would seem to seek to combine the best features of many existing types with some modern innovations, so as to produce a more or less standardised craft adapted for all inland waterways. The design is by no means original, and would seem to owe much to the wood-oil lighter.

First introduced in 1939 under Government auspices, these junks are apparently coming into service in considerable numbers. Further modifications and alterations may yet be made as a result of practical experience before the type is finally settled. The conservative junkmen consider that the junks in their present form are too heavy.

Like all other junks, they vary considerably in unessentials. The illustration in Plate No. 149 shows a characteristic junk of this type, measuring 66½ feet long, with a beam of 13 feet and a depth of 5 feet.

The solidly built hull of cypress, or *pai-mu*, is strengthened by a kelson [1] and two side kelsons [2] at the turn of the bilge, and on to these the bottom planks of *ch'ing-kang* are secured. There are numerous traverse bulkheads and usually three "coffer-dams," [3] each fitted with a manhole door.[4] These coffer-dams, which are occasionally to be found in the larger type of junk, are very small compartments which are always kept free of cargo, and have two small apertures leading into the neighbouring main cargo-holds on either side. Their function is to drain off any seepage or water which may have found its way into the holds, so that it may be conveniently bailed out.

The high spoon-bow terminates in a heavy traverse stem beam,[5] fitted with thole pin fair-leads. This cross-beam projects 6 inches on either bow and provides one of the main characteristics of the vessel. Two heavy hardwood bitts[6] are firmly secured to the structure by being cut away at deck-level into a deep wedge and, after passing through the deck planks, are slotted through a timber which is joined to the bulkhead. Their position, however, varies somewhat. The flush-deck of *pai-mu* has a low coaming, which aft of the deck-house gives place to a bulwark. In lieu of the usual removable planks, a large part of the deck amidships is occupied by a low hatch coaming, which varies in extent and width, but always covers a considerable portion of the deck. The hatch covers,[7] which are removable in sections, are watertight. Another modern feature of the boat is the conspicuous marks in roman figures cut into each bow and painted, together with a foreign registration number.

The stern, which is wide in shape, has a considerable rise, and a small portion of it is decked-in, roofed with matting, and provided with doors, although it is often only large enough to contain a huge square bed.[8] The house, which starts abaft the mast, extends for a short distance to the conning position,[9] which presents no variation from the normal. The light *sha-mu* pole mast is stepped against the bulkhead in the usual manner; similarly the rudder, the simple galley-stove on the port side, and the "stick in the mud" anchor[10] are all in the traditional style.

1940 prices.

The crew usually consists of seven men, and the cost of the junk is approximately $2,000.

撒網捉魚船

THE LAGOON FISHER

Quite a different type of craft is the lagoon fisher. This boat is about 12 feet long and 3 feet beam, and designed entirely for the still waters of the Chungking lagoon.

This type of boat is usually rowed by an old woman, with an eagle eye for flotsam and jetsam. Ships anchored in the lagoon—particularly gunboats—always have a number of these craft clustered round waiting for something to fall overboard, which, according to the custom of the Yangtze, becomes the property of the first to reach it.

Garbage of all kinds is highly prized and has varied uses. For example, orange peel is retrieved, dried in the sun, threaded on string, and finally becomes medicine. Empty tins, cardboard boxes, and paper always find a buyer.

The real work of the lagoon fisher, however, is cast-net or otter fishing. Both methods require the utmost skill. The former is carried out by one man, who stands in the bow with the net gathered in his left hand. The net, which may be made of hemp, but is more often of "Szechwan hemp," which is really abutilon, is circular in shape and weighted at the circumference with small pieces of lead. The fisherman, turning his face in the desired direction, transfers the net from left to right hand and, with a widespread sweeping movement, casts the net right forward, so that it falls at least 8 feet clear of the bow and opens up into a perfect circle as it sinks below the surface.

Various methods of fishing are described in Part One, pages 134–38.

Despite his skill, very few fish are ever seen to be landed by this or any other method of fishing, and river fish is a prized and expensive commodity in Chungking.

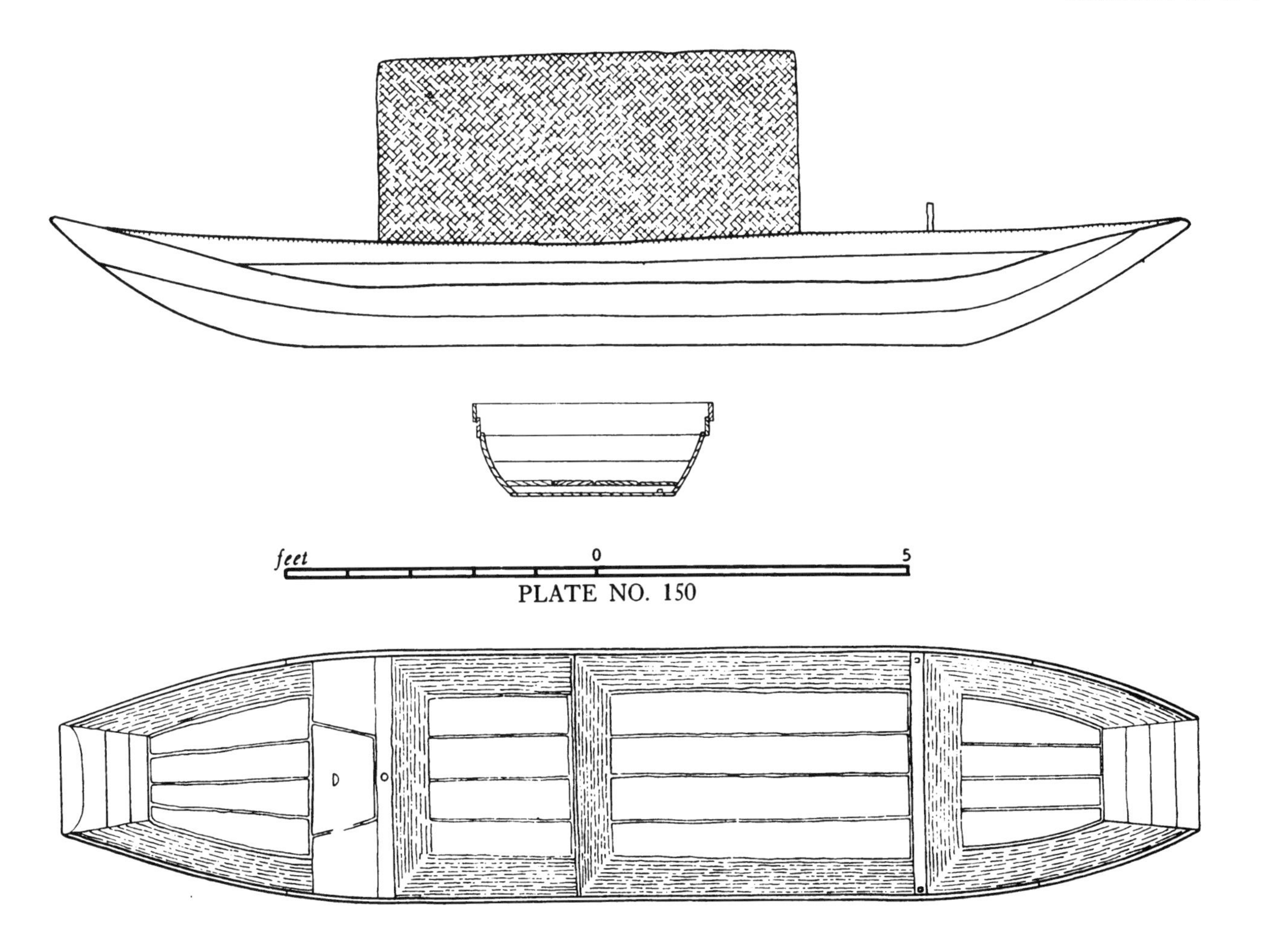

PLATE NO. 150

Otter-fishing is also carried out in the same sort of small sampan in the still waters of some of the lagoons of the Upper Yangtze.

Fishing with an otter.

The boat drifts slowly while a fisherman casts his net in the manner already described. He is assisted, however, by one or more trained otters which are attached to small, light bamboos by means of an iron chain fixed to a sort of leather harness. The fishing-net ends in a long neck with an aperture through which, after the net has been cast, the otter is inserted and performs its task of stirring the fish out of the mud and crevices of the bottom of the lagoon, so that they get enmeshed in the net when it is drawn tight. Otter, net, and fish are then all hauled on board together.

Hope springs eternal, and despite the fact that very few fish are ever caught, the otter remains a valuable and expensive ally of the fisherman, a well-trained animal costing as much as $50. The sampan, when used for fishing by either method, is controlled by a man standing in the stern, who operates two miniature oars. The coffer-dam between the two foremost bulkheads contains a small water-tank, fitted with a trap-door, inside which any captured fish are kept just sufficiently alive to remain technically "fresh."

In Chungking the practice is for the otter to dive over the side at the word of command and hunt the fish into the net. What it does below the surface is not quite clear, but it is often to be seen emerging independently of the net with a fish in its mouth, which it readily gives up to its owner.

Such animals are said to be worth as much as $200 each. They are obviously very well treated and on excellent terms with their masters.

From Mr. Worcester's notes: These otters are described as tame, but are so only to their masters who feed and handle them with the greatest confidence.

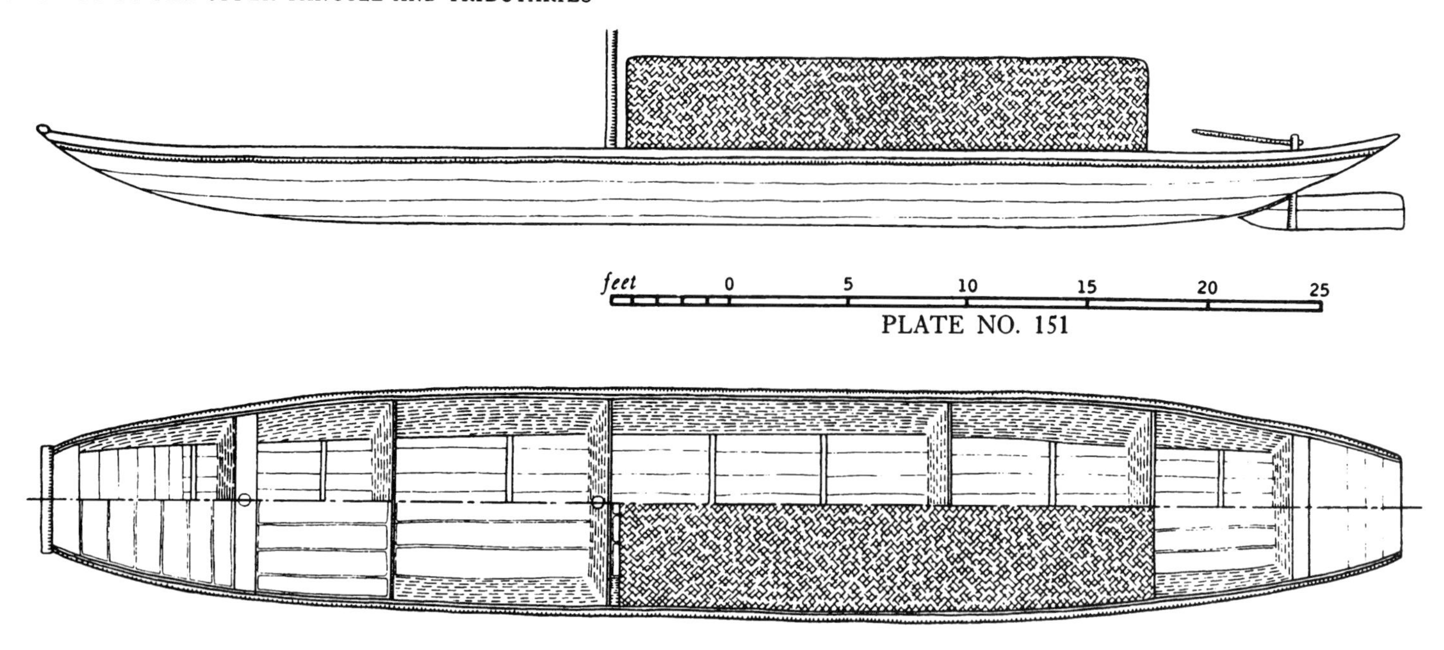

PLATE NO. 151

扒窩子 THE PA-WO-TZŬ

The *pa-wo-tzŭ*, as illustrated in Plate No. 151, is the largest type of junk which trades up the numerous small creeks which enter the Yangtze, and it is rather surprising that so large a craft is used for this purpose, for she measures 58 feet with a beam of 9½ feet. The shallow waters she has to negotiate are indicated by her draught, which, when fully loaded with 67 piculs, is only about 6 inches; indeed, her total depth is only 3 feet.

Of simple construction, she is built of *pai-mu* with *ch'ing-kang* for the bottom, and has six bulkheads and six half-frames.

Actually this particular craft trades with the two small towns of Kaotan (高 灘) and Linshui (鄰 水), up a creek, or small tributary, known as the Yuling (雨 林). These towns act as focal points for foodstuffs from the surrounding countryside, and also for pigs, of which as many as 30 can be carried, stowed in pairs athwartships. This cargo is taken to Chungking, and the junks return with salt and sugar. Occasionally cargoes of stones are carried.

From Mr. Worcester's notes: The prevailing fashionable colour for pigs in Szechwan seems to be white, and the Chinese, who waste absolutely nothing, have built up a very profitable industry by cleaning, grading, and selling the white pig bristles, which are used in making toothbrushes. On climbing the grimy streets of steps anywhere in Chungking one may see women and children sorting pigs' bristles into tiny bunches, and inserting them with startling swiftness and dexterity into the bone frames of toothbrushes for use in China.

A square sail is often used, but tracking and oars are the more usual means of propulsion.

Additional Types or Variations of Which No Plans are Available.

The *kua-tzŭ-ch'uan* (掛 子 船), or passenger-boat,* used to be the most comfortable means of travel in Szechwan. These craft varied in size, and were primarily designed for passenger accommodation, but they also carried cargo. They were turret-built, and very similar to the *ma-yang-tzŭ*.

Finally, mention must be made of the fleet of over 50 post-boats, which carried about 1,800 tons of mail per year between Ichang and Chungking. These craft, though quite small, were noted for their record passages. They carried on gallantly in all weathers, in exceptional floods, during times of famine or civil war, and, despite hampering restrictions, maintained their high standard of speed and efficiency.

* A model of this junk appears in the Maze collection of Chinese junk models in the Science Museum, London.

THE UPPER YANGTZE BAMBOO RAFTS

The bamboo rafts of the Upper Yangtze are not remarkable. They consist of large, medium, and small sized bamboos lashed together in the form of large, medium, and small sized rafts.

Drifting down with the stream, they take full advantage of any swift water that may be available, and travel from one bank of the river to the other in order to keep in the greatest current. The only interest which attaches to them is their method of achieving this object, which is accomplished by means of what may be described as a "water-rake." This consists of a belt made of six pieces of split bamboo retained in place by cross-weaving, the whole being bent into an oval form,[1] 4½ feet by 3 feet, and 6 inches deep. This is attached to a 15-foot bamboo,[2] which, running through the oval, bisects it, and is secured there by two bamboo pegs,[3] which pass through holes[4] in the pole. The water-rake is hurled with a sweeping movement into the river as far as possible and then drawn towards the raft.

Considerable skill and technique—more than is apparent—are required to navigate the raft to the best advantage, and suitable progress is governed by the direction in which the rake is thrown and the operator's position on the raft.

No ropes or other gear are carried, except for the occasional use of an improvised oar in the form of a plank lashed to a bamboo. This absence of other mechanical aid necessitates great nicety in judgment, particularly in the matter of rounding-to or avoiding obstacles which do not get out of the way. A knowledge of pace is another essential.

The rafts are formed of small bundles of bamboos and are arranged so as to converge into a long, narrow point which may be termed the bow, although it must not be assumed that they necessarily travel bow first. Extra bundles superimposed make a higher and drier stance for the crew. It is an easy matter to enlarge the raft by simply adding more bundles.

In the larger rafts, improvised bow and stern sweeps are sometimes employed, as well as a make-shift oar on each side. The crew range from one man in the smallest raft to as many as six in the largest variety. Sometimes unimportant cargo may be transported, such as bales of straw, and an occasional passenger may be seen.

These rafts, travelling with the current at high speed and, broadly speaking, out of control, are given a wide berth by all other craft.

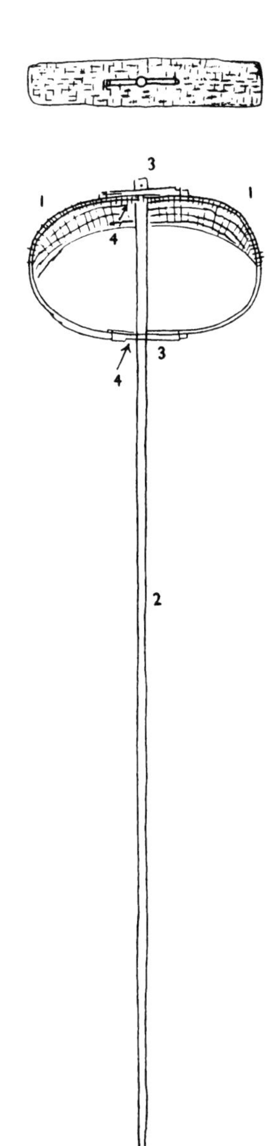

The water rake.

THE KIALING RIVER (嘉 陵 江)

THE Kialing River is a tributary of the Yangtze, which it joins at Chungking. It drains the whole of the north-eastern portion of Szechwan by means of its three confluents—the Suiningho, the Paoningho (保 寧 河), and the Küho, or Suitingho (渠 或 綏 定 河), which all unite at or near Hochow (合 州), 50 miles above Chungking. In the low-river season from December to April, the general character of the river consists of a series of deep reaches separated by shallow bars of rock and shingle, over which the stream, running rapidly, forms races which make navigation difficult. The water is fairly clear, more especially in winter. The river throughout is subject to very rapid fluctuations in height, particularly at Hochow, where the extreme range is about 40 feet.

The country traversed by this river and its tributaries is immensely rich agriculturally and minerally, and a variety of produce comes down this, the Yangtze's most important tributary.

The limits of junk navigation are Shunkiang (順 江), on the Suiningho; Suiting, on the Suitingho or Küho; and Kwangyüan (廣 元), on the Paoningho, the latter affluent being navigable for the longest distance. These places can still be reached throughout the winter, either by a smaller type of junk or by the larger junks not so heavily loaded.

THE LAO-HUA-CH'IU

This junk, Plate No. 152, which generally plies on the Suiningho, is a typical general cargo carrier, in that it is turret-built, with a very considerable tumble home throughout the whole length of the ship. This is so marked as to give an angular, blistered appearance.[1]

Its over-all measurements are 125 feet by 17 feet beam, which establish it as the largest junk on this river and the longest in the Upper Yangtze areas. The bottom planks are of *ch'ing-kang* and the sides of *pai-mu* or *huang-lien.*

Lighter in structure than usual, this junk is built on well-proportioned lines, tapering at bow and stern, and rising with a graceful sweep to a high stern.

The deck is flush throughout, and the square-shaped flat bow is provided with a small coaming.[2] Two solid hardwood bollards [3] are secured in the usual wedge-footed fashion on the foremost bulkhead, just forward of the "stick in the mud" anchor.[4] A pair of larger bollards [5] are situated about 3 feet apart on the fourth bulkhead. These permit one of the two tracking-lines to be made fast farther aft when necessary, as, for instance, when rounding a sharp bend of the river.

A tall *sha-mu* mast [6] is stepped in the ordinary way, and abaft of it is the central roomy deck-house where the crew live, and in which the only fitting is the simple galley-stove on the port side, connected to a right-angled brick chimney

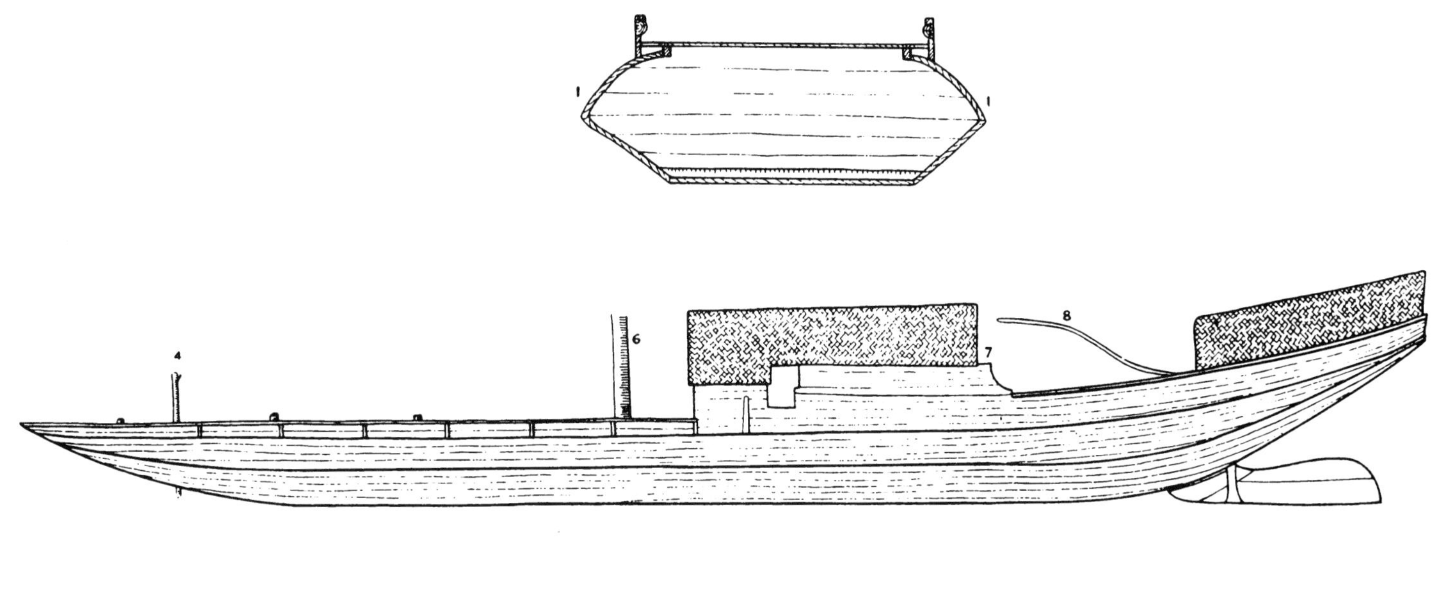

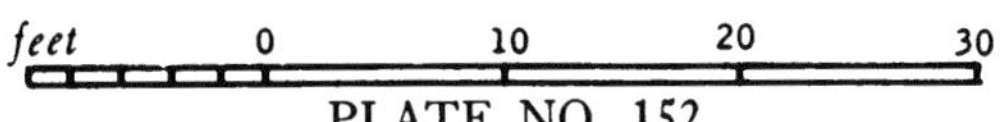

PLATE NO. 152

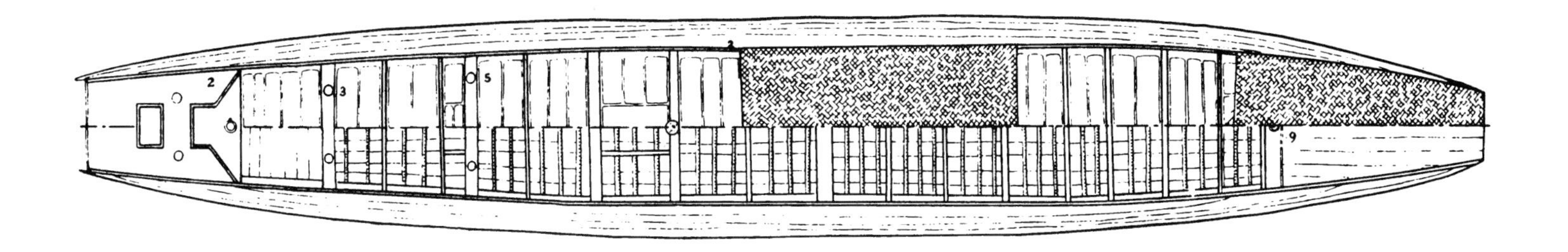

which ends at the level of the mat roof. Simplicity is the key-note. There are no elaborate food or grain lockers, but merely a rough shelf and a wooden box containing chow-bowls.

The whole junk can be enclosed by means of a removable fore-deck awning of matting. Aft of the house is the usual open space with bulwarks and the plank-bridge site [7] for conning the vessel. The extra long tiller [8] is always made of *mu-tzŭ-mu* (木 子 木) and reinforced with two spars.

Just abaft the rudder post [9] all the remaining after portion is decked-in to form two communicating cabins. An attempt at adornment is here seen in the varnished fret-wood windows, the niche for the Patron God, and four long black and gold plaques.

The foremost cabin contains a bed, a cupboard, and a manhole giving access to the rudder post. The after cabin, being in the sharply raised portion of the stern, is reached by a high step and is mainly filled by a large bed athwart the stern window, which opens with two upright shutters.

This particular junk, as described, was religiously orthodox, for in addition to the Junk God and the invocations, a cock was regularly sacrificed before each up-bound trip, and the feathers, stuck on with blood to portions of the rounded arch of the deck-house beams, were still to be seen.

It will be remembered that these are the type of junks which often have an umbrella, or *fêng-pao*, lashed to the masthead to "keep off the rain."

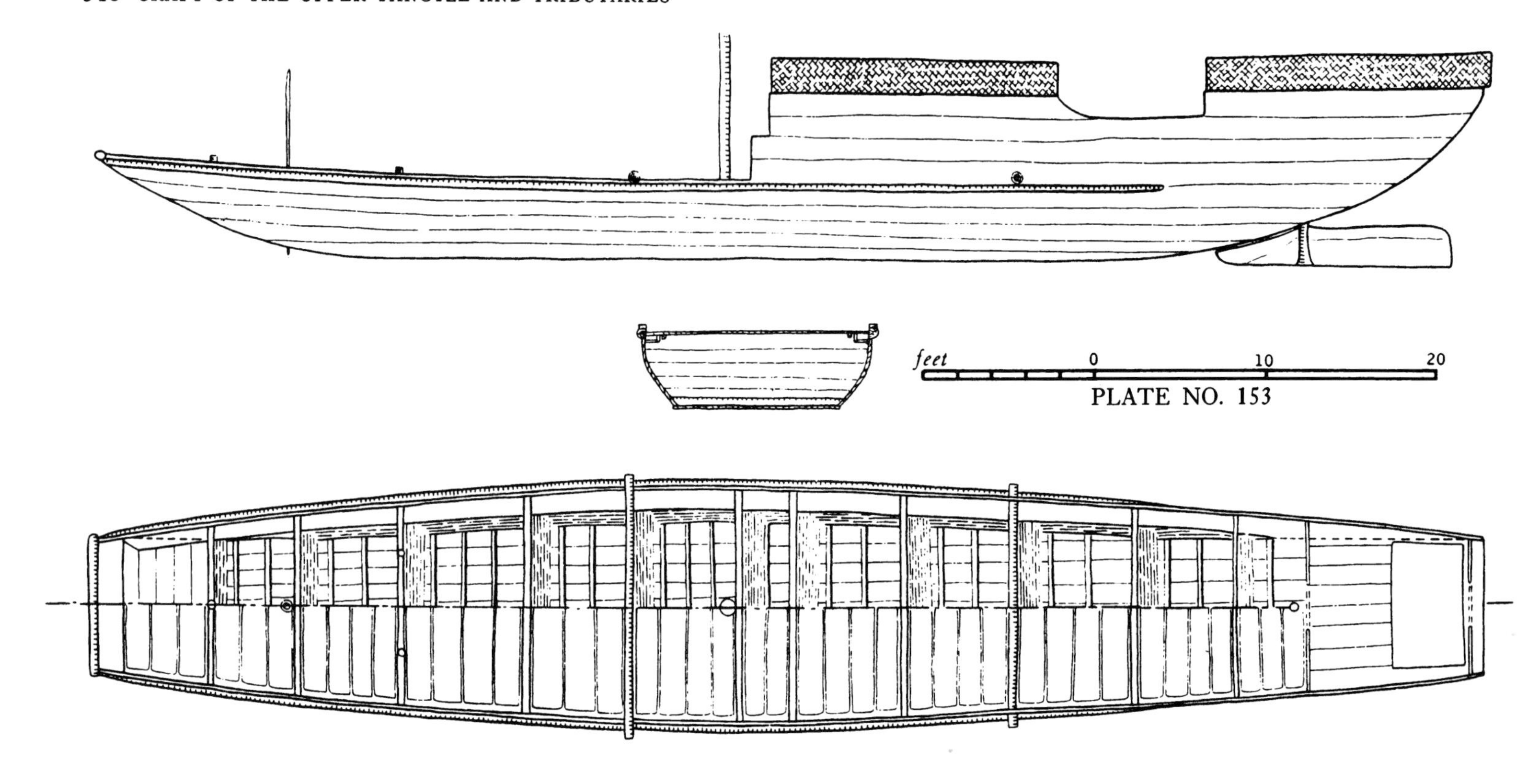

PLATE NO. 153

THE TO-LUNG-TZŬ

The normal trade route of the *to-lung-tzŭ* is between Chungking and Hochow, and above when circumstances permit. These are large, heavy craft built on the characteristic lines of a great many of the bigger junks of the Upper Yangtze. To the lay mind there is little to be discerned between this type and the *shao-ma-yang*, Plate No. 130, the *nan-ho-ch'uan*, Plate No. 166, and other varieties of these two, which follow their prototypes closely with only a few minor variations.

A typical specimen of the *to-lung-tzŭ*, as illustrated in Plate No. 153, is 93 feet long by 14 feet beam, with a depth of 4 feet, and is built of *ch'ing-kang* for the bottom boards and cypress for the rest of the planking.

The square, wide, flat bow ends in one of the heavy projecting cross-beams, of which there are three in all. Some of these craft have a 1-foot high bulwark on the forecastle extending back to the large open deck-house which begins abaft the mast, and is joined to the after-house by quite a high bulwark. This after-house contains a good cabin which, starting just abaft the rudder-head, covers an area of 10 feet by 8 feet and has a large window looking out over the stern. The customary River God is in a niche over the door.

The heavy rudder has a long, curved tiller leading to the conning position. The *sha-mu* mast is stepped in the normal way. A tall hardwood bollard is situated on the first bulkhead, and farther aft is a pair of shorter bitts for use in the same way as in the *lao-hua-ch'iu*, that is to say, in order that one of the two tracking-lines may be moved farther aft to negotiate a particularly sharp bend in the river.

The galley on the port side has a short, curved, brick chimney which ends at roof level. There is a standing crew of about six men, and 18 trackers are required for the upward journey. These craft are largely used for passenger traffic.

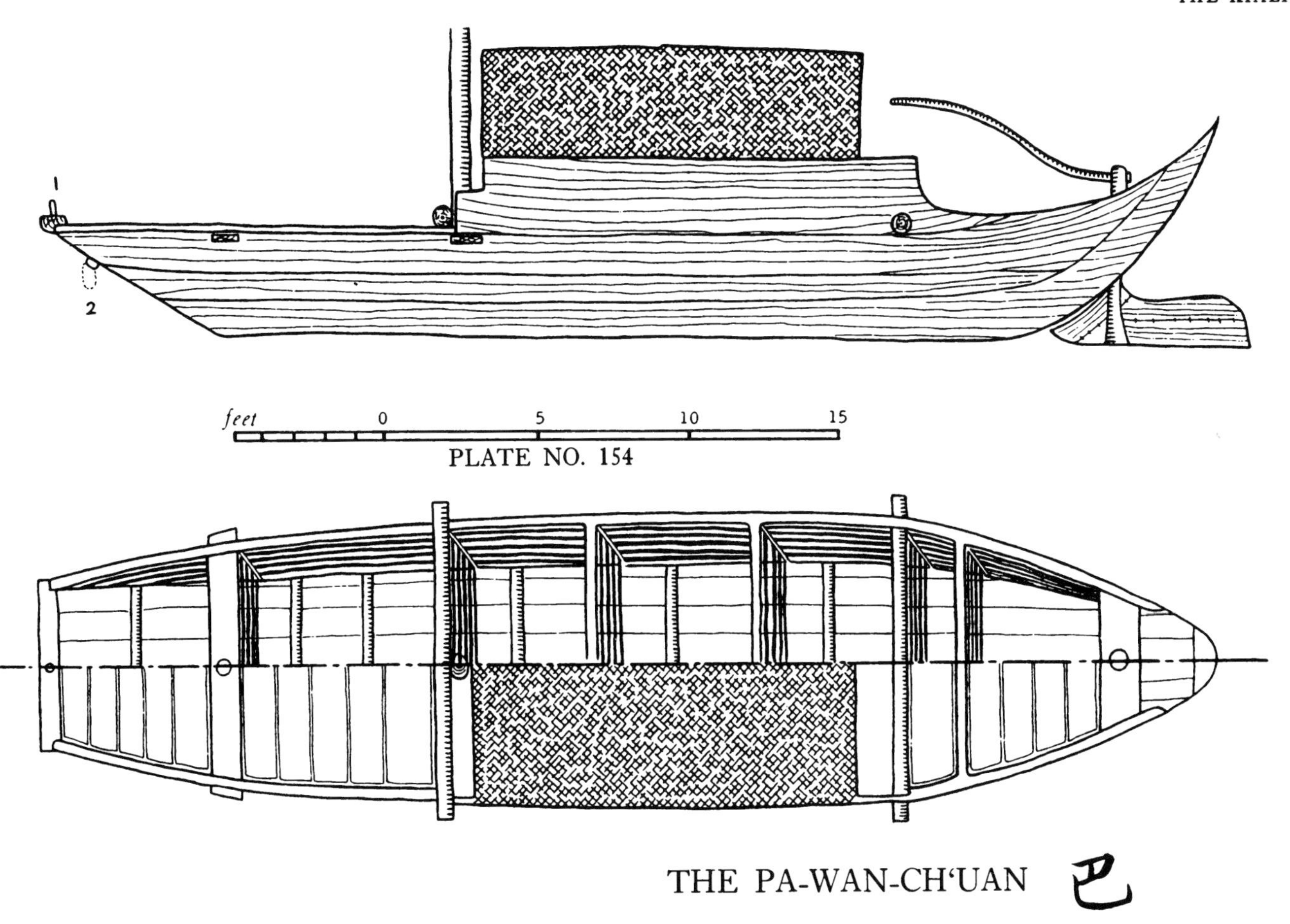

PLATE NO. 154

THE PA-WAN-CH'UAN 巴灣船

The *pa-wan-ch'uan* is sometimes known as the *huang-tou-k'o* (黃豆殼), or "yellow bean pod," on account of the similarity in its shape to that vegetable. Although mainly operating on the Kialing, it is one of the commonest types of junk to be met with at and around Chungking and in the adjacent tributaries. It varies considerably in length and small details of structure. A very general size is that illustrated in Plate No. 154, which measures 40 feet, with a beam of 9 feet and a depth of 3½ feet, being very beamy for its length. It is, moreover, very easy to distinguish because of its high, curiously tapered stern, though this may vary in size and height.

The deck-house, comprising about one-third of the length of the boat, is placed amidships but farther aft than forward. It is in every respect primitive and devoid of any elaboration. The strictest economy obtains throughout: the galley has degenerated into a mere charcoal brazier, and even the junkmen's God here takes the form of a short, sturdy thole pin[1] in the bow, though this representation of the divinity they propitiate receives the same obeisance and respect as the more elaborate plaster images in the larger junks and would appear to afford equal satisfaction.

The smaller varieties of the type do not even have a mast, but proceed under oars or tracking. Trackers for the journey up the Kialing are engaged for $20 per trip, which usually takes a month. The number of annual trips ranges from one to three, though as many as six can be taken if to Hochow only. The crew are all men from the Kialing River district.

An interesting method of bringing the junk up all standing, or turning short round, is achieved by means of a pole slipped through a grass-rope strop[2] secured to what might be described as a built-in wooden ring-bolt, set at a slight angle under the overhang of the bow. The pole, when driven into the bed of the river, acts as an instant brake.

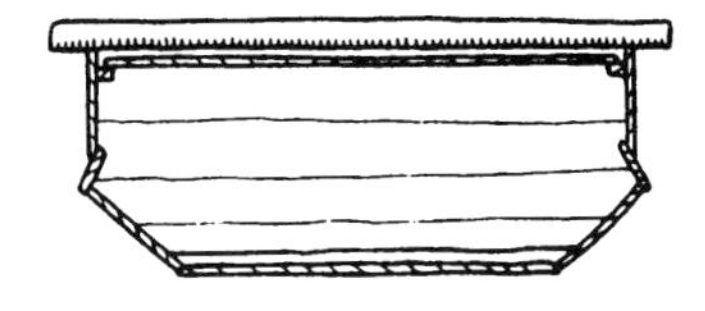

金銀錠 THE CHIN-YIN-TING

These queer craft are named *chin-yin-ting*, or the "gold and silver ingot," from their shape, which bears some resemblance to sycee, or the semi-spheroidal ingot of silver. They ply on the Suitingho, the eastern affluent of the Kialing River, and penetrate as far up as it is navigable, carrying up eight packets of salt, each weighing 175 catties, and returning to Chungking with medicines.

This type, which is very uniform in design and fairly common in Chungking, is illustrated in Plate No. 155. The over-all measurement is 33½ feet, with a beam of 7½ feet at the broadest point, which is about 6 feet from the stern. They are very easily recognised by reason of their bow and stern, which rise gently and taper—the former gently and the latter abruptly—until both finally narrow to a mere 8 inches across. This constitutes the narrowest bow on the Upper Yangtze.

Lightly built of *pai-mu* throughout, the workmanship is rough, and the minimum amount of nails is used, actually only about one to every foot of planking. Economy is also served by half sections of cross-beams abaft the house. The removable house occupies much more room than is usual. There is no mast, and propulsion is by oars and tracking.

The crew consists of three men and four trackers. When past navigable use, the craft are in great demand as foundations for floating dwellings, and in spite of their small size, they can accommodate two families complete with the usual live stock.

In the second-hand market, despite its name, the "gold and silver ingot" is only valued at $60.

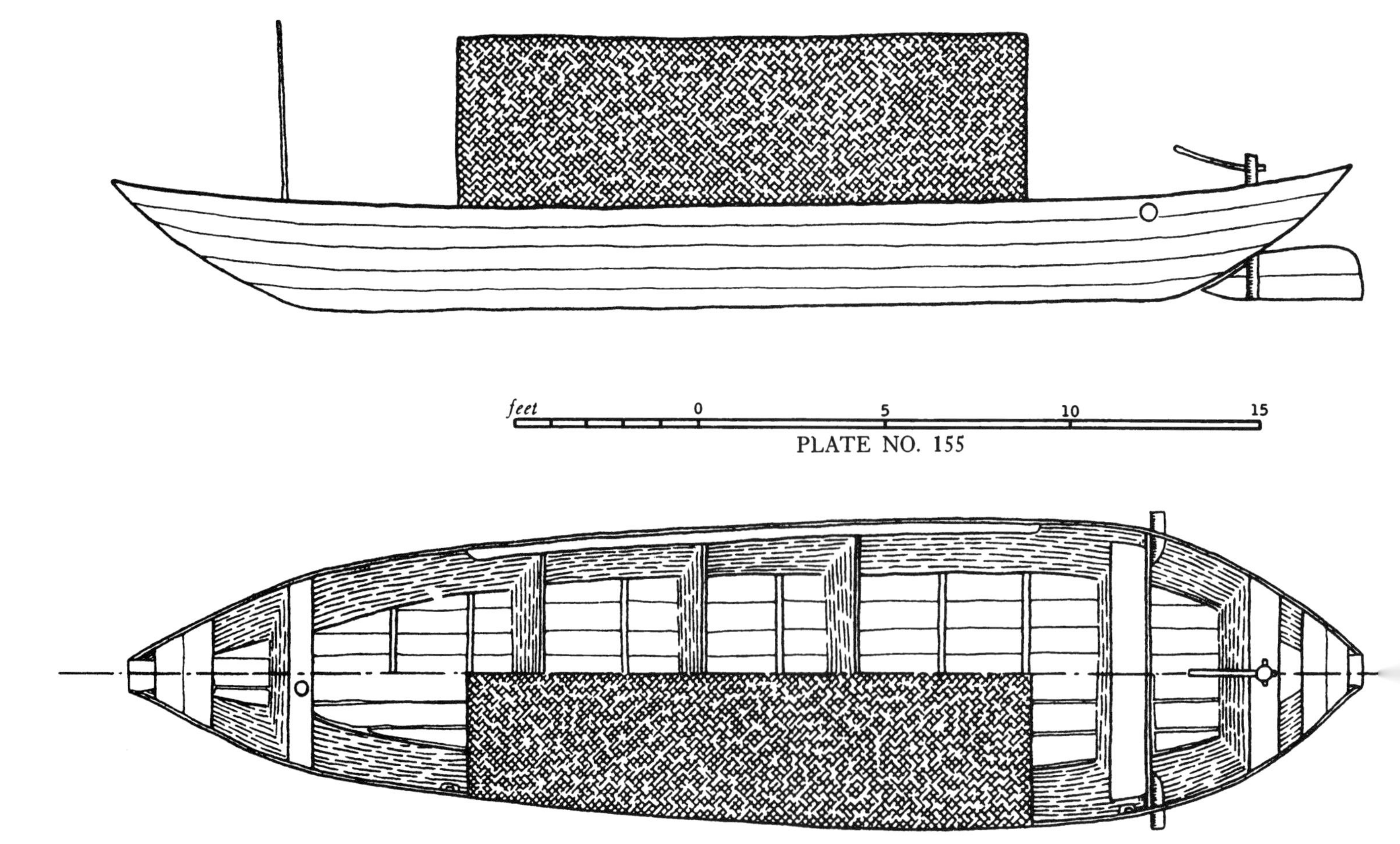

PLATE NO. 155

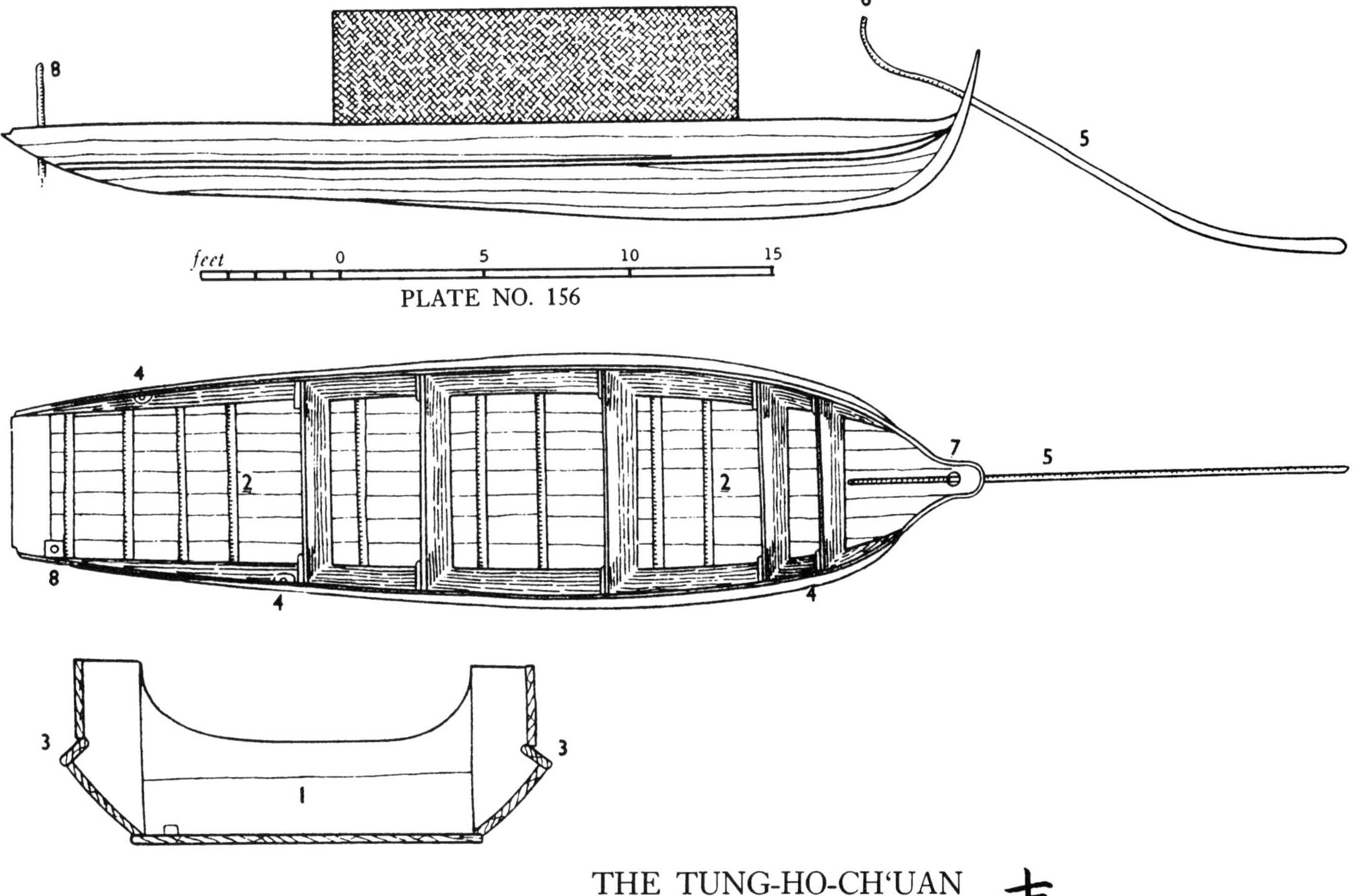

PLATE NO. 156

THE TUNG-HO-CH'UAN 東河船

The *tung-ho-ch'uan*, Plate No. 156, is a flat-bottomed, light-draught cargo carrier, designed for the shoal-water upper reaches of the Suitingho, the easternmost affluent of the Kialing River.

Normally measuring about 35 feet and 8½ feet beam, this type is sturdily built and, for its size, admirably adapted to carry a maximum load on a minimum draught. The construction of what may be termed "half-bulkheads"[1] and "half-frames"[2] is typical of all smaller Upper Yangtze craft. In this case there are five of the former strengtheners and nine of the latter.

A cross section on Plate No. 156 shows the "half-bulkhead,"[1] and also illustrates the method of combining the essential light-draught quality demanded with the additional cargo space. This is provided by a sudden increase in beam,[3] almost like a blister, with a sharp tumble home below the water-line.

There is neither mast nor rudder. Propulsion is effected by three oars.[4] The two foremost oars are worked by two men, while the after oar is operated by the laodah, who works it with his right hand while controlling the stern-sweep,[5] with its turned-up loom,[6] with his left hand. This substitute[5] for a rudder passes through a circular hole[7] in the distinctive, high, narrow, pointed stern. A cheek-piece, similar to that shown in Plate No. 147 (Chungking sampan), has a deep slot cut in its projecting side. This engages in a wooden cross-piece which, bisecting the aperture in the stern, acts as a bearing-pin.

The "stick in the mud"[8] anchor is placed to one side, right in the bow, so as to be clear of cargo being embarked. A small removable mat house is usually fitted amidships. A marked feature of these junks, which gives a curious lift to the outline of the hull, is the light-draught construction forward.

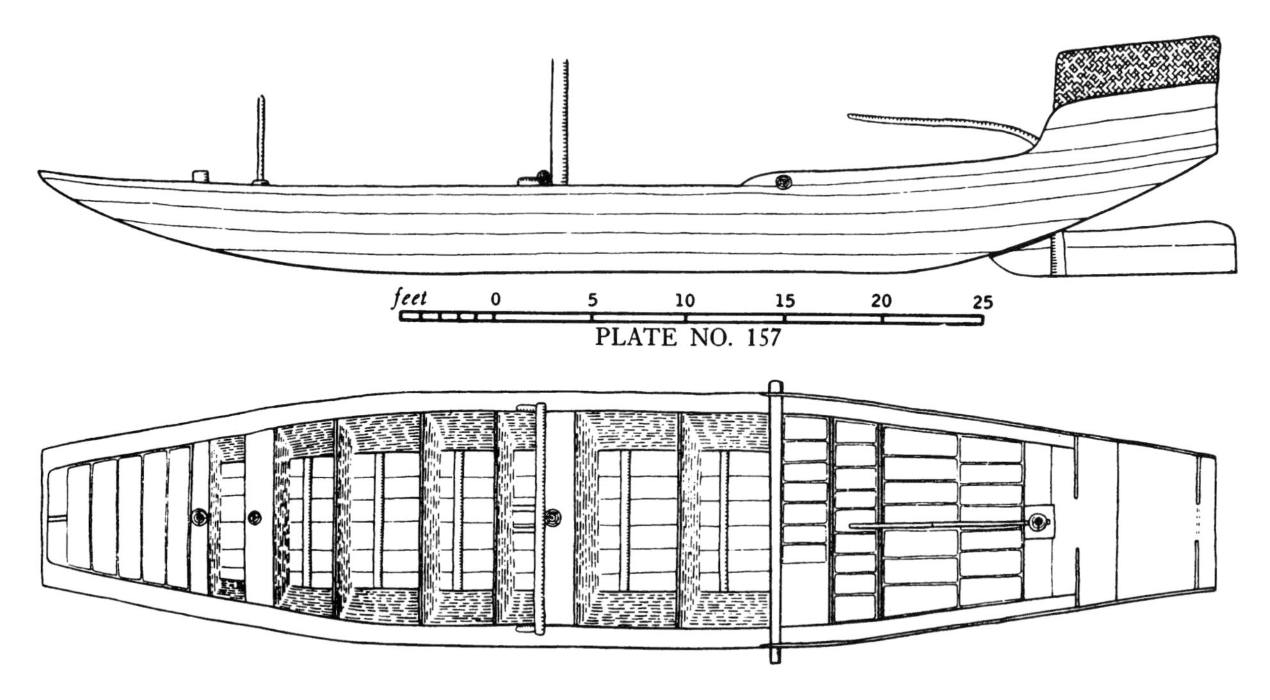

PLATE NO. 157

廠邊邊 THE CH'ANG-PIEN-PIEN

The *ch'ang-pien-pien*, as illustrated in Plate No. 157, is a typical example of a medium-sized coal carrier on the Little River. This boat measures 60½ feet, with a beam of 12½ feet and a depth of 4½ feet, although when fully loaded with 14 tons of coal the free-board is little more than a few inches.

Built with *ch'ing-kang* bottom and *pai-mu* sides, this type is of very strong construction, as is necessary for carrying a dead-weight cargo such as coal, and there are numerous bulkheads with half-frames between.

This junk is one of the most common types to be seen at Chungking. Indeed, their numbers are so great that they have to wait their turn at the mines up the Kialing River for sometimes as long as two weeks before obtaining a cargo.

It is interesting to compare this junk with the Chungking sampan, Plate No. 147, page 536.

The short mast is for tracking purposes only, for this type of craft is propelled by eight oars when down bound, and the rowers act as trackers on the upward journey. A few additional men are engaged to assist in getting the boat over a rapid.

Additional Types or Variations of Which No Plans are Available.

The Paishui, or Pikow River (白水或碧口河), has a very short course in Szechwan territory, as, after crossing the frontier from Kansu (甘肅), it is soon absorbed in the waters of the Kialing, junction with which is effected at Chaohwahsien (昭化縣).

This tributary of the Kialing is little more than a mountain stream traversing a series of gorges from Pikow (碧口) to within a few miles of Chaohwahsien. A few large boats, known as the medicine or tobacco junks, laden with 25,000 catties of tobacco venture down; but the river is practically unnavigable, and these boats on reaching Kwangyüan are broken up and do not attempt to get back again.

The Tsŭ and the Siang River coal-junk, Part Three, page 426, is also broken up on arrival at destination.

No iron nails are used in their construction, it being said that a loadstone on the route would cause the junk to be sucked under and lost. A more probable reason, however, is that nails are expensive and the wooden pegs that are used in lieu are quite efficient enough to last the trip. The junks, moreover, as a further economy, are caulked with moss instead of oakum or bamboo shavings.

CHUNGKING TO PINGSHAN

ON leaving Chungking the river curves round to the west between the shingle bank of the airport and the extensive sand and shingle flats off Hai-Tang-Chi. Opposite the south wall of the city and between these obstructions, the channel narrows to about 300 yards at low water. At high levels, however, the width of the river here is two-thirds of a mile. The country to the west is broken, and the river curves round a chain of high, grey sandstone hills running north and south with some considerable upheaval of the strata.

For the first 15 miles the trend is mostly to the south. The general character of the scenery is more open and much cultivated, with low hills near the stream, which winds and curves up as far as Suifu, 134 miles away. The country is still traversed by cross ranges, and the nature of the river is much influenced accordingly. Oranges are grown extensively in groves along the slopes on both banks, gold washing is to be seen, and later on there are extensive workings of coal. The character of the rock is silicious grit, with a fine red sandstone and a fair amount of conglomerate of varying solidity.

The river is now much shallower, and long sandy gravel beaches are common. Although the fall in the level of the river is greater than in the gorges, the bed of the stream is not encumbered with such prominent reefs, and the rapids are, therefore, easier to negotiate; moreover they have no tongue, as is the case with the rapids below Chungking. Such difficulties of navigation as they present therefore are now due to narrow and tortuous channels, to lack of water, and to the fact that the current always seems to set towards any submerged danger. The strength of the current varies from 2 to 2½ knots to 6 in the rapids at low water and 8 knots in the summer.

About four miles above the large village of Yü-Tung-Chen is a remarkable rock island named Hsiao-nan-hai-shih, Stone of the Small South Sea. It rises to a high pinnacle crowned with the inevitable temple set among trees. A change in the character of the river banks occurs at the gorge of Tan-jao-hsia running east and west for two miles. The cliff which gives its name to the gorge rises sheer from the left bank for 100 feet and is of a blue tint. Above here the river turns south, the banks fall away again, and orange groves become more numerous. The first tributary of any size to enter the Yangtze above the Kialingho at Chungking is the Kikiang at Kiangkow, or Chic-chiang-kow, a large village in a bay on the right bank. The Kikiang is said to be navigable for about 60 miles. Some miles further on, past a flat stretch of country, are some hills with ancient cliff dwellings.

The first town of any size is Kiangtsing, with a pagoda up-river beyond it on a hill. Village succeeds village; shingle banks, islands, and races follow each other. On the left bank is a town which derives its name from yet a third pair of the stone gates of the Upper Yangtze known as Shih-men. The two large rocks in this case are 200 yards apart on opposite banks of the river.

The second bad rapid on this stretch of water is that known as Lien-shih-san-t‘an. It is formed by a large shingle island near the right bank and rocks on the other side, which leave a channel only 30 yards wide. This rapid disappears at mid-level. Mountains now come into view, as the river swings from south-west to north-west, and an outstanding peak named Pi-chia-shan is noticeable.

A pagoda on the left bank is a pointer to the town of Ho-kiang, which has been likened to that of Fowchow. Like that town it is situated on the right bank, and on the left bank of an important tributary coming into it from the south to join the Yangtze. Both towns, too, are walled and stand on a sloping hillside. The affluent is the Chih-shui, variously known by several other names. It is 200 yards wide at its mouth and navigable for junks for about 70 miles, after which a difficult rapid necessitates lightening or transhipment of cargo. It forms a valuable waterway into the province of Kweichow.

Above Ho-kiang the river winds to the north-east for seven miles, and then turns west. The scenery is varied and pleasing with hills, ravines, and waterfalls and two conspicuous arches a few miles above Ho-kiang. Pagodas and towers also lend their decorative note to the landscape.

Above a difficult race, the Hsiaomit'an, which runs on each side of a shingle bank in mid-stream, the river makes a horseshoe bend, which extends to above the important town of Luchow. The Yangtze, in its sinuous course and at points below and above, exposes deep beds of gravel of great thickness on the right bank, as the deeper channels meander from side to side.

Luchow is a fair-sized town with the usual crenellated walls around it and the pagoda in its centre. It stands on the left bank of the Yangtze and on the right bank of T'o or Lu River at its junction with the main stream. This clear-water stream, called the Chin T'ang or River of Gold and Sugar, the Nei-chiang-ho and, in its upper reaches, the Chung-chiang, is about 300 miles long, but is navigable for only about a third of its length. It is said to be liable to a few sudden and dangerous freshets in the summer, which stop all navigation for a time. It flows through country immensely rich in agricultural produce and mineral deposits including, as its name implies, a limited quantity of gold. All up the narrow valley of the river may be seen the little matshed huts of gold washers, who are busy washing the tiny particles of gold from the fine black sand residue caught in the screen below their "cradles." Sugar cane is grown in abundance in the valley, and there are many refineries along the banks. Other exports are rice, tobacco, and timber, but the chief export from the interior, the one from which the town derives its main importance, is salt. About 60 miles up the river is a small affluent coming from the west, which affords direct water communicating with the famous salt wells of Tzeliutsing, one of the oldest, as well as the greatest, of China's engineering feats.

On leaving Luchow the river rounds the point into a wide westerly reach about three miles long. At the end of this bend is the small town of Lan-tsien-pa on the right bank, and opposite it a sturdy wall has been constructed leading from the Yangtze to the T'o River for the protection of the latter. The telegraph line to India also crosses the Yangtze here, a strange and anachronistic reminder of the insidious advance of modern science and civilization into the wildest and most remote regions. In the 70 mile stretch up to Suifu there are several villages and small towns and three walled cities. The scenery becomes very striking and is varied by ravines, chains of hills, advancing and retreating, and rocky banks alternating with shingle flats.

The next tributary to enter the Yangtze is the Na-ch'i-ho, 80 yards wide at its junction and reportedly navigable by junks for about 50 miles. As always, where any fair-sized stream enters the Yangtze, there is a town at its confluence, in this case the small walled town of Na-ch'i-hsien, on the right bank of the Yangtze and also of the Na-ch'i-ho, which divides it from its commercial suburb. The Yangtze here is nearly 600 yards broad, but shallow.

A shingle isle named Ta-chung-pa, a small stream called the Ya-lu-chi, and the rapid of Yeh-chu-ya with quite a line of breakers at its head, are followed in succession by another brook entering the river from the south and the detached rocks of Hsiang-lu-shih, or Burning Furnace. Above are the cliffs of Hsiao-hsin-chi-kou with more cliff dwellings with the hill of Niu-nao-shan, or Cow's Udder, to the south-west.

The second walled town before reaching Suifu is Chiang-an-hsien, 50 feet above the right bank in an attractive mountainous setting and with a fine pagoda. The chief local industry is a line of bamboo carvings. As usual with walled towns there is an affluent adjacent, the An-ning Ho. The bamboos grown in the vicinity are not only used for the fancy carved oddments, but are made into quanting poles, sounding bamboos, and boat-hooks. The houses that now form the hamlets near the river are of humbler type. Such trees as can be seen are more varied. Cedars are now common; and there are pines, ashes, and bamboos.

Above Chiang-an-hsien the river curves round in a long loop and widens to accommodate two large islands, one being both cultivated and inhabited. It narrows again later to pass between Lung-tung-shan, a hill crowned with a pagoda, and a shingle bank on the left bank; not far below the last walled town before Suifu is Nan-chih-hsien on the left bank. The rock formation here is limestone and red and grey sandstone in horizontal strata or dipping towards the south-east. A tower and bizarre-shaped rocks named Ting-ting-shih are the distinguishing features of this locality. Above the town there are whirlpools and disturbed waters owing to a transverse shingle bank three miles up-stream.

Two more rapids, the Kuo-pin-t'an and Hei-shih-t'an, improve with rising water; and the river turns past a pretty village to the town of Li-chuang, with some handsome pagodas and a picturesque pavilion. The river here is much hemmed in by shingle flats at low water.

Coal again crops up in considerable quantity and six miles below Suifu are the mines of Pa-ko-shan, where good bituminous coal is found. After another village with its neighbouring stream and the inevitable pagoda marking the approach to a town of any consequence, Suifu is reached, the last important town on the Yangtze or, as it is now, the Kinsha or River of Golden Sand. The usual confluence of waters marks the site and explains the existence of this busy trade and transhipment centre. The affluent in this case is the Min-kiang, which was for long considered by the Chinese to be the true continuation of the Yangtze instead of the Kinsha. The Min River, to be described later, descends from the north-west to join the Yangtze at its left bank. At Suifu the Yangtze narrows from about 400 to 500 yards to 250 yards. The Min and the Yangtze are of equal width; the former, however, has a shingle bank extending from its left shore which serves to narrow the channel at low water. Like most of the affluents of the Yangtze, the Min is a clear-water stream, in striking contrast to the main river, which here in its upper reaches is still muddy, though the colour is normally a light yellow except when in freshets it is stained red with the mud brought down the Kinsha from above Suifu.

There is a hill at the confluence and a pagoda opposite the town, which is situated 130 feet above low water level on the edge of the rugged and mountainous regions to the west. Behind and to the east are hills, which are used as burial grounds. The general nature of the rock is micaceous sandstone, and iron is to be found nearby. Suburbs extend to the north and south of the walled portion of the town, which measures two miles in circumference and lies parallel on two sides to the two rivers with deep water along both frontages. On approaching from the river, the Ho-kiang gate at the east corner and a pagoda are notable features; and just outside, at the point, are a fine archway and an interesting temple to the Emperor Yü. The town is said to date back at least 2,000 years to the time when it was set up as the capital of a state by the Emperor Yuan ti of the Han Dynasty.

In addition to the trade down the Min River from the populous and fertile Chengtu plain, trade from the south-western province of Yunnan converges on Suifu, and also from the very far western trade centre of Ning-yüan-fu in the Chien-chang valley lying to the south-west in the region of the most southern loops of the Kinsha.

The Chien-chang region is richly fertile and produces three crops a year, while the fruit trees are also prolific. One of the chief industries here is the trade in wax insects and thousands of pickers invade the country each year to collect the insects which breed in this valley. The eggs, which are laid in the branches of ash or privet, are picked and despatched each April to the wax district, some 200 miles to the north-east. The coolies work in relays so as to complete the journey in six days and thus to arrive before the insects hatch. The cone-shaped scales full of eggs are then replaced on ash or privet trees, where the eggs come to maturity and the insects continue to deposit wax on the underside of the branches over a period of about four months. The wax is then collected, skimmed off, and formed into hard cakes. It is used to coat the softer wax of Chinese candles, to polish semi-precious stones and furniture and to add gloss to cloth or high-grade paper.

On leaving Suifu the Yangtze preserves much of the same character; only it remains narrower, and after the first two miles of flat country the banks are steeper as the country rises rapidly towards the mountainous western region. The high lands approach the right bank, until at the village of Pai-shu-chi seven miles above Suifu the river is confined in a long rocky defile, down which the current descends with force. Many races and whirlpools make navigation difficult. The rock formations are reddish sandstone, and coal occurs in considerable quantities.

About 13 miles above Suifu is the fair-sized town of An-pien, which shows a striking departure from custom in that it is on the left bank and not at the confluence of the Yangtze with a side stream, the Ta-kwan-ho, which enters from the south.

The Yangtze now curves to the west and soon enters a 2½-mile-long gorge named An-pien-hsia, with walls some 500 feet high. Coal is here extensively worked. Rapids of varying strength according to the water level succeed each other. The villages are mostly concerned with the mining industry. The coal produced in this area is excellent steam coal, probably better than any other found on the river. The river is closely hemmed in by mountains, which are cultivated right up to their summits. Fir and fruit trees grow plentifully. There is one more straight reach, where coal is worked, and the village of Hui-i-chi appears situated at the mouth of a side stream. After some meanderings, mostly in a westerly direction, Pingshan is reached. It is a small town with nothing remarkable about it except the fact that it marks the limit of continuous junk navigation for a distance of 1,700 miles from the sea on the fifth largest river in the world.

THE KIKIANG AND THE CHIHSHUIHO

THE Ki River enters the Yangtze on the right, or south, bank close by a large village named Kiangtsing (江 津), or Kikiangkow (綦 江 口), meaning Ki River mouth. This river is navigable by large junks at high water for about 60 miles, up to the town of Kikiang, with loads of from 20,000 to 30,000 catties. At low river they can only load to one-half this amount. A considerable amount of salt is conveyed this way into Kweichow.

An affluent of this river, known as the Sanki, or Sung River (三 溪 或 松 江), is navigable by smaller craft as far up as Sungkan (松 坎), about 85 to 90 miles from the Yangtze. Above this point rafts are the only means of communication.

At least two well-defined types of craft are built for the navigation of this river, and a very noticeable feature is that, although both are totally different in design, yet both are almost precisely the same length. They both show, moreover, by their general lines and appearance, that they have been constructed for use in shoal water and are well adapted to negotiate the many obstacles in the river-bed which make navigation of the Ki River slow and difficult.

Locally the Chihshuiho is known as the Jenhwaiho (仁 懷 河) or Hokiang-siaoho. This quite important tributary, which provides communication with the province of Kweichow, is navigable up to the small walled town of Yunghwaiting (永 懷 亭), about 42 miles from its mouth, where it is about 200 yards broad. During the winter the rapids and shallows make navigation difficult.

This river rises not far from the source of the Kungt'anho in the hills south of the Yangtze, where the three far western provinces of Yunnan, Kweichow, and Szechwan meet, and, indeed, it more or less follows the frontier line between the two latter provinces.

Flowing between precipitous limestone gorges, it finally empties itself at the south-east side of the town of Hokiang (合 江) into the waters of the Upper Yangtze, which, above Suifu, take on the name of Kinsha (金 沙), or River of Golden Sand.

The main exports down the Chihshuiho are wood, charcoal, bamboo, and medicines, while salt and yarn are carried up stream.

Above the town of Yunghwaiting, a transhipment centre, specially constructed junks operate on the Chihshuiho. They are said to be obliged to discharge their cargo in order to negotiate a particularly difficult rapid named Pint'an (品 灘), 20 miles above Yunghwaiting. Their limit of navigation is about 10 miles above Pint'an.

It is probable that above this point more isolated navigable stretches recur, as is so often the case with the tributaries of the Upper Yangtze where no through navigation is possible.

The junkmen affirm that a small type of "crooked-stern" junk, similar to that in use in the Kungt'anho, is used in the upper reaches to surmount the many rapids. This report, if true, is of particular interest, for the head waters of the river are close to each other.

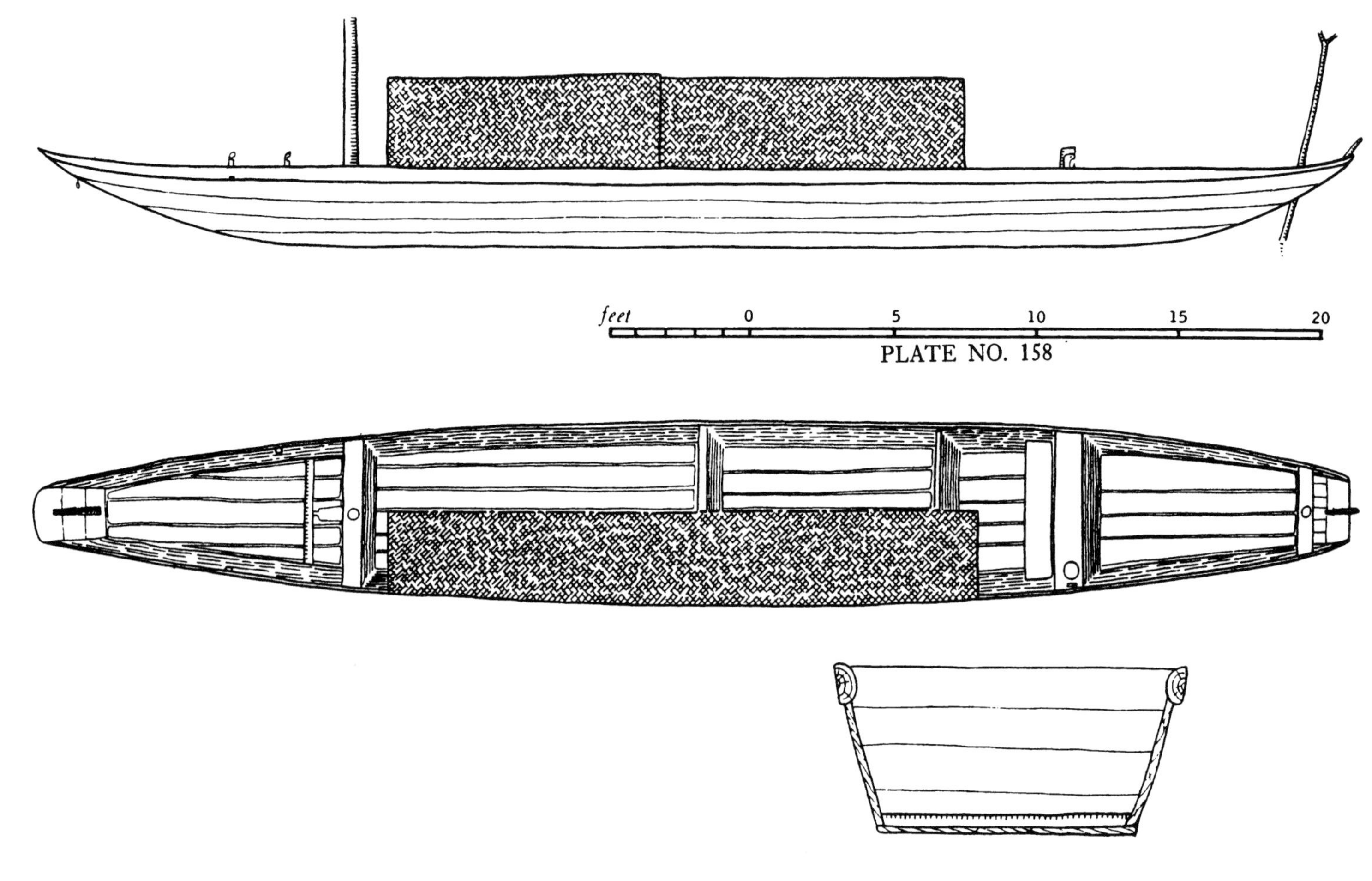

PLATE NO. 158

小河船 THE HSIAO-HO-CH'UAN

This is a very light-draught species of coal carrier, Plate No. 158, with an over-all length of 47 feet, a beam of 6 feet, and a depth of 3 feet. The *pai-mu* wood hull is divided into four bulkheads, with no frames of any kind, and is built on slender lines.

These boats are often to be seen in Chungking. They carry 1,000 catties of coal from the mines on the Ki River and return light. Usually they travel in convoys of four.

They are equipped with a mast and a large, heavy, square mat sail, but they rely for the most part on their oars for propulsion. The crew consists of three men: the laodah, who works the long stern-sweep and an oar, and two men, who each operates an oar in the fore part of the vessel.

The "stick in the mud" anchor is situated in the stern, which suggests, as in the case of the Wushan "fan-tail" junk, that there are decided fluctuations in the level of the Ki River and also the presence of an up current at times.

三板船 THE SAMPAN-CH'UAN

This craft, Plate No. 159, which measures 46 feet, with a beam of 9 feet, is built on square punt-like lines, and its main distinguishing features, which prevent confusion with the *pa-wan-ch'uan*, of which it is a variety, are a marked triangular-shaped flattening-in of the hull at bow and stern for a distance of about 6 feet and also a definite difference in the shape of the stern, which is square and broad.

The bottom is made of *ch'ing-kang*; the hull, of cypress. There are four bulkheads and eight half-frames. There is one cross-beam [1] built into the structure and situated aft of the house; it is used to secure the braces and also the tracking-lines from the mast.

The tiller [2] is typical of this class of vessel, and, after following the line of the deck for a foot or two, curves sharply upwards. It is said that this curve is obtained by a steaming process, but it seems not unlikely that the wood is more often grown to shape.

The shallow-draught type of rudder projects far beyond the small overhang of the stern, which curves roundly up to the same level as the slightly rising blunt bow. Both bow and stern are exactly the same in breadth, and both end in a cross-beam. A pair of bitts [3] are placed on either side of a "stick in the mud" anchor [4] on the first bulkhead. The small house, which starts abaft the mast, has built-up sides and is roofed with matting.

These junks are coal carriers, and the bottom boards are placed on the top of the cargo throughout its length—usually leaving a mere 2 or 3 feet head room in the living-space inside the house.

The laodah does not stand on a plank, as is usual in all other Upper Yangtze craft, but on the deck, below which all cargo is stowed. His view forward, therefore, is alwavs through the house.

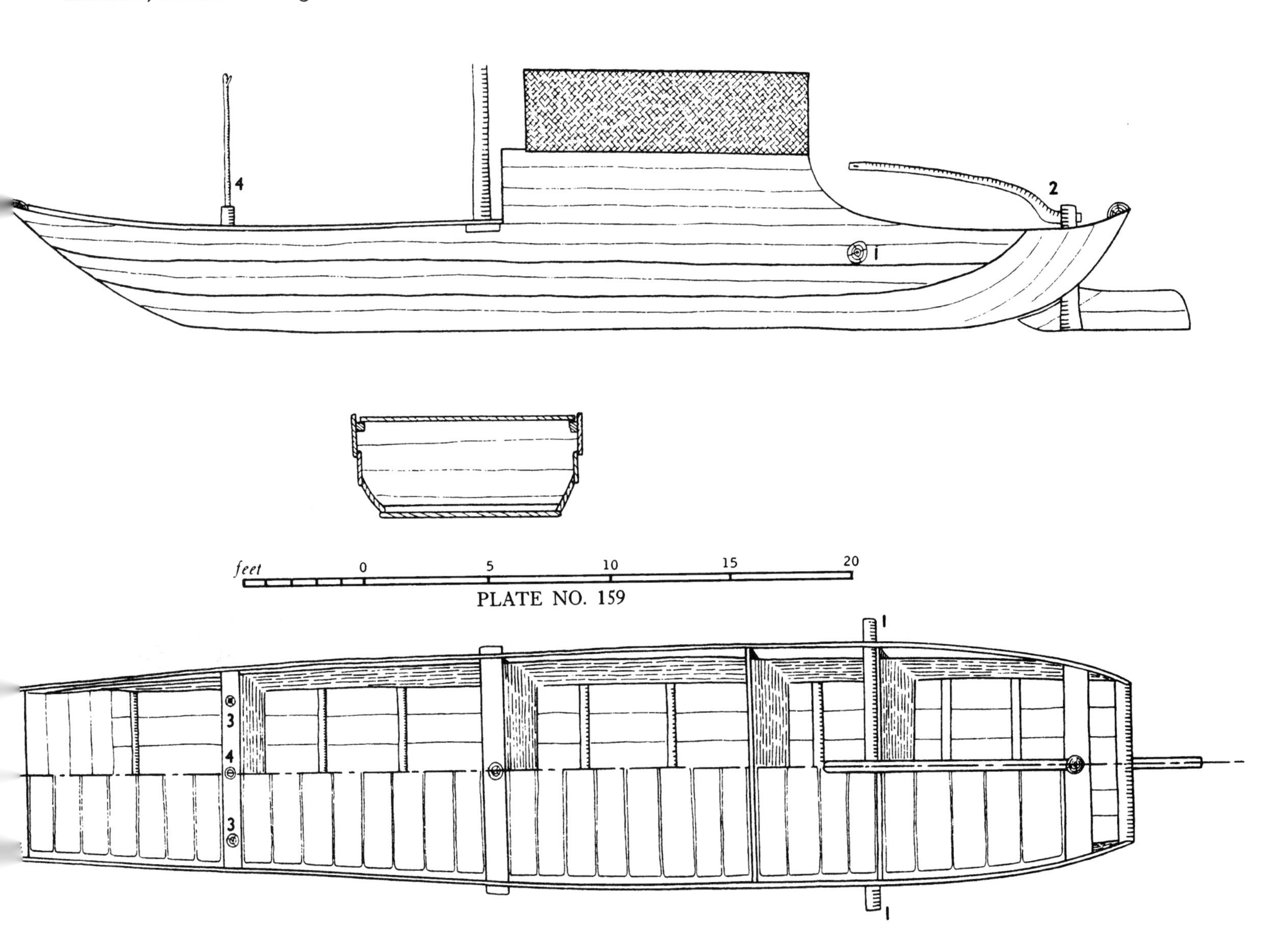

PLATE NO. 159

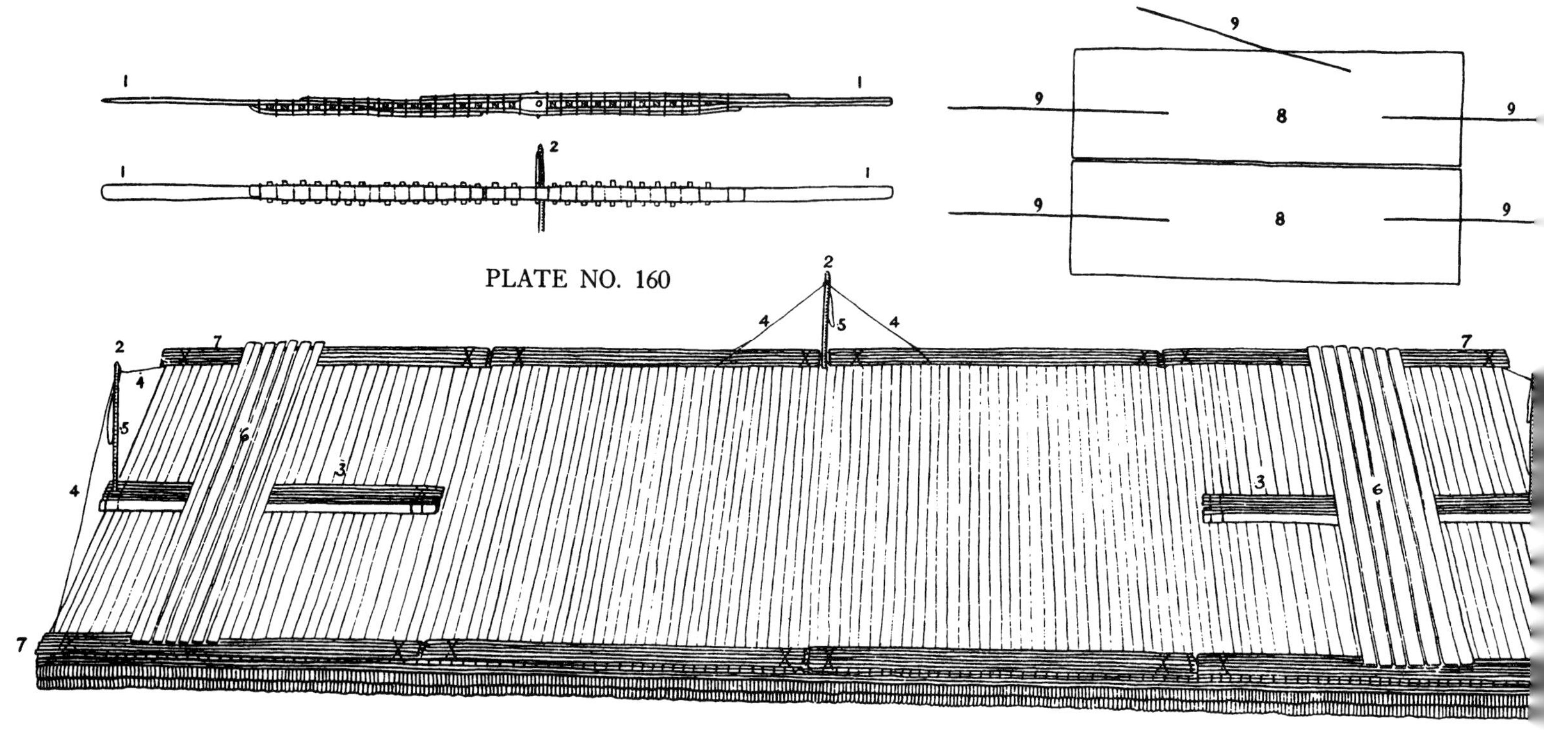

PLATE NO. 160

杉木筏子

THE SHA-MU RAFT OF THE CHIHSHUIHO

The *sha-mu* plank raft, as illustrated in Plate No. 160, measures 58 feet long, with a beam of 15 feet, and is the largest size of raft able to come down the Chihshui River from the town of that name. The draught in winter is about 2 feet, but during the high-water season rafts are built to draw as much as 7 feet. Two men can build a raft in 10 days.

The rafts travel down singly, and on arrival at the mouth of the river at Hokiang join up into pairs lashed alongside each other, and so continue their voyage down the Yangtze to Chungking, where they are broken up and sold.

There is nothing remarkable about their construction, which consists of bundles of *sha-mu* planks lashed together and placed athwartships. Deck planks are laid also athwartships, across the top of these, and secured to fore and aft strengthening pieces along the sides, about 6 inches inboard and 6 inches high, forming a small continuous coaming.

Everything on board is made of *sha-mu* except the cooking-stove and the straw bedding on which the crew of four men sleep in an improvised "house," which is no more than a *sha-mu* plank lean-to.

The distinctive feature of this craft is the type of sweep [1] employed, which, like everything else on board, is improvised from *sha-mu* planks of varying sizes, thicknesses, and lengths, lashed together at frequent intervals. Through these lashings wedges are driven between the planks to tighten the component parts and maintain rigidity. This apparently haphazard method produces an exceedingly strong implement, and, for all its clumsy appearance, it is balanced with great care, and the result is a most practical, economical, and simple job.

The three identical sweeps operate one at each extremity of the raft and one on the beam. The thole pins [2] at each end are 3-foot high poles driven into the deck planks, where they are kept in position by partners [3] composed of *sha-mu* planks lashed to the deck. All three thole pins [2] are fitted with guys [4] and a bamboo-rope grummet,[5] from which the sweep is slung. A few planks [6] laid athwartships over the coaming [7] and thole-pin partners act as a small raised platform for the men at the bow and stern sweeps.

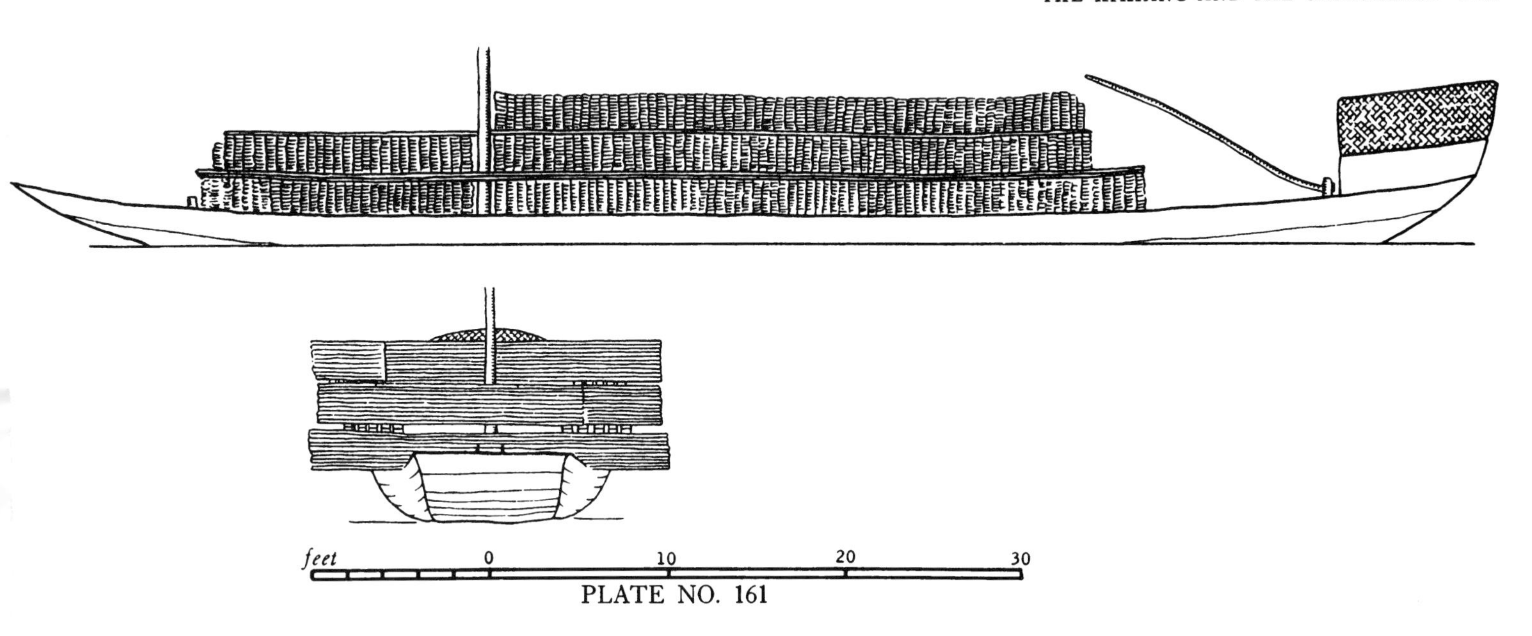

PLATE NO. 161

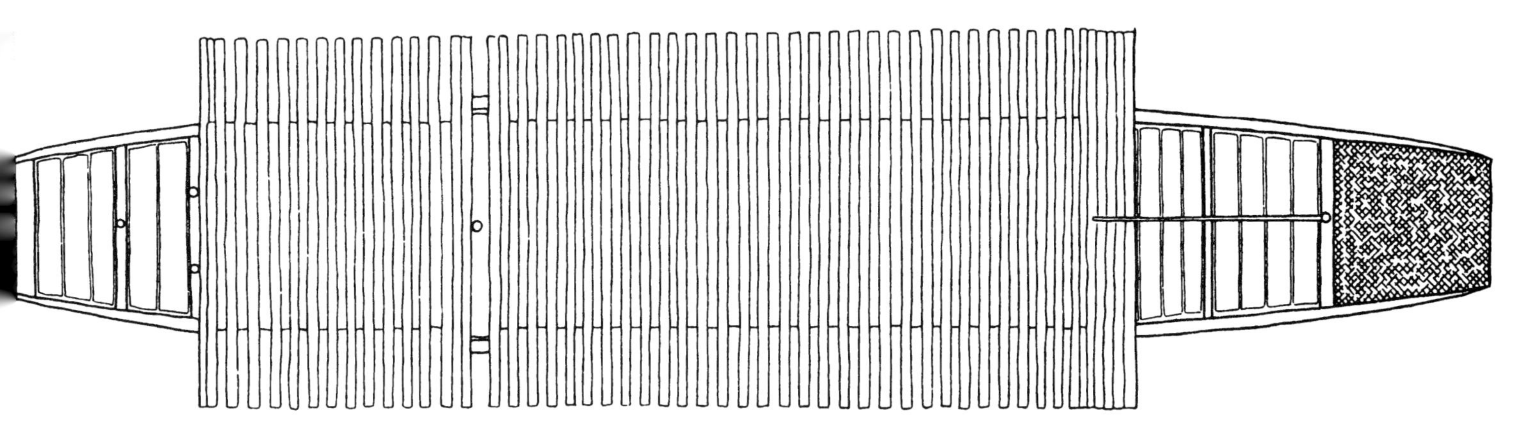

THE TIMBER CARRIER

The timber carrier of the Upper Yangtze is very distinctive, not only on account of its very remarkable beam, but also because the small living quarters in the only built-up house are right aft.

The junk illustrated in Plate No. 161 is 85 feet long, with a beam of 15 feet, and is actually a less beamy type than usual. The outstanding feature in the construction is the fact that there are only three bulkheads. This provides uninterrupted stowage room for balks of timber to be laid in the hold. The sawn planks comprising the rest of the cargo are stowed athwartships in regular ascending rows, each tier of 10 deep being separated from the next by fore and aft planks.

In spite of their heavy build and cumbersome arrangement of superimposed cargo, these junks can be manœuvred with apparent ease. They are propelled by four oars on each side and have a sweep on the quarter. The mast is used for sailing up stream and, of course, for tracking.

These craft bring wood, mostly *sha-mu*, to Chungking from Hokiang, a town at the mouth of the Chihshuiho, and other timber, chiefly *pai-mu*, from Hochow, on the Kialing River.

THE T'o or Lu River, also called the Fushun (富順) and the Kintangho (金糖河), that is to say, the River of Gold and Sugar, rises in the Min Mountains (岷山) and flows for about 300 miles to join the Yangtze at Luchow, forming a useful highway to tap some of the natural wealth of Szechwan. Like the Minkiang, it affords direct communication with the plain of Chengtu (成都).

The narrow valley through which it flows is potentially rich, producing, as its name indicates, sugar cane and small quantities of gold from its shingle banks. Moreover, rice and salt are shipped in large quantities. About 60 miles above Luchow a small tributary leads to the prolific salt wells of Tzeliutsing (自流井).

The story of the salt wells of Tzeliutsing is told in Part One, pages 139–47.

In summer the T'o River can be navigated for about 250 miles as far as Hsüankow (漩口) by large junks. In winter, however, only small junks can reach so far. At Hanchow (漢州) a canal is said to join the upper reaches of the Luho (瀘河) with those of the Minkiang above Chengtu, the capital of Szechwan, though it is only navigable by sampans or similar craft. There are many rapids all along the T'o River.

A junk very rarely seen in Chungking is the *tung-kua-ch'uan* (東瓜船), a sugar carrier from the T'o Valley. Other types now obsolete, which formerly plied on this river, are the *kuo-ch'an-t'ou* (鍋鏟頭), a large salt and general cargo carrier, and the *mao-yü-ch'iu* (毛魚秋), which was a larger variation of the willow leaf junk, or *liu-yeh-ch'uan*, before the final evolution from this type of the present *chung-yüan-po*.

THE CHUNG-YÜAN-PO

These junks, which are very uniform in type, vary considerably in size and are of comparatively recent design, for they only date back about 50 years. Before that time the only junks controlled by the same guild were the *liu-yeh-ch'uan* (柳葉船), or "willow leaf junks," so named on account of their shape, which tapers at bow and stern.

These willow leaf junks, which still function above Luchow on the T'o River, trade with Kintang (金堂), a town situated on the cross-country channel connecting the T'o River and Minkiang, not far from Chengtu. In the high-water season they can get up the Minkiang as far as Kwanhsien (灌縣). They are small craft, with a short mast and stern-sweep instead of a rudder, and not more than 5 tons capacity. As this was considered inadequate, the *chung-yüan-po* was evolved to bring larger cargoes down the T'o Valley, much of which is transhipped from the willow leaf junk. Both types carry tobacco, sugar, and salt, and operate under the auspices of the Chungking-Kintang Guild, on whose books there are actually as many as 5,000 *chung-yüan-po* junks registered. The largest *chung-yüan-po* salt junks can carry well over 100 tons, while the sugar junks carry up to 60 tons.

The *chung-yüan-po* also navigate up the Yangtze as far as Suifu as well as down to Chungking, and even occasionally down to Shasi and up the Kialing

River to Kwanyuan. The main centres for building these junks, which are made of *nan-mu* with *ch'ing-kang* for the bottom, are Luchow and Nuikiang on the T'o River and Kintang near Chengtu.

A typical specimen, as illustrated in Plate No. 162, measures 94 feet, with a beam of 14 feet and a depth of 5 feet, and is a graceful, light-draught vessel of eminently pleasing lines. The stern, which is the main distinguishing feature, ascends slightly and tapers to a long, narrow point.

Principally intended to ply in shallow waters, she shows the favourite method of combining light draught with extra cargo capacity, which is provided in the shape of blistered sides. An unusual feature, however, is the joining of the side planks to the deck planks by means of a wooden angle piece.[1] Strength throughout the boat is afforded by 11 full bulkheads.

The 30-foot house starts abaft the mast and ends at the tenth bulkhead. Instead of a whole cross-beam across this bulkhead, economy has been served by a compromise, for two quarter portions[2] only—2 feet in length—are secured to the top of the bulkhead. The projecting outboard ends of this sham cross-beam are used for making fast the braces and tracking-lines.

The sail in general use is the square sail, so common on the Upper Yangtze. When these junks venture below Wanhsien they use a lug-sail, and it is maintained that they adapt the square sail to this purpose by folding down one corner and withdrawing the horizontal bamboo battens. The idea, though surprising, is not improbable and shows economical ingenuity.

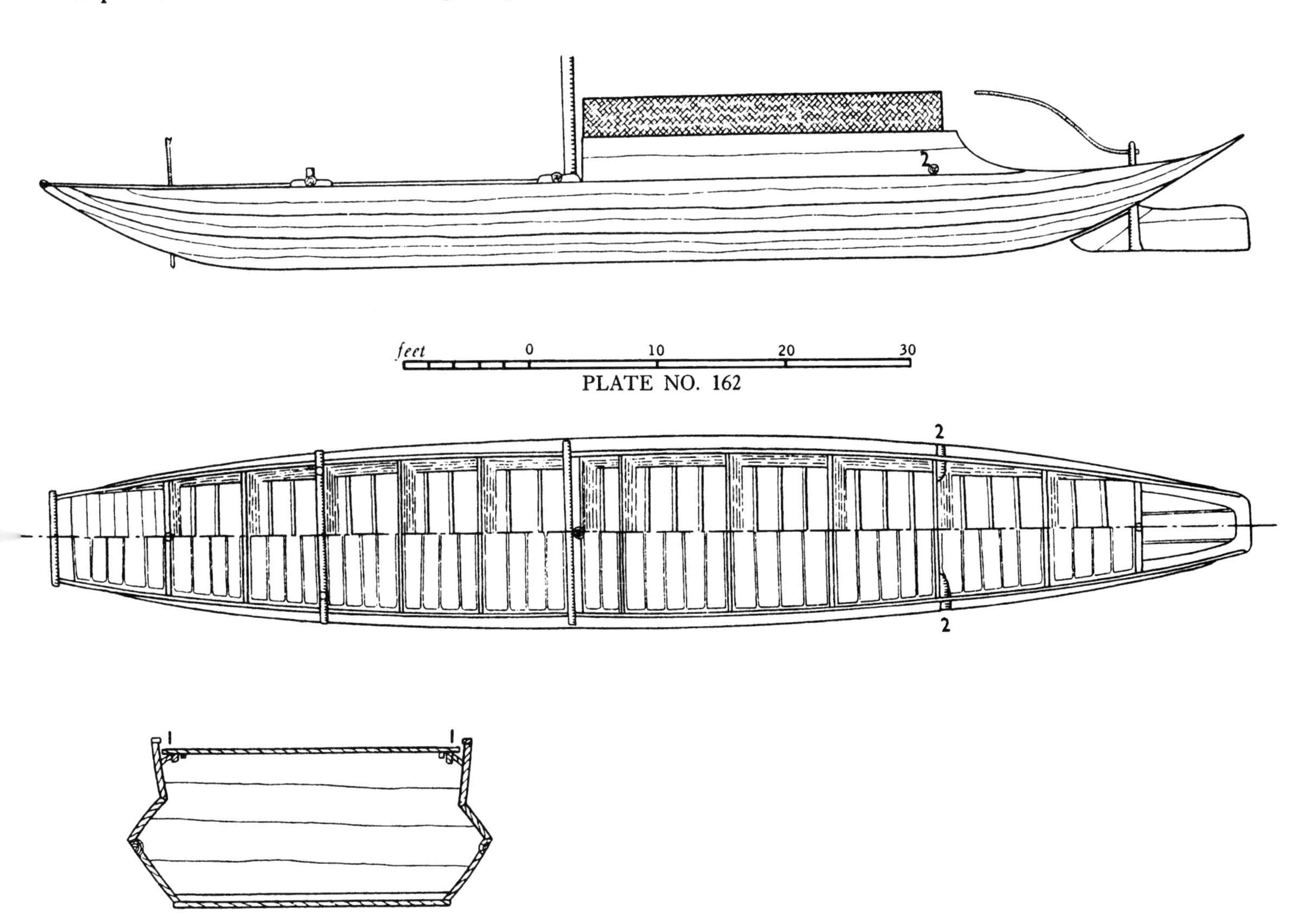

PLATE NO. 162

THE COAL JUNK: A VARIETY OF THE CHUNG-YÜAN-PO

This type of junk, which has a large range in size, is a square-shaped double-ender of about 40 feet long, with a beam of 12 feet and not much lift in the stern. It preserves the main characteristics of build in that it has the distinctive angular blister which, running its whole length, disappears into the structure of the hull a few feet short of bow and stern.

Two deck-beams extend outboard on either side, one being lashed just before the mast—its purpose apparently being to provide a securing place for the tacks of the sail—and the other aft for making fast the tracking-lines. There are usually eight watertight compartments. The mast is stepped in the third of these against a bulkhead and between two heel-chocks; these exactly fit the compartment and so prevent any lateral movement. The heel of the mast on the bottom of the boat is kept from forward movement by a bamboo-rope grummet passing round it and through holes pierced in the watertight compartment—a most unseamanlike practice. Further security is provided at deck-level, where the mast is socketed into the transom.

The two large midship compartments are never decked-in as are the others, and act as an extension of the living quarters when the junk is without cargo. In spite of the fact that their whole cargo is coal, these junks are kept remarkably clean once it is discharged. The bilges are kept free from coal by dunnage in the form of bamboo gratings which fit the apertures left between the floor-boards. The built-up deck-house, just abaft the mast, covers about one-fourth of the total length. All the matting roof, which is supported on curved frames, is removable. A modicum of comfort is provided for the owner in a large square bed, built up like a small cabin under the stern roofing.

The galley, as usual, is a cement coal-stove on the port side just before the mast. These junks go up light and return with coal.

THE CROOKED-BOW SALT JUNK OF TZELIUTSING

The Chinese have shown themselves to be expert boat-builders, for all their craft are eminently suited to the waters in which they are designed to operate. Few types are more interesting than the *lu-ch'uan* (櫓 船), or oar boat.

As its name implies, one of its features is the enormous sweep, which may even be longer than the boat itself, but the most outstanding of many peculiarities is the crooked construction of the bow, designed to negotiate the rapids on the Yentsingho (鹽 井 河), or Salt Well River.*

The Weiyüanho (威 遠 河) and the Junghsienho (榮 縣 河) unite a few miles above Tzeliutsing and proceed, as the Yentsingho, to the T'o or Lu River (沱 江). On this short stretch of 120 *li*, or about 40 miles,† there are four formidable rapids. The first is a weir at Chungt'an (重 灘); the second at Hsien-t'an (仙 灘) consists of a rapid and weir; the third at Yent'an (沿 灘) is the worst obstacle of all; and finally there is a dam and rapid at Laoyat'an (老 鴉 灘).

The crooked-stern junks of Fowchow (涪 州) have attracted the attention of travellers passing by that town and have acquired a limited and rather local fame, but the crooked-bow junks of Tzeliutsing seem to have contrived to exist without attracting the slightest wonder, or, indeed, much notice, even in their

* Also known as the Tzeliutsingho (自 流 井 河) or, shortly, as the Tsingho (井 河).

† In 川 鹽 紀 要, written by Mr. Ling Chên Han (林 振 翰) of Ningteh of the Fukien province, the distance is given as 180 *li*, or 60 miles.

Crooked-bow junks moving down river.

own home port. Exhaustive research produces at most two or three casual references to these craft in travel books, all of which make the mistake of alluding to them as "crooked-stern junks." True, the port side of the curious, high, rounded taffrail is slightly raised, the member forming the site for the sweep does not extend the full way, and a perfect illusion of wryness is imparted by the planks of the square stern being set at an angle instead of vertically; but the essential crookedness of these craft lies in the bow, which makes them unique.

As is generally the case with an unusual form of construction in Szechwan, the credit or blame for the eccentricity is attributed to supernatural intervention. In the case of the oar boat, the design is assigned to Lu Pan (魯 班), the Carpenter god.

A tale is told in Tzeliutsing that Lu Pan (魯 班) built several types of junks for that turbulent little river, the Yentsingho, none of which, however, was successful. One day while he was engaged on a new design, a large hawk swooped down close to him, and he noticed how, as it came out of its dive, it banked at an angle. This inspired Lu Pan to build the bow of the junk leaning obliquely to one side, while the planks forming the stern were slanted to match, after the manner in which the feathers of the hawk's tail were disposed as it flew away from him. The junk when completed proved the most successful of all his efforts, and the type has been perpetuated ever since.

Lu Pan is worshipped by the carpenters, and his name is a household word in Szechwan. For instance, a novice at the trade, in being warned not to show off before an expert, is told "not to swing his axe at the door of Lu Pan."

As *lu-ch'uan*, or oar boat, is such an inadequate description of this craft, it will in future pages be called the crooked-bow junk, a name descriptive of what, it may be surmised, is probably the only type of craft of its kind in existence.

The crooked-bow junks are built on the banks of the Yentsingho, mainly at Tzeliutsing itself, at a cost, in 1941, of $2,400 each. There are said to have been 3,000 of these craft in 1926, and even now there are believed to be over 2,000, a number still greatly in excess of requirements, which serves to keep up the price of exporting salt.

The crooked-bow junks are built on slender and pleasing lines, tapering gently to bluff bow and rounded stern. Despite their graceful appearance they are, however, of exceptionally strong construction, as, indeed, is essential for their passage up and down the dangerous rapids. The length is supposed to be standard, that is to say, 57 English feet, but they are sometimes a little longer. The junks work in convoys of five, each group being known as a *tsai* (載). The leader, or flagship, as she might be called, of each group is known as *tso-ch'uan* (座 船) and is always slightly larger than the others. They all draw only a few inches when light and 1 foot when loaded.

It is noticeable that for use in comparatively deep rapids the Chinese have in nearly every case designed vessels with an underwater line, or flare, more or less rounded, and this deep draught makes for greater stability in broken water. As the rapids of the Yentsingho, however, are abnormally shallow in the low-water season, the craft built to negotiate them must draw the minimum of water and are therefore probably, with the exception of rafts, the lightest cargo carriers in the world. To achieve this end they are flat-bottomed and, moreover, represent more markedly than any other Upper Yangtze craft a vessel in its very simplest form, that is to say, a long four-sided box. This method of construction indicates its ancient origin, and the primitive manner in which the building is still carried out supports the junkmen's claim that they have been thus fashioned without change in design for many hundreds of years, very likely dating back at least to the time of the first needs of water-borne export of salt from the wells.

The basically simple methods of construction used have therefore a special interest. The first operation is to lay six planks side by side on the ground. These, which are the bottom planks, are normally of *sung-mu* (松 木), or pine-wood, although sometimes *ch'ing-kang* (青 杠), or oak, is used instead. Though they are not uniform in size, these planks usually measure about 20 feet in length, with a thickness of 1½ inches, and are about 1 foot broad, further lengths being scarfed as necessary to bring the total up to the length of the boat.

The first two planks are laid one on the other, and with the aid of a wooden set-square, straight lines are drawn across the edges of both at intervals of about three to the foot, right down their length, to mark the site for the holes to be drilled to receive the nails. The second plank is then laid on the third, on to which the guiding lines are produced so as to ensure that the nail holes will coincide. The third plank now acts as a pattern for the fourth, and so on, until all six are marked and the holes duly drilled. The bottom planks are now "pinned" to each other, that is to say, 3-inch wrought-iron double-ended nails are inserted in the holes and all the planks knocked together to form a solid whole.

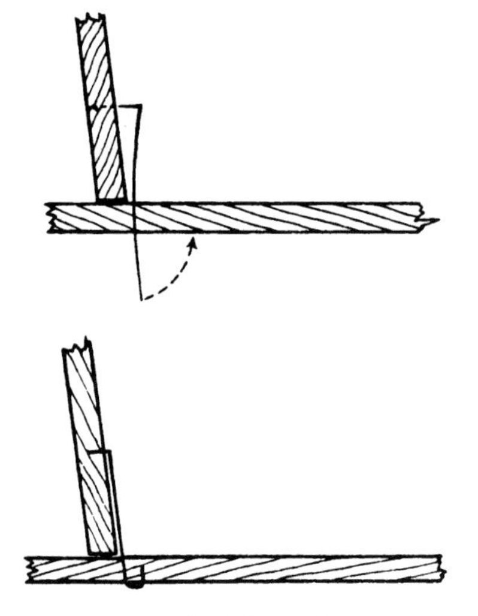
Method of fastening.

The foremost and aftermost bulkheads, made of *nan-mu* (楠 木)—a fine-grained yellow hardwood obtained from a tree of the laurel family,—are next placed in position a few inches in from either extremity and are "spiked" to the bottom planks. This is done by inserting an L-shaped wrought-iron spike or dog through a hole bored in the bottom planks, as shown in the diagram.
The L-shaped portion is then hammered home into the bulkhead, while the other extremity is clinched 180° back on itself into the bottom surface of the plank. The result is a fastening which it is almost impossible to dislodge.

The foremost and aftermost bulkheads are not erected at right angles to the bottom planks but at an angle of about 5° out of the vertical, leaning forward and aft respectively, for reasons which will later be apparent. All the intermediate bulkheads, sometimes consisting of a single plank, are now erected in the positions they are to occupy in the boat, each being "pinned" and "spiked" in the same manner as in the case of the first and last bulkheads.

The boat is now turned upside down, ready to receive the side planks of the hull. These, which consist of four long, heavy planks of *nan-mu* on either side, are joined together in the same manner as the bottom planks of the junk. The planks vary in number from three to five according to the width available, but four is most usual. The topmost planks of the hull are gently curved amidships so as to form an upward wave in the centre of the boat. When assembled, the two sides of the hull are lifted into position and securely nailed to the bulkheads, commencing amidships and gradually working outwards to bow and stern.

It will be remembered that the foremost and aftermost bulkheads were not erected absolutely vertical, and, as the bow and stern both taper somewhat abruptly at the first and last bulkheads, the action of heaving the side planks down to these bulkheads by means of a Spanish windlass naturally forces the two bulkheads to assume an upright position, in which they are nailed to the side planks.

Deck-beams rest on all the bulkheads, their ends being let into the topmost side planks and retained there by the planks resting on the carling shelf, making the junk very strong in construction.

It must be appreciated that the work of the Yentsingho shipwrights, though ingeniously conceived and skilfully carried out, is of the crudest. This necessarily makes the caulkers' task a formidable one. Gaping apertures between the planks, deficiencies in the wood, careless clinching of nails, and other minor errors of omission and commission not only demand a lavish use of chunam (油 灰) and bamboo shavings, but frequently graving pieces have to be inserted to fill up the larger holes.

As may be seen in Plate No. 163, there are 10 full bulkheads and two half-bulkheads, one in the second and the other in the tenth compartment. The foremost of the two half-bulkheads is reinforced with a 2-inch frame.[1] A small, full bulkhead,[2] more in the nature of a strengthening piece, is situated half-way up the turn of the bow in the foremost compartment. Additional strength is imparted to the fourth compartment by means of the mast-partners. The same is achieved by fore and aft removable deck-beams,[3] fitted between the bulkheads in the first two, the fourth, and the last four compartments. The only one of these deck-beams worthy of note is the small 3-foot one [4] in the foremost compartment, which is fitted obliquely in the crooked bow, not for symmetry, presumably, but so as to clear the foremost single bollard.[19] In true Szechwan tradition, moreover, there is only one way in which it will go in.

A coffer-dam [5] (a term used for want of a better) is situated abaft the sixth bulkhead. This is an uncommon position for a single coffer-dam, which in riverine craft is normally in the fore part of the vessel. The coffer-dam, which is usually to be found in the larger types of junks, is a small compartment always kept free of cargo, having two small apertures, or limbers, leading into the neighbouring main cargo-holds on either side. Their function is to drain off any seepage of water which may have found its way into the holds so that it may be conveniently bailed out.

In former days monetary transactions were conducted in the shape of cash, that is to say, small brass coins of low value with a hole through the middle, by means of which they could be threaded to form "strings of cash." In order to accommodate sufficient of this bulky wealth for daily needs, food, payment to trackers, and so forth, a shelf was made, filling up one side of the coffer-dam. The cash are no longer carried, and the shelf has long since been discontinued, but every new junk is still conservatively built with the supporting slats [6] for the shelf, a relic of the primitive form of safe and evidence of the old traditional honesty of the Chinese in that neither bolt nor lock was used.

The tall rounded mat-house [7] begins at the fourth bulkhead and extends aft to beyond the sixth bulkhead. There is little comfort or accommodation, as there is only one crude bunk,[8] and a small cooking-stove,[9] which, contrary to the usual Upper Yangtze tradition, is on the starboard side.

The two compartments [10] contained within the house are never decked-in. The fifth, or central, bulkhead has a section measuring 2 feet high by 2½ feet broad cut out amidships,* so that the fore and aft gang-plank,[11] which runs the length of the house, has a 1-foot dip in the middle. This permits of ample headroom in the central part of the house alone. The cut-out portion of the bulkhead is fitted with flanges, so as to slide back into the bulkhead when it is required to close the gate, but in point of fact this is never done, and the removable knee-high door is always kept slung up out of the way in the house under the matting, yet another instance of the conservative methods of the junk builder, who adheres so closely to the accepted type as to continue making fittings which are never used in the way for which they were intended.

* See Fig. 2, page 571.

All the other compartments, with the exception of the third, are decked-in with athwartship *sha-mu* (杉 木) planking. The open third compartment has, at

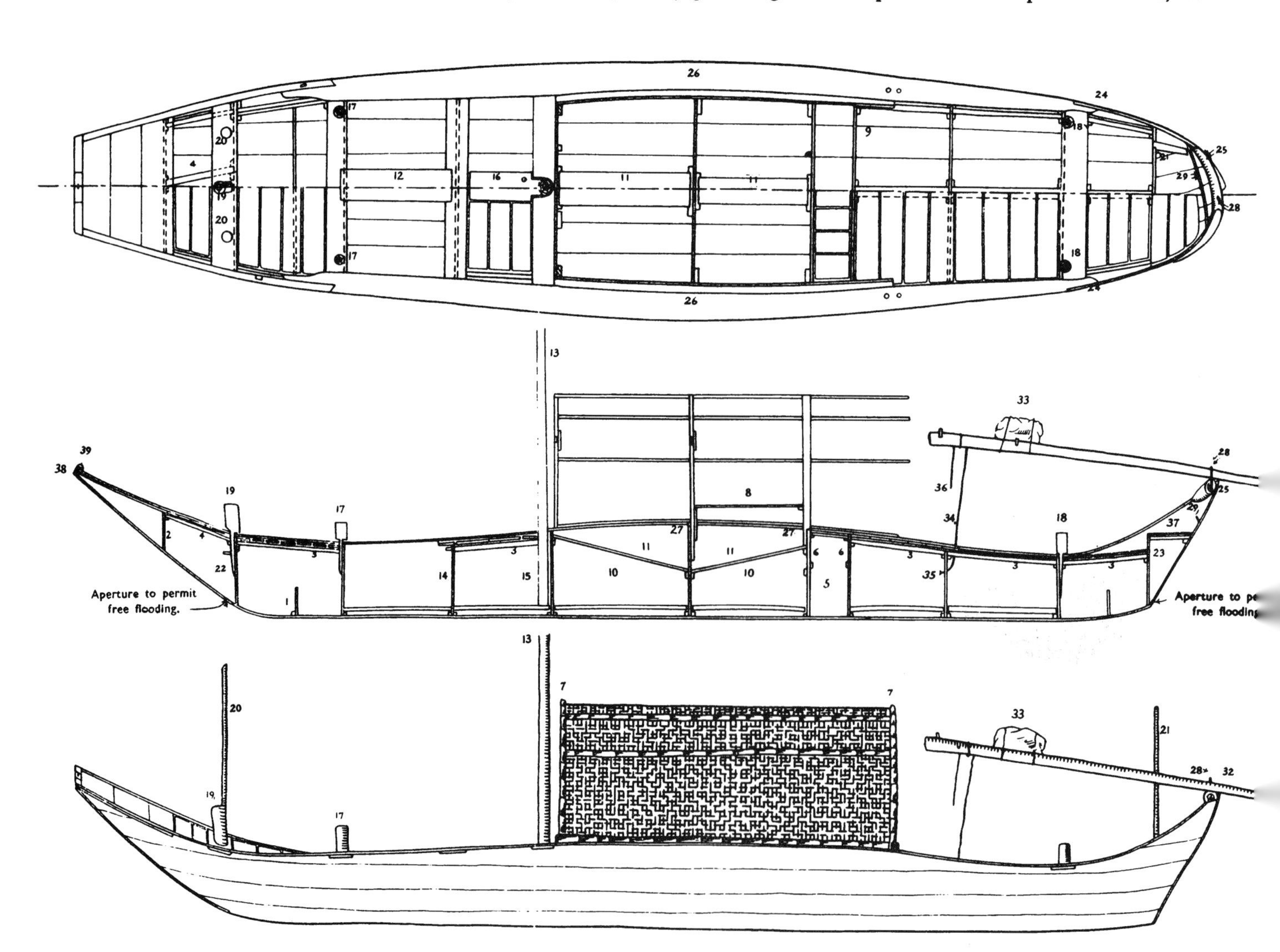

deck-level, a small fore and aft central gangway [12] and four loose *sha-mu* poles, two on each side of it, upon which deck cargo is placed. The poles are shaped to obviate rolling.

The full load consists of 90 baskets each weighing 290 pounds of soft salt and 120 baskets each weighing 210 pounds of lump salt. All the compartments are fitted with dunnage in the form of six fore and aft *sha-mu* poles, whereon the salt baskets are stowed. When loaded, not only are all holds full, but a considerable number of baskets are carried on the fore-deck, and every available inch of space is utilised—even the house is filled up nearly to the roof. A through gangway, however, is left from the bow right through the house, not only as a passage way, but to permit the laodah, standing aft at the big sweep, a view ahead which, restricted as it may be, seems to be adequate.

The tracking-mast [13] is made of *sha-mu*, and is stepped into two parallel fore and aft chocks, the office of which is to distribute the weight between the third [14] and fourth bulkheads.[15] It is held upright to the level of the deck by a mast-case (*following page*), and strengthened above that by mast-partners. Absolute rigidity is ensured by means of a 4-foot fore and aft plank,[16] fitting snugly between the third and fourth bulkheads. This method of stepping the mast is quite commonly found with the plank resting on top of the half-frames, but as this craft has full bulkheads practically throughout, the plank rests upon them, that is to say, at deck-level, and therefore constitutes a somewhat unusual form of fitting. Back stays are rove through the masthead and are set up to ring bolts on either side of the after ends of the house. These stays also serve to steady a standing iron gin-block with an iron sheave, which is used to elevate the tow-rope when occasion demands. Details of these fittings will be found on page 570.

There are two small forward bollards [17] on the second bulkhead, and two of similar size and design are to be found on the ninth bulkhead,[18] considerably farther aft than is usual. All are of tough *pai-mu* (柏 木) and are fitted in a similar manner to the single, larger foremost bollard.[19] This strong post is admirably adapted to take the exceptional strain for which it was designed, as will appear later. It is situated right forward in the centre of the first bulkhead and flanked on either side by two "stick in the mud" anchors [20] of the class so much in use on the Upper Yangtze. The latter usually consist of a square, or sometimes round, boxed-in navel pipe, through which a pole ending in a cross-haft is rammed into the soft mud of the river-bed so as to anchor the vessel, a stone being often hung from the cross-haft to lend extra weight. In the crooked-bow junks, however, a very curious and interesting feature is that the apertures are not boxed-in, but merely consist of two horseshoe-shaped holes cut into the bottom of the second bow planks at the turn of the bow in the first watertight compartment.*

* See Fig. 1, page 571.

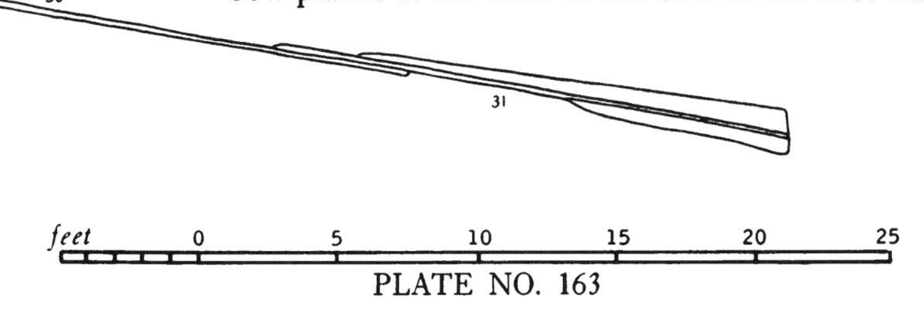

PLATE NO. 163

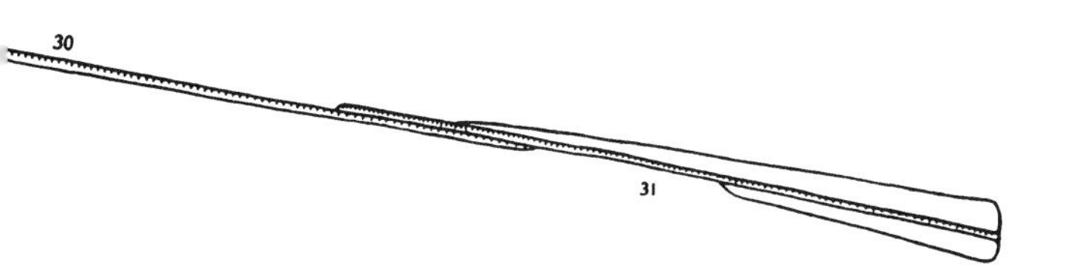

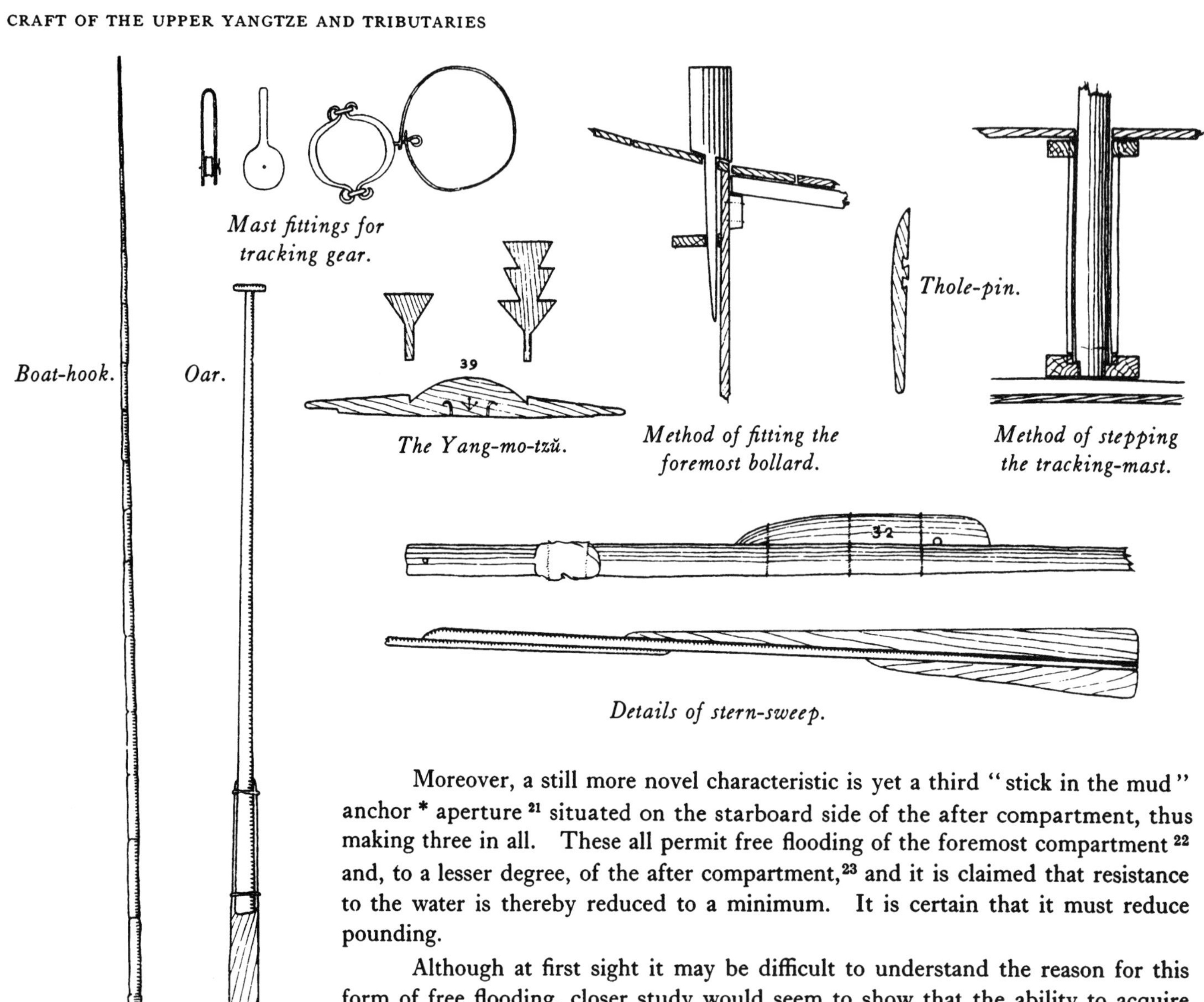

Moreover, a still more novel characteristic is yet a third "stick in the mud" anchor * aperture [21] situated on the starboard side of the after compartment, thus making three in all. These all permit free flooding of the foremost compartment [22] and, to a lesser degree, of the after compartment,[23] and it is claimed that resistance to the water is thereby reduced to a minimum. It is certain that it must reduce pounding.

Although at first sight it may be difficult to understand the reason for this form of free flooding, closer study would seem to show that the ability to acquire and discharge water ballast at either extremity in a rapid must impart a valuable steadying influence and reduce oscillation. The advantage of this simple automatic device is that it comes into operation just at the most necessary time to counteract the effect of buffeting, for the boat is balanced by this alternate emptying and filling at either end.†

The gunwale, starting from the bow, is scarfed between the first and second bulkheads into a much wider gunwale, 1 foot wide increasing to 1½ feet amidships. Abaft the ninth bulkhead it is again scarfed into a narrow portion,[24] which tapers until it is lost in the curved top of the transom. This tapering ends unsymmetrically in the *lu-tan* (櫓 担), or site for the sweep.[25] The wider section of the gunwale [26] forms a convenient gangway outside the house for quanting. It is supported on a carling shelf,[27] and at intervals below decks by hanging knees at the bulkheads. An oddly interesting feature of all these junks is that the gunwale has a marked wave in it, for it has a built-up rise amidships of about a foot, giving the vessel a hogged appearance. This rather ugly peculiarity is most carefully adhered to. It is possibly designed to give the quanter additional leverage, and, as it is cambered, it tends to protect the cargo in the rapids when seas are liable to be shipped.

The *lu-tan* [25] consists of a curved trunk of *nan-mu*, grown to shape, but extending across only two-thirds of the transom. In this the iron bearing-pin [28] is sunk. Immediately below is a piece of wood [29] set obliquely across the inner face of the stern planks and serving as a shelf as well as reinforcement. The slanting arrangement of the planking of the stern may be seen in Fig. 3, ***right.***

* To the writer's knowledge this is not only the sole instance in Upper Yangtze craft of "stick in the mud" anchors at both bow and stern, but also is the only case where as many as three of these devices are fitted.

† The practice of having the foremost compartment free flooding is also found in some sea-going junks, notably the *wang-tow*, a fishing-junk working out of Hongkong.

The starboard wing-plank, very narrow at its join with the bottom planks, widens and narrows again in a curve on its outer edge, but the most eccentric feature about it is that this wing-piece terminates on the transom at a markedly higher level than the other stern planks, thus accentuating the crooked aspect of the outboard face (see Fig. 3, *right*). This is known as the *yen-tzŭ-pan* (燕 子 板), or swallow plank. The junkmen say that it is purely decorative and has no use beyond satisfying their remarkable æsthetic ideas.

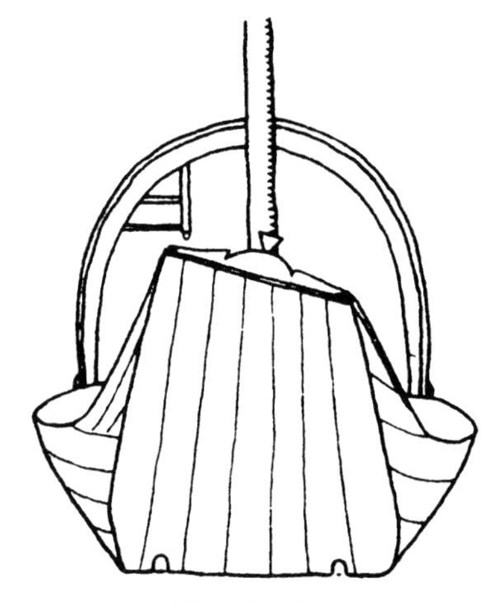

Fig. 1. Bow.

The *sha-mu* sweep,[30] which consists of a long pole with two (sometimes only one) shorter sections joined at either extremity,[31] measures 57 feet, which is roughly the same over-all measurement as of the junk itself, but is occasionally a little longer. Where the loom joins the neck is a shaped cheek-piece,[32] which takes into the bearing-pin [28] (*sketched at left*). The sweep is beautifully balanced by means of an abnormally large stone [33] made fast to the top of the loom. A rope [34] secured to the bulkhead [35] passes through the deck planks and round the sweep. The running part of this rope [36] is held by the laodah, its function being to aid him in holding the sweep in the required position. In a bad rapid the sweep's full complement consists of six men, who brace their shoulders against it for leverage, and extra men have to be stationed on the after platform,[37] bearing down on the sweep with their full weight to prevent it from being displaced from the bearing-pin. It is odd that no device has been adopted to achieve this end without recourse to man-power.

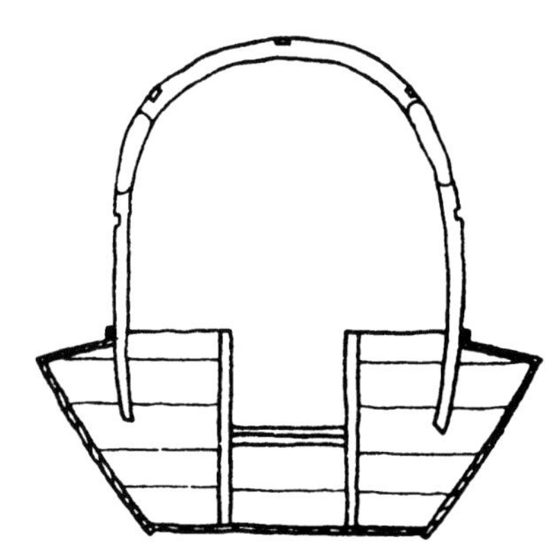

Fig. 2. Amidships.

The high bow, essential for work in rapids, is built up with shorter planks. It terminates in a transverse beam laid over the assembled ends of the deck planks, the topmost side planks, the ascending bow planks, and the scarfed gunwale, thus making a total of five thicknesses meeting at the bow.[38] Instead of the pole-shaped transverse stem-beam so common on the Upper Yangtze and its affluents, the bow in this type is surmounted by a piece of hardwood of unusual shape let into the gunwale [39] (*sketched at left*). This is called the *yang-mo-tzŭ* (羊 模 子), and serves as an object of reverence. Similar stem-post formations are to be found on the Middle Yangtze, where they are known as *ling-p'ai* (靈 牌) and are also regarded as objects of worship by the junkmen, who make their customary sacrifices before them.

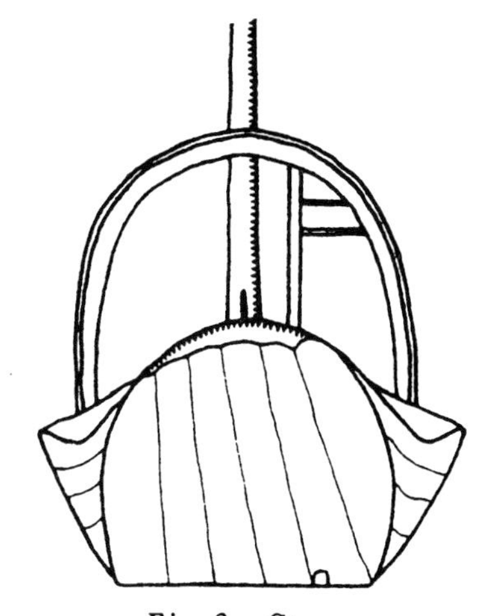

Fig. 3. Stern.

In the crooked-bow junks, the inner facing of the *yang-mo-tzŭ* is ornamented with a crudely chiselled device resembling a central broad arrow flanked by two pot hooks; these latter are called the *mei-mao-ting* (眉 毛 釘), or eyebrows. Occasional variations in the *yang-mo-tzŭ* occur, for it may be added to in serrated tiers up to as many as five.

The most outstanding of all the uncommon features of these craft is, of course, the crookedness of the bow, which tapers from the water-line upwards. On the port side the height from water-line to stem-head is 4 feet 8 inches, while on the starboard side it is 5 feet 11 inches. The angle of ascent is also markedly different, and the planking, as it runs at right angles to the stem-head, is therefore aslant, although to a lesser degree than the stern planking. Seen from the end-on view, this gives the vessel a most odd appearance, as if she had a heavy list to port (see Fig. 1, *right*).

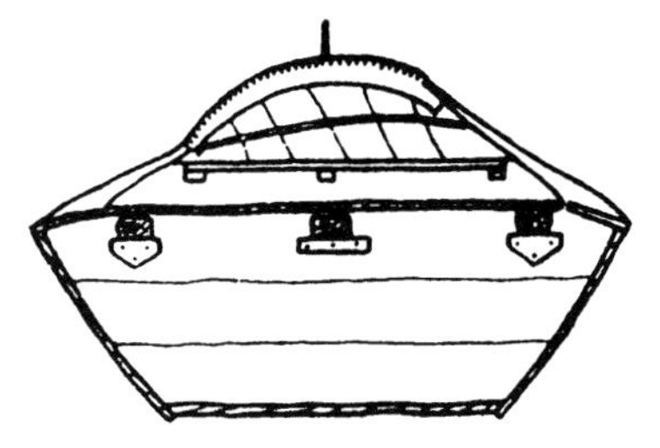

Fig. 4. Stern.
(view from forward.)

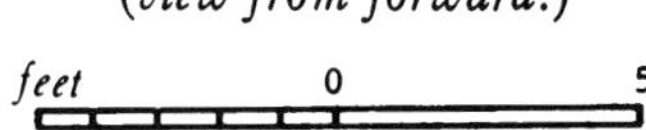

The closest questioning of the junkmen and trackers as to the reason for this novel form of construction was on the whole disappointingly fruitless, for the majority of them had no ideas on the subject at all. A few vaguely affirmed that the channel in some places is so narrow, being little more than sufficient for the junks to pass through, and so steeply bounded by rocks that a cut-away and distorted shaping of the bow averts collision. Others, who seemed better informed, claimed that the bow formation alters the balance of the junk so as to deflect the current in such a manner as to gain the fullest advantage from it when proceeding down stream, while, when proceeding up stream, it facilitates towing and makes for easier handling in the sharp turns of the rapids. The free flooding device already referred to doubtless plays its part here too.

The claim that the whole balance of the vessel is so affected by her unsymmetrical lines as favourably to influence her passage through the water raises an interesting problem and one difficult to solve. Before lightly dismissing such claims, however, it must be remembered that the ancient Chinese methods of trial and error have always been carried out with some ingenious, if unusual, end in view, which has presumably always been attained, albeit by methods strange to Western eyes. Moreover, in favour of the balance theory, it should never be forgotten that the Chinese understand the art of balance better than any other nation in the world, for, in a country where every form of produce and merchandise is mainly carried by man, the principles of balance are intuitively known and appreciated and the knowledge fully exploited.

From Mr. Worcester's notes: The most important reason of all is that when tracking the junk will proceed on a perfectly straight course without the aid of rudder or sweep, even with the tracking line broad on the bow. This is yet another example of true Chinese ingenuity in solving very difficult problems in a supremely simple manner.

From personal observation on board a crooked-stern junk, both in rapids and in calm water, it would appear that there is some justification for much of what the Chinese claim. Unquestionably, when proceeding down river in the quiet reaches, the elevation of the starboard side of the bow enables the quanter to get a better purchase on his pole.

The rapids of the Yentsingho are of such a nature that they have to be negotiated by crossing from the left to the right bank of the river when descending, and conversely when ascending. The peculiar type of bow would appear to be mainly designed to meet the requirements of the upward journey, for, as the trend of the channel through the rapids is then always from right bank to left bank, the distorted port bow serves to maintain the trim of the vessel and ensures that the tow-rope will always lead clear of any fouling on that bow. This could ordinarily be achieved by mastheading the tracking-line, but such a procedure would be dangerous, if not disastrous, in a rapid.

Normally a light tracking-line is used. This is attached to an interrupted iron ring and a parrel fitted with halyards. The halyards are rove through an iron gin-block at the masthead, so that the ring may be maintained at any desired height on the mast to suit the conditions obtaining and the height of the trackers' path as well as to "masthead" the tracking-lines when overtaking another craft.

Each *tsai* (載), or group, of five junks has a permanent staff of seven men, that is to say, a helmsman for each junk, a laodah in charge of the group, and a flotilla cook. Additional men are hired as required for periods ranging from a fraction of an hour to a couple of weeks or the whole journey up river. On the down-river trip the numbers hired are usually two or three men for the passage of the Chungt'an, four or five for the Hsient'an, six or eight for the formidable Yent'an, and three or four for the Laoyat'an. On the upward journey each junk requires from 50 to 70 trackers.

Dams are built at each rapid so as to maintain sufficient water in the low-water season. These dams are opened after the suitable dates have been selected by a joint meeting of the representatives of the Salt Administration, the Rapids Controlling Bureau, and the Junk Guild. During the low-water season the last dam at the Laoyat'an cannot be opened, and this necessitates discharging the cargo and reloading it into other junks below the dam. High water is also unsuitable for navigation, which is entirely interrupted from July to August.

When the large crooked-bow junks are loaded either direct or by means of ferry-boats, bamboo baskets of salt are stacked up in every available corner. The craft then leave Tzeliutsing overnight in convoys of four with intervals of half a cable between each.

Early the next morning the leading junks begin to arrive at Chungt'an. This obstacle consists at low water of a rocky ledge crossing the river, into which wooden boards have been built to form a dam, leaving an aperture slightly more than that of the beam of the junks. Although there is no particular danger, great care is necessary to keep each boat in the axis of the current when approaching the weir, over which there is a fall of probably 3 feet at dead low water. Before making the passage two or three men are taken on board to assist the helmsman.

Once fairly in the current the junk gathers considerable speed, and the combined efforts of all the men are necessary to wield the heavy stern-sweep. After passing the weir the surplus men wade ashore and proceed to the next boat.

The long line of junks then drifts slowly down with the current to the Hsient'an. On arrival they bank-in and await their turn. This at low level is, indeed, a formidable rapid, and the passage down it is a most exciting and thrilling experience, yielding a sensation of utter helplessness, for there is no turning back once the craft has started her mad rush down the rapid.

A crooked-bow junk coming down a rapid.

Again two or three extra hands board each boat, which moves slowly with the current, 200 feet astern of the next ahead, and crosses from the left bank through a flagged channel to mid-river at the point A (see Page 574). Here a dam extends two-thirds of the way across the river, essentially the same as at Chungt'an, and similarly leaving only a narrow aperture capable of admitting one junk at a time. Gradually gaining momentum, the junk appears to be heading directly for the dam, but partly by the force of the water and partly by the action of the great stern-sweep, it is suddenly diverted as it strikes the axis of the current, and at the point B curves round the end of the dam to come finally to rest, banked-in, at the point C. Here it again awaits its turn for the ordeal of the main Hsient'an.

Keeping perfect station, the boats leave in succession from the point C, where they have been lying. Each boat's crew now consists of four men at the sweep and a bowman with a boat-hook. Having gained a speed of about 6 knots, the boat arrives at the point D, where a long line of men can be seen wading out to meet the boats in mid-stream.

As each boat rushes past, three men nonchalantly slip on board. Instantly one takes up his station at the foremost bollard, while the two others leap to the stern-sweep to direct and assist the men already there. These three are local pilots, of which there are a total of 96, and they receive $1 for each junk they pilot. Trained by their fathers for the hereditary work, they start their careers at the age of 12.

From the point C to D, and thence to G, is a straight course, and the boat is now travelling at a very high speed. Across the surface of the river is a perfect shoal of scattered rocks that seem to bar all passage through them, but as the junk gets nearer, an opening between two of the largest groups of rocks can be seen. What, however, is not apparent is how the boat on arrival at the point G can

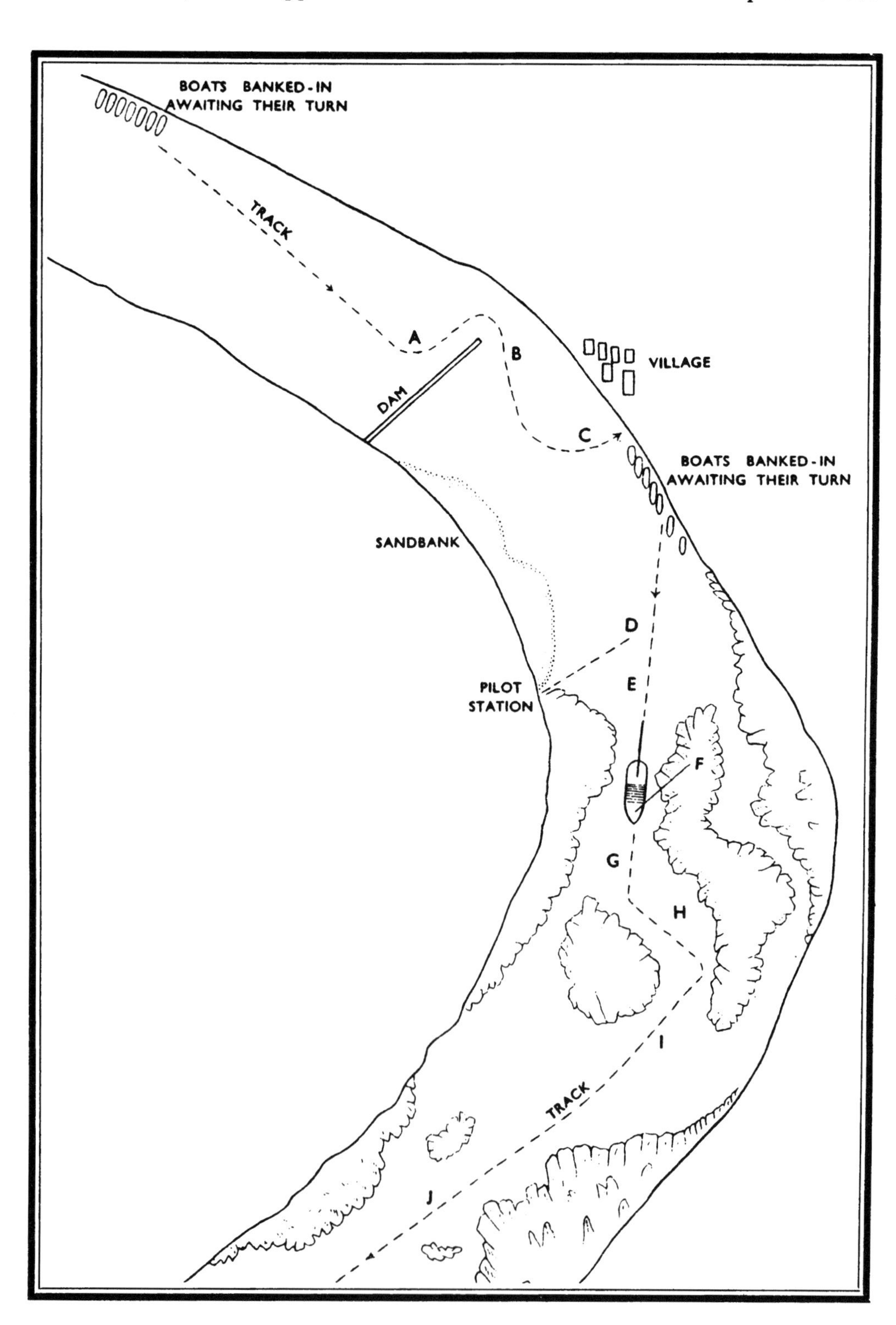

The Hsient'an at low level. (Sketch plan—not to scale.)

possibly be turned almost at right angles, where the channel is only a few feet broader than the junk itself, and where the stream is at its maddest.

The men at the stern-sweep direct their entire attention to keeping a straight course through the various eddies and races. The sweep is kept in the water and is used as a rudder. There is a moment of tension as the boat, moving with what appears to be the speed of an express train, heads directly for a rock some 2 feet above the avalanche of seething waters.

The river flows down with a mighty swing, and the rocks at a distance of 2 or 3 feet seem to be flying in the opposite direction. The supreme moment has arrived, and the bowman braces himself for his important *rôle*. As the junk flashes past the point F, a man standing on the rock neatly hands him the end of a bamboo rope which is, at the other end, made fast to the rock. In a few seconds the bowman has cast three turns round the foremost bollard, and as swiftly starts to surge the rope in short, sharp motions, that is to say, he allows it to slacken in jerks. So deftly does he perform this operation that the 50-foot length of rope slips smoothly and quickly round the bollard until it finally runs out and falls over the side. On being asked what would happen if the bowman failed to grasp the rope, the junkmen replied that the man on the rock had been passing the rope in just this manner for 20 years, that no accident had ever occurred, and that there seemed to them no reason why one ever should. This rope, which is renewed after five boats have passed down, takes only about 15 seconds to run out, but the restraint has been just sufficient to alter the course of the boat from headlong collision with the ugly jagged-looking rock round which the current foams.

True, the boat is still in the grip of the rapid and appears to be steering a course directly for another rock and utter destruction. The safety of the junk now depends entirely on the men at the sweep, which not only acts as a rudder, but can be used as a powerful lever. The five men bend all the weight of their shoulders against the heavy loom, and with a single movement wrench the junk round at the critical moment when a crash seems inevitable. To achieve this, the sweep must be put over once only and at precisely the right moment, when the junk is only a few feet off the rock. Diverted as if on a pivot, the junk now careers away in comparative safety, still at a fairly high speed, through the narrow gutterway, with the dangers fast disappearing astern.

The current slackens somewhat at the point I, where the junk emerges into an open stretch, but as the channel narrows, she again commences to fly down the lower part of the rapid until eventually she enters a long, even reach, which, after the point J, becomes smooth water.

In the low-water season the pilots do not wait to reach the bank, but, when sufficient way is off the junk, these intrepid men slip off the junk into the icy water in the same unobtrusive way as when they boarded her.

Lying snugly banked-in in a convoy, or hauled up on the bank for repairs, the crooked-bow junks of Tzeliutsing display in their odd yet trim outlines evidence of that antiquity of design which probably reaches back with little fundamental change to the time of the origin of the salt wells themselves some 1,700 years ago; but to be fully appreciated they should be seen in operation in the wild waters of the little river for which they were designed.

To the sailor's eye there is little to surpass in interest and beauty the sight of a well-handled crooked-bow junk descending the rapids of the Yentsingho at dead low water.

鹽船

THE TZELIUTSING SALT SAMPAN

When water conditions are favourable, the salt junks can berth opposite the town of Tzeliutsing and load their cargoes direct. During the low-water season, however, they have to bank in about a mile below the town, and the salt is brought to them from the factories in open-decked boats known as the *yen-ch'uan* (鹽船), or salt-boats, which are 43 feet long, of 8 feet beam, and 2½ feet in depth (Plate No. 164).

These craft are exceedingly interesting, because, although they are never called upon to negotiate rapids and carry the salt only for a distance of little more than a mile, yet they are true to the local tradition in that they all have crooked bows. Indeed, they are in most respects miniatures of the larger salt junks. They have the same long, slender lines, and, in some form or other, embody most of the peculiarities of the crooked-bow junks. The bow itself is less crooked, for the difference in level between the two gunwales is only 4 inches. The stern planks are similarly set at an angle, and the wave amidships is also present, though it is indicated rather than stressed. The gunwales are scarfed into wider amidship portions in the same manner. There are nine watertight compartments and, as in the junks, the foremost and after compartments are free flooding through the apertures for the "stick in the mud" anchors, of which there are two, one at each extremity. The whole sampan is undecked with the exception of the first compartment and small platforms in bow and stern for the quanters. No explanation is forthcoming from the junkmen as to why this pattern has been adhered to for these ferry craft.

From Mr. Worcester's notes: The first port of call after leaving Tzeliutsing is at Tengtsingkwan on the T'o River, some 100 *li* above Luchow. Here the salt is transhipped into Upper Yangtze junks, usually the *chung-yüan-po*, or willow leaf junks, so named on account of their shape, which tapers at bow and stern.
There is no break of cargo after Tengtsingkwan until Chungking is reached, where the salt is either disposed of locally or transhipped into larger junks at Tangkiato, some 25 *li* below that city.
Salt destined for ports on the Kungt'anho is again transhipped at Fowchow into the famous *wai-p'i-ku*, or crooked-stern junks.

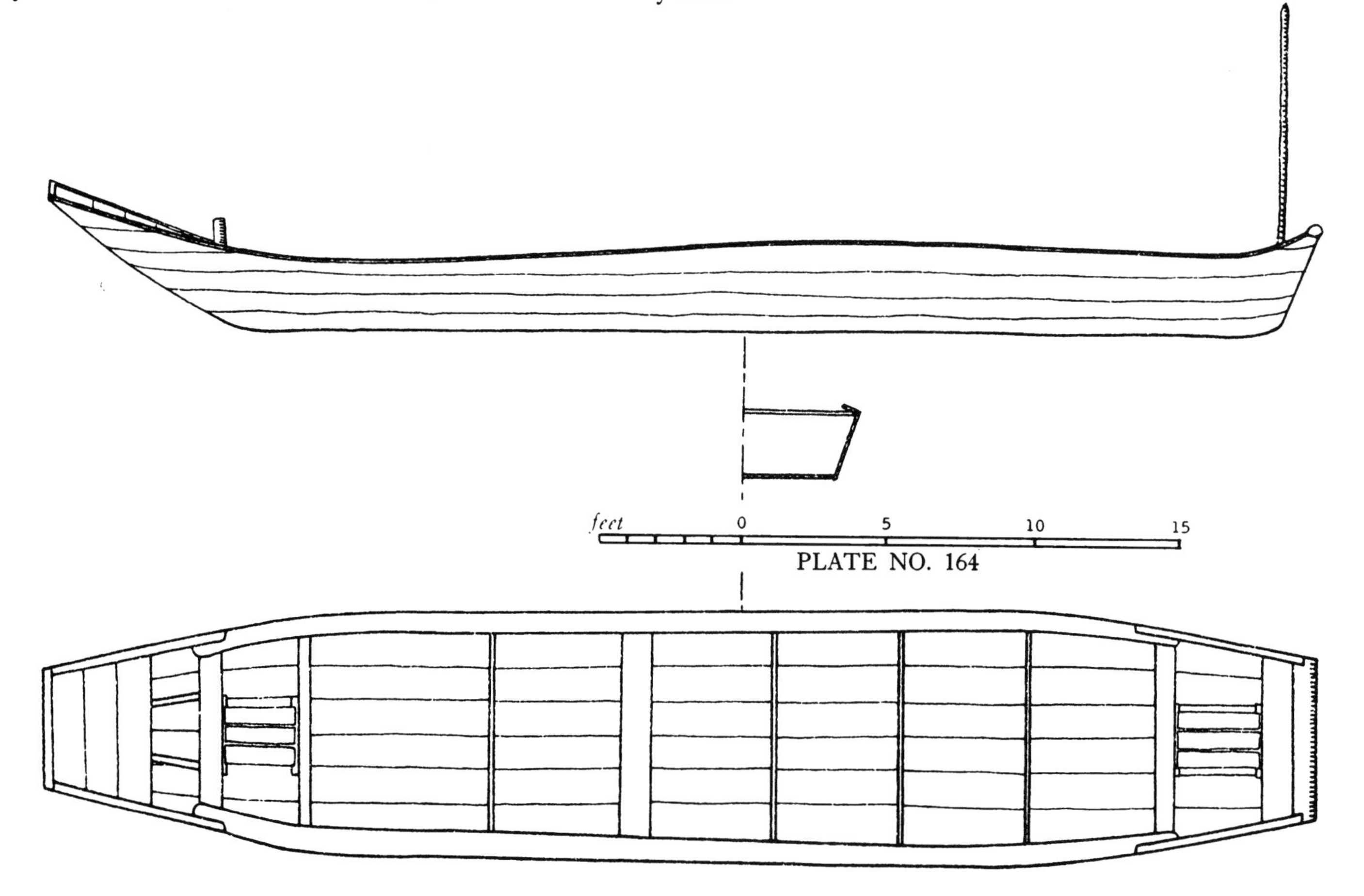

PLATE NO. 164

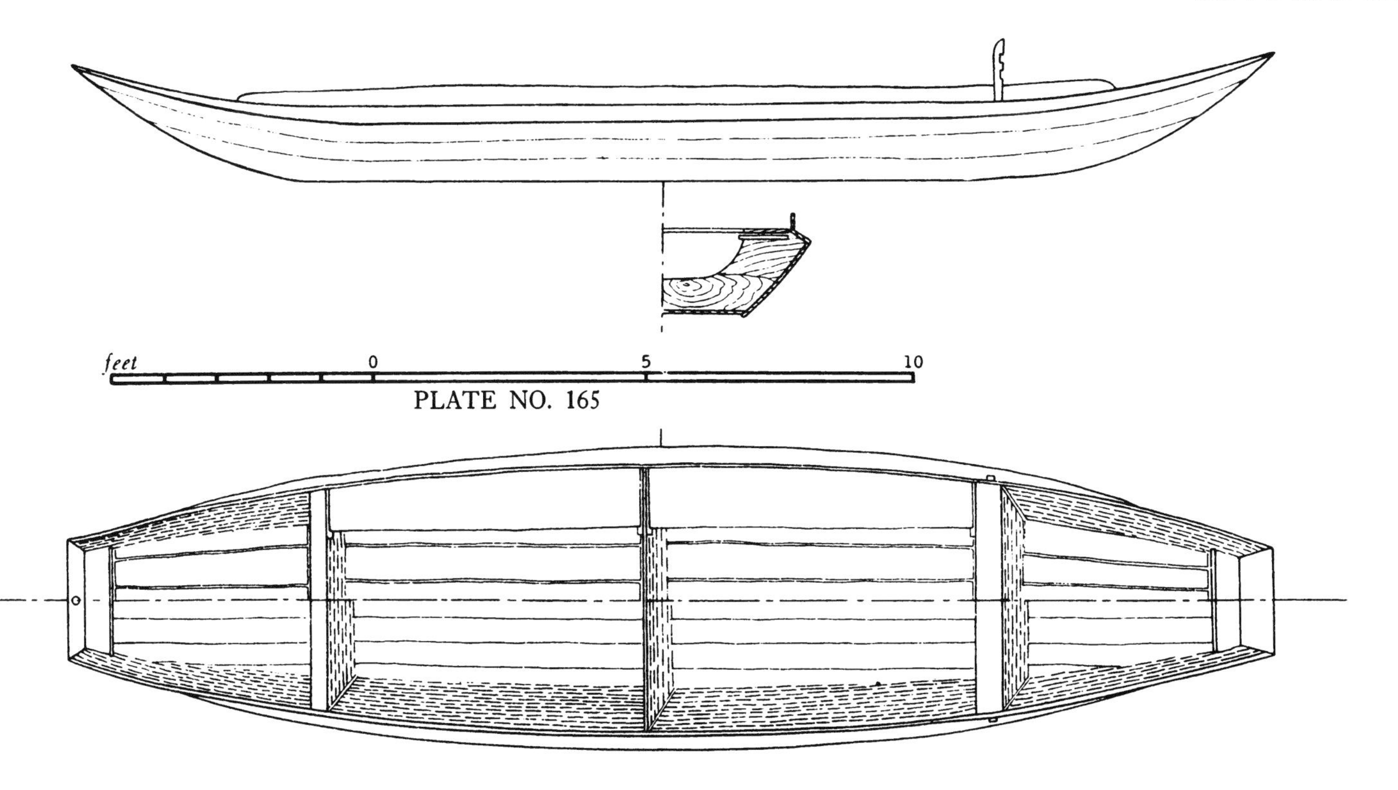

PLATE NO. 165

THE TZELIUTSING FERRY SAMPAN

The *kuo-ho-ch'uan*(過 河 船), or ferry sampan, is a beamy type of craft with a slight rise to a tapered bow and stern. It is found very generally in all the quiet reaches of the Yentsingho and, of course, mainly at Tzeliutsing itself. It serves as a dual-purpose cargo and passenger carrier, either across the river or for short distances up and down.

Notwithstanding small local differences in detail, these boats vary little as a class. The sampan as illustrated in Plate No. 165 measures 22 feet 6 inches, with a beam of 5 feet 6 inches, and a depth of 1 foot 8 inches. It is built of *nan-mu* (楠 木) throughout. There are two full bulkheads, and the third, which is amidships, may be termed a three-quarter bulkhead.

The design clearly shows that it is intended for use in still waters. There is no sweep, and propulsion by oars is carried out by a man in a standing position in the after compartment.

THE MINKIANG

From Mr. Worcester's notes: In the upper reaches of the Mingkiang, according to Ernest Henry Wilson, the celebrated naturalist, skin coracles, broadly oval in shape, navigate short reaches, and can easily be carried by one man. He describes them as being like the pictures of those used by the ancient Britons before the Roman invasion. Large enough to carry two passengers, they are made of cow-hide stretched over tough, light, wood ribs, and are steered by a man in the stern operating a paddle. They descend in wide circles or half-circles.

THE Minkiang, also known as the Fu-ho, is always considered by the Chinese to be the parent stream of the Yangtze. Probably this idea emanated from the fact that the Kinsha is only navigable for 58 miles above Suifu, whereas junks can travel up the Min River as far as Kiangkow, 133 miles above Suifu, and at high water levels can proceed another 25 miles to Chengtu. Another contributing factor to the Chinese opinion that the Min is the main stream is that it is far more important as a trade artery, flowing as it does past the provincial capital of Chengtu, and tapping the fertile area of the Red basin. Finally there seems ample evidence for believing that as the upper reaches of the Kinsha in ancient times ran into the Red River, the continuation of the Yangtze only extended for a comparatively short distance above Pingshan and there was then not so much relative distance in the length of the Min River and the Kinsha of these days, which then as now drained a wild and mountainous region of small interest or value to the commercially minded Chinese.

The Min probably derives its name from the Minshan Range not far from its origin. Its source is situated near the edge of the Tibetan plateau, more than 13,000 feet above the sea. It consists of a brook which rises from nine springs at a place called Tchangla, a day's march north of Sungpan. A temple marks the importance of the site in Chinese eyes. This little stream flows between artificial banks through the centre of Tchangla and thence down to Sungpan, 9,500 feet above the sea, an important trading city marking the frontier between China and Tibet. The Min then descends through a 100-mile long gorge until it finally emerges from the Szechwan alps onto the Chengtu plain at the mountain town of Kwanhsien.

This most picturesque and attractive city stands at the clear-cut boundary between east and west Szechwan, and has all the diverse features of a frontier settlement. Here the Chinese, the tribesmen, and Tibetans mingle in the streets.

Wooden carrying frame.

Immense loads are carried by coolies over incredibly long distances. In the central basin the load is divided into two, each weighing more than 40 pounds and slung from either end of a carrying bamboo. A coolie thus laden will, in easy country, comfortably cover 20 miles or even more in a day. In mountainous provinces, however, and over the borders this normal method is abandoned in favour of the back-load system. This ingenious device consists of a wooden frame. This is quite easily adjusted by slipping the arms through the harness which holds it securely to the wearer. The load is secured compactly to the frame, which has the advantage of distributing the weight evenly between the shoulders. It usually projects well above the man's head at a forward angle. The loads carried in this way are enormous. Two hundred pounds are an ordinary load, and frequently coolies will carry as much as 300 pounds over a bad mountain path at a steady rate of six or seven miles a day. The bearer carries a long sturdy pole with a T-shaped handle, which he braces against the lowest bar of the framework when he wishes to rest by the roadside.

In this manner they bring down medicinal herbs, skins, wool, deer horns, musk and coke, and take back salt, cotton, sugar, tools, straw sandals and tea, the latter often in the peculiar form of "stick tea." A coolie with a load of this kind of tea would seem to the uninitiated to be carrying a quantity of brush wood. Yaks often are driven down to the gates of Kwanhsien, but this marks the limit of their departure from the mountain wilds. From the Chinese side, the tide of western civilization reaches thus far and no further; the limit is marked by the motor road from Chengtu, along which a battered bus passes two or three times a week.

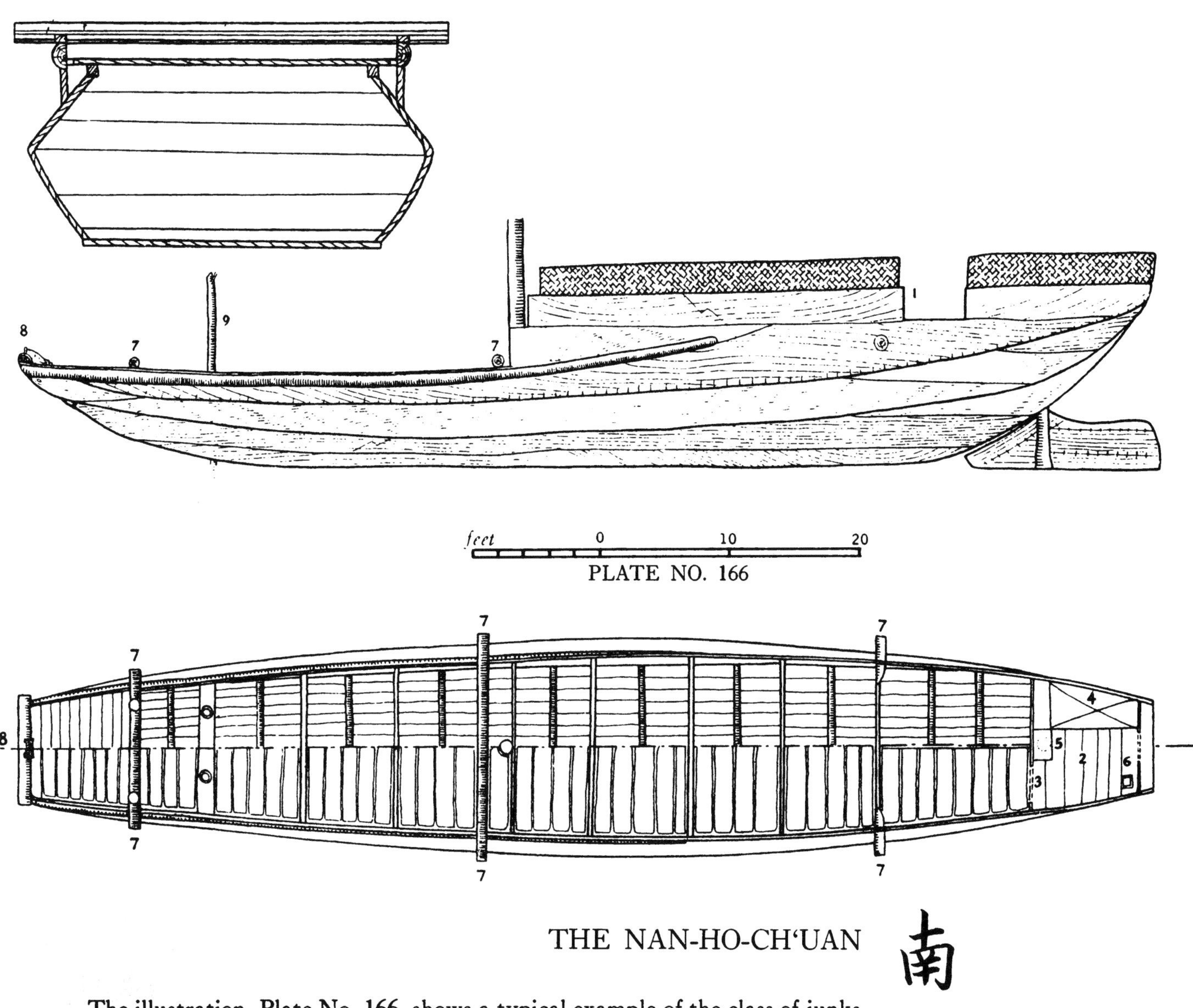

PLATE NO. 166

THE NAN-HO-CH'UAN

南河船

The illustration, Plate No. 166, shows a typical example of the class of junks known as the *nan-ho-ch'uan*, which vary considerably in size, though in little else.

They are generally built below Kiating, where much of the wood is grown of which they are made—*nan-mu*, a species of fine yellow wood. This Minkiang junk, one of the largest of its kind, is 86 feet long, with a beam of 12½ feet and a depth of 6 feet, and is flush-decked and divided into watertight compartments, the cargo being stowed between the second and seventh bulkheads. The deck is composed of removable thwartship planks 14 inches wide.

The single, large deck-house covers all the portion abaft the mast, interrupted by an aperture with sliding roof to enable the helmsman to obtain a clear view from the conning position[1] when the junk is under way.

All forward of this is a roomy compartment which forms the living and sleeping quarters of the crew, who when under way are augmented by between 30 and 50 men hired for the trip. The only furniture in this compartment is an

L-shaped series of lockers with room for chow-bowls and small personal effects of the crew, and beneath is an enormous bin containing rice. These lockers are secured to the foremost bulkhead, on the other side of which is the galley.

Aft of this house there is, in some junks, a cabin [2] for the owner partitioned off with a door [3] on the port side, and in the centre of this bulkhead is a paper window surmounted by three niches like a dovecot, in which is housed an image of Yang, the River God or Patron Saint. Above again is a wooden scroll on which is written in golden characters, with a black ground, a propitious sentence, such as "with fair wind and happiness." Inside the owner's cabin is a bunk,[4] and a table ingeniously built in over the rudder-head,[5] above which hangs a varnished board which acts as a pay sheet and accounts record of the junk.

The large stern-windows, filled in with paper, occupy the whole breadth of the junk, and are ornamented with a minute gallery, below being washing arrangements, with a square chute [6] for water and rubbish and a locker for personal belongings.

Three heavy hardwood cross-beams [7] are built into the structure of the junk. The centre beam is just forward of the mast, and carries at its extremities a small wooden frame holding a bearing-pin upon which the yulohs operate. The foremost hardwood cross-beam carries a massive pair of bitts.

A neat contrivance is the bow roller-cum-crutches [8] for the bow-sweep, which in breadth exactly fits the sweep and enables it to be run in or out quickly and easily. There are two "stick in the mud" anchors.[9]

A curious and distinguishing feature of this type of junk is the long irregular wale which, starting at the bow, follows the upper edge of the fore-deck, and on meeting the deck-house rises upwards for a short distance and then becomes lost in the superstructure.

When the *nan-ho-ch'uan* is exclusively used as a salt carrier it is sometimes called the *ch'iao-yen-ch'uan* (橋眼船).

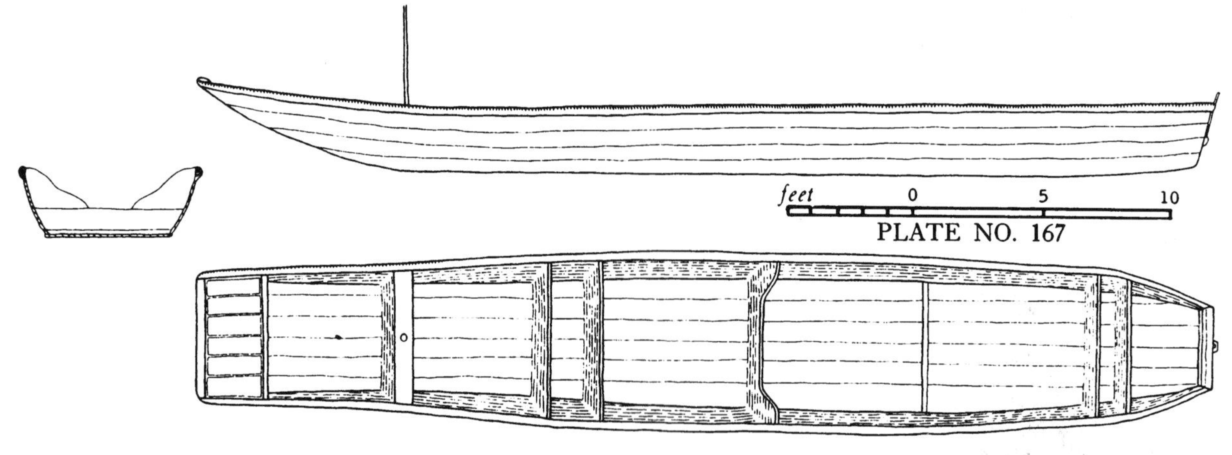

PLATE NO. 167

船

THE HSIAO-MU-CH'UAN

A more or less standard type of small cargo junk called the *hsiao-mu-ch'uan*, or small wooden boat, is able to reach Chengtu during the greater portion of the year, but differs in size according to the state of the water. The *hsiao-mu-ch'uan*, as illustrated in Plate No. 167, is 40 feet long, with a beam of 7 feet and a draught, unloaded, of about 4 inches.

Its breadth is just sufficient to entitle it to the term of junk. It is a crudely built boat made of *ch'ing-kang* for the bottom and *nan-mu* for the hull, and has six bulkheads, one half-bulkhead, and two frames.

The two outstanding features about this type are, firstly, the lift to the stern which overhangs the water and has a small wooden becket on the outer face to take the bearing-pin, and, secondly, the small temporary mat house, which is in the nature of a lean-to and which, small as it is, accommodates the five men of the crew. This house is removed when the junk is under way.

The type illustrated has neither mast nor rudder, and the methods of propulsion include use of the oars, poling in shallow reaches, and even pushing by the crew, who walk in the water for the purpose.

The 4-inch wide gunwales, which start from the bow and slant outboard, cease at the fourth bulkhead, and become long built-in poles for the remainder of the length of the boat.

The only interesting point about these craft is that they are able to navigate the upper reaches of the Minkiang below Chengtu longer than any other type—except, of course, the Ya River rafts.

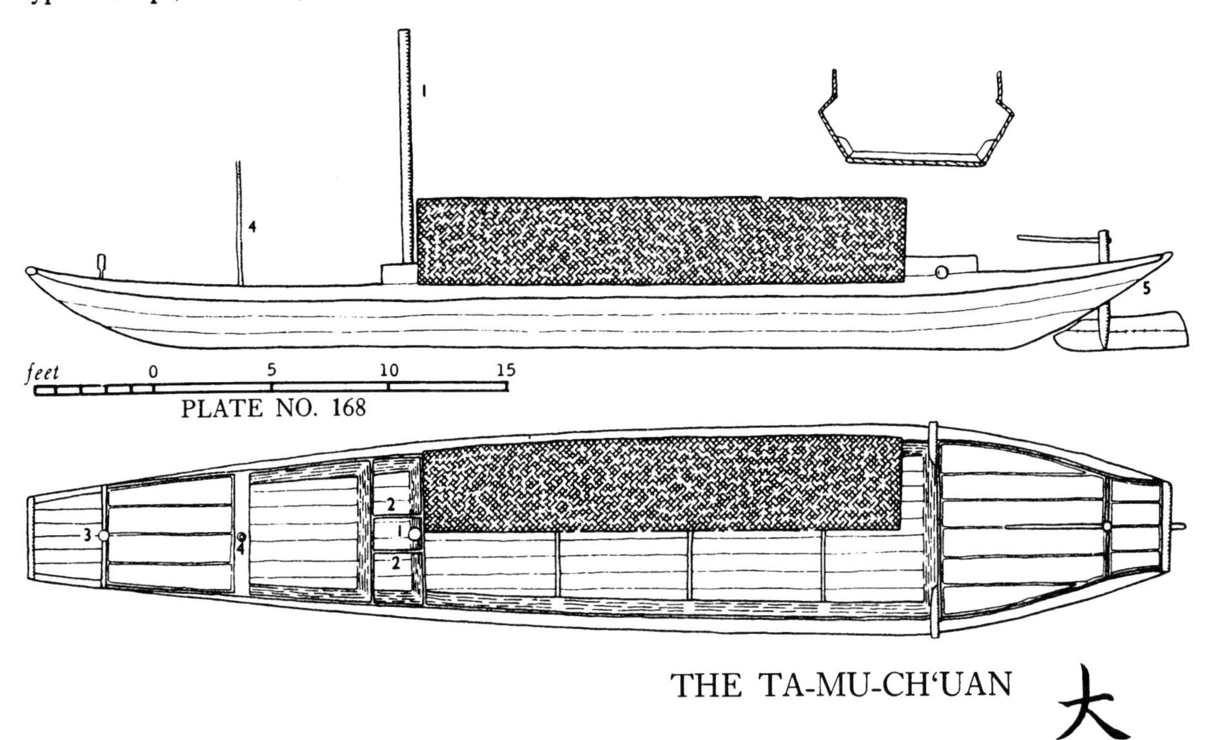

PLATE NO. 168

THE TA-MU-CH'UAN 大木船

The *ta-mu-ch'uan*, or large wooden boat, and the *hsiao-mu-ch'uan*, or small wooden boat, are the main cargo carriers up to Chengtu.

The *hsiao-mu-ch'uan* navigates the Minkiang at all seasons of the year up to Kiangkow, and as soon as the rising water permits, proceeds up to Chengtu. The *ta-mu-ch'uan*, which requires rather more water, varies in size considerably. The boat illustrated, however, measures 47½ feet long.

There is nothing outstanding about this type, except that the long, narrow, slightly upraised bow widens very gradually till the maximum beam of 7½ feet is reached aft, at a point 10 feet from the stern.

The main lines of construction follow the accepted pattern in the Chengtu district, that is to say, forward and after compartments decked-in, centre well with three frames given up to the cargo, and one or more coffer-dams. In this case there is one, wherein the short tracking-mast [1] is stepped between mast-partners.[2] A bollard,[3] a "stick in the mud" anchor,[4] and a rudder[5] complete the equipment of this useful but uninteresting vessel.

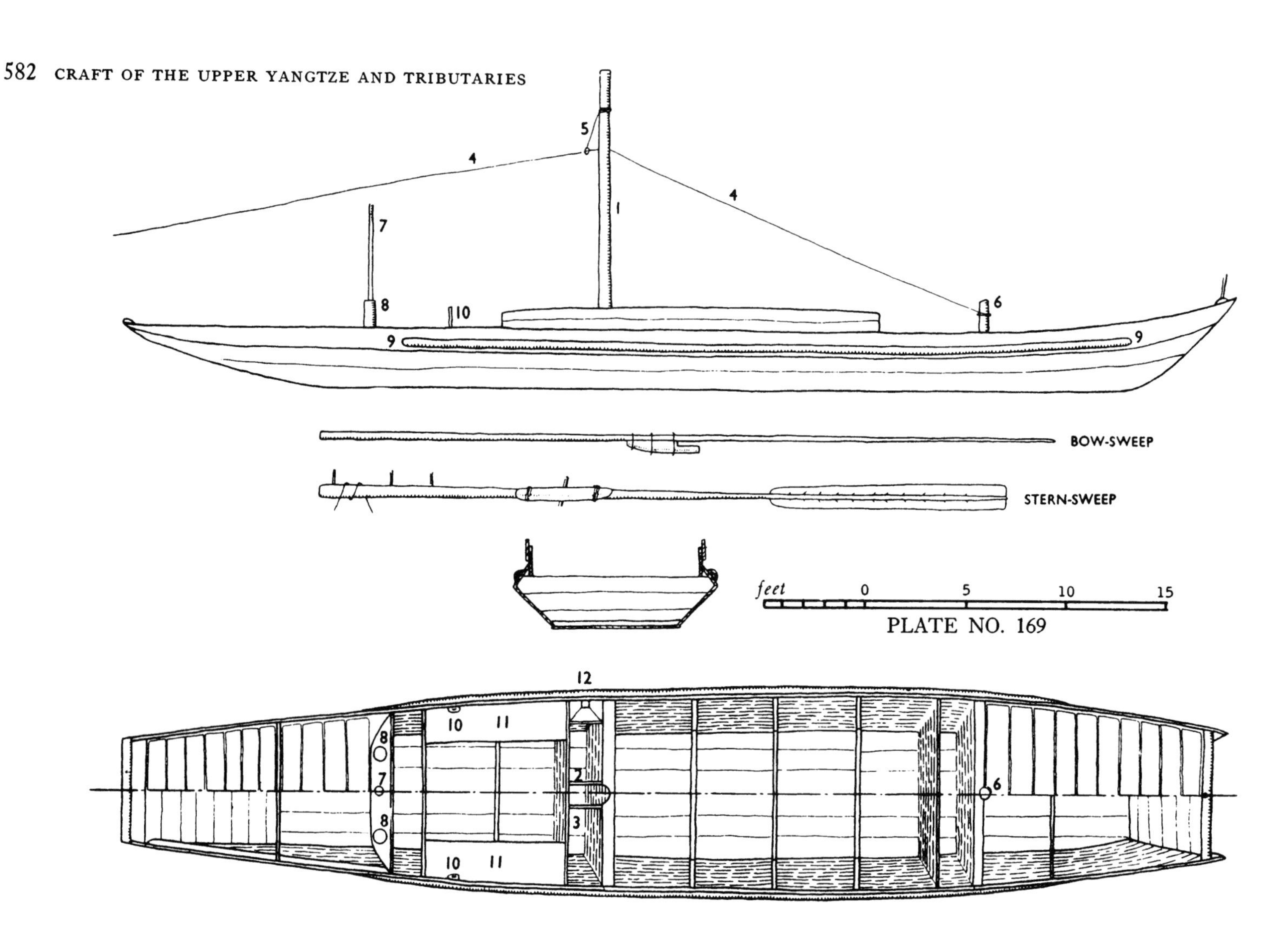

PLATE NO. 169

THE SHA-CH'UAN

The *sha-ch'uan*, or sand-boat, is so called from the name of its port of origin, Paisha (白 沙), or White Sands. Its main interest lies in the fact that it is the only type of boat used on the upper reaches of the Minkiang, where it plies up to the point where navigation for junks ceases—about 30 *li* above Kwanhsien.

This type is essentially built for work in shallow rapids, and is of light though strong construction. It measures 55 feet by 10 feet, with a depth of 3 feet, and has six bulkheads (four of which are arranged in pairs in the form of two coffer-dams) and six full frames.

The chief distinguishing characteristic is the flat, long, low bow, which overhangs the water to a marked degree. The stern rises gently to the small cross-beam, which ends within the slightly projecting sides of the hull.

The short tracking-mast [1] is stepped in the forward coffer-dam between mast-partners,[2] [3] and the tracking-line,[4] supported by a small pennant,[5] is firmly secured to the after-bollard.[6]

The "stick in the mud" anchor [7] is situated on the first main bulkhead rather farther aft than usual, and is flanked by low bitts.[8] A long split pole in the form of a wale extends down most of the sides, just below the sharply tilted gunwale.

The crew usually consists of about 11 men, of whom nine are used as trackers when up bound. Sometimes these boats go down as far as Kiating.

When descending the very shallow rapids above Kwanhsien, the boat travels with the current at a very high speed. Four men are stationed at the stern-sweep and four more at the bow-sweep. Just forward of the mast the whole compartment is given up to the two men at the oars, for which there are two thole pins.[10] These two men stand on small raised platforms,[11] while a third is stationed on the starboard side in the coffer-dam behind them, with a square wooden bailer which he empties down a specially constructed scupper.[12] The cargo is usually coal.

THE MINKIANG CAR-FERRY 汽車過渡船

The extensive construction of roadways in the interior of China has brought its own problem of transport across the numerous rivers and waterways. When, for reasons of time, labour, and expense, bridges are not yet established, this problem has been solved by the use of a new type of craft, a wooden car-ferry. These fall into two main categories: those for use in very narrow and shoal waters, and the sturdier type for the deep and broader rivers. A good example of the former type is the car-ferry which conveys road traffic across the shallow, placid waters of the T'o River at Peimuchen (椑 木 鎮), near Niukiang, on the Chungking–Chengtu high road. This ferry draws only a very few inches, yet is said to be capable of carrying two large fully-loaded motor-lorries at the same time. The cars enter by the bow or stern by means of two sets of specially constructed planks, which first lead up to the heavy cross-beam in which the boat terminates, and then down to the bottom level of the ferry in a gentle form of switch-back. These planks are kept in place by an easily removable iron band which half encircles the cross-beam. The ferry crosses the stream under oars and a stern-sweep.

The second type, the Min ferry, as illustrated in Plate No. 170, takes cars across the outer channel of the Minkiang, about 5 miles below Kwanhsien on

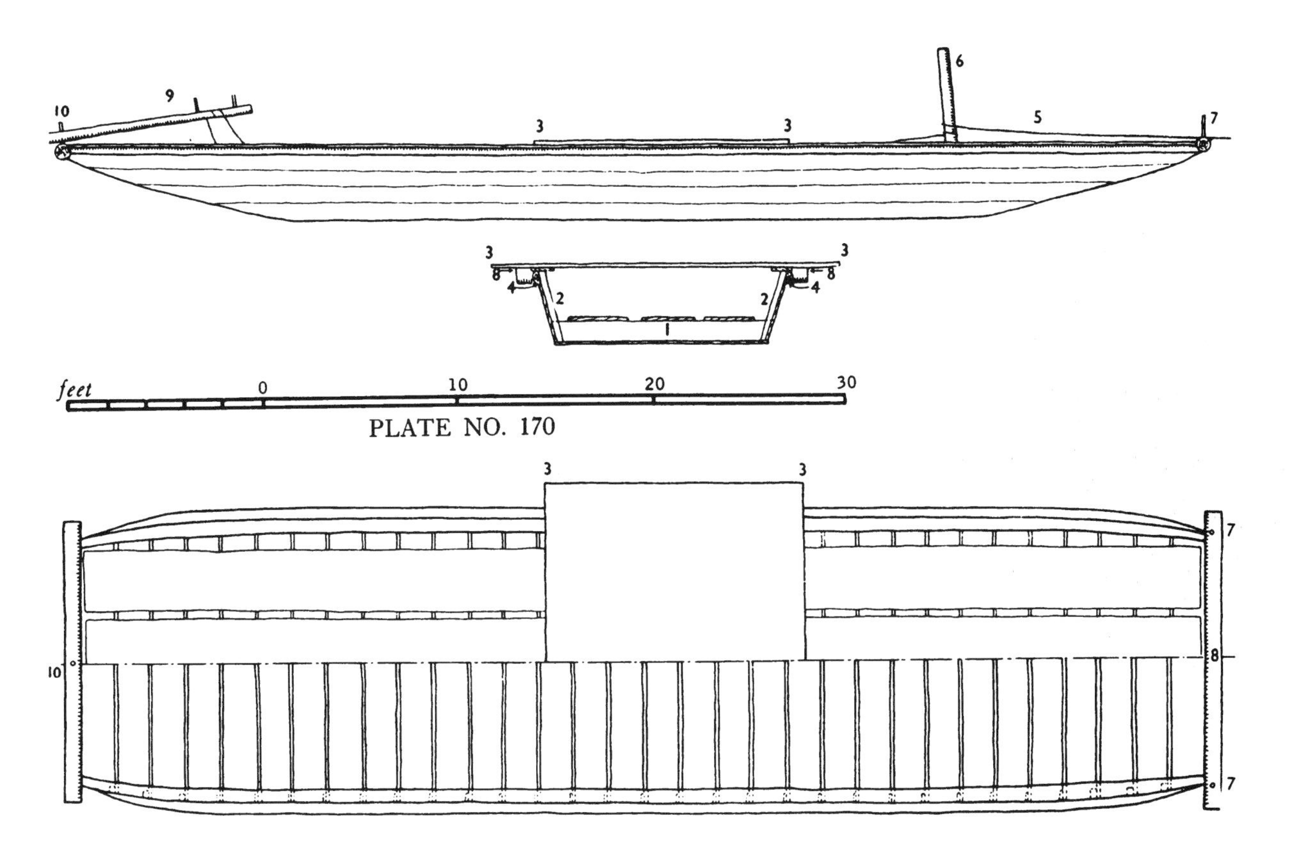

PLATE NO. 170

the road to Chingchengshan (青 城 山). This large, sturdily built, and clumsy craft measures 59 feet long, with a beam of 15 feet and a depth of 4 feet. There are 31 frames of more than ordinary strength, for they stand 13 inches high [1] from the bottom and are 4½ inches deep [2] on the sides of the hull.

Cars are driven on board up a wooden runway supported on a trestle in the water, and enter over the side amidships on to planks [3] laid athwartships over the gunwales,[4] but projecting considerably on both sides.

The method of crossing the river is simple and ingenious, and is accomplished without any effort at all, as the current is used to the full.

About 200 yards up stream a collection of large stones or boulders in bamboo cages has been built up in the shallow bed of the river in the rough form of a pier.

To this holdfast is attached one end of a bamboo rope,[5] which is secured at deck-level to a tall, strong, removable bollard.[6] The rope is kept clear of the water and any passing craft by being rove through three grummets on three other lines which are suspended at right angles to it and cross the river at regular intervals between the ferry stages and the holdfast. These cross-lines are elevated on six bamboo trestles, so as to allow other craft to pass beneath them and the main rope.

To cross the stream, the bowman lifts the rope [5] when it is slack and places it outside the shore side of the pair of pins [7] on the heavy cross-beam.[8] The laodah in control of the stern-sweep,[9] which operates on an iron bearing-pin,[10] gives the craft a cant with his sweep, which, placing her at an angle to the axis of the stream, utilises the force of the current as it strikes on the bow to carry her swiftly to the opposite ferry stage.

水老鴉捉魚船

THE CHENGTU CORMORANT FISHING-PUNT

This type of craft is designed for use on the network of waterways surrounding Chengtu. The punt, a double-ender, measures 16 feet long, with a beam of 2 feet and a depth of 8 inches. When carrying a crew of two men, a large fishing-basket, and a landing-net, the draught seldom exceeds 3 inches.

Lightly constructed of *nan-mu*, it contains seven half-frames and two or three perches for the birds. It is astonishing that any craft of such slender and shallow proportions should also be able to support two men.

feet 0 5

PLATE NO. 171

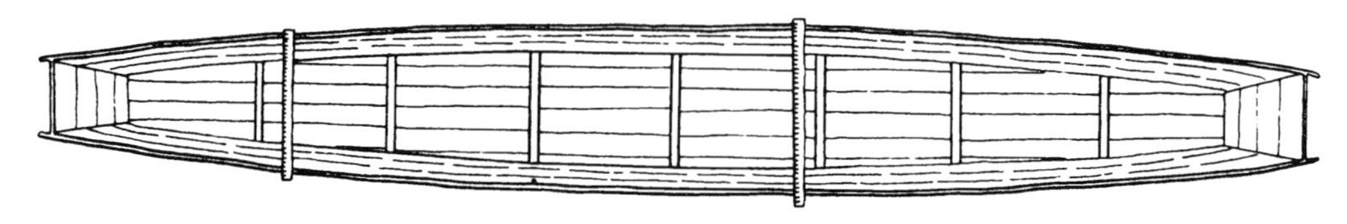

From Mr. Worcester's notes: The Chinese make great use of the cormorant in fishing and have done so from time immemorial. These birds are reared in captivity from the time they are hatched.

The method of propulsion is by poling, and the pole also serves as a gangway-cum-main-derrick for any bird that has secured a fish. The pole is inclined at an angle for the bird to climb onto from the water, when it is then hoisted bodily into the boat. The patient bird is then immediately relieved of its catch, after which it is pushed overboard again to dive for more fish.

When on duty the cormorants wear a tight rattan ring round their throats to prevent their swallowing any fish. The owner claimed that two birds working in co-operation, as they can be trained to do, are capable of landing fish up to 1½ feet in length.

With profitless patience and industry these long-suffering birds continue to retrieve fish with the greatest dexterity from early morning to late afternoon for their taskmasters, who reward them with a fish meal. When the day's work is concluded, the cormorants may be seen at their ease on their perches, or on the gunwales of their sampans, with their wings extended to the full, gently waving them to and fro in the air to dry.

The cormorant may be said to be on competing terms with the various other Chinese methods of fishing, if not the most successful exponent of all. The price of each fully trained bird is said to be as high as $50, but this may be a fisherman's story.

At first the fledglings are fed on eel's blood mixed with bean curd, but as they grow to the age of discretion their diet takes the form of small fish and the entrails of larger ones. In about three or four months the young birds are ready to start the training that enables them to earn their own living and, incidentally, that of their masters. As they reach maturity they become extraordinarily tame but the look of frustration seldom leaves their eyes. It would be interesting to know if they ever get used to what must be the exasperating sequel to their skill, that of being disgorged of their prey. It is amusing to watch young and imperfectly trained birds under instruction. When it happens that one of them catches a large fish he is pursued by the remainder of the class, each bent on relieving him of the prize. This undisciplined behavour is immediately corrected by the fisherman who beats the water with a long stick and restores order. Although scores of cormorants may be fishing in a small area, each knows his own boat and seldom makes a mistake as to where and to whom he belongs.

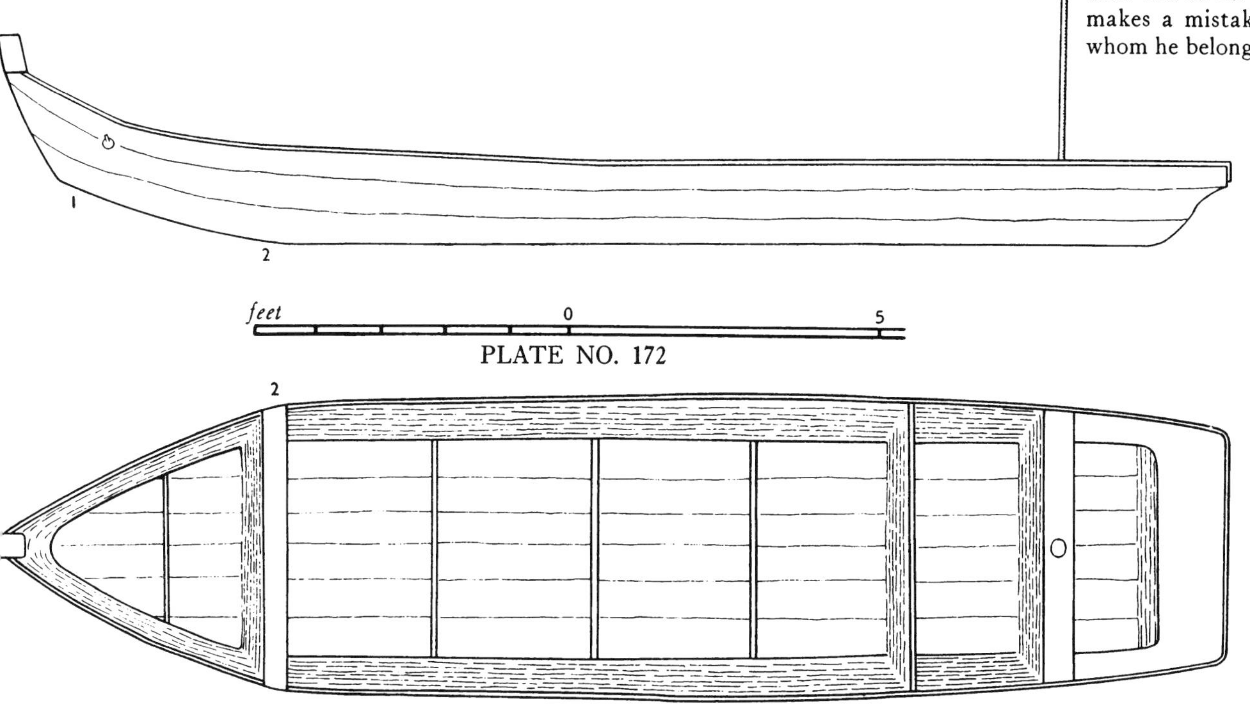

PLATE NO. 172

THE PLEASURE BOAT

小花船

The name *hsiao-hua-ch'uan*, or small pleasure boat, is given by the inhabitants of Chengtu to this curious craft. The reason for its name seems as obscure as the reason for the peculiar bow.[1]

The main purpose of a sharp bow is to enable the craft to cut through the water with greater ease. In this type the cutting edge is well above the water-line, which meets the square portion below the first bulkhead.[2]

The boat measures 19½ feet by 4½ feet, and the type is quite common on the Fu River at Chengtu. Despite its name, it is often to be seen laden with coal.

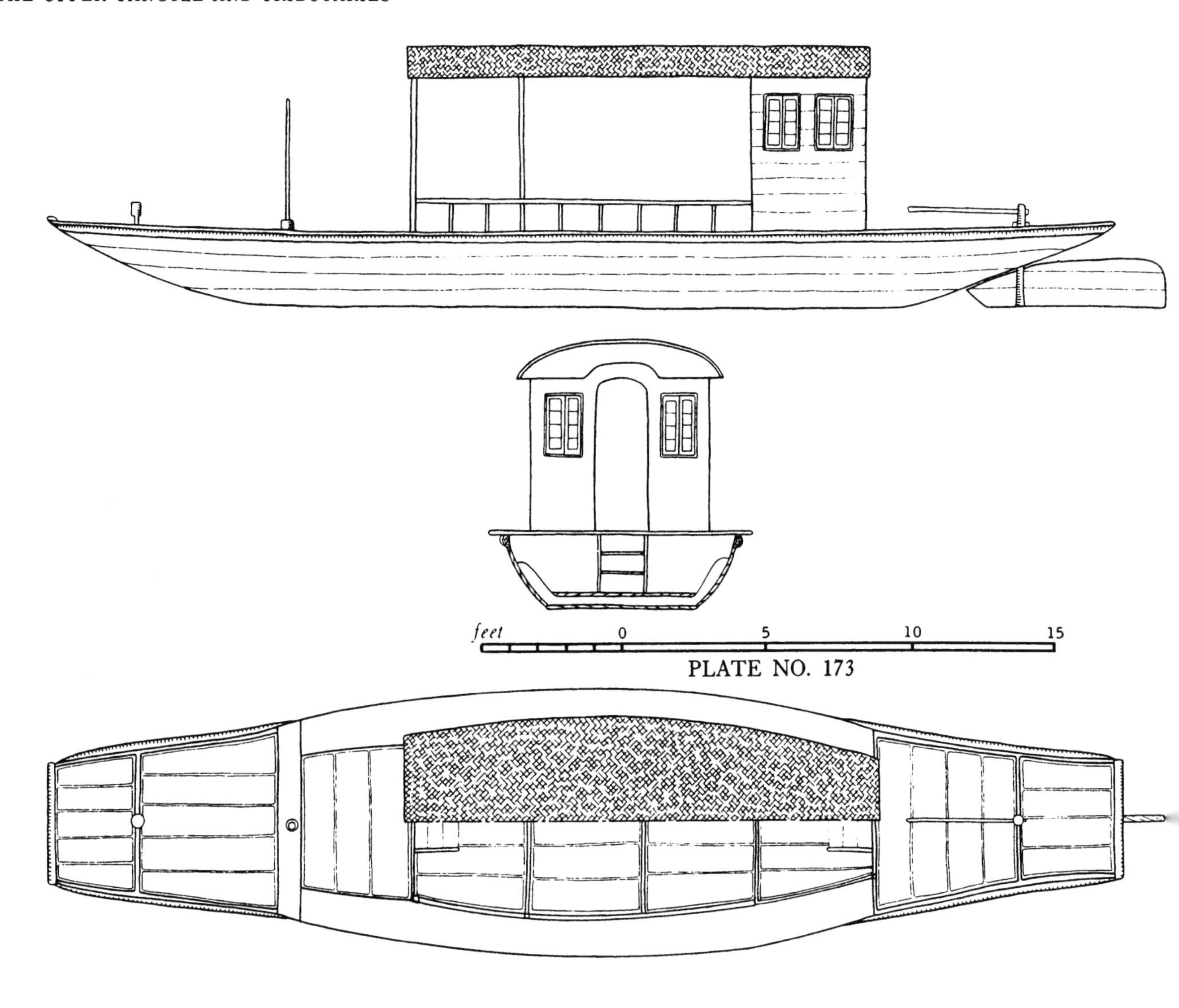

PLATE NO. 173

花船 THE HUA-CH'UAN

The *hua-ch'uan*, or flower boat, as it is locally termed, is designed for use on the numerous waterways surrounding Chengtu, where, for the modest sum of 25 cents per person, the inhabitants can, in summer, temporarily escape the heat of the town and enjoy the cool evening air afloat.

The boat as illustrated measures 37 feet and has an over-all beam of 9 feet. There are six bulkheads and four frames. It can accommodate nine passengers on each side. As they sit on bamboo chairs, facing inboard, they can derive little pleasure from the obstructed view, which in summer is further screened by lowered bamboo blinds. All the boat is decked-in, with the exception of the central portion contained within the deck-house, which is roofed with matting and has small railings on both sides. Outside these railings runs a 1-foot wide projecting gunwale, which narrows to normal proportions at bow and stern. This provides an uninterrupted gangway for the crew, which consists of two men at the oars and a laodah-ticket-collector. The small, after, built-up portion of the house is said to be for the use of lady passengers.

Hostilities with Japan.

The present hostilities have provided a new use for these craft. They have all been chartered by rich merchants for transporting their families and valuables out of the danger zone during air-raids. When the first alarm is given, these clumsy craft can be seen, loaded to the gunwales, making for the safety of the outlying waterways and canals.

THE MINKIANG WOOD RAFT

The Minkiang descends from the 12,000 feet high plateau in the north to the city of Sungpan on the Tibetan border, and flows thence down to the Chengtu Plain, which it enters by a cleft in the Tibetan Range at Kwanhsien, 2,500 feet above sea-level.

These heights and drops explain the torrential current and rapids of the Upper Minkiang. Logs from the mountain regions are floated separately down, some coming from almost inaccessible places many days journey away by foot.

These logs of various kinds of timber, comprising all lengths and shapes but mostly about the size of railway sleepers, although more solid and thicker, bump and crash their way down river, and arrive marked with the scars of their battle with the rocks and current, their ends being hammered and beaten to bluntness.

About 5 miles above Kwanhsien, where an affluent joins the Minkiang in a picturesque mountain setting, is the village of Paisha,[1] or White Sands (see sketch below). Here the logs are collected after their tempestuous passage and stacked into piles until, in late spring or early summer, after the irrigation dike[2] at Kwanhsien is opened, they are made up into rafts for their last journey to Chengtu.

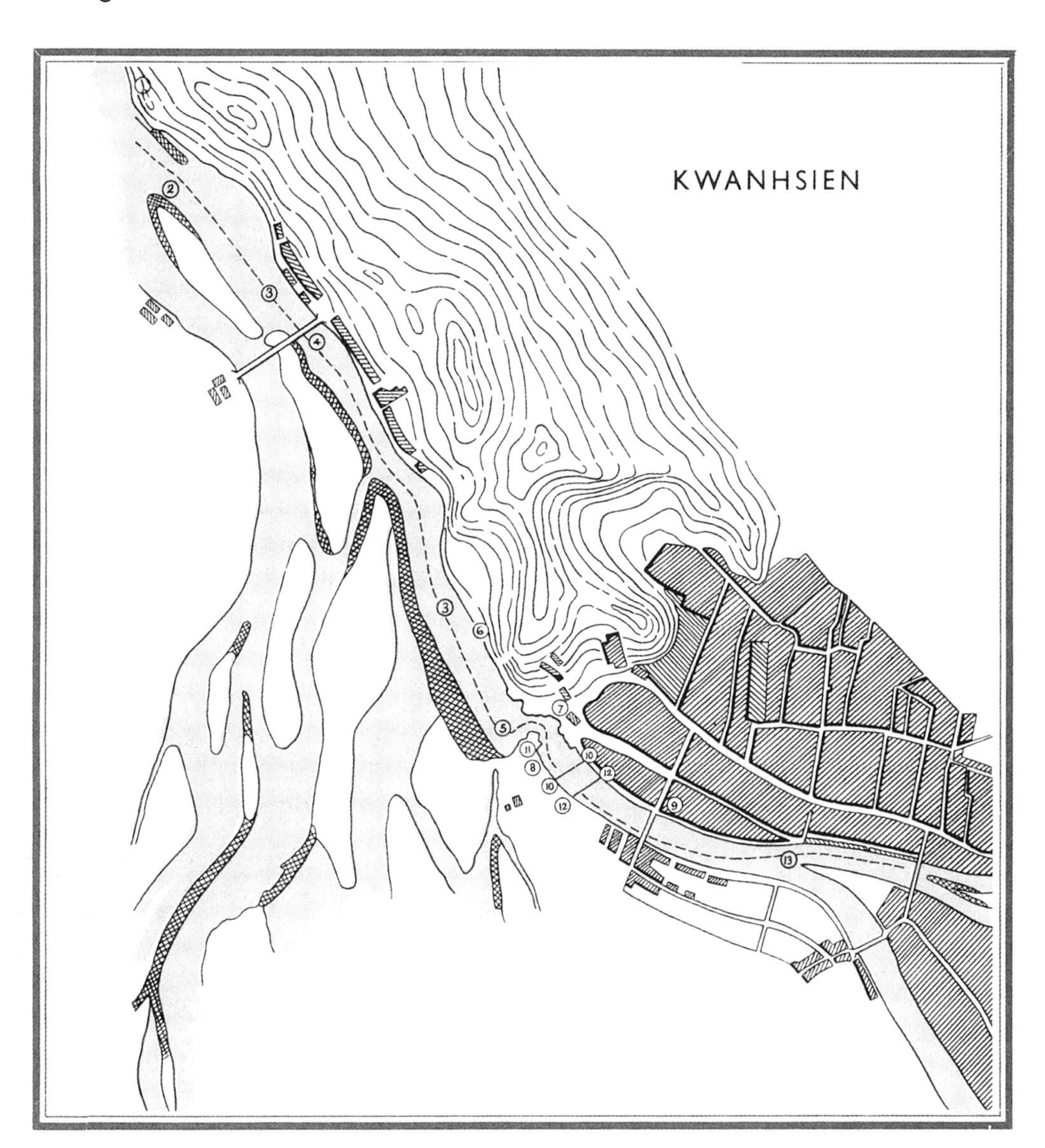

1. *From Paisha.*
2. *Position of Irrigation Dams on Fishes Mouth.*
3. *Inner Channel.*
4. *The Bamboo Bridge.*
5. *and 7. Li Ping's Cut.*
6. *River Gauge.*
8. *Whirlpool.*
9. *South Gate.*
10. *Life Saving Station.*
11. *Fu Lung Kuan Temple.*
12. *Lower Life Saving Station.*
13. *Division of Channels.*

These rafts, which vary in size from 25 feet long by 10 feet wide to 50 feet by 15 feet, are crudely assembled of balks, poles, and planks arranged in layers in an irregular rectangular shape, and lashed together with bamboo rope. At either end an improvised framework is built up for about 2 feet in the form of a trestle, through which the bow and stern sweeps are operated. A small oar is also worked from amidships.

Although they are mainly intended to be broken up for use in Chengtu, yet advantage is taken of their passage by using them to transport coal and a little general cargo. They take two days to reach Chengtu, and tie up *en route* at night. No illustrations or plans are here given, as there is little of interest in their general construction and shape.

There is, however, considerable interest and excitement attached to the first few miles of their journey (see map, page 587). From Paisha [1] the river runs swiftly over a boulder-strewn bed,[2] and the inner channel,[3] hugging the left bank, continues under a bamboo bridge [4] with three obstructing stone piers on the left bank of the river. No sooner have these obstacles been negotiated than the inner channel takes what is almost a right-angle bend [5] under the cliffs south-west of the town and approaches the narrow 40-yard bottle-neck of Paopingkow, or Mouth of the Precious Vase, which was cut through the rock by Li Ping about the third century, B.C.

There are many traditions connected with this event, most of them centring round a mythical Dragon, which had the disconcerting gift of being able to change itself into 72 different forms. Li Ping, who was himself no novice in the magic arts, used various disguises to combat the Dragon, which was responsible for the annual floods in that district.

From Mr. Worcester's notes: Li Ping was not a mythical figure; he was a conservancy engineer of high capacity and distinction known to history for his great work in the third century, B.C., in irrigating the Chengtu Plain and turning it from what was once a barren district into one of the richest and most thickly populated areas in China.

Li Ping transformed himself into a rhinoceros, adorned with a white sash to distinguish him from the Dragon, which had instantly assumed the same shape. Excellent service was rendered by Li Ping's second son, Êrh Lang (二 郎), who greatly alarmed the Dragon by painting his face dark blue. He seems to have derived the inspiration for this from Kuan Yin (觀 音), the Goddess of Mercy, who appeared to him as an old woman selling indigo.

With the combined help of the gods, his sons, and the local inhabitants, who were armed with bows and arrows, Li Ping was at last enabled to capture the Dragon, which was imprisoned in the river under an iron tablet [6] and retained there by lock and chain, and, in reply to its question as to when it would regain its freedom, was told "when stones are in blossom, and horns grow on horses' heads."

A temple stands on the Litui, or Separated Hill, on the right bank of the Cut, to commemorate the heroes of this epic battle, and is known as the Fu Lung Kuan (伏 龍 觀),[11] or Crouching Dragon Temple. Two iron bars,[6] dating to 1376 and 1863, the successors of scores of such, are in the bed of the river on the left bank, above the Cut, with a modern bench-mark, installed in 1936, above them.

Every low-water season when the inner channel is dammed, 8 to 10 feet of sand, boulders, and shingle, brought down by the current, are excavated from the river-bed till these marks are exposed. Inside the Paopingkow [7] is a river gauge, with 12 divisions carved on the cliff of the left bank. If the water-level sinks below the "11" mark it is considered insufficient for the irrigation of the Chengtu Plain and more water is released at the dam.

As the river, at summer level, rounds the bend to enter the Cut,[5] the swift current, meeting opposition in a projecting pinnacle below the Litui,

The Li Ping Cut, showing the "Elephant's Trunk" below the Temple.

likened by the Chinese to an elephant's trunk, causes a very dangerous whirlpool.[8] This was always attributed to the agitated lashing of the imprisoned Dragon's tail.

The stream then runs like a mill-race past the south gate of Kwanhsien.[9] The navigation by rafts of this short and difficult stretch, from Paisha to just below the second bridge outside the town of Kwanhsien, is carried out by a specially trained crew of 20 men, who are paid 50 cents a head per trip and who, after completing the passage and handing the raft over to its own crew, walk back and pilot another, making two or even three trips a day.

With a current reaching a maximum of 15 feet per second, and the whirlpool deflecting the raft and causing it to gyrate wildly, these men need all their courage and promptitude to deal with such conditions.

A life-saving station [10] has been inaugurated just past the most dangerous point, opposite the Temple of Fu Lung Kuan,[11] and another about 50 yards lower down.[12] These consist of a group of six bamboo ropes stretched from shore to shore, on each of which are rove a number of strong rattan rings. From these are suspended hemp ropes, each terminating in another rattan ring, and suspended just above the water-level.

When a raft comes to grief by colliding with the cliff,[8] which quite often occurs, the men are washed overboard. This inexpensive life-saving apparatus has therefore been instrumental in saving many lives, for the men have merely to clutch on to a ring and are then pulled to the shore by means of an in-haul on the upper ring. An out-haul returns the ring to its place after use. Men are stationed on both banks, and by manipulating the in and out hauls can almost place a ring in a struggling man's hand. After such an accident, the raft is collected farther down river and repaired.

Just east of the south gate of Kwanhsien the artificially made branch of the river is again artificially divided into two channels.[13] The rafts pursue the north-east channel which flows to the north gate of Chengtu, and once the adventurous passage of Li Ping's Cut has been accomplished, the remainder of the journey across the gently sloping plain to Chengtu is comparatively peaceful and uneventful.

THE YA RIVER

THE Yaho unites with the Tungho about 3 miles above Kiating, or Pearl of the West, where a mile or so beyond the west gate of the city both waters join the Minkiang.

The Yaho is a swift-running stream thickly bestrewn with boulders, shingle, and sandbanks. It rises in the Hung Shan (洪 山), the mountainous country north of Yachow (雅 州), and its waters, shallow in winter and tumultuously swift in summer, are always hazardous, and can only be navigated with great risk by junks at high water for, at most, 30 miles above Kiatingfu, to Hungyahsien (洪 雅 縣).

The importance of the Tibetan trade was such, however, that it was found imperative to negotiate the 100 miles of intractable waterway up to Yachow, situated at a level of 800 feet above Kiating. This gradient explains the swiftness of the rapids, of which there are 33, and places the Yaho in the class of a mountain torrent rather than a river.

Though boats are in use at various ferry points, the river is so unsuitable for ordinary navigation that cargo is conveyed up and down by rafts which ply from Yachow and Changpehsha (長 白 沙) to Kiating, and up to Chengtu, and even occasionally go down to Suifu. They take five days in the low-water season to go from Chengtu to Kiating, and three days in summer.

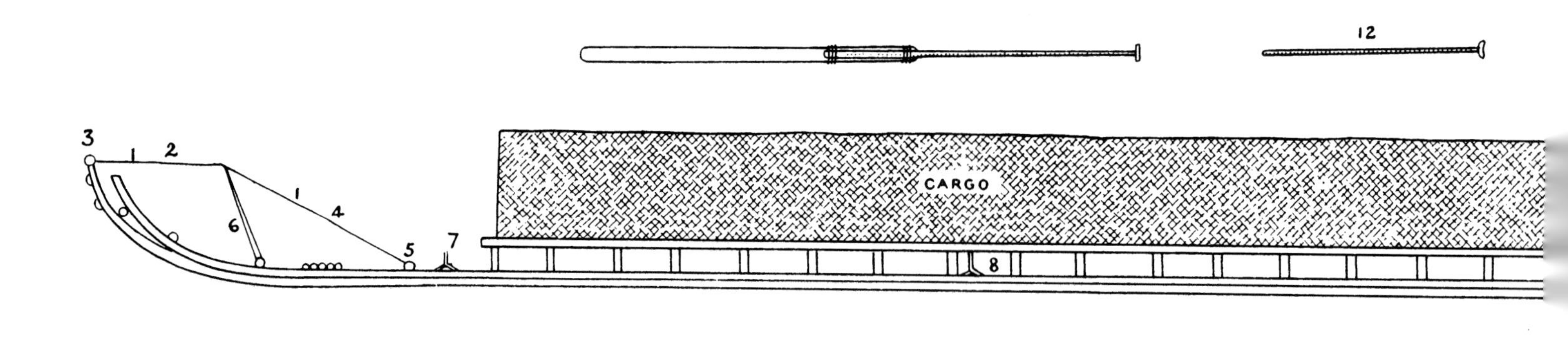

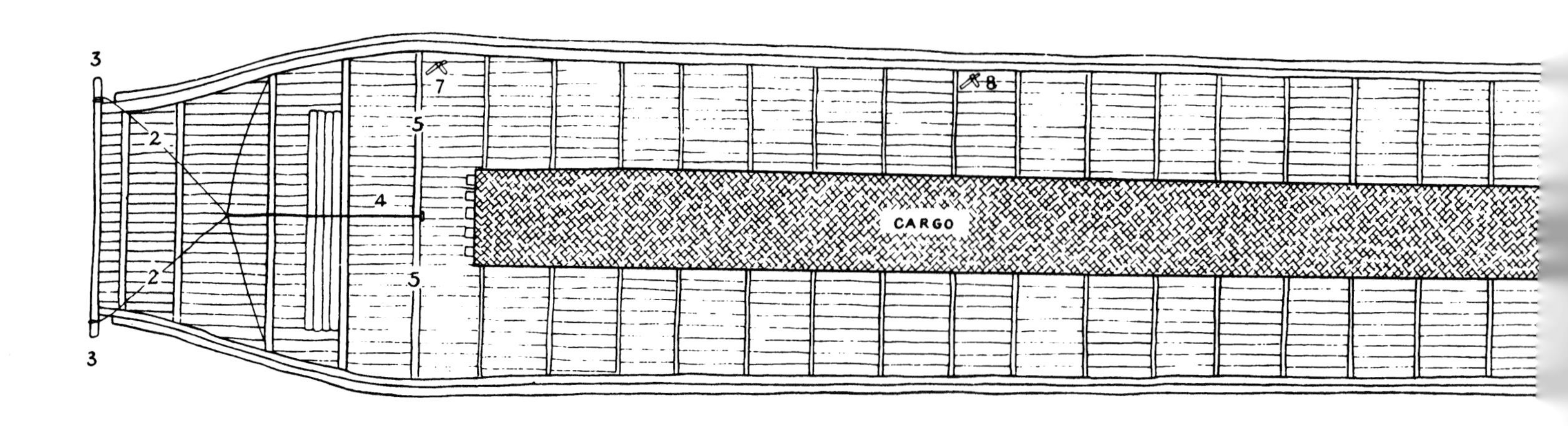

THE BAMBOO CARGO-CARRYING RAFT

The Yachow raft, or *fa-tzŭ* (筏 子), though primitive, is of very ancient origin or adoption, and may be described as the lightest-draught general cargo carrier of the Yangtze, and quite possibly of the world, in that its loaded draught is often as little as 3 inches and never exceeds 6 inches, this being largely due to the extra buoyancy afforded by the hollow watertight cylinders of the bamboos.

The *fa-tzŭ*, which is quite unsinkable, consists of a long, narrow platform of immense strength and flexibility, and embodies a number of very ingenious yet eminently practical devices for surmounting the difficulties it has to meet. Its most outstanding characteristic is the turned-up bow, which is designed so as to enable the raft to slide over the rocks, even though they may be almost breaking surface.

There is considerable variation in length, the smallest rafts being about 2 *chang*—these have the bow only very slightly raised—and the largest 10 *chang*. They are built at Kiating or Yachow, and only take about two weeks to make at a cost of about $600. The type illustrated in Plate No. 174 is therefore the largest, being 10 *chang* or 110 feet long, with a maximum beam of 12½ feet, which diminishes somewhat at bow and stern. It is built throughout of the culms of the giant bamboo (*Dendrocalamus giganteus*), known as *nan-chu* (南 竹), which is the largest of all the bamboos in Western Szechwan, and grows to a height of 60 to 80 feet, with a maximum diameter of 10 or 12 inches. This species, with its large core and light wood, is most supremely suitable. The bamboos used appear to be carefully selected, for they are of uniform diameter, that is to say, 5 inches, but are of unequal lengths, so that the end-to-end joins

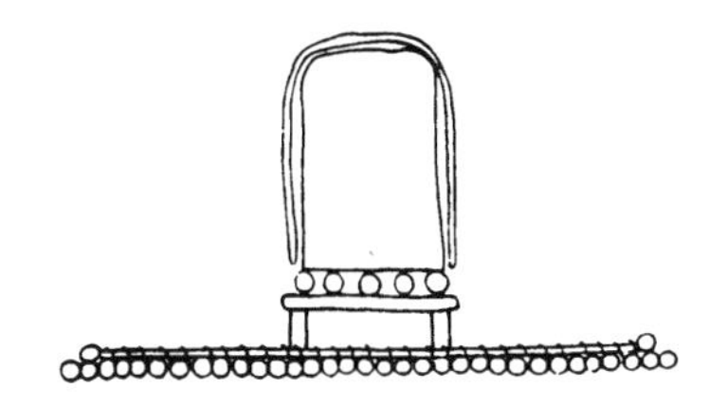

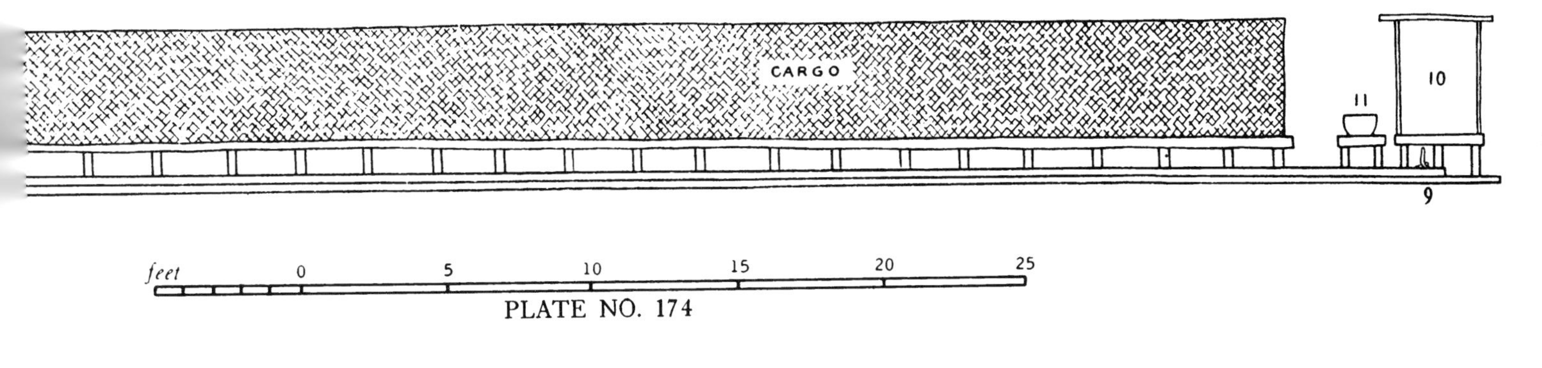

PLATE NO. 174

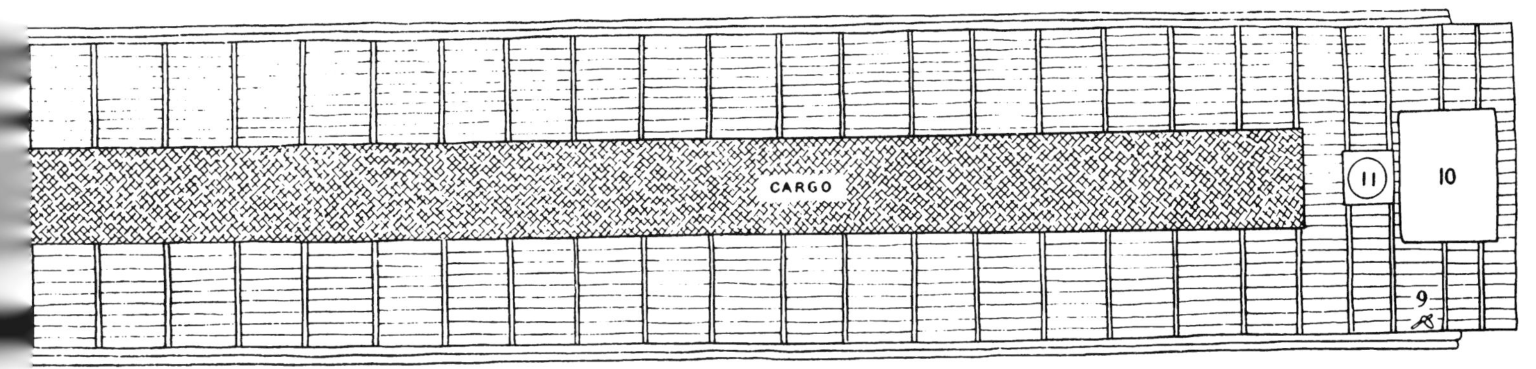

occur at irregular intervals. The outer siliceous skin is removed and the nodes hardened over a hot fire. Heat is also used to bend those canes intended for the bow, which are then weighted with stones to curve them to the upturned shape.

Due to the smoking process, the canes acquire a blackened appearance, further intensified by the practice of wood-oiling them once a year in the low-water season, when the whole raft is dismantled for overhaul and reassembled. This unusual colour of the bamboos, together with the fact that they have had their outer surface planed off, gives the raft the appearance of being made of timber.

The bamboos are laid side by side and securely lashed with cane withes to numerous cross-beams or frames, not a single nail being used in the whole construction; these frames are of less diameter, and are of the natural green bamboo without any treatment. The irregular length of the bamboos, as previously stated, ensures that no two joins ever coincide, and the raft is not, as commonly believed, made in separate sections joined together. Nevertheless, the utmost flexibility is achieved, for the rafts can yield both traversely and laterally when passing over a semi-submerged obstacle.

Protection and additional strength is provided by a continuous fender on each side from bow to stern. This fender is the width of two bamboos, and carries a third superimposed on the inner one. Unlike the floor of the raft, these joins are fished with strips of bamboo securely lashed, and extending for 1 foot on either side of the join. The over-all breadth of the fender is 10 inches.

The upturned bow is supported by a fibre-rope bridle,[1] strengthened with rattan frappings [2] leading from either side of the projecting *nan-mu* cross-beam at the bow [3] to a central fore and aft iron bar, [4] terminating in a hook and situated on the fifth frame,[5] to which it is made fast by a lashing.

In order to ensure a better lead, the bridle rests on a towing-horse [6] 4 feet above the deck. Below this is a small low platform of five bamboos laid athwartships, from where the laodah cons the raft.

Situated on the fifth frame [5] by the starboard side is a thole pin.[7] The problem of securing it has been cleverly solved by employing an alder stump about 2½ feet high, the two natural roots being lashed to the bottom-board bamboos, while a third artificial leg is provided in the shape of a wooden wedge with a tenon through the tree trunk and locked with a wooden pin. Eight frames farther down on the starboard side is a second exactly similar tree trunk,[8] and a third [9] is right aft on the last but one frame on the port side. No satisfactory explanation could be obtained for the number and position of these original thole pins for the three oars, but there is doubtless some very excellent reason.

A long, narrow, raised platform runs down most of the length of the raft, starting at the sixth frame and ending on the fifth frame from aft. This platform is elevated 1 foot off the deck, and rests on short, stout, upright sections of bamboo. It consists of five bamboos laid lengthways on the supports. On this, which is the only moderately dry place on the raft, which is usually awash when under way, the 7 tons of cargo is stacked to a height of something under 4 feet and covered with matting.

The stern, which narrows slightly, is flat, and has a small matshed [10] lean-to shelter for the normal crew of seven or eight men. Here, too, the galley, which consists of a brazier,[11] is situated on the third frame from aft. The raft is towed up river by the bow, and in shoal water these efforts are augmented by some of the crew entering the water and pushing by means of an 8-foot pole[12] ending in a cross-piece, so shaped as to accommodate a man's shoulder, the whole being not unlike a crutch. The rafts usually travel in company in order that the crews may assist each other over the more difficult rapids.

The average rate of progress when tracking up to Yachow is 5 to 10 miles a day, and the journey takes anything from two to four weeks, though the whole 100 miles may, on the downward trip, be accomplished in 20 running hours.

A curious and noticeable feature when travelling is the loud and crackling noise which forms a continuous accompaniment to the raft's progress when passing through shoal water over the shingle bed of the river. This noise reverberates, and is accentuated by the hollow bamboos, which act as sounding-boards.

The rafts are uniformly kept in excellent condition. Any damage sustained is instantly and easily repaired by substituting a new length of bamboo. It is obvious that the crew take a pride in their craft, and the result is that these rafts last for years, as they are always being renewed piecemeal.

The Ya River raft is probably the oldest type of craft on the Yangtze to-day, but, unlike the more modern types, it is likely to continue to ply, for there is no adequate substitute for this interesting and ingenious cargo carrier.

EPILOGUE

In 1946, after nearly three years in a Japanese concentration camp, I left China, my work still unfinished. Then, through the great kindness of Mr. L. K. Little, the new Inspector General, I was invited to return to complete the task set for me by Sir Frederick Maze.

While seeing my books through the press in Shanghai, I worked in a room just beneath the huge printing presses of the Statistical Department of the Chinese Customs. Over the rumble of the machines, the printers called loudly and insistently to each other, and the overseers added their voices to the general din. The vibrations of the presses shook the building, and the photograph of Sir Robert Hart, "The Great Inspector General," which hung on my office wall, oscillated so violently he appeared to have chronic Parkinson's disease. My visitors found all this noise distracting, but to me it was music.

In any case, the air was filled with a different, sinister rumbling, not of printing presses but of politics. The Communists were at the door; indeed, their propaganda slogans could almost be heard. Even the most casual observer could see that sooner, rather than later, the whole country would be overrun by them.

Part Two of this work was published, and a few hundred copies reached England and America, but the new Government prohibited further export on the grounds of security. It was then, with sadness rather than satisfaction, that I again left China, for the last time. As I walked down the familiar Bund, I remembered the words of Sir Bruce Hart the day I joined the Service: "China, you know, is in the melting pot!" I did not understand what he meant until I reached China. The words were still true the day I left the country 33 years later; one could sense the change that had come.

For thousands of years, Chinese civilization has taught filial piety and respect to superiors, and the Chinese people have abided by strict codes of ethics in propriety, sound judgement, and discrimination. For centuries the Chinese have taught the fundamental virtue of "Jên," for which our nearest equivalent is "humanity." Was all this to be swept away, like paper boats on the river?

The colourful history of an ancient land and people is disappearing in the pressing flood of turmoil and change. The melancholy truth is that the culture and civilization of China, which has endured for centuries, is indeed being swept down the river.

In this great field—or should I say sea—of junk lore, I feel I have merely scratched the surface; but I would be proud indeed if this small contribution of mine were to be the means of its becoming more generally understood and perhaps of tempting someone with a knowledge of the classics and the arts of China—and some knowledge of ships, too—to take up the torch of Chinese nautical research where I here lay it down.

I will end with the words of the writer whom I have already quoted in the Prologue:

> So these things being done . . . I also will here make an end of my narration. Which if I have done well, and as it becometh the history, it is what I desired, but, if not so perfectly, it must be pardoned me. For as it is hurtful to drink always wine or always water, but pleasant to use sometimes the one and sometimes the other; so if the speech be always nicely framed, it will not be grateful to the readers. But here it shall be ended.

JUNK MODELS

Accurate scale models of the crooked-bow and crooked-stern junks have now been made, of which the photographs reproduced in the following pages should be of interest to all students of ships in general and of Chinese nautical lore in particular. Each model is accurate in every minute detail, and was constructed in the port of origin by the actual local junk builders who make the junks themselves.

In the Mediterranean and Mesopotamian areas, sculptures and bas-reliefs form a source of our knowledge of the craft of the ancients. Well-informed authorities claim that it is known to be a fact that ships were navigating the great rivers of the Near East 9,000 years ago. Although representations of those craft are lacking, reasonably accurate pictures and carvings of boats, and even of sailing ships, were found in Egyptian tombs, which portray types in use nearly 5,000 years ago and, moreover, give a detailed account of the wood employed. Later, actual models of ships were placed in the tombs.

Countless models of varying degrees of accuracy exist, portraying later types in the evolution of shipbuilding in Europe. Even where the authenticity or reliability of the models may be in question, there is available a wealth of contemporary data giving the fullest details as to the lengths, breadths, riggings, etc., whereby those long-gone vessels may be reconstructed with considerable accuracy.

Nothing of the kind has been found in China. Chinese literature is singularly devoid of pictorial or written reference to junks, and foreign research, so busy in other fields, has hitherto contributed little to the world's knowledge of the fascinating subject of Chinese craft.

No other nation can boast of so long a succession of historians as the Chinese. From the time of Confucius, who was born about 550 B.C. and first collected the ancient records and formed them into a history, to the present day, every age has had its historians. It is as curious as regrettable, therefore, that they should have paid so little attention to the history of the shipping of China, which represents one of her largest and most important industries.

Excluding the imaginary or symbolic craft in old Chinese paintings and woodcuts, the only notable portrayal of early Chinese ships seems to be that in a fresco in one of the caves at Ajanta, in India. Warrington Smyth* writes of how this junk figures in Torr's Ancient Ships, and speaks of it as a "perfect representation of a three-masted North China junk." Models of junks of very indeterminate age are often found in Chinese temples, but these, too, are more or less symbolic—interesting but inaccurate, and not, of course, built to scale.

In the latter part of the last century the Chinese model-maker made his appearance for the benefit of the tourist, and he, together with the silversmith and the ivory carver, produced many picturesque, if not altogether accurate, representations of junks which have since evolved into the conventional, if erroneous, types so often to be seen in the shops of Shanghai.

Unlike a drawing, which however inaccurate may yet present a faithful impression of a ship, a model, since it deals with three dimensions, increases the possibility of error, whereby not only is all true likeness destroyed, but the result is made infinitely more misleading than a bad drawing.

Casual model-making of this sort is, of course, prevalent everywhere, but is nowhere more in evidence than in China, where not only is the idea of a scale

* "Mast and Sail in Europe and Asia," by H. Warrington Smyth.

model unknown to the Chinese carpenter, but almost invariably a due sense of proportion is lacking. Add to this a lively imagination, and the effect is a mere conventional work of art with little, if any, relation to reality.

So long as it is regarded in this light, it has a value for decorative purposes, but when, as sometimes happens, such a model finds its way into museums, the danger is that in after years it may be taken as a truthful representation of an obsolete vessel.

As no contemporary scale models of ships seem to exist prior to the seventeenth century, accurate scale model-making may be said to be a comparatively modern art. It is, however, still old enough to leave some doubt as to which is the oldest extant example of the art.

There is a Stewart Three-decker at Hamble which Keble Chatterton is inclined to consider might be that of the *Prince Royal*, launched in 1610, and rebuilt and renamed the *Resolution*. This, of course, is no proof of the age of the model, which may be later seventeenth century. A. G. Vercoe says: " the oldest contemporary model of an English warship is that of the *Fairfax*, built in 1653."

In an interesting article,* R.C. Anderson writes of a model now in the Rogers Collection at Annapolis. This model, he says, represents a ship of about 1650, and although its accuracy is superficially marred by rigging and alterations proper to a century later, he gives it as his opinion that it is probably a genuine contemporary model, in which case it would antedate the Model No. 1 of the National Maritime Museum and the Stockholm Three-decker, both of the 1650's, and would be thus entitled to first place as the oldest known English scale model.

There remains the field of reconstruction from available information. One of the most notable examples of this is the scale model made from the Viking ship discovered in 1880 in the burial ground at Gogstad, near Sandefjord.

Except perhaps for the Louvre in Paris and the Belfast and Liverpool Museums, it is difficult, if not impossible, to find any accurate models of Chinese craft in other museums than the Science Museum, London, which has recently been furnished with a collection of large-scale models of representative types of Chinese sea-going junks. These are apparently the nucleus of the first scientific attempt at nautical research in China, and have a double value, for they not only faithfully represent existing craft of unusual interest, but, when the changelessness of the various classes of junks is remembered, point to doubtless ancient origins to which the builders have adhered for centuries.

This is particularly true in respect of the two models of curious salt craft depicted herein. The junks represented, plying as they do on obscure tributaries of the Yangtze in the heart of Western China, are far from the modifying effects of any outside influence from the rest of the world, for even the Chinese launch, known as the chicken-boat, has not yet ventured up these rivers.

Surrounded, moreover, by a semi-superstitious aura, since their design is believed to be due to divine inspiration, there would appear to have been little incentive to introduce changes into these craft, particularly as they efficiently perform all that is demanded of them. It seems probable, therefore, that those scale models are unique in faithfully representing types of craft in use in much their present form at a very remote period in history.

THE model of the crooked-bow junk, as illustrated here, has, besides the interest attaching to its peculiar formation, the additional novelty of being a craft of which so far as can be ascertained not even the most inaccurate attempt has ever been made to represent it in model form.

Built on the banks of the Yentsingho, at Tzeliutsing, the port of origin of

For further research on this subject, the following books are recommended: "Ship Models," E. Keble Chatterton; "The Story of the Ship," G. M. Boumphrey; "English Warships in the Days of Sail," A. Guy Vercoe.

* "The Mariners Mirror." The Quarterly Journal of the Society for Nautical Research. London, April 1941 Vol. 27, No. 2.

Scale model of the crooked-bow junk.

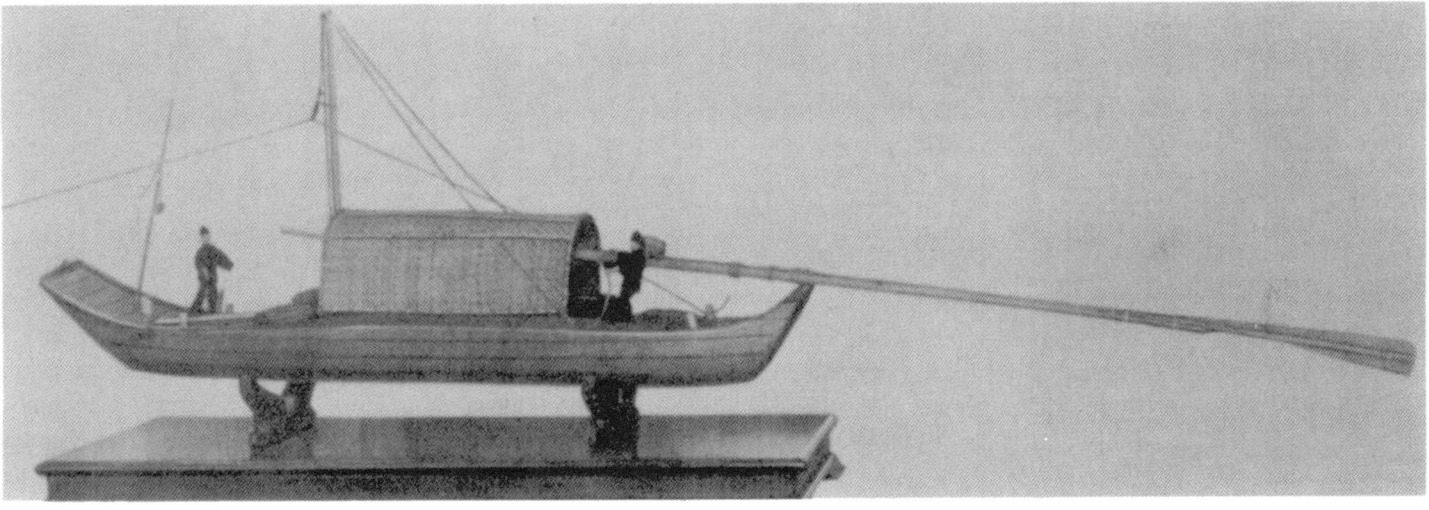

the craft it portrays, this model was made by the actual junk builders, who have been engaged for generations in making its prototypes.

The junk carpenters, who were, incidentally, very sceptical as to the desirability of such unproductive labour, were entirely unversed in the art of model-making, so it was necessary to provide them with cardboard patterns cut from carefully drawn-up plans. Such patterns were provided of all the component parts, and from these the carpenters made the final faithful copies in wood.

Made to the scale of 1 inch to the foot, this model measures 4 feet 9 inches in length, and represents Salt Junk No. 1091, a *tsai* (載), or leader of a group of five junks.

All the appurtenances, furnishings, and fittings have been made to scale, and nothing of the least importance has been omitted. The model is especially interesting, as it embodies many features which it would be difficult, if not impossible, to give in a plan, and therefore shows these strange craft in all their details.

Scale model of the crooked-stern junk.

The model of the crooked-stern junk, illustrated here, was built at Fowchow, and, like the model of the crooked-bow junk of Tzeliutsing, was made by two of the actual junk builders, who have for generations been making its prototypes.

There have been many attempts to make models of this queer craft, but they have always originated from Chinese model-makers, who have in no way kept even approximately to scale or bothered to be accurate in detail. Such obvious errors have included a mast and sails, oars of the wrong pattern, sweep on the wrong side, and so on. Such models, though picturesque, are quite valueless as reliable representations.

From a naval architectural point of view, therefore, this model is of great interest, and is, moreover, unique, in that it was not only built in the port of origin of the species, but that the workshop was on board its prototype. By a happy coincidence a full-sized craft was also under construction on the foreshore nearby and kept pace with the work on the model, both being completed in the astonishingly short period of two weeks.

As in the case of the crooked-bow model, the carpenters, who had never even heard of scale model-making, had to be provided with cardboard patterns of the various structural portions of the junk from which to shape their wooden copies.

Note.—Both these models have been added to the Maze collection of junk models in the Science Museum, London.

Built to the same scale as the model of the crooked-bow junk, that is to say, 1 inch to the foot, this model is 7 feet long, and represents a medium-sized junk with a length of 84 feet and a beam of 16 feet. Like the original, it is made mainly of *hung-ch'un* (紅 椿), a very attractive hardwood obtainable only on the Kungt'anho and much in favour with the Fowchow carpenters, because it yields readily to their curious methods of bending under fire. The bulkheads are made of *pai-mu* (柏 木), the bridge of *fêng-hsiang* (楓 香).

It will be noticed that in the photograph half the matting roof has been removed to allow the arrangements of the interior to be clearly seen.

The crooked stern itself is built on the *huang-shan* (黃 鱔), or yellow eel, principle. Timber for timber and plank for plank, all have their scale prototypes down to the last wrought-iron clamp and clinched nail. No detail has been too small to reproduce to scale, and the cooking-stove, grindstone, bunks, bedding, strops, bamboo rope, oars, sweeps, trackers' harness, and furnishings are exactly similar to those in daily use in the original crooked-stern junks of the Kungt'anho.

It is appropriate here to mention the junk-model makers of Ichang, who have now established their miniature craft as one of the well-known products of the Upper Yangtze. The industry, as such, is of recent growth, and owes its existence to an incident about the year 1909, when Captain Plant, in his pioneer days on the Upper Yangtze, happened to notice some children playing with a junk model by the river bank at Hsint'an. Captain Plant not only purchased the model, but ordered more to be made, and so started the industry.

Inquiry into the history of that first model proves it to have been built by one Hsiung (熊), son of a wealthy family at Hsint'an and descended from a line of junkowners. His father, however, had purchased an official title during the Ch'ing dynasty, and Hsiung, the son, developed into a young man of leisure, with a taste for gorgeous garments, and seems to have employed his idle moments in making junk models. These were originally designed to float, and were used at first purely for amusement. Later, however, it came about that junkowners would accept toy junks from their crews as a token of good fortune, and if a junk was wrecked, they would sacrifice a model to their River God, or even sometimes worship or pay reverence to the model itself. Taking on a semi-religious character as they then did, a mystic significance was attached to the building of the models, which was only done by still innocent, adolescent boys.

Liu-tzŭ-ch'uan, *Hunan police boat.*

Kua-tzŭ-ch'uan, *passenger-boat.*

The model-making family of the Hsiung was followed by the Tu (杜), many of whom are now still functioning as pilots on the Upper Yangtze. The industry at present is mainly carried out by two men at Ichang: one a descendant of the original Hsiung, and the other a dumb man of the name of Lung (龍).

These model makers, and one cannot but render the fullest praise to their craftsmanship, have provided miniatures of the ancient traditional types which, good as they are and pleasing to the eye, yet embody some artistic inaccuracies and are not altogether faithful reproductions of the junks they purport to portray—in other words, they are not scale models. Moreover, many of their types are purely imaginary.

They have acquired a collection of photographs of junks from all over China and invite their patrons to make their own selection therefrom, and being business men first and riggers afterwards, if their clients so require, they willingly incorporate the characteristics of any one junk in those of another without even having seen either. It would not offend their sense of the fitness of things to add the five masts of the Pechili trader to a model of the Fowchow "crooked-stern" junk to satisfy the wishes of a fastidious patron from Chicago. The models of the *ma-yang-tzŭ* and the "dragon" boat are excellent; the "crooked-stern" junk, however, is little more than a caricature.

The material used is the same as that of the majority of Upper Yangtze junks, namely, cypress-wood. A skilled worker can produce a finished model of about 12 inches long in about a week to 10 days at a price ranging from $10 to $15. The present small demand for these attractive toys, coupled with the high cost of living, has caused a big falling-off in the trade.

A sad sign of the times has crept even into their industry, for they are now turning out amazingly clever kerosene-oil tin models of steamers.

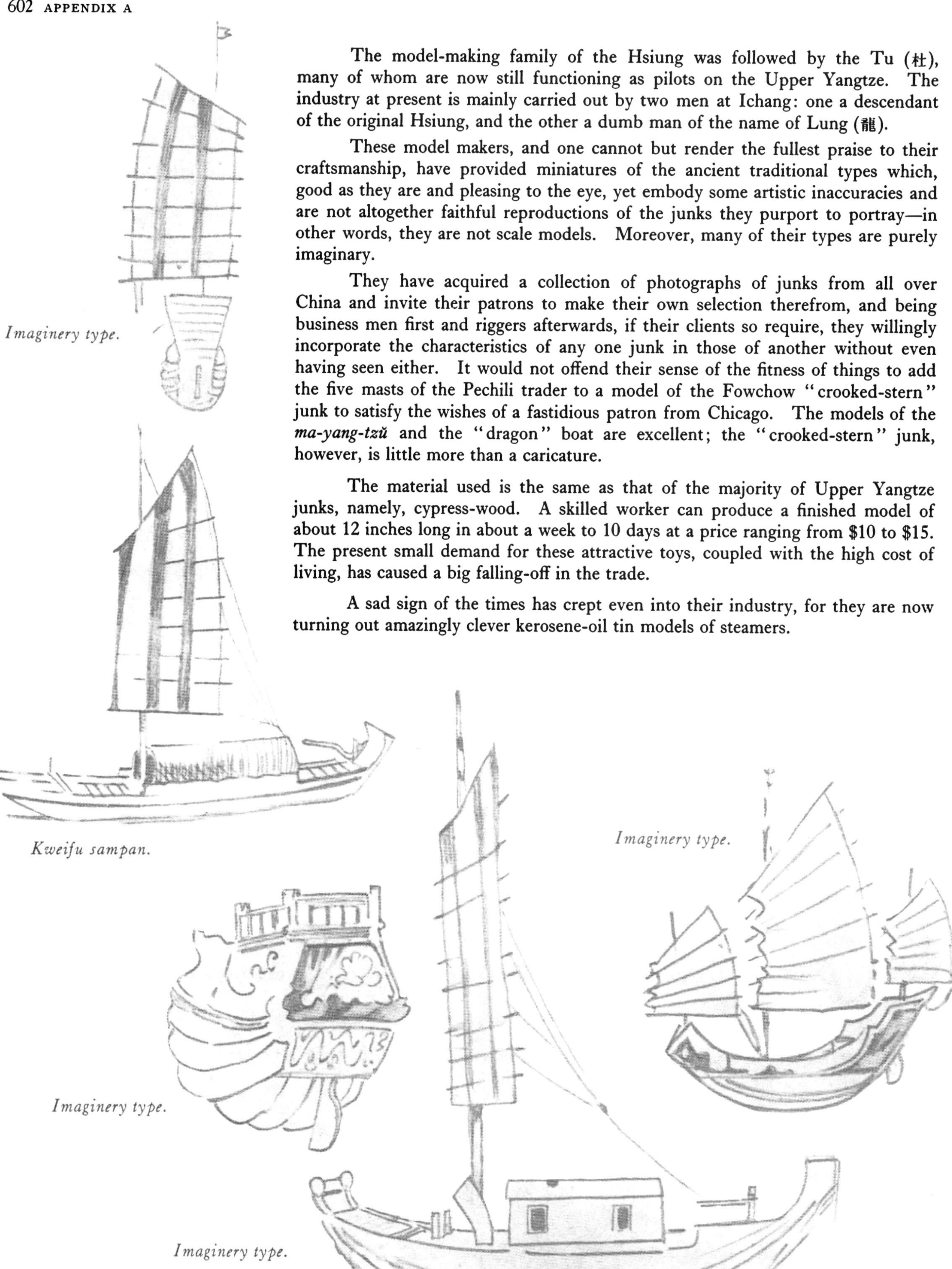

Imaginery type.

Kweifu sampan.

Imaginery type.

Imaginery type.

Imaginery type.

THE KEYING

The most famous of Chinese junks from a Western point of view was probably the *Keying*, and her claim to fame rests on more than one count. Not only was she the first ship of Chinese construction to make the journey from China to America and thence to London under sail, but she was the first and probably the only junk to be visited by a European crowned head, for Queen Victoria went on board her when she was lying on show in the Thames, where she arrived on the 28th March 1848. The "Mariner's Mirror," October 1922, describes her as "not differing essentially in important points of construction from typical junks of the larger class."

Contemporary drawings in the "Illustrated London News" of the 20th May 1848, together with the astonishing descriptions supplied by the pamphlets and newspapers of the time, represent a type of junk which, if it ever really existed, is certainly extinct to-day, for the craft bears no resemblance to any class now to be seen in China.

The type to which she most nearly approximates, and that only to a degree, is the Foochow junk, although the perforated rudder and two stern galleries are suggestive of other South China ports. There is a possibility that she may have been some type of war junk or even a built-up composite craft specially adapted for the particular voyage for which she was purchased at Canton by a few enterprising Englishmen, of whom the moving spirit and Commander was Captain Charles A. Kellett. Others were: G. Burton, Mate; S. Revett, Second Mate; T. A. Lane, and Lapraik. Including these, the vessel was manned by 12 Englishmen and between 26 and 30 Chinese under a Chinese Captain named So Yin Sang Hsi. The Chinese law of that day, whereby it was said to be a capital offence to sell a vessel to a foreigner, was circumvented by their wearing Chinese dress as a disguise and pretending that local yachting was their only motive.

The *Keying*, presumably named after the Chinese Commissioner then in office at Canton, was 160 feet long. Her breadth was given as 33 feet and the depth of the hold as 16 feet; but a printed description in the Marine Collection at South Kensington gives the beam as 25.5 feet and depth as only 12 feet. Conflicting tonnage figures were also given, namely, 800 tons, 750 tons, and 700 tons.

The hull, which was said to be of teak, was constructed with "15 compartments, several of which were watertight." It was said that "the caulking was a cement of burnt, powdered oyster shells and chinan-tree oil, said to dry very hard and to be not liable to start." The wood-oil tree is here masquerading under a fanciful name. Very curious claims were made as to the method of construction, for it was said that "the timbers were raised last instead of first, then the doubling and clamping was done above and below decks; two large beams or string-pieces were ranged below fore and aft to keep the other beams in place." If this were really the case it would show a method of shipbuilding never practised by the Chinese to-day.

The gunwale was said to be so wide that it could be used for walking fore and aft, and "the lower wales projected 3 feet." These projections do not, however, appear in the contemporary pictures. The main deck was "arched," and there were in addition a "raised quarter-deck; two poops, the first containing cabins; and a raised forecastle with a high veranda above that again"; also the quarter galleries already mentioned. The main saloon measured 30 by 25 feet with a height of 12 feet. The raised bow of the drawings presents a very strange factor which in no way fits in with the traditional Chinese types of junks.

There were three hardwood masts. The foremast measured 75 feet with a diameter of 1.5 feet at deck level, the mainmast 90 feet with a diameter of 3.3 feet, and the mizzen-mast 50 feet. As there was no keelson, there were no mast steps. "The mainmast ended 4 feet from the bottom and was kept in place by a toggle." Another description said that the fore and main masts were "toggled to two large pieces of wood which answered as partners; to these are added two heavy pieces of wood as chocks, which are intended to keep the huge spars in their places. The foremast raked forward and is supported by a large piece of wood on the after part. The mizzen-mast was placed out of the centre line in order to enable the tiller to work when the junk was in shoal water." The mainmast was hooped or woolded in some kind of way and was not quite straight. The upper or main yard measured 67 feet and the lower yard or boom 60 feet. The sails were of matting. The mainsail was said to have a spread of 11,000 square feet, to weigh nearly 9 tons, and to take two hours to hoist.

The hardwood iron-bound hoisting rudder was slung in the ordinary Chinese manner, without gudgeons or pintles, and retained in place by "bamboo and grass ropes" passing under the hull. It weighed from 7½ to 8 tons, drew 23 or 24 feet, and was worked by 15 to 20 men on a luff tackle. In fine weather, however, two men were sufficient to steer her.

An interesting feature was the collection of what was described as Treaty Port flags of Canton, Ningpo, Shanghai, Amoy, and Foochow. The vane at the masthead was a fish worked in rattan and matting and inscribed " Good luck to the junk."

The windlass was of hardwood. Two anchors were carried. These were made of hardwood with iron-shod flukes and were lashed with bamboo. The stock consisted of three pieces fished with rattan. The shanks of the anchors were about 30 feet long.

The junk left Hongkong on the 6th December 1846. She was at anchor for about six weeks in the Java Sea and Sunda Straits with light southerly and south-westerly winds. The worst weather of the whole voyage was in the Indian Ocean, off Mauritius. On the 22nd March 1847 she experienced a south-westerly gale, and on the 30th March rounded the Cape and made St. Helena on the 17th April. She left this port on the 23rd April, bound for England. Owing to the head winds now encountered, shortage of food, and the mutinous state of the crew, it was decided to change their plans and make for New York, which was reached on the 9th July. She was exhibited there and at Boston for several months. While in America the *Keying* was arrested for debt, as the 26 men of the Chinese crew had not been paid by the Chinese Captain, and they demanded to be sent back to Canton, as they claimed they had been engaged for only eight months. A court decision was made in favour of the crew, the sale of the vessel was ordered, and the Captain instructed to pay each man $100 or $200 according to his rank.

Nevertheless, however, the matter was finally settled; the *Keying* left Boston for England on the 17th February 1848, being towed out for 60 miles. She now met with bad weather the whole way, including a strong gale on the 28th February. Two boats were washed away and the fore-sail split. One rudder rope parted on the 25th February and the other on the 5th March, when the rudder took charge. Repairs were effected after about six hours. At some time, probably then, Revett, the Second Mate, was drowned while over the side seeing to the rudder. Under these trying conditions the junk gave excellent proof of her seaworthy qualities and, it was said, " never shipped a drop of water."

This medal was struck to commemorate the arrival of the Keying *in London in 1848. It is of white metal, 1.75 inches across, and is now displayed in the British Museum.*

St. Aubin, Jersey, was reached on the 15th March. She left again on the 25th in tow of the s.s. *Monarch* and arrived off Gravesend on the 28th March 1848 after a roundabout voyage of 16 months across two oceans.

She proceeded up the Thames to London and moored at the bottom of Exeter Street, Strand, surrounded by a palisade and put on view for the public. Interest in China had been started in 1843 by a Chinese Exhibition at Hyde Park Corner which seems to have come from America. The advent of the *Keying* accentuated this interest. She sailed, apparently under her own canvas, to Liverpool and was exhibited there and at other ports. Her end was that of other famous and adventurous ships.

On her return to the Mersey she was sold for breaking up to Redhead, Harland, & Brown. Her teak planking was used for building two ferry-boats, work-boxes, and other small souvenirs.

This information has been gleaned from an article by H. H. Brindley in the "Mariner's Mirror" for October 1922. As he points out, no scientific account of the vessel appears to have been written, and much of the contemporary information fails in technical clearness.

It is a great pity that, when such a junk was available for extensive survey, always a problem with the Chinese, reliable data was not collected as to the structure of this interesting ship, so that an accurate description of at least one junk of 100 years ago might have been preserved for posterity.

NAUTICAL CHRONOLOGICAL TABLE

Showing the sequence of the chief events in nautical history and the most important inventions connected therewith from the earliest times of the world's history to the present day, but dealing more particularly with Chinese vessels and events.

Many of the earlier events and dates are of so legendary a character and are so often contradictory according to the various authorities that they must be accepted as an approximate guide only, and as interesting evidence of their origin rather than as accurate and infallible information.

B.C.

5000 Terra cotta model of Egyptian canoe.

4000 Extensive trade between Crete and Egypt. Drawings of ships are to be found on vases.

3500 Silver model of a canoe at Ur of the Chaldees.

3000 The dawn of the rudder. Egyptian boats at this time were steered by a large stern paddle.

2852 Fu Hsi taught the Chinese people the art of shipbuilding and fishing.

2697 Invention of the "south-pointing chariot," popularly called the compass, by Huang Ti, and development of junkbuilding.

2600 Sails make their appearance in Egypt during the fifth dynasty and in the Eastern Mediterranean.

2348 The Ark of Noah.

2205 The Emperor Yü crossed a mud flat on a *chiao*. The Great Chinese Flood. Chinese shipbuilding receives impetus. I Ti produced the first wine in China. Boats with oarsmen, in the oldest monuments of Egypt, shown paddling with their faces towards the bow.

2000 First use of anchors in China, according to Giles. Boats of Egypt shown with single square sail.

1766–1122 Traditionally accepted date of Shang dynasty of China. Period during which the Shang oracle bones were inscribed with pictographs showing boats. The shaping of boats by means of fire and with metal tools. Caulking, rowing, and loading cargo.

1400 First reference to oars in China. The Greeks and Phœnicians come out with powerful fleets.

1350 Models of boats placed in Tutankhamen's tomb. Reed fishing-boats used in Egypt.

1250 Egyptian crews represented unmistakably rowing with their faces towards the stern. Boom discarded. Sheets and brails introduced.

1204 *The Argo*, claimed by the Greeks to be the oldest ship.

1200 Chinese penetrated down to the Yangtze cape.

1130 The Duke Chou gave "south-pointing chariots" to foreign envoys.

1122 First distinct mention of fishing in China. (Werner.) First mention of boat-builders in China, in the class known as the "hundred artisans."

1012 Hiram, King of Tyre, mentions rafts when writing to King Solomon.

850 Homer. Greek anchors consist of stones.

786 The first double-ended ship built by Tyrians.

785 Prophet Isaiah mentions fishing, and suggests pisciculture was known to Egyptians. Isaiah XIX, v, 10.

700 Chinese dictionary mentions boats generally, and especially ferries and rafts.

600 Iron anchors known in Europe. Sails make their appearance in Mesopotamia.

588 Prophet Ezekiel describes the ships of Tyre, and mentions sails, oars, rowers, and pilots. Ezekiel XXVII, v, 6.

551–479 Confucius. Mentions boats and their fittings.

500 Map made for Aristagoras, Tyrant of Miletus (minutely described by Herodotus). The *Paralus* and *Salaminia*, Athenian State galleys, the first ships mentioned by name in authentic history.

472 Reference in the Chinese classics to the Navy of the feudal State of Yüeh.

400 Ch'ü Yüan, of "dragon" boat fame. Boats on Tigris (described by Herodotus). Tacking discovered in Egypt.

332 Siege of Tyre. Probable first use of iron chain in lieu of rope.

325 Chinese silks were sold in Greek markets.

300 First reference in Chinese dictionary to bumkin for yuloh. Greek and Roman coins show anchors with all features of present day.

219 Emperor Shih Huang sends a mission in search of the "Isles of the Blest."

214 First mention of northern junks when "ships laden with iron were sunk" to provide foundations for the Great Wall.

213 Burning of the Books.

206 Han Emperor was rowed in boat with oars on Yangtze.

200 Roman corn ships reach high standard of development.

143 Model of ship mentioned in First Book of Maccabees, XIII, v, 29.

140 Chinese sea expedition, carrying cargo of silks and gold, goes to Conjeveran, near Madras.

132 Piracy first mentioned in Chinese history.

59 Livy definitely mentions flukes of an anchor, implying there were two.

56 Use of iron anchor chains and skin or hide sails by the Veneti of Brittany recorded by Cæsar.

55 Cæsar invades Britain.

10 Chinese ships carry on an extensive trade from Korea and Indo-China.

11 Arc de Triomphe at Orange, erected by Tiberius (d. A.D. 37), shows anchor with rope and block.

18 Chinese Dictionary "Fang Yen" mentions boats in general; also rafts and ferries.

47 The barbarian tribe of Ngai-Lao descended the Yangtze on rafts to attack the Lu To tribe.

63 Anchors, sails, rudders, and lead-line mentioned in Acts in connection with the ship of St. Paul. The Romans introduce the artemon: half mast, half bowsprit.

100 "Shuo Wên" (dictionary) mentions boats. "Shih Ming" (dictionary) mentions sails for the first time; also masts, rudders, *lu*, tow-ropes.

121 Earliest reference in a Chinese dictionary to lodestone.

165 A commercial embassy arrived by sea, sent by Marcus Aurelius. The mission travelled to China *via* Burma.

225 A merchant from Rome said to have reached Nanking, at that time the capital of Wu.

280 "History of the Three Kingdoms" written. Mention of stone anchors.

400 Various Buddhist pilgrims left China to visit India by sea.

417 Fa Hsien describes the ships he travelled in from India to China. He speaks of anchors, and implies stone ones.
446 Emperor Wen Ti sent an expedition against pirates.
543 "Yü P'ien" (dictionary) mentions iron anchors in China for the first time.
560 Carpenter's string line-marker mentioned in Chinese classics.
618 Persian traders are stated to have come to China by sea.
651 Embassy from Arabia reaches Peking by way of Canton.
652 Foreign influences arriving by sea were said to have effected changes in the design of southern junks.
733–792 General Li Kao invented paddle-wheels.
787 Arab ships arrive in Chinese ports.
789 Viking age commences.
897 First recorded use of the word anchor in England by King Alfred.
960 Geomancer's compass introduced.
1120 Bayeux tapestry: ships shown under oars and sails.
1127 Earliest known representation of a rudder in Europe (slung from stern-post).
1135 General Yang Yao said to have used paddle-wheel junks in Tungting Lake.
1242 Seal of Elbing, in Germany, depicting certain use of a stern rudder.
1265 Marco Polo sets out for the court of Kublai Khan. Describes junks.
1300 Discovery of the compass attributed to Flavius, or John of Amalfi.
1318 Friar Odoric sets out on his travels in China. Describes junks.
1324 Ibn Batuta sent on an embassy to China. Describes Chinese oars.
1325 Seal of Poole, depicting certain use of a stern rudder in England.
1368 Ming Emperor sends an expedition to the Eastern Seas, visiting Aden.
1375 Catalan Map introduces the Chinese mat sail to Europe.
1435 Christopher Columbus born.
1500 Port-holes invented by Descharges, a French builder, of Brest.
1540 First use of word lorcha, by Pinto.
1550 Warfare between Knights of Malta and Turks and Algerian pirates.
1552 Book of woodcuts of Chinese junks published.
1555 First mention of junks in European literature.
1578 Drake sails round the world.
1588 Defeat of Spanish Armada.
1596 Probably the first authentic picture of a Chinese junk, drawn by H. Van Linschoten, of Amsterdam.
1620 The *Mayflower* of the Pilgrim Fathers.
1677 First use of the word lug-sail in England. "London Gazette," 119414.
1686 First reference to lug-sail in Europe.
1740 Commodore Anson's *Centurion* reaches China.
1792 Sir George Staunton describes Chinese junks.
1811 Rope cable replaced by chain in British Navy.
1829 The East Indiamen.
1843 Convoying by lorchas introduced as protection against pirates.
1848 Junk *Keying* visits America and England. Is visited by Queen Victoria.
1872 *Aden*, the first steamer under Chinese flag.
1905 Office of the Director General of Grain Transport in China abolished.

SYNOPTICAL TABLE OF CHINESE DYNASTIES

A greater appreciation of the subjects appearing in this book will be enjoyed by those readers who keep on hand the following list of dynasties.

ANCIENT PERIOD.

Neolithic Culture [新石器時代]	*circa* 4000–3000 B.C.
Hsia (Black Pottery) [夏 (黑陶)]	2205–1766 B.C.
Shang (Oracle Bones) [商 (甲骨文)]	1766–1122 B.C.
Chou (the Five Classics) [周]	1122–255 B.C.
Ch'in [秦]	255–206 B.C.
Han, or Western Han, or Former Han [漢]	206 B.C.–A.D. 25
Later Han, Eastern Han, or Minor Han [東漢]	A.D. 25–221

MIDDLE PERIOD.

The Three Kingdoms [三國]	A.D. 221–265
Chin (Eastern and Western) [晉]	A.D. 265–420
Division into North and South [南北朝]	A.D. 420–589
Sui [隋]	A.D. 589–618
T'ang [唐]	A.D. 618–907
Five Dynasties [五代]	A.D. 907–960
Sung and Southern Sung [宋及南宋]	A.D. 960–1280
Liao (Kitan Tartars) [遼]	A.D. 916–1125
Western Liao [西遼]	A.D. 1125–1168
Chin (Golden Tartars) [金]	A.D. 1115–1260
Yüan (Mongols) [元]	A.D. 1260–1368

MODERN PERIOD.

Ming [明]	A.D. 1368–1644
Ch'ing [淸]	A.D. 1644–1911

2

MASTHEAD DEVICES

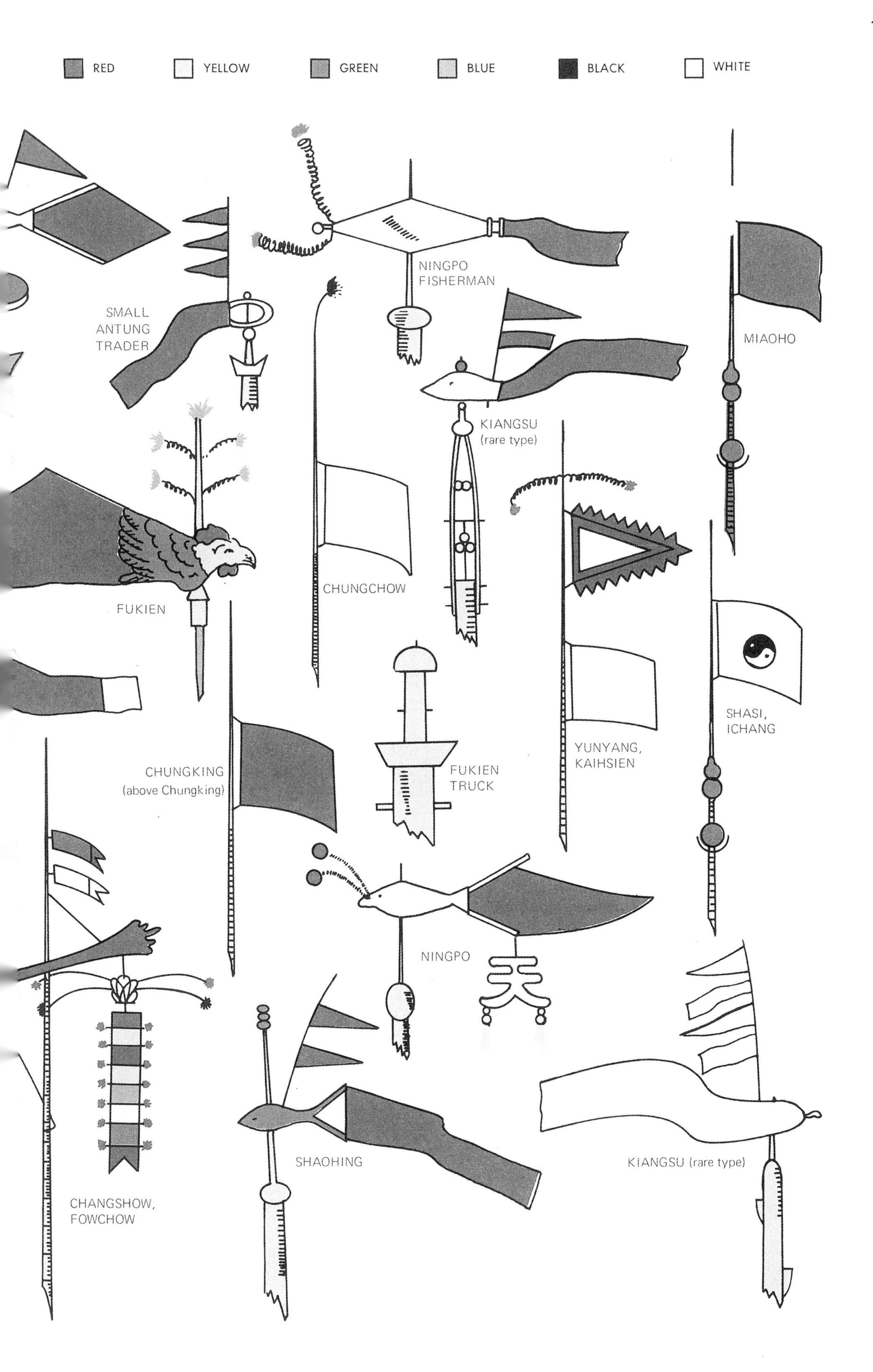
RED
YELLOW
GREEN
BLUE
BLACK
WHITE
SMALL ANTUNG TRADER
NINGPO FISHERMAN
MIAOHO
KIANGSU (rare type)
FUKIEN
CHUNGCHOW
SHASI, ICHANG
YUNYANG, KAIHSIEN
CHUNGKING (above Chungking)
FUKIEN TRUCK
NINGPO
CHANGSHOW, FOWCHOW
SHAOHING
KIANGSU (rare type)

CHINESE WAR VESSELS AND THEIR STATIONS, 1851*

Description of Vessel.	Shingking Outer.	Shantung Outer.	Kiangnan Outer.	Kiangnan Inner.	Fukien Outer.	Fukien Inner.	Chekiang Outer.	Chekiang Inner.	Kwangtung Outer.	Kwangtung Inner.	Kiangsi Inner.	Hupeh Inner.	Hunan Inner.
Chen-ch'uan, fighting vessels	10	..	..	..	..	..	..	..	..	..	..	68	50
Tsang-ch'uan, vessels with nets	..	..	..	..	..	..	..	..	2	..	..	..	..
Kan-tsang-ch'uan, chasers	..	4	2	..	10	..	10	..	..	..	..	..	..
Sha-ch'uan, flat-bottomed	..	6	17	14	..	..	..	6	..	..	..	..	..
Ku-ch'uan (unexplained)	..	..	..	..	..	..	..	..	5	..	..	..	..
Shwang-pung-ch'uan, two-masted	..	2	..	..	2	..	..	..	..	..	..	..	..
Ku-ch'uan (unexplained)	..	..	..	..	..	..	..	..	..	..	..	..	..
Ta-ku (unexplained)	..	..	38	12	..	..	..	..	..	..	..	..	..
Shwang-pung-ku, two-masted	..	..	2	..	1	..	..	..	..	..	..	..	..
Ku-tsau	..	..	..	..	..	..	..	..	..	4	..	..	..
Tsiau-ch'uan, going particular beats	..	..	31	27	..	63	..	14	..	..	..	..	..
Siau-ch'uan, small	..	..	37	10	..	10	..	..	..	..	..	..	..
Sz-lu-ch'uan, with four sculls	..	..	..	10	..	..	..	..	..	..	..	..	..
Kw'ai-ch'uan, fast-sailing with four sculls	..	..	..	..	..	..	49	..	..	..	..	..	..
Hai-tsiau, sea-going with four sculls	..	..	..	16	..	11	..	..	..	..	..	..	..
Lu-tsiau, worked with sculls	..	..	..	4	..	..	..	..	..	..	..	..	..
Tungngan-ch'uan, of that district	..	..	4	..	222	..	139	..	..	..	..	..	..
Hu-ch'uan (unexplained)	..	..	16	52	..	..	4	..	..	..	39	..	..
Ta-hu (unexplained)	..	..	..	2	..	..	..	..	..	..	..	..	..
Siau-hu (unexplained)	..	..	..	53	..	..	..	..	..	..	..	..	..
Kw'ai-hu (unexplained)	..	..	..	..	..	..	..	18	..	..	..	..	..
Siun-ch'uan, cruisers	..	..	5	218	..	..	..	15	..	126	10	18	..
Kw'ai-tsiau-siun, fast cruisers	..	..	2	..	..	..	..	..	..	..	..	..	..
Hai-tsiau-siun, sea-going cruisers	..	..	4	..	..	..	..	..	..	..	..	..	..
Siau-siun, small cruisers	..	..	..	..	..	18	..	57	..	..	..	..	..
Pah-tsiang-siun, eight-oared cruisers	..	..	..	..	..	..	24	2	..	..	..	..	..
Chung-siun, middle-class cruisers	..	..	..	..	..	..	..	40	..	..	..	..	..
Mi-ting, grain-boats	..	..	..	..	30	..	30	..	135	..	..	..	..
Chan-pan-ch'uan, fir-built vessels	..	..	..	..	1	..	..	..	..	..	..	..	..
Hang-yang-ch'uan, vessels to cross	..	..	..	..	1	..	..	..	..	..	..	..	..
Tiau-ch'uan, fishing vessels	..	..	..	..	..	..	56	..	..	..	..	..	..
Yang-poh-ch'uan, anchoring at sea	..	..	..	..	..	..	1	..	..	..	..	..	..
Tsiang-ch'uan, vessels with oars	..	..	..	12	..	..	..	..	..	51	..	..	..
Pah-tsiang, vessels with eight oars	..	..	..	..	..	35	..	..	..	..	..	..	..
Luh-tsiang, vessels with six oars	..	..	..	..	..	8	..	..	..	18	..	..	..
Sz-tsiang, vessels with four oars	..	..	..	..	..	5	..	..	..	..	..	..	..
Kw'ai-tsiang, fast boats with oars	..	..	..	..	..	..	..	..	..	26	..	..	..
Pung-ch'uan, vessels broad in beam	..	..	..	..	..	2	..	..	..	..	..	..	..
Pung-tsai, small vessels broad in beam	..	..	..	..	..	..	..	..	12	..	..	..	..
Pung-kw'ai, fast vessels broad in beam	..	..	..	..	..	..	2	..	2	..	..	..	..
Wu-pi, black-bottomed	..	..	..	..	..	..	..	..	..	..	..	..	..
Hwa-tso, flower-boats	..	..	..	..	..	3	..	..	..	..	..	..	..
Kih-tiau, quick-leaping	..	..	..	..	..	..	..	..	..	35	..	..	..
Lu-ch'uan, vessels with sculls	..	..	..	..	..	..	..	..	..	6	..	..	..
Lu-tsiang, vessels with sculls and paddles	..	..	..	..	..	..	..	..	..	..	..	..	..
Kw'ai-ch'uan, fast vessels	..	..	..	20	..	..	..	18	..	7	..	..	..
Ta-kw'ai, large vessels	..	..	..	6	..	..	..	..	..	..	..	..	..
Siau-kw'ai, small vessels	..	..	..	20	..	..	..	..	..	..	..	..	..
Tsiang-lu-kw'ai, with oars and sculls	..	..	..	22	..	..	..	..	..	..	..	..	..
Kw'ai-ma, fast horse	..	..	..	..	..	..	..	..	..	2	..	..	..
Total of All Denominations	10	12	158	498	267	155	315	170	156	275	49	86	50

*The "Chinese Repository," Vol. XX, page 379.

NAUTICAL GLOSSARY

The small glossary of nautical terms used in this book is for the benefit of those who, though interested in all floating craft, may be unfamiliar with, or rusty in, the very specialized jargon of sailors. These Western terms have, in default of others, been necessarily used to describe junk details of construction and gear, which may not always correspond exactly with the Western prototypes.

About : the situation of a vessel after she has gone round and trimmed sails on the opposite tack.

Artifact : a prehistoric scrap heap. The simple products of human workmanship, especially applied to aboriginal art.

Batten : a small spar, usually of bamboo, secured to, and extending across, a sail so as to extend the leech.

Bawley : a shallow-draught, wide beamed, cutter rigged, Thames Estuary fishing-boat. One of its characteristics is that it has no main boom.

Beam : the breadth of a vessel taken at its widest point.

Bearding : the angular fore-part of the rudder, in juxtaposition with the stern-post. Also the corresponding bevel of the stern-post.

Becket : a short length of small rope with an eye at one end. When the other end is passed through the eye and secured by a knot, it forms the rope circle known as a becket.

Bilge : the nearly horizontal portion of the ship's side; bottom on either side of the keel, where such exists.

Bitt : usually used in the plural. One of the strong posts firmly fastened in the deck for securing ropes or cables.

Bollard : a post, always of wood unless otherwise stated, to which ropes are secured.

Bonnet : an additional part laced to the foot of a sail in fine weather to increase its size.

Boom : a spar used to extend the foot of a sail.

Bridle : usually applied to a small length of rope. It has many nautical uses, but may be best described as a rope serving to connect in two parts to a single rope or object, the idea being to distribute the strain or improve the lead.

Bulkhead : a partition built up in a vessel to separate various portions below deck.

Bumkin : from the Dutch *boomken*, little tree. A short boom, of great strength, projecting from the side or stern of a vessel.

Carlines : short beams running fore and aft, between the transverse beams, which they bind securely together.

Carvel-built : a method of building a boat with the planks of the hull laid edge to edge and caulked so as to present a flush and smooth surface.

Centre-board : a deep plate of wood which is hoisted up or lowered through a case built over a longitudinal aperture in the bottom of a junk, for the purpose of giving greater draught of water.

Clinch : to fix a nail securely, especially by bending and beating back or flattening the point or end which has passed through a plank.

Coaming : a raised piece of woodwork running round any opening in the deck to prevent water from getting below.

Coffer-dam : a small compartment always kept free of cargo, having two small apertures, or limbers, leading into the neighbouring main cargo-holds on either side. Its function is to receive any seepage of water which may have found its way into the holds so that it may be conveniently bailed out.

Cotter : a pin or tapered piece of wood or metal used to fasten together parts of a structure. It is driven into an opening through one of the parts.

Dog : a clamp for supporting something, or fastening or holding it in place.

Dunnage : light material stowed among and beneath the cargo of a vessel to protect it from chafing and getting wet.

Euphroe : a crowfoot deadeye—long cylinderical blocks with a number of small holes in them to receive the legs or lines composing the crowfoot.

Fake : to lay a rope in fakes or coils.

Fish : to fasten a piece of wood, technically called a fish, upon a beam, mast, etc., so as to strengthen it; to mend a spar with a fish or fishes.

Flare : the gradual swell, or flare upwards and outwards, of a vessel's hull. Usually applies to the bow.

Frame : the bends of timbers constituting the shape of the ship's body.

Frap : to bind tightly by means of lashings.

Freeboard : the side of the vessel from the water-line to the gunwale.

Futtock : one of the crooked wooden timbers scarfed together to form the lower part of the compound rib of a vessel.

Graving piece : a small piece of wood inserted to repair a defect in a plank.

Grummet : from old French *gromette*, a curb; a ring of rope sometimes twisted, seized, or tied with small yarn.

Gunwale : a continuous horizontal planking running along the ship's side and binding the heads of the timbers or ribs.

Handspike : a wooden bar used as a lever or crow.

Hogged : drooping at stem and stern.

Junk : The term "junk" according to the Customs definition* refers to a sailing vessel of Oriental build and rig. Sailing vessels of any other, including lorchas, come within the category of sailing vessels of foreign type, and are subject, like steamers, to General Regulations, but are not allowed to trade under I.W.S.N. Regulations. A Chinese-flag lorcha, however, may apply for permission to change its status to that of junk, and thus become subject to Junk Regulations.

Knee-piece : a shaped piece of wood with an angular bend designed to fasten parts of a ship together. It is especially used to secure beams to ribs.

Lanyard : a short rope or line to which anything may be attached.

Laodah : literally, "old great." The shipmaster.

Limber : one of a series of holes cut through the floor timbers (in a junk, through the bottom of the ribs and bulkheads). These holes permit the free passage of water from one compartment to another for drainage.

Loom : the shaft, that is to say, the part between the blade and the handle of an oar; also limited to that part of the oar between the thole-pin, or rowlock, and the hands in rowing.

Lumber iron : a forked crutch or stanchion fixed upright to hold oars, spars, or sails when they are not in use.

Parrel : a collar of metal or twisted rope, or even bamboo, normally used to keep the yard in to—that is, close to—the mast.

Partners : pieces of wood placed horizontally on either side of the aperture for the mast, which serve to strengthen the deck and distribute the strain.

Puff-puff : a type of craft introduced by the Japanese, chiefly fishermen. These boats are always powered motor-boats with the same type of hull as those operating in the coastal waters of Japan. They have evolved from Japanese junks and sampans.

Quant : to propel a boat with a quant or pole.

Quarter : that portion of the ship's side between the stern and the beam abaft the middle section.

Rake : a fore and aft inclination of mast or spars or stem and stern, from the vertical.

Rib : one of the curved frame-timbers of a vessel which rise from the keel to the top of its side. To the ribs are fastened the side planks forming the hull.

Roach : a cutting away in a curve of the edge of a sail, especially in the leech or foot, to prevent chafing, or to secure a better fit.

Rudder, fenestrated : an unbalanced rudder having numerous rhomboidal openings, regularly or irregularly reticulated, from the notion that the eddying of the water through the holes causes more resistance than a plain surface.

Sampan : literally, three planks. Generally applied to all Chinese open, or half-decked, boats of 30 to 40 feet measurement.

Scarf : a join by which two timbers are connected longitudinally into a continuous piece, the ends being halved, notched, or cut away so as to fit into each other with mutual overlapping.

Scupper : a hole at deck-level in the ship's side to carry off water from the deck.

Seize : to secure two ropes or a turn of a rope on itself by lashing or fastening with several turns of fine rope, cord, or yarn.

Sennit : braided cordage woven from three or more strands in flat, round, or square form.

Snub : to check the way of a ship suddenly by means of a rope wound round a post; to bring up a vessel.

Stanchion : an upright bar, stay, prop, or support; a sort of small pillar of wood or iron.

Stoppers : short pieces of rope, usually knotted at one or both ends, which are used to suspend any weighty body or to retain a cable in a fixed position.

Strake : continuous line of planking in the side of a vessel running from stem to stern. There are seven or more varieties of strakes, all named according to their position.

Strop : a ring or band of iron, rope, hide, or bamboo, with the ends bound or fastened together.

Tabernacle : a perpendicular square trunk, open at the after end, made to take the lower part of the mast. If the mast is stepped on deck (as in the case of those junks which have to pass under bridges) the heel of the mast is pivoted on a bolt passing through the wings, or sides, of the tabernacle above the deck.

* "Code of Customs Regulations and Procedure," page 133.

Tackle, feeding part of : that part running through the sheave, in opposition to the standing part.

Tackle, standing part of : that part which is made fast to the mast, deck, block, or euphroe, in contradistinction to that pulled upon, which is called the fall, running part, or feeding part.

Thole : a vertical pin or peg in the side of a boat against which in rowing the oar presses as the fulcrum.

Timber : *see* Rib.

Toggle : a short hardwood pin which acts as a fastener when passed through an eye or loop of rope, or round its own part.

Transom : one or more traverse beams across the stern and supporting the extremities of the deck. The aftermost athwartship bulkhead giving shape to and supporting the stern.

Wale : the strake running beneath and supporting the outer edge of the gunwale; sometimes called the rubbing streak. *See also* Strake.

Wall knot (known also as a wale knot) : a knot made by interlaying and interweaving the strands at the end of a rope so as to prevent unravelling, or to act as a stopper.

The following nautical terms may be of interest as showing how fond the Western sailor is of naming parts of his ship after objects of everyday life ashore :

Bight, Blade, Bucket, Buttons, Feather, Knees, Shoulder, Scull, Stretcher, Apron, Bonnet, Braces, Bridle, Cap, Cat-head, Cat, Cat's-paw, Cot, Cradle, Crib, Crowfoot, Crow's-nest, Crown, Diamond, Dog, Driver, Earring, Fox, Goose-neck, Goose-wing, Horse, Hose, Hounds, Jewel, Mouse, Puddings, Rabbit, Ribband, Saddle, Steer, Sheaves, Sheets, Shoe, Sister, Stays, Stirrup, Truck, Watch, Whip, Yard, Fiddle, Bed, Bear, Bearding.

INDEX

(*Italicized page numbers indicate an illustration or drawing*)

ABOUT THE AUTHOR

George Raleigh Gray Worcester (1890–1969) termed himself a sailor by profession. Born in England in 1890, he entered the Royal Navy in the days of sail and rounded the Horn as a midshipman. Although he turned his back on salt water in 1919, the balance of his professional life was spent within sight and sound of water of some sort. He left the Navy to join the Marine Department of the Chinese Maritime Customs Service, and during his thirty years as river inspector he assisted in surveying, marking, and opening the Yangtze to steam navigation to a point 1,450 miles from the sea. In his wanderings up and down the coast and rivers of China, he developed a deep interest in, and affection for, the junkmen and their craft.